P9-DIH-548

GARDNER'S
ART
THROUGH THE
AGES

THE WESTERN PERSPECTIVE

VOLUME I

SIXTEENTH EDITION

FRED S. KLEINER

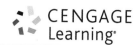

CENGAGE
Learning·

Australia • Brazil • Mexico • Singapore • United Kingdom • United States

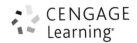

Gardner's Art through the Ages: The Western Perspective, Volume I, Sixteenth Edition
Fred S. Kleiner

Product Director: Marta Lee-Perriard

Product Manager: Vanessa Manter

Product Assistant: Teddy Coutracos

Marketing Manager: Laura Kuhlman

Senior Content Manager: Lianne Ames

IP Analyst: Ann Hoffman

Senior IP Project Manager: Betsy Hathaway

Production Service and Layout: Joan Keyes, Dovetail Publishing Services

Compositor: Cenveo® Publisher Services

Art Director: Sarah Cole

Text Designer: Alisha Webber

Cover Designer: Sarah Cole

Cover Image: Canali Photobank

© 2021, 2017, 2014 Cengage Learning, Inc.

Unless otherwise noted, all content is © Cengage.

ALL RIGHTS RESERVED. No part of this work covered by the copyright herein may be reproduced or distributed in any form or by any means, except as permitted by U.S. copyright law, without the prior written permission of the copyright owner.

For product information and technology assistance, contact us at
Cengage Customer & Sales Support, 1-800-354-9706
or **support.cengage.com**.

For permission to use material from this text or product,
submit all requests online at **www.cengage.com/permissions**.

Library of Congress Control Number: 2019948292

Student Edition:
ISBN: 978-0-357-37038-4

Loose-leaf Edition:
ISBN: 978-0-357-37045-2

Cengage
200 Pier 4 Boulevard
Boston, MA 02210
USA

Cengage is a leading provider of customized learning solutions with employees residing in nearly 40 different countries and sales in more than 125 countries around the world. Find your local representative at **www.cengage.com**.

Cengage products are represented in Canada by Nelson Education, Ltd.

To learn more about Cengage platforms and services, register or access your online learning solution, or purchase materials for your course, visit **www.cengage.com**.

Printed in the United States of America
Print Number: 01   Print Year: 2019

ABOUT THE COVER ART

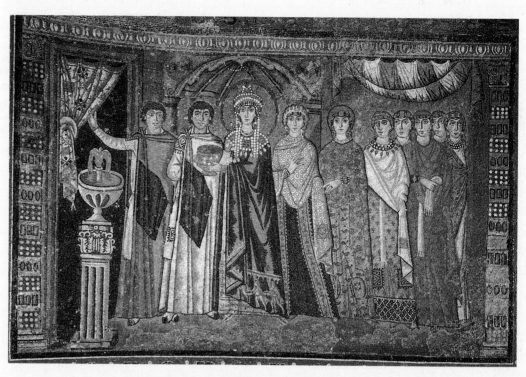

Theodora and attendants, mosaic on the south wall of the apse, San Vitale, Ravenna, Italy, ca. 547.

San Vitale is the most spectacular building in Ravenna, the Byzantine Empire's outpost in northern Italy. Dedicated by Bishop Maximianus in 547 in honor of Saint Vitalis, the second-century Christian martyr who died at the hands of the Romans at Ravenna, the church makes an unforgettable impression on all who have entered it and marveled at its intricate design and magnificent mosaics.

The most unexpected of those mosaics is the one in the apse depicting Empress Theodora, which faces the mosaic depicting Emperor Justinian, Maximianus, and their attendants. The two panels together show the emperor and empress taking part in the Eucharist. Justinian carries the bowl containing the bread, and Theodora the golden cup with the wine. Neither one ever visited Ravenna, however. Their participation in the liturgy at San Vitale is pictorial fiction. Justinian's presence underscores that his authority extended over his territories in Italy. The inclusion of Theodora is more surprising and testifies to her enormous stature at the Byzantine court.

Of humble origin, Theodora, who was 15 years younger than Justinian, initially attracted his attention because of her beauty, but she soon became his most trusted adviser. A contemporary described Theodora as "the most intelligent of all and of all times." During the Nika revolt in Constantinople in 532, when all of her husband's ministers counseled flight from the city, Theodora, by the sheer force of her personality, persuaded Justinian and his generals to hold their ground—and they succeeded in suppressing the uprising. In the mosaic, the artist underscored Theodora's elevated rank by decorating the border of her garment with a representation of the three magi, suggesting that the empress belongs in the company of the three monarchs bearing gifts who approached the newborn Jesus.

Artworks honoring women are far less common in the history of art than works celebrating men and their achievements, and until recently male artists outnumbered their female counterparts by a wide margin, but women artists as well as paintings, sculptures, and even buildings commemorating women figure prominently in this 16th edition of the groundbreaking introduction to art and architecture first published in 1927 by Helen Gardner of the Art Institute of Chicago.

BRIEF CONTENTS

CONTENTS

v

PREFACE

I take great pleasure in introducing the extensively revised and expanded 16th edition of *Gardner's Art through the Ages: The Western Perspective,* which, like the 15th edition, is a hybrid art history textbook—the first, and still the only, introductory survey of the history of art of its kind. This innovative new kind of "Gardner" retains all of the best features of traditional books on paper while harnessing 21st-century technology to increase by 25% the number of works examined—without increasing the size or weight of the book itself and at only nominal additional cost to students.

When Helen Gardner published the first edition of *Art through the Ages* in 1926, she could not have imagined that nearly a century later, instructors all over the world would still be using her textbook (available even in a new Chinese edition, the third time this classic textbook has been translated into Chinese) in their classrooms. Indeed, if she were alive today, she would not recognize the book that, even in its traditional form, long ago became—and remains—the world's most widely read introduction to the history of art and architecture. I hope that instructors and students alike will agree that this new edition lives up to the venerable Gardner tradition and even exceeds their high expectations.

The 16th edition follows the 15th in incorporating an innovative new online component called MindTap™, which includes, in addition to a host of other features (enumerated below), MindTap Bonus Images (with zoom capability) and descriptions of more than 200 additional important works of all eras, from prehistory to the present. The printed and online components of the hybrid 16th edition are very closely integrated. For example, each MindTap Bonus Image appears as a thumbnail in the traditional textbook, with abbreviated caption, to direct readers to MindTap for additional content, including an in-depth discussion of each image. The integration extends also to the maps, index, glossary, and chapter summaries, which seamlessly merge the printed and online information.

KEY FEATURES OF THE 16TH EDITION

In this new edition, in addition to revising the text of every chapter to incorporate the latest research and methodological developments and dividing the former chapter on European and American art from 1900 to 1945 into two chapters, I have added several important features while retaining the basic format and scope of the previous edition. Once again, the hybrid Gardner boasts roughly 1,600 photographs, plans, and drawings, nearly all in color and reproduced according to the highest standards of clarity and color fidelity, including hundreds of new images, among them a new series of superb photos taken by Jonathan Poore exclusively for *Art through the Ages* during a photographic campaign in England in 2016

(following similar forays into France, Tuscany, Rome, and Germany for the 14th and 15th editions). MindTap also includes custom videos made on these occasions at each site by Sharon Adams Poore. This extraordinary proprietary Cengage archive of visual material ranges from ancient temples and aqueducts in Rome and France; to medieval, Renaissance, and Baroque churches in England, France, Germany, and Italy and 18th-century landscape architecture in England; to such postmodern masterpieces as the Pompidou Center and the Louvre Pyramid in Paris, the Neue Staatsgalerie in Stuttgart, and the Gherkin in London. The 16th edition also features the highly acclaimed architectural drawings of John Burge prepared exclusively for Cengage, as well as Google Earth coordinates for all buildings and sites and all known provenances of portal objects. Together, these exclusive photographs, videos, and drawings provide readers with a visual feast unavailable anywhere else.

Once again, scales accompany the photograph of every painting, statue, or other artwork discussed—another innovative feature of the Gardner text. The scales provide students with a quick and effective way to visualize how big or small a given artwork is and its relative size compared with other objects in the same chapter and throughout the book—especially important given that the illustrated works vary in size from tiny to colossal.

Also retained in this edition are the Quick-Review Captions (brief synopses of the most significant aspects of each artwork or building illustrated) that students have found invaluable when preparing for examinations. These extended captions accompany not only every image in the printed book but also all the digital images in MindTap, where they are also included in a set of interactive electronic flashcards. Each chapter also again ends with the highly popular full-page feature called *The Big Picture,* which sets forth in bullet-point format the most important characteristics of each period or artistic movement discussed in the chapter. Also retained from the 15th edition are the timelines summarizing the major artistic and architectural developments during the era treated (again in bullet-point format for easy review) and a chapter-opening essay called *Framing the Era,* which discusses a characteristic painting, sculpture, or building and is illustrated by four photographs.

Another pedagogical tool not found in any other introductory art history textbook is the *Before 1300* section that appears at the beginning of the second volume of the paperbound version of the book. Because many students taking the second half of a survey course will not have access to Volume I, I have provided a special (expanded) set of concise primers on architectural terminology and construction methods in the ancient and medieval worlds, and on mythology and religion—information that is essential for understanding the history of Western art after 1300. The subjects of these special essays are Greco-Roman Temple Design and the Classical Orders; Arches and Vaults; Basilican Churches; Central-Plan Churches; the Gods and Goddesses of Mount Olympus; the Life of

Jesus in Art; and Early Christian Saints and Their Attributes. *Before 1300* also is included in MindTap for all courses.

Feature boxes once again appear throughout the book as well. These features fall under nine broad categories, one of which is new to the 16th edition:

Architectural Basics boxes provide students with a sound foundation for the understanding of architecture. These discussions are concise explanations, with drawings and diagrams, of the major aspects of design and construction. The information included is essential to an understanding of architectural technology and terminology.

Materials and Techniques essays explain the various media that artists have employed from prehistoric to modern times. Because materials and techniques often influence the character of artworks, these discussions contain essential information on why many monuments appear as they do.

Religion and Mythology boxes introduce students to the principal elements of the world's great religions, past and present, and to the representation of religious and mythological themes in painting and sculpture of all periods and places. These discussions of belief systems and iconography give readers a richer understanding of some of the greatest artworks ever created.

Art and Society essays treat the historical, social, political, cultural, and religious context of art and architecture. In some instances, specific monuments are the basis for a discussion of broader themes.

Written Sources boxes present and discuss key historical documents illuminating important monuments of art and architecture throughout the world. The passages quoted permit voices from the past to speak directly to the reader, providing vivid and unique insights into the creation of artworks in all media.

In the *Artists on Art* boxes, artists and architects throughout history discuss both their theories and individual works.

The Patron's Voice essays underscore the important roles played by the individuals and groups who paid for the artworks and buildings in determining the character of those monuments.

Problems and Solutions essays are designed to make students think critically about the decisions that went into the making of every painting, sculpture, and building from the Old Stone Age to the present. These discussions address questions of how and why various forms developed; the problems that painters, sculptors, and architects confronted; and the solutions they devised to resolve them.

New to the 16th edition are boxes titled *A Second Opinion,* in which an individual work of art that is the subject of current debate or has recently been reinterpreted is discussed. These essays underscore for students that the history of art and architecture is not a static discipline and that scholars are constantly questioning and rethinking traditional interpretations of paintings, sculptures, and buildings.

Other noteworthy features retained from the 15th edition are the extensive (updated) bibliography of books in English; a glossary containing definitions of all italicized terms introduced in both the printed and online texts. The host of state-of-the-art resources in the 16th edition version of MindTap for *Art through the Ages* are enumerated on page xv.

ACKNOWLEDGMENTS

A work as extensive as a comprehensive history of Western art could not be undertaken or completed without the counsel of experts in all areas of world art. As with previous editions, Cengage has enlisted dozens of art historians to review every chapter of *Art through the Ages* in order to ensure that the text lives up to the Gardner reputation for accuracy as well as readability. I take great pleasure in acknowledging here the important contributions to the 16th edition made by the following: Bradley Bailey, Saint Louis University; Amy Bloch, University at Albany; Anne-Marie Bouché, Florida Gulf Coast University; Betty Brownlee, Macomb Community College; Caroline Bruzelius, Duke University; Petra Chu, Seton Hall University; Kathy Curnow, Cleveland State University; Paola Demattè, Rhode Island School of Design; Sarah Dillon, Kingsborough City College, City University of New York; Eduardo de Jesús Douglas, University of North Carolina-Chapel Hill; Sonja Drimmer, University of Massachusetts Amherst; Ingrid Furniss, Lafayette College; Karen Hope Goodchild, Wofford College; Christopher Gregg, George Mason University; Melinda Hartwig, Emory University; Joe Hawkins, Hagley Park; Peter Holliday, California State University, Long Beach; Craig Houser, City College of New York/City University of New York; Margaret Jackson, University of New Mexico; Mark J. Johnson, Brigham Young University; Lynn Jones, Florida State University; Tanja L. Jones, University of Alabama Tuscaloosa; Nancy Klein, Texas A&M; Peri Klemm, California State University, Northridge; Yu Bong Ko, Dominican College; Paul Lavy, University of Hawai'i at Manoa; John Listopad, California State University, Sacramento; Gary Liu Jr., University of Hawaii at Manoa; Nancy Bea Miller, Montgomery County Community College; Michelle Moseley-Christian, Virginia Tech University; Evan Neely, Pratt Institute; Huiping Pang, University of Iowa; Benjamin Paul, Rutgers University; Julie-Anne Plax, University of Arizona; Stephanie Porras, Tulane University; Sharon Pruitts, East Carolina University; Kurt Rahmlow, University of North Texas; Julie Risser, Minneapolis College of Art and Design; Robyn Roslak, University of Minnesota-Duluth; Susan Elizabeth Ryan, Louisiana State University; Nicholas Sawicki, Lehigh University; Nancy Serwint, Arizona State University; Kerri Cox Sullivan, University of Texas, Austin; James R. Swensen, Brigham Young University; David S. Whitley, University of California, Los Angeles/ASM Affiliates; Margaret L. Woodhull, University of Colorado Denver.

I am especially indebted to the following for creating the instructor and student materials for the 16th edition: Anne McClanan, Portland State University; Kerri Cox Sullivan, University of Texas, Austin.

I am also happy to have this opportunity to express my gratitude to the extraordinary group of people at Cengage involved with the editing, production, and distribution of *Art through the Ages.* Some of them I have now worked with on various projects for two decades and feel privileged to count among my friends. The success of the Gardner series in all of its various permutations depends in no small part on the expertise and unflagging commitment of these dedicated professionals, especially Vanessa Manter, senior product manager; Laura Hildebrand, senior content manager; Lianne Ames, senior content manager; Paula Dohnal, learning designer; Ann Hoffman, intellectual property analyst; Betsy Hathaway, senior intellectual property project manager; Laura Kuhlman, marketing manager; Sarah Cole, senior designer; as well as Sharon Adams Poore, former product manager for art; Cate Barr, former senior art director; Jillian Borden, former senior marketing manager; and Sayaka Kawano, former product assistant. I also express my deep gratitude to the incomparable group of learning consultants who have passed on to me the welcome advice offered by the hundreds of instructors they speak to daily.

It is a special pleasure also to acknowledge my debt to the following out-of-house contributors to the 16th edition: the peerless quarterback of the entire production process, Joan Keyes, Dovetail Publishing Services; Michele Jones, copy editor extraordinaire; Susan Gall, eagle-eyed proofreader; Alisha Webber, text and cover designer; Lumina Datamatics, photo researchers; Jay and John Crowley, Jay's Publisher Services; Cenveo Publisher Services; and Jonathan Poore and John Burge, for their superb photos and architectural drawings.

I conclude this long (but no doubt incomplete) list of acknowledgments with an expression of gratitude to my colleagues at Boston University and to the thousands of students and hundreds of teaching fellows in my art history courses since I began teaching in 1975. From them I have learned much that has helped determine the form and content of *Art through the Ages* and made it a much better book than it otherwise might have been.

Fred S. Kleiner

CHAPTER-BY-CHAPTER CHANGES IN THE 16TH EDITION

The 16th edition is extensively revised and expanded, as detailed below. Instructors will find a very helpful figure number transition guide on the online instructor companion site.

Introduction: What Is Art History? Added the head of the portrait of Augustus as pontifex maximus from the Via Labicana, Rome.

1: Art in the Stone Age. Revised and expanded discussion of chronology and current theories about Paleolithic art, including a new A Second Opinion essay "The Meaning of Paleolithic Art." New Art and Society essay "The Neolithic Temple at Göbekli Tepe." New photographs of the passage grave at Newgrange and the circles of trilithons at Stonehenge.

2: Ancient Mesopotamia and Persia. Added the Babylonian *Queen of the Night,* the Kalhu panel of Assyrians besieging a citadel, and a bull protome capital from Achaemenid Susa. Revised chronology of Sumerian art and expanded discussion of the Royal Cemetery at Ur with a new A Second Opinion essay "The *Standard of Ur.*" Revised discussion and dating of the Sasanian palace at Ctesiphon. New photographs of the cylinder seal of Puabi, the portrait head of an Akkadian ruler, the lamassu from the palace of Sargon II, and the Nineveh panel of Ashurbanipal hunting lions.

3: Egypt from Narmer to Cleopatra. Added the colossal head of Senusret III in Kansas City. New A Second Opinion essay "Akhenaton." New photographs of the columnar entrance corridor of the funerary precinct of Djoser at Saqqara, the exterior and interior of the Temple of Ramses II at Abu Simbel, the Temple of Amen-Re and the hypostyle hall at Karnak, Thutmose's portrait of Nefertiti, the sunken relief in Berlin of the family of Akhenaton, and the sphinx of Taharqo in the British Museum.

4: The Prehistoric Aegean. New A Second Opinion essay "Cycladic Statuettes." New photographs of the Hagia Triada sarcophagus, the Akrotiri *Spring Fresco,* the corbel-vaulted gallery in the fortification walls of Tiryns, the Lion Gate and the interior of the Treasury of Atreus at Mycenae, and the Mycenaean painted female head in the Athens National Archaeological Museum.

5: Ancient Greece. Added a second centauromachy metope, the horse of Selene from the east pediment, the river god Ilissos and Iris from the west pediment, and the peplos ceremony of the east frieze of the Parthenon; and the lion hunt pebble mosaic from Pella. New A Second Opinion essay "The *Alexander Mosaic.*" New photographs of the west pediment of the Temple of Artemis, Corfu;

the *Charioteer of Delphi*; the herm of Pericles in the Vatican; metope 28, Helios and Dionysos and the three goddesses of the east pediment, and the horsemen and maidens of the Panathenaic procession frieze of the Parthenon; the Temple of Athena Nike and the caryatids of the Erechtheion on the Athenian Acropolis; the Tomb of the Diver, Paestum; the *Farnese Hercules*; and the Stoa of Attalos in the Athenian agora.

6: The Etruscans. New Framing the Era essay "The Portal to the Etruscan Afterlife." New A Second Opinion essay "The *Capitoline Wolf.*" New photographs of the Tomb of the Augurs and the *Capitoline Wolf.*

7: The Roman Empire. Added the portraits of a Republican priest in the Vatican Museums and of Pompey the Great in Venice. New Framing the Era essay "The Roman Emperor as World Conqueror." New A Second Opinion essay "The Arch of Constantine." New photographs of the Temple of Portunus, Rome; the Temple of Vesta, Tivoli; the funerary relief of the Gessii in Boston; the funerary procession relief from Amiternum; the gardenscape from the Villa of Livia at Primaporta; the Ara Pacis Augustae, Rome (general view and Tellus panel); the Pont-du-Gard, Nîmes; the Porta Maggiore, Rome; the facade of the Colosseum, Rome; the portrait of a Flavian woman in the Museo Capitolino; the spoils relief of the Arch of Titus, Rome; four details of the spiral frieze of the Column of Trajan, Rome; the portrait of Hadrian in the Palazzo Massimo; the exterior of the Pantheon, Rome; the apotheosis and decursio reliefs of the Column of Antoninus Pius, Rome; the portrait of Caracalla in Berlin; the portrait of Trajan Decius in the Museo Capitolino; the portrait of Philip the Arabian in the Vatican Museums; the *Ludovisi Battle Sarcophagus*; the Temple of Venus, Baalbek; and the Arch of Constantine, Rome.

8: Late Antiquity. Added the baptistery of the Christian community house at Dura-Europos, the Anastasis Rotunda of the Church of the Holy Sepulchre in Jerusalem, and the mosaics of the chancel arch of Santa Maria Maggiore in Rome. New Framing the Era essay "Polytheism and Monotheism at Dura-Europos." New A Second Opinion essay "The Via Latina Catacomb." New photographs of the Dura-Europos baptistery, the Santa Maria Antiqua sarcophagus, two details of the Catacomb of Commodilla in Rome, and the ivory diptych of the Symmachi.

9: Byzantium. Added the pedestal of the Theodosian obelisk in the Constantinople hippodrome. New A Second Opinion essay "The *Vienna Genesis.*" New photographs of the apse of San Vitale at Ravenna, the interior of the Cappella Palatina at Palermo, and the exterior of the church of Saint Catherine at Thessaloniki.

10: The Islamic World. New A Second Opinion essay "The Rock of the Dome of the Rock." New photographs of the exterior and interior of the Dome of the Rock, the Umayyad palace at Mshatta, and the pyxis of al-Mughira.

11: Early Medieval Europe. New Framing the Era essay "Missionaries and the Beauty of God's Words." New A Second Opinion essay "The Lindisfarne Saint Matthew." New Problems and Solutions essay "How to Illustrate a Psalm." New photographs of the Oseberg ship, San Juan Bautista at Baños de Cerrato, and the bronze doors of St. Michael's at Hildesheim.

12: Romanesque Europe. New Framing the Era essay "The Blessed and the Damned on Judgment Day." New Written Sources essay "The Burning of Canterbury Cathedral." Two new Problems and Solutions essays "Stone Vaulting in Romanesque Churches" and "How to Illuminate a Nave." New A Second Opinion essay "The Rebirth of Large-Scale Sculpture in Romanesque Europe." New photographs of the west tympanum *Last Judgment* at Autun (three new details), the *Tower of Babel* on the nave vault of Saint-Savin-sur-Gartempe, the interior and atrium of Sant'Ambrogio at Milan, and the nave of Durham Cathedral.

13: Gothic Europe North of the Alps. Added the head of Moses from the west facade of Saint-Denis; Wells and Exeter Cathedrals; and a discussion of the Decorated style of English Gothic architecture. New Framing the Era essay "The Birth of Gothic." New Art and Society essay "Louis IX, the Saintly King." New A Second Opinion essay "Gothic Cathedrals and Gothic Cities." New photographs of Chartres Cathedral (aerial view and nave), Reims Cathedral (west

facade), Sainte-Chapelle in Paris (interior), Salisbury Cathedral (west facade, statue of Bishop Poore, and nave), Gloucester Cathedral (choir and tomb of Edward II), the exterior of the Chapel of Henry VII in Westminster Abbey, Nicholas of Verdun's *Shrine of the Three Kings,* and the choir of Cologne Cathedral.

14: Late Medieval Italy. New Framing the Era essay "Duccio di Buoninsegna." New A Second Opinion essay "Pietro Cavallini." New Problems and Solutions essay "Cityscapes and Landscapes as Allegories." Two new photographs of Pietro Cavallini's *Last Judgment* in Santa Cecilia in Trastevere.

ABOUT THE AUTHOR

Fred S. Kleiner

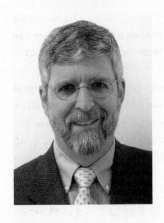

FRED S. KLEINER (Ph.D., Columbia University) has been the author or coauthor of *Gardner's Art through the Ages* beginning with the 10th edition in 1995. He has also published more than a hundred books, articles, and reviews on Greek and Roman art and architecture, including *A History of Roman Art,* also published by Cengage Learning. Both *Art through the Ages* and the book on Roman art have been awarded Texty prizes as the outstanding college textbook of the year in the humanities and social sciences, in 2001 and 2007, respectively. Professor Kleiner has taught the art history survey course since 1975, first at the University of Virginia and, since 1978, at Boston University, where he is currently professor of the history of art and architecture and classical archaeology and has served as department chair for five terms, most recently from 2005 to 2014. From 1985 to 1998, he was editor-in-chief of the *American Journal of Archaeology*.

Long acclaimed for his inspiring lectures and devotion to students, Professor Kleiner won Boston University's Metcalf Award for Excellence in Teaching as well as the College Prize for Undergraduate Advising in the Humanities in 2002, and he is a two-time winner of the Distinguished Teaching Prize in the College of Arts & Sciences Honors Program. In 2007, he was elected a Fellow of the Society of Antiquaries of London, and, in 2009, in recognition of lifetime achievement in publication and teaching, a Fellow of the Text and Academic Authors Association.

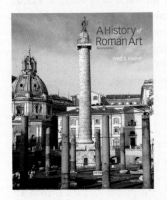

Also by Fred Kleiner: *A History of Roman Art, Second Edition* (Cengage Learning 2018; ISBN 9781337279505), winner of the 2007 Texty Prize for a new college textbook in the humanities and social sciences. In this authoritative and lavishly illustrated volume, Professor Kleiner traces the development of Roman art and architecture from Romulus's foundation of Rome in the eighth century BCE to the death of Constantine in the fourth century CE, with special chapters devoted to Pompeii and Herculaneum, Ostia, funerary and provincial art and architecture, and the earliest Christian art, with an introductory chapter on the art and architecture of the Etruscans and of the Greeks of South Italy and Sicily.

RESOURCES FOR STUDENTS AND INSTRUCTORS

MINDTAP FOR *ART THROUGH THE AGES*

MindTap for *Gardner's Art through the Ages: The Western Perspective,* 16th edition, helps students engage with course content and achieve greater comprehension. Highly personalized, fully online, and completely mobile-optimized, the MindTap learning platform presents authoritative Cengage content, assignments, and services.

Students

MindTap guides you through your course via a learning path where you can annotate readings and take quizzes. Concepts are brought to life with zoomable versions of close to 1,600 images; videos to reinforce concepts and expand knowledge of particular works or art trends; numerous study tools, including mobile-optimized image flashcards; a glossary complete with an audio pronunciation guide; and more!

Instructors

You can easily tailor the presentation of each MindTap course and integrate activities into a learning management system. The Resources for Teaching folder in MindTap and the Instructor Companion Site hold resources such as instructions on how to use the online test bank; Microsoft PowerPoint slides with high-resolution images, which can be used as is or customized by importing personal lecture slides or other material; YouTube playlists organized by chapter; course learning objectives; and more.

MINDTAP MOBILE

Gardner's Art through the Ages: The Western Perspective, 16th edition, is now more accessible than ever with the MindTap Mobile App, empowering students to learn on their terms—anytime, anywhere, online or off.

- The MindTap eReader provides convenience as students can read or listen to their eBook on their smartphone, take notes, and highlight important passages.
- Students have instant access to ready-made flashcards to engage with key concepts and images and confidently prepare for exams.
- Notifications keep students connected. Due dates are never forgotten with MindTap Mobile course notifications, which push assignment reminders, score updates, and instructor messages directly to students' smartphones.

LECTURE NOTES & STUDY GUIDES

The Lecture Notes & Study Guide for each chapter is a lecture companion that allows students to take notes alongside the images shown in class. This resource includes reproductions of the images from the reading, with full captions and space for note-taking either on a computer or on a printout. It also includes a chapter summary, key terms list, and learning objectives checklist.

GOOGLE EARTH

Take a virtual tour of art through the ages! Resources for the 16th edition include Google Earth coordinates for all works, monuments, and sites discussed in the reading, encouraging students to make geographical connections between places and sites. Instructors can use these coordinates to start lectures with a virtual journey to locations all over the globe or take aerial screenshots of important sites to incorporate into lecture materials.

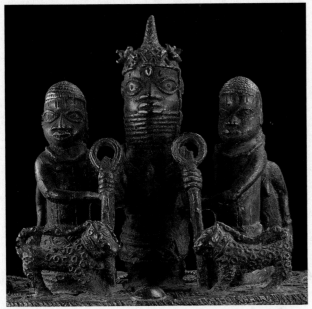

▲ **I-1a** Art historians seek to understand not only why artworks appear as they do but also why those works exist at all. Who paid this African artist to make this altar? Can the figures represented provide the answer?

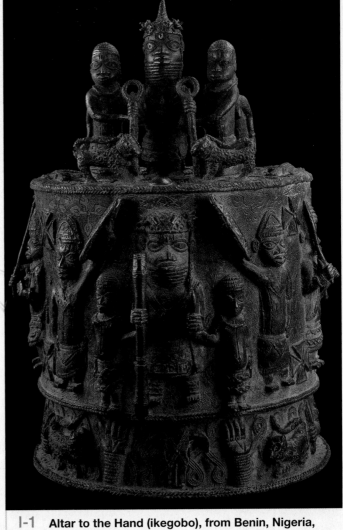

I-1 **Altar to the Hand (ikegobo), from Benin, Nigeria, ca. 1735–1750. Bronze, 1′ 5½″ high. British Museum, London (gift of Sir William Ingram).**

1 in.

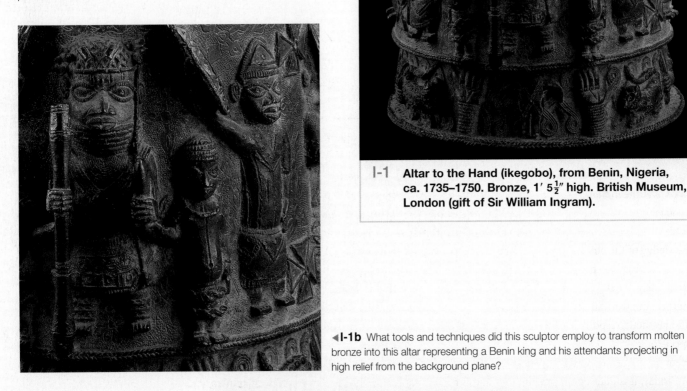

◄ **I-1b** What tools and techniques did this sculptor employ to transform molten bronze into this altar representing a Benin king and his attendants projecting in high relief from the background plane?

► **I-1c** At the bottom of the altar is a band with hands and other symbols, but no artist's signature or date. How can art historians determine when an unlabeled work such as this one was made and by and for whom?

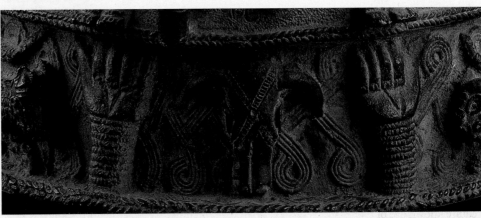

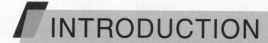

WHAT IS ART HISTORY?

What is art history? Except when referring to the modern academic discipline, people do not often juxtapose the words *art* and *history*. They tend to think of history as the record and interpretation of past human events, particularly social and political events. By contrast, most think of art, quite correctly, as part of the present—as something people can see and touch. Of course, people cannot see or touch history's vanished human events, but a visible, tangible artwork is a kind of persisting event. One or more artists made it at a certain time and in a specific place, even if no one now knows who, when, where, or why. Although created in the past, an artwork continues to exist in the present, long surviving its times. The earliest known paintings and sculptures were created almost 40,000 years ago, but they can be viewed today, often in glass cases in museums built only during the past few years.

Modern museum visitors can admire these objects from the remote past and countless others produced over the millennia—whether a large painting on canvas by a 17th-century French artist (FIG. I-12), a wood portrait from an ancient Egyptian tomb (FIG. I-15), an illustrated book by a medieval German monk (FIG. I-8), or an 18th-century bronze altar glorifying an African king (FIG. I-1)—without any knowledge of the circumstances leading to the creation of those works. The beauty or sheer size of an object can impress people, the artist's virtuosity in the handling of ordinary or costly materials can dazzle them, or the subject depicted can move them emotionally. Viewers can react to what they see, interpret the work in the light of their own experience, and judge it a success or a failure. These are all valid aesthetic responses. (*Aesthetics* is the branch of philosophy that addresses the nature of beauty, especially in art.) But the enjoyment and appreciation of artworks in museum settings are relatively recent phenomena, as is the creation of artworks solely for museum-going audiences to view.

Today, it is common for artists to work in private studios and to create paintings, sculptures, and other objects to be offered for sale by commercial art galleries. This is what American artist CLYFFORD STILL (1904–1980) did when he created his series of paintings (FIG. I-2) of pure color titled simply with the year of their creation. Usually, someone whom the artist has never met will purchase the artwork and display it in a setting that the artist has never seen. This practice is not a new phenomenon in the history of art—an ancient potter decorating a vase for sale at a village market stall probably did not know who would buy the pot or where it would be housed—but it is not at all typical. In fact, it is exceptional. Throughout history, most artists created paintings, sculptures, and other objects for specific patrons and settings and to fulfill a specific purpose, even if today no one knows the original contexts of those artworks. A museum visitor can appreciate the visual and tactile qualities of these objects, but without knowing the circumstances of their creation, that modern viewer cannot understand why they were made or why they appear as they do. Art *appreciation* and aesthetic judgments in general do not require knowledge of the historical context of an artwork (or a building). Art *history* does.

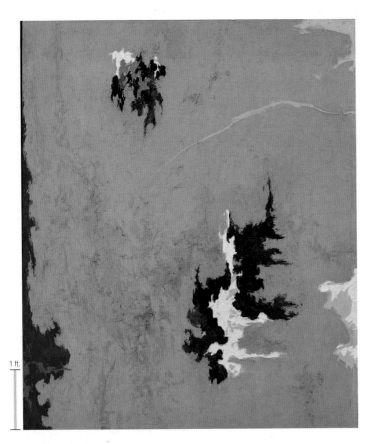

1 ft.

I-2 CLYFFORD STILL, *1948-C*, 1948. Oil on canvas, 6′ 8 $\frac{7}{8}$″ × 5′ 8 $\frac{3}{4}$″. Hirshhorn Museum and Sculpture Garden, Smithsonian Institution, Washington, D.C. (purchased with funds of Joseph H. Hirshhorn, 1992).

Clyfford Still painted this abstract composition without knowing who would purchase it or where it would be displayed, but throughout history, most artists created works for specific patrons and settings.

Thus a central aim of art history is to determine the original context of artworks. Art historians seek to achieve a full understanding not only of why these "persisting events" of human history look the way they do but also of why the artistic events happened at all. What unique set of circumstances gave rise to the construction of a particular building or led an individual patron to commission a certain artist to fashion a singular artwork for a specific place? The study of history is therefore vital to art history. And art history is often indispensable for a thorough understanding of history. In ways that other historical documents may not, art objects and buildings can shed light on the peoples who made them and on the times of their creation. Furthermore, artists and architects can affect history by reinforcing or challenging cultural values and practices through the objects they create and the structures they build. Although the two disciplines are not the same, the analysis of art and architecture is inseparable from the study of history.

The following pages introduce some of the distinctive subjects that art historians address and the kinds of questions they ask, and explain some of the basic terminology they use when answering these questions. Readers armed with this arsenal of questions and terms will be ready to explore the multifaceted world of art through the ages—and to form their own opinions and write knowledgably about artworks and buildings in all places and at all times. This is the central aim of this book.

ART HISTORY IN THE 21ST CENTURY

Art historians study the visual and tangible objects that humans make and the structures they build. Scholars traditionally have classified these works as architecture, sculpture, the pictorial arts (painting, drawing, printmaking, and photography), and the craft arts, or arts of design. The craft arts comprise utilitarian objects, such as ceramics, metalwork, textiles, jewelry, and similar accessories of ordinary living—but the fact that these objects were used does not mean that they are not works of art. In fact, in some times and places, these so-called minor arts were the most prestigious artworks of all. Artists of every age have blurred the boundaries among these categories, but this is especially true today, when multimedia works abound.

Beginning with the earliest Greco-Roman art critics, scholars have studied objects that their makers consciously manufactured as "art" and to which the artists assigned formal titles. But today's art historians also study a multitude of objects that their creators and owners almost certainly did not consider to be "works of art"—for example, the African altar illustrated on the opening page of this introductory chapter (FIG. I-1). Likewise, few ancient Romans would have regarded a coin bearing their emperor's portrait as anything but money. Today, an art museum may exhibit that coin in a locked case in a climate-controlled room, and scholars may subject it to the same kind of art historical analysis as a portrait by an acclaimed Renaissance or modern sculptor or painter.

The range of objects that art historians study is constantly expanding and now includes, for example, computer-generated images, whereas in the past almost anything produced using a machine would not have been regarded as art. Most people still consider the performing arts—music, drama, and dance—as outside art history's realm because these arts are fleeting, impermanent media. But during the past few decades, even this distinction between "fine art" and "performance art" has become blurred. Art historians, however, generally ask the same kinds of questions about what they study, whether they employ a restrictive or expansive definition of art.

The Questions Art Historians Ask

How Old Is It? Before art historians can write a history of art, they must be sure that they know the date of each work they study. Thus an indispensable subject of art historical inquiry is *chronology*, the dating of art objects and buildings. If researchers cannot determine a monument's age, they cannot place the work in its historical context. Art historians have developed many ways to establish, or at least approximate, the date of an artwork.

Physical evidence often reliably indicates an object's age. The material used for a statue or painting—bronze, plastic, or oil-based pigment, to name only a few—may not have been invented before a certain time, indicating the earliest possible date (the *terminus post quem*: Latin, "point after which") that someone could have fashioned the work. Or artists may have ceased using certain materials—such as specific kinds of inks and papers for drawings—at a known time, providing the latest possible date (the *terminus ante quem*: Latin, "point before which") for objects made of those materials. Sometimes the material (or the manufacturing technique) of an object or a building can establish a very precise date of production or construction. The study of tree rings, for instance, usually can determine within a narrow range the date of a wood statue or a timber roof beam.

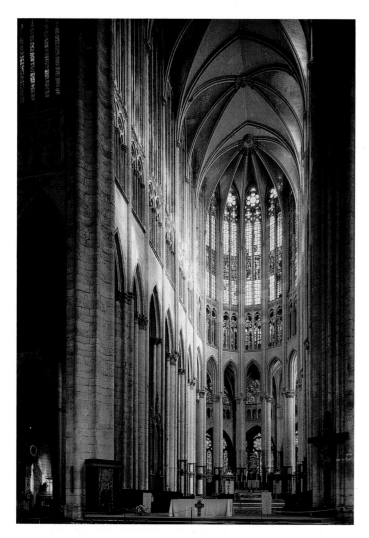

I-3 Choir of Beauvais Cathedral (looking east), Beauvais, France, rebuilt after 1284.

The style of an object or building often varies from region to region. This cathedral has towering stone vaults and large colored-glass windows typical of 13th-century French architecture.

Documentary evidence can help pinpoint the date of an object or building when a dated written document mentions the work. For example, official records may note when church officials commissioned a new altarpiece—and how much they paid to which artist.

Internal evidence can play a significant role in dating an artwork. A painter or sculptor might have depicted an identifiable person or a kind of hairstyle or garment fashionable only at a certain time. If so, the art historian can assign a more accurate date to that painting or sculpture.

Stylistic evidence is also very important. The analysis of *style*—an artist's distinctive manner of producing an object—is the art historian's special sphere. Unfortunately, because it is a subjective assessment, an artwork's style is by far the most unreliable chronological criterion. Still, art historians find stylistic evidence a very useful tool for establishing chronology.

What Is Its Style? Defining artistic style is one of the key elements of art historical inquiry, although the analysis of artworks solely in terms of style no longer dominates the field the way it once did. Art historians speak of several different kinds of artistic styles.

Period style refers to the characteristic artistic manner of a specific era or span of years, usually within a distinct culture, such as

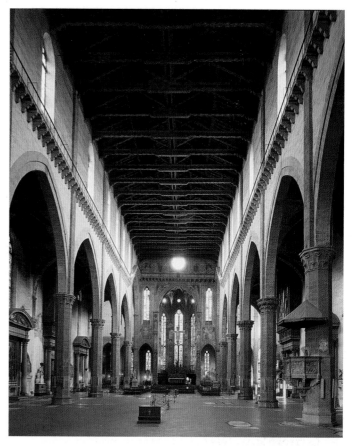

I-4 Interior of Santa Croce (looking east), Florence, Italy, begun 1294.

In contrast to Beauvais Cathedral (FIG. I-3), this contemporaneous Florentine church conforms to the quite different regional style of Italy. The building has a low timber roof and small windows.

"Archaic Greek" or "High Renaissance." But many periods do not display any stylistic unity at all. How would someone define the artistic style of the second or third decade of the new millennium in North America? Far too many crosscurrents exist in contemporary art for anyone to describe a period style of the early 21st century—even in a single city such as New York.

Regional style is the term that art historians use to describe variations in style tied to geography. Like an object's date, its *provenance,* or place of origin, can significantly determine its character. Very often two artworks from the same place made centuries apart are more similar than contemporaneous works from two different regions. To cite one example, usually only an expert can distinguish between an Egyptian statue carved in 2500 BCE (FIG. 3-13) and one created 2,000 years later (FIG. 3-37). But no one would mistake an Egyptian statue of 500 BCE for one of the same date made in Greece (FIG. 5-35) or Africa (FIG. 19-4).

Considerable variations in a given area's style are possible, however, even during a single historical period. In late medieval Europe, French architecture differed significantly from Italian architecture. The interiors of Beauvais Cathedral (FIG. I-3) and the church of Santa Croce (Holy Cross, FIG. I-4) in Florence typify the architectural styles of France and Italy, respectively, at the end of the 13th century. The rebuilding of the east end of Beauvais Cathedral began in 1284. Construction commenced on Santa Croce only 10 years later. Both structures employ the *pointed arch* characteristic of this era, yet the two churches differ strikingly. The French church has towering stone ceilings and large expanses of colored-glass windows, whereas the Italian building has a low timber roof and small,

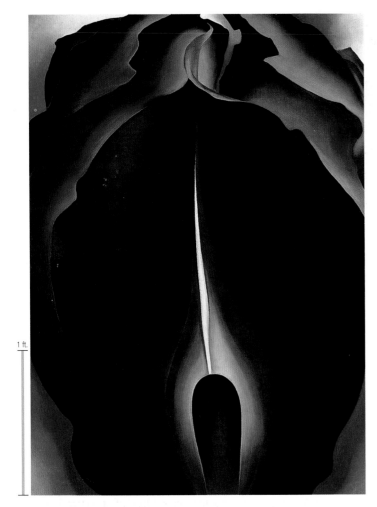

1 ft.

I-5 GEORGIA O'KEEFFE, *Jack-in-the-Pulpit No. 4,* 1930. Oil on canvas, 3′ 4″ × 2′ 6″. National Gallery of Art, Washington, D.C. (Alfred Stieglitz Collection, bequest of Georgia O'Keeffe).

O'Keeffe's paintings feature close-up views of petals and leaves in which the organic forms become powerful abstract compositions. This approach to painting typifies the artist's distinctive personal style.

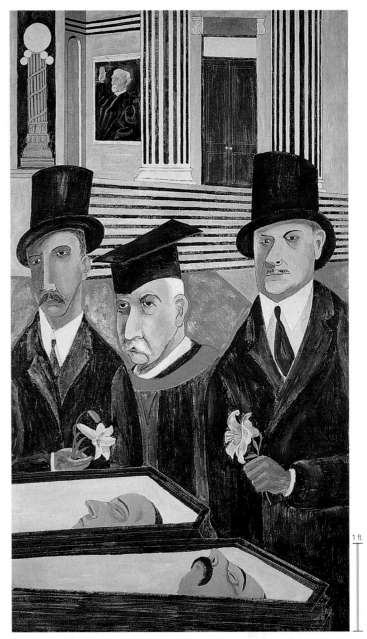

1 ft.

I-6 BEN SHAHN, *The Passion of Sacco and Vanzetti,* 1931–1932. Tempera on canvas, 7′ $\frac{1}{2}$″ × 4′. Whitney Museum of American Art, New York (gift of Edith and Milton Lowenthal in memory of Juliana Force).

O'Keeffe's contemporary, Shahn developed a style markedly different from hers. His paintings are often social commentaries on recent events and incorporate readily identifiable people.

widely separated clear windows. Because the two contemporaneous churches served similar purposes, regional style mainly explains their differing appearance.

Personal style, the distinctive manner of individual artists or architects, often decisively explains stylistic discrepancies among paintings, sculptures, and buildings of the same time and place. For example, in 1930, American painter GEORGIA O'KEEFFE (1887–1986) produced a series of paintings of flowering plants. One of them— *Jack-in-the-Pulpit No. 4* (FIG. I-5)—is a sharply focused close-up view of petals and leaves. O'Keeffe captured the growing plant's slow, controlled motion while converting the plant into a powerful *abstract* composition of lines, forms, and colors (see the discussion of art historical vocabulary in the next section). Only a year later, another American artist, BEN SHAHN (1898–1969), painted *The Passion of Sacco and Vanzetti* (FIG. I-6), a stinging commentary on social injustice inspired by the trial and execution of two Italian anarchists, Nicola Sacco and Bartolomeo Vanzetti. Many people believed that Sacco and Vanzetti had been unjustly convicted of killing two men in a robbery in 1920. Shahn's painting compresses time in a symbolic representation of the trial and its aftermath. The two executed men lie in their coffins. Presiding over them are the three members of the commission (headed by a college president

wearing academic cap and gown) who declared that the original trial was fair and cleared the way for the executions. Behind, on the wall of a stately government building, hangs the framed portrait of the judge who pronounced the initial sentence. Personal style, not period or regional style, sets Shahn's canvas apart from O'Keeffe's. The contrast is extreme here because of the very different subjects that the artists chose. But even when two artists depict the same subject, the results can vary widely. The *way* that O'Keeffe painted flowers and the *way* that Shahn painted faces are distinctive and unlike the styles of their contemporaries. (See the "Who Made It?" discussion on page 6.)

The different kinds of artistic styles are not mutually exclusive. For example, an artist's personal style may change dramatically

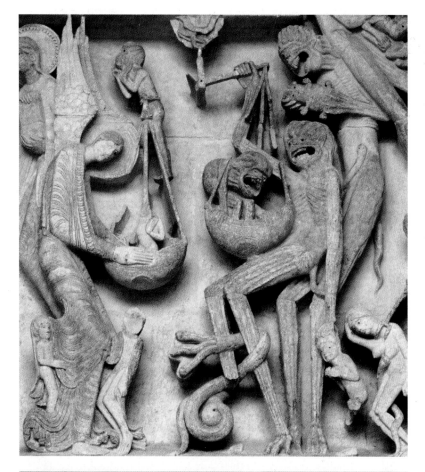

I-7 **GISLEBERTUS**, weighing of souls, detail of *Last Judgment* (FIG. 12-1), west tympanum of Saint-Lazare, Autun, France, ca. 1120–1135.

In this high relief portraying the weighing of souls on Judgment Day, Gislebertus used disproportion and distortion to dehumanize the devilish figure yanking on the scales of justice.

during a long career. Art historians then must distinguish among the different period styles of a particular artist, such as the "Rose Period" (FIG. 29-10A) and the "Cubist Period" (FIG. 29-14) of the prolific 20th-century artist Pablo Picasso.

What Is Its Subject? Another major concern of art historians is, of course, subject matter, encompassing the story or narrative; the scene presented; the action's time and place; the persons involved; and the environment and its details. Some artworks, such as modern abstract paintings (FIG. I-2), have neither traditional subjects nor even settings. The "subject" is the artwork itself—its colors, textures, composition, and size. But when artists represent people, places, or actions, viewers must identify these features to achieve a complete understanding of the work. Art historians traditionally separate pictorial subjects into various categories, such as religious, historical, mythological, *genre* (daily life), portraiture, *landscape* (a depiction of a place), *still life* (an arrangement of inanimate objects), and their numerous subdivisions and combinations.

Iconography—literally, the "writing of images"—refers both to the content, or subject, of an artwork, and to the study of content in art. By extension, it also includes the study of *symbols,* images that stand for other images or encapsulate ideas. In Christian art, two intersecting lines of unequal length or a simple geometric cross can serve as an emblem of the religion as a whole, symbolizing the cross of Jesus Christ's crucifixion. A symbol also can be a familiar object that an artist has imbued with greater meaning. A balance or scale, for example, may symbolize justice or the weighing of souls on Judgment Day (FIG. I-7).

Artists may depict figures with unique *attributes* identifying them. In Christian art, for example, each of the authors of the biblical Gospel books, the four evangelists (FIG. I-8), has a distinctive attribute. People can recognize Saint Matthew by the winged man associated with him, John by his eagle, Mark by his lion, and Luke by his ox.

Throughout the history of art, artists have used *personifications*—abstract ideas codified in human form. Because of the fame of the colossal statue set up in New York City's harbor in 1886, people everywhere visualize Liberty as a robed woman wearing a rayed crown and holding a torch. Four different personifications appear

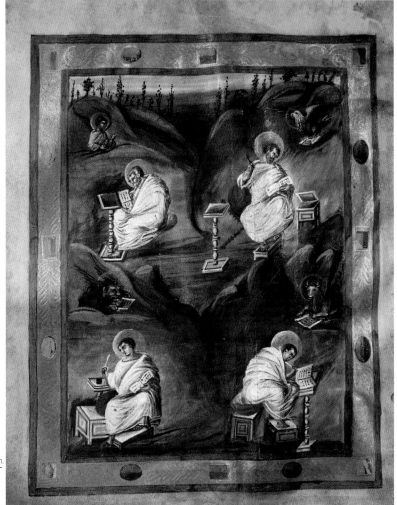

I-8 The four evangelists, folio 14 verso of the *Aachen Gospels,* ca. 810. Ink and tempera on vellum, $1' \times 9\frac{1}{2}''$. Domschatzkammer, Aachen.

Artists depict figures with attributes in order to identify them for viewers. The authors of the four Gospels have distinctive attributes—winged man (Matthew), eagle (John), lion (Mark), and ox (Luke).

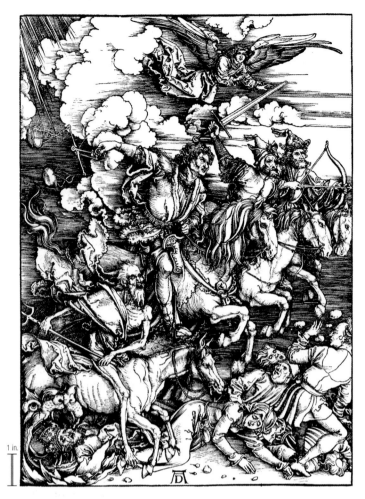

I-9 ALBRECHT DÜRER, *The Four Horsemen of the Apocalypse*, ca. 1498. Woodcut, 1′ 3$\frac{1}{4}$″ × 11″. Metropolitan Museum of Art, New York (gift of Junius S. Morgan, 1919).

Personifications are abstract ideas codified in human form. Here, Albrecht Dürer represented Death, Famine, War, and Pestilence as four men on charging horses, each one carrying an identifying attribute.

common (but by no means universal) today, in the history of art, countless works exist whose artists remain unknown. Because personal style can play a major role in determining the character of an artwork, art historians often try to attribute anonymous works to known artists. Sometimes they assemble a group of works all thought to be by the same person, even though none of the objects in the group is the known work of an artist with a recorded name. Art historians thus reconstruct the careers of artists such as the "Achilles Painter" (FIG. 5-58), the anonymous ancient Greek artist whose masterwork is a depiction of the hero Achilles. Scholars base their attributions on internal evidence, such as the distinctive way that an artist draws or carves drapery folds, earlobes, or flowers. It requires a keen, highly trained eye and long experience to become a *connoisseur,* an expert in assigning artworks to "the hand" of one artist rather than another. Attribution is subjective, of course, and ever open to doubt. For example, for a half-century through 2014, scholars involved with the Rembrandt Research Project debated attributions to the famous 17th-century Dutch painter Rembrandt van Rijn (FIG. 25-15)—and the debate continues today.

Sometimes a group of artists works in the same style at the same time and place. Art historians designate such a group as a *school.* "School" in this sense does not mean an educational institution or art academy. The term connotes only shared chronology, style, and geography. Art historians speak, for example, of the Dutch school of the 17th century and, within it, of subschools such as those of the cities of Haarlem, Utrecht, and Leyden.

Who Paid for It? The interest that many art historians show in attribution reflects their conviction that the identity of an artwork's maker is the major reason why the object looks the way it does. For them, personal style is of paramount importance. But in many times and places, artists had little to say about what form their work would take. They toiled in obscurity, doing the bidding of their *patrons,* those who paid them to make individual works or employed them on a continuing basis. The role of patrons in dictating the content and shaping the form of artworks is also an important subject of art historical inquiry.

In the art of portraiture, to name only one category of painting and sculpture, the patron has often played a dominant role in deciding how the artist represented the subject, whether that person was the patron or another individual, such as a spouse, son, or mother. Many Egyptian pharaohs (for example, FIG. 3-13) and some Roman emperors insisted that artists depict them with unlined faces and perfect youthful bodies no matter how old they were when portrayed. In these cases, the state employed the sculptors and painters, and the artists had no choice but to portray their patrons in the officially approved manner. This is why Augustus, who lived to age 76, looks so young in his portraits (FIG. I-10; compare FIG. 7-27). Although Roman emperor for more than 40 years, Augustus demanded that artists always represent him as a young, godlike head of state.

All modes of artistic production reveal the impact of patronage. Learned monks provided the themes for the sculptural decoration of medieval church portals (FIG. I-7). Renaissance princes and popes dictated the subject, size, and materials of artworks destined for display in buildings also constructed according to their specifications. An art historian could make a very long list of commissioned works, and it would indicate that patrons have had diverse tastes and needs throughout history and consequently have demanded different kinds of art. Whenever a patron contracts with an artist or architect to paint, sculpt, or build in a prescribed manner, personal style often becomes a very minor factor in the ultimate appearance

in *The Four Horsemen of the Apocalypse* (FIG. I-9) by German artist ALBRECHT DÜRER (1471–1528). The late-15th-century print is a terrifying depiction of the fateful day at the end of time when, according to the Bible's last book, Death, Famine, War, and Pestilence will annihilate the human race. Dürer personified Death as an emaciated old man with a pitchfork. Famine swings the scales for weighing human souls (compare FIG. I-7). War wields a sword, and Pestilence draws a bow.

Even without considering style and without knowing a work's maker, informed viewers can determine much about the work's period and provenance by iconographical and subject analysis alone. In *The Passion of Sacco and Vanzetti* (FIG. I-6), for example, the two coffins, the trio headed by an academic, and the robed judge in the background are all pictorial clues revealing the painting's subject. The work's date must be after the trial and execution (the terminus post quem), probably while the event was still newsworthy. And because the two men's deaths caused the greatest outrage in the United States, the painter–social critic was probably an American.

Who Made It? If Ben Shahn had not signed his painting of Sacco and Vanzetti, an art historian could still assign, or *attribute* (make an *attribution* of), the work to him based on knowledge of the artist's personal style. Although signing (and dating) works is quite

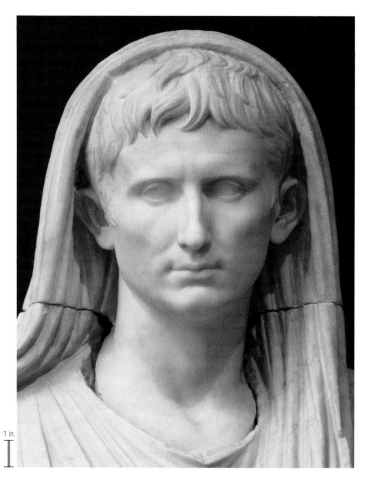

1 in.

I-10 **Head of the statue of Augustus as pontifex maximus, from Via Labicana, Rome, Italy, late first century BCE. Marble, statue 6′ 10″ high; detail 1′ 4½″. Palazzo Massimo alle Terme, Museo Nazionale Romano, Rome.**

Patrons frequently dictate the form that their portraits will take. Emperor Augustus demanded that he always be portrayed as a young, godlike head of state even though he lived to age 76.

of the painting, statue, or building. In these cases, the identity of the patron reveals more to art historians than does the identity of the artist or school. The portrait of Augustus illustrated here (FIG. I-10)—showing the emperor wearing a hooded *toga* in his official capacity as *pontifex maximus* (chief priest of the Roman state religion)—was the work of a virtuoso sculptor, a master wielder of hammer and chisel. But scores of similar portraits of this Roman emperor also exist today. They differ in quality but not in kind from this one. The patron, not the artist, determined the character of these artworks. Augustus's public image never varied. *Art through the Ages* highlights the involvement of patrons in the design and production of sculptures, paintings, and buildings throughout the text and in a series of boxed essays called *The Patron's Voice.*

The Words Art Historians Use

As in all fields of study, art history has its own specialized vocabulary consisting of hundreds of words, but certain basic terms are indispensable for describing artworks and buildings of any time and place. They make up the essential vocabulary of *formal analysis,* the visual analysis of artistic form, and are used whenever one talks or writes about art and architecture. Definitions and discussions of the most important art historical terms follow.

Form and Composition. *Form* refers to an object's shape and structure, either in two dimensions (for example, a portrait painted on canvas) or in three dimensions (such as a statue carved from a marble block). Two forms may take the same shape but differ in their color, texture, and other qualities. *Composition* refers to how an artist *composes* (organizes) forms in an artwork, either by placing shapes on a flat surface or by arranging forms in space.

Material and Technique. To create art forms, artists shape materials (pigment, clay, marble, gold, and many more) with tools (pens, brushes, chisels, and so forth). Each of the materials and tools available has its own potentialities and limitations. Part of all artists' creative activity is to select the *medium* and instrument most suitable to the purpose—or to develop new media and tools, such as bronze and concrete in antiquity and cameras and computers in modern times. The processes that artists employ, such as applying paint to canvas with a brush, and the distinctive, personal ways that they handle materials constitute their *technique.* Form, material, and technique interrelate and are central to analyzing any work of art.

Line. Among the most important elements defining an artwork's shape or form is *line.* A line can be understood as the path of a point moving in space, an invisible line of sight. More commonly, however, artists and architects make a line visible by drawing (or chiseling) it on a *plane,* a flat surface. A line may be very thin, wirelike, and delicate. It may be thick and heavy. Or it may alternate quickly from broad to narrow, the strokes jagged or the outline broken. When a continuous line defines an object's outer shape, art historians call it a *contour line.* All of these line qualities are present in Dürer's *Four Horsemen of the Apocalypse* (FIG. I-9). Contour lines define the basic shapes of clouds, human and animal limbs, and weapons. Within the forms, series of short broken lines create shadows and textures. An overall pattern of long parallel strokes suggests the dark sky on the frightening day when the world is about to end.

Color. Light reveals all colors. Light in the world of the painter and other artists differs from natural light. Natural light, or sunlight, is whole or *additive light.* As the sum of all the wavelengths composing the visible *spectrum,* it may be disassembled or fragmented into the individual colors of the spectral band. The painter's light in art—the light reflected from pigments and objects—is *subtractive light.* Paint pigments produce their individual colors by reflecting a segment of the spectrum while absorbing all the rest. Green pigment, for example, subtracts or absorbs all the light in the spectrum except that seen as green.

Hue is the property giving a color its name. Although the spectrum colors merge into each other, artists usually conceive of their hues as distinct from one another. Color has two basic variables—the apparent amount of light reflected and the apparent purity. A change in one must produce a change in the other. Some terms for these variables are *value* or *tonality* (the degree of lightness or darkness) and *intensity* or *saturation* (the purity of a color, its brightness or dullness).

Artists call the three basic colors—red, yellow, and blue—the *primary colors.* The *secondary colors* result from mixing pairs of primaries: orange (red and yellow), purple (red and blue), and green (yellow and blue). *Complementary colors* represent the pairing of a primary color and the secondary color created from mixing the two other primary colors—red and green, yellow and purple, and blue and orange. They "complement," or complete, each other, one absorbing the colors that the other reflects.

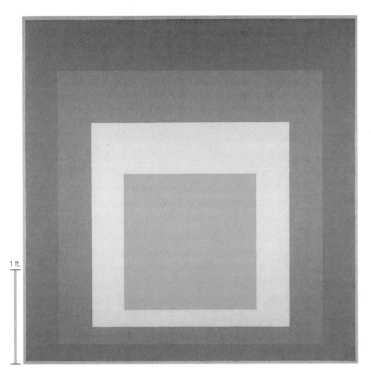

1 ft.

I-11 JOSEF ALBERS, *Homage to the Square: "Ascending,"* 1953. Oil on composition board, 3′ 7½″ × 3′ 7½″. Whitney Museum of American Art, New York.

Albers created hundreds of paintings using the same composition but employing variations in hue, saturation, and value in order to reveal the relativity and instability of color perception.

Artists can manipulate the appearance of colors, however. One artist who made a systematic investigation of the formal aspects of art, especially color, was JOSEF ALBERS (1888–1976), a German-born artist who emigrated to the United States in 1933. In connection with his studies, Albers created the series *Homage to the Square*—hundreds of paintings, most of which are color variations on the same composition of concentric squares, as in the illustrated example (FIG. I-11). The series reflected Albers's belief that art originates in "the discrepancy between physical fact and psychic effect."[1] Because the composition in most of these paintings remains constant, the works succeed in revealing the relativity and instability of color perception. Albers varied the hue, saturation, and value of each square in the paintings in this series. As a result, the sizes of the squares from painting to painting appear to vary (although they remain the same), and the sensations emanating from the paintings range from clashing dissonance to delicate serenity. Albers explained his motivation for focusing on color juxtapositions:

> They [the colors] are juxtaposed for various and changing visual effects. . . . Such action, reaction, interaction . . . is sought in order to make obvious how colors influence and change each other; that the same color, for instance—with different grounds or neighbors—looks different. . . . Such color deceptions prove that we see colors almost never unrelated to each other.[2]

Texture. The term *texture* refers to the quality of a surface, such as rough or shiny. Art historians distinguish between true texture—that is, the tactile quality of the surface—and represented texture, as when painters depict an object as having a certain texture even though the pigment is the true texture. Sometimes artists combine different materials of different textures on a single surface, juxtaposing paint with pieces of wood, newspaper, fabric, and so forth. Art historians refer to this mixed-media technique as *collage.* Texture is, of course, a key determinant of any sculpture's character. People's first impulse is usually to handle a work of sculpture—even though museum signs often warn "Do not touch!" Sculptors plan for this natural human response, using surfaces varying in texture from rugged coarseness to polished smoothness. Textures are often intrinsic to a material, influencing the type of stone, wood, plastic, clay, or metal that a sculptor selects.

Space, Mass, and Volume. *Space* is the bounded or boundless "container" of objects. For art historians, space can be the real three-dimensional space occupied by a statue or a vase or contained within a room or courtyard. Or space can be *illusionistic,* as when painters depict an image (or illusion) of the three-dimensional spatial world on a two-dimensional surface.

Mass and *volume* describe three-dimensional objects and space. In both architecture and sculpture, mass is the bulk, density, and weight of matter in space. Yet the mass need not be solid. It can be the exterior form of enclosed space. Mass can apply to a solid Egyptian pyramid or stone statue; to a church, synagogue, or mosque (architectural shells enclosing sometimes vast spaces); and to a hollow metal statue or baked clay pot. Volume is the space that mass organizes, divides, or encloses. It may be a building's interior spaces, the intervals between a structure's masses, or the amount of space occupied by a three-dimensional object such as a statue, pot, or chair. Volume and mass describe both the exterior and interior forms of a work of art—the forms of the matter of which it is composed and the spaces immediately around the work and interacting with it.

Perspective and Foreshortening. *Perspective* is one of the most important pictorial devices for organizing forms in space. Throughout history, artists have used various types of perspective to create an illusion of depth or space on a two-dimensional surface. The French painter CLAUDE LORRAIN (1600–1682) employed several perspective devices in *Embarkation of the Queen of Sheba* (FIG. I-12), a painting of a biblical episode set in a 17th-century European harbor with an ancient Roman ruin in the left foreground—an irrationally anachronistic combination that the art historian can explain only in the context of the cultural values of the artist's time and place. In Claude's painting, the figures and boats on the shoreline are much larger than those in the distance, because decreasing the size of an object makes it appear farther away. The top and bottom of the port building at the painting's right side are not parallel horizontal lines, as they are in a real building. Instead, the lines converge beyond the structure, leading the viewer's eye toward the hazy, indistinct sun on the horizon. These three perspective devices—the reduction of figure size, the convergence of diagonal lines, and the blurring of distant forms—have been familiar features of Western art since they were first employed by the ancient Greeks. It is important to state, however, that all kinds of perspective are only pictorial conventions, even when one or more types of perspective may be so common in a given culture that people accept them as "natural" or as "true" means of representing the natural world.

These perspective conventions are by no means universal. In *Waves at Matsushima* (FIG. I-13), a Japanese seascape painting on

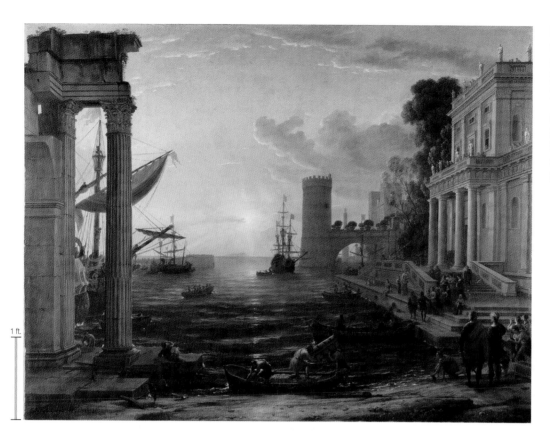

I-12 CLAUDE LORRAIN, *Embarkation of the Queen of Sheba*, 1648. Oil on canvas, 4' 10" × 6' 4". National Gallery, London.

To create the illusion of a deep landscape, Claude Lorrain employed perspective, reducing the size of and blurring the most distant forms. All diagonal lines converge on a single point.

a six-part folding screen, OGATA KORIN (1658–1716) ignored these Western "tricks" for representing deep space on a flat surface. A Western viewer might interpret the left half of Korin's composition as depicting the distant horizon, as in the French painting, but the sky is an unnatural gold, and the clouds filling that unnaturally colored sky are almost indistinguishable from the waves below. The rocky outcroppings decrease in size with distance, but all are in sharp focus, and there are no shadows. The Japanese artist was less concerned with locating the boulders and waves and clouds in space than with composing shapes on a surface, playing the swelling curves of waves and clouds against the jagged contours of the rocks. Neither the French nor the Japanese painting can be said to project "correctly" what viewers "in fact" see. One painting is not a "better" picture of the world than the other. The European and Asian artists simply approached the problem of picture making differently.

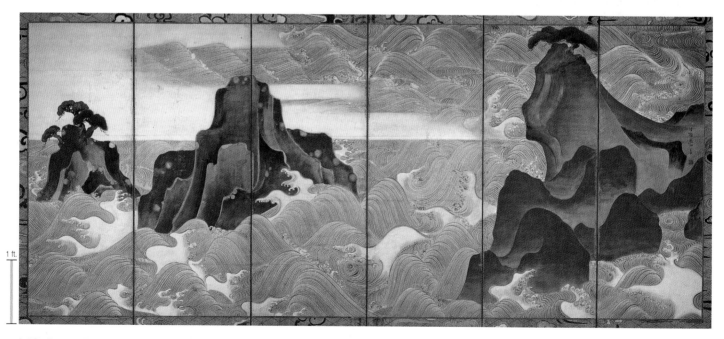

I-13 OGATA KORIN, *Waves at Matsushima*, Edo period, Japan, ca. 1700–1716. Six-panel folding screen, ink, colors, and gold leaf on paper, 4' 11⅛" × 12' 7⅞". Museum of Fine Arts, Boston (Fenollosa-Weld Collection).

Asian artists rarely employed Western perspective (FIG. I-12). Korin was more concerned with creating an intriguing composition of shapes on a surface than with locating boulders, waves, and clouds in space.

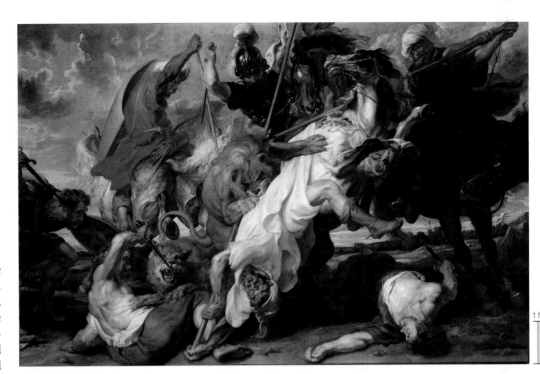

I-14 PETER PAUL RUBENS, *Lion Hunt*, 1617–1618. Oil on canvas, 8′ 2″ × 12′ 5″. Alte Pinakothek, Munich.

Foreshortening—the representation of a figure or object at an angle to the picture plane—is a common device in Western art for creating the illusion of depth. Foreshortening is a type of perspective.

Artists also represent single figures in space in varying ways. When Flemish artist PETER PAUL RUBENS (1577–1640) painted *Lion Hunt* (FIG. I-14), he used *foreshortening* for all the hunters and animals—that is, he represented their bodies at angles to the picture plane. When in life one views a figure at an angle, the body appears to contract as it extends back in space. Foreshortening is a kind of perspective. It produces the illusion that one part of the body is farther away than another, even though all the painted forms are on the same plane. Especially noteworthy in *Lion Hunt* are the gray horse at the left, seen from behind with the bottom of its left rear hoof facing viewers and most of its head hidden by its rider's shield, and the fallen hunter at the painting's lower right corner, whose barely visible legs and feet recede into the distance.

The artist who carved the portrait of the ancient Egyptian official Hesire (FIG. I-15) for display in Hesire's tomb did not employ foreshortening. That artist's purpose was to present the various human body parts as clearly as possible, without overlapping. The lower part of Hesire's body is in profile to give the most complete view of the legs, with both the heel and toes of each foot visible. The frontal torso, however, enables viewers to see its full shape, including both shoulders, equal in size, as in nature. (Compare the shoulders of the hunter on the gray horse or those of the fallen hunter in *Lion Hunt*'s left foreground.) The result—an "unnatural" 90-degree twist at the waist—provides a precise picture of human body parts, if not an accurate picture of how a standing human figure really looks. Rubens and the Egyptian sculptor used very different means of depicting forms in space. Once again, neither is the "correct" manner.

Proportion and Scale. *Proportion* concerns the relationships (in terms of size) of the parts of persons, buildings, or objects. People can judge "correct proportions" intuitively ("that statue's head seems the right size for the body"). Or proportion can be a mathematical relationship between the size of one part of an artwork or building and the other parts within the work. Proportion in art implies using a *module*, or basic unit of measure. When an artist or architect uses a formal system of proportions, all parts of a building, body, or other entity will be fractions or multiples of the module. A module might be the diameter of a *column*, the height of a human head, or any other component whose dimensions can be multiplied or divided to determine the size of the artwork's or building's other parts.

In certain times and places, artists have devised *canons*, or systems, of "correct" or "ideal" proportions for representing human figures, constituent parts of buildings, and so forth. In ancient Greece, many sculptors formulated canons of proportions so strict and all-encompassing that they calculated the size of every body part in advance, even the fingers and toes, according to mathematical ratios.

Proportional systems can differ sharply from period to period, culture to culture, and artist to artist. Part of the task that art history

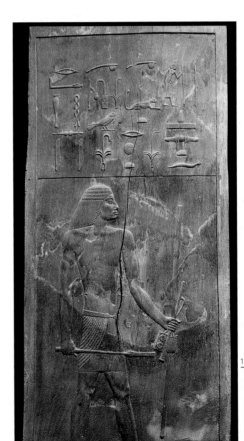

I-15 Hesire, relief from his tomb at Saqqara, Egypt, Dynasty III, ca. 2650 BCE. Wood, 3′ 9″ high. Egyptian Museum, Cairo.

Egyptian artists combined frontal and profile views to give a precise picture of the parts of the human body, as opposed to depicting how an individual body appears from a specific viewpoint.

students face is to perceive and adjust to these differences. In fact, many artists have used disproportion and distortion deliberately for expressive effect. In the medieval French depiction of the weighing of souls on Judgment Day (FIG. I-7), the devilish figure yanking down on the scale has distorted facial features and stretched, lined limbs with animal-like paws for feet. Disproportion and distortion make him appear "inhuman," precisely as the sculptor intended.

In other cases, artists have used disproportion to focus attention on one body part (often the head) or to single out a group member (usually the leader). These intentional "unnatural" discrepancies in proportion constitute what art historians call *hierarchy of scale,* the enlarging of elements considered the most important. On the bronze altar from Nigeria illustrated here (FIG. I-1), the sculptor varied the size of each figure according to the person's social status. Largest, and therefore most important, is the Benin king, depicted twice, each time flanked by two smaller attendant figures and shown wearing a multistrand coral necklace emblematic of his high office. The king's head is also disproportionately large compared to his body, consistent with one of the Benin ruler's praise names: Great Head.

One problem that students of art history—and professional art historians too—confront when studying illustrations in art history books is that although the relative sizes of figures and objects in a painting or sculpture are easy to discern, it is impossible to determine the absolute size of the work reproduced because they all are printed at approximately the same size on the page. Readers of *Art through the Ages* can learn the exact size of all artworks from the dimensions given in the captions and, more intuitively, from the scales positioned at the lower left or right corner of each illustration.

Carving and Casting. Sculptural technique falls into two basic categories, *subtractive* and *additive. Carving* is a subtractive technique. The final form is a reduction of the original mass of a block of stone, a piece of wood, or another material. Wood statues were once tree trunks, and stone statues began as blocks pried from mountains. The unfinished marble statue illustrated here (FIG. I-16) by renowned Italian artist MICHELANGELO BUONARROTI (1475–1564) clearly reveals the original shape of the stone block. Michelangelo thought of sculpture as a process of "liberating" the statue within the block. All sculptors of stone or wood cut away (subtract) "excess material." When they finish, they "leave behind" the statue—in this example, a twisting nude male form whose head Michelangelo never freed from the stone block.

In additive sculpture, the artist builds up the forms, usually in clay around a framework, or *armature.* Or a sculptor may fashion a *mold,* a hollow form for shaping, or *casting,* a fluid substance such as bronze or plaster. The ancient Greek sculptor who made the bronze statue of a warrior found in the sea near Riace, Italy, cast the head (FIG. I-17) as well as the limbs, torso, hands, and feet (FIG. 5-36)

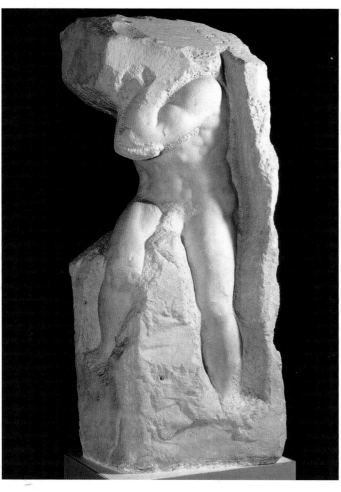

1 ft.

I-16 MICHELANGELO BUONARROTI, unfinished statue, 1527–1528. Marble, 8′ 7½″ high. Galleria dell'Accademia, Florence.

Carving a freestanding figure from stone or wood is a subtractive process. Michelangelo thought of sculpture as a process of "liberating" the statue contained within the block of marble.

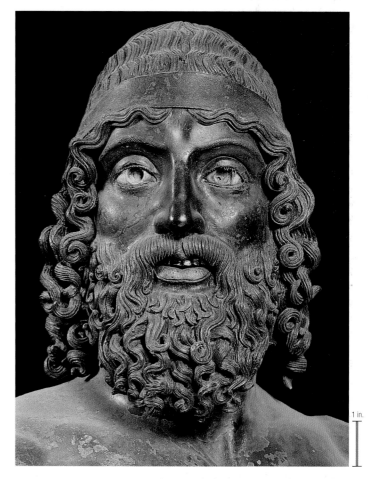

1 in.

I-17 Head of a warrior, detail of a statue (FIG. 5-36) from the sea off Riace, Italy, ca. 460–450 BCE. Bronze, full statue 6′ 6″ high. Museo Archeologico Nazionale, Reggio Calabria.

The sculptor of this life-size statue of a bearded Greek warrior cast the head, limbs, torso, hands, and feet in separate molds, then welded the pieces together and added the eyes in a different material.

in separate molds and then *welded* them together (joined them by heating). Finally, the artist added features, such as the pupils of the eyes (now missing), in other materials. The warrior's teeth are silver, and his lower lip is copper.

Relief Sculpture. *Statues* and *busts* (head, shoulders, and chest) that exist independent of any architectural frame or setting and that viewers can walk around are *freestanding sculptures,* or *sculptures in the round,* whether the artist produced the piece by carving (FIG. I-10) or casting (FIG. I-17). In *relief sculpture,* the subjects project from the background but remain part of it. In *high-relief* sculpture, the images project boldly. In some cases, such as the medieval weighing-of-souls scene (FIG. I-7), the *relief* is so high that not only do the forms cast shadows on the background, but some parts are even in the round, which explains why some pieces—for example, the arms of the scales—broke off centuries ago. In *low-relief,* or *bas-relief,* sculpture, such as the portrait of Hesire (FIG. I-15), the projection is slight. Artists can produce relief sculptures, as they do sculptures in the round, either by carving or casting. The altar from Benin (FIG. I-1) is an example of bronze-casting in high relief (for the figures on the cylindrical altar) as well as in the round (for the king and his two attendants on the top).

Architectural Drawings. Buildings are groupings of enclosed spaces and enclosing masses. People experience architecture both visually and by moving through and around it, so they perceive architectural space and mass together. These spaces and masses can be represented graphically in several ways, including as plans, sections, elevations, and cutaway drawings.

A *plan,* essentially a map of a floor, shows the placement of a structure's masses and, therefore, the spaces they circumscribe and enclose. A *section,* a kind of vertical plan, depicts the placement of the masses as if someone cut through the building along a plane. Drawings showing a theoretical slice across a structure's width are *lateral sections.* Those cutting through a building's length are *longitudinal sections.* Illustrated here are the plan and lateral section of Beauvais Cathedral (FIG. I-18), which readers can compare with the photograph of the church's *choir* (FIG. I-3). The plan shows the

choir's shape and the location of the *piers* dividing the *aisles* and supporting the *vaults* above, as well as the pattern of the crisscrossing vault *ribs.* The lateral section shows not only the interior of the choir with its vaults and tall *stained-glass* windows but also the structure of the roof and the form of the exterior *flying buttresses* holding the vaults in place.

Other types of architectural drawings appear throughout this book. An *elevation* drawing is a head-on view of an external or internal wall. A *cutaway* combines in a single drawing an exterior view with an interior view of part of a building.

This overview of the art historian's vocabulary is not exhaustive, nor have artists used only painting, drawing, sculpture, and architecture as media over the millennia. Ceramics, jewelry, textiles, photography, and computer graphics are just some of the numerous other arts. All of them involve highly specialized techniques described in distinct vocabularies. As in this introductory chapter, new terms are in *italics* when they first appear. Many are defined and discussed again in greater detail in the boxed essays called *Architectural Basics* and *Materials and Techniques.* In addition, the comprehensive glossary at the end of the book contains definitions of all italicized terms.

Art History and Other Disciplines

By its very nature, the work of art historians intersects with the work of others in many fields of knowledge, not only in the humanities but also in the social and natural sciences. Today, art historians must go beyond the boundaries of what the public and even professional art historians of previous generations traditionally considered the specialized discipline of art history. In short, art historical research has always been interdisciplinary in nature, but never more than in the 21st century. To cite one example, in an effort to

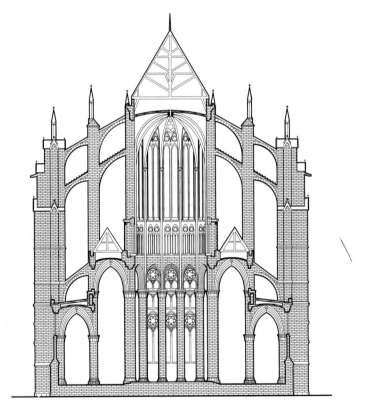

I-18 Plan (*left*) and lateral section (*right*) of Beauvais Cathedral, Beauvais, France, rebuilt after 1284.

Architectural drawings are indispensable aids for the analysis of buildings. Plans are maps of floors, recording the structure's masses. Sections are vertical "slices" across a building's width or length.

unlock the secrets of a particular statue, an art historian might conduct archival research hoping to uncover new documents shedding light on who paid for the work and why, who made it and when, where it originally stood, how people of the time viewed it, and a host of other questions. Realizing, however, that the authors of the written documents often were not objective recorders of fact but observers with their own biases and agendas, the art historian may also use methodologies developed in such fields as literary criticism, philosophy, sociology, and gender studies to weigh the evidence that the documents provide.

At other times, rather than attempting to master many disciplines at once, art historians band together with other specialists in multidisciplinary inquiries. Art historians might call in chemists to date an artwork based on the composition of the materials used, or might ask geologists to determine which quarry furnished the stone for a particular statue. X-ray technicians might be enlisted in an attempt to establish whether a painting is a forgery. Of course, art historians often reciprocate by contributing their expertise to the solution of problems in other disciplines. A historian, for example, might ask an art historian to determine—based on style, material, iconography, and other criteria—if any of the portraits of a certain king date after his death. Such information would help establish the ruler's continuing prestige during the reigns of his successors. Some portraits of Augustus (FIG. I-10), the founder of the Roman Empire, postdate his death by decades, even centuries, as do the portraits of several deceased U.S. presidents on coins and paper currency produced today. The study of art history, then, demands collaboration among scholars, and never more than in today's "global village."

DIFFERENT WAYS OF SEEING

The history of art can be a history of artists and their works, of styles and stylistic change, of materials and techniques, of images and themes and their meanings, and of contexts and cultures and patrons. The best art historians analyze artworks from many viewpoints. But no art historian (or scholar in any other field), no matter how broad-minded in approach and no matter how experienced, can be truly objective. Like the artists who made the works illustrated and discussed in this book, art historians are members of a society, participants in its culture. How can scholars (and museum visitors and travelers to foreign locales) comprehend cultures unlike their own? They can try to reconstruct the original cultural contexts of artworks, but they are limited by their distance from the thought patterns of the cultures they study and by the obstructions to understanding—the assumptions, presuppositions, and prejudices peculiar to their own culture—that their own thought patterns raise. Art historians may reconstruct a distorted picture of the past because of culture-bound blindness.

A single instance underscores how differently people of diverse cultures view the world and how various ways of seeing can result in sharp differences in how artists depict the world. Illustrated here are two contemporaneous portraits of a 19th-century Maori chieftain (FIG. I-19)—one by an Englishman, JOHN HENRY SYLVESTER (active early 19th century), and the other by the New Zealand chieftain himself, TE PEHI KUPE (d. 1829). Both reproduce the chieftain's facial *tattoo*. The European artist (FIG. I-19, *left*) included the head and shoulders and downplayed the tattooing. The tattoo pattern is one aspect of the likeness among many, no more or less important than the chieftain's European attire. Sylvester also recorded his subject's momentary glance toward the right and the play of light on his hair, fleeting aspects having nothing to do with the figure's identity.

By contrast, Te Pehi Kupe's self-portrait (FIG. I-19, *right*)—made during a trip to Liverpool, England, to obtain European arms to take back to New Zealand—is not a picture of a man situated in space and bathed in light. Rather, it is the chieftain's statement of the supreme importance of the tattoo design announcing his rank among his people. Remarkably, Te Pehi Kupe created the tattoo patterns from memory, without the aid of a mirror. The splendidly composed insignia, presented as a flat design separated from the body and even from the head, is Te Pehi Kupe's image of himself. Only by understanding the cultural context of each portrait can art historians hope to understand why either representation appears as it does.

As noted at the outset, the study of the context of artworks and buildings is one of the central concerns of art historians. *Art through the Ages* seeks to present a history of art and architecture that will help readers understand not only the subjects, styles, and techniques of paintings, sculptures, buildings, and other art forms created in all parts of the world during 40 millennia but also their cultural and historical contexts. That story now begins.

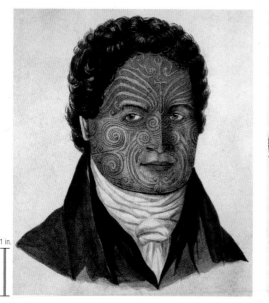

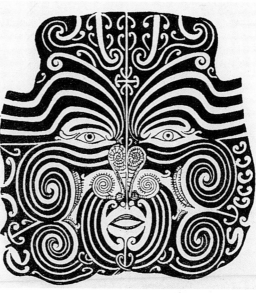

I-19 *Left:* JOHN HENRY SYLVESTER, *Portrait of Te Pehi Kupe*, 1826. Watercolor, $8\frac{1}{4}'' \times 6\frac{1}{4}''$. National Library of Australia, Canberra (Rex Nan Kivell Collection). *Right:* TE PEHI KUPE, *Self-Portrait*, 1826. From Leo Frobenius, *The Childhood of Man: A Popular Account of the Lives, Customs and Thoughts of the Primitive Races* (Philadelphia: J. B. Lippincott, 1909), 35, fig. 28.

These strikingly different portraits of the same Maori chief reveal the different ways of seeing by a European artist and an Oceanic one. Understanding the cultural context of artworks is vital to art history.

1 in.

▼ 1-1a The species of animals depicted in the cave paintings of France and Spain are not among those that Paleolithic humans typically consumed as food. The meaning of these paintings is the subject of debate.

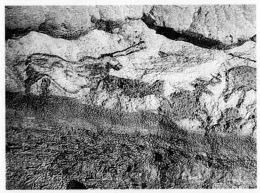

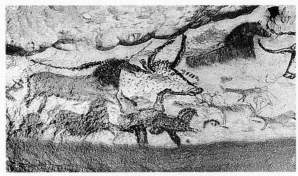

▲ 1-1b The Lascaux animals are inconsistent in size and move in different directions. Some are colored silhouettes; others are outline drawings. They were probably painted at different times by different painters.

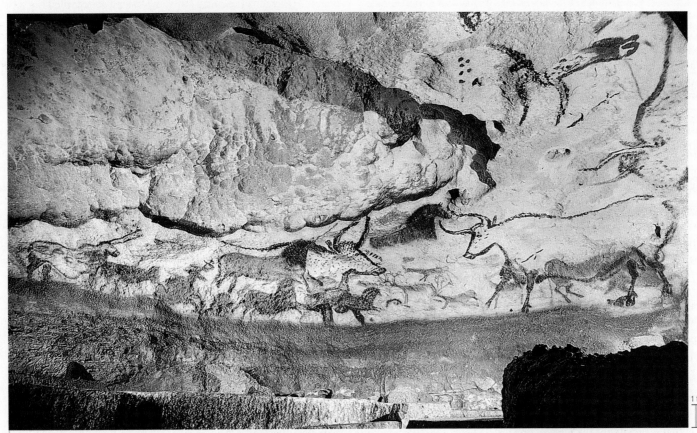

1 ft.

1-1 **Left wall of the Hall of the Bulls in the cave at Lascaux, France, ca. 16,000–14,000 BCE. Largest bull 11′ 6″ long.**

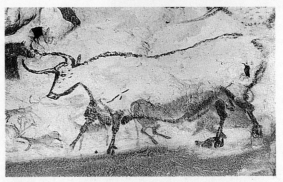

▲ 1-1c Prehistoric painters consistently represented animals in strict profile, the only view showing the head, body, tail, and all four legs. But at Lascaux, both horns are included to give a complete picture of the bull.

ART IN THE STONE AGE /1

The Dawn of Art

The Old Stone Age, or *Paleolithic* period (from the Greek *paleo,* "old," and *lithos,* "stone"), which began around 40,000 BCE at the latest, was arguably the most important era in the entire history of art. It was then that humans invented the concept of recording the world around them in pictures, often painted on or carved into the walls of caves.

The oldest and best-known painted caves are in southern France and northern Spain (MAP 1-1). The most famous is the cave at Lascaux. More than 17,000 years ago, prehistoric painters covered many of the walls of the cave with images of animals. The main chamber (FIG. 1-1), nicknamed the Hall of the Bulls, is an unusually large space and easily accessible, but many of the paintings at Lascaux and in other caves are almost impossible to reach. Even in the Hall of the Bulls, the people who congregated there could only have viewed the paintings in the flickering light of primitive lamps. The representations of animals cannot have been merely decorative, but what meaning they carried for those who made and viewed them is fiercely debated. Bulls and horses, the most commonly depicted species, were not diet staples in the Old Stone Age. Why, then, did the painters choose to represent these particular animals? Many explanations have been put forward, but there is no generally accepted answer to the question.

By contrast, art historians have reached secure conclusions about the working methods and conceptual principles of the world's first artists by closely studying the Lascaux paintings and others like them. The immediate impression that a modern viewer gets of a rapidly moving herd is almost certainly false. The "herd" consists of several different species of animals of various sizes moving in different directions. Also, two fundamentally different approaches to picture making are on display. Many of the animals are colored silhouettes, whereas others are outline drawings. These differences in style and technique suggest that different painters created the images at different times, perhaps over the course of generations. The Hall of the Bulls is not one painting but many, created by many different painters.

Nonetheless, at Lascaux and elsewhere for thousands of years, all painters depicted animals in the same way: in strict profile, the only view of these beasts wherein the head, body, tail, and all four legs are visible. Often, as at Lascaux, the bulls' horns are shown from the front, not in profile, because two horns are part of the concept "bull." Only much later in the history of art did painters become concerned with how to depict animals and people from a fixed viewpoint or develop an interest in recording the environment around the figures. The paintings created at the dawn of art are in many ways markedly different in kind from all that followed.

PALEOLITHIC ART

Humankind originated in Africa in the very remote past. From that great continent also has come the earliest evidence of human recognition of pictorial images in the natural environment—a three-million-year-old pebble (FIG. 1-1A) found at Makapansgat in South Africa. The first examples of what people generally call "art" are much more recent, however. They date to around 40,000 to 30,000 BCE during the Paleolithic period. This era was of unparalleled importance in human history and in the history of art. It was during the Old Stone Age that humans first consciously manufactured pictorial images. The works that the earliest artists produced are remarkable not simply for their existence but also for their astonishing variety. They range from simple shell necklaces to human and animal forms in ivory, clay, and stone to life-size *mural* (wall) paintings and sculptures in caves. During the Paleolithic period, humankind went beyond the *recognition* of human and animal forms in the natural environment to the *representation* (literally, the presenting again—in different and substitute form—of something observed) of humans and animals. The immensity of this achievement cannot be overstated.

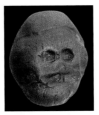

⊿1-1A Pebble resembling a face, Makapansgat, ca. 3,000,000 BCE.

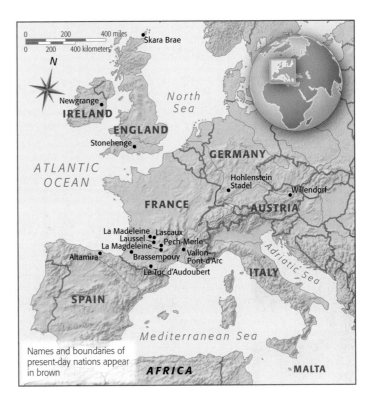

MAP 1-1 Stone Age sites in Europe.

Africa

Some of the earliest paintings yet discovered come from Africa, where, as noted, the first humans evolved. The most important Paleolithic African artworks were discovered in a cave in Namibia near the southern tip of the continent (MAP 19-1).

Apollo 11 Cave.   Between 1969 and 1972, scientists working in the Apollo 11 Cave in Namibia found seven fragments of what are usually referred to as painted stone plaques, but are really fragments that fell from the cave's ceiling. The approximate date of the charcoal from the archaeological layer containing the Namibian fragments is 28,000 BCE. The paintings depict several recognizable images of animals, including a striped beast, possibly a zebra, and a rhinoceros. Of special interest is the example illustrated here (FIG. 1-2), which seems to be a feline with human feet, one of many examples in Paleolithic art of composite human-animals. In all of the Apollo 11 paintings, the forms are carefully rendered, and all of the animals are represented in the identical way (see "How to Represent an Animal," page 17).

Europe

Even older than the Namibian cave paintings—and far better known—are some of the first sculptures and paintings of western Europe (MAP 1-1), although examples of great antiquity have also been found in Southeast Asia.

Hohlenstein-Stadel.   One of the oldest sculptures ever discovered is an extraordinary ivory statuette (FIG. 1-3), which may date back as far as 40,000 BCE. Found in 1939 in fragments inside a cave at Hohlenstein-Stadel in Germany, the statuette, carved from the tusk of a woolly mammoth, is nearly a foot tall—a truly huge image for its era. Long thought to have been created about 30,000 years ago, the recent discovery of hundreds of additional tiny fragments has pushed the date back about 10,000 years based on *radiocarbon dating* of the bones found in the same excavation level. (Radiocarbon dating, an important technology used in archaeological research, is a measure of the rate of degeneration of carbon 14 in organic materials.) The statuette thus testifies to a very early date for the development of the human brain, because the subject of

ART IN THE STONE AGE

40,000–20,000 BCE	20,000–9000 BCE	9000–5000 BCE	5000–2300 BCE
Early Paleolithic	**Later Paleolithic and Mesolithic**	**Early Neolithic**	**Later Neolithic**
▪ Hunter-gatherers create the first sculptures and paintings, long before the invention of writing ▪ The works range in scale from tiny figurines, such as the *Venus of Willendorf*, to almost life-size paintings and relief sculptures, such as the murals in the Chauvet Cave	▪ Painters cover the walls and ceilings of caves at Altamira and Lascaux with profile representations of animals ▪ Sculptors carve images of nude women on the walls of the cave at La Magdeleine	▪ In Anatolia and Mesopotamia, the earliest villages take shape and agriculture begins ▪ Neolithic builders erect a pillared shrine at Göbekli Tepe and stone towers and fortification walls at Jericho ▪ Sculptors fashion large-scale painted plaster human figures at Ain Ghazal ▪ Painters depict coherent narratives at Çatal Höyük	▪ Neolithic builders in Ireland and Britain erect megalithic passage graves and henges at Newgrange, Stonehenge, and elsewhere ▪ The stone temples of Malta incorporate sophisticated curved and rectilinear forms

How to Represent an Animal

Like every artist in every age in every medium, the Paleolithic painter of the feline-animal (FIG. 1-2) found in the Apollo 11 Cave in Namibia had to answer two questions before beginning work: *What* shall be my subject? and *How* shall I represent it? In Paleolithic art, the almost universal answer to the first question was an animal. Bison, horse, woolly mammoth, and ibex are the most common. In fact, Paleolithic painters

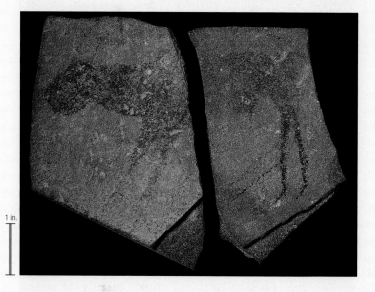

and sculptors depicted humans infrequently, and men almost never. In equally stark contrast to today's world, there was also agreement on the best answer to the second question. During at least the first 35,000 years of the history of art, artists represented virtually every animal in every painting in the same manner: in strict profile. Why?

The profile is the only view of an animal in which the head, body, tail, and all four legs are visible. The frontal view conceals most of the body, and a three-quarter view shows neither the front nor side fully. Only the profile view is completely informative about the animal's shape, and that is why Stone Age painters universally chose it.

A very long time passed before artists placed any premium on "variety" or "originality" either in subject choice or in representational manner. These are quite modern notions in the history of art. The aim of the earliest painters was to create a convincing image of their subject, a kind of pictorial definition of the animal capturing its very essence, and only the profile view met their needs.

1-2 Feline with human feet, from the Apollo 11 Cave, Namibia, ca. 28,000 BCE. Charcoal on stone, $5'' \times 4\frac{1}{4}''$. State Museum of Namibia, Windhoek.

As in almost all paintings for thousands of years, in this very early example from Africa the painter represented the animal in strict profile so that the head, body, tail, and all four legs are clearly visible.

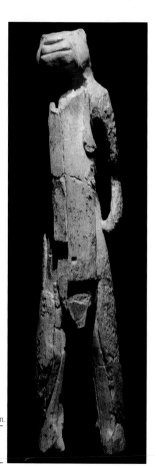

1-3 Human with feline (lion?) head, from Hohlenstein-Stadel, Germany, ca. 40,000–35,000 BCE. Woolly mammoth ivory, $11\frac{5}{8}''$ high. Ulmer Museum, Ulm.

One of the world's oldest preserved sculptures is this large ivory figure of a human with a feline head. It is uncertain whether the work depicts a composite creature or a human wearing an animal mask.

the work is not something that the Paleolithic sculptor could see and copy but something that existed only in the artist's vivid imagination. The ivory figurine represents a human (whether male or female cannot be determined) with a feline (lion?) head. Composite creatures with animal heads and human bodies (and vice versa) are familiar in the art of ancient Mesopotamia and Egypt (compare, for example, FIGS. 2-7 and 3-1). In those civilizations, surviving texts usually enable historians to name the figures and

describe their role in religion and mythology. But for Stone Age representations, no one knows what their makers had in mind. Some scholars identify the animal-headed humans as sorcerers, whereas others describe them as magicians wearing masks. Similarly, some researchers have interpreted Paleolithic representations of human-headed animals as humans wearing animal skins. Others think that the images of composite animal-humans reproduce the visions seen by *shamans* during trances (see "The Meaning of Paleolithic Art," page 21). In the absence of any contemporaneous written explanations—this was a time before writing, before (or pre-) history—experts and amateurs alike can only speculate on the purpose and function of statuettes such as the one from Hohlenstein-Stadel.

Art historians are certain, however, that these sculptures were important to those who created them, because manufacturing an ivory figure, especially one a foot tall, was a complicated process. First, the hunter or the sculptor had to remove the tusk from the dead animal by cutting into the tusk where it joined the head. Then the sculptor cut the ivory to the desired size and rubbed it into its approximate final shape with sandstone. Finally, the carver used a sharp stone blade to shape the body, limbs, and head, and a stone *burin* (a pointed *engraving* tool) to *incise* (scratch or engrave) lines into the surfaces, as on the Hohlenstein-Stadel creature's arms. Experts estimate that this large figurine required about 400 hours (about two months of uninterrupted working days) of skilled work.

Willendorf. The composite feline-human from Germany is exceptional both for its very early date and its subject. The vast majority of Stone Age sculptures depict either animals or humans. In the earliest

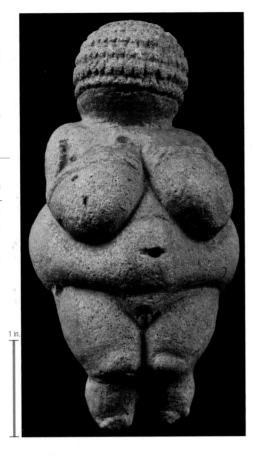

1-4 Nude woman (*Venus of Willendorf*), from Willendorf, Austria, ca. 28,000–25,000 BCE. Limestone, 4¼″ high. Naturhistorisches Museum, Vienna.

The anatomical exaggerations in this tiny figurine from Willendorf are typical of Paleolithic representations of women, whose child-bearing capabilities ensured the survival of the species.

art, humankind consists almost exclusively of women as opposed to men. Paleolithic painters and sculptors almost invariably showed them nude, although historians generally assume that during the Ice Age, both women and men wore garments covering parts of their bodies. When archaeologists first encountered these statuettes of women, they dubbed them "Venuses" after the Greco-Roman goddess of beauty and love, whom later artists usually depicted nude. The nickname is inappropriate and misleading. Indeed, it is doubtful that the Paleolithic figurines represent deities of any kind.

One of the oldest and most famous Paleolithic female images is the tiny limestone figurine of a woman that long ago became known as the *Venus of Willendorf* (FIG. 1-4) after its *findspot* (place of discovery) in Austria. Its cluster of almost ball-like shapes is unusual, the result in part of the sculptor's response to the natural shape of the stone selected for carving. The anatomical exaggeration has suggested to many observers that this and similar statuettes served as fertility images. But other Paleolithic figurines depicting women with far more slender proportions exist, and the meaning of these images is as elusive as everything else about the world's earliest art. Yet the preponderance of female over male figures seems to indicate a preoccupation with women, whose child-bearing capabilities ensured the survival of the species.

One thing at least is clear: the sculptor of the Willendorf woman did not aim for *naturalism* (fidelity to nature) in shape and proportion. As is true of most Paleolithic figures, this statuette has no facial features. A similar but even smaller ivory figurine found in 2008 in a cave at Hohle Fels, near Ulm, Germany, contemporaneous with or perhaps even several thousand years older than the Hohlenstein-Stadel statuette, lacks any head at all. The ivory head (FIG. 1-4A) of a woman from Brassempouy, France, is a notable exception. The carver of the Willendorf figurine suggested only a mass of curly hair or, as some researchers have argued, a hat woven from plant fibers—evidence for the art of textile manufacture at a very early date. In either

case, the emphasis is on female anatomy. The breasts of the Willendorf woman are enormous, far larger in proportion than the tiny forearms and hands resting on them. The carver also took pains to scratch into the stone the outline of the pubic triangle. Sculptors often omitted this detail in other early figurines, leading some scholars to question the function of these figures as fertility images. Whatever the purpose of these statuettes, the makers' intent seems to have been to represent not a specific woman but the female form.

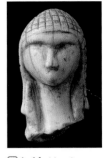

⏏**1-4A** Head of a woman(?), Brassempouy, ca. 25,000–20,000 BCE.

Laussel. Probably later in date than the Willendorf statuette is a female figure (FIG. 1-5) from Laussel in France. The Willendorf and Hohlenstein-Stadel figures are *sculptures in the round* (*freestanding sculptures*). The Laussel woman is one of the earliest *relief sculptures* known. The sculptor employed a stone *chisel* to cut into the relatively flat surface of a large rock in order to create an image projecting from the background. Today, the Laussel relief is on display in a museum, divorced from its original context, a detached piece of what once was a much more imposing work. When discovered, the Laussel woman (who is about

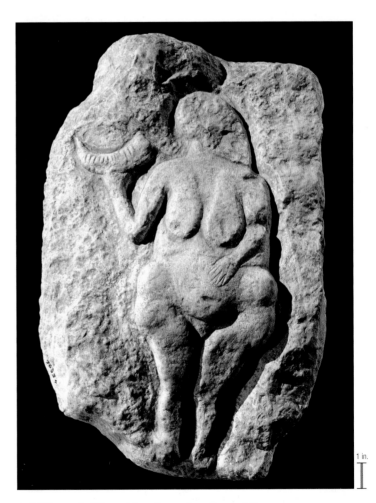

1-5 Woman holding a bison horn, from Laussel, France, ca. 25,000–20,000 BCE. Painted limestone, 1′ 6″ high. Musée d'Aquitaine, Bordeaux.

One of the oldest known relief sculptures depicts a woman who holds a bison horn and whose left arm draws attention to her belly. Scholars continue to debate the meaning of the gesture and the horn.

$1\frac{1}{2}$ feet tall, more than four times larger than the Willendorf statuette) was part of a great stone block measuring about 140 cubic feet. The carved block stood in the open air in front of a Paleolithic rock shelter. Rock shelters were a common type of dwelling for early humans, along with huts and the mouths of caves. The Laussel relief is one of many examples of open-air art in the Old Stone Age. The popular notions that early humans

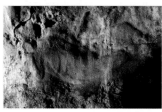

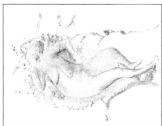

① **1-5A** Reclining woman, La Magdeleine, ca. 12,000 BCE.

dwelled exclusively in caves and that all Paleolithic art comes from mysterious dark caverns are false. Reliefs depicting nude women do, however, occur inside Old Stone Age caves. Perhaps the most interesting is the pair of reclining nude women (FIG. 1-5A) on the wall of a corridor in a cave at La Magdeleine, France.

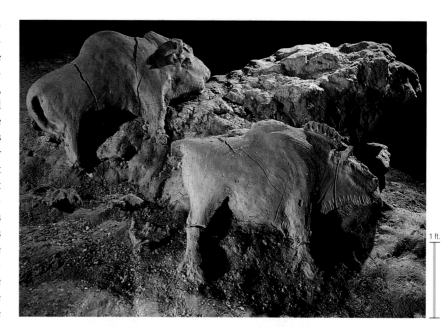

1-6 Two bison, reliefs in the cave at Le Tuc d'Audoubert, France, ca. 15,000–10,000 BCE. Clay, right bison $2' \frac{7}{8}''$ long.

Representations of animals are far more common than those of humans in Paleolithic art. The sculptor built up these clay bison using a stone spatula-like smoothing tool and fingers to shape the details.

After chiseling out the female body and incising the details with a sharp burin, the Laussel sculptor applied red ocher, a naturally colored mineral, to the body. (Traces of red ocher coloration also remain on parts of the Willendorf woman's body.) Contrary to modern misconceptions, ancient artists usually painted stone sculptures (compare FIG. 5-63A). The Laussel woman has the same bulbous forms as the earlier Willendorf figurine, with a similar exaggeration of the breasts, abdomen, and hips. The head is once again featureless, but the arms have taken on greater importance. The left arm draws attention to the midsection and pubic area, and the raised right hand holds what most scholars identify as a bison horn with 13 incised lines. Debate continues, however, about the meaning of the horn and its incisions as well as the gesture of the left hand.

Le Tuc d'Audoubert. Paleolithic sculptors sometimes created reliefs by building up forms out of clay instead of cutting into stone blocks or cave walls. Sometime 12,000 to 17,000 years ago in the low-ceilinged circular space at the end of a succession of cave chambers at Le Tuc d'Audoubert, a master sculptor modeled a pair of bison (FIG. 1-6) in clay against a large, irregular freestanding rock. The two bison, like the much older painted feline (FIG. 1-2) from the Apollo 11 Cave, are in strict profile. Each is about 2 feet long. They are among the largest Paleolithic sculptures known. The sculptor brought the clay from elsewhere in the cave complex and used both hands to form the overall shape of the animals. The next step was to smooth the surfaces with a spatula-like tool. Finally, the sculptor used fingers to shape the eyes, nostrils, mouths, and manes. The cracks in the two reliefs resulted from the drying process and probably appeared within days of the clay sculptures' completion.

La Madeleine. As already noted, sculptors fashioned the ivory tusks of woolly mammoths into human (FIG. 1-4A), animal, and composite human-animal (FIG. 1-3) forms from very early times. Stone Age carvers also used antlers as a sculptural medium. The bison (FIG. 1-7) found at La Madeleine in France is what remains

of an *atlatl* (a device that enables hunters to throw a spear farther and with greater velocity) carved from a reindeer antler. Although only 4 inches long, the engraved antler is more detailed than the two much larger bison at Le Tuc d'Audoubert. The sculptor used a sharp burin to incise lines for the Madeleine bison's mane, horns, eye, ear, nostrils, mouth, tongue, and facial hair. Especially interesting is the engraver's decision to represent the bison with its head turned and licking its flank. The small size and irregular shape of the antler, rather than a desire to record a characteristic anecdotal activity, may have been the primary motivation for this space-saving device.

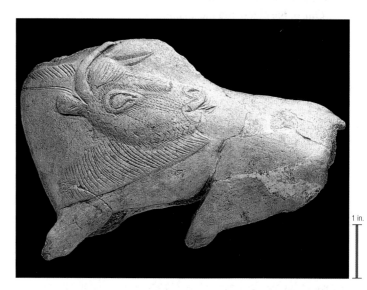

1-7 Bison licking its flank, fragmentary atlatl, from La Madeleine, France, ca. 12,000 BCE. Reindeer antler, $4\frac{1}{8}''$ long. Musée d'Archéologie nationale, Saint-Germain-en-Laye.

This fragment of an atlatl was carved from a reindeer antler. The sculptor turned the bison's head a full 180 degrees to maintain the profile view and incised the details with a stone burin.

Painting in the Dark

The caves of Altamira (FIG. 1-8), Lascaux (FIGS. 1-1, 1-9A, and 1-10), and other sites in prehistoric Europe are a few hundred to several thousand feet long. They are often choked, sometimes almost impassably, by mineral deposits, such as stalactites and stalagmites. Far inside these caverns, well removed from the cave mouths that early humans often chose for habitation, painters sometimes made pictures on the walls and ceilings. How did the world's first *muralists* paint bison and other animals on surfaces far from any source of natural light? What tools and materials did the Paleolithic painters of France and Spain use, and how did they make them?

To illuminate the cave walls and ceilings while working, Paleolithic painters lit fires on cave floors and used torches as well as stone lamps filled with marrow or fat, with a wick, perhaps of moss. For drawing, they used chunks of charcoal and red and yellow ocher. For painting, they ground these same natural materials into powders that they mixed with water before applying. Recent analyses of the pigments used show that Paleolithic painters employed many different minerals, attesting to a technical sophistication surprising at so early a date.

Large, flat stones served as *palettes*. The painters made brushes from reeds, bristles, or twigs and may have used a blowpipe of reed or hollow bone to spray pigments on out-of-reach surfaces. Some caves have natural ledges on the rock walls on which the painters could have stood in order to reach the upper surfaces of the naturally formed chambers and corridors. One gallery wall in the Lascaux cave complex has holes that once probably anchored a scaffold made of saplings lashed together.

Despite the difficulty of making the tools and pigments, modern attempts at replicating the techniques of Paleolithic painting have demonstrated that skilled workers could cover large surfaces with images in less than a day.

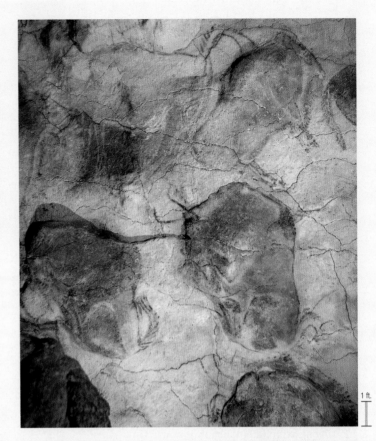

1 ft.

1-8 Bison, detail of a painted ceiling in the cave at Altamira, Spain, ca. 13,000–11,000 BCE. Standing bison 5′ 2½″ long.

Paleolithic painters used stone lamps to provide light in the dark caves. They made brushes from reeds and twigs or used reed or bone blowpipes to spray ground ocher pigments onto out-of-reach surfaces.

Whatever the reason, it is noteworthy that the sculptor turned the neck a full 180 degrees to maintain the strict profile that Stone Age sculptors and painters insisted on for the sake of clarity and completeness (see "How to Represent an Animal," page 17).

Altamira. The works examined here thus far, whether portable or fixed to rocky outcroppings or cave walls, are all small, with the exception of the paintings in the Lascaux Hall of the Bulls (FIG. 1-1). The Lascaux animals dwarf all the other illustrated examples, as do the other "herds" of painted animals roaming the walls and ceilings of other caves in southern France and northern Spain, where some of the most spectacular examples of Paleolithic art have been discovered. An amateur archaeologist accidentally found the first known examples of cave paintings at Altamira, Spain, in 1879. Don Marcelino Sanz de Sautuola (1831–1888) was exploring a cavern on his estate where he had previously collected specimens of flint and carved bone. Maria, his young daughter, was with him when they reached a chamber some 85 feet from the cave's entrance. Because it was dark (see "Painting in the Dark," above) and the ceiling of the debris-filled chamber was only a few inches above the father's head, the child was the first to notice, due to her lower vantage point, the shadowy forms of bison (FIG. 1-8, a detail of a much larger painting approximately 60 feet long).

Sanz de Sautuola was certain that the paintings in his cave dated to prehistoric times. Professional archaeologists, however, doubted the authenticity of these works, and at the 1880 Congress on Prehistoric Archaeology in Lisbon, they officially dismissed the Altamira paintings as forgeries. But by the close of the century, explorers had discovered other caves with painted walls partially covered by mineral deposits that would have taken thousands of years to accumulate. This finally persuaded skeptics that the world's oldest paintings were of an age far more remote than anyone had imagined. Examples of Paleolithic painting now have been found at more than 200 Spanish and French sites. Nonetheless, art historians still regard painted caves as rare because the images in them, even if they number in the hundreds, span a period of some 20,000 to 30,000 years.

The bison at Altamira are 13,000 to 14,000 years old, but the painters of Paleolithic Spain approached the problem of representing an animal in essentially the same way as the painter of the Namibian murals (FIG. 1-2), who worked in Africa some 15,000 years before. Every one of the Altamira bison is in profile, whether alive and standing or curled up on the ground—probably dead, although some scholars dispute this. (One suggestion is that these bison are giving birth.) To maintain the profile in the latter case, the painter had to adopt a viewpoint above the animal, looking down, rather than the view of a person standing on the ground.

The Meaning of Paleolithic Art

Ever since the discovery in 1879 of the first cave paintings, scholars have wondered why the hunters of the Old Stone Age decided to cover the surfaces of dark caverns with animal images such as those found at Lascaux (FIG. 1-1), Altamira (FIG. 1-8), and Pech-Merle (FIG. 1-9). Researchers have proposed various theories, including that the painted and engraved animals were mere decoration, but this explanation cannot account for the inaccessibility of many of the representations. In fact, the remote locations of many images, and indications that the caves were used for centuries, are precisely why many experts have suggested that prehistoric peoples attributed magical properties to the images they painted and sculpted. According to this argument, by confining animals to the surfaces of their cave walls, Paleolithic communities believed they were bringing the beasts under their control. Some scholars have even hypothesized that rituals or dances were performed in front of the images and that these rites served to improve the luck of the community's hunters. Others have suggested that the animal representations may have served as teaching tools to instruct new hunters about the character of the various species that they would encounter, or even were targets for spears.

By contrast, other experts have argued that the magical purpose of the paintings and reliefs was not to facilitate the *destruction* of bison and other species. Instead, they believe that the world's first painters and sculptors created animal images to assure the *survival* of the herds on which Paleolithic peoples depended for their food supply and for their clothing. A central problem for both the hunting-magic and food-creation theories is that the staple foods of Old Stone Age diets did not include the animals most frequently portrayed. For example, faunal remains show that the Altamirans ate red deer, not bison.

Other scholars have sought to reconstruct an elaborate belief system based on the cave paintings and sculptures, suggesting, for example, that the animals are deities or ancestors that Paleolithic humans revered. Some researchers have equated certain species with men and others with women and postulated various meanings for the dots, squares, and other signs accompanying some images.

Almost all of these theories have been discredited over time, but the idea persists that the images in the Paleolithic caves are tied to magic. This would explain, for example, the numerous cases of images painted over older images: when the magic no longer worked, a new image was created.

Most researchers now believe that the images of animals—and, more rarely, of composite human-animals—in the Paleolithic caves of France and Spain are records of the visions seen by shamans during ritual trances. The many instances of painted and sculpted images that were inspired by natural surface configurations, as at Pech-Merle (FIG. 1-9) and La Magdeleine (FIG. 1-5A), are consistent with the idea that at least some of the shamanic visions were prompted by unique rock formations in the caves themselves and that the murals and reliefs are pictures of those visions.

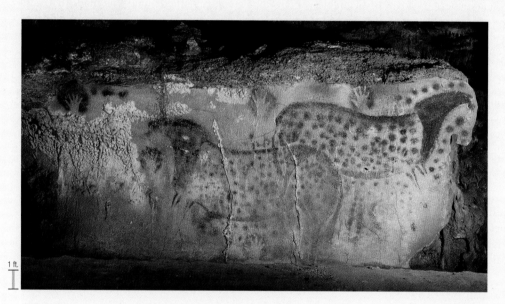

1-9 Spotted horses and negative hand imprints, wall painting in the cave at Pech-Merle, France, ca. 23,000–22,000 BCE. 11′ 2″ long.

The purpose and meaning of Paleolithic art are uncertain, but the fact that one of the horse heads at Pech-Merle was inspired by the natural rock formation suggests a connection to shamanic visions.

Modern critics often refer to the Altamira animals as a "group" of bison, but that is very likely a misnomer. The several bison in FIG. 1-8 do not stand on a common *ground line* (a painted or carved baseline on which figures appear to stand in paintings and reliefs), unlike many of the animals at Lascaux (FIG. 1-1), nor do they share a common orientation. They seem almost to float above viewers' heads, like clouds in the sky. And the painter provided an "aerial view" of the dead(?) bison, whereas the observer views the others from a position on the ground. The painting has no setting, no background, no indication of place. *Where* the animals are or how they relate to one another, if at all, was of no concern to the Paleolithic painters of Altamira. Instead, several *separate* images of bison adorn the ceiling, perhaps painted at different times spanning generations, and each is as complete and informative as possible.

Pech-Merle.   No one knows why animals play a central, indeed a nearly exclusive, role in the caves at Altamira, Lascaux (FIG. 1-1), and elsewhere in Paleolithic Europe. That these paintings of different animal species did have meaning to Stone Age peoples cannot, however, be doubted. In fact, signs consisting of checks, dots, squares, or other arrangements of lines often accompany the pictures of animals, and these must have communicated messages understood by the Stone Age men and women who viewed them. In short, the cave paintings may document the earliest forms of what we call writing—an invention usually attributed to the Sumerians (see "Writing," page 32).

Painted human hands also are common. At Pech-Merle (FIG. 1-9), the hands accompany representations of spotted horses. (The "spots" also surround the horses and may not be spots at all but stones or signs.) Most of the painted hands in Paleolithic caves are "negative." That is, the painter placed one hand against the wall and then brushed or blew or spat pigment around it. Occasionally, the painter dipped a hand in the pigment and then pressed it against the wall, leaving a "positive" imprint. Like the abstract motifs, these handprints must have served a purpose. Some researchers consider them "signatures" of cult or community members or, less likely, of individual painters. One clue is that some of the painted hands have incomplete fingers, leading some scholars to postulate that the fingers were folded back and that these are hand signals (often used by hunters) to convey specific meanings, unfortunately indecipherable today but underscoring that Paleolithic painting is not simple "art for art's sake" (see "The Meaning of Paleolithic Art," page 21).

The mural paintings at Pech-Merle also furnish some insight into the reasons that Paleolithic peoples chose subjects for specific places in a cave. One of the horses (at the right in FIG. 1-9) may have been inspired by the rock formation in the wall surface resembling a horse's head and neck. Old Stone Age painters and sculptors frequently and skillfully used the naturally irregular surfaces of caves to help give the illusion of real presence to their forms, as they did at La Magdeleine (FIG. 1-5A) and at Altamira (FIG. 1-8), where many of the bison paintings cover bulging rock surfaces.

Lascaux. Perhaps the most impressive collection of Paleolithic animal paintings is in the Hall of the Bulls (FIG. 1-1) at Lascaux. The large chamber, away from the cave entrance and mysteriously dark, has good acoustics, and would have provided an excellent setting for the kinds of rituals that many archaeologists assume took place in front of the paintings. One noteworthy aspect of the Lascaux murals is that they exhibit, side by side, the two basic approaches to drawing and painting found repeatedly in the history of art—silhouettes and outlines—indicating that different painters created these pictures, probably at different times. The Lascaux bulls also show a convention of representing horns in what art historians call *twisted perspective*, or a *composite view*, because viewers see the heads in profile but the horns from the front. Thus the painter's approach

is not strictly or consistently optical (seen from a fixed viewpoint). Rather, the approach is descriptive of the fact that cattle have two horns. Two horns are part of the concept "bull." In strict optical-perspective profile, only one horn would be visible, but to paint the animal in that way would amount to an incomplete definition of it.

Paintings of animals appear throughout the cave complex at Lascaux, including in the so-called Axial Gallery, which features a representation of a running, possibly pregnant horse (FIG. 1-9A) surrounded by what may be arrows or traps. But the most perplexing painting at Lascaux and perhaps in all Paleolithic art is deep in a well

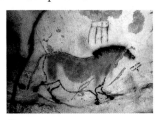

⚲ **1-9A** Running horse, Lascaux, ca. 16,000–14,000 BCE.

shaft. In this mural (FIG. 1-10), man (as opposed to woman) makes one of his earliest appearances in the history of art. At the left, and moving to the left, is a now-extinct woolly rhinoceros. Beneath its tail are two rows of three dots of uncertain significance. At the right is a bison, also facing left but with less realistic proportions, probably the work of someone else. The second painter nonetheless successfully suggested the bristling rage of the animal, whose bowels are hanging from it in a heavy coil. Between the two beasts is a bird-faced (masked?) man (compare FIG. 1-3) with outstretched arms and hands having only four fingers. The painter depicted the man with far less care and detail than either animal, but made the hunter's gender explicit by the prominent penis. The position of the man is ambiguous. Is he wounded or dead or merely tilted back and unharmed? Do the bird-topped atlatl and spear belong to him? Is it he or the rhinoceros that gravely wounded the bison—or neither? Which animal, if either, has knocked the man down, if indeed he is on the ground? Are these three images related at all? Modern viewers can be sure of nothing, but if the painters placed the figures beside each other to tell a story, this is evidence for the creation of a complex narrative *composition* (how the motifs are arranged on the surface) involving humans and animals at a much earlier date than

1-10 Woolly rhinoceros, wounded man, and disembow-eled bison, painting in the well of the cave at Lascaux, France, ca. 16,000–14,000 BCE. Bison 3′ 4½″ long.

If these paintings of two animals and a bird-faced (masked?) man deep in a Lascaux well shaft depict a hunting scene, they constitute the earliest example of narrative art ever discovered.

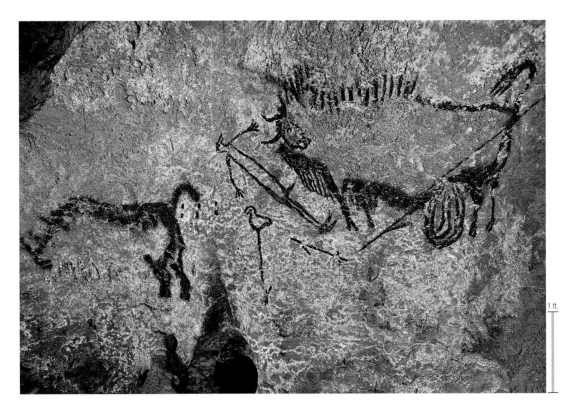

1 ft.

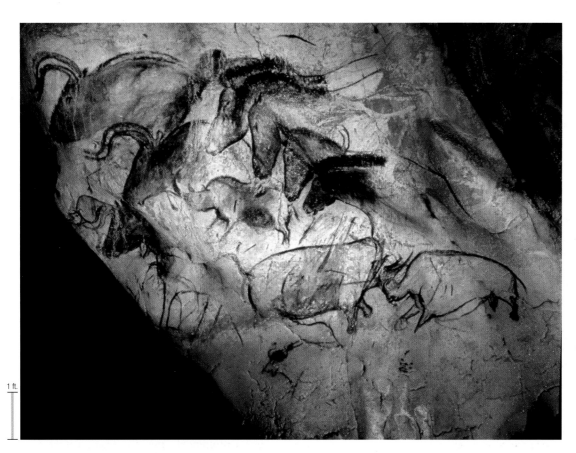

1 ft.

1-11 Aurochs, horses, and woolly rhinoceroses, wall painting in the Chauvet Cave, Vallon-Pont-d'Arc, France, ca. 34,000–32,000 BCE. Right rhinoceros 3′ 4″ long.

Radiocarbon dating of the Chauvet Cave indicates that its paintings are the oldest known, even though they exhibit advanced features, such as overlapping animal horns and, possibly, narrative content.

anyone had imagined only a few generations ago. Yet it is important to remember that even if the painter(s) intended to tell a story, very few people would have been able to "read" it. The mural, in a deep shaft, is very difficult to reach and could have been viewed only in flickering lamplight.

Chauvet Cave.　One of the most spectacular archaeological finds of the past century poses a problem of a different kind. In December 1994, a French team led by Jean-Marie Chauvet discovered Paleolithic mural paintings (FIG. 1-11) in a cave at Vallon-Pont-d'Arc. To determine the date of the Chauvet Cave paintings, French scientists used radiocarbon dating of the charcoal in the black pigments. The tests revealed that the mural paintings dated around 34,000 to 32,000 BCE and were much older than any previously discovered.

This unexpectedly early date immediately forced scholars to reevaluate the scheme of "stylistic development" from simple to more complex forms that historians of Stone Age art had accepted for decades. In the Chauvet Cave, in contrast to Lascaux (FIG. 1-1), the painters depicted the horns of the aurochs (extinct long-horned wild oxen) naturalistically, one behind the other, not in the twisted perspective normally used in Paleolithic art. Moreover, although the two woolly rhinoceroses at the lower right of FIG. 1-11 may be independent paintings, they appear to attack each other, suggesting that the painter intended a narrative. This would be another "first" in either painting or sculpture. If the paintings are more than twice as old as those of Lascaux and Altamira (FIG. 1-8), the assumption that Paleolithic art "evolved" from simple to more sophisticated representations is wrong. The issues raised by the Chauvet Cave exemplify the frustration—and the excitement—of studying the art of an age so remote that almost nothing remains and almost every new find causes art historians to reevaluate what they had previously taken for granted.

NEOLITHIC ART

Around 9000 BCE, the ice that covered much of northern Europe during the Paleolithic period melted as the climate warmed. The sea level rose more than 300 feet, separating England from continental Europe, and Spain from Africa. The reindeer migrated north, and the woolly mammoth disappeared. The Paleolithic gave way to a transitional period, usually called the *Mesolithic* (Middle Stone Age).

Then, for several thousand years at different times in different parts of the globe, a great new age, the *Neolithic* (New Stone Age), dawned.* Human beings began to domesticate plants and animals and to settle in fixed abodes. Their food supply assured, many groups changed from hunters to herders to farmers and finally to townspeople. Wandering hunters settled down to organized community living in villages surrounded by cultivated fields.

The basis for the conventional division of the Stone Age into three periods is the development of stone implements. However, a different kind of distinction may be made between an age of food gathering and an age of food production.

In this scheme, the Paleolithic period corresponds roughly to the age of food gathering. Intensified food gathering and the taming of the dog are the hallmarks of the Mesolithic period. In the Neolithic period, agriculture and livestock became humankind's major food sources. The transition to the Neolithic was nothing less than a revolution. It occurred first in Anatolia and Mesopotamia.

---

*This chapter treats the Neolithic art of Europe, Anatolia, and Mesopotamia only. For the Neolithic art of Africa, see Chapter 19; for Asia, see Chapters 15, 16, and 17.

Anatolia and Mesopotamia

The remains of the oldest known settled communities lie in the grassy foothills of the Antilebanon, Taurus, and Zagros mountains in present-day Turkey, Syria, Iraq, and Iran (MAP 1-2). These regions provided the necessary preconditions for the development of agriculture. Species of native plants, such as wild wheat and barley, were plentiful, as were herds of animals (goats, sheep, and pigs) that could be domesticated. Sufficient rain occurred for the raising of crops. When village farming life was well developed, some settlers, attracted by the greater fertility of the soil and perhaps also by the need to find more land for their rapidly growing populations, moved into the valleys and deltas of the Tigris and Euphrates Rivers.

In addition to systematic agriculture, the new village societies of the Neolithic Age originated weaving, metalworking, pottery, and counting and recording with clay tokens. These innovations spread with remarkable speed throughout Anatolia (roughly equivalent to present-day Turkey) and Mesopotamia (primarily present-day Syria and Iraq). Settled farming communities, such as Jarmo in Iraq and Çatal Höyük in southern Anatolia, date to the mid-seventh millennium BCE. The remarkable fortified town of Jericho, before whose walls the biblical Joshua appeared thousands of years later, is even

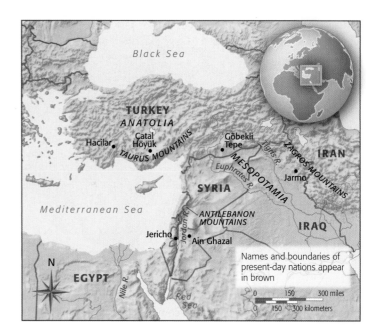

MAP 1-2 Neolithic sites in Anatolia and Mesopotamia.

ART AND SOCIETY

The Neolithic Temple at Göbekli Tepe

One of the most important archaeological discoveries of the past few decades is the Anatolian Neolithic site of Göbekli Tepe in southeastern Turkey near Sanliurfa. Excavated since 1995 by the German Archaeological Institute in cooperation with the Sanliurfa Museum, the hilltop site appears to have been a religious, or at least a ceremonial, center rather than a habitation site.

The excavated area consists of about 20 circular structures with monolithic T-shaped stone pillars (FIG. 1-12) set at right angles into the walls. At the center of the rooms are two additional similarly shaped pillars. The pillars served as roof supports. There are no doorways, and visitors to the site probably entered the circular rooms through the roof.

Many of the pillars are covered with shallow reliefs depicting a wide array of animals, birds, and insects. Some of the reliefs include human arms and hands. The interpretation of the representations is uncertain, but the animals and other forms must be connected to the rituals that took place at the site.

If the German archaeologists' dating and interpretation are correct, Göbekli Tepe overturns one of the most basic assumptions about prehistoric societies. It now appears possible, even likely, that hunter-gatherers erected stone temples long before farmers established permanent village communities. The history of art and architecture—and of civilization—must now be rewritten.

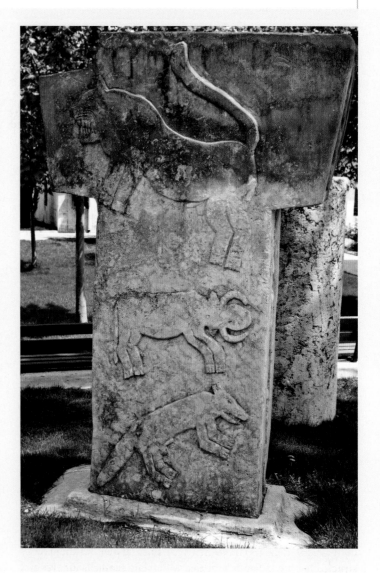

1-12 T-shaped stone pillar with animal reliefs, from Göbekli Tepe, Turkey, ca. 9000 BCE. Sanliurfa Museum, Sanliurfa.

Göbekli Tepe appears to be the world's oldest religious complex, comprising about 20 circular structures whose roofs were supported by T-shaped pillars decorated with a wide variety of animals, birds, and insects.

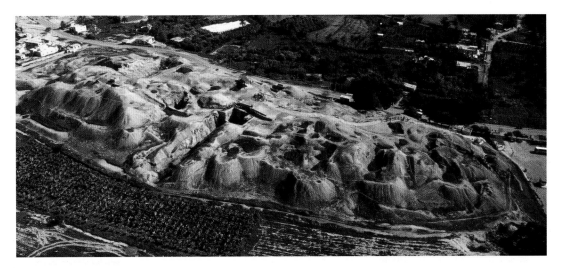

Protecting Neolithic Jericho were 5-foot-thick walls and at least one tower 30 feet high and 33 feet in diameter constructed of stone laid without mortar— an outstanding technological achievement.

older. Archaeologists are constantly uncovering surprises, and the exploration of new sites each year is compelling them to revise their views about the emergence of Neolithic society. Especially noteworthy are the ongoing excavations at Göbekli Tepe in southeastern Turkey (see "The Neolithic Temple at Göbekli Tepe," page 24). Of those sites known for some time, Jericho, Ain Ghazal, and Çatal Höyük together probably offer the most representative picture of the rapid and exciting transformation of human society and of art during the Neolithic period.

Jericho. By 7000 BCE, agriculture was well established from Anatolia to ancient Palestine and Iran. Its advanced state by this date presupposes a long development. Indeed, the very existence of a major settlement such as Jericho gives strong support to this assumption. Jericho, situated on a plateau in the Jordan River Valley with an unfailing spring, was the site of a small village as early as the ninth millennium BCE. This village underwent spectacular development around 8000 BCE, when the inhabitants established a new Neolithic settlement (FIG. 1-13) covering about 10 acres. Its mudbrick houses sat on round or oval stone foundations and had roofs of branches covered with earth.

As Jericho's wealth grew, the need for protection against marauding nomads resulted in the first known permanent stone fortifications. By 7500 BCE, a wide rock-cut ditch and a 5-foot-thick wall surrounded the town, which probably had a population exceeding 2,000. Set into the circuit wall, which has been preserved to a height of almost 13 feet, was a 30-foot-tall circular tower (FIG. 1-13, *bottom center*) constructed of roughly shaped stones laid without mortar (*dry masonry*). Almost 33 feet in diameter at the base, the tower has an inner stairway leading to its summit. Not enough of the site has been excavated to determine whether this tower was solitary or one of several similar towers forming a complete defense system. In either case, a stone structure as large as the Jericho tower was a tremendous technological achievement and a testimony to the Neolithic builders' ability to organize a significant workforce.

Sometime around 7000 BCE, Jericho's inhabitants abandoned their fortified site, but new settlers arrived in the early seventh millennium and established a farming community of rectangular mudbrick houses on stone foundations with plastered and painted floors and walls. Several of the excavated buildings contained statuettes of animals and women and seem to have served as shrines. The new villagers buried their dead beneath the floors of their houses with the craniums detached from their skeletons and their features reconstructed in plaster. Subtly modeled with inlaid seashells for eyes and

painted hair, these reconstructed heads appear strikingly lifelike. One head (FIG. 1-14) features a painted mustache, distinguishing it from the others. The Jericho skulls constitute the world's earliest known "portrait gallery," but the artists' intention was certainly not portraiture in the modern sense. The plastered skulls must have served a ritualistic purpose. The community of several hundred Neolithic farmers who occupied Jericho at this time honored and

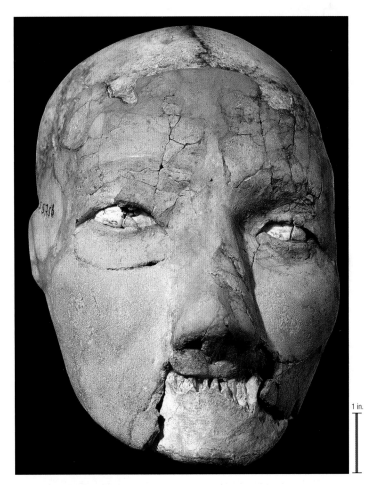

1 in.

1-14 Human skull with restored features, from Jericho, ca. 7200–6700 BCE. Features modeled in plaster, painted, and inlaid with seashells. Life-size. Archaeological Museum, Amman.

Neolithic Jericho farmers removed the skulls of their dead before burial, modeled them with plaster, and inlaid the eyes to create lifelike "portraits" of their ancestors, whom they may have worshiped.

1-15 Human figure, from Ain Ghazal, Jordan, ca. 6750–6250 BCE. Plaster, painted and inlaid with bitumen, 3′ 5⅜″ high. Musée du Louvre, Paris.

The dozens of large painted plaster statuettes (some with two heads and with details added in paint or inlaid with bitumen) found at Ain Ghazal are the earliest large-scale sculptures known.

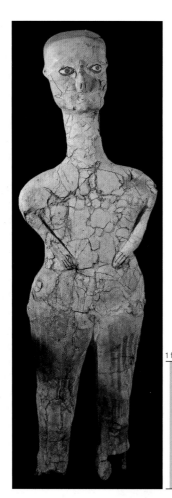

perhaps worshiped their ancestors as intercessors between the living and the world beyond. They may have believed that the dead could exert power over the living and that they had to offer sacrifices to their ancestors to receive favorable treatment. These skulls were probably the focus of rites in honor of those ancestors.

Ain Ghazal. A second important Neolithic settlement in ancient Palestine was Ain Ghazal, near the modern Jordanian capital of Amman. Occupied from around 7200 to 5000 BCE, the site featured houses of irregularly shaped stones with plastered floors and walls painted red. The most striking finds, however, are two caches containing three dozen plaster statuettes (FIG. 1-15) and busts, some with two heads, datable to ca. 6500 BCE. The sculptures, which appear to have been ritually buried, are white plaster built up over a core of reeds and twine, with black bitumen, a tarlike substance, for the pupils of the eyes. Some of the figures have painted clothing. Only rarely did the sculptors indicate the gender of the figures. Whatever their purpose, the size (as much as 3 feet tall) and sophisticated technique of the Ain Ghazal statuettes and busts sharply differentiate the Neolithic figurines from tiny and often faceless Paleolithic sculptures such as the Willendorf woman (FIG. 1-4) and even the foot-tall Hohlenstein-Stadel ivory feline-headed human (FIG. 1-3).

1-16 Deer hunt, detail of a wall painting from level III, Çatal Höyük, Turkey, ca. 6000 BCE. Museum of Anatolian Civilization, Ankara.

This Neolithic painter depicted human figures as a composite of frontal and profile views, the most descriptive picture of the shape of the human body. This format would become the rule for millennia.

The Ain Ghazal statues mark the beginning of the long history of large-scale sculpture in Mesopotamia.

Çatal Höyük. During the past half century, archaeologists also have made remarkable discoveries in Turkey, not only at Göbekli Tepe (FIG. 1-12) but also at Hacilar and especially Çatal Höyük (FIG. 1-15A), the site of a flourishing Neolithic culture on the central Anatolian plain between ca. 7500 and 6000 BCE. Although animal husbandry was well established, hunting continued

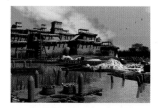

1-15A Restored view of Çatal Höyük, ca. 6000 BCE.

to play an important part in the early Neolithic economy of Çatal Höyük. The importance of hunting as a food source is reflected in the wall paintings of the site's older decorated rooms, where hunting scenes predominate. In style and concept, however, the deer hunt mural (FIG. 1-16) at Çatal Höyük is worlds apart from the wall paintings that the hunters of the Paleolithic period produced. Perhaps what is most strikingly new about the Çatal Höyük painting and similar Neolithic examples is the regular appearance of the human figure—not only singly but also in large, coherent groups with a wide variety of poses, subjects, and settings. As noted earlier, humans rarely figured in Paleolithic cave paintings, and pictorial narratives are almost unknown. Even the "hunting scene" (FIG. 1-10) in the well at Lascaux is questionable as a narrative. By contrast, human themes and concerns and action scenes with humans dominating animals are central subjects of Neolithic paintings.

In the Çatal Höyük mural, the painter depicted an organized hunting party, not a series of individual figures. The representation of the hunters is a rhythmic repetition of basic shapes, but the painter took care to distinguish important descriptive details (bows, arrows, and garments), and the heads have clearly defined noses, mouths, chins, and hair. The Neolithic painter placed all the heads in profile for the same reason that Paleolithic painters universally chose the profile view for representations of animals (see "How to Represent an Animal," page 17). Only the side view of the human head shows

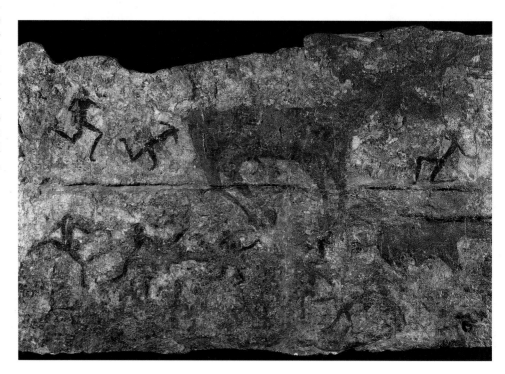

all its shapes clearly. However, at Çatal Höyük the painter presented the torsos from the front—again, the most informative viewpoint—whereas the profile view was the choice for the legs and arms. This composite view of the human body is highly artificial—the human body cannot make an abrupt 90-degree shift at the hips—but it well describes the parts of a human body, as opposed to how a body appears from a particular viewpoint. In fact, the head of each hunter is also shown in a composite view, because the eyes are frontal, not profile. If the painter had placed a profile eye in the profile head, the eye would not "read" as an eye at all, because it would not have its distinctive oval shape. Art historians call this characteristic early approach to representation *conceptual representation* (as opposed to *optical representation*—the portrayal of people, animals, and objects seen from a fixed point) because the artists who painted and carved figures in this manner did not seek to record the immediate, fleeting aspects of the human body. Instead, they rendered the human form's distinguishing and fixed properties. The fundamental shapes of the head, arms, torso, and legs, not their accidental appearance, dictated the artists' selection of the composite view as the best way to represent the human body, just as Paleolithic painters represented bulls' bodies from the side but their horns from the front (FIG. 1-1). This conceptual approach to depicting the human form would become the rule for the next 6,000 years.

The technique of painting also changed dramatically from the Paleolithic to the Neolithic Age. The Çatal Höyük painters used brushes to apply their pigments to a background of dry white plaster.

The careful preparation of the wall surface contrasts sharply with the typical direct application of pigment to the irregularly shaped walls and ceilings of Old Stone Age caves.

Europe

In Europe, where Paleolithic paintings and sculptures abound, no evidence exists for comparably developed early Neolithic towns. However, in succeeding millennia, perhaps as early as 4000 BCE, the local populations of several European regions constructed imposing monuments employing massive rough-cut stones. The very dimensions of the stones, some as high as 17 feet and weighing as much as 50 tons, have prompted historians to call them *megaliths* (great stones) and to designate Neolithic architecture employing them as *megalithic*.

Newgrange. One of the most impressive megalithic monuments in Europe is also one of the oldest. The megalithic tomb at Newgrange in Ireland, north of Dublin, may date to as early as 3200 BCE and is one of the oldest funerary monuments in Europe. It takes the form of a *passage grave*—that is, a tomb with a long stone corridor leading to a burial chamber beneath a great *tumulus* (earthen burial mound). Some mounds contain more than one passage grave. Similar graves have been found also in England, France, Spain, and Scandinavia. All attest to the importance of honoring the dead in Neolithic society. The Newgrange tumulus is 280 feet in diameter and 44 feet tall. Its passageway is 62 feet long, and it and the primitive *dome* over the main chamber (FIG. 1-17) are early examples of *corbeled vaulting* (see "Corbeled Arches, Vaults, and Domes," page 97, and FIG. 4-18). At Newgrange, the huge megaliths forming the vaulted passage and the dome are held in place by their own weight without mortar, each stone countering the thrust of neighboring stones. Decorating some of the megaliths are incised spirals and other motifs (not visible in FIG. 1-17). A special feature of the Newgrange tomb is that at the winter solstice, the sun illuminates the passageway and the burial chamber.

Hagar Qim. By the end of the fourth millennium BCE, Neolithic civilization had spread to the most remote parts of Europe, including, in the far north, Skara Brae (FIG. 1-17A) in the Orkney Islands, and,

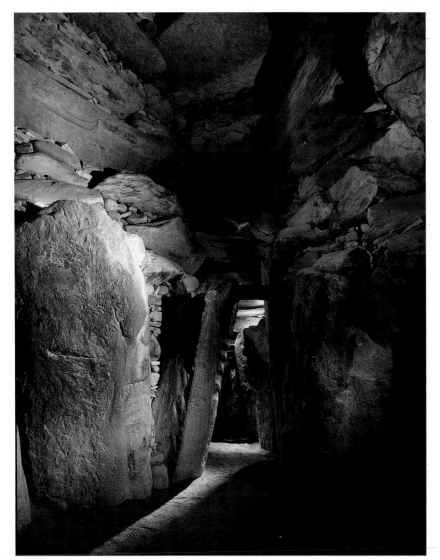

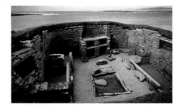

⚐ **1-17A** House 1, Skara Brae, ca. 3100–2500 BCE.

1-17 Main chamber with corbeled dome of the passage grave, Newgrange, Ireland, ca. 3200–2500 BCE.

The Newgrange passage grave is an early example of corbeled vaulting. The huge stones (megaliths) of the dome of the main burial chamber beneath the tumulus are held in place by their own weight.

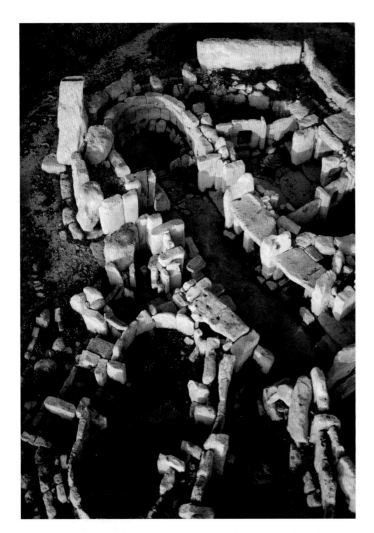

1-18 Aerial view of the ruins of Hagar Qim (looking east), Malta, ca. 3200–2500 BCE.

The 5,000-year-old stone temple at Hagar Qim on the remote island of Malta is very sophisticated for its date, especially in the way that the Neolithic builders incorporated both rectilinear and curved forms.

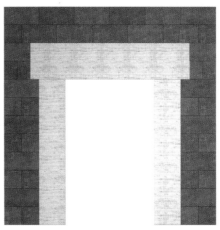

1-19 Post-and-lintel construction (John Burge).

The simplest and oldest method of spanning a passageway is to set up two upright blocks (posts), which support a horizontal beam (lintel), a technique used in both prehistoric Europe and Egypt.

of rectilinear and curved forms, including multiple *apses* (semicircular recesses). Inside the Hagar Qim temple, archaeologists found altars (hence the identification of the structure as a religious shrine) and several stone statues of headless nude women—one standing, the others seated. The level of architectural and sculptural sophistication seen on this isolated island at so early a date is extraordinary.

Stonehenge.   The most famous megalithic monument in Europe is Stonehenge (FIG. 1-20) on the Salisbury Plain in southern England. A *henge* is an arrangement of megalithic stones in a circle, often surrounded by a ditch. The type is almost exclusively limited to Britain. Stonehenge is a complex of rough-cut sarsen (a form of sandstone) stones and smaller "bluestones" (various volcanic rocks) built in several stages over at least several hundred years. The final henge consists of concentric post-and-lintel circles. Huge sarsen megaliths form the outer ring, which is almost 100 feet in diameter. Inside is a ring of bluestones encircling a horseshoe (open end facing east) of *trilithons* (three-stone constructions)—five lintel-topped pairs of the largest sarsens, each weighing 45 to 50 tons. Standing apart and to the east (outside the view in FIG. 1-20) is the "heel stone," which, for a person looking outward from the center of the complex, would have marked the point where the sun rose at the summer solstice. Stonehenge, perhaps originally a funerary site where Neolithic peoples cremated their dead, seems in its latest phase to have been a kind of astronomical observatory. According to a recent theory, it also served as a center of healing that attracted the sick and dying from throughout the region. In any case, the henge itself is now known to be just one part of a much larger ritual complex.

Whatever role they played in society, the megalithic tombs, temples, houses, and henges of Europe are enduring testaments to the rapidly developing intellectual powers of Neolithic humans as well as to their capacity for heroic physical effort.

in the far south, Malta. The megalithic temple (FIG. 1-18) of Hagar Qim is one of many constructed on Malta between 3200 and 2500 BCE. The Maltese builders erected their temples by piling carefully cut stone blocks in *courses* (stacked horizontal rows). To construct the doorways at Hagar Qim, the builders employed the *post-and-lintel system* (FIG. 1-19) in which two upright stones (posts) support a horizontal block (*lintel* or *beam*). The layout of this and other Neolithic Maltese temples is especially noteworthy for the combination

1-20 Circle of trilithons (looking southwest), Stonehenge, Salisbury Plain, Wiltshire, England, ca. 2550–1600 BCE. Circle 97′ in diameter; trilithons 24′ high.

Stonehenge's circles of trilithons functioned as an astronomical observatory within a larger ritual complex. The sun rises over its "heel stone" at the summer solstice. Some of the megaliths weigh 50 tons.

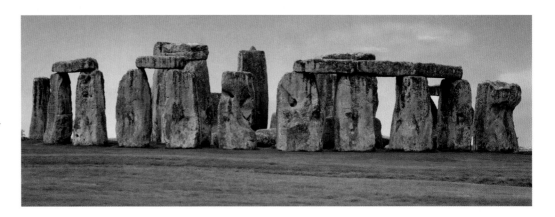

Art in the Stone Age

Paleolithic (Old Stone Age) Art ca. 40,000–9000 BCE

- The first sculptures and paintings antedate the invention of writing by tens of thousands of years. Paleolithic humans' decision to represent the world around them initiated an intellectual revolution of enormous consequences.

- Scholars debate why humans began to paint and carve images and what role those images played in the lives of Paleolithic peoples. All that is certain is that animals, not humans, dominate Paleolithic art, and that women were far more common subjects than men.

- Some archaeologists believe that Stone Age hunters performed rituals in front of the animal images, which aided them in killing their prey. By contrast, other scholars think that the purpose of the images was to ensure the fertility of the species on which humans depended for food and clothing. Many researchers now believe that the Paleolithic cave paintings record the visions seen by shamans during trances.

- The works created by Paleolithic sculptors and painters range in size from tiny portable figurines, such as the stone image of a woman from Willendorf, to large, sometimes over-life-size, carved and painted representations of animals on the walls of the caves of Lascaux, Pech-Merle, Altamira, and elsewhere in southern France and northern Spain. Sometimes, the choice of subject was inspired by irregularities in natural rock formations that seemed to resemble animals or humans.

- The earliest known sculptures, such as the feline-human from Hohlenstein-Stadel, date to 40,000 to 35,000 BCE. The oldest paintings known, established by radiocarbon dating, are in the Chauvet Cave at Vallon-Pont-d'Arc.

- Paleolithic artists regularly depicted animals in profile in order to present a complete picture of each beast, including its head, body, tail, and all four legs. This format persisted for millennia.

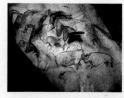

Chauvet Cave, ca. 35,000 BCE

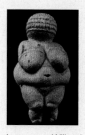

Nude woman, Willendorf, ca. 28,000–25,000 BCE

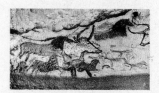

Lascaux Cave, ca. 16,000–14,000 BCE

Neolithic (New Stone Age) Art ca. 9000–2300 BCE

- Around 9000 BCE, the ice that had covered much of northern Europe for millennia receded. The Neolithic Age emerged first in Anatolia and Mesopotamia, roughly corresponding to present-day Turkey, Syria, and Iraq.

- The Neolithic Age revolutionized human life with the beginning of agriculture and the formation of the first settled communities, such as that at Çatal Höyük in Anatolia, where archaeologists have uncovered an extensive town with numerous shrines.

- Some Neolithic towns—for example, Jericho in the Jordan River Valley—also had fortified stone circuit walls.

- The excavation of a religious complex with decorated stone pillars at Göbekli Tepe in Anatolia indicates that Neolithic people constructed stone temples long before they established permanent village communities.

- In art, the Neolithic period brought the birth of large-scale sculpture, notably the painted plaster figurines from Ain Ghazal and the restored life-size skulls from Jericho.

- In painting, coherent narratives became common, and artists began to represent human figures as composites of frontal and profile views—a formula that would remain universal for millennia.

- Neolithic technology spread gradually from Anatolia and Mesopotamia to Europe, where it continued longer in remote places—for example, Stonehenge in England.

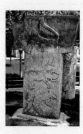

Stone pillar, Göbekli Tepe, ca. 9000 BCE

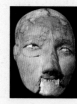

Painted and inlaid skull, Jericho, ca. 7200–6700 BCE

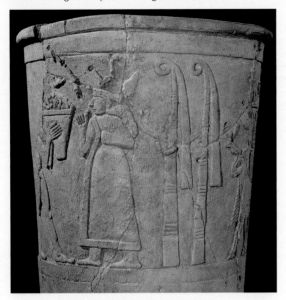

▼ **2-1a** The *Warka Vase* is the first great work of narrative relief sculpture known. It represents a religious ceremony in honor of Inanna in which a priest-king brings votive offerings to deposit in the goddess's shrine.

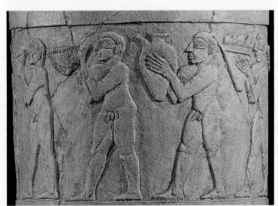

▲ **2-1b** The Sumerians were probably the first to use pictures to tell coherent stories. This sculptor placed the figures in three registers. Humans are shown in composite views standing on a common ground line.

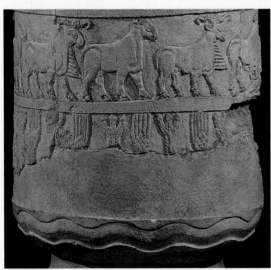

▼ **2-1c** As in prehistoric art, representations of animals in Mesopotamian art are always strict profile views, save for the animals' eyes, which are seen from the front, as are also sometimes an animal's two horns.

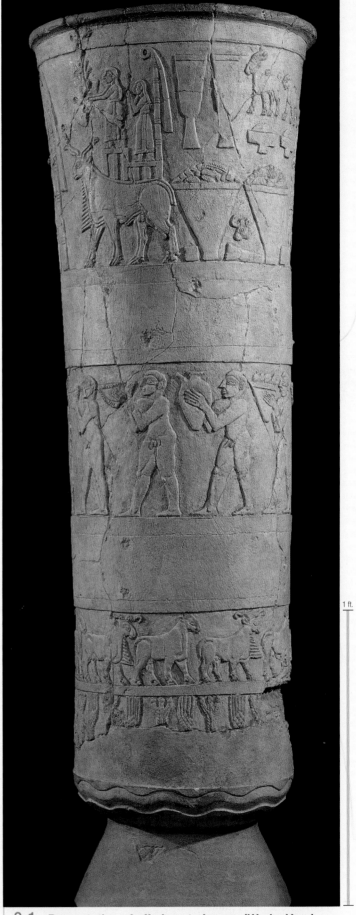

1 ft.

2-1 **Presentation of offerings to Inanna (*Warka Vase*), from the Inanna temple complex, Uruk (modern Warka), Iraq, ca. 3300 BCE. Alabaster, 3′ ¼″ high. National Museum of Iraq, Baghdad.**

ANCIENT MESOPOTAMIA AND PERSIA /2

Pictorial Narration in Ancient Sumer

In ancient Sumer, "the cradle of civilization" in Mesopotamia, humans first learned how to use the wheel and plow and how to control floods and construct irrigation canals. In the fourth millennium BCE, the Sumerians also invented writing and were the first to establish complex urban societies, called *city-states,* and to use pictures to tell coherent stories, far surpassing Stone Age artists' tentative efforts at pictorial narration.

The *Warka Vase* (FIG. 2-1), found within the Inanna temple complex at Uruk (modern Warka, Iraq), is the first great work of narrative relief sculpture known. Its depiction of a religious ceremony honoring Inanna incorporates all of the pictorial conventions that would dominate narrative art for the next 2,800 years. The artist divided the pictorial field into three bands (called *registers,* or *friezes*) and placed all the figures on a common *ground line,* a strict compositional format that marks a significant break with the more haphazard figure placement of Stone Age art. The lowest band shows crops above a wavy line representing water. Then comes a register with alternating ewes and rams. Agriculture and animal husbandry were the staples of the Sumerian economy, but the produce and the female and male animals are also fertility symbols. They underscore that Inanna blessed Uruk's inhabitants with good crops and increased herds.

A procession of naked men moving in the opposite direction of the animals fills the band at the center of the vase. The men carry baskets and jars overflowing with the earth's abundance. They will present their bounty to the goddess as a *votive offering* (gift of gratitude to a deity usually made in fulfillment of a vow). In the uppermost (and tallest) band of the *Warka Vase* is a female figure with a tall horned headdress next to two reed posts with streamers, the sign of the goddess Inanna. (Some scholars think that the woman is a priestess and not the goddess herself.) Facing her is a nude male figure bringing a large vessel brimming with offerings to be deposited in the goddess's shrine, and behind him (not visible in FIG. 2-1a), a man wearing a tasseled skirt and an attendant carrying his long train. Near the man is the *pictograph* (a simplified picture standing for a word) for the Sumerian official whom scholars ambiguously call a "priest-king"—that is, both a religious and secular leader. Some art historians interpret the scene as a symbolic marriage between the priest-king and the goddess, ensuring her continued goodwill—and reaffirming the leader's exalted position in society. The greater height of the priest-king and Inanna (or her priestess) compared with the offering bearers indicates their greater importance, a convention called *hierarchy of scale,* which the Sumerians also pioneered.

MESOPOTAMIA

When humans first gave up the dangerous and uncertain life of the hunter and gatherer for the more predictable and stable life of the farmer and herder, the change in human society was so significant that historians justly have dubbed it the Neolithic Revolution. This fundamental change in the nature of daily life first occurred in Mesopotamia—the Greek name for "the land between the [Tigris and Euphrates] rivers." The foothills surrounding the Mesopotamian valley form a huge arc from the mountainous border between Turkey and Syria through Iraq to Iran's Zagros Mountains (MAP 2-1). Often called the Fertile Crescent, Mesopotamia is the presumed locale of the biblical Garden of Eden (Gen. 2.10–15) and the region that gave birth to three of the world's great modern faiths—Judaism, Christianity, and Islam. This land "between the rivers" has, consequently, long been of interest to historians. Not until the 19th century, however, did systematic excavation open the public's eyes to the extraordinary art and architecture of ancient Mesopotamia.

After the first discoveries in Syria and Iraq, the major museums of Europe and North America began to avidly collect Mesopotamian art. The most popular 19th-century acquisitions were the stone reliefs depicting warfare and hunting (FIGS. 2-22, 2-22A, and 2-23) and the colossal statues of monstrous man-headed winged bulls (FIG. 2-20) from the palaces of the Assyrians, rulers of a northern Mesopotamian empire during the ninth to the seventh centuries BCE. But nothing extracted from the earth during the 19th century garnered as much attention as the treasure of gold objects, jewelry, musical instruments (FIGS. 2-6 and 2-7), and other artworks (FIGS. 2-8, 2-9, and 2-10) that British archaeologist Sir Leonard Woolley (1880–1960) discovered in the 1920s at the Royal Cemetery at Ur in southern Iraq. The interest in the lavish third-millennium Sumerian cemetery that he excavated rivaled the fascination with the 1922 discovery of the tomb of the Egyptian boy-king Tutankhamen (FIGS. 3-33, 3-34, and 3-35).

Sumer

The discovery of the treasures of ancient Ur put the Sumerians once again in a prominent position on the world stage, from which they had been absent for more than 4,000 years. Ancient Sumer, which roughly corresponds to southern Iraq today, comprised a dozen or so independent city-states under the protection of different Mesopotamian deities (see "The Gods and Goddesses of Mesopotamia," page 34). The Sumerian rulers were the gods' representatives on earth and the stewards of their earthly treasure.

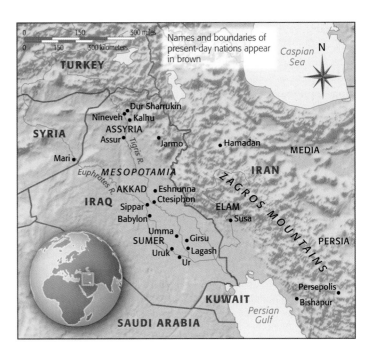

MAP 2-1 Ancient Mesopotamia and Persia.

The rulers and priests directed all communal activities, including canal construction, crop collection, and food distribution. Because the Sumerians developed agriculture to such an extent that only a portion of the population had to produce food, some members of the community were free to specialize in other activities, including manufacturing, trade, and administration. Specialization of labor is the hallmark of the first complex urban societies. In the city-states of ancient Sumer, activities that once had been individually initiated became institutionalized for the first time. The city-state, whether ruled by a single person or a council chosen from among the leading families, assumed such functions as defense against enemies and the whims of nature, roles previously the responsibility of individuals and their extended families. The city-state was one of the many Sumerian innovations that transformed the ancient world.

Writing. Another Sumerian invention of enormous importance was writing. The oldest written documents known are Sumerian records of administrative acts and commercial transactions. At first, around 3400 to 3200 BCE, the Sumerians made inventories of cattle, food, and other items by drawing pictographs, often in boxes, in soft clay with a sharp tool, or *stylus*. The clay hardened into

ANCIENT MESOPOTAMIA AND PERSIA

3500–2332 BCE	2332–2150 BCE	2150–1600 BCE	1600–612 BCE	604–559 BCE	330 BCE–636 CE
Sumerian	**Akkadian**	**Neo-Sumerian and Babylonian**	**Hittite and Assyrian**	**Neo-Babylonian and Achaemenid**	**Greco-Roman and Sasanian**
▪ The Sumerians found the first city-states and invent writing ▪ Sumerian builders construct the oldest Mesopotamian temples on lofty platforms ▪ Sumerian artists present narratives in register format	▪ The Akkadians are the first Mesopotamian rulers to call themselves kings and have themselves depicted in art with divine attributes ▪ Akkadian sculptors create the earliest preserved hollow-cast metal statues	▪ Neo-Sumerian builders erect the largest extant ziggurat at Ur ▪ Gudea of Lagash rebuilds temples and commissions portraits ▪ Babylonian king Hammurabi sets up a stele recording his laws	▪ The Hittites sack Babylon and fortify their capital at Hattusa ▪ Assyrian kings rule a vast empire from citadels guarded by lamassu ▪ Extensive relief cycles celebrate Assyrian military campaigns and lion hunts	▪ Nebuchadnezzar II rebuilds Babylon, home of the ziggurat called the Tower of Babel in the Bible ▪ The Achaemenids build a huge palace complex at Persepolis	▪ After conquest by Alexander the Great, Mesopotamia and Persia are absorbed into the Greco-Roman world ▪ Sasanian kings challenge Rome from their capital at Ctesiphon

breakable, yet nearly indestructible, tablets. Thousands of these tablets, dating back nearly five millennia, exist today. By 3000 to 2900 BCE, the Sumerians had further simplified the pictographic signs by reducing them to a group of wedge-shaped (*cuneiform*) signs read from top to bottom and right to left (FIGS. 2-8 and 2-11 are early examples; see also FIGS. 2-13, 2-16, 2-17, and 2-18). The development of cuneiform marked the beginning of writing, as historians strictly define it. The surviving cuneiform tablets testify to the far-flung network of Sumerian contacts reaching from southern Mesopotamia eastward to the Iranian plateau, northward to Assyria, and westward to Syria. Trade was essential to the Sumerians, because despite Sumer's fertile soil, the land was poor in such vital natural resources as metal, stone, and wood.

The Sumerians also produced great literature. Their most famous work, known from fragmentary cuneiform texts, is the late-third-millennium BCE *Epic of Gilgamesh,* which antedates the Greek poet Homer's *Iliad* and *Odyssey* by some 1,500 years. It recounts the heroic story of Gilgamesh, legendary king of Uruk and slayer of the monster Huwawa. Translations of the Sumerian epic into several other ancient languages attest to the fame of the original version.

White Temple, Uruk. The layout of Sumerian cities reflected the central role of the gods in daily life. The main temple to each state's chief god was its most important structure and the city's nucleus. In fact, the temple complex was a kind of city within a city, where a staff of priests and scribes carried on official administrative and commercial business as well as oversaw all religious functions.

The outstanding preserved example of early Sumerian temple architecture is the 5,000-year-old White Temple (FIGS. 2-2 and 2-3) at Uruk, a city that in the late fourth millennium BCE was about 500 acres in size and had a population of about 40,000. Usually only the foundations of early Mesopotamian temples remain. The White Temple is a rare exception. Sumerian builders did not have easy access to stone quarries and instead formed mud bricks for the

superstructures of their temples and other buildings. Mud brick is a durable building material, but unlike stone, it deteriorates with exposure to water. Almost all the Sumerian mud-brick structures have eroded over the course of time. The Sumerians nonetheless erected towering works, such as the Uruk temple, several centuries before the Egyptians built their famous stone pyramids. The construction of grandiose shrines when stone was unavailable says a great deal about the Sumerians' desire to provide inspiring settings for the worship of their deities.

Enough of the White Temple at Uruk remains to permit a fairly reliable reconstruction (FIG. 2-3). The temple (whose white gypsum-coated walls suggested its modern nickname) stands atop a lofty platform 43 feet above street level at the city's highest point, called Kullaba. A stairway on one side leads to the top, but does not end in front of any of the temple doorways, necessitating two or three angular changes in direction. This *bent-axis plan* is the standard arrangement for Sumerian temples, a striking contrast to the linear approach that the Egyptians preferred for their temples and tombs (compare FIGS. 3-10 and 3-20).

As in other Sumerian temples, the corners of the White Temple are oriented to the cardinal points of the compass. The building, probably dedicated to Anu, the sky god, is of modest proportions (61 by 16 feet). By design, Sumerian temples did not accommodate large throngs of worshipers but only a select few, the priests and perhaps the leading community members. The White Temple had several chambers. The central hall, or *cella,* was the divinity's room and housed a stepped altar. The Sumerians referred to their temples as "waiting rooms," a reflection of their belief that the deity would descend from the heavens to appear before the priests in the cella. It is unclear whether the Uruk temple had a roof, and if it did, what kind.

The Sumerian notion of the gods residing above the world of humans is central to most of the world's religions. Moses ascended Mount Sinai to receive the Ten Commandments from the Hebrew

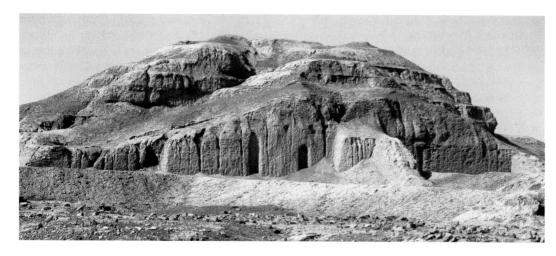

2-2 **White Temple, Uruk (modern Warka), Iraq, ca. 3300 BCE.**

Using only mud bricks, the Sumerians erected towering temple platforms several centuries before the Egyptians built stone pyramids. This temple was probably dedicated to Anu, the sky god.

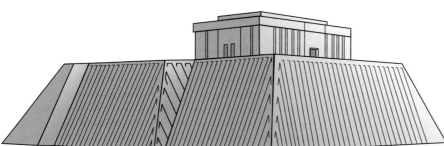

2-3 **Restored view of the White Temple, Uruk (modern Warka), Iraq, ca. 3300 BCE.**

The 5,300-year-old White Temple at Uruk is the outstanding example of early Sumerian religious architecture. In its central hall (cella), the Sumerian priests would await the apparition of the deity.

The Gods and Goddesses of Mesopotamia

The Sumerians and their successors in Mesopotamia worshiped numerous deities, mostly nature gods. Listed here are the Mesopotamian gods and goddesses discussed in this chapter.

- **Anu,** the god of the sky and of the city of Uruk, was the chief deity of the Sumerians. One of the earliest Mesopotamian shrines, the White Temple at Uruk (FIGS. 2-2 and 2-3), may have been dedicated to his worship.
- **Enlil** was Anu's son and lord of the winds and the earth. He eventually replaced his father as king of the gods.
- **Inanna** was the Sumerian goddess of love and war. Later known as **Ishtar,** she was the most important female deity in all periods of Mesopotamian history. As early as the fourth millennium BCE, the Sumerians constructed a sanctuary to Inanna at Uruk. Amid the ruins, excavators uncovered sculptures (FIGS. 2-1 and 2-4) connected with her worship.
- **Nanna,** also known as **Sin,** was the moon god and chief deity of Ur, where the Sumerians erected his most important shrine (FIG. 2-14).
- **Utu,** the sun god, later known as **Shamash,** was especially revered at Sippar. On a Babylonian relief (FIG. 2-18) of ca. 1780 BCE, King Hammurabi presents his laws to Shamash, whom the sculptor depicted as a bearded god wearing a horned headdress. Flames radiate from the sun god's shoulders.
- **Ningirsu** was the local god of Lagash and Girsu. He helped Eannatum, one of the early rulers of Lagash, defeat an enemy army. The *Stele of the Vultures* (FIG. 2-11) of ca. 2600–2500 BCE records Ningirsu's role in the victory. Gudea (FIGS. 2-16 and 2-17), one of Eannatum's Neo-Sumerian successors, built a great temple around 2100 BCE in honor of Ningirsu after the god instructed him to do so in a dream.
- **Marduk** was the chief god of the Babylonians.
- **Nabu,** Marduk's son, was the Babylonian god of writing and wisdom.
- **Adad** was the Babylonian god of storms. Adad's sacred bull and Marduk and Nabu's dragon adorn the sixth-century BCE Ishtar Gate (FIG. 2-24) at Babylon.

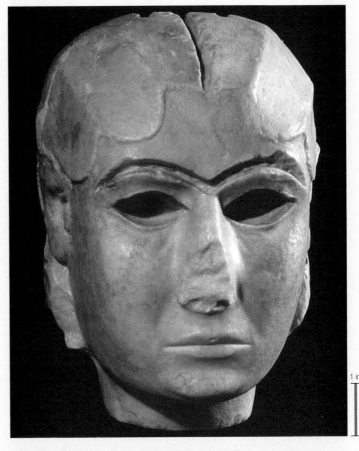

1 in.

2-4 Female head (Inanna?), from the Inanna temple complex, Uruk (modern Warka), Iraq, ca. 3300 BCE. Marble, 8″ high. National Museum of Iraq, Baghdad.

The Sumerians imported the marble for this head at great cost. It may represent the goddess Inanna and originally had inlaid colored shell or stone eyes and brows, and a wig, probably of gold leaf.

- **Ashur** was the local deity of Assur, the city that took his name. Sometimes identified with Enlil, Ashur became the king of the Assyrian gods.

God, and the Greeks placed the home of their gods and goddesses on Mount Olympus. The elevated placement of Mesopotamian temples on giant platforms reaching to the sky is consistent with this widespread religious concept. The loftiness of the Sumerian temple platforms made a profound impression on the peoples of ancient Mesopotamia. The tallest, at Babylon, was about 270 feet high. Known to the Hebrews as the Tower of Babel, it became the centerpiece of a biblical story about the arrogant and disrespectful pride of humans (see "Babylon, City of Wonders," page 50).

Inanna. A fragmentary white marble female head (FIG. 2-4) from Uruk is also an extraordinary achievement at so early a date. The head, one of the treasures of the National Museum of Iraq in Baghdad, disappeared during the Iraq War of 2003, but was later recovered, along with other priceless items (FIGS. 2-1 and 2-12). The Sumerians lacked a ready source of fine stones suitable for carving sculptures, and consequently used stone sparingly. The glossy hard stone selected for this head had to be brought to Uruk at great cost. In fact, the "head" is really only a face with a flat back. It has drilled holes for attachment to the rest of the head and the body, which may have been of wood, and would have been much less costly. Although found in the sacred precinct of the goddess Inanna, the subject is unknown. Many have suggested that the face is an image of Inanna, although others think that it portrays a mortal woman, perhaps a priestess.

Often the present condition of an artwork can be very misleading, and this female head from Uruk is a dramatic example. Its original appearance would have been much more vibrant than the pure white fragment preserved today. Colored shell or stone filled the deep recesses for the eyebrows and the large eyes. The groove

Sumerian Votive Statuary

The Sumerians, innovators in so many areas, were also the first to adopt the practice of placing in their shrines votive offerings representing the donors of the gods' gifts. Because there was no established tradition for depicting donors, the Sumerians had to invent a new pictorial formula. The votive statuettes from Eshnunna are among the earliest examples. Carved of soft gypsum and inlaid with shell and black limestone, the statuettes range in size from well under a foot to about 30 inches tall. The two largest figures from the group are shown here (FIG. 2-5). All of the statuettes represent mortals rather than deities. They hold the small

beakers the Sumerians used to make a *libation* (ritual pouring of liquid) in honor of the gods. (Archaeologists found hundreds of these goblets in the temple complex at Eshnunna.) The men wear belts and fringed skirts. Most have beards and shoulder-length hair. The women wear long robes, with the right shoulder bare.

Similar figurines have been unearthed at other sites. Some stand, as do the Eshnunna statuettes. Others are seated—for example, the figurine portraying Urnanshe (FIG. 2-5A) from the Ishtar temple at Mari in Syria. Many bear inscriptions giving valuable information, such as the name of the donor or the god. The texts inscribed on some statuettes are specific prayers to the deity on the owner's behalf. With their heads tilted upward, the figures represented in these statuettes wait in the Sumerian "waiting room" for the divinity to appear.

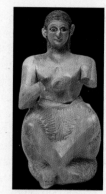

2-5A Urnanshe seated, from Mari, ca. 2450 BCE.

The Sumerian sculptors employed simple forms, primarily cones and cylinders, for the figures. The statuettes, even those bearing the names of individuals (for example, Urnanshe), are not portraits in the strict sense of the word, but the sculptors did distinguish physical types. At Eshnunna, the sculptors portrayed at least one child, because next to the woman in FIG. 2-5 are the remains of two small legs. Most striking is the disproportionate relationship between the inlaid oversized eyes and the tiny hands, which represents a conscious decision on the part of the sculptors to vary the size of the parts of the body—a kind of hierarchy of scale within a single figure complementing the hierarchy of scale among figures in a group. Scholars have explained the exaggeration of the eye size in various ways. Because the purpose of these votive figures was to offer constant prayers to the gods on their donors' behalf, the open-eyed stares most likely symbolize the eternal wakefulness necessary to fulfill their duty.

1 ft.

2-5 **Statuettes of two worshipers, from the Square Temple at Eshnunna (modern Tell Asmar), Iraq, ca. 2900–2750 BCE. Gypsum, shell, and black limestone. Man 2′ 4¼″ high, woman 1′ 11¼″ high. National Museum of Iraq, Baghdad.**

The oversized eyes probably symbolize the perpetual wakefulness of these substitute worshipers offering prayers to the deity. The beakers that the figures hold were used to pour libations for the gods.

at the top of the head anchored a wig, probably made of gold leaf. The hair strands engraved in the metal would have fallen in waves over the forehead and sides of the face. The bright coloration of the eyes, brows, and hair likely overshadowed the soft modeling of the cheeks and mouth. The missing body was probably clothed in expensive fabrics and bedecked with jewels.

Eshnunna Statuettes. The *Warka Vase* (FIG. 2-1), also from the Inanna sanctuary of Uruk, provides some insight into the rituals in honor of the goddess. Further clues about Sumerian religious beliefs and votive practices come from sculptures deposited in Sumerian

sanctuaries, especially the extensive group of statuettes (FIG. 2-5) reverently buried beneath the floor of a temple at Eshnunna (modern Tell Asmar) during remodeling of the structure (see "Sumerian Votive Statuary," above).

Royal Cemetery, Ur. Agriculture and trade brought considerable wealth to some of the city-states of ancient Sumer. Nowhere is this more evident than in the burial ground that the excavators of Ur dubbed the Royal Cemetery. Ur was one of the major Sumerian city-states and the home of the biblical Abraham. In the third millennium BCE, the leading families of Ur placed their dead in vaulted chambers beneath the earth. Scholars still debate whether the deceased individuals were true kings and queens or merely aristocrats, priests, and priestesses, but they were laid to rest in regal fashion. The archaeologists who explored the Ur cemetery uncovered gold helmets and daggers with handles of lapis lazuli (a rich azureblue stone), gold beakers and bowls, jewelry of gold and lapis lazuli, musical instruments, chariots, and other luxurious items inlaid with lapis lazuli, red limestone, and shells. Some of these materials had to be obtained at great cost from far away. Lapis lazuli, for example, was imported from Afghanistan. The luxury goods in the Royal Cemetery tombs testify not only to the wealth of those buried there but also to the wide trade network of the Sumerians. The excavators also found dozens of bodies in the richest tombs—a retinue of musicians, servants, charioteers, and soldiers who died, probably by voluntarily drinking poison, in order to accompany the "kings and queens" into the afterlife.

Bull-Headed Harps. One of the most important tombs in the Royal Cemetery of Ur was the burial place of "Queen" Puabi, wife of "King" Meskalamdug. (Many historians prefer to designate her more conservatively and ambiguously as Lady Puabi, perhaps a high priestess of the moon god Nanna.) From Puabi's tomb comes a fragmentary harp that has been reconstructed (FIG. 2-6) on the basis of representations of similar instruments (for example, FIG. 2-10, *top right*). A magnificent bull's head fashioned of gold leaf over a wood core caps the sound box of Puabi's harp. The hair and beard of the bull are of lapis lazuli, as is the inlaid background of the sound box, which features figures of shell and red limestone.

The excavators unearthed a similar harp in the adjacent burial of Meskalamdug, which they dubbed the King's Grave. That harp also has a costly inlaid sound box (FIG. 2-7). In the uppermost of the four panels is a heroic figure embracing two man-bulls in a *heraldic composition* (symmetrical on either side of a central figure). Below are a jackal wearing a dagger and carrying a laden table, a lion holding a vase and cup, an onager (wild ass) playing a harp steadied by a (dancing?) bear, a jackal playing a zither, a scorpion-man, and a goat bearing goblets. The artist represented all of the animals in profile, consistent with an approach to depicting four-legged creatures that was then some 30,000 years old (see "How to Represent an Animal," page 17). The hero in the uppermost zone and the scorpion-man at the bottom, like the Neolithic deer hunters (FIG. 1-16) at Çatal Höyük and the figures on the *Warka Vase* (FIG. 2-1), are equally characteristically a composite of frontal and profile views.

The meaning of the scenes on this sound box is unclear. Some scholars have suggested, for example, that the depicted creatures inhabit the land of the dead and that the narrative has a funerary

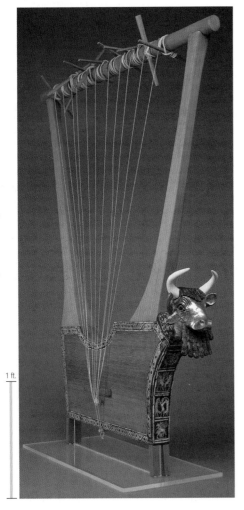

2-6 Bull-headed harp with inlaid sound box, from the tomb of Puabi (tomb 800), Royal Cemetery, Ur (modern Tell Muqayyar), Iraq, ca. 2550 BCE. Wood, gold, lapis lazuli, red limestone, and shell, 3′ 8⅛″ high. British Museum, London.

A bearded bull's head fashioned of gold leaf and lapis lazuli over a wood core adorns this harp from the tomb of Puabi, perhaps a queen of Ur. The inlaid sound box features four narrative scenes.

1 ft.

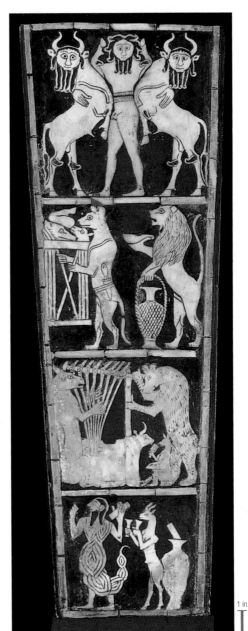

2-7 Sound box of a bull-headed harp, from the burial pit of Meskalamdug (grave 789), Royal Cemetery, Ur (modern Tell Muqayyar), Iraq, ca. 2550 BCE. Wood, lapis lazuli, and shell, 1′ 7″ high. University of Pennsylvania Museum of Archaeology and Anthropology, Philadelphia.

The four inlaid panels on the sound box of the harp found in Meskalamdug's burial pit at Ur represent a Gilgamesh-like hero between man-bulls, and animals acting out scenes of uncertain significance.

1 in.

Mesopotamian Seals

Archaeologists (and farmers and treasure hunters) have unearthed seals in great numbers at sites throughout Mesopotamia. Generally made of stone, Mesopotamian seals of ivory, glass, and other materials also survive. The seals take two forms: flat *stamp seals* and *cylinder seals.* The latter have a hole drilled lengthwise through the center of the cylinder so that they could be strung and worn around the neck or suspended from the wrist. Cylinder seals were prized possessions, signifying high positions in society. When elite individuals died, their families frequently buried them with their seals to carry into the afterlife. The cylinder seal illustrated here (FIG. 2-8) was found in the tomb of Puabi in the Royal Cemetery at Ur and bears her name in cuneiform.

The primary function of cylinder seals, however, like the earlier stamp seals, was not to serve as items of adornment or signifiers of wealth and prestige. The Sumerians (and other ancient Mesopotamian peoples) used both stamp and cylinder seals to authenticate documents and protect storage jars and doors against tampering. The oldest seals predate the invention of writing and conveyed their messages with pictographs that certified ownership. Later seals often bore long cuneiform inscriptions and recorded the names and titles of rulers, bureaucrats, and deities. Although sealing is increasingly rare today, the tradition lives on whenever someone seals an envelope with a lump of wax and then stamps it with a monogram or other identifying mark. Customs officials often still seal packages and sacks with official stamps when goods cross national borders.

In Mesopotamia, artists incised designs in both stamp and cylinder seals, producing a raised pattern when the owner pressed the seal into soft clay. (Cylinder seals largely displaced stamp seals because they could be rolled over the clay and could thus cover a greater area more quickly.) FIG. 2-8 reproduces both Puabi's seal and a modern impression made from it. Note how cracks in the stone cylinder become raised lines in the impression and how the engraved figures, chairs, and cuneiform characters appear in relief. Continuous rolling of the seal over a clay strip results in a repeating design, as the impression of Puabi's seal demonstrates at the left and right ends.

The miniature reliefs that the seals produce are a priceless source of information about Mesopotamian religion and society. Without them, archaeologists would know much less about how Mesopotamians dressed and dined; what their shrines looked like; how they depicted their gods, rulers, and mythological figures; how they fought wars; and what role women played in society. Clay seal impressions excavated in architectural contexts shed a welcome light on the administration and organization of Mesopotamian city-states. Finally, Mesopotamian seals are an invaluable resource for art historians, providing them with thousands of miniature examples of relief sculpture spanning three millennia.

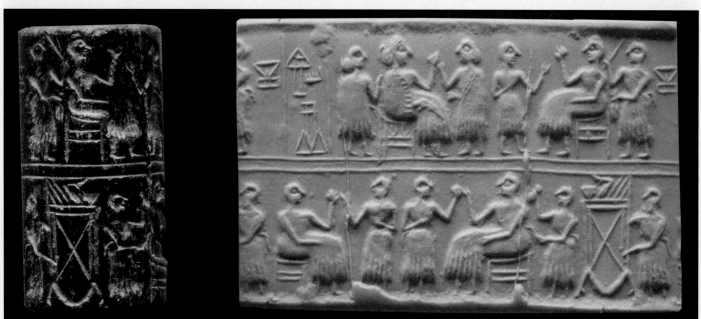

1 in.

2-8 Banquet scene, cylinder seal (*left*) and its modern impression (*right*), from the tomb of Puabi (tomb 800), Royal Cemetery, Ur (modern Tell Muqayyar), Iraq, ca. 2550 BCE. Lapis lazuli, 1 $\frac{7}{8}$″ high, 1″ diameter. British Museum, London.

The Mesopotamians used seals to identify and secure goods. Artists incised designs into stone cylinders that could be rolled over clay to produce miniature artworks such as this banquet scene.

significance. In any event, the sound box is a very early instance of the recurring theme in both literature and art of animals acting as people. Later examples include Aesop's fables in ancient Greece, medieval bestiaries, and, in modern times, Walt Disney's cartoon animal actors.

Cylinder Seals. The excavators of the Ur cemetery found Puabi's remains on a bier in her tomb, wearing an elaborate headdress and jewelry of gold, silver, lapis lazuli, carnelian, and agate. Near her body were pins to fasten her garment and three *cylinder seals,* one of which (FIG. 2-8) gives her name in cuneiform script.

The *Standard of Ur*

Art historians usually refer to the two long sides of the *Standard of Ur* as the "war side" and the "peace side," but there is little agreement about the relationship between the two narratives. The artist, working expertly with very small cut pieces of shell and stone, created two narratives divided into three horizontal bands. Each narrative reads from bottom to top, contrary to the way cuneiform is read. The explanation no doubt is that the artist wanted to place the most important figure in each narrative at the top center.

The story on the war side (FIG. 2-9) begins with four four-wheeled carts, each pulled by a team of four onagers—the earliest known representation of war chariots, which dramatically changed the nature of

ancient combat. Each chariot has a driver and an armed soldier. Art historians debate whether the artist intended to depict four different chariots or a single chariot gaining speed as it moves along the band from left to right. The artist depicted all of the overlapping onagers in strict profile. Beneath the legs of the onagers are the bodies of enemies, with blood pouring from the wounds they incurred during the battle. Above, foot soldiers (shown in composite view with frontal eyes in their profile heads) gather up and lead away captured foes. In the uppermost register, soldiers bring bound captives (whom the victors have stripped naked to degrade them) to a kinglike figure, who has stepped out of his chariot. His central place in the composition and his greater stature (his head breaks through the border at the top) set him apart from all the other figures.

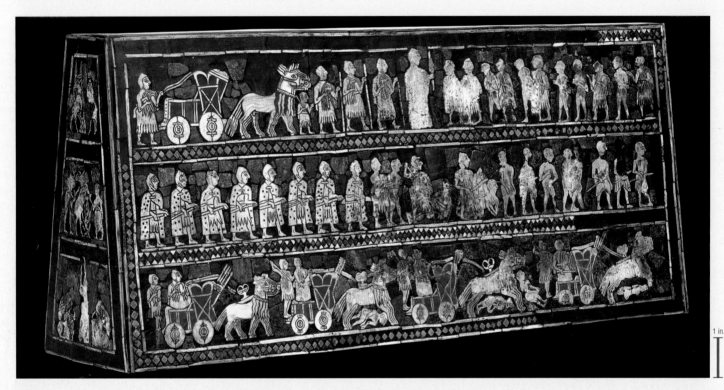

2-9 War side of the *Standard of Ur*, from tomb 779, Royal Cemetery, Ur (modern Tell Muqayyar), Iraq, ca. 2550–2400 BCE. Wood, lapis lazuli, shell, and red limestone set into bitumen, $7\frac{7}{8}'' \times 1' \, 6\frac{1}{2}''$. British Museum, London.

Using a mosaic-like technique, this Sumerian artist depicted a battlefield victory in three registers. The narrative reads from bottom to top, and the size of the figures varies with their importance in society.

The seal is typical of the period, consisting of a cylindrical piece of stone engraved to produce a raised impression when rolled over clay (see "Mesopotamian Seals," page 37). In the upper zone, a woman, probably Puabi, and a man sit and drink from beakers, attended by servants. Below, male attendants serve two more seated men. As in other Sumerian artworks, all the human figures are in composite views with large frontal eyes in profile heads, and the seated dignitaries are larger in scale to underscore their elevated position in the social hierarchy (compare, for example, FIG. 2-10).

Standard of Ur. Not the costliest object found in the "royal" graves, but probably the most significant from the viewpoint of the history of art, is the *Standard of Ur* (FIGS. 2-9 and 2-10). This small wood box inlaid with shell, lapis lazuli, and red limestone has broad rectangular faces and narrow trapezoidal ends. It was found in a third tomb in the Ur cemetery on the ground next to a man's shoulder, and Woolley, the excavator, thought that the object was originally mounted on a pole. He postulated that the box was a kind of military standard—hence its nickname. The "standard" may instead have been the sound box of a musical instrument, but no consensus

The peace side (FIG. 2-10) of the *Standard of Ur* portrays a banquet. In the lowest band, men carry provisions on their backs, and in the middle register, attendants transport animals and fish. At the top, seated dignitaries and a larger-than-life personage (third from the left; probably a king, whose head interrupts the upper border) attend the feast. At the top right are two entertainers. A musician plays a harp, and a long-haired *eunuch* (castrated male) sings; compare FIG. 2-5A.

Art historians have usually interpreted this banquet as a celebration after the victorious battle represented on the other side of the box. But even if that is the case, the provisions for the feast are not the spoils of war but the fruits of the Ur economy gathered from different corners of the realm.

In fact, this traditional interpretation should probably yield to a more nuanced "second opinion." The two sides may not constitute two episodes in an unfolding narrative. Instead, they are more likely to be independent scenes illustrating the two principal roles of a Sumerian ruler—the mighty warrior who defeats enemies of his city-state, and the chief administrator ("priest-king") who, with the blessing of the gods, assures the bountifulness of the land in peacetime (compare FIG. 2-1).

The absence of an inscription prevents connecting either of the scenes with a specific event or person, but the *Standard of Ur* undoubtedly is a very early example of historical narrative, even if only of a generic kind.

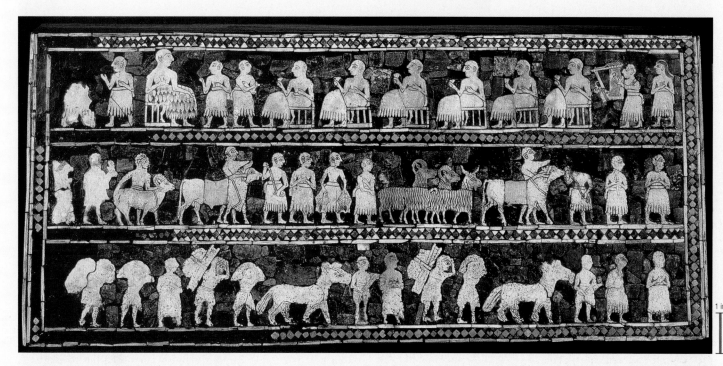

2-10 Peace side of the *Standard of Ur,* from tomb 779, Royal Cemetery, Ur (modern Tell Muqayyar), Iraq, ca. 2550–2400 BCE. Wood, lapis lazuli, shell, and red limestone set into bitumen, $7\frac{7}{8}'' \times 1' 6\frac{1}{2}''$. British Museum, London.

The entertainers at this banquet of Sumerian nobility include a musician playing a bull-headed harp of a type found in royal graves at Ur (FIG. 2-6). The long-haired, bare-chested singer is a court eunuch.

has ever been reached about its function. Varying interpretations have also been voiced about the narrative scenes that account for the box's fame today and its importance in the history of art (see "The *Standard of Ur,*" pages 38–39).

Stele of the Vultures. The city-states of ancient Sumer were often at war with one another, and the *Standard of Ur* is but one of many Sumerian artworks that have warfare as a principal subject. Another example is the so-called *Stele of the Vultures* (FIG. 2-11) from Girsu. A *stele* (pl. *stelae*) is a carved stone slab

erected to commemorate a historical event or, in some cultures, to mark a grave. The Girsu stele presents a labeled historical narrative, one of the earliest known (compare FIGS. 3-2 and 3-3). Cuneiform inscriptions fill almost every blank space and inform the viewer that the *Stele of the Vultures* celebrates the victory of Eannatum, the *ensi* ("ruler"; king?) of Lagash, over the neighboring city-state of Umma. The stele has reliefs on both sides and takes its modern name from a fragment depicting a gruesome scene of vultures carrying off the severed heads and arms of the defeated enemy soldiers. Another fragment shows the giant figure of the local god Ningirsu holding

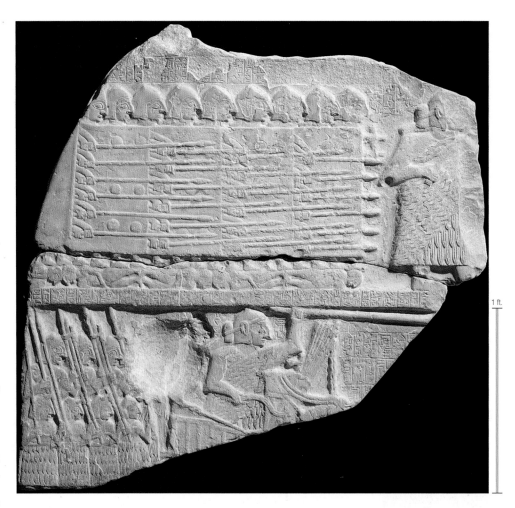

2-11 Battle scenes, fragment of the victory stele of Eannatum (*Stele of the Vultures*), from Girsu (modern Telloh), Iraq, ca. 2550–2500 BCE. Limestone, fragment 2′ 6″ high; full stele 5′ 11″ high. Musée du Louvre, Paris.

Cuneiform inscriptions on this stele describe Eannatum's victory over Umma with the aid of the god Ningirsu. This fragment shows Eannatum leading his troops into battle on foot and in a chariot.

1 ft.

tiny enemies in a net and beating one of them on the head with a mace—a striking contrast to the *Standard of Ur* (FIG. 2-9), where no gods are present and the victory is achieved by men alone.

The fragment in FIG. 2-11 depicts Eannatum leading an infantry battalion into battle (*above*) and attacking from a war chariot (*below*). The foot soldiers protect themselves by forming a wall of shields—there are far more hands and spears than heads and feet—and trample naked enemies as they advance (compare FIG. 2-9). (The fragment representing vultures devouring corpses belongs just to the right in the same register.) Both on foot and in a chariot, Eannatum is larger than everyone else, save for Ningirsu on the other side of the stele. The artist presented the ensi as the fearless general who paves the way for his army. Many Girsu attackers nonetheless lost their lives, and the inscription reports that Eannatum himself sustained wounds in the campaign, although the sculptor always portrayed the ensi as unharmed. In art, the outcome was never in doubt, because Ningirsu fought with the men of Lagash.

Despite its fragmentary state, the *Stele of the Vultures,* like the *Standard of Ur,* is an extraordinary find, not only as a very early effort to record historical events in relief (and to commemorate those events in a permanent public monument—another Sumerian "first") but also for the insight it yields about Sumerian society. Through both words and pictures, the stele provides information about warfare and the special nature of the Sumerian ruler. Eannatum was greater in stature than other men, and Ningirsu watched over him. According to the text, the ensi was born from the god Enlil's semen, which Ningirsu implanted in his mother's womb. When Eannatum incurred injuries in battle, the god shed tears for him. The inscription also says that it was Ningirsu who chose Eannatum to rule Lagash and preside over all aspects of the city-state, both in war and in peace. This also seems to have been the role of the ensi in the other cities of ancient Sumer.

Akkad

In 2332 BCE, the loosely linked group of Sumerian city-states came under the domination of a great ruler, Sargon of Akkad (r. 2332–2279 BCE). Archaeologists have yet to locate the site of Akkad, but the city was in the vicinity of Babylon. The Akkadians were Semitic in origin—that is, they were a Mesopotamian people who spoke a language related to Hebrew and Arabic. Their language, Akkadian, was very different from the language of Sumer, but they used the Sumerians' cuneiform characters for their written documents. Under Sargon (whose name means "true king") and his followers, the Akkadians introduced a new concept of royal power based on unswerving loyalty to the ruler rather than to the city-state. Naram-Sin (r. 2254–2218 BCE; FIG. 2-13), Sargon's grandson, regarded the governors of his cities as mere royal servants, and called himself King of the Four Quarters—in effect, ruler of the earth, akin to a god.

Akkadian Portraiture. A magnificent copper head (FIG. 2-12) of an Akkadian king embodies this new concept of absolute monarchy. Found at Nineveh, the head is all that survives of a statue knocked over in antiquity, perhaps when the Medes, a people who occupied the land south of the Caspian Sea (MAP 2-1), sacked the city in 612 BCE. But the damage to the portrait was not the result solely of the statue's toppling. There are also signs of deliberate mutilation. To make a political statement, the attackers gouged out the eyes (once inlaid with precious or semiprecious stones), broke off the lower part of the beard, and slashed the ears of the royal portrait. Later parallels for this kind of political vandalism abound—for example (in the same region), the destruction of images of Saddam Hussein after the Iraqi ruler's downfall in 2003.

Even in its mutilated state, however, the Akkadian portrait conveys the king's majestic serenity, dignity, and authority. The portrait is also remarkable for the masterful way that the sculptor balanced naturalism and abstract patterning. The artist carefully observed and recorded the Akkadian's distinctive features—the profile of the

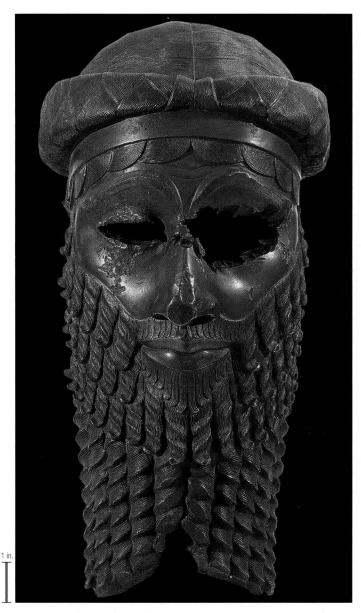

1 in.

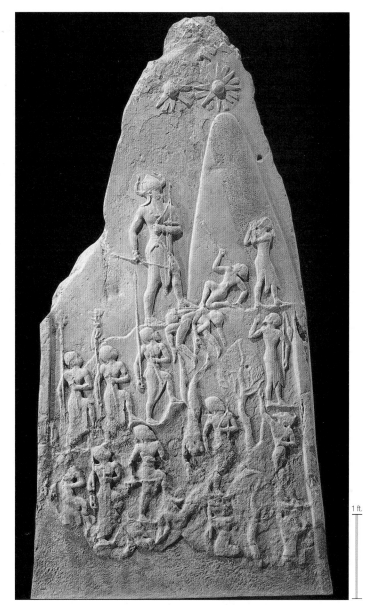

1 ft.

2-12 Head of an Akkadian ruler, from the Temple of Ishtar, Nineveh (modern Kuyunjik), Iraq, ca. 2250–2200 BCE. Copper, 1′ 2 3/8″ high. National Museum of Iraq, Baghdad.

The sculptor of this oldest extant life-size hollow-cast head captured the distinctive features of the ruler while also displaying a keen sense of abstract pattern. Vandals damaged the head in antiquity.

2-13 Victory stele of Naram-Sin, set up at Sippar, Iraq, 2254–2218 BCE; found at Susa, Iran. Pink sandstone, 6′ 10 5/8″ high. Musée du Louvre, Paris.

To commemorate his conquest of the Lullubi, Naram-Sin set up this stele showing him leading his army up a mountain. The sculptor staggered the figures, abandoning the traditional register format.

nose and the long, curly beard—and brilliantly communicated the differing textures of flesh and hair, even the contrasting textures of the mustache, beard, and braided hair on the top of the head. The coiffure's triangles, lozenges, and overlapping disks of hair and the great arching eyebrows that give such character to the portrait reveal that the sculptor was also sensitive to formal pattern.

No less remarkable is the fact that this is the oldest known life-size, hollow-cast metal sculpture. Hollow-casting is a production technique requiring great skill and many steps, including the forming of molds, casting, welding, engraving, and polishing (see "Hollow-Casting Life-Size Bronze Statues," page 129).

Naram-Sin Stele. The godlike sovereignty claimed by the kings of Akkad is also evident in the victory stele (FIG. 2-13) set up by Naram-Sin at Sippar. The stele commemorates the Akkadian ruler's

defeat of the Lullubi, a people of the Iranian mountains to the east. It carries two inscriptions, one in honor of Naram-Sin and one naming the Elamite king who captured Sippar in 1157 BCE and took the stele as booty back to Susa in southwestern Iran (MAP 2-1), the stele's findspot. The sculptor depicted Naram-Sin leading his army up the slopes of a wooded mountain. His routed enemies fall, flee, die, or beg for mercy. The king stands alone, far taller than his men, treading on the bodies of two of the fallen Lullubi. He wears the horned helmet signifying divinity—the first representation of a king as a god in Mesopotamian art. At least three favorable stars (the stele is damaged at the top), symbols of the gods, shine on his triumph.

By storming the mountain, Naram-Sin seems also to be scaling the ladder to the heavens, the same idea that lies behind the Mesopotamian temples on their elevated platforms. His troops march up

Enheduanna, Priestess and Poet

In the man's world of ancient Akkad, one woman stands out prominently—Enheduanna, daughter of King Sargon and priestess of the moon god Nanna at Ur. Her name appears in several inscriptions, and she was the author of a series of hymns in honor of the goddess Inanna. Enheduanna's is the oldest recorded name of a poet, male or female—indeed, the earliest known name of an author of any literary work in world history.

The most important surviving object associated with Enheduanna is the alabaster disk (FIG. 2-14) found in several fragments in the residence of the priestess of Nanna at Ur. The reverse bears a cuneiform inscription identifying Enheduanna as the "wife of Nanna" and "daughter of Sargon, king of the world." It also credits Enheduanna with erecting an altar to Nanna in his temple. The dedication of the relief to the moon god explains its unusual round format, which corresponds to the shape of the full moon. The front of the disk shows four figures approaching a four-story temple platform. The first figure is a nude man who is either a priest or Enheduanna's assistant. He pours a libation into a plant stand. The second figure, taller than the rest and wearing the headgear of a priestess, is Enheduanna herself. She raises her right hand in a gesture of greeting and respect for the god (compare FIG. 2-18). Two figures, probably female attendants, follow her.

Artworks created to honor women are rare in Mesopotamia and in the ancient world in general, but they are by no means unknown. The Sumerians, for example, buried Puabi of Ur in her own tomb filled with a treasure of jewelry, metal vessels, musical instruments (FIG. 2-6), and cylinder seals (FIG. 2-8), accompanied by 10 female retainers to attend her in the afterlife. The works created in honor of Puabi and Enheduanna are among the oldest known, but they pale in comparison with

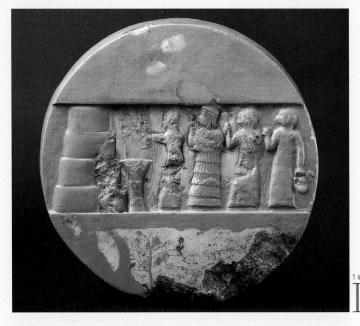

1 in.

2-14 Votive disk of Enheduanna, from Ur (modern Tell Muqayyar), Iraq, ca. 2300–2250 BCE. Alabaster, diameter $10\frac{1}{8}$". University of Pennsylvania Museum of Archaeology and Anthropology, Philadelphia.

Enheduanna, daughter of Sargon of Akkad and priestess of Nanna at Ur, is the first author whose name is known. She is the tallest figure on this votive disk, which she dedicated to the moon god.

the monuments erected in the mid-second millennium BCE in honor of Queen Hatshepsut of Egypt (see "Hatshepsut, the Woman Who Would Be King," page 72).

---

the mountain behind him in orderly files, suggesting the discipline and organization of the king's forces. By contrast, his enemies are in disarray, depicted in a great variety of postures. One falls head-long down the mountainside. The Akkadian artist adhered to older conventions in many details, especially by enlarging the size of the king, portraying him and his soldiers in composite views, and placing a frontal two-horned helmet on Naram-Sin's profile head. But the sculptor showed daring innovation in creating a landscape setting for the story and placing the figures on successive levels within that landscape. Among extant Mesopotamian works, this is the first time an artist rejected the standard format of telling a story in a series of horizontal registers, the compositional formula that had been the rule for a millennium. The traditional frieze format was the choice, however, for an alabaster disk (FIG. 2-14) that is in other respects an equally distinctive find (see "Enheduanna, Priestess and Poet," above).

2-15 Ziggurat (looking southwest), Ur (modern Tell Muqayyar), Iraq, begun ca. 2100 BCE.

The ziggurat at Ur is one of the largest in Mesopotamia. It has three (restored) ramp-like stairways of a hundred steps each that originally ended at a gateway to a brick temple, which does not survive.

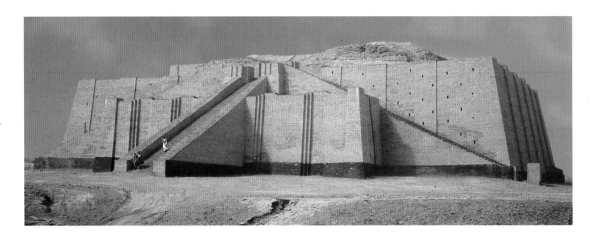

Gudea of Lagash

A central figure of the Neo-Sumerian age was Gudea of Lagash. More than two dozen portraits of him survive, many with inscriptions revealing Gudea's reasons for commissioning the portraits and setting them up where he did. All of Gudea's statues stood in temples where they could render perpetual service to the gods and intercede with the divine powers on his behalf. Although a powerful ruler, Gudea rejected the regal trappings of Sargon of Akkad and his successors, as well as their pretensions of divinity, in favor of a return to the Sumerian model of the ruler as the agent of the gods in the service of his people. Gudea's portraits follow the votive tradition of the Eshnunna (FIG. 2-5) and Mari (FIG. 2-5A) statuettes. Like the earlier examples, many of his statues bear inscriptions with messages to the gods of Sumer. They constitute one of the most extensive examples of "the patron's voice" in the ancient world.

In these inscriptions, Gudea often addresses the viewer directly. One inscribed portrait statue from Girsu says, "I am the one loved by my master [Ningirsu, the god of Girsu]; may my life be long." Another, also from Girsu, as if in answer to the first, says, "To Gudea, the one who built the temple, he [Ningirsu] has given long life."* Some of the inscriptions clarify why Gudea was portrayed as he was. For example, his large chest is a sign that the gods have given him fullness of life, and his muscular arms reveal his god-given strength. Other inscriptions explain that his large eyes signify that his gaze is perpetually fixed on the gods (see "Sumerian Votive Statuary," page 35, and FIG. 2-5).

Gudea built or rebuilt, at great cost, all the temples in which he placed his statues. One characteristic portrait (FIG. 2-16) depicts Gudea as a pious ruler seated with his hands clasped in front of him in a gesture of prayer. The statue is of special interest because Gudea has a temple plan drawn on a tablet on his lap. It is the plan for a new temple dedicated to Ningirsu. Gudea buried accounts of his building enterprises in the temple foundations. The surviving texts describe how the Neo-Sumerians prepared and purified the sites, obtained the materials, and dedicated the completed temples. They also record Gudea's dreams of the gods asking him to erect temples in their honor, promising him prosperity if he fulfilled his duty. In one of these dreams, Ningirsu addresses Gudea:

> When, O faithful shepherd Gudea, thou shalt have started work for me on Eninnu, my royal abode [Ningirsu's new temple], I will call up in heaven a humid wind. It shall bring the abundance from on high. . . . All the great fields will bear for thee; dykes and canals will swell for thee; . . . good weight of wool will be given in thy time.†

One of Gudea's portraits (FIG. 2-17) differs from the rest in depicting the ensi holding a jar from which water flows freely in two streams, one

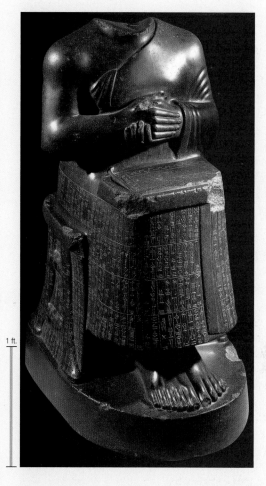

2-16 Gudea seated, holding the plan of a temple, from Girsu (modern Telloh), Iraq, ca. 2150 BCE. Diorite, 3' $\frac{5}{8}$" high. Musée du Louvre, Paris.

Gudea built or rebuilt many temples and placed statues of himself in them. The inscription on this seated portrait states that Gudea has on his lap a plan of the new temple he erected to Ningirsu.

running down each side of his cloak. Fish swim in the coursing water. In Mesopotamian art, gods and goddesses often hold similar overflowing vessels (FIG. 2-17A), which symbolize the prosperity they bring to their people. This small statue (less than half life-size) is the only known instance in which a Mesopotamian ruler is so depicted. For that reason and because the statue is made of calcite instead of the costly imported diorite used for Gudea's other portraits (FIG. 2-16), some scholars have questioned the authenticity of this piece. But the cuneiform inscription—which states that Gudea dedicated the statue in the temple he built in honor of the goddess Geshtinanna, the divine interpreter of dreams—is genuine, and so too must be the statue.

*Translated by Claudia E. Suter, *Gudea's Temple Building: The Representation of an Early Mesopotamian Ruler in Text and Image* (Groningen: Styx, 2000), 149.
†Translated by Thorkild Jacobsen, in Henri Frankfort, *The Art and Architecture of the Ancient Orient*, 5th ed. (New Haven, Conn.: Yale University Press, 1996), 98.

Third Dynasty of Ur

Around 2150 BCE, a mountain people, the Gutians, brought an end to Akkadian power. The cities of Sumer, however, soon united in response to the alien presence, drove the Gutians out of Mesopotamia, and established a Neo-Sumerian state ruled by the kings of Ur. Historians call this period the Neo-Sumerian age or the Third Dynasty of Ur.

Ziggurat, Ur. The most imposing extant Neo-Sumerian monument is the 50-foot-high mud-brick *ziggurat* (FIG. 2-15) at Ur, begun by the founder of the Third Dynasty, Ur-Namma (r. 2112–2095 BCE), and completed by his son and successor, Shulgi (r. 2094–2047 BCE). A millennium later than Uruk's more modest White Temple (FIGS. 2-2 and 2-3), the Ur ziggurat is the oldest preserved tiered temple platform (compare FIG. 2-14, *left*). (The platform of the White Temple is commonly, if incorrectly, called a

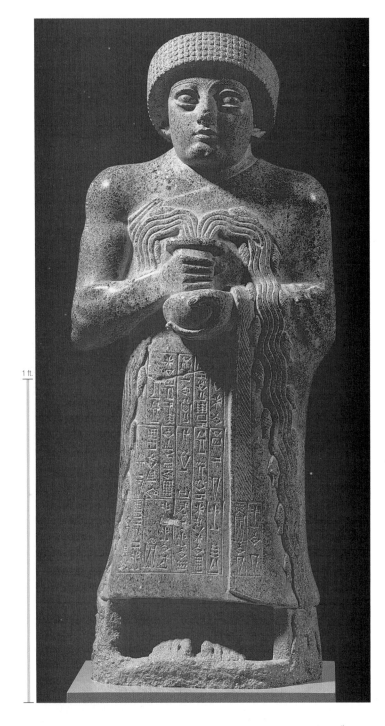

1 ft.

2-17 Gudea standing, holding an overflowing water jar, from the Temple of Geshtinanna, Girsu (modern Telloh), Iraq, ca. 2100 BCE. Calcite, 2′ 3/8″ high. Musée du Louvre, Paris.

The overflowing water jar that Gudea holds symbolizes the prosperity that he brings to the people of Lagash. In Mesopotamian art, normally only gods and goddesses are the sources of life-giving water.

ziggurat. It is a single-story platform.) The Neo-Sumerian builders used baked bricks laid in bitumen, an asphaltlike substance, for the facing of the entire monument. (Today, most of the bricks are part of the modern reconstruction.) Three ramplike stairways of a hundred steps each converge on a tower-flanked gateway. From there, another flight of steps (which has not been rebuilt) probably led to the temple in honor of the god Nanna that once crowned the ziggurat, the corners of which are aligned to the cardinal points.

Gudea of Lagash. Of all the preserved sculptures of the Third Dynasty of Ur, the most notable and numerous are those portraying Gudea, the ensi of Lagash around 2100 BCE. His statues show him seated (FIG. 2-16) or standing (FIG. 2-17), hands usually tightly clasped, head shaven, sometimes wearing a brimmed sheepskin hat, and always dressed in a long garment that leaves one shoulder and arm exposed. He has a youthful face with large, arching, herringbone-patterned eyebrows framing wide-open eyes. Almost all of his portraits are of polished diorite, a rare and costly dark stone that had to be imported from present-day Oman. Diorite is also extremely hard and difficult to carve. Underscoring the prestige of the material—which in turn lent prestige to Gudea's portraits—is an inscription on one of his statues: "This statue . . . is made neither of silver nor from lapis lazuli, nor copper, nor tin, nor bronze, but of diorite."[1] Indeed, the inscriptions on Gudea's portraits furnish a rare explicit record in the second millennium BCE or earlier of a patron's motivations for commissioning artworks (see "Gudea of Lagash," page 43).

Babylon

The resurgence of Sumer was short-lived. The last of the kings of the Third Dynasty of Ur fell at the hands of the Elamites, who ruled the territory east of the Tigris River. In the following two centuries, the traditional Mesopotamian political pattern of several independent city-states existing side by side reemerged. One of those city-states was Mari, home of Urnanshe (FIG. 2-5A) in the third millennium, and ruled by Zimri-Lin (r. 1779–1757 BCE; FIG. 2-17A) in the 18th century BCE. Another was Babylon, the probable provenance of one of the most fascinating surviving Mesopotamian artworks—the plaque acquired by the British Museum in 2003 and nicknamed *Queen of the Night* (FIG. 2-17B).

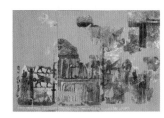

⏴ **2-17A** Investiture of Zimri-Lim, Mari, ca. 1775–1760 BCE.

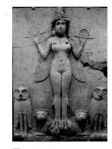

⏴ **2-17B** *Queen of the Night,* ca. 1800–1750 BCE.

Hammurabi. Babylon's most powerful king was Hammurabi (r. 1792–1750 BCE), who reestablished a centralized government in southern Mesopotamia in the area known as Babylonia, after its chief city. Hammurabi was famous in antiquity for his conquests, but he is best known today for his laws, which he enacted more than a thousand years before Draco provided Athens with its first comprehensive law code and when parts of Europe were still in the Stone Age. Hammurabi's laws prescribed penalties for everything from adultery and murder to the cutting down of a neighbor's trees (see "Hammurabi's Laws," page 45, and FIG. 2-18).

Hammurabi's stele is noteworthy artistically as well. At the top, the sculptor depicted the sun god Shamash in the familiar convention of combined front and side views, but with two important exceptions. Shamash's great headdress with its four pairs of horns is in true profile so that only four, not all eight, of the horns are visible. Also, the artist seems to have tentatively explored the notion of *foreshortening*—a means of suggesting depth by representing a figure or object at an angle, instead of frontally or in profile. Shamash's beard is a series of diagonal rather than horizontal lines, suggesting

Hammurabi's Laws

In the early 18th century BCE, the Babylonian king Hammurabi formulated a set of nearly 300 laws for his people. Two earlier sets of Sumerian laws survive in part, but Hammurabi's are the only laws known in great detail, thanks to the chance survival of a tall black basalt stele (FIG. 2-18) that an Elamite king carried off (along with the Naram-Sin stele [FIG. 2-13]) as war booty to Susa in 1157 BCE.

At the top of Hammurabi's stele is a representation in high relief of the Babylonian king in the presence of Shamash, the flame-shouldered sun god. Hammurabi raises his hand in respect as the god extends to his earthly representative the rod and ring symbolizing authority. The objects are builders' tools—measuring rods and coiled rope. They connote the ruler's capacity to build the social order and to measure people's lives—that is, to render judgments and enforce laws.

The collection of Hammurabi's judicial pronouncements is inscribed on the Susa stele in Akkadian in 3,500 lines of cuneiform characters. Hammurabi's laws governed all aspects of Babylonian life, from commerce and property to murder and theft to marital infidelity, inheritances, and the treatment of slaves.

Here is a small sample of the infractions described and the penalties imposed, which vary with the person's standing in society and notably deal with the rights and crimes of women as well as men:

- If a man puts out the eye of another man, his eye shall be put out.
- If he kills a man's slave, he shall pay one-third of a *mina*.
- If someone steals property from a temple, he will be put to death, as will the person who receives the stolen goods.
- If a married woman dies before bearing any sons, her dowry shall be repaid to her father, but if she gave birth to sons, the dowry shall belong to them.
- If a man strikes a freeborn woman so that she loses her unborn child, he shall pay ten *shekels* for her loss. If the woman dies, his daughter shall be put to death.
- If a man is guilty of incest with his daughter, he shall be exiled.

2-18 **Stele with the laws of Hammurabi, set up at Babylon, Iraq, ca. 1780 BCE; found at Susa, Iran. Basalt, 7′ 4″ high. Musée du Louvre, Paris.**

Crowning the stele recording Hammurabi's laws is a representation of the flame-shouldered sun god Shamash extending to the Babylonian king the symbols of his authority to govern and judge.

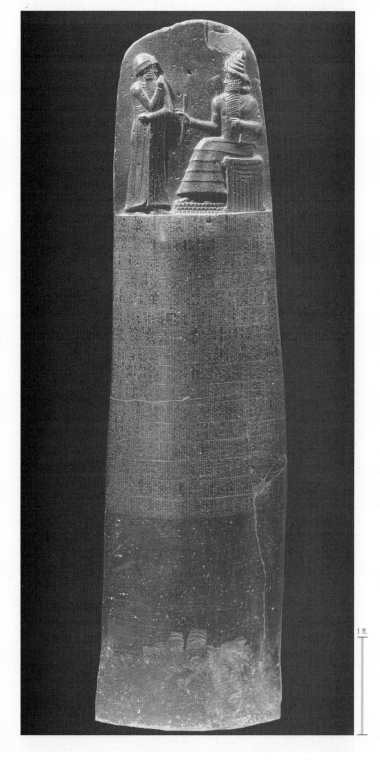

1 ft.

its recession from the picture plane. The sculptor also depicted the god's throne at an angle, further enhancing the illusion of spatial recession.

Elam

The Babylonian Empire toppled in the face of an onslaught by the Hittites, an Anatolian people whose heavily fortified capital was at Hattusa (FIG. 2-18A) near modern Boghazköy, Turkey. After sacking Babylon around 1595 BCE, the Hittites abandoned Mesopotamia and returned to their homeland, leaving Babylon in the hands of the Kassites. To the east of Babylon was Elam, which appears in the Bible as early as Genesis 10:22. At the Elamite capital of Susa in present-day Iran, archaeologists have discovered

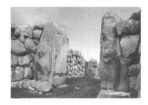

2-18A Lion Gate, Hattusa, ca. 1400 BCE.

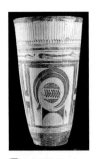

2-18B Beaker with animal decoration, Susa, ca. 4000 BCE.

painted pottery (FIG. 2-18B) dating as far back as the Neolithic period.

Elam reached the height of its political and military power during the second half of the second millennium BCE. At that time, the Elamites were strong enough to plunder Babylonia and carry off the stelae of Naram-Sin (FIG. 2-13) and Hammurabi (FIG. 2-18) and triumphantly display them as war spoils in Susa.

Napir-Asu. A life-size bronze-and-copper statue (FIG. 2-19) of Queen Napir-Asu, wife of one of the most powerful Elamite kings, Untash-Napirisha (r. ca. 1345–ca. 1305 BCE), is

one of the most important finds from Susa. Discovered in the Ninhursag temple, the statue weighs 3,760 pounds even in its fragmentary and mutilated state, because the sculptor, incredibly, cast the statue with a solid bronze core inside a hollow-cast copper shell (see "Hollow-Casting," page 129). The bronze core increased the cost of the statue enormously, but the queen wished her portrait to be a permanent, immovable votive offering in the temple where archaeologists found it. In fact, the Elamite inscription on the queen's skirt explicitly asks the gods to protect the statue:

> He who would seize my statue, who would smash it, who would destroy its inscription, who would erase my name, may he be smitten by the curse of [the gods], that his name shall become extinct, that his offspring be barren, that [Ishtar], the great goddess, shall sweep down on him. This is Napir-Asu's offering.[2]

Napir-Asu's portrait thus falls within the votive tradition dating back to the third-millennium BCE Eshnunna (FIG. 2-5) and Mari (FIG. 2-5A) figurines (see "Sumerian Votive Statuary," page 35). In the Elamite statue, the Mesopotamian instinct for cylindrical volume is again evident. The tight silhouette, strict frontality, and firmly crossed hands held close to the body are all enduring characteristics common to the Sumerian statuettes. Yet within these rigid conventions of form and pose, the Elamite artist incorporated features based on close observation. The sculptor conveyed the feminine softness of arm and bust, the grace and elegance of the long-fingered hands, the supple bend of the wrist, the ring and bracelets, and the gown's patterned fabric. The loss of the head is especially unfortunate. The figure presents a portrait of the ideal queen. The hands crossed over the belly may allude to fertility and the queen's role in assuring peaceful dynastic succession.

Assyria

During the first half of the first millennium BCE, the fearsome Assyrians vanquished the various peoples who succeeded the Babylonians and Hittites, including the Elamites, whose capital of Susa they sacked in 641 BCE. The Assyrians took their name from Assur, the city east of the Tigris River in the Zagros Mountains of northern Iraq dedicated to the god Ashur. At the height of their power, the Assyrians ruled an empire that extended from the Tigris River to the Nile and from the Persian Gulf to Asia Minor.

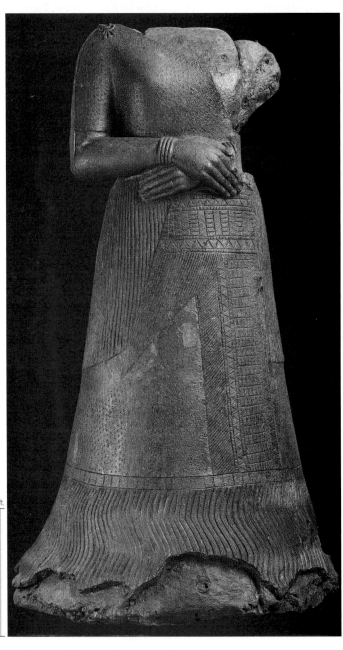

1 ft.

2-19 Statue of Queen Napir-Asu, from the Ninhursag temple, Susa, Iran, ca. 1340–1300 BCE. Bronze and copper, 4′ 2¾″ high. Musée du Louvre, Paris.

This life-size bronze-and-copper statue of the wife of a powerful Elamite king weighs 3,760 pounds. The queen wanted her portrait to stand in a temple at Susa as an immovable votive offering to the deity.

Palace of Sargon II. The Assyrian kings cultivated an image of themselves as merciless to anyone who dared oppose them, but forgiving to those who submitted to their will. Ever mindful of possible attack, the Assyrians constructed their palaces as fortified citadels (FIG. 2-19A) guarded by monstrous guardian figures (see "How Many Legs Does a Lamassu Have?" page 47, and FIG. 2-20). They profusely decorated these complexes with mural paintings (FIG. 2-21) and relief sculptures (FIGS. 2-22, 2-22A, and 2-23) exalting royal power.

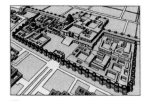

2-19A Citadel of Sargon II, Dur Sharrukin, ca. 721–705 BCE.

Palace of Ashurnasirpal II. Unfortunately, few Assyrian paintings exist today. A notable exception is the panel (FIG. 2-21) depicting King Ashurnasirpal II (r. 883–859 BCE) and his retinue

How Many Legs Does a Lamassu Have?

Guarding the gate of the Dur Sharrukin palace (FIG. 2-19A) of Sargon II (r. 721–705 BCE) and many of the other Assyrian royal complexes were colossal limestone monsters (FIG. 2-20), which the Assyrians probably called lamassu. These winged, man-headed bulls (or lions in some instances) served to ward off the king's enemies.

The task of moving and installing these immense stone sculptures was so difficult that several reliefs in the palace of Sargon's successor, Sennacherib (r. 705–681 BCE), celebrate that feat, showing scores of men dragging *lamassu* figures with the aid of ropes and sledges.

Transporting these mammoth sculptures (nearly 14 feet tall in the case of the two lamassu guarding the gateway of Sargon's Dur Sharrukin palace) was not the only problem the Assyrian sculptors had to confront. The artists also had to find a satisfactory way to represent a composite beast no one had ever seen, and they had to make the monster's unfamiliar form intelligible from every angle. They came up with a solution that may seem strange to modern eyes, but one consistent with the pictorial conventions of the age and perfectly suited to the problem.

The Assyrian lamassu sculptures are partly in the round, but the sculptors nonetheless conceived them as high reliefs on adjacent sides of a corner. They combine the front view of the animal at rest with the side view of it in motion. Seeking to present a complete picture of the lamassu from both the front and the side, the sculptors of all the extant Assyrian guardian statues gave each of the monsters five legs—two seen from the front, four seen from the side. The Assyrian lamassu sculptures, therefore, are yet another case of a conceptual picture of an animal or person and of all its important parts, as opposed to an optical view of the composite monster as it would stand in the real, versus the pictorial, world.

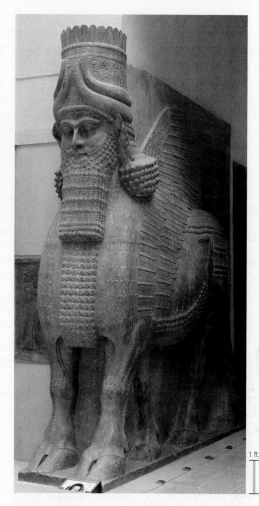

2-20 Lamassu (man-headed winged bull), from the citadel of Sargon II, Dur Sharrukin (modern Khorsabad), Iraq, ca. 721–705 BCE. Limestone, 13′ 10″ high. Musée du Louvre, Paris.

Ancient sculptors insisted on complete views of animals. This four-legged composite monster that guarded an Assyrian palace has five legs—two when seen from the front and four in profile view.

1 ft.

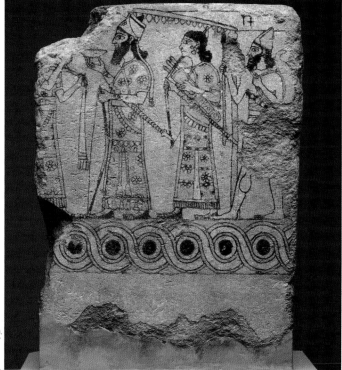

1 in.

paying homage to the gods. It comes from the king's northwest palace at Kalhu. The painting medium is *glazed* brick, a much more durable format than direct painting on plastered mud-brick walls, the technique used a millennium earlier in Zimri-Lim's palace at Mari (FIG. 2-17A). The Assyrian painter first applied lines and colors to a clay panel and then baked the clay in a kiln, fusing the colors to the clay.

The Kalhu panel shows Ashurnasirpal—his name means "Ashur guards the heir"—delicately holding a cup. With it, he will make a libation in honor of the protective Assyrian gods. The artist represented the king as taller than everyone else, befitting his rank, and rendered the figures in outline, devoting special attention to the patterns of the rich fabrics they wear. The king and the attendant behind him are in consistent profile view, but the painter adhered to the convention of showing the eye from the front in a profile head. Painted scenes such as this hint at the original appearance (before the color

2-21 Ashurnasirpal II with attendants and soldier, from the northwest palace of Ashurnasirpal II, Kalhu (modern Nimrud), Iraq, ca. 875–860 BCE. Glazed brick, 11¾″ high. British Museum, London.

Paintings on glazed bricks adorned the walls of Assyrian palaces. This rare example shows Ashurnasirpal II paying homage to the gods. The artist represented the king as taller than his attendants.

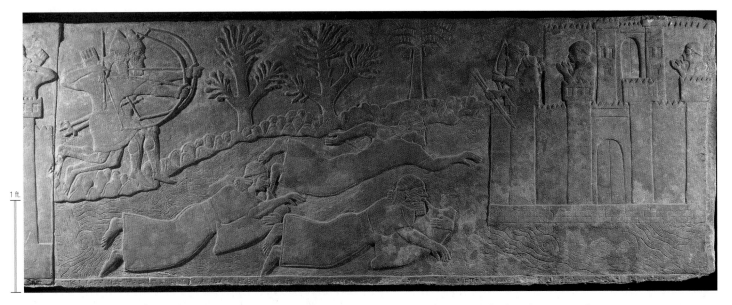

2-22 Assyrian archers pursuing enemies, relief from the northwest palace of Ashurnasirpal II, Kalhu (modern Nimrud), Iraq, ca. 875–860 BCE. Gypsum, 2′ 10⅝″ high. British Museum, London.

Extensive reliefs exalting the king and recounting his great deeds have been found in several Assyrian palaces. This one depicts Ashurnasirpal II's archers driving the enemy into the Euphrates River.

disappeared) of the stone reliefs (FIGS. 2-22, 2-22A, and 2-23) in Assyrian palaces, although the reliefs probably featured a wider range of hues than those available to the ceramic painter.

Ashurnasirpal's Kalhu palace also boasts one of the earliest and most extensive cycles of Assyrian relief sculptures, which, in their degree of documentary detail, are without parallel in the ancient world before the Roman Empire (see "The Roman Emperor as World Conqueror," page 181). The Assyrian reliefs, however, in contrast to their Roman imperial counterparts decorating grandiose public monuments, were viewed only by the royal entourage and privileged visitors in the innermost parts of the palace complexes.

The Assyrian reliefs are painted gypsum panels that sheathed the lower parts of the mud-brick palace walls below brightly colored plaster. Rich textiles on the floors contributed to the luxurious ambience. Every relief bore an inscription naming Ashurnasirpal and describing his accomplishments. Two of the reliefs are illustrated here.

The first (FIG. 2-22) shows Assyrians driving the enemy's forces into the Euphrates River. In the second relief (FIG. 2-22A),

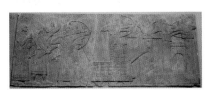

⌐⌐**2-22A** Assyrians besieging a fort, Kalhu, ca. 875–860 BCE.

the Assyrian army lays siege on an enemy citadel. The river scene probably depicts an episode that occurred in 878 BCE. Two of Ashurnasirpal's archers shoot arrows at the fleeing foe. Three enemy soldiers are in the water. One swims with an arrow in his back. The other two attempt to float to safety by inflating animal skins. Their destination is a fort where their compatriots await them. The artist showed the fort as if it were in the middle of the river, but it was, of course, on land, perhaps at some distance from where the escapees entered the water. The artist's purpose was to tell the story clearly and economically. Ancient sculptors and painters often compressed distances and enlarged the human actors so that they would stand out from their environment. For example, literally interpreted, this relief presents the defenders of the fort as too tall to walk through its archway. (Compare Naram-Sin and his men scaling a mountain, FIG. 2-13.) The sculptor also combined different viewpoints in the same frame, just as the figures are composites of frontal and profile views. The spectator views the river from above, and the men, trees, and fort from the side. The artist also made other adjustments for clarity. The archers' bowstrings are in front of their bodies but behind their heads in order not to hide the soldiers' faces. (The men will snare their heads in their bows when they launch their arrows.) All these liberties with optical reality, however, result in a vivid and easily legible retelling of a decisive moment in the king's victorious campaign. That was the sculptor's primary goal.

Palace of Ashurbanipal. Two centuries later, other Assyrian artists carved hunting reliefs (FIG. 2-23) for the Nineveh palace of the conqueror of Elamite Susa, Ashurbanipal (r. 668–627 BCE), whose name means "Ashur is creator of the son." The Greeks called him Sardanapalus, and the French painter Eugène Delacroix immortalized the Assyrian king in the 19th century in one of the most dramatic canvases (FIG. 27-15) of the Romantic era in Europe. The Assyrians, like many other societies before and after, regarded prowess in hunting as a manly virtue on a par with success in warfare. The royal hunt did not take place in the wild, however, but in a controlled environment, ensuring the king's safety and success.

In FIG. 2-23, lions released from cages in a large enclosed arena charge the king, who, in his chariot and with his attendants, thrusts a spear into a savage lion. The animal leaps at the king even though it already has two arrows in its body. All around the royal chariot is a pathetic trail of dead and dying animals, pierced by what appear to be far more arrows than needed to kill them. Blood streams from some of the lions, but they refuse to die. The artist brilliantly depicted the straining muscles, the swelling veins, the muzzles' wrinkled skin, and the flattened ears of the powerful and defiant beasts.

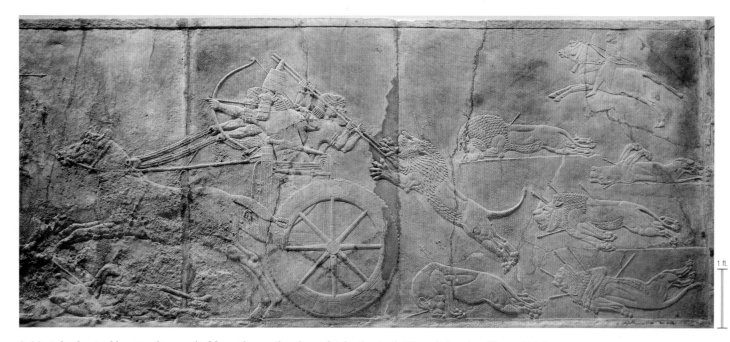

2-23 Ashurbanipal hunting lions, relief from the north palace of Ashurbanipal, Nineveh (modern Kuyunjik), Iraq, ca. 645–635 BCE. Gypsum, 5′ 4″ high. British Museum, London.

In addition to ceremonial and battle scenes, the hunt was a common subject of Assyrian palace reliefs. The Assyrians viewed prowess in hunting lions as a manly royal virtue on a par with victory in warfare.

Modern sympathies make this scene of carnage a kind of heroic tragedy, with the lions as protagonists. It is unlikely, however, that the king's artists had any intention other than to glorify their ruler by showing the king of men pitted against and repeatedly besting the king of beasts. Portraying Ashurbanipal's beastly foes as possessing courage and nobility as well as the power to kill made the king's accomplishments that much grander.

The Assyrian Empire was never very secure, however, and most of its kings had to fight revolts throughout Mesopotamia. Assyria's conquest of Elam in the seventh century BCE and frequent rebellions in Babylonia apparently overextended its resources. During the last years of Ashurbanipal's reign, the empire began to disintegrate. Under his successors, it collapsed from the simultaneous onslaught of the Medes from the east and the resurgent Babylonians from the south. Neo-Babylonian kings held sway over the former Assyrian Empire until the Persian conquest.

Neo-Babylonia

The most renowned of the Neo-Babylonian kings was Nebuchadnezzar II (r. 605–562 BCE), whose exploits are recounted in the Bible's Book of Daniel. Nebuchadnezzar restored Babylon to its rank as one of the great cities of antiquity. The Greeks and Romans counted "the hanging gardens of Babylon" among the Seven Wonders of the ancient world, and the Bible immortalized the city's enormous ziggurat as the Tower of Babel (see "Babylon, City of Wonders," page 50).

Ishtar Gate. Nebuchadnezzar's Babylon was a mud-brick city, but dazzling blue-glazed bricks adorned the most important monuments, such as the 47-foot-high Ishtar Gate (FIG. 2-24)—actually a pair of gates, one of which has been restored and

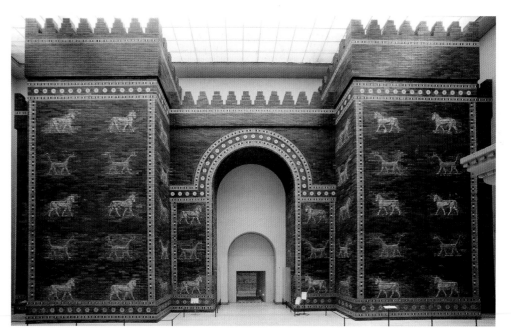

2-24 Ishtar Gate (restored), Babylon, Iraq, ca. 575 BCE. Vorderasiatisches Museum, Staatliche Museen zu Berlin, Berlin.

Nebuchadnezzar II's Babylon was one of the ancient world's greatest cities and boasted the biblical Tower of Babel. Its Ishtar Gate featured glazed-brick reliefs of Marduk and Nabu's dragon and Adad's bull.

Babylon, City of Wonders

The uncontested list of the Seven Wonders of the ancient world was not codified until the 16th century. But already in the second century BCE, Antipater of Sidon, a Greek poet, compiled a roster of seven must-see monuments, including six of the seven later Wonders. All of the Wonders were of colossal size and constructed at great expense. The oldest were of great antiquity, nearly 2,500 years old in Antipater's day: the pyramids of Gizeh (FIG. 3-8), which he described as "man-made mountains." Only one site on Antipater's list could boast two Wonders: Babylon, with its "hanging gardens" and "impregnable walls." The wondrous gardens were not in Babylon, however, but part of the Assyrian king Sennacherib's "palace without rival" at Nineveh. Later list makers preferred to distribute the Seven Wonders among seven different cities (not including Nineveh). Most of these Wonders date to Greek times—the Ephesos of Saint Paul, with its 60-foot-tall *columns*; Phidias's colossal gold-and-ivory statue of Zeus at Olympia; the "Mausoleum" at Halikarnassos, the gigantic tomb (FIG. 5-63C) of the fourth-century BCE ruler Mausolus; the Colossus of Rhodes, a bronze statue of the Greek sun god 110 feet tall; and the lighthouse at Alexandria, perhaps the tallest building in the ancient world. The "Babylonian" gardens were the only Wonder in the category of landscape architecture.

Several ancient texts describe the wondrous hanging gardens, although none of the authors had traveled to Babylon. Quintus Curtius Rufus, for example, basing his account on earlier, unfortunately unreliable, sources, reported in the mid-first century CE:

> On the top of the citadel are the hanging gardens, a wonder celebrated in the tales of the Greeks. . . . Columns of stone were set up to sustain the whole work, and on these was laid a floor of squared blocks, strong enough to hold the earth which is thrown upon it to a great depth, as well as the water with which they irrigate the soil; and the structure supports trees of such great size that the thickness of their trunks equals a measure of eight cubits [about 12 feet]. They tower to a height of fifty feet, and they yield as much fruit as if they were growing in their native soil. . . . To those who look upon [the trees] from a distance, real woods seem to be overhanging their native mountains.*

Not qualifying as a Wonder, but in some ways no less impressive (and far more real), was Babylon's Marduk ziggurat, erected by King Nebuchadnezzar, who also constructed Babylon's Ishtar Gate (FIG. 2-24). Called the Etemenanki (Sumerian, Home of the Foundation Platform of Heaven and Earth) by the Babylonians, the ziggurat was immortalized in the Bible (Gen. 11:1–9) as the Tower of Babel. The Babylonians considered their city to be the center of the world and the Etemenanki the *axis mundi,* the symbolic pole connecting the earth with the heavens, a concept with close parallels in other civilizations—for example, in the Indus Valley of South Asia (FIG. 15-6). According to the Bible, men's arrogant desire to build a tower to Heaven angered God. The Lord put an end to it by causing the workers to speak different languages, preventing them from communicating with one another. The fifth-century BCE Greek historian Herodotus described the Babylonian temple complex:

> In the middle of the sanctuary [of Marduk] has been built a solid tower . . . which supports another tower, which in turn supports another, and so on: there are eight towers in all. A stairway has been constructed to wind its way up the outside of all the towers; halfway up the stairway there is a shelter with benches to rest on, where people making the ascent can sit and catch their breath. In the last tower there is a huge temple. The temple contains a large couch, which is adorned with fine coverings and has a golden table standing beside it, but there are no statues at all standing there. . . . [The Babylonians] say that the god comes in person to the temple [compare the Sumerian notion of the temple as a "waiting room"] and rests on the couch; I do not believe this story myself.†

The fictional hanging gardens of Babylon are a cautionary tale about the accuracy of written sources, which are indispensable for the study of the history of art and architecture, but must be examined critically before being accepted at face value.

*Quintus Curtius 5. 1. 31–35. Translated by John C. Rolfe, *Quintus Curtius I* (Cambridge, Mass.: Harvard University Press, 1971), 337–339.

†Herodotus 1.181–182. Translated by Robin Waterfield, *Herodotus: The Histories* (New York: Oxford University Press, 1998), 79–80.

installed in the Vorderasiatisches (Near Eastern) Museum in Berlin. The Ishtar Gate consists of a large *arcuated* (arch-shaped) opening flanked by towers, and features glazed bricks with reliefs of animals, real and imaginary. The Babylonian builders molded and glazed each brick separately, then set them in proper sequence on the wall. On the Ishtar Gate, profile figures of Marduk and Nabu's dragon and Adad's bull alternate. Lining the processional way leading up to the gate were reliefs of Ishtar's sacred lion, glazed in yellow, brown, and red against a lapis lazuli blue background.

PERSIA

Although Nebuchadnezzar—the "king of kings" in the Book of Daniel (2:37)—had boasted in an inscription that he "caused a mighty wall to circumscribe Babylon . . . so that the enemy who would do evil would not threaten," Cyrus of Persia (r. 559–529 BCE) captured the city in 539 BCE. Cyrus, who may have been descended from an Elamite line, was the founder of the Achaemenid dynasty and traced his ancestry back to a mythical King Achaemenes.

Achaemenid Empire

Babylon was but one of the Achaemenids' conquests. Egypt fell to them in 525 BCE, and by 480 BCE they boasted the largest empire the world had yet known, extending from the Indus River in South Asia to the Danube River in northeastern Europe. If the Greeks had not succeeded in turning back the Persians in 479 BCE, they would have taken control of southeastern Europe as well. The Achaemenid line ended with the death of Darius III in 330 BCE, after his defeat at the hands of Alexander the Great (FIG. 5-70).

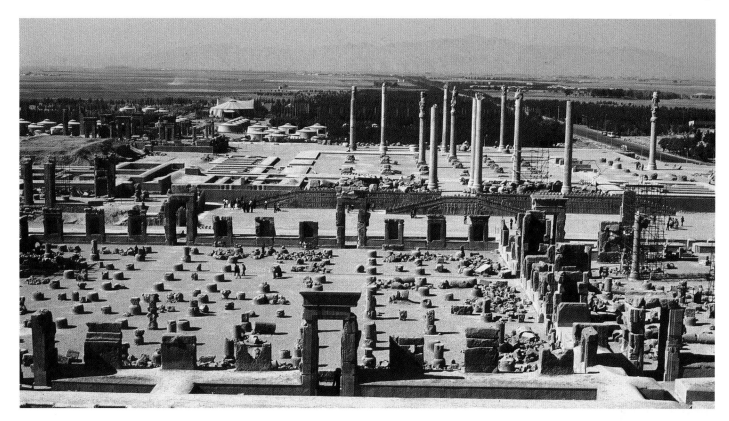

2-25 Aerial view of the palace (*above*: looking west with the apadana in the background) and three columns of the apadana with animal protomes (*right*), Persepolis, Iran, ca. 521–465 BCE.

The heavily fortified complex of Persian royal buildings on a high plateau at Persepolis included extensive sculpted friezes (FIG. 2-27) and a royal audience hall, or apadana, with 36 colossal columns.

Persepolis. The most important source of knowledge about Persian art and architecture is the ceremonial and administrative complex within the citadel at Persepolis (FIG. 2-25), which the successors of Cyrus, Darius I (r. 522–486 BCE) and Xerxes (r. 486–465 BCE), built between 521 and 465 BCE. Situated on a high plateau, the heavily fortified complex of royal buildings stood on a wide platform overlooking the plain. Alexander the Great razed the site in 330 BCE in a gesture symbolizing the destruction of Persian imperial power. Some said it was an act of revenge for the Persian sack of the Athenian Acropolis in 480 BCE (see "Early and High Classical Periods," page 125). Nevertheless, even in ruins, the Persepolis citadel is impressive.

The approach to the citadel led through a monumental gateway called the Gate of All Lands, a reference to the harmony among the peoples of the vast Persian Empire. Assyrian-inspired colossal man-headed winged bulls flanked the great entrance. Broad ceremonial stairways provided access to the platform and the immense (1,173-square-foot) royal audience hall, or *apadana,* in which at least 10,000 guests could stand at one time. Although the hall had mud-brick walls, the floors were paved in stone or brick, and the apadana's chief feature—its forest of 36 colossal columns—was entirely of stone.

The columns (FIG. 2-25, *right*) consisted of tall *bases* with a ring of palm leaves, 57-foot *shafts* with *flutes,* and enormous *capitals* composed of stacked *volutes* (see "Doric and Ionic Orders," page 116, for the architectural terminology) topped by polished and painted back-to-back animal *protomes* (the head, forelegs, and

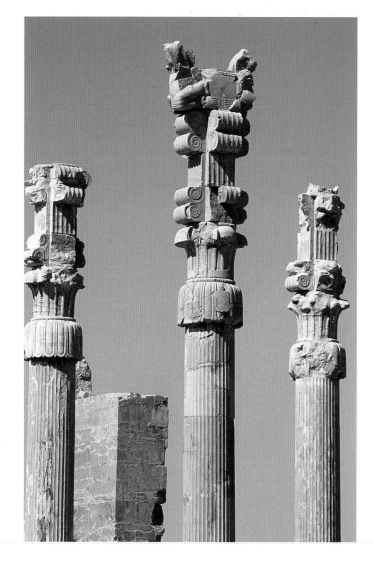

2-26 Column capital with bull protomes, from the apadana of the palace of Darius I, Susa, Iran, ca. 510 BCE. Limestone, 7′ high. Musée du Louvre, Paris.

The 65-foot columns of the Susa apadana drew on Mesopotamian, Greek, and Egyptian models, but are unique in form. The back-to-back protomes resting on the volutes of the capitals supported huge cedar beams.

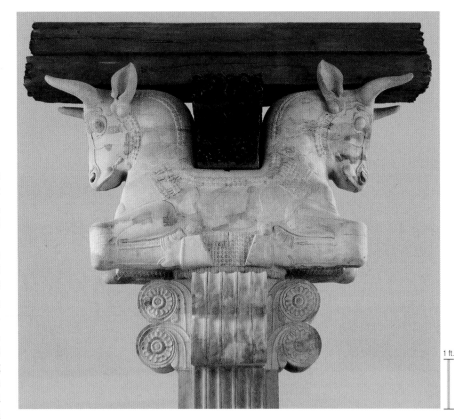

part of the body). Similar columns and capitals (FIG. 2-26) filled the apadana of Darius I's palace at Susa. The Achaemenid capitals are unique in form, but the designers drew on Greek, Egyptian, and Mesopotamian traditions.

The capitals with animal protomes in the Susa apadana are about 7 feet tall, bringing the total height of each of the 36 columns in the hall to 65 feet, including the bases. The Persepolis and Susa capitals incorporate several different animals—*griffins* (eagle-headed winged lions), bulls, lions, and composite man-headed bulls. The architects may have wanted to suggest that the Persian king had captured the fiercest animals and monsters to hold up the roof of his palace. The choice of paired protomes may have symbolized that the Persian cosmos was in equilibrium. The back-to-back protomes of each capital form a ∪-shaped socket that held massive cedar beams (imported from Lebanon), which in turn supported a timber roof sealed with mud plaster. The illustrated Susa capital (FIG. 2-26) was reconstructed from fragments of several different capitals, which explains the variation in the color of the gray limestone.

The reliefs (FIG. 2-27) decorating the walls of the terrace and staircases leading to the Persepolis apadana represent processions of royal guards, Persian nobles and dignitaries, and representatives from 23 subject nations, including Medes, Elamites, Babylonians, Egyptians, and Nubians, bringing tribute to the king. Every emissary wears a characteristic costume and carries a typical regional

2-27 Persians and Medes, detail of the processional frieze on the east side of the terrace of the apadana of the palace (FIG. 2-25), Persepolis, Iran, ca. 521–465 BCE. Limestone, 8′ 4″ high.

The reliefs decorating the walls of the terrace and staircases leading up to the Persepolis apadana (FIG. 2-25) included depictions of representatives of 23 nations bringing tribute to the Persian king.

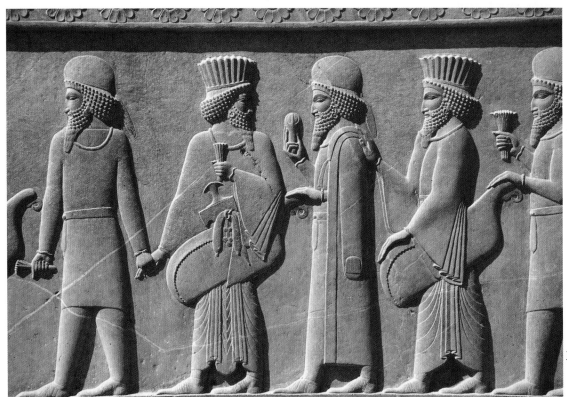

gift for the conqueror. The section of the procession reproduced here represents Persian nobles (in pleated skirts) and Medes wearing their distinctive round caps, knee-length tunics, and trousers. The carving of the Persepolis reliefs is technically superb, with subtly modeled surfaces and crisply chiseled details. Traces of paint prove that the reliefs were brightly colored.

Although the Assyrian palace reliefs may have inspired those at Persepolis, the Persian sculptures differ in style. The forms are more rounded, and they project more from the background. Some of the details, notably the treatment of drapery folds, echo forms characteristic of Archaic Greek sculpture (compare FIG. 5-11), and Greek influence seems to be one of the many ingredients of Achaemenid style. Persian art testifies to the active exchange of ideas and artists among all the civilizations of Persia, Mesopotamia, and the Mediterranean at this date. In an inscription from the Susa palace, Darius I boasts of the diverse origin of the stonemasons, carpenters, and sculptors who constructed and decorated the complex. He names Medes, Egyptians, Babylonians, and Ionian Greeks. This heterogeneous workforce created a new and coherent style that perfectly suited the expression of Persian imperial ambitions.

Achaemenid Rhyton. When the Achaemenid kings entertained guests, they served them food and drink in tableware of costly materials. Indeed, the Persians were famous for their luxurious cups and plates of gold and silver. Herodotus (*Histories,* 9.80), for example, recounted how after the Greeks defeated the Persians at the Battle of Plataea in 479 BCE, they entered the Persian camp and found tents filled with gold bowls and goblets and wagons overflowing with gold and silver basins. In fact, this opulent collection was merely what the Persian king Xerxes brought with him on a military campaign.

When Alexander the Great sacked Persepolis, he discovered even greater riches, including gold objects similar to the *rhyton* (conical pouring vessel) in the form of a winged lion illustrated here (FIG. 2-28). Although found at Hamadan in Iran instead of Persepolis or Susa, the rhyton must closely resemble the magnificent items that graced the tables of the Achaemenid royal house. Its shape is typical of these elaborate service pieces: a conical, trumpet-like container for wine, hammered (*repoussé*) from a thin sheet of gold inserted at a right angle into an animal protome (compare FIG. 2-26) also crafted in repoussé. In this case, the protome is a winged lion, one of the many composite beasts popular in Mesopotamian art from the Sumerian era through the seventh century CE. Around the lip of the rhyton is a lotus-and-palmette band that has close parallels on painted Greek vases (compare FIGS. 5-23, 5-23A, and 5-59) and in Greek architectural decoration. The Hamadan rhyton is thus another example of the varied stylistic and iconographical roots of Persian art.

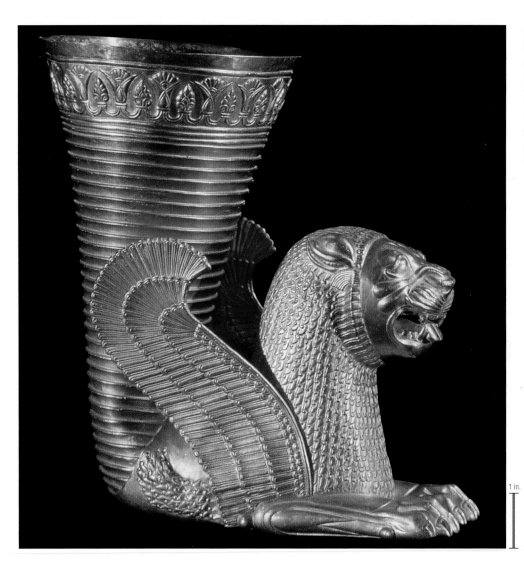

2-28 Rhyton in the form of a winged lion, from Hamadan, Iran, fifth to third century BCE. Gold, $8\frac{3}{8}''$ high. Archaeological Museum of Iran, Tehran.

This hammered-gold conical pouring vessel with a winged-lion protome is a characteristic example of the luxurious items that graced the tables of Achaemenid royal palaces.

1 in.

Sasanian Empire

Alexander the Great's conquest of the Achaemenid Empire in 330 BCE marked the beginning of a long period of first Greek and then Roman rule of large parts of Mesopotamia and Persia, beginning with one of Alexander's former generals, Seleucus I (r. 312–281 BCE), founder of the Seleucid dynasty. In the third century CE, however, a new power rose up in Persia that challenged the Romans and sought to force them out of Asia. The new rulers called themselves Sasanians. They traced their lineage to a legendary figure named Sasan, said to be a direct descendant of the Achaemenid kings. The first Sasanian king, Ardashir I (r. 211–241), founded the New Persian Empire in 224 CE after he defeated the Parthians (another of Rome's eastern enemies).

Bishapur and Ctesiphon. The son and successor of Ardashir, Shapur I (r. 241–272), was an accomplished general who further extended Sasanian territory. In 260, he even captured the Roman emperor Valerian (r. 253–260)—a singular feat, which he immortalized in a series of reliefs (for example, FIG. 2-28A) at Bishapur, Iran. Traditionally also thought to have been the work of Shapur I is the great palace (FIG. 2-29) at Ctesiphon, the capital that his father had established near modern Baghdad in Iraq. The construction of the palace is now attributed by most scholars to Khosrow I (r. 531–579), a Sasanian king who lived three centuries later. The central feature of the Ctesiphon palace, known locally as the Taq-I Kisra, is the monumental *iwan*, or brick audience hall, covered by a *vault* (here, a deep arch over an oblong space) that comes almost to a point more than 100 feet above the ground. A series of horizontal bands made up of *blind arcades* (a series of arches without openings, applied as wall decoration) divide the *facade* (building front) to the left and right of the iwan.

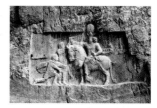

⊡ **2-28A** Triumph of Shapur I, Bishapur, ca. 260 CE.

The New Persian Empire endured more than 400 years, until the Arabs drove the Sasanians out of Mesopotamia in 636 CE, just four years after the death of Muhammad. But the prestige of Sasanian art and architecture long outlasted the empire. Eight centuries after Khosrow I built his palace at Ctesiphon, Islamic architects in Cairo (FIG. 10-25) still considered its soaring iwan as the standard for judging their own engineering feats.

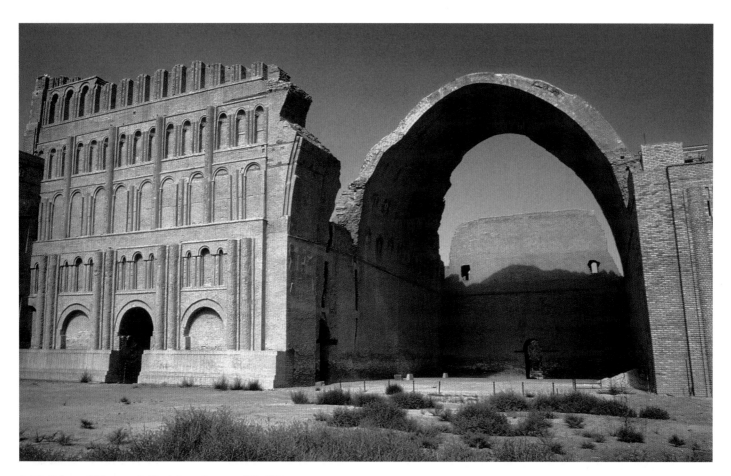

2-29 Palace of Khosrow I, Ctesiphon, Iraq, ca. 531–579 CE.

The Sasanians were the last great pre-Islamic civilization of Mesopotamia and Persia. Their palace at Ctesiphon, near Baghdad, features a brick audience hall (iwan) covered by an enormous pointed vault.

Mesopotamia and Persia

Sumerian Art ca. 3500–2332 BCE

- The Sumerians founded the world's first city-states in the valley between the Tigris and Euphrates Rivers and invented writing in the fourth millennium BCE.

- They were also the first to build communal religious shrines on towering platforms, such as Uruk's mud-brick White Temple, and to place figures in registers to tell coherent stories, as on the *Standard of Ur*.

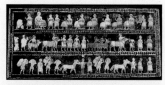

Standard of Ur, ca. 2550–2400 BCE

Akkadian Art ca. 2332–2150 BCE

- The Akkadians were the first Mesopotamian rulers to call themselves kings of the world and to assume divine attributes. The earliest recorded name of an author is Enheduanna, an Akkadian priestess of the god Nanna.

- Akkadian artists may have been the first to cast hollow life-size metal sculptures and to place figures at different levels in a landscape setting, as on the stele erected by Naram-Sin to celebrate his victory over the Lullubi.

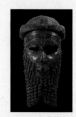

Akkadian ruler, ca. 2250–2200 BCE

Neo-Sumerian and Babylonian Art ca. 2150–1600 BCE

- During the Third Dynasty of Ur, the Sumerians rose again to power and constructed one of Mesopotamia's largest tiered temple platforms, or ziggurats, at Ur.

- Gudea of Lagash (r. ca. 2150 BCE) built numerous temples and placed portraits of himself in them as votive offerings to the gods.

- Babylon's greatest king, Hammurabi (r. 1792–1750 BCE), formulated wide-ranging laws for the empire he ruled. Babylonian artists were among the first to experiment with foreshortening.

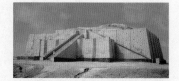

Ziggurat, Ur, begun ca. 2100 BCE

Assyrian and Neo-Babylonian Art ca. 900–539 BCE

- At the height of their power, the Assyrians ruled an empire that extended from the Persian Gulf to the Nile and Asia Minor.

- Assyrian palaces were fortified citadels with gates guarded by monstrous lamassu. Paintings and reliefs depicting official ceremonies and the king battling enemies and hunting lions decorated the walls of the ceremonial halls.

- In the sixth century BCE, Babylon was thought to be home to two of the Seven Wonders of the ancient world. The Ishtar Gate, with its colorful glazed brick reliefs, gives an idea of Babylon's magnificence under Nebuchadnezzar II (r. 605–562 BCE).

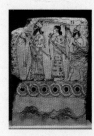

Palace of Ashurnasirpal II, Kalhu, ca. 875–860 BCE

Achaemenid and Sasanian Art ca. 559–330 BCE and 224–636 CE

- The capital of the Achaemenid Persians was at Persepolis, where Darius I (r. 522–486 BCE) and Xerxes (r. 486–465 BCE) built a huge palace complex with an audience hall that could accommodate 10,000 guests. Painted reliefs of subject nations bringing tribute adorned the terraces.

- The Sasanians, enemies of Rome, ruled the New Persian Empire from their palace at Ctesiphon until the Arabs defeated them four years after the death of Muhammad.

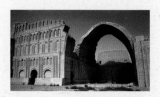

Palace of Khosrow I, Ctesiphon, ca. 531–579 CE

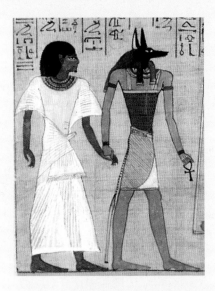

◄3-1a At the left, Anubis, the Egyptian god of embalming, shown with a man's body and a jackal's head, grasps the deceased Hunefer's left hand and leads him into the hall of judgment.

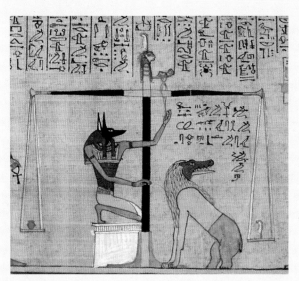

▶3-1b Anubis weighs Hunefer's heart against a feather, the hieroglyph of Maat, the goddess of truth and right doing. The monstrous Ammit will devour the heart if it weighs more than the feather.

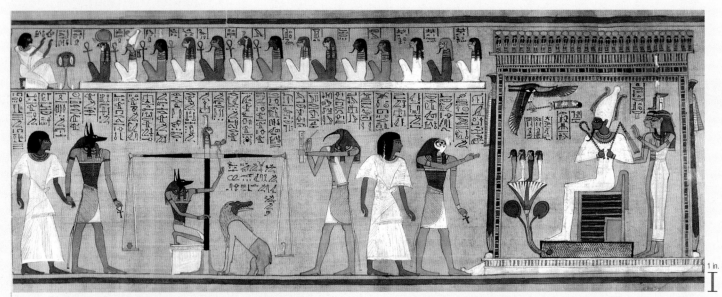

3-1 **Judgment of Hunefer, detail of an illustrated *Book of the Dead,* from the tomb of Hunefer, Thebes, Egypt, 19th Dynasty, ca. 1290–1275 BCE.** Painted papyrus scroll, 1′ 3½″ high; full scroll 18′ ½″ long. British Museum, London.

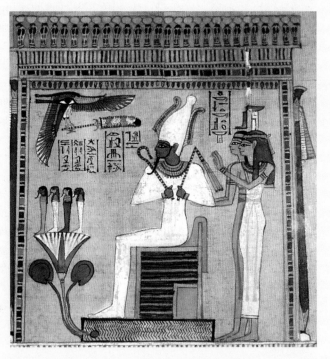

▶3-1c After the scales declare him worthy, Hunefer is led before the enthroned green-faced god Osiris and his sisters, Isis and Nephthys, to receive the award of eternal life, the goal of every Egyptian.

EGYPT FROM NARMER TO CLEOPATRA /3

Life after Death in Ancient Egypt

Blessed with abundant sources of stone of different hues suitable for carving statues and fashioning building blocks, the ancient Egyptians left to posterity a profusion of spectacular monuments spanning three millennia. Many of them glorified the gods and were set up by the Egyptian kings, whom the Egyptians believed were also divine and could serve as intermediaries with the gods. Indeed, the Egyptians devoted enormous resources to erecting countless monuments and statues to honor their god-kings during their lifetimes, and to constructing and furnishing magnificent tombs to serve as the divine kings' eternal homes in the afterlife.

Those who were not of royal birth could also aspire to an afterlife. Egyptians believed in the eternal existence of a person's *ka,* or life force, which continued to inhabit the corpse after an individual died. For this reason, those who could afford it lavishly furnished their tombs for the "next life." In those tombs, archaeologists have discovered not only stone and metal objects but also a vast number of items fashioned from perishable materials rarely preserved elsewhere, including illustrated *papyrus* scrolls such as the *Book of the Dead* (FIG. 3-1) found in the tomb of Hunefer, the royal scribe and steward of Seti I (r. 1306–1290 BCE).

Hunefer's scroll is a collection of spells and prayers needed to secure a happy afterlife. Illustrated scrolls (some are 70 feet long) containing these texts were essential items in the tombs of well-to-do Egyptians. At the top left of the section reproduced here, Hunefer kneels in adoration before a row of seated Egyptian deities. Below, Anubis, the jackal-headed god of embalming, leads the deceased into the hall of judgment. The god then adjusts the scales to weigh Hunefer's heart against a feather, the *hieroglyph* of the name of the goddess Maat and a symbol for truth and right doing. Because the dead man's heart weighs less than the feather, he merits eternal life. Otherwise, Ammit, the hybrid crocodile-hippopotamus-lion monster, who watches the weighing, would have eaten Hunefer's heart, and he would die a second time. To the right, the ibis-headed god Thoth records the proceedings.

Finally, having been judged favorably by the scales, Hunefer is brought by Osiris's son, the falcon-headed Horus, into the presence of the enthroned green-faced Osiris and his sisters, Isis and Nephthys, to receive the award of eternal life. This was the goal of every Egyptian and the concept that dictated the form and content of much of Egyptian art and architecture from its beginnings in the fourth millennium BCE and for several thousand years thereafter.

EGYPT AND EGYPTOLOGY

The backbone of Egypt was, and still is, the Nile River, which, through its annual floods, supported all life in that ancient land (MAP 3-1). Even more so than the Tigris and Euphrates Rivers of Mesopotamia (MAP 2-1), the Nile defined the cultures that developed along its banks. Originating deep in Africa, the world's longest river flows through regions that may not receive a single drop of rainfall in a decade. Yet crops thrive from the rich soil that the Nile brings thousands of miles from the African hills. In antiquity, the land bordering the Nile consisted of marshes dotted with island ridges. Amphibious animals swarmed in the marshes, where the Egyptians hunted them through tall forests of papyrus and rushes (FIGS. 3-15 and 3-28A). The fertility of Egypt was famous. When the Kingdom of the Nile became a province of the Roman Empire after the death of Queen Cleopatra (r. 51–30 BCE), it served as the granary of the Mediterranean world.

During the Middle Ages, the detailed knowledge that the Romans possessed about the Egyptians and their gods was largely forgotten (see "The Gods and Goddesses of Egypt," page 60). With the Enlightenment of the 18th century, scholars began to piece together Egypt's history from references in the Bible, from the fifth-century BCE Greek historian Herodotus and other Greco-Roman authors, and from preserved portions of a third-century BCE history of Egypt written in Greek by Manetho, an Egyptian high priest. Manetho described the succession of Egyptian rulers, dividing them into the still-useful groups called dynasties, based on a line of hereditary rulers or the changing location of the royal residence. Unfortunately, Manetho's chronology is inaccurate, and today historians still do not agree on the absolute dates of the kings. The chronologies that scholars have proposed for the earliest Egyptian dynasties can vary by as much as two centuries. Only after 664 BCE (26th Dynasty) are the exact years of individual reigns certain.[1]

The modern discipline of Egyptology dates to the late 18th century, when archaeological exploration of the land of the Nile began in earnest. In 1799, on a military expedition to Egypt, Napoleon Bonaparte (1769–1821) took with him a large team of scholars, linguists, antiquarians, and artists. In 1804, they published *Description of Egypt,* a groundbreaking collaborative work based on the massive amount of data that the scientific expedition collected.

Rosetta Stone. Most noteworthy was the chance discovery of the famed *Rosetta Stone,* now in the British Museum, which provided the key to deciphering Egyptian hieroglyphic writing. The stone bears an inscription in three sections: one in Greek, which Napoleon's team easily read; one in *demotic* (Late Egyptian); and one in formal hieroglyphic. On the assumption that the text

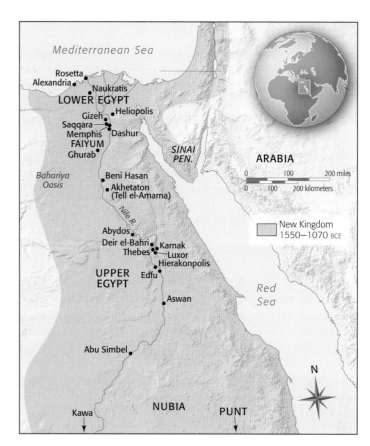

MAP 3-1 Ancient Egypt.

was the same in all three sections, Jean-François Champollion (1790–1832) and other scholars attempted to decipher the two non-Greek sections. Eventually, they deduced that the hieroglyphs were not simply pictographs but the signs of a once-spoken language whose traces survived in Coptic, the language of Christian Egypt. The ability to read hieroglyphic inscriptions revolutionized the study of Egyptian civilization and art.

PREDYNASTIC AND EARLY DYNASTIC PERIODS

The prehistoric beginnings of Egyptian civilization predate writing and are consequently obscure. Nevertheless, tantalizing remains of tombs, paintings, pottery, and other artifacts attest to the existence of a sophisticated culture on the banks of the Nile around 3500 BCE. Egyptologists refer to this era as the Predynastic period.

EGYPT FROM NARMER TO CLEOPATRA

3500–2575 BCE	2575–2134 BCE	2040–1640 BCE	1550–1070 BCE	1000–30 BCE
Predynastic and Early Dynastic	**Old Kingdom**	**Middle Kingdom**	**New Kingdom**	**First Millennium BCE**
■ Egyptians produce narrative reliefs and paintings, including some of the earliest preserved labeled historical artworks, such as the Narmer palette ■ Imhotep, the first artist whose name is recorded, builds the stepped pyramid and funerary complex of King Djoser	■ Sculptors formulate the canonical Egyptian statuary types expressing the eternal nature of divine kingship ■ Workers quarry millions of blocks of stone for the construction of the three Fourth Dynasty pyramids at Gizeh	■ Egyptian sculptors introduce a new, more realistic and emotional, kind of royal portrait ■ Rock-cut tombs become the preferred form of Egyptian burial monument for wealthy private patrons	■ Architects construct grandiose pylon temples featuring hypostyle halls with clerestory lighting ■ Akhenaton introduces a new religion and new art forms during the short-lived religious and artistic revolution of the Amarna period	■ Traditional modes of Egyptian art and architecture continue under foreign (Kushite and Greek) rule

Painting and Sculpture

In Predynastic times, Egypt was divided geographically and politically into Upper Egypt (the southern, upstream part of the Nile Valley), a narrow tract of grassland that encouraged hunting, and Lower (northern) Egypt, where the rich soil of the Nile Delta islands promoted agriculture and animal husbandry. The major finds of Predynastic art come from Upper Egypt, especially Abydos and Hierakonpolis, where archaeologists discovered a tomb dating between 3500 and 3200 BCE that boasts the most extensive preserved series of early Egyptian mural paintings (FIG. 3-1A).

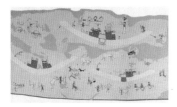
⟳ 3-1A Tomb 100, Hierakonpolis, ca. 3500–3200 BCE.

Palette of King Narmer. The Predynastic period ended with the unification of Upper and Lower Egypt, which historians once thought occurred during the First Dynasty kingship of Menes, identified by some Egyptologists with Narmer, by others with Aha. King Narmer's image and name appear on both sides of a ceremonial *palette* (stone slab with a circular depression) found at Hierakonpolis. The palette (FIGS. 3-2 and 3-3) is one of the earliest extant historical (versus prehistorical) artworks, but Egyptologists still debate exactly what event(s) it depicts. No longer regarded as commemorating the founding of the first of Egypt's 31 dynasties around 2920 BCE (the last ended in 332 BCE), the scenes probably record selected events that took place during the unification of the two kingdoms. Historians now believe that the formation of the "Kingdom of the Two Lands" occurred over several centuries.

Narmer's palette is an elaborate version of a utilitarian object commonly used in the Predynastic period to prepare eye makeup, which Egyptian men and women used to protect their eyes against irritation and the glare of the sun as well as to enhance their appearance. The palette is important not only as a document marking the transition from the prehistoric to the historical period in ancient Egypt but also as one of the earliest examples of the formula for figure representation that characterized most Egyptian art for 3,000 years. At the top of each side of the palette are two heads of a cow

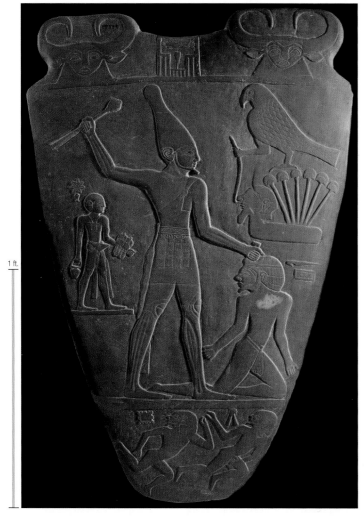

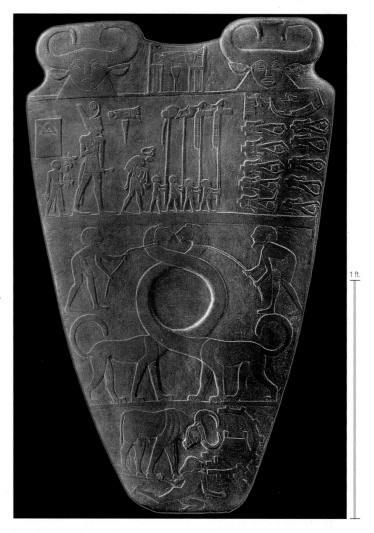

1 ft.

3-2 Back of the palette of King Narmer, from Hierakonpolis, Egypt, Predynastic, ca. 3000–2920 BCE. Slate, 2′ 1″ high. Egyptian Museum, Cairo.

Narmer's palette is one of the earliest labeled historical artworks. On this side, the king, wearing the crown of Upper Egypt, is the largest figure in the composition. He slays a captured Lower Egyptian enemy.

3-3 Front of the palette of King Narmer, from Hierakonpolis, Egypt, Predynastic, ca. 3000–2920 BCE. Slate, 2′ 1″ high. Egyptian Museum, Cairo.

Narmer, now wearing the crown of Lower Egypt, reviews beheaded enemy bodies. At the center of the palette, the intertwined animal necks may symbolize the unification of the two kingdoms.

⟳ Every thumbnail image has a corresponding full-size MindTap Bonus Image and content in the MindTap reader for this chapter. **59**

The Gods and Goddesses of Egypt

The worldview of the Egyptians was distinct from the outlook of their neighbors in the ancient Mediterranean, Mesopotamian, and Persian worlds. Egyptians believed that before the beginning of time, the primeval waters, called *Nun,* existed alone in the darkness. At the moment of creation, a mound rose out of the limitless waters—just as muddy mounds emerge from the Nile after the annual flood recedes. On this mound, the creator god, *Amen,* later identified with the god of the sun (*Re*), appeared and brought light to the world. In later times, the Egyptians symbolized the original mound as a pyramidal stone called the *ben-ben.*

Amen, the supreme god, also created the first of the other gods and goddesses of Egypt. According to one version of the myth, the creator masturbated and produced *Shu* and *Tefnut,* the primary male and female forces in the universe. They coupled to give birth to *Geb* (Earth) and *Nut* (Sky), who bore Osiris, Seth, Isis, and Nephthys. The eldest, *Osiris,* was the god of order, whom the Egyptians revered as the king who brought civilization to the Nile valley. His brother, *Seth,* was his evil opposite, the god of chaos. Seth murdered Osiris and cut him into pieces, which he scattered across Egypt. *Isis,* the sister and consort of Osiris, with the help of *Nephthys,* Seth's wife, succeeded in collecting Osiris's body parts, and with her powerful magic brought him back to life. The resurrected Osiris fathered a son with Isis—*Horus,* who avenged his father's death and displaced Seth as king of Egypt. Osiris then became the lord of the Underworld. The Egyptians identified all their living kings with Horus, then with Osiris after they died. Horus appears in art either as a falcon, considered the noblest bird of the sky, or as a falcon-headed man. (However, the Egyptians did not believe that their gods had composite human-animal forms. The animal-headed images in FIG. 3-1 and elsewhere in Egyptian art are merely pictorial conventions descriptive of the various gods' characteristics.)

Other Egyptian deities include *Mut,* the consort of the sun god Amen, and *Khonsu,* the moon god, who was their son. *Thoth,* another lunar deity and the god of knowledge and writing, appears in art as an ibis, a baboon, or an ibis-headed man crowned with the crescent moon and the moon disk. When Seth tore out Horus's falcon eye (*wedjat*), Thoth restored it. The Egyptians associated Thoth too with rebirth and the afterlife. *Hathor,* daughter of Re, was a divine mother of the Egyptian king, nourishing him with her milk. Egyptian artists represented her (and her predecessor goddess, *Bat*) as a cow-headed woman or as a woman with a cow's horns. *Anubis,* a jackal or jackal-headed deity, was the god of the dead and of embalming. *Maat,* another daughter of Re, was the goddess of truth and justice. Her feather measured the weight of the deceased's heart on Anubis's scales to determine whether the individual would be blessed in the afterlife.

with a woman's face, whom scholars have traditionally identified as the goddess Hathor, the divine mother of all Egyptian kings, but who is probably Hathor's predecessor, the sky goddess Bat. Between the heads is a hieroglyph giving Narmer's name (catfish = *nar*; chisel = *mer*) within a frame representing the royal palace.

On the back (FIG. 3-2) of the palette, the king, wearing the high, white conical crown of Upper Egypt and attended by his official foot washer, who carries his sandals, is shown slaying a captured enemy. The slaying motif closely resembles the group at the lower left of the Hierakonpolis mural (FIG. 3-1A) and became the standard pictorial formula signifying the inevitable triumph of the Egyptian god-kings over their foes (compare FIG. 3-38). Above and to the right, the king appears again in his role as the "Living Horus"—here as a falcon with one human arm. The falcon-king takes captive a man-headed hieroglyph with papyrus plants growing from it, which stands for the king's victory over the land of Lower Egypt. Below the king are two fallen enemies.

On the front (FIG. 3-3), the elongated necks of two felines form the circular depression that would have held eye makeup in an ordinary palette not made for display. The intertwined necks of the animals (a motif common in Mesopotamian art) may be a symbolic reference to Egypt's unification. In the uppermost register, Narmer, now wearing Lower Egypt's red crown topped by its distinctive wiry projection, reviews the beheaded bodies of the enemy. The dead are seen from above, a viewpoint reminiscent of the Paleolithic paintings (FIG. 1-8) on the ceiling of the Altamira cave in Spain representing bison lying on the ground. The Egyptian artist depicted each body with its severed head neatly placed between its legs. By virtue of his superior rank, the king, on both sides of the palette, performs his ritual task alone and towers over his men and the enemy. In the lowest band, a great bull, symbolizing the king's superhuman strength, knocks down the fortress walls of a rebellious city (also seen in an "aerial view").

As in Mesopotamian art (compare, for example, FIGS. 2-7 and 2-8), the Egyptian artist's portrayal of Narmer combines profile views of his head, legs, and arms with frontal views of his eye and torso. Although the proportions of the human figure would vary over the centuries, this composite representation of the body's parts became standard in Egyptian art as well. In the Hierakonpolis painting (FIG. 3-1A), the artist scattered the figures across the wall more or less haphazardly. On Narmer's palette, the sculptor subdivided the surface into registers and inserted the pictorial elements into their organized setting in a neat and orderly way. The horizontal lines separating the narratives also define the ground supporting the figures. This was the preferred mode for narrative art in Mesopotamia as well. Narmer's palette and other Predynastic works established this compositional scheme as the norm in Egypt for millennia. Egyptian artists who departed from this convention did so deliberately, usually to express the absence of order, as in a chaotic battle scene (for example, FIG. 3-35).

Architecture

Narmer's palette is a commemorative artwork. Far more typical of Egyptian art is the Predynastic mural (FIG. 3-1A) from tomb 100 at Hierakonpolis. In fact, the contents of Egyptian tombs provide the principal, if not the exclusive, evidence for reconstructing Egyptian culture. The majority of monuments that the Egyptians left behind were dedicated to ensuring safety and happiness in the next life (see "Mummification and Immortality," page 61).

Mummification and Immortality

The Egyptians did not make the sharp distinction between body and soul that is basic to many religions. Rather, they believed that from birth a person possessed a kind of other self—the ka—which, on the death of the body, could inhabit the corpse and live on. For the ka to live securely, however, the body had to remain as nearly intact as possible. To ensure that it did, the Egyptians developed the technique of embalming (*mummification*) to a high art. Although they believed that the god Anubis invented embalming to preserve the body of the murdered Osiris (see "The Gods and Goddesses of Egypt," page 60, and FIG. 7-60A), Egyptians did not practice mummification systematically until the Fourth Dynasty, when they also buried their dead in underground chambers beneath large brick or stone tombs (FIG. 3-4).

The details of the 70-day mummification process developed and changed over time, but the essential elements remained constant. The first step was the surgical removal of the lungs, liver, stomach, and intestines through an incision in the left flank. The Egyptians thought that these organs were most subject to decay, and wrapped them individually and placed them in four containers known as *canopic jars* for eventual deposit in the burial chamber with the corpse. (The jars take their name from the port of Canopus, where the Greeks believed that the Egyptians worshiped human-headed jars as personifications of Osiris. Those jars were not, however, used in embalming.) Egyptian surgeons extracted the brain through the nostrils and then discarded it because they did not attach any special significance to that organ. But they left in place the heart, necessary for life and also regarded as the seat of intelligence. (In FIG. 3-1, Hunefer's heart is weighed against Maat's feather to determine whether he is worthy of eternal life.)

Next, the body was treated for 40 days with natron, a naturally occurring salt compound that dehydrated the body. Then the embalmers filled the corpse with resin-soaked linens, and closed and covered the incision with a representation of the wedjat eye of Horus, a powerful *amulet* (a device to ward off evil and promote rebirth). Finally, they treated the body with lotions and resins and wrapped it tightly with hundreds of yards of linen bandages to maintain its shape. The Egyptians often placed other amulets within the bandages or on the corpse. The most important were heart *scarabs* (gems in the shape of beetles), which bore spells to ensure that the heart would not tip the scales against the deceased at judgment time (FIG. 3-1). Masks (FIG. 3-34) usually covered the faces of the deceased.

The Egyptian practice of mummification endured for thousands of years, even under Greek and Roman rule. Roman *mummies* with painted portraits (FIGS. 7-60A, 7-61, and 7-61A) have been popular attractions in museums worldwide for a long time, but the discovery in 1996 of a cemetery at Bahariya Oasis in the desert southwest of Cairo greatly expanded their number. The site, which archaeologists call the Valley of the Golden Mummies, extends for at least four square miles. The largest tomb found to date contained 32 mummies, but another held 43, some stacked on top of others because the tomb was used for generations and space ran out.

Preserving the deceased's body by mummification was only the first requirement for immortality in ancient Egypt. Food and drink also had to be provided, as did clothing, utensils, and furniture. Nothing that had been enjoyed on Earth was to be lacking. The Egyptians also placed statuettes called *ushabtis* (Arabic, "answerers") in the tomb. These figurines performed any labor required of the deceased in the afterlife, answering whenever his or her name was called.

Beginning in the third millennium BCE, the Egyptians also set up statues of the dead (for example, FIGS. 3-13A, 3-14, 3-14A, and 3-14B) in their tombs. The statues were meant to guarantee the permanence of the person's identity by providing substitute dwelling places for the ka in case the mummy disintegrated. Wall paintings and reliefs (for example, FIGS. 3-15, 3-16, 3-28, and 3-28A) recorded the recurring round of human activities. The Egyptians hoped and expected that the images and inventory of life, collected and set up within the protective stone walls of the tomb, would ensure immortality.

Mastabas. The standard tomb type in early Egypt was the *mastaba* (Arabic, "bench"), a rectangular brick or stone structure with sloping sides erected over an underground burial chamber (FIG. 3-4). The form probably developed from earthen mounds that had covered even earlier burials. Although mastabas originally housed single burials, as in FIG. 3-4, they later became increasingly complex in order to accommodate members of several families. The main feature of these tombs, other than the burial chamber itself, was the chapel, which had a false door through which the ka could join the world of the living and partake in the meals placed on an offering table. Some mastabas also had a *serdab*, a small room housing a statue of the deceased.

Imhotep and Djoser. One of the most renowned figures in Egyptian history was IMHOTEP, master builder for King Djoser (r. 2630–2611 BCE) of the Third Dynasty. Imhotep's is the first recorded name of an artist anywhere in the world. A man of legendary talent, Imhotep also served as Djoser's official seal bearer and as high priest of the sun god Re. After his death, the Egyptians deified Imhotep as the son of the god Ptah and in time probably inflated

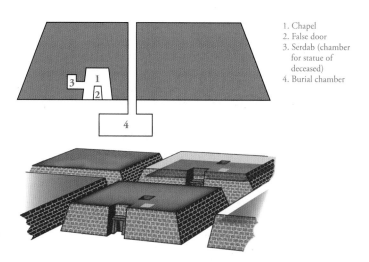

1. Chapel
2. False door
3. Serdab (chamber for statue of deceased)
4. Burial chamber

3-4 Section (*top*) and restored view (*bottom*) of typical Egyptian mastaba tombs.

Egyptian mastabas had underground chambers, which housed the mummified body, portrait statues, and offerings to the deceased. Scenes of daily life often decorated the interior walls.

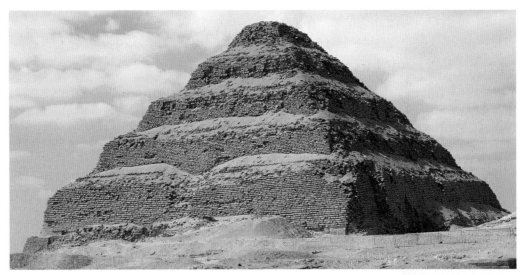

3-5 IMHOTEP, stepped pyramid (looking northwest) of Djoser, Saqqara, Egypt, Third Dynasty, ca. 2630–2611 BCE.

Imhotep, the first artist whose name is recorded, built the first stone pyramid during the Third Dynasty for King Djoser. The god-king's pyramid resembles a series of stacked mastabas of diminishing size.

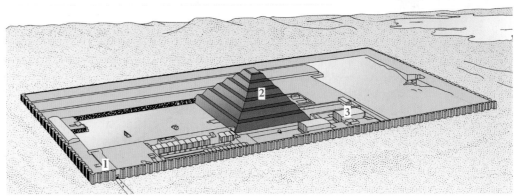

3-6 Restored view of the mortuary precinct of Djoser, Saqqara, Egypt, Third Dynasty, ca. 2630–2611 BCE. (1) entrance hall, (2) stepped pyramid, (3) north palace.

Djoser's pyramid was the centerpiece of an immense funerary complex that included buildings connected with his funerary cult. Underground galleries resembling a palace were the king's home in the afterlife.

the list of his achievements. Nonetheless, architectural historians accept Manetho's attribution to Imhotep of the stepped pyramid (FIG. 3-5) of Djoser at Saqqara. Saqqara was the ancient *necropolis* (Greek, "city of the dead") of Memphis, Egypt's capital at the time. Built before 2600 BCE, Djoser's pyramid is one of the oldest stone structures in Egypt and the first stone pyramid. Begun as a large mastaba with each of its faces oriented toward one of the cardinal points of the compass, the tomb was enlarged at least twice before assuming its ultimate shape. About 200 feet high in its final form, Djoser's stepped pyramid is the first truly grandiose Egyptian tomb. Composed of a series of mastabas of diminishing size, stacked one atop another, it resembles a Mesopotamian ziggurat (FIG. 2-15). Unlike a ziggurat, however, Djoser's pyramid is a tomb, not a temple platform, and its dual function was to protect the mummified king and his possessions and to symbolize, by its gigantic presence, his absolute and godlike power. Beneath Djoser's pyramid was a network of several hundred underground rooms and galleries cut out of the Saqqara bedrock. The vast subterranean complex resembles a palace. It was to be the king's home in the afterlife.

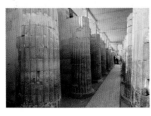

3-6A Entrance hall, Djoser precinct, Saqqara, ca. 2630–2611 BCE.

Djoser's pyramid stands near the center of an immense (37-acre) rectangular enclosure (FIG. 3-6) surrounded by a wall of white limestone 34 feet high and 5,400 feet long. The huge precinct, with its protective walls and tightly regulated access (FIGS. 3-6, no. 1, and 3-6A), stands in sharp contrast to the roughly contemporaneous

Sumerian Royal Cemetery at Ur, where no barriers kept people away from the burial area. Nor did the Mesopotamian cemetery have a temple for the worship of the deified dead. At Saqqara, a funerary temple stands against the northern face of Djoser's pyramid (FIG. 3-6, no. 2) so that after his death, the divine king could join with the northern star. Priests performed daily rituals at the temple in celebration of the immortal ruler.

Djoser's funerary temple was but one of many buildings arranged around several courts. Most of the others were dummy structures with stone walls enclosing fills of rubble, sand, or gravel. The buildings imitated in stone various types of temporary structures made of plant stems and mats erected in Upper and Lower Egypt to celebrate the Jubilee Festival, which perpetually reaffirmed the royal existence in the hereafter. The translation into stone of structural forms previously made out of plants may be seen in the columns (FIG. 3-7) of the north palace (FIG. 3-6, no. 3) of Djoser's funerary precinct. The columns end in *capitals* that take the form of the papyrus blossoms of Lower Egypt. The column shafts resemble papyrus stalks. Djoser's columns are not freestanding, as are most later columns. They are *engaged columns* (that is, attached to walls), but are nonetheless the earliest known stone columns in the history of architecture.

OLD KINGDOM

The Old Kingdom is the first of the three great periods of Egyptian history, called the Old, Middle, and New Kingdoms, respectively. Many Egyptologists now begin the Old Kingdom with Sneferu (r. 2575–2551 BCE), the first king of the Fourth Dynasty, although

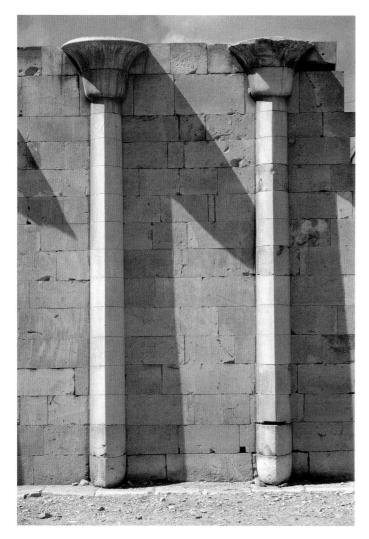

3-7 Detail of the facade of the north palace (FIG. 3-6, no. 3) of the mortuary precinct of Djoser, Saqqara, Egypt, Third Dynasty, ca. 2630–2611 BCE.

The earliest known stone columns are in Djoser's funerary precinct. Those on the north palace facade are engaged (attached) to the walls and have shafts and capitals resembling papyrus plants.

the traditional division of kingdoms places Djoser and the Third Dynasty in the Old Kingdom. It ended with the breakup of the Eighth Dynasty around 2134 BCE.

Architecture

The divine rulers of the Old Kingdom amassed great wealth and expended it on grandiose architectural projects, of which the most spectacular were the Fourth Dynasty pyramids of Gizeh, the oldest of the Seven Wonders of the ancient world (see "Babylon, City of Wonders," page 50). The prerequisites for membership in the elite club of Wonders were colossal size and enormous cost.

Gizeh. The Egyptians constructed the three major pyramids (FIG. 3-8) at Gizeh over the course of about 75 years (see "Building the Pyramids of Gizeh," page 64) to serve as the tombs of the Fourth Dynasty kings Khufu (r. 2551–2528 BCE; FIG. 3-9), Khafre (r. 2520–2494 BCE), and Menkaure (r. 2490–2472 BCE). They represent the culmination of an architectural evolution that began with

the mastaba (FIG. 3-4), but the classic pyramid form is not simply a refinement of the stepped pyramid (FIG. 3-5). The new tomb shape probably reflects the influence of Heliopolis, the seat of the powerful cult of Re, whose emblem was a pyramidal stone, the ben-ben (see "The Gods and Goddesses of Egypt," page 60). The pyramids are symbols of the sun. The Pyramid Texts, inscribed on the burial chamber walls of royal pyramids beginning with the Fifth Dynasty pyramid of Unas (r. 2356–2323 BCE), refer to the sun's rays as the ladder that the god-king uses to ascend to the heavens.

> Ho, Unas! You have not gone away dead: You have gone away alive.[2]
>
> So, you shall go forth, Unas, to the sky and step up on it in this its identity of the ladder.[3]
>
> [Unas] has flown . . . to the sky amidst his brothers the gods. . . . Unas's seat is with you, Sun.[4]

The pyramids were where Egyptian kings were reborn in the afterlife, just as the sun is reborn each day at dawn.

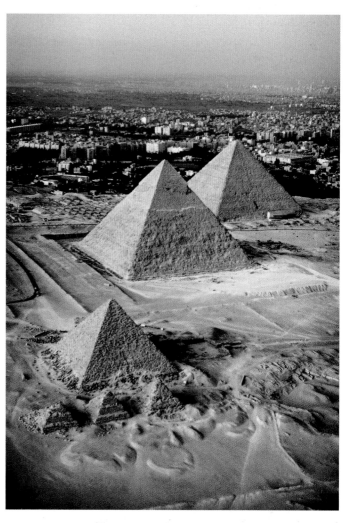

3-8 Aerial view of the Fourth Dynasty pyramids (looking north), Gizeh, Egypt. *From bottom:* pyramid of Menkaure, ca. 2490–2472 BCE; pyramid of Khafre, ca. 2520–2494 BCE; and Great Pyramid of Khufu, ca. 2551–2528 BCE.

The three pyramids of Gizeh took the shape of the ben-ben, the emblem of the sun god Re. The sun's rays were the ramp that the Egyptian kings used to ascend to the heavens after their death and rebirth.

Building the Pyramids of Gizeh

The Fourth Dynasty pyramids (FIG. 3-8) across the Nile from modern Cairo are on every list of Wonders of the ancient world. How did the Egyptians solve the myriad problems they encountered in constructing these colossal tombs?

As with all building projects of this type, the erection of the Gizeh pyramids was a complex process that began with surveying and leveling the construction site. Next, skilled masons had to quarry the millions of stone blocks needed—in this case, primarily from the Gizeh limestone plateau itself. Teams of workers had to cut into the rock and remove large blocks of roughly equal size using stone or copper chisels and wood mallets and wedges. Often, the artisans had to cut deep tunnels to find high-quality stone free of cracks and other flaws. To remove a block, the stonemasons cut channels by pounding diorite balls against the rock on the sides and partly underneath. Then they pried the stones free from the bedrock with wood levers. New tools for this difficult work had to be manufactured constantly because the chisels and mallets broke or became dull very quickly.

After workers liberated the stones, the rough blocks had to be transported to the building site. There, the Egyptian stonemasons shaped the blocks to the exact dimensions required, with smooth faces (*dressed masonry*) for a perfect fit. Small blocks could be carried on a man's shoulders or on the back of a donkey, but the Egyptians moved the massive blocks for the pyramids using wood sleds. The artisans dressed the blocks by chiseling and pounding the surfaces and, in the last stage, by rubbing and grinding the surfaces with fine polishing stones. Architectural historians call this kind of construction *ashlar masonry*—carefully cut and regularly shaped blocks of stone piled in successive horizontal rows, or *courses.*

To set the ashlar blocks in place, workers under the direction of master builders such as Hemiunu (FIG. 3-14B), who supervised the construction of Khufu's pyramid (FIG. 3-9), erected rubble ramps against the core of the pyramid. They adjusted the ramps' size and slope as work progressed and the tomb grew in height. Scholars debate whether the Egyptians used simple linear ramps inclined at a right angle to one face of the pyramid, or zigzag or spiral ramps akin to staircases. Linear ramps would have had the advantage of simplicity and would have left three sides of the pyramid unobstructed. But zigzag ramps placed against one side of the structure or spiral ramps winding around the pyramid would have greatly reduced the slope of the incline and would have made dragging the blocks easier. Some scholars also have suggested a combination of straight and spiral ramps, and one recent theory posits a system of spiral ramps within, instead of outside, the pyramid.

The Egyptians used ropes and levers both to lift and to lower the stones, guiding each block into its designated place. Finally, the pyramid received a casing of white limestone blocks (FIG. 3-9, no. 1), cut so

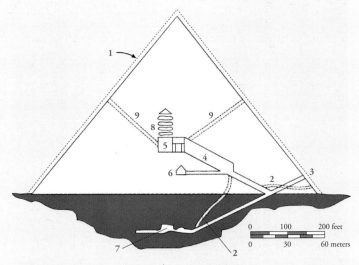

1. Silhouette with original facing stone
2. Thieves' tunnels
3. Entrance
4. Grand gallery
5. King's chamber
6. So-called Queen's chamber
7. False tomb chamber
8. Relieving blocks
9. Air shafts(?)

3-9 Section of the Great Pyramid of Khufu, Gizeh, Egypt, Fourth Dynasty, ca. 2551–2528 BCE.

Khufu's pyramid is the largest at Gizeh. Constructed of roughly 2.3 million blocks of stone weighing an average of 2.5 tons, the structure is an almost solid mass of stone quarried from the Gizeh plateau itself.

precisely that the eye could scarcely detect the joints. The reflection of sunlight on the facing would have been dazzling, underscoring the pyramid's solar symbolism. Some casing stones are still in place at the peak of the pyramid of Khafre (FIG. 3-11).

Of the three Fourth Dynasty pyramids at Gizeh, the tomb of Khufu (FIGS. 3-9 and 3-10, no. 7), known as the Great Pyramid, is the oldest and largest. Except for the galleries and burial chamber, it is an almost solid mass of limestone masonry. At the base, the length of one side of Khufu's tomb is approximately 775 feet, and its area is some 13 acres. Its present height is about 450 feet (originally 480 feet). Roughly 2.3 million blocks of stone, each weighing an average of 2.5 tons, make up the fabric of the aptly named Great Pyramid. Some of the stones at the base weigh about 15 tons.

The three immense Gizeh pyramids attest to the extraordinary engineering and mathematical expertise of the Egyptians of the mid-third millennium BCE as well as to the Old Kingdom builders' mastery of masonry construction and ability to mobilize, direct, house, and feed a huge workforce engaged in one of the most labor-intensive enterprises ever undertaken.

Imhotep may have conceived Djoser's stepped pyramid as a giant stairway. As with the Saqqara pyramid, the four sides of each of the Gizeh pyramids are oriented to the cardinal points of the compass. But the funerary temples associated with the three Gizeh pyramids are not on the north side, facing the stars of the northern sky, as was Djoser's temple. The Gizeh temples are on the east side, facing the rising sun and underscoring their connection with Re.

From the remains surrounding the pyramid of Khafre at Gizeh, archaeologists have been able to reconstruct an entire funerary complex (FIG. 3-10). The complex included the pyramid itself, with the god-king's burial chamber; the *mortuary temple* adjoining the pyramid on the east side, where priests made offerings to the deceased and stored cloth, food, and ceremonial vessels; the roofed *causeway* (raised road) leading to the mortuary temple; and the *valley temple*

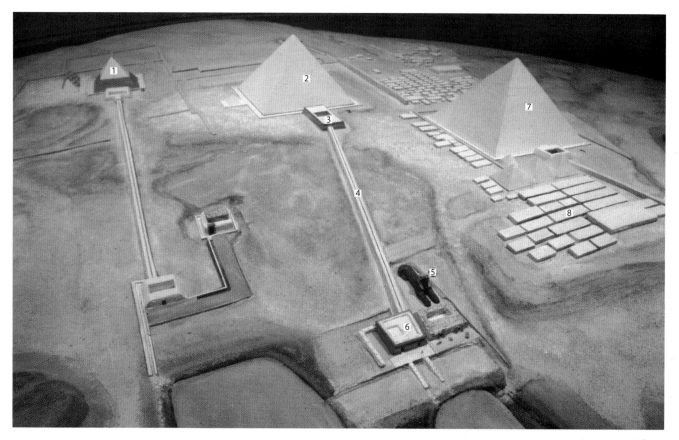

3-10 Model of the pyramid complex, Gizeh, Egypt. Harvard University Semitic Museum, Cambridge. (1) pyramid of Menkaure, (2) pyramid of Khafre, (3) mortuary temple of Khafre, (4) causeway, (5) Great Sphinx, (6) valley temple of Khafre, (7) Great Pyramid of Khufu, (8) pyramids of the royal family and mastabas of nobles.

Like Djoser's pyramid (FIG. 3-6), the Gizeh pyramids were not isolated tombs but parts of funerary complexes with a valley temple, a covered causeway, and a mortuary temple adjoining the tomb.

at the edge of the floodplain. Many Egyptologists believe that the complex served not only as the king's tomb and temple but also as his palace in the afterlife.

Great Sphinx. Beside the causeway and dominating the valley temple of Khafre rises the Great Sphinx (FIG. 3-11). Carved from a spur of rock in the Gizeh quarry, the colossal statue—the largest in Egypt, Mesopotamia, or Persia—is probably an image of Khafre (originally complete with the king's ceremonial beard and *nemes* headdress with *uraeus* cobra), although some scholars think that it portrays Khufu and predates the construction of Khafre's complex. Whomever it portrays, the *sphinx*—a lion with a human head—was an appropriate image for a king. The composite form suggests that the Egyptian king combined human intelligence with the fearsome strength and authority of the king of beasts.

3-11 Great Sphinx (with pyramid of Khafre in the background), Gizeh, Egypt, Fourth Dynasty, ca. 2520–2494 BCE. Sandstone, 65′ high.

Carved out of the Gizeh stone quarry, the Great Sphinx is of colossal size. The sphinx has the body of a lion and the head of a king (probably Khafre) and is associated with the sun god.

How to Portray a God-King

The Egyptian kings were divine beings, not mortal rulers, and the sculptors of the Old Kingdom needed to formulate a distinctive way to portray them in order to differentiate them from other men—beyond simply representing them wearing royal regalia. The solution they devised proved so satisfactory that, with the exception of some Middle and New Kingdom portraits discussed later in this chapter (FIGS. 3-17 and 3-29), the formula persisted for millennia.

In the portrait (FIG. 3-12) from his valley temple at Gizeh, King Khafre wears a simple kilt and sits rigidly upright on a throne formed of

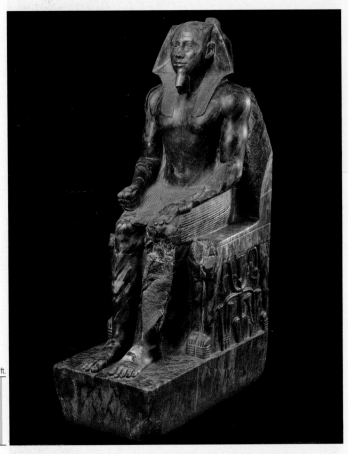

3-12 Khafre enthroned, from Gizeh, Egypt, Fourth Dynasty, ca. 2520–2494 BCE. Diorite, 5′ 6″ high. Egyptian Museum, Cairo.

This portrait from his pyramid complex depicts Khafre as an enthroned divine ruler with a perfect body. The formality of the pose creates an aura of eternal stillness, appropriate for the timeless afterlife.

two stylized lions' bodies. Intertwined lotus and papyrus plants—symbolic of the united Egypt—appear between the throne's legs. Khafre has the royal false beard fastened to his chin and wears the royal linen headdress. The headdress covers his forehead and falls in pleated folds over his shoulders. Behind Khafre's head is the falcon (compare FIG. 3-2) that identifies the king as the "Living Horus."

As befitting a divine ruler, the sculptor portrayed Khafre with a well-developed, flawless body and a perfect face, regardless of his real age and appearance. Khafre's portrait is not a true likeness and was not intended to be. The purpose of Egyptian royal portraiture was not to reproduce the distinctive shapes of bodies or to record individual features, as was the case, for example, in Republican Rome (FIG. 7-8). Old Kingdom sculptors sought to create idealized images that communicated the divine nature of Egyptian kingship. Nevertheless, each king's portraits incorporated enough distinctive facial traits to enable his ka to know where to reside.

The enthroned Khafre radiates serenity. The sculptor created this effect in part by giving the figure great compactness and solidity, with few projecting, breakable parts. The form of the statue expresses its purpose: to last for eternity. Khafre's body is one with the simple slab that forms the back of the king's throne. His arms follow the bend of his body and rest on his thighs, and his legs are close together. Part of the original stone block still connects the king's legs to his chair. Khafre's pose is frontal and, except for the hands, *bilaterally symmetrical* (the same on either side of an axis, in this case the vertical axis). The sculptor suppressed all movement and with it the notion of time, creating an aura of eternal stillness.

Some extant reliefs and paintings (FIG. 3-12A) show Egyptian sculptors at work and provide detailed information about the successive stages of carving a statue. To produce Khafre's statue, the artist first drew the front, back, and two profile views of the seated king on the four vertical faces of the stone block. Next, apprentices chiseled away the excess stone on each side. Finally, the master sculpted the parts of Khafre's body, the falcon, and so forth. The polished surface was achieved by *abrasion* (rubbing or grinding). This method

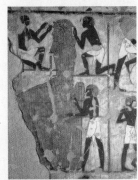

3-12A Sculptors at work, Thebes, ca. 1425 BCE.

of creating statuary accounts in large part for the blocklike look of the standard Egyptian statue, but that is not the necessary result of this carving method. Other sculptors, both ancient and modern, with different aims, have transformed stone blocks into dynamic, twisting human forms (for example, FIGS. I-16 and 5-85).

Sculpture

Old Kingdom sculptors were called upon to produce statues in significant numbers because they fulfilled an important function in Egyptian tombs as substitute abodes for the ka if the embalmed corpse deteriorated (see "Mummification and Immortality," page 61). Egyptian sculptors worked with wood, clay, and other materials, but most of the many preserved funerary statues are of stone.

Khafre.   Perhaps the finest example of Old Kingdom royal portraiture (see "How to Portray a God-King," above) is the seated statue of Khafre illustrated here (FIG. 3-12), one of a series of similar statues carved for the god-king's valley temple (FIG. 3-10, no. 6) near the Great Sphinx. The stone is diorite, an exceptionally hard dark stone brought some 400 miles down the Nile from royal quarries in the south. (The Neo-Sumerian ruler Gudea [see "Gudea of Lagash," page 43, and FIG. 2-16] so admired diorite that he imported it to faraway Girsu.)

Menkaure. The seated statue, although a popular choice for royal portraits, is one of only a small number of standard types that Old Kingdom sculptors employed to represent the human figure. Another is the image of a person or deity standing, either alone or in a group—for example, the two-figure group (FIG. 3-13) of Menkaure and a female figure, usually identified as one of his wives, probably the queen Khamerernebty, but perhaps the goddess Hathor. The statue once stood in the valley temple of Menkaure's pyramid complex at Gizeh. Here, too, the figures remain wedded in part to the stone block. In many Old Kingdom portraits, the stone backdrop is as high and wide as the figures and the back of the statue is an unarticulated slab. Those portraits could be classified as *high-relief* sculptures rather than freestanding statues.

Menkaure's pose—duplicated in countless other Egyptian statues—is rigidly frontal with the arms hanging straight down and close to his well-built body. He clenches his hands into fists with the thumbs forward and advances his left leg slightly. But no shift occurs in the angle of the hips to correspond to the uneven distribution of weight. Khamerernebty(?) stands in a similar position. Her right arm, however, circles the king's waist, and her left hand gently rests on his left arm. This frozen stereotypical gesture indicates their marital status or, if king and goddess, their shared divinity. The two figures show no other sign of affection or emotion and look not at each other but out into space. As in the seated statue of Khafre (FIG. 3-12), the artist's aim was not to portray vibrant living figures but to suggest the timeless nature of the stone statue that might need to serve as an eternal substitute home for the ka.

Seated Scribe. Traces of paint remain on the portrait of Menkaure. Egyptian artists painted most of their statues, although sometimes sculptors left the natural color of the stone exposed, enhancing the sense of abstraction and timelessness. Striking examples of painted sculpture are the seated statues of Rahotep and Nofret (FIG. 3-13A) and the statue found at Saqqara portraying a Fourth Dynasty scribe (FIG. 3-14). Despite the stiff upright postures of all these statues and the frontality of head and body, the coloration lends a lifelike quality to the stone images.

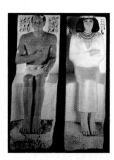

⬈**3-13A** Rahotep and Nofret, Maidum, ca. 2575–2550 BCE.

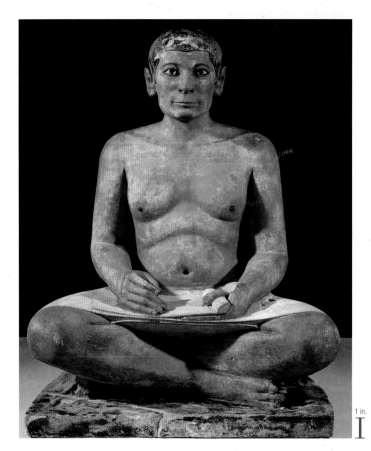

3-13 Menkaure and Khamerernebty(?), from Gizeh, Egypt, Fourth Dynasty, ca. 2490–2472 BCE. Graywacke, 4′ 6½″ high. Museum of Fine Arts, Boston.

The statue of Menkaure and his wife (or Hathor?) displays the conventional postures used for Old Kingdom royal statues. The formalized embrace denotes the close association of the two figures.

3-14 Seated scribe, from Saqqara, Egypt, Fourth Dynasty, ca. 2500 BCE. Painted limestone, 1′ 9″ high. Musée du Louvre, Paris.

The idealism that characterizes the portraiture of the Egyptian god-kings did not extend to the depiction of non-elite individuals. The sculptor portrayed this seated scribe with clear signs of aging.

The head of the Saqqara scribe displays an extraordinary sensitivity. With a penetration and sympathy seldom achieved at this early date, the sculptor conveyed the personality of a sharply intelligent and alert individual. The scribe sits directly on the ground, not on a throne or even on a chair. Although he occupied a position of honor in a largely illiterate society and performed a variety of official duties, the scribe was not as exalted a figure in the Egyptian hierarchy as the king, whose divinity made him superhuman. Consequently, his portrait is not idealized. Quite the contrary. For example, the sculptor reproduced the scribe's sagging chest muscles and protruding belly. These signs of age would have been disrespectful and wholly inappropriate in a depiction of an Egyptian god-king or members of his family (see "How to Portray a God-King," page 66). But the statue of the scribe is not a true portrait either. Rather, it is a composite of conventional types. Obesity, for example, characterizes many nonroyal Old Kingdom male portraits (for example, FIGS. 3-14A and especially 3-14B), perhaps because it attested to the comfortable life of the person represented and his relatively high position in society.

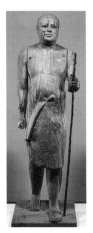

⤢ **3-14A** Kaaper, Saqqara, ca. 2450–2350 BCE.

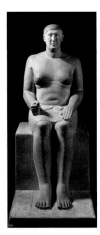

⤢ **3-14B** Hemiunu, Gizeh, ca. 2550–2530 BCE.

Tomb of Ti. In Old Kingdom tombs, images of the deceased also frequently appear in relief sculpture and in mural painting, sometimes singly (FIG. I-15), sometimes in a narrative context. The painted limestone relief scenes decorating the walls of the mastaba of a Fifth Dynasty official named Ti typify the subjects that Old Kingdom patrons favored for the adornment of their final resting places. Depictions of the deceased at his funerary meal and scenes of agriculture and hunting fill Ti's tomb. The Egyptians associated farming and hunting as well as dining with providing nourishment for the ka in the hereafter, but the subjects also had powerful symbolic overtones. In ancient Egypt, success in the hunt, for example, was a metaphor for triumph over the forces of evil.

On one wall (FIG. 3-15) of his tomb, Ti, his men, and his boats move slowly through the marshes, hunting hippopotami and birds in a dense growth of towering papyrus. The sculptor delineated the reedy stems of the plants with repeated fine grooves that fan out gracefully at the top into a commotion of frightened birds and stalking foxes. The water beneath the boats, signified by a pattern of wavy lines, is crowded with hippopotami and fish. Ti's men seem frantically busy with their spears, whereas Ti, depicted twice their size, stands aloof. The

3-15 Ti watching a hippopotamus hunt, relief in the mastaba of Ti, Saqqara, Egypt, Fifth Dynasty, ca. 2450–2350 BCE. Painted limestone, 4′ high.

In Egypt, a successful hunt was a metaphor for the triumph over evil. In this painted tomb relief, the deceased stands aloof from the hunters busily spearing hippopotami. Ti's size reflects his high rank.

basic conventions of Egyptian figure representation—used a half millennium earlier for the palette of King Narmer (FIG. 3-2)—appear again here. As in the Predynastic work, the artist exaggerated the size of Ti to announce his rank, and combined frontal and profile views of Ti's body to show its most characteristic parts clearly. This approach to representation was well suited for Egyptian funerary art because it emphasizes the essential nature of the deceased, not his accidental appearance. Ti's conventional pose contrasts with the realistically rendered activities of his tiny servants and with the naturalistically carved and painted birds and animals among the papyrus buds. Ti's immobility suggests that he is not an actor in the hunt. He does not *do* anything. He simply *is,* a figure apart from time and an impassive observer of life, like his ka.

The idealized image of Ti is typical of Egyptian relief sculpture. Egyptian artists regularly ignored the endless variations in body types of real human beings. Painters and sculptors did not sketch their subjects from life but applied a strict *canon,* or system of proportions, to the human figure. They first drew a grid on the wall. Then they placed various human body parts at specific points on the network of squares. The height of a figure, for example, was a fixed number of squares, and the head, shoulders, waist, knees, and other parts of the body also had a predetermined size and place within the scheme. This approach to design continued for more than 2,500 years. Specific proportions might vary from workshop to workshop and change over time, but the principle of the canon persisted.

On another wall (FIG. 3-16) of Ti's mastaba, goats tread in seeds in the upper register, and, below, cattle ford a canal in the Nile. Here too, the scenes should be interpreted on a symbolic as well as a literal level. The fording of the Nile, for example, was a

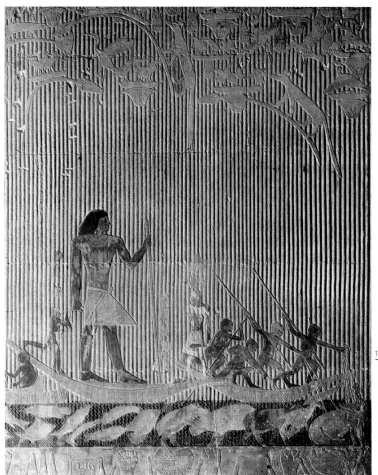

1 ft.

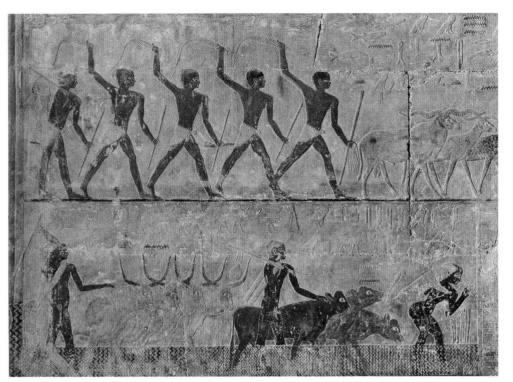

The fording of the Nile was a metaphor for the passage to the afterlife. These reliefs combine stereotypical poses for humans and animals with unconventional postures and anecdotal details.

Senusret III. One of Mentuhotep II's successors was Senusret III (r. 1878–1859 BCE), who fought four brutal military campaigns in Nubia (MAP 3-1). Although Egyptian armies devastated the land and poisoned the wells, Senusret never fully achieved secure control over the Nubians. In Egypt itself, he attempted, with greater success, to establish a more powerful central government.

Senusret's portraits are of special interest because they represent a sharp

metaphor for the deceased's passage from life to the hereafter. Ti is absent from the scenes, and all the men and animals participate in the narrative. Despite the sculptor's repeated use of similar poses for most of the human and animal figures, the reliefs are full of anecdotal details. Especially charming is the group at the lower right. A youth, depicted in a complex unconventional posture, carries a calf on his back. The animal, not a little afraid, turns its head back a full 180 degrees (compare FIG. 1-7) to seek reassurance from its mother, who returns the calf's gaze. Scenes such as this demonstrate that Egyptian artists could be close observers of daily life. The suppression of the anecdotal (that is, of the time-bound) from their representations of the deceased both in relief and in the round was a deliberate choice. Egyptian artists' primary purpose was not storytelling but to suggest the deceased's eternal existence in the afterlife as a reflection of his life on earth.

break from Old Kingdom practice. Although the king's preserved statues have idealized bodies, the sculptors brought a stunning and unprecedented realism to the rendition of the king's features. This new approach to portraying the Egyptian king is evident in the colossal head of Senusret (FIG. 3-17) in the Nelson-Atkins Museum of Art. The king, wearing the traditional nemes headdress, appears

MIDDLE KINGDOM

About 2150 BCE, the Egyptians challenged the power of the weak kings of the Sixth Dynasty, and for more than a century the land was in a state of civil unrest and near anarchy. But in 2040 BCE, the king of Upper Egypt, Mentuhotep II (r. 2050–1998 BCE), managed to unite Egypt again under a single ruler and established the Middle Kingdom (11th to 14th Dynasties), which lasted 400 years.

Sculpture

Although in most respects Middle Kingdom sculptors adhered to the conventions established during the Old Kingdom, portraying both men and women in the familiar seated (FIG. 3-16A) and standing poses, there were some notable innovations.

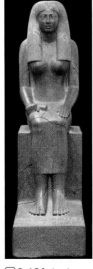

⟋ 3-16A Lady Sennuwy, Kerma, ca. 1960–1916 BCE.

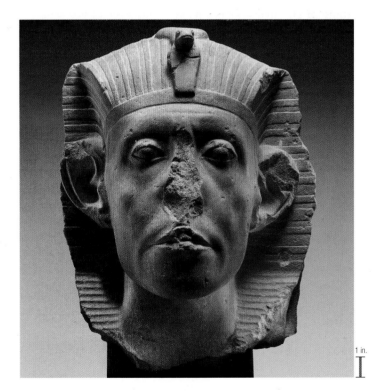

1 in.

3-17 Head of Senusret III, 12th Dynasty, ca. 1860–1850 BCE. Red quartzite, 1′ 5¾″ high. Nelson-Atkins Museum of Art, Kansas City (William Rockhill Nelson Trust purchase).

Senusret III's portraits exhibit an unprecedented realism. The king's brooding expression reflects the mood of the time and contrasts sharply with the impassive faces of Old Kingdom pharaohs.

as a mature man with protruding ears; round eyes with heavy lids; a lined forehead; loose, aging flesh; and a downturned mouth. His pessimistic expression reflects the dominant mood of the time, echoed in Middle Kingdom literature. The portrait is very different in kind from the typically impassive faces of the Old Kingdom, and some art historians have interpreted the signs of age and emotion as projecting weakness. However, the intended message was probably that the king is old and wise—but possessing youthful physical vigor. This combination of older head and younger body, with a similar composite message, also characterizes many portraits of the Roman Republic (FIG. 7-9).

Architecture

Senusret III's tomb, at Dashur, is a mud-brick pyramid, the preferred form for royal burials. More characteristic of Middle Kingdom funerary architecture are the rock-cut tombs of wealthy private patrons. This kind of tomb, documented also in the Old Kingdom, largely replaced the mastaba as the standard Egyptian tomb type.

Beni Hasan. Some of the best-preserved Middle Kingdom tombs are those of local officials at Beni Hasan. Hollowed out of the cliffs, the most elaborate examples, such as the 12th Dynasty tomb of

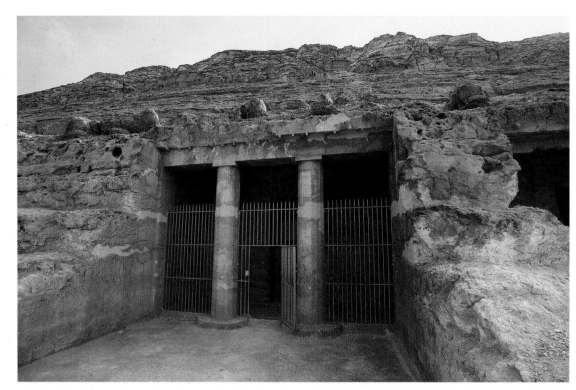

3-18 **Tomb of Khnum-hotep II (tomb 3), Beni Hasan, Egypt, 12th Dynasty, ca. 1900–1880 BCE.**

The tombs of Beni Hasan are characteristic of the Middle Kingdom. Hollowed out of the cliffs, these nonroyal tombs often have a shallow columnar porch, which leads into a columned hall and burial chamber.

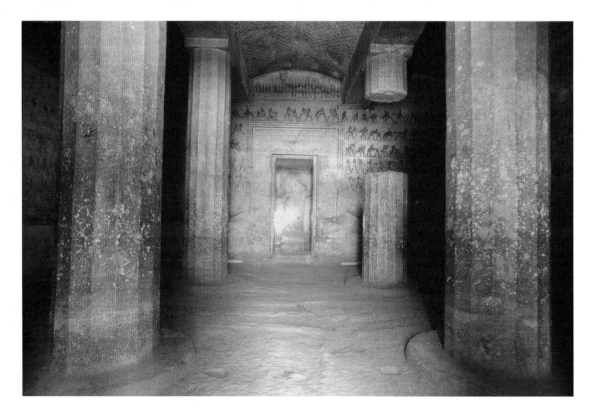

3-19 **Interior hall of the rock-cut tomb of Amenemhet (tomb 2), Beni Hasan, Egypt, 12th Dynasty, ca. 1900–1880 BCE.**

Stonemasons carved the columnar hall of Amenemhet's tomb out of the living rock, which explains the suspended broken column at the rear. The shafts have flutes, a form that Greek architects later emulated.

Khnumhotep II (FIG. 3-18), have a shallow columnar porch, which leads into a columned hall and then into a burial chamber featuring rock-cut statues of the deceased in niches, and paintings and painted reliefs on the walls. In the neighboring tomb of Amenemhet (FIG. 3-19), the columns in the hall serve no supporting function because, like the porch columns, they are continuous parts of the rock fabric. (Note the broken column in the rear suspended from the ceiling like an icicle.) The column shafts have *flutes,* like those in the entrance corridor (FIG. 3-6A) of Djoser's mortuary precinct at Saqqara. The Beni Hasan columns are more refined versions of Imhotep's earlier columns, which still look like bundles of reeds. The Middle Kingdom columns closely resemble later Greek columns of the Doric order (FIG. 5-13, *left*), and there is no doubt that the Greeks knew about and emulated many aspects of Egyptian architecture. Archaeologists believe that the kind of *fluting* used for the Beni Hasan column shafts derived from the carving of softwood trunks with the rounded cutting edge of the adze.

NEW KINGDOM

The Middle Kingdom collapsed when the Hyksos descended on Egypt from the Syrian and Mesopotamian uplands. They ruled the Nile Delta and Lower Egypt during what historians call the Second Intermediate Period until, in the mid-16th century, native Egyptian kings of the 17th Dynasty rose up in revolt. Ahmose I (r. 1550–1525 BCE), final conqueror of the Hyksos and first king of the 18th Dynasty, ushered in the New Kingdom, the most glorious period in Egypt's long history, when the Egyptian kings became known as *pharaohs,* the term commonly, if incorrectly, used to refer to Egyptian rulers of all periods. During the New Kingdom, Egypt extended its borders by conquest from the Euphrates River in the northeast deep into Nubia to the south (MAP 3-1). The capital remained at Memphis, but Thebes in Upper Egypt rose to prominence in large part due to the growing importance of the god worshiped there—Amen-Re. Thebes became a great metropolis with magnificent palaces, tombs, and temples along both banks of the Nile.

Architecture

If the most impressive monuments of the Old Kingdom are its pyramids, those of the New Kingdom are its grandiose temples. Some of these temples were built to worship the state gods, but others were mortuary temples, which provided the pharaohs with a place for worshiping their patron gods during their lifetimes and then served as temples in their own honor after their death. The greatest mortuary temples arose along the Nile in the Thebes district during the 18th and 19th Dynasties.

Deir el-Bahri. The most distinctive New Kingdom royal mortuary temple (FIG. 3-20) is at Deir el-Bahri, erected by and for the female pharaoh Hatshepsut, one of the most remarkable women of the ancient world (see "Hatshepsut, the Woman Who Would Be King," page 72). Some Egyptologists attribute the temple to SENENMUT (FIG. 3-27), Hatshepsut's chancellor, described in two inscriptions as the queen's architect. His association with this project is uncertain, however. Hatshepsut's temple rises from the valley floor in three column-lined terraces connected by ramps on the central axis. It is striking how well Senenmut(?) designed the complex to complement its natural setting. The long horizontals and verticals of the *colonnades* and their rhythm of light and dark repeat the pattern of the limestone cliffs above.

As imposing as it is today, Hatshepsut's mortuary temple was once part of an even larger complex with a causeway connecting it to a now-lost valley temple. The multilevel funerary temple proper incorporated shrines to Hathor, Anubis, and the most important state god of the New Kingdom, the composite Amen-Re, as well as to Hatshepsut and her father, Thutmose I. As many as 200 statues in the round portraying the queen in various guises were on display throughout the vast complex. On the lowest terrace, to either side of the processional way, statues repeatedly represented Hatshepsut as a sphinx. On the uppermost level, the royal sculptors depicted the female pharaoh standing, seated, and as Osiris (compare FIG. 3-23A). At least eight colossal kneeling statues in red granite lined the way to the entrance of the Amen-Re sanctuary. The

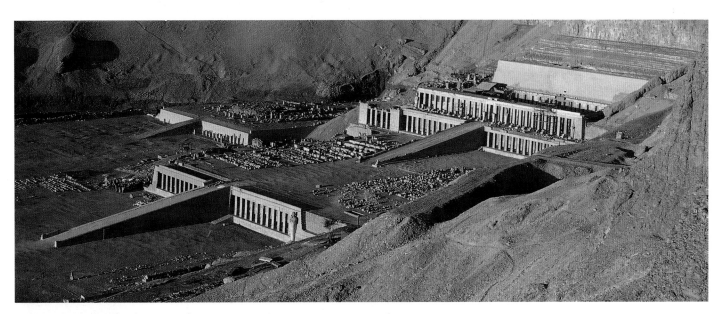

3-20 **Mortuary temple of Hatshepsut (looking southwest), Deir el-Bahri, Egypt, 18th Dynasty, ca. 1473–1458 BCE.**

Hatshepsut was the first great female monarch whose name is recorded. Her immense funerary temple incorporated shrines to Amen-Re, whom she claimed was her father, and to Hathor and Anubis.

Hatshepsut, the Woman Who Would Be King

In 1479 BCE, Thutmose II, the fourth pharaoh of the 18th Dynasty (r. 1492–1479 BCE), died. His principal wife (and half sister), Queen Hatshepsut (r. 1473–1458 BCE), had not given birth to any sons who survived, so the title of king went to Thutmose III, son of Thutmose II by another of his wives. Hatshepsut became regent for the boy-king. Within a few years, however, the queen proclaimed herself pharaoh and insisted that her father, Thutmose I, had chosen her as his successor during his lifetime. Underscoring her claim, one of the reliefs decorating Hatshepsut's enormous funerary complex (FIG. 3-20) depicts Thutmose I crowning his daughter as king in the presence of the Egyptian gods. Other reliefs (FIG. 3-22) represent her many achievements during her reign.

Hatshepsut is the first great female monarch whose name has been recorded. (In the 12th Dynasty, Sobekneferu was crowned king of Egypt, but she reigned for only a few years.) As pharaoh for two decades, Hatshepsut ruled what was then the most powerful and prosperous empire in the world.

Hatshepsut commissioned numerous building projects, and sculptors produced portraits of the female pharaoh in great numbers for display in those complexes. Unfortunately, Thutmose III (r. 1458–1425 BCE), for reasons still not fully understood, late in his reign ordered Hatshepsut's portraits destroyed. Her surviving portraits are of two types. In those carved before she consolidated power, Hatshepsut appears as a woman with delicate features, a slender frame, and breasts. In her latest portraits, such as the one illustrated here (FIG. 3-21), Hatshepsut uniformly wears the costume of the male pharaohs, with royal headdress and kilt, and in some cases even a false ceremonial beard. Inscriptions of this time refer to Hatshepsut as "*His* Majesty."

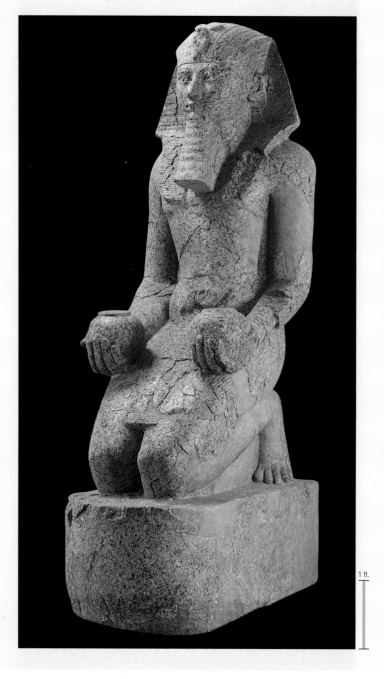

3-21 **Hatshepsut with offering jars, from the upper court of her mortuary temple, Deir el-Bahri, Egypt, 18th Dynasty, ca. 1473–1458 BCE. Red granite, 8′ 6″ high. Metropolitan Museum of Art, New York.**

Hatshepsut's successor destroyed many of her portraits. Conservators reassembled this one, which depicts the queen as a male pharaoh, consistent with inscriptions calling her "His Majesty."

1 ft.

statue reproduced here (FIG. 3-21) suffered the same fate as most of Hatshepsut's portraits during the reign of Thutmose III. Vandals smashed it and threw the pieces in a dump, but conservators skillfully reassembled the portrait. Hatshepsut holds a globular offering jar in each hand as she takes part in a ritual in honor of the gods. (A king kneels only before a god, never a mortal.) She wears the royal male nemes headdress and the pharaoh's ceremonial beard (compare FIGS. 3-12, 3-13, and 3-34). The agents of Thutmose III hacked off the uraeus cobra that once adorned the front of the headdress. The figure is also anatomically male, consistent with the queen's formal assumption of the title of king and with the many inscriptions addressing her as a man (see "Hatshepsut," above).

Complementing the array of portrait statues was an extensive series of reliefs glorifying Hatshepsut and her reign—the first great tribute to a woman's achievements in the history of art. In the middle colonnade of the second level, for example, painted limestone reliefs commemorated Hatshepsut's divine birth. Hatshepsut claimed to be the daughter of Amen-Re, who had assumed the form of the pharaoh Thutmose I in order to impregnate her mother, the king's principal wife. Other reliefs depicted the impressive engineering feat of transporting huge granite *obelisks* (tall *monolithic*—one-piece—*pillars* with pyramidal tops, symbols of the sun god Re) from the Aswan quarries to the temple of Amen-Re (FIG. 3-24) at Karnak. (Several Roman emperors later transported many of the Egyptian obelisks to Rome, where they remain prominent landmarks in the modern city; FIGS. 7-49, 24-4, and 24-7.)

The relief illustrated here (FIG. 3-22) is one of those documenting Hatshepsut's successful expedition to Punt, famed for its gold,

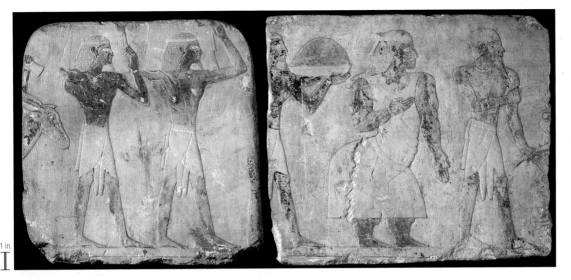

3-22 King and queen of Punt and attendants, relief from the mortuary temple of Hatshepsut, Deir el-Bahri, Egypt, 18th Dynasty, ca. 1473–1458 BCE. Painted limestone, 1′ 3″ high. Egyptian Museum, Cairo.

Painted limestone reliefs throughout Hatshepsut's mortuary temple complex celebrated her reign, her divine birth, and her successful expedition to the kingdom of Punt on the Red Sea.

1 in.

myrrh, and other exotic natural resources. The reliefs record the sea journey, the precious cargo of gold and frankincense trees that the Egyptians brought back with them, as well as the people, animals, and houses that the Egyptians found in Punt. In this detail, bare-chested men carry the local goods that Hatshepsut's men will load onto their ships. Leading the procession are two figures that art historians traditionally identify as the king and queen of Punt. The Egyptian sculptor depicted the queen as an obese and misshapen woman. Scholars debate whether this is an accurate portrayal or an exaggeration designed to underscore the foreignness of the Punt queen.

Abu Simbel. The sheer size of Hatshepsut's mortuary temple never fails to impress visitors, and this is no less true of the immense rock-cut temple (FIG. 3-23) of Ramses II (r. 1290–1224 BCE) at Abu Simbel in Nubia, territory that Ahmose I acquired after his victory over the Hyksos. The temple was dedicated to the worship of the pharaoh's divine essence and the three chief gods of that era— Amen-Re, Ptah, and Re-Horakhty—and was carefully designed so that at the summer and winter solstices, the rising sun illuminates the king's image inside. The temple has a remarkable modern history. In 1968, to save the Nubian monument from submersion in the Aswan High Dam reservoir, engineers cut the temple into sections and reassembled it nearly 700 feet away, resting against a new artificial mountain they had constructed—an amazing achievement in its own right.

Ramses, Egypt's last great warrior pharaoh, ruled for two-thirds of a century, an extraordinary accomplishment even in peacetime in an era when life expectancy was far shorter than it is today. The king, proud of his many campaigns to restore the

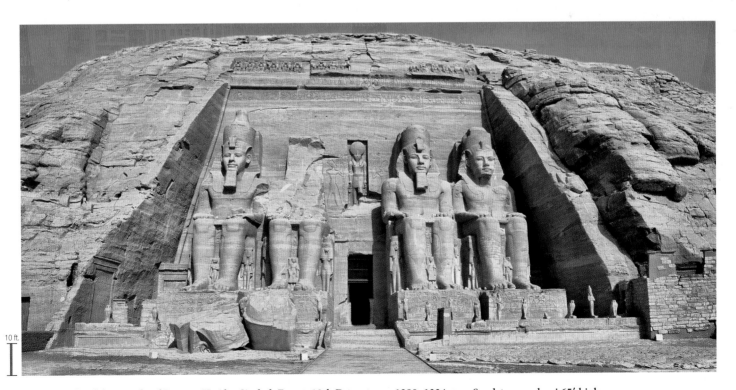

10 ft.

3-23 Facade of the temple of Ramses II, Abu Simbel, Egypt, 19th Dynasty, ca. 1290–1224 BCE. Sandstone, colossi 65′ high.

Four rock-cut images of Ramses II dominate the facade of this New Kingdom temple at Abu Simbel in Nubia. The colossal portraits are a dozen times the height of a man, even though the pharaoh is seated.

empire, proclaimed his greatness by placing four colossal images of himself on the temple facade. The portraits are 65 feet tall—almost a dozen times the height of an ancient Egyptian, even though the pharaoh is seated. They face toward Nubia and served to intimidate the Egyptian's southern neighbor. Spectacular as Ramses's colossi are, the rock-cut statues nonetheless lack the refinement of earlier periods, because the sculptors sacrificed detailed carving to overwhelming size. This trade-off is characteristic of colossal statuary of every period and every place (compare FIG. 16-16). The immense rock-cut interior (FIG. 3-23A) of the Abu Simbel temple also makes an indelible impression.

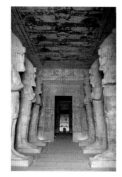

⟦🡕⟧ **3-23A** Interior of temple of Ramses II, Abu Simbel, ca. 1290–1224 BCE.

Ramses, like other pharaohs, had many wives, and he fathered scores of sons. The pharaoh honored the most important members of his family with grandiose monuments of their own. At Abu Simbel, for example, north of his temple, Ramses ordered the construction of a temple for his principal wife, Nefertari. Huge rock-cut statues—four standing images of the king and two of the queen—dominate the temple's facade. For his sons, Ramses constructed an enormous underground tomb complex in the Valley of the Kings at Thebes, which an American team rediscovered in 1987. Robbers looted the tomb within a half century of its construction, but archaeologists have yet to find the royal burial chambers in the complex, so the tomb may yet yield important artworks.

Karnak. Distinct from the New Kingdom temples that primarily honor pharaohs and queens are the edifices built for the worship of one or more of the gods. Successive kings often added to these sanctuaries until they reached gigantic size. The temple of Amen-Re (FIG. 3-24) at Karnak, for example, begun during the Middle Kingdom, was largely the work of 18th Dynasty pharaohs, including Thutmose I and III and Hatshepsut, but Ramses II (19th

Dynasty) also contributed sections, and other pharaohs added chapels to the complex at least as late as the fourth century BCE. Enclosing the 247-acre complex and shutting it off from the outside world was a perimeter wall 39 feet high and 26 feet thick. Inside, next to the temple proper, was an artificial sacred lake (FIG. 3-24, center)—a reference to the primeval waters before creation (see "The Gods and Goddesses of Egypt," page 60). The temple of Amen-Re rises from the earth as the original sacred mound rose from the waters at the beginning of time.

The Karnak temple and similar New Kingdom temples, such as the equally huge one at nearby Luxor (FIG. 3-24A), all had similar *axial plans.* A typical *pylon temple* (the name derives from the sanctuaries' simple and massive gateways, or *pylons,* with sloping walls forming two wings flanking a central doorway) is bilaterally symmetrical along a single axis that runs from an approaching avenue through a colonnaded court and hall and then into the sanctuary proper. Axial plans are characteristic of much of

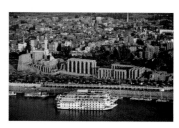

⟦🡕⟧ **3-24A** Temple of Amen-Re, Luxor, begun early 14th century BCE.

Egyptian architecture. Narrow corridors on the longitudinal axis are also the approaches to the Gizeh pyramids (FIG. 3-10) and to Hatshepsut's multilevel mortuary temple (FIG. 3-20). Marking the end of the statuary-lined approach to a New Kingdom temple was the monumental facade of the pylon (FIG. 3-24, *right*). The pylon faced the Nile, from which festival processions arrived by boat, and served as a symbolic barrier between the chaotic world and the sacred ordered precinct within. New Kingdom sculptors routinely covered pylons with reliefs glorifying their rulers (FIG. 3-38), especially in their role as defenders of order who defeat all who pose a threat to Egypt's stability. Beyond the pylon was an open court with columns on two or more sides, followed by a hall (FIG. 3-24, *center*) between the court and sanctuary, its long axis placed at a right angle to the corridor of the entire building complex. Only the pharaohs and the priests could enter the mysterious dark inner shrine

3-24 Restored view of the temple of Amen-Re (looking southeast), Karnak, Egypt, major construction 15th–13th centuries BCE (Jean Claude Golvin).

The vast Karnak temple complex contains a pylon temple with a bilaterally symmetrical axial plan and an artificial lake associated with the primeval waters of the Egyptian creation myth.

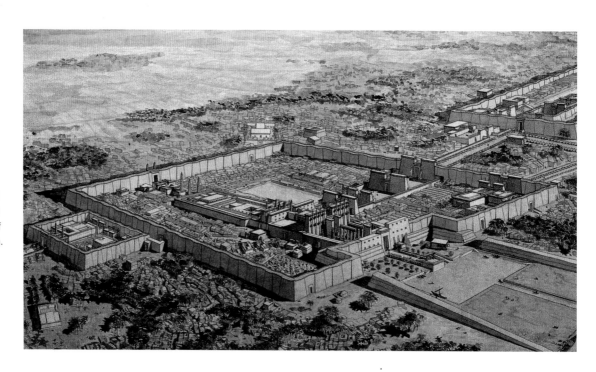

Illuminating Buildings before Lightbulbs

Until the invention of the electric lightbulb, one of the central problems all architects had to confront was how to illuminate a roofed interior without depending solely on torches and lamps, which were fire hazards. As early as the Old Kingdom, in the valley temple of Khafre at Gizeh, Egyptian architects experimented with a way to admit natural light using a device called the *clerestory.* One of the most effective examples of clerestory lighting is in the hypostyle hall (FIGS. 3-25 and 3-26) of the New Kingdom pylon temple at Karnak (FIG. 3-24).

Filling Karnak's gigantic (58,000-square-foot) hypostyle hall are massive columns, which support a roof of stone slabs carried on lintels. The 134 sandstone columns have bud-cluster or bell-shaped capitals resembling lotus or papyrus, the plants symbolizing Upper and Lower Egypt. The 12 central columns are 75 feet high, and the capitals are 22 feet in diameter at the top, large enough to hold a hundred people. The Egyptians, who used no mortar, depended on precise cutting of the joints and the weight of the huge stone blocks to hold the columns in place. The two central rows of columns are taller than those at the sides. The purpose of raising the roof's central section was to create a clerestory, an elevated additional story with openings enabling sunlight

to filter into the interior, although the Karnak hall's stone grilles (FIG. 3-26) would have blocked much of the light.

The clerestory is evidently an Egyptian innovation, and its significance cannot be overstated. Clerestories played a key role in the history of architecture until very recently.

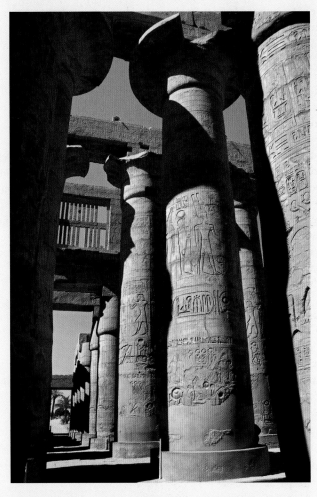

3-26 **Columns and clerestory of the hypostyle hall of the temple of Amen-Re, Karnak, Egypt, 19th Dynasty, ca. 1290–1224 BCE.**

Columns crowd the hypostyle hall of the Amen-Re temple. The tallest are 66 feet high and have capitals that are 22 feet in diameter. The columns support a roof of stone slabs carried on lintels.

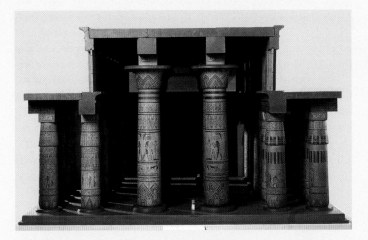

3-25 **Model of the hypostyle hall, temple of Amen-Re, Karnak, Egypt, 19th Dynasty, ca. 1290–1224 BCE. Metropolitan Museum of Art, New York.**

The two central rows of columns of Karnak's hypostyle hall are taller than the rest. Raising the roof's central section created a clerestory that admitted light through windows with stone grilles.

at the culmination of the sacred path. The darkness called to mind the moment of creation out of the primeval waters. A chosen few were admitted to the great columnar *hypostyle hall* (a hall with a roof resting on columns; FIGS. 3-25 and 3-26), shrouded in semi-darkness but with light admitted through a *clerestory* illuminating the axial corridor (see "Illuminating Buildings before Lightbulbs," above). The majority of the people could proceed only as far as the sun-drenched open court.

Sculpture and Painting

Although the Egyptians lavishly decorated the great temple complexes of the New Kingdom with statues and painted reliefs, many of the finest examples of statuary and mural painting adorned tombs, as in the Old and Middle Kingdoms.

Senenmut and Nefrura. *Block statues* were popular during the New Kingdom because their large flat surfaces were well suited for

design concentrates attention on the heads. The sculptor treated the two bodies as a single polished cubic block with smoothly rounded corners. Senenmut holds the pharaoh's daughter by Thutmose II in his "lap" and envelops the girl in his cloak. The work is one of many surviving statues depicting Senenmut with the princess, which enhanced the chancellor's stature through his association with the pharaoh's daughter (he was her tutor) and, by implication, with Hatshepsut herself.

Tomb of Nebamun. Some of the best-preserved mural paintings of the New Kingdom come from the Theban tomb of Nebamun (FIGS. 3-28 and 3-28A). The painting technique, also employed in earlier Egyptian tombs, is *fresco secco* (dry fresco), in which artists let the plaster dry before painting on it. This procedure, in contrast to true fresco painting on wet plaster (see "Fresco Painting," page 428), enabled slower and more meticulous work than painting on fresh plaster, which had to be completed before the plaster dried. As the many third- and fourth-millennium BCE Egyptian murals attest, fresco secco is a very durable medium, even though, unlike in true fresco painting, the colors do not fuse with the wall surface.

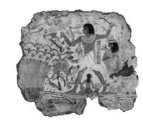

🔎 **3-28A** Fowling scene, tomb of Nebamun, Thebes, ca. 1400–1350 BCE.

Nebamun, whose official titles were "scribe and counter of grain," was a wealthy man who could afford to hire highly skilled painters to decorate his tomb. One of the preserved fresco fragments (FIG. 3-28) from Nebamun's tomb shows noblewomen watching and apparently participating in a musical performance in which two nimble and almost nude girls dance in front of the guests at a commemorative funerary ceremony. At these banquets, the guests consumed great quantities of wine and beer to enable them, in their drunken state, to commune with the dead. (The painter took care to include the ample supply of wine jars at the right.) Stylistically, the fresco is significant in showing that New Kingdom artists did not always adhere to the old norms for figural representation. Nebamun's painter recorded the dancers' overlapping figures, their facing in opposite directions, and their rather complicated gyrations, producing a pleasing intertwined motif at the same time. The profile view of the dancers is consistent with their lower stature in the Egyptian hierarchy. The New Kingdom

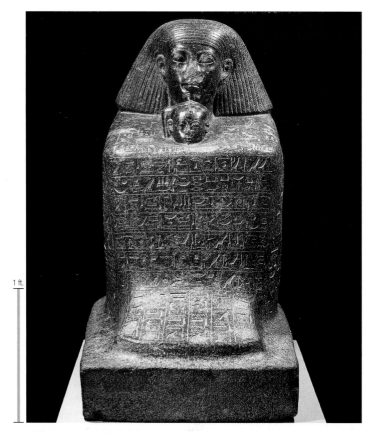

3-27 Senenmut with Princess Nefrura, from Thebes, Egypt, 18th Dynasty, ca. 1470–1460 BCE. Granite, 3′ ½″ high. Ägyptisches Museum, Staatliche Museen zu Berlin, Berlin.

Hatshepsut's chancellor holds the queen's daughter in his "lap" and envelops her in his cloak. New Kingdom block statues exhibit a radical simplification of form and are well suited for lengthy inscriptions.

lengthy inscriptions and because their simple shapes were easier to carve and less susceptible to damage. These works display an even more radical simplification of form than was common in Old Kingdom statuary, but they performed the same function—the provision of an eternal home for the deceased's ka. In the statue illustrated here (FIG. 3-27) depicting Senenmut, Hatshepsut's chancellor and possible lover, with her daughter, Nefrura, the streamlined

3-28 Musicians and dancers, detail of a mural from the tomb of Nebamun, Thebes, Egypt, 18th Dynasty, ca. 1400–1350 BCE. Fresco secco, 1′ × 2′ 3″. British Museum, London.

This fresco in Nebamun's tomb represents entertainers at a funerary banquet. The artist experimented with frontal views of faces and bodies—a relaxation of the Old Kingdom's strict rules of representation.

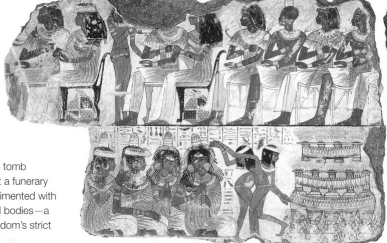

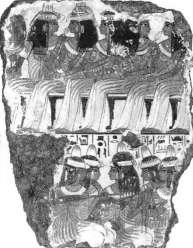

Akhenaton

When the 18th Dynasty pharaoh Akhenaton instituted his overhaul of Egyptian religion in the mid-14th century BCE, he deleted the name of Amen from all inscriptions and even from his own name and that of his father, Amenhotep III (r. 1390–1352 BCE). He emptied the traditional temples, enraged the priests, and moved his court downriver from Thebes to present-day Amarna, a site he named Akhetaton (Horizon of Aton). The pharaoh claimed to be both the son and sole prophet of Aton. To him alone did the god reveal himself. Moreover, in stark contrast to earlier practice, painters and sculptors represented Akhenaton's god neither in animal nor in human form (nor in composite human-animal form; compare FIG. 3-1) but simply as the sun disk emitting life-giving rays (FIG. 3-32).

The pharaohs who followed Akhenaton reestablished the Theban cult and priesthood of Amen at Karnak (FIG. 3-24) and elsewhere, and they restored Amen's temples and inscriptions. Akhenaton's brief religious revolution was soon undone, and his new city largely abandoned.

During the brief heretical episode of Akhenaton, profound changes also occurred in Egyptian art. A colossal statue (FIG. 3-29) of Akhenaton, one of several from Karnak toppled and buried after his death, retains the standard frontal pose of traditional Egyptian royal portraits. But the effeminate body, with its curving contours, and the long face with full lips and heavy-lidded eyes are a far cry indeed from the heroically proportioned figures of the pharaoh's predecessors (compare FIG. 3-13). Akhenaton's body is curiously misshapen, with weak arms, a narrow waist, protruding belly, wide hips, and fatty thighs.

What is the explanation for this new royal imagery? Many Egyptologists have turned to modern physicians for the answer. The doctors have tried to explain Akhenaton's physique by attributing a variety of illnesses to the pharaoh, but they have been unable to agree on a diagnosis. And their premise—that the statue is a faithful depiction of a physical deformity—is probably faulty, just as the misshapen body of the queen of Punt (FIG. 3-22) may be an artistic convention and not anatomically accurate. Some art historians have expressed a second opinion.

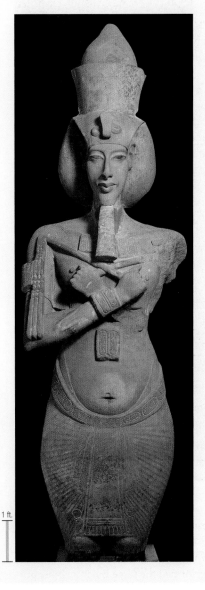

1 ft.

3-29 **Akhenaton, colossal statue from the temple of Aton, Karnak, Egypt, 18th Dynasty, ca. 1353–1335 BCE. Sandstone, 13′ high. Egyptian Museum, Cairo.**

Akhenaton initiated both religious and artistic revolutions. This androgynous figure is a deliberate reaction against tradition. It may be an attempt to portray the pharaoh as Aton, the sexless sun disk.

They think that Akhenaton's portrait is a deliberate artistic reaction against the established style, paralleling the suppression of traditional religion. They argue that because Akhenaton was the child and image of Aton on earth, his artists tried to formulate a new androgynous image of the pharaoh as the manifestation of Aton, the sexless sun disk. Confirmation for this view can be found in the representation of other members of the royal family (FIG. 3-32), whose body types also break sharply with tradition.

artist reserved the composite view for Nebamun and his family. Of the four seated women, the two at the left are represented conventionally, but the other two face the observer in what is a rarely attempted frontal pose. They clap and beat time to the dance, while one of them plays the reeds. The painter took careful note of the soles of their feet as they sit cross-legged, and suggested the movement of the women's heads by the loose arrangement of their hair strands. This informality also constitutes a relaxation of the Old Kingdom's strict rules of representation.

The frescoes in Nebamun's tomb testify to the luxurious life of the Egyptian nobility, filled with good food and drink, fine musicians, lithe dancers, and leisure time to hunt and fish in the marshes (FIG. 3-28A). Still, as in the earlier tomb of Ti, the scenes should be read both literally and allegorically. Although Nebamun enjoys himself in the afterlife, the artist symbolically asked viewers to recall how he got there. Hunting scenes reminded Egyptians of Horus, the son of Osiris, hunting down his father's murderer, Seth, the god of disorder (see "The Gods and Goddesses of Egypt," page 60). Successful hunts were metaphors for triumphing over

death and disorder, ensuring a happy existence in the afterlife. Music and dance were sacred to Hathor, who aided the dead in their passage to the other world. The sensual women at the banquet are a reference to fertility, rebirth, and regeneration.

Akhenaton and the Amarna Period

Not long after his family laid Nebamun to rest in his tomb at Thebes, a revolution occurred in Egyptian religion and society. In the mid-14th century BCE, Amenhotep IV, later known as Akhenaton (r. 1353–1335 BCE), abandoned the worship of most of the Egyptian gods in favor of Aton, identified with the sun disk, whom the pharaoh declared to be the universal and only god (see "Akhenaton," above).

Nefertiti and Tiye. Akhenaton's religious revolution was accompanied by a break with artistic tradition, seen both in portraiture (FIGS. 3-29, 3-30, and 3-31) and relief sculpture (FIG. 3-32). The new

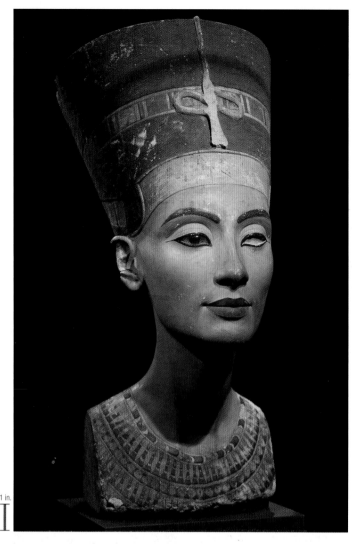

3-30 THUTMOSE, bust of Nefertiti, from Amarna, Egypt, 18th Dynasty, ca. 1353–1335 BCE. Painted limestone, 1' 8" high. Ägyptisches Museum, Staatliche Museen zu Berlin, Berlin.

Found in the sculptor's workshop, Thutmose's bust of Nefertiti portrays Akhenaton's influential wife as an elegant beauty with a thoughtful expression and a long, delicately curved neck.

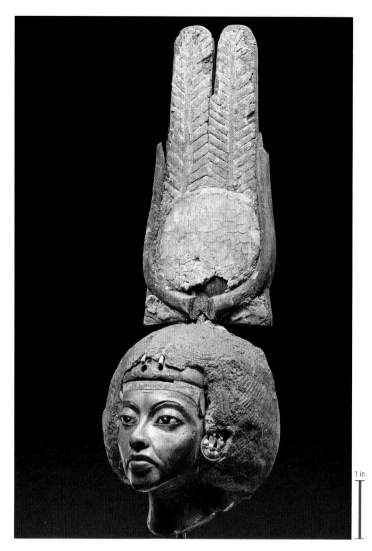

3-31 Portrait of Tiye, from Ghurab, Egypt, 18th Dynasty, ca. 1353–1335 BCE. Yew wood, gold, silver, alabaster, faience, and lapis lazuli, $8\frac{7}{8}$" high. Ägyptisches Museum, Staatliche Museen zu Berlin, Berlin.

This portrait of Akhenaton's mother is carved of dark yew wood, possibly to match the queen's complexion. The tall gold crown with the sun disk and cow horns was added during her son's reign.

Amarna style is on display in a painted limestone bust (FIG. 3-30) of Akhenaton's queen, Nefertiti (The Beautiful One Has Come). The portrait exhibits an expression of entranced musing and an almost mannered sensitivity and delicacy of curving contour. Excavators discovered the bust in the Amarna workshop of the sculptor THUTMOSE. It appears to be a deliberately unfinished model very likely by the master's own hand. The left eye socket still lacks the inlaid eye, making the face a kind of before-and-after demonstration piece. With this elegant bust, Thutmose may have been alluding to a heavy flower on its slender stalk by exaggerating the weight of the crowned head and the length of the almost serpentine neck. The sculptor seems to have adjusted the likeness of his subject to meet the era's standard of spiritual beauty.

By contrast, the miniature head (FIG. 3-31) of Queen Tiye, mother of Akhenaton, is a moving portrait of old age. Although not of royal birth, Tiye was the daughter of a high-ranking official and became the chief wife of Amenhotep III. Archaeologists unearthed her portrait, carved of dark yew wood (possibly to match her complexion), at Ghurab with other objects connected with the funerary cult of Amenhotep III. A sculptor probably remodeled the portrait

during her son's reign to eliminate all reference to deities of the old religion. That is when the head acquired the present wig of plaster and linen with small blue beads and the tall crown consisting of cow horns, Aton's sun disk, and a pair of feathers. This type of crown is worn only by goddesses in Egyptian art, and it indicates that Tiye, like Egypt's god-kings, is divine. Nonetheless, Akhenaton's mother appears as an older woman with lines and furrows, consistent with the new relaxation of artistic rules in the Amarna age. The sculptor inlaid her heavy-lidded slanting eyes with alabaster and ebony, and painted the lips red. The earrings (one is hidden by the later wig) are of gold and lapis lazuli. The wig covers what was originally a silver-foil headdress. A gold band still adorns the forehead, and the tall crown is also made of hammered gold.

Both Nefertiti and Tiye figured prominently in the art and life of the Amarna age. Tiye, for example, regularly appeared in art beside her husband during his reign, and she apparently played an important role in his administration as well as her son's. Letters survive from foreign rulers advising the young Akhenaton to seek his mother's counsel in the conduct of international affairs. Nefertiti,

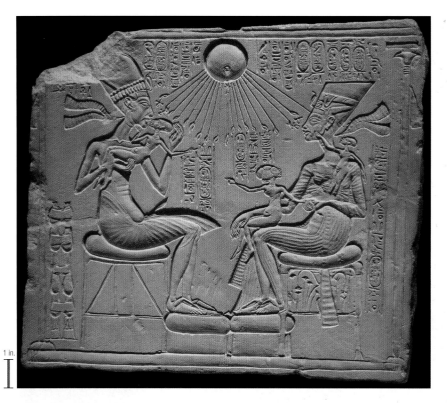

1 in.

3-32 Akhenaton and Nefertiti with three daughters, from Amarna, Egypt, 18th Dynasty, ca. 1353–1335 BCE. Limestone, 1′ ¼″ high. Ägyptisches Museum, Staatliche Museen zu Berlin, Berlin.

In this sunken relief, the Amarna artist provided a rare intimate look at the royal family in a domestic setting. Akhenaton, Nefertiti, and three of their six daughters bask in the life-giving rays of Aton, the sun disk.

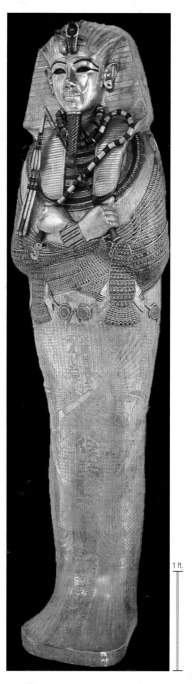

1 ft.

too, was an influential woman. She frequently appears in reliefs of this period in which she not only equals her husband in size but also sometimes wears pharaonic headgear.

Family of Akhenaton. A relief stele (FIG. 3-32), perhaps from a private shrine, provides a rare look at this royal family. The style is familiar from the colossus of Akhenaton (FIG. 3-29) and the portrait head of Nefertiti (FIG. 3-30). Undulating curves have replaced rigid lines, and the figures possess the prominent bellies that characterize figures of the Amarna period. The pharaoh, his wife, and three of their six daughters bask in the rays of Aton, the sun disk, which end in hands holding the *ankh,* the sign of life. The mood is informal and anecdotal. Akhenaton lifts one of his daughters in order to kiss her. Another daughter sits on Nefertiti's lap and gestures toward her father, while the youngest daughter reaches out to touch a pendant on her mother's crown. This kind of intimate portrayal of the pharaoh and his family is unprecedented in Egyptian art, but it typifies the radical upheaval in art that accompanied Akhenaton's religious revolution.

The Akhenaton family portrait is a *sunken relief.* In this technique, the sculptor chisels deep outlines below the stone's surface instead of cutting back the stone around the figures to make them project from the surface. Sunken reliefs are much less subject to damage than high reliefs and, when used on columns, such as those in Karnak's hypostyle hall (FIG. 3-26), have the additional advantage of maintaining the shafts' contours.

The Tomb of Tutankhamen and the Post-Amarna Period

The most famous figure of the Post-Amarna period is Tutankhamen (r. 1333–1323 BCE), who was probably Akhenaton's son by a minor wife. Tutankhamen ruled for a decade and died at age 18. (Although some have speculated foul play, examination of the king's mummy in 2005 ruled out murder.) Tutankhamen was a very unimportant figure in Egyptian history, however. The public remembers him today solely because in 1922, Howard Carter (1874–1939), a British archaeologist, discovered the boy-king's tomb with its fabulously rich treasure of sculpture, furniture, and jewelry largely intact.

Tutankhamen's Mummy. The principal item that Carter found in Tutankhamen's tomb was the enshrined body of the pharaoh himself. The royal mummy reposed in the innermost of three coffins, nested one within the other. The innermost coffin (FIG. 3-33) is the most luxurious of the three. Made of beaten gold (about a quarter ton of it) and inlaid with semiprecious stones such as lapis lazuli, turquoise, and carnelian, it is a supreme monument to the sculptor's and goldsmith's crafts. The portrait mask, which covered the king's face, is also made of gold with inlaid semiprecious stones.

3-33 Innermost coffin of Tutankhamen, from his tomb at Thebes, Egypt, 18th Dynasty, ca. 1323 BCE. Gold with inlay of enamel and semiprecious stones, 6′ 1″ long. Egyptian Museum, Cairo.

The boy-king Tutankhamen owes his fame today to his treasure-laden tomb. His mummy was encased in three nested coffins. The innermost one, made of gold, portrays the pharaoh as Osiris.

3-34 Death mask of Tutankhamen, from the innermost coffin in his tomb at Thebes, Egypt, 18th Dynasty, ca. 1323 BCE. Gold with inlay of semiprecious stones, 1′ 9¼″ high. Egyptian Museum, Cairo.

The treasures in Tutankhamen's tomb include this mummy mask portraying the teenaged pharaoh with idealized features and wearing the traditional false beard and uraeus cobra headdress.

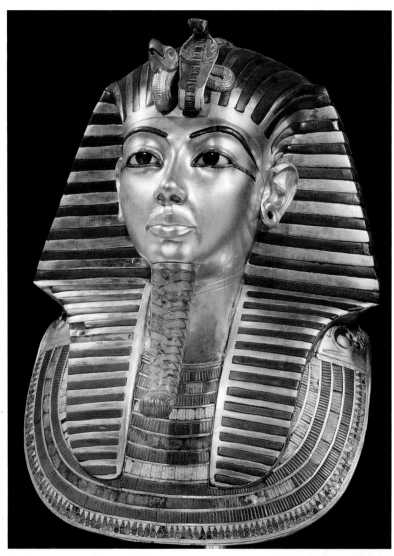

It is a sensitive portrayal of the serene adolescent king dressed in his official regalia, including the nemes headdress and false beard (FIG. 3-34). The general effect of the mask and the tomb treasures as a whole is one of grandeur and richness expressive of Egyptian power, pride, and limitless wealth.

Tutankhamen at War. Although Tutankhamen died young, recent research suggests that he fought in several wars. But even if he had never commanded an army, his position as king required that artists represent him as a conqueror, and he appears as a victorious general on a painted wood chest deposited in his tomb. The lid panel shows the king as a successful hunter pursuing droves of fleeing animals in the desert. On the side panels, the pharaoh, larger than all other figures, rides in a war chariot pulled by spirited, plumed horses. On the side illustrated here (FIG. 3-35), he draws his bow against a cluster of bearded Asian enemies (he battles Africans on the other side), who fall in confusion before him. (The absence of a ground line in an Egyptian painting or relief often implies chaos and death.) Tutankhamen slays the enemy, like game, in great numbers. Behind him are three tiers of smaller war

3-35 Painted chest, from the tomb of Tutankhamen, Thebes, Egypt, 18th Dynasty, ca. 1333–1323 BCE. Wood, 1′ 8″ long. Egyptian Museum, Cairo.

In this representation of Tutankhamen triumphing over Asian enemies, the artist contrasted the orderly registers of Egyptian chariots with the chaotic pile of foreign soldiers who fall before the king.

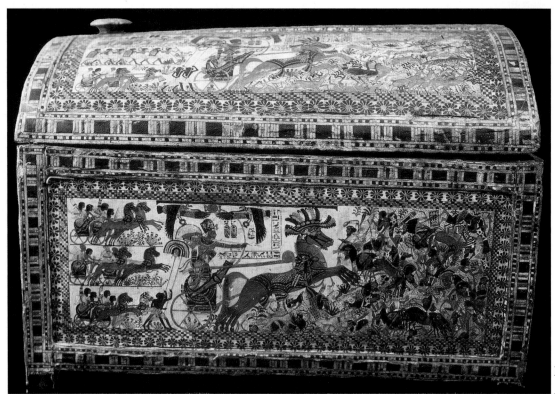

chariots, which serve to magnify the king's figure and to increase the count of his warriors. The themes are traditional, but the fluid, curvilinear forms are features reminiscent of the Amarna style.

FIRST MILLENNIUM BCE

During the first millennium BCE, Egypt lost the commanding role it had once played in the ancient world. Egypt's fertile lands and immense riches had long made it desirable territory. Foreign powers invaded and occupied the land, and the empire dwindled away until, beginning in the fourth century BCE, Alexander the Great of Macedon and his Greek successors and, eventually, the emperors of Rome replaced the pharaohs as rulers of the Kingdom of the Nile.

Kingdom of Kush

One of those foreign powers was Egypt's gold-rich neighbor to the south, the kingdom of Kush, part of which is in present-day Sudan. Called Nubia by the Romans, perhaps from the Egyptian word for "gold," Kush appears in Egyptian texts as early as the Old Kingdom. During the New Kingdom, the pharaohs colonized Nubia and appointed a viceroy of Kush to administer the Kushite kingdom, which included Abu Simbel (FIG. 3-23) and controlled the major trade route between Egypt and sub-Saharan Africa. But in the eighth century BCE, the Nubians conquered Egypt and established themselves as the 25th Dynasty.

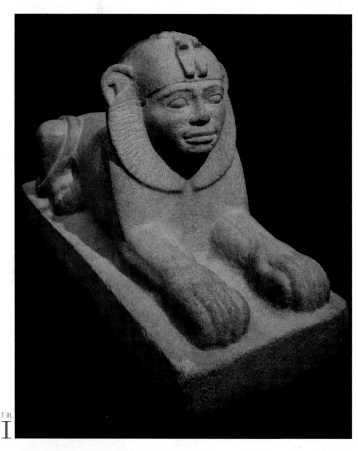

3-36 Taharqo as a sphinx, from temple T, Kawa, Sudan, 25th Dynasty, ca. 680 BCE. Granite, 1′ 4″ × 2′ 4¾″. British Museum, London.

The Nubian kings who ruled Egypt during the 25th Dynasty adopted traditional Egyptian statuary types, such as the sphinx, but sculptors incorporated the Kushite pharaohs' distinctly African features.

Taharqo.   Around 680 BCE, the Kushite pharaoh Taharqo (r. 690–664 BCE) constructed a temple at Kawa and placed a portrait of himself in it. Emulating traditional Egyptian types, the sculptor portrayed Taharqo as a sphinx (FIG. 3-36; compare FIG. 3-11) with the ears, mane, and body of a lion but with a human face and a headdress featuring two uraeus cobras. The king's name is inscribed on his chest, and his features are distinctly African, although, as in most pharaonic portraits, they record a physiognomic and ethnic type and should not be considered a specific likeness.

Thebes

The Kushite 25th Dynasty fell in turn to the Assyrians, who sacked Thebes in 660 BCE. At this time, a rich and powerful man named Mentuemhet was mayor of the city.

Mentuemhet.   In addition to his role as chief magistrate, Mentuemhet was the Fourth Prophet (priest) of Amen, and according to the inscriptions on works that he commissioned, he was responsible for restoring the temples that the Assyrians had razed. Reflecting his wealth and position, Mentuemhet placed numerous portrait statues of himself in those temples and also in the tomb he constructed in a prominent place in the Theban necropolis. More than a dozen of Mentuemhet's portraits survive, including the somewhat under-life-size granite statue illustrated here (FIG. 3-37).

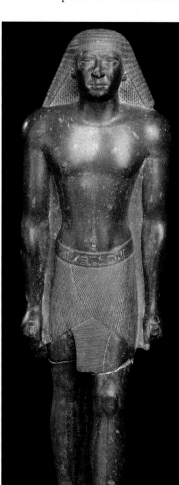

3-37 Portrait statue of Mentuemhet, from Karnak, Egypt, 26th Dynasty, ca. 660–650 BCE. Granite, 4′ 5″ high. Egyptian Museum, Cairo.

This late portrait of the mayor of Thebes combines a realistic face with the idealized body and conventional pose of Old Kingdom statuary, a testimony to the longevity of artistic modes in Egypt.

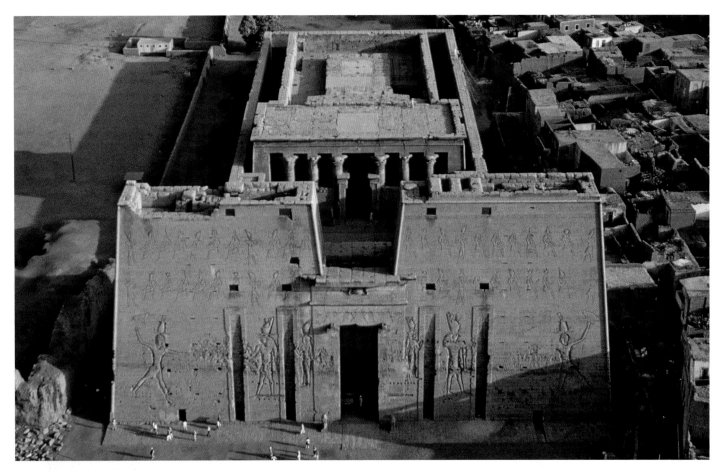

3-38 Temple of Horus (looking east), Edfu, Egypt, ca. 237–47 BCE.

The pylon temple at Edfu is more than a thousand years later than that at Karnak (FIG. 3-24), but it adheres to the same basic architectural scheme. Egyptian artistic forms tended to have very long lives.

The Theban mayor's portrait statues are typical of Egyptian sculpture at about the time the Greeks first encountered the art of the Nile region. The pose is traditional, and Mentuemhet has the trim, muscular body of a young man characteristic of Old Kingdom royal statues, but he wears a Middle Kingdom kilt and a New Kingdom wig. This eclecticism is typical of later Egyptian art. So too is the treatment of the face, which is much more realistic than most earlier representations of elite men and frankly portrays Mentuemhet's advanced age. The sculptor removed the slab of stone that forms a backdrop to most earlier royal portraits, but left the stone block intact between the arms and the torso and between the legs, an artistic decision that contributes significantly to the immobile look of the statue, so appropriate for a timeless image of the deceased in his eternal afterlife.

After Alexander

As Mentuemhet's portrait demonstrates, Egyptian artistic conventions, once formulated, tended to have very long lives. This is also true of architecture, even after Alexander the Great brought Greek rule and Greek culture to the Kingdom of the Nile.

Temple of Horus, Edfu. The temple of Horus (FIG. 3-38) at Edfu, built during the third, second, and first centuries BCE, still follows the basic pylon temple scheme that architects worked out more than a thousand years before (compare the New Kingdom temples at Karnak, FIG. 3-24, and Luxor, FIG. 3-24A).

The great entrance pylon at Edfu is especially impressive. The broad surface of its massive facade, with its characteristic sloping walls, is broken only by the doorway and its overshadowing *moldings* at the top and sides, deep channels to hold great flagstaffs, and over-lifesize sunken reliefs. The reliefs celebrate King Ptolemy XIII (r. 51–47 BCE), coruler with (and younger brother and husband of) Egypt's last queen, Cleopatra VII (r. 51–30 BCE). Cleopatra, who outlived her brother-husband by nearly two decades, was one of Egypt's most important female pharaohs and patrons of art and architecture.

On the Edfu pylon, Horus and Hathor witness a gigantic Ptolemy XIII smiting diminutive enemies—a motif first used in Egyptian reliefs and paintings in Predynastic times (FIGS. 3-1A and 3-2). The Edfu temple is eloquent testimony to the persistence of age-old Egyptian architectural and pictorial types even under Greek rule.

Indeed, the exceptional longevity of formal traditions in Egypt is one of the marvels of the history of art. It attests to the invention of an artistic vocabulary so satisfactory that it endured in Egypt for millennia. Everywhere else in the ancient Mediterranean world, stylistic change was the only common denominator.

Egypt from Narmer to Cleopatra

Predynastic and Early Dynastic ca. 3500–2575 BCE

- The unification of Upper and Lower Egypt into a single kingdom under the rule of a divine king occurred around 3000–2920 BCE. The palette of King Narmer probably commemorates events from the wars leading to the formation of the "Kingdom of the Two Lands." This and other Predynastic works established the basic principles of most Egyptian representational art for 3,000 years.

- Imhotep, the first artist in history whose name is known, was the earliest master of monumental stone architecture. He designed the funerary complex and stepped pyramid of King Djoser (r. 2630–2611 BCE) at Saqqara.

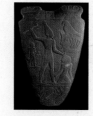

Palette of King Narmer,
ca. 3000–2920 BCE

Old Kingdom ca. 2575–2134 BCE

- The Old Kingdom was the first golden age of Egyptian art and architecture, the time when three kings of the Fourth Dynasty erected the pyramids at Gizeh, the oldest of the Seven Wonders of the ancient world. The pyramids were emblems of the sun on whose rays the god-kings ascended to the heavens when they died.

- Old Kingdom sculptors created seated and standing statuary types in which all movement was suppressed in order to express the eternal nature of divine kingship. These types would dominate Egyptian art for 2,000 years.

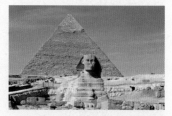

Pyramid of Khafre and Great Sphinx,
Gizeh, ca. 2520–2494 BCE

Middle Kingdom ca. 2040–1640 BCE

- After an intermediate period of civil war, Mentuhotep II (r. 2050–1998 BCE) reestablished central rule and founded the Middle Kingdom.

- The major artistic innovation of this period was a new kind of royal portrait with heightened realism and emotional content.

- Rock-cut tombs in which sculptors hewed both the facade and interior chambers out of the living rock replaced the mastaba as the standard Egyptian burial monument.

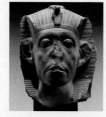

Senusret III, ca. 1860–1850 BCE

New Kingdom ca. 1550–1070 BCE

- During the New Kingdom, Egypt extended its borders to the Euphrates River in the east and deep into Nubia in the south.

- The most significant architectural innovation of this period was the axially planned pylon temple incorporating an immense gateway, columnar courtyards, and a hypostyle hall with clerestory lighting.

- Powerful pharaohs such as Hatshepsut (r. 1473–1458 BCE) and Ramses II (r. 1290–1224 BCE) erected gigantic temples in honor of their patron gods and themselves.

- Akhenaton (r. 1353–1335 BCE) abandoned the traditional Egyptian religion in favor of Aton, the sun disk, and initiated a short-lived artistic revolution in which undulating curves and anecdotal content replaced the cubic forms and impassive stillness of earlier Egyptian art.

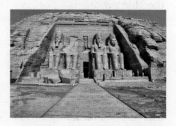

Temple of Ramses II, Abu Simbel,
ca. 1290–1224 BCE

First Millennium BCE 1000–30 BCE

- After the demise of the New Kingdom, Egypt's power in the ancient world declined, and the Nile came under the control of foreigners. These included the Kushite kings of Nubia and, after 332 BCE, Alexander the Great and his Greek successors. In 30 BCE, Egypt became a province of the Roman Empire.

- The traditional forms of Egyptian art and architecture lived on even under foreign rule.

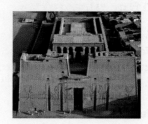

Temple of Horus, Edfu,
ca. 237–47 BCE

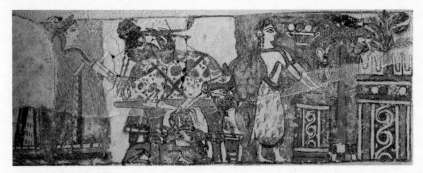

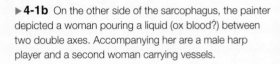 **4-1a** The Hagia Triada sarcophagus provides insight into Minoan rituals. On one side, four women (with light skin) and a dark-skinned male double-flute player take part in a ceremony involving a sacrificial ox.

4-1b On the other side of the sarcophagus, the painter depicted a woman pouring a liquid (ox blood?) between two double axes. Accompanying her are a male harp player and a second woman carrying vessels.

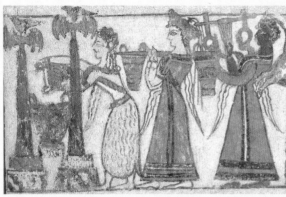

4-1c Three men (with dark skin) moving in the opposite direction carry sculptures of two sacrificial animals and a model of a boat, offerings to the deceased man shown standing in front of his tomb.

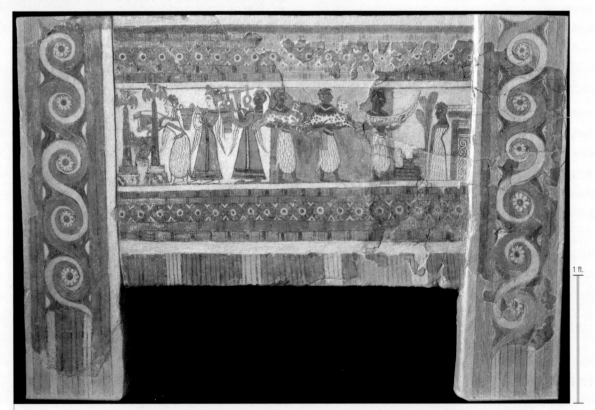

1 ft.

4-1 **Sarcophagus, from Hagia Triada (Crete), Greece, ca. 1450–1400 BCE. Painted limestone, 4′ 6″ long. Archaeological Museum, Iraklion.**

THE PREHISTORIC AEGEAN /4

Greece in the Age of Heroes

When, in the eighth century BCE, Homer immortalized in the *Iliad* and the *Odyssey* the great war between the Greeks and the Trojans and the subsequent adventure-packed journey home of Odysseus, the epic poet was describing a time long before his own—a golden age of larger-than-life heroes. Since the late 19th century, archaeologists have gradually uncovered impressive remains of that heroic age, including the palaces of the legendary King Minos at Knossos (FIG. 4-4) on Crete and of King Agamemnon at Mycenae (FIG. 4-19) on the Greek mainland. But they have also recovered thousands of less glamorous objects and inscriptions that provide a contemporaneous view of life in the prehistoric Aegean unfiltered by the romantic lens of Homer and later writers.

One of the most intriguing finds to date is the painted *Minoan* (named after King Minos) *sarcophagus* (FIG. 4-1) from Hagia Triada on the southern coast of Crete. The paintings adorning the sides of the small coffin are closely related in technique, color scheme, and figure style to the much larger frescoes (FIGS. 4-7 and 4-8) on the walls of Minoan palaces, but the subject is foreign to the royal repertoire. Befitting the function of the sarcophagus as a burial container, the paintings illustrate the funerary rites in honor of a man. They furnish welcome information about Minoan religion, which still remains obscure despite more than a century of excavation on Crete.

On one long side of the sarcophagus, four women and a male double-flute player take part in a ritual centered on an ox tied up on a table. One of the women makes an offering at an altar. In contrast to this unified narrative, the other side is divided into two scenes. At the left, a woman pours liquid (perhaps the blood of the sacrificial ox) from a jar into a large vessel on a stand between two double axes. Behind her, a second woman carries two more jars, and a male figure plays the harp. Consistent with the common convention in many ancient cultures, all of the women have light skin and the men dark skin (compare FIG. 3-13A). To their right, three men carry two sculpted sacrificial animals and a model of a boat to offer to a dead man, whom the painter represented as standing in front of his tomb, just as the biblical Lazarus, raised from the dead, will later appear in medieval art.

The precise meaning of the sarcophagus paintings is uncertain, but there is no doubt that they document well-established Minoan rites in honor of the dead, which included the sacrifice of animals accompanied by music and the deposit of gifts in the tomb. Until scholars can decipher the written language of the Minoans, artworks such as the Hagia Triada sarcophagus will be the primary tools for reconstructing life on Crete, and in Greece as a whole, during the millennium before the birth of Homer.

GREECE BEFORE HOMER

In the *Iliad,* Homer describes the might and splendor of the Greek armies poised before the walls of Troy.

> Clan after clan poured out from the ships and huts onto the plain . . . innumerable as the leaves and blossoms in their season . . . the Athenians from their splendid citadel, . . . the citizens of Argos and Tiryns of the Great Walls . . . troops . . . from the great stronghold of Mycenae, from wealthy Corinth, . . . from Knossos, . . . Phaistos, . . . and the other troops that had their homes in Crete of the Hundred Towns.[1]

The Greeks had come from far and wide, from the mainland and the islands (MAP 4-1), to seek revenge against Paris, the Trojan prince who had abducted Helen, wife of King Menelaus of Sparta. The *Iliad,* composed around 750 BCE, is the first great work of Greek literature. Until about 1870, the world regarded Homer's epic poem as pure fiction. Scholars paid little heed to the bard as a historian, instead attributing the profusion of names and places in his writings to the rich abundance of his imagination. The prehistory of Greece remained shadowy and lost in an impenetrable world of myth.

Troy and Mycenae. In the late 1800s, however, Heinrich Schliemann (1822–1890), a wealthy German businessman turned archaeologist, proved that scholars had not given Homer his due. Between 1870 and his death 20 years later, Schliemann (whose methods later archaeologists have harshly criticized) uncovered some of the very cities that Homer named. In 1870, he began work at Hissarlik on the northwestern coast of Turkey, which a British archaeologist, Frank Calvert (1828–1908), had postulated was the site of Homer's Troy. Schliemann dug into a vast mound and found a number of fortified cities built on the remains of one another. Fire had destroyed one of them in the 13th century BCE. This, scholars now agree, was the Troy of King Priam and his son Paris.

Schliemann continued his excavations at Mycenae on the Greek mainland, where, he believed, King Agamemnon, Menelaus's brother, had once ruled. Here his finds were even more startling, among them a massive fortress-palace with an imposing gateway (FIG. 4-19) and a circle of royal graves (FIG. 4-21A); other tombs featuring stone domes beneath earthen mounds (FIGS. 4-20 and 4-21); quantities of gold jewelry, drinking cups, and masks (FIG. 4-22); and inlaid bronze weapons (FIG. 4-23). Schliemann's discoveries revealed a magnificent civilization far older than the famous vestiges of Classical Greece that had remained visible in Athens and elsewhere. Subsequent excavations proved that Mycenae had not been the only center of this fabulous civilization.

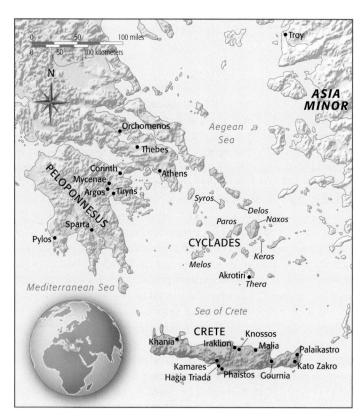

MAP 4-1 The prehistoric Aegean.

Minoan Crete. Another legendary figure was Minos, the king of Knossos on the island of Crete, who exacted from Athens a tribute of youths and maidens to be fed to the *Minotaur,* a creature half bull and half man that inhabited a vast labyrinth. In 1900, an Englishman, Arthur Evans (1851–1941), began work at Knossos, where he uncovered a palace (FIGS. 4-4 and 4-5) resembling a maze. Evans named the people who had constructed it *Minoans* after their mythological king. Other archaeologists soon discovered further evidence of the Minoans at Phaistos (FIG. 4-11), Hagia Triada (FIGS. 4-1 and 4-14), and other sites, including Gournia, which Harriet Boyd Hawes (1871–1945), an American archaeologist (and one of the first women of any nationality to direct a major excavation), explored between 1901 and 1904.

More recently, archaeologists have excavated important Minoan remains at many other locations on Crete. They have also explored contemporaneous sites on other islands in the Aegean Sea (named after Aegeus, father of King Theseus of Athens), most notably Thera (FIGS. 4-9, 4-9A, and 4-10). Together, the buildings,

THE PREHISTORIC AEGEAN

3000–2000 BCE	2000–1700 BCE	1700–1400 BCE	1400–1200 BCE
■ Early Cycladic sculptors create marble figurines for placement in graves to accompany the dead into the afterlife	■ Minoans construct major palaces on Crete during the Old Palace period ■ Cretan ceramists produce Kamares Ware painted pottery	■ Minoans construct large administrative complexes with extensive fresco decoration during the second (New Palace) period on Crete ■ Minoan potters manufacture Marine Style vases, and sculptors carve small-scale images of gods ■ Volcanic eruption buries Akrotiri, 1628 BCE ■ Mycenaeans bury their dead in shaft graves with gold funerary masks and cups and inlaid daggers	■ Mycenaeans erect fortification walls around their citadels at Mycenae, Tiryns, and elsewhere, and build tombs featuring corbeled domes ■ The oldest known large-scale sculptures in Greece appear at Mycenae ■ Mycenaean civilization comes to an end with the destruction of their palace-citadels, ca. 1200 BCE

A SECOND OPINION

Cycladic Statuettes

One way that the ancient world is fundamentally different from the world today is that ancient art is largely anonymous and undated. The systematic signing and dating of artworks—a commonplace feature in the contemporary art world—has no equivalent in antiquity. That is why the role of archaeology in the study of ancient art is so important. Only the scientific excavation of ancient artworks can establish their context. Exquisite and strikingly "modern" sculptures, such as the marble Cycladic figurines illustrated in FIGS. 4-2 and 4-3, may be appreciated as masterpieces when displayed in splendid isolation in glass cases in museums or private homes. But to understand the role that these or any other artworks played in ancient society—in many cases, even to determine the date of an object—the art historian must learn the *provenance* (place of origin) of the piece. Only when the context of an artwork is known can anyone go beyond an appreciation of its formal qualities and begin to analyze its place in art history and its role in the society that produced it.

The extraordinary popularity of Cycladic figurines in recent decades has had unfortunate consequences. Clandestine treasure hunters, anxious to meet the insatiable demand of collectors, have plundered many sites and smuggled their finds out of Greece to sell to the highest bidder on the international art market. This looting has destroyed entire prehistoric cemeteries and towns.

It also poses a serious dilemma for the study of Cycladic art. Attempts have been made to establish a chronology for the Cycladic statuettes, even to attribute most examples to different workshops. The largest and most unusual pieces, of course, figure prominently in the effort to write a coherent history of Cycladic art. However, two British scholars have expressed a cautionary second opinion.* They have calculated that only about 10 percent of the known Cycladic marble statuettes (including the two discussed here) come from secure archaeological contexts. Many of the rest could be forgeries produced after World War II, when developments in modern art fostered a new appreciation of these abstract renditions of human anatomy and created a

4-2 **Figurine of a woman, from Syros (Cyclades), Greece, ca. 2600–2300 BCE. Marble, 1′ 6″ high. National Archaeological Museum, Athens.**

Most Cycladic statuettes depict nude women. This one comes from a grave, but whether it represents the deceased is uncertain. The sculptor rendered the female body schematically as a series of triangles.

boom in demand for "Cycladica" among collectors. For some categories of Cycladic sculptures—those of unusual type or size—not a single piece with a documented provenance exists. Those groups may be 20th-century inventions—made by sophisticated forgers using marble from the same quarries and replicas of ancient tools—designed to fetch even higher prices in the marketplace due to their rarity. Consequently, most of the conclusions that art historians have drawn about Cycladic sculpture are highly speculative and suspect. The importance of the information that the original contexts would have provided cannot be overestimated. That information, however, can probably never be recovered.

*David W. J. Gill and Christopher Chippindale, "Material and Intellectual Consequences of Esteem for Cycladic Figures," *American Journal of Archaeology* 97 (1993): 601–659.

paintings, sculptures, and other finds on the Greek mainland and on the Aegean islands attest to the wealth and sophistication of the people who occupied Greece in that once-obscure heroic age celebrated in later Greek mythology.

Aegean Archaeology Today. Archaeologists know much more today about the prehistoric societies of the Aegean than they did a generation ago. Arguably more important for the understanding of Aegean prehistory than the art objects that tourists flock to see in the museums of Athens and Iraklion (near Knossos) are the many documents that archaeologists have found written in scripts conventionally called Linear A and Linear B. The progress made during the past several decades in deciphering Linear B texts has provided a welcome corrective to the romantic treasure-hunting approach of Schliemann and Evans. Scholars now recognize Linear B as an early form of Greek, and they have begun to reconstruct Mycenaean civilization by referring to records made at the time and not just to Homer's heroic account. Archaeologists now also know that humans inhabited Greece as far back as the early Paleolithic period and that village life was firmly established in Greece and on Crete in Neolithic times.

The heyday of the ancient Aegean, however, did not arrive until the second millennium BCE, well after the emergence of the river valley civilizations of Mesopotamia, Egypt, and South Asia.

The prehistoric Aegean has three geographic areas, and each has its own distinctive artistic identity. *Cycladic* art is the art of the Cyclades islands (so named because they "circle" around Delos), as well as of the adjacent islands in the Aegean, excluding Crete. *Minoan* art encompasses the art of Crete. *Helladic* art is the art of the Greek mainland (*Hellas* in Greek). Archaeologists subdivide each area chronologically into early, middle, and late periods, designating the art of the Late Helladic period *Mycenaean* after Agamemnon's great citadel of Mycenae.

CYCLADIC ART

Marble was abundantly available in the superb quarries of the Aegean islands, especially on Naxos, and the sculptors of the Early Cycladic period produced large quantities of marble statuettes (FIGS. 4-2 and 4-3) of distinctive form. Today, collectors revere those Cycladic figurines (see "Cycladic Statuettes," above) because of their striking abstract forms, which call to mind some modern sculptures (FIGS. 30-00 and 30-00A).

Syros Woman. Most of the Cycladic sculptures represent nude women, as do many of their Stone Age predecessors in the Aegean, Anatolia, Mesopotamia, and western Europe (FIG. 1-4). The Cycladic examples often depict women with their arms folded across their abdomens. The sculptures, which excavators have found both in graves and in settlements, vary in height from a few inches to almost life-size. The statuette illustrated here (FIG. 4-2) comes from a grave on the island of Syros and is about a foot-and-a-half tall—but only about a half-inch thick. Using obsidian tools, the sculptor carved the figurine and then polished the surface with emery. The Cycladic artist's rendition of the human body is highly schematic. Large, simple triangles dominate the form—the head, the body itself (which tapers from exceptionally broad shoulders to tiny feet), and the incised triangular pubis. Other examples have more rounded forms, but the feet always have the toes pointed downward, so the figurines cannot stand upright. All of the statuettes must have been placed on their backs in the grave—lying down, like the deceased.

Archaeologists speculate whether the Syros statuette and the many other similar Cycladic figurines known today represent dead women or fertility figures or goddesses. Whether those depicted are mortals or deities, the sculptors took pains to emphasize the breasts as well as the pubic area. In the Syros statuette, a slight swelling of the belly may suggest pregnancy (compare FIG. 1-5). Traces of paint found on some of the Cycladic figurines indicate that at least parts of these sculptures were colored. The now almost featureless faces would have had painted eyes and mouths in addition to the sculpted noses. Red and blue necklaces and bracelets, as well as painted dots on the cheeks and necks (compare FIG. 4-26), characterize a number of the surviving figurines.

Keros Musician. Fewer Cycladic statuettes represent men. The most elaborate of the male figurines portray seated musicians, such as the harp player (FIG. 4-3) from Keros. Wedged between the echoing shapes of chair and instrument, he may be playing for the deceased in the afterlife, although, again, the meaning of these sculptures remains elusive. The harpist reflects the same preference for simple geometric shapes and large, flat planes as do the female figures. Still, the artist showed a keen interest in recording the elegant shape of what must have been a prized possession: the harp with a duck-bill or swan-head ornament. (Compare the form of Sumerian harps, FIGS. 2-6 and 2-10, *top right*.)

One woman's grave contained figurines of both a musician and a reclining woman. The burial of a male figure together with the body of a woman suggests that the harp players are not images of dead men, but it does not prove that the female figurines represent dead women. The musician might be entertaining the deceased herself, not her image, or be engaged in commemorative rites honoring the dead. (The harp player on the Hagia Triada *sarcophagus* [FIG. 4-1b] may indicate some continuity in funerary customs and beliefs from the Cycladic to the Minoan period in the Aegean.) Given the absence of written documents in Greece at this date, as everywhere else in prehistoric times, and the lack of contextual information for most Cycladic sculptures, art historians cannot be sure of the meaning of these statuettes. It is likely, in fact, that the same form took on different meanings in different contexts.

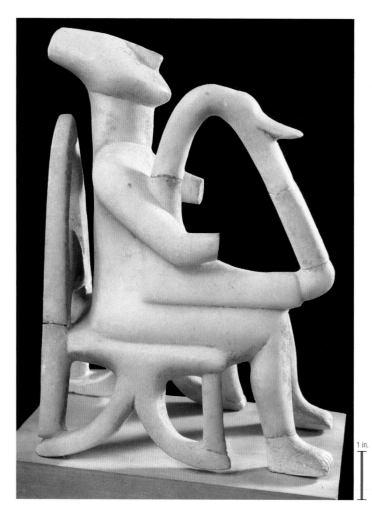

1 in.

4-3 Male harp player, from Keros (Cyclades), Greece, ca. 2600–2300 BCE. Marble, 9″ high. National Archaeological Museum, Athens.

The meaning of all Cycladic figurines is elusive, but this seated musician may be playing for the deceased in the afterlife. The statuette displays simple geometric shapes and flat planes.

MINOAN ART

During the third millennium BCE, both on the Aegean islands and on the Greek mainland, most settlements were small and consisted only of simple buildings. Rarely were the dead buried with costly offerings such as the Cycladic statuettes just examined. By contrast, the hallmark of the opening centuries of the second millennium (the Middle Minoan period on Crete) is the construction of large palaces.

Architecture

The first, or Old Palace, period ended abruptly around 1700 BCE, when fire destroyed these grand structures, probably following an earthquake. Rebuilding began almost immediately, and archaeologists consider the ensuing Late Minoan (New Palace) period the golden age of Crete, an era when the first great Western civilization emerged. Although conventionally called palaces, the rebuilt structures may not have served as royal residences. They were administrative, commercial, and religious centers with courtyards for pageants, ceremonies, and games, and dozens of offices, shrines, and storerooms for the collection and distribution of produce and

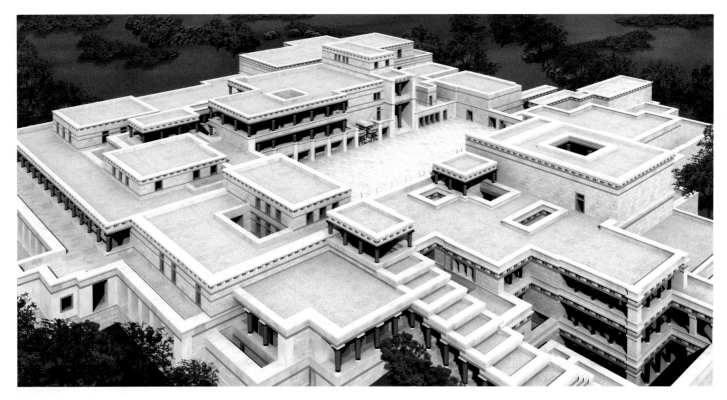

4-4 Restored view of the palace (looking northwest), Knossos (Crete), Greece, ca. 1700–1370 BCE (John Burge).

The Knossos palace, the largest on Crete, was the legendary home of King Minos. Its layout features a large central court surrounded by scores of residential and administrative units.

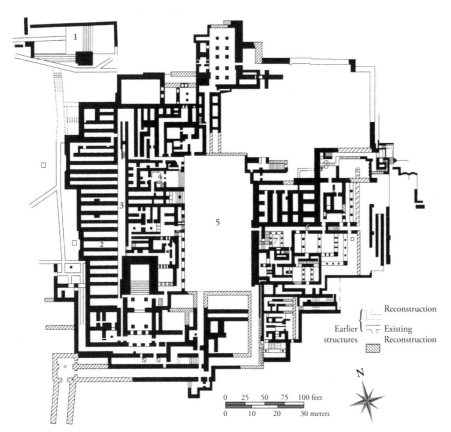

Reconstruction

Earlier { Existing
structures { Reconstruction

4-5 Plan of the palace, Knossos (Crete), Greece, ca. 1700–1370 BCE. (1) "theater," (2) magazines, (3) north-south corridor, (4) throne room, (5) central court, (6) east-west corridor, (7) grand stairwell.

The mazelike plan of the Knossos palace gave rise to the Greek myth of the Cretan labyrinth inhabited by the Minotaur, a half-man, half-bull monster that King Theseus of Athens slew.

goods. These huge complexes were the centers of Minoan life. The principal "palaces" on Crete are at Knossos, Phaistos, Malia, Kato Zakro, and Khania. The Minoans laid out all of them along similar lines. The size and number of these important centers, as well as the rich finds they have yielded, attest to the power and prosperity of the Minoans.

Knossos. The largest Cretan palace—at Knossos (FIGS. 4-4 and 4-5)—was the legendary home of King Minos. Here, the hero Theseus hunted the bull-man Minotaur in his labyrinth. According to the myth, after defeating the monster, Theseus found his way out of the mazelike complex only with the aid of the king's daughter, Ariadne. She had given Theseus a spindle of thread to mark his path through the labyrinth and safely find his way out again. In fact, the English word *labyrinth* derives from the intricate plan and scores of rooms of the Knossos palace. The *labrys* ("double ax") serves as a recurring motif in the Minoan palace and in Minoan art generally (FIG. 4-1b), referring to sacrificial slaughter. The labyrinth was the "House of the Double Ax."

The Knossos palace was a rambling structure built against the upper slopes and across the top of a low hill that rises from a fertile plain. All around the palace proper were mansions and villas of the Minoan elite. The central feature of the palace was its great rectangular court (FIG. 4-5, no. 5). The builders carefully planned

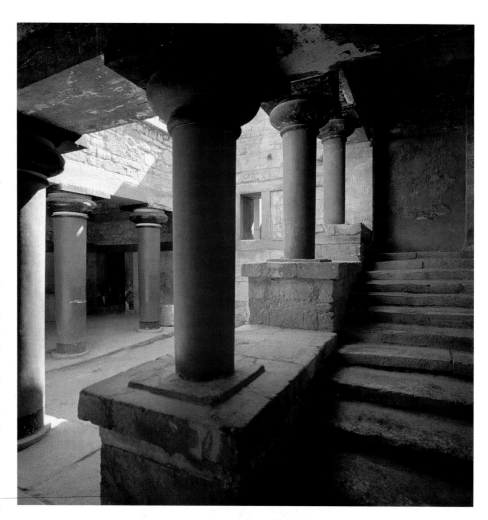

4-6 Stairwell in the residential quarter of the palace (FIG. 4-5, no. 7), Knossos (Crete), Greece, ca. 1700–1370 BCE.

The Knossos palace was complex in elevation as well as plan. It had at least three stories on all sides of the court. Minoan columns taper from top to bottom, the opposite of Egyptian and Greek columns.

the structure with clusters of rooms of similar function grouped around this primary space. On the west side of the court, a north-south corridor (FIG. 4-5, no. 3) separates official and ceremonial rooms from the magazines (no. 2), where the Minoans stored wine, grain, oil, and honey in large jars. On the east side of the court, a smaller east-west corridor (no. 6) separates the administrative areas (to the south) from the workrooms (to the north). At the northwest corner of the palace is a theater-like area (no. 1) with steps on two sides that may have served as seats. This arrangement is a possible forerunner of the later Greek theater (FIG. 5-71). Its purpose is unknown, but the feature also appears in the Phaistos palace.

The Knossos palace was complex in elevation as well as plan. Around the central court, there were as many as three stories, and on the south and east sides, where the terrain sloped off sharply, the palace had four or five stories. Interior light and air wells, some with staircases (FIGS. 4-5, no. 7, and 4-6), provided necessary illumination and ventilation. The Minoans also addressed such issues as drainage of rainwater. At Knossos, a remarkably efficient system of terracotta (baked clay) pipes lies under the enormous building.

The Cretan palaces were sturdy structures, with thick walls composed of rough, unshaped fieldstones embedded in clay. For corners and around door and window openings, the builders used large stone blocks, especially for the walls facing the central court. The painted wood columns (which Evans restored in cement at Knossos) have distinctive capitals and shafts (FIG. 4-6). The bulbous, cushionlike Minoan capitals resemble those of the later Greek Doric order (FIG. 5-13, *left*), but the column shafts—essentially stylized inverted tree trunks—taper from a wide top to a narrower base, the opposite of both Egyptian and later Greek columns.

Painting

Mural paintings liberally adorned the palace at Knossos, constituting one of its most striking features. The brightly painted walls and the red shafts and black capitals of the wood columns produced an extraordinarily rich effect. The paintings depict many aspects of Minoan life (bull-leaping, processions, and ceremonies) and of nature (birds, animals, flowers, and marine life).

La Parisienne. From a ceremonial scene of uncertain significance comes the fragment dubbed *La Parisienne* (*The Parisian Woman*; FIG. 4-7) on its discovery because of the elegant dress, elaborate coiffure, and full rouged lips of the young woman depicted.

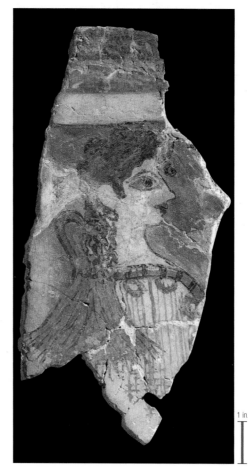

4-7 Minoan woman or goddess (*La Parisienne*), from the palace, Knossos (Crete), Greece, ca. 1500 BCE. Fragment of a fresco, 10″ high. Archaeological Museum, Iraklion.

Frescoes decorated the Knossos palace walls. This fragment depicts a woman or a goddess—perhaps a statue—with a large frontal eye in her profile head, as in Mesopotamian and Egyptian art.

1 in.

Some have identified her as a priestess taking part in a religious ritual, but because the figure has no arms, it is more likely a statue of a goddess. Although the representation is still convention-bound (note especially the oversized frontal eye in the profile head), the charm and freshness of the mural are undeniable. Unlike the Egyptians, who painted in *fresco secco* (dry fresco), the Minoans coated the rough fabric of their rubble walls with a fine white lime plaster and were apparently the first to use a true *buon fresco* method in which the painter applies the pigments while the walls are still wet (see "Fresco Painting," page 428). The color consequently becomes chemically bonded to the plaster after it dries. The Minoan painters therefore had to execute their work rapidly, in contrast to Egyptian practice, which permitted slower, more deliberate work.

Bull-Leaping. Another fresco (FIG. 4-8) from the palace at Knossos depicts the Minoan ceremony of bull-leaping, in which young men grasped the horns of a bull and vaulted onto its back—a perilous and extremely difficult acrobatic maneuver. Excavators recovered only fragments of the full composition. (The dark patches are original; the rest is a modern restoration.) The Minoan artist provided no setting, instead focusing all attention on the three protagonists and the fearsome bull. The young women have fair skin and the leaping youth has dark skin, in accordance with the widely accepted ancient convention for distinguishing male and female, as on the Hagia Triada sarcophagus (FIG. 4-1; compare FIGS. 3-13A and 5-20A). The painter brilliantly suggested the powerful charge of the bull (which has all four legs off the ground) by elongating the animal's shape and using sweeping lines to form a funnel of energy, beginning at the very narrow hindquarters of the bull and culminating in its large, sharp horns. The highly animated human figures also have stylized shapes, with typically Minoan pinched waists. Although the profile pose with frontal eye was a familiar convention in Egypt and Mesopotamia, the elegant Cretan figures, with their long, curly hair and proud and self-confident bearing, have no parallels in the art of other early cultures. In contrast to the angularity of the figures in Egyptian wall paintings, the curving lines that the Minoan artist employed suggest the elasticity of living and moving beings.

Thera. Much better preserved than the Knossos frescoes are the mural paintings that Greek archaeologists have discovered in their ongoing excavations at Akrotiri on the island of Thera in the Cyclades, some 60 miles north of Crete. In the Late Cycladic period, Thera was artistically (and possibly also politically) within the Minoan orbit. The Akrotiri murals are invaluable additions to the fragmentary and frequently misrestored frescoes from Crete. The excellent condition of the Theran paintings is due to an enormous volcanic explosion on the island that buried Akrotiri in volcanic pumice and ash, making it a kind of Pompeii of the prehistoric Aegean (see "The Theran Eruption and the Chronology of

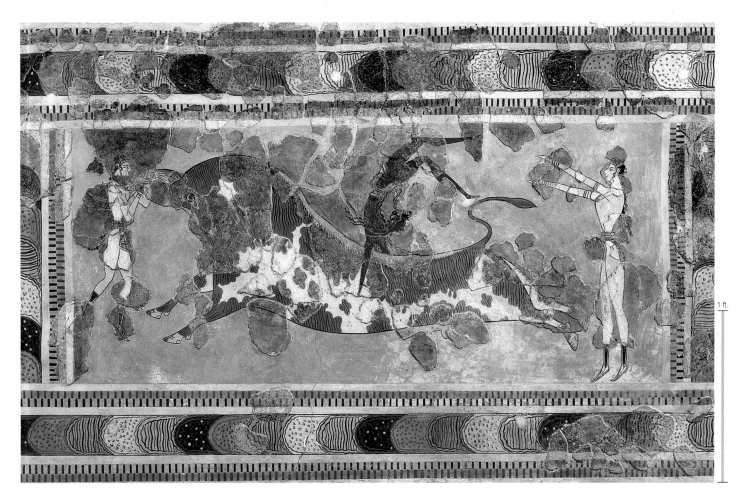

1 ft.

4-8 Bull-leaping, from the palace, Knossos (Crete), Greece, ca. 1500 BCE. Fresco, 2′ 8″ high, including border. Archaeological Museum, Iraklion.

The subjects of the Knossos frescoes are often ceremonial scenes, such as this one of bull-leaping. The women have fair skin and the man has dark skin, a common convention in ancient painting.

The Theran Eruption and the Chronology of Aegean Art

Today, ships bound for the beautiful Greek island of Thera (formerly Santorini), with its picture-postcard white houses, churches, shops, and restaurants, weigh anchor in a bay beneath steep cliffs. Until about 20,000 BCE, however, Thera had gentler slopes. Then, suddenly, a volcanic eruption blew out the center of the island, leaving behind the crescent-shaped main island and several lesser islands grouped around a bay that roughly corresponds to the shape of the gigantic ancient volcano. The volcano erupted again, thousands of years later, during the zenith of Aegean civilization.

The later explosion buried the site of Akrotiri, which Greek excavators have been gradually uncovering since 1967, under a layer of pumice more than a yard deep in some areas and by an even larger volume of volcanic ash (*tephra*) often exceeding 5 yards in depth, even after nearly 37 centuries of erosion. Tephra filled whole rooms, and boulders spewed forth by the volcano pelted the walls of some houses. Closer to the volcano's cone, the tephra is almost 60 yards deep in places. In fact, the force of the eruption was so powerful that sea currents carried the pumice, and wind blew the ash, throughout much of the eastern Mediterranean, not only to Crete, Rhodes, and Cyprus but also as far away as Turkey, Egypt, Syria, and Israel.

A generation ago, most scholars embraced the theory formulated by Spyridon Marinatos (1901–1974), an eminent Greek archaeologist, that the otherwise unexplained demise of Minoan civilization on Crete around 1500 BCE was the by-product of the volcanic eruption on Thera. According to Marinatos, devastating famine followed the rain of ash that fell on Crete. But archaeologists now know that after the eruption, life went on in Crete, if not on Thera.

Teams of researchers, working closely in an impressive and most welcome interdisciplinary effort, have determined that a major climatic event occurred during the last third of the 17th century BCE. In addition to collecting evidence from Thera, they have studied tree rings at sites in Europe and in North America for evidence of retarded growth and have examined ice cores in Greenland for peak acidity layers. The scientific data pinpoint a significant disruption in weather patterns in 1628 BCE. Most scholars now believe that the cause of this disruption was the cataclysmic volcanic eruption on Thera. The date of the Aegean catastrophe remains the subject of much debate, however, and many archaeologists favor placing the eruption in the 16th century BCE. In either case, the date of Thera's destruction has profound consequences for determining the chronology of Aegean art. If the Akrotiri frescoes (FIGS. 4-9, 4-9A, and 4-10) date between 1650 and 1625 BCE, they are at least 150 years older than scholars thought not long ago, and are much older than the Knossos palace murals (FIGS. 4-7 and 4-8).

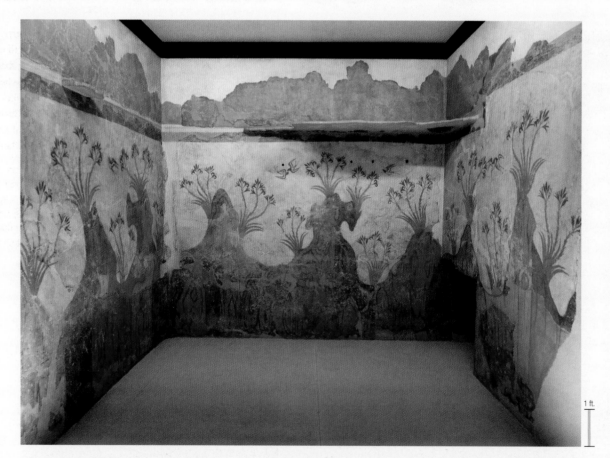

1 ft.

4-9 Landscape with swallows (*Spring Fresco*), south and west walls of room Delta 2, Akrotiri, Thera (Cyclades), Greece, ca. 1650–1625 BCE. Fresco, 7′ 6″ high. Reconstructed in National Archaeological Museum, Athens.

Aegean muralists painted true frescoes, which required rapid execution. In this wraparound landscape, the painter used vivid colors and undulating lines to capture the essence of nature.

Aegean Art," page 92, and "An Eyewitness Account of the Eruption of Mount Vesuvius," page 191). The Akrotiri frescoes decorated the walls of houses and shrines, not the walls of a great palace, such as Minos's at Knossos, and therefore the number of painted walls from the site is especially impressive.

The almost perfectly preserved mural painting from Akrotiri known as the *Spring Fresco* (FIG. 4-9) is the largest and most complete prehistoric example of a pure landscape painting. *Landscapes* (pictures of a natural setting in its own right, without any narrative content) and seascapes (FIG. 4-9A) are key elements of many of the mural paintings found at Akrotiri. In each case, however, the artist's aim was not to render the rocky island terrain real-

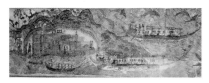

4-9A *Miniature Ships Fresco,* Akrotiri, ca. 1650–1625 BCE.

istically but rather to capture its essence. In FIG. 4-9, the irrationally undulating and vividly colored rocks, the graceful lilies swaying in the cool island breezes, and the darting swallows express the vigor of growth, the delicacy of flowering, and the lightness of birdsong and flight. In the lyrical language of curving line, the artist celebrated the rhythms of nature. The *Spring Fresco* represents the polar opposite of the first efforts at mural painting in the caves of Paleolithic Europe (see "The Dawn of Art," page 15), where animals (and occasionally humans) appeared as isolated figures with no indication of setting.

Crocus Gatherers. A rocky landscape is also the setting for the figures depicted in room 3 of building Xeste 3 at Akrotiri. The room probably served as a shrine in which girls took part in puberty initiation rites. Frescoes decorated the walls on two levels. In one section (not illustrated), a young girl with a bleeding foot sits on a rock. Approaching her from behind is a bare-breasted woman carrying a necklace, probably a gift for the bleeding girl. In the section reproduced here (FIG. 4-10), two elegantly dressed young women bedecked with bracelets and hoop earrings gather crocuses. One has a shaved head with a serpentine lock of hair at the back, indicating that she is a young girl. Crocus flowers produce saffron, used for the yellow dye of some of the garments that the figures wear. Saffron may also have been used as a painkiller for menstrual cramps. In another section of the mural (not illustrated), girls carry baskets full of the flowers they have picked. They bring the flowers to a woman seated on a stepped platform. Scholars have identified the woman, who is flanked by a blue monkey and a *griffin* (a mythical winged lion with an eagle's head), as a goddess rather than a mortal, but the precise meaning of the scenes depicted in the fresco remains uncertain.

Minoan Pottery. Nature as a preferred subject for paintings is documented on Minoan pottery, even before the period of the new Cretan palaces. During the Middle Minoan period, Cretan ceramists fashioned sophisticated shapes using newly introduced potters' wheels, and decorated their vases in a distinctive and fully polychromatic style. These Kamares Ware vessels, named for the

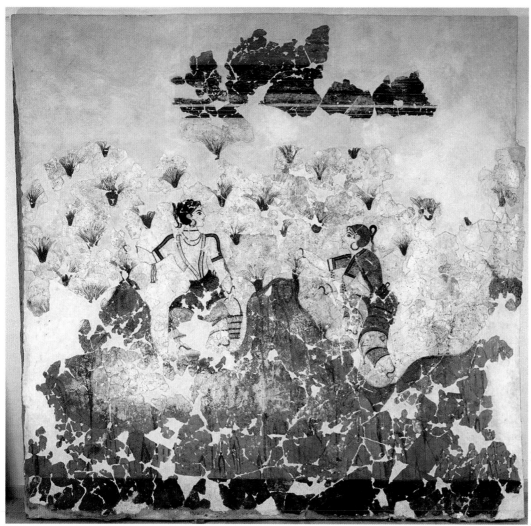

4-10 Crocus gatherers, detail of the east wall of room 3 of building Xeste 3, Akrotiri, Thera (Cyclades), Greece, ca. 1650–1625 BCE. Fresco, $8' \frac{1}{8}''$ high. Reconstructed in National Archaeological Museum, Athens.

In a room at Akrotiri probably used for puberty rites, young girls pick crocus flowers in a rocky landscape recalling the *Spring Fresco* (FIG. 4-9) and present them to a seated goddess (not shown).

1 ft.

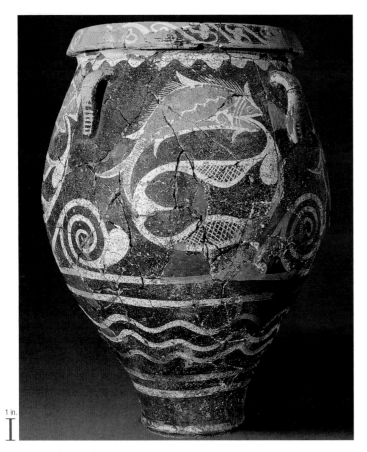

1 in.

4-11 Kamares Ware jar, from Phaistos (Crete), Greece, ca. 1800–1700 BCE. 1′ 8″ high. Archaeological Museum, Iraklion.

Kamares Ware vases have creamy white and reddish-brown decoration on a black background. This jar combines a fish (and a net?) with curvilinear abstract patterns, including spirals and waves.

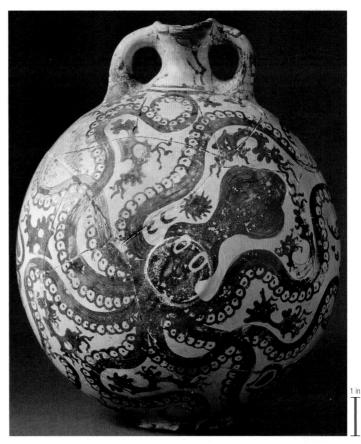

1 in.

4-12 Marine Style octopus flask, from Palaikastro (Crete), Greece, ca. 1500 BCE. 11″ high. Archaeological Museum, Iraklion.

Marine Style vases have dark figures on a light ground. On this octopus flask, the tentacles of the sea creature reach out over the curving surface of the vessel to fill the shape perfectly.

cave on the slope of Mount Ida where they were first discovered, have been found in quantity at Phaistos and Knossos. Some examples come from as far away as Egypt and testify to the expansive trade network of the Minoans. On the jar shown here (FIG. 4-11), as on other Kamares vases, the painter applied creamy white and reddish-brown decoration to a rich black ground. The central motif is a great leaping fish and perhaps a fishnet surrounded by a host of curvilinear abstract patterns, including waves and spirals. The swirling lines evoke life in the sea, and both the abstract and the natural forms beautifully complement the shape of the vessel.

The sea and the creatures inhabiting it also inspired the Late Minoan octopus flask (FIG. 4-12) from Palaikastro decorated in what art historians have dubbed the Marine Style. The tentacles of the octopus reach out over the curving surfaces of the vessel, embracing the piece and emphasizing its volume. The flask is a masterful realization of the relationship between the vessel's decoration and its shape, always an issue for the vase painter. This later jar, which is contemporaneous with the new palaces at Knossos and elsewhere, differs markedly from its Kamares Ware predecessor in color. Not only is the octopus vase more muted in tone, but the Late Minoan artist also reversed the earlier scheme and placed dark silhouettes on a light ground. Dark-on-light coloration remained the norm for about a millennium in Greece, until about 530 BCE, when light figures and a dark background emerged once again, albeit in a very different form, as the preferred manner (see "The Invention of Red-Figure Painting," page 121).

Sculpture

In contrast to the contemporaneous civilizations of Mesopotamia and Egypt, Minoan Crete has yielded no trace of temples or life-size statues of gods, kings, or monsters. Large painted wood images may once have existed—*La Parisienne* (FIG. 4-7) may be a depiction of one of them—but what remains of Minoan sculpture is uniformly small in scale.

Snake Goddess. One of the most striking finds from the palace at Knossos is the *faience* (low-fired opaque glasslike silicate) statuette popularly known as the *Snake Goddess* (FIG. 4-13). Reconstructed from many pieces and in large part modern in its present form, it is one of several similar figurines that some scholars believe may represent mortal priestesses rather than a deity. The prominently exposed breasts suggest, however, that these figurines stand in the long line of prehistoric fertility images usually considered divinities. The Knossos woman holds snakes in her hands and, as reconstructed, supports a tamed leopardlike feline on her head. When archaeologists discovered the statuette, the feline was not associated with the other fragments. If it was part of the figurine, the implied power over the animal world would be appropriate for a deity. The frontality of the figure is reminiscent of Egyptian and Mesopotamian statuary, but the costume, with its open bodice and flounced skirt, is distinctly Minoan. If the statuette represents a goddess, then the Minoan is yet another example of a culture

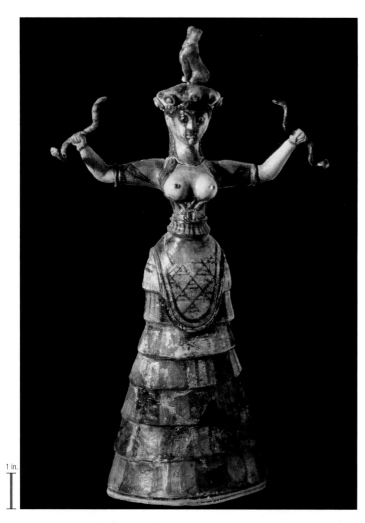

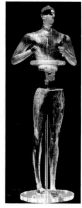

fashioning its gods in the image of its people. Another Cretan example is the gold-and-ivory statuette (FIG. 4-13A) of a nude youthful god from Palaikastro.

4-13A
Young god(?), Palaikastro, ca. 1500–1450 BCE,

Harvesters Vase. The finest surviving example of Minoan relief sculpture is the so-called *Harvesters Vase* (FIG. 4-14) from Hagia Triada. Only the upper half of the ostrich-egg-shaped body and neck of the vessel remain. Missing are the lower parts of the harvesters (or, as some think, sowers) and the ground on which they stand, as well as the gold leaf that originally covered the relief figures. Formulaic scenes of sowing and harvesting were staples of Egyptian funerary art (FIG. 3-16), but the Minoan artist shunned static repetition in favor of a composition filled with individually characterized figures bursting with energy. The relief shows a riotous crowd of young men singing and shouting as they go to or return from the fields. The artist vividly captured the youths' forward movement and lusty exuberance.

Although most of the "harvesters" conform to the age-old convention of combined profile and frontal views, the relief sculptor singled out one figure (FIG. 4-14, *right of center*) from his companions. He shakes a *sistrum* (a percussion instrument or rattle) to beat time, and the artist depicted him in full profile with his lungs so inflated with air that his ribs show. This is one of the first instances in the history of art of a sculptor showing a keen interest in the underlying muscular and skeletal structure of the human body. The Minoan artist's painstaking study of human anatomy is a singular achievement, especially given the size of the *Harvesters Vase*, barely 5 inches at its greatest diameter. Equally noteworthy is how the sculptor recorded the tension and relaxation of facial muscles with astonishing exactitude, not only for this figure but for his nearest companions as well. This degree of animation of the human face is without precedent in ancient art.

Minoan Decline. Scholars dispute the circumstances ending the Minoan civilization, although most now believe that Mycenaeans had already moved onto Crete and established themselves at Knossos at the end of the New Palace period. From the palace at Knossos, these intruders appear to have ruled the island for at least a half century, perhaps much longer. Parts of the palace continued to be occupied until its final destruction around 1200 BCE, but its importance as a cultural center faded soon after 1400 BCE, as the focus of Aegean civilization shifted to the Greek mainland.

4-13 *Snake Goddess,* from the palace, Knossos (Crete), Greece, ca. 1600 BCE. Faience, 1′ 1½″ high. Archaeological Museum, Iraklion.

This figurine may represent a priestess, but it is more likely a bare-breasted goddess. The snakes in her hands (and the feline on her head, if it belongs) imply that she has power over the animal world.

4-14 *Harvesters Vase,* from Hagia Triada (Crete), Greece, ca. 1500 BCE. Steatite, originally with gold leaf, greatest diameter 5″. Archaeological Museum, Iraklion.

The relief sculptor of the singing young farmers on this small stone vase was one of the first artists in history to represent the underlying muscular and skeletal structure of the human body.

PROBLEMS AND SOLUTIONS

Fortified Palaces for a Hostile World

In contrast to the Minoans, whose sprawling palaces (FIGS. 4-4 and 4-5) were unprotected by enclosing walls, the Mycenaeans were fearsome warriors who inhabited a hostile world. The palatial administrative centers of their Cretan predecessors did not provide useful models for royal residences on the mainland. Consequently, the Mycenaeans had to develop an independent solution for housing—and protecting—their kings and their families and attendants.

Construction of the citadels of Tiryns (FIGS. 4-15 and 4-16) and Mycenae (FIG. 4-19) began about 1400 BCE. Both burned (along with all the other Mycenaean strongholds) between 1250 and 1200 BCE when northern invaders overran the Mycenaeans, they fell victim to internal warfare, or they suffered a natural catastrophe—or a combination of these factors. Homer called Tiryns the city "of the great walls." In the second century CE, when Pausanias, author of an invaluable Roman guidebook to Greece, visited the long-abandoned site, he marveled at the towering fortifications and considered the walls of Tiryns to be as spectacular as the pyramids of Egypt. Indeed, the Greeks of the historical age believed that mere humans could not have erected these enormous edifices. They attributed the construction of the great Mycenaean citadels to the mythical *Cyclopes,* a race of one-eyed giants. Architectural historians still employ the term *Cyclopean masonry* to refer to the huge, roughly cut stone blocks forming the massive fortification walls of Tiryns and other Mycenaean sites.

The Mycenaean engineers who designed the circuit wall of Tiryns compelled would-be attackers to approach the palace (FIG. 4-15) within the walls via a long ramp that forced the soldiers (usually right-handed; compare FIG. 4-27) to expose their unshielded sides to the Mycenaean defenders above. Then—if they got that far—the enemy forces had to pass through a series of narrow gates that also could be defended easily.

Inside, at Tiryns as elsewhere, the most important element in the palace plan was the *megaron,* or reception hall and throne room, of the *wanax* (Mycenaean king). The main room of the megaron had a throne against the right wall and a central hearth bordered by four Minoan-style wood columns serving as supports for the roof. A vestibule with a columnar facade preceded the throne room. The remains of the megarons at Tiryns and Mycenae are scant, but at Pylos, home of Homer's King Nestor (and the Griffin Warrior), archaeologists found sufficient evidence to enable them to visualize the original appearance of its megaron, complete with mural and ceiling paintings (FIG. 4-18A).

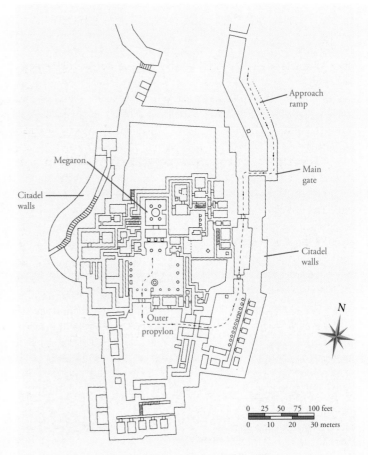

4-15 **Plan of the palace and southern part of the citadel, Tiryns, Greece, ca. 1400–1200 BCE.**

The plan of the Mycenaean fortress at Tiryns incorporated an entrance ramp designed to expose attacking soldiers' unprotected right sides to the spears and arrows of the defending Mycenaean warriors.

4-16 **Aerial view of the citadel (looking east), Tiryns, Greece, ca. 1400–1200 BCE.**

In the *Iliad,* Homer called the fortified citadel of Tiryns the city "of the great walls." Its huge, roughly cut stone blocks are examples of Cyclopean masonry, named after the mythical one-eyed giants.

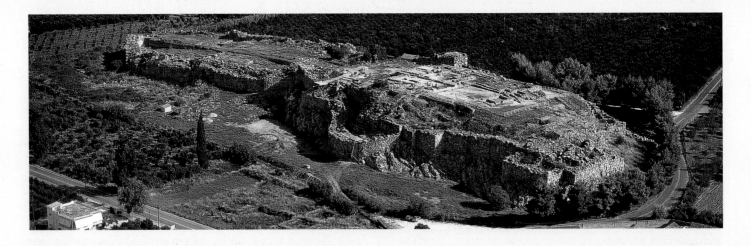

Corbeled Arches, Vaults, and Domes

The simplest method of spanning a passageway, documented in Neolithic times and in Old Kingdom Egypt, is the post-and-lintel system (FIG. 1-19).

A more sophisticated construction technique is the *corbeled arch* (FIG. 4-17), which, when extended, forms a *corbeled vault,* seen in primitive form at the citadel of Tiryns in the galleries (FIG. 4-18) of its fortified wall circuit.

At Tiryns, the Mycenaean builders piled the large, irregular blocks in horizontal courses and then cantilevered them inward until the two walls met in a *pointed arch.* The Mycenaeans used no mortar. The vault is held in place only by the weight of the blocks (often several tons each), by the smaller stones used as wedges, and by the clay filling some of the empty spaces. This crude but effective vaulting scheme possesses an earthy monumentality. It is easy to see how a later age came to believe that the uncouth Cyclopes were responsible for these massive but unsophisticated fortifications.

The corbeling principle was also used in antiquity to construct *relieving triangles* above horizontal lintel blocks, as in Mycenae's Lion Gate (FIG. 4-19) and Treasury of Atreus (FIG. 4-20), and stone domes. The finest example of a *corbeled dome* in the ancient world is the burial chamber (FIG. 4-21) of the Treasury of Atreus. The Mycenaean builders probably constructed the vault using rough-hewn blocks. But after they set the stones in place, the stonemasons had to finish the surfaces with great precision to make them conform to both the horizontal and vertical curvature of the wall. Hence, although the principle involved is no different from that of the corbeled gallery of Tiryns, the problem of constructing a complete dome is far more complicated, and the execution of the vault in the Treasury of Atreus is much more sophisticated than that of the vaulted gallery at Tiryns. About 43 feet high, this Mycenaean dome was at the time the largest vaulted space without interior supports that had ever been built. The achievement was not surpassed until the Romans constructed the Pantheon (FIG. 7-51) almost 1,500 years later using a new technology—concrete construction—unknown to the Mycenaeans or their Greek successors.

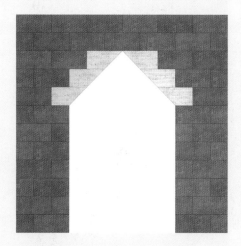

4-17 Corbeled-arch construction (John Burge).

Builders construct a corbeled arch by piling stone blocks in horizontal courses and then cantilevering them inward until the walls meet in a pointed arch. The stones are held in place by their own weight.

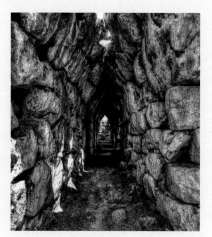

4-18 Corbel-vaulted gallery in the circuit wall of the citadel, Tiryns, Greece, ca. 1400–1200 BCE.

In this long gallery within the circuit walls of Tiryns, the Mycenaeans piled irregular Cyclopean blocks in horizontal courses and then cantilevered them until the two walls met in a corbeled arch.

MYCENAEAN ART

The origin of the Mycenaeans is also a subject of continuing debate among archaeologists and historians. The only certainty is the presence of these forerunners of the Greeks on the mainland about the time of the construction of the old palaces on Crete—that is, about the beginning of the second millennium BCE. By the middle of that millennium, a distinctive Mycenaean culture was flourishing—one that filled a prior artistic vacuum on the mainland. Archaeologists and historians have discussed the reasons for the sudden flourishing of Mycenaean art and architecture, but the phenomenon must reflect newfound wealth. Many scholars believe that the Mycenaeans were mercenaries who fought for the Egyptians and returned home with rich war booty. That the Mycenaeans accumulated great wealth and that their leaders were successful warriors was reconfirmed in 2015 when a team from the University of Cincinnati discovered at Pylos the extraordinarily rich burial of a man now known as the Griffin Warrior. The dramatic discoveries of Schliemann and his successors have fully justified Homer's characterization of mid-second-millennium BCE Mycenae as "rich in gold," even if today's archaeologists no longer view the Mycenaeans solely through the eyes of Homer. The Minoans also possessed gold, but they derived their wealth from a wide network of trading partners instead of from plunder. And that is only one of the many differences between these two great prehistoric Aegean cultures.

Architecture

The destruction of the Cretan palaces left the Late Helladic mainland culture supreme. Although historians refer to this civilization as Mycenaean, Mycenae was but one of several large citadel complexes. Archaeologists have also unearthed Mycenaean remains at Tiryns, Orchomenos, Pylos, and elsewhere (MAP 4-1), and a section of a Mycenaean fortification wall is still in place on the Acropolis of Athens, where Theseus ruled as king. The best-preserved and most impressive Mycenaean remains are those of the citadels at Tiryns and Mycenae (see "Fortified Palaces for a Hostile World," page 96).

Tiryns. The walls of the Tiryns citadel (FIGS. 4-15 and 4-16) average about 20 feet in thickness and impress visitors today as much as they did in antiquity, when they were thought to be the work of giants. In one section, the Tiryns circuit walls incorporate a long

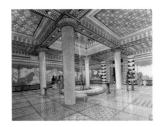

⬈**4-18A** Megaron, Palace of Nestor, Pylos, ca. 1300 BCE.

gallery (FIG. 4-18) covered by *corbeled vaults* (see "Corbeled Arches, Vaults, and Domes," page 97). The severity of the exterior aspect of the Mycenaean citadels did not, however, extend to their interiors, where frescoed walls (FIG. 4-18A) were commonplace, as in the Cretan palaces. Sculptural decoration was nonetheless rare. Agamemnon's Mycenae was the exception.

Lion Gate, Mycenae. The so-called Lion Gate (FIG. 4-19) is the outer gateway of the stronghold at Mycenae. It is protected on the left by a wall built on a natural rock outcropping and on the right by a projecting bastion of large blocks. Any approaching enemies would have had to enter this 20-foot-wide channel and face Mycenaean defenders above them on both sides. The gate itself consists of two great upright monoliths (posts) capped with a huge horizontal lintel (FIG. 1-19). Above the lintel, the masonry courses form a *corbeled arch* (FIG. 4-17), leaving an opening that lightens the weight that the lintel carries. Filling this *relieving triangle* is a great limestone slab with two lions in high relief facing a central Minoan-type column. The whole

design admirably matches its triangular shape, harmonizing in dignity, strength, and scale with the massive stones forming the walls and gate. Similar groups appear in miniature on Cretan seals, but the concept of placing monstrous guardian figures at the entrances to palaces, tombs, and sacred places has its origin in Mesopotamia and Egypt (FIGS. 2-18A and 2-20; a notable later example is FIG. 3-11). At Mycenae, the sculptors fashioned the animals' heads separately. Because those heads are lost, some scholars have speculated that the "lions" may be composite beasts, possibly sphinxes or griffins.

Treasury of Atreus. The Mycenaeans erected the Lion Gate and the adjoining fortification wall circuit a few generations before the presumed date of the Trojan War. At that time, elite families buried their dead outside the citadel walls in beehive-shaped tombs covered by enormous earthen mounds. Nine such tombs remain at Mycenae and scores more at other sites. The best preserved of these *tholos tombs* is Mycenae's so-called Treasury of Atreus (FIG. 4-20), which in the Greco-Roman era people mistakenly believed was the repository of the treasures of Atreus, father of Agamemnon and Menelaus. A long passageway (*dromos*) leads to a doorway surmounted by a relieving triangle similar to that in the roughly contemporaneous Lion Gate, but without figural ornamentation. Both the doorway and the relieving triangle, however, once

4-19 Lion Gate (looking east), Mycenae, Greece, ca. 1300–1250 BCE. Limestone, relief panel 9′ 6″ high.

The largest sculpture in the prehistoric Aegean is this relief of confronting lions that fills the relieving triangle of Mycenae's main gate. The gate itself consists of two great monolithic posts and a huge lintel.

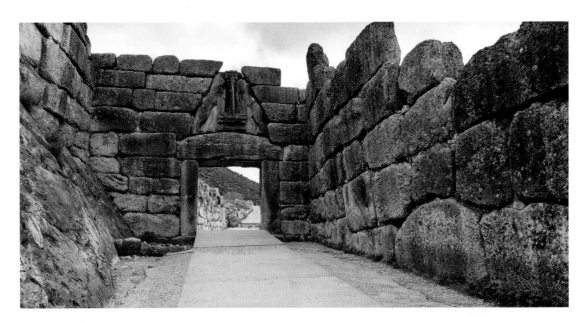

4-20 Exterior of the Treasury of Atreus (looking west), Mycenae, Greece, ca. 1300–1250 BCE.

The best-preserved Mycenaean tholos tomb is named after Homer's King Atreus. An earthen mound covers the burial chamber, reached through a doorway at the end of a long dromos (passageway).

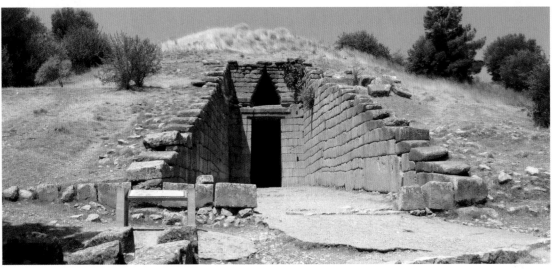

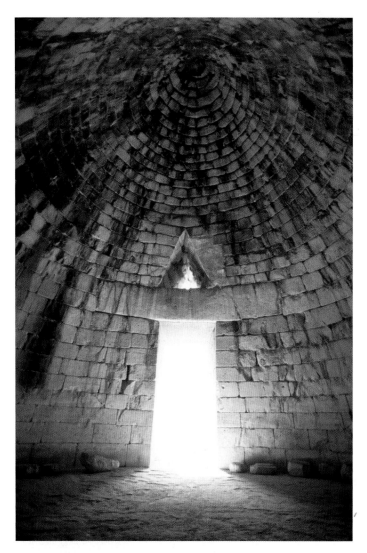

4-21 Interior of the Treasury of Atreus (looking east toward entrance), Mycenae, Greece, ca. 1300–1250 BCE.

The beehive-shaped tholos of the Treasury of Atreus consists of corbeled courses of stone blocks laid on a circular base. The 43-foot-high dome was the largest in the world for almost 1,500 years.

had engaged columns on each side, preserved in fragments today. The burial chamber, or *tholos* (FIG. 4-21), consists of a series of stone corbeled courses laid on a circular base to form a lofty dome (see "Corbeled Arches, Vaults, and Domes," page 97).

Metalwork, Sculpture, and Painting

The Treasury of Atreus was thoroughly looted long before its modern rediscovery, but archaeologists have unearthed spectacular grave goods elsewhere at Mycenae (and in the grave of the Griffin Warrior at Pylos). Just inside the Lion Gate, Schliemann uncovered what archaeologists call Grave Circle A (FIG. 4-21A). It predates the Lion Gate and the walls of Mycenae by some three centuries, and encloses six deep shafts that served as tombs for the kings and their families. The royal corpses that the Mycenaeans lowered into their deep graves had masks covering the

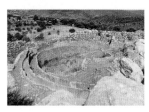

4-21A Grave Circle A, Mycenae, ca. 1600 BCE.

men's faces, recalling the Egyptian funerary practice (see "Mummification and Immortality," page 61). Jewelry adorned the bodies of the women, and weapons and gold cups accompanied the men into the afterlife.

Masks and Daggers. The Mycenaeans used the *repoussé* technique to fashion the masks that Schliemann found—that is, goldsmiths hammered the shape of each mask from a single sheet of metal and pushed the features out from behind. Art historians have often compared the mask illustrated here (FIG. 4-22) to Tutankhamen's gold mummy mask (FIG. 3-34), but it is important to remember that the Mycenaean metalworker was one of the first in Greece to produce a sculpted image of the human face at life-size. By contrast, Tutankhamen's mask stands in a long line of large-scale Egyptian sculptures going back more than a millennium. No one knows whether the Mycenaean masks were intended as portraits, but the artists took care to record different physical types. The masks found in Grave Circle A portray youthful faces as well as mature ones. The mask shown in FIG. 4-22, with its full beard, must depict a mature man, perhaps a king—although not Agamemnon, as Schliemann wished. If Agamemnon was a real king, he lived some 300 years after the death of the man buried in Grave Circle A. Clearly the Mycenaeans were "rich in gold" long before Homer's heroes fought at Troy.

Also found in Grave Circle A were several magnificent bronze dagger blades inlaid with gold, silver, and *niello* (a black metallic alloy), again attesting to the wealth of the Mycenaean kings as

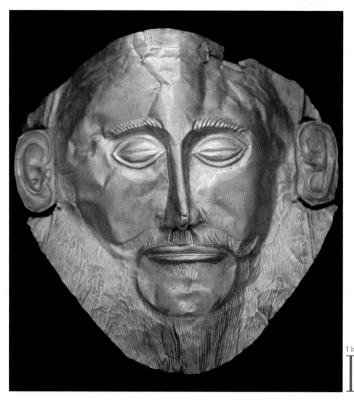

1 in.

4-22 Funerary mask, from Grave Circle A (FIG. 4-21A), Mycenae, Greece, ca. 1600–1500 BCE. Beaten gold, 1′ high. National Archaeological Museum, Athens.

Homer described the Mycenaeans as "rich in gold." This beaten-gold (repoussé) mask of a bearded man comes from a royal shaft grave. It is one of the first attempts at life-size sculpture in Greece.

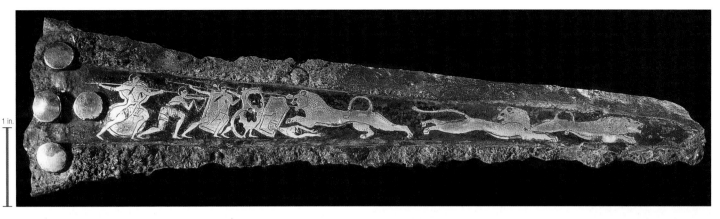

4-23 Inlaid dagger blade with lion hunt, from Grave Circle A (FIG. 4-21A), Mycenae, Greece, ca. 1600–1500 BCE. Bronze, inlaid with gold, silver, and niello, 9″ long. National Archaeological Museum, Athens.

The burial goods in Grave Circle A included costly weapons. The lion hunters on this bronze dagger are Minoan in style, but the metalworker borrowed the subject from Egypt and Mesopotamia.

well as to their warlike nature. On one side of the largest and most elaborate dagger (FIG. 4-23) from Circle A is a scene of four hunters attacking a lion that has struck down a fifth hunter, while two other lions flee. The other side (not illustrated) depicts lions attacking deer. The slim-waisted, long-haired figures are Minoan in style, but the artist borrowed the subject from the repertoire of Egypt and Mesopotamia. (There were no lions in Greece at this date.) It is likely that a Minoan metalworker made the dagger for a Mycenaean patron who admired Minoan art, but whose tastes in subject matter differed from those of his Cretan counterparts.

Vapheio Cups. Excavations at other Mycenaean sites have produced several additional luxurious objects decorated with Minoan-style figures. Chief among them is the pair of gold drinking cups from a tholos tomb at Vapheio. The Vapheio cup illustrated here (FIG. 4-24), also made using the repoussé technique, is probably the work of a Cretan goldsmith. Both cups represent hunters attempting to capture wild bulls—probably for the bull games (FIG. 4-8)

staged in the courtyards of the Cretan palaces. The men have long hair, bare chests, and narrow waists, and they closely resemble the figures on the Minoan *Harvesters Vase* (FIG. 4-14) and the hunters on the dagger blade (FIG. 4-23) from Grave Circle A. The other cup (not illustrated) depicts hunters trying to snare bulls in nets. One bull has already been trapped. The artist's choice of an unusual contorted posture for the bull effectively suggests the animal's struggle to free itself. To either side, a bull gallops away from the trap. One of them tramples his would-be captor.

Most art historians think that the goldsmith depicted three successive episodes in the hunters' attempt to capture a bull using a cow as bait. If so, the story reads from right to left. First, the bull follows the decoy cow. Then (at the right in FIG. 4-24), the bull and cow "converse." Finally, a hunter sneaks up behind the bull and succeeds in catching its left hind leg in a noose. Whatever the significance of the theme, the setting in a carefully delineated landscape of trees and rocks is noteworthy, as is the exceptional technical and artistic quality of the cups.

4-24 Hunter capturing a bull, drinking cup from Vapheio, near Sparta, Greece, ca. 1600–1500 BCE. Gold, $3\frac{1}{2}$″ high. National Archaeological Museum, Athens.

The cups from a tholos tomb at Vapheio are probably the work of a Cretan goldsmith. They complement the finds in Grave Circle A at Mycenae and suggest that gold objects were common in elite Mycenaean burials.

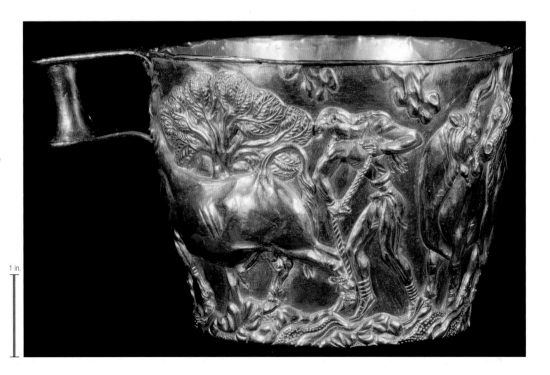

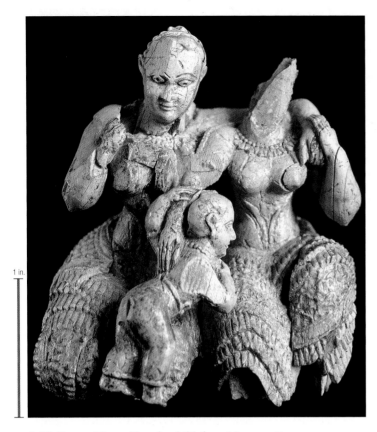

1 in.

4-25 Two goddesses(?) and a child, from Mycenae, Greece, ca. 1400–1250 BCE. Ivory, 2¾″ high. National Archaeological Museum, Athens.

Made of rare imported ivory, perhaps by a Cretan artist, this statuette may represent deities later paralleled in Greek mythology, but their identity and even the gender of the child are uncertain.

Ivory Goddesses. Gold was not the only luxurious material that elite Mycenaean patrons demanded for the objects they commissioned. For a shrine within the palace at Mycenae, a master sculptor carved an intricately detailed group of two women and a child (FIG. 4-25) from a single piece of costly imported ivory. The women's costumes with breasts exposed have the closest parallels in Minoan art (FIG. 4-13), and this statuette, like the Vapheio cups, is probably of Cretan manufacture. The intimate and tender theme also is foreign to the known Mycenaean repertoire, in which scenes of hunting and warfare dominate.

The identity of the three figures remains a mystery. Some scholars have suggested that the two women are the "two queens" mentioned in inscriptions found in the excavation of the Mycenaean palace at Pylos (FIG. 4-18A). Others have speculated that the two women are deities, Mycenaean forerunners of the Greek agricultural goddesses Demeter and Persephone (see "The Gods and Goddesses of Mount Olympus," page 107), and that the child is Triptolemos, the hero who spread the gift of agriculture to the Greeks. That myth, however, probably postdates the Mycenaean era.

Life-Size Statuary. In the second millennium BCE, large-scale figural art was very rare on the Greek mainland, as on Crete, other than the paintings that once adorned the walls of Mycenaean palaces (FIG. 4-18A). The triangular relief of the Lion Gate (FIG. 4-19) at Mycenae is exceptional, as is the painted plaster head (FIG. 4-26) of a woman or goddess—or, perhaps, a sphinx—found at Mycenae.

The white flesh tone indicates that the head is female. The hair and eyes are dark blue, almost black, and the lips, ears, and headband are red. The artist decorated the cheeks and chin with red circles surrounded by a ring of red dots, recalling the facial paint or tattoos recorded on Early Cycladic figurines of women. Although the large, staring eyes give the face a menacing, if not terrifying, expression appropriate for a guardian figure such as a sphinx, the closest parallels to this work in the prehistoric Aegean are terracotta images of goddesses. This head may therefore be a fragment of a very early life-size *cult statue* in Greece, many times the height of the Palaikastro youth (FIG. 4-13A).

Were it not for this plaster head and a few other exceptional pieces, art historians might have concluded, wrongly, that the Mycenaeans had no large-scale freestanding statuary—a reminder that it is always dangerous to generalize from the chance remains of an ancient civilization. Nonetheless, Mycenaean life-size statuary must have been rare, and no large stone statue has ever been found in the prehistoric Aegean world, in striking contrast to Egypt and Mesopotamia. After the collapse of Mycenaean civilization and for the next several hundred years, no attempts at large-scale statuary in any material are evident in the Aegean until, after the waning of the so-called Dark Ages, Greek sculptors became exposed to the great sculptural tradition of Egypt.

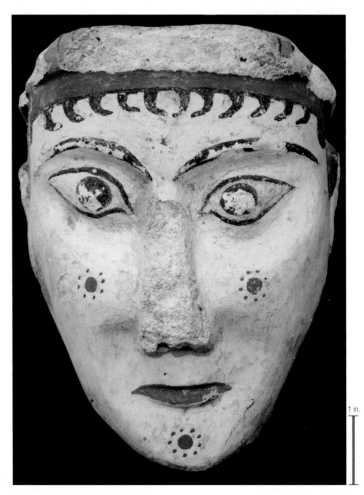

1 in.

4-26 Female head, from Mycenae, Greece, ca. 1300–1250 BCE. Painted plaster, 6½″ high. National Archaeological Museum, Athens.

This painted white plaster head of a woman with staring eyes may be a fragment of a very early life-size statue of a goddess in Greece, but some scholars think that it is the head of a sphinx.

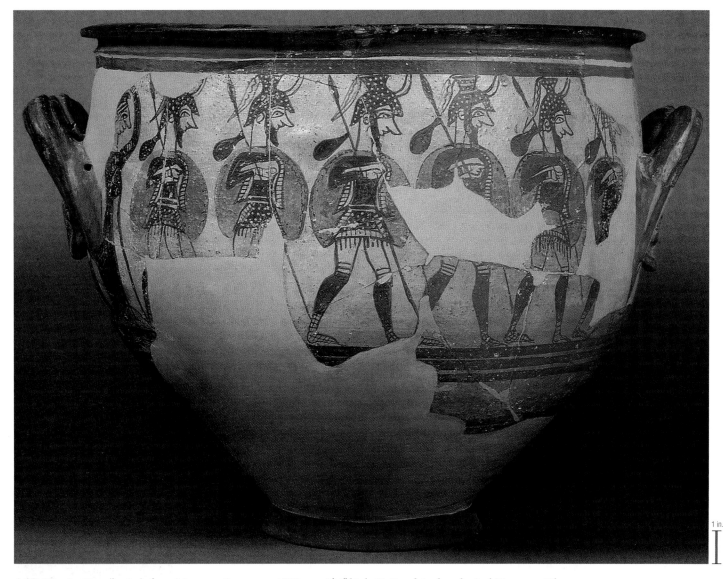

4-27 *Warrior Vase* (krater), from Mycenae, Greece, ca. 1200 BCE. 1′ 4″ high. National Archaeological Museum, Athens.

This bowl for mixing wine and water shows a woman bidding farewell to heavily armed Mycenaean warriors depicted using both silhouette and outline and a combination of frontal and profile views.

Warrior Vase. An art form that did continue throughout the period after the downfall of the Mycenaean palaces was vase painting. One of the latest examples of Mycenaean painting is the *krater* (bowl for mixing wine and water) commonly called the *Warrior Vase* (FIG. 4-27) after its prominent frieze of soldiers marching off to war. At the left, a woman bids farewell to the column of heavily armed warriors moving away from her. The painting on this vase has no indication of setting and lacks the landscape elements that commonly appear in earlier Minoan and Mycenaean art. Although the painter depicted the soldiers using both silhouette and outline, all repeat the same pattern of combined frontal and profile views, a

far cry from the variety and anecdotal detail of the lively procession shown on the Minoan *Harvesters Vase* (FIG. 4-14).

This simplification of narrative has parallels in the increasingly schematic and abstract treatment of marine life on other painted vases. The octopus, for example, eventually became a stylized motif composed of concentric circles and spirals that are almost unrecognizable as a sea creature. By Homer's time, the greatest days of Aegean civilization were but a distant memory, and the men and women of Crete and Mycenae—Minos and Ariadne, Agamemnon and Helen—had assumed the stature of heroes from a lost golden age.

The Prehistoric Aegean

Early Cycladic Art ca. 3000–2000 BCE

- The islands of the Aegean Sea boast excellent marble quarries, and marble statuettes are the major surviving artworks of the Cyclades during the third millennium BCE.

- Unfortunately, little is known about the function of the Cycladic figurines because few have secure provenances. Most of the statuettes represent nude women with their arms folded across their abdomens. They probably came from graves and may represent the deceased, but others—for example, musicians—almost certainly do not. Whatever their meaning, these statuettes mark the beginning of the long history of marble sculpture in Greece.

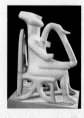

Harp player, Keros, ca. 2600–2300 BCE

Middle and Late Minoan Art ca. 1700–1200 BCE

- The construction of the first palaces on Crete occurred during the Old Palace period (ca. 2000–1700 BCE), but the golden age of Crete was the Middle and Late Minoan periods. The Minoan "palaces" were administrative, commercial, and religious centers that may not have been royal residences.

- The greatest Minoan palace was at Knossos. A vast multistory structure arranged around a central court, the Knossos palace was so complex in plan that it gave rise to the myth of the Minotaur in the labyrinth of King Minos.

- The major pictorial art form in the Minoan world was fresco painting. The murals depicted rituals (such as bull-leaping), landscapes, seascapes, and other subjects. Some of the best examples, such as the *Spring Fresco,* come from Akrotiri on the island of Thera, buried during the volcanic eruption of 1628 BCE.

- Vase painting also flourished. Sea motifs—the octopus, for example—were popular subjects.

- Surviving examples of Minoan sculpture are of small scale. They include statuettes of "snake goddesses" and reliefs on small objects, for example, the *Harvesters Vase.*

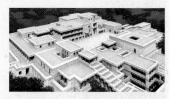

Palace, Knossos, ca. 1700–1370 BCE

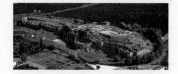

Spring Fresco, Akrotiri, ca. 1650–1625 BCE

Mycenaean (Late Helladic) Art ca. 1600–1200 BCE

- As early as 1600–1500 BCE, the Mycenaeans, who with their Greek allies later waged war on Troy, buried their kings in deep shaft graves in which the excavator, Heinrich Schliemann, also found gold funerary masks and bronze daggers inlaid with gold and silver.

- By 1400 BCE, the Mycenaeans had occupied Crete, and between 1400 and 1200 BCE, they erected great citadels on the mainland at Mycenae, Tiryns, and elsewhere with "Cyclopean" walls of huge, irregularly shaped stone blocks. The Greeks of the historical period did not believe that mere humans could have constructed these fortifications.

- Masters of corbel vaulting, the Mycenaeans also erected beehive-shaped tholos tombs. The best example—the Treasury of Atreus—boasts the largest dome in the pre-Roman world.

- The oldest preserved large-scale sculptures in Greece, most notably Mycenae's Lion Gate, date to the end of the Mycenaean period.

- The Mycenaeans also excelled in small-scale ivory carving, metalworking, and pottery painting. Many of the Mycenaean objects known today may have been the work of Cretan artists, however.

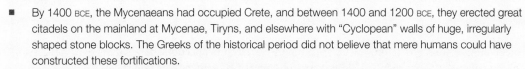

Citadel, Tiryns, ca. 1400–1200 BCE

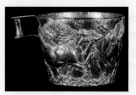

Gold drinking cup, Vapheio, ca. 1600–1500 BCE

5-1a The reliefs depicting Greeks battling semihuman centaurs are allegories of the triumph of civilization and rational order over barbarism and chaos—and of the Greek defeat of the Persians in 479 BCE.

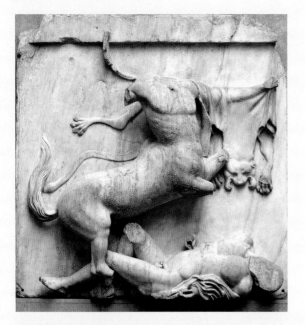

5-1b The costliest part of the Parthenon's lavish sculptural program was inside— Phidias's colossal gold-and-ivory statue depicting Athena holding the personification of Victory (of the Greeks over the Persians).

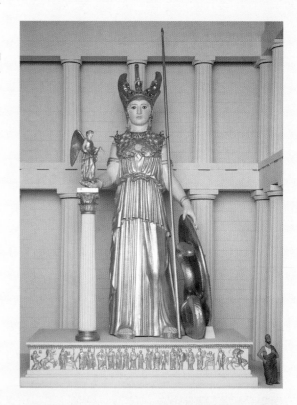

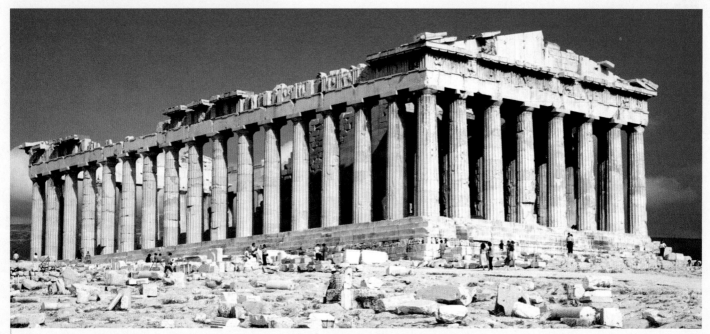

5-1 IKTINOS, **Parthenon (looking southeast), Acropolis, Athens, Greece, 447–438 BCE.**

5-1c An unusual feature of the Parthenon is the addition of an inner frieze depicting a cavalcade of Athenian citizens during a religious festival—the first depiction of a human event on a Greek temple.

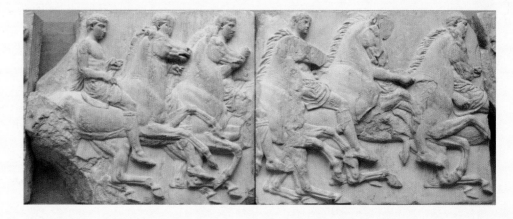

ANCIENT GREECE /5

The Perfect Temple

Although the Greeks borrowed many ideas, motifs, conventions, and skills from the artists and architects of the older Egyptian and Mesopotamian civilizations, they quickly developed an independent artistic identity. Their many innovations in painting, sculpture, and architecture became the foundation of the Western tradition in the history of art. Indeed, no building type has ever had a longer and more profound impact on the later history of architecture than the Greek temple, which was itself a multimedia monument, richly adorned with painted statues and reliefs.

The most famous Greek building today is the Parthenon (FIG. 5-1), considered by many to be the "perfect temple," although, ironically, it lacks some of the key features of all other Greek temples. Erected on the Acropolis of Athens in the mid-fifth century BCE, the Parthenon represents the culmination of a century-long effort by Greek architects to design a building with ideal proportions. Applying the thinking of the influential philosopher Pythagoras of Samos, who believed that beauty resided in harmonic numerical ratios, the architect IKTINOS calculated the dimensions of every part of the Parthenon in terms of a fixed proportional scheme. Thus the ratio of the length to the width of the building, the number of columns on the long versus the short sides, and even the relationship between the diameter of a column and the space between neighboring columns conformed to an all-encompassing mathematical formula.

The Athenians did not, however, construct the Parthenon to solve a purely formal problem of architectural design. Nor did the shrine honor Athena Parthenos (Athena the Virgin) alone. The Parthenon also celebrated the Athenian people, who a generation earlier had led the Greeks to victory over the Persians after they had sacked the Acropolis in 480 BCE. Under the direction of PHIDIAS, a team of gifted sculptors lavishly decorated the building with statues and reliefs that in many cases alluded to that triumph. For example, the sculptural program included reliefs depicting nude Greek warriors battling with the part-horse, part-human *centaurs*—an allegory of the triumph of civilization (that is, Greek civilization) over barbarism (in this case, the Persians). And the Athenians themselves are the subject of the Parthenon's inner frieze—the first time that a human event was depicted on a Greek temple. The costliest and most prestigious sculpture Phidias reserved for himself: the colossal gold-and-ivory statue of Athena inside, which depicted the warrior goddess holding the winged personification of Victory—an unmistakable reference to the Greek defeat of the Persians.

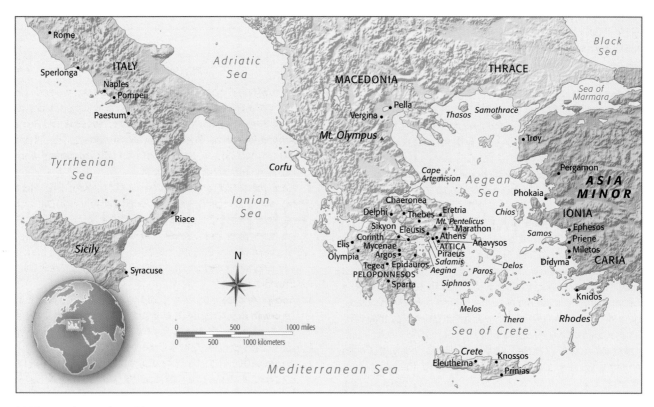

MAP 5-1 The Greek world.

THE GREEKS AND THEIR GODS

Ancient Greek art occupies a special place in the history of art through the ages. Many of the cultural values of the Greeks, especially the exaltation of humans as the "measure of all things," remain fundamental principles of Western civilization today. This humanistic worldview led the Greeks to create the concept of democracy (rule by the *demos,* the people) and to make groundbreaking contributions in the fields of art, literature, philosophy, mathematics, and science. Because ancient Greek ideas are so completely part of modern Western habits of mind, most people are scarcely aware that the concepts originated in Greece 2,500 years ago.

The Greeks, or *Hellenes,* as they called themselves, were the product of an intermingling of Aegean and Indo-European peoples who established independent city-states, or *poleis* (singular, *polis*). The Dorians of the north, who many believe brought an end to Mycenaean civilization, settled in the Peloponnesos (MAP 5-1). The Ionians settled the western coast of Asia Minor (modern Turkey) and the islands of the Aegean Sea, possibly because they were native to Asia Minor, developing out of a mixed stock of settlers between

the 11th and 8th centuries BCE. Whatever the origins of the various regional populations, in 776 BCE the separate Greek-speaking city-states held their first athletic games in common at Olympia, a sanctuary dedicated to Zeus, king of the Greek gods (see "The Gods and Goddesses of Mount Olympus," page 107). From then on, despite their differences and rivalries, the Greeks regarded themselves as citizens of *Hellas,* joined by a common culture and language distinct from "barbarians" who did not speak Greek.

Just as the Greeks saw themselves as unique, so too their gods were distinct from those of neighboring civilizations. Unlike Mesopotamian and Egyptian deities, the Greek gods and goddesses were conceived in human form and differed from men and women only in being immortal. Humans, conversely, had the potential to become gods by fulfilling heroic ideals. The same ideals of perfection that the designers of the Parthenon (FIG. 5-1) sought in architecture applied to ideals of beauty in individuals. Greek sculptors and painters focused on portraying ideal beauty in human form.

The sculptures, paintings, and buildings discussed in this chapter come from cities all over Greece and their many colonies abroad

ANCIENT GREECE

900–600 BCE	600–480 BCE	480–400 BCE	400–323 BCE	323–30 BCE
Geometric and Orientalizing	**Archaic**	**Early and High Classical**	**Late Classical**	**Hellenistic**
■ Greek artists revive figure painting during the Geometric period ■ Eastern motifs enter Greek sculpture and painting during the Orientalizing period	■ Greek architects erect the first peripteral Doric and Ionic temples ■ Greek sculptors carve life-size stone statues with "Archaic smiles" ■ Greek ceramists perfect black- and, later, red-figure vase painting	■ Sculptors introduce weight shift in Greek statuary ■ Polykleitos formulates his canon of proportions for statues of ideal humans ■ Pericles rebuilds the Athenian Acropolis after the Persian sack	■ Praxiteles and other sculptors humanize the Greek gods and goddesses ■ Corinthian capitals are introduced in Greek architecture ■ Lysippos is appointed the official court artist of Alexander the Great	■ Hellenistic kingdoms replace Athens as leading cultural centers ■ Artists explore new subjects in sculpture and painting ■ Architects break the rules of the Classical orders

The Gods and Goddesses of Mount Olympus

The names of scores of Greek gods and goddesses appear as early as the eighth century BCE in Homer's epic tales of the war against Troy (*Iliad*) and of the adventures of the Greek hero Odysseus on his long journey home (*Odyssey*). The poet Hesiod enumerated even more names, especially in his *Theogony* (*Genealogy of the Gods*), composed around 700 BCE.

The Greek deities most often represented in art are all ultimately the offspring of the two key elements of the Greek universe: Earth (*Gaia/Ge*; all names appear here in their Greek and Latin forms respectively) and Heaven (*Ouranos/Uranus*). Earth and Heaven mated to produce 12 *Titans,* including Ocean (*Okeanos/Oceanus*) and his youngest brother *Kronos* (*Saturn*). Kronos castrated his father in order to rule in his place, married his sister *Rhea,* and then swallowed all his children as they were born, because a prophecy said that one of them would seek in turn to usurp him. When *Zeus* (*Jupiter*) was born, Rhea deceived Kronos by feeding him a stone wrapped in clothes in place of the infant. After growing to manhood, Zeus forced Kronos to vomit up Zeus's siblings. Together they overthrew their father and the other Titans, and ruled the world from their home on Mount Olympus, Greece's highest peak.

This cruel and bloody tale of the origin of the Greek gods has parallels in Mesopotamian and Egyptian mythology and is clearly pre-Greek in origin, one of many Greek borrowings from the East. The Greek version of the creation myth, however, appears infrequently in painting and sculpture. Instead, the later 12 Olympian gods and goddesses figure most prominently in art—not only in antiquity but also in the Middle Ages, the Renaissance, and up to the present.

ZEUS AND HIS SIBLINGS

- **Zeus (Jupiter)** King of the gods, Zeus ruled the sky and allotted the sea to his brother Poseidon and the Underworld to his other brother, Hades. His weapon was the thunderbolt, and with it he led the other gods to victory over the giants, who had challenged the Olympians for control of the world.
- **Hera (Juno)** Wife and sister of Zeus, Hera was the goddess of marriage.
- **Poseidon (Neptune)** Poseidon, one of the three sons of Kronos and Rhea, was lord of the sea. He controlled waves, storms, and earthquakes with his three-pronged pitchfork (*trident*).
- **Hestia (Vesta)** Sister of Zeus, Poseidon, and Hera, Hestia was goddess of the hearth.
- **Demeter (Ceres)** Third sister of Zeus, Demeter was the goddess of grain and agriculture.

ZEUS'S CHILDREN

- **Ares (Mars)** God of war, Ares was the son of Zeus and Hera and the lover of Aphrodite. His Roman counterpart, Mars, was the father of the twin founders of Rome, Romulus and Remus.
- **Athena (Minerva)** Goddess of wisdom and warfare, Athena was a virgin (*parthenos* in Greek), born not from a woman's womb but from the head of her father, Zeus.
- **Hephaistos (Vulcan)** God of fire and of metalworking, Hephaistos, son of Zeus and Hera, fashioned the armor Achilles wore in battle against Troy. He also provided Zeus his scepter and Poseidon his trident, and was the "surgeon" who split open Zeus's head to facilitate the birth of Athena. Hephaistos was born lame and, uncharacteristically for a god, ugly. His wife, Aphrodite, was unfaithful to him.
- **Apollo (Apollo)** God of light and music, Apollo was the son of Zeus with **Leto/Latona**, daughter of one of the Titans. His epithet, *phoibos,* means "radiant," and the young, beautiful Apollo was sometimes identified with the sun (**Helios/Sol**).
- **Artemis (Diana)** Sister of Apollo, Artemis was goddess of the hunt and of wild animals. As Apollo's twin, she was occasionally regarded as the moon (**Selene/Luna**).
- **Aphrodite (Venus)** Daughter of Zeus and **Dione** (daughter of Okeanos and one of the *nymphs*—the goddesses of springs, caves, and woods), Aphrodite was the goddess of love and beauty. In one version of her myth, she was born from the foam (*aphros* in Greek) of the sea. She was the mother of Eros with Ares and of the Trojan hero Aeneas with a mortal named Anchises.
- **Hermes (Mercury)** Son of Zeus and another nymph, Hermes was the fleet-footed messenger of the gods and possessed winged sandals. He was also the guide of travelers, including the dead journeying to the Underworld. He carried the herald's rod (*kerykeion/caduceus*) and wore a winged traveler's hat.

SOME NON-OLYMPIAN DEITIES

- **Hades (Pluto)** One of the children of Kronos who fought with his brothers against the Titans, Hades was equal in stature to the Olympians but never resided on Mount Olympus. He was the god of the dead and lord of the Underworld (also called Hades).
- **Dionysos (Bacchus)** The son of Zeus and a mortal woman, Dionysos was the god of wine.
- **Eros (Amor or Cupid)** The son of Aphrodite and Ares, Eros was the winged child-god of love.
- **Asklepios (Aesculapius)** The son of Apollo and a mortal woman, Asklepios was the Greek god of healing, whose serpent-entwined staff is the emblem of modern medicine.

(MAP 5-1), but Athens, where the plays of Aeschylus, Sophocles, and Euripides were first performed and where many of the most famous artists and architects worked, has justifiably become symbolic of ancient Greek culture. There, Socrates engaged his fellow citizens in philosophical argument, and Plato formulated his prescription for the ideal form of government in his *Republic.* Complementing the rich intellectual life of Athens was a strong interest in athleticism. Through athletics, Athenian men balanced intellectual and physical perfection to achieve an ideal of humanistic education, well expressed in the familiar phrase "a sound mind in a sound body."

Although deserving, a high estimation of Greek art and culture should not blind anyone to the realities of Hellenic life and society. Athenian "democracy," for example, was a political reality for only one segment of the demos. Of the roughly 500,000 people who lived in Athens in the year 309, only about 2 percent were male citizens, who alone had the right to vote. The rest were women, children, foreigners, and slaves. Slavery was a universal institution among the Greeks, as among other ancient peoples. Likewise, Greek women were in no way the equals of Greek men. Well-born women normally remained secluded in their homes, emerging usually only for weddings, funerals, and religious festivals, in which they played prominent roles. Otherwise, they took little part in public or political life. Despite the fame of the poet Sappho, only a handful of female artists' names are known, and none of their works survive. The existence of slavery and the exclusion of women from public life are both reflected in Greek art. Freeborn men and women often appear with their slaves in large-scale public sculpture. The *symposium* (a dinner party that only men and prostitutes attended) is a popular subject on painted vases used in private homes.

GEOMETRIC AND ORIENTALIZING PERIODS

The destruction of the Mycenaean palaces around 1200 BCE brought with it the disintegration of the traditional social order in the prehistoric Aegean. The disappearance of powerful kings and their retinues led to the loss of the knowledge of how to cut masonry, construct citadels and tombs, paint frescoes, and sculpt in stone. Depopulation, poverty, and an almost total loss of contact with the outside world characterized the succeeding centuries, sometimes called the Dark Age of Greece. Only in the eighth century BCE did economic conditions improve and the population begin to grow again. This era was in its own way a heroic age, when the Greeks established the Olympic Games and wrote down Homer's epic poems, formerly passed orally from bard to bard. During the eighth century BCE, the Greeks broke free of their isolation and once again began to trade with cities in both the east and the west.

Geometric Art

The eighth century also brought the return of the human figure to Greek art—not in large-scale statuary, which was exceedingly rare even in Mycenaean Greece, but in small bronze figurines and in paintings on ceramic pots.

Dipylon Krater. One of the earliest examples of Greek figure painting is a huge *krater* (FIG. 5-2) found in the Dipylon cemetery of Athens. The vase marked the grave of a man who died around 740 BCE. At well over 3 feet tall, the krater is a considerable technical achievement and a testament both to the potter's skill and to the wealth and position of the deceased's family in the community. The bottom of the great vessel is open, perhaps to enable visitors to the grave to pour libations in honor of the dead, perhaps simply to provide a drain for rainwater, or both.

The artist covered much of the krater's surface with precisely painted abstract angular motifs in horizontal bands. Especially prominent is the *meander,* or key, pattern around the rim of the krater. The decoration of most early Greek vases consists exclusively of abstract motifs—hence the designation of this formative phase of Greek art as the *Geometric* period. On this krater, however, although abstract motifs abound, the painter reserved the widest part of the vase for two bands of human figures and horse-drawn chariots rather than for geometric ornament.

Befitting the vase's function, the scenes depict the mourning for a man laid out on his bier and the grand chariot procession

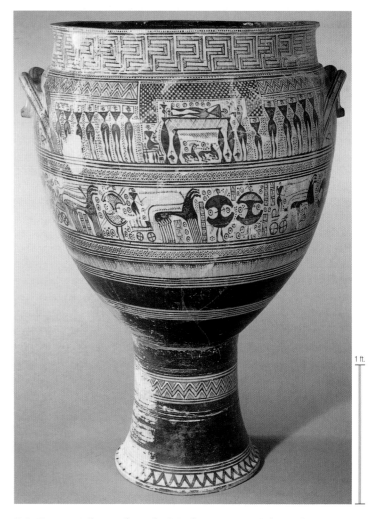

5-2 **Geometric krater, from the Dipylon cemetery, Athens, Greece, ca. 740 BCE. 3′ 4½″ high. Metropolitan Museum of Art, New York.**

Figure painting returned to Greek art in the Geometric period, named for the abstract motifs on vases such as this funerary krater featuring a mourning scene and procession in honor of the deceased.

in his honor, scenes that appear frequently on other large Geometric vessels that served as grave markers—for example, the 5-foot-tall *amphora* (two-handled storage jar; FIG. 5-2A) by the DIPYLON PAINTER, so named because this vase, his masterpiece, stood in the Dipylon cemetery, where it marked the grave of a woman. On both the amphora and the krater, all empty space around the figures is filled with circles and M-shaped ornaments, negating any sense that the mourners or soldiers inhabit open space. The human figures, animals, and furniture are as two-dimensional as the geometric shapes elsewhere on the vessel. In the upper band, the shroud, raised to reveal the corpse, is a flat, abstract checkerboard-like backdrop. The figures are composite silhouettes constructed of triangular (frontal) torsos with attached profile arms, legs, feet, and heads with a single large frontal eye in the center, following the age-old convention. To distinguish male from female, the painter added a penis protruding from the deceased's right thigh. The mourning women, who tear their hair out in grief, have breasts indicated as short lines beneath

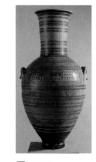

⟑ 5-2A
DIPYLON PAINTER, Geometric funerary amphora, ca. 750 BCE.

their armpits. In both cases, the artist's concern was specifying gender, not representing human anatomy accurately. Below, the warriors look like walking shields, and, in the old conceptual manner, the two wheels of the chariots appear side by side. The horses have the correct number of heads and legs but seem to share a common body, another indication that representing spatial depth was not the artist's purpose. Despite the highly stylized and conventional manner of representation, this krater and the Dipylon Painter's amphora (FIG. 5-2A) mark a significant turning point in the history of Greek art. Not only did the human figure reenter the painter's repertoire, but the Geometric artists also revived the art of storytelling in pictures. It is no coincidence that the rebirth of narrative art in Geometric Greece occurred at the same time that Homer's epic poems were codified in written form.

Herakles and Nessos.   One of the most impressive surviving Geometric sculptures is a characteristically small solid-cast bronze group (FIG. 5-3) made up of two schematic figures locked in a hand-to-hand struggle. The man is a hero, probably Herakles (see "Herakles, the Greatest Greek Hero," page 126). His opponent is a centaur, possibly Nessos, who had volunteered to carry the hero's bride across a river but then assaulted her. Whether or not the pair is Herakles and Nessos, the mythological nature of the group is certain. The repertoire of the Geometric artist was not limited to scenes inspired by daily life (and death). Composite monsters

were staples of the artistic cultures of Mesopotamia and Egypt, and renewed contact with the East may have inspired the human-animal monsters of Geometric Greece.

The centaur, however, is a purely Greek invention—and one that posed a problem for the artist, who had, of course, never seen such a creature. The Geometric artist conceived the centaur as a man in front and a horse in back, a rather unconvincing configuration in which the forelegs and hind legs belong to different species. In this example, the sculptor rendered the figure of the hero and the human part of the centaur in a similar fashion. Both have beards and wear helmets, but (contradictory to nature) the man is larger than the horse to indicate that he will be the victor. Like other Geometric male figures, both painted and sculpted, this hero is nude, in contrast to the foreign statuettes that might have inspired the Greek works. Greek youths exercised without their clothes and even competed nude in the Olympic Games from very early times. Here, at the beginning of Greek figural art, the Hellenic instinct for the natural beauty of the human figure is evident. So too is a second theme that characterizes Greek art throughout the centuries: in the struggle between humans and animals, man wins the day, and reason always overcomes chaos.

Orientalizing Art

During the seventh century BCE, the pace and scope of Greek trade and colonization accelerated, and Greek artists became exposed more than ever before to Eastern artworks, especially small portable objects such as Syrian ivory carvings. The closer contact had

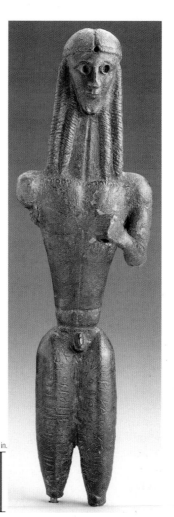

a profound effect on the development of Greek art. Indeed, so many motifs borrowed from or inspired by Egyptian and Mesopotamian art entered the Greek pictorial vocabulary at this time that art historians have dubbed the seventh century BCE the *Orientalizing* period.

Mantiklos Apollo.   One of the masterworks of the early seventh century BCE is the *Mantiklos Apollo* (FIG. 5-4), a small bronze statuette dedicated to Apollo by an otherwise unknown man named Mantiklos. Scratched into the thighs of the figure is a message to the deity: "Mantiklos dedicated me as a tithe to the

5-4 *Mantiklos Apollo,* **statuette of a youth dedicated by Mantiklos to Apollo, from Thebes, Greece, ca. 700–680 BCE. Bronze, 8″ high. Museum of Fine Arts, Boston.**

Mantiklos dedicated this statuette to Apollo, and it probably represents the god. The treatment of the body reveals the interest that seventh-century BCE Greek artists had in representing human anatomy.

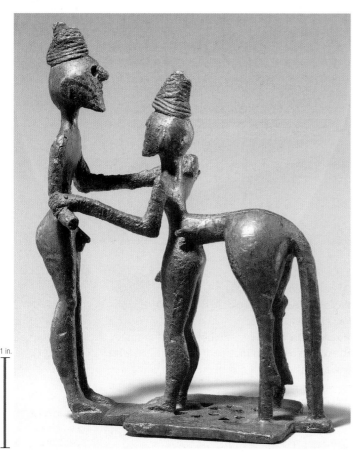

1 in.

5-3 **Hero and centaur (Herakles and Nessos?), from Olympia(?), Greece, ca. 750–730 BCE. Bronze, 4½″ high. Metropolitan Museum of Art, New York (gift of J. Pierpont Morgan, 1917).**

Sculpture of the Geometric period is small in scale, and the figures have simple, stylized shapes. This statuette depicts a hero battling a centaur—an early example of mythological narrative.

Greek Vase Painting

The techniques that Greek ceramists used to shape and decorate fine vases required great skill, acquired over many years as apprentices in the workshops of master potters. During the sixth and fifth centuries BCE, when the art of vase painting was at its height in Greece, both potters and painters frequently signed their work. These signatures reveal the pride of the artists. In the ancient world, the Greeks were unique in celebrating individual artists as creative geniuses and in systematically recording artists' names for posterity. Many artists achieved great renown even during their lifetimes. No earlier civilization held artists in such high esteem (Egypt's deification of Imhotep was exceptional)—nor would any later culture bestow such high regard on painters, sculptors, and other artisans until the Renaissance in Italy 2,000 years later.

The signatures on Greek vases also might have functioned as "brand names" for a large export market. The products of the workshops in Corinth and Athens in particular were highly prized and have been found all over the Mediterranean world. For example, the Corinthian Orientalizing amphora shown here (FIG. 5-5) was found on Rhodes, an island at the opposite side of the Aegean from mainland Corinth (MAP 5-1). The Etruscans of central Italy (MAP 6-1) were especially good customers. Athenian vases, with their distinctive red-orange clay, were staples in Etruscan tombs, and all of the illustrated sixth-century BCE examples came from Etruscan sites. Other painted Athenian pots have been unearthed as far away as France, Russia, and the Sudan.

The first step in manufacturing a Greek vase was to remove any impurities found in the natural clay and then to knead it, like dough, to remove air bubbles and make it flexible. The Greeks used dozens of different kinds and shapes of pots, and produced most of them in several parts. Potters constructed the vessel's body by placing the clay on a rotating horizontal wheel. While an apprentice turned the wheel by hand, the potter pulled up the clay with the fingers to form the desired shape. The master or the apprentice modeled the handles separately and attached them to the vase body by applying *slip* (liquefied clay) to the joints.

Painting was usually the job of a specialist, although many potters decorated their own work. (Today, most people tend to regard painters as more elevated artists than potters, but in ancient Greece, the potters owned the shops and employed the painters.) Art historians customarily refer to the "pigment" that vase painters applied to the clay surface as *glaze,* but the black areas on Greek pots are neither pigment nor glaze but a slip of finely sifted clay that originally was of the same rich red-orange color as the clay of the pot. In the three-phase firing process that Athenian ceramists used, the first (oxidizing) phase turned both pot and slip red. During the second (reducing) phase, the potter shut off the oxygen supply into the kiln, and both pot and slip turned black. In the final (reoxidizing) phase, the pot's coarser material reabsorbed oxygen and became red again, while the smoother, silica-laden slip did not and remained black. After long experimentation, Greek ceramists developed a velvety jet-black "glaze" of this kind, produced in kilns heated to temperatures as high as 950° Celsius (about 1742° Fahrenheit). The firing process was the same whether the painter worked in black-figure or in the later red-figure technique (see "The Invention of Red-Figure Painting," page 121). In fact, Athenian vase painters sometimes employed both manners on the same vessel (FIGS. 5-21 and 5-22). A special advantage of the Greek manufacturing process is that the painted decoration fused with the clay fabric of the pot. Black- and red-figure pottery can be broken, but the colors cannot fade.

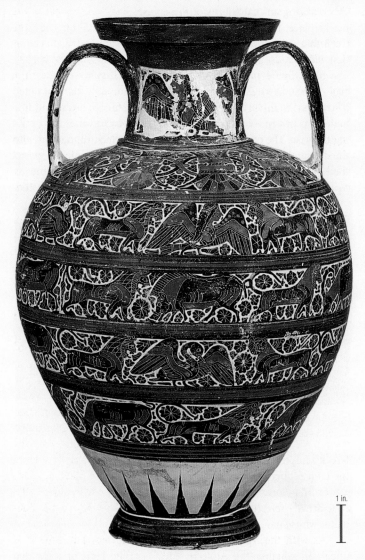

5-5 Corinthian black-figure amphora with animal friezes, from Rhodes, Greece, ca. 625–600 BCE. 1′ 2″ high. British Museum, London.

The Corinthians invented the black-figure technique of vase painting in which artists incised linear details into black-glaze silhouettes. This early example features Orientalizing animals.

far-shooting Lord of the Silver Bow; you, Phoibos [Apollo], might give some pleasing favor in return." Because the Greeks conceived their gods in human form, it is uncertain whether the figure represents the youthful Apollo or Mantiklos (or neither). But if the left hand at one time held a bow, the statuette is certainly an image of the deity. In any case, the purpose of the votive offering is clear. Equally apparent is the increased interest that Greek artists at this time had in reproducing details of human anatomy, such as the pectoral and abdominal muscles, which define the stylized triangular torso. The sculptor also took care to represent the long hair framing the unnaturally elongated neck. The triangular face once had inlaid eyes, and the figure may have worn a separately fashioned helmet pegged into the hole and groove at the top of the head.

Orientalizing Amphora. Dominated by the Greek city-state of Corinth, a thriving trade in exported ceramics arose in the late seventh century BCE. The Corinthian amphora illustrated here (FIG. 5-5) typifies the new Greek fascination with the Orient. In a series of bands recalling the organization of Geometric painted vases, animals such as the native boar appear beside exotic lions and panthers and composite creatures inspired by Eastern monsters such as the sphinx and lamassu—in this instance, the *siren* (part bird, part woman) prominently displayed on the amphora's neck. The Orientalizing animal friezes of these vases had wide appeal in the marketplace, but so too did the new ceramic technique that the Corinthians invented. Art historians call this type of vase decoration *black-figure painting* (see "Greek Vase Painting," page 110). The black-figure painter first put down black silhouettes on the clay surface, as in Geometric times, but then used a sharp, pointed instrument to incise linear details within the forms, usually adding highlights in white or purplish red over the black figures before firing the vase. The combination of the weighty black silhouettes with the delicate detailing against the pale, creamy Corinthian clay and the bright polychrome overlay proved to be irresistible. Athenian painters soon copied the technique that the Corinthians pioneered.

Daedalic Art. The founding of the Greek trading colony of Naukratis in Egypt (MAP 3-1) before 630 BCE brought the Greeks into direct contact with the impressive stone architecture of the Egyptians. Soon after, Greek builders began to erect the first stone edifices since the fall of the Mycenaean kingdoms. One of the oldest is Temple A—noteworthy too for its extensive sculptural adornment (FIG. 5-5A)—at Prinias on Crete. Once the heart of Minoan civilization, Crete was also a center of innovation during the Orientalizing period. There, an early Greek sculptor carved the limestone statuette popularly known as the *Lady of Auxerre* (FIG. 5-6) after the French town that is her oldest recorded location. The *Lady of Auxerre* is the masterpiece of the style usually referred to as *Daedalic*, after the legendary artist Daedalus, whose name means "the skillful one."

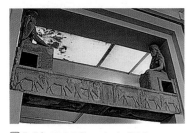

⏎ **5-5A** Lintel, Temple A, Prinias, ca. 625 BCE.

As with the figure that Mantiklos dedicated (FIG. 5-4), it is uncertain whether the Auxerre "lady" is a goddess or a maiden (*kore;* plural, *korai*). In contrast to the nude figures of men, she is clothed, as are all images of goddesses and women of this period. Yet her unadorned head (the goddesses of Temple A at Prinias wear headdresses; FIG. 5-5A) and the placement of her right hand across her chest in what is probably a gesture of prayer indicate that this is a kore. Evidence suggests that the findspot of the *Lady of Auxerre* was a cemetery at Eleutherna in Crete, which would confirm that the statue represents a deceased woman and not a goddess. The style is much more naturalistic than in Geometric times, but the love of abstract shapes is still evident. Note, for example, the triangular flat-topped head framed by long strands of hair that form triangles complementary to the shape of the face, and the decoration of the long skirt with its incised concentric squares, once brightly

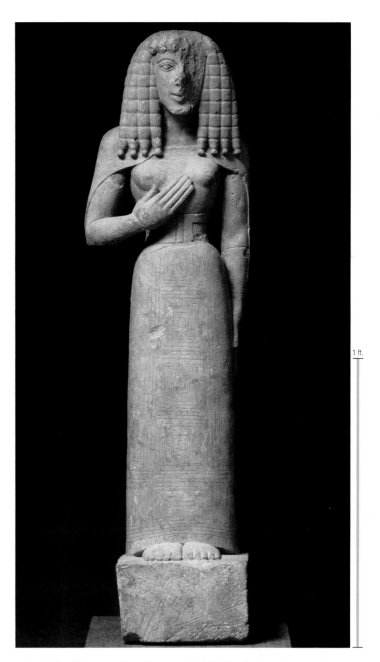

5-6 *Lady of Auxerre,* from Crete, probably Eleutherna, Greece, ca. 650–625 BCE. Limestone, 2′ 1½″ high. Musée du Louvre, Paris.

Carved on Crete, this praying kore (maiden) typifies the Daedalic sculptural style of the seventh century BCE with its triangular face and hair and lingering Geometric fondness for abstract pattern.

painted, as were all Greek stone statues. The modern notion that Greco-Roman statuary was pure white is mistaken. The Greeks did not, however, color their statues garishly. They left the flesh in the natural color of the stone, which they waxed and polished, and painted the eyes, lips, hair, and drapery in *encaustic* (see "Encaustic Painting," page 223, and FIG. 5-63A). In this technique, the painter mixed the pigment with hot wax and applied it to the statue to produce a durable coloration.

ARCHAIC PERIOD

In addition to his status as a great sculptor, Daedalus reputedly built the labyrinth (FIG. 4-5) in Crete to house the Minotaur and also designed a temple at Memphis in Egypt. The historical Greeks attributed to him almost all the great achievements in early sculpture and architecture. The legend that Daedalus worked in Egypt reflects the enormous influence of Egyptian art and architecture on the Greeks, not only during the Orientalizing age of the seventh century BCE but also in the succeeding *Archaic* period, which lasted from 600 to 480 BCE.

Statuary

According to the first-century BCE Greek historian Diodorus Siculus, Daedalus used the same compositional patterns for his statues as the Egyptians used for their own.[1] The earliest surviving large-scale stone statues of the Greeks do, in fact, follow very closely the standard Egyptian format.

New York Kouros. One of the earliest Greek examples of life-size statuary (FIG. 5-7) is the marble *kouros* ("youth"; plural, *kouroi*) now in New York, which emulates the stance of Egyptian statues (FIG. 3-13). In both Egypt and Greece, the figure is rigidly frontal with the left foot advanced slightly. The arms are held beside the body, and the fists are clenched with the thumbs forward. Like most Egyptian statues, the New York kouros also had a funerary function. It stood over a grave in the countryside of Attica, the region around Athens, possibly in the same cemetery as the later statue of Kroisos (FIG. 5-9). Statues such as this one replaced the huge vases (FIGS. 5-2 and 5-2A) of Geometric times as the preferred form of grave marker in the sixth century BCE. The Greeks also used kouroi as votive offerings in sanctuaries. The kouros type, because of its generic quality, could be employed in several different contexts.

Despite the adherence to Egyptian prototypes, Greek kouros statues differ from their models in two important ways. First, the Greek sculptors liberated the figures from the stone block. The Egyptian obsession with permanence was alien to the Greeks, who were preoccupied with finding ways to represent motion rather than stability in their sculpted figures. Second, the kouroi are nude (this kouros wears only a choke necklace), and in the absence of identifying attributes, they, like Mantiklos's bronze statuette (FIG. 5-4), are formally indistinguishable from Greek images of deities with their perfect bodies exposed for all to see.

The New York kouros shares many traits with the *Mantiklos Apollo* and other Orientalizing works such as the *Lady of Auxerre,* especially the triangular shape of head and hair and the flatness of the face—hallmarks of the Daedalic style. Eyes, nose, and mouth all sit on the front of the head, and ears on the sides. The long hair forms a flat backdrop behind the head. The placement of the various anatomical parts is the result of the sculptor's having drawn these features on four independent sides of the marble block, following the same workshop procedure used in Egypt for millennia. The New York kouros also has the slim waist of earlier Greek statues and exhibits the same love of pattern. The pointed arch of the rib cage, for example, echoes the V-shaped ridge of the hips, which suggests but does not accurately reproduce the rounded flesh and muscle of the human body.

Calf Bearer. A generation later than the New York kouros is the statue (FIG. 5-8) of a *moschophoros,* or calf bearer, found in fragments on the Athenian Acropolis. Its inscribed base (not visible in the photograph) states that an otherwise unknown man named Rhonbos, son of Palos, dedicated the statue to Athena. Rhonbos is almost certainly the calf bearer himself, bringing an offering to the goddess. He stands in the left-foot-forward manner of the kouroi,

but he is bearded and therefore no longer a youth. He wears a thin cloak (once painted to set it off from the otherwise nude body). No one dressed this way in ancient Athens. The sculptor adhered to the artistic convention of male nudity and attributed to the calf bearer the noble perfection that nudity imparts, yet indicated that this mature gentleman is clothed, as any respectable citizen would be in this context. The Archaic sculptor's love of pattern is evident once again in the handling of the difficult problem of representing man and animal together. The calf's legs and the man's arms form a bold X that unites the two bodies both physically and formally.

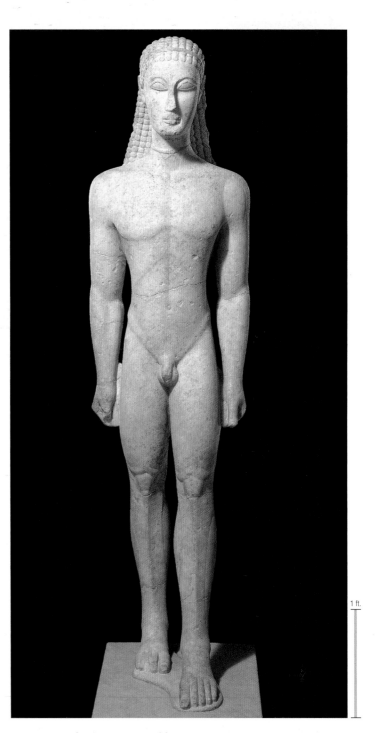

5-7 Kouros, from Attica, possibly Anavysos, Greece, ca. 600 BCE. Marble, 6′ $\frac{1}{2}$″ high. Metropolitan Museum of Art, New York.

The sculptors of the earliest life-size statues of kouroi (young men) adopted the Egyptian pose for standing figures (FIG. 3-13), but the kouroi are nude and liberated from the stone block.

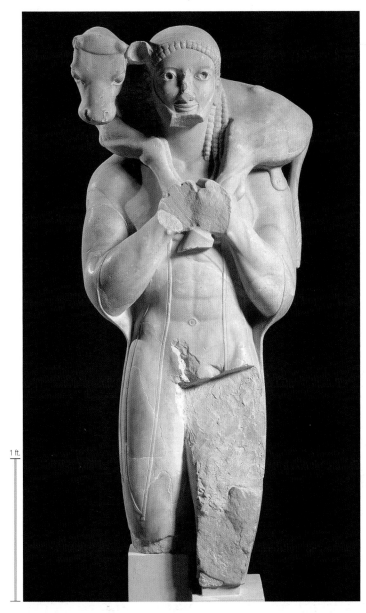

5-8 Calf bearer, dedicated by Rhonbos on the Acropolis, Athens, Greece, ca. 560 BCE. Marble, restored height 5′ 5″; fragment 3′ 11½″ high. Acropolis Museum, Athens.

This statue of a bearded man bringing a calf to sacrifice to Athena is one of the first to employ the so-called Archaic smile—probably the Greek sculptor's way of indicating that a person is alive.

The calf bearer's face differs markedly from those of earlier Greek statues (and those of Egypt and Mesopotamia) in one notable way. The man smiles—or at least seems to. From this time on, Archaic Greek statues always smile, even in the most inappropriate contexts (see, for example, FIG. 5-28, which shows a dying warrior with an arrow in his chest—yet grinning broadly). Art historians have interpreted this so-called *Archaic smile* in various ways, but the happy face should not be taken literally. Rather, the Archaic smile is the way that Greek sculptors of this era indicated that the person portrayed is alive. By adopting this convention, Greek artists signaled that their intentions were very different from those of their Egyptian counterparts.

Anavysos Kouros. Sometime around 530 BCE, a young man named Kroisos died a hero's death in battle, and, to commemorate

his life, his family erected a kouros statue (FIG. 5-9) over his grave at Anavysos, not far from Athens. Fortunately, some of the paint remains, giving a good sense of the statue's original appearance. The inscribed base invites visitors to "stay and mourn at the tomb of dead Kroisos, whom raging Ares destroyed one day as he fought in the foremost ranks." The smiling statue is no more a portrait of a specific youth than is the New York kouros. But two generations later, without rejecting the Egyptian stance, the Greek sculptor rendered the human body in a far more naturalistic manner. The head is no longer too large for the body, and the face is more rounded, with swelling cheeks replacing the flat planes of the earlier work. The long hair does not form a stiff backdrop to the head but falls naturally over the back, and the V-shaped ridges of the New York kouros have become rounded, fleshy hips.

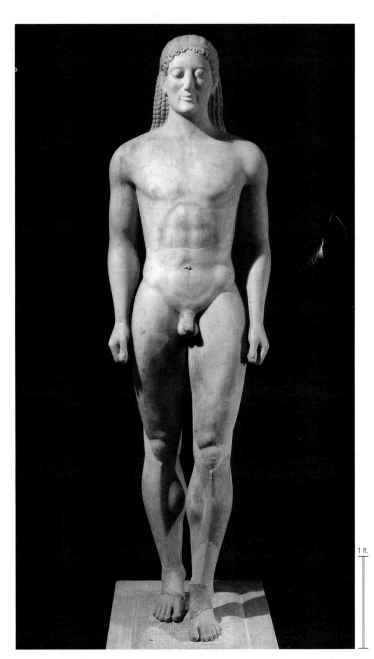

5-9 Kroisos, from Anavysos, Greece, ca. 530 BCE. Marble, 6′ 4″ high. National Archaeological Museum, Athens.

This later kouros stood over the grave of Kroisos, a young man who died in battle. The statue displays more naturalistic proportions and more rounded modeling of face, torso, and limbs.

Peplos Kore. A stylistic "sister" to the Anavysos kouros is the statue of a woman traditionally known as the *Peplos Kore* (FIG. 5-10) because until recently scholars thought that this kore wore a peplos. A *peplos* is a simple, long, woolen belted garment. Careful examination of the statue has revealed, however, that she wears four different garments, one of which only goddesses wore. The attribute that the goddess held in her missing left hand would immediately have identified her. Whichever goddess she is, the contrast with the *Lady of Auxerre* (FIG. 5-6) is striking. Although in both cases the drapery conceals the entire body save for head, arms, and feet, the sixth-century BCE sculptor rendered the soft female form much more naturally. This softer treatment of the flesh also sharply differentiates later korai from kouroi, which have hard, muscular bodies.

Traces of paint remain on the *Peplos Kore* because the statue lay buried for more than two millennia, which protected the painted surface from the destructive effects of exposure to the atmosphere and bad weather. The Persians had knocked over this statue, Rhonbos's (FIG. 5-8), and many other votive offerings in Athena's sanctuary during their sack of the Acropolis in 480 BCE. Shortly thereafter, the Athenians buried all the damaged Archaic sculptures, which accounts for the preservation of the coloration today.

Kore in Ionian Dress. By the late sixth century BCE, the light linen Ionian *chiton,* worn in conjunction with a heavier *himation* (mantle), was the garment of choice for fashionable women. Archaic sculptors of korai in Ionian dress (FIG. 5-11) delighted in rendering the intricate patterns created by the cascading folds of thin, soft material. The asymmetry of the folds greatly relieves the stiff frontality of the body and makes the figure appear much more lifelike than the typical kouros. The sculptor achieved added variety by showing the kore grasping part of her chiton in her left hand (unfortunately broken off) to lift it off the ground in order to take a step forward. This is the equivalent of the advanced left foot of the kouroi and became standard for statues of korai. Despite the varied surface treatment of brightly colored garments on the korai, the kore postures are as fixed as those of their male counterparts.

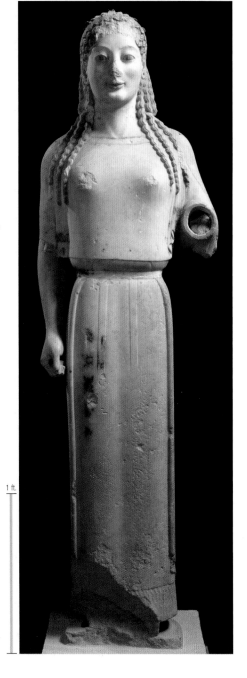

5-10 *Peplos Kore,* from the Acropolis, Athens, Greece, ca. 530 BCE. Marble, 4′ high. Acropolis Museum, Athens.

Unlike men, women are always clothed in Archaic statuary. This kore is a votive statue representing a goddess wearing four garments. She held her identifying attribute in her missing left hand.

1 ft.

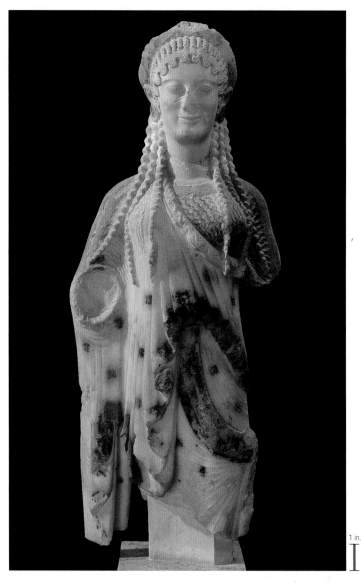

1 in.

5-11 Kore in Ionian dress, from the Acropolis, Athens, Greece, ca. 520–510 BCE. Marble, 1′ 9″ high. Acropolis Museum, Athens.

Archaic sculptors delighted in rendering the intricate asymmetrical patterns created by the cascading folds of garments, such as the Ionian chiton and himation worn by this smiling Acropolis kore.

Greek Temple Plans

Although Greek temple plans (FIG. 5-12) vary, in all cases what strikes the eye first is the remarkable order, compactness, and symmetry of the design, reflecting the Greeks' sense of proportion and their effort to achieve ideal forms in terms of numerical relationships and geometric rules (see "The Perfect Temple," page 105).

The core of the ancient Greek temple plan was the *naos, or cella,* a windowless room that usually housed the cult statue of the deity. In front of the naos was a *pronaos,* or porch, often with two columns between the *antae,* or extended walls (columns *in antis*). A smaller second room might be placed behind the cella (FIG. 5-15) to store votive offerings, but in its canonical form, the Greek temple had a porch at the rear (*opisthodomos*) set against the blank back wall of the cella. The second porch served only a decorative purpose, satisfying the Greek passion for balance and symmetry.

Around this core, Greek builders might erect a colonnade across the front of the temple (*prostyle*; FIG. 5-52), across both front and back (*amphiprostyle*; FIG. 5-55), or, more commonly, all around the cella and its porch(es) to form a *peristyle,* as in FIG. 5-12 (compare FIGS. 5-1 and 5-14). Single (*peripteral*) colonnades were the norm, but double (*dipteral*) colonnades were features of especially elaborate temples (FIGS. 5-75 and 5-76).

The Greeks' insistence on balance and order guided their experiments with the proportions of temple plans. The earliest temples tended

to be long and narrow, with the proportion of the ends to the sides roughly expressible as a ratio of 1:3. From the sixth century BCE on, the ratio of front to side was closer to but not usually exactly 1:2. That is, Classical temples tended to be a little longer than twice their width. To the Greek mind, proportion in architecture and sculpture was comparable to harmony in music (see "Polykleitos's Prescription for the Perfect Statue," page 131). Both were reflections and embodiments of the beauty and perfection of the cosmos.

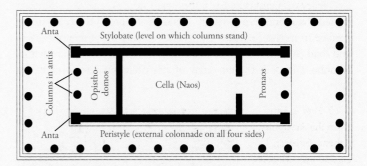

5-12 Plan of a typical Greek peripteral temple.

The canonical Greek temple plan is compact and symmetrical. The core of the building—the cella—housed the deity's statue. The altar was outside, on the east, where the worshipers assembled.

Architecture and Architectural Sculpture

The earliest Greek temples do not survive because their builders constructed them of wood and mud brick. Pausanias, the author of a famous second-century CE guidebook to Greece, noted that in the even-then-ancient Temple of Hera at Olympia, one oak column was still in place.[2] (Stone columns had replaced the others.) For Archaic and later Greek temples, however, Greek builders used more permanent materials—limestone or, where it was available, marble, which was more beautiful and durable (and more expensive). In Greece proper, if not in its western colonies, marble was readily available. Bluish-white Hymettian marble came from Mount Hymettus, just east of Athens, and glittering white Pentelic marble from Mount Pentelicus, northeast of the city. Fine white marble was also quarried on some of the Aegean Islands, especially Paros.

As early as the Orientalizing seventh century BCE, the Greeks had built at Prinias a stone temple (FIG. 5-5A) embellished with stone sculptures, but the Cretan temple was small and simple, without the familiar, later external ring of columns (FIG. 5-1). In the Archaic age of the sixth century BCE, when the Greeks began to travel and trade widely in the Mediterranean, they became familiar with Egyptian columnar halls, such as those at Luxor (FIG. 3-24A) and Karnak (FIGS. 3-24, 3-25, and 3-26). It was then that Greek architects began to build the columnar stone temples that have become synonymous with Greek architecture and influenced countless later structures in the Western world.

The Canonical Greek Temple. Greek temples differed in function from most later religious shrines. The altar lay outside the

temple—at the east end, facing the rising sun—and the Greeks gathered to worship outside, not inside, the building. The temple proper housed the so-called *cult statue* of the deity, the grandest of all votive offerings. In both its early and its mature manifestations, the Greek temple (see "Greek Temple Plans," above, and FIG. 5-12) was the house of the god or goddess, not of his or her followers.

Figural sculpture played a major role in the exterior program of the Greek temple from early times, partly to embellish the god's shrine, partly to tell something about the deity represented within, and partly to serve as a votive offering. But Greek architects also conceived the building itself, with its finely carved *capitals* and moldings, as sculpture, abstract in form and possessing the power of sculpture to evoke human responses. To underscore the commanding importance of the sculptured temple and its inspiring function in public life, the Greeks usually erected their temples on elevated sites, often on a hill above the city (*acropolis* means "high city").

Most of the sculptural ornament was on the upper part of the building, in the *frieze* and *pediments* (see "Doric and Ionic Orders," page 116). The Greeks painted their architectural sculptures (FIGS. 5-17 and 5-27), as they did their freestanding statues (FIG. 5-63A), and usually placed sculpture only in the building parts that had no structural function. This is true particularly of the *Doric order* (FIG. 5-13, *left*), in which decorative sculpture appears only in the "voids" of the *metopes* and pediments. In the *Ionic order* (FIG. 5-13, *right*), builders were willing to decorate the entire frieze and sometimes even the lower part of the column. Occasionally, Ionic architects replaced columns with female figures, known as *caryatids* (FIGS. 5-17 and 5-54). The Greeks also painted capitals, decorative moldings, and other architectural elements. The original

Doric and Ionic Orders

Architectural historians describe the elevation (FIG. 5-13) of a Greek temple in terms of the platform, the colonnade, the *entablature* (the section between the columns and the roof), and the roof. In the Archaic period, two basic systems, or *orders,* evolved—the *Doric* and the *Ionic,* which differ both in the nature of the details and in the relative proportions of the parts. The orders are like sentences in a language, which are constructed according to rules of grammar and syntax. Placing a Doric frieze above an Ionic colonnade would be comparable to using a plural verb with a singular subject in a sentence.

The names of the two orders derive from the Greek regions where they were most commonly employed. The Doric, formulated on the mainland, remained the preferred style there and in Greece's western colonies. The Ionic was the order of choice in the Aegean Islands and on the western coast of Asia Minor. The geographical distinctions are by no means absolute. The Ionic order, for example, was a frequent choice for buildings in Athens (where, according to some ancient authors, the Athenians considered themselves Ionians who never migrated).

In both orders, the columns rest on the *stylobate,* the uppermost course of the platform. Metal clamps held together the stone blocks in each horizontal course, and metal dowels joined the blocks of different courses vertically. The columns have two or three parts, depending on the order: the *shaft,* usually marked with vertical channels (*flutes*); the *capital* ("head"); and, in the Ionic order, the *base.* Greek column shafts, in contrast to Minoan and Mycenaean examples, taper gradually from bottom to top. They usually are composed of separate *drums* joined by metal dowels to prevent turning as well as shifting, although occasionally the Greeks erected *monolithic* (single-piece) columns.

Greek column capitals have two elements. The lower part (the *echinus*) varies with the order. In the Doric, it is convex and cushionlike, similar to the echinus of Minoan (FIG. 4-6) and Mycenaean (FIG. 4-19) capitals. In the Ionic, it is small and supports a bolster ending in scroll-like spirals (the *volutes*). The upper element, present in both orders, is a block (the *abacus*) that provides the immediate support for the entablature. The abacus takes different shapes in the Doric and Ionic systems.

The entablature has three parts: the *architrave,* the main weight-bearing and weight-distributing element; the *frieze;* and the *cornice,* a molded horizontal projection that together with two sloping (*raking*) cornices forms a triangle framing the *pediment.* In the Ionic order, the architrave is usually subdivided into three horizontal bands. Doric architects subdivided the frieze into *triglyphs* and *metopes,* whereas Ionic builders left the frieze open to provide a continuous field for relief sculpture.

The Doric order is massive in appearance, its sturdy columns firmly planted on the stylobate. Compared with the weighty and severe Doric, the Ionic order seems light, airy, and much more decorative. Its columns are more slender and rise from molded bases.

The most obvious differences between the two orders are, of course, the capitals—the Doric, severely plain, and the Ionic, highly ornamental.

DORIC ORDER

IONIC ORDER

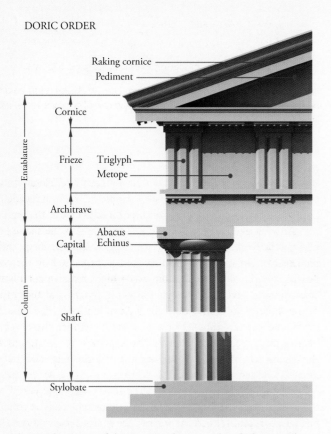
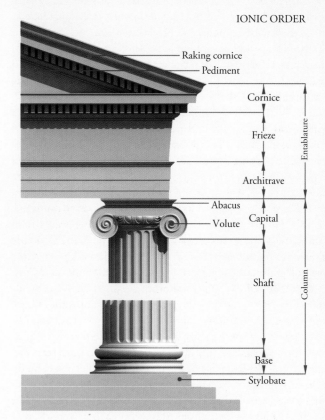

5-13 **Elevations of the Doric and Ionic orders (John Burge).**

The major differences between the Doric and Ionic orders are the form of the capitals and the treatment of the frieze. The Doric frieze is subdivided into triglyphs and metopes.

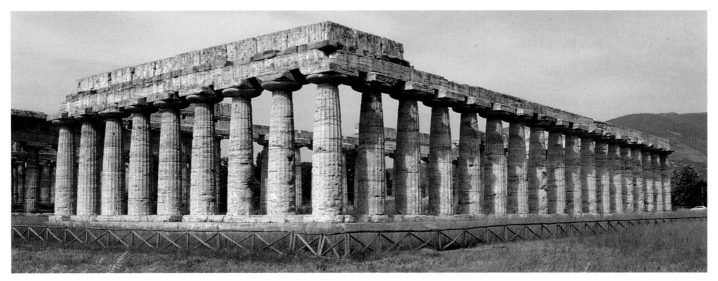

5-14 Temple of Hera I ("Basilica," looking northeast), Paestum, Italy, ca. 550 BCE.

The peristyle of this huge early Doric temple consists of heavy, closely spaced, cigar-shaped columns with bulky, pancakelike capitals, characteristic features of Archaic Greek architecture.

appearance of Greek temples was therefore quite different than their gleaming white, if ruined, state today.

Although the Greeks used color for emphasis and to relieve what might have seemed too bare, Greek architects primarily sought clarity and balance. To the Greeks, it was unthinkable to use surfaces in the way that the Egyptians used their gigantic columns—as fields for complicated ornamentation (FIGS. 3-25 and 3-26). The history of Greek temple architecture is the history of Greek architects' efforts to find the most satisfactory (that is, what they believed were most perfect) proportions for each part of the building and for the structure as a whole.

Basilica, Paestum. The premier example of early Greek efforts at Doric temple design is not in Greece but in one of their many settlements in Italy, at Paestum (Greek Poseidonia), south of Naples. The huge (80-by-170-foot) Archaic temple (FIG. 5-14) erected there around 550 BCE retains its entire peripteral colonnade, but most of the frieze and pediment, and the entire roof, have vanished. Called the "Basilica" by early investigators, who believed that it resembled the Roman columnar hall building type, the structure was a shrine to the goddess Hera. Today, the Basilica is known as the Temple of Hera I to distinguish it from its neighbor, the later Temple of Hera II (FIG. 5-30). The misnomer is partly due to the building's plan (FIG. 5-15), which differs from that of most other Greek temples. The unusual feature, found only in early Archaic temples, is the central row of columns dividing the *cella* into two aisles. Placing columns underneath the *ridge beam* (the timber beam running the length of the building below the peak of the gabled roof) might seem the logical way to provide interior support for the roof structure, but it had several disadvantages. The row of columns on the cella's axis precluded a central cult statue. Further, in order to correspond with the interior, the temple's facade required an odd number of columns (nine in this case). At Paestum, there are also three columns in antis instead of the standard two, which in turn ruled out a central doorway for viewing the statue. (This design, however, was well suited for two statues, and some scholars have speculated

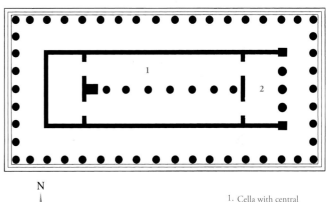

N

0 10 20 30 40 50 feet
0   5   10   15 meters

1. Cella with central row of columns
2. Pronaos with three columns in antis

5-15 Plan of the Temple of Hera I, Paestum, Italy, ca. 550 BCE.

The Hera temple's plan also reveals its early date. The building has an odd number of columns on the facade and a single row of columns in the cella, leaving no place for a central cult statue.

that the Paestum cella housed statues of Zeus and Hera.) In any case, the architect chose to employ a simple 1:2 ratio of facade and flank columns, and erected 18 columns on each side of the temple.

Another early aspect of the Paestum temple is the shape of its heavy, closely spaced columns (FIG. 5-14) with their large, bulky, pancakelike Doric capitals, which seem compressed by the overbearing weight of what probably was a high, massive entablature. The columns have a pronounced swelling (*entasis*) at the middle of the shafts, giving them a profile akin to that of a cigar. The columns and capitals thus express in a vivid manner their weight-bearing function. One reason for the heaviness of the design and the narrowness of the spans between the columns might be that the Archaic builders were afraid that thinner and more widely spaced columns would result in the superstructure's collapse. In later Doric temples (FIGS. 5-1, 5-25, and 5-30), the builders placed the columns farther apart and refined the forms. The shafts became more slender, the entasis subtler, the capitals smaller, and the entablature lighter. Greek architects sought the ideal proportional relationship among the parts of their buildings. The sculptors of Archaic kouroi and korai grappled with similar problems. Architecture and sculpture developed in a parallel manner during the sixth century BCE.

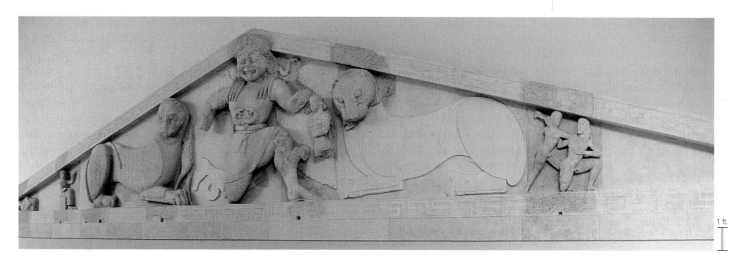

5-16 West pediment, Temple of Artemis, Corfu, Greece, ca. 600–580 BCE. Limestone, greatest height 9′ 4″. Archaeological Museum, Corfu.

The hideous Medusa and two panthers at the center of this early pediment served as temple guardians. To either side, and much smaller, are scenes from the Trojan War and the battle of gods and giants.

Temple of Artemis, Corfu. Architects and sculptors frequently worked together, as at Corfu (ancient Corcyra), where, soon after 600 BCE, the Greeks constructed a large Doric temple in honor of Artemis. Corfu is an island off the western coast of Greece and was an important stop on the trade route between the mainland and the Greek settlements in Italy (MAP 5-1). Prosperity made possible the erection of one of the earliest stone peripteral temples in Greece, one also lavishly embellished with sculpture. Sculptors decorated the metopes with reliefs (unfortunately very fragmentary today) and filled both pediments with huge high-relief sculptures (more than 9 feet tall at the center). It appears that the pediments on both ends of the temple were decorated in an identical manner. The west pediment (FIG. 5-16) is better preserved.

Designing figural decoration for a pediment was never an easy task for the Greek sculptor because of the pediment's awkward triangular shape. The central figures had to be of great size. By contrast, as the pediment tapered toward the corners, the available area became increasingly cramped. At the center of the Corfu pediment is the *gorgon* Medusa, a demon with a woman's body and a bird's wings. Medusa also had a hideous face and snake hair, and anyone who gazed at her turned to stone. The Corfu sculptor depicted her in the conventional Archaic bent-leg, bent-arm, pinwheel-like posture that signifies running or, for a winged creature, flying. To her left and right are two great felines. Together they serve as temple guardians, repulsing all enemies from the sanctuary of the goddess. Similar panthers stood sentinel on the lintel (FIG. 5-5A) of the seventh-century BCE temple at Prinias. The Corfu felines are in the tradition of the guardian lions of Mycenae (FIG. 4-19) and the beasts that stood guard at the entrances to Hittite and Assyrian palaces (FIGS. 2-18A and 2-20). Medusa herself is also an *apotropaic* figure—that is, she protects the temple and wards off evil. The triad of Medusa and the felines recalls as well Mesopotamian heraldic human-and-animal compositions (FIG. 2-10). The Corfu figures are, in short, still further examples of the Orientalizing manner in early Greek sculpture.

Between Medusa and the two felines are two smaller figures—the human Chrysaor at her left and the winged horse Pegasus at her right (only the rear legs remain, next to Medusa's right foot). Chrysaor and Pegasus were Medusa's children. According to legend, they

sprang from her head when the Greek hero Perseus severed it with his sword. Their presence here on either side of the living Medusa is therefore a chronological impossibility. The Archaic artist's interest was not in telling a coherent story but in identifying the central figure by depicting her offspring. Narration was, however, the purpose of the much smaller groups situated in the pediment corners. To the viewer's right is Zeus, brandishing his thunderbolt and slaying a kneeling giant. In the extreme corner (not preserved) was a dead giant. The *gigantomachy* (battle of gods and giants) was a popular theme in Greek art of all periods and was a metaphor for the triumph of reason and order over chaos. In the pediment's left corner is one of the Trojan War's climactic events: Achilles's son, Neoptolemos, kills the enthroned King Priam. The fallen figure to the left of this group may be a dead Trojan.

The master responsible for the Corfu pediments was a pioneer, and the composition shows all the signs of experimentation. The lack of narrative unity in the Corfu pediment and the figures' extraordinary diversity of scale eventually gave way to pedimental designs in which all the figures are the same size and act out a single event. But the Corfu designer already had shown the way. That sculptor realized, for example, that the area beneath the raking cornice could be filled with gods and heroes of similar size by employing a combination of standing, leaning, kneeling, seated, and lying figures. The Corfu master also discovered that animals could be very useful space fillers because, unlike humans, they have one end taller than the other.

Siphnian Treasury, Delphi. With the sixth century BCE also came the construction of grandiose Ionic temples on the Aegean Islands and the west coast of Asia Minor. Yet the gem of Archaic Ionic architecture and architectural sculpture is not a temple but a *treasury* erected by the citizens of Siphnos in the Sanctuary of Apollo (FIG. 5-16A) at Delphi. Greek treasuries were small buildings set up by individual city-states for the safe storage of their votive offerings. At Delphi, many Greek poleis expressed

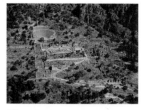

⊞ **5-16A** Sanctuary of Apollo, Delphi.

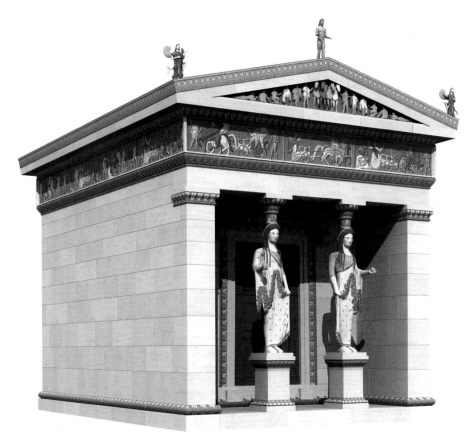

5-17 Restored view of the Siphnian Treasury, Sanctuary of Apollo, Delphi, Greece, ca. 530 BCE (John Burge).

Treasuries were storehouses for a city's votive offerings. The Ionic treasury that the Siphnians erected in Apollo's sanctuary had caryatids in the porch, and sculptures in the pediment and frieze.

surviving fragments now on display in the Delphi museum have enabled archaeologists to reconstruct the treasury's original appearance (FIG. 5-17). Wealth from the island's gold and silver mines made such a luxurious building possible. In the porch, where one would expect to find fluted Ionic columns, far more elaborate caryatids were employed instead. Caryatids are rare, even in Ionic architecture, but they are unknown in Doric architecture, where they would have been discordant elements in that much more severe order. The Siphnian statue-columns resemble korai dressed in Ionian chitons and himations (FIG. 5-11). They are generic women, not portraits of individuals, but scholars continue to debate whom the caryatids represent. Like most korai, the statue-columns may simply be elite women who are paying homage to the deity.

Another Ionic feature of the Siphnian Treasury is the continuous sculptured frieze on all four sides of the building. The north frieze represents the popular theme of the gigantomachy, but it is a much more detailed rendition than that in the corner of the Corfu pediment (FIG. 5-16, *right*). In the section reproduced here (FIG. 5-18), Apollo and Artemis pursue a fleeing giant at the center, while behind them one of the lions pulling an attacking chariot bites into a giant's midsection. Paint originally enlivened the crowded composition, and painted labels identified the various protagonists, as they do on Archaic black-figure vases (for example, FIGS. 5-19 and 5-20). The sculptors placed metal weapons in the hands of some figures. The effect must have been dazzling. On one of the shields, the sculptor inscribed his name (unfortunately lost), a clear indication of pride in accomplishment.

their civic pride by erecting these templelike but nonperipteral structures. Athens built one with Doric columns in the porch and sculptured metopes in the frieze. The Siphnians equally characteristically employed the Ionic order for their Delphic treasury. The

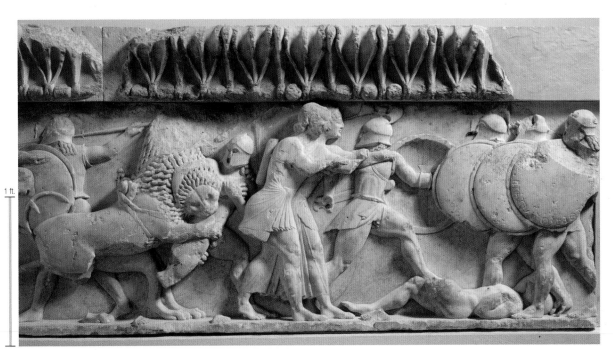

1 ft.

5-18 Giganto-machy, detail of the north frieze of the Siphnian Treasury, Delphi, Greece, ca. 530 BCE. Marble, 2′ 1″ high. Archaeological Museum, Delphi.

Greek friezes were brightly painted (FIG. 5-17). As in Archaic vase painting, the Siphnian frieze also had painted labels identifying the various gods and giants. Some of the figures held metal weapons.

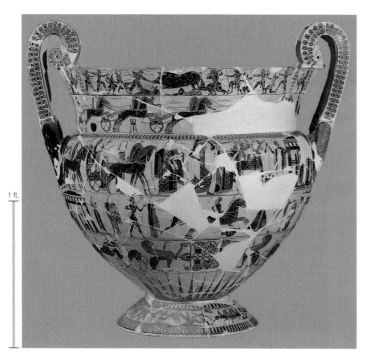

5-19 **KLEITIAS** and **ERGOTIMOS**, *François Vase* (Athenian black-figure volute krater), from Chiusi, Italy, ca. 570 BCE. 2′ 2″ high. Museo Archeologico Nazionale, Florence.

The painter and potter both signed this huge early black-figure krater. The vase has more than 200 mythological figures in five registers, the same format as on Geometric and Orientalizing vases.

Vase Painting

By the mid-sixth century BCE, the Athenians, having learned the black-figure technique from the Corinthians (FIG. 5-5), had taken over the export market for fine painted ceramics (see "Greek Vase Painting," page 110).

François Vase. The masterpiece of early Athenian black-figure painting is the *François Vase* (FIG. 5-19), named for the excavator who discovered it (in hundreds of fragments) in an Etruscan tomb at Chiusi. The vase is a new kind of krater with volute-shaped handles, probably inspired by costly metal prototypes. The signatures of both its painter ("KLEITIAS painted me") and potter ("ERGOTIMOS made me") appear twice among the more than 200 figures in five registers. Labels abound, naming humans and animals alike, even some inanimate objects. The painter devoted only the lowest band to the Orientalizing repertoire of animals and sphinxes. The others feature a selective encyclopedia of Greek mythology, focusing on the exploits of Peleus and his son, Achilles, the great hero of Homer's *Iliad,* and of Theseus, the legendary king of Athens. Among the most prominent scenes depicted is the battle between the Lapiths (a northern Greek tribe) and centaurs (*centauromachy*; FIG. 5-19A)

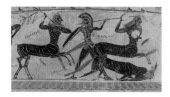

⬈5-19A KLEITIAS and ERGOTIMOS, centauromachy, ca. 570 BCE.

after a wedding celebration at which the man-beasts, who were invited guests, got drunk and attempted to abduct the Lapith maidens and young boys. Theseus, also on the guest list, was chief among the centaurs' Greek adversaries.

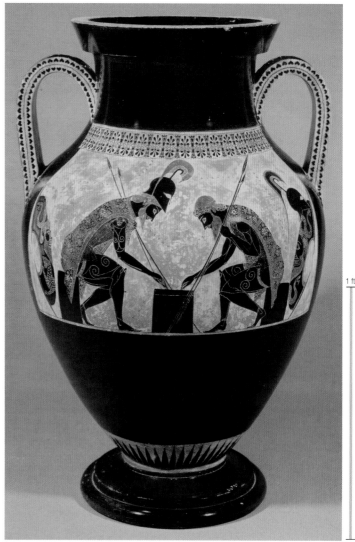

5-20 **EXEKIAS**, Achilles and Ajax playing a dice game (Athenian black-figure amphora), from Vulci, Italy, ca. 540–530 BCE. 2′ high. Musei Vaticani, Rome.

The dramatic tension, coordination of figural poses with vase shape, and intricacy of the engraved patterns of the cloaks are hallmarks of Exekias, the greatest master of black-figure painting.

Exekias. The acknowledged master of the black-figure technique was an Athenian named EXEKIAS, whose vases were not only widely exported but copied as well. Perhaps his greatest work is an amphora (FIG. 5-20) found in an Etruscan tomb at Vulci, which Exekias signed as both painter and potter. Unlike Kleitias, Exekias did not divide the surface of the vase into a series of horizontal bands. Instead, he placed large figures in a single framed panel. At the left is Achilles, fully armed, the mightiest Greek soldier in the war against Troy. He appears again on another of Exekias's amphoras (FIG. 5-20A) battling Penthesilea, queen of the Amazons. Here, Achilles plays a dice game with his comrade Ajax during a lull in the Trojan conflict. Out of the lips of Achilles comes the word *tesara* ("four"). Ajax calls out *tria*

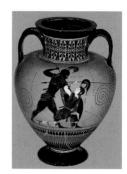

⬈5-20A EXEKIAS, Achilles killing Penthesilea, ca. 540–530 BCE.

The Invention of Red-Figure Painting

By 530 BCE, master ceramists such as Exekias (FIGS. 5-20 and 5-20A) had taken the art of black-figure painting to a level never surpassed, but that painting technique, invented in the seventh century BCE (FIG. 5-5), presented severe limitations for artists who wished to break free of the conventions of figure drawing that had dominated art production since the third millennium BCE. The need for a new ceramic painting technique with greater versatility than black-figure, with its dark silhouettes and incised details, was pressing. The solution was red-figure painting. Its inventor was the ceramist whom art historians call the ANDOKIDES PAINTER—that is, the anonymous painter who decorated the vases signed by the potter Andokides.

The differences between the black-figure and red-figure techniques can best be studied on a series of experimental vases with the same composition painted on both sides, once in black-figure and once in red-figure. Andokides and other Athenian potters produced these so-called *bilingual vases* only for a short time. An especially interesting example is an amphora (FIGS. 5-21 and 5-22) featuring copies of the Achilles and Ajax panel (FIG. 5-20) by Exekias. The red-figure side is the work of the Andokides Painter. Most art historians attribute the black-figure side to a colleague in the same workshop nicknamed the LYSIPPIDES PAINTER, who was probably a pupil of Exekias. In neither black-figure nor red-figure did Exekias's emulators capture the intensity of the master's rendition of the same subject, and the treatment of details is decidedly inferior. Yet the new red-figure technique had obvious advantages over the old black-figure manner.

Red-figure is the opposite of black-figure. What was previously black became red, and vice versa. The artist used the same black glaze for the figures, but instead of using the glaze to create silhouettes, the painter outlined the figures and then colored the background black. The ceramist reserved the red clay for the figures themselves and used a soft brush instead of a stiff metal graver to draw the interior details. This gave the red-figure painter much greater flexibility. The artist could vary the thickness of the lines and even build up the glaze to give relief to curly hair or dilute it to create brown shades, thereby expanding the chromatic range of the Greek vase painter's craft. The Andokides Painter—many scholars think that he is the potter Andokides himself—did not yet appreciate the full potential of his own invention. Still, he created a technique that, in the hands of other, more skilled artists, such as Euphronios (FIGS. 5-23 and 5-23A), helped revolutionize the art of drawing.

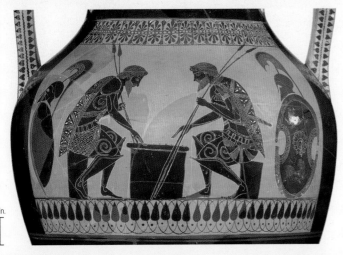

5-21 LYSIPPIDES PAINTER, *Achilles and Ajax playing a dice game* (black-figure side of an Athenian bilingual amphora), from Orvieto, Italy, ca. 525–520 BCE. Amphora, 1′ 9″ high; detail 8 1/4″ high. Museum of Fine Arts, Boston.

Around 530 BCE, Greek ceramists invented the red-figure technique. Some of the earliest examples are "bilingual" vases—that is, vases with the same scene on both sides, one in black-figure and one in red-figure.

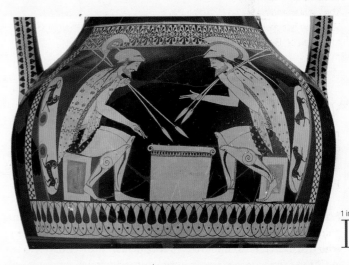

5-22 ANDOKIDES PAINTER, *Achilles and Ajax playing a dice game* (red-figure side of an Athenian bilingual amphora), from Orvieto, Italy, ca. 525–520 BCE. Amphora, 1′ 9″ high; detail 8$\frac{1}{4}$″ high. Museum of Fine Arts, Boston.

The red-figure painter uses a soft brush instead of a metal graver and can vary the thickness of the interior lines. The glaze can also be diluted to create shades of brown and expand the color range.

("three"). Although Ajax has taken off his helmet, both men hold their spears. Their shields are nearby. Each man is ready for action at a moment's notice. This depiction of "the calm before the storm" is the antithesis of the Archaic preference for dramatic action. The gravity and tension that will characterize much Classical Greek art of the next century, but that are generally absent in Archaic art, already may be seen in this vase.

Exekias had no equal as a black-figure painter. This is evident in such details as the extraordinarily intricate engraving of the patterns on the heroes' cloaks and in the brilliant composition. The arch formed by the backs of the two warriors echoes the shape of the rounded shoulders of the amphora. The shape of the vessel is echoed again in the void between the heads and spears of Achilles and Ajax. Exekias also used the spears to lead the viewer's eye toward the thrown dice, where the heroes' gazes are fixed. Of course, Achilles's and Ajax's eyes do not really look down at the table but stare out from their profile heads in the old manner. For all his brilliance, Exekias was still wedded to many of the old conventions.

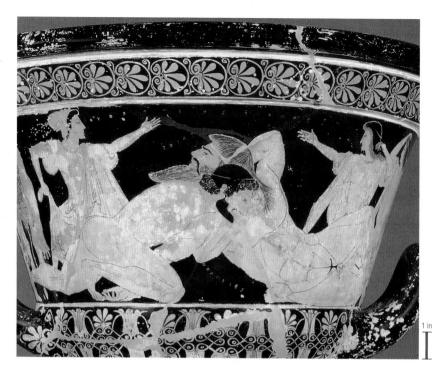

5-23 Euphronios, Herakles wrestling Antaios (detail of an Athenian red-figure calyx krater), from Cerveteri, Italy, ca. 510 BCE. Krater 1′ 7″ high; detail 7¾″ high. Musée du Louvre, Paris.

Euphronios rejected the age-old composite view for his depiction of Herakles and the giant Antaios and instead attempted to reproduce the way the human body appears from a specific viewpoint.

Real innovation in figure drawing would have to await the invention of a new ceramic painting technique: *red-figure painting*. The first examples of red-figure painting came from the studio of the potter ANDOKIDES (see "The Invention of Red-Figure Painting," page 121).

Euphronios. One of the earliest masters of red-figure painting was EUPHRONIOS, whose krater depicting the struggle between Herakles and Antaios (FIG. 5-23) reveals the exciting possibilities of the new technique. Antaios was a Libyan giant, a son of Earth, and he derived his power from contact with the ground. To defeat him, Herakles had to lift him into the air and strangle him while no part of the giant's body touched the earth. In Euphronios's representation of the myth, the two wrestle on the ground, and Antaios still possesses enormous strength. Nonetheless, Herakles has the upper hand. The giant's face is a mask of pain. His eyes roll, and he bares his teeth. His right arm is paralyzed, with the fingers limp.

On this krater, as on his other masterworks—including the most expensive vase ever purchased, a krater cosigned by the pot-

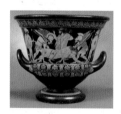

⍐ **5-23A** EUPHRONIOS, death of Sarpedon, ca. 515 BCE.

ter EUXITHEUS (FIG. **5-23A**)—Euphronios used the new red-figure technique brilliantly. For example, he took advantage of the ability to dilute the glaze and produced a golden brown hue for Antaios's hair—intentionally contrasting the giant's unkempt hair with the neat coiffure and carefully trimmed beard of the emotionless Greek hero. The artist also used thinned glaze to delineate the muscles of both figures. But rendering human anatomy convincingly was not his only interest. Euphronios also wished to show that his figures occupy space. He deliberately rejected the conventional composite posture for the human figure, which communicates so well the shape of the individual parts of the human body, and attempted instead to reproduce how a particular human body is *seen*. He presented, for example, not only Antaios's torso but also his right thigh from the front. The lower leg disappears behind the giant, and only part of the right foot is visible. The viewer must mentally make the connection between the upper leg and the foot. Unlike his Archaic and pre-Greek predecessors, Euphronios did not create a two-dimensional panel filled with figures in stereotypical postures. His panel is a window into a mythological world with protagonists moving in three-dimensional space—a revolutionary new conception of what a picture is supposed to be.

Euthymides. A preoccupation with the art of drawing per se is evident in a remarkable amphora (FIG. **5-24**) painted by EUTHYMIDES, a rival of Euphronios's. The subject is appropriate for a wine storage jar—three tipsy revelers. But the theme was little

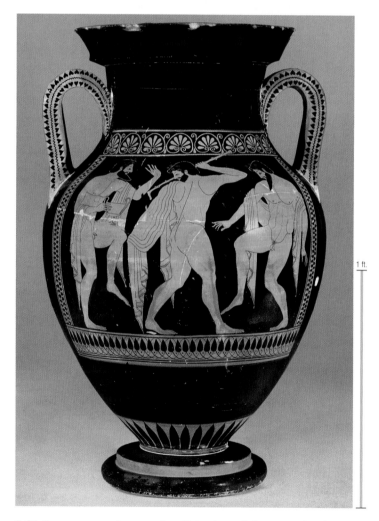

5-24 EUTHYMIDES, three revelers (Athenian red-figure amphora), from Vulci, Italy, ca. 510 BCE. 2′ high. Staatliche Antikensammlungen, Munich.

Euthymides chose this theme as an excuse to represent bodies in unusual positions, including a foreshortened three-quarter rear view. He claimed to have surpassed Euphronios as a draftsman.

more than an excuse for the artist to experiment with the representation of unusual positions of the human form. It is no coincidence that the bodies do not overlap, for each is an independent figure study. Euthymides cast aside the conventional frontal and profile composite views. Instead, he painted torsos that are not two-dimensional surface patterns but *foreshortened*—that is, drawn in a three-quarter view with a compression of the parts of the figure farther away. Most noteworthy is the central figure, shown from the rear with a twisting spinal column and buttocks in three-quarter view. Earlier artists had no interest in attempting to depict figures seen from behind and at an angle because those postures not only are incomplete views but also do not show the "main" side of the human body. For Euthymides, however, the challenge of drawing a figure from this unusual viewpoint was a reward in itself. With understandable pride he proclaimed his achievement by adding to the formulaic signature "Euthymides painted me" the phrase "as never Euphronios [could do!]."

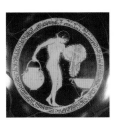

⬀ **5-24A** Onesimos, girl preparing to bathe, ca. 490 BCE.

Other vase painters also challenged themselves to outdo their contemporaries in representing the human form. For example, Onesimos successfully drew a young woman's nude torso from a three-quarter view (FIG. 5-24A).

Aegina and the Transition to the Classical Period

The years just before and after 500 BCE were also a time of dynamic transition in architecture and architectural sculpture. Some of the changes were evolutionary in nature, others revolutionary. Both kinds are evident in the Doric temple at Aegina dedicated to Aphaia, a local nymph.

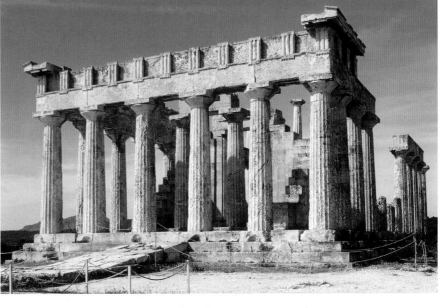

5-25 Temple of Aphaia (looking southwest), Aegina, Greece, ca. 500–490 BCE.

In this refined early-fifth-century BCE temple design (compare FIG. 5-14), the Doric columns are more slender and widely spaced, and there are only 6 columns on the facade and 12 on the flanks.

Temple of Aphaia, Aegina. The temple (FIG. 5-25) sits on a prominent ridge with dramatic views out to the sea. The peripteral colonnade consists of 6 Doric columns on the facade and 12 on the flanks. This is a much more compact structure than Paestum's impressive but ungainly Archaic temple (FIG. 5-14), even though the ratio of width to length is similar. Doric architects had learned a great deal in the half century that elapsed between the construction of the two temples. The columns of the Aegina temple are more widely spaced and more slender. The capitals create a smooth transition from the vertical shafts below to the horizontal architrave above. Gone are the Archaic flattened echinuses and bulging shafts of the Paestum columns. The Aegina architect also refined the internal elevation and plan (FIG. 5-26). In place of a single row of columns down the center of the cella is a double colonnade, and each row has two stories. This arrangement enabled the Aeginetans to place a statue on the central axis, and, because of the open space

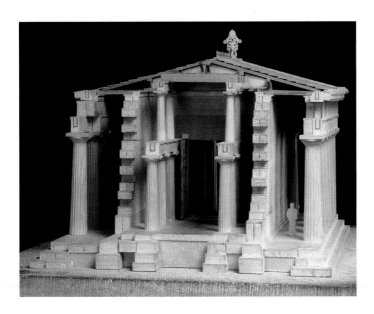

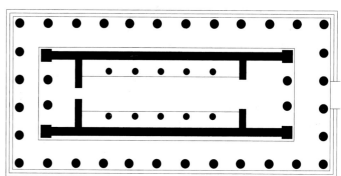

5-26 Model showing the internal elevation (*left*) and plan (*above*) of the Temple of Aphaia, Aegina, Greece, ca. 500–490 BCE. Model: Glyptothek, Munich.

Later Doric architects also modified the plan of their temples (compare FIG. 5-15). The Aegina temple's cella has two colonnades of two stories each (originally with a statue of the deity between them).

between the pair of columns in the pronaos, worshipers standing in front of the building had an unobstructed view of that cult image.

Painted life-size statuary (FIG. 5-27) filled both pediments, in contrast to the high reliefs characteristic of most Archaic temple pediments. The theme of both statuary groups was the battle of Greeks and Trojans, but the sculptors depicted different episodes. The compositions were nonetheless almost identical, with Athena at the center of the bloody combat. She is larger than all the other figures because she is superhuman, but all the mortal heroes are the same size, regardless of their position in the pediment. Unlike the Corfu west pediment (FIG. 5-16), which is an early, experimental design, the Aegina pediments feature a unified theme and consistent scale. The Aegina master was able to keep the size of the figures constant by using the whole range of body postures from upright (Athena) to leaning, falling, kneeling, and prone (Greeks and Trojans).

Workmen set the Aegina pedimental statues in place around 490 BCE, as soon as construction of the temple concluded. Many scholars believe that the statues at the eastern end were damaged and replaced with a new group a decade or two later, although some think that both groups date after 480 BCE. In either case, it is revealing to compare the eastern and western figures. The sculptor of the west pediment's dying warrior (FIG. 5-28) still conceived the statue in the Archaic mode. The warrior's torso is rigidly frontal, and he looks out directly at the spectator—with his face set in an Archaic smile despite the bronze arrow puncturing his chest. He is like a mannequin in a store window whose arms and legs have been arranged by someone else for effective display. There is no sense whatsoever of a thinking and feeling human being.

The comparable figure (FIG. 5-29) in the east pediment is fundamentally different. This warrior's posture is more natural and more complex, with the torso placed at an angle to the viewer (compare FIG. 5-23). Moreover, he reacts to his wound as a

flesh-and-blood human would. He knows that death is inevitable, but he still struggles to rise once again, using his shield for support. He does not look out at the spectator. This dying warrior is solely concerned with his plight, not with the viewer. No more than a decade separates the two statues, but they belong to different eras. The eastern warrior is not a creation of the Archaic world, when sculptors imposed anatomical patterns (and smiles) on statues. This statue belongs to the Classical world, where statues move as

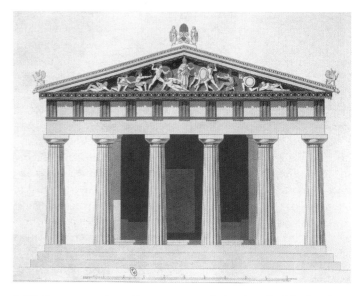

5-27 GUILLAUME-ABEL BLOUET, restored view (1828) of the facade of the Temple of Aphaia, Aegina, Greece, ca. 500–490 BCE.

The Aegina designer solved the problem of composing figures in a pediment by using the whole range of body postures from upright to prone. The restored view suggests how colorful Greek temples were.

5-28 Dying warrior, from the west pediment of the Temple of Aphaia, Aegina, Greece, ca. 490 BCE. Marble, 5′ 2½″ long. Glyptothek, Munich.

The statues of the west pediment of the early-fifth-century BCE temple at Aegina exhibit Archaic features. This fallen warrior still has a rigidly frontal torso and an Archaic smile on his face.

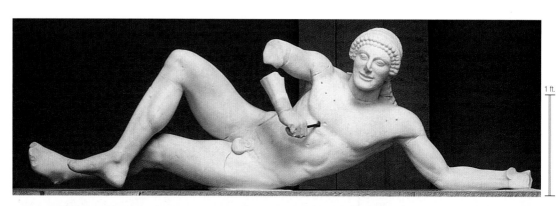

5-29 Dying warrior, from the east pediment of the Temple of Aphaia, Aegina, Greece, ca. 480 BCE. Marble, 6′ 1″ long. Glyptothek, Munich.

The eastern dying warrior already belongs to the Classical era. His posture is more natural, and he exhibits a new self-consciousness. Concerned with his own pain, he does not face the viewer.

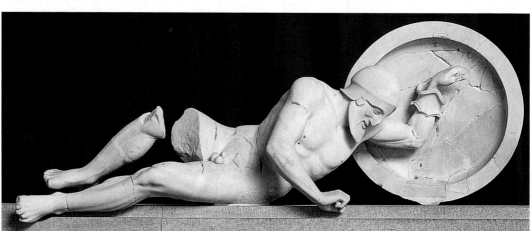

humans move and possess the self-consciousness of real men and women. This constitutes a radical change in the conception of the nature of statuary. In sculpture, as in painting, the Classical revolution had occurred.

EARLY AND HIGH CLASSICAL PERIODS

Art historians date the beginning of the Classical* age from a historical event: the defeat of the Persian invaders of Greece by the allied Hellenic city-states. Shortly after the Persians occupied and sacked Athens in 480 BCE, the Greeks won a decisive naval victory over the invaders at Salamis. It had been a difficult war, and at times it appeared that Asia would swallow up Greece and that the Persian king Xerxes would rule over all. When the Persians destroyed Miletos, a Greek city on the western coast of present-day Turkey, in 494 BCE, they killed the male inhabitants and sold the women and children into slavery. The narrow escape of the Greeks from domination by Asian "barbarians" nurtured a sense of Hellenic identity so strong that from then on, European civilization would be distinct from the civilization of Asia, even though they continued to interact. Typical of the time were the views of the great dramatist Aeschylus (ca. 525–456 BCE), who celebrated, in his *Oresteia* trilogy, the triumph of reason and law over barbarous crimes, blood feuds, and mad vengeance. As a veteran himself of the epic battle of Marathon, Aeschylus repudiated in majestic verse all the slavish and inhuman traits of nature that the Greeks at that time of crisis associated with the Persians.

*In *Art through the Ages,* the adjective "Classical," with uppercase *C,* refers specifically to the Classical period of ancient Greece, 480–323 BCE. Lowercase "*classical*" refers to Greco-Roman antiquity in general—that is, the period treated in Chapters 5, 6, and 7.

Architecture and Architectural Sculpture

Historians universally consider the decades following the removal of the Persian threat the high point of Greek civilization. This is the era of the dramatists Sophocles and Euripides, as well as Aeschylus; the historian Herodotus; the statesman Pericles; the philosopher Socrates; and many of the most famous Greek architects, sculptors, and painters.

Temple of Zeus, Olympia. The first great monument of Classical art and architecture is the Temple of Zeus at Olympia, site of the Olympic Games. The architect was LIBON OF ELIS, who began work on the temple about 470 BCE and completed it by 457 BCE. Today the structure is in ruins, its picturesque tumbled columns an eloquent reminder of the effect of the passage of time on even the grandest monuments that humans have built. A good sense of its original appearance can be gleaned, however, from a slightly later Doric temple (FIG. 5-30) at Paestum modeled closely on the Olympian shrine of Zeus—the temple usually identified as Hera's second at the site (the Temple of Hera II) but possibly a shrine dedicated to Apollo. The plans and elevations of both temples follow the pattern of the Temple of Aphaia (FIG. 5-26) at Aegina: an even number of columns (six) on the short ends, two columns in antis, and two rows of columns in two stories inside the cella. But the Temple of Zeus was more lavishly decorated than even the Aphaia temple. Statues filled both pediments, and narrative reliefs adorned the six metopes over the doorway in the pronaos and the matching six of the opisthodomos.

The Olympia metopes are thematically connected with the site, for they depict the 12 labors of Herakles (see "Herakles, the Greatest Greek Hero," page 126), the legendary founder of the Olympic

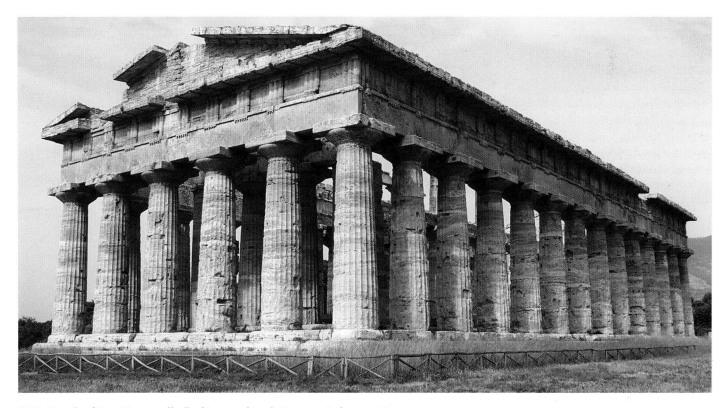

5-30 **Temple of Hera II or Apollo (looking northeast), Paestum, Italy, ca. 460 BCE.**

The model for the second Hera(?) temple at Paestum was Libon's Zeus temple at Olympia. The Paestum temple reflects the Olympia design, but lacks the pedimental sculpture of its model.

Herakles, the Greatest Greek Hero

Greek heroes were a class of mortals intermediate between ordinary humans and the immortal gods. Most often the children of gods, some were great warriors, such as those Homer celebrated for their exploits at Troy. Others went from one fabulous adventure to another, ridding the world of monsters and generally benefiting humankind. The Greeks worshiped many of their heroes after their death, especially in the cities with which they were most closely associated.

The greatest Greek hero was Herakles (the Roman Hercules), born in Thebes, the son of Zeus and Alkmene, a mortal woman. Zeus's jealous wife, Hera, hated Herakles and sent two serpents to attack him in his cradle, but the infant strangled them. Later, Hera caused the hero to go mad and kill his wife and children. As punishment, he was condemned to perform 12 great labors. In the first, he defeated the legendary lion of Nemea and ever after wore its pelt. The lion's skin and his weapon, a club, are Herakles's distinctive attributes (FIGS. 5-63A, 5-66, and 7-58A). The hero's last task was to obtain the golden apples that the goddess Gaia gave to Hera at her marriage (FIG. 5-31). They grew from a tree in the garden of the Hesperides at the western edge of the ocean, where a dragon guarded them.

After completion of the 12 seemingly impossible tasks, Herakles was awarded immortality. Athena, who had watched over him carefully throughout his life and assisted him in performing the labors, introduced him into the realm of the gods on Mount Olympus. According to legend, it was Herakles who established the Olympic Games.

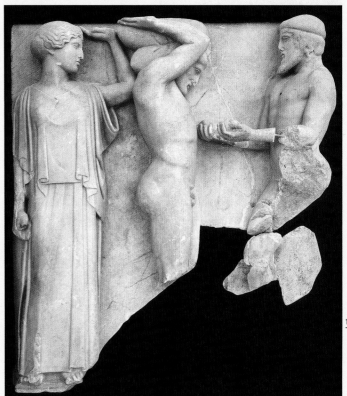

5-31 **Athena, Herakles, and Atlas with the apples of the Hesperides, metope from the Temple of Zeus, Olympia, Greece, ca. 470–456 BCE. Marble, 5′ 3″ high. Archaeological Museum, Olympia.**

Herakles founded the Olympic Games, and his 12 labors were the subjects of the 12 metopes of the Zeus temple. This one shows the hero holding up the sky (with Athena's aid) for Atlas.

Games. In the metope illustrated here (FIG. 5-31), Herakles holds up the sky (with the aid of the goddess Athena—and a cushion) in place of Atlas, who had undertaken the dangerous journey to fetch the golden apples of the Hesperides for the hero. Herakles will soon transfer the load back to Atlas (at the right, still holding the apples), but at the moment the sculptor chose to depict, each of the very high relief figures stands quietly with serene dignity. In both attitude and dress (a simple Doric peplos for Athena), these Olympia figures display a severity that contrasts sharply with the smiling and elaborately clad figures of the Late Archaic period. Consequently, many art historians call this Early Classical phase of Greek art the *Severe Style*.

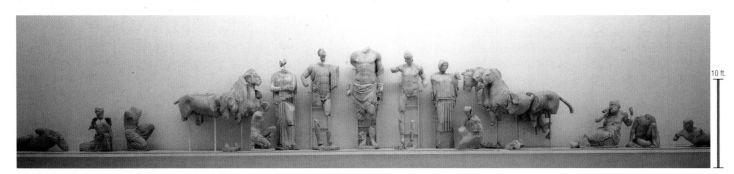

5-32 **Chariot race of Pelops and Oinomaos, east pediment, Temple of Zeus, Olympia, Greece, ca. 470–456 BCE. Marble, 87′ wide. Archaeological Museum, Olympia.**

The east pediment of the Zeus temple depicts the legendary chariot race across the Peloponnesos from Olympia to Corinth. The actors in the pediment faced the starting point of Olympic chariot races.

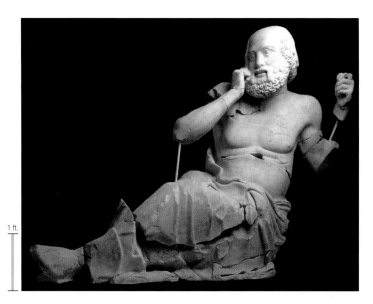

5-33 **Seer, from the east pediment (FIG. 5-32) of the Temple of Zeus, Olympia, Greece, ca. 470–456 BCE. Marble, 4′ 6″ high. Archaeological Museum, Olympia.**

The balding seer in the Olympia east pediment is a rare depiction of old age in Classical sculpture. He has a shocked expression because he foresees the tragic outcome of the chariot race.

The subject of the Temple of Zeus's east pediment (FIG. 5-32) is the chariot race between Pelops (from whom the Peloponnesos region takes its name) and King Oinomaos. The story, which had deep local significance, is a sinister one. Oinomaos had one daughter, Hippodameia, and a prophecy foretold that he would die if she married. Consequently, Oinomaos challenged any suitor who wished to make Hippodameia his bride to a chariot race from Olympia to Corinth. If the suitor won, he also won the hand of the king's daughter. But if he lost, Oinomaos killed him. The outcome of each race was inevitable, however, because Oinomaos possessed the divine horses of his father, Ares.

To ensure his victory when all others had failed, Pelops resorted to bribing the king's groom, Myrtilos, to rig the royal chariot so that it would collapse during the race. Oinomaos was killed and Pelops won his bride, but he drowned Myrtilos rather than pay his debt to him. Before he died, Myrtilos brought a curse on Pelops and his descendants. This curse led to the murder of Pelops's son, Atreus, and to events that figure prominently in some of the greatest Greek tragedies of the Classical era, Aeschylus's three plays known collectively as the *Oresteia*: the sacrifice by Atreus's son, Agamemnon, of his daughter, Iphigeneia; the slaying of Agamemnon by Aegisthus, lover of Agamemnon's wife, Clytaemnestra; and the murder of Aegisthus and Clytaemnestra by Orestes, the son of Agamemnon and Clytaemnestra.

Indeed, the pedimental statues (FIG. 5-32), which appropriately faced toward the starting point of all Olympic chariot races, are posed as though they are actors on a stage—Zeus in the center, Oinomaos and his wife on one side, Pelops and Hippodameia on the other, and their respective chariots to each side. All are quiet. The horrible events known to every spectator have yet to occur. Only one man reacts—a seer (FIG. 5-33) who knows the future. He is a remarkable figure. Unlike the gods, heroes, and noble youths and maidens who are the almost exclusive subjects of Archaic and Classical Greek statuary, this seer is a rare depiction of old age.

He has a balding, wrinkled head and sagging musculature—and a shocked expression on his face. This is a true show of emotion, unlike the stereotypical Archaic smile, and is without precedent in earlier Greek sculpture and not a regular feature of Greek art until the Hellenistic age.

In the west pediment (FIG. 5-33A), Apollo (FIG. 5-34), the central figure, is also at rest, but all around him is a chaotic scene of Greeks battling centaurs. This mixture of calm, even pensive, figures and others involved in violent action also characterizes most of the narrative reliefs of the 12 metopes (FIG. 5-31) of the Zeus temple.

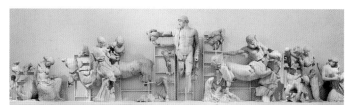

⬀ 5-33A West pediment, Temple of Zeus, Olympia, ca. 470–456 BCE.

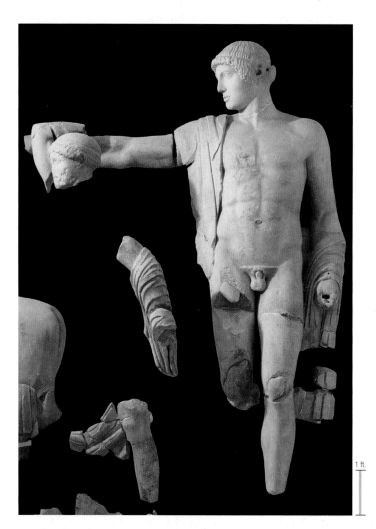

5-34 **Apollo, from the west pediment (FIG. 5-33A) of the Temple of Zeus, Olympia, Greece, ca. 470–456 BCE. Marble, restored height 10′ 8″. Archaeological Museum, Olympia.**

The model of calm rationality, Apollo, with a commanding gesture of his right hand, attempts to bring order out of the chaotic struggle all around him between the Lapiths and the beastly centaurs.

Statuary

The hallmark of Early Classical statuary is the abandonment of the rigid and unnatural Egyptian-inspired pose of Archaic statues. The figures in the Olympia pediments exemplify this radical break with earlier practice, but the change occurred even earlier—at the very moment that Greece was under attack by the Persians.

Kritios Boy. Although it is well under life-size, the marble statue known as the *Kritios Boy* (FIG. 5-35)—because art historians once thought it was the work of the sculptor Kritios—is one of the most important statues in the history of art. Never before had a sculptor been concerned with portraying how a human being (as opposed to a stone image) truly stands. Real people do not stand in the stiff-legged pose of the kouroi and korai or their Egyptian predecessors. Humans shift their weight and the position of the torso around the vertical (but flexible) axis of the spine. When humans move, the body's elastic musculo-skeletal structure dictates a harmonious, smooth motion of all its parts. The sculptor of the *Kritios Boy* was the first, or one of the first, to grasp this anatomical fact and to represent it in statuary. The youth dips his right hip slightly to the right, indicating the shifting of weight onto his left leg. His right leg is bent, at ease. The head, which no longer exhibits an Archaic smile, also turns slightly to the right and tilts, breaking the unwritten rule of frontality that dictated the form of virtually all earlier statues. This weight shift separates Classical from Archaic Greek statuary.

Riace Bronzes. An unknown sculptor carried the innovations of the *Kritios Boy* even further in the bronze statue (FIG. 5-36) of a warrior found in the sea near Riace, at the "toe" of the Italian "boot." It is one of a pair of statues that divers accidentally discovered in the cargo of a ship that sank in antiquity on its way from Greece probably to Rome, where Greek sculpture was much admired. Known as the *Riace Bronzes,* the two statues had to undergo several years of cleaning and restoration after nearly two millennia of sub-mersion in salt water, but they are nearly intact. The statue shown here lacks only its shield, sword, and helmet. It is a masterpiece of hollow-casting (see "Hollow-Casting Life-Size Bronze Statues," page 129), with inlaid eyes, silver teeth and eyelashes, and copper lips and nipples (FIG. I-17). The weight shift is more pronounced than in the *Kritios Boy.* The warrior's head turns more forcefully to the right, his shoulders tilt, his hips swing more markedly, and his arms have been freed from the body. Natural motion in space has replaced Archaic frontality and rigidity.

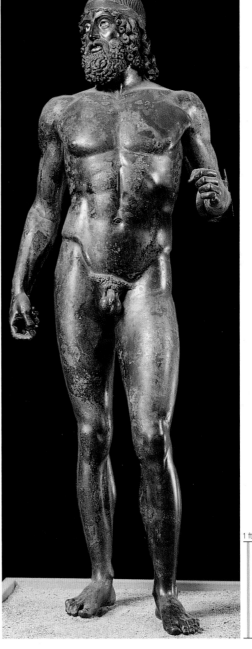

5-36 **Warrior, from the sea off Riace, Italy, ca. 460–450 BCE. Bronze, 6′ 6″ high. Museo Archeo-logico Nazionale, Reggio Calabria.**

The bronze Riace warrior statue has inlaid eyes, silver teeth and eyelashes, and copper lips and nipples (FIG. I-17). The weight shift is more pronounced than in the earlier marble *Kritios Boy* (FIG. 5-35).

5-35 *Kritios Boy,* **from the Acropolis, Athens, Greece, ca. 480 BCE. Marble, 3′ 10″ high. Acropolis Museum, Athens.**

This is the first statue to show how a person naturally stands. The Severe Style sculptor depicted the weight shift from one leg to the other. The head turns slightly, and the youth no longer smiles.

1 ft.

1 ft.

Hollow-Casting Life-Size Bronze Statues

Large-scale bronze statues such as the Riace warrior (FIG. 5-36), the Delphi charioteer (FIG. 5-38), and the Artemision god (FIG. 5-39) required great technical skill to produce. They could not be manufactured using a single simple mold like those used by Geometric and Archaic sculptors for their small-scale figurines (FIGS. 5-3 and 5-4). Weight, cost, and the tendency of large masses of bronze to distort when cooling made life-size castings in solid bronze impractical, if not impossible. Instead, Greek *foundry* workers hollow-cast large statues by the *lost-wax* (*cire perdue,* in French) method (FIG. 5-37). The lost-wax process entailed several steps and had to be repeated many times, because sculptors typically cast life-size and larger statues in parts—head, arms, hands, torso, and so forth. Even the long locks of hair of the Riace warrior (FIG. I-17) were cast separately from the rest of the head. The same is true for the hair over the ears of the *Charioteer of Delphi.*

First, the sculptor fashioned a full-size clay model of the intended statue. Then an assistant formed a clay master mold around the model and removed the mold in sections. When dry, the various pieces of the master mold were reassembled for each separate body part. Next, assistants applied a layer of beeswax to the inside of each mold. When the wax cooled, the sculptor removed the mold, revealing a hollow wax model in the shape of the original clay model. The artist could then correct or refine details—for example, engrave fingernails on the wax hands or individual locks of hair in a beard.

In the next stage, an assistant applied a final clay mold (*investment*) to the exterior of the wax model and poured liquid clay inside the model. Apprentices then hammered metal pins (*chaplets*) through the new mold to connect the investment with the clay core (FIG. 5-37, *left*). Next, the wax was melted out ("lost") and molten bronze poured into the mold in its place (FIG. 5-37, *right*). When the bronze hardened and assumed the shape of the wax model, the bronze-caster removed the investment and as much of the core as possible, completing the hollow-casting process. The last step was to fit together and solder the individually cast pieces, smooth the joins and any surface imperfections, inlay the eyes, and add teeth, eyelashes, and accessories such as swords and wreaths. Life-size bronze statues produced in this way were very costly but highly prized.

5-37 **Two stages of the lost-wax method of bronze casting (after Sean A. Hemingway).**

Left: Chaplets connect a clay mold (investment), wax model, and clay core. *Right:* With the wax melted out, the molten bronze is poured into the mold to form the cast bronze head.

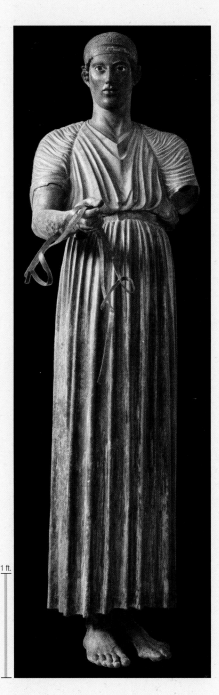

1 ft.

5-38 **Charioteer (*Charioteer of Delphi*), from a group dedicated by Polyzalos of Gela in the Sanctuary of Apollo (FIG. 5-16A), Delphi, Greece, ca. 470 BCE. Bronze, 5′ 11″ high. Archaeological Museum, Delphi.**

The charioteer was part of a large bronze group that also included a chariot, a team of horses, and a groom. The assemblage required hundreds of individually cast pieces soldered together.

Charioteer of Delphi. A bronze statuary group that equals or exceeds the Riace warrior in technical quality is the chariot group set up a decade or two earlier at Delphi (FIG. 5-16A) by the tyrant Polyzalos of Gela (Sicily) to commemorate his brother Hieron's victory in the Delphic Pythian Games. Almost all that remains of the large group composed of the Sicilian driver, the chariot, the team

of horses, and a young groom is the bronze charioteer popularly known as the *Charioteer of Delphi* (FIG. 5-38). He stands in an almost Archaic pose, but the turn of the head and feet in opposite directions as well as a slight twist at the waist are in keeping with the Severe Style. The moment that the sculptor chose for depiction was not during the frenetic race but after, when the charioteer modestly held his horses quietly in the winner's circle. He grasps the reins in his outstretched right hand (the lower left arm, cast separately, is missing), and he wears the standard charioteer's garment, girdled high and held in at the shoulders and the back to keep it from flapping. The folds emphasize both the verticality and calm of the figure and recall the flutes of a Greek column. The fillet that holds the charioteer's hair in place is inlaid with silver. The eyes are glass paste, shaded by delicate lashes individually cut from a sheet of bronze and soldered to the head.

Artemision Zeus. The male human form in motion is, by contrast, the subject of another Early Classical bronze statue (FIG. 5-39), which, like the Riace warrior, divers found in an ancient shipwreck, in this case off the coast of Greece itself at Cape Artemision. The bearded god once hurled a weapon held in his right hand, probably a thunderbolt, in which case he is Zeus. A less likely suggestion is that this is Poseidon with his trident (see "Gods and Goddesses," page 107). Both arms are boldly extended, and the right heel is raised off the ground, underscoring the lightness and tensile strength of hollow-cast life-size statues.

Myron, *Diskobolos*. A bronze statue similar to the Artemision Zeus was the renowned *Diskobolos* (*Discus Thrower*) by the Early Classical master MYRON. The original is lost. Only marble copies (FIG. 5-40) survive, made in Roman times, when demand so far exceeded the supply of Greek statues that a veritable industry was born to meet the call for Greek statuary to display in public places and private villas alike. Usually, the copies were of less costly painted marble, which presented a very different appearance from shiny bronze. In most cases, the copyist also had to add an intrusive tree trunk to support the great weight of the stone statue, and to place struts between arms and body to strengthen weak points. The copies rarely approach the quality of the originals, and the Roman sculptors sometimes took liberties with their models according to their own tastes and needs. Occasionally, for example, sculptors created a mirror image of the original for a specific setting. Nevertheless, the copies are indispensable today. Without them it would be impossible to reconstruct the history of Greek sculpture after the Archaic period.

Myron's *Discus Thrower* is a vigorous action statue, like the Artemision Zeus, but the sculptor posed the body in an almost

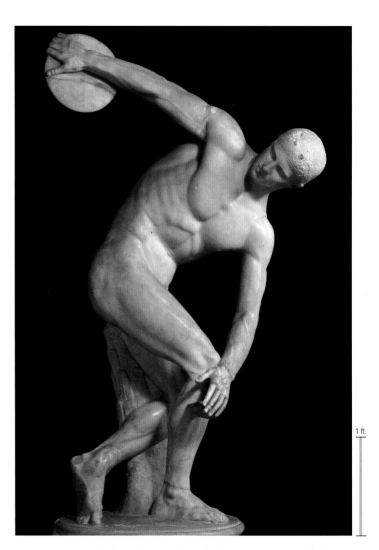

5-39 Zeus (or Poseidon?), from the sea off Cape Artemision, Greece, ca. 460–450 BCE. Bronze, 6′ 10″ high. National Archaeological Museum, Athens.

In this statue, the god—probably Zeus hurling a thunderbolt—boldly extends both arms and raises his right heel off the ground, underscoring the lightness and stability of hollow-cast bronze statues.

5-40 MYRON, *Diskobolos* (*Discus Thrower*), from the Esquiline hill, Rome, Italy. Roman copy of a bronze statue of ca. 450 BCE. Marble, 5′ 1″ high. Palazzo Massimo alle Terme, Museo Nazionale Romano, Rome.

This marble copy of Myron's lost bronze statue captures how the sculptor froze the action of discus throwing and arranged the nude athlete's body and limbs so that they form two intersecting arcs.

Polykleitos's Prescription for the Perfect Statue

In his treatise simply called the *Canon,* Polykleitos of Argos (FIG. 5-41) sought to define what constituted a perfect statue, one that could serve as the standard by which all other statues might be judged. How does one make a "perfect statue"? What principles guided the Greek master in formulating his canon?

One of the most influential philosophers of the ancient world was Pythagoras of Samos, who lived during the latter part of the sixth century BCE. A famous geometric theorem still bears his name. Pythagoras also is said to have discovered that harmonic chords in music are produced on the strings of a lyre at regular intervals that may be expressed as ratios of whole numbers—for example, 2:1, 3:2, 4:3. He and his followers, the Pythagoreans, believed more generally that underlying harmonic proportions could be found in all of nature, determining the form of the cosmos as well as of things on earth, and that beauty resided in harmonious numerical ratios.

Following this reasoning, Polykleitos concluded that the way to create a perfect statue would be to design it according to an all-encompassing mathematical formula. The treatise in which the Argive sculptor recorded the proportions he used is unfortunately lost, but Galen of Pergamon, a renowned Greek physician who lived during the second century CE, summarized the sculptor's philosophy as follows:

> [Beauty arises from] the commensurability [*symmetria*] of the parts, such as that of finger to finger, and of all the fingers to the palm and the wrist, and of these to the forearm, and of the forearm to the upper arm, and, in fact, of everything to everything else, just as it is written in the *Canon* of Polykleitos. . . . Polykleitos supported his treatise [by making] a statue according to the tenets of his treatise, and called the statue, like the work, the *Canon.**

This is why Pliny the Elder, whose first-century CE multivolume *Natural History* is one of the most important sources for the history of Greek art, maintained that Polykleitos "alone of men is deemed to have rendered art itself [that is, the theoretical basis of art] in a work of art."[†]

Polykleitos's belief that a successful statue resulted from the precise application of abstract principles is reflected in an anecdote (probably a later invention) told by the third-century CE Roman historian Aelian:

> Polykleitos made two statues at the same time, one which would be pleasing to the crowd and the other according to the principles of his art. In accordance with the opinion of each person who came into his workshop, he altered something and changed its form, submitting to the advice of each. Then he put both statues on display. The one was marvelled at by everyone, and the other was laughed

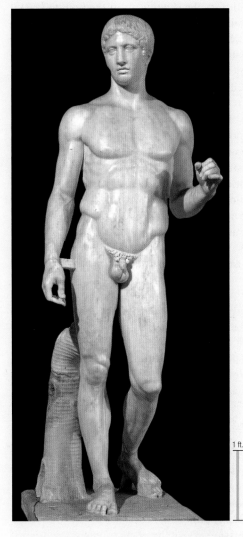

5-41 POLYKLEITOS, *Doryphoros* (*Spear Bearer*). Roman copy from the palaestra, Pompeii, Italy, of a bronze statue of ca. 450–440 BCE. Marble, 6′ 11″ high. Museo Archeologico Nazionale, Naples.

Polykleitos sought to portray the perfect man and to impose order on human movement. He achieved his goals through harmonic proportions and a system of cross-balancing for all parts of the body.

1 ft.

at. Thereupon Polykleitos said, "But the one that you find fault with, you made yourselves; while the one that you marvel at, I made."[‡]

Galen, Pliny, and Aelian are only three of the many Greek and Roman authors who wrote about Greek art and artists. Although none of those writers was an art historian in the modern sense, the existence in the Greco-Roman world of theoretical treatises by artists and of a tradition of art criticism is noteworthy and without parallel in antiquity or during the Middle Ages.

*Galen, *De placitis Hippocratis et Platonis,* 5. Translated by J. J. Pollitt, *The Art of Ancient Greece: Sources and Documents* (New York: Cambridge University Press, 1990), 76.
†Pliny the Elder, *Natural History,* 34.55. Translated by Pollitt, 75.
‡Aelian, *Varia historia,* 14.8. Translated by Pollitt, 79.

Archaic manner, with profile limbs and a nearly frontal chest, suggesting the tension of a coiled spring. Like the arm of a pendulum clock, the right arm of the *Diskobolos* has reached the apex of its arc, but has not yet begun to swing down again. Myron froze the action and arranged the body and limbs to form two intersecting arcs (one from the discus to the left hand, one from the head to the right knee), creating the impression of a tightly stretched bow a moment before the archer releases the string. This tension, however, is not mirrored in the athlete's face, which remains expressionless. Once

again, as in the warrior statue (FIG. 5-29) from the Aegina east pediment, the head is turned away from the spectator. In contrast to Archaic athlete statues, the Classical *Diskobolos* does not perform for the spectator but concentrates on the task at hand.

Polykleitos, *Doryphoros.* One of the most frequently copied Greek statues was the *Doryphoros* (*Spear Bearer*) by POLYKLEITOS, the sculptor whose work exemplifies the intellectual rigor of Classical art. The best marble replica (FIG. 5-41) stood in a *palaestra* (gymnasium) at Pompeii, where it served as a model for Roman athletes. The *Doryphoros* embodied Polykleitos's vision of the ideal statue of a nude male athlete or warrior. (The *Spear Bearer* may also have held a shield.) In fact, the sculptor made it as a demonstration piece to accompany a treatise on the subject. *Spear Bearer* is a modern descriptive title for the statue. The name that Polykleitos assigned to it was *Canon* (see "Polykleitos's Prescription for the Perfect Statue," page 131).

The *Doryphoros* is the culmination of the evolution in Greek statuary from the Archaic kouros to the *Kritios Boy* to the Riace warrior. The weight shift is more pronounced than ever before in a standing statue, but Polykleitos was not content with simply rendering a figure that stands naturally. His aim was to impose order on human movement, to make it "beautiful," to "perfect" it. He achieved this through *contrapposto* ("counterbalance"). What appears at first to be a casually natural pose is, in fact, the result of an extremely complex and subtle organization of the figure's various parts. Note, for instance, how the straight-hanging arm echoes the rigid supporting leg, providing the figure's right side with the columnar stability needed to anchor the left side's dynamically flexed limbs. If read anatomically, however, the tensed and relaxed limbs may be seen to oppose each other diagonally—the right arm and the left leg are relaxed, and the tensed supporting leg opposes the flexed arm, which held a spear. In like manner, the head turns to the right while the hips twist slightly to the left. And although the *Doryphoros* seems to take a step forward, he does not move. This dynamic asymmetrical balance, this motion while at rest, and the resulting harmony of opposites are the essence of the Polykleitan style.

The Athenian Acropolis

While Polykleitos was formulating his *Canon* in Argos, the Athenians, under the leadership of Pericles (ca. 495–429 BCE), were at work on one of the most ambitious building projects ever undertaken: the reconstruction of the Acropolis after the Persian sack. In September 480 BCE, the Athenian commander Themistocles decisively defeated the Persian navy off the island of Salamis, southwest of Athens, and forced it to retreat to Asia. Athens, despite the damage it suffered at the hands of the army of Xerxes, emerged from the war with enormous power and prestige. In 478 BCE, while the Persian devastation was still fresh in everyone's memory, the Greeks formed an alliance for mutual protection against any renewed threat from the East. The new confederacy came to be known as the Delian League, because its headquarters were on the sacred island of Delos, midway between the Greek mainland and the coast of Asia Minor. Although at the outset each league member had an equal vote, Athens was "first among equals," providing the allied fleet commander and determining which cities were to furnish ships and which were instead to pay an annual tribute to the treasury at Delos.

Continued fighting against the Persians kept the Delian alliance intact, but Athens gradually assumed a dominant role. In 454 BCE, the league's treasury was transferred to Athens, ostensibly for security reasons. Pericles, who was only in his teens when the Persians laid waste to the Acropolis, was by midcentury the recognized leader of the Athenians, and he succeeded in converting the alliance into an Athenian empire. Tribute continued to be paid, but the Athenians did not spend the surplus reserves for the common good of the allied Greek states. Instead, Pericles expropriated the money to underwrite his enormously costly grand plan to embellish the Acropolis of Athens.

The reaction of the allies—in reality the subjects of Athens—was predictable. Plutarch, who wrote a biography of Pericles in the early second century CE, reported not only the wrath of the Greek victims of Athenian tyranny but also the protest voiced against Pericles's decision even in the Athenian assembly. Greece, Pericles's enemies said, had been dealt "a terrible, wanton insult" when Athens used the funds contributed out of necessity for a common war effort to "gild and embellish itself with images and extravagant temples, like some pretentious woman decked out with precious stones."[3] That the Delian League was the source of the funds used for the Acropolis building program is important to keep in mind when examining those great and universally admired buildings erected to realize Pericles's vision of his polis reborn from the ashes of the Persian sack. They are not the glorious fruits of Athenian democracy but are instead the by-products of tyranny and the abuse of power. Too often art and architectural historians do not ask how patrons, whether public or private, paid for the monuments they commissioned. The answer can be very revealing—and very embarrassing.

Portrait of Pericles. A number of extant Roman marble sculptures are copies of a famous bronze portrait statue of Pericles by KRESILAS, who was born on Crete but worked in Athens. The

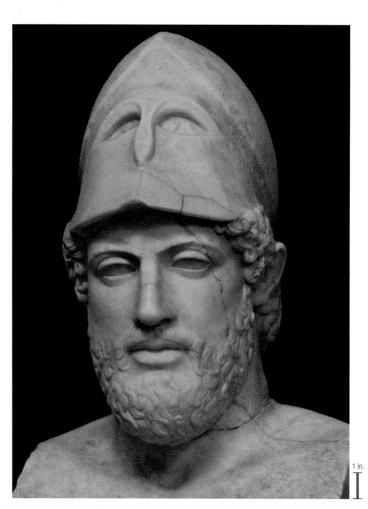

5-42 KRESILAS, *Pericles*. Head of a Roman herm copy of the bronze statue of ca. 429 BCE. Marble, full herm 6′ high; detail 1′ 6″ high. Musei Vaticani, Rome.

In his portrait of Pericles, Kresilas was said to have made a noble man appear even nobler. Classical Greek portraits were not likenesses but idealized images in which humans appeared godlike.

Athenians set up the portrait on the Acropolis, probably immediately after their leader's death in 429 BCE. Kresilas depicted Pericles in heroic nudity, and his portrait must have resembled the Riace warrior (FIG. 5-36). The copies reproduce the head only, sometimes in the form of a *herm* (FIG. 5-42)—that is, a sculpted head on a square pillar. The inscription on the Vatican herm (not visible in the photograph) reads "Pericles, son of Xanthippos, the Athenian." Pericles wears the helmet of a *strategos* (general), the elective position he held 15 times. The Athenian leader was said to have had an abnormally elongated skull, and Kresilas recorded this feature (while also concealing it) by providing a glimpse through the helmet's eye slots of the hair at the top of the head. This, together with the unblemished features of Pericles's aloof face and, no doubt, his body's perfect physique, led Pliny to assert that Kresilas had the ability to make noble men appear even more noble in their portraits. This praise was apt because the Acropolis statue was not a portrait in the modern sense of a record of unique features, but an image of an individual that conformed to the Classical ideal of beauty. Pliny refers to Kresilas's "portrait" as "the Olympian Pericles," because the statue made Pericles appear almost godlike.[4]

Periclean Acropolis. The centerpiece of the Periclean building program on the Acropolis (FIG. 5-43) was the Parthenon (FIGS. 5-1 and 5-44, no. 1), a magnificent marble building dedicated to Athena Parthenos that had neither a priestess nor an altar for her worship. The Parthenon was therefore not a temple in the strict sense. Construction began in 447 BCE and proceeded rapidly despite the complexity of the project. By 438 BCE, the building campaign was complete, although work on the Parthenon's ambitious sculptural ornamentation continued until 432 BCE. In 437 BCE, the Parthenon stonemasons commenced construction of the Propylaia (FIG. 5-44, no. 2), the grand new western gateway to the Acropolis (the only accessible side of the natural plateau). Work ceased, however, in 432 BCE at the outbreak of the Peloponnesian War between Athens and Sparta and never resumed. Two later temples, the Erechtheion (no. 4) and the Temple of Athena Nike (no. 5), built after Pericles died, were probably also part of the original project. The greatest Athenian architects and sculptors of the Classical period focused their attention on the construction and decoration of these four buildings.

That these ancient buildings exist at all today is something of a miracle. In the Middle Ages, the Parthenon, for example, became a Byzantine and later a Roman Catholic church and then, after the Ottoman conquest of Greece, a mosque. With each rededication, religious officials remodeled the building. The Christians early on removed the colossal statue of Athena inside. The churches had a great curved *apse* at the east end housing the altar. The Ottomans added a *minaret* (tower used to call Muslims to prayer). In 1687, the Venetians besieged the Acropolis. One of their rockets scored a direct hit on the ammunition depot that the Ottomans had installed in part of the Parthenon. The resultant explosion blew out the building's center. To make matters worse, the Venetians subsequently tried to remove some of the statues from the Parthenon's pediments. In more than one case, the workmen dropped the statues, which smashed on the ground. From 1801 to 1803, while Greece was part of the Ottoman Empire, Thomas Bruce (1766–1841), Lord Elgin, brought most of the surviving sculptures to England. For the past two centuries, they have been on exhibit in London's British Museum, although Greece has appealed many times for the return of the "Elgin Marbles" and has even built a new museum near the Acropolis to house them, but the British have refused to repatriate the Acropolis sculptures. In the ongoing debate about who owns the Elgin Marbles, proponents of both sides have passionately advanced compelling arguments.

Today, a uniquely modern blight threatens the Parthenon and the other buildings of the Periclean age. The corrosive emissions of factories and automobiles are decomposing the ancient marbles. A comprehensive campaign has been under way for decades to

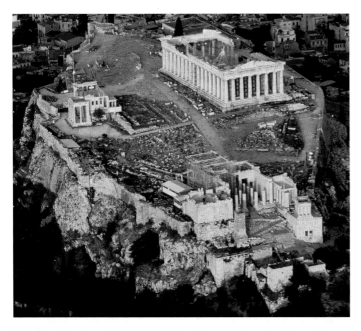

5-43 Aerial view of the Acropolis (looking southeast), Athens, Greece.

Under the leadership of Pericles, the Athenians undertook the costly project of reconstructing the Acropolis after the Persian sack of 480 BCE. The funds came from the Delian League treasury.

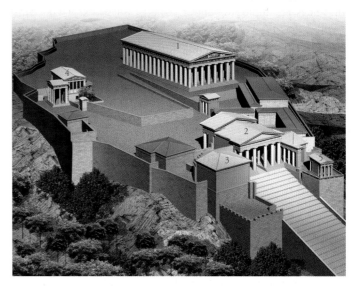

5-44 Restored view of the Acropolis, Athens, Greece (John Burge). (1) Parthenon, (2) Propylaia, (3) pinakotheke, (4) Erechtheion, (5) Temple of Athena Nike.

The fifth-century BCE transformation of the Acropolis under Pericles consisted of a new entranceway (the Propylaia) and three shrines (the Parthenon, the Erechtheion, and the Temple of Athena Nike).

protect the columns and walls from further deterioration. What little original sculpture remained in place when modern restoration began is now in the new museum's climate-controlled rooms.

Parthenon: Architecture. Despite the ravages of time and humans, most of the Parthenon's peripteral colonnade (FIG. 5-1) is still standing (or has been reerected), and art historians know a great deal about the building and its sculptural program. The architect was Iktinos, assisted, according to some sources, by KALLIKRATES, who may have played the role of contractor, supervising the construction of the building. The statue of Athena (FIG. 5-46) in the cella was the work of Phidias, who was also the overseer of the temple's sculptural decoration. In fact, Plutarch stated that Phidias was in charge of the entire Acropolis project.[5]

Just as the contemporaneous *Doryphoros* (FIG. 5-41) may be seen as the culmination of nearly two centuries of searching for the ideal proportions of the various human body parts, so, too, the Parthenon may be viewed as the ideal solution to the Greek architect's quest for perfect proportions in Doric temple design (see "The Perfect Temple," page 105), even if the building did not function as a temple proper. Its well-spaced columns, with their slender shafts, and the capitals, with their straight-sided conical echinuses, are the ultimate refinement of the bulging and squat Doric columns and compressed capitals of the Archaic Hera temple (FIG. 5-14) at Paestum. The Parthenon architects and Polykleitos were kindred spirits in their belief that beautiful proportions resulted from strict adherence to harmonic numerical ratios, whether in a temple more than 200 feet long or a life-size statue of a nude man. For the Parthenon, the controlling ratio for the symmetria of the parts may be expressed algebraically as $x = 2y + 1$. Thus, for example, the temple's plan (FIG. 5-45) called for 8 columns on the short ends and 17 on the long sides, because $17 = (2 \times 8) + 1$. The stylobate's ratio of width to length is 4:9, because $9 = (2 \times 4) + 1$. This ratio also characterizes the proportion of one column's diameter at the bottom to the distance between the centers of two adjacent column drums (the *interaxial*), and so forth.

The Parthenon's harmonious design and the mathematical precision of the sizes of its constituent elements tend to obscure the fact that the building is quite irregular in shape. Throughout the structure are pronounced deviations from the strictly horizontal and vertical lines assumed to be the basis of all Greek post-and-lintel designs. The stylobate, for example, curves upward at the center on the sides and both facades, forming a kind of shallow dome, and this curvature carries up into the entablature. Moreover, the peristyle columns lean inward slightly. Those at the corners have a diagonal inclination and are also about 2 inches thicker than the rest. If their lines continued, they would meet about 1.5 miles above the temple. These deviations from the norm meant that virtually every Parthenon block and drum had to be carved according to the special set of specifications dictated by its unique place in the structure. This was obviously a daunting task, and the builders must have had a reason for introducing these so-called refinements in the Parthenon. Some modern observers note, for example, how the curving of horizontal lines and the tilting of vertical ones create a dynamic balance in the building—a kind of architectural contrapposto—and give it a greater sense of life.

The oldest recorded explanation of the Parthenon's "refinements" is that of Vitruvius, a Roman architect of the late first century BCE (see "Vitruvius's *Ten Books on Architecture*," page 204). Vitruvius claimed to have had access to Iktinos's treatise on the Parthenon (again, note the kinship with the *Canon* of Polykleitos), and his rationale for the deviations therefore carries a lot of weight. Vitruvius maintained that these adjustments were made to compensate for optical illusions, noting, for example, that if a stylobate is laid out on a level surface, it will appear to sag at the center. He also recommended that the corner columns of a building should be thicker because they are surrounded by light and would otherwise appear thinner than their neighbors.

The Parthenon is "irregular" in other ways as well. One of the ironies of this most famous of all Doric buildings is that it incorporates Ionic elements. Although the cella (FIG. 5-46) had a two-story Doric colonnade, the back room (which housed the goddess's treasury and the tribute collected from the Delian League) had four tall and slender Ionic columns as sole supports for the superstructure (FIG. 5-45). And whereas the temple's exterior had a standard Doric frieze (FIGS. 5-47 and 5-47A), the inner frieze (FIGS. 5-50 and 5-50A) that ran around the top of the cella wall was Ionic. Perhaps this fusion of Doric and Ionic elements reflects the Athenians' belief that the Ionians of the Aegean Islands and Asia Minor were descendants of Athenian settlers and were therefore their kin. (The Ionians take their name from Ion, the grandson of King Erechtheus of Athens.) Or it may be Pericles and Iktinos's way of suggesting that Athens was the leader of *all* the Greeks. In any case, a mix of Doric and Ionic features characterizes the fifth-century BCE buildings of the Acropolis as a whole.

5-45 Plan of the Parthenon, Acropolis, Athens, Greece, with diagram of the sculptural program (after Andrew Stewart), 447–432 BCE.

A team of sculptors directed by Phidias lavishly decorated the Parthenon with statues in both pediments, figural reliefs in all 92 Doric metopes, and an inner 524-foot sculptured Ionic frieze.

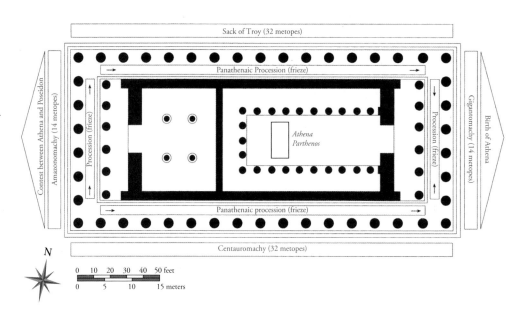

Sack of Troy (32 metopes)

Panathenaic Procession (frieze)

Contest between Athena and Poseidon

Amazonomachy (14 metopes)

Procession (frieze)

Athena Parthenos

Procession (frieze)

Gigantomachy (14 metopes)

Birth of Athena

Panathenaic procession (frieze)

Centauromachy (32 metopes)

N

0 10 20 30 40 50 feet

0 5 10 15 meters

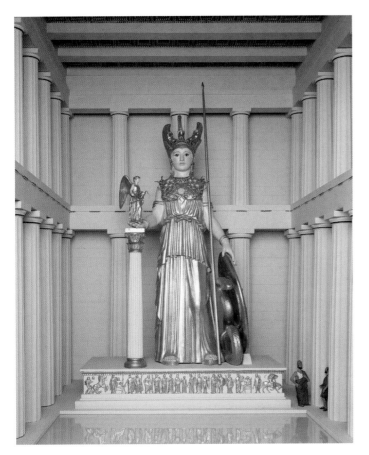

5-46 PHIDIAS, *Athena Parthenos,* in the cella of the Parthenon, Acropolis, Athens, Greece, ca. 438 BCE. Model of the lost chryselephantine statue. Royal Ontario Museum, Toronto.

Inside the cella of the Parthenon stood Phidias's 38-foot-tall gold-and-ivory *Athena Parthenos* (the Virgin). The goddess is fully armed and holds Nike (Victory) in her extended right hand.

Athena Parthenos. The decision to incorporate two sculptured friezes in the Parthenon's design is symptomatic of the enormous investment the Athenians made in the building project. This Pentelic marble shrine was more lavishly adorned than any Greek temple before it, Doric or Ionic. A mythological scene appears in every one of the 92 Doric metopes, and every inch of the 524-foot-long Ionic frieze depicts a procession and cavalcade. Dozens of larger-than-life-size statues filled both pediments. And inside was the most expensive item of all—Phidias's *Athena Parthenos,* a colossal gold-and-ivory (*chryselephantine*) statue of the virgin goddess. Art historians know a great deal about Phidias's lost statue from descriptions by Greek and Latin authors and from Roman copies. A model (FIG. 5-46) gives a good idea of its appearance and setting. Athena stood 38 feet tall, and to a large extent Iktinos designed the Parthenon around her. To accommodate the statue's huge size, the cella had to be wider than usual. This, in turn, dictated the width of the facade—eight columns at a time when six columns were the norm (FIGS. 5-25 and 5-30).

Athena was fully armed with shield, spear, and helmet, and she held Nike (the winged female personification of Victory) in her extended right hand. No one doubts that this Nike referred to the victory of 479 BCE. The memory of the Persian sack of the Acropolis was still vivid, and the Athenians were intensely conscious that by driving back the Persians, they had saved their civilization from the Eastern "barbarians" who had committed atrocities at Miletos. In

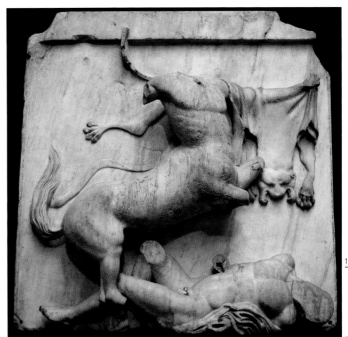

5-47 Centauromachy, metope 28 from the south side of the Parthenon, Acropolis, Athens, Greece, ca. 447–438 BCE. Marble, 4′ 8″ high. British Museum, London.

The Parthenon's centauromachy metopes allude to the Greek defeat of the Persians. Here the sculptor brilliantly distinguished the vibrant living centaur from the lifeless Greek corpse.

fact, Phidias's *Athena Parthenos* incorporated multiple allusions to the Persian defeat. On the thick soles of Athena's sandals was a representation of a centauromachy. High reliefs depicting the battle of Greeks and Amazons (*Amazonomachy*), in which Theseus drove the Amazons out of Athens, emblazoned the exterior of her shield. On the shield's interior, Phidias painted a gigantomachy. Each of these mythological contests was a metaphor for the triumph of order over chaos, of civilization over barbarism, and of Athens over Persia.

Parthenon: Metopes. Phidias took up these same themes again in the Parthenon's metopes. The best-preserved metopes (FIGS. 5-47 and 5-47A)—although the paint on these and all the other Parthenon marbles long ago disappeared—are those of the south side, which depicted the battle of Lapiths and centaurs, a combat in which Theseus played a major role. On one extraordinary slab (FIG. 5-47), a triumphant centaur rises up on its hind legs, exulting over the crumpled body of the Greek whom the horseman has defeated. The relief is so high that parts are fully in the round. Some have broken off. The sculptor brilliantly distin-

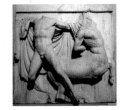

🔊 5-47A Centauromachy metope, Parthenon, ca. 447–438 BCE.

guished the vibrant, powerful form of the living beast from the lifeless corpse on the ground. In other metopes, the Greeks have the upper hand, but the full set suggests that the battle was a difficult one against a dangerous enemy and that losses as well as victories occurred. The same was true of the war against the Persians, and the centauromachy metopes—and also the gigantomachy, Amazonomachy, and Trojan War metopes—are allegorical references to the Greek-Persian conflict of the early fifth century BCE.

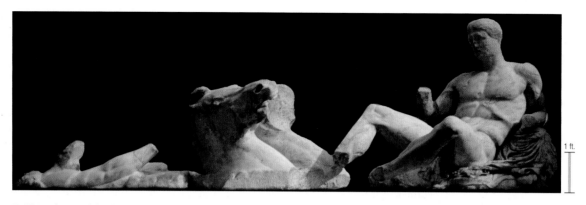

5-48 Helios and his horses, and Dionysos (Herakles?), from the east pediment of the Parthenon, Acropolis, Athens, Greece, ca. 438–432 BCE. Marble, greatest height 4′ 3″. British Museum, London.

The east pediment of the Parthenon depicts the birth of Athena. At the left, Helios and his horses emerge from the pediment's floor, suggesting the sun rising above the horizon at dawn.

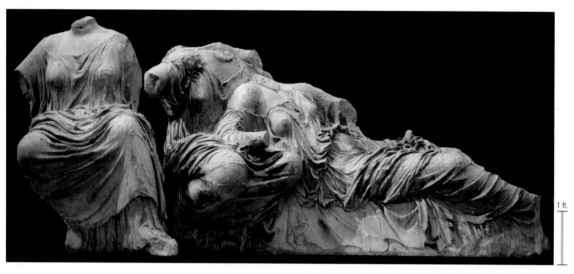

5-49 Three goddesses (Hestia, Dione, and Aphrodite?), from the east pediment of the Parthenon, Acropolis, Athens, Greece, ca. 438–432 BCE. Marble, greatest height 4′ 5″. British Museum, London.

The statues of Hestia, Dione, and Aphrodite conform perfectly to the shape of the Parthenon's east pediment. The thin and heavy folds of the garments alternately reveal and conceal the body forms.

Parthenon: Pediments. The subjects of the two pediments were especially appropriate for a building that celebrated Athena—and the Athenians. The east pediment (FIGS. 5-48, 5-49, and 5-49A) depicted the birth of the goddess. At the west (FIGS. 5-49B and 5-49C) was the contest between Athena and Poseidon to determine which one would become the city's patron deity. Athena won, giving her name to the polis and its citizens. It is significant that in the story and in the pediment, the Athenians are the judges of the relative merits of the two gods. The selection of this theme for the Parthenon reflects the same arrogance that led to the use of Delian League funds to adorn the Acropolis.

The Christians removed the center of the east pediment when they added an apse to the Parthenon at the time of its conversion into a church. What remains are the spectators to the left and the right who witnessed Athena's birth on Mount Olympus. At the far left (FIG. 5-48) are part of the head and arms of Helios (the Sun) and his chariot horses rising from the pediment floor. Next to them is a powerful male figure usually identified as Dionysos or possibly Herakles, who entered the realm of the gods on completion of his 12 labors (see "Herakles," page 126). At the right

(FIG. 5-49) are three goddesses, probably Hestia, Dione, and Aphrodite (see "Gods and Goddesses," page 107), and either Selene (the Moon) or Nyx (Night) and more horses (FIG. 5-49A), this time sinking below the pediment's floor. Here, Phidias, who must have designed the composition even if his assistants executed it, discovered an entirely new way to deal with the awkward

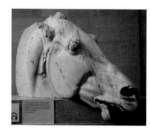

5-49A Horse of Selene or Nyx, Parthenon, ca. 438–432 BCE.

triangular frame of the pediment. Its floor is now the horizon line, and the charioteers and their horses move through it effortlessly.

The reclining figures next to the horses on each side of the pediment beautifully fill the space beneath the raking cornice. Dionysos/Herakles and Aphrodite in the lap of her mother, Dione, are imposing Olympian presences yet totally relaxed organic forms. The Athenian sculptors fully understood not only the surface appearance of human anatomy, both male and female, but also the mechanics of how muscles and bones make the body move. The

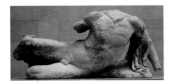

⬈5-49B River god, Parthenon, ca. 438–432 BCE.

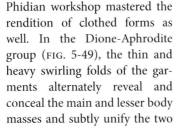

⬈5-49C Iris, Parthenon, ca. 438–432 BCE.

Phidian workshop mastered the rendition of clothed forms as well. In the Dione-Aphrodite group (FIG. 5-49), the thin and heavy swirling folds of the garments alternately reveal and conceal the main and lesser body masses and subtly unify the two figures. The articulation and integration of the bodies produce a wonderful variation of surface and play of light and shade. The statues of the west pediment (FIGS. 5-49B and 5-49C) are equally remarkable.

Parthenon: Ionic Frieze. In many ways, the most noteworthy part of the Parthenon's sculptural decoration is the inner Ionic frieze (FIGS. 5-50 and 5-50A). Scholars still debate its subject, but most agree that it represents the Panathenaic Festival procession that took place every four years in Athens. If this identification is correct, the Athenians judged themselves fit for inclusion in the Parthenon's iconographical program—a remarkable decision, because no Greek temple had ever featured a human event in its decoration. It is another example of the Athenians' extraordinarily high sense of self-worth.

The procession began at the Dipylon Gate, passed through the *agora* (central square), and ended on the Acropolis, where the Athenians placed a new peplos on an ancient wood statue of Athena. That statue (probably similar in general appearance to the *Lady of Auxerre*, FIG. 5-6) had been housed in the Archaic temple that the Persians razed in 480 BCE, but the Athenians removed it

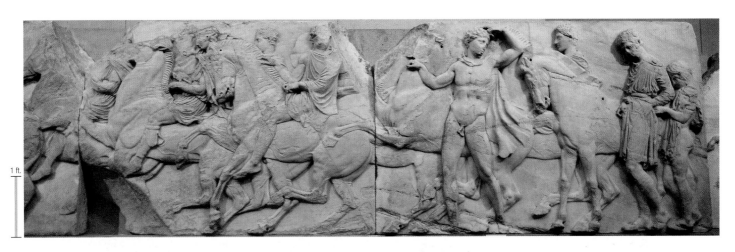

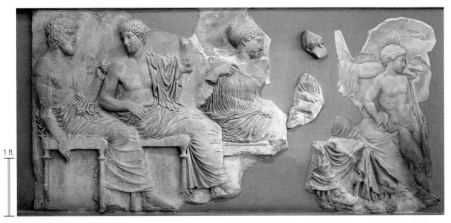

5-50 Three details of the Panathenaic Festival procession frieze, from the Parthenon, Acropolis, Athens, Greece, ca. 447–438 BCE. Marble, 3′ 6″ high. *Top:* horsemen (north frieze), British Museum, London. *Center:* Poseidon, Apollo, Artemis, Aphrodite, and Eros (east frieze), Acropolis Museum, Athens. *Bottom:* elders and maidens (east frieze), Musée du Louvre, Paris.

The Parthenon's Ionic frieze represents the Panathenaic procession of citizens on horseback and on foot under the gods' watchful eyes. The Parthenon celebrated the Athenians as much as Athena.

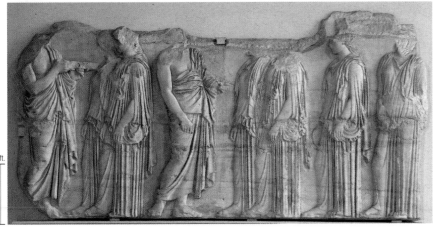

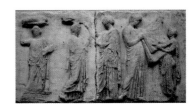

⬈5-50A Peplos ceremony, Parthenon, ca. 447–438 BCE.

before the attack for security reasons and eventually installed it in the Erechtheion (FIG. 5-53, no. 1). On the Parthenon frieze, the procession begins on the west side—that is, at the temple's rear, the side facing the gateway to the Acropolis. It then moves in parallel lines down the long north and south sides of the building and ends at the center of the east frieze (FIG. 5-50A), over the doorway to the cella housing Phidias's statue (FIGS. 5-45 and 5-46). It is noteworthy that the upper part of the frieze is in higher relief than the lower part so that the more distant and more shaded upper zone is as legible from the ground as the lower part of the frieze. This is another instance of how the Parthenon's builders took optical effects into consideration.

The frieze vividly communicates the procession's acceleration and deceleration. At the outset, on the west side, marshals gather, and youths mount their horses (FIG. 5-50, *top*). In the north and south friezes, the momentum picks up as the cavalcade moves from the lower town to the Acropolis, accompanied by musicians, jar carriers, and animals destined for sacrifice. On the east side, seated gods and goddesses (FIG. 5-50, *center*), the invited guests, watch the procession slow almost to a halt (FIG. 5-50, *bottom*) as it nears its goal at the shrine of Athena's ancient wood idol. Most remarkable of all is the role assigned to the Olympian deities. They do not take part in the festival or determine its outcome, but are merely spectators. Aphrodite, in fact, extends her left arm to draw her son Eros's attention to the Athenians, just as today a parent at a parade would point out important people to a child. Indeed, the Athenian people *were* important—self-important, one might say. They were the masters of an empire, and in Pericles's famous funeral oration for Athenians who lost their lives in the war against Persia, the leader painted a picture of Athens that elevated its citizens almost to the stature of gods. The Parthenon celebrated the greatness of Athens and the Athenians as much as it honored Athena.

Propylaia. Even before all the sculptures were in place on the Parthenon, work began on a grandiose new entrance to the Acropolis, the Propylaia (FIG. 5-51). The architect entrusted with this important commission was MNESIKLES. The site was a difficult one, on a steep slope, but Mnesikles succeeded in disguising the change in ground level by splitting the building into eastern and western sections (FIG. 5-44, no. 2), each one resembling a Doric temple

facade, hence the name Propylaia. (*Propylaia* is Greek for "gates," rather than "gate.") Practical considerations dictated that the space between the central pair of columns on each side be enlarged. This was the path that the vehicles and animals of the Panathenaic Festival procession took, and they required a wide ramped causeway. To either side of the central ramp were stairs for pedestrian traffic. Inside, tall, slender Ionic columns supported the split-level roof. Once again an Athenian architect mixed the two orders on the Acropolis. But as Iktinos did for the Parthenon, Mnesikles chose the Doric order for the stately exterior.

Mnesikles's full plan for the Propylaia was never executed. Of the side wings that were part of the original project, the northwest one (FIG. 5-44, no. 3) is of special importance in the history of art. In Roman times, it housed a *pinakotheke* ("picture gallery"). In it were displayed paintings on wood panels by some of the major artists of the fifth century BCE. It is uncertain whether this was the wing's original function. If it was, the Propylaia's pinakotheke, although not an independent building, is the first recorded structure built for the specific purpose of displaying paintings, and it is the forerunner of modern museums.

Erechtheion. In 421 BCE, work finally began on the temple that was to replace the Archaic Athena temple that the Persians had destroyed. The new structure, the Erechtheion (FIG. 5-52), built to the north of the old temple's remains, was to be a multiple shrine, however. It honored Athena and housed the ancient wood image of the goddess that was the goal of the Panathenaic Festival procession. But it also incorporated shrines to a host of other gods and demigods who loomed large in the city's legendary past. Among these were Erechtheus, an early king of Athens, during whose reign the ancient statuette of Athena was said to have fallen from the heavens, and Kekrops, another king of Athens, who served as judge of the contest between Athena and Poseidon (and who is present at the contest in the Parthenon's west pediment). In fact, the site chosen for the new temple was the very spot where that contest occurred. Poseidon had staked his claim to Athens by striking the Acropolis rock with his trident and producing a salt-water spring. The imprint of his trident remained for Athenians of the historical period (and visitors to the Acropolis today) to see on the north side of the Erechtheion. Nearby, Athena had miraculously caused an

5-51 MNESIKLES, Propylaia (looking west), Acropolis, Athens, Greece, 437–432 BCE.

Mnesikles disguised the change of ground level by splitting the Propylaia into eastern and western sections. Each facade resembles a Doric temple, but with a wider space between the central columns.

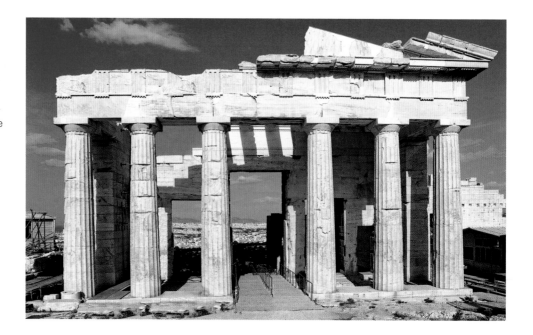

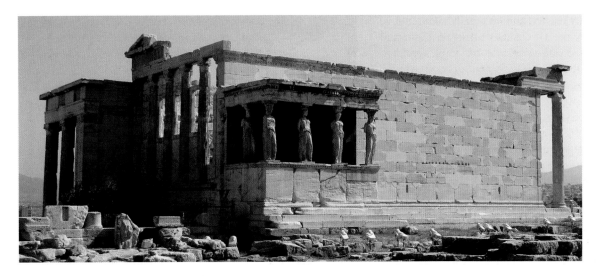

The Erechtheion is in many ways the antithesis of the Doric Parthenon directly across from it. An Ionic temple, it has some of the finest decorative details of any ancient Greek building.

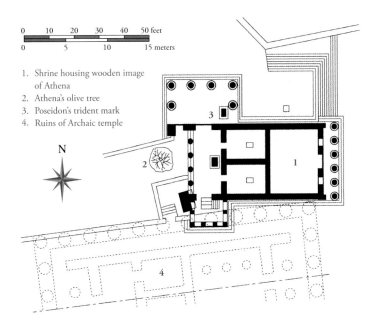

0 10 20 30 40 50 feet
0 5 10 15 meters

1. Shrine housing wooden image of Athena
2. Athena's olive tree
3. Poseidon's trident mark
4. Ruins of Archaic temple

N

5-53 Plan of the Erechtheion, Acropolis, Athens, Greece, ca. 421–405 BCE.

The asymmetrical form of the Erechtheion is unique for a Greek temple. It reflects the need to incorporate preexisting shrines into the plan, including those of the kings Erechtheus and Kekrops.

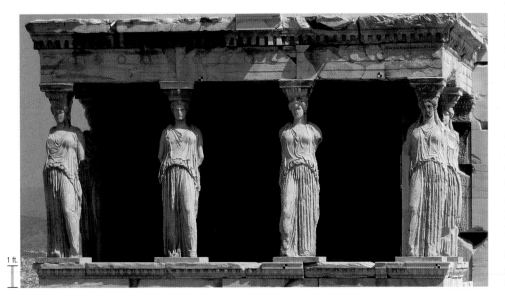

1 ft.

5-54 Caryatids of the south porch of the Erechtheion, Acropolis, Athens, Greece, ca. 421–405 BCE. Plaster casts of marble statues, 7′ 7″ high. Original statues in the Acropolis Museum, Athens, and the British Museum, London.

The south porch of the Erechtheion features updated Classical versions (with weight-shift stances) of the Archaic caryatids of the porch of the Siphnian Treasury (FIG. 5-17) at Delphi.

olive tree to grow. A tree still stands at the west end of the temple. In antiquity, Athena's tree reminded the citizens of the goddess's victory over Poseidon.

The asymmetrical plan (FIG. 5-53) of the Ionic Erechtheion is unique for a Greek temple and the antithesis of the simple and harmoniously balanced plan of the Doric Parthenon across the way. Its irregular form reflected the need to incorporate the tomb of Kekrops and other preexisting shrines, the trident mark, and the olive tree into a single complex. The unknown architect responsible for the building also had to struggle with the problem of uneven terrain. The area could not be leveled by terracing because that would disturb the ancient sacred sites. As a result, the Erechtheion has four sides of very different character, and each side rests on a different ground level.

Perhaps to compensate for the awkward character of the building as a whole, the architect took great care with the Erechtheion's decorative details. The Ionic capitals were inlaid with gold, rock crystal, and colored glass, and the frieze received special treatment. The stone chosen was the gray-blue limestone of Eleusis to contrast with the white Pentelic marble of the walls and columns and the marble relief figures attached to the dark frieze.

The Erechtheion's most striking and famous feature is its south porch (FIG. 5-54), where the architect replaced Ionic columns with caryatids, as on the Siphnian Treasury (FIG. 5-17) at Delphi. The Archaic caryatids resemble sixth-century BCE korai, and their Classical counterparts equally characteristically look like Phidian-era statues. Although the caryatids exhibit the weight shift that was standard for the fifth century BCE, the flutelike

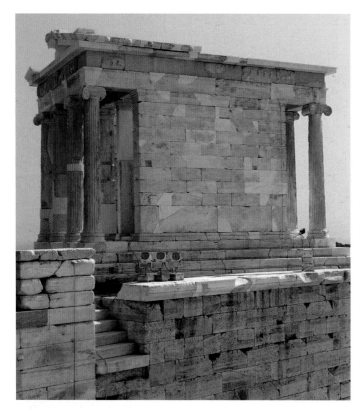

5-55 KALLIKRATES, Temple of Athena Nike (looking southwest), Acropolis, Athens, Greece, ca. 427–424 BCE.

The Ionic temple at the entrance to the Acropolis is an unusual amphiprostyle building. It celebrated Athena as bringer of victory, and one of the friezes depicts the Persian defeat at Marathon.

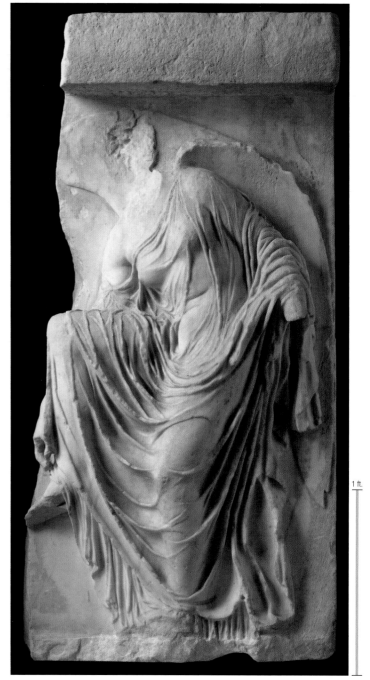

1 ft.

5-56 Nike adjusting her sandal, from the south side of the parapet of the Temple of Athena Nike, Acropolis, Athens, Greece, ca. 410 BCE. Marble, 3′ 6″ high. Acropolis Museum, Athens.

Dozens of images of winged Victory adorned the parapet on three sides of the Athena Nike temple. The sculptor carved this Nike with garments that appear almost transparent.

drapery folds concealing their stiff, weight-bearing legs underscore their role as architectural supports. The figures have enough rigidity to suggest the structural column and just the degree of flexibility needed to suggest the living body.

Temple of Athena Nike. Another Ionic building on the Athenian Acropolis is the small Temple of Athena Nike (FIG. 5-55), designed by Kallikrates, who worked with Iktinos on the Parthenon and may have been responsible for that temple's Ionic elements. The Athena Nike temple, rebuilt in 2012 after having been dismantled for restoration, is amphiprostyle (see "Greek Temple Plans," page 115) with four columns on both the east and west facades. It stands on what used to be a Mycenaean bastion near the Propylaia and greets all visitors entering Athena's great sanctuary. Like the Parthenon, this temple commemorated the victory over the Persians—and not just in its name. The sculptors devoted part of the frieze to a representation of the decisive battle at Marathon, which turned the tide against the Persians—a human event, as in the Parthenon's Panathenaic Festival procession frieze. But on the Athena Nike temple, the Athenians chronicled a specific occasion, not a recurring event involving anonymous citizens.

Around the building, at the bastion's edge, was a *parapet* (a low wall) decorated with exquisite reliefs, today displayed in the new Acropolis Museum. The theme of the balustrade matched that of the temple proper—victory. Dozens of images of Nike adorned the parapet, always in different attitudes. Sometimes she erects trophies bedecked with Persian spoils. Other times she brings forward sacrificial bulls for Athena. One relief (FIG. 5-56) shows Nike adjusting

her sandal—an awkward posture that the sculptor rendered elegant and graceful. The artist carried the style of the Parthenon pediments (FIGS. 5-49 and 5-49C) even further and created a figure whose garments cling so tightly to the body that they seem almost transparent, as if drenched with water. The sculptor was, however, interested in much more than revealing the supple beauty of the young female body. The drapery folds form intricate linear patterns unrelated to the body's anatomical structure and have a life of their own as abstract designs.

The Hegeso Stele

In Geometric times, huge painted vases (FIGS. 5-2 and 5-2A) marked the graves of wealthy Athenians. In the Archaic period, the Greeks placed kouroi (FIGS. 5-7 and 5-9) and, to a lesser extent, korai, or stelae ornamented with relief depictions of the deceased over their graves. The stele (FIG. 5-57) erected in the Dipylon cemetery at the end of the fifth or beginning of the fourth century BCE to commemorate the death of Hegeso, daughter of Proxenos, is in this tradition. An inscription giving the names of the daughter and father is on the cornice of the pediment crowning the stele. *Pilasters* (flat engaged columns) at left and right complete the architectural framework.

Hegeso is the well-dressed woman seated on an elegant chair (with footstool). She examines a piece of jewelry (once rendered in paint, not now visible) selected from a box that a servant girl brings to her. The maid's simple unbelted chiton contrasts sharply with the more elaborate attire of her mistress. The garments of both women reveal the body forms beneath them. The faces are serene, without a trace of sadness. Indeed, the sculptor depicted both mistress and maid during a characteristic shared moment out of daily life. Only the epitaph reveals that Hegeso is the one who has departed.

The simplicity of the scene on the Hegeso stele is deceptive, however. This is not merely a bittersweet scene of tranquil domestic life before an untimely death. The setting itself is significant—the secluded women's quarters of a Greek house, from which Hegeso rarely would have emerged. Contemporaneous grave stelae of men regularly show them in the public domain, often as warriors. The servant girl is not so much the faithful companion of the deceased in life as she is Hegeso's possession, like the jewelry box. The slave girl may look at her mistress, awaiting her next command, but Hegeso has eyes only for her ornaments. Both slave and jewelry attest to the wealth of Hegeso's father, unseen but prominently cited in the epitaph. (It is noteworthy that there is no mention of the mother's name.) Indeed, even the jewelry box carries a deeper significance, for it probably represents the dowry that Proxenos would have provided to his daughter's husband when she left her father's home to enter her husband's home. In the patriarchal society of ancient Greece, the dominant position of men is manifest even when only women are depicted.

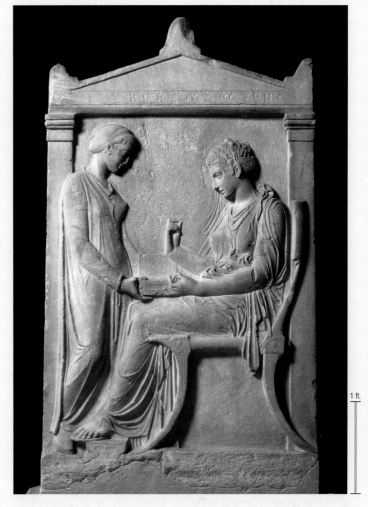

5-57 Grave stele of Hegeso, from the Dipylon cemetery, Athens, Greece, ca. 400 BCE. Marble, 5′ 2″ high. National Archaeological Museum, Athens.

On her tombstone, Hegeso examines jewelry from a box that her servant girl holds. Mistress and maid share a serene moment out of daily life. Only the epitaph reveals that Hegeso is the one who died.

Hegeso Stele. Although the decoration of the great building projects on the Acropolis must have occupied most of the finest sculptors of Athens during the second half of the fifth century BCE, other commissions were available in the city, notably for tombstones in the Dipylon cemetery. There, around 400 BCE, an Athenian family set up in memory of a woman named Hegeso a beautiful and touching grave stele (FIG. 5-57) in the style of the Temple of Athena Nike parapet reliefs. The stele's subject—a young woman in her home, attended by her maid (see "The Hegeso Stele," above)—and its composition have close parallels in Classical vase painting.

Painting

In the Classical period, some of the most renowned artists were the painters of large wood panels displayed in public buildings, both secular and religious. Those works were by nature perishable, and all of the great panels of the masters are unfortunately lost. Nonetheless, Greek vases of this period, especially those painted using the *white-ground painting* technique (see "White-Ground Painting," page 142), give some idea of the polychrome nature of Classical panel paintings.

Polygnotos. The leading panel painter of the first half of the fifth century BCE was Polygnotos of Thasos, whose works adorned important buildings in both Athens and Delphi. One of these was the pinakotheke of Mnesikles's Propylaia, but the most famous was a building in the Athenian agora that came to be called the Stoa Poikile (Painted Portico; compare FIG. 5-78). Descriptions of Polygnotos's paintings make clear that he introduced a revolutionary compositional format. Before Polygnotos, figures stood on a common ground line at the bottom of the picture plane, whether they appeared in horizontal bands or vertical panels. Polygnotos placed his figures on different

White-Ground Painting

White-ground painting takes its name from the chalky white slip used to provide a background for the painted figures. The Andokides Painter (FIG. 5-22) was one of the first to experiment with white-ground painting in the sixth century BCE, but the method became popular only toward the middle of the fifth century BCE. One of the best examples of the white-ground technique is the *lekythos* (flask to hold perfumed oil) illustrated here (FIG. 5-58), painted around 440 BCE by the ACHILLES PAINTER. White-ground is essentially a variation of the red-figure technique. First, the painter covered the pot with a slip of very fine white clay, then applied black glaze to outline the figures, and diluted brown, purple, red, and white to color them. The artist could use other colors—for example, the yellow that the Achilles Painter chose for the garments of both figures on this lekythos—but these had to be applied after firing because the Greeks did not know how to make them withstand the intense heat of the kiln.

Despite the obvious attractions of the technique, the impermanence of the expanded range of colors discouraged white-ground painting on everyday vessels, such as drinking cups and kraters. In fact, Greek artists explored the full polychrome possibilities of the white-ground technique almost exclusively on *lekythoi*, which families commonly placed in graves as offerings to the deceased. For vessels designed for short-term use, the fragile nature of white-ground painting was of little concern.

The Achilles Painter, like the REED PAINTER (FIG. 5-58A) later in the century, selected a scene appropriate for the funerary purpose of a lekythos. A youthful warrior takes leave of his wife. The red scarf, mirror, and jug hanging on the wall behind the woman indicate that the setting is the interior of their home. The motif of the seated woman is strikingly similar to that of Hegeso on her grave stele (FIG. 5-57), but here the woman is the survivor. It is her husband, preparing to go to war with helmet, shield, and spear, who will depart, never to return. On his shield is a large painted eye, roughly life-size. Greek shields often bore decorative devices such as the horrific face of Medusa, intended to ward off evil and frighten the enemy (compare FIG. 5-16). This eye undoubtedly recalls that tradition, but for the Achilles Painter it was little more than an excuse to display superior drawing skills. Since the late sixth

century BCE, Greek painters had abandoned the Archaic habit of placing frontal eyes on profile faces and attempted to render the eyes in profile. The Achilles Painter's mastery of this difficult problem in foreshortening is on exhibit here.

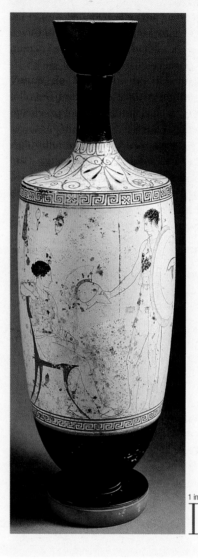

5-58 ACHILLES PAINTER, warrior taking leave of his wife (Athenian white-ground lekythos), from Eretria, Greece, ca. 440 BCE. 1′ 5″ high. National Archaeological Museum, Athens.

White-ground painters applied the colors after firing because most colored glazes could not withstand the kiln's heat. The Achilles Painter here displayed his mastery of drawing an eye in profile.

1 in.

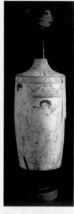

⏴5-58A REED PAINTER, warrior seated at his tomb, ca. 410–400 BCE.

levels, staggered in tiers in the manner of Ashurbanipal's lion hunt relief (FIG. 2-23) of two centuries before. He also incorporated landscape elements into his paintings, making his pictures true windows onto the world and not simply surface designs peopled with foreshortened figures. Polygnotos's abandonment of a single ground line was as momentous a break from the past as Early Classical Greek sculptors' rejection of frontality in statuary.

Niobid Painter. Polygnotos's influence is evident on a red-figure krater (FIG. 5-59) painted around the middle of the fifth century BCE by the NIOBID PAINTER—so named because one side of this krater depicts the massacre of the Niobids, the children of Niobe. Niobe, who had at least a dozen children, had boasted that she was superior to the goddess Leto, who had only two offspring, Apollo and Artemis. To punish her *hubris* (arrogant pride) and teach the

lesson that no mortal could be superior to a god or goddess, Leto sent her two children to slay all of Niobe's many sons and daughters. On the Niobid Painter's krater, the horrible slaughter occurs in a schematic landscape setting of rocks and trees. The painter placed the figures on several levels, and they actively interact with their setting. One slain son, for example, not only has fallen upon a rocky outcropping but is partially hidden by it. The Niobid Painter also drew the son's face in a three-quarter view, something even Euphronios and Euthymides never attempted.

Phiale Painter. Further insight into the appearance of the lost panel paintings of the fifth century BCE comes from a white-ground krater (FIG. 5-60) by the PHIALE PAINTER. The subject is Hermes handing over his half brother, the infant Dionysos, to Papposilenos (Grandpa-Satyr). The other figures represent the nymphs in

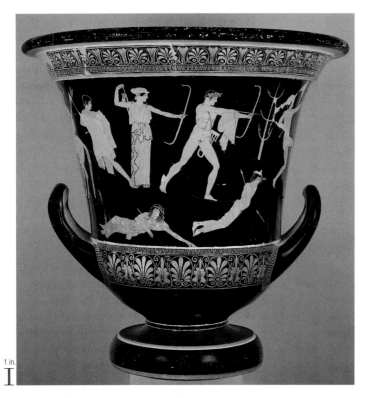

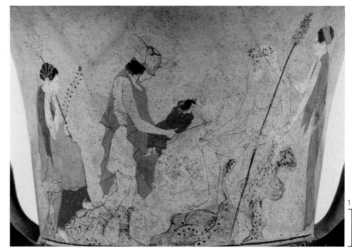

5-60 PHIALE PAINTER, Hermes bringing the infant Dionysos to Papposilenos (Athenian white-ground calyx krater), from Vulci, Italy, ca. 440–435 BCE. Krater 1′ 2″ high; detail 6½″ high. Musei Vaticani, Rome.

In the Phiale Painter's white-ground representation of Hermes and the infant Dionysos at Nysa, the use of diluted brown to color and shade the rocks may reflect the panel paintings of Polygnotos.

5-59 NIOBID PAINTER, Artemis and Apollo slaying the children of Niobe (Athenian red-figure calyx krater), from Orvieto, Italy, ca. 450 BCE. 1′ 9″ high. Musée du Louvre, Paris.

The placement of figures on different levels in a landscape on this red-figure krater depicting the massacre of the Niobids reflects the compositions of the panel paintings of Polygnotos of Thasos.

the shady glens of Nysa, where Zeus had sent Dionysos, one of his numerous natural sons, to be raised, safe from the possible wrath of his wife, Hera. Unlike the decorators of funerary lekythoi, the Phiale Painter used for this krater only colors that could survive the firing in a Greek kiln—red, brown, purple, and a special snowy white reserved for the flesh of the nymphs and for the hair, beard,

and shaggy body of Papposilenos. The use of diluted brown wash to color and shade the rocks may reflect the coloration of Polygnotos's landscapes. This vase and the Niobid krater together provide a shadowy idea of the character of Polygnotos's lost paintings.

Tomb of the Diver, Paestum. Although all the panel paintings of the masters disappeared long ago, some Greek mural paintings survive. An early example is in the Tomb of the Diver at Paestum. Covering the four walls of this small, coffinlike tomb are symposium scenes of the kind that appear regularly on Greek vases. On the tomb's cover slab (FIG. 5-61), a youth dives from a stone platform into a body of water. The scene most likely symbolizes the plunge from this life into the next. Trees resembling those of the Niobid krater are included within the decorative frame.

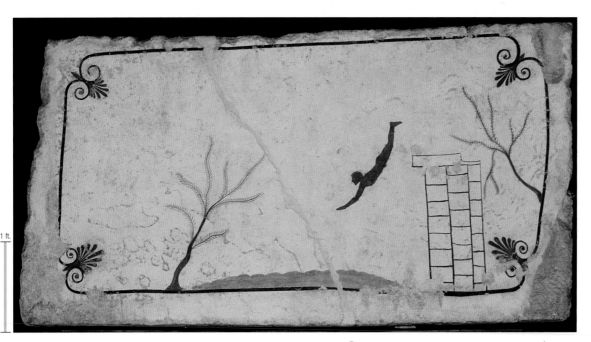

5-61 Youth diving, cover slab of the Tomb of the Diver, from the Tempe del Prete necropolis, Paestum, Italy, ca. 480–470 BCE. Fresco, 3′ 4″ high. Museo Archeologico Nazionale, Paestum.

This tomb in Italy is a rare example of Classical mural painting. The diving scene most likely symbolizes the deceased's plunge into the Underworld. The trees resemble those on the Niobid krater (FIG. 5-59).

LATE CLASSICAL PERIOD

The Peloponnesian War, which began in 431 BCE, ended in 404 BCE with the decisive defeat of a plague-weakened Athens. The victor, Sparta, and then Thebes undertook the leadership of Greece, both unsuccessfully. In the middle of the fourth century BCE, a threat from without caused the rival Greek states to put aside their disagreements and unite for their common defense, as they had earlier against the Persians. But at the battle of Chaeronea in 338 BCE, the Greek cities suffered a devastating loss and had to give up their independence to the Macedonian king Philip II (r. 359–336 BCE). Philip was assassinated in 336, and his son, Alexander III (r. 336–323 BCE), better known simply as Alexander the Great, succeeded him. Alexander led a powerful army on an extraordinary campaign that overthrew the Persian Empire (the ultimate revenge for the Persian invasion of Greece in the early fifth century), wrested control of Egypt, and even reached India (see "The Great Stupa at Sanchi," page 443).

Sculpture

The fourth century BCE in Greece was thus a time of political upheaval, which had a profound impact on the psyche of the Greeks and on the art they produced. In the fifth century BCE, Greeks had generally believed that rational human beings could impose order on their environment, create "perfect" statues such as the *Canon* of Polykleitos, and discover the "correct" mathematical formulas for constructing buildings such as the Parthenon. The Parthenon frieze celebrated the Athenians as a community of citizens with shared values. The Peloponnesian War and the unceasing strife of the fourth century BCE brought an end to the serene idealism of the previous century. Disillusionment and alienation followed. Greek thought and Greek art began to focus more on the individual and on the real world of appearances instead of on the community and the ideal world of perfect beings and perfect shrines.

Praxiteles. The new approach to art is immediately apparent in the work of PRAXITELES, one of the three greatest sculptors of the Late Classical period. Praxiteles did not reject the favored statuary themes of the High Classical period, and his Olympian gods and goddesses retained their superhuman beauty. But in his hands, those deities lost some of their solemn grandeur and took on a worldly sensuousness. Nowhere is this new humanizing spirit more evident than in the statue of Aphrodite (FIG. 5-62) that Praxiteles sold to the Knidians after another city had rejected it. The lost original, carved from Parian marble, is known only through copies of Roman date, but Pliny considered it "superior to all the works, not only of Praxiteles, but indeed in the whole world." It made Knidos famous, and many people sailed there just to see the statue in its round temple (compare FIG. 5-72), where "it was possible to view the image of the goddess from every side." According to Pliny, some visitors were "overcome with love for the statue."[6]

The *Aphrodite of Knidos* caused such a sensation in its time because Praxiteles took the unprecedented step of representing the goddess of love completely nude. Female nudity was rare in earlier Greek art and had been confined almost exclusively to paintings on vases designed for *symposia* and household use. The women so depicted also were usually not noblewomen or goddesses but courtesans or slave girls—for example, the one whom Onesimos depicted on a red-figure drinking cup (FIG. 5-24A). No one had ever dared place a statue of an undressed goddess inside a temple.

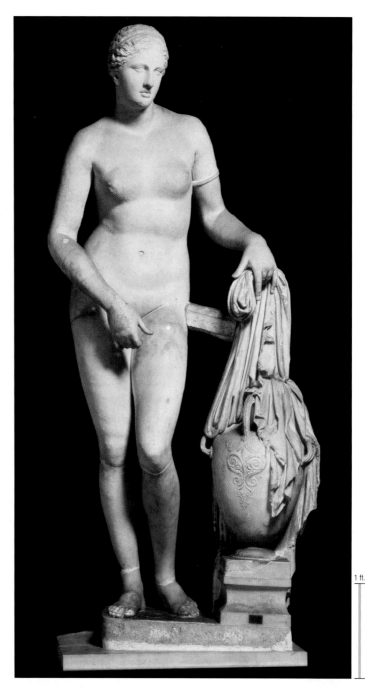

5-62 PRAXITELES, *Aphrodite of Knidos*. Roman copy of a marble statue of ca. 350–340 BCE. Marble, 6′ 8″ high. Musei Vaticani, Rome.

This first nude statue of a Greek goddess caused a sensation. But Praxiteles was also famous for his ability to transform marble into soft and radiant flesh. His Aphrodite had "dewy eyes."

Moreover, Praxiteles's Aphrodite is not a cold and remote image. In fact, the goddess engages in a trivial act out of everyday life. She has removed her garment and draped it over a large *hydria* (water pitcher), and is about to step into the bath.

Although shocking in its day, the *Aphrodite of Knidos* is not overtly erotic (the goddess modestly shields her pelvis with her right hand), but she is quite sensuous. Lucian, writing in the second century CE, noted that she had a "welcoming look" and a "slight smile" and that Praxiteles was renowned for his ability to transform marble into soft and radiant flesh. Lucian mentioned, for example, the "dewy quality of Aphrodite's eyes."[7] Unfortunately, the rather mechanical Roman copies do not capture the quality of the master's

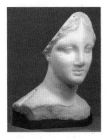

5-62A Head of a woman, Chios, ca. 320–300 BCE.

modeling of the stone, but some originals of the period do—for example, a female head (FIG. 5-62A) from Chios.

The Praxitelean "touch" is also evident in a statue once thought to be by the hand of the renowned artist himself but now generally considered either a copy of the highest quality or an original work by a son or grandson of Praxiteles with the same name. The statue of Hermes and the infant Dionysos (FIG. 5-63) found in the Temple of Hera at Olympia brings to the realm of life-size statuary the theme that the Phiale Painter had chosen for a white-ground krater (FIG. 5-60) a century earlier. Hermes has stopped to rest in a forest on his journey to Nysa to entrust the upbringing of Dionysos to Papposilenos and the nymphs. Hermes leans on a tree trunk (here it is an integral part of the composition and not a copyist's addition), and his slender body forms a sinuous, shallow S-curve that is the hallmark of many of Praxiteles's statues. He gazes dreamily into space while he dangles a bunch of grapes (now missing) as a temptation for the infant, who is to become the Greek god of the vine. This is the kind of tender human interaction between an adult and a child that one encounters frequently in life but that had been absent from Greek statuary before the fourth century BCE.

The quality of the carving is superb. The modeling is deliberately smooth and subtle, producing soft shadows that follow the planes as they flow almost imperceptibly one into another. All that is missing to give a complete sense of the "look" of a Praxitelean statue is the original paint, which a specialist, not the sculptor, applied to the statue (compare FIG. 5-63A). The delicacy of the marble facial features stands in sharp contrast to the metallic precision of Polykleitos's bronze *Doryphoros* (FIG. 5-41). The High Classical sculptor even subjected the *Spear Bearer*'s locks of hair to the laws of symmetry, and the hair does not violate the skull's perfect curve. The comparison of these two statues reveals the sweeping changes in artistic attitude and intent that took place from the fifth to the fourth century BCE. In the statues of Praxiteles, the deities of Mount Olympus still possess a beauty that mortals can aspire to, although not achieve, but they are no longer aloof. Praxiteles's gods have stepped off their pedestals and entered the world of human experience.

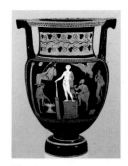

5-63A Artist painting a statue of Herakles, ca. 350–320 BCE.

Skopas. In the Archaic period and throughout most of the Early and High Classical periods, Greek sculptors generally shared common goals, but in the Late Classical period of the fourth century BCE, distinctive individual styles emerged. The dreamy, beautiful divinities of Praxiteles had enormous appeal, and the master had many followers (FIG. 5-62A). Other sculptors, however, pursued very different interests. One of these was SKOPAS OF PAROS, an architect as well as a sculptor, who designed a temple at Tegea (fragments of the pedimental sculptures remain; FIG. 5-63B) and contributed to the decoration of one of the Seven Wonders of the ancient world (see "Babylon," page 50), the Mausoleum (FIG. 5-63C) at Halikarnassos. Although Skopas's sculptures reflect the general Late Classical trend toward the humanization of the Greek gods and heroes, his hallmark was intense emotionalism. No statue by Skopas survives, but a grave stele found near the Ilissos River

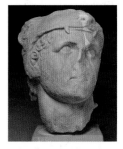

5-63B Herakles, Temple of Athena Alea, Tegea, ca. 340 BCE.

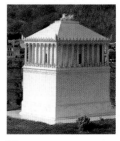

5-63C Mausoleum, Halikarnassos, ca. 353–340 BCE.

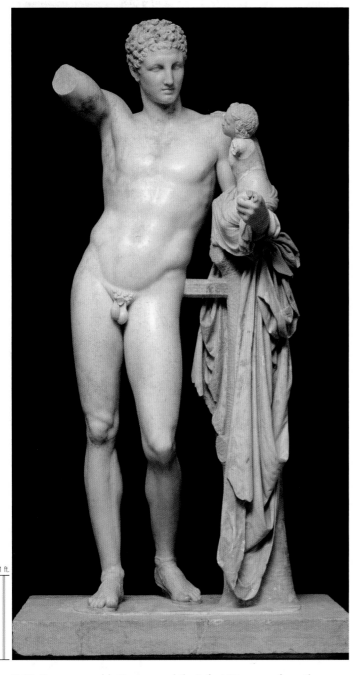

1 ft.

5-63 PRAXITELES(?), Hermes and the infant Dionysos, from the Temple of Hera, Olympia, Greece. Copy of a marble statue by Praxiteles of ca. 340 BCE or an original work of ca. 330–270 BCE by a son or grandson. Marble, 7′ 1″ high. Archaeological Museum, Olympia.

Praxiteles humanized the Olympian deities. This Hermes is as sensuous as the sculptor's Aphrodite. The god gazes dreamily into space while he dangles grapes to tempt the infant wine god.

in Athens exhibits the psychological tension for which the master's works were famous.

The Ilissos stele (FIG. 5-64) was originally set into an architectural frame similar to that of the earlier Hegeso stele (FIG. 5-57). A comparison of the two works is revealing. In the later stele, the relief is much higher, with parts of the figures carved fully in the round. The major difference, however, is the pronounced change in mood, which reflects Skopas's innovations. The Late Classical work makes a clear distinction between the living and the dead and depicts overt mourning. The deceased is a young hunter who, like the other figures, has the large, deeply set eyes and fleshy overhanging brows that characterized Skopas's sculptures (compare FIG. 5-63B). At his feet, a small boy, either his servant or perhaps a younger brother, sobs openly. The hunter's dog also droops its head in sorrow. Beside the youth, an old man, undoubtedly his father, leans on a walking stick and, in a gesture reminiscent of that of the Olympia seer (FIG. 5-33), ponders the irony of fate that has taken the life of his powerful son yet preserved him, the father, in his frail old age. Most remarkable of all, the hunter himself looks out at the viewer, inviting sympathy and creating an emotional bridge between the spectator and the artwork inconceivable in the art of the High Classical period.

Lysippos. The third great Late Classical sculptor, LYSIPPOS OF SIKYON, won such renown that Alexander the Great selected him to create his official portrait. (Alexander could afford to employ the best because the Macedonian kingdom enjoyed vast wealth. For example, King Philip was able to hire the leading thinker of his age, Aristotle, as the young Alexander's tutor.) Lysippos introduced a new canon of proportions in which the bodies were more slender than those of Polykleitos and the heads roughly one-eighth the height of the body rather than one-seventh, as in the previous

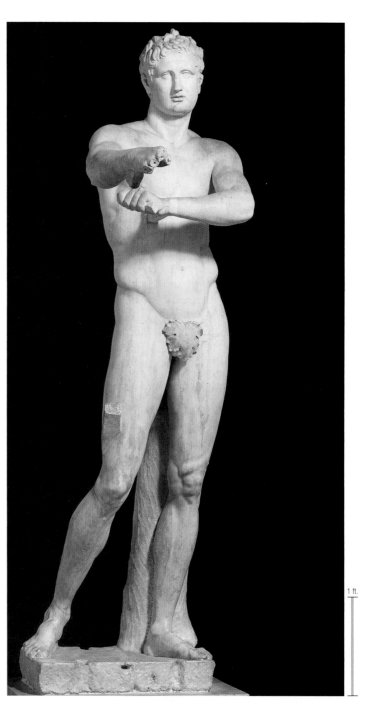

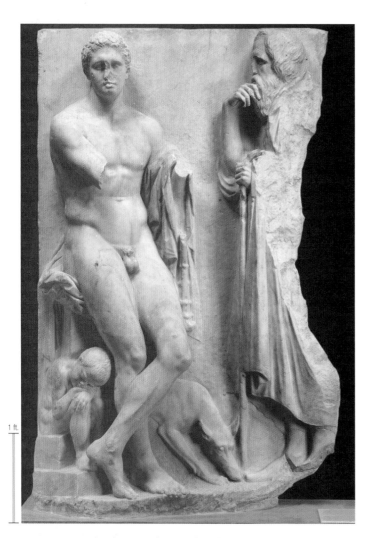

5-64 Grave stele of a young hunter, found near the Ilissos River, Athens, Greece, ca. 340–330 BCE. Marble, 5′ 6″ high. National Archaeological Museum, Athens.

The emotional intensity of this stele representing an old man mourning the loss of his son as well as the figures' large, deeply set eyes with fleshy overhanging brows reflect the style of Skopas of Paros.

5-65 LYSIPPOS, *Apoxyomenos* (*Scraper*), from Trastevere, Rome, Italy. Roman copy of a bronze statue of ca. 330 BCE. Marble, 6′ 9″ high. Musei Vaticani, Rome.

Lysippos introduced a new canon of proportions and a nervous energy to his statues. He also broke down the dominance of the frontal view and encouraged viewing his statues from multiple angles.

century. One of Lysippos's most famous works, a bronze statue of an *apoxyomenos* (an athlete scraping oil from his body after exercising)—known, as usual, only from Roman copies in marble (FIG. 5-65)—exhibits the new proportions. A comparison with Polykleitos's *Doryphoros* (FIG. 5-41) reveals more than a change in physique, however. A nervous energy, lacking in the balanced form of the *Doryphoros,* runs through Lysippos's *Apoxyomenos.* The *strigil* (scraping tool) is about to reach the end of the right arm, and at any moment the athlete will switch it to the other hand so that

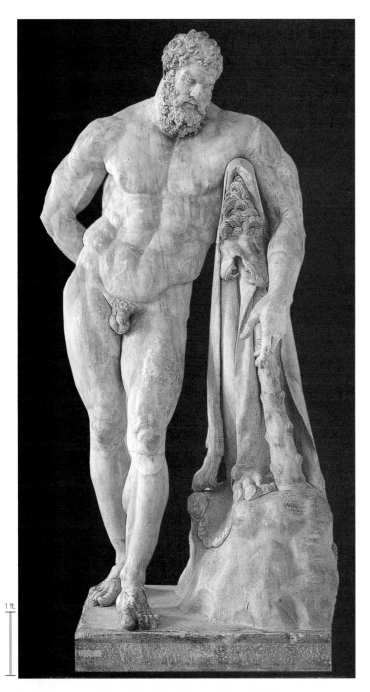

5-66 LYSIPPOS, Weary Herakles (*Farnese Hercules*). Roman statue from the Baths of Caracalla (FIG. 7-65), Rome, Italy, signed by GLYKON OF ATHENS, based on a bronze statue of ca. 320 BCE. Marble, 10′ 5″ high. Museo Archeologico Nazionale, Naples.

Lysippos's portrayal of Herakles after the hero obtained the golden apples of the Hesperides ironically shows the muscle-bound hero as so weary that he must lean on his club for support.

he can scrape his left arm. At the same time, he will shift his weight and reverse the positions of his legs. Lysippos also began to break down the dominance of the frontal view in statuary and encouraged the observer to view his athlete from multiple angles. Because Lysippos represented the apoxyomenos with his right arm boldly thrust forward, the figure breaks out of the shallow rectangular box that defined the boundaries of earlier statues. To comprehend the action, the observer must move to the side and view Lysippos's work at a three-quarter angle or in full profile.

To grasp the full meaning of another of Lysippos's works, a statue depicting the weary Herakles, the viewer must walk around it. Once again, the original is lost. The most impressive of the surviving statues (FIG. 5-66) based on the Lysippan original is nearly twice life-size. It stood in the Baths of Caracalla in Rome, where, like the marble copy of Polykleitos's *Doryphoros* (FIG. 5-41) from the Roman palaestra at Pompeii, Lysippos's muscle-bound Greek hero provided inspiration for Romans who came to the baths to exercise. (The Roman sculptor GLYKON OF ATHENS signed the statue, but did not mention Lysippos. The educated Roman public needed no label to identify the famous work.) The exaggerated muscular development of Herakles is poignantly ironic, however. Lysippos depicted the hero as so weary that he must lean on his club for support. Without that prop, Herakles would topple over. Lysippos and other fourth-century BCE artists rejected stability and balance as goals for statuary.

Herakles holds the golden apples of the Hesperides in his right hand behind his back—unseen unless the viewer walks around the statue. Lysippos's subject is thus the same as that of the metope (FIG. 5-31) of the Early Classical Temple of Zeus at Olympia, but the fourth-century BCE Herakles is no longer serene. Instead of expressing joy, or at least satisfaction, at having completed one of the impossible 12 labors, he is almost dejected. Exhausted by his physical efforts, he can think only of his pain and fatigue. Lysippos's portrayal of Herakles in this statue is an eloquent testimony to Late Classical sculptors' interest in humanizing the Greek gods and heroes. In this respect, despite their divergent styles, Praxiteles, Skopas, and Lysippos followed a common path.

Alexander the Great and Macedonian Court Art

Alexander the Great's favorite book was the *Iliad,* and his own life very much resembled an epic saga, full of heroic battles, exotic locales, and unceasing drama. Alexander was a man of singular character, an inspired leader with boundless energy and an almost foolhardy courage. He personally led his army into battle on the back of Bucephalus (FIG. 5-70), the wild and mighty steed that only he could tame and ride.

Alexander's Portraits. Ancient sources reveal that Alexander believed that only Lysippos had captured his essence in a portrait, and thus only he was authorized to sculpt the king's image. Lysippos's most famous portrait of the Macedonian king was a full-length, heroically nude bronze statue of Alexander holding a lance and turning his head toward the sky. According to Plutarch, an epigram inscribed on the base stated that the statue depicted Alexander gazing at Zeus and proclaiming, "I place the earth under my sway; you, O Zeus, keep Olympus." Plutarch also reported that Lysippos's portrait immortalized Alexander's "leonine" hair and "melting glance."[8] The Lysippan original is lost, and because

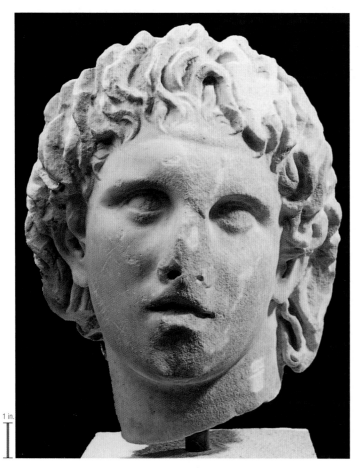

5-67 Head of Alexander the Great, from Pella, Greece, third century BCE. Marble, 1′ high. Archaeological Museum, Pella.

Lysippos was the official portrait sculptor of Alexander the Great. This third-century BCE sculpture has the sharp turn of the head and thick mane of hair of Lysippos's statue of Alexander with a lance.

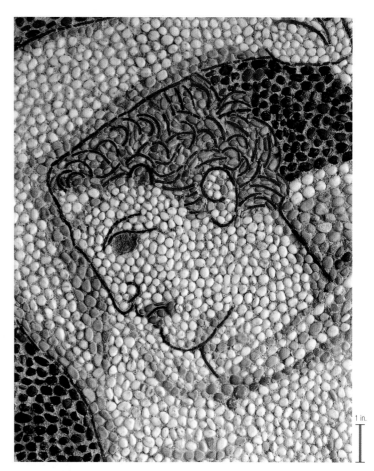

5-68 Detail of a lion hunt, from Pella, Greece, ca. 330–300 BCE. Pebble mosaic, figural panel 5′ 4¼″ high; detail 1′ high. Archaeological Museum, Pella.

The floor mosaics at Pella, the Macedonian capital, are of the early type made with naturally colored pebbles. The use of shading suggests that the Pella mosaics reflect contemporaneous panel painting.

Alexander was portrayed so many times and long after his death, it is difficult to determine which of the many surviving images is most faithful to the fourth-century BCE portrait. A leading candidate is a third-century BCE marble head (FIG. 5-67) from Pella, the capital of Macedonia and Alexander's birthplace. It has the sharp turn of the head and thick mane of hair that were key ingredients of Lysippos's portrait. The Pella sculptor's treatment of the features also is consistent with the style of the later fourth century BCE. The deep-set eyes and parted lips recall the manner of Skopas (FIG. 5-63B), and the delicate handling of the flesh brings to mind the faces of Praxitelean statues (FIG. 5-63). Although not a copy, this head very likely approximates the young king's official portrait and provides insight into Alexander's personality as well as Lysippos's art.

Pella Mosaics. The luxurious life of the Macedonian aristocracy is evident from the costly objects found in Macedonian graves and from the abundance of mosaics uncovered in houses at Pella. The Macedonian mosaics are *pebble mosaics* (see "Mosaics," page 256). The floors consist of small stones of various colors collected from beaches and riverbanks and set into a thick coat of cement. One of the finest pebble mosaics uncovered in the Pella excavations depicts a lion hunt. A detail of one of the two hunters (FIG. 5-68) is reproduced here to showcase the character of this early mosaic technique. The placement of light figures against

a dark ground has much in common with red-figure painting. In the pebble mosaic, however, thin strips of lead define most of the contour lines and some of the interior details. Subtle gradations of yellow, brown, and red, as well as black, white, and gray pebbles, suggest the interior volumes. The mosaicist used shading to model the musculature of the hunters as well as their billowing cloaks and the lion's body. The use of light and dark to suggest volume is rare on Greek painted vases, although examples exist. Panel painters, however, commonly used shading, the Greek term for which was *skiagraphia* (literally, "shadow painting"). The Greeks attributed the invention of shading to an Athenian painter of the fifth century BCE named Apollodoros. The Pella lion hunt, with its sparse landscape setting, probably reflects contemporaneous panel painting.

Hades and Persephone. Excavations at Vergina have provided valuable additional information about Macedonian art and about Greek mural painting. One of the most important finds is a painted tomb (possibly the tomb of Philip II) with a fresco (FIG. 5-69) representing Hades, lord of the Underworld, abducting Persephone, the daughter of Demeter, the goddess of grain. The mural is remarkable for its intense drama and for the painter's use of foreshortening and shading. Hades holds the terrified seminude Persephone in his left arm and steers his racing chariot with his right as Persephone's garments and hair blow in the wind. The artist depicted the

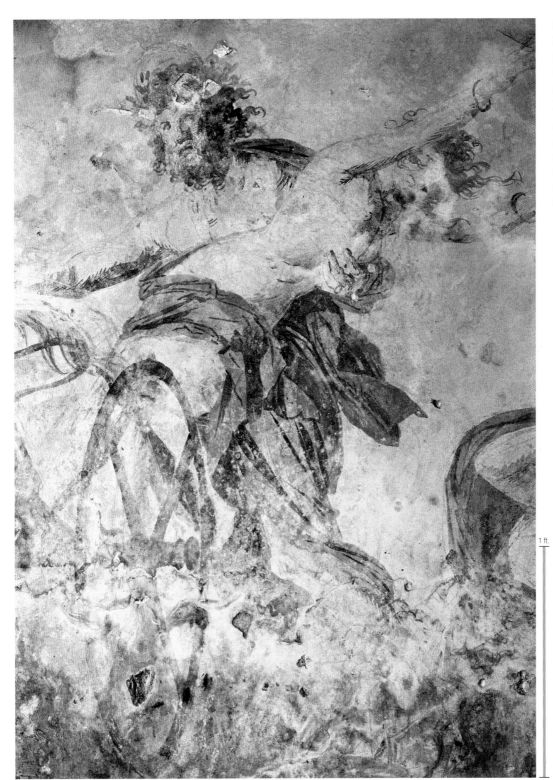

5-69 Hades abducting Persephone, detail of a wall painting in tomb 1, Vergina, Greece, ca. 336 BCE. Fresco, detail 3′ 3½″ high.

The intense drama, three-quarter views, and shading in this representation of the lord of the Underworld kidnapping Demeter's daughter are characteristics of mural painting at the time of Alexander.

1 ft.

heads of both figures and even the chariot's wheels in three-quarter views. The chariot, in fact, seems to be bursting into the viewer's space. Especially noteworthy is the way the painter used short, dark brushstrokes to suggest shading on the underside of Hades's right arm, on Persephone's torso, and elsewhere. Although fragmentary, the Vergina mural is a precious document of the almost totally lost art of large-scale wall and panel painting in ancient Greece.

Battle of Issus. Further insight into developments in painting at the time of Alexander comes from a large late-second-century BCE mosaic (FIG. 5-70) that decorated the floor of a room in a lavishly appointed Roman house at Pompeii. The mosaicist was a master of a later mosaic technique employing *tesserae* (cubical pieces of glass or tiny stones cut to the desired size and shape) instead of pebbles (see "Mosaics," page 256). The subject is a great battle between the armies of Alexander the Great and the Achaemenid Persian king Darius III (r. 336–330 BCE), probably the Battle of Issus in southeastern Turkey. The mosaic is probably a copy of a late-fourth-century BCE Greek painting (see "The *Alexander Mosaic*," page 150).

The *Alexander Mosaic*

The *Alexander Mosaic* (FIG. 5-70), which depicts the humiliating defeat of Darius III by Alexander the Great, is one of the masterpieces of the mosaicist's art. Art historians believe that it is a reasonably faithful copy of a Greek panel painting of the late fourth century BCE. Proposed dates for the original range from 333 to 316 BCE—that is, in the decade before or after Alexander's death in 323 BCE.

The panel is notable for the artist's technical mastery of problems that had long fascinated Greek painters. Even Euthymides would have marveled at the Late Classical painter's depiction of the rearing horse seen in a three-quarter rear view below Darius. The subtle modulation of the horse's rump through shading in browns and yellows is much more accomplished than the comparable attempts at shading in the Pella mosaic (FIG. 5-68) or the Vergina mural (FIG. 5-69). Other details are even more impressive. The Persian to the right of the rearing horse has fallen to the ground and raises, backward, a dropped Macedonian shield to protect himself from being trampled. The painter recorded the reflection of the man's terrified face on the polished surface of the shield. Everywhere in the scene, men, animals, and weapons cast shadows on the ground. This interest in the reflection of insubstantial light on a shiny surface, and in the absence of light (shadows), stands in sharp contrast to earlier painters' preoccupation with the clear presentation of weighty figures seen against a blank background. This master artist truly opened a window onto a world filled not only with figures, trees, and sky but also with light. This new, distinctly Greek notion of what a painting should be characterizes most of the history of art in the Western world from the Renaissance on.

Perhaps most impressive about the painting, however, is the psychological intensity of the drama unfolding before the viewer's eyes. Alexander, riding Bucephalus, leads his army into battle, recklessly one might say, without even a helmet to protect him. He drives his spear through one of Darius's trusted "Immortals," who swore to guard the king's life, while the Persian's horse collapses beneath him. The Macedonian king is only a few yards away from Darius, and Alexander directs his gaze at the Persian king, not at the man impaled on his now-useless spear. Darius has called for retreat. In fact, his charioteer is already whipping the horses and speeding the king to safety. Before he escapes, Darius looks back at Alexander and in a pathetic gesture reaches out toward his brash foe. But the victory has slipped from his hands.

Who was the painter who created this memorable record of Alexander's triumph over Darius? Most art historians believe that the *Alexander Mosaic* is a replica of the *Battle of Issos,* a work that Pliny judged to be "inferior to none" and that he stated was painted for King Cassander (r. 305–297 BCE) by Philoxenos of Eretria.* However, another ancient source describes a painting of Alexander in battle by Helen of Alexandria that was on display in the emperor Vespasian's Temple of Peace in Rome. Some scholars contend that the model for the *Alexander Mosaic* was her painting, not Philoxenos's. A third hypothesis is that the artist was the most renowned Greek painter of all—Apelles, two of whose portraits of Alexander were on view in the Forum of Augustus in Rome.

Unfortunately, this is a problem that has no solution because no original Greek panel painting survives from antiquity. Consequently, in contrast to Greek vase paintings, it is impossible to define the individual style of any of the famous Greek painters whose names are known.

*Pliny, *Natural History,* 35.110.

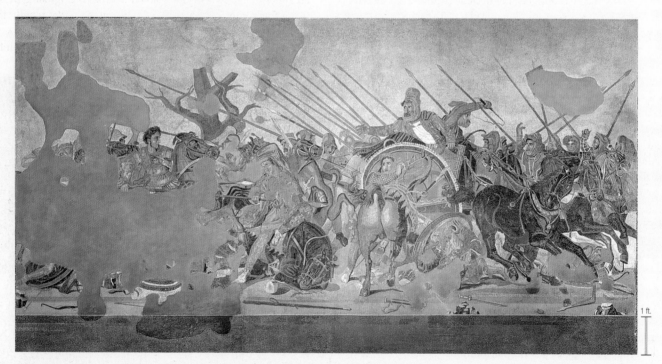

5-70 PHILOXENOS OF ERETRIA(?), *Battle of Issus.* Roman copy (*Alexander Mosaic*) from the House of the Faun, Pompeii, Italy, ca. 120–100 BCE, of a panel painting of ca. 333–316 BCE. Tessera mosaic, 8′ 10″ × 16′ 9″. Museo Archeologico Nazionale, Naples.

Battle of Issus reveals the Greek painter's mastery of foreshortening, of modeling figures in color, and of depicting reflections and shadows. The artist also captured the psychological intensity of warfare.

Architecture

In architecture, as in sculpture and painting, the Late Classical period was a time of innovation and experimentation.

Theater of Epidauros. In ancient Greece, actors did not perform plays repeatedly over months or years as they do today, but only during sacred festivals. Greek drama was closely associated with religious rites and was not pure entertainment. In the fifth century BCE, for example, the Athenians staged performances of the tragedies of Aeschylus, Sophocles, and Euripides during the Dionysos festival in the theater dedicated to the god on the southern slope of the Acropolis. Yet it is Epidauros, in the Peloponnesos, that boasts the finest theater (FIG. 5-71) in Greece. Constructed shortly after the birth of Alexander, the theater is still the setting for performances of ancient Greek dramas. The architect was POLYKLEITOS THE YOUNGER, possibly a later-generation member of the famous fifth-century BCE sculptor's family.

The precursor of the formal Greek theater was a circular patch of earth where actors performed sacred rites, songs, and dances. This circular hard and level surface later became the orchestra of the theater. *Orchestra* literally means "dancing place." The actors and the chorus performed there, and, at Epidauros, an altar to Dionysos stood at the center of the circle. The spectators sat on a slope overlooking the orchestra—the *theatron,* or "place for seeing." When the Greek theater took architectural shape, the builders always situated the auditorium (*cavea,* Latin for "hollow place, cavity") on a hillside. The cavea at Epidauros, composed of wedge-shaped sections (*cunei,* singular *cuneus*) of stone benches separated by stairs, is somewhat greater than a semicircle in plan. The auditorium is 387 feet in diameter, and its 55 rows of seats accommodated about 12,000 spectators. They entered the theater via a passageway between the seating area and the scene building (*skene*), which housed dressing rooms for the actors and also formed a backdrop for the plays. The design is simple but perfectly suited to its function. Even in antiquity, the Epidauros theater was famous for the harmony of its proportions. Although spectators sitting in some of the seats would have had a poor view of the skene, all had unobstructed views of the orchestra. Because of the open-air cavea's excellent acoustics, everyone could hear the actors and chorus.

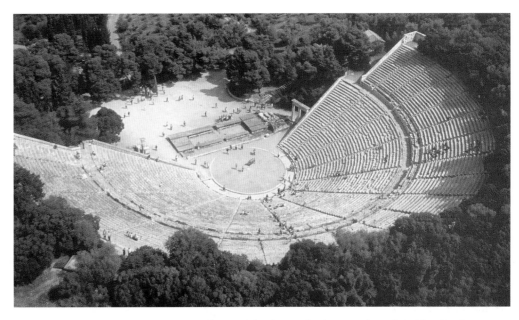

5-71 POLYKLEITOS THE YOUNGER, aerial view of the theater (looking southwest), Epidauros, Greece, ca. 350 BCE.

The Greeks always situated theaters on hillsides to support the cavea of stone seats overlooking the circular orchestra. The Epidauros theater is the finest in Greece. It could seat 12,000 spectators.

Corinthian Capitals. The theater at Epidauros is about 500 yards southeast of the sanctuary of Asklepios, and Polykleitos the Younger worked there as well. He was the architect of the *tholos,* the circular shrine that probably housed the sacred snakes of the healing god. That building lies in ruins today, but the Greek archaeological service is in the process of reconstructing it. One can get an approximate idea of the Epidauros tholos's original appearance from the somewhat earlier and already partially rebuilt tholos (FIG. 5-72) at Delphi designed by THEODOROS OF PHOKAIA. Both *tholoi* had an exterior colonnade of Doric columns, but the interior

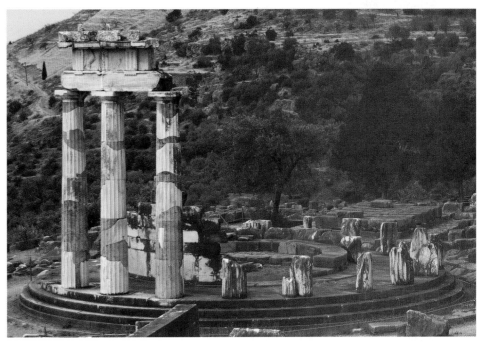

5-72 THEODOROS OF PHOKAIA, tholos (looking northwest), Delphi, Greece, ca. 375 BCE.

The tholos at Delphi, although in ruins, is the best-preserved example of a round temple of the Classical period. It had Doric columns on the exterior and Corinthian columns inside.

The Corinthian Capital

The Corinthian capital (FIG. 5-73) is more ornate than either the Doric or Ionic (FIG. 5-13). It consists of a double row of acanthus leaves, from which tendrils and flowers emerge, wrapped around a bell-shaped echinus. Although architectural historians often cite this capital as the distinguishing feature of the Corinthian order, strictly speaking no Corinthian order exists. The new capital type was simply a substitute for the Ionic order's volute capital.

The sculptor Kallimachos invented the Corinthian capital during the second half of the fifth century BCE. Vitruvius recorded the circumstances that supposedly led to its creation:

> A maiden who was a citizen of Corinth . . . died. After her funeral, her nurse collected the goblets in which the maiden had taken delight while she was alive, and after putting them together in a basket, she took them to the grave monument and put them on top of it. In order that they should remain in place for a long time, she covered them with a tile. Now it happened that this basket was placed over the root of an acanthus. As time went on the acanthus root, pressed down in the middle by the weight, sent forth, when it was about springtime, leaves and stalks; its stalks growing up along the sides of the basket and being pressed out from the angles because of the weight of the tile, were forced to form volute-like curves at their extremities. At this point, Kallimachos happened to be going by and noticed the basket with this gentle growth of leaves around it. Delighted with the order and the novelty of the form, he made columns using it as his model and established a canon of proportions for it.*

Kallimachos worked on the Acropolis in Pericles's great building program. Many scholars believe that a Corinthian column supported the outstretched right hand of Phidias's *Athena Parthenos* (FIG. 5-46) because one appears in some of the Roman copies of the lost statue. In any case, the earliest preserved Corinthian capital dates to the time of Kallimachos. The new type was rarely used before the mid-fourth century BCE, however, and did not become popular until Hellenistic and especially Roman times. Later architects favored the Corinthian capital because of its ornate character and because it eliminated certain problems of both the Doric and Ionic orders.

The Ionic capital, unlike the Doric, has two distinct profiles—the front and back (with the volutes) and the sides. The volutes always faced outward on a Greek temple, but architects met with a vexing problem at the corners of their buildings, which had two adjacent "fronts." They solved the problem by placing volutes on both outer faces of the corner capitals—as on the Temple of Athena Nike (FIG. 5-55)—but that was an awkward solution.

Doric design rules also presented problems for Greek architects at the corners of buildings. Doric friezes had to satisfy three supposedly inflexible rules:

- A triglyph must be exactly over the center of each column.
- A triglyph must be over the center of each *intercolumniation* (the space between two columns).
- Triglyphs at the corners of the frieze must meet so that no space is left over.

These rules are contradictory, however. If the corner triglyphs must meet, then they cannot be placed over the center of the corner column (FIGS. 5-1, 5-25, and 5-30).

The Corinthian capital eliminated both problems. Because the capital's four sides have a similar appearance, corner Corinthian capitals do not have to be modified, as do corner Ionic capitals. And because the Corinthian "order" incorporates an Ionic frieze, architects do not have to contend with corner triglyphs.

*Vitruvius, *De architectura*, 4.1.8–10. Translated by J. J. Pollitt, *The Art of Ancient Greece: Sources and Documents* (New York: Cambridge University Press, 1990), 193–194.

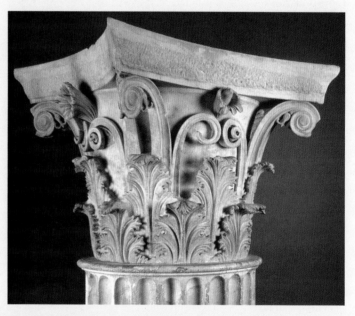

5-73 POLYKLEITOS THE YOUNGER, **Corinthian capital, from the tholos, Epidauros, Greece, ca. 350 BCE. Archaeological Museum, Epidauros.**

Corinthian capitals, invented by the fifth-century BCE sculptor Kallimachos, are more ornate than Doric and Ionic capitals. They feature a double row of acanthus leaves with tendrils and flowers.

columns had molded *bases* and *Corinthian capitals* (see "The Corinthian Capital," above), an invention of the second half of the fifth century BCE.

Greek architects did not readily embrace the Corinthian capital, however. Until the second century BCE, Greek builders used Corinthian capitals only for the interiors of sacred buildings, as at Delphi and Epidauros. The earliest instance of a Corinthian capital on the exterior of a Greek building is the Choragic Monument of Lysikrates (FIG. 5-74), which is not really a building at all. Lysikrates had sponsored a chorus in a theatrical contest in 334 BCE, and after his chorus won, he erected a monument to commemorate the victory. The monument consists of a cylindrical drum resembling a

HELLENISTIC PERIOD

Alexander the Great's conquest of Mesopotamia and Egypt ushered in a new cultural age that historians and art historians alike call *Hellenistic*. The Hellenistic period opened with the death of Alexander in 323 BCE and lasted nearly three centuries, until the double suicide of Queen Cleopatra of Egypt and her Roman consort, Mark Antony, in 30 BCE after their decisive defeat at the battle of Actium by Antony's rival Augustus. That year, Augustus made Egypt a province of the Roman Empire.

The cultural centers of the Hellenistic period were the court cities of the Greek kings who succeeded Alexander and divided his far-flung empire among themselves. Chief among them were Antioch in Syria, Alexandria in Egypt (named after Alexander, and the site of his tomb), and Pergamon in Asia Minor (MAP 5-1). An international culture united the Hellenistic world, and its language was Greek. Hellenistic kings became enormously rich, and they prided themselves on their libraries, art collections, scientific enterprises, and skills as critics and connoisseurs, as well as on the learned men they could assemble at their courts. The world of the small, austere, and heroic city-state passed away, as did the power and prestige of its center, Athens. A cosmopolitan ("citizen of the world," in Greek) civilization, much like today's, replaced it.

Architecture

The greater variety, complexity, and sophistication of Hellenistic culture called for an architecture on a grandiose scale and of wide diversity, something far beyond the requirements of the Classical polis, even beyond that of Athens at the height of its power. Building activity shifted from the old centers on the Greek mainland to the opulent cities of the Hellenistic monarchs in the East.

Temple of Apollo, Didyma.   Great scale, a theatrical element of surprise, and a willingness to break the traditional rules of Greek temple design characterize one of the most ambitious projects of the Hellenistic period, the Temple of Apollo (FIG. 5-75) at Didyma. The Hellenistic temple replaced the Archaic temple at the site razed by the Persians in 494 BCE when they sacked nearby Miletos. Construction began around 300 BCE under the direction of two architects native to the area, PAIONIOS OF EPHESOS and DAPHNIS OF MILETOS. So vast was the undertaking, however, that work on the temple continued off and on for more than 500 years—and still the project was never completed.

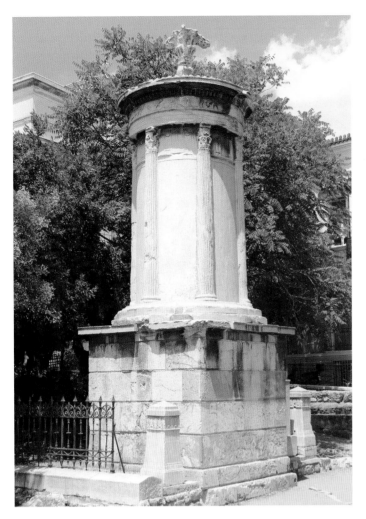

5-74 **Choragic Monument of Lysikrates, Athens, Greece, 334 BCE.**

The first known use of Corinthian capitals on the exterior of a building is on the monument erected by Lysikrates in Athens to commemorate the victory his chorus won in a theatrical contest.

tholos, set on a square base. Engaged Corinthian columns adorn the drum of Lysikrates's monument, and a huge Corinthian capital sits atop the roof. The freestanding capital once supported the victor's trophy, a bronze *tripod,* a deep basin on a tall three-legged stand, traditionally associated with Apollo, the patron god of music.

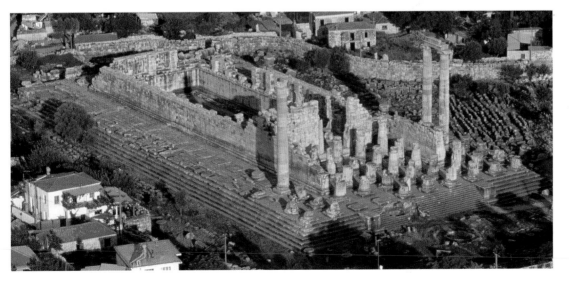

5-75 PAIONIOS OF EPHESOS and DAPHNIS OF MILETOS, **aerial view of the Temple of Apollo (looking east), Didyma, Turkey, begun ca. 300 BCE.**

A theatrical element of surprise is one of the key features of Didyma's immense Early Hellenistic Ionic Apollo temple—a building project so ambitious that it continued for more than five centuries.

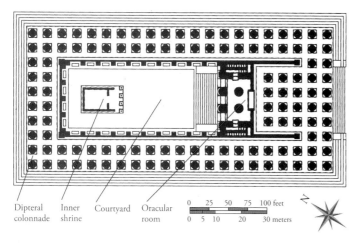

Dipteral   Inner   Courtyard   Oracular
colonnade   shrine   room

0   25   50   75   100 feet
0   5   10   20   30 meters

5-76 Paionios of Ephesos and Daphnis of Miletos, plan of the Temple of Apollo, Didyma, Turkey, begun ca. 300 BCE.

Apollo's temple at Didyma was hypaethral (open to the sky) and featured a dipteral (double peripteral) colonnade framing an interior courtyard with a small shrine that housed a statue of Apollo.

The temple had a double peripteral (dipteral) colonnade (FIG. 5-76) and an unusually broad facade of 10 Ionic columns almost 65 feet tall. The sides had 21 columns, consistent with the Classical formula for perfect proportions used for the Parthenon ($21 = [2 \times 10] + 1$), but nothing else about the design is Classical. One anomaly immediately apparent to anyone who approached the building was that it had no pediment and no roof—it was *hypaethral*, or open to the sky. Also, the grand doorway to what should have been the temple's cella was nearly 5 feet off the ground and could not be entered. The explanation for the peculiar elevated doorway is that it served as a kind of stage where the oracle of Apollo could be announced to those assembled in front of the temple. Further, the unroofed dipteral colonnade did not surround a traditional cella. The columns were instead an elaborate frame for a central courtyard in which was a small prostyle shrine with a statue of Apollo inside. Entrance to the interior court was through two smaller doorways to the left and right of the great portal and down two narrow vaulted tunnels that could accommodate only a single file of people. From these dark and mysterious lateral passageways, worshipers emerged into the clear light of the courtyard, which also had a sacred spring and laurel trees in honor of Apollo. Opposite Apollo's inner temple, a stairway some 50 feet wide rose

PROBLEMS AND SOLUTIONS

Hippodamos's Plan for the Ideal City

When the Greeks finally expelled the Persians from Asia Minor in 479 BCE, they returned to cities in near ruin. Reconstruction of Miletos began after 466 BCE, but the Classical city did not follow the plan of its Archaic predecessor. Hippodamos of Miletos, whom Aristotle singled out as the father of rational city planning, was the designer of the new Miletos as well as Piraeus, the port city of Athens. Hippodamos had to address the question of what an ideal city plan should be. His solution was to impose a strict grid of streets on the site, regardless of the terrain, so that all streets met at right angles.

Although such *orthogonal plans* predate Hippodamos and can be found in Archaic Greece and Etruscan Italy (FIG. 6-2A) as well as in ancient Mesopotamia and Egypt, the Greek city planner became so famous that his name has ever since been synonymous with urban grid plans. The so-called *Hippodamian plan* was not, however, solely a grid of streets. Hippodamos also designated separate quarters for public, private, and religious functions. A "Hippodamian city" was logically as well as regularly planned. This desire to impose order on nature and to assign a proper place in the whole to

5-77 Restored view of Priene, Turkey, fourth century BCE and later (John Burge).

Despite its irregular terrain, Priene had a strict grid plan conforming to the principles of Hippodamos of Miletos, whom Aristotle singled out as the father of rational city planning.

each of the city's constituent parts was very much in keeping with the philosophical principles of the fifth century BCE. Hippodamos's formula for the ideal city was another manifestation of the same outlook that produced Polykleitos's *Canon* and the Parthenon.

Hippodamian planning was still the norm in Late Classical and Hellenistic Greece. The city of Priene (FIG. 5-77), also in Asia Minor, was laid out during the fourth century BCE. It had fewer than 5,000 inhabitants. (Hippodamos thought 10,000 was the ideal number. Fifth-century BCE Athens had a population of 150,000 to 200,000.) Situated on sloping ground, many of its narrow north-south streets were little more than long stairways. Uniformly sized city blocks, the standard planning unit, were nonetheless imposed on the irregular terrain. More than one unit was reserved for major structures, such as the Temple of Athena and the theater. The central agora occupied six blocks.

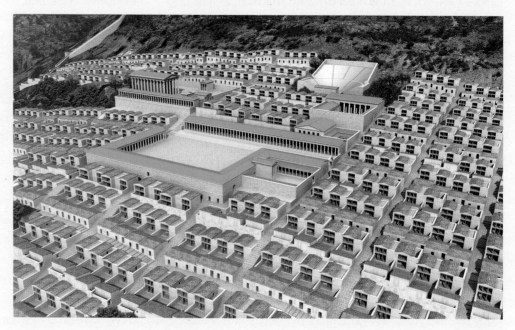

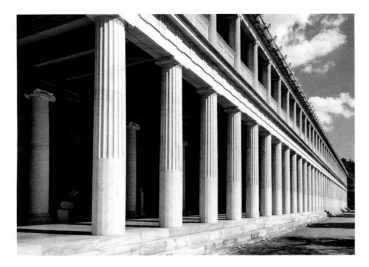

5-78 Stoa of Attalos II (looking southeast), Agora, Athens, Greece, ca. 150 BCE.

The Stoa of Attalos II in the Athenian agora has been meticulously restored. Greek stoas were covered colonnades that housed shops and civic offices. They were also ideal vehicles for shaping urban spaces.

majestically toward three portals leading into the oracular room that also opened onto the front of the temple. This complex spatial planning marked a sharp departure from Classical Greek architecture, which stressed a building's exterior almost as a work of sculpture and left its interior relatively undeveloped.

Stoas and City Planning. One of the most important—and certainly the most versatile—secular Greek buildings was the *stoa.* These covered colonnades, or *porticos,* which often housed shops and civic offices, were ideal vehicles for shaping urban spaces, and they were staples of Late Classical and Hellenistic cities (see "Hippodamos's Plan for the Ideal City," page 154). Priene (FIG. 5-77) had stoas framing each side of its agora, and even the marketplace of Athens, an ancient city notable for its haphazard, unplanned development, was eventually framed to the east and south by stoas placed at right angles to one another. These new porticos joined the famous Painted Stoa in the Athenian agora, which housed paintings

by Polygnotos and other Classical masters, and where the Hellenistic philosopher Zeno and his successors taught. The *Stoic* school of Greek philosophy took its name from that building.

The finest of the new Athenian stoas was the Stoa of Attalos II (FIG. 5-78), a gift to the city by a grateful alumnus, the king of Pergamon (r. 159–138 BCE), who had studied at Athens in his youth. The stoa has been meticulously reconstructed under the direction of the American School of Classical Studies at Athens and today has a second life as a museum housing eight decades of finds from the Athenian agora, as well as the offices of the American excavation team. The stoa has two stories, each with 21 shops opening onto the colonnade. The facade columns are Doric on the ground level and Ionic on the second story. The mixing of the two orders on a single facade had occurred even in the Late Classical period. But it became increasingly common in the Hellenistic period, when respect for the old rules of Greek architecture was greatly diminished and a desire for variety and decorative effects often prevailed. Practical considerations also governed the form of the Stoa of Attalos II. The columns are far more widely spaced than in Greek temple architecture, to enable easy access. Also, the builders left the lower third of every Doric column shaft unfluted to guard against damage from constant traffic.

Pergamon

Pergamon, the kingdom of Attalos II, was born in the early third century BCE after the breakup of Alexander's empire. Founded by Philetairos (r. 282–263 BCE), the Pergamene kingdom embraced almost all of western and southern Asia Minor. Upon the death in 133 BCE of its last king, Attalos III (r. 138–133 BCE), Pergamon was bequeathed to Rome, which by then was the greatest power in the Mediterranean world. The Attalids enjoyed immense wealth and expended much of it on the embellishment of their capital city, especially its acropolis. Located there were the royal palace, an arsenal and barracks, a great library and theater, an agora, and the sacred precincts of Athena and Zeus.

Altar of Zeus. The Altar of Zeus at Pergamon, erected about 175 BCE, is the most famous Hellenistic sculptural ensemble. The monument's west front (FIG. 5-79) has been reconstructed in

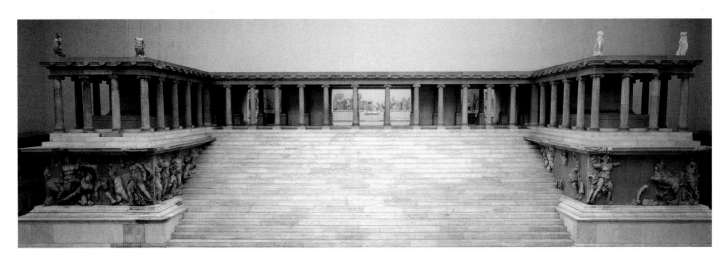

5-79 Reconstructed west front of the Altar of Zeus, Pergamon, Turkey, ca. 175 BCE. Pergamonmuseum, Staatliche Museen zu Berlin, Berlin.

The gigantomachy frieze of Pergamon's monumental Altar of Zeus is almost 400 feet long. The battle of gods and giants alluded to the victory of King Attalos I over the Gauls of Asia Minor.

Athena battling Alkyoneos, detail of the gigantomachy frieze, Altar of Zeus (FIG. 5-79), Pergamon, Turkey, ca. 175 BCE. Marble, 7′ 6″ high. Pergamonmuseum, Staatliche Museen zu Berlin, Berlin.

The tumultuous battle scenes of the Pergamon altar have an emotional power unparalleled in earlier Greek art. Violent movement, swirling draperies, and vivid depictions of suffering fill the frieze.

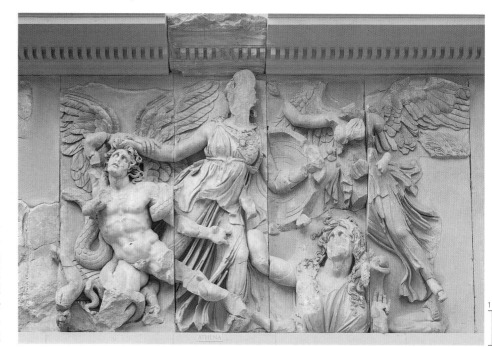

Berlin. The altar proper was on an elevated platform, framed by an Ionic stoa-like colonnade with projecting wings on either side of a broad central staircase. All around the altar platform was a sculptured frieze almost 400 feet long, populated by about a hundred larger-than-life-size figures. The subject is the battle of Zeus and the gods against the giants. It is the most extensive representation that Greek artists ever attempted of that epic conflict for control of the world. The gigantomachy also appeared on the shield of Phidias's *Athena Parthenos* and on the east metopes of the Parthenon, because the Athenians wished to draw a parallel between the defeat of the giants and the defeat of the Persians. In the third century BCE, King Attalos I (r. 241–197 BCE) had successfully turned back an invasion of the Gauls in Asia Minor. The gigantomachy of the Altar of Zeus alluded to that Attalid victory over those barbarians. The Pergamene designers also used the gigantomachy frieze to establish a connection with Athens, whose earlier defeat of the Persians was by then legendary, and with the Parthenon, which the Hellenistic Greeks already recognized as a Classical monument—in both senses of the word. The figure of Athena (FIG. 5-80), for example, closely resembles the Athena from the Parthenon's east pediment. While Gaia, the earth goddess and mother of the giants, emerges from the ground and looks on with horror, Athena grabs the hair of the giant Alkyoneos as Nike flies in to crown her. Zeus (not illustrated) derives from the Poseidon of the west pediment.

The Pergamene frieze is not a dry series of borrowed motifs, however. On the contrary, its tumultuous narrative has an emotional intensity without parallel in earlier sculpture. The battle rages everywhere, even spilling onto the steps used to reach Zeus's altar (FIG. 5-79). Violent movement, swirling draperies, and vivid depictions of death and suffering fill the frieze. Wounded figures writhe in pain, and their faces reveal their anguish. Deep carving creates dark shadows. The figures project from the background like bursts of light. Art historians have justly described these features as *baroque,* borrowing the term from 17th-century Italian sculpture (see "'Baroque' Art and Architecture," page 712). Indeed, there perhaps can be no greater contrast than between the Pergamene gigantomachy frieze and the comparable frieze (FIG. 5-18) of the Archaic Siphnian Treasury at Delphi.

Dying Gauls. On the Altar of Zeus, Pergamene sculptors presented the victory of Attalos I over the Gauls in mythological disguise. An earlier Pergamene statuary group explicitly depicted the defeat of the barbarians. Roman copies of some of these figures show that Hellenistic sculptors carefully studied and reproduced

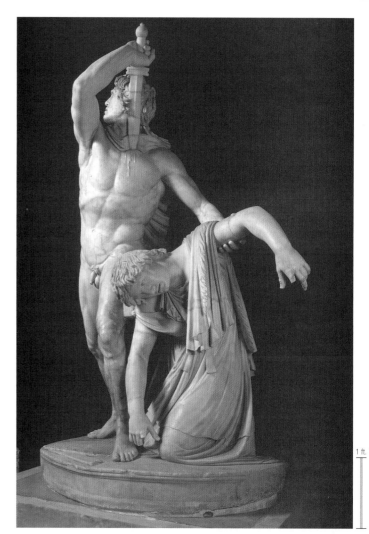

5-81 EPIGONOS(?), **Gallic chieftain killing himself and his wife.** Roman copy of a bronze statue of ca. 230–220 BCE. Marble, 6′ 11″ high. Palazzo Altemps, Museo Nazionale Romano, Rome.

The defeat of the Gauls was also the subject of Pergamene statuary groups. The centerpiece of one group was a chieftain committing suicide after taking his wife's life. He preferred death to surrender.

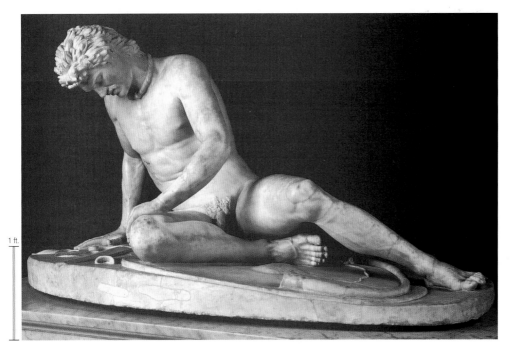

5-82 Epigonos(?), dying Gaul. Roman copy of a bronze statue of ca. 230–220 BCE. Marble, 3′ $\frac{1}{2}$″ high. Museo Capitolino, Musei Capitolini, Rome.

A Pergamene sculptor depicted this defeated Gallic trumpeter and the other Gauls as barbarians with bushy hair, mustaches, and neck bands, but also as noble foes who fought to the death.

the distinctive features of the foreign Gauls, most notably their long, bushy hair and mustaches and the *torques* (neck bands) they frequently wore. The Pergamene victors were apparently not part of this group. The viewer saw only their Gallic foes and their noble and moving response to defeat.

In what was probably the center-piece of the group, a heroic Gallic chieftain (FIG. 5-81) defiantly drives a sword into his own chest just below the collarbone, preferring suicide to surrender. He already has taken the life of his wife, who, if captured, would have been sold as a slave. In the best Lysippan tradition, the group can be fully appreciated only by walking around it. From one side, the observer sees the Gaul's intensely expressive face, from another his powerful torso, and from a third the woman's limp, lifeless body. The man's twisting posture, the almost theatrical gestures, and the emotional intensity of the suicidal act are hallmarks of the Pergamene baroque style and have close parallels in the later frieze of Zeus's altar.

The third Gaul from this group is a trumpeter (FIG. 5-82) who collapses upon his large oval shield as blood pours from the gash in his chest. He stares at the ground with a pained expression. The Hellenistic figure recalls the dying warrior (FIG. 5-29) from the east pediment of the Temple of Aphaia at Aegina, but the pathos and drama of the suffering Gaul are far more pronounced. As in the suicide group and the gigantomachy frieze, the sculptor rendered the male musculature in an exaggerated manner. Note the tautness of the chest and the bulging veins of the left leg—implying that the unseen Pergamene warrior who has struck down this noble and savage foe must have been an extraordinarily powerful man. If this figure is the *tubicen* ("trumpeter") that Pliny mentioned as the work of the Pergamene master EPIGONOS,[9] then Epigonos may be the sculptor of the entire group and the creator of the dynamic Hellenistic baroque style.

Statuary

In different ways, Praxiteles, Skopas, and Lysippos had already taken bold steps in redefining the nature of Greek statuary. Still, Hellenistic sculptors went further, both in terms of style and in expanding the range of subjects considered suitable for large-scale public sculpture.

Nike of Samothrace. One of the masterpieces of Hellenistic baroque sculpture is the statue of winged Victory set up in the Sanctuary of the Great Gods on the island of Samothrace. The *Nike of Samothrace* (FIG. 5-83) has just alighted on the prow of a Greek warship. She raises her (missing) right arm to crown the naval

5-83 Nike alighting on a warship (*Nike of Samothrace*), from Samothrace, Greece, ca. 190 BCE. Marble, Nike 8′ 1″ high. Musée du Louvre, Paris.

Victory lands on a ship's prow to crown a naval victor. Her wings still beat, and the wind sweeps her drapery. The statue's placement in a fountain of splashing water heightened the dramatic visual effect.

victor, just as Nike places a wreath on Athena's head on the Altar of Zeus (FIG. 5-80). But the Pergamene relief figure seems calm by comparison. The Samothracian Nike's wings still beat, and the wind sweeps her drapery (compare the earlier attempt to suggest wind-blown clothing in the figure of Iris [FIG. 5-49C] in the Parthenon's west pediment). Nike's himation bunches in thick folds around her right leg, and her chiton is pulled tightly across her abdomen and left leg.

The statue's setting amplified this theatrical effect. The sculptor set the war galley in the upper basin of a two-tiered fountain. In the lower basin were large boulders. The fountain's flowing water created the illusion of rushing waves hitting the prow of the ship. The statue's reflection in the shimmering water below accentuated the sense of lightness and movement. The sound of splashing water added another dimension to the visual drama. Art and nature combined here to create one of the most successful sculptures ever fashioned. In the *Nike of Samothrace* and other works in the Hellenistic baroque manner, sculptors resoundingly rejected the Polykleitan conception of a statue as an ideally proportioned, self-contained entity on a bare pedestal. The Hellenistic statues interact with their environment and appear as living, breathing, and intensely emotive human (or divine) presences.

Venus de Milo. In the Hellenistic period, sculptors regularly followed Praxiteles's lead in undressing Aphrodite, but they also openly explored the eroticism of the nude female form. The famous *Venus de Milo* (FIG. 5-84) is a larger-than-life-size marble statue of Aphrodite found on Melos together with its inscribed base (now lost) signed by the sculptor ALEXANDROS OF ANTIOCH-ON-THE-MEANDER. In this statue, the goddess of love is more modestly draped than the *Aphrodite of Knidos* (FIG. 5-62), but is more overtly sexual. Her left hand (separately preserved) holds the apple that Paris awarded her when he judged her the most beautiful goddess. Her right hand may have lightly grasped the edge of her drapery near the left hip in a halfhearted attempt to keep it from slipping farther down her body. The sculptor intentionally designed the work to tease the spectator, instilling this partially draped Aphrodite with a sexuality absent from Praxiteles's entirely nude image of the goddess. Other Hellenistic sculptors (FIG. 5-84A), especially when creating works for private patrons, went even further in depicting the goddess of love as an object of sexual desire.

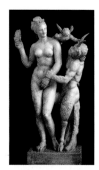

⏁ **5-84A** Aphrodite, Eros, and Pan, ca. 100 BCE.

Barberini Faun. Archaic statues smile at the viewer, and even when Classical statues look away, they are always awake and alert. Hellenistic sculptors often portrayed sleep (FIG. 5-84B). The suspension of consciousness and the entrance into the fantasy world of dreams—the antithesis of the Classical ideals of

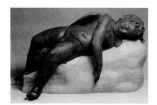

⏁ **5-84B** Sleeping Eros, ca. 150–100 BCE.

rationality and discipline—had great appeal for them. This newfound interest is evident in a marble statue (FIG. 5-85) of a drunken, restlessly sleeping *satyr* (a semihuman follower of Dionysos) known as the *Barberini Faun,* after Cardinal Francesco Barberini (1597–1679), who acquired the statue when it was unearthed in Rome in the 17th century. Barberini hired Gianlorenzo Bernini, the great Italian Baroque sculptor (FIGS. 24-1, 24-6, 24-6A, and 24-7), to restore the statue. Bernini no doubt felt that this dynamic statue in the Pergamene manner was the work of a kindred spirit. The satyr has consumed too much wine and has thrown down his panther skin on a convenient rock, then fallen into a disturbed, intoxicated sleep. His brows are furrowed, and one can almost hear him snore.

Eroticism also comes to the fore in this statue. Although men had been represented naked in Greek art for hundreds of years, Archaic kouroi and Classical athletes and gods do not exude

5-84 ALEXANDROS OF ANTIOCH-ON-THE-MEANDER, Aphrodite (*Venus de Milo*), from Melos, Greece, ca. 150–125 BCE. Marble, 6′ 7″ high. Musée du Louvre, Paris.

Displaying the eroticism of many Hellenistic statues, this Aphrodite is more overtly sexual than the Knidian Aphrodite (FIG. 5-62). The goddess's slipping garment teases the spectator.

1 ft.

sexuality. Sensuality surfaced in the works of Praxiteles and his followers in the fourth century BCE. But the dreamy and supremely beautiful Hermes playfully dangling grapes before the infant Dionysos (FIG. 5-63) has nothing of the blatant sexuality of the *Barberini Faun,* whose wantonly spread legs focus attention on his genitals. Homosexuality was common in the male world of ancient Greece. It is not surprising that when Hellenistic sculptors began to explore the sexuality of the human body, they turned their attention to men as well as women. In the Greek world, the "male gaze" was directed at both sexes.

Defeated Boxer. Although Hellenistic sculptors tackled an expanded range of subjects, they did not abandon traditional themes, such as the Greek athlete. Nevertheless, they often treated the old subjects in novel ways. This is certainly true of the magnificent bronze statue (FIG. 5-86) of a seated boxer, a Hellenistic original found in Rome and perhaps at one time part of a group. The boxer is not a victorious young athlete with a perfect face and body but a heavily battered, defeated veteran whose upward glance may have been directed at the man who had just beaten him. Too many punches from powerful hands wrapped in leather thongs—Greek boxers did not use the modern sport's cushioned gloves—have distorted the boxer's face. His nose is broken, as are his teeth. He has smashed "cauliflower" ears. Inlaid copper blood drips from the cuts on his forehead, nose, and cheeks. How different is this rendition of a powerful bearded man from that of the noble Riace warrior (FIGS. I-17 and 5-36) of the Early Classical period. The Hellenistic sculptor appealed not to the intellect but to the emotions when striving to evoke compassion for the pounded hulk of a once-mighty fighter.

Old Market Woman. The realistic bent of much Hellenistic sculpture—the very opposite of the Classical period's idealism—is evident above all in a series of statues of old men and women from the lowest rungs of the social order. Shepherds, fishermen, and drunken beggars are common—the kinds of people pictured earlier on red-figure vases but never before thought worthy of life-size statuary. One of the finest preserved statues of this type depicts a haggard old woman bringing chickens and a basket of fruits and vegetables to sell in the market or, according to a recent interpretation suggested by the ivy wreath in her hair, bringing gifts to the

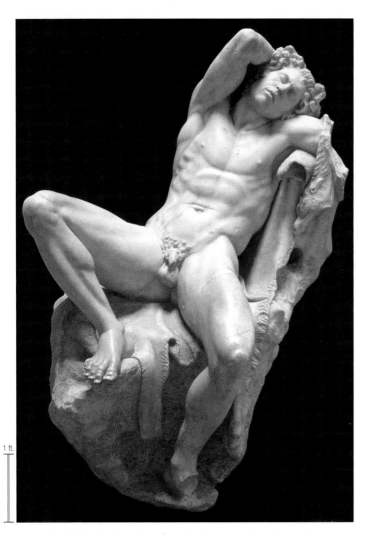

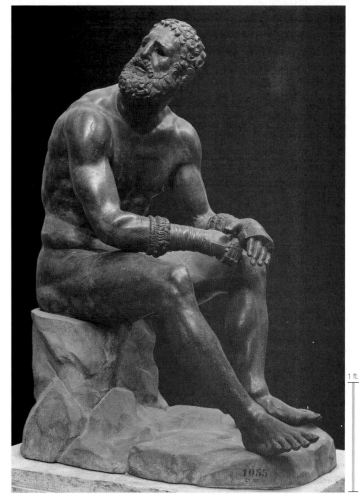

5-85 Sleeping satyr (*Barberini Faun*), from Castel Sant'Angelo, Rome, Italy, ca. 230–200 BCE. Marble, 7′ 1″ high. Glyptothek, Munich.

Here, a Hellenistic sculptor represented a restlessly sleeping, drunken satyr, a semihuman in a suspended state of consciousness—the antithesis of the Classical ideals of rationality and discipline.

5-86 Seated boxer, from the Baths of Constantine, Quirinal hill, Rome, Italy, ca. 100–50 BCE. Bronze, 4′ 2″ high. Palazzo Massimo alle Terme, Museo Nazionale Romano, Rome.

Even when Hellenistic artists treated traditional themes, they approached them in novel ways. This bronze statue depicts an older, defeated boxer with a broken nose and battered ears.

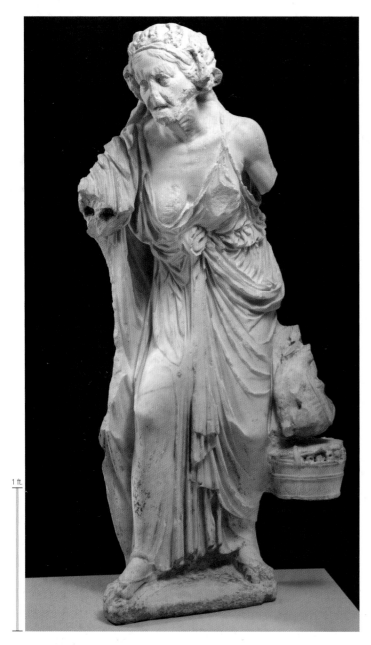

5-87 Old market woman. Roman copy(?) of a marble statue of
ca. 150–100 BCE. Marble, 4′ 1⅝″ high. Metropolitan Museum of Art,
New York.

Consistent with the realism of much Hellenistic art, many statues portray the
elderly of the lowest rungs of society. Earlier Greek artists did not consider
them suitable subjects for statuary.

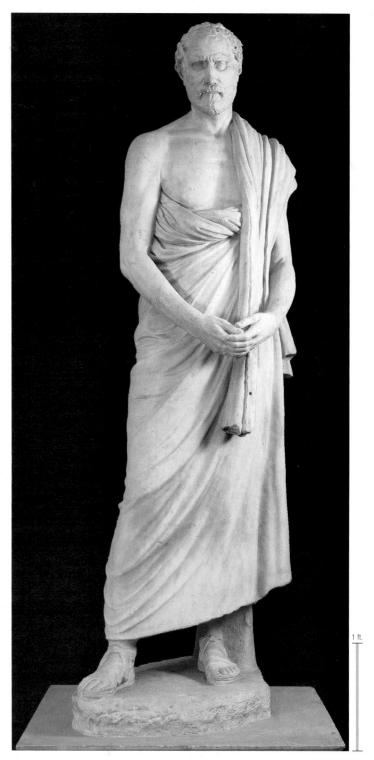

5-88 POLYEUKTOS, Demosthenes. Roman copy of a bronze
original of ca. 280 BCE. Marble, 6′ 7½″ high. Ny Carlsberg Glyptotek,
Copenhagen.

One of the earliest Hellenistic portraits, frequently copied, was Polyeuktos's
representation of the great orator Demosthenes as a frail man who possessed great courage and moral conviction.

god Dionysos at one of his festivals (FIG. 5-87). In either case, the
woman's face is wrinkled and her body bent with age. Whatever
the purpose of this and similar statues, they attest to an interest in
social realism absent in earlier Greek statuary.

Statues of the aged and the ugly are, of course, the polar opposites of the images of the young and the beautiful that dominated
Greek art until the Hellenistic age, but they are consistent with the
period's changed character. The Hellenistic world was a cosmopolitan place, and the highborn could not help but encounter the
poor and a growing number of foreigners (non-Greek "barbarians") on a daily basis. Hellenistic art reflects this different social
climate in the depiction of a much wider variety of physical types,

including different ethnicities. The sensitive portrayal of Gallic warriors with their shaggy hair, strange mustaches, and gold torques
(FIGS. 5-81 and 5-82) has already been noted. Africans, Scythians,
and others, formerly only the occasional subject of vase painters,
also entered the realm of large-scale sculpture in Hellenistic art.

Demosthenes. These sculptures of foreigners and the urban poor, however realistic, are not portraits. Rather, they are sensitive studies of physical types. But the growing interest in the individual beginning in the Late Classical period did lead in the Hellenistic era to the production of true likenesses of specific persons. In fact, one of the great achievements of Hellenistic artists was the redefinition of portraiture. In the Classical period, Kresilas won fame for having made the noble Pericles appear even nobler in his portrait (FIG. 5-42). By contrast, in Hellenistic times, sculptors sought not only to record the true appearance of their subjects in bronze and stone but also to capture the essence of their personalities in likenesses both accurate and moving.

One of the earliest of these, perhaps the finest of the Hellenistic age and frequently copied in Roman times, was a bronze portrait statue of Demosthenes (FIG. 5-88) by POLYEUKTOS. The original, commissioned in 280 BCE, 42 years after the great orator's death, stood in the Athenian agora. Demosthenes was a frail man and in his youth even suffered from a speech impediment, but he had enormous courage and great moral conviction. A veteran of the disastrous battle against Philip II at Chaeronea, he repeatedly tried to rally opposition to Macedonian imperialism, both before and after Alexander's death.

In the end, when it was clear that the Macedonians would capture him, he took his own life by drinking poison.

Polyeuktos rejected Kresilas's and Lysippos's notions of the purpose of portraiture and did not attempt to portray a supremely confident leader with a magnificent physique. His Demosthenes has an aged and slightly stooped body. The orator clasps his hands nervously in front of him as he looks downward, deep in thought. His face is lined, his hair is receding, and his expression is one of great sadness. Whatever physical discomfort Demosthenes felt is here joined by an inner pain, his deep sorrow over the tragic demise of democracy at the hands of the Macedonian conquerors.

Hellenistic Art under Roman Patronage

In the opening years of the second century BCE, the Roman general Flamininus defeated the Macedonian army and declared the old poleis of Classical Greece free once again. The city-states never regained their former glory, however. Greece became a Roman province in 146 BCE. When, 60 years later, Athens sided with King Mithridates VI of Pontus (r. 120–63 BCE) in his war against Rome, the general Sulla crushed the Athenians. Thereafter, although Athens retained some of its earlier prestige as a center of culture and learning, politically it was merely another city in the ever-expanding Roman Empire. Nonetheless, Greek artists continued to be in great demand, both to furnish the Romans with an endless stream of copies of Classical and Hellenistic masterpieces and to create new statues in Greek style for Roman patrons.

Laocoön. One work of this type is the famous group (FIG. 5-89) of the Trojan priest Laocoön and his sons, unearthed in Rome in 1506 in the presence of the great Italian Renaissance artist Michelangelo. The marble group, long believed to be an original of the second century BCE, was found in the remains of the palace of the emperor Titus (r. 79–81 CE), exactly where Pliny had seen it more than 14 centuries

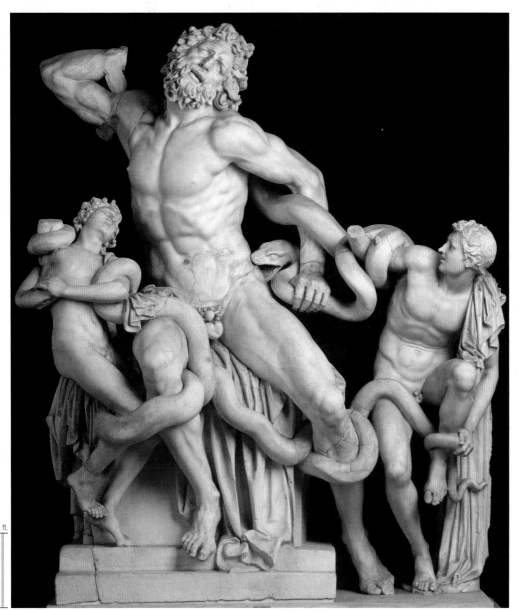

1 ft.

5-89 ATHANADOROS, HAGESANDROS, and POLYDOROS OF RHODES, Laocoön and his sons, from Rome, Italy, early first century CE. Marble, 7′ 10½″ high. Musei Vaticani, Rome.

Hellenistic style lived on in Rome. Although stylistically akin to Pergamene sculpture, this statue of sea serpents attacking Laocoön and his two sons matches the account given only in the *Aeneid*.

before. Pliny attributed the statue to three sculptors—ATHANADOROS, HAGESANDROS, and POLYDOROS OF RHODES—who most art historians now think worked in the early first century CE. These artists probably based their group on a Hellenistic masterpiece, perhaps depicting Laocoön and only one son. The Rhodian sculptors may have added the son at Laocoön's left (note the greater compositional integration of the other two figures) to match the Roman poet Vergil's account in the *Aeneid*. Vergil vividly described the strangling of Laocoön and his *two* sons by sea serpents while sacrificing at an altar. The gods who favored the Greeks in the war against Troy had sent the serpents to punish Laocoön for having tried to warn his compatriots about the danger of bringing the Greeks' wood horse within the walls of their city.

In Vergil's graphic account, Laocoön suffered in terrible agony. Athanadoros, Hagesandros, and Polydoros communicated the torment of Vergil's priest and his sons in spectacular fashion in the marble group. The three Trojans writhe in pain as they struggle to free themselves from the death grip of the serpents. One bites into Laocoön's left hip as the priest lets out a ferocious cry. The serpent-entwined figures recall the suffering giants of the great frieze of the Altar of Zeus at Pergamon, and Laocoön himself is strikingly similar to Alkyoneos (FIG. 5-80), Athena's opponent. In fact, many scholars believe that a Pergamene statuary group of the second century BCE was the inspiration for the Rhodian artists.

Sperlonga. That the work seen by Pliny and displayed in the Vatican Museums today was made for Romans rather than Greeks was confirmed in 1957 by the discovery of fragments of several Hellenistic-style groups illustrating scenes from Homer's *Odyssey*. Archaeologists found the sculptures in a grotto that served as the picturesque summer banquet hall of the seaside villa of the Roman emperor Tiberius (r. 14–37 CE) at Sperlonga, some 60 miles south of Rome. One of these groups—depicting the monster Scylla attacking Odysseus's ship—bears the signatures of the same three sculptors whom Pliny cited as the creators of the Laocoön group. Another group, installed around a central pool in the grotto, depicted the blinding of the Cyclops Polyphemos by Odysseus and his comrades, an incident also set in a cave in the Homeric epic. The figure of Odysseus (FIG. 5-90) from this theatrical group is one of the finest sculptures of antiquity. The hero's cap can barely contain his swirling locks of hair. Even Odysseus's beard seems to be swept up in the emotional intensity of the moment. The parted lips and the deep shadows produced by sharp

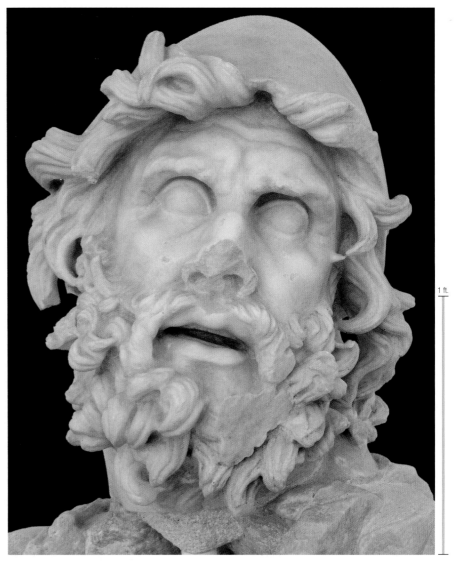

1 ft.

5-90 ATHANADOROS, HAGESANDROS, and POLYDOROS OF RHODES, head of Odysseus, from the villa of Tiberius, Sperlonga, Italy, early first century CE. Marble, 2′ 1¼″ high. Museo Archeologico, Sperlonga.

This emotionally charged depiction of Odysseus was part of a mythological statuary group that the three Laocoön sculptors made for a grotto at the emperor Tiberius's seaside villa at Sperlonga.

undercutting add drama to the head, which complemented Odysseus's agitated body.

At Tiberius's villa in Sperlonga and in Titus's palace in Rome, the baroque style of Hellenistic sculpture lived on long after Greece ceased to be a political force. When Rome inherited the Pergamene kingdom from the last of the Attalids in 133 BCE, it also became heir to the Greek artistic legacy. What Rome adopted from Greece it passed on to the medieval and modern worlds. If Greece can claim to be the inventor of the European spirit, Rome was its propagator and amplifier.

Ancient Greece

Geometric and Orientalizing Art ca. 900–600 BCE

- Homer lived during the eighth century BCE, the era when the city-states of Classical Greece took shape, the Olympic Games were founded (776 BCE), and the Greeks began to trade with their neighbors to both east and west. At the same time, the human figure returned to Greek art in simplified bronze statuettes and as composite silhouettes amid other abstract motifs on Geometric vases.

- Increasing contact with the civilizations of Egypt and Mesopotamia inspired the so-called Orientalizing phase (ca. 700–600 BCE) of Greek art, when Eastern monsters began to appear on black-figure vases.

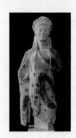

Geometric krater, ca. 740 BCE

Archaic Art ca. 600–480 BCE

- Around 600 BCE, the first life-size stone statues appeared in Greece. Archaic kouroi emulated the frontal poses of Egyptian statues, but artists depicted the young men nude, the way Greek athletes competed at Olympia. During the sixth century BCE, Greek sculptors refined the proportions and added "Archaic smiles" to the faces of their statues, both male and female, to make them seem more lifelike.

- The Archaic age also brought the codification of the Doric and Ionic orders and the construction of the first stone temples with peripteral colonnades.

- Greek ceramists perfected black-figure painting and then, around 530 BCE, red-figure painting, which encouraged experimentation with foreshortening.

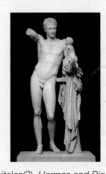

Kore, Athenian Acropolis, ca. 520–510 BCE

Early and High Classical Art ca. 480–400 BCE

- The Classical period opened with the Persian sack of the Athenian Acropolis in 480 BCE and the Greek victory a year later. During the Early Classical period (480–450 BCE), sculptors revolutionized statuary by introducing weight shift to their figures.

- In the High Classical period (450–400 BCE), Polykleitos developed a canon of proportions for the perfect statue. Iktinos similarly applied mathematical formulas to temple design in the shared belief that beauty resulted from the use of harmonic numbers.

- Under the patronage of Pericles and the artistic directorship of Phidias, the Athenians rebuilt the Acropolis after 447 BCE. The Parthenon and its sculptures and those of Polykleitos have defined what it means to be "Classical" ever since.

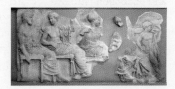

East frieze, Parthenon, Athens, ca. 447–438 BCE

Late Classical Art ca. 400–323 BCE

- In the aftermath of the Peloponnesian War, which ended in 404 BCE, Greek artists, though still adhering to the philosophy that humans are the "measure of all things," began to focus more on the real world of appearances than on the ideal world of perfect beings. Late Classical sculptors humanized the remote deities, athletes, and heroes of the fifth century BCE. Praxiteles injected sensuality into his images, even representing Aphrodite nude. Lysippos depicted Herakles as muscle-bound but so weary that he needed to lean on his club for support.

- In architecture, the ornate Corinthian capital became increasingly popular, breaking the monopoly of the Doric and Ionic orders.

- The period closed with Alexander the Great, who transformed the Mediterranean world politically and ushered in a new artistic age as well.

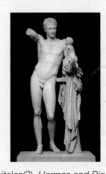

Praxiteles(?), *Hermes and Dionysos*, ca. 340 BCE

Hellenistic Art ca. 323–30 BCE

- The Hellenistic age extended from the death of Alexander until the death of Cleopatra, when Egypt became a province of the Roman Empire.

- In art, both architects and sculptors broke most of the rules of Classical design. At Didyma, for example, the Temple of Apollo had no roof and contained a smaller temple within it. Hellenistic sculptors explored new subjects, such as aged, bent women, and Gauls with strange mustaches and necklaces, and treated traditional subjects in new ways—for example, athletes with battered bodies and faces, and openly erotic goddesses. Artists delighted in depicting violent movement and unbridled emotion.

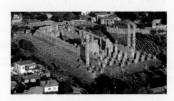

Temple of Apollo, Didyma, begun ca. 300 BCE

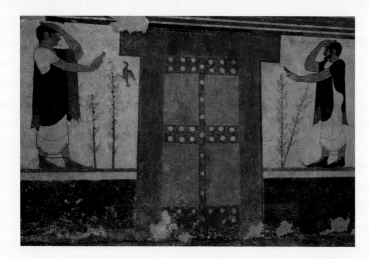

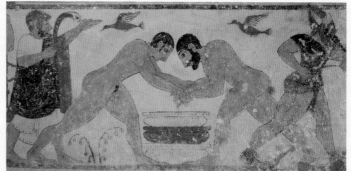

6-1a The large door is probably the symbolic entrance to the Underworld. Two men extend one arm toward the door and place one hand against the forehead in a double gesture signifying salute and mourning.

▶6-1b On the right wall, the Etruscan painter depicted the funerary games in honor of the deceased. The man with a curved staff is not a Roman augur with a lituus but the umpire at a wrestling match.

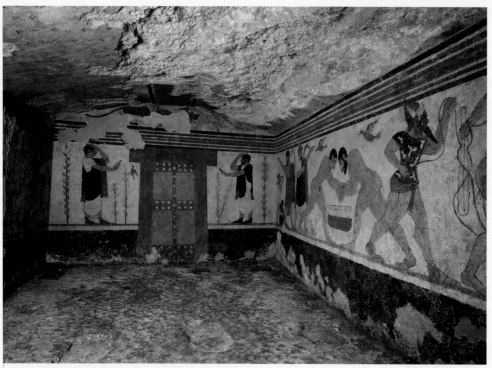

6-1 **Interior of the Tomb of the Augurs, Monterozzi necropolis, Tarquinia, ca. 520 BCE.**

▶6-1c A masked phersu, unique to Etruria, oversees a gruesome contest—perhaps a precursor of Roman gladiatorial games—between a club-wielding man, whose head is covered by a sack, and a fearsome dog.

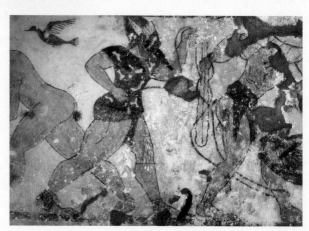

THE ETRUSCANS /6

The Portal to the Etruscan Afterlife

"The Etruscans, as everyone knows, were the people who occupied the middle of Italy in early Roman days, and whom the Romans, in their usual neighborly fashion, wiped out entirely." So opens D. H. Lawrence's witty and sensitive *Etruscan Places* (1929), one of the earliest modern essays to place a high value on Etruscan art and treat it as much more than a debased form of Greek art. ("Most people despise everything B.C. that isn't Greek, for the good reason that it ought to be Greek if it isn't," Lawrence quipped.) Fortunately, scholars and the public at large soon also came to admire the Etruscans, and it has been a long time since anyone had to argue for the importance and originality of Etruscan art. Indeed, although influenced by Greek art, Etruscan art differs in many fundamental ways.

The Tomb of the Augurs (FIG. 6-1), datable around 520 BCE, makes that point forcefully. It is one of thousands of underground tombs laboriously carved out of the bedrock at the important Etruscan city of Tarquinia, at a time when the Greeks still buried their dead in simple graves with a statue or stele as a commemorative marker. The Etruscan tomb also has fresco paintings on all four walls, an art form virtually unknown in sixth-century BCE Greece. And although the Tarquinian painters adopted many Late Archaic Greek stylistic features, the subjects they represented are distinctly Etruscan.

At the center of the rear wall is a large door, probably the symbolic portal to the Underworld and the afterlife. Two facing men extend one arm toward the door and place one hand against the forehead in a double gesture signifying salute and mourning. At the far end of the right wall is a man in a purple robe, a mark of his elevated stature, and two attendants. One carries a chair, the official seat of the man's high office. The other sleeps, or more likely weeps, crouched on the ground. The official is likely the one who has died. The rest of the right wall as well as the left and front walls depict the funerary games in honor of the dead man. To the right of the official and his attendants is a man with a curved staff similar to the *lituus* of the Roman priests called *augurs,* hence the modern name of the tomb. Etruscan priests studied the flight patterns of birds to predict the future. But this Etruscan "augur" is really an umpire at a wrestling match. To the right, a masked man labeled *phersu* (another phersu is at the far end of the left wall) controls a fearsome dog on a leash, which also entangles and restrains the legs of a club-wielding man. A sack covers the man's head, rendering him an almost helpless victim of the dog, which has already drawn blood. Some historians regard this gruesome contest as a direct precursor of Roman gladiatorial shows. In any case, Etruscan art and architecture unquestionably provided the models for the earliest Roman painters, sculptors, and architects.

ETRURIA AND THE ETRUSCANS

The heartland of the Etruscans (who called themselves Rasenna) was the territory between the Arno and Tiber rivers of central Italy (MAP 6-1). The lush green hills still bear their name—Tuscany, the land of the people whom the Romans called Etrusci or Tusci, the region centered on Florence. So, too, do the blue waters that splash against the western coastline of the Italian peninsula, for the Greeks referred to the Etruscans as Tyrsenoi or Tyrrhenoi and gave their name to the Tyrrhenian Sea. Both ancient and modern commentators have debated whether the Etruscans were an indigenous people or immigrants. Their language, although written in a Greek-derived script, is unrelated to the Indo-European linguistic family and remains largely undeciphered. The fifth-century BCE Greek historian Herodotus claimed that the Etruscans came from Lydia in Asia Minor and that Tyrsenos was their king—hence their Greek name. But Dionysius of Halikarnassos, a first-century BCE Greek historian, maintained that the Etrusci were native Italians. Some modern researchers have theorized that the Etruscans emigrated to Italy from the north.

No doubt some truth exists in each theory. The Etruscans of historical times—the Rasenna—were very likely the result of a gradual fusion of native and immigrant populations. This mixing of peoples occurred in the early first millennium BCE during the *Villanovan* period, named for an archaeological site near present-day Bologna. At that time—contemporaneous with the Geometric period in Greece—the Etruscans emerged as a people with an art-producing culture related to but distinct from those of other Italic peoples and from the civilizations of Greece and the Orient.

During the eighth and seventh centuries BCE, the Etruscans, as highly skilled seafarers, enriched themselves through trade abroad. By the sixth century BCE, they controlled most of northern and central Italy. Their most powerful cities included Tarquinia, Cerveteri, Vulci, and Veii. These and the other Etruscan cities never united to form a state, however, so it is inaccurate to speak of an Etruscan "nation" or "kingdom," but only of Etruria, the territory that the Etruscans occupied. Any semblance of unity among the independent Etruscan cities was based primarily on common linguistic ties and religious beliefs and practices.

EARLY ETRUSCAN ART

Although art historians now universally acknowledge the distinctive character of Etruscan painting, sculpture, and architecture, they still usually divide the history of Etruscan art into periods mirroring those of Greek art. The seventh century BCE is the Orientalizing period of Etruscan art (followed by the Archaic, Classical, and Hellenistic periods).

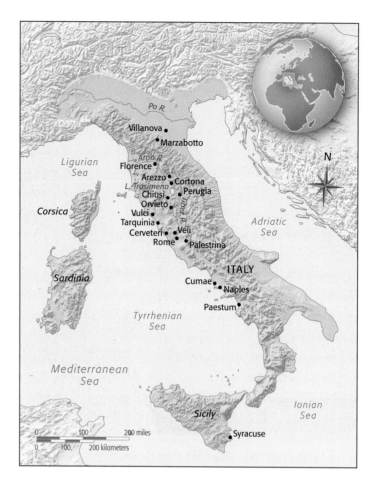

MAP 6-1 Italy in Etruscan times.

Orientalizing Art

During the Orientalizing period, the Etruscans successfully mined iron, tin, copper, and silver, creating great wealth and, in the process, transforming Etruscan society. Villages with agriculture-based economies gave way in the seventh century BCE to prosperous cities engaged in international commerce. Wealthy families could afford to acquire foreign goods, and the Etruscan elite quickly developed a taste for luxury objects incorporating Eastern motifs. To satisfy the demand, local artisans, inspired by imported goods, produced magnificent objects for both homes and tombs. As in Greece at the same time, the locally manufactured Orientalizing artifacts cannot be mistaken for their foreign models.

Regolini-Galassi Tomb. About 650–640 BCE, a wealthy Etruscan family in Cerveteri stocked the Regolini-Galassi Tomb (named after its excavators) with bronze cauldrons and gold jewelry

---

THE ETRUSCANS

900–600 BCE	600–480 BCE	480–89 BCE
Villanovan and Orientalizing	**Archaic**	**Classical and Hellenistic**
▪ The Etruscans emerge as a distinct artistic culture during the Villanovan period (ca. 900–700 BCE) ▪ During the seventh century BCE, trade with Mesopotamia inspires the incorporation of monsters and other Orientalizing motifs in Etruscan funerary goods	▪ The Etruscans construct temples of mud brick and wood, with columns and stairs only on the front and terracotta statuary on the roof ▪ At Cerveteri, the Etruscans bury their dead beneath huge earthen tumuli in multichambered tombs resembling houses ▪ Tarquinian tombs feature fresco paintings depicting banquets and funerary games	▪ Etruscan artists excel in bronze-casting, engraving mirrors and cistae, and carving stone sarcophagi ▪ Etruscan architects construct arcuated gateways, often with engaged columns or pilasters framing the arched passageway

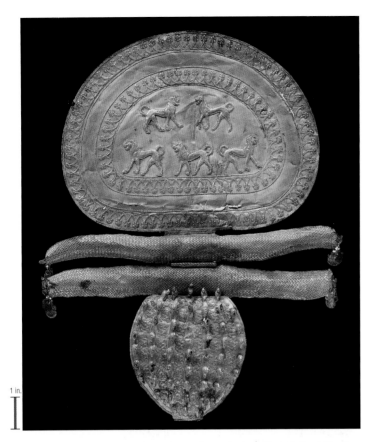

6-2 Fibula with Orientalizing lions, from the Regolini-Galassi Tomb, Sorbo necropolis, Cerveteri, Italy, ca. 650–640 BCE. Gold, 1′ ½″ high. Musei Vaticani, Rome.

This huge gold pin found with other Orientalizing jewelry in a Cerveteri tomb combines repoussé and granulation and is the work of an Etruscan artist, but the lions are Egyptian and Mesopotamian motifs.

produced in Etruria but of Orientalizing style. The most spectacular of the many luxurious objects found in the tomb is a gold *fibula* (clasp or safety pin; FIG. 6-2) of unique shape used to fasten a woman's gown at the shoulder. The gigantic disk-shaped fibula is in the Italic tradition, but the five lions striding across its surface

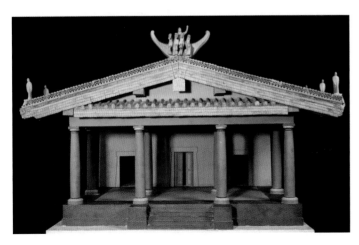

6-3 Model of a typical Etruscan temple of the sixth century BCE, as described by Vitruvius. Istituto di Etruscologia e di Antichità Italiche, Università di Roma, Rome.

Etruscan temples resembled Greek temples, but had widely spaced, unfluted wood columns placed only at the front, walls of sun-dried mud brick, and a narrow staircase at the center of the facade.

RELIGION AND MYTHOLOGY

Etruscan Counterparts of Greco-Roman Gods and Heroes

Etruscan	Greek	Roman
Tinia	Zeus	Jupiter
Uni	Hera	Juno
Menrva	Athena	Minerva
Apulu	Apollo	Apollo
Artumes	Artemis	Diana
Hercle	Herakles	Hercules

are motifs originating in the Orient. The technique, also emulating Eastern imports, is masterful, combining repoussé and *granulation* (the fusing of tiny metal balls, or granules, to a metal surface). The Regolini-Galassi fibula equals or exceeds in quality anything that might have served as a model.

The jewelry from the Regolini-Galassi Tomb also includes a gold *pectoral* that covered a deceased woman's chest, and two gold circlets that may be earrings, although they are large enough to be bracelets. A taste for this kind of ostentatious display is frequently the hallmark of newly acquired wealth, and this was certainly the case in seventh-century BCE Etruria.

Archaic Art and Architecture

The art and architecture of Greece also impressed Etruscan artists looking eastward for inspiration. Still, however eager those artists may have been to emulate Greek works, their distinctive Etruscan temperament always manifested itself.

Etruscan Temples. In religious architecture, for example, the differences between Etruscan temples and their Greek prototypes outweigh the similarities. Because of the materials that Etruscan builders employed, usually only the foundations of their temples have survived. (The same is true of Etruscan civic and domestic structures, but the extant foundations at the Etruscan site of Marzabotto [FIG. 6-2A] establish that the Etruscans laid out their towns according to a rational grid plan. Fortunately, the scant remains of Etruscan temples are supplemented by the Roman architect Vitruvius's treatise on architecture written near the end of the first century BCE (see "Vitruvius's *Ten Books on Architecture*," page 204). In it, Vitruvius provided an invaluable chapter on Etruscan temple design.

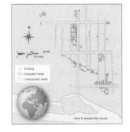

⬈ **6-2A** Marzabotto, early fifth century BCE.

Archaeologists have constructed a model (FIG. 6-3) of a typical Archaic Etruscan temple based on the preserved foundations of Etruscan temples and on Vitruvius's account. Sixth-century BCE Etruscan temples resembled contemporaneous Greek stone gable-roofed temples, but had wood columns, a tile-covered timber roof, and walls of sun-dried mud brick. Entrance was possible only via a narrow staircase at the center of the front of the temple, which sat on a high podium, the only part of the building made of stone.

Etruscan Artists in Rome

In 616 BCE, according to the traditional chronology, Tarquinius Priscus of Tarquinia became Rome's first Etruscan king. He ruled for almost 40 years. His grandson, Tarquinius Superbus ("the Arrogant"), was Rome's last king. Outraged by his tyrannical behavior, the Romans drove him from power in 509 BCE. Before his expulsion, however, Tarquinius Superbus embarked on a grand program to embellish the city.

The king's most ambitious undertaking was the construction on the Capitoline Hill of a magnificent temple, roughly 60 yards long and almost as wide, for the joint worship of Jupiter, Juno, and Minerva. For this grandiose commission, Tarquinius summoned architects, sculptors, and workers from all over Etruria. Rome's first great religious shrine was therefore Etruscan in patronage, manufacture, and form. The architect's name is unknown, but several sources preserve the identity of the Etruscan sculptor brought in to adorn the temple—Vulca of Veii, who may also have made a statue of the god Apulu (FIG. 6-4) for his native city. Pliny the Elder described Vulca's works as "the finest images of deities of that era . . . more admired than gold."* The Romans entrusted Vulca with creating the statue of Jupiter that stood in the central cella (one for each of the three deities) in the Capitoline temple. He also fashioned the enormous terracotta statuary group of Jupiter in a four-horse chariot, which he mounted on the roof at the highest point, directly over the center of the temple facade. The fame of Vulca's red-faced (painted terracotta) portrayal of Jupiter was so great that when Roman generals paraded in triumph through Rome after a battlefield victory, they would paint their faces red in emulation of the ancient statue. (The model of a typical three-cella Etruscan temple in FIG. 6-3 also serves to give an approximate idea of the appearance of the Capitoline Jupiter temple and of Vulca's roof statue.)

Vulca is the only Etruscan artist named in any ancient text, but the signatures of other Etruscan artists appear on extant artworks. One of these is Novios Plautios (FIG. 6-13), who also worked in Rome, although a few centuries later. By then the Etruscan kings of Rome were a distant memory, and the Romans had captured Veii and annexed its territory.

*Pliny, Natural History, 35.157.

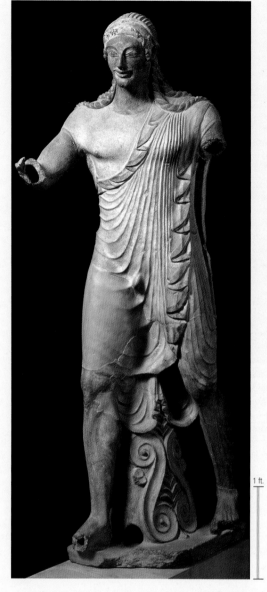

6-4 Apulu (*Apollo of Veii*), from the roof of the Portonaccio temple, Veii, Italy, ca. 510–500 BCE. Painted terracotta, 5′ 11″ high. Museo Nazionale di Villa Giulia, Rome.

This statue of Apulu was part of a group depicting a Greek myth. Distinctly Etruscan, however, are the god's vigorous motion and gesticulating arms and the placement of the statue on a temple rooftop.

1 ft.

The proportions also differed markedly. Greek temples were about twice as long as wide. According to Vitruvius, and confirmed by the archaeological record, the typical ratio for Etruscan temples was 6:5. Greek and Etruscan architects also arranged the columns in distinct ways. The columns in Etruscan temples were usually all at the front of the building, creating a deep porch occupying roughly half the podium and setting off one side of the structure as the main side. By contrast, the front and rear of Greek temples were indistinguishable, and builders placed steps and columns on all sides (FIG. 5-12). The Etruscan temple was not meant to be seen as a sculptural mass from all directions, as Greek temples were. Rather, it had a strong frontality directing visitors to the axial entrance.

Furthermore, although the columns of Etruscan temples resembled Greek Doric columns (FIG. 5-13, *left*), *Tuscan columns* were made of wood, were unfluted, and had bases. Also, because of the lightness of the timber superstructure, fewer, more widely spaced columns were the rule in Etruscan temples. Unlike their Greek counterparts, Etruscan temples also frequently had three cellas—one for each of their chief gods: Tinia, Uni, and Menrva (see "Etruscan Counterparts of Greco-Roman Gods and Heroes," page 167). Pedimental statuary was also rare in Etruria. The Etruscans normally placed life-size narrative statuary (in terracotta instead of stone) along the roof-ridges of their temples rather than in the pediments, as was the Greek custom.

Apollo of Veii. The finest surviving Etruscan temple statue is a life-size image of Apulu (FIG. 6-4), which displays the energy and excitement that characterize Archaic Etruscan art in general. The statue comes from the rooftop of a temple in the Portonaccio sanctuary at Veii. Popularly known as the *Apollo of Veii*, it is but one of a group of at least four painted terracotta figures that adorned the temple's ridge beam. The statues depicted one of the 12 labors of Herakles (see "Herakles," page 126). Apulu confronted Hercle for possession of the hind of Ceryneia, a wondrous gold-horned animal sacred to the god's sister Artumes. The bright paint and the rippling folds of Apulu's garment call to mind Archaic Greek korai

The "Audacity" of Etruscan Women

At the instigation of the emperor Augustus at the end of the first century BCE, Titus Livy wrote a history of Rome from its legendary founding in 753 BCE to his own day. In the first book of his great work, Livy recounted the tale of Tullia, daughter of Servius Tullius, an Etruscan king of Rome in the sixth century BCE. The princess had married the less ambitious of two brothers of the royal Tarquinius family, while her sister had married the bolder of the two princes. Together, Tullia and her brother-in-law, Tarquinius Superbus (see "Etruscan Artists in Rome," page 168), arranged for the murder of their spouses. They then married each other and plotted the overthrow and death of Tullia's father. After the king's murder, Tullia made a show of driving her carriage over her father's corpse, spraying herself with his blood. (The Romans still call the road where the evil deed occurred the Street of Infamy.) Livy, though condemning Tullia's actions, placed them in the context of the famous "audacity" of Etruscan women.

The independent spirit and relative freedom women enjoyed in Etruscan society similarly horrified other Greco-Roman male authors. The stories the fourth-century BCE Greek historian Theopompus heard about the debauchery of Etruscan women appalled him. Etruscan women personified immorality for Theopompus, but much of what he reported is untrue. Etruscan women did not, for example, exercise naked alongside Etruscan men. But archaeological evidence confirms the accuracy of at least one of his "slurs": Etruscan women did attend banquets and recline with their husbands on a common couch (FIGS. 6-5, 6-9, and 6-9A). Aristotle also remarked on this custom. It was so foreign to the Greeks that it both shocked and frightened them. Only men, boys, slave girls, and prostitutes attended Greek symposia. The wives remained at home, excluded from most aspects of public life. In Etruria, in striking contrast to Greece, women also regularly attended sporting events with men. Etruscan paintings and reliefs document this as well.

Etruscan inscriptions also reflect the higher status of women in Etruria as compared to Greece. They often give the names of both the father and mother of the person commemorated (for example, the inscribed portrait of Aule Metele, FIG. 6-17), a practice unheard of in Greece (witness the grave stele of "Hegeso, daughter of Proxenos," FIG. 5-57). Etruscan women, moreover, retained their own names (Ramtha Visnai, FIG. 6-16A) and could legally own property independently of their husbands. The frequent use of inscriptions on Etruscan mirrors and other toiletry items (FIG. 6-13) buried with women seems to attest to a high degree of female literacy as well.

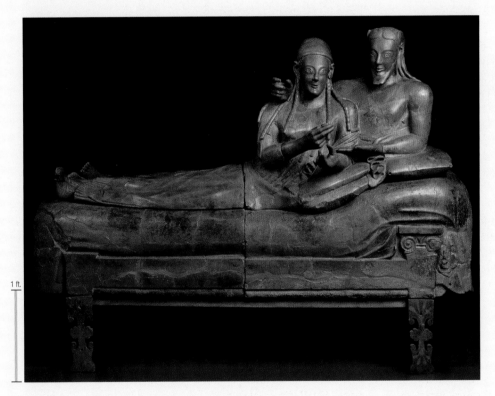

6-5 Sarcophagus with reclining couple, from the Banditaccia necropolis, Cerveteri, Italy, ca. 520 BCE. Painted terracotta, $3' 9\frac{1}{2}'' \times 6' 7''$. Museo Nazionale di Villa Giulia, Rome.

Sarcophagi in the form of a husband and wife on a dining couch have no parallels in Greece. The artist's focus on the upper half of the figures and the emphatic gestures are Etruscan hallmarks.

1 ft.

in Ionian garb (FIG. 5-11). But Apulu's vigorous striding motion, gesticulating arms, fanlike calf muscles, rippling drapery, and animated face are distinctly Etruscan. Some scholars have attributed the Apulu statue to Vulca of Veii, the most famous Etruscan sculptor of the time (see "Etruscan Artists in Rome," page 168). The statue's discovery in 1916 was instrumental in prompting a reevaluation of the originality of Etruscan art.

Cerveteri Sarcophagus. Statues in terracotta were not confined to temples and other public structures in Etruria. One of the masterworks of Archaic Etruscan sculpture, a terracotta sarcophagus (FIG. 6-5), comes from a tomb, as do so many other important Etruscan artworks. Found at Cerveteri, the sarcophagus takes

the form of a husband and wife reclining on a banqueting couch. It consists of four separately cast and fired sections, once brightly painted. Although the man and woman on the couch are life-size, the sarcophagus contained only the ashes of the husband or wife, or perhaps both. Cremation was the most common means of disposing of the dead in Archaic Italy. This kind of funerary monument has no parallel at this date in Greece, where there were no tombs big enough to house large sarcophagi. The Greeks buried their dead in simple graves marked by a stele or a statue. Moreover, although banquets were common subjects on Greek vases (which, by the late sixth century BCE, the Etruscans imported in great quantities and regularly deposited in their tombs; see "Greek Vase Painting," page 110), only men dined at Greek symposia. The image of a

Houses of the Dead
in a City of the Dead

Many ancient civilizations did not permit families to bury their dead within the boundaries of cities. They strictly separated the city of the living from the cemetery or *necropolis* (Greek, "city of the dead"). The Etruscan solution to the problem of disposing of the remains of their deceased in *extramural* (outside the walls) cities of the dead was to construct tombs that mirrored the layout and furnishings of Etruscan houses of the living. Today, tourists can visit dozens of these "houses of the dead" in the Banditaccia necropolis at Cerveteri.

The Cerveteri tumuli (FIG. 6-6) resemble Mycenaean tholos tombs, such as the Treasury of Atreus (FIG. 4-20). But whereas the Mycenaeans built their tombs with masonry blocks and then covered the burial chambers with an earthen mound, each Etruscan tumulus stood over one or more subterranean multichambered tombs cut out of the dark local limestone called tufa. The largest burial mounds at Cerveteri are of truly colossal size, exceeding 130 feet in diameter and reaching nearly

50 feet in height. Arranged in an orderly manner along a network of streets spread over 200 acres, the Banditaccia tombs truly constitute a city of the dead.

The aptly named Tomb of the Shields and Chairs (FIGS. 6-7 and 6-7A) is one of the most elaborate in the Banditaccia necropolis. Sculptors carved out of the tufa bedrock six beds and two high-backed chairs with footstools, as well as door frames and ceiling beams, in imitation of the wood furniture and timber architecture of Archaic Etruscan homes. Evidence from other tombs suggests that terracotta figures of the deceased were probably placed on the sculpted chairs. Reliefs of 14 shields adorn the walls.

The technique recalls that of rock-cut Egyptian tombs such as Amenemhet's (FIG. 3-19) at Beni Hasan and highlights the very different values of the Etruscans and the Greeks. The Greeks employed stone for the shrines of their gods, but only rarely built monumental tombs for their dead. The Etruscans' temples no longer stand because they were constructed of wood and mud brick, but the grand subterranean tombs of Cerveteri are as permanent as the bedrock itself.

6-6 Tumuli in the Banditaccia necropolis, Cerveteri, Italy, seventh to second centuries BCE.

In the Banditaccia necropolis at Cerveteri, the Etruscans buried several generations of families in multichambered rock-cut underground tombs covered by great earthen mounds (tumuli).

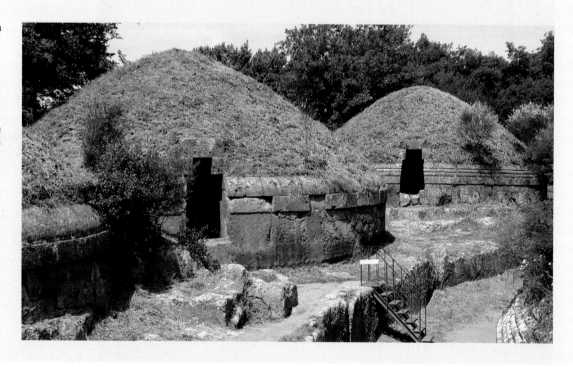

husband and wife sharing the same banqueting couch is uniquely Etruscan (see "The 'Audacity' of Etruscan Women," page 169).

The man and woman on the Cerveteri sarcophagus are as animated as the *Apollo of Veii* (FIG. 6-4), even though they are at rest. The woman may have held a perfume flask and a pomegranate in her hands, the man an egg (a symbol of regeneration; compare FIG. 6-9). They are the antithesis of the stiff and formal figures encountered in Egyptian funerary sculpture (compare FIGS. 3-13 and 3-13A). Also typically Etruscan, and in sharp contrast to Greek statues of similar date with their emphasis on proportion and balance, is the manner in which the Cerveteri sculptor rendered the upper and lower parts of each body. The artist shaped the legs only summarily, and the transition to the torso at the waist is unnatural. The sculptor's interest focused on the upper half of the figures,

especially on the vibrant faces and gesticulating arms. The Cerveteri banqueters and the Veii Apulu speak to the viewer in a way that Archaic Greek statues, with their closed contours and calm demeanor, never do.

Banditaccia Necropolis. The exact findspot of the Cerveteri sarcophagus is unrecorded, but it came from the Banditaccia necropolis, where, beginning in the seventh century BCE, wealthy Etruscan families constructed enormous tombs (FIG. 6-6) in the form of a mound, or *tumulus,* a practice documented much earlier in Mycenaean Greece (see "Houses of the Dead in a City of the Dead," above). Two of the most elaborate Cerveteri tombs are the Tomb of the Shields and Chairs (FIGS. 6-7 and 6-7A) and the Tomb of the Reliefs (FIG. 6-8), both of which accommodated several

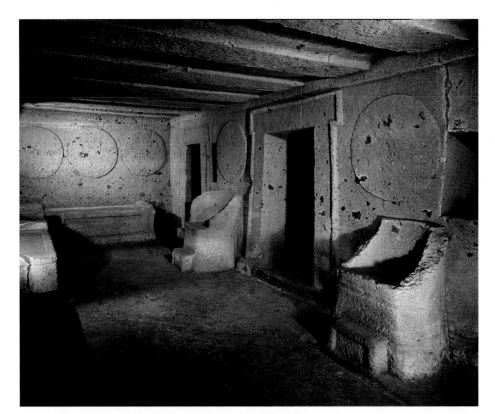

Terracotta statues of the deceased probably "sat" in the chairs cut out of the bedrock of this subterranean tomb chamber. The tomb's plan (FIG. 6-7A) follows that of a typical Etruscan house.

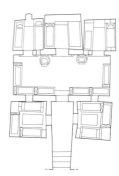

⌖ 6-7A Plan, Tomb of the Shields and Chairs, ca. 550–500 BCE.

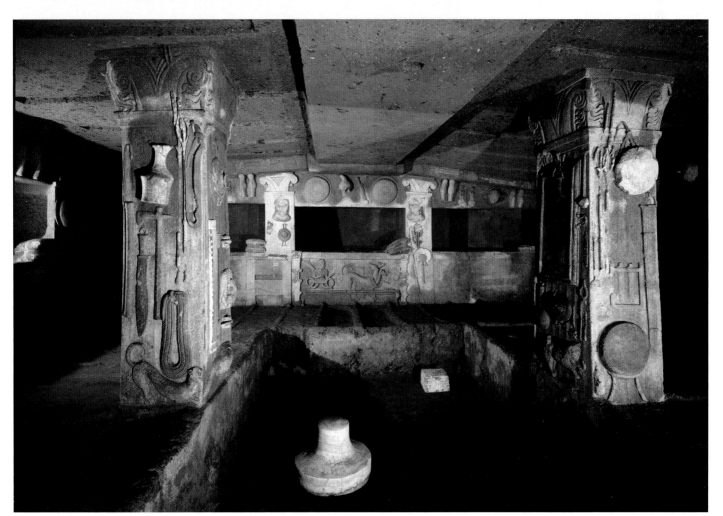

6-8 Interior of the Tomb of the Reliefs, Banditaccia necropolis, Cerveteri, Italy, late fourth or early third century BCE.

The Tomb of the Reliefs takes its name from the painted stucco reliefs covering its walls and piers. The stools, mirrors, drinking cups, and other items are reminders of the houses of the living.

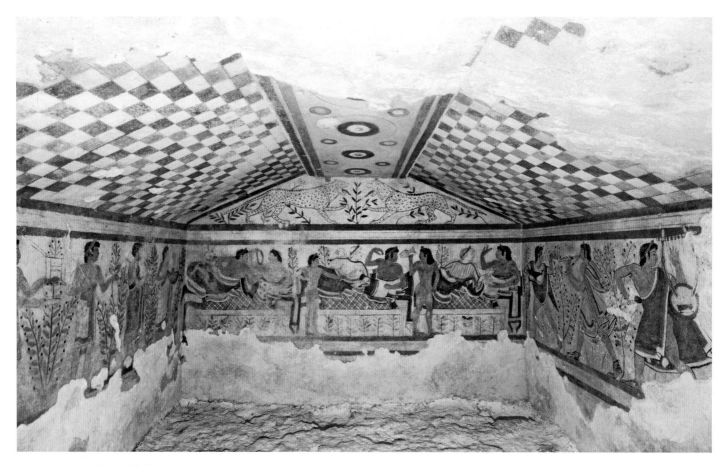

6-9 Interior of the Tomb of the Leopards, Monterozzi necropolis, Tarquinia, Italy, ca. 480 BCE.

The paintings in the Tomb of the Leopards, named after the guardian beasts in the rear pediment, depict banqueting couples, servants, and musicians. The egg that one man holds is a symbol of regeneration.

generations of a single family. The Etruscans created the elaborate interiors of both tombs by gouging the burial chambers out of the bedrock. In the Tomb of the Reliefs, they covered the sculpted walls and piers with painted stucco reliefs, hence the tomb's modern name. The stools, mirrors, drinking cups, pitchers, and knives effectively suggest a domestic context, underscoring the connection between Etruscan houses of the dead and those of the living. Other reliefs—for example, the helmet and shields over the main funerary couch (the pillows are also shallow reliefs)—are signs of the elite status of this Cerveteri family. The three-headed dog beneath the same couch is Cerberus, guardian of the gate to the Underworld, a reference to the passage from this life to the next.

Tarquinia. Large underground burial chambers hewn out of the natural rock were also the norm in the Monterozzi necropolis at Tarquinia. Earthen mounds may once have covered the Tarquinian tombs too, but the tumuli no longer exist. In contrast to Cerveteri, the subterranean rooms at Tarquinia lack carvings imitating the appearance of Etruscan houses. In approximately 200 tombs, however, paintings decorate the walls, as in the Tomb of the Augurs (FIG. 6-1). Painted tombs are nonetheless statistically rare, the privilege of only the wealthiest Tarquinian families. Archaeologists have succeeded in locating such a large number of them because they use periscopes to explore tomb interiors from the surface before considering time-consuming and costly excavation. Consequently, art historians have an almost unbroken record of mural painting in Etruria from Archaic to Hellenistic times.

Tomb of the Leopards. Two important tombs—the Tomb of the Leopards (FIG. 6-9) and the Tomb of the Triclinium (FIG. 6-9A)—are about 40 years later than the Tomb of the Augurs. The Leopards tomb takes its name from the beasts that guard the burial chamber from their perch within the pediment of the rear wall. The confronting felines are reminiscent of the panthers on each side of Medusa in the pediment (FIG. 5-16) of the Temple

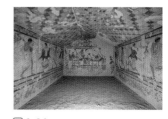

⏎6-9A Tomb of the Triclinium, Tarquinia, ca. 480–470 BCE.

of Artemis at Corfu. But mythological figures, whether Greek or Etruscan, are uncommon in Tarquinian murals, and none appear in the Augurs, Leopards, or Triclinium tombs. In the Tomb of the Leopards, banqueting couples (the men with dark skin, the women with light skin, in conformity with the age-old convention; compare FIGS. 3-13A, 4-1, 4-8, and 5-20A) are the subject. They are painted versions of the terracotta sarcophagus (FIG. 6-5) from Cerveteri. Pitcher- and cup-bearers serve the guests, and musicians entertain them. The banquet takes place in the open air or perhaps in a tent set up for the occasion. In characteristic Etruscan fashion, the banqueters, servants, and entertainers all make exaggerated gestures with unnaturally enlarged hands. The man on the couch at the far right on the rear wall holds up an egg, a reference to rebirth in the afterlife. The tone is joyful, rather than somber. The banqueters do not contemplate death. They celebrate the good life of the privileged Etruscan elite.

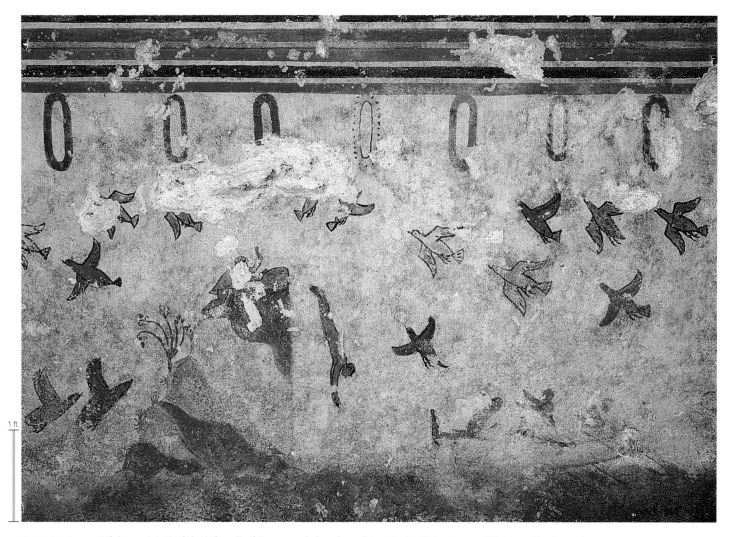

6-10 Diving and fishing, detail of the left wall of the second chamber of the Tomb of Hunting and Fishing, Monterozzi necropolis, Tarquinia, Italy, ca. 530–520 BCE. Fresco, detail 5′ 6$\frac{1}{2}$″ high.

Scenes of young men enjoying the pleasures of nature cover the walls of this Tarquinian tomb. The Etruscan diving scene predates a similar landscape painting (FIG. 5-61) in a Greek tomb at Paestum.

In stylistic terms, the Etruscan figures are comparable to those on sixth-century BCE Greek vases before Late Archaic painters became preoccupied with the problem of foreshortening. Etruscan painters were somewhat backward in this respect, but in other ways they outpaced their counterparts in Greece, especially in their interest in representing the natural world. In the Tomb of the Leopards, the "landscape" is but a few trees and shrubs placed between the entertainers (and leopards) and behind the banqueting couches. But in at least one Tarquinian tomb, the natural environment was the painters' chief interest.

Tomb of Hunting and Fishing. In the Tomb of Hunting and Fishing, scenes of Etruscans enjoying the pleasures of nature decorate all the walls of the main chamber. In the detail reproduced here (FIG. 6-10), a youth dives off a rocky promontory, while others fish from a boat. Brightly painted birds fly freely overhead. On another wall, youthful hunters aim their slingshots at the birds. The scenes of hunting and fishing recall the paintings in Egyptian tombs (FIGS. 3-15 and 3-28A) and may indicate knowledge of that Eastern funerary tradition. The multicolored rocks evoke those of the Akrotiri *Spring Fresco* (FIG. 4-9), but art historians know of nothing similar in contemporaneous Greek art save the Tomb of the Diver

at Paestum (FIG. 5-61). That exceptional Greek work, however, is from a Greek tomb in Italy about a half century later than the Tarquinian tomb. In fact, the Paestum painter probably based the diving motif on older Etruscan designs, undermining the outdated art historical judgment that Etruscan art was merely derivative and that Etruscan artists never set the standard for Greek artists.

LATER ETRUSCAN ART

The fifth century BCE was a golden age in Greece, but not in Etruria. In 509 BCE, the Romans expelled the last of their Etruscan kings, Tarquinius Superbus (see "Etruscan Artists in Rome," page 168), and replaced the monarchy with a republican form of government. In 474 BCE, the allied Greek forces of Cumae and Syracuse won a victory over the Etruscan fleet off Cumae, effectively ending Etruscan dominance of the seas—and with it Etruscan prosperity.

Classical Art

These events had important consequences in the world of art and architecture. The number of grandiose Etruscan tombs, for example, decreased sharply, and the quality of the furnishings declined

The *Capitoline Wolf*

The statue known as the *Capitoline Wolf* (FIG. 6-11) is a somewhat larger than life-size hollow-cast bronze image of the she-wolf that, according to legend, nursed Romulus and Remus after they were abandoned as infants. When the twins grew to adulthood, they quarreled, and Romulus killed his brother. On April 21, 753 BCE, Romulus founded Rome and became the city's first king. Scholars have long believed that the statue of the she-wolf that is today one of the most popular exhibits in the Capitoline Museums in Rome was made for the new Roman Republic after the expulsion of Tarquinius Superbus and became the new government's totem.

All art historians agree that the *Capitoline Wolf* is not a work of Roman art, which had not yet developed a distinct identity. Most still attribute the statue to an Etruscan workshop. (The suckling infants are 15th-century additions.) However, in the course of conservation and repair work in 1997–2000, the restorer, Anna Maria Carruba, discovered that the *Capitoline Wolf* was cast using the lost-wax method, a technique well known in antiquity (see "Hollow-Casting Life-Size Bronze Statues," page 129) and regularly employed by the Etruscans (FIGS. 6-12 and 6-17), but Carruba also determined that the she-wolf was cast in a single mold instead of being assembled from separately cast pieces—a practice unknown in antiquity for bronze statues of this size. The closest stylistic parallels are also not ancient but medieval, especially with regard to the decorative treatment of the she-wolf's hair. The new evidence weighs heavily in favor of the later date, making the *Capitoline Wolf* a masterpiece not of Etruscan bronze-casting but the product of a 12th-century CE Italian foundry.

Whether ancient or medieval, the sculptor brilliantly characterized the she-wolf physically and psychologically. The body is tense, with spare flanks, gaunt ribs, and taut, powerful legs. The lowered neck and head, alert ears, glaring eyes, and ferocious muzzle capture the psychic intensity of the fierce and protective mother as danger approaches. Few sculptures or paintings in the history of art can match this profound characterization of animal temperament.

6-11 *Capitoline Wolf,* from Rome, Italy, ca. 500–480 BCE or 12th century CE. Bronze, 2' 7½" high. Palazzo dei Conservatori, Musei Capitolini, Rome.

This bronze statue of the she-wolf that nursed the infants Romulus and Remus, founders of Rome, was long thought to be an Etruscan masterpiece, but it probably dates to the late Middle Ages.

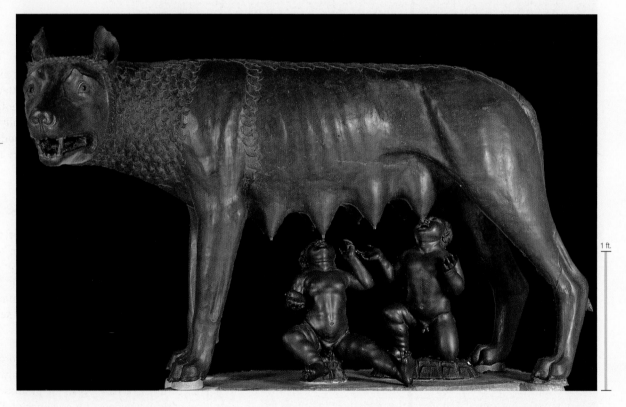

markedly. No longer did the Etruscan elite fill their tombs with gold jewelry and imported Greek vases or decorate the walls with paintings of the first rank. But art did not cease in Etruria. Indeed, in the areas in which Etruscan artists excelled, especially the casting of statues in bronze and terracotta, they continued to produce impressive works, even though fewer in number. That number may be even smaller than traditionally thought because one of the masterpieces of this era, the *Capitoline Wolf* (FIG. 6-11), has recently been attributed to a medieval Italian workshop (see "The *Capitoline Wolf*," above).

Chimera of Arezzo. An unquestioned masterpiece of Etruscan bronze-casting is the Late Classical *Chimera of Arezzo* (FIG. 6-12), found at Arezzo in 1553 and inscribed *tinscvil* (Etruscan, "gift to [the god] Tinia"), indicating that the chimera was a votive offering in a sanctuary. The *chimera* is a monster of Greek invention with a lion's head and body and a serpent's tail (restored in this case). A second head, that of a goat, grows out of the lion's left side. The goat's neck bears the wound that the Greek hero Bellerophon inflicted when he hunted and slew the mythical beast. As rendered by the Etruscan sculptor, the chimera, although injured and

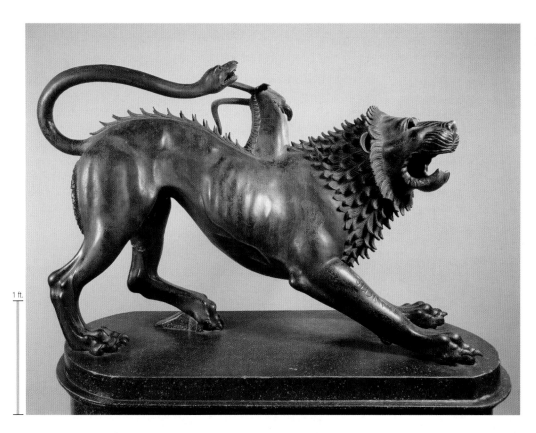

6-12 *Chimera of Arezzo,* from Arezzo, Italy, first half of fourth century BCE. Bronze, 2′ 7½″ high. Museo Archeologico Nazionale, Florence.

The chimera was a composite monster, slain by the Greek hero Bellerophon. In this Late Classical Etruscan statue, the artist depicted the wounded beast poised to attack and growling ferociously.

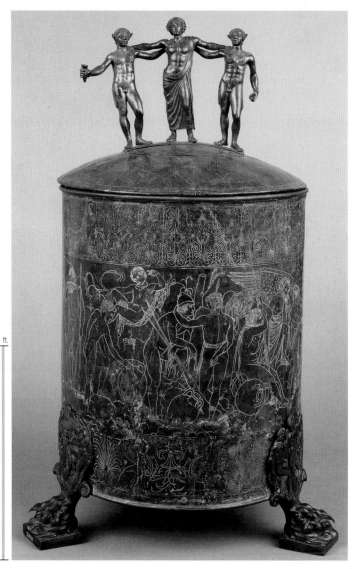

bleeding, refuses to surrender. The monster's muscles are stretched tightly over its rib cage as it prepares to attack, and a ferocious cry emanates from its open jaws. Some scholars have postulated that the statue was part of a group originally including Bellerophon, but the chimera could easily have stood alone. The menacing gaze upward toward an unseen adversary need not have been answered.

Hellenistic Art and the Rise of Rome

At about the time that an Etruscan sculptor cast the *Chimera of Arezzo,* Rome began to appropriate Etruscan territory. Veii fell to the Romans in 396 BCE after a terrible 10-year siege. The Tarquinians forged a peace treaty with the Romans in 351 BCE, but by the beginning of the next century, Rome had annexed Tarquinia too, and in 273 BCE, the Romans conquered Cerveteri.

Ficoroni Cista. An inscription on the *Ficoroni Cista* (FIG. 6-13) reflects Rome's growing power in central Italy. In the fourth century BCE, Etruscan artists began to produce large numbers of *cistae* (cylindrical containers for a woman's toiletry articles) made of sheet bronze with cast handles and feet and elaborately engraved

6-13 NOVIOS PLAUTIOS, *Ficoroni Cista,* from Palestrina, Italy, late fourth century BCE. Bronze, 2′ 6″ high. Museo Nazionale di Villa Giulia, Rome.

Novios Plautios made this container for a woman's toiletry articles in Rome and engraved it with the Greek myth of the Argonauts. The composition is probably an adaptation of a Greek painting.

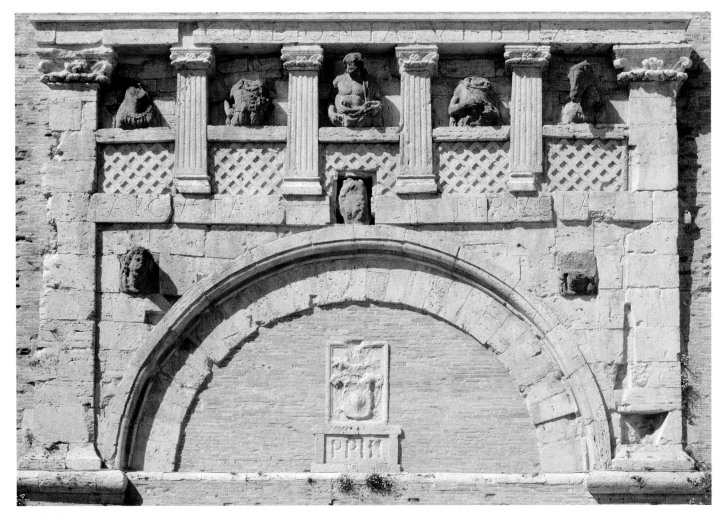

6-14 Porta Marzia, Perugia, Italy, second century BCE.

The Porta Marzia was one of the gates in Perugia's walls. The use of fluted pilasters or engaged columns to frame arches typifies Etruscan builders' adaptation of Greek architectural motifs.

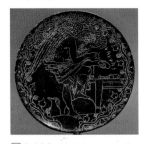

⤴ **6-13A** Chalchas examining a liver, ca. 400–375 BCE.

bodies. Along with engraved bronze mirrors (FIG. **6-13A**), they were popular gifts for both the living and the dead. The *Ficoroni Cista,* found at Palestrina, takes its name from an Italian collector, Francesco de' Ficoroni. The inscription on the cista's handle states that Dindia Macolnia, a local noblewoman, gave the cista (the largest found to date) to her daughter and that the artist was NOVIOS PLAUTIOS. According to the inscription, his workshop was not in Palestrina but in Rome, which by this date was becoming an important cultural, as well as political, center.

The engraved frieze of the *Ficoroni Cista* depicts an episode from the Greek story of the expedition of the Argonauts (the crew of the ship *Argo*) in search of the Golden Fleece. Art historians generally agree that the composition is an adaptation of a lost Greek panel painting, perhaps one on display in Rome (like the presumed model for the *Alexander Mosaic,* FIG. 5-70)—another testimony to the growing wealth and prestige of the city that was once ruled by Etruscan kings. The Greek source for Novios Plautios's engraving is

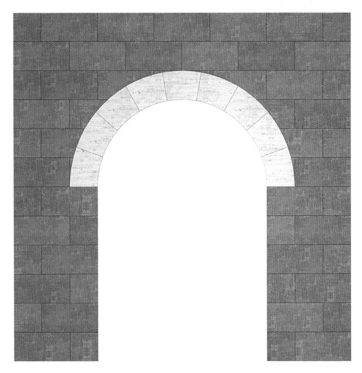

6-15 Arch construction (John Burge).

The Etruscans, and later the Romans, often constructed arches, which consist of a series of trapezoidal voussoirs held in place by being pressed against each other. The central voussoir is called a keystone.

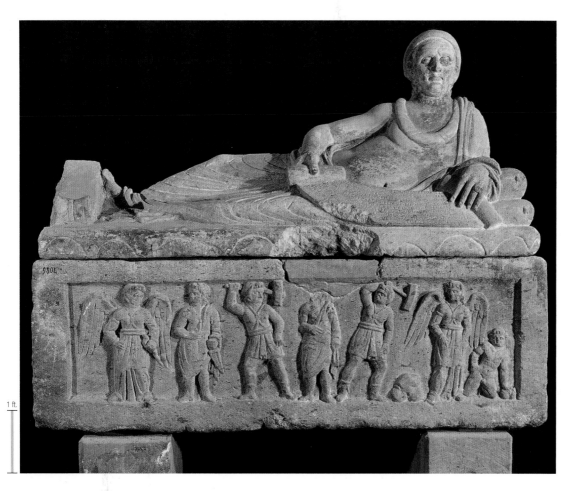

6-16 Sarcophagus of Lars Pulena, from Tarquinia, Italy, ca. 220–180 BCE. Tufa, 6′ 6″ long. Museo Archeologico Nazionale, Tarquinia.

Images of the deceased on late Etruscan sarcophagi are more somber than those on Archaic examples (FIG. 6-5), but Lars Pulena proudly displays a list of his life's achievements on an open scroll.

evident in the figures seen entirely from behind or in three-quarter view and in the placement of the protagonists on several levels in the Polygnotan manner (compare FIG. 5-59).

Porta Marzia. In the third century BCE, the Etruscans of Perugia formed an alliance with Rome and were spared the destruction that Veii, Cerveteri, and other Etruscan cities suffered. Portions of Perugia's ancient walls still stand, as do some of its gates. One of these, known as the Porta Marzia (Gate of Mars), was dismantled during the Renaissance, but the upper part of the gate (FIG. 6-14) is preserved, embedded in a later wall. A series of trapezoidal stone *voussoirs* held in place by being pressed against each other (FIG. 6-15) form the arcuated gateway. The central voussoir is called a *keystone*. Arches of similar construction have been documented earlier in Greece as well as in Mesopotamia (FIG. 2-24), but Italy, first under the Etruscans and later under the Romans, is where arcuated gates and freestanding ("triumphal") arches became a major architectural type.

The use of *pilasters* to frame the rounded opening of the Porta Marzia typifies the Etruscan adaptation of Greek motifs. Arches bracketed by *engaged columns* or pilasters have a long and distinguished history in Roman and later times. In the Porta Marzia, sculpted half-figures of Jupiter and his sons Castor and Pollux and their steeds look out from between the fluted pilasters. The divine twins had appeared miraculously on a battlefield in 484 BCE to turn the tide in favor of the Romans. The presence of these three deities above the arched passageway of the Porta Marzia may reflect the new Roman practice of erecting triumphal arches with gilded bronze statues on top.

Lars Pulena. In Hellenistic Etruria, the descendants of the magnificent Archaic terracotta sarcophagus (FIG. 6-5) from Cerveteri were coffins of local stone. The leading production center was Tarquinia, and that is where, during the late third or early second century BCE, an Etruscan sculptor carved the sarcophagus (FIG. 6-16) containing the remains of Lars Pulena. The scene sculpted on the front of the coffin shows the deceased in the Underworld between two *charuns* (Etruscan death demons) swinging hammers. Two *vanths* (winged female demons) stand to the left and right. The representation signifies that Lars Pulena has successfully made the journey to the afterlife. Above, the deceased reclines on a couch, as do the couple on the Cerveteri sarcophagus and their counterparts in the Tomb of the Leopards and the Tomb of the Triclinium (FIGS. 6-9 and 6-9A), but this Etruscan gentleman is not at a festive banquet, and his wife is not present. The somber expression on his middle-aged face contrasts sharply with the smiling, confident faces of the Archaic era when Etruria enjoyed its greatest prosperity. Similar heads—realistic but generic types, not true portraits—can be found on most later Etruscan sarcophagi (FIG. 6-16A) and in tomb paintings. They are symptomatic of the economic and political decline of the once-mighty Etruscan city-states. Nonetheless, Lars Pulena was a proud man. He wears a fillet on his head and a wreath around his neck, and he displays

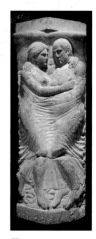

6-16A Sarcophagus of Ramtha Visnai and Arnth Tetnies, ca. 350–300 BCE.

a partially unfurled scroll inscribed with his name and those of his ancestors as well as a record of his life's accomplishments.

Aule Metele. One of the latest extant works produced for an Etruscan patron is the bronze statue (FIG. 6-17) portraying the magistrate Aule Metele raising his arm to address an assembly—hence his modern nickname *Arringatore* (*Orator*). This life-size statue, which dates to the early first century BCE, proves that Etruscan artists continued to be experts at bronze-casting long after the heyday of Etruscan prosperity. The time coincides with the Roman achievement of total domination of Etruria. The so-called Social War ended in 89 BCE with the conferring of Roman citizenship on all of Italy's inhabitants. In fact, Aule Metele—identifiable because the sculptor inscribed the magistrate's Etruscan name and those of his father and mother on the hem of his garment—wears the short *toga* and high, laced boots of a Roman magistrate. His head, with its close-cropped hair and signs of age in the face, resembles portraits produced in Rome at the same time. This orator is Etruscan in name only. If the origin of the Etruscans remains the subject of debate, the question of their demise has a ready answer. Aule Metele and his compatriots became Roman citizens, and Etruscan art became Roman art.

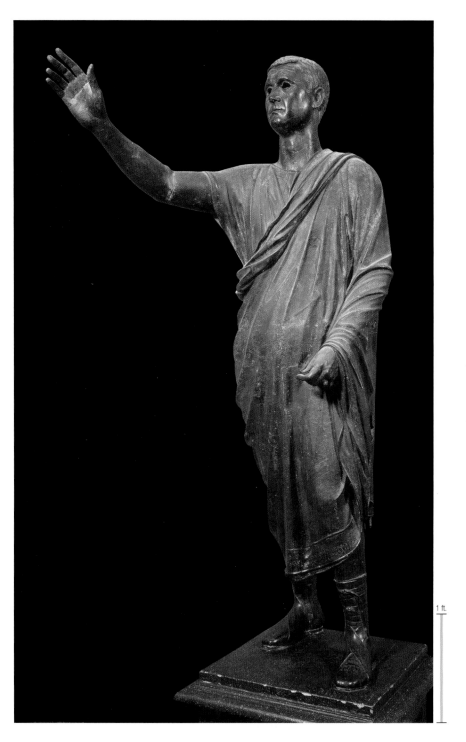

6-17 Aule Metele (*Arringatore*), from Cortona, Italy, early first century BCE. Bronze, 5′ 7″ high. Museo Archeologico Nazionale, Florence.

This life-size bronze statue portraying Aule Metele is Etruscan in name only. The orator wears the short toga and high boots of a Roman magistrate, and the portrait style is Roman as well.

1 ft.

The Etruscans

Villanovan and Orientalizing Art ca. 900–600 BCE

- During the Villanovan period of the early first millennium BCE, the Etruscans emerged as a people with a culture distinct from those of other Italic peoples and the Greeks. Their language, although written in a Greek-derived script, is unrelated to the Indo-European linguistic family.

- In the seventh century BCE, the Etruscans traded metals from their mines for foreign goods and began to produce jewelry and other luxury objects decorated with motifs modeled on those found on imports from Mesopotamia. The Regolini-Galassi Tomb at Cerveteri contained a treasure trove of Orientalizing Etruscan jewelry.

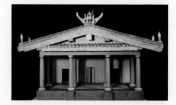

Regolini-Galassi fibula, Cerveteri, ca. 650–640 BCE

Archaic Art ca. 600–480 BCE

- Etruscan power in Italy was strongest during the sixth century BCE. Etruscan kings even ruled Rome until 509 BCE, when the Romans expelled Tarquinius Superbus and established the Roman Republic.

- The Etruscans admired Greek art and architecture, but did not copy Greek works. They constructed their temples of wood and mud brick instead of stone and placed the columns and stairs only at the front. Terracotta statuary decorated the roof.

- Most surviving Etruscan artworks come from underground tomb chambers. In the Banditaccia necropolis at Cerveteri, great earthen mounds (tumuli) covered tombs such as the Tomb of the Shields and Chairs, which has a sculptured interior imitating a house of the living. Some of the tombs housed terracotta statues, including sarcophagi of married couples.

- At Tarquinia, painters covered the tomb walls with large-scale frescoes, often depicting banquets attended by both men and women, as in the Tomb of the Leopards and the Tomb of the Triclinium. The murals in some tombs depict funerary games (Tomb of the Augurs) and landscapes (Tomb of Hunting and Fishing).

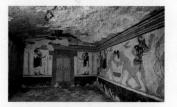

Model of an Etruscan temple, sixth century BCE

Tomb of the Augurs, Tarquinia, ca. 520 BCE

Classical and Hellenistic Art ca. 480–89 BCE

- The Greek victory over the Etruscan fleet off Cumae in 474 BCE ended Etruscan domination of the sea and marked the beginning of the decline of Etruria. Rome destroyed Veii in 396 BCE and conquered Cerveteri in 273 BCE. All of Italy became Romanized by 89 BCE.

- Later Etruscan tombs are not as richly furnished as those of the Archaic period, but Classical and Hellenistic Etruscan sculptors continued to excel in bronze-casting and engraving. The *Chimera of Arezzo* and the *Ficoroni Cista* are Late Classical masterworks.

- A more somber mood characterizes many Late Classical and Hellenistic Etruscan artworks—for example, the sarcophagus of Lars Pulena.

- Later Etruscan architecture is noteworthy for the widespread use of the stone arch, often framed with Greek pilasters or engaged columns, as on the Porta Marzia at Perugia.

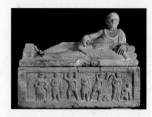

Sarcophagus of Lars Pulena, ca. 220–180 BCE

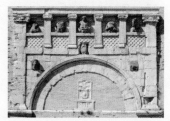

Porta Marzia, Perugia, second century BCE

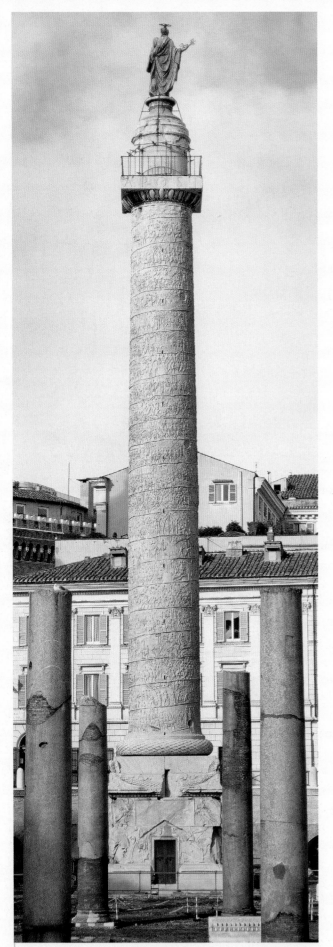

7-1　Column of Trajan (looking northwest), Forum of Trajan (FIG. 7-44), Rome, Italy, dedicated 112 CE.

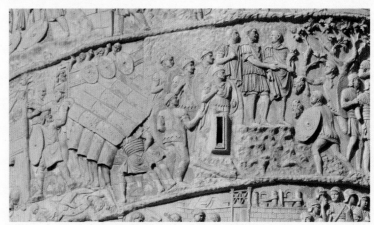

▲7-1a Trajan's soldiers storm a Dacian fortress with their shields joined to form a protective turtle-shell. The battle won, the soldiers present to the emperor the severed heads of the enemy as evidence of their success.

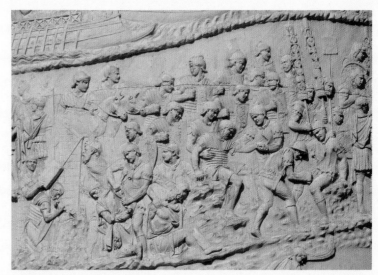

▲ 7-1b This unexpected detail of the frieze shows the Romans tending to their wounded—an acknowledgment that victory did not come easily, but also giving the impression that this is a balanced record of the war.

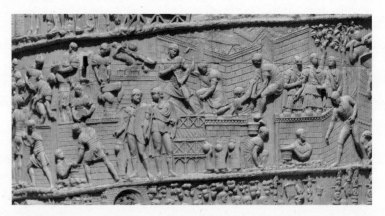

▲ 7-1c Most of the scenes do not depict battles but rather the routine business of warfare, such as road building and fort construction. The common denominator is Trajan's personal direction of all aspects of the war.

THE ROMAN EMPIRE /7

The Roman Emperor as World Conqueror

The name "Rome" almost invariably conjures images of power and grandeur, of mighty armies and fearsome gladiators, of marble cities and far-flung roads. Indeed, at the death of the emperor Trajan in 117 CE, the "eternal city" was the capital of the greatest empire the world had ever known. For the first time in history, a single government ruled an empire extending from the Strait of Gibraltar to the Nile, from the Tigris and Euphrates Rivers to the Rhine, Danube, Thames, and beyond (MAP 7-1). The Romans presided over prosperous cities and frontier outposts on three continents, ruling virtually all of Europe, North Africa, and West Asia. Trajan, perhaps Rome's greatest general, had led the imperial army to victory in both the East and West, bringing vast new territories under Roman dominion. To celebrate his successes—at home as well as abroad—in an era long before newspapers, television, and the Internet, Trajan, like his predecessors and successors as emperor of Rome, marshaled the power of art and architecture to communicate his version of events to the citizenry.

A case in point is the 128-foot-tall column (FIG. 7-1) that Trajan erected in Rome to commemorate the defeat of Dacia (roughly equivalent to present-day Romania). Although frequently imitated, the Column of Trajan was the first of its kind. Its distinguishing new feature was the 625-foot frieze that winds around the shaft 23 times from bottom to top and presents the emperor's two military campaigns against the Dacians in the manner of a modern documentary film.

Three details are illustrated here. In the top section, a group of Roman soldiers storms a Dacian fortress with their shields raised and joined to form a turtle-shell umbrella to protect them. To the right, the battle won, Trajan, flanked by two lieutenants, views the severed Dacian heads that his soldiers have brought to him as evidence of the successful completion of their mission. The middle detail comes as a surprise. It shows the Romans tending to their wounded after a battle—an admission that the Dacian victory did not come easily. But it also suggests to the viewer that this is a balanced pictorial record of the war, even if that record is sharply skewed to glorify Trajan and his men. Also unexpected is the third detail showing the construction of a fort. In fact, most of the scenes on the Column of Trajan do not depict battles, but the routine business of warfare, including the transportation of supplies and the building of roads and bridges. The common denominator, however, is the presence of Trajan almost everywhere. His personal direction of all aspects of the Dacian campaigns—and in expanding Rome's empire on all fronts—is one of the central messages of the Column of Trajan.

ROME, *CAPUT MUNDI*

The Roman Empire was unlike any other ancient civilization. Within its borders lived millions of people of numerous races, religions, languages, and cultures: Britons and Gauls, Greeks and Egyptians, Africans and Syrians, Jews and Christians, to name but a few. Of all early cultures, the Roman most closely approximated today's world in its multicultural character.

Roman monuments of art and architecture are the most conspicuous and numerous remains of antiquity worldwide. In Europe, the Middle East, and Africa today, Roman temples and basilicas have an afterlife as churches. The powerful concrete vaults of ancient Roman buildings form the cores of modern houses, stores, restaurants, factories, and museums. Bullfights, sports events, operas, and rock concerts are staged in Roman amphitheaters. Ships dock in what were once Roman ports, and Western Europe's highway system still closely follows the routes of Roman roads. Ancient Rome also lives on in the Western world in concepts of law and government, in languages, in the calendar—even in the coins used daily.

The art of the ancient Romans speaks a language that almost every Western viewer today can readily understand. Indeed, the diversity and complexity of Roman art foreshadowed the art of the modern world. The Roman use of art, especially portraits and narrative reliefs (FIG. 7-1), to manipulate public opinion is similar to the carefully crafted imagery of contemporary political campaigns. And the Roman mastery of concrete construction began an architectural revolution still felt today.

The center of the far-flung Roman Empire was the city on the Tiber River that, according to legend, Romulus founded on April 21, 753 BCE. Hundreds of years later, it would become the *caput mundi,* the "head [capital] of the world," but in the eighth century BCE, Rome consisted only of small huts clustered together on the Palatine Hill overlooking what was then uninhabited marshland. In the Archaic period, Rome was essentially an Etruscan city, both politically and culturally. Its first great shrine, the Temple of Jupiter *Optimus Maximus* (Best and Greatest) on the Capitoline Hill, was built by an Etruscan king, designed by an Etruscan architect, made of wood and mud brick in the Etruscan manner, and

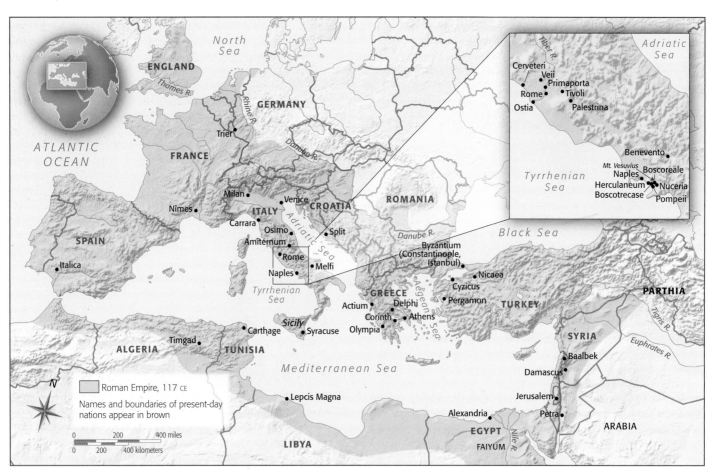

MAP 7-1 The Roman Empire at the death of Trajan in 117 CE.

THE ROMAN EMPIRE

753–27 BCE	27 BCE–14 CE	14–96 CE	96–192 CE	192–337 CE
Monarchy and Republic	**Augustus**	**Julio-Claudians and Flavians**	**High Empire**	**Late Empire**
▪ Republican architects mix Hellenistic and Etruscan features ▪ Sculptors depict patricians in superrealistic portraits ▪ Painters decorate walls in the First and Second Styles	▪ Augustan artists and architects revive the Classical style ▪ Augustan painters introduce the Third Style of Roman mural painting	▪ Neronian and Flavian architects realize the full potential of concrete ▪ Neronian painters develop the Fourth Style of Pompeian painting	▪ Trajan extends the Empire and builds a new forum in Rome ▪ Hadrian builds the Pantheon ▪ Domination of the Classical style erodes under the Antonines	▪ Late Antique style takes root under the Severans ▪ Portraits of soldier emperors display an unprecedented psychic intensity ▪ Constantinian art bridges antiquity and the Middle Ages

Who's Who in the Roman World

MONARCHY (753–509 BCE)

Latin and Etruscan kings ruled Rome from the city's founding by Romulus, its first king, until the revolt against Tarquinius Superbus (exact dates of rule unreliable).

REPUBLIC (509–27 BCE)

The Republic lasted from the expulsion of Tarquinius Superbus until the bestowing of the title of Augustus on Octavian, the grandnephew of Julius Caesar and victor over Mark Antony in the civil war that ended the Republic. Some major figures of this period are

- Marcellus, b. 268(?), d. 208 BCE; consul
- Marius, b. 157, d. 86 BCE; consul
- Sulla, b. 138, d. 79 BCE; consul and dictator
- Pompey, b. 106, d. 48 BCE; consul (FIG. 7-9A)
- Julius Caesar, b. 100, d. 44 BCE; consul and dictator (FIG. 7-10)
- Mark Antony, b. 83, d. 30 BCE; consul

EARLY EMPIRE (27 BCE–96 CE)

The Early Empire began with the rule of Augustus and his Julio-Claudian successors and continued until the end of the Flavian dynasty. Selected emperors and their dates of rule (with names of the most influential empresses in parentheses) are

- Augustus (Livia), r. 27 BCE–14 CE (FIGS. I-10, 7-27, and 7-28)
- Tiberius, r. 14–37
- Caligula, r. 37–41
- Claudius (Agrippina the Younger), r. 41–54
- Nero, r. 54–68

- Vespasian, r. 69–79 (FIG. 7-38)
- Titus, r. 79–81 (FIGS. 7-40A and 7-42)
- Domitian, r. 81–96

HIGH EMPIRE (96–192 CE)

The High Empire began with the rule of Nerva and the Spanish emperors, Trajan and Hadrian, and ended with the last emperor of the Antonine dynasty. The emperors (and empresses) of this period are

- Nerva, r. 96–98
- Trajan (Plotina), r. 98–117 (FIG. 7-45A)
- Hadrian (Sabina), r. 117–138 (FIG. 7-48)
- Antoninus Pius (Faustina the Elder), r. 138–161 (FIG. 7-56)
- Marcus Aurelius (Faustina the Younger), r. 161–180 (FIG. 7-58)
- Lucius Verus, coemperor with Marcus Aurelius, r. 161–169
- Commodus, r. 180–192 (FIG. 7-58A)

LATE EMPIRE (193–337 CE)

The Late Empire began with the Severan dynasty and included the so-called soldier emperors of the third century; the tetrarchs; and Constantine, the first Christian emperor. Emperors (and empresses) discussed in this chapter are

- Septimius Severus (Julia Domna), r. 193–211 (FIGS. 7-62 and 7-64)
- Caracalla (Plautilla), r. 211–217 (FIGS. 7-62 and 7-63)
- Severus Alexander, r. 222–235
- Philip the Arabian, r. 244–249 (FIG. 7-67A)
- Trajan Decius, r. 249–251 (FIG. 7-67)
- Trebonianus Gallus, r. 251–253 (FIG. 7-68)
- Aurelian, r. 270–275
- Diocletian, r. 284–305 (FIG. 7-72)
- Constantine I, r. 306–337 (FIGS. 7-77, 7-78, and 7-79)

---

decorated with terracotta statuary fashioned by an Etruscan sculptor (see "Etruscan Artists in Rome," page 168).

REPUBLIC

In 509 BCE, the Romans overthrew Tarquinius Superbus, the last of Rome's Etruscan kings, and established a constitutional government. The new Roman Republic vested power mainly in a *senate* (literally, "a council of elders," *senior* citizens) and in two elected *consuls* (see "Who's Who in the Roman World," above). Under extraordinary circumstances, a *dictator* could be appointed for a limited time and specific purpose, such as commanding the army during a crisis. All leaders came originally from among the wealthy landowners, or *patricians*, but later also from the *plebeian* class of small farmers, merchants, and freed slaves.

Before long, the descendants of Romulus conquered Rome's neighbors one by one: the Etruscans and the Gauls to the north, the Samnites and the Greek colonists to the south. Even the Carthaginians of North Africa, who under Hannibal's dynamic leadership had destroyed some of Rome's legions and almost brought down the Republic, fell before the mighty Roman armies.

Architecture

The year 211 BCE was a turning point both for Rome and for Roman art. Breaking with precedent, Marcellus, conqueror of the fabulously wealthy Sicilian Greek city of Syracuse, brought back to Rome not only the usual spoils of war—captured arms and armor, gold and silver coins, and the like—but also the city's artistic patrimony. Thus began, in the words of the historian Livy, "the craze for works of Greek art."[1]

Exposure to Greek sculpture and painting and to the splendid marble temples of the Greek gods increased as the Romans expanded their conquests beyond Italy. Greece became a Roman province in 146 BCE, and in 133 BCE the last king of Pergamon willed his kingdom to Rome. Nevertheless, although the Romans developed a virtually insatiable taste for Greek "antiques," the influence of Etruscan art and architecture persisted. The artists and architects of the Roman Republic drew on both Greek and Etruscan traditions for their paintings, sculptures, and buildings.

Temple of Portunus. The mixing of Greek and Etruscan forms is the primary characteristic of the Republican-era Temple of Portunus,

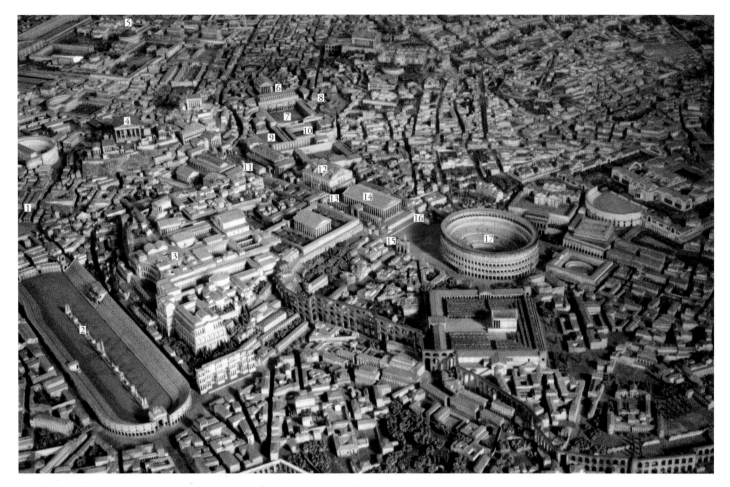

7-2 Model of the city of Rome during the fourth century CE. Museo della Civiltà Romana, Rome. (1) Temple of Portunus, (2) Circus Maximus, (3) Palatine Hill, (4) Temple of Jupiter Capitolinus, (5) Pantheon, (6) Column of Trajan, (7) Forum of Trajan, (8) Markets of Trajan, (9) Forum of Julius Caesar, (10) Forum of Augustus, (11) Forum Romanum, (12) Basilica Nova, (13) Arch of Titus, (14) Temple of Venus and Roma, (15) Arch of Constantine, (16) Colossus of Nero, (17) Colosseum.

By the fourth century CE, the city of Rome was densely packed with temples, fora, triumphal arches, theaters, baths, racetracks, aqueducts, markets, private homes, and apartment houses.

the Roman god of harbors, on the east bank of the Tiber River in Rome (FIGS. 7-2, no. 1, and 7-3). Its plan follows the Etruscan pattern with a high podium and a flight of steps only at the front (FIG. 6-3). As in Etruscan temples, the only freestanding columns are in the deep porch, but the temple's ratio of length to width is closer to that of Greek temples. The Portunus temple is also built of stone (local tufa and travertine), overlaid originally with *stucco* in imitation of Greek marble. The columns are not Tuscan but Ionic, complete with flutes and bases, and there is a matching Ionic frieze. Moreover, in an effort to approximate a peripteral Greek temple yet maintain the basic Etruscan plan, the architect added a series of engaged Ionic half columns to the sides and back of the cella. The result was a *pseudo-peripteral* temple. Although the design combines Etruscan and Greek elements, the resultant mix is distinctively Roman.

7-3 Temple of Portunus (looking southwest), Rome, Italy, ca. 75 BCE.

Republican temples combined Etruscan plans and Greek elevations. This pseudoperipteral stone temple employs the Ionic order, but it has a staircase and freestanding columns only at the front.

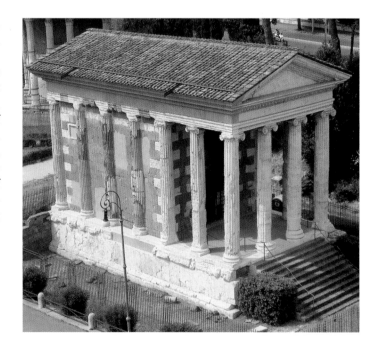

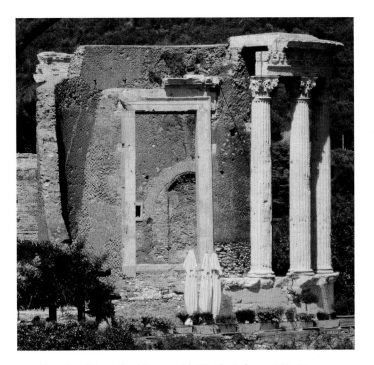

7-4 Temple of Vesta (looking north), Tivoli, Italy, ca. 100–80 BCE.

The round temple type is unknown in Etruria. The models for Tivoli's Temple of Vesta were Greek tholoi (FIG. 5-72), but the Roman building has a frontal orientation and a concrete cella.

Temple of Vesta. The Romans' admiration for the Greek temples they encountered in their conquests also led to the importation into Republican Italy of a temple type unknown in Etruscan architecture—the round, or *tholos,* temple. At Tivoli, east of Rome, on a dramatic site overlooking a deep gorge, a Republican architect erected a Greek-inspired round temple (FIG. 7-4) early in the first century BCE. The circular plan is standard for shrines of Vesta, and she was probably the deity honored here. The temple has Corinthian columns and a frieze carved with garlands held up by ox heads, also in emulation of Greek models. The stone is not marble, however, but travertine, a high-quality variety of limestone from quarries at Tivoli itself. In contrast to Greek tholoi (FIG. 5-72), the Vesta temple has a high podium that can be reached only via a narrow stairway leading to the cella door. This arrangement introduced an Etruscan-style axial alignment not found in Greek round temples, where, as in Greek rectangular temples, steps continue all around the structure. Also in contrast to the Greeks, the Roman builders did not construct the cella wall using masonry blocks. Instead, they used a new material of recent invention: *concrete.*

Sanctuary of Fortuna. The most impressive and innovative use of concrete during the Republic was in the Sanctuary of Fortuna Primigenia (FIG. 7-5), the goddess of good fortune, at Palestrina, southeast of Rome. Spread out over several terraces leading up the hillside to a tholos at the peak of an ascending triangle, the layout

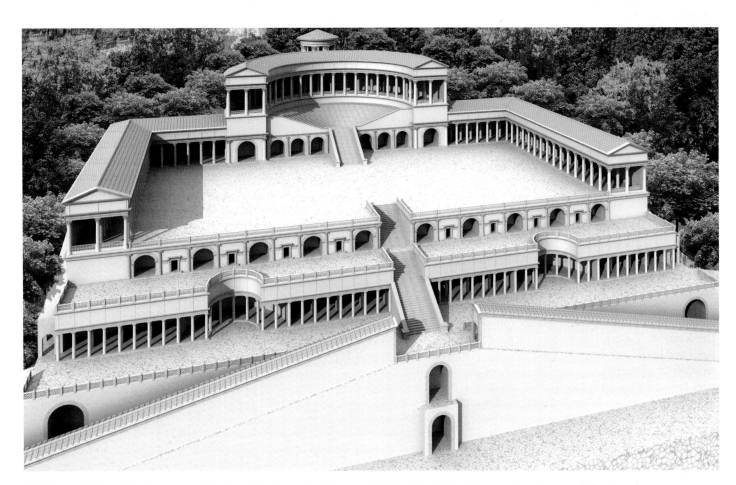

7-5 Restored view of the Sanctuary of Fortuna Primigenia (looking north), Palestrina, Italy, late second century BCE (John Burge).

Concrete construction made possible Fortuna's hillside sanctuary at Palestrina with its terraces, ramps, shops, and porticos spread out over several levels. A tholos temple crowned the complex.

Roman Concrete Construction

The history of Roman architecture would be very different had the Romans been content to use the same building materials that the Greeks, Etruscans, and other ancient peoples did. Instead, the Romans developed *concrete* construction (FIG. 7-6), which revolutionized architectural design. Roman builders mixed concrete according to a changing recipe of lime mortar, volcanic sand, water, and small stones (*caementa,* from which the English word "cement" derives). After mixing the concrete, the builders poured it into wood frames and left it to dry. When the concrete hardened completely, they removed the wood molds, revealing a solid mass of great strength, though rough in appearance. The Romans often covered the coarse concrete surfaces with stucco or with marble *revetment* (facing). Despite this lengthy procedure, concrete walls were much less costly to construct than walls of imported Greek marble or even local tufa and travertine.

The advantages of concrete go well beyond cost, however. It is possible to fashion concrete shapes unachievable in masonry construction, especially huge vaulted and domed rooms without internal supports. The new medium enabled Roman architects to design buildings in revolutionary ways by focusing not on solid walls and ceilings but on the volumes of space they enclose.

The most common types of Roman concrete vaults and domes are

- **Barrel Vaults** Also called the *tunnel vault,* the *barrel vault* is an extension of a simple arch, creating a semicylindrical ceiling over parallel walls. Pre-Roman builders constructed barrel vaults using traditional ashlar masonry (FIG. 2-24), but those earlier vaults were less stable than concrete barrel vaults. As with arches (FIG. 6-15), if even a single block of a cut-stone vault comes loose, the whole vault may collapse. Also, masonry barrel vaults can be illuminated only by light entering at either end of the tunnel. Using concrete, Roman builders could place windows at any point in a barrel vault, because once the concrete hardens, it forms a seamless sheet of "artificial stone" in which the openings do not lessen the vault's structural integrity. Whether made of stone or concrete, barrel vaults require *buttressing* (lateral support) of the walls below the vaults to counteract their downward and outward *thrust.*

- **Groin Vaults** A *groin* (or *cross*) *vault* is formed by the intersection at right angles of two barrel vaults of equal size. Besides appearing lighter than the barrel vault, the groin vault needs less buttressing. Whereas the barrel vault's thrust is continuous along the entire length of the supporting wall, the groin vault's thrust is concentrated along the groins, the lines at the juncture of the two barrel vaults. Buttressing is needed only at the points where the groins meet the vault's vertical supports, usually *piers.* This system leaves the area between the piers open, enabling light to enter. Builders can construct groin vaults as well as barrel vaults using stone blocks, but stone groin vaults have the same structural limitations as stone barrel vaults do compared to their concrete counterparts.

  When a series of groin vaults covers an interior hall (for example, FIG. 7-47), the open lateral arches of the vaults form the equivalent of a *clerestory* of a traditional timber-roofed structure (for example, FIGS. 8-18 and 8-25). A *fenestrated* (with openings or windows) sequence of groin vaults has a major advantage over a timber clerestory: concrete vaults are relatively fireproof, always an important consideration because throughout history, fires have been common occurrences (see "The Burning of Canterbury Cathedral," page 353).

- **Hemispherical Domes** The largest domed space in the ancient world for more than a millennium was the corbeled, beehive-shaped tholos (FIG. 4-21) of the Treasury of Atreus at Mycenae. The Romans were able to surpass the Mycenaeans by using concrete to construct hemispherical domes, which usually rested on concrete cylindrical *drums.* If a barrel vault is a round arch extended in a line, then a hemispherical dome is a round arch rotated the full circumference around the central, vertical axis of a circle. Masonry domes, like masonry vaults, cannot accommodate windows without threat to their stability. Concrete domes, by contrast, can be opened up even at their apex with a circular *oculus* ("eye"), enabling light to reach the vast space beneath (for example, FIGS. 7-35 and 7-51).

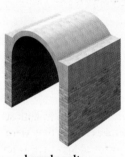

barrel vault

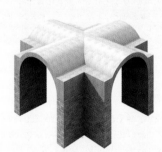

groin vault

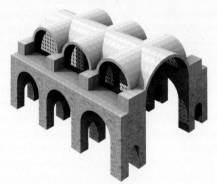

fenestrated sequence of groin vaults

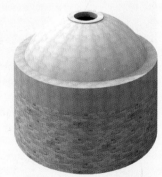

hemispherical dome with oculus

7-6 Roman concrete vaults (John Burge).

Concrete enabled Roman builders to revolutionize the history of architecture by shaping spaces in novel ways. The major types of concrete vaulting are the barrel and groin vault and the hemispherical dome.

Roman Ancestor Portraits

In Republican Rome, ancestor portraits separated the old patrician families not only from the plebeian middle and lower classes of working citizens and former slaves but also from the newly wealthy and powerful of more modest origins. The case of Marius, a renowned Republican general who lacked a long and distinguished genealogy, is revealing. When his patrician colleagues in the Senate ridiculed him as a man who had no *imagines* (portrait masks) in his home, he resorted to defending himself by saying that his battle scars were his masks, the proof of his nobility.

Patrician pride in genealogy was unquestionably the motivation for a unique portrait statue (FIG. 7-7), datable to the late first century BCE, in which a man wearing a *toga,* the badge of Roman citizenship, holds in each hand a bust of one of his male forebears. (The head of the man is ancient, but does not belong to this statue.) The two heads he holds, which are probably likenesses of his father and grandfather, are characteristic examples of Republican portraiture of the first century BCE (compare FIG. 7-8). The heads may be reproductions of wax or terracotta portraits. Marble or bronze heads would have been too heavy to support with one hand. They are not, however, wax imagines, because they are sculptures in the round, not masks. The statue nonetheless would have had the same effect on the observer as the spectacle of parading ancestral portraits at a patrician funeral.

Polybius, a Greek author who wrote a history of Rome in the middle of the second century BCE, described these patrician funerals in detail:

> For whenever one of the leading men among [the Romans] dies . . . they place a likeness of the dead man in the most public part of the house [the atrium; FIG. 7-15, no. 2], keeping it in a small wooden shrine. The likeness is a mask [*imago*] especially made for a close resemblance. . . . And whenever a leading member of the family dies, they introduce [the wax masks] into the funeral procession, putting them on men who seem most like them in height and as regards the rest of their general appearance. . . . It is not easy for an ambitious and high-minded young man to see a finer spectacle than this. For who would not be won over at the sight of all the masks together of those men who had been extolled for virtue as if they were alive and breathing?*

*Polybius, *History of Rome,* 6.5. Translated by Harriet I. Fowler, *Ancestor Masks and Aristocratic Power in Roman Culture* (Oxford: Clarendon Press, 1996), 309.

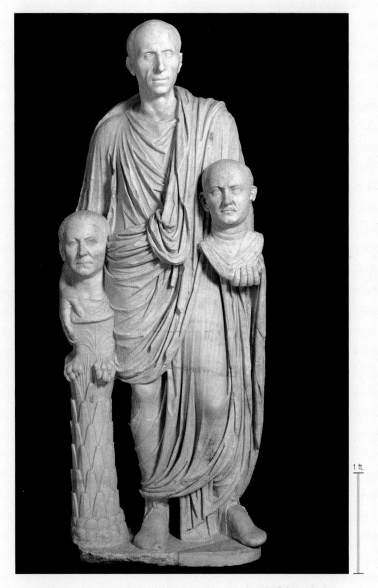

7-7 Man with portrait busts of his ancestors, from Rome, Italy, late first century BCE. Marble, 5′ 5″ high. Centro Montemartini, Musei Capitolini, Rome.

Reflecting the importance that patricians placed on genealogy, this toga-clad man proudly displays the portrait busts of his father and grandfather. Both are characteristically realistic likenesses.

---

reflects the new Republican familiarity with the terraced sanctuaries of the Hellenistic East. The construction method, however, was distinctly Roman.

The builders used concrete *barrel vaults* (see "Roman Concrete Construction," page 186) of enormous strength to support the imposing terraces and to cover the great ramps leading to the grand central staircase, as well as to give shape to the shops aligned on two levels that sold food and souvenirs to those who came to the festivals in honor of the goddess. In this way, Roman engineers transformed the entire hillside, subjecting nature itself to human will and rational order.

Sculpture

The patrons of Republican temples and sanctuaries were in almost all cases men from old and distinguished families. Often they were victorious generals, like Marcellus, the conqueror of Syracuse, who used the spoils of war to finance public works. These aristocratic patricians were fiercely proud of their lineage. They kept likenesses of their ancestors in wood cupboards in their homes and paraded them at the funerals of prominent relatives (see "Roman Ancestor Portraits," above). Portraiture was one way that the patrician class celebrated its elevated position in society.

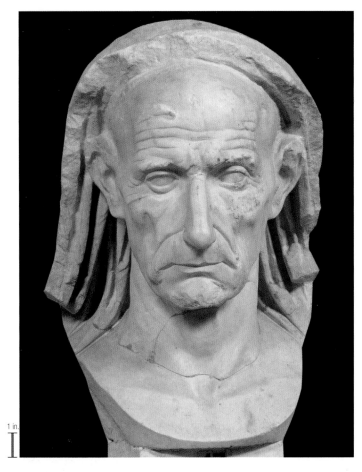

7-8 Head of a Republican priest, ca. 50–30 BCE. Marble, 1′ 2⅝″ high (without modern bust). Musei Vaticani, Rome.

Veristic (superrealistic) portraits of old men from distinguished families were the norm during the Republic. The sculptor of this head painstakingly recorded every detail of the elderly priest's face.

Verism. The subjects of these portraits were almost exclusively men (and, occasionally, women) of advanced age, for generally only elders held power in the Republic. These patricians did not ask sculptors to make them appear nobler than they were, as Kresilas portrayed Pericles (FIG. 5-42). Instead, they requested images memorializing their distinctive features, in the tradition of the treasured household *imagines*. One of the most striking of these so-called *veristic* (superrealistic) portraits is the head (FIG. 7-8) of a Republican priest now in the Vatican Museums. (Roman priests drew part of their toga over their head to form a hood while performing their sacred duties; compare FIG. I-10.) The sculptor painstakingly recorded his bald head and the lines, bulges, and folds of his aged face, not wanting to miss the slightest detail of the priest's unique appearance. Scholars debate whether Republican veristic portraits were truly blunt records of individual features or exaggerated types designed to make a statement about personality: serious, experienced, determined, loyal to family and state—the most admired virtues during the Republic.

Tivoli General. The priest's head illustrates that the Romans believed that the head or bust alone (FIGS. 7-7 and 7-11) was enough to constitute a portrait. The Greeks, by contrast, believed that head and body were inseparable parts of an integral whole, so

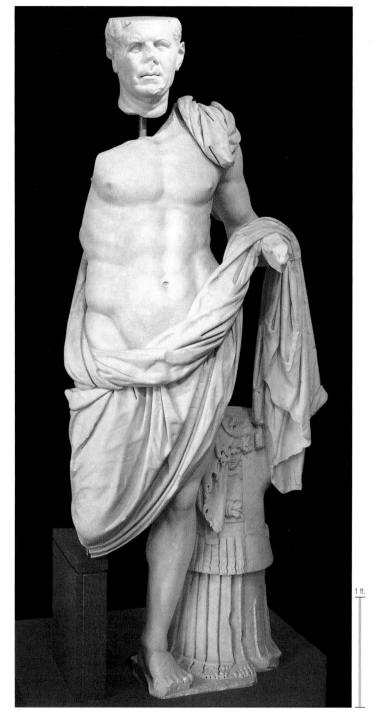

7-9 Portrait of a Roman general, from the Sanctuary of Hercules, Tivoli, Italy, ca. 75–50 BCE. Marble, 6′ 2″ high. Palazzo Massimo alle Terme, Museo Nazionale Romano, Rome.

The sculptor based this life-size portrait of a general on idealized Greek statues of heroes and athletes, but the man's head is a veristic likeness. The combination is typical of Republican portraiture.

their portraits were always full length (FIG. 5-88), although Roman copies often reproduced only the head (FIG. 5-42). In fact, Republican sculptors often placed veristic heads on bodies to which they could not possibly belong, as in the seminude portrait statue (FIG. 7-9) from Tivoli representing a Republican general. The *cuirass* (leather breastplate) at his side, which acts as a prop for the heavy marble statue, is the emblem of his rank. But the general does not appear as he would in life. Although he has a typically Republican stern and lined face, the head sits atop a powerful, youthful body. The sculptor modeled the portrait on the statues of Greek athletes and heroes the Romans admired so much and often copied. The incorporation of references to Greek art in these portrait statues evoked the notion of patrician cultural superiority. To be portrayed nude also suggested that the person possessed a heroic character. To modern eyes, the juxtaposition of a veristic head and an idealized body may seem incongruous and discordant, but the purpose of the portrait was to characterize different aspects of the man portrayed—and the sculptor succeeded admirably.

Julius Caesar. Beginning early in the first century BCE, the Roman desire to advertise distinguished ancestry led to the placement of portraits of illustrious forebears on Republican coins. These ancestral portraits supplanted the earlier Roman tradition (based on Greek convention) of using images of divinities on coins. No Roman, however, not even Pompey "the Great" (FIG. 7-9A), who likened himself to Alexander the Great, dared to place his own likeness on a coin until 44 BCE, when Julius Caesar, shortly before his assassination on the Ides of March, issued coins featuring his portrait and his newly acquired title, *dictator perpetuo* ("dictator for life"). The *denarius* (the standard Roman silver coin, from which the word *penny* ultimately derives) illustrated here (FIG. 7-10) records Caesar's aging face and receding hairline in conformity

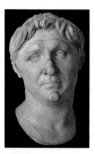

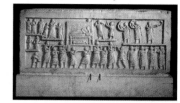

⏴**7-9A** Pompey the Great, ca. 70–60 BCE.

with the Republican veristic tradition. But placing the likeness of a living person on a coin violated all the norms of Republican propriety. Henceforth, Roman coins, which circulated throughout the vast territories under Roman control, would be used to mold public opinion in favor of the ruler by announcing his achievements—both real and fictional.

Non-Elite Portraiture. In stark contrast to patricians, who traditionally displayed portraits of themselves and their ancestors in homes and public places, slaves and former slaves could not possess any family portraits, because, under Roman law, their parents and grandparents were not people but property. Freed slaves, however, often ordered figural reliefs (FIGS. 7-10A and 7-11) for their tombs to commemorate their new status as Roman citizens (see "Art for Freed Slaves," page 190).

⏴**7-10A** Funerary procession, Amiternum, ca. 50–1 BCE.

POMPEII AND THE CITIES OF VESUVIUS

On August 24, 79 CE (according to Pliny the Younger, but more likely a month or two later, based on new archaeological evidence), Mount Vesuvius, a long-dormant volcano, suddenly erupted (see "An Eyewitness Account of the Eruption of Mount Vesuvius," page 191). Many prosperous towns around the Bay of Naples (the ancient Greek city of Neapolis), among them Pompeii, were buried in a single day. The eruption was a catastrophe for the inhabitants of the Vesuvian cities, but a boon for archaeologists and art historians. When researchers first systematically explored the buried cities in the 18th century, the ruins had lain largely undisturbed for nearly 1,700 years, enabling a reconstruction of the art and life of Roman towns of the Late Republic and Early Empire to a degree impossible anywhere else.

Civic Architecture

Walking through Pompeii today is an unforgettable experience. The streets, with their heavy flagstone pavements and sidewalks, are still there, as are the stepping-stones pedestrians used to cross the streets without having to step in puddles. Ingeniously, the city planners placed these stones in such a way that vehicle wheels could straddle them, enabling supplies to be brought directly to the shops, taverns, and bakeries. Tourists still can visit the impressive concrete-vaulted rooms of Pompeii's public baths, sit in the seats of its theater and amphitheater, enter private homes with statue-filled gardens and dining- and bedrooms with elaborate frescoes, even walk among the tombs outside the city's walls. Pompeii is an archaeological time capsule and has been called the living city of the dead for good reason.

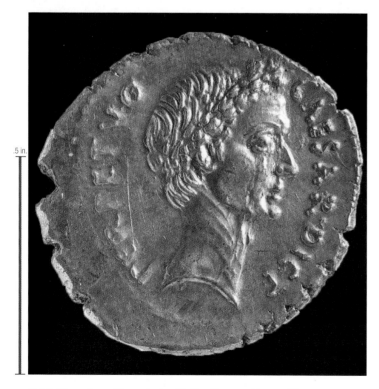

7-10 Denarius with portrait of Julius Caesar, 44 BCE. Silver, diameter $\frac{3}{4}''$. American Numismatic Society, New York.

Julius Caesar was the first to place his own portrait on Roman coinage during his lifetime. This denarius, issued just before his assassination, shows the dictator with a deeply lined face and neck.

Forum. The center of civic life in any Roman town was its *forum* (plural, *fora*), or public square. Usually located at the city's geographical center at the intersection of the main north-south street, the *cardo,* and the main east-west avenue, the *decumanus,* as at

Art for Freed Slaves

Historians and art historians alike tend to focus on the lives and monuments of famous individuals, but some of the most interesting remains of ancient Roman civilization are the artworks that ordinary people commissioned, especially former slaves—*freedmen* and *freedwomen*. Slavery was common in the Roman world. Indeed, at the end of the Republic, there were approximately two million slaves in Italy—roughly one slave for every three citizens. The very rich might own hundreds of slaves, but slaves could also be found in all but the poorest households. The practice was so much a part of Roman society that even slaves often became slave owners when their former masters freed them. Some gained freedom in return for meritorious service, others as bequests in their masters' wills. Most slaves died as slaves in service to their original or new owners.

The most noteworthy artworks that Roman freedmen and freedwomen commissioned are the stone reliefs that regularly adorned their tomb facades. One of these reliefs (FIG. **7-11**) depicts two men and a woman, all named Gessius or Gessia. At the left is Gessia Fausta and at the right, Gessius Primus. Both are the freed slaves of Publius Gessius,

the freeborn citizen in the center, shown wearing a soldier's cuirass and portrayed in the standard Republican superrealistic fashion (FIGS. 7-7 and 7-8). As slaves, this couple had no legal standing. They were the property of Publius Gessius. According to Roman law, however, after gaining freedom the ex-slaves became people (though they still could not serve in the Roman army). These stern frontal portraits proclaim their new status as members of Roman society—and their gratitude to Publius Gessius for granting them their freedom.

As was the custom, the ex-slaves bear their patron's name. Therefore, whether they are sister and brother, wife and husband, or unrelated is unclear. The inscriptions on the relief, however, explicitly state that Gessius Primus provided the funds for the monument in his will and that Gessia Fausta, the only survivor of the three, directed the work. The relief thus depicts the living and the dead side by side, indistinguishable without the accompanying inscriptions. This theme is common in Roman art and proclaims that death does not break the bonds formed in life and that families will be reunited in the afterlife, as the emperor Antoninus Pius (FIG. 7-56) and an anonymous circus official (FIG. 7-43A) expected to rejoin their wives after they too died.

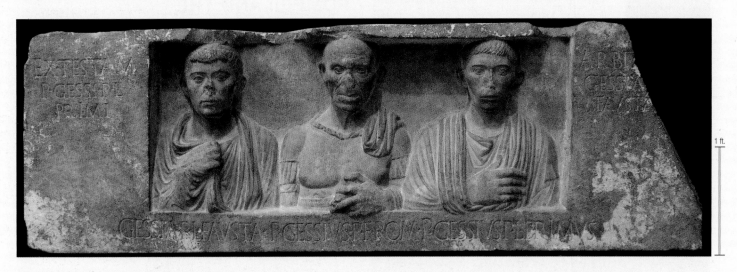

7-11 Funerary relief with portraits of the Gessii, from Rome(?), Italy, ca. 30 BCE. Marble, 2′ 1½″ high. Museum of Fine Arts, Boston.

Roman freedmen often placed reliefs depicting themselves and their former owners on the facades of their tombs. The portraits and inscriptions celebrated their freedom and new status as citizens.

Timgad (FIG. 7-43), the forum was nevertheless generally closed to all but pedestrian traffic. Pompeii's forum (FIG. 7-12, no. 1) lies in the southwest corner of the expanded Roman city, but at the heart of the original town.

The forum, originally just an open area, took on monumental form only after the town became a Roman colony in 80 BCE. Inspired by Hellenistic architecture, the Romans erected two-story colonnades on three sides of the long and narrow plaza. At the north end, they constructed a *Capitolium* (FIG. 7-12, no. 2)—a temple honoring the three chief Roman gods, Jupiter, Juno, and Minerva. Pompeii's Capitolium is of standard Republican type, constructed of tufa covered with fine white stucco and combining

an Etruscan plan with Corinthian columns. It faces into the civic square, dominating the area. This contrasts with the siting of Greek temples (FIGS. 5-43 and 5-44), which stood in isolation and could be approached and viewed from all sides, like colossal statues on giant stepped pedestals. Roman fora, like Etrusco-Roman temples, have a chief side, a focus of attention.

The area within the porticos of the forum at Pompeii was empty, except for statues portraying local dignitaries and, later, Roman emperors. This is where the citizens conducted daily commerce and held festivities. All around the square, behind the colonnades, were secular and religious structures, including the town's administrative offices. Most important was the *basilica* at the

An Eyewitness Account of the Eruption of Mount Vesuvius

One of the world's most famous archaeological sites is Pompeii, which owes its preservation today to the devastating volcanic eruption of Mount Vesuvius in 79 CE. The Oscans, one of the many early Italic population groups, were the first to settle at Pompeii, but toward the end of the fifth century BCE, the Samnites took over the town. Under the influence of their Greek neighbors, the Samnites greatly expanded the original settlement and gave monumental shape to the city center (FIG. 7-12). Pompeii fought with other Italian cities on the losing side against Rome in the so-called Social War (from the Latin word for "allies"—*socii*) that ended in 89 BCE, and in 80 BCE the Roman consul Sulla founded a new Roman colony on the site, with Latin as its official language. The colony's population had grown to between 10,000 and 15,000 when, in February 62 CE, an earthquake shook the city, causing extensive damage. Vesuvius erupted 17 years later, bringing an end to the life of the city and all its inhabitants who did not flee in time.

Pliny the Elder, whose *Natural History* is one of the most important sources for the history of Greek art, was among those who tried to rescue others from danger when Vesuvius erupted. Overcome by the volcano's fumes, he died. His nephew, Pliny the Younger (ca. 61–ca. 112 CE), a government official under the emperor Trajan, left an account of the eruption and his uncle's demise:

> [The volcanic cloud's] general appearance can best be expressed as being like a pine . . . for it rose to a great height on a sort of trunk and then split off into branches. . . . Sometimes it looked white, sometimes blotched and dirty, according to the amount of soil and ashes it carried with it. . . . The buildings were now shaking with violent shocks, and seemed to be swaying to and fro as if they were torn from their foundations. Outside, on the other hand, there was the danger of falling pumice-stones, even though these were light and porous. . . . Elsewhere there was daylight, [but around Vesuvius, people] were still in darkness, blacker and denser than any night that ever was. . . . When daylight returned . . . two days after the last day [my uncle] had been seen, his body was found intact and uninjured, still fully clothed and looking more like sleep than death.*

*Betty Radice, trans., *Pliny the Younger: Letters and Panegyricus*, vol. 1 (Cambridge, Mass.: Harvard University Press, 1969), 427–433.

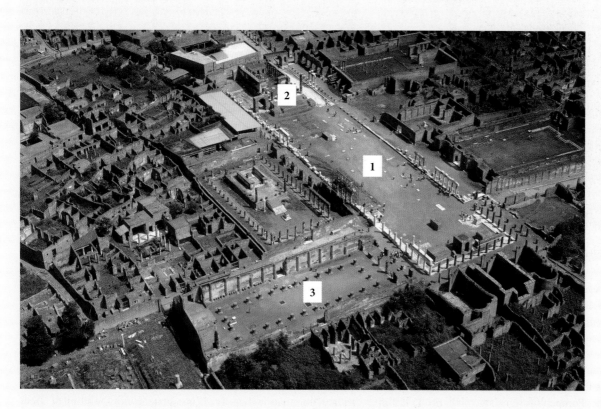

7-12 Aerial view of the forum (looking northeast), Pompeii, Italy, 80 BCE–79 CE. (1) forum, (2) Capitolium, (3) basilica.

Before the Vesuvian eruption, the forum was the center of civic life at Pompeii. At the north end was the city's main temple, the Capitolium, and at the southwest corner, the basilica (law court).

southwest corner (FIG. 7-12, no. 3). It is the earliest well-preserved building of its kind. Also constructed by the Roman colonists, the basilica was Pompeii's law court and chief administrative building. In plan, it resembled the forum itself: long and narrow, with two stories of internal columns dividing the space into a central *nave* and flanking *aisles*. This scheme had a long afterlife in architectural history and will be familiar to anyone who has ever entered a church (compare, for example, FIG. 8-18).

Amphitheater. Shortly after the Romans took control of Pompeii, two of the town's officials, Quinctius Valgus and Marcus Porcius, used their own funds (a common expectation of wealthy

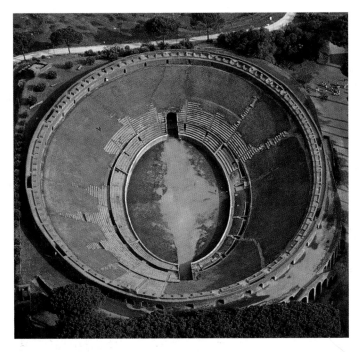

7-13 Aerial view of the amphitheater (looking southeast), Pompeii, Italy, ca. 70 BCE.

Pompeii's amphitheater is the oldest known and an early example of Roman concrete technology. In the arena, bloody gladiatorial combats and wild animal hunts took place before 20,000 spectators.

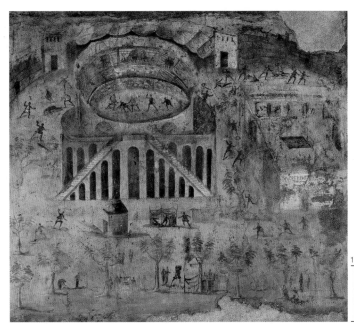

7-14 Brawl in the Pompeii amphitheater, wall painting from House I,3,23, Pompeii, Italy, ca. 60–79 CE. Fresco, 5′ 7″ × 6′ 1″. Museo Archeologico Nazionale, Naples.

This wall painting records a brawl that broke out in the Pompeii amphitheater in 59 CE. The painter included the awning (velarium) that could be rolled down to shield the spectators from sun and rain.

magistrates) to erect a large amphitheater (FIG. 7-13) at the southeastern end of town. The earliest permanent amphitheater known, it could seat some 20,000 spectators—more than the entire population of the town even a century and a half after its construction. The donors would have had choice reserved seats in the new entertainment center. In fact, seating was by civic and military rank. The Roman social hierarchy was therefore on display at every event.

The word *amphitheater* means "double theater," and Roman amphitheaters resemble two Greek theaters put together. Amphitheaters nonetheless stand in sharp contrast, both architecturally and functionally, to Greco-Roman theaters, where actors performed comedies and tragedies. Amphitheaters were where the Romans staged bloody gladiatorial combats and wild animal hunts (see "Spectacles in the Colosseum," page 207). Greek theaters were always on natural hillsides (FIG. 5-71), but supporting an amphitheater's continuous elliptical cavea required building an artificial mountain. Only concrete, unknown to the Greeks, could easily meet that challenge. In the Pompeii amphitheater, shallow concrete barrel vaults form a giant retaining wall holding up the earthen mound and stone seats. Barrel vaults running all the way through the elliptical mountain of earth form the tunnels leading to the arena, the central area where the violent contests took place. (*Arena* is Latin for "sand," which soaked up the blood of the wounded and killed.)

A painting (FIG. 7-14) found in one of Pompeii's houses records a brawl that occurred in the amphitheater during a gladiatorial contest in 59 CE. The fighting—between the Pompeians and their neighbors, the Nucerians—left many seriously wounded and led to the banning of games in the amphitheater for a decade. (The ban was lifted in 62 CE to help revive the city's economy after the earthquake.) The painting shows the cloth awning (*velarium*) that could be rolled down from the top of the cavea to shield spectators

from sun and rain. Also featured are the distinctive external double staircases (FIG. 7-13, *lower right*) that enabled large numbers of people to enter and exit the cavea in an orderly fashion.

Domestic Architecture

The evidence from Pompeii regarding Roman domestic architecture is unparalleled anywhere else and is the most precious byproduct of the volcanic eruption of 79 CE (see "The Roman House," page 193).

House of the Vettii. One of the best-preserved houses at Pompeii, partially rebuilt by the Italian excavators, is the House of the Vettii, an old second-century BCE house remodeled and repainted (FIG. 7-22) after the earthquake of 62 CE. A photograph (FIG. 7-16) taken in the fauces shows the impluvium in the center of the atrium; the opening in the roof above; and, in the background, the peristyle garden (FIG. 7-16A) with its marble tables and splendid mural paintings dating to the last years of the Vesuvian city. At that time, two brothers, Aulus Vettius Restitutus and Aulus Vettius Conviva, owned the house. They were freedmen who probably had made their fortune as merchants. Their wealth enabled them to purchase and furnish the kind of fashionable townhouse that in an earlier era only patricians could have acquired.

Painting and Mosaic

The houses of Pompeii and neighboring cities and the *villas* in the countryside around Mount Vesuvius have yielded a treasure trove of mural paintings—the most complete record of the changing fashions in interior decoration found anywhere in the ancient world. The sheer quantity of these paintings tells a great deal about

The Roman House

The Roman house (FIG. 7-15) was not only a place to live. It played an important role in societal rituals. In the Roman world, individuals were frequently bound to others in a patron-client relationship whereby a wealthier, better-educated, and more powerful *patronus* would protect the interests of a *cliens,* sometimes large numbers of them. The size of a patron's clientele was one measure of his standing in society. Being seen in public accompanied by a crowd of clients was a badge of honor. In this system, a plebeian might be bound to a patrician, a freed slave to a former owner, or even one patrician to another. Regardless of rank, all clients were obligated to support their patron in political campaigns and to perform specific services on request, as well as to call on and salute the patron at the patron's home.

A client calling on a patron would enter the typical Roman *domus* ("private house") through a narrow foyer (*fauces,* the "jaws" of the house), which led to a large central reception area, the *atrium* (plural, *atria*), which, in the case of an old patrician family's house, would feature cupboards with wax ancestor masks (see "Roman Ancestor Portraits," page 187). The rooms flanking the fauces could open onto the atrium, as in FIG. 7-15, or onto the street, in which case the owner could operate or rent them as shops. The roof over the atrium was partially open to the sky, not only to admit light but also to channel rainwater into a basin (*impluvium*) below to be stored in cisterns for household use. Opening onto the atrium were small bedrooms called *cubicula* ("cubicles"; singular, *cubiculum*). At the back were two recessed areas (*alae,* "wings") and the patron's *tablinum,* or home office; one or more *triclinia* ("dining rooms"; singular, *triclinium*); a kitchen; and sometimes a small garden.

Extant houses—for example, the House of the Vettii (FIG. 7-16)—display endless variations of the same basic plan, dictated by the owners' personal tastes and means, the size and shape of the lot, and so forth, but all Roman houses of this type were inward-looking in nature. The design shut off the street's noise and dust, and all internal activity

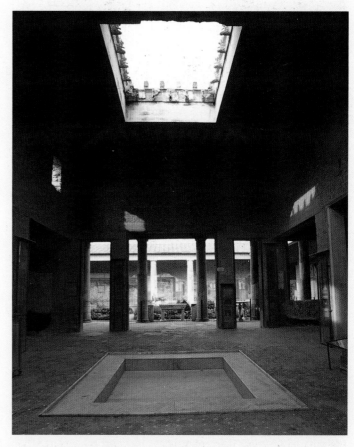

7-16 **Atrium of the House of the Vettii, Pompeii, Italy, mid-second century BCE, rebuilt 62–79 CE.**

The house of the Vettius brothers was of the later Hellenized type with a peristyle garden behind the atrium. The impluvium below the open roof collected rainwater for domestic use.

focused on the brightly illuminated atrium at the center of the residence. This basic module (only the front half of the typical house in FIG. 7-15) resembles the plan of the typical Etruscan house as reflected in the tombs of Cerveteri (FIGS. 6-7 and 6-7A). The early Roman house, like the early Roman temple, grew out of the Etruscan tradition.

During the second century BCE, when Roman architects were beginning to construct stone temples with Greek columns, the Roman house also took on Greek airs. Builders added a garden framed by a *peristyle* (FIG. 7-16A) behind the Etruscan-style house, providing a second internal source of illumination as well as a pleasant setting for meals served in a summer triclinium. The axial symmetry of the plan meant that on entering the fauces of the house, a visitor had a view through the atrium directly into the colonnaded garden (as in FIG. 7-16), which often boasted a fountain or pool, marble statuary, mural paintings, and mosaic floors (FIG. 5-70).

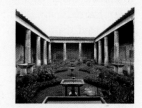

⊿**7-16A** Peristyle, House of the Vettii, second century BCE.

Private houses of this type were typical of Pompeii and other Italian towns, but they were very rare in cities such as Rome, where the masses lived instead in multistory apartment houses (FIG. 7-54).

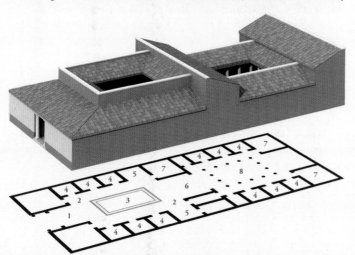

7-15 **Restored view and plan of a typical Roman private house (domus) of the Late Republic and Early Empire (John Burge).**
(1) fauces, (2) atrium, (3) impluvium, (4) cubiculum, (5) ala, (6) tablinum, (7) triclinium, (8) peristyle.

Older Roman houses closely followed Etruscan models and had atria and small gardens, but during the Late Republic and Early Empire, peristyles with Greek columns became common.

both the prosperity and the tastes of the times. How many homes today, even of the very wealthy, have custom-painted murals in nearly every room? Roman wall paintings were true frescoes (see "Fresco Painting," page 428), with the colors applied while the plaster was still damp. The process was painstaking. First, the painter prepared the wall by using a trowel to apply several layers of plaster (mixed with marble dust if the patron could afford it). Only then could painting begin. Finally, when the painter completed work and the surface dried, an assistant polished the wall to achieve a lustrous finish.

In the early years of exploration at Pompeii and nearby Herculaneum, interest in Roman wall paintings focused almost exclusively on the figural panels that formed part of the overall mural designs, especially those depicting Greek myths. The excavators cut the panels out of the walls and transferred them to the royal collection in Naples. In time, more enlightened archaeologists put an end to the practice of cutting pieces out of the walls and began to give serious attention to the mural designs as a whole. Toward the end of the 19th century, August Mau (1840–1909), a German art historian, turned scholars' attention to the overall compositions of the Roman wall paintings. He divided the various mural painting schemes into four "Pompeian Styles." Mau's classification system, although later refined and modified in detail, was an important contribution to the study of Roman art and still serves as the basis for describing Roman frescoes.

First Style. In Mau's *First Style,* the decorator's aim was to imitate costly marble panels using painted stucco relief. The fauces (FIG. 7-17) of an old mansion at Herculaneum, the so-called Samnite House, greets visitors with a stunning illusion of walls faced with marbles imported from quarries all over the Mediterranean. This approach to wall decoration is comparable to the modern practice, employed in private libraries and corporate meeting rooms alike, of using inexpensive manufactured materials to approximate the look and shape of genuine wood paneling. The practice was not, however, uniquely Roman. First Style walls are well documented in Greece from the late fourth century BCE on. The use of the First Style in Italian houses is yet another example of the Hellenization of Republican architecture.

Second Style. The First Style never went completely out of fashion, but after 80 BCE, a new approach to mural design became more popular. The *Second Style* is in most respects the antithesis of the First Style. Some scholars have argued that the Second Style also has precedents in Greece, but most believe that it is a Roman invention. Certainly, the Second Style evolved in Italy, where it was the preferred manner until around 15 BCE, when Roman painters introduced the Third Style. Second Style painters did not aim to create the illusion of an elegant marble wall, as First Style painters sought to do. Rather, they wanted to dissolve a room's confining walls and replace them with the illusion of an imaginary three-dimensional world.

Villa of the Mysteries. An early example of the new style is the room (FIG. 7-18) that gives its name to the Villa of the Mysteries at Pompeii. Many archaeologists believe that this chamber was used to celebrate, in private, the rites of the Greek god Dionysos (Roman Bacchus). Dionysos was the focus of an unofficial mystery religion popular among women in Italy at this time. The precise nature of the Dionysiac rites is unknown, but the figural cycle in the Villa of the Mysteries, illustrating mortals (all female save for one boy)

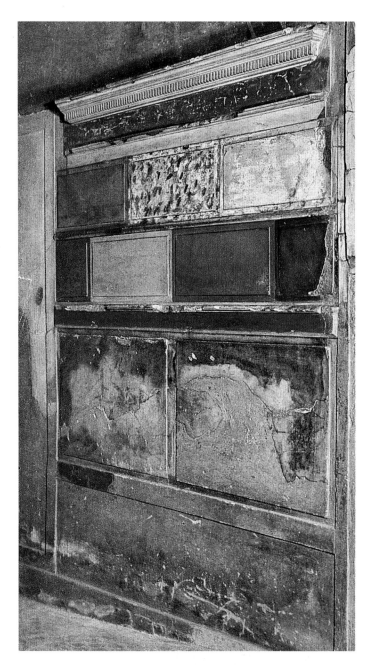

7-17 First Style wall painting in the fauces of the Samnite House, Herculaneum, Italy, late second century BCE.

In First Style murals, the aim was to imitate costly marble panels using painted stucco relief. The style is Greek in origin and another example of the Hellenization of Republican architecture.

interacting with mythological figures, probably provides some evidence of the cult's initiation rites. In these rites, young women were united in marriage with Dionysos, emulating Ariadne, the daughter of King Minos who helped Theseus find his way out of the Knossos labyrinth (FIGS. 4-4 and 4-5).

The backdrop for the nearly life-size figures is a series of painted panels imitating marble revetment, just as in the First Style but without the modeling in relief. In front of this painted marble wall, the artist created the illusion of a shallow ledge on which the human and divine actors move around the room. Especially striking is the way some of the figures interact across the corners of the room. For example, a seminude winged woman at the far right of the rear wall lashes out with her whip across the space of the room

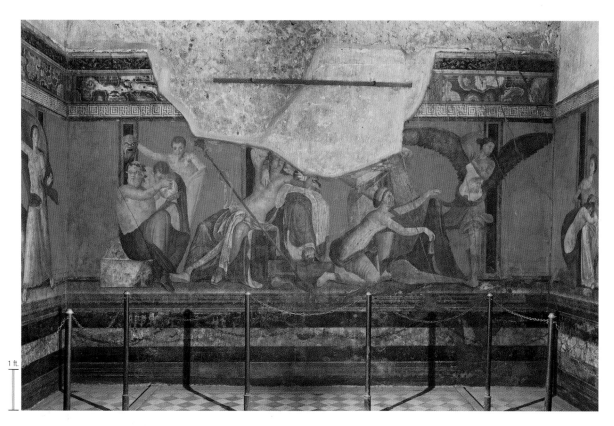

Second Style painters created the illusion of an imaginary three-dimensional world on the walls of Roman houses. The figures in this room are acting out the initiation rites of the Dionysiac mysteries.

1 ft.

at a kneeling woman with a bare back (the initiate and bride-to-be of Dionysos) on the left end of the right wall. Nothing comparable to this room existed in Hellenistic Greece. Despite the presence of Dionysos, satyrs, and other Greek mythological figures, this is a Roman design.

Boscoreale. In the early Second Style Dionysiac mystery frieze, the spatial illusionism is confined to the painted platform that projects into the room. But in mature Second Style designs, Roman painters created a three-dimensional setting that also extends beyond the wall, as in a cubiculum (FIG. 7-19) from the Villa of

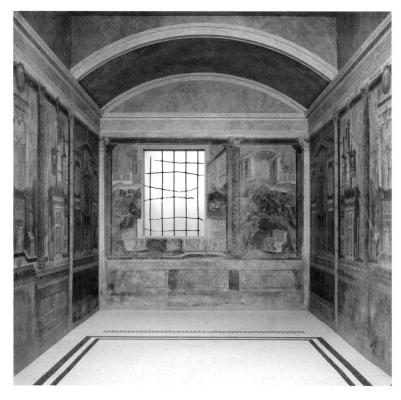

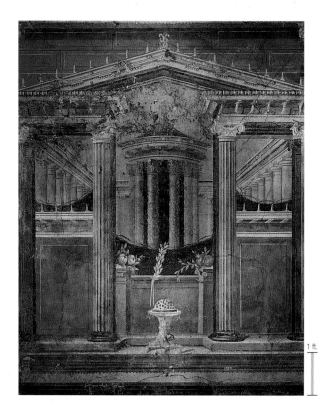

1 ft.

7-19 Second Style wall paintings (general view, *left,* and detail of tholos, *right*), from cubiculum M of the Villa of Publius Fannius Synistor, Boscoreale, Italy, ca. 50–40 BCE. Fresco, 8′ 9″ high. Metropolitan Museum of Art, New York.

In this Second Style bedroom, the painter opened up the walls with vistas of towns, temples, and colonnaded courtyards. The convincing illusionism is due in part to the use of linear perspective.

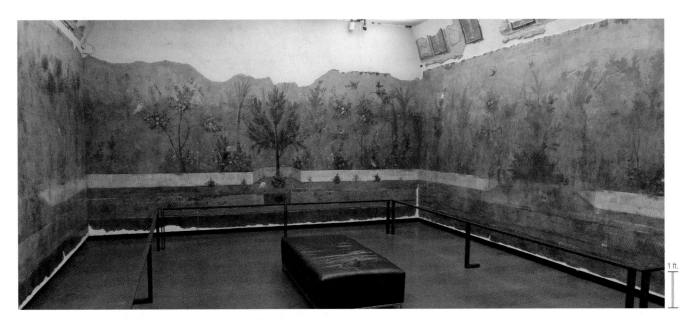

7-20 Gardenscape, Second Style wall paintings, from the summer triclinium of the Villa of Livia, Primaporta, Italy, ca. 30–20 BCE. Fresco, 6′ 7″ high. Palazzo Massimo alle Terme, Museo Nazionale Romano, Rome.

The ultimate example of a Second Style "picture-window" wall is this gardenscape in Livia's villa. To suggest recession, the painter used atmospheric perspective, intentionally blurring the distant forms.

Publius Fannius Synistor at Boscoreale, near Pompeii. The excavators removed the frescoes soon after their discovery, and today they are part of a reconstructed Roman bedroom in the Metropolitan Museum of Art in New York. All around the room, the Second Style painter opened up the walls with vistas of Italian towns, marble tholos temples, and colonnaded courtyards. Painted doors (FIG. 7-19, *left,* near the far right corner of the room; compare FIG. 6-1) and gates (FIG. 7-19, *right*) invite the viewer to walk through the wall into the magnificent world the painter created.

In this cubiculum, the Boscoreale muralist, like many other Roman painters around the Bay of Naples, demonstrated familiarity with *linear perspective,* often incorrectly said to be an innovation of Italian Renaissance artists (see "Linear Perspective," page 599). In this kind of perspective, all the receding lines in a composition converge on a single *vanishing point* along the painting's central axis to show depth and distance. Ancient writers state that Greek painters of the fifth century BCE first used linear perspective for the design of Athenian stage sets (hence its Greek name, *skenographia,* "scene painting"). In the Boscoreale cubiculum, the painter most successfully employed skenographia in the far corners, where a low gate leads to a peristyle framing a round temple (FIG. 7-19, *right*). Although, by Renaissance standards, linear perspective was often inconsistently executed, it was a favored tool of Second Style painters seeking to transform the

usually windowless walls of Roman houses into "picture-window" vistas that expanded the apparent space of the rooms.

Primaporta. The ultimate example of a Second Style picture-window mural (FIG. 7-20) comes from the villa of the emperor Augustus's third wife, Livia (FIG. 7-28), at Primaporta, just north of Rome. There, in a barrel-vaulted subterranean summer triclinium, imperial painters decorated all four walls with a lush gardenscape. The only architectural element is the flimsy fence of the garden

7-21 Third Style wall painting, from cubiculum 15 of the Villa of Agrippa Postumus, Boscotrecase, Italy, ca. 10 BCE. Fresco, 7′ 8″ high. Metropolitan Museum of Art, New York.

In the Third Style, Roman painters decorated walls with delicate linear fantasies sketched on monochromatic backgrounds. Here, a tiny floating landscape on a black ground is the central motif.

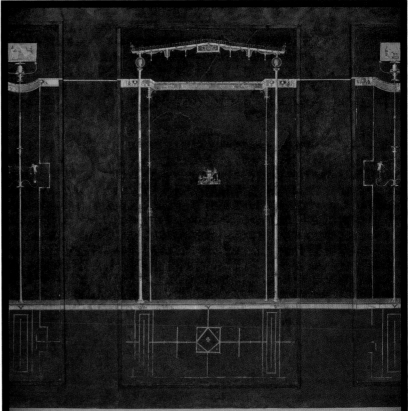

itself. To suggest recession, the painter employed another kind of perspective, *atmospheric perspective,* in which the illusion of depth is achieved by the increasingly blurred appearance of objects in the distance. At Primaporta, the muralist precisely painted the fence, trees, and birds in the foreground, whereas the details of the dense foliage in the background are indistinct. Among the wall paintings examined so far, only the landscape fresco (FIG. 4-9) from Akrotiri offers a similar wraparound view of nature devoid of human actors (in contrast to the Etruscan Tomb of Hunting and Fishing; FIG. 6-10). But the Theran fresco's white sky and red, yellow, and blue rock formations do not create a successful illusion of a world filled with air and light just a few steps away.

Third Style. The Primaporta gardenscape is the polar opposite of First Style designs, which reinforce, rather than deny, the heavy presence of confining walls. But tastes changed rapidly in the Roman world, as in society today. Not long after Livia hired painters to decorate her villa, Roman patrons began to favor mural designs that reasserted the primacy of the wall surface. In Mau's *Third Style,* artists no longer attempted to replace the walls with three-dimensional worlds of their own creation. Nor did they seek

to imitate the appearance of the marble walls of Hellenistic palaces. Instead they adorned walls with delicate linear fantasies sketched on predominantly *monochromatic* (one-color) backgrounds.

Boscotrecase. One of the earliest examples of the Third Style—dating around 10 BCE—is cubiculum 15 (FIG. 7-21) in the Villa of Agrippa Postumus at Boscotrecase. Nowhere did the artist use illusionistic painting to penetrate the wall. In place of the stately columns of the Second Style are insubstantial and impossibly thin *colonnettes* supporting featherweight canopies barely reminiscent of pediments. In the center of this delicate and elegant architectural frame is a tiny floating landscape painted directly on the jet-black ground. It is hard to imagine a sharper contrast with the panoramic gardenscape at Livia's villa. On other Third Style walls, landscapes and mythological scenes appear in frames, like modern easel paintings hung on walls. Never could these framed panels be mistaken for windows opening onto a world beyond the room. Not everyone approved of the new mural style. One of those who disliked the Third Style was the Augustan architect Vitruvius, author of the most important extant ancient treatise on architecture (see "Vitruvius's *Ten Books on Architecture,*" page 204).

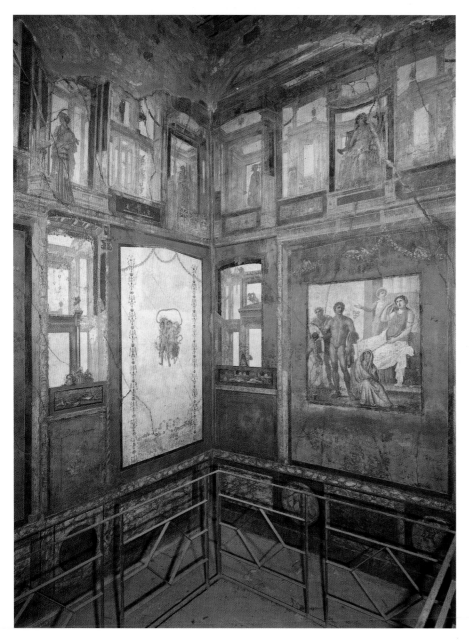

Fourth Style. A taste for illusionism returned in the *Fourth Style* of mural painting, which became popular in the 50s CE. Characterized by the reintroduction of architectural vistas seen through the painted walls, the Fourth Style nonetheless cannot be confused with the Second Style. In the later style, the views of buildings are irrational fantasies, as in the Ixion Room (FIG. 7-22) of the House of the Vettii (FIG. 7-16) at Pompeii. In this late Fourth Style design dating to just before the eruption of Mount Vesuvius, the painter rejected the quiet elegance of the Third Style in favor of a crowded and complex multicolor composition. The decorative scheme of the Vettius brothers' triclinium opening onto the peristyle (FIG. 7-16A) of their Pompeian house is a kind of summation of all the previous mural schemes, another instance of the mixing of styles noted earlier as characteristic of Roman art in general. The lowest zone, for example, is one of the most successful imitations anywhere of costly multicolored imported marbles, despite the fact that the painter created the illusion without recourse to relief, as in the First Style. The large white panels in the corners of the room, with their delicate floral frames and floating central motifs, would fit naturally into the most elegant Third Style design. Unmistakably Fourth Style, however, are the fragmentary architectural vistas of the central and upper

7-22 Fourth Style wall paintings in the Ixion Room (triclinium P) of the House of the Vettii (FIG. 7-16), Pompeii, Italy, ca. 70–79 CE.

Late Fourth Style murals are often multicolored, crowded, and confused compositions with a mixture of architectural views, framed mythological panels, and First and Third Style motifs.

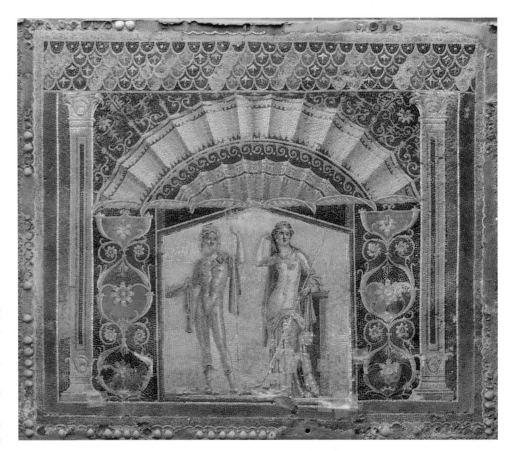

7-23 Neptune and Amphitrite, wall mosaic in the summer triclinium of the House of Neptune and Amphitrite, Herculaneum, Italy, ca. 62–79 CE.

In the ancient world, mosaics usually decorated floors, but this example adorns a wall. The sea deities Neptune and Amphitrite fittingly overlook cascading water in an elaborate private fountain.

zones of the walls. They are unrelated to one another and do not constitute a unified cityscape beyond the wall. Moreover, the figures depicted would tumble into the room if they took a single step forward.

The Ixion Room takes its name from the mythological panel painting at the center of the rear wall. Ixion had attempted to seduce Zeus's wife, Hera, and the king of the gods punished Ixion by binding him to a perpetually spinning wheel. The panels on the two side walls also have Greek myths as subjects. The Ixion Room is a kind of private art gallery. Many art historians believe that lost Greek panel paintings were the models for the many mythological paintings on Third and Fourth Style walls. The mythological paintings on Pompeian walls attest to the Romans' continuing admiration for Greek artworks three centuries after Marcellus brought the treasures of Syracuse to Rome. But few (if any) of these mythological paintings can be described as true copies of famous Greek works. Unlike the replicas of Greek statues that have been found throughout the Roman world, including Pompeii (FIG. 5-41), these panels seem to be merely variations on standard compositions. The themes chosen no doubt reflected the individual owners' tastes and the impression they wished to make on their guests.

Wall Mosaics. Mythological themes were on occasion also the subject of Roman mosaics. In the ancient world, mosaics usually covered floors. For example, the *Battle of Issus* mosaic (FIG. 5-70) was the floor of an *exedra* (recessed area) opening onto a peristyle in the biggest house at Pompeii, the so-called House of the Faun, named for a Hellenistic-style bronze statue in the larger of its two atria. But occasionally Roman mosaics decorated walls and even ceilings, foreshadowing the extensive use of wall and vault mosaics in the Middle Ages (see "Mosaics," page 256). An early example of a wall mosaic (FIG. 7-23) is in the House of Neptune and Amphitrite at Herculaneum. The statuesque figures of the sea god and his wife appropriately presided over the flowing water of the fountain in the courtyard in front of them, where the house's owners and guests enjoyed outdoor dining in warm weather.

Private Portraits. The subjects that Roman patrons preferred for mural paintings and mosaics were diverse, as expected in private contexts. Although mythological compositions were immensely popular, Roman homeowners commissioned a vast range of other subjects for the walls of their houses and villas. As noted, landscape paintings frequently appear on Second, Third, and Fourth Style

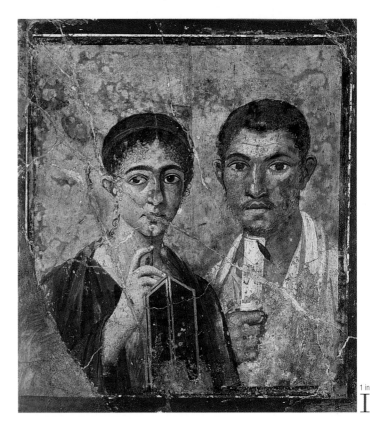

1 in.

7-24 Portrait of Terentius Neo(?) and his wife, wall painting from House VII, 2, 6, Pompeii, Italy, ca. 70–79 CE. Fresco, 1′ 11″ × 1′ 8½″. Museo Archeologico Nazionale, Naples.

This husband and wife wished to present themselves to their guests as thoughtful and well read. The portraits are individualized likenesses, but the poses and attributes are conventional.

walls. Paintings and mosaics depicting scenes from history include the *Battle of Issus* (FIG. 5-70) and the brawl in the Pompeii amphitheater (FIG. 7-14). Given the Roman custom of keeping masks of illustrious ancestors in atria, it is not surprising that painted portraits also appear in Pompeian houses. The double portrait of a

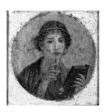

7-24A Woman with stylus, Pompeii, ca. 55–70 CE.

husband and wife illustrated here (FIG. 7-24) originally formed part of a Fourth Style wall of an exedra opening onto the atrium of the house owned by the baker Terentius Neo. He holds a scroll, and the woman holds a *stylus* (writing instrument) and wax writing-tablet, standard attributes in Roman marriage portraits (FIG. 7-24A). The scroll and stylus suggest the fine education of those depicted—even if, as was sometimes true, the individuals were minimally educated or even illiterate. (The Roman satirist Juvenal [ca. 55–ca. 140 CE] wryly noted around 120 CE that "there are many parts of Italy . . . in which no man puts on a toga until he is dead."[2]) By contrast, the heads are not standard types but sensitive studies of the couple's individual faces. Both the man and woman seem to be of equal standing in the eyes of the artist. In fact, the woman is in the foreground, overlapping the man's right shoulder. Such a portrait would have been inconceivable in ancient Greece.

Menander. Rarer on Pompeian walls are portraits of famous men and women of earlier eras, but several examples survive. The most famous is the seated portrait of the Greek poet Menander (FIG. 7-25) on the right wall of an exedra facing the peristyle in the House of the Menander, which takes its modern name from this mural. On the open scroll that the poet holds in his left hand is a label identifying him as Menander, "the first to write New Comedy." On the opposite wall, poorly preserved, is a portrait of a bearded man with theatrical masks—possibly Euripides, but definitely a tragedian as a counterpart to the writer of comic plays across from him. The portrait of Menander is probably an enlarged version of the kind of author portrait that art historians believe was a standard feature of ancient books, comparable to the photographs of authors that appear inside or on the dust jackets of modern books. These portraits of ancient authors seated at their writing tables had a long afterlife in the countless medieval Gospel books with full-page illustrations of the Gospel authors, the four evangelists (FIGS. 11-8, 11-13, 11-14, and 12-16A).

Still-Life Painting. Another genre that Roman mural painters explored was *still-life* painting (the representation of inanimate objects, artfully arranged). A still life with peaches and a carafe (FIG. 7-26), a detail of a Fourth Style wall from the House of the Stags in Herculaneum, is one of the finest extant examples. The painter was a master of illusionism and devoted as much attention to the shadows and highlights on the fruit, the stem and leaves, and the glass jar as to the objects themselves. Roman still lifes of this type are without precedent and have few successors until the 17th-century Dutch studies of food and other inanimate objects (FIGS. 25-1, 25-22, and 25-23).

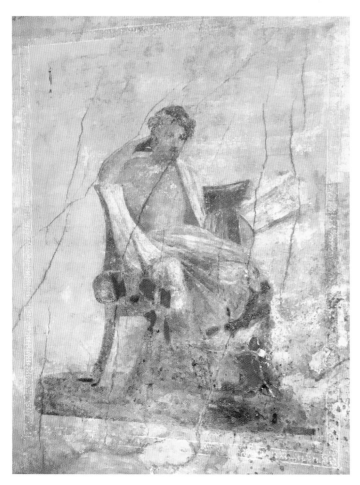

7-25 Seated portrait of the Greek poet Menander, detail of a Fourth Style mural painting in exedra 23 of the House of the Menander, Pompeii, ca. 62–79 CE.

This image of Menander is an enlarged version of the kind of author portrait that was a standard feature of ancient books. Classical author portraits had an afterlife in medieval portrayals of the four evangelists.

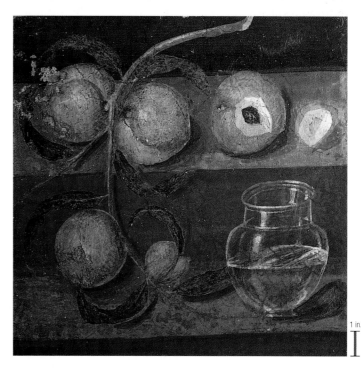

1 in.

7-26 Still life with peaches, detail of a Fourth Style wall painting, from the House of the Stags, Herculaneum, Italy, ca. 62–79 CE. Fresco, 1′ 2″ × 1′ 1½″. Museo Archeologico Nazionale, Naples.

The Roman interest in illusionism explains the popularity of still-life paintings. This painter paid scrupulous attention to the play of light and shadow on different shapes and textures.

Role Playing in Roman Portraiture

In every town throughout the vast Roman Empire, portraits of the emperors and empresses and their families were on display—in fora, basilicas, baths, and markets; in front of temples; atop triumphal arches—anywhere a statue could be placed. The rulers' heads varied little from Britain to Syria. All were replicas of official images, either imported or scrupulously copied by local artists. But the imperial sculptors combined portrait heads with many different statuary types. The type chosen depended on the position the person held in Roman society or the various fictitious guises that members of the imperial family assumed. Portraits of Augustus, for example, show him not only as armed general (FIG. 7-27) but also as priest with hooded head (FIG. I-10), toga-clad magistrate, traveling commander on horseback, and heroically nude warrior, and in the guise of various Roman gods, including Jupiter, Apollo, and Mercury. Nero, Augustus's most notorious successor, had himself portrayed as Sol, the sun god, in a colossal gilded-bronze statue (see "The Golden House of Nero," page 206). Commodus, a late-second-century CE emperor, considered himself Hercules reincarnate and appeared in the guise of that Greek hero in his portraits (FIG. 7-58A).

Role playing was not the exclusive prerogative of emperors and princes but extended to their wives, daughters, sisters, and mothers. Portraits of Livia (FIG. 7-28) depict her as many goddesses, including Ceres, Juno, Venus, and Vesta. She also appeared as the personification of Health, Justice, and Piety. In fact, it was common for imperial women to be represented on Roman coins as goddesses or as embodiments of feminine virtue. Faustina the Younger, for example, the wife of Marcus Aurelius and mother of 13 children, including Commodus, frequently took on the roles of Venus and Fecundity, among many others. Some portraits of Julia Domna (FIG. 7-62), Septimius Severus's wife, equated her with Juno, Venus, Peace, or Victory.

Ordinary citizens also engaged in role playing. Many assumed literary pretensions in the painted portraits (FIGS. 7-24 and 7-24A) they commissioned for the walls of their homes. Others likened themselves to Greek heroes (FIG. 7-59) or Roman deities (FIG. 7-60) on their coffins. The common people followed the lead of the emperors and empresses.

7-27 **Portrait of Augustus as imperator (general), from Primaporta, Italy, early-first-century CE copy of a bronze original of ca. 20 BCE. Marble, 6′ 8″ high. Musei Vaticani, Rome.**

The models for Augustus's idealized portraits, which depict him as a never-aging youth, were Classical Greek statues (FIG. 5-41). This portrait presents the armor-clad emperor in his role as general.

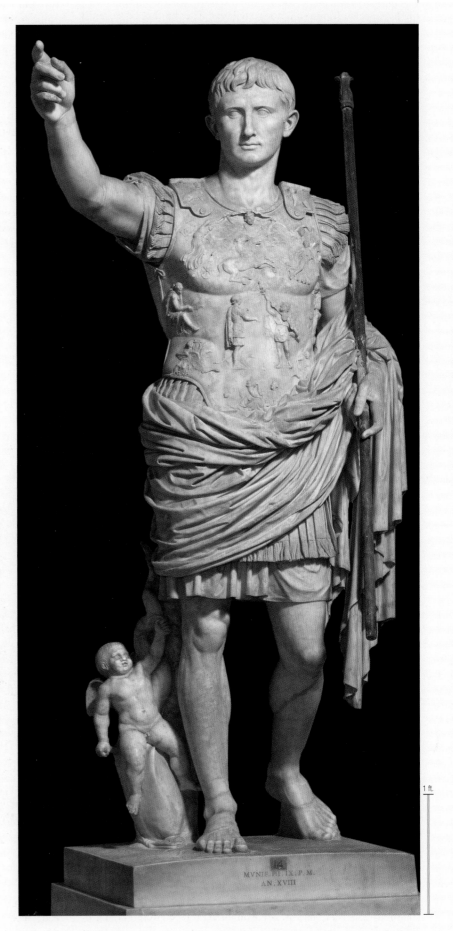

1 ft.

EARLY EMPIRE

The murder of Julius Caesar on the Ides of March, 44 BCE, plunged the Roman world into a bloody civil war. The fighting lasted until 31 BCE, when Octavian, Caesar's grandnephew and adopted son, crushed the naval forces of Mark Antony and Queen Cleopatra of Egypt at Actium in northwestern Greece. Antony and Cleopatra committed suicide, and in 30 BCE, Egypt, once the wealthiest and most powerful kingdom of the ancient world, became another province in the ever-expanding Roman Empire.

Historians mark the passage from the Roman Republic to the Roman Empire from the day in 27 BCE when the Senate conferred the title of *Augustus* (the Majestic, or Exalted, One; r. 27 BCE–14 CE) on Octavian. The Empire was ostensibly a continuation of the Republic, with the same constitutional offices, but in fact Augustus, whom the Senate recognized as *princeps* ("first citizen"), occupied all the key positions. He was consul and *imperator* ("commander in chief"; root of the word *emperor*) and even, after 12 BCE, *pontifex maximus* ("chief priest"). These offices gave Augustus control of all aspects of Roman public life.

Pax Romana. With powerful armies keeping order on the Empire's frontiers and no opposition at home, Augustus brought peace and prosperity to a war-weary Mediterranean world. Known in his day as the *Pax Augusta* (Augustan Peace), the peace that Augustus established prevailed for two centuries. It came to be called simply the *Pax Romana* (Roman Peace). During this time, the emperors commissioned a huge number of public works throughout the Empire: roads and bridges, theaters and amphitheaters, and bathing complexes, all on an unprecedented scale. The erection of imperial portrait statues and monuments covered with inscriptions and reliefs recounting the rulers' great deeds reminded people everywhere that the emperors were the source of peace and prosperity. These portraits and reliefs, however, often presented a picture of the emperors and their achievements that bore little resemblance to historical fact. Their purpose was not to provide an objective record but to mold public opinion. The Roman emperors and the artists they employed have had few equals in the effective use of art and architecture for propagandistic ends.

Augustus and the Julio-Claudians

When Augustus vanquished Antony and Cleopatra at Actium and became undisputed master of the Mediterranean world, he was not yet 32 years old. The rule by elders that had characterized the Roman Republic for nearly 500 years came to an abrupt end. Suddenly, Roman portraitists had to produce images of a youthful head of state. But Augustus was not merely young. The Senate had declared Caesar a god after his death, and Augustus, though never claiming to be a god himself, widely advertised himself as the son of a god. His portraits were designed to present the image of a godlike leader who miraculously never aged. Although Augustus lived until 14 CE, even official portraits made near the end of his life show him as a handsome youth (FIG. I-10). Such fictional likenesses might seem ridiculous today, when everyone can easily view photographs of world leaders as they truly appear, but in antiquity few people ever saw the emperor. His official image was all that most knew. It therefore could be manipulated at will.

Augustus as General. The portraits of Augustus depict him in his many different roles in the Roman state (see "Role Playing in Roman Portraiture," page 200), but the models for many of them

were Classical Greek statues—one aspect of Augustus's programmatic effort to present himself as the ruler who would place Rome on a par with, or as greater than, Athens in the era that had already come to be viewed as a Golden Age. The statue (FIG. 7-27) of the emperor found at his wife Livia's villa at Primaporta (FIG. 7-20) portrays Augustus as imperator, standing like Polykleitos's *Doryphoros* (FIG. 5-41), but with his right arm raised to address his troops in the manner of the orator Aule Metele (FIG. 6-17). Augustus's head, although depicting a recognizable individual, also emulates the idealized Polykleitan youth's head in its overall shape, the sharp ridges of the brows, and the tight cap of layered hair. Augustus is not nude, however, and the details of the statue carry political messages. The reliefs on his cuirass advertise an important diplomatic victory—the return of the Roman legionary banners that the Parthians had captured from a Republican general—and the Cupid at Augustus's feet proclaims his divine descent. Caesar's family, the Julians, traced their ancestry back to Venus. Cupid was the goddess's son (see "The Gods and Goddesses of Mount Olympus," page 107).

Livia. A marble portrait (FIG. 7-28) of Livia reveals that the imperial women of the Augustan age shared the emperor's eternal youthfulness. Although the empress sports the latest Roman coiffure, with the hair rolled over the forehead and knotted at the nape of the neck, her blemish-free skin and sharply defined features derive from images of Classical Greek goddesses. Livia outlived Augustus by 15 years, dying at age 87. In her portraits, the coiffure changed with the introduction of each new fashion, but her face remained ever young, befitting her exalted position in the Roman state.

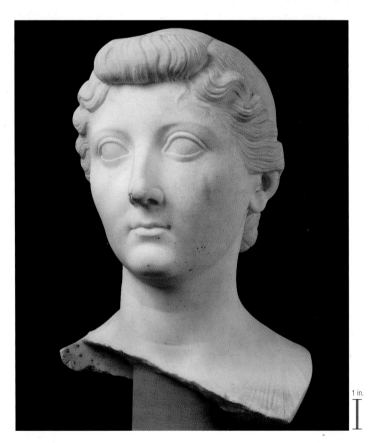

1 in.

7-28 Portrait bust of Livia, from Arsinoe, Egypt, early first century CE. Marble, 1′ 1½″ high. Ny Carlsberg Glyptotek, Copenhagen.

Although Livia sports the latest Roman coiffure, her youthful appearance and sharply defined features derive from images of Greek goddesses. She died at 87, but never aged in her portraits.

The *Res Gestae* of Augustus

Shortly before he died, the emperor Augustus reflected on his achievements during his 76 years and summarized them for posterity in a lengthy document called the *Res Gestae Divi Augusti* (*Achievements of the Deified Augustus*). The *Res Gestae* recounts Augustus's successes in all of the many arenas in which he made his mark—political, military, religious, economic, social, and artistic.

The document opens with Augustus's claim to have restored liberty to the Republic by freeing the Roman people from the tyranny of Mark Antony. He goes on to enumerate the wars he fought and the territories he added to the Empire, including Egypt; the triumphs and numerous other honors the Senate awarded him, including those he chose to decline; and the many occasions on which he distributed gifts of cash or grain to the people. He also describes the extensive building program he undertook, including a temple for the worship of the deified Julius Caesar in the Republican Forum Romanum (FIG. 7-2, no. 11); two new fora bearing the names of Caesar and Augustus (nos. 9 and 10); the restoration of the temple of Jupiter Capitolinus (no. 4) and the theater of Pompey; an altar celebrating the Augustan Peace (FIG. 7-29); and roads, aqueducts, and bridges throughout Italy.

The following selections highlight the fictive nature of Augustan constitutional government, the emperor's role as a great patron of architecture, and his professed modesty in not taking credit for some of his achievements.

[W]hen I had extinguished the flames of civil war, after receiving by universal consent the absolute control of affairs, I transferred the republic from my own control to the will of the senate and the Roman people. For this service I was given the title of Augustus by decree of the senate. . . . After that time I took precedence of all in rank [*princeps*], but of power I possessed no more than those who were my colleagues in any magistracy. [6.34]

The Capitolium and the theater of Pompey, both works involving great expense, I rebuilt without any inscription of my own name. . . . I rebuilt in the city eighty-two temples of the gods, omitting none which at that time stood in need of repair. [4.20]

When I returned from Spain and Gaul . . . the senate voted in honor of my return the consecration of an altar to Pax Augusta in the Campus Martius. [2.12]*

*All passages translated by Frederick W. Shipley, *Res gestae divi Augusti*, rev. ed. (Cambridge, Mass.: Harvard University Press, 1979), 365, 379, 399, 401.

7-29 West facade of the Ara Pacis Augustae (Altar of the Augustan Peace), Rome, Italy, 13–9 BCE.

Augustus sought to present his new order as a Golden Age equaling that of Athens under Pericles. The Ara Pacis celebrates the emperor's most important achievement, the establishment of peace.

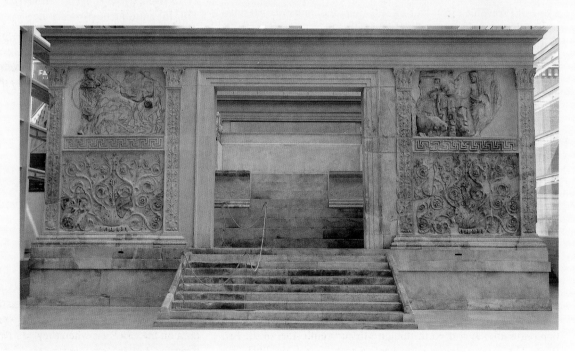

Ara Pacis Augustae. On Livia's birthday in 9 BCE, the Senate dedicated the Ara Pacis Augustae (Altar of the Augustan Peace; FIG. 7-29), the monument celebrating the emperor's most significant achievement, the establishment of peace (see "The *Res Gestae* of Augustus," above). Figural reliefs and acanthus tendrils adorn the altar's marble precinct walls. Four panels on the east and west ends depict carefully selected mythological subjects, including a relief (FIG. 7-29, *right*) of Aeneas making a sacrifice. Aeneas was the son of Venus and one of Augustus's forefathers. The connection between the emperor and Aeneas was a key element of Augustus's political ideology for his new Golden Age. It is no coincidence that Vergil wrote the *Aeneid* during Augustus's rule. Vergil's epic poem glorified the young emperor by celebrating the founder of the Julian line.

A second panel (FIG. 7-30), on the other end of the altar enclosure, depicts a seated matron with two lively babies on her lap. Her identity is uncertain. Art historians usually call her Tellus (Mother Earth), although some scholars have identified her as Pax (Peace), Ceres (goddess of grain), or even Venus. Whoever she is, she embodies the fruits of the Pax Augusta. All around her, the bountiful earth is in bloom, and animals of different species live peacefully together. Personifications of refreshing breezes (note their windblown drapery) flank her. One rides a bird, the other a sea creature.

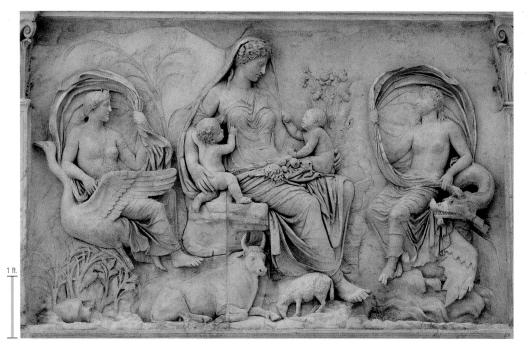

7-30 Female personification (Tellus?), panel on the east facade of the Ara Pacis Augustae, Rome, Italy, 13–9 BCE. Marble, 5′ 3″ high.

This female personification with two babies on her lap embodies the fruits of the Pax Augusta. All around her, the bountiful earth is in bloom, and animals of different species live together peacefully.

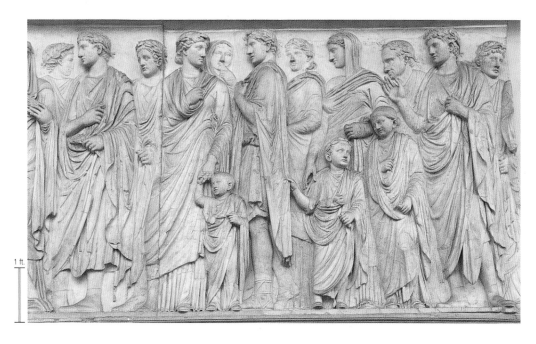

7-31 Procession of the imperial family, detail of the south frieze of the Ara Pacis Augustae, Rome, Italy, 13–9 BCE. Marble, 5′ 3″ high.

Although inspired by the frieze (FIG. 5-50, *bottom*) of the Parthenon, the Ara Pacis processions depict recognizable individuals, including children, some of whom are the sons of foreign kings.

Earth, sky, and water are all elements of this picture of peace and fertility in the Augustan cosmos.

Processions of the imperial family (FIG. 7-31) and other important dignitaries appear on the long north and south sides of the Ara Pacis. The inspiration for these parallel friezes was very likely the Panathenaic procession frieze (FIG. 5-50, *bottom*) of the Parthenon. As with his portraits, Augustus sought to present his new order as a Golden Age equaling that of Athens under Pericles. The emulation of Classical models thus made a political as well as an artistic statement.

Even so, the Roman procession is very different in character from its presumed Greek model. On the Parthenon, anonymous figures act out an event that recurred every four years. The frieze stands for all Panathenaic Festival processions. The Ara Pacis depicts a specific event—probably the inaugural ceremony of 13 BCE when work on the altar began—and recognizable historical figures. Among those portrayed are children, who restlessly tug on their elders' garments and talk to one another when they should be quiet on a solemn occasion—in short, children who act like children and not like miniature adults, as they frequently do in the history of art. Their presence lends a great deal of charm to the procession, but that is not why the imperial sculptors included children on the Ara Pacis when they had never before appeared on any Greek or Roman state monument. Augustus was concerned about a decline in the birthrate among the Roman nobility, and he enacted a series of laws designed to promote marriage, marital fidelity, and raising children. The portrayal of men with their families on the Altar of Peace served as a moral exemplar. Moreover, some of the children are the sons of foreign kings who had pledged their allegiance to the emperor. Their inclusion in the frieze underscored the message of Augustan Peace. Augustus used relief sculpture as well as portraiture to further his political and social agendas.

Forum of Augustus. Augustus's most ambitious project in the capital was the construction of a new forum (FIG. 7-2, no. 10) next to Julius Caesar's forum (no. 9), which Augustus completed (see "*Res Gestae*," page 202). The temples and porticos in both fora were

Vitruvius's *Ten Books on Architecture*

Little is known about the Augustan architect Vitruvius, including his full name. He was probably born in the 70s BCE, either in Campania (the area around the Bay of Naples) or in Rome, and most likely wrote his *De architectura* (*On Architecture*) between 25 and 15 BCE—that is, in the years following Augustus's defeat of Mark Antony and the establishment of the Pax Augusta. There are few mentions of Vitruvius's architectural treatise in other extant ancient Greek or Latin texts, but his *Ten Books on Architecture* became the handbook of classical architecture during the Renaissance, and it has remained so to the present day.

De architectura is noteworthy both for what it includes and what it does not. One of the treatise's most interesting features is Vitruvius's insistence on the broad training an architect must receive, not only in engineering and architectural design but in the liberal arts. As a how-to manual, it focuses on traditional means of construction and on the classical orders (FIG. 5-13) as used in Greek, Etruscan (FIG. 6-3), and Roman

buildings. Vitruvius's tastes were quite conservative and fully in accord with the classicism of the Augustan building program in the capital (FIG. 7-29) and in the provinces (FIG. 7-32). In the preface to Book I, Vitruvius dedicated his treatise to Augustus, citing the emperor's interest in "the construction of suitable buildings" in the new era of peace that he brought to the Romans. Vitruvius rarely refers, for example, to concrete vaulting, the most innovative mode of Roman construction, and he complained bitterly about the latest developments in mural painting of the Third Style (FIG. 7-21), which he described as examples of

depraved taste. For monsters are now painted in frescoes rather than reliable images of definite things. Reeds are set up in place of columns, as pediments, little scrolls, striped with curly leaves and volutes, candelabra hold up the figures of aediculae [pediment-capped niches], and above the pediments of these, several tender shoots, sprouting in coils from roots, have little statues nestled in them for no reason, or shoots split in half, some holding little statues with human heads, some with the heads of beasts. No, these things do not exist nor can they exist nor have they ever existed, and thus this new fashion [the Third Style] has brought things to such a pass that bad judges have condemned the right practice of the arts [the Second Style] as lack of skill.*

*Vitruvius, *De architectura*, 7.5.3–4. Translated by Ingrid D. Rowland, *Vitruvius. Ten Books on Architecture* (New York: Cambridge University Press, 1999), 91.

7-32 **Maison Carrée (looking northwest), Nîmes, France, ca. 1–10 CE.**

This well-preserved Corinthian pseudoperipteral temple in France, modeled on the temple in the Forum of Augustus in Rome, exemplifies the Augustan classical architectural style.

white marble from Carrara. Prior to the opening of those quarries in the second half of the first century BCE, marble had to be imported at great cost from abroad, and the Romans used it sparingly. The ready availability of Italian marble under Augustus made possible the emperor's famous boast that he found Rome a city of brick and transformed it into a city of marble.

The extensive use of Carrara marble for public monuments (including the Ara Pacis) must be seen as part of Augustus's program to make his city the equal of Periclean Athens. In fact, the Forum of Augustus incorporated several explicit references to Classical Athens and to the Acropolis in particular, most notably copies of the caryatids (FIG. 5-54) of the Erechtheion in the upper story of the porticos. The forum also evoked Roman history. The porticos contained dozens of portrait statues, including images of all the major figures of the Julian family going back to Aeneas. Augustus's forum became a kind

of public atrium filled with ancestor portraits. His family history thus became part of the Roman state's official history.

Maison Carrée. The Forum of Augustus is in ruins today, but many scholars believe that some of the stonemasons from that project also constructed the so-called Maison Carrée (Square House; FIG. 7-32) at Nîmes in southern France (Roman Gaul). This exceptionally well preserved Corinthian pseudoperipteral temple, which dates to the opening years of the first century CE, is the best surviving example of Augustan classicism in architecture (see "Vitruvius's *Ten Books on Architecture*," above), paralleling the emperor's preference for emulating Classical models in statuary and relief sculpture.

Pont-du-Gard. An earlier Augustan project in France was the construction over the Gard River near Nîmes of the great

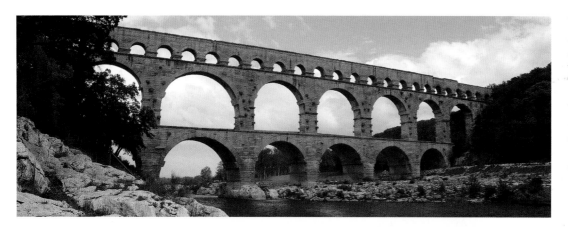

Roman engineers constructed roads and bridges throughout the Empire. This aqueduct-bridge brought water from a distant mountain spring to Nîmes—about 100 gallons a day for each inhabitant.

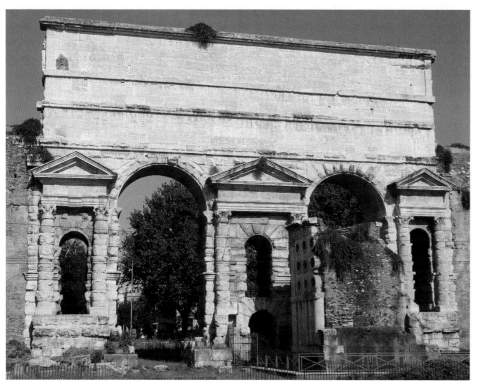

7-34 East facade of the Porta Maggiore, Rome, Italy, ca. 50 CE.

This double gateway, which supports the water channels of two important aqueducts, is the outstanding example of Roman rusticated (rough) masonry, which was especially popular under Claudius.

Porta Maggiore. The demand for water in the capital required the construction of many aqueducts. The emperor Claudius (r. 41–54 CE) erected a grandiose gate, the Porta Maggiore (FIG. 7-34), at the point where two of Rome's water lines (and two major intercity roads) converged. Its huge *attic* (uppermost story) bears a lengthy dedicatory inscription concealing the stacked conduits of both aqueducts. The gate is the outstanding example of the Roman *rusticated* (rough) masonry style. Instead of using the precisely shaped blocks that Greek and Augustan architects preferred, the designer of the Porta Maggiore combined smooth and rusticated surfaces. These created an exciting, if eccentric, facade with crisply carved (*dressed masonry*) pediments resting on engaged columns composed of rusticated drums.

Nero's Golden House. In 64 CE, when Nero (r. 54–68 CE), stepson and successor of Claudius, was emperor, a great fire destroyed large sections of Rome. Afterward, Nero enacted a new building code requiring greater fireproofing, resulting in the widespread use of concrete and more opportunities for Roman architects to explore the possibilities opened up by the still relatively new building material. The fire also enabled the emperor to construct a luxurious new palace on a huge confiscated plot of fire-ravaged land near the Forum Romanum. Nero chose two brilliant architect-engineers, SEVERUS and CELER, to design and build his new home (see "The Golden House of Nero," page 206). The palace they constructed for the emperor had scores of rooms, many adorned with frescoes (FIG. 7-34A) in the early Fourth Style, others with marble paneling or painted and gilded stucco reliefs. Structurally, most of these rooms, although made of concrete, are unremarkable. One octagonal hall (FIG. 7-35), however, stands apart from the rest and testifies to Severus and Celer's bold new approach to architectural design.

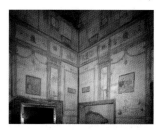

7-34A Room 78, Domus Aurea, 64–68 CE.

aqueduct-bridge known today as the Pont-du-Gard (FIG. 7-33). In the fourth century BCE, the Romans began to build *aqueducts* to carry water from mountain sources to their city on the Tiber River. As Rome's power spread through the Mediterranean world, its engineers constructed aqueducts, roads, and bridges to serve colonies throughout the far-flung empire. The Pont-du-Gard aqueduct provided about 100 gallons of water a day for each inhabitant of Nîmes from a source some 30 miles away. The water flowed over the considerable distance mostly by gravity alone, which required channels built with a continuous gradual decline over the entire route from source to city. The three-story Pont-du-Gard maintained the height of the water channel where the water crossed the river. Each large arch spans some 82 feet and consists of blocks weighing up to two tons each. The bridge's uppermost level is a row of smaller arches, three above each of the large openings below. They carry the water channel itself. The harmonious proportional relationship between the larger and smaller arches reveals that the Roman hydraulic engineer who designed the aqueduct-bridge also had a keen aesthetic sense.

The Golden House of Nero

Nero's Domus Aurea, or Golden House, was a vast and notoriously extravagant country villa in the heart of Rome. The Roman biographer Suetonius (ca. 69–ca. 135 CE) described it vividly:

> The entrance-hall was large enough to contain a huge statue [of Nero in the guise of Sol, the sun god; FIG. 7-2, no. 16], 120 feet high; and the pillared arcade ran for a whole mile. An enormous pool, like a sea, was surrounded by buildings made to resemble cities, and by a landscape garden consisting of plowed fields, vineyards, pastures, and woodlands—where every variety of domestic and wild animal roamed about. Parts of the house were overlaid with gold and studded with precious stones and mother-of-pearl. All the dining-rooms had ceilings of fretted ivory, the panels of which could slide back and let a rain of flowers, or of perfume from hidden sprinklers, shower upon [Nero's] guests. The main dining-room was circular, and its roof revolved, day and night, in time with the sky. Sea water, or sulphur water, was always on tap in the baths. When the palace had been decorated throughout in this lavish style, Nero dedicated it, and condescended to remark: "Good, now I can at last begin to live like a human being!"*

Suetonius's description is a welcome reminder that the Roman ruins that millions of tourists flock to see are but a dim reflection of the magnificence of the original structures. Only in rare instances, such as the Pantheon, with its marble-faced walls and floors (FIG. 7-51), can visitors experience anything approaching the architects' intended effects. Even there, much of the marble paneling is of later date, and the gilding is missing from the dome.

*Suetonius, *Nero*, 31. Translated by Robert Graves, *Suetonius: The Twelve Caesars* (New York: Penguin, 1957; illustrated edition, 1980), 197–198.

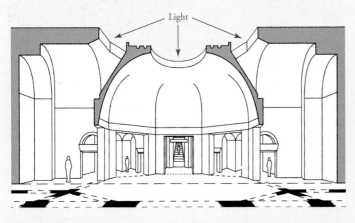

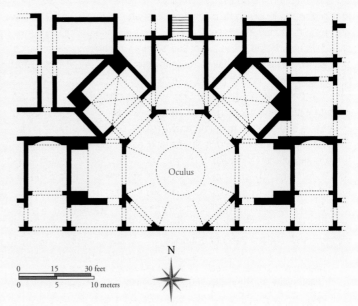

Oculus

7-35 SEVERUS and CELER, section (*left*) and plan (*right*) of the octagonal hall (room 85) of the Domus Aurea of Nero, Rome, Italy, 64–68 CE.

Nero's architects illuminated this octagonal room by placing an oculus in its concrete dome, and ingeniously lit the rooms around it by leaving spaces between their vaults and the dome's exterior.

The ceiling of the octagonal room is a dome that modulates from an eight-sided to a hemispherical form as it rises toward the oculus. Radiating outward from the five inner sides (the other three, directly or indirectly, face the outside) are smaller, rectangular rooms, three covered by barrel vaults, two others (marked on the plan [FIG. 7-35, *right*] by X's composed of broken lines) by the earliest known concrete groin vaults (FIG. 7-6). Severus and Celer ingeniously lit these satellite rooms by leaving spaces between their vaulted ceilings and the central dome's exterior. But the most significant aspect of the design is that here, for the first time, the architects appear to have thought of the walls and vaults not as limiting space but as shaping it.

Today, the octagonal hall is deprived of its stucco decoration and marble *incrustation* (veneer). The concrete shell stands bare, but this serves to focus the visitor's attention on the design's spatial complexity. Anyone walking into the domed hall perceives that the space is defined not by walls but by eight angled piers. The openings between the piers are so large that the rooms beyond look like extensions of the central hall. The grouping of spatial units of different sizes and proportions under a variety of vaults creates a dynamic three-dimensional composition that is both complex and unified. Nero's architects were not only inventive but also progressive in their recognition of the malleable nature of concrete, a material not limited to the rectilinear forms of traditional architecture.

The Flavians

Facing certain assassination as a result of his outrageous behavior, Nero committed suicide in 68 CE, bringing the Julio-Claudian dynasty to an end. A year of renewed civil strife followed. The man who emerged triumphant in this brief but bloody conflict was Vespasian (r. 69–79 CE), a general who had served under Claudius and Nero. Vespasian, whose family name was Flavius, had two sons, Titus (r. 79–81 CE) and Domitian (r. 81–96 CE). Both became emperor in turn after their father's death. The Flavian dynasty ruled Rome for more than a quarter century.

Spectacles in the Colosseum

A favorite pastime throughout the Roman Empire was going to the amphitheater to see two immensely popular kinds of spectacles: gladiatorial combats and animal hunts.

Gladiators were professional fighters, usually slaves who had been purchased to train in gladiatorial schools as hand-to-hand combatants. Their owners, seeking to turn a profit, rented them out for performances. Beginning with Domitian, however, all gladiators who competed in Rome were owned by the state to ensure that they could not be used as a private army to overthrow the government. Although every gladiator faced death each time he entered the arena, some had long careers and achieved considerable fame. Others—for example, criminals or captured enemies—entered the amphitheater without any training and without any defensive weapons. Those "gladiatorial games" were a form of capital punishment coupled with entertainment for the masses.

The participants in wild animal hunts (*venationes*) were also professionals, but often the hunts, like the gladiatorial games, were executions in thin disguise involving helpless prisoners who were easy prey for the animals. Sometimes no one entered the arena with the animals. Instead, skilled archers in the stands shot the beasts with arrows. Other times animals would be pitted against other animals—bears versus bulls, lions versus elephants, and the like—to the delight of the crowds.

The Colosseum (FIGS. 7-36 and 7-37) was the largest and most important amphitheater in the world, and the kinds of spectacles staged there were costlier and more impressive than those held anywhere else. Some ancient accounts, such as the one quoted here, even mention the flooding of the Colosseum so that naval battles could be staged in the arena. Many scholars, however, doubt that the arena could be made watertight or that ships could maneuver in the space available.

The games celebrating Titus's inauguration of the Colosseum in 80 were especially lavish. In the early third century, the historian Dio Cassius (ca. 164–235 CE) described them:

There was a battle between cranes and also between four elephants; animals both tame and wild were slain to the number of nine thousand; and women . . . took part in dispatching them. As for the men, several fought in single combat and several groups contended together both in infantry and naval battles. For Titus suddenly filled [the arena] with water and brought in horses and bulls and some other domesticated animals that had been taught to behave in the liquid element just as on land. He also brought in people on ships, who engaged in a sea-fight there. . . . On the first day there was a

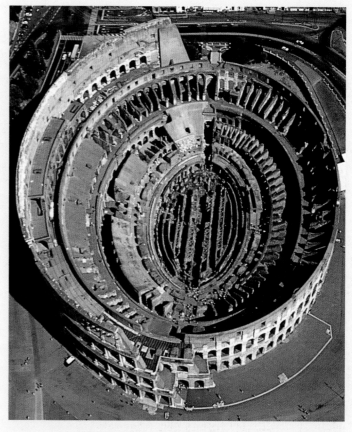

7-36 Aerial view of the Colosseum (Flavian Amphitheater; looking east), Rome, Italy, ca. 70–80 CE.

A complex system of concrete barrel vaults once held up the seats in the world's largest amphitheater, where 50,000 spectators could watch gladiatorial combats and wild animal hunts.

gladiatorial exhibition and wild-beast hunt. . . . On the second day there was a horse-race, and on the third day a naval battle between three thousand men, followed by an infantry battle. . . . These were the spectacles that were offered, and they continued for a hundred days.*

*Dio Cassius, *Roman History*, 66.25. Translated by Earnest Cary, *Dio's Roman History*, vol. 8 (Cambridge, Mass.: Harvard University Press, 1925), 311, 313.

Colosseum. The Flavians left their mark on the capital in many ways, not the least being the construction of the Colosseum (FIGS. 7-2, no. 17; 7-36; and 7-37), the gigantic amphitheater that, for most people, still represents Rome more than any other building. The Flavian Amphitheater, as it was then known, was one of Vespasian's first undertakings after becoming emperor. The decision to build the Colosseum was politically shrewd. The site chosen was the artificial lake on the grounds of Nero's Domus Aurea, which engineers drained to make way for the new entertainment center. By building his amphitheater there, Vespasian reclaimed for the public the land that Nero had confiscated for his private pleasure, and provided Romans with the largest arena for gladiatorial combats and other lavish spectacles ever constructed. The Colosseum takes its name, however, not from its size—although it could hold more than 50,000 spectators—but from its location beside the Colossus of Nero (FIG. 7-2, no. 16), the 120-foot-tall statue at the entrance to his urban villa. Vespasian did not live to see the Colosseum in use. But his elder son, Titus, completed and formally dedicated the amphitheater in the year 80 with great fanfare (see "Spectacles in the Colosseum," above).

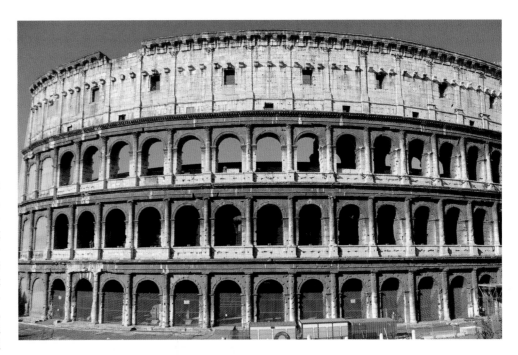

7-37 North facade of the Colosseum (Flavian Amphitheater), Rome, Italy, ca. 70–80 CE.

For the facade of the Colosseum, an unknown architect mixed Roman arches and Greek columns—Tuscan on the lowest story, then Ionic and Corinthian. Wood poles held up a velarium over the cavea.

The Colosseum, like the much earlier Pompeian amphitheater (FIG. 7-13), could not have been built without concrete. Concrete engineering had, however, advanced rapidly during the century and a half since the Pompeians constructed the earliest known amphitheater. In the Colosseum, instead of an earthen mound, a complex system of barrel-vaulted corridors held up the enormous oval seating area. This concrete "skeleton" is exposed today because in the centuries following the fall of Rome, the Colosseum served as a convenient quarry for ready-made building materials. All of its marble seats were hauled away (the remaining ones are restorations of the Fascist era in Rome), revealing the network of vaults below (FIG. 7-36). Also visible today but hidden in antiquity are the arena substructures, which in their present form date to the third century CE. They housed waiting rooms for the gladiators, animal cages, and machinery for raising and lowering stage sets as well as animals and humans. Cleverly designed lifting devices brought beasts from their dark dens into the arena's bright light. Above the seats, a great velarium, as at Pompeii (FIG. 7-14), once shielded the spectators.

The exterior travertine shell (FIG. 7-37) is approximately 160 feet high, the height of a modern 16-story building. In antiquity, 76 numbered gateways provided efficient entrance and exit paths leading to and from the cavea, where, as at Pompeii, the spectators sat according to their place in the social hierarchy. The decor of the exterior, however, had nothing to do with function. The architect divided the facade into four bands, with large arched openings piercing the lower three. Ornamental Greek orders frame the arches in the standard Roman sequence for multistory buildings: from the ground up, Tuscan, Ionic, and then Corinthian. The diverse proportions of the orders formed the basis for this progression, with the Tuscan viewed as capable of supporting the heaviest load. Corinthian pilasters (and between them the brackets for the wood poles that held up the velarium; compare FIG. 7-14) circle the uppermost story.

The use of engaged columns and a lintel to frame the openings in the Colosseum's facade is a variation of the scheme used on the Etruscan Porta Marzia (FIG. 6-14) at Perugia. The Romans commonly used this scheme from Late Republican times on—for example, at Palestrina (FIG. 7-5). Just as the Roman pseudoperipteral temple combines Greek orders with an Etruscan plan, this manner of decorating a building's facade mixed Greek orders with an architectural form foreign to Greek post-and-lintel architecture—the arch. The Roman practice of framing an arch with an applied Greek order had no structural purpose, but it added variety to the surface. In the Colosseum, it also unified a multistory facade by casting a net of verticals and horizontals over it.

Flavian Portraiture. Vespasian was an unpretentious career army officer who desired to distance himself from Nero's self-indulgent misrule. His portraits (FIG. 7-38) reflect his much simpler tastes. They also made an important political statement. Breaking

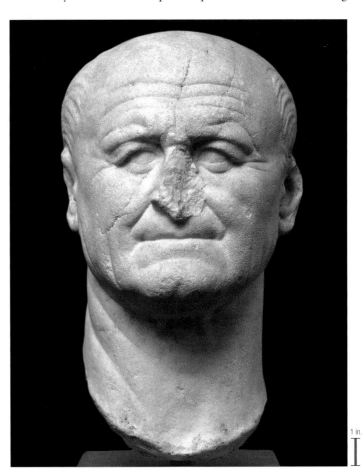

1 in.

7-38 Portrait of Vespasian, ca. 75–79 CE. Marble, 1′ 4″ high. Ny Carlsberg Glyptotek, Copenhagen.

Vespasian's sculptors revived the veristic tradition of the Republic to underscore the elderly new emperor's Republican values in contrast to Nero's self-indulgence and extravagance.

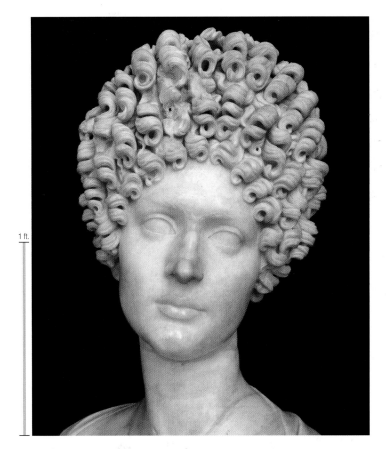

7-39 Portrait of a Flavian woman, from Rome, Italy, ca. 90 CE. Marble, 2′ 1⅜″ high (without modern bust). Museo Capitolino, Musei Capitolini, Rome.

The Flavian sculptor reproduced the elaborate coiffure of this elegant woman by drilling deep holes for the corkscrew curls, and carved the rest of the hair and the face with hammer and chisel.

with the tradition that Augustus established of depicting the Roman emperor as godlike and eternally youthful, Vespasian's sculptors resuscitated the veristic tradition of the Republic (FIG. 7-8), probably at his specific direction. The emperor's portraits frankly recorded his receding hairline and aging, leathery skin—proclaiming Vespasian's traditional Republican values in contrast to Nero's undisciplined behavior and excessive spending.

Numerous portraits of people of all ages survive from the Flavian period, in contrast to the Republic, when few but the elderly were deemed worthy of depiction. The purpose of the portrait of a young woman illustrated here (FIG. 7-39) was not to project Republican virtues but to present the sitter as beautiful—in terms of current fashion rather than by emulating the idealized images of Greek goddesses. The portrait is especially notable for the virtuoso way the sculptor rendered the elaborate Flavian coiffure, with its corkscrew curls punched out using a drill instead of a chisel. The sculptor brilliantly set off the dense mass of hair from the softly modeled and highly polished skin of the face and elegant, swanlike neck. The drill played an increasing role in Roman sculpture in succeeding periods, and when long hair and full beards became fashionable for men, sculptors used drills for their portraits as well.

Arch of Titus. When Titus died in 81 CE, only two years after becoming emperor, his younger brother, Domitian, succeeded him. Domitian erected an arch (FIGS. 7-2, no. 13, and 7-40) in Titus's honor on the Sacred Way leading into the Republican Forum

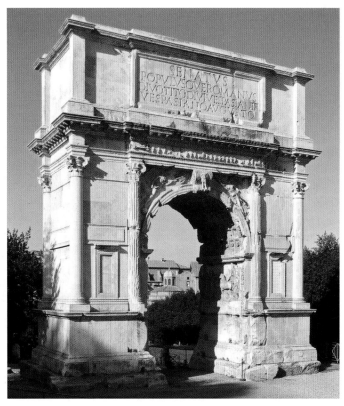

7-40 East facade of the Arch of Titus, Rome, Italy, after 81 CE.

Domitian built this arch on the road leading into the Roman Forum to honor his brother, the emperor Titus, who became a god after his death. Victories fill the spandrels of the arcuated passageway.

Romanum (FIG. 7-2, no. 11). This type of freestanding arch, the so-called *triumphal arch,* has a long history in Roman art and architecture, beginning in the second century BCE. The term is something of a misnomer, however, because Roman arches did not celebrate only military victories. Usually crowned by gilded bronze statues, they commemorated a wide variety of events, ranging from victories abroad to the building of roads and bridges at home (FIG. 7-44A).

The Arch of Titus is a typical early triumphal arch in having only one passageway. As on the Colosseum, engaged columns frame the arcuated opening. The capitals are not Greek, however, but Roman *Composite capitals,* an ornate combination of Ionic volutes and Corinthian acanthus leaves. The new type became popular at about the same time as the Fourth Style in Roman painting. Reliefs depicting personified Victories (winged women, as in Greek art) fill the *spandrels* (the area between the arch's curve and the framing columns and frieze). The dedicatory inscription on the attic states that the Senate erected the arch to honor the god Titus, son of the god Vespasian. To underscore Titus's divinity, at the center of the vault of the passageway is a relief (FIG. 7-40A) showing Titus's *apotheosis* (ascent to Heaven). The Senate normally proclaimed Roman emperors gods after

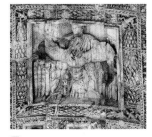

7-40A Apotheosis of Titus, after 81 CE.

they died, unless they ran afoul of the senators and were damned. The statues of those who suffered *damnatio memoriae* were torn down, and their names were erased from public inscriptions. This was Nero's fate.

7-41 Spoils of Jerusalem, relief panel in the passageway of the Arch of Titus, Rome, Italy, after 81 CE. Marble, 7′ 10″ high.

The reliefs inside the bay of the Arch of Titus commemorate the emperor's conquest of Judaea. Here, Roman soldiers carry in triumph the spoils taken from the Jewish temple in Jerusalem.

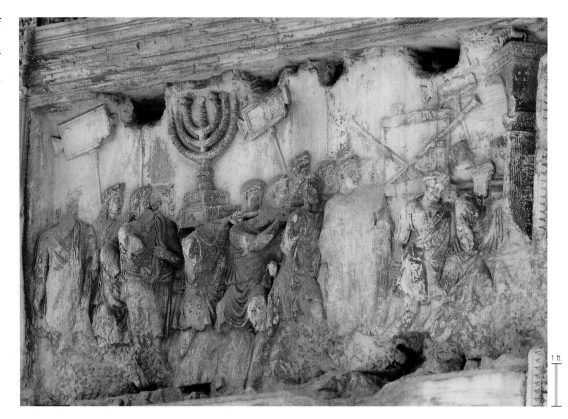

7-42 Triumph of Titus, relief panel in the passageway of the Arch of Titus, Rome, Italy, after 81 CE. Marble, 7′ 10″ high.

Victory crowns Titus in his triumphal chariot. Also present are Honor and Valor in this first known instance of the intermingling of human and divine figures in a Roman historical relief.

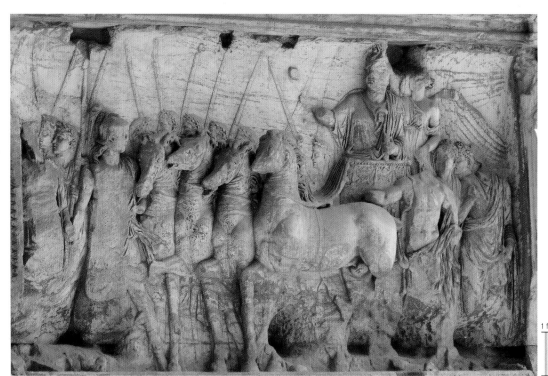

Inside the passageway of the Arch of Titus are two great relief panels. They represent the triumphal parade of Titus down the Sacred Way after his return from the conquest of Judaea at the end of the Jewish War in 70 CE. One of the reliefs (FIG. 7-41) depicts Roman soldiers carrying the spoils—including the sacred seven-branched candelabrum, the *menorah* (compare FIG. 8-4A)—from the Jewish temple in Jerusalem. Despite considerable damage to the relief, the illusion of movement is convincing. The parade emerges from the left background into the center foreground and disappears through the obliquely placed arch in the right background. The energy and swing of the column of soldiers suggest a rapid march. The sculptor rejected the Classical low-relief style of the Ara Pacis (FIG. 7-31) in favor of extremely deep carving, which produces strong shadows. The heads of the forward figures have broken off because they stood free from the block. Their high relief emphasized their different placement in space compared with the heads in low relief, which are intact. The play of light and shadow across the protruding foreground and receding background figures enhances the sense of movement.

On the other side of the passageway, the panel (FIG. 7-42) shows Titus in his triumphal chariot. The seeming historical accuracy of the spoils panel, which closely corresponds to the contemporaneous description of Titus's triumph by the Jewish historian Josephus (37–ca. 100 CE), gave way in this panel to allegory. Victory rides with Titus in the four-horse chariot and places a wreath on his head. Below her is a bare-chested youth who is probably a personification of honor (*Honos*). A female personification of valor (*Virtus*) leads the horses. These allegorical figures transform the relief from a record of Titus's battlefield success into a celebration of imperial virtues. A comparable intermingling of divine and human figures characterizes the Dionysiac frieze (FIG. 7-18) of the Villa of the Mysteries at Pompeii, but the Arch of Titus panel is the first known instance of divine beings interacting with humans on an official Roman historical relief. (On the Ara Pacis [FIG. 7-29], Aeneas and Tellus appear in separate framed panels, carefully segregated from the procession of living Romans.) The Arch of Titus, however, does not honor the living emperor but the deified Titus, who has entered the realm of the Roman gods. But soon afterward, this kind of interaction between mortals and immortals became a staple of Roman narrative relief sculpture, even on monuments erected in honor of emperors during their lifetimes.

HIGH EMPIRE

In the second century CE, under Trajan, Hadrian, and the Antonines, the Roman Empire reached its greatest geographic extent (MAP 7-1) and the height of its power. Rome's might was unchallenged in the Mediterranean world, although the Germanic peoples in Europe, the Berbers in Africa, and the Parthians and Persians in the East constantly applied pressure. Within the Empire's secure boundaries, the Pax Romana meant unprecedented prosperity for all who came under Roman rule.

Trajan

Domitian's extravagant lifestyle and ego resembled Nero's. He demanded to be addressed as *dominus et deus* ("lord and god"), and so angered the Senate that he was assassinated in 96 CE. The senators chose the elderly Nerva (r. 96–98 CE), one of their own, as emperor. Nerva ruled for only 16 months, but before he died he established a pattern of succession by adoption that endured for almost a century. Nerva picked Trajan, a capable and popular general born in Italica, Spain, as the next emperor. Under Trajan, the first non-Italian to rule Rome, imperial armies brought Roman rule to ever more distant areas (see "The Roman Emperor as World Conqueror," page 181), and the imperial government took on ever greater responsibility for its people's welfare by instituting a number of farsighted social programs. Trajan was so popular that the Senate granted him the title *Optimus* (the Best), an epithet he shared with Jupiter (who was said to have instructed Nerva to choose Trajan as his successor). In time, Trajan, along with Augustus, became the yardsticks for measuring the success of later emperors, who strove to be *felicior Augusto, melior Traiano* ("luckier than Augustus, better than Trajan").

Timgad. In 100 CE, as part of his program to extend and strengthen Roman rule on three continents, Trajan founded a new colony for army veterans at Timgad (FIG. 7-43), in what is today Algeria. Like other colonies, Timgad became the physical

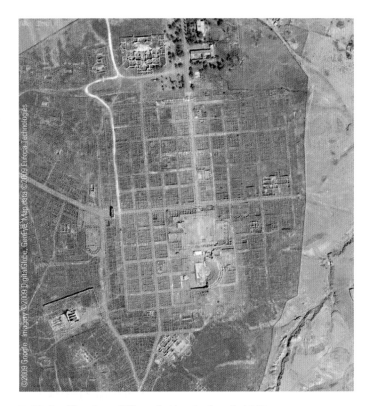

7-43 Satellite view of Timgad, Algeria, founded 100 CE.

The plan of Trajan's new colony of Timgad in North Africa features a strict grid scheme, with the forum at the intersection of the two main thoroughfares, the cardo and the decumanus.

embodiment of Roman authority and civilization for the local population. Roman engineers laid out the town with great precision, on the pattern of a Roman military encampment, or *castrum,* although some scholars think that the castrum plan followed the scheme of Roman colonies, not vice versa. Unlike the sprawling unplanned cities of Rome and Pompeii, Timgad is a square divided into equal quarters by its two colonnaded main streets, the cardo and the decumanus, which cross at right angles. The forum is at the point where the two avenues intersect, and imposing gateways marked the ends of both streets. The quarters are subdivided into square blocks, and the forum and public buildings, such as the theater and baths, occupy areas sized as multiples of these blocks. The Roman plan is a modification of the Hippodamian plan of Greek cities (see "Hippodamos's Plan for the Ideal City," page 154), though more rigidly ordered. The Romans laid out most of their new settlements in the same manner, regardless of whether they were in Africa, Mesopotamia, or Britain. This uniformity expresses concretely the centralized power of the Roman Empire at its height. But even the Romans could not regulate human behavior completely. As the satellite view reveals, when the population of Timgad grew sevenfold and burst through the Trajanic colony's walls, the colonists abandoned rational planning, and the city and its streets branched out haphazardly.

Forum of Trajan. Trajan completed several major building projects in Rome, including the remodeling of the Circus Maximus (FIGS. 7-2, no. 2, and 7-43A), Rome's giant chariot-racing stadium, and the

7-43A Funerary relief of a circus official, ca. 110–130 CE.

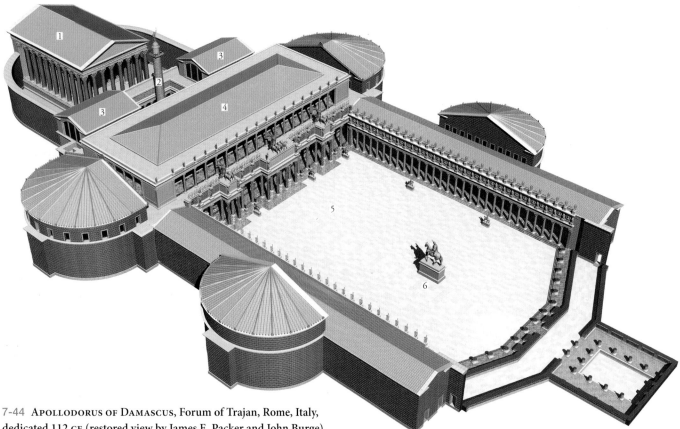

7-44 APOLLODORUS OF DAMASCUS, Forum of Trajan, Rome, Italy, dedicated 112 CE (restored view by James E. Packer and John Burge). (1) Temple of Trajan, (2) Column of Trajan, (3) libraries, (4) Basilica Ulpia, (5) forum, (6) equestrian statue of Trajan.

Funded by the spoils from two Dacian wars, Rome's largest forum featured a basilica with clerestory lighting, two libraries, a commemorative column (FIG. 7-1), and a temple of the deified Trajan.

construction of a vast new bathing complex near the Colosseum, constructed on top of Nero's Golden House. His most important undertaking, however, was a huge new forum (FIGS. 7-2, no. 7, and 7-44), roughly twice the size of the century-old Forum of Augustus (FIG. 7-2, no. 10)—even excluding the enormous adjoining market complex.

The new forum glorified Trajan's victories in his two wars against the Dacians in present-day Romania, the spoils of which paid for Trajan's building program in the capital. The architect was Trajan's chief military engineer during the Dacian wars, APOLLODORUS OF DAMASCUS. Apollodorus's plan incorporated the main features of most early fora (FIG. 7-12), except that a huge basilica (FIG. 7-44, no. 4), not a temple, dominated the colonnaded open square. The temple (FIG. 7-44, no. 1; completed after the emperor's death and dedicated to the newest god in the Roman pantheon—Trajan himself) stood instead behind the basilica facing two libraries and a giant commemorative column (FIGS. 7-1 and 7-44, no. 2). Entry to Trajan's forum was through an impressive gateway resembling a triumphal arch. (Trajan also erected freestanding triumphal arches in Rome and elsewhere in Italy—for example, at Benevento; FIG. 7-44A.) Inside the forum were other reminders of Trajan's military prowess. A larger-than-life-size gilded-bronze equestrian statue (FIG. 7-44,

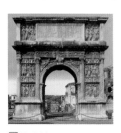

7-44A Arch of Trajan, Benevento, ca. 114–118 CE.

no. 6) of the emperor on horseback, trampling a terrified Dacian, stood at the center of the great court in front of the basilica. Statues of captive Dacians stood above the columns of the forum porticos. (Some were reused on the Arch of Constantine; FIG. 7-76.)

The Basilica Ulpia (Trajan gave his family name, Ulpius, to the structure) was a much larger and far more ornate version of the basilica adjoining the forum of Pompeii (FIG. 7-12, no. 3). As shown in FIG. 7-44, no. 4, it had *apses,* or semicircular recesses, on each short end. Two aisles flanked the nave on each side. In contrast to the Pompeian basilica, the Basilica Ulpia was entered through doorways on the long side facing the forum. The building was vast: about 400 feet long (without the apses) and 200 feet wide. Light entered through clerestory windows, made possible by elevating the timber-roofed nave above the colonnaded aisles, an idea developed first by the Egyptians (see "Illuminating Buildings before Lightbulbs," page 75).

Column of Trajan. Behind the ruins of the Basilica Ulpia still stands, almost perfectly preserved, the 128-foot-tall Column of Trajan (FIG. 7-1), which once had a heroically nude statue of the emperor at the top. (The present statue of Saint Peter dates to the 16th century.) The tall pedestal, decorated with captured Dacian arms and armor, encloses a chamber that originally served as Trajan's tomb.

The Column of Trajan is most noteworthy, however, for its spiral frieze (FIG. 7-45), which was often copied in antiquity, during the Middle Ages (FIG. 11-26A), and even as late as the 19th century. That frieze was probably the brainchild of Apollodorus of Damascus. It was the architect's solution to the problem of how to incorporate a pictorial record of Trajan's military campaigns in a monument—a freestanding column—ill-suited for narrative relief sculpture except on its pedestal.

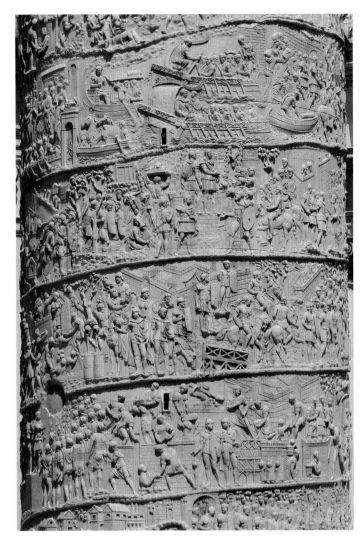

7-45 Detail of the spiral frieze of the Column of Trajan (FIG. 7-1), Forum of Trajan, Rome, Italy, dedicated 112 CE.

The spiral frieze of Trajan's Column tells the story of the Dacian wars in 150 episodes. The reliefs depict all aspects of the campaigns, from battles to sacrifices to road and fort construction.

Carving the frieze was a complex process. First, the stonemasons had to fashion enormous marble column drums, hollowed out to accommodate an internal spiral staircase running the entire length of the column shaft. The sculptors carved the relief scenes after the drums were in place to ensure that the figures and buildings lined up perfectly. The sculptors carved the last scenes in the narrative first, working from the top to the bottom of the shaft so that falling marble chips or a dropped chisel would not damage the reliefs below.

Art historians have likened the sculptured frieze winding around the column to an illustrated scroll (FIG. 3-1) of the type housed in the neighboring libraries (FIG. 7-44, no. 3) of the Forum of Trajan. The reliefs recount Trajan's two Dacian campaigns in more than 150 episodes, in which some 2,500 figures appear. The band increases in width as it winds to the top of the column in order to make the upper portions easier to see. Throughout, the relief is very low so as not to distort the contours of the shaft. Paint enhanced the legibility of the figures, but it still would have been very difficult for anyone to follow the narrative from beginning to end.

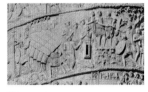

7-45A Battle and aftermath, Column of Trajan, 112 CE.

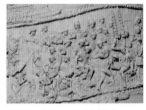

7-45B Wounded Romans, Column of Trajan, 112 CE.

Easily recognizable compositions such as those found on coin reverses and on historical relief panels—Trajan addressing his troops, sacrificing to the gods, and so on—fill most of the frieze. The narrative is not a reliable chronological account of the Dacian wars, as once thought. The sculptors nonetheless accurately recorded the general character of the campaigns. Notably, battle scenes (FIG. 7-45A) and their aftermath (FIG. 7-45B) take up only about a quarter of the frieze. As is true of modern military

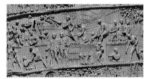

7-45C Fort construction, Column of Trajan, 112 CE.

operations, the Romans spent more time constructing forts (FIG. 7-45C), transporting men and equipment, and preparing for battle than fighting.

Markets of Trajan. On the Quirinal Hill overlooking the forum, Apollodorus built the Markets of Trajan (FIGS. 7-2, no. 8, and 7-46) to house both shops and

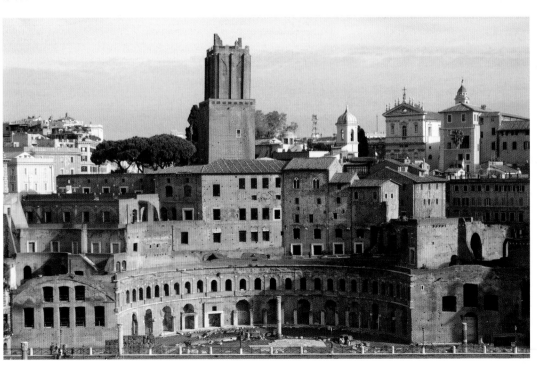

7-46 APOLLODORUS OF DAMASCUS, Markets of Trajan (looking northeast), Rome, Italy, ca. 100–112 CE.

Apollodorus of Damascus used brick-faced concrete to transform the Quirinal Hill overlooking Trajan's forum into a vast multilevel complex of barrel-vaulted shops and administrative offices.

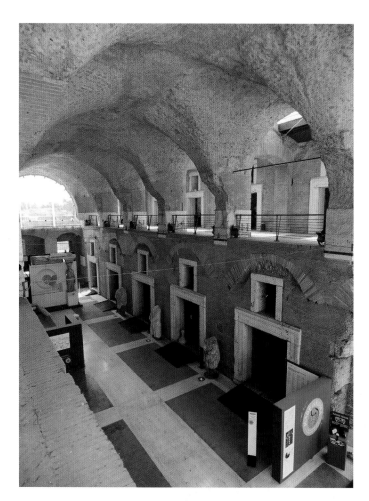

7-47 APOLLODORUS OF DAMASCUS, interior of the great hall, Markets of Trajan, Rome, Italy, ca. 100–112 CE.

The great hall of Trajan's markets resembles a modern shopping mall. It housed two floors of shops, with the upper ones set back and lit by skylights. Concrete groin vaults cover the central space.

administrative offices. As earlier at Palestrina (FIG. 7-5), concrete made possible the transformation of a natural slope into a multilevel complex. Trajan's architect was a master of this modern medium as well as of the traditional stone-and-timber post-and-lintel architecture of the forum below. The basic unit was the *taberna*, a single-room shop covered by a barrel vault. Each taberna had a wide doorway, usually with a window above it. The shops were on several levels. They opened either onto a concave semicircular facade winding around one of the forum's large exedras (FIG. 7-46), onto a paved street farther up the hill, or onto a great indoor market hall (FIG. 7-47) resembling a modern shopping mall. The hall housed two floors of shops, with the upper shops set back on each side and lit by skylights. Light from the same sources reached the ground-floor shops through arches beneath the great umbrella-like groin vaults (FIG. 7-6) covering the hall. (Today, as FIG. 7-47 reveals, the hall serves as a museum housing finds from the area, including those from the fora of Augustus and Trajan.)

Hadrian

Hadrian, Trajan's chosen successor and fellow Spaniard, was a connoisseur and lover of all the arts, as well as an author, architect, and avid hunter (FIG. 7-47A). He greatly admired Greek culture and traveled widely as emperor, often in the Greek East. Everywhere he went, local officials set up statues and arches in his honor. That is why more portraits of Hadrian exist today than of any other emperor except Augustus. Hadrian, who was 41 years old at the time of Trajan's death and who ruled for more than two decades, always appears in his portraits as a mature man, but one who never ages. Those likenesses—for example, the marble bust illustrated here (FIG. 7-48)—more closely resemble Kresilas's portrait of Pericles (FIG. 5-42) than those of any Roman emperor before him. Fifth-century BCE statues had provided the prototypes for the idealized official portraits of Augustus (FIG. 7-27), but the Augustan models were Greek images of youthful athletes (FIG. 5-41). The models for Hadrian's artists were Classical statues of bearded adults (FIG. 5-36). Hadrian's beard was a Greek affectation at the time, but thereafter beards became the norm for all Roman emperors for more than a century and a half.

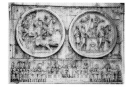

7-47A Hadrianic hunting tondi, ca. 130–138 CE.

Pantheon. Work began on the Pantheon (FIGS. 7-2, no. 5; 7-49; 7-50; and 7-51), the temple of all the gods, soon after Hadrian became emperor (or possibly shortly before, as indicated by the use of some Trajanic bricks in the building's construction). The Pantheon is one of the best-preserved buildings of antiquity, and also one of the most influential designs in architectural history. Hadrian

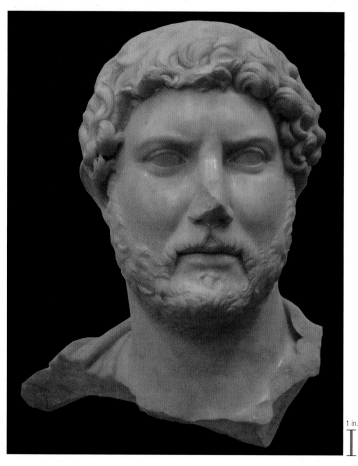

1 in.

7-48 Portrait bust of Hadrian, from Rome, Italy, ca. 117–120 CE. Marble, 1′ 4¾″ high. Palazzo Massimo alle Terme, Museo Nazionale Romano, Rome.

Hadrian, a lover of all things Greek, was the first Roman emperor to wear a beard. His artists modeled his idealizing official portraits on Classical Greek statues such as Kresilas's Pericles (FIG. 5-42).

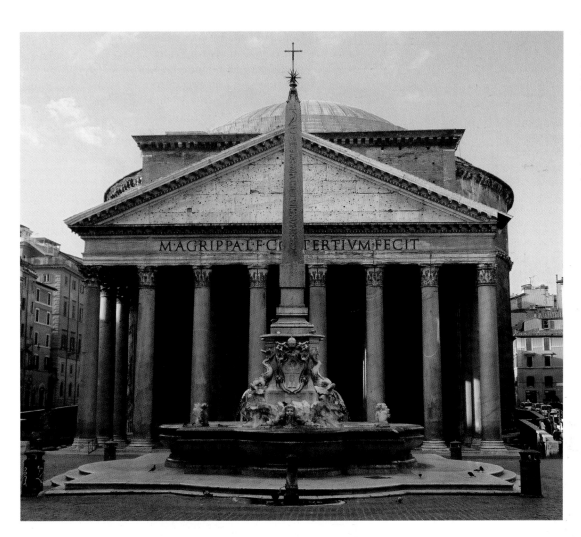

The Pantheon's traditional facade masked its revolutionary cylindrical drum and its huge hemispherical dome. The interior symbolized both the orb of the earth and the vault of the heavens.

did not take credit for the building, however, preferring, as Augustus did before him (see "*Res Gestae,*" page 202), to dedicate the temple in the name of Marcus Agrippa, who had erected an earlier Pantheon on this site in the late first century BCE. Unfortunately, neither the inscription on the Pantheon facade nor any historical source gives the name of the brilliant architect who in this building revealed the full potential of concrete, both as a construction material and as a means of shaping architectural space.

The original approach to the temple was from a columnar courtyard, and, like a temple in a Roman forum, the Pantheon stood at one narrow end of the enclosure (FIG. 7-50, *left*). Its facade of eight Corinthian columns—almost all that could be seen

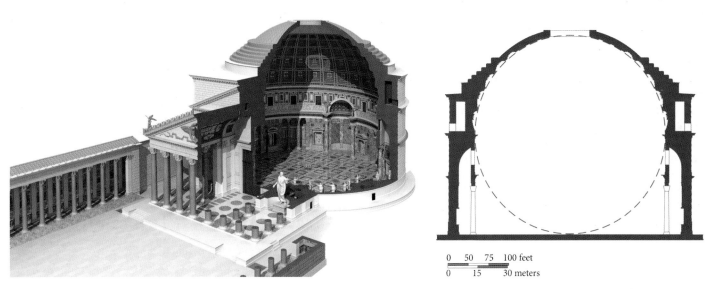

0	50	75	100 feet
0	15		30 meters

7-50 **Restored cutaway view** (*left*) **and lateral section** (*right*) **of the Pantheon, Rome, Italy, completed 125 CE** (John Burge).

Originally, the approach to Hadrian's "temple of all gods" was from a columnar courtyard. Like a temple in a Roman forum (FIG. 7-12), the Pantheon stood at one narrow end of the enclosure.

The Ancient World's Largest Dome

If the design of the dome (FIGS. 7-50 and 7-51) of Hadrian's Pantheon (FIG. 7-49) is geometric simplicity itself (a dome whose diameter and height from the floor are equal), executing that design took all the ingenuity of Hadrian's engineers. The builders were faced with the problem of constructing the largest dome in the world up to that time—a feat not surpassed until the 16th century. Their solution was to build up the cylindrical drum level by level using concrete of varied composition. Extremely hard and durable basalt went into the mix for the foundations, and the recipe gradually changed until, at the top of the dome, featherweight pumice replaced stones to lighten the load. The dome's thickness also decreases as it nears the oculus, the circular opening 30 feet in diameter that is the only light source for the interior. The use of *coffers* (sunken decorative panels) lessened the dome's weight without weakening its structure, further reduced its mass, and even provided a handsome pattern of squares within the vast circle. Renaissance drawings suggest that each coffer once had a glistening gilded-bronze rosette at its center, enhancing the symbolism of the dome as the starry heavens.

Below the dome, much of the original marble veneer of the walls, niches, and floor has survived. In the Pantheon, visitors can appreciate, as almost nowhere else (compare FIG. 7-66), how magnificent the interiors of Roman concrete buildings could be. But despite the luxurious skin of the Pantheon's interior, on first entering the structure, visitors do not focus on the walls but on the vastness of the space they enclose. In pre-Roman architecture, the form of the enclosed space was determined by the placement of the solids, which did not so much shape space as interrupt it. Roman architects were the first to conceive of architecture in terms of units of space that could be shaped by the enclosures. The Pantheon's interior is a single unified, self-sufficient whole, uninterrupted by supporting solids, and capped by a dome through the oculus of which the visitor sees the drifting clouds, the blue sky, the sun—and the realm of the gods.

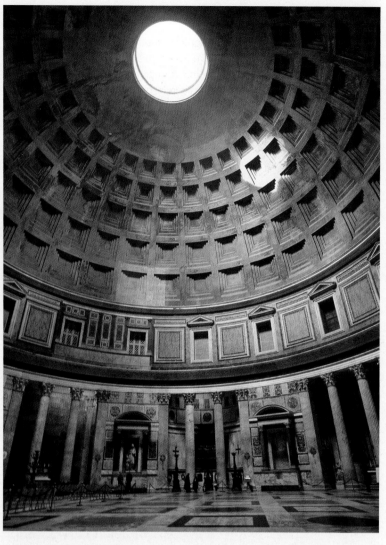

7-51 Interior of the Pantheon (looking south), Rome, Italy, completed 125 CE.

The coffered dome of the Pantheon is 142 feet in diameter and 142 feet high. Light entering through its oculus forms a circular beam that moves across the dome as the sun moves across the sky.

from the ancient ground level, which was lower than today's—was a bow to tradition. Everything else about the Pantheon was revolutionary. Behind the columnar porch is an immense concrete cylinder covered by a huge hemispherical dome (FIG. 7-51), unseen from the portico. That dome is 142 feet in diameter (see "The Ancient World's Largest Dome," above), and its top is an identical 142 feet from the floor (FIG. 7-50, *right*). The design is thus based on the intersection of two circles (one horizontal, the other vertical). The interior space can be imagined as the orb of the earth, and the dome as the vault of the heavens. The unknown architect enhanced this impression by using light not merely to illuminate the darkness but to create drama and underscore the symbolism of the building's shape. On a sunny day, the light passing through the oculus forms a circular beam, a disk of light that moves across the dome in the course of the day as the sun moves across the sky itself. Escaping from the noise and heat of a Roman summer day into the

Pantheon's cool, calm, and mystical immensity is an experience not to be missed.

Hadrian's Villa. Although some have speculated that Hadrian himself was the architect of the Pantheon, that is extremely unlikely. The emperor was, however, an amateur architect, and he became deeply involved with the development of the country villa he owned at Tivoli. One of his projects there was the construction of a pool and an artificial grotto, called the Canopus and Serapeum (FIG. 7-52), respectively. Canopus was an Egyptian city connected to Alexandria by a canal. Its most famous temple was dedicated to the god Serapis. However, nothing about the Tivoli design derives from Egyptian architecture. The grotto at the end of the pool is made of concrete and has an unusual pumpkin-shaped dome that Hadrian probably designed himself (see "Hadrian and Apollodorus of Damascus," page 217). Yet, in keeping with the persistent mixing of styles in

Hadrian and Apollodorus of Damascus

Dio Cassius, the third-century CE senator who described the games celebrating the opening of the Colosseum (see "Spectacles in the Colosseum," page 207) in his history of Rome from its founding to his day, recounted a revealing anecdote about Hadrian and Apollodorus of Damascus, architect of the Forum of Trajan (FIG. 7-44):

> Hadrian first drove into exile and then put to death the architect Apollodorus who had carried out several of Trajan's building projects. . . . When Trajan was at one time consulting with Apollodorus about a certain problem connected with his buildings, the architect said to Hadrian, who had interrupted them with some advice, "Go away and draw your pumpkins. You know nothing about these problems." For it so happened that Hadrian was at that time priding himself on some sort of drawing. When he became emperor he remembered this insult and refused to put up with Apollodorus's outspokenness. He sent him [his own] plan for the temple of Venus

and Roma [FIG. 7-2, no. 14], in order to demonstrate that it was possible for a great work to be conceived without his [Apollodorus's] help, and asked him if he thought the building was well designed. Apollodorus sent a [very critical] reply. . . . [The emperor did not] attempt to restrain his anger or hide his pain; on the contrary, he had the man slain.*

The story says a great deal about both the absolute power that Roman emperors wielded and how seriously Hadrian took his architectural designs. But perhaps the most interesting detail is the description of Hadrian's drawings of "pumpkins." These must have been drawings of concrete domes similar to the one in the Serapeum (FIG. 7-52) at Hadrian's Tivoli villa. Such vaults were too adventurous for Apollodorus, or at least for a public building in Trajanic Rome, and Hadrian had to try them out later at home at his own expense.

*Dio Cassius, *Roman History*, 69.4.1–5. Translated by J. J. Pollitt, *The Art of Rome, c. 753 B.C.–A.D. 337: Sources and Documents* (New York: Cambridge University Press, 1983), 175–176.

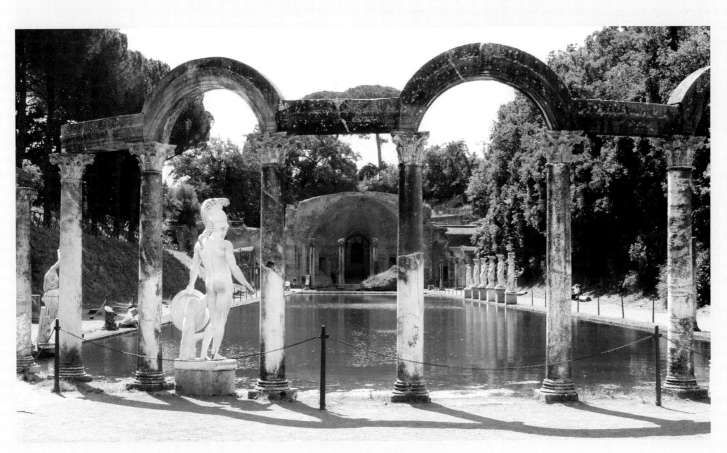

7-52 **Canopus and Serapeum (looking south), Hadrian's Villa, Tivoli, Italy, ca. 125–128 CE.**

Hadrian was an architect and may have personally designed some buildings at his private villa at Tivoli. The Serapeum features the kind of pumpkin-shaped concrete dome that the emperor favored.

Roman art and architecture as well as with Hadrian's love of Greek art, traditional Greek columns and marble copies of famous Greek statues, including the Erechtheion caryatids (FIG. 5-54), lined the pool. The Corinthian colonnade at the curved end of the pool is, however, of a type unknown in Classical Greek architecture. The colonnade is not a portico, just a decorative columnar frame at the curved end of the Canopus. Between alternating pairs of columns topped by traditional horizontal lintels are *arcuated lintels* (arch-shaped lintels), also unknown in Greek architecture. This simultaneous respect for Greek forms and willingness to break the rules

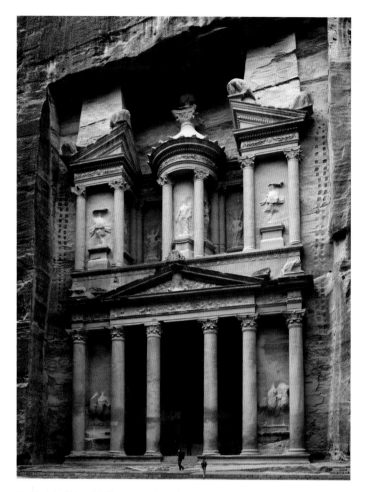

7-53 Al-Khazneh (Treasury, looking east), Petra, Jordan, second century CE (?).

This rock-cut tomb facade is a prime example of Roman "baroque" architecture. The designer used Greek architectural elements in a purely ornamental fashion and with a studied disregard for Classical rules.

of Greek design typifies much Roman architecture of the High and Late Empire.

Al-Khazneh. An even more extreme example of what many have called Roman "baroque" architecture (because of the striking parallels with 17th-century Italian buildings; see "'Baroque' Art and Architecture," page 712) is the tomb nicknamed Al-Khazneh, the "Treasury" (FIG. 7-53), at Petra, Jordan, often dated to the second century CE but possibly much earlier. It is one of the most elaborate of many tomb facades cut into the sheer rock faces of the local rose-colored mountains. As at Hadrian's Tivoli villa, the architect used Greek architectural elements in a purely ornamental fashion and with a studied disregard for Classical rules.

The Treasury's facade is more than 130 feet high and consists of two stories. The lower story resembles a temple facade with six columns, but the columns are unevenly spaced, and the pediment is only wide enough to cover the four central columns. On the upper level, a temple-within-a-temple sits atop the lower temple. Here the facade and roof split in half to make room for a central tholoslike cylinder, which contrasts sharply with the rectangles and triangles of the rest of the design. On both levels, the rhythmic alternation of deep projection and indentation creates dynamic patterns of light

and shadow. At Petra, as at Tivoli, the architect used the vocabulary of Greek architecture, but the syntax, or arrangement of elements, is new and distinctively Roman. In fact, the design recalls some of the architectural fantasies painted on the walls of Roman houses—for example, the tholos seen through columns surmounted by a broken pediment (FIG. 7-19, *right*) in the Second Style cubiculum from Boscoreale.

Ostia

The average Roman, of course, did not own a luxurious country villa and was not buried in a grand tomb. About 90 percent of Rome's population of close to one million lived in multistory apartment blocks (*insulae*). After the great fire of 64 CE, these were brick-faced concrete buildings. The rents were not inexpensive, as the law of supply and demand in real estate was just as valid in antiquity as it is today. Juvenal, whose satires are an indispensable source of information about daily life in imperial Rome, commented that people willing to give up chariot races and the other diversions that Rome had to offer could purchase a fine home in the countryside "for a year's rent in a dark hovel" in a city so noisy that "the sick die mostly from lack of sleep."[3] Conditions were much the same for the inhabitants of Ostia, Rome's harbor city. After its new port opened under Trajan, Ostia's fortunes boomed, and so did its population. A burst of building activity began under Trajan

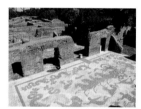

7-53A Baths of Neptune mosaic, Ostia, ca. 140 CE.

and continued under Hadrian and throughout the second century CE. Visitors to Ostia today can see temples, a theater, public baths (FIG. 7-53A), warehouses, and apartment houses that all mirror buildings of similar date in Rome.

Apartment Houses. The most common buildings in second-century Ostia were its multistory insulae (FIG. 7-54). Shops occupied the ground floors. Above were up to four floors of apartments. Although many of the apartments were large and had frescoed walls and ceilings, as in the aptly named Insula of the Painted Vaults (FIG. 7-54A), they had neither the space nor the light of the typical Pompeian private domus (see "The Roman House," page 193). In place of peristyles, insulae had only narrow light wells or small courtyards. Consequently, instead of looking inward, large numbers of windows faced the

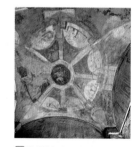

7-54A Insula of the Painted Vaults, Ostia, ca. 200–220 CE.

city's noisy streets. The residents cooked their food in the hallways. Only deluxe apartments had private toilets. Others shared latrines, often on a different floor from their apartments. Still, these insulae were more similar to modern apartment houses (which also sometimes have shops on the ground floor) than any other ancient building type.

Another strikingly modern feature of these multifamily residences is their brick facades, which were not concealed by stucco or marble veneers. When builders desired to incorporate a Classical motif, they added brick pilasters or engaged columns, but always left the brick exposed. Ostia and Rome have many examples

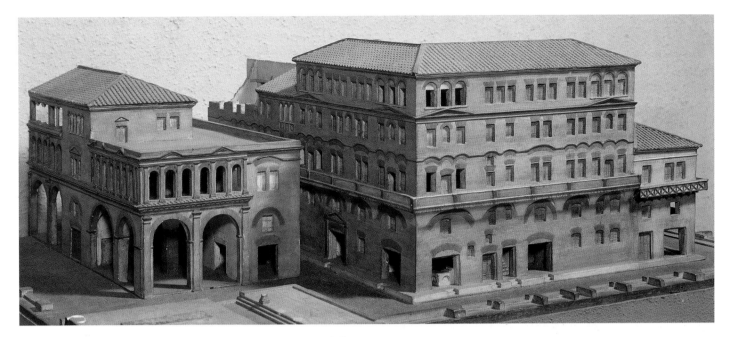

7-54 Model of an insula, Ostia, Italy, second century CE. Museo della Civiltà Romana, Rome.

Rome and Ostia were densely populated cities, and most Romans lived in multistory brick-faced concrete insulae (apartment houses) with shops on the ground floor. Private toilet facilities were rare.

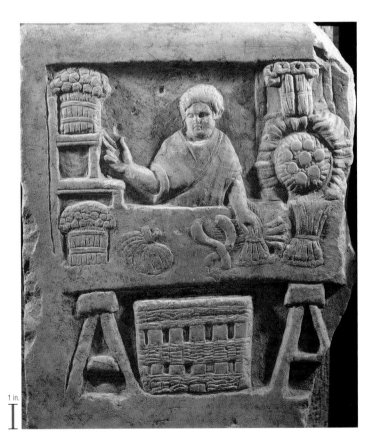

1 in.

7-55 Funerary relief of a vegetable vendor, from Ostia, Italy, second half of second century CE. Painted terracotta, 1′ 5″ high. Museo Archeologico Ostiense, Ostia.

Terracotta plaques illustrating the activities of middle-class merchants frequently adorned Ostian tomb facades. In this relief of a vegetable seller, the artist tilted the counter to display the produce clearly.

of apartment houses, warehouses, and tombs with intricate moldings and contrasting colors of brick. In the second century CE, brick came to be appreciated as attractive facing material in its own right.

Isola Sacra. Brick-faced concrete was also the preferred medium for the tombs in Ostia's Isola Sacra cemetery. The Ostian tombs were not the final resting places of the very wealthy. Rather, they were communal houses of the dead for middle-class families. The tombs resembled the multifamily insulae of most Ostians. Small painted terracotta plaques immortalizing the activities of merchants and professional people frequently adorned the facades of those tombs. A characteristic example (FIG. 7-55) depicts a vegetable seller behind a counter. The artist had little interest in the Classical-revival style that the emperors favored, and tilted the counter forward so that the observer could see the produce clearly. Comparable scenes of daily life appear on Roman funerary reliefs from sites throughout Europe. They were as much a part of the Roman artistic legacy to the later history of Western art as the emperors' monuments, which until recently were the almost exclusive interest of art historians.

The Antonines

Early in 138 CE, Hadrian adopted the 51-year-old Antoninus Pius (r. 138–161 CE). At the same time, he required Antoninus to adopt Marcus Aurelius (r. 161–180 CE) and Lucius Verus (r. 161–169 CE), thereby assuring a peaceful succession for at least another generation. When Hadrian died later in the year, the Senate proclaimed him a god, and Antoninus Pius became emperor. Antoninus ruled the Roman world with distinction for 23 years.

Column of Antoninus Pius. Shortly after Antoninus's death and deification, his adopted sons and new coemperors erected a memorial column in his honor. Atop the column was a gilded bronze portrait statue of Antoninus. The pedestal had a dedicatory inscription on the front and sculpted reliefs on the other three

7-56 Apotheosis of Antoninus Pius and Faustina, relief on the rear of the pedestal of the Column of Antoninus Pius, Rome, Italy, ca. 161 CE. Marble, 8′ 1½″ high. Musei Vaticani, Rome.

This representation of the joint apotheosis of Antoninus Pius and Faustina is firmly in the Classical tradition with its elegant, well-proportioned figures, personifications, and single ground line.

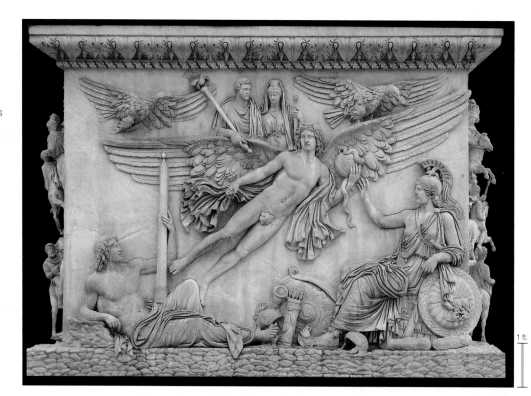

1 ft.

7-57 Decursio, pedestal of the Column of Antoninus Pius, Rome, Italy, ca. 161 CE. Marble, 8′ 1½″ high. Musei Vaticani, Rome.

In contrast to the apotheosis scene (FIG. 7-56), the decursio reliefs break sharply with Classical art conventions. The ground is the whole surface of the relief, and the figures stand on floating patches of earth.

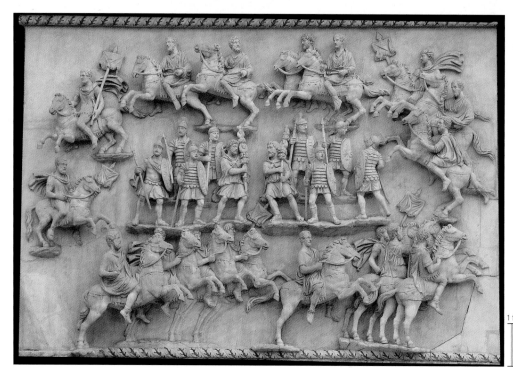

1 ft.

sides. The back (FIG. 7-56) depicts the apotheosis of Antoninus and his wife, Faustina the Elder. On the adjacent sides are two identical representations of the *decursio* (FIG. 7-57), or ritual circling of the imperial funerary pyre. The two figural compositions are very different. The apotheosis relief remains firmly in the Classical tradition with its elegant, well-proportioned figures, personifications, and single ground line corresponding to the panel's lower edge. The Campus Martius (Field of Mars), personified as a youth holding the Egyptian obelisk that was an important local landmark, reclines at the lower left corner. Roma (Rome personified) leans on a shield decorated with the she-wolf suckling Romulus and Remus (compare FIG. 6-11). Roma waves farewell to the couple being lifted into

the realm of the gods on the wings of a personification of uncertain identity. Scenes of apotheosis (FIG. 7-40A) had been standard in imperial art since Augustus. New to the pictorial repertoire, however, was the fusion of time that the joint apotheosis represents. Faustina had died 20 years before her husband. By depicting the two as ascending together, the artist wished to suggest that Antoninus had been faithful to his wife for two decades and that now they would be reunited in the afterlife—a common conceit in Roman non-elite funerary art (FIG. 7-43A).

The decursio reliefs (FIG. 7-57) break even more strongly with Classical convention. The figures are much stockier than those in the apotheosis relief, and the sculptor did not conceive the panel as a window onto the world. The ground is the whole surface of the relief, and marching soldiers and galloping horses alike stand on floating patches of earth. This, too, had not occurred before in imperial art, only in the art of freedmen (FIG. 7-10A). After centuries of following the rules of Classical design, elite Roman artists and patrons finally were becoming dissatisfied with them. When seeking a new direction, they adopted some of the non-Classical conventions of the art of the lower classes. This stylistic shift, still tentative and used for only one of the compositions on Antoninus's column pedestal, nonetheless represents a major turning point in the history of Roman art.

Marcus Aurelius. Another break with the past occurred in the official portraits of Marcus Aurelius, although his images retain the pompous trappings of imperial iconography. In a larger-than-life-size gilded-bronze equestrian statue (FIG. 7-58), the emperor

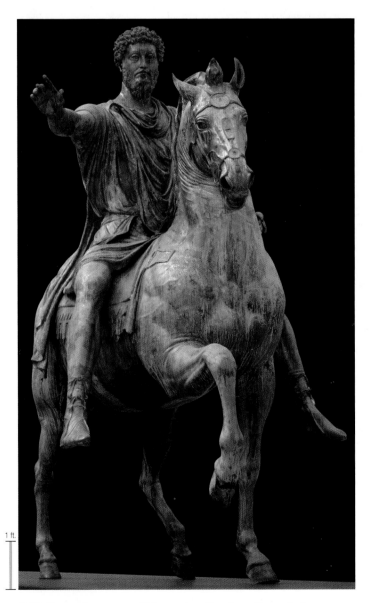

7-58 Equestrian statue of Marcus Aurelius, from Rome, Italy, ca. 175 CE. Bronze, 11′ 6″ high. Palazzo dei Conservatori, Musei Capitolini, Rome.

In this equestrian portrait of Marcus Aurelius as omnipotent conqueror, the emperor stretches out his arm in a gesture of clemency. An enemy once cowered beneath the horse's raised foreleg.

possesses a superhuman grandeur and is much larger in relation to his horse than any normal human would be. Marcus stretches out his right arm in a gesture that is both a greeting and an offer of clemency. Beneath the horse's raised right foreleg, an enemy once cowered, begging the emperor for mercy. The statue is a rare example of an imperial equestrian portrait, but the type was common in antiquity. For example, an equestrian statue of Trajan stood in the middle of his forum (FIG. 7-44, no. 6). Marcus's portrait survived the wholesale melting down of ancient bronze statues during the Middle Ages because it was mistakenly thought to portray Constantine, the first Christian emperor of Rome. Perhaps more than any other statuary type, the equestrian portrait expresses the Roman emperor's majesty and authority.

This message of supreme confidence is not, however, conveyed by the portrait head of Marcus's equestrian statue or any of the other portraits of the emperor in the years just before his death. Portraits of aged emperors were not new (FIG. 7-38), but Marcus's were the first in which a Roman emperor appeared weary, saddened, and even worried. For the first time, the strain of constant warfare on the frontiers and the burden of ruling a worldwide empire show in the emperor's face. The Antonine sculptor ventured beyond Republican verism, exposing the ruler's character, his thoughts, and his soul for all to see, as Marcus revealed them himself in his *Meditations,* a deeply moving philosophical treatise setting forth the emperor's personal worldview. This too was a major turning point in the history of ancient art, and, coming as it did when relief sculptors were also challenging the Classical style (FIG. 7-57), it marked the beginning of the end of Classical art's domination in the Greco-Roman world.

From Cremation to Burial. Other profound changes were taking place in Roman art and society at this time. Under Trajan and Hadrian and especially during the rule of the Antonines, Romans began to favor burial over cremation. This reversal of funerary practices may reflect the influence of Christianity and other Eastern religions, whose adherents believed in an afterlife for the human body, as did the ancient Egyptians (see "Mummification and Immortality," page 61). Although the emperors themselves continued to be cremated in the traditional Roman manner, many private citizens opted for burial. Thus they required larger containers for their remains than the ash urns that were the norm until the second century CE. This in turn led to a sudden demand for sarcophagi, which are more similar to modern coffins than any other ancient type of burial container.

Orestes Sarcophagus. Greek mythology was one of the most popular subjects for the decoration of these sarcophagi. In many cases, especially in the late second and third centuries CE, Roman men and women identified themselves on their coffins with Greek heroes and heroines, whose heads often were portraits of the deceased. These private patrons were following the model of imperial portraiture, in which emperors and empresses frequently masqueraded as gods and goddesses and heroes and heroines (see "Role Playing in Roman Portraiture," page 200, and FIG. 7-58A, a portrait of Commodus, son and successor of Marcus Aurelius, in the guise of Hercules). An early example of the type (although it lacks any

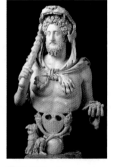

7-58A Commodus as Hercules, ca. 190–192 CE.

7-59 Sarcophagus with the myth of Orestes, from Rome, Italy, ca. 140–150 CE. Marble, 2′ 7½″ high. Cleveland Museum of Art, Cleveland.

Under the Antonines, Romans began to favor burial over cremation, and sarcophagi became very popular. Themes from Greek mythology, such as the tragic saga of Orestes, were common subjects.

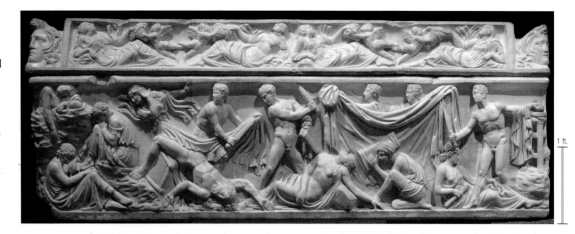

1 ft.

7-60 Asiatic sarcophagus with kline portrait of a woman, from Rapolla, near Melfi, Italy, ca. 165–170 CE. Marble, 5′ 7″ high. Museo Nazionale Archeologico del Melfese, Melfi.

The Romans produced sarcophagi in several regions. Western sarcophagi have carvings on the front and sides. Eastern sarcophagi, such as this one with a woman's portrait on the lid, feature reliefs also on the back.

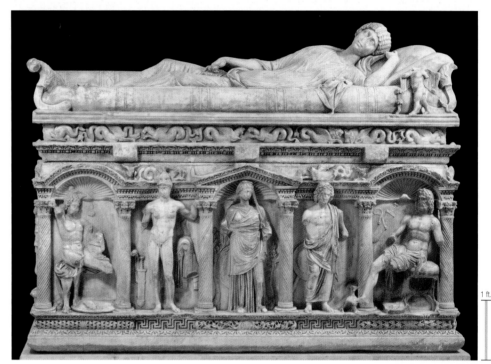

1 ft.

portraits) is a sarcophagus (FIG. 7-59) now in Cleveland, one of many decorated with the story of the tragic Greek hero Orestes. All the examples of this type use the same basic composition. Orestes appears more than once in every case. Here, at the center, Orestes slays his mother, Clytaemnestra, and her lover, Aegisthus, to avenge their murder of his father, Agamemnon. At the right, Orestes takes refuge at Apollo's sanctuary at Delphi (symbolized by the god's *tripod*).

The repetition of sarcophagus compositions indicates that Roman sculptors had access to pattern books. In fact, sarcophagus production was a major industry during the High and Late Empire. Several important regional manufacturing centers existed. The sarcophagi produced in the Latin West, such as the Cleveland Orestes sarcophagus, differ in format from those made in the Greek-speaking East. Western sarcophagi have reliefs only on the front and sides, because they were placed in floor-level niches inside Roman tombs. Eastern sarcophagi have reliefs on all four sides and stood in the center of the burial chamber. This contrast parallels the essential difference between the Etrusco-Roman and the Greek temple. The former was set against the back wall of a forum or sanctuary and was approached from the front, whereas the latter could be reached (and viewed) from every side.

Melfi Sarcophagus. An elaborate sarcophagus (FIG. 7-60) of the Eastern type—found at Rapolla, near Melfi in southern Italy, but manufactured in Asia Minor—attests to the vibrant export market for these luxury items in Antonine times. The characteristically Asiatic decoration of all four sides of the marble box consists of statuesque images of Greek deities and heroes in architectural frames. The figures portrayed include Venus and the legendary beauty, Helen of Troy. The lid

portrait, which carries on the tradition of Etruscan sarcophagi (FIGS. 6-5, 6-16, and 6-16A), is also a feature of the most expensive Western Roman coffins. Here, the deceased woman reclines on a *kline,* or couch. (The triclinium [FIG. 7-15, no. 7], or dining room of a Roman house, takes its name from the standard arrangement of one dining couch on each of three walls of the room.) With her are her faithful little dog (only its forepaws remain at the left end of the lid) and Cupid (at the right). The winged infant god mournfully holds a downturned torch, a reference to the death of a woman whose beauty rivaled that of his mother, Venus, and of Homer's Helen.

Mummy Portraits. In Egypt, as noted, burial had been practiced for millennia. Even after Augustus reduced the Kingdom of the Nile to a Roman province in 30 BCE, Egyptians continued to bury their dead in mummy cases (for example, FIG. 7-60A). In Roman times, however, painted wood panels depicting the deceased

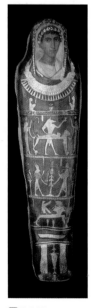

⎙7-60A Mummy of Artemidorus, ca. 100–120 CE.

Iaia of Cyzicus and the Art of Encaustic Painting

The names of very few Roman artists survive, and the known names tend to be those of artists and architects who directed major imperial building projects (Severus and Celer, Domus Aurea; Apollodorus of Damascus, Forum of Trajan), worked on a gigantic scale (Zenodorus, Colossus of Nero), or made precious objects for famous patrons (Dioscurides, gem cutter for Augustus).

An interesting exception to this rule is Iaia of Cyzicus. Information about Roman artists is scant in ancient literature, and descriptions of works by female artists is rarer still. But Pliny the Elder has a lot to say about Iaia, a female painter from Asia Minor who worked in Italy during the Republic and painted a self-portrait, an artistic genre for which there is little evidence before the 15th century (FIG. 20-12 is an early example).

> Iaia of Cyzicus, who remained a virgin all her life, painted at Rome during the time when M. Varro [116–27 BCE; a renowned Republican scholar and author] was a youth, both with a brush and with a cestrum on ivory, specializing mainly in portraits of women; she also painted a large panel in Naples representing an old woman and a portrait of herself done with a mirror. Her hand was quicker than that of any other painter, and her artistry was of such high quality that she commanded much higher prices than the most celebrated painters of the same period.*

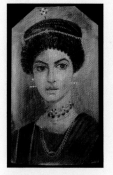

⊅ **7-60B** Young woman, Hawara, ca. 110–120 CE.

The *cestrum* mentioned by Pliny is a small spatula used in *encaustic* painting, a technique of mixing colors with hot wax and then applying them to the surface. Pliny knew of encaustic paintings of considerable antiquity, including those of the fifth-century BCE master Polygnotos of Thasos. The best evidence for the technique comes, however, from Roman Egypt, where mummy cases routinely incorporated encaustic portraits on wood panels (FIGS. 7-60A, **7-60B**, and 7-61).

Artists applied encaustic to marble (FIG. 5-63A) as well as to wood. According to Pliny, when Praxiteles was asked which of his statues he preferred, the fourth-century BCE Greek artist, perhaps the ancient world's greatest marble sculptor, replied: "Those that Nikias painted."† This anecdote underscores the importance of coloration in ancient statuary.

*Pliny the Elder, *Natural History,* 35.147–148. Translated by J. J. Pollitt, *The Art of Rome, c. 753* B.C.–A.D. *337: Sources and Documents* (New York: Cambridge University Press, 1983), 87.
†Pliny the Elder, *Natural History,* 35.133.

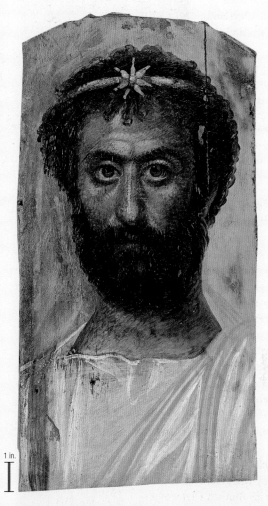

7-61 Mummy portrait of a priest of Serapis, from Hawara (Faiyum), Egypt, ca. 140–160 CE. Encaustic on wood, $1' 4\frac{3}{4}''$ × $8\frac{3}{4}''$. British Museum, London.

In Roman times, the Egyptians continued to bury their dead in mummy cases, but painted portraits replaced the traditional masks. The painting medium is encaustic—colors mixed with hot wax.

1 in.

---

often replaced the traditional stylized portrait masks (see "Iaia of Cyzicus and the Art of Encaustic Painting," above). Many scholars have postulated that these portraits, which date mostly to the second and third centuries, were painted while the subjects were still alive and then cut down to fit into the mummy cases. However, CAT scans of intact mummies associated with painted portraits have revealed a correspondence between the age of the deceased and the apparent age of the person in the portrait. Therefore, the portraits were created for insertion into mummy cases and were not "recycled" portraits from the homes of the deceased.

One of the hundreds of Roman mummy portraits unearthed in the cemeteries of the Faiyum district depicts a priest of the Egyptian god Serapis (FIG. 7-61). The priest's curly hair and beard closely emulate the Antonine fashion in Rome, but the corkscrew curls of hair on his forehead are distinctive to images of Serapis and his followers. The mummy portrait exhibits the painter's masterful use of the brush and spatula to depict different textures and the play of light over the soft and delicately modeled face. The Faiyum mummies enable art historians to trace the history of portrait painting after Mount Vesuvius erupted in 79 CE. (Compare, for example, FIGS. 7-24 and 7-24A with FIGS. 7-61 and 7-61A.)

LATE EMPIRE

By the time of Marcus Aurelius, two centuries after Augustus established the Pax Romana, Roman power was beginning to erode. The Roman legions found it increasingly difficult to keep order on the frontiers, and even within the Empire, many challenged the authority of Rome. The assassination of Marcus's son Commodus (FIG. 7-58A) in 192 CE brought the Antonine dynasty to an end. The economy was in decline, and the efficient imperial bureaucracy was disintegrating. Even the official state religion was losing ground to Eastern cults, Christianity among them. The Late Empire was a pivotal era in world history, during which the classical world and its multitude of gods gradually gave way to the Christian Middle Ages.

The Severans

Civil conflict followed Commodus's death. When it ended, an African-born general named Septimius Severus (r. 193–211 CE) was master of the Roman world. He succeeded in establishing a new dynasty that ruled the Empire for nearly a half century.

Severan Portraiture. Anxious to establish his legitimacy after the civil war, Septimius Severus adopted himself into the Antonine dynasty, declaring that he was Marcus Aurelius's son. It is not surprising, then, that to underscore his fictional lineage, the official portraits of the emperor in bronze and marble depict him with the long hair and beard of his Antonine "father"—whatever Severus's actual appearance may have been. That is also how Severus appears in the only preserved painted portrait (FIG. 7-62) of an emperor. Discovered in Egypt and painted in *tempera* (pigments in egg yolk) on wood (as were many of the mummy portraits from Faiyum), the portrait is of *tondo* (circular) format. It shows Severus with his wife, Julia Domna, the daughter of a Syrian priest, and their two sons, Caracalla and Geta. Painted likenesses of the imperial family must have been quite common in Italy and the provinces, but their perishable nature explains their almost total loss.

The Severan family portrait is of special interest for two reasons beyond its survival. Severus's hair is tinged with gray, suggesting that his marble portraits—which, like all marble sculptures in antiquity, were painted—also may have revealed his advancing age in this way. (The same was very likely true of the marble likenesses of the elderly Marcus Aurelius.) The group portrait is also notable because of the erasure of Geta's face. When Caracalla (r. 211–217 CE) succeeded his father as emperor, he ordered his younger brother murdered and had the Senate damn Geta's memory. (Caracalla also arranged the death of his own wife, Plautilla, and his influential father-in-law in order to consolidate his power.) The Severan family portrait is an eloquent testimony to that damnatio memoriae and to the long arm of Roman authority, which reached all the way to Egypt in this case. This kind of defacement of a rival's image is not unique to ancient Rome, but the Roman government employed damnatio memoriae as a political tool more often and more systematically than any other civilization.

Caracalla. In the Severan painted tondo, the artist portrayed Caracalla as a boy with long, curly Antonine hair. The portraits of Caracalla as emperor are very different. In the bust in Berlin illustrated here (FIG. 7-63), Caracalla appears in heroic nudity save for a mantle over one shoulder and a *baldric* across his chest. His hair and beard, although still curly, are much shorter—initiating a new fashion in male coiffure during the third century CE. More remarkable, however, is the moving characterization of Caracalla's ruthless personality, a further development from the groundbreaking introspection of Marcus Aurelius's portraits. Caracalla's brow is knotted—the ∨ of his forehead forms an ✕ with the lines running from his nostrils

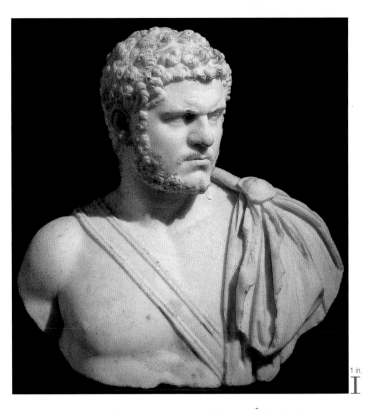

1 in.

7-62 Painted portrait of Septimius Severus and his family, from Egypt, ca. 200 CE. Tempera on wood, 1′ 2″ diameter. Altes Museum, Staatliche Museen zu Berlin, Berlin.

The only known painted portrait of an emperor shows Septimius Severus with gray hair. With him are his wife, Julia Domna, and their two sons, but Geta's head was removed after his damnatio memoriae.

7-63 Bust of Caracalla, ca. 211–217. Marble, 1′ 10¾″ high. Altes Museum, Staatliche Museen zu Berlin, Berlin.

Caracalla's portraits introduced a new fashion in male coiffure, but are more remarkable for the dramatic turn of the emperor's head and the moving characterization of his personality.

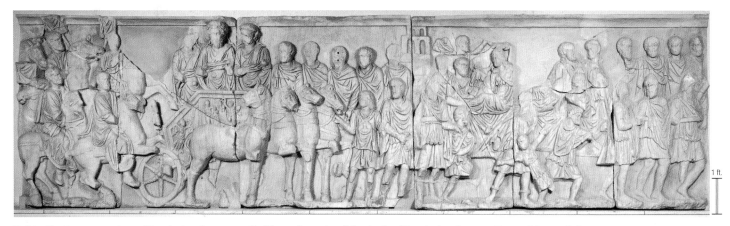

7-64 Chariot procession of Septimius Severus, relief from the attic of the Arch of Septimius Severus, Lepcis Magna, Libya, 203 CE. Marble, 5′ 6″ high. Castle Museum, Tripoli.

This relief from a triumphal arch exemplifies a new non-naturalistic aesthetic—the Late Antique style. Septimius Severus and his two sons face the viewer even though their chariot is moving to the right.

to the corners of his mouth—and he abruptly turns his head over his left shoulder. The sculptor probably intended the facial expression and the dramatic movement to suggest energy and strength, but it appears to modern viewers as if Caracalla suspects danger from behind. The emperor had reason to be fearful. An assassin's dagger felled him in the sixth year of his rule. Assassination would be the fate of many Roman emperors during the turbulent third century CE.

Lepcis Magna. The hometown of the Severans was Lepcis Magna, on the Mediterranean coast of what is now Libya. In the late second and early third centuries CE, the Severans constructed a modern harbor there, as well as a new forum, basilica, arch, and other monuments. The Lepcis Arch of Septimius Severus has friezes on the attic on all four sides. One (FIG. 7-64) depicts the chariot procession of the emperor and his two sons on the occasion of their homecoming in 203. Unlike the triumph panel (FIG. 7-42) on the Arch of Titus in Rome, this relief gives no sense of rushing motion. Rather, it has a stately stillness. The chariot and the horsemen behind it move forward, but the emperor and his sons are frozen in place and face the viewer. Also different is the way the figures in the second row, whether on horseback or on foot, have no connection with the ground. The sculptor elevated them above the heads of those in the first row so that they could be seen more clearly.

Both the frontality and the floating figures were new to official Roman art in Antonine and Severan times, but both appeared long before in the private art of freed slaves (FIGS. 7-10A and 7-11). Once these non-Classical elements were embraced by sculptors in the emperor's employ, they had a long afterlife, largely (although never totally) displacing the Classical style that the Romans adopted from Greece. As is often true in the history of art, the emergence of this new aesthetic was a by-product of a period of social, political, and economic upheaval. Art historians call this new non-naturalistic, more abstract style the *Late Antique* style.

Baths of Caracalla. The Severans were also active builders in the capital. The Baths of Caracalla (FIG. 7-65) in Rome were the greatest in a long line of bathing and recreational complexes constructed, beginning with Augustus, with imperial funds to win the public's favor. Caracalla's baths dwarfed the typical baths of cities and towns

such as Ostia (FIG. 7-53A) and Pompeii. All the rooms had thick brick-faced concrete walls up to 140 feet high, covered by enormous concrete vaults. The design was symmetrical along a central axis, facilitating the Roman custom of taking sequential plunges in warm-, hot-, and cold-water baths in, respectively, the *tepidarium, caldarium,* and *frigidarium.* The caldarium (FIG. 7-65, no. 4) was a huge circular chamber with a concrete drum even taller than the Pantheon's (FIGS. 7-50 and 7-51) and a dome almost as large. Caracalla's 50-acre bathing complex also included landscaped gardens, lecture halls, libraries, colonnaded exercise courts (*palaestras*), and a giant swimming pool (*natatio*). Archaeologists estimate that up to 1,600 bathers

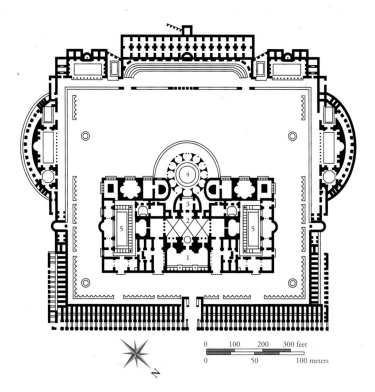

7-65 Plan of the Baths of Caracalla, Rome, Italy, 212–216 CE. (1) natatio, (2) frigidarium, (3) tepidarium, (4) caldarium, (5) palaestra.

Caracalla's baths could accommodate 1,600 bathers. They resembled a modern health spa and included libraries, lecture halls, and exercise courts in addition to bathing rooms and a swimming pool.

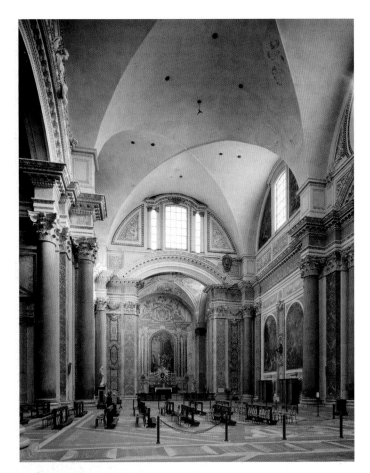

7-66 Frigidarium, Baths of Diocletian, Rome, Italy, ca. 298–306 (remodeled by Michelangelo Buonarroti as the nave of Santa Maria degli Angeli, 1563).

The groin-vaulted nave of the church of Santa Maria degli Angeli in Rome was once the frigidarium of the Baths of Diocletian. It gives an idea of the lavish adornment of imperial Roman baths.

at a time could enjoy this Roman equivalent of a modern health spa. A branch of one of the city's major aqueducts supplied water, and furnaces circulated hot air through hollow floors and walls throughout the bathing rooms. (The Romans were pioneers in central heating, as in so many other areas.)

The Baths of Caracalla also featured stucco-covered vaults, marble-faced walls, marble statuary, and mosaic floors—both black-and-white (compare FIG. 7-53A) and polychrome. One of the statues on display was the 10-foot-tall marble version of Lysippos's Herakles (FIG. 5-66), whose muscular body must have inspired Romans to exercise vigorously. The concrete vaults of the Baths of Caracalla collapsed long ago, but visitors can approximate the original appearance of the central bathing hall, the frigidarium, by entering the nave (FIG. 7-66) of the church of Santa Maria degli Angeli in Rome, which was once the frigidarium of the later Baths of Diocletian. The Renaissance interior (remodeled in the 18th century) of that church has, of course, many features foreign to a Roman bath, including a painted altarpiece. The ancient mosaics and marble revetment are long gone, but the present-day interior—with its rich wall treatment, colossal columns with Composite capitals, immense groin vaults, and clerestory lighting—provides a better sense of what it was like to be in a Roman imperial bathing complex than does any other building in the world. It takes a powerful imagination to visualize the original appearance of Roman concrete buildings from the pathetic ruins of brick-faced walls and

fallen vaults at ancient sites today, but Santa Maria degli Angeli—and the Pantheon (FIG. 7-51)—make the task much easier.

The Soldier Emperors

The Severan dynasty ended with the murder of Severus Alexander (r. 222–235 CE). The next half century was one of almost continuous civil war. The Roman legions declared as emperor one general after another, only to have each murdered in turn by another general a few years or even a few months later. (In the year 238, two coemperors selected by the Senate were dragged from the imperial palace and murdered in public after only three months of rule.) In such unstable times, no emperor could begin ambitious architectural projects. The only significant building activity in Rome during the era of the "soldier emperors" occurred under Aurelian (r. 270–275 CE). He constructed a new defensive circuit wall for the capital—a military necessity and a poignant commentary on the decay of Roman power.

Trajan Decius. If architects went hungry in third-century Rome, engravers and sculptors had much to do. The mint produced great quantities of coins (in debased metal) to ensure that the troops could be paid with money stamped with the current emperor's portrait and not with the likeness of his predecessor or rival. Each new ruler set up portrait statues and busts everywhere he could to

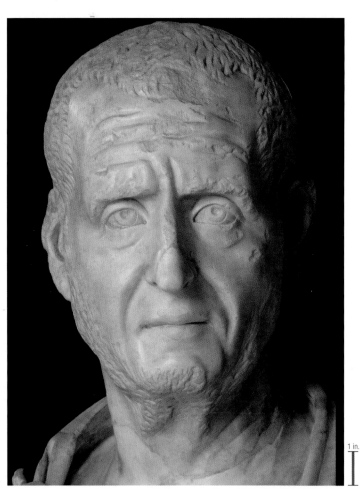

1 in.

7-67 Portrait bust of Trajan Decius, 249–251 CE. Marble, 1′ 2″ high (without modern bust). Museo Capitolino, Musei Capitolini, Rome.

This portrait of a short-lived soldier emperor depicts an older man with bags under his eyes and a sad expression. The eyes glance away nervously, seemingly reflecting the anxiety of an insecure ruler.

assert his authority, although few are preserved because of these rulers' brief reigns and the many decrees of damnatio memoriae. The sculpted portraits that do survive from the third century CE are among the most moving ever made, as notable for their emotional content as they are for their technical virtuosity. Portraits of Trajan Decius (r. 249–251 CE; FIG. 7-67) show the emperor best known for persecuting Christians as an old man with bags under his eyes and a sad expression. The eyes glance away nervously rather than engage the viewer directly, revealing the anxiety of a man who knows he can do little to restore order to an out-of-control world. The sculptor modeled the marble as if it were pliant clay, compressing the sides of the head at the level of the eyes, etching the hair and beard into the stone, and chiseling deep lines in the forehead and around the mouth. The portrait seems to reveal the anguished soul of the man and of the times, but it and the many like it present a problem in interpretation. It is hard to believe that the soldier emperors approved being represented as weak and troubled.

Trebonianus Gallus. Portraits of Decius's short-lived predecessor, Philip the Arabian (r. 244–249 CE), and successor, Trebonianus Gallus (r. 251–253 CE), also exist today. Philip's busts (FIG. **7-67A**) are marble and typical of the era, but the portrait of Trebonianus illustrated here (FIG. **7-68**) is a larger-than-life-size bronze statue. Trebonianus appears in heroic nudity, as had so many emperors and generals (FIG. 7-9) before him. His physique, however, is not that of the strong but graceful Greek athletes whom Augustus and his successors admired so much. Instead, his is a wrestler's body with massive legs and a swollen trunk. The heavyset body dwarfs the head, with its nervous expression. In this portrait, the Greek ideal of the keen mind in the harmoniously proportioned body gave way to an image of brute force—an image well suited to the age of the soldier emperors.

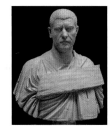

⟨🖾⟩**7-67A** Philip the Arabian, 244–249 CE.

Ludovisi Battle Sarcophagus. By the third century CE, burial of the dead had become so widespread that even the imperial family practiced it in place of cremation. Sarcophagi were more popular than ever. The unusually large sarcophagus illustrated here (FIG. 7-69) was discovered in Rome in 1621 and purchased by

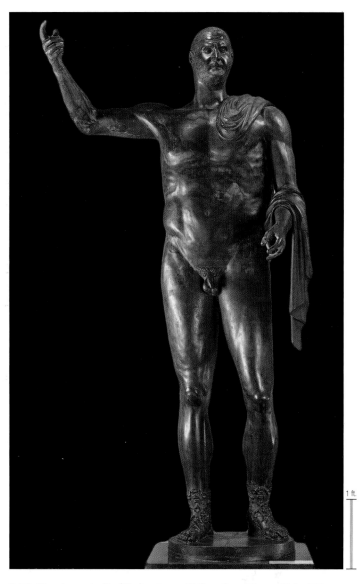

7-68 Heroic portrait of Trebonianus Gallus, from Rome, Italy, 251–253 CE. Bronze, 7′ 11″ high. Metropolitan Museum of Art, New York.

In this over-life-size statue, Trebonianus Gallus projects an image of brute force. He has the massive physique of a powerful wrestler, in contrast to the lean bodies of Greek athletes and earlier emperors.

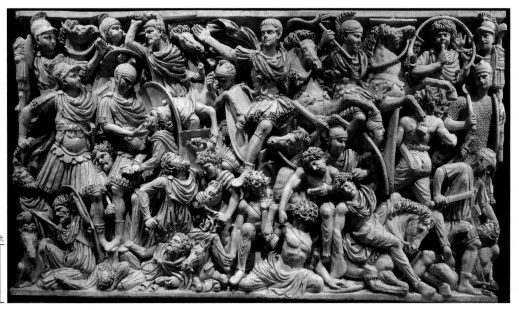

7-69 Battle of Romans and barbarians (*Ludovisi Battle Sarcophagus*), from Rome, Italy, ca. 250–260 CE. Marble, 5′ high. Palazzo Altemps, Museo Nazionale Romano, Rome.

A chaotic scene of battle between Romans and barbarians decorates the front of this sarcophagus. The sculptor piled up the writhing, emotive figures in an emphatic rejection of Classical perspective.

7-70 Sarcophagus of a philosopher, ca. 270–280 CE. Marble, 4′ 11″ high. Musei Vaticani, Rome.

On many third-century CE sarcophagi, the deceased appears as a learned intellectual. Here, the seated philosopher is the central frontal figure. His two female muses also have portrait features.

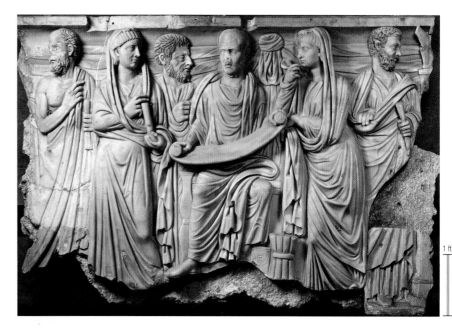

1 ft.

Cardinal Ludovico Ludovisi (1595–1632), a great collector of antiquities. On the front of the *Ludovisi Battle Sarcophagus* is a chaotic scene of Romans fighting one of their northern foes, probably the Goths. The sculptor spread the writhing and highly emotive figures evenly across the entire relief, with no illusion of space behind them. This piling of figures is an even more emphatic rejection of Classical perspective than was the use of floating ground lines in the decursio panel (FIG. 7-57) of the Column of Antoninus Pius. It underscores the increasing dissatisfaction of Late Antique artists with the Classical style.

Within this dense mass of intertwined bodies, the central horseman stands out vividly. He wears no helmet and thrusts out his open right hand to demonstrate that he holds no weapon. Several scholars have identified him as one of the sons of Trajan Decius. In an age when the Roman army was far from invincible and Roman emperors were continuously assassinated by other Romans, the young general on the *Ludovisi Battle Sarcophagus* boasts that he is a fearless commander assured of victory. His self-assurance may stem from his having embraced one of the increasingly popular Oriental mystery religions. On the youth's forehead, the sculptor carved the emblem of Mithras, the Persian god of light, truth, and victory over death.

Philosopher Sarcophagus. The insecurity of the times led some Romans to seek solace in philosophy. On many third-century sarcophagi, the deceased assumed the role of the learned intellectual. One especially large example (FIG. 7-70) depicts a seated Roman philosopher holding a scroll. Two standing women (also with portrait features) gaze at him from left and right, confirming his importance. In the background are other philosophers, students or colleagues of the central deceased teacher. The two women may be the deceased's wife and daughter, two sisters, or some other combination of family members. The composition, with a frontal central figure and two subordinate flanking figures, is typical of the Late Antique style (compare FIG. 7-64). This type of sarcophagus became popular for Christian burials. Sculptors used the wise-man motif to portray not only the deceased (FIG. 8-7) but also Christ flanked by saints (FIG. 8-8, *top center*).

Baalbek. Significant deviations from the norms of Classical art also are evident in third-century architecture. At Baalbek in present-day

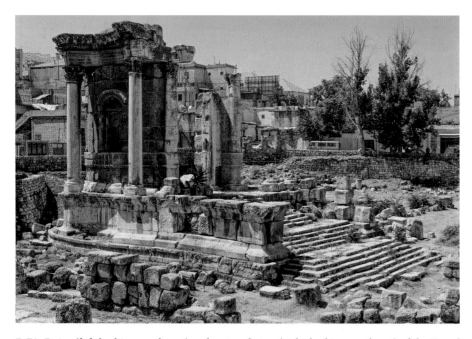

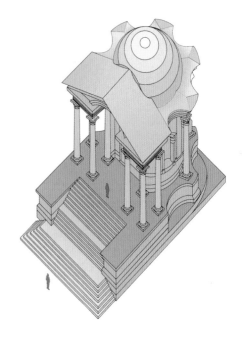

7-71 Ruins (*left,* looking southwest) and restored view (*right,* looking northeast) of the Temple of Venus, Baalbek, Lebanon, mid-third century CE.

This "baroque" temple violates almost every rule of Classical design. It has a scalloped platform and entablature, five-sided Corinthian capitals, and a facade with an arch inside the pediment.

Tetrarchic Portraiture

With the establishment of the tetrarchy in 293 CE, the sculptors in the emperors' employ suddenly had to grapple with a new problem—namely, how to represent four individuals who oversaw different regions of a vast empire but were equal partners in power. Although in life the four tetrarchs were rarely in the same place, in art they usually appeared together, both on coins and in statues. Artists did not try to capture their individual appearances and personalities—the norm in portraiture of the preceding soldier emperors (FIGS. 7-67, 7-67A, and 7-68)—but sought instead to represent the power-sharing nature of the tetrarchy itself.

The finest extant tetrarchic portraits are the two pairs of porphyry (purple marble) statues (FIG. 7-72) that have since medieval times adorned the southwestern corner of the great church (FIG. 9-26) dedicated to Saint Mark in Venice. (Originally, they adorned the shafts of two columns, probably in Byzantium, present-day Istanbul, Turkey.) In this and similar tetrarchic group portraits, it is impossible to name the rulers. Each of the four emperors has lost his identity as an individual and been absorbed into the larger entity of the tetrarchy. All the tetrarchs are identically clad in cuirass and cloak. Each grasps a sheathed sword in his left hand. With their right arms, the corulers embrace one another in an overt display of concord. The figures, like those on the decursio relief (FIG. 7-57) of the Column of Antoninus Pius, have large cubical heads and squat bodies. The drapery is schematic, the bodies are shapeless, and the faces are emotionless masks, distinguished only by the beards of two of the tetrarchs (the older Augusti, differentiating them from the younger Caesars). Other than the presence or absence of facial hair, each pair is as alike as freehand carving can achieve.

In this group portrait, carved eight centuries after Greek sculptors first freed the human form from the rigidity of the Egyptian-inspired kouros stance, an artist or artists once again conceived the human figure in iconic terms. Idealism, naturalism, individuality, and personality have disappeared.

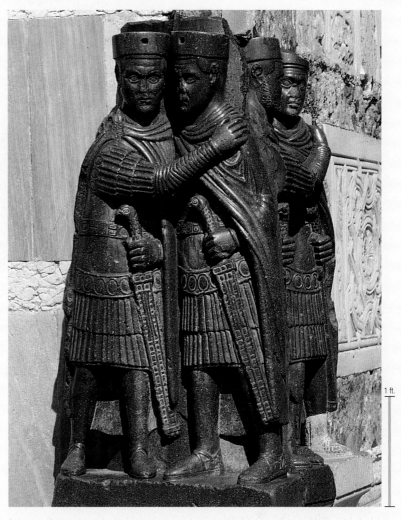

1 ft.

7-72 Portraits of the four tetrarchs, from Constantinople, ca. 300 CE. Porphyry, 4′ 3″ high. Saint Mark's, Venice.

Diocletian established the tetrarchy to bring order to the Roman world. In group portraits, artists always depicted the four corulers as nearly identical partners in power, not as distinct individuals.

Lebanon, the architect of the Temple of Venus (FIG. 7-71), following in the "baroque" tradition of the Petra Treasury (FIG. 7-53), ignored almost every rule of Classical design. Although made of stone, the building, with its circular domed cella set behind a gabled columnar facade, is in many ways a critique of the concrete Pantheon (FIG. 7-49), which by then had achieved the status of a "classic." Many features of the Baalbek temple intentionally depart from the norm. The platform, for example, is scalloped all around the cella. The columns—the only known instance of five-sided Corinthian capitals with corresponding pentagonal bases—support a matching scalloped entablature (which serves to buttress the shallow stone dome). These concave forms and those of the niches in the cella walls play off against the cella's convex shape. Even the "traditional" facade of the Baalbek temple is eccentric. The unknown architect inserted an arch within the triangular pediment. Many centuries later, the Venus temple would inspire the design of a "Temple of Apollo" (FIG. 26-32A) on the grounds of an English private estate.

Diocletian and the Tetrarchy

In an attempt to restore order to the Roman Empire, Diocletian (r. 284–305 CE), whose troops proclaimed him emperor, decided to share power with his potential rivals. In 293, he established the *tetrarchy* (rule by four) and adopted the title of Augustus of the East. The other three *tetrarchs* were a corresponding Augustus of the West, and Eastern and Western Caesars (whose allegiance to the two Augusti was cemented by marriage to their daughters). The four coemperors ruled without strife until Diocletian retired in 305, and they often appeared together in group portraits (FIG. 7-72) to underscore their harmonious partnership (see "Tetrarchic Portraiture," above). Without Diocletian's leadership, however, the tetrarchic form of government collapsed, and renewed civil war followed. Nonetheless, the division of the Roman Empire into eastern and western spheres persisted throughout the Middle Ages, setting the Greek East (Byzantium) apart from the Latin West.

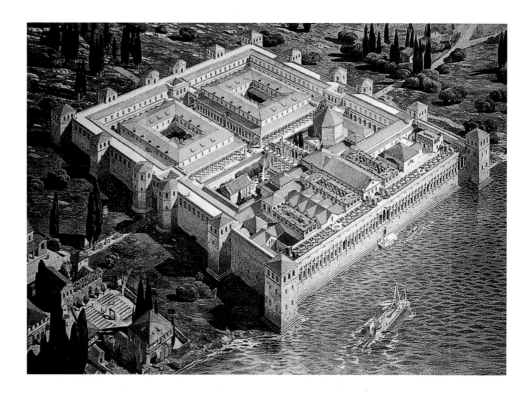

7-73 Restored view of the palace of Diocletian, Split, Croatia, ca. 298–306.

Diocletian's palace resembled a fortified Roman city (compare FIG. 7-43). Within its high walls, two avenues intersected at the forumlike colonnaded courtyard leading to the emperor's residential quarters.

Palace of Diocletian. When Diocletian abdicated in 305, he returned to his birthplace, Dalmatia (roughly the former Yugoslavia), where he built a palace (FIG. 7-73) at Split on the Adriatic coast. Just as Aurelian had felt it necessary to girdle Rome with fortress walls, Diocletian instructed his architects to provide him with a walled suburban palace. The fortified complex, which covers about 10 acres, has the layout of a Roman castrum, complete with watchtowers flanking the gates. It gave the retired emperor a sense of security in the most insecure of times.

Within the high walls, two avenues (comparable to the cardo and decumanus of a Roman city; FIG. 7-43) intersected at the palace's center. Where a city's forum would have been situated, Diocletian's palace had a colonnaded court leading to the entrance to the imperial residence, which had a templelike facade with an arch within its pediment, as in Baalbek's Temple of Venus (FIG. 7-71). Diocletian presented himself as if he were a god in his temple when he appeared before those who gathered in the court to pay homage to him. On one side of the court was a Temple of Jupiter. On the other side was Diocletian's domed octagonal *mausoleum* (FIG. 7-73, *center right*), which towered above all the other structures in the complex. Domed tombs of this type became very popular in Late Antiquity, not only for mausoleums but eventually also for churches, especially in the Byzantine Empire (FIGS. 9-10 and 9-11). In fact, Diocletian's mausoleum is a church today.

Constantine

An all-too-familiar period of conflict followed the short-lived concord among the tetrarchs that ended with Diocletian's abdication. This latest war among rival Roman armies lasted two decades. The eventual victor was Constantine I, son of Constantius Chlorus, Diocletian's Caesar of the West. After the death of his father, Constantine (r. 306–337 CE), later called Constantine the Great, invaded Italy. In 312 CE, in a decisive battle at Rome's Milvian Bridge, he defeated and killed Maxentius and took control of the capital. Constantine attributed his victory to the aid of the Christian god. The next year, he and Licinius, Constantine's

coemperor in the East, issued the Edict of Milan, ending the persecution of Christians.

In time, Constantine and Licinius became foes, and in 324 Constantine defeated and executed Licinius near Byzantium. Constantine, now unchallenged ruler of the whole Roman Empire, founded a "New Rome" at Byzantium and named it Constantinople (City of Constantine). In 325, at the Council of Nicaea, Christianity became the de facto official religion of the Roman Empire. From this point on, the ancient cults declined rapidly. Constantine dedicated Constantinople on May 11, 330, "by the commandment of God," and in 337 the emperor was baptized on his deathbed. For many scholars, the transfer of the seat of power from Rome to Constantinople and the recognition of Christianity mark the end of antiquity and the beginning of the Middle Ages.

Constantinian art is a mirror of this transition from the ancient to the medieval world. In Rome, for example, Constantine was a builder in the grand tradition of the emperors of the first, second, and early third centuries, erecting public baths, a basilica on the road leading into the Roman Forum, and a triumphal arch. But he was also the patron of the city's first churches (see "The First Churches," page 248).

Basilica Nova. Constantine's basilica in the Roman Forum was called the Basilica Nova (New Basilica) and was the first major building project in the forum since the Severans. Its ruins (FIGS. 7-2, no. 12, and 7-74) never fail to impress tourists with their size and mass. The original structure was 300 feet long and 215 feet wide. Brick-faced concrete walls 20 feet thick supported coffered barrel vaults in the aisles. These vaults also buttressed the groin vaults of the nave, which was 115 feet high. Marble slabs and stuccoes covered the walls and floors. The reconstruction effectively suggests the immensity of the interior. Noteworthy too is the *fenestration* of the groin vaults (FIG. 7-6), a lighting system akin to the clerestory of a traditional stone-and-timber basilica. The architect here applied to basilica design the lessons learned in the design and construction of earlier Roman buildings, such as Trajan's great market hall (FIG. 7-47) and the Baths of Caracalla and Diocletian (FIG. 7-66).

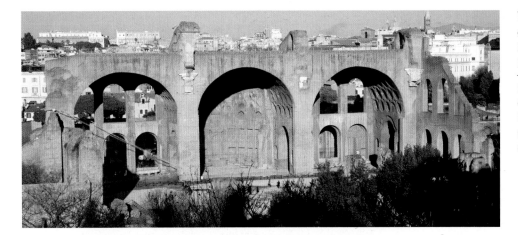

Roman builders applied the lessons learned constructing baths and market halls to the Basilica Nova, in which fenestrated concrete groin vaults replaced the clerestory of a stone-and-timber basilica.

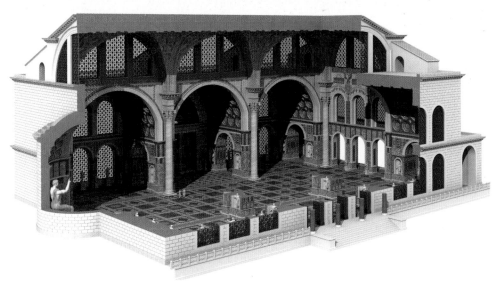

basilica-like audience hall, the Aula Palatina, as part of his new palace complex. The Trier *aula* measures about 190 feet long and 95 feet wide. Inside (FIG. **7-75**, *left*), the hall was very simple, unlike the contemporaneous Basilica Nova in Rome. Its flat, coffered wood ceiling is some 95 feet above the floor. The interior has no aisles, only a wide space with two stories of large windows that provide ample light. At the narrow north end, a *chancel arch* divides the main hall from the semicircular apse (which also has a flat ceiling). The Aula Palatina's interior is quite severe, although mosaics and marble plaques originally covered the arch and apse to provide a magnificent frame for the enthroned emperor.

Aula Palatina. Few architects, however, followed suit. At Trier on the Moselle River in Germany, the imperial seat of Constantius Chlorus as Caesar of the West, Constantine built a traditional

The exterior (FIG. 7-75, *right*) of the Trier basilica is also austere, with brick walls enlivened somewhat by highlighting in grayish-white stucco. The use of lead-framed panes of glass for

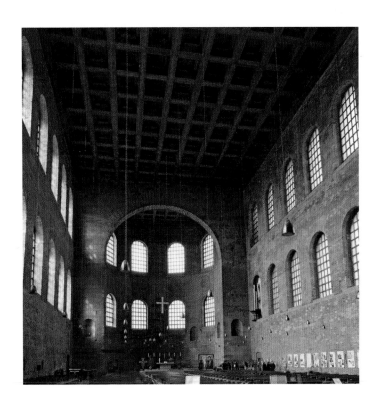

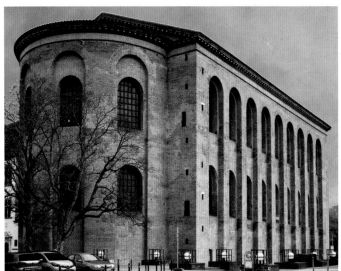

7-75 Interior (*left,* looking north) and exterior (*above,* looking southeast) of the Aula Palatina, Trier, Germany, early fourth century CE.

The austere brick exterior of Constantine's Aula Palatina at Trier is typical of later Roman architecture. The interior resembles a timber-roofed basilica with an apse, but there are no aisles.

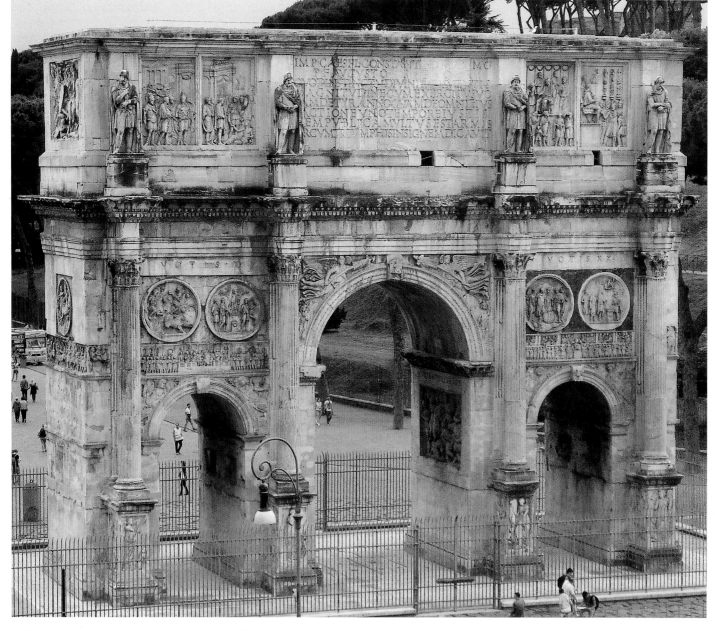

7-76 Arch of Constantine (looking southwest), Rome, Italy, 312–315 CE.

Much of the sculptural decoration of Constantine's arch came from monuments of Trajan, Hadrian, and Marcus Aurelius. Sculptors recut the heads of the earlier emperors to substitute Constantine's features.

the windows enabled the builders to give life and movement to the blank exterior surfaces. The design of the exterior of the Aula Palatina has close parallels in many Early Christian churches (FIG. 8-19).

Arch of Constantine. Between 312 and 315, the Senate erected a grandiose triple-passageway arch (FIGS. 7-2, no. 15; 7-76; and 7-77) next to the Colosseum to commemorate Constantine's defeat of Maxentius. The arch was the largest erected in Rome since the end of the Severan dynasty. The builders, however, took much of the sculptural decoration from earlier monuments of Trajan, Hadrian (FIG. 7-47A), and Marcus Aurelius, and all of the columns and other architectural elements date to an earlier era. As a result, art historical evaluations of the Arch of Constantine differ sharply (see "The Arch of Constantine," page 233).

Colossus of Constantine. Until Constantine's victory over Maxentius, his portraits conformed to the tetrarchic mode, but once he secured control of Rome, the portraits he commissioned took on a very different look, resuscitating the Augustan image of a perpetually youthful head of state. The most impressive of the emperor's preserved portraits is an 8½-foot-tall head (FIG. 7-78), one of several fragments of a colossal enthroned statue of the emperor set up in the western apse of the Basilica Nova (FIG. 7-74, *bottom*). The emperor's image dominated the interior of the basilica in much the same way that statues of Greco-Roman divinities loomed over awestruck mortals in temple cellas (compare FIG. 5-46).

The statue's head and limbs were marble, but it had a brick core and a wood torso covered with bronze. The emperor held an orb (possibly surmounted by the cross of Christ), the symbol of global power, in his extended left hand. The sideways glance of

The Arch of Constantine

The Arch of Constantine (FIG. 7-76) presents one of the greatest interpretive problems in ancient art. Most of the sculptural ornament consists of reused sculptures, or *spolia* ("spoils"), and the reliefs that are of Constantinian date have traditionally been judged to be of inferior quality. Consequently, the arch has often been cited as the primary example of the lack of creativity and technical skill and of what one eminent art historian called the "decline of form"* that paralleled the deteriorating economy of the third and fourth centuries CE.

By contrast, some scholars have argued that the reuse of earlier sculptures was not an act of desperation but an attempt to associate Constantine with the "good emperors" of the second century CE. One of the arch's few Constantinian reliefs (FIG. 7-47A, *bottom*) underscores that message. It shows Constantine on the speaker's platform in the Roman Forum between statues of Hadrian and Marcus Aurelius. Moreover, Constantine's sculptors refashioned the second-century reliefs to honor him by recutting the heads of the earlier emperors with his features. They also added labels to the old reliefs, such as *Liberator Urbis* (Liberator of the City) and *Fundator Quietus* (Bringer of Peace), references to the downfall of Maxentius and the end of civil war.

The "decline of form" is a valid judgment only if the Classical style is used as the yardstick of artistic excellence. In another Constantinian relief (FIG. 7-77), the emperor distributes largesse to grateful citizens, who approach him from right and left. Constantine is a frontal and majestic presence, elevated on a throne above the recipients of his generosity. The figures are squat in proportion, as are the tetrarchs (FIG. 7-72). They move, not according to any Classical principle of naturalistic motion, but rather with the mechanical and repeated stances and gestures of puppets. The relief is very shallow, the forms are not fully modeled, and the details are incised. The frieze is less a narrative of action than a picture of actors frozen in time. Is this a "decline of form"? Perhaps not. In this relief, the viewer can instantly distinguish the all-important imperial donor (the largest figure, enthroned at the center) from his attendants (to the left and right above) and the recipients of the largesse (below), both of smaller stature than the emperor. The composition's rigid formality, determined by the rank of those portrayed, reflects a new set of values that supplanted the Classical notion that a picture is a window onto a world of anecdotal action. Comparing this Constantinian relief with a Byzantine icon (FIG. 9-19) reveals that the compositional principles of the Late Antique style became those of early medieval art. They were very different from, but not "better" or "worse" than, those of Greco-Roman art.

The Arch of Constantine is the quintessential monument of its era, exhibiting a respect for the past in its use of second-century spolia while rejecting the norms of Classical design in its frieze and thereby paving the way for the iconic art of the Middle Ages.

*Bernard Berenson, *The Arch of Constantine: or, The Decline of Form* (London: Chapman & Hall, 1954).

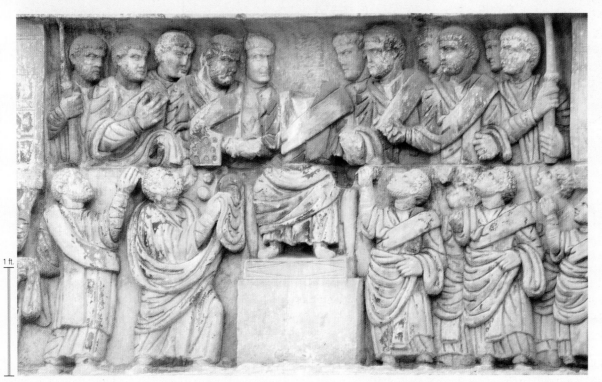

7-77 **Constantine distributing largesse, detail of the north frieze of the Arch of Constantine, Rome, Italy, 312–315 CE. Marble, 3′ 4″ high.**

This Constantinian frieze is less a narrative of action than a picture of actors frozen in time. The composition's rigid formality reflects the new values that would come to dominate medieval art.

1 ft.

third-century portraits is absent, replaced by a frontal mask with enormous eyes set into the broad and simple planes of the head (FIG. 7-78). Constantine's personality is lost in this immense image of eternal authority. The colossal size, the likening of the emperor to Jupiter, the eyes directed at no person or thing of this world—all combine to produce a formula of overwhelming power appropriate to Constantine's exalted position as absolute ruler.

Constantinian Coins. No examination of Constantinian art is complete without a discussion of his coins, because they reveal

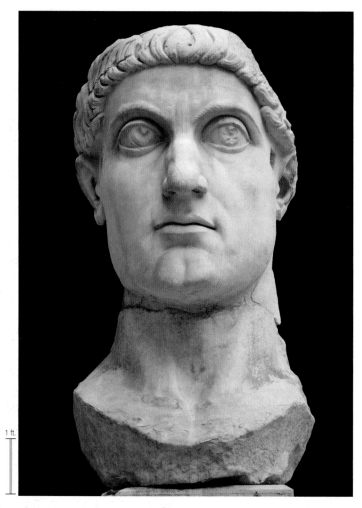

7-78 Portrait of Constantine, from the Basilica Nova, Rome, Italy, ca. 315–330 CE. Marble, 8′ 6″ high. Palazzo dei Conservatori, Musei Capitolini, Rome.

Constantine's portraits revive the Augustan image of a perpetually youthful ruler. This colossal head is one fragment of an enthroned Jupiter-like statue of the emperor holding the orb of world power.

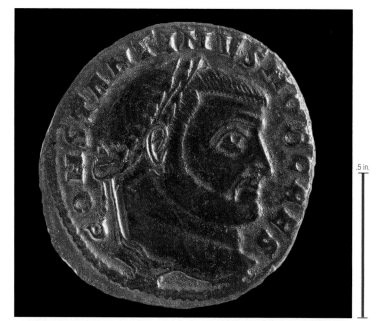

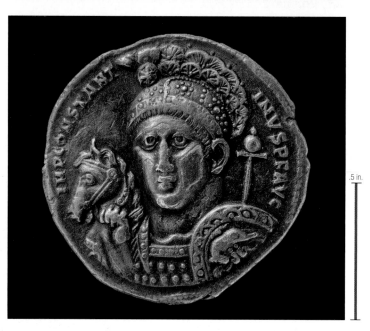

7-79 Two coins with portraits of Constantine. *Top*: nummus, 307 CE. Billon, diameter 1″. American Numismatic Society, New York. *Bottom*: medallion, ca. 315 CE. Silver, diameter 1″. Staatliche Münzsammlung, Munich.

These two coins underscore that portraits of Roman emperors were rarely true likenesses. On the earlier coin, Constantine appears as a bearded tetrarch. On the later coin, he appears eternally youthful.

both the essential character of Roman imperial portraiture and the special nature of the works he commissioned. Two are illustrated here. The first (FIG. 7-79, *top*) dates shortly after the death of Constantine's father, when Constantine was in his early 20s and his position was still insecure. Here, in his official portrait, he appears considerably older, because he adopted the imagery of the tetrarchs. Indeed, were it not for the accompanying label identifying this Caesar as Constantine, it would be impossible to know whom the coin engraver portrayed. Eight years later (FIG. 7-79, *bottom*)—after the defeat of Maxentius and the Edict of Milan—Constantine, now the unchallenged Augustus of the West, is clean-shaven and looks his real age, having rejected the mature tetrarchic look in favor of youth. These two coins should dispel any uncertainty about the often fictive nature of imperial portraiture and the ability of Roman emperors to choose any official image that suited their needs. In Roman art, "portrait" is often not synonymous with "likeness."

The later coin is also an eloquent testimony to the dual nature of Constantinian rule. The emperor appears in his important role as imperator, dressed in armor, wearing an ornate helmet, and carrying a shield bearing the enduring emblem of the Roman state—the she-wolf nursing Romulus and Remus (compare FIG. 6-11 and Roma's shield in FIG. 7-56). Yet he does not carry the traditional eagle-topped scepter of the Roman emperor. Rather, he holds a cross crowned by an orb. At the crest of his helmet, at the front, just below the grand plume, is a disk containing the *Christogram*, the monogram made up of *chi* (X), *rho* (P), and *iota* (I), the initial letters of Christ's name in Greek (compare the shield held by a soldier in FIG. 9-13). The artist portrayed Constantine as both Roman emperor and soldier in the army of the Lord. The coin, like Constantinian art in general, belongs to both the ancient and the medieval worlds.

The Roman Empire

Monarchy and Republic 753–27 BCE

- According to legend, Romulus founded Rome on April 21, 753 BCE. In the sixth century BCE, Etruscan kings ruled the city, and Roman art was Etruscan in character.

- In the centuries following the establishment of the Republic in 509 BCE, Rome conquered its neighbors in Italy and then moved into Greece, gaining exposure to Greek art and architecture.

- Republican temples combined Etruscan plans with the Greek orders, and houses had peristyles with Greek columns. The Romans, however, pioneered the use of concrete as a building material.

- The First Style of mural painting derived from Greece and imitates marble revetment, but the illusionism of the Second Style is distinctly Roman.

- Republican portraits usually depicted elderly patricians. The superrealistic likenesses celebrated traditional Roman values.

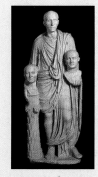

Man with ancestor busts, late first century BCE

Early Empire 27 BCE–96 CE

- Augustus (r. 27 BCE–14 CE), the first Roman emperor, defeated Mark Antony and Cleopatra at Actium in 31 BCE and established the Pax Augusta, the beginning of the Pax Romana.

- Augustan art revived the Classical style with frequent references to Periclean Athens. Augustus's ambitious building program made lavish use of marble, and his portraits always represented him as an idealized youth.

- Under the Julio-Claudians (r. 14–68 CE), builders began to realize the full potential of concrete in buildings such as the Golden House of Nero.

- The Flavian emperors (r. 69–96 CE) built the Colosseum, the largest amphitheater in the world, and other grandiose buildings in Rome. The Arch of Titus celebrated the Flavian victory in Judaea and Titus's apotheosis.

- The eruption of Mount Vesuvius in 79 CE buried Pompeii and Herculaneum. During the quarter century before the disaster, painters decorated the walls of houses in the Third and Fourth Styles.

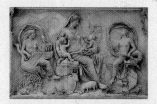

Ara Pacis Augustae, Rome, 13–9 BCE

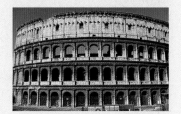

Colosseum, Rome, ca. 70–80 CE

High Empire 96–192 CE

- The Roman Empire reached its greatest extent under Trajan (r. 98–117 CE). The emperor's new forum and markets transformed the civic center of Rome. The Column of Trajan commemorated his two campaigns in Dacia in a 625-foot-long spiral frieze.

- Hadrian (r. 117–138 CE), emulating Greek statesmen and philosophers, was the first emperor to wear a beard. His Pantheon is a triumph of concrete technology and boasts the ancient world's largest dome.

- Under the Antonines (r. 138–192 CE), the dominance of Classical art began to erode, and imperial artists introduced new compositional schemes in relief sculpture and a psychological element in portraiture.

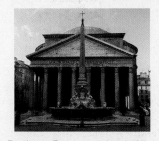

Pantheon, Rome, completed 125 CE

Late Empire 193–337 CE

- In the art of the Severans (r. 193–235 CE), the non-naturalistic Late Antique style took root. Artists represented the emperor as a central frontal figure disengaged from the action around him.

- During the chaotic era of the soldier emperors (r. 235–284 CE), artists portrayed the short-lived emperors in portraits displaying an unprecedented psychic intensity.

- Diocletian (r. 284–305 CE) reestablished order by sharing power. Statues of the tetrarchs portray the four coemperors as identical and equal rulers, not as individuals.

- Constantine (r. 306–337 CE) restored one-man rule, ended persecution of Christians, and transferred the capital of the Empire from Rome to Constantinople in 330. The abstract formality of Constantinian art paved the way for the iconic art of the Middle Ages.

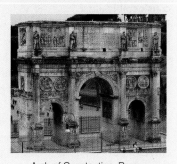

Arch of Constantine, Rome, 312–315 CE

▼**8-1a** The Dura synagogue murals surprised scholars because the Second Commandment prohibits Jews from worshiping images. This detail shows the prophet Samuel anointing the future King David.

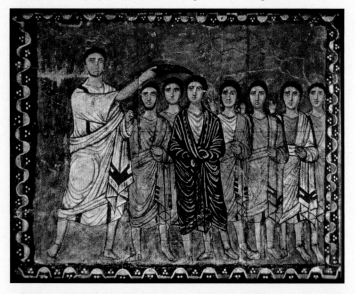

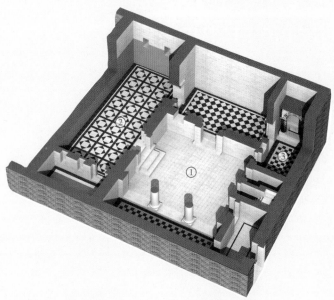

▲**8-1b** The Christians also had a place for community worship at Dura—a modest remodeled Roman house with a central courtyard, a meeting hall, and a baptistery. It could accommodate about 70 people.

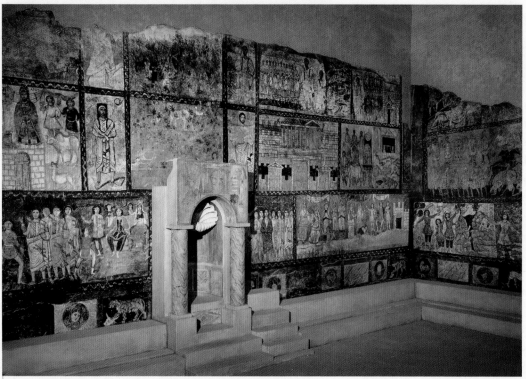

8-1 **Interior of the synagogue, Dura-Europos, Syria, with wall paintings of biblical themes, ca. 245–256. Tempera on plaster. Reconstruction in National Museum of Damascus, Damascus.**

▶**8-1c** The frescoes of the Dura baptistery are the earliest known Christian iconographical program. The representations include Jesus as the Good Shepherd and New Testament miracles and parables.

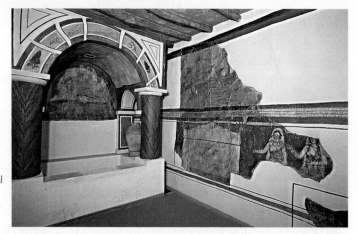

LATE ANTIQUITY /8

Polytheism and Monotheism at Dura-Europos

During the third and fourth centuries, a rapidly growing number of Romans rejected *polytheism* (belief in multiple gods) in favor of *monotheism* (the worship of a single all-powerful god). This period of religious upheaval—Late Antiquity—is one of the most significant in history, marking the transition from the ancient Roman Empire to medieval Christian Europe and Byzantium.

These religious crosscurrents may be seen in microcosm in a distant outpost of the Roman Empire on a promontory overlooking the Euphrates River in Syria (MAP 8-1). Called Europos by the Greeks and Dura by the Romans, the town probably was founded by one of the successors of Alexander the Great. By the end of the second century BCE, Dura-Europos was in the hands of the Parthians. Trajan captured the city in 115 CE, but Dura reverted to Parthian control shortly thereafter. In 165, under Marcus Aurelius, the Romans retook the city. Dura-Europos fell in 256 to Rome's new enemy in the East, the Sasanians (FIGS. 2-28A and 2-29). The Romans abandoned the town, leaving its buildings largely intact. Excavations of this "Pompeii of the desert" have revealed the remains of more than a dozen different religious shrines, including many for the polytheistic religions of the Mediterranean and Mesopotamia as well as one each for Judaism and Christianity.

The *synagogue* (Jewish house of worship) at Dura-Europos was a converted private house with a central courtyard and a main room (FIG. 8-1) with a niche for the *Torah* (the scroll containing the *Pentateuch,* the first five books of the Hebrew Bible) at the center of one long wall. The synagogue is remarkable not only for its very existence in a Roman garrison town but also for its extensive cycle of mural paintings. The Christian community at Dura-Europos also had a place to gather for worship and to conduct important ceremonies. Like the synagogue, the Christian meetinghouse was a remodeled private residence. It consisted of a central courtyard, a meeting hall, and a *baptistery* for initiating newborns and converts into the Christian religion. The baptistery, like the synagogue, had frescoes on its walls.

These modest shrines stand in striking contrast to the grand temples of the Roman gods. Without the approval of the state, both Jews and Christians remained small in number during the first three centuries CE. The Christians especially suffered from persecution by the Roman authorities, which ended only in 311, when Galerius issued an edict of toleration. A new chapter in the history of Christianity opened in 313, when Constantine, who embraced the Christians' God as the source of his power rather than a threat to it, issued the Edict of Milan. That proclamation established Christianity as a legal religion with equal or superior standing to the traditional Roman cults.

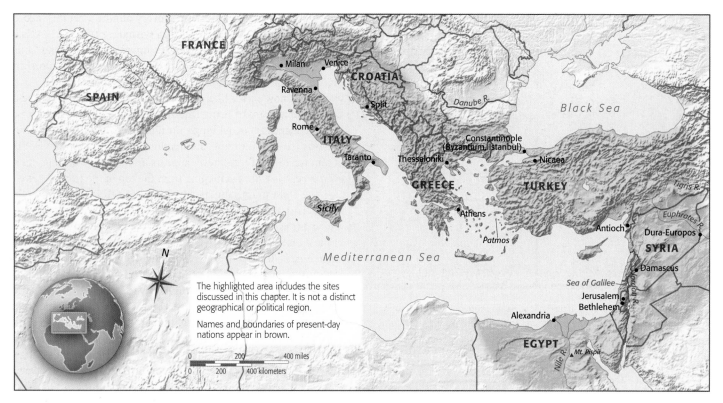

MAP 8-1 The Mediterranean world in Late Antiquity.

The highlighted area includes the sites discussed in this chapter. It is not a distinct geographical or political region.

Names and boundaries of present-day nations appear in brown.

THE LATE ANTIQUE WORLD

The Roman Empire was home to an extraordinarily diverse population. In Rome alone on any given day, someone walking through the city's various quarters would have encountered people of an astonishing range of social, ethnic, racial, linguistic, and religious backgrounds. This multicultural character of Roman society became only more pronounced as the Romans expanded their territories throughout Europe, Africa, and Mesopotamia (MAP 7-1). Chapter 7 focused on the public and private art and architecture of those Romans through the time of Constantine who worshiped the traditional gods and embraced the values of the classical world.* This chapter treats Late Antique Jewish and Christian artworks, created both before and after Constantine, as well as post-Constantinian examples of the persistence of classical subjects (and of the classical style) through the early sixth century.† It is important to note at the outset that the Judeo-Christian sculptures, paintings, mosaics, and other artworks discussed in this chapter are no less Roman than imperial portraits, statues of gods and heroes, or sarcophagi

with mythological scenes. Indeed, the artists may in some cases have been the same. But although they are Roman in style and technique, the Jewish and Christian sculptures, paintings, and buildings of Late Antiquity differ significantly in subject and often in function from contemporaneous Roman art and architecture. They are pivotal works in the history of art through the ages and constitute the bridge between ancient and medieval art and architecture.

FROM THE SOLDIER EMPERORS TO THE SACK OF ROME

Very little is known about the art of the first Christians. When art historians speak about "Early Christian art," they are referring to the earliest preserved artworks with Christian subjects, not to the art of

*In *Art through the Ages*, the adjective "Classical," with uppercase C, refers specifically to the Classical period of ancient Greece, 480–323 BCE. Lowercase "classical" refers to Greco-Roman antiquity in general—that is, the period treated in Chapters 5, 6, and 7.

†In this and succeeding chapters, all dates are CE unless otherwise indicated.

LATE ANTIQUITY

235–306	306–337	337–527
Soldier Emperors to Constantine	**Constantine**	**Sons of Constantine to Justinian**
■ Syrian artists paint biblical scenes on the walls of the Dura-Europos synagogue ■ The murals in the baptistery of Dura's Christian community house are the earliest preserved Christian pictorial program ■ Late Antique sarcophagi and catacomb paintings are also among the first efforts at the establishment of a standard iconography for Christian subjects	■ Constantine erects Christian shrines in Rome, Jerusalem, and Bethlehem, and at other sites throughout the Roman Empire ■ Roman basilicas instead of temples serve as models for the first churches in Rome, including Old Saint Peter's, which stood, like many other Early Christian shrines, above the grave of a Christian martyr ■ Constantine moves his capital to Constantinople and dedicates it as the New Rome on the site of Greek Byzantium	■ Construction of basilican churches as well as central-plan mausolea and martyria—for example, Santa Costanza in Rome—continues ■ The luxury arts of metalwork, ivory carving, and manuscript illumination flourish ■ Mosaics become a major medium for church decoration ■ A new aesthetic focused on the spiritual rather than the physical world emerges in Late Antique art ■ Theodosius establishes Christianity as the state religion, and Honorius moves the capital of the Western Roman Empire to Ravenna

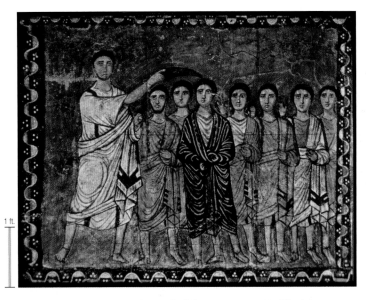

8-2 **Samuel anoints David, detail of the main interior wall of the synagogue, Dura-Europos, Syria, ca. 245–256. Tempera on plaster, 4′ 7″ high.**

The figures in this scene from the book of Samuel lack volume, stand in frontal rows, and exhibit stylized gestures—features characteristic of Late Antique art, regardless of subject matter.

Christians living in the time of Jesus. The same is true, of course, for Jewish art of the time of Abraham. Most of the oldest extant examples of Jewish and Christian art date to the period from the soldier emperors of the mid-third century to the sack of Rome in 410.

Dura-Europos

Among the earliest preserved artworks depicting Jewish and Christian subjects, the most important adorned the walls of the synagogue and baptistery of Dura-Europos (see "Polytheism and Monotheism at Dura-Europos," page 237).

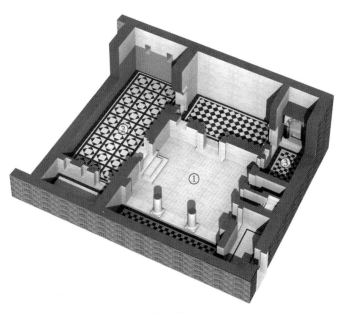

8-3 **Restored cutaway view of the Christian community house (looking southwest), Dura-Europos, Syria, ca. 240–256 (John Burge). (1) former courtyard of private house, (2) meeting hall, (3) baptistery.**

The Christian community at Dura-Europos met in a remodeled private home that could accommodate only about 70 people. The converted house had a central courtyard, a meeting hall, and a baptistery (FIG. 8-4).

Synagogue Paintings. The discovery almost a century ago of the elaborate mural cycle in the Dura synagogue (FIG. 8-1) initially surprised scholars because they had assumed that the Second Commandment (Exodus 20:4–6), which prohibits Jews from worshiping images, precluded the display of figural scenes in houses of worship. It now seems likely that narrative scenes such as those at Dura were features of many Late Antique synagogues as well as of Hebrew manuscripts, although no illustrated Bible of this period survives (see "Manuscript Illumination," page 252). God (YHWH, or Yahweh in the Torah) never appears in the Dura paintings, however, except as a hand emerging from the top of the framed panels.

The Dura murals are mostly devoid of action, even when the subject is a narrative theme. The artists told the stories through stylized gestures, and the figures, which have expressionless features, in most cases lack both volume and shadow. The painting illustrating the episode in the Book of Samuel in which Samuel anoints David (FIG. 8-2) exemplifies this Late Antique style, also seen in the friezes of the Arch of Septimius Severus (FIG. 7-64) at Lepcis Magna and the Arch of Constantine (FIG. 7-77) in Rome. The scene is on the main wall just to the right of the Torah niche. The prophet anoints the future king of Israel, as David's six older brothers look on. The painter drew attention to Samuel by depicting him larger than all the rest, a familiar convention in Late Antique art. David and his brothers are frontal figures looking out at the viewer. They seem almost weightless. Some bodies do not have legs to support them. The painter distinguished David from his brothers by the purple toga he wears. Purple was the color associated with the Roman emperor, and the Dura artist borrowed the imperial toga from Roman state art to signify David's royalty.

Christian Community House. The place where Christians gathered at Dura was also a remodeled home (FIG. 8-3). Its meeting hall (no. 2)—created by breaking down the partition between two rooms on the south side of the courtyard (no. 1)—could accommodate no more than about 70 people at a time. It had a raised platform at one end where the leader of the congregation sat or stood. The baptistery (no. 3), a small room 22 feet long and 10 feet wide with a font at the west end, was on the opposite side of the courtyard. This modest room is, nonetheless, of great importance because it was decorated with the oldest known Christian iconographical program (FIG. 8-4).

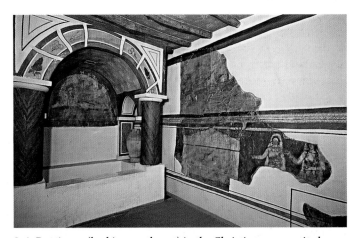

8-4 **Baptistery (looking northwest) in the Christian community house (FIG. 8-3), Dura-Europos, Syria, ca. 240–256. Reconstructed in the Yale University Art Gallery, New Haven.**

The frescoes of the Dura baptistery are the oldest surviving Christian iconographical program. The representations include Jesus as the Good Shepherd and New Testament miracles and parables.

The baptistery frescoes include, on the long wall, representations of two of Christ's miracles—the healing of the paralytic and Jesus (and Peter) walking on water (see "The Life of Jesus in Art," pages 244–245) and the parable of the wise and foolish virgins. Above the font is Christ as the Good Shepherd, a popular Early Christian motif (FIGS. 8-6, 8-7, and 8-24) that can be traced back to Archaic Greek art, but there the calf bearer (FIG. 5-8) was a bearded man offering his animal in sacrifice to Athena. In Early Christian art, Christ is the youthful and loyal protector of the Christian flock. He said to his disciples, "I am the good shepherd; the good shepherd gives his life for the sheep" (John 10:11). In the Christian motif, the sheep on Christ's shoulders is not a sacrificial offering. It is one of the lost sheep Christ has retrieved, and it symbolizes a sinner who has strayed and been rescued. Near the baptismal font is a painting of a woman at a well, recently identified as the Virgin Mary learning that she is "blessed among women" because she will give birth to the Son of God. The Dura fresco of Mary is the earliest known depiction of Jesus's mother in the history of art.

Rome

Most of the Jewish and Early Christian art in Rome dates to the third and fourth centuries and is found in the *catacombs*—vast subterranean networks of *galleries* (passageways) and chambers designed as cemeteries for burying Christians and, to a lesser extent, Jews (FIG. 8-4A) and others. The name derives from the Latin *ad catacumbas*, which

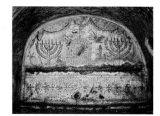

⟨↗⟩ **8-4A** Villa Torlonia Catacomb, Rome, third century.

A SECOND OPINION

The Via Latina Catacomb

Discovered in 1955, the catacomb in the Via Dino Compagni on the ancient Via Latina outside the walls of Rome features an extensive series of high-quality mural paintings. Of unusually regular plan, the underground complex probably was the private burial place of a small number of families of considerable means. According to many scholars, some of these families must have been Christian, others possibly Jewish, and some traditional Roman, based on the subjects chosen for the murals, which range from Old Testament themes—for example, Moses and the Israelites crossing the Red Sea—to the miracles of Christ to Greco-Roman mythology.

In place of the long galleries of modest loculi that characterize most catacombs, the Via Latina Catacomb consists of a series of elaborate cubicula with groin vaults, columns, pediments, cornices, and niches carved out of the bedrock and then decorated with mural paintings. The frescos in cubiculum N (FIG. 8-5) celebrate the greatest Greco-Roman hero, Hercules (see "Herakles," page 126). The setting of the story in the main niche is Hades. (The three-headed guardian dog of the Underworld, Cerberus, establishes the location; compare FIG. 6-8.) The painter depicted Hercules rescuing Alcestis from the Underworld and presenting her to her husband, Admetus, seated at the right. The side walls of the niche illustrate two of the hero's seemingly impossible 12 labors: the multiheaded hydra of Lerna, and the golden apples of the Hesperides (compare FIG. 5-31), the last of his labors, after which the gods awarded Hercules immortality.

Does the presence of mythological scenes in the same burial complex as biblical themes featuring both Hebrew prophets and Jesus mean that the Via Latina Catacomb housed the remains of adherents of different faiths? Not necessarily. About the time that painters were decorating this catacomb (ca. 320–360), the Church officially incorporated the Hebrew Bible—called the Old Testament by Christians—into the full Bible as we know it today. The Jewish subjects were thus merged into a coherent Christian "story line" in which the events of the Old Testament were seen as predictive forerunners of those of the New Testament (see "Old Testament Subjects in Christian Art," page 242).

Traditional Greco-Roman mythological themes also took on new meaning for Christians. In the Via Latina Catacomb, the patrons

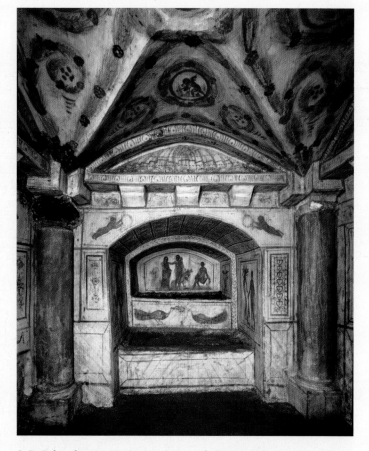

8-5 Cubiculum N, Via Latina Catacomb, Rome, Italy, ca. 320–360.

The commingling of mythological and Old and New Testament subjects in the mural decoration of this unusually elaborate catacomb typifies Late Antique art. Cubiculum N celebrates the hero Hercules.

undoubtedly chose the labors of Hercules to highlight the hero's role as conqueror of death and savior of humankind, establishing Hercules as an ancient counterpart to Christ. The commingling of religious iconography and artistic traditions in this catacomb typifies the world of Late Antiquity and of fourth-century Rome in particular.

means "in the hollows." The Christian and Jewish communities tunneled the catacombs out of the tufa bedrock, much as the Etruscans created the underground tomb chambers (FIGS. 6-7 and 6-8) in the Cerveteri necropolis. The catacombs are less elaborate than the Etruscan tombs, but much more extensive. The known catacombs in Rome (others exist elsewhere) ring the outskirts of the city. Their combined galleries run for 60 to 90 miles. From the second through the fourth centuries, these burial complexes were in constant use, accommodating as many as four million bodies.

In accordance with Roman custom, the dead had to be buried outside a city's walls on private property. Families often pooled funds in a burial association, or *confraternity*. Each of the now-labyrinthine catacombs was initially of modest extent. First, the builders dug a gallery 3 to 4 feet wide around the perimeter of the burial ground at a convenient level below the surface. In the walls of these galleries, they cut *loculi* (stacked openings, like shelves, to receive the bodies of the dead). Often, small rooms carved out of the rock, called *cubicula* (as in Roman houses of the living), served as mortuary chapels. Once the original perimeter galleries were full of loculi and cubicula, the excavators cut other galleries at right angles to them. This process continued as long as lateral space permitted, at which point the confraternities opened lower levels connected by staircases to those above. Some Roman catacomb systems extend as deep as five levels. When adjacent burial areas belonged to members of the same confraternity, or by gift or purchase fell into the same hands, the owners opened passageways between the respective cemeteries. The galleries thus spread laterally, and gradually acquired a vast extent.

After Christianity received official approval under Constantine, churches rose on the land above Rome's Christian catacombs so that the pious could worship openly at the burial sites of some of the earliest Christian *martyrs* (men and women who chose to die rather than deny their religious beliefs), whom the Church had declared *saints* (see "Early Christian Saints and Their Attributes," pages 246–247).

Via Latina Catacomb. As already noted, Late Antique Jewish and Christian works of art do not differ from contemporaneous Roman artworks in style or technique, only in subject. Some catacomb paintings, including many of those in a fourth-century catacomb on the Via Latina in Rome, even depict traditional Greco-Roman myths (see "The Via Latina Catacomb," page 240).

Peter and Marcellinus. It is not surprising, therefore, that the painted ceiling (FIG. 8-6) of a cubiculum in the Catacomb of Saints Peter and Marcellinus in Rome is similar in format to the painted vaults (FIG. 7-54A) of some third-century apartment houses at Ostia that have a circular frame with a central medallion and *lunettes* (semicircular frames) around the circumference. In the corners of the catacomb fresco are the heads of the personified Four Seasons, another borrowing from the repertoire of classical art.

The lunettes in the Peter and Marcellinus cubiculum contain the key episodes from the biblical story of Jonah. Sailors throw him from his ship on the left. He emerges on the right from the "whale." (The Greek word is *ketos* ("sea dragon"), and that is how the artist represented the monstrous marine creature that swallowed Jonah; compare the sea dragon on the Ara Pacis—FIG. 7-30, *right*.) At the bottom, safe on land, Jonah contemplates the miracle of his salvation and the mercy of God. His figure is based on representations, common on Roman sarcophagi, of the Greek hero Endymion, who was beloved by Selene, the moon goddess, who asked Zeus to grant Endymion eternal youth. Jonah was a popular figure in Early Christian painting and sculpture, especially in funerary contexts. The Christians honored him as a *prefiguration* (prophetic forerunner) of Christ, who rose from death as Jonah had been delivered from the belly of the ketos, also after three days. Old Testament miracles prefiguring Christ's resurrection abound in the catacombs and in Early Christian art in general (see "Old Testament Subjects in Christian Art," page 242).

A man, a woman, and at least one child occupy the compartments between the Jonah lunettes. They are *orants* (praying figures),

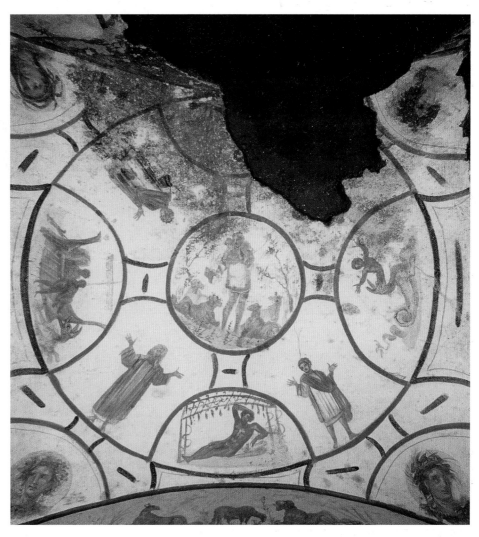

8-6 The Good Shepherd, the story of Jonah, orants, and Seasons, frescoed ceiling of a cubiculum in the Catacomb of Saints Peter and Marcellinus, Rome, Italy, early fourth century.

Christian catacomb paintings often mixed Old and New Testament themes. Jonah was a popular subject because he emerged safely from a sea monster after three days, prefiguring Christ's resurrection.

Old Testament Subjects in Christian Art

When the Christians codified the Bible in its familiar form in the fourth century, they incorporated the Hebrew Torah and other writings, and designated the Jewish books as the "Old Testament" in contrast to the Christian books of the "New Testament." From the beginning, the Old Testament played an important role in Christian life and Christian art, in part because Jesus was a Jew and so many of the first Christians were converted Jews, but also because Christians came to view many of the persons and events of the Old Testament as *prefigurations* of New Testament persons and events.

Christ himself established the pattern for this kind of biblical interpretation, called *typology,* when he compared Jonah's spending three days in the belly of the sea dragon (usually translated as "whale" in English) to the comparable time that he would be entombed in the earth before his resurrection (Matt. 12:40). Saint Augustine (354–430) confirmed the validity of this typological approach to the Old Testament when he stated that "the New Testament is hidden in the Old; the Old is clarified by the New."* Thus the events recounted in the Hebrew Bible figured prominently in Early Christian art in all media. Biblical tales of Jewish faith and salvation were especially common in funerary contexts, but appeared also in churches and on household objects.

The following are three of the most popular Old Testament stories depicted in Early Christian art:

- **Adam and Eve** (FIG. 8-8, *bottom, second from left*) Eve, the first woman, tempted by a serpent, ate the forbidden fruit of the tree of knowledge, and fed some to Adam, the first man. As punishment, God expelled Adam and Eve from Paradise. This "Original Sin" ultimately led to Christ's sacrifice on the cross so that all humankind could be saved. Christian theologians often consider Christ the new Adam and his mother, Mary, the new Eve.

- **Sacrifice of Isaac** (FIG. 8-8, *top left*) God instructed Abraham, the father of the Hebrew nation, to sacrifice Isaac, his only son with his wife, Sarah, as proof of his faith. (The mother of Abraham's first son, Ishmael, was Sarah's handmaiden.) When it became clear that Abraham would obey, the Lord sent an angel to restrain him and provided a ram for sacrifice in Isaac's place. Christians view this episode as a prefiguration of the sacrifice of God's only son, Jesus.

- **Jonah** (FIGS. 8-6, *lunettes,* and 8-7, *left*) The Old Testament prophet Jonah had disobeyed God's command. In his wrath, the Lord caused a storm while Jonah was at sea. Jonah asked the sailors to throw him overboard, and the storm subsided. A sea dragon then swallowed Jonah, but God answered his prayers, and the monster spat Jonah out after three days, foretelling Christ's resurrection.

*Augustine, *City of God,* 16.26.

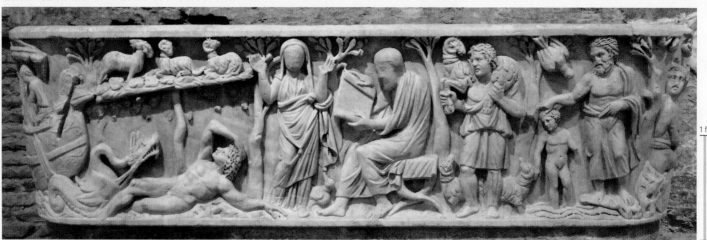

8-7 Sarcophagus with philosopher, orant, and Old and New Testament scenes, ca. 270. Marble, 1′ 11¼″ × 7′ 2″. Santa Maria Antiqua, Rome.

This Early Christian sarcophagus depicts the salvation of Jonah, Christ as Good Shepherd, and the baptism of Christ. The two figures with unfinished heads were to become portraits of the deceased.

raising their arms in the ancient attitude of prayer. Together they make up a cross-section of the Christian family seeking a heavenly afterlife, although they may be generic portraits of the owners of the cubiculum. The central medallion shows Christ as the Good Shepherd, whose powers of salvation the painter underscored by placing the four episodes of the Jonah story around him.

Santa Maria Antiqua Sarcophagus. Most Christians rejected cremation because they believed in the resurrection of the body, and the wealthiest Christian faithful favored impressive marble sarcophagi, as did well-to-do non-Christian Romans. Many of these coffins have survived in the catacombs and elsewhere. As one might expect, the most common themes painted on the walls and vaults of the Roman subterranean cemeteries were also the subjects that appeared most frequently on Early Christian sarcophagi. Often, the decoration of the marble coffins was a collection of significant Old and New Testament themes, just as on the painted ceiling (FIG. 8-6) in the Catacomb of Saints Peter and Marcellinus.

On the front of a sarcophagus (FIG. 8-7) in Santa Maria Antiqua in Rome, the story of Jonah occupies the left third. At the center are an orant and a seated philosopher, the latter a motif, like the reclining Jonah motif, borrowed directly from Roman sarcophagi (FIG. 7-70) and popular also in Roman painting (FIG. 7-25) and statuary. The heads of both the praying woman and the seated man reading a scroll are unfinished. Roman workshops often produced sarcophagi before knowing who would purchase them. The sculptors added the portraits at the time of burial, if they added them at all. This practice underscores the universal appeal of the themes chosen.

At the right are two different, yet linked, representations of Jesus—as the Good Shepherd and as a child receiving baptism in the Jordan River in the presence of the dove of the Holy Spirit, though he really was baptized as an adult (see "The Life of Jesus in Art," pages 244–245). In the early centuries of Christianity, baptism was usually delayed almost to the moment of death because it cleansed the Christian of all sin. One of those who was baptized on his deathbed was Emperor Constantine. On this sarcophagus, the newly baptized child Jesus turns his head away from John and toward the Good Shepherd and one of the sheep at his feet—

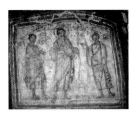

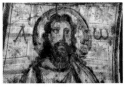

⏽ 8-7A Catacomb of Commodilla, Rome, ca. 370–385.

perhaps the sculptor's way of suggesting Jesus's future ministry.

Early Christian artists almost invariably represented Christ either as the Good Shepherd or as a teacher. Only after Christianity became the Roman Empire's official religion in 380 did Christ commonly take on in art such imperial attributes as the halo, the purple robe, and the throne, which denoted rulership. Eventually, artists depicted Christ with the beard of a mature adult—as in the late-fourth-century Catacomb of Commodilla (FIG. 8-7A) in Rome. The bearded Christ soon became the standard, if not the exclusive, "portrait" of the Savior, supplanting the youthful imagery of most Early Christian portrayals.

Junius Bassus Sarcophagus. We do not know who purchased the Santa Maria Antiqua sarcophagus, but the blank portrait heads prove that it was a stock piece. Other patrons, however, had the wealth and interest to commission costly custom marble coffins. One of them was Junius Bassus, the mid-fourth-century city prefect of Rome who converted to Christianity and, according to the inscription on his sarcophagus (FIG. 8-8), was baptized just before his death in 359. He is a prominent example of a mid-fourth-century patrician who grew up immersed in traditional Roman culture and initially paid homage to the old Roman gods. It is not surprising, then, that he chose to be buried in a richly decorated sarcophagus that included images of the major divinity that he revered at the time of his death—Jesus.

The reliefs on Junius Bassus's sarcophagus are only on the front and two short sides in the western Roman manner (FIG. 7-59). The front has 10 figural scenes in two registers of five compartments, each framed by columns, as on Asiatic sarcophagi (FIG. 7-60). However, the deceased does not appear in any of those compartments. Instead, Old and New Testament stories fill the niches. Jesus has pride of place and appears in the central compartment of each register: enthroned between Saints Peter and Paul (see "Early Christian Saints," pages 246–247), and entering Jerusalem on a donkey. Both compositions owe a great deal to official Roman art. In the upper zone, Christ, like an enthroned Roman emperor, sits above the sky god, who holds a billowing mantle over his head, indicating that Christ is ruler of the cosmos. The scene below derives in part from representations of Roman emperors entering conquered cities on horseback, but the sculptor here emphasized humility, not majesty. Jesus's steed and the absence of imperial attributes stand in stark and doubtless intentional contrast to the models the sculptor must have used as compositional sources.

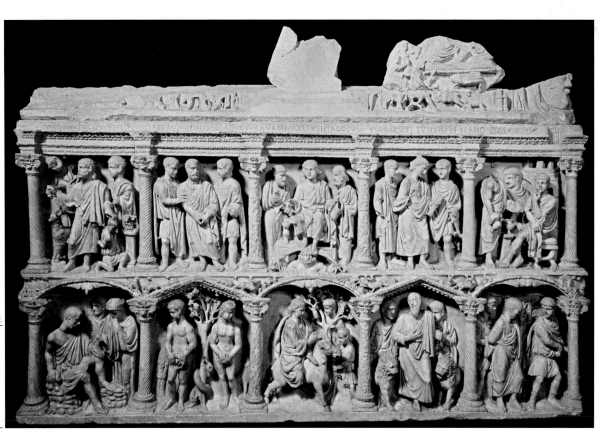

8-8 Sarcophagus of Junius Bassus, from Rome, Italy, ca. 359. Marble, $3' \, 10\frac{1}{2}'' \times 8'$. Museo Storico del Tesoro della Basilica di San Pietro, Rome.

Episodes from the Old Testament appear beside scenes from the life of Jesus on this lavishly decorated sarcophagus. Jesus is in the center of the upper register, flanked by the saints Peter and Paul.

1 ft.

The Life of Jesus in Art

Christians believe that Jesus of Nazareth is the son of God, the prophesied *Messiah* (Savior, *Christ*) of the Jews. His life—his miraculous birth from the womb of a virgin mother, his preaching and miracle working, his execution by the Romans and subsequent ascent to Heaven—has been the subject of countless artworks from Late Antiquity through the present day. The primary literary sources for these representations are the Gospels of the New Testament attributed to the four evangelists (Saints Matthew, Mark, Luke, and John; see "The Four Evangelists," page 331); later apocryphal works; and medieval theologians' commentaries on these texts.

The life of Jesus dominated the subject matter of Christian art to a far greater extent than Greco-Roman religion and mythology ever did classical art. Whereas images of athletes, portraits of statesmen and philosophers, narratives of war and peace, genre scenes, and other secular subjects were staples of the classical tradition, Christian iconography held a near monopoly in the art of the Western world during the Middle Ages.

Although during certain periods artists rarely, if ever, depicted many of the events of Jesus's life, the cycle as a whole has been one of the most frequent subjects of Western art, even after the widespread revival of classical and secular themes during the Renaissance. Thus it is useful to summarize at the outset the entire cycle of events as they usually appear in artworks.

INCARNATION AND CHILDHOOD

The first "cycle" of the life of Jesus consists of the events of his conception (incarnation), birth, infancy, and childhood.

- *Annunciation to Mary* (FIGS. 9-34 and 21-21) The archangel Gabriel announces to the Virgin Mary that she will miraculously conceive God's son, Jesus. Artists sometimes indicated God's presence at the Incarnation by a dove, the symbol of the Holy Spirit, the third "person" of the *Trinity* with God the Father and Jesus.

- *Visitation* (FIGS. 13-25 and 20-4, *left*) The pregnant Mary visits Elizabeth, her older cousin, who is pregnant with the future John the Baptist. Elizabeth is the first to recognize that the baby in Mary's womb is the son of God, and they rejoice.

- *Nativity* (FIG. 14-3), *Annunciation to the Shepherds* (FIG. 11-32), and *Adoration of the Shepherds* (FIG. 20-16) Jesus is born at night in Bethlehem and placed in a manger. Mary and her husband, Joseph, marvel at the newborn in a stable or, in Byzantine art, in a cave. An angel announces the birth of the Savior to shepherds in the field, who rush to adore the infant Jesus.

- *Adoration of the Magi* (FIG. 21-17) A bright star alerts three wise men (*magi*) in the East that the king of the Jews has been born. They travel 12 days to find the holy family and present precious gifts to the infant Jesus.

- *Presentation in the Temple* (FIGS. 10-36 and 20-4, *right*) In accordance with Jewish tradition, Mary and Joseph bring their firstborn son to the temple in Jerusalem, where the aged Simeon, who God said would not die until he had seen the Messiah, recognizes Jesus as the prophesied savior of humankind.

- *Massacre of the Innocents* and *Flight into Egypt* (FIG. 24-15) King Herod, fearful that a rival king has been born, orders the massacre of all infants in Bethlehem, but an angel warns the holy family, and they escape to Egypt.

- *Dispute in the Temple* Joseph and Mary travel to Jerusalem for the feast of *Passover* (the celebration of the release of the Jews from bondage to the pharaohs of Egypt). Jesus, only 12 years old at the time, engages in learned debate with astonished Jewish scholars in the temple, foretelling his ministry.

PUBLIC MINISTRY

The public-ministry cycle comprises the teachings of Jesus and the miracles he performed.

- *Baptism* (FIGS. 8-24A and 12-27) Jesus's public ministry begins with his baptism by John the Baptist in the Jordan River, where the dove of the Holy Spirit appears and God's voice is heard proclaiming that Jesus is his son.

- *Apostles* and *Miracles* In the course of his teaching and travels, Jesus enlists 12 disciples (see "Early Christian Saints," pages 246–247) to serve as his messengers (apostles), including the fisherman Peter and the tax collector Matthew (FIG. 24-17). Jesus performs many miracles, revealing his divine nature. These include acts of healing and raising the dead, turning water into wine, walking on water and calming storms, and creating wondrous quantities of food. In the miracle of the loaves and fishes (FIG. 8-26), for example, Jesus transforms a few loaves of bread and a handful of fish into enough food to feed several thousand people.

- *Delivery of the Keys to Peter* (FIG. 21-41) Jesus chooses the apostle Peter (whose name means "rock") as the leader of the Christian community. Jesus declares that Peter is the rock on which his church will be built, and symbolically delivers to Peter the keys to the kingdom of Heaven.

- *Transfiguration* (FIG. 9-16) Jesus scales a high mountain and, in the presence of Peter and two other disciples, James and John the Evangelist, transforms into radiant light. God, speaking from a cloud, again discloses that Jesus is his son.

- *Cleansing of the Temple* Jesus returns to Jerusalem, where he finds money changers and merchants conducting business in the temple. He rebukes them and drives them out of the sacred precinct.

PASSION

The passion (from Latin *passio,* "suffering") cycle includes the episodes leading to Jesus's death, resurrection, and ascent to Heaven.

- **Entry into Jerusalem** (FIGS. 8-8 and 14-11A) On the Sunday before his crucifixion (Palm Sunday), Jesus rides into Jerusalem on a donkey, accompanied by disciples. Crowds of people enthusiastically greet Jesus and place palm fronds in his path.

- **Last Supper** (FIG. 22-4) and **Washing of the Disciples' Feet** (FIG. 11-30A) In Jerusalem, Jesus celebrates Passover with his disciples. During this final meal with his followers, Jesus foretells his imminent betrayal, arrest, and death, and he invites the disciples to remember him when they eat unleavened bread (symbol of his body) and drink wine (his blood). This ritual became the central feature of the celebration of *Mass* (*Eucharist*) in the Catholic Church. Jesus also sets an example of humility for his apostles by washing their feet.

- **Agony in the Garden** Jesus goes to the Mount of Olives in the Garden of Gethsemane, where he struggles to overcome his human fear of death by praying for divine strength. The apostles who accompanied him there fall asleep despite his request that they stay awake with him while he prays.

- **Betrayal** and **Arrest** (FIG. 14-12) The disciple Judas Iscariot agrees to betray Jesus to the Jewish authorities in return for 30 pieces of silver. Judas leads the soldiers to Jesus and identifies the "king of the Jews" by kissing him, whereupon the soldiers arrest Jesus. Later, a remorseful Judas hangs himself from a tree (FIG. 8-16).

- **Trials of Jesus** (FIG. 9-17B) and **Denial of Peter** The soldiers bring Jesus before Caiaphas, the Jewish high priest, who interrogates Jesus about his claim to be the Messiah. Meanwhile, the disciple Peter thrice denies knowing Jesus, as Jesus predicted he would. Jesus is then brought before the Roman governor of Judaea, Pontius Pilate, on the charge of treason because he had proclaimed himself as the Jews' king. Pilate asks the crowd to choose to free either Jesus or Barabbas, a murderer. The people select Barabbas, and the judge condemns Jesus to death. Pilate then washes his hands, symbolically relieving himself of responsibility for the mob's decision.

- **Flagellation** (FIG. 21-43) and **Mocking** The Roman soldiers who hold Jesus captive whip (*flagellate*) him and mock him by dressing him as king of the Jews and placing a crown of thorns on his head.

- **Carrying of the Cross, Raising of the Cross** (FIG. 25-2), and **Crucifixion** (FIGS. 9-24 and 23-2) The Romans force Jesus to carry the cross on which he will be crucified from Jerusalem to Mount Calvary (Golgotha, the "Place of the Skull," Adam's burial place). Jesus falls three times, and his robe is stripped from him along the way. Soldiers erect the cross—often labeled in art *INRI* (the initial letters of "Jesus of Nazareth, King of the Jews" in Latin)—and nail his hands and feet to it. Jesus's mother, John the Evangelist, and Mary Magdalene mourn at the foot of the cross, while the Roman soldiers torment Jesus. One of them (the centurion Longinus) stabs the Savior in the side with a spear. After suffering great pain, Jesus dies. The Crucifixion occurred on a Friday, and Christians celebrate the day each year as Good Friday.

- **Deposition** (FIG. 20-13), **Lamentation** (FIGS. 9-29 and 14-10), and **Entombment** (FIGS. 12-30C and 24-17B) Joseph of Arimathea and Nicodemus remove Jesus's body from the cross (the Deposition). Sometimes those present at the Crucifixion look on. They then take Jesus to the tomb that Joseph had purchased for himself, and Joseph, Nicodemus, the Virgin Mary, John the Evangelist, and Mary Magdalene mourn over the dead Jesus (the Lamentation). (When in art the isolated figure of the Virgin Mary cradles her dead son in her lap, it is called a *Pietà* (FIGS. 13-52 and 22-12)—Italian for "pity.") In portrayals of the entombment, his followers lower Jesus into a sarcophagus in the tomb.

- **Descent into Limbo** (FIG. 9-32) During the three days he spends in the tomb, Jesus descends into Hell, or Limbo, and triumphantly frees the souls of the righteous, including Adam, Eve, Moses, David, Solomon, and John the Baptist. In Byzantine art, the label *Anastasis* (Greek, "resurrection") often identifies this episode, although the event precedes Jesus's own emergence from the tomb and reappearance on earth.

- **Resurrection** (FIG. 21-25) and **Three Marys at the Tomb** (FIG. 9-18A) On the third day (Easter Sunday), Jesus rises from the dead and leaves the tomb while the Roman guards sleep. The Virgin Mary, Mary Magdalene, and Mary, the mother of James, visit the tomb but find it empty. An angel informs them of Jesus's resurrection.

- **Noli Me Tangere** (FIG. 9-18A), **Supper at Emmaus,** and **Doubting of Thomas** (FIG. 12-9B) During the 40 days between Jesus's resurrection and his ascent to Heaven, he appears on several occasions to his followers. Jesus warns Mary Magdalene, weeping at his tomb, with the words "Don't touch me" (*Noli me tangere* in Latin), but he tells her to inform the apostles of his return. At Emmaus, he eats supper with two of his astonished followers. Later, Christ invites Thomas, who cannot believe that Jesus has risen, to touch the wound in his side that he received at his crucifixion.

- **Ascension** (FIG. 9-18) On the 40th day, on the Mount of Olives, with his mother and apostles as witnesses, Jesus gloriously ascends to Heaven in a cloud.

Early Christian Saints and Their Attributes

A distinctive feature of Christianity is the veneration accorded to *saints* (from the Latin word for "holy"—*sanctus*), a practice dating to the second century. Most of the earliest Christian saints were *martyrs* who died for their faith at the hands of the Roman authorities, often after suffering cruel torture. During the first millennium of the Church, the designation of sainthood, or *canonization,* was an informal process, but in the late 12th century, Pope Alexander III (r. 1159–1181) ruled that only the papacy could designate individuals as saints, and only after a lengthy and detailed review of the life, character, deeds, and miracles of the person under consideration. A preliminary stage is *beatification,* the official determination that a deceased individual is a *beatus* (blessed person).

In Christian art, saints almost always have *haloes* around their heads. To distinguish individual saints, artists commonly depicted them with one or more characteristic *attributes*—often the means of their martyrdom, although saintly attributes take a wide variety of forms.

The most important saints during the centuries before Constantine's Edict of Milan were contemporaries of Jesus, but several later martyrs also received widespread veneration and continue to do so today. They may be classified in several categories.

FAMILY OF JESUS AND MARY

- *Anne* The parents of the Virgin Mary were Anne and Joachim, a couple childless after 20 years of marriage. Angels separately announced to them that Anne would give birth, and the couple celebrated the news by embracing at Jerusalem's Golden Gate. That meeting became a popular subject for artists, as did the depiction of the birth of the Virgin (FIGS. 14-15 and 21-26) as a parallel to the Nativity of Jesus (see "The Life of Jesus," pages 244–245).

- *Elizabeth* A cousin of Anne, Elizabeth was also an elderly barren woman. The angel Gabriel announced to her husband, the priest Zacharias, that she would give birth to a son named John. Six months later, Gabriel informed Mary that she would become the mother of the son of God (the Annunciation), whereupon Mary visited Elizabeth, and in Elizabeth's womb the future John the Baptist leaped for joy at the approach of the Mother of God. In depictions of the Visitation (FIG. 13-25), Elizabeth is a veiled matron. Sometimes, artists depicted the infants Jesus and John the Baptist and the two mothers together (FIG. 22-3).

- *Joseph* Although a modest craftsman, Joseph was a descendant of King David. An elderly widower, he was chosen among several suitors to wed the much younger Mary when his staff miraculously blossomed (FIG. 22-7). He married Mary even after learning of her pregnancy because an angel informed him of her chastity and that the child in her womb was the son of God. Joseph probably died before Christ's passion. He appears in artworks as a carpenter (FIG. 20-8) and as foster father and protector of Jesus in scenes of Jesus's infancy, such as the Nativity (FIGS. 14-3 and 14-4) and the flight into Egypt (FIG. 24-15). His principal attributes are the flowering staff and carpentry tools.

- *John the Baptist* Elizabeth's son, John, became a preacher in the wilderness with many followers. He promoted baptism as a means of cleansing Jews of their sins in preparation for the coming of the Messiah (Savior) prophesied in the Hebrew scriptures. When he baptized Jesus in the Jordan River, the dove of the Holy Spirit descended to identify Jesus as the Lamb of God. Later, John denounced the marriage of Herod Antipas (r. 4 BCE–39 CE) to Herodias, his niece and brother's wife. John met his death when Herodias's daughter, Salome, demanded John's head on a platter (FIGS. 21-8 and 28-26) and Herod ordered his decapitation, making John the earliest Christian martyr. John most often appears in art as a bearded hermit baptizing a much younger Jesus (FIG. 8-7), even though John was only six months older. His attribute is a lamb.

APOSTLES

During the course of his ministry, Jesus called 12 men to be his *apostles* (from the Greek for "messenger") to spread the news of the coming of the son of God. The first two—Andrew and John the Evangelist—were followers of John the Baptist. Andrew introduced his brother Simon to Jesus, who renamed him Peter. The others were John's brother James, Philip, Bartholomew, Matthew, Thomas, James "the Lesser," Jude, Simon "the Zealot," and Judas Iscariot. All 12 apostles were present at the Last Supper (FIGS. 21-22, 22-4, and 22-50). After Judas's betrayal and suicide (FIG. 8-16), the remaining 11 witnessed the Ascension (FIG. 9-18) and then chose another follower of Jesus, Matthias, to replace Judas. On the day of Pentecost (FIG. 12-15), the Holy Spirit assigned the 12 apostles the mission of spreading the Gospel throughout the world. All but John the Evangelist eventually suffered martyrdom.

Four of the apostles figure prominently in the history of art:

- *Peter* The "prince of apostles," Peter was a fisherman whom Jesus made a "fisher of men." Jesus designated Peter as the rock on which he would found his Church and presented him with the keys to the kingdom of Heaven (FIG. 21-41). The keys are Peter's chief attribute (FIG. 23-6). He was the leader of the Christian community in Rome—its first bishop and the head of the long line of popes. Peter died in Rome around 64 under Nero—crucified upside down because Peter insisted that he was unworthy to die as Jesus did. Peter figures prominently in pictorial cycles of the ministry and passion of Jesus, including, for example, Masaccio's *Tribute Money* (FIG. 21-18), in which he retrieves a coin from a fish's mouth to pay the tax collector, and scenes of the betrayal of Jesus (for example, FIG. 14-10A), in which he cuts off the ear of the high priest's servant. He was one of three apostles present at the Transfiguration (FIG. 9-16).

- *John the Evangelist* Another fisherman, John was the youngest apostle and "the disciple whom Jesus loved." With Peter and James, John witnessed Jesus's transfiguration, and he was present at the miracle of the loaves and fishes (FIG. 8-26). John sat next to Jesus at the Last Supper (FIG. 22-4) and was the only apostle who did not desert Jesus at the Crucifixion (FIGS. 9-24 and 23-2). From the cross, Jesus entrusted Mary to John's care. He was also one of two apostles who became *evangelists*—those who recorded Jesus's life in the Gospels (see "The Four Evangelists," page 331). During his exile on the Greek island of Patmos (FIG. 25-32), John also wrote the Book of Revelation. His attribute is an eagle.

■ *Matthew* The second evangelist among the apostles, Matthew was a Jewish tax collector. Called Levi when Jesus summoned him in Capernaum to serve as his disciple (FIGS. 24-17 and 25-7), Matthew appears most frequently in art as a seated robed figure writing his Gospel (FIGS. 11-13 and 11-14). Different accounts report that he was either stabbed to death or beheaded while saying Mass. His attribute is a winged man.

■ *James* The brother of John the Evangelist and also a fisherman, James the Greater was the first apostle to be martyred—by beheading at the order of Herod Agrippa I (r. 41–44). With Peter and John, he was one of the inner circle of apostles and witnessed Jesus's transfiguration. According to tradition, before his martyrdom he preached the Gospel in Spain. His tomb is at Santiago de Compostela (FIG. 12-6B), which became the most important pilgrimage site in Europe after Rome (see "Pilgrimage Roads in France and Spain," page 350). James's attribute is a scallop shell, the emblem of pilgrims to his Spanish shrine.

OTHER EARLY SAINTS

Several other saints who died before Constantine ended the persecution of Christians have also frequently been the subjects of artworks:

■ *Paul* A Roman citizen by birth, Paul had been a Jew named Saul who fervently opposed Christian teaching until Christ spoke to him in a blinding burst of light on the road to Damascus (FIG. 24-17A). The priest Ananias restored Paul's sight and baptized him. Converted, Paul became the "Apostle to the Gentiles," preaching the Gospel to non-Jews as well as Jews. He traveled widely, establishing churches in all the communities he visited. His *Epistles* are the foundation of Christian theology. In Rome, Paul became a close associate of Peter and was beheaded under Nero. In Early Christian art, he holds a scroll and often appears with Peter flanking Christ (FIG. 8-8), although, unlike the original apostles, Paul never met Jesus. In later representations, he may hold the sword of his martyrdom (FIG. 23-6).

■ *Mark* The two evangelists who were not apostles were disciples of Paul. Mark (FIG. 21-5) accompanied Paul on his first missionary journey and was with him and Peter in Rome at the time of their executions. Mark later became the first bishop of Alexandria, where he was martyred under Nero or Vespasian by being dragged with a rope around his neck through the city's streets. His remains, which the Venetians acquired in 828, are in the Basilica of Saint Mark (FIG. 9-26). His attribute—a lion (see "The Four

Evangelists," page 331, and FIG. 12-16A)—is the emblem of Venice to this day.

■ *Luke* A close companion of Paul on several missionary journeys, Luke was a Gentile physician who, in addition to being a Gospel author, also painted a portrait of Mary and the infant Jesus (FIGS. 20-1 and 23-14A) and became the patron saint of artists as well as doctors. Tradition says that he never married and died peacefully at the age of 84. His attribute is an ox.

■ *Mary Magdalene* Born in Magdala on the Sea of Galilee, Mary Magdalene became one of Jesus's most devoted followers. Often identified with the sinner who washed Jesus's feet with her tears and dried them with her hair, Mary was one of the few disciples present at the Crucifixion (FIGS. 9-18A and 23-2). She was the first to arrive at Christ's empty tomb. The resurrected Savior instructed Mary to inform the others that he had risen, but warned her, "Do not touch me!" (FIG. 9-18A). Tradition records that the penitent Mary Magdalene lived to old age in the wilderness. The Magdalene's *relics* are in the church dedicated to her at Vézelay (FIG. 12-15) in France. Her major attribute is her long hair (FIG. 21-11A).

■ *Lawrence* Born in Spain, Lawrence became one of seven *deacons* (church officials charged with distributing alms to the poor) under Pope Sixtus II (r. 257–258). He died in 258 during the persecution under Valerian. Lawrence's attribute is a gridiron because tradition holds that the Romans roasted him on a grill three days after the pope's martyrdom. The Escorial palace complex (FIG. 23-25) near Madrid is dedicated to Saint Lawrence and has a gridiron plan.

■ *George* A Christian soldier in the Roman army, George saved a town and a princess by slaying a dragon after 15,000 of the townspeople converted to Christianity. He was beheaded in 303 under Diocletian after refusing to renounce his faith. In art, George wears military garb (FIG. 21-6) and is often portrayed on horseback fighting a dragon (FIG. 21-7). He was a very popular saint among late medieval Crusaders.

■ *Theodore* Another soldier-martyr (FIG. 13-19) under Diocletian, Theodore refused to worship the Roman gods, and set fire to a temple of Cybele, for which he stood trial and was convicted and burned to death in a furnace. His relics are in Chartres Cathedral (FIG. 13-12).

■ *Anthony Abbot* The founder of *monasticism,* Anthony was a pious Egyptian Christian who fled to the desert in 286 to escape persecution and became an ascetic hermit who attracted many followers and founded a *monastery* on Mount Pispir in 311. While Anthony was in the desert, he was tempted by a lewd woman, but he resisted (FIGS. 20-24 and 23-2). Horrible demons also tormented him. He died in 356, more than 100 years old. Artists portrayed Anthony as an elderly man with a long beard and a T-shaped staff because a T-cross was the symbol of Alexandrian Christians.

The Old Testament scenes include the salvation tale of Daniel, unscathed by flanking lions, saved by his faith (FIG. 8-8, lower row, to the right of the Entry into Jerusalem), and of special significance, the Genesis stories of Abraham and Isaac (top left) and Adam and Eve (lower row, second from left), which Christians believe foretell events in the life of their savior. Christians view Abraham's willingness to sacrifice Isaac as a parallel to God's sacrifice of his own son, Jesus. Adam and Eve's sin of eating the apple in the Garden of Eden ultimately necessitated that sacrifice for the salvation of humankind. Note how the Early Christian sculptor approached the representation of Adam and Eve. Unlike classical nudes, these figures are embarrassed by their nakedness—an essential element of the biblical account.

The Crucifixion, however, does not appear on Junius Bassus's sarcophagus and was rarely depicted in Early Christian art. (FIGS. 8-16 and 8-19B are exceptions in the fifth century.) Artists emphasized Christ's exemplary life as teacher and miracle worker, not his suffering and death as a condemned mortal criminal at the hands of the Romans. Nonetheless, this sculptor alluded to the Crucifixion in the scenes in the two compartments at the upper right of the sarcophagus. They depict Jesus being led before Pontius Pilate for judgment (see "The Life of Jesus in Art," pages 244–245), which resulted in the execution of Jesus, but he triumphantly overcame death. Junius Bassus hoped for a similar salvation.

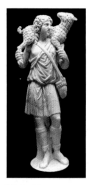

8-8A Christ as the Good Shepherd, ca. 300–350.

Freestanding Statuary. Apart from the reliefs on privately commissioned sarcophagi such as the Santa Maria Antiqua sarcophagus (FIG. 8-7) and that of the city prefect Junius Bassus (FIG. 8-8), large-scale sculpture became increasingly uncommon in the fourth century. Roman emperors and other officials continued to set up portraits, and sculptors still carved and cast statues of Greco-Roman gods and mythological figures, but the number of freestanding sculptures decreased sharply. Two exceptional Early Christian statuettes portraying Christ are today in the Vatican (FIG. 8-8A) and the Roman National Museum (FIG. 8-8B) and were probably commissioned by recent Roman converts who, unlike Jews and Christians, had no qualms about possessing "idols" portraying divinities.

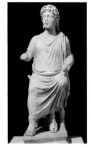

8-8B Christ seated, ca. 350–375.

The First Churches. Before Constantine, Christians conducted some ceremonies in the catacombs, but regular services took place in private community houses of the type found at Dura-Europos (FIG. 8-3). Once Christianity achieved imperial sponsorship in the early fourth century, an urgent need suddenly arose to construct churches (see "What Should a Church Look Like?" page 249). Constantine claimed that the Christians' God had guided him to victory over Maxentius, and he thereafter protected and advanced Christianity throughout his empire. As Roman emperor, he was of course obliged to safeguard the traditional culture, and he was (for his time) a builder on a grand scale in the heart of the city (FIGS. 7-74 and 7-76). But Constantine, eager to provide buildings to house the Christian rituals and venerated burial places, especially the memorials of founding saints (*martyria*), also was the first major patron of Christian architecture. He constructed elaborate churches, memorials, and *mausolea* not only in Rome

but also in Ostia, Naples, and other Italian cities; in North Africa and Syria; in Constantinople, the emperor's "New Rome" in the East; and in Palestine—most notably in Bethlehem, the birthplace of Jesus, and Jerusalem, the site of his crucifixion and entombment. Constantine's Church of the Holy Sepulchre

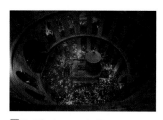

8-8C Anastasis Rotunda, Jerusalem, 326–335.

(FIG. 8-8C) marks the location both of the cross (Golgotha) and of Jesus's empty tomb (see "The Life of Jesus," pages 244–245).

Old Saint Peter's. The greatest of Constantine's churches in Rome was Old Saint Peter's (FIGS. 8-9 and 8-10), probably begun as early as 319. The present-day church (FIGS. 22-25, 24-3, and 24-4), one of the masterpieces of Italian Renaissance and Baroque architecture, is a replacement for the Constantinian structure. Old Saint Peter's stood on the western side of the Tiber River, on a terrace on the irregular slope of the Vatican Hill over the ancient cemetery in which Constantine and Pope Sylvester (r. 314–335) believed that Peter, the founder of the Christian community in Rome, had been buried (see "Early Christian Saints," pages 246–247). In keeping with Roman burial practice, Peter's grave, like those of all Christian martyrs, was on the city's outskirts. The decision to erect Peter's church on the Vatican Hill also enabled Constantine to locate the new Christian shrine away from the city center to avoid any confrontation between Rome's Christians and those who continued to worship the old gods.

Excavations in the Roman cemetery beneath Saint Peter's have in fact revealed a second-century martyrium erected in honor of Peter at his reputed grave. Capable of housing 3,000 to 4,000 worshipers at one time, the immense church (its nave was 300 feet long) enshrined Peter's tomb, one of the most hallowed sites in Christendom, second only to the Holy Sepulchre (FIG. 8-8C) in Jerusalem, the site of Christ's resurrection. The project also fulfilled the figurative words of Christ himself, when he said, "Thou art Peter, and upon this rock I will build my church" (Matt. 16:18). Peter was Rome's first bishop and the head of the long line of popes extending to the present. (Saint Peter's, however, is not the *cathedral* of Rome—the bishop's church, from the Latin word for seat or throne, *cathedra*—despite its location in Vatican City.)

Old Saint Peter's followed the pattern of Roman basilicas in most respects (see "What Should a Church Look Like?" page 249), but a special feature of this Constantinian church was the *transept,* or transverse aisle, an area perpendicular to the nave between the nave and apse (FIG. 8-10). Over the archway leading into the transept was an inscription stating that "Constantine, victor, built this hall." The transept housed Saint Peter's *relics,* which attracted hordes of pilgrims. (Relics are body parts, clothing, or objects associated with a saint or Christ himself; see "The Veneration of Relics," page 349.) Transepts were, however, rare additions to Early Christian basilicas. The transept became a standard element of church design in the West only much later (compare, for example, FIGS. 12-5 and 12-6), when it also took on, with the nave and apse, the symbolism of the Christian cross. Saint Peter's basilica also had an open colonnaded courtyard in front of the narthex, very much like the forum proper in the Forum of Trajan (FIG. 7-44, no. 5), but called an *atrium* (compare FIGS. 8-9 and 12-24), like the central room in a Roman private house (FIG. 7-15, no. 2).

Compared with Roman temples, which usually displayed statuary in pediments on their facades, most Early Christian basilicas

What Should a Church Look Like?

When Constantine conferred official recognition on Christianity and became its first imperial sponsor, Christians could finally begin openly to construct buildings in which to celebrate the Christian *liturgy* (the official ritual of public worship). But what form should these new buildings—*churches,* not temples—take? The Christians, understandably, did not want their houses of worship to mimic the form of polytheistic shrines, but practical considerations also contributed to their rejection of the classical temple type. Greco-Roman temples housed only statues of deities and votive offerings. The priests and worshipers stood outside, where the rituals were performed at open-air altars. Therefore, Late Antique architects would have found it difficult to adapt the classical temple to accommodate large numbers of people within it. Roman *basilicas* and audience halls, by contrast, were ideally suited as places for congregation, and Christian architects readily selected these secular building types as models for the first churches, including the official church of Rome's bishop (Saint John Lateran) and the enormous church Constantine constructed over the site of Saint Peter's tomb in what is today Vatican City.

Indeed, the elevation (FIG. 8-9) and plan (FIG. 8-10) of Old Saint Peter's resemble those of Roman meeting and audience halls, such as the Basilica Ulpia (FIG. 7-44, no. 4) in the Forum of Trajan and Constantine's own Aula Palatina (FIG. 7-75) at Trier, rather than the design of any Greco-Roman temple. Like most Roman basilicas, Old Saint Peter's had a wide central *nave* with flanking *aisles* and an *apse* at the end. And, as in the Roman basilicas, the new churches had *clerestory* windows above the *nave arcade* to provide natural illumination to complement the light of candelabras. But unlike Roman basilicas, which sometimes had doorways on one long side opening onto an aisle (FIG. 7-44, no. 4), Early Christian basilicas all have a *longitudinal plan* (FIGS. 8-9, 8-18, and 8-25). Worshipers entered the basilica through a *narthex,* or vestibule. When they emerged in the nave, they had an unobstructed view of the altar and the officiating priest in the apse, framed by the *chancel arch.* Thus the Christians turned to an old building type and modified it as the perfect solution to a new problem.

One feature of the typical Greco-Roman temple was retained, however. Constantine's churches also faced east toward the rising sun. By the end of the fourth century, the orientation of basilican churches was reversed, with the entrance facade on the west and the apse at the east end, which has remained the norm ever since.

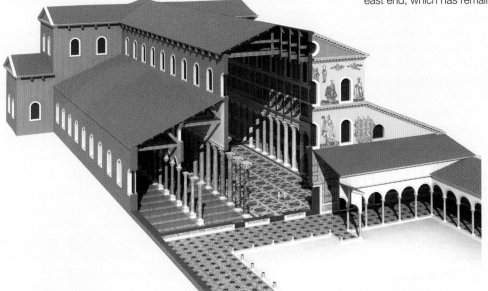

8-9 Restored cutaway view of Old Saint Peter's (looking northwest, with later mosaics decorating the east facade), Rome, Italy, begun ca. 319 (John Burge).

Built by Constantine, the first imperial patron of Christianity, this huge church stood over Saint Peter's grave. The building's plan and elevation resemble those of Roman basilicas, not temples.

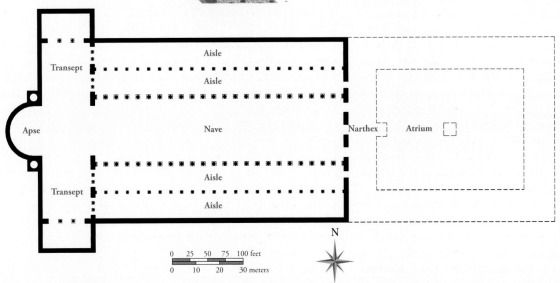

8-10 Restored plan of Old Saint Peter's, Rome, Italy, begun ca. 319.

Old Saint Peter's closely followed the plan of a Roman basilica and had a 300-foot-long nave with flanking aisles leading to an apse, but unlike other early churches, it also had a transept and an atrium.

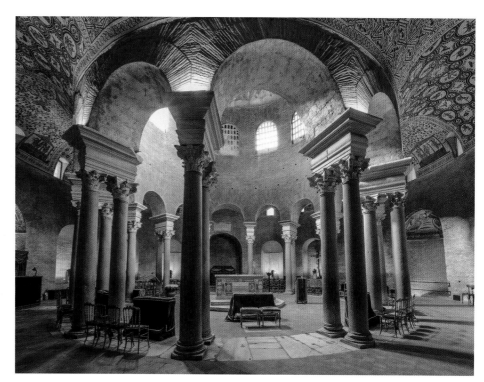

8-11 Interior of Santa Costanza (looking southwest), Rome, Italy, ca. 337–351.

Built as the mausoleum of Constantine's daughter, Santa Costanza later became a church. Its central plan, featuring a domed interior, would become the preferred form for Byzantine churches.

were quite austere on the exterior. Inside, however, were frescoes and mosaics, marble columns (*spolia* taken from older Roman buildings, as was customary at the time), and costly ornaments. The *Liber Pontificalis,* or *Book of the Pontiffs* (*Popes*), compiled by an anonymous sixth-century author, lists Constantine's gifts to Old Saint Peter's. They included altars, chandeliers, candlesticks, pitchers, goblets, and plates fashioned of gold and silver and sometimes embellished with jewels and pearls, as well as jeweled altar cloths for use in the Mass and gold foil to sheathe the vault of the apse. A huge marble *baldacchino* (domical canopy over an altar), supported by four spiral porphyry columns, marked the spot of Saint Peter's tomb.

Santa Costanza. The rectangular basilican church design was long the favorite of the Western Christian world. But Early Christian architects also adopted another classical architectural type: the *central-plan* building, in which the parts are of equal or almost equal dimensions around the center. Roman central-plan buildings were usually round or polygonal domed structures. Byzantine architects developed this form to massive proportions and amplified its theme in numerous ingenious variations. In the West, builders generally used the central plan for structures adjacent to the main basilicas, such as mausolea, baptisteries, and private chapels, rather than for churches, as in the East.

A highly refined example of the central-plan design is Santa Costanza (FIGS. 8-11 and 8-12), built on the northern outskirts of Rome in the mid-fourth century as the mausoleum for Constantina, the emperor Constantine's daughter. The mausoleum, later converted into a church, housed Constantina's unusually large porphyry sarcophagus and stood next to the basilican church of Saint Agnes, erected over the catacomb in which she was buried. Santa Costanza's distant antecedents were the tholos tombs (FIGS. 4-20 and 4-21) of the Mycenaeans, but the immediate predecessors were the domed structures of the Romans, such as the Pantheon (FIG. 7-51) and especially imperial mausolea such as Diocletian's (FIG. 7-73) at Split. At Santa Costanza, the architect modified the interior design of those Roman buildings to accommodate an *ambulatory,* as in the Anastasis Rotunda (FIG. 8-8C) of the Church of the Holy Sepulchre in Jerusalem. Santa Costanza's ambulatory is a ringlike barrel-vaulted corridor separated from the central domed cylinder by a dozen pairs of columns—the earliest instance of a dome resting on a colonnade.

Like Early Christian basilicas, Santa Costanza has a severe brick exterior. Its interior was once richly adorned with mosaics, although most are lost. Old and New Testament themes appeared side by side, as in the catacombs and on Early Christian sarcophagi. The Santa Costanza mosaic program, however, also included subjects common

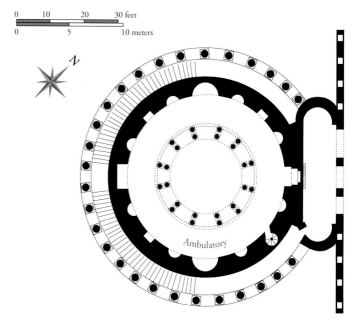

8-12 Plan of Santa Costanza, Rome, Italy, ca. 337–351.

Santa Costanza has antecedents in the domed temples (FIG. 7-51) and mausolea (FIG. 7-73) of the Romans, but its dome resting on 12 pairs of columns framed by a vaulted ambulatory is new.

in Roman funerary art, although they lent themselves to a Christian interpretation. In one section (FIG. 8-13, *center*) of the mosaic in the ambulatory vault, for example, are scenes of putti harvesting grapes and making wine. (Similar scenes decorate Constantina's sarcophagus.) A portrait bust is at the center of a rich vine scroll. A second bust appears in another section of the mosaic vault, but both are heavily restored, and the identification of the pair as Constantina and her husband is uncertain. In the Roman world, wine was primarily associated with Bacchus, but for a Christian, the vineyards brought to mind the wine of the Eucharist and the blood of Christ. As early as the third century, however, mosaics of explicitly Christian content had been used in tombs—for example, in the Mausoleum of the Julii

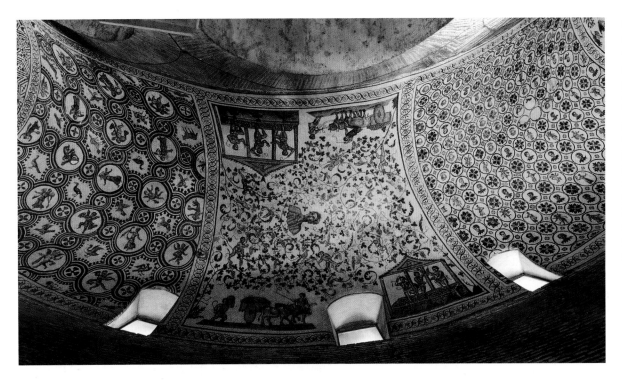

The ambulatory mosaics of Santa Costanza depict putti harvesting grapes and making wine, motifs associated with Bacchus, but for a Christian, the scenes evoked the Eucharist and Christ's blood.

in the ancient cemetery beneath Saint Peter's in Rome, where Christ, in the guise of Sol Invictus (FIG. 8-13A), the Invincible Sun, drives his chariot across the heavens.

Luxury Arts

Throughout history, artists have produced so-called minor arts—jewelry, metalwork, cameos, ivories, among other crafts—alongside the "major arts" of sculpture and painting. Although the traditional terminology unfortunately suggests a difference in importance or quality, "minor" refers only to size. Indeed, the artists who fashioned jewelry, carved ivories and cameos, and produced gold and silver vessels by casting or hammering (*repoussé*) employed the costliest materials known. Some of these artists—for example, Dioscurides, official gem cutter of the emperor Augustus—are among the few Roman artists working in any medium whose names survive. In Late Antiquity and the Middle Ages, the minor arts—more appropriately called "luxury arts"—enjoyed high status, and they figure prominently in the history of art through the ages.

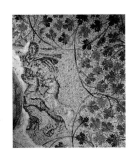

⌐**8-13A** Christ as Sol Invictus, late third century.

Mildenhall Treasure. Especially prized in Late Antiquity were items of tableware fashioned out of precious metals (as were their counterparts in earlier ages—for example, the gold Achaemenid rhyton [FIG. 2-28] from Hamadan and the Mycenaean drinking cups [FIG. 4-24] from Vapheio). An especially rich hoard of silver tableware dating to the mid-fourth century came to light in 1942 when a farmer plowing his fields near Mildenhall, England, discovered what was quickly dubbed the "Mildenhall Treasure." The hoard consists of 34 silver pieces, including bowls, platters, ladles, and spoons, and must have been the proud possession of a wealthy local family.

The most spectacular item is a large platter known as the "Great Dish" (FIG. 8-14). At the center is the bearded head of the god Oceanus, framed by a ring of *Nereids* (sea nymphs, daughters

of Nereus, a Greek sea god). A larger outer band celebrates the consumption of wine and features a drinking contest between Bacchus (with his left foot resting on a panther) and Hercules, who is so drunk that two satyrs struggle to support him. Three of the spoons bear the Greek letters *chi, rho, alpha,* and *omega*—explicit references to Christ (compare FIG. 8-7A)—but the figural decoration of all the items in the treasure consists of characters from classical

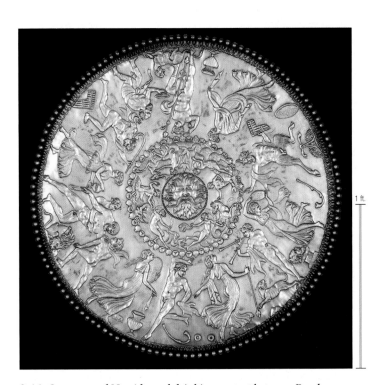

8-14 Oceanus and Nereids, and drinking contest between Bacchus and Hercules, "Great Dish," from Mildenhall, England, mid-fourth century CE. Silver, 1′ 11¾″ diameter. British Museum, London.

Part of a hoard of silver tableware owned by a Christian family, this large platter nonetheless features sea deities and a drinking contest between Bacchus, the Roman god of wine, and Hercules.

Manuscript Illumination

Rare as Late Antique books are, they are far more numerous than their classical predecessors. An important invention during the Early Roman Empire was the *codex* (plural, *codices*), which greatly aided the dissemination of *manuscripts* (handwritten books, from the Latin *manu scriptus*) as well as their preservation. A codex is much like a modern book, composed of separate leaves (*folios*) enclosed within a cover and bound together at one side. The new format, with pages with fronts (*recto*) and backs (*verso*), superseded the long manuscript scroll (*rotulus*) of the Egyptians (FIG. 3-1), Greeks, Etruscans, and Romans. (The Etruscan magistrate Lars Pulena [FIG. 6-16]; the philosophers on Roman and Early Christian sarcophagi [FIGS. 7-70 and 8-7]; and Christ himself in his role as lawgiver [FIGS. 8-8 and 8-8B] all hold rotuli in their hands.) Much more durable *vellum* (calfskin) and *parchment* (lamb and other animal skins), which provided better surfaces for painting, also replaced the comparatively brittle *papyrus* used for ancient scrolls. As a result, luxuriousness of ornamentation became increasingly typical of Christian sacred books, and at times the material beauty of the pages and their illustrations overwhelm or usurp the spiritual beauty of the text. Art historians refer to the luxurious painted books produced before the invention of the printing press as *illuminated manuscripts,* from the Latin *illuminare,* meaning "to adorn, ornament, or brighten." The oldest preserved examples (FIGS. 8-15, 9-17, 9-17A, and 9-17B) date to the fifth and sixth centuries.

Illuminated books were costly to produce, and the process involved many steps. Numerous artisans performed very specialized tasks, beginning with the curing and cutting (and sometimes the dyeing; FIGS. 9-17, 9-17A, and 9-17B) of the animal skin, followed by the sketching of lines to guide the scribe and to set aside spaces for illumination, the lettering of the text, the addition of pigment and gold leaf for paintings, and finally the binding of the pages and attachment of covers, buckles, and clasps. The covers could be even more extravagant than the book itself. Many preserved covers are fashioned of gold and decorated with jewels, ivory carvings, and repoussé reliefs (FIG. 11-16).

8-15 *Old Farmer of Corycus,* folio 7 verso of the *Vatican Vergil,* ca. 400–420. Tempera on parchment, $1' \frac{1}{2}'' \times 1'$. Biblioteca Apostolica Vaticana, Rome.

The earliest surviving painted Latin manuscript is a collection of the poet Vergil's works. This page includes part of the text of the *Georgics* and a pastoral scene reminiscent of Roman landscape murals.

mythology. The hoard attests to the survival of the Roman gods and of classical iconography during the Late Antique period, even in Christian contexts.

Vatican Vergil. Although few examples survive, illustrated books were popular in the ancient world. The long tradition of placing pictures in *manuscripts* began in Egypt (FIG. 3-1) and continued in Greek and Roman times and throughout the Middle Ages (see "Manuscript Illumination," above). The oldest preserved painted Greek or Latin manuscript is the *Vatican Vergil,* which dates from the early fifth century and is among the earliest preserved illustrated books. It originally contained more than 200 pictures illustrating all of Vergil's works. Today only 50 painted *folios* (pages) of the *Aeneid* and *Georgics* survive. The manuscript is important not only because of its age. The *Vatican Vergil* is a prime example of traditional Roman iconography and of the classical style long after Theodosius banned worship of the old gods—underscoring, as does the Mildenhall Treasure, that European art did not become exclusively "Early Christian" even after the Roman emperors abandoned their old gods in favor of the new monotheistic religion.

The page illustrated here (FIG. 8-15) includes a section of text from the *Georgics* at the top and a framed illustration below. Vergil recounts his visit to a modest farm near Taranto in southern Italy belonging to an old man from Corycus in Asia Minor. In the illustration, the old farmer sits at the left. His rustic farmhouse is in the background, rendered in three-quarter view. The farmer speaks about the pleasures of the simple life in the country—a recurrent theme in Latin poetry—and on his methods of gardening. His audience is two laborers and, at the far right, Vergil himself in the guise of a farmhand. The style is reminiscent of Pompeian landscapes, with quick touches that suggest space and atmosphere. In fact, the dark red frame has close parallels in the Third and Fourth Styles of Roman mural painting (compare FIG. 7-34A).

Suicide of Judas and Crucifixion. Among the other important luxury arts of Late Antiquity was ivory carving, which has a much longer history in the ancient world than metalwork and book illustration (see "Ivory Carving," page 253). In the early fifth century, a Roman or northern Italian master sculptor produced an extraordinary series of ivory plaques recounting the suffering and

Ivory Carving

Ivory has been prized since the earliest times, when sculptors fashioned the tusks of Ice Age European mammoths into pendants, beads, and other items for body adornment, and, occasionally, statuettes (FIGS. 1-3 and 1-4A). The primary ivory sources in the historical period have been the elephants of India and especially Africa, where the species is larger than the Asian counterpart and the tusks longer, heavier, and of finer grain. African elephant tusks 5 to 6 feet in length and weighing 10 pounds are common, but tusks of male elephants can be 10 feet long or more and weigh well over 100 pounds. Objects carved from hippopotamus ivory have been found as well. Carved ivories are familiar, if precious, finds at Mesopotamian and Egyptian sites, and ivory objects were also coveted in the prehistoric Aegean (FIGS. 4-13A and 4-25) and throughout the classical world. Most frequently employed then for household objects, small votive offerings, and gifts to the deceased,

ivory also could be used in grandiose statues such as Phidias's *Athena Parthenos* (FIG. 5-46).

In the Greco-Roman world, people admired ivory both for its beauty and because of its exotic origin. Elephant tusks were costly imports, and Roman generals proudly displayed them in triumphal processions when they paraded the spoils of war before the people. (In FIG. 9-4, a barbarian brings tribute to a Byzantine emperor in the form of an ivory tusk.) Adding to the expense of the material itself was that only highly skilled artisans were capable of working in ivory. The tusks were very hard and of irregular shape, and the ivory workers needed a full toolbox of saws, chisels, knives, files, and gravers close at hand to cut the tusks into blocks for statuettes or thin plaques decorated with relief figures and ornamentation.

In Late Antiquity and the early medieval period, artists chose ivory most frequently for book covers, chests and boxes (FIG. 8-16), and diptychs (FIGS. 8-17 and 9-2). A *diptych* is a pair of hinged tablets, usually of wood, with a wax layer on the inner sides for writing letters and other documents. (The women in two painted portraits from Pompeii [FIGS. 7-24 and 7-24A] and the court scribe recording Jesus's trial in the *Rossano Gospels* [FIG. 9-17B] all hold wood diptychs.) Diptychs fashioned from ivory generally were reserved for ceremonial and official purposes— for example, to announce the election of a consul or a marriage between two wealthy families or to commemorate the death of an elevated member of society.

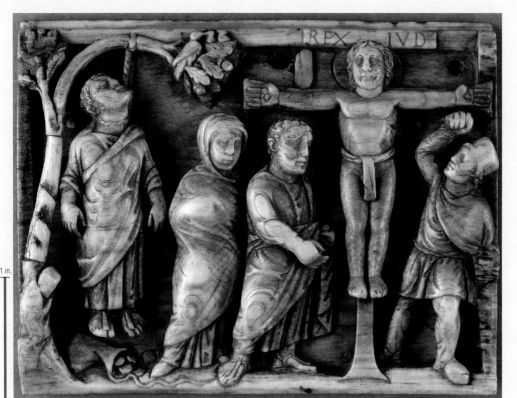

8-16 *Suicide of Judas and Crucifixion of Christ,* **plaque from a box, early fifth century. Ivory, $3'' \times 3\frac{7}{8}''$. British Museum, London.**

This plaque from a luxurious ivory box is one of the first known representations of Christ's crucifixion. The Savior is a beardless youth who experiences no pain. At the left, Judas, his betrayer, hangs himself.

triumph of Christ. The plaques were affixed to the sides of a small box. The narrative begins with Pilate washing his hands, Jesus carrying the cross on the road to Calvary, and the denial of Peter, all compressed into a single panel. The plaque illustrated here, *Suicide of Judas and Crucifixion of Christ* (FIG. 8-16), is the next in the sequence. It shows, at the left, Judas hanging from a tree with his open bag of silver dumped on the ground beneath his feet. The Crucifixion is at the right. The Virgin Mary and the apostle John are to the left of the cross. On the other side, Longinus thrusts his spear into the side of the "king of the Jews" (the inscribed letters *REX IVD* appear above Jesus's head). The two remaining panels show two Marys and two soldiers at the open doors of a tomb with an

empty coffin within, and the doubting Thomas touching the wound of the risen Christ.

The series is one of the oldest cycles of passion scenes preserved today. It dates to the period when artists were beginning to establish the standard iconographical types for medieval narratives of Christ's life. On these plaques, Jesus always appears as a beardless youth. In the Crucifixion scene (FIG. 8-16, *right*), one of the earliest known renditions of the subject in the history of art (compare FIG. 8-19B), the Savior exhibits a superhuman indifference to pain. Jesus is a muscular, nearly nude, heroic figure who appears virtually weightless. He does not *hang* from the cross. He is *displayed* on it—a divine being with open eyes who will be resurrected, not

1 in.

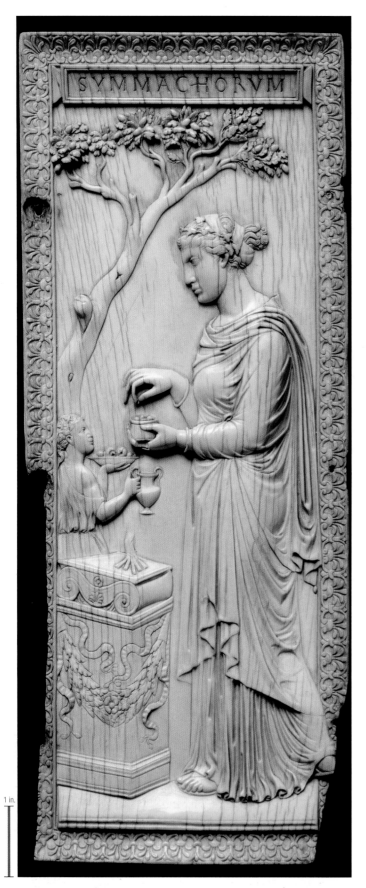

8-17 Woman sacrificing at an altar, right leaf of the diptych of the Nicomachi and the Symmachi, ca. 400. Ivory, $11\frac{3}{4}'' \times 5\frac{1}{2}''$. Victoria & Albert Museum, London.

Even after Theodosius banned all cults of the old gods in 391, some Roman families still practiced the ancient rites. The sculptor who carved this ivory plaque also carried on the classical artistic style.

the mortal condemned to death by Pontius Pilate (see "The Life of Jesus," pages 244–245). The striking contrast between the powerful frontal unsuffering Jesus on the cross and the limp, hanging body of his betrayer with his snapped neck is highly effective, both visually and symbolically.

Diptych of the Symmachi. As noted earlier, although Constantine endorsed Christianity and dedicated his New Rome in the East to the Christian God, not everyone converted to the new religion, even after Theodosius banned all ancient cults and closed all temples in 391. An ivory plaque (FIG. 8-17), probably produced in Rome around 400, strikingly exhibits the endurance of the traditional Roman gods and of the classical style on the eve of Alaric's sack of the "eternal city" in 410. The ivory, one of a pair of leaves of a diptych, commemorates two powerful Roman families of the senatorial class, the Nicomachi and the Symmachi, and may mark the passing within a decade of two prominent male members of the two families. Whether or not the diptych refers to any specific event(s), the Nicomachi and the Symmachi here ostentatiously reaffirmed their faith in the old gods. Certainly, they favored the aesthetic ideals of the classical past, as exemplified by the stately processional friezes of the Greek Parthenon (FIG. 5-50, *bottom*) and the Roman Ara Pacis (FIG. 7-31).

The leaf inscribed "of the Symmachi" (FIG. 8-17) represents a woman, assisted by an attendant, sacrificing at an altar in front of a tree. She wears ivy in her hair and seems to be celebrating the rites of Bacchus—the same wine god featured on the Mildenhall silver platter (FIG. 8-14). Some scholars dispute the identity of the divinity honored, but no one questions that the deity is one of the Roman gods whose worship had been banned. The other diptych panel (not illustrated), inscribed "of the Nicomachi," also shows a woman at an open-air altar. She holds a torch pointing to the ground, a sign of mourning (compare Cupid on the lid of the Melfi sarcophagus; FIG. 7-60). On both panels, the graceful line, the relaxed poses, and the mood of spiritual serenity reveal an artist who practiced within a still-vital classical tradition that idealized human beauty as its central focus. The great senatorial magnates of Rome, who resisted the empire-wide imposition of the Christian faith at the end of the fourth century, probably deliberately sustained the classical tradition, which was never fully extinguished in the Middle Ages.

FROM THE SACK OF ROME TO JUSTINIAN

The basilican solution that Constantinian architects formulated for church design (see "What Should a Church Look Like?" page 249) has dominated ecclesiastical architecture in the Western world to the present day. Unfortunately, no fourth-century church survives in its original form, least of all the radically redesigned dome-capped Saint Peter's (FIGS. 22-25, 24-3, and 24-4) in the Vatican. But some fifth-century basilicas that followed the Constantinian pattern still stand relatively unchanged over the past 16 centuries.

Rome

Santa Sabina. Some idea of the character, if not the scale, of the timber-roofed interior of Old Saint Peter's can be gleaned from the interior of Santa Sabina (FIGS. 8-18 and 8-19) in Rome. Built a century later, the church, which sits atop the Aventine Hill with a

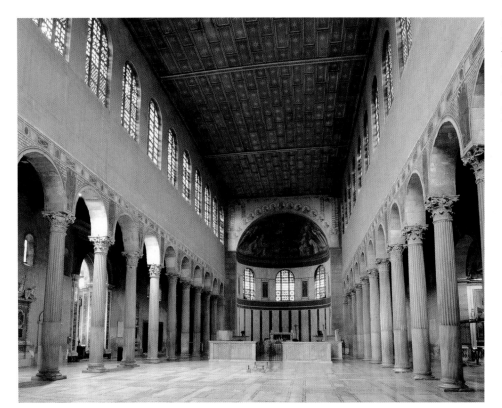

8-18 **Interior of Santa Sabina (looking northeast), Rome, Italy, 422–432.**

Santa Sabina and other Early Christian basilican churches are timber-roofed and illuminated by clerestory windows. The nave arcade produces a steady rhythm that focuses all attention on the apse.

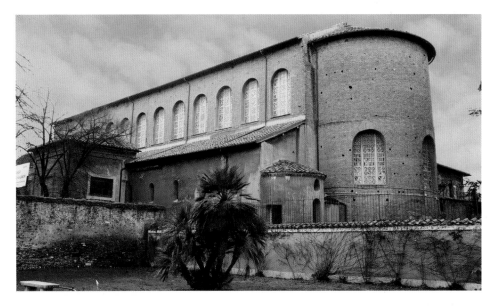

8-19 **Exterior of Santa Sabina (looking west), Rome, Italy, 422–432.**

Although mosaics and frescoes commonly adorned the interiors of Early Christian basilicas, Santa Sabina and other early churches had plain brick exteriors like the Aula Palatina (FIG. 7-75) at Trier.

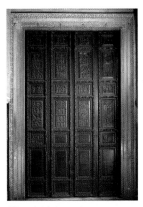

⬈ **8-19A** West doors, Santa Sabina, Rome, ca. 432.

distant view of Saint Peter's from the southeast, still retains its Early Christian character, as well as its original carved wood doors (FIGS. **8-19A** and **8-19B**). The Corinthian columns of its nave arcade (FIG. 8-18) produce a steady rhythm that focuses all attention on the chancel arch and the apse, which frame the altar. In the fifth century, the clerestory windows piercing the thin upper wall above the colonnade would have admitted sunlight not only to illuminate the interior for the performance of the Christian liturgy but also, importantly, to make visible the frescoes

and mosaics that commonly adorned the nave and apse of Early Christian churches (compare FIG. 8-25). Outside (FIG. 8-19), Santa Sabina has the plain brick walls typical of the earliest basilican churches as well as Constantine's Aula Palatina (FIG. 7-75, right) at Trier.

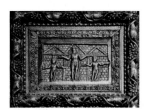

⬈ **8-19B** *Crucifixion,* Santa Sabina, Rome, ca. 432.

Santa Maria Maggiore. Another Roman fifth-century basilican church, although later extensively remodeled, is Santa Maria Maggiore, the first major church in the West dedicated to the Virgin Mary. Construction of the church began in 432, the year after the Council of Ephesus officially designated Mary as *Theotokos* ("bearer of god" in Greek). The council, which had been convened to debate whether Mary had given birth to the man Jesus or to God as a man,

Mosaics

As an art form, *mosaic* had a rather simple and utilitarian beginning, seemingly invented primarily to provide inexpensive but durable flooring. Originally, mosaicists set small beach pebbles, unaltered from their natural form and color, into a thick coat of cement. Artisans soon discovered, however, that the stones could be arranged in decorative patterns. At first, these *pebble mosaics* were uncomplicated and confined to geometric shapes. Generally, the artists used only black and white stones. Examples of this type, dating to the eighth century BCE, have been found at Gordion in Asia Minor. Eventually, artists arranged the stones to form more complex pictorial designs, and by the fourth century BCE, the technique had developed to a high level of sophistication. Mosaicists depicted elaborate figural scenes using a broad range of colors—red, yellow, and brown in addition to black, white, and gray—and shaded the figures, clothing, and setting to suggest volume. Thin strips of lead provided linear definition (FIG. 5-68).

By the middle of the third century BCE, artists had invented a new kind of mosaic that enabled the best mosaicists to create designs more closely approximating true paintings. The new technique employed *tesserae* (Latin for "cubes" or "dice"). These tiny cut stones gave artists much greater flexibility because their size and shape could be adjusted, eliminating the need for lead strips to indicate contours and interior details. More gradual gradations of color also became possible (FIG. 5-70), and by using tiny tesserae for complex areas, such as faces, and larger cubes for garments and the background, mosaicists finally could aspire to rival the achievements of painters.

In Early Christian mosaics, the tesserae are usually made of glass, which reflects light and makes the surfaces sparkle. Ancient mosaicists occasionally used glass tesserae, but the Romans preferred opaque marble pieces. Mosaics quickly became a popular, if expensive, means of decorating walls and vaults in Early Christian buildings, although less costly mural paintings were more common. The mosaics caught the light flooding through the windows in vibrant reflection, producing sharp contrasts and concentrations of color that could focus attention on a composition's central, most relevant features. Early Christian mosaics were not meant to incorporate the subtle tonal changes that a naturalistic painter's approach would require. Artists "placed," rather than blended, colors. Bright, hard, glittering texture, set within a rigorously simplified pattern, became the rule. For mosaics situated high on a chancel arch (FIG. 8-20), over the nave colonnade (FIGS. 8-21 and 8-26), in an apse or ambulatory vault (FIG. 8-13), or in a dome (FIGS. 8-24A and 8-27), far above the observer's head, the painstaking use of tiny tesserae seen in Roman floor and wall mosaics (FIGS. 5-70 and 7-23) would be pointless. Early Christian mosaics,

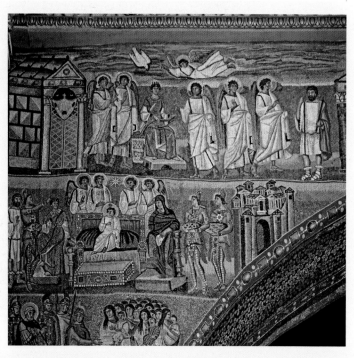

8-20 *Annunciation* and *Adoration of the Magi,* mosaics in the left spandrel of the chancel arch of Santa Maria Maggiore, Rome, Italy, 432–440.

Befitting a church dedicated to the Virgin, Mary plays a dominant role in the mosaic program of the apse and the chancel arch. Two of the scenes represent the Annunciation and the adoration of the magi.

designed to be seen from a distance, usually consist of larger tesserae. The mosaicists also set the cubes unevenly so that their surfaces could catch and reflect the light. Artists favored simple designs for optimal legibility. For several centuries, mosaic, in the service of Christian theology, was the medium of some of the supreme masterpieces of medieval art.

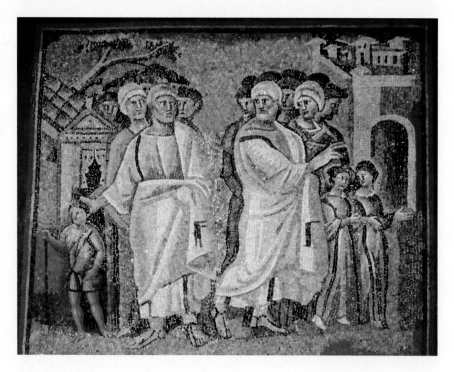

8-21 *The Parting of Abraham and Lot,* mosaic in the nave of Santa Maria Maggiore, Rome, Italy, 432–440.

In this tessera mosaic depicting the parting of Abraham and Lot as set out in the book of Genesis, the artist included the yet-unborn Isaac because of his importance as a prefiguration of Christ.

ruled that the divine and human coexisted in Christ and that Mary had indeed given birth to the son of God.

Santa Maria Maggiore is noteworthy above all for the fifth-century cycle of nave mosaics depicting Old and New Testament stories. Mosaic decoration (see "Mosaics," page 256) played an important role in the interiors of Early Christian buildings of all types, but in churches, mosaics did not just provide a beautiful setting for the Mass. They also were vehicles for instructing the congregation about biblical events and Christian dogma, especially in an age of widespread illiteracy.

Befitting a church dedicated to the Virgin, Mary plays a dominant role in the mosaic program. In fact, the Mother of God will rarely again figure so prominently in Western art until the Gothic age 800 years later (see "The Virgin in Gothic France," page 385). According to the dedicatory inscription of Pope Sixtus III (r. 432–440), a mosaic representing Mary flanked by saints originally filled the apse. The Mother of God was also central to the iconographical program of the chancel arch, which illustrated episodes from the New Testament. In the detail illustrated here (FIG. 8-20), the upper register shows Mary as an enthroned regal figure accompanied by angels as she receives from Gabriel and the dove of the Holy Spirit the news that she will give birth to God's son. Below, the infant Jesus is the center of attention, but both he and Mary sit on thrones as the magi present their gifts.

Abraham and Lot. The mosaics above Santa Maria Maggiore's nave colonnade depict Old rather than New Testament themes. One of them—*The Parting of Abraham and Lot* (FIG. 8-21)—dramatically represents the story of Abraham and his nephew Lot as set forth in Genesis, the Bible's opening book. Agreeing to disagree, Lot leads his family and followers to the right, toward the city of Sodom, while Abraham heads for Canaan, moving toward a basilica-like building (symbolizing Christianity in the form of a church) on the left. Lot's is the evil choice, and the instruments of the evil (his two daughters) stand in front of him. The figure of the yet-unborn Isaac, the instrument of good (and, as noted earlier, a prefiguration of Christ), stands before his father, Abraham—a violation of the unity of time and space in order to communicate Christian dogma pictorially.

The cleavage of the two groups is emphatic, and the mosaicist represented each group using a shorthand device employed earlier

in ancient art called a *head cluster,* in which the artist represents more heads than bodies to suggest a crowd. The figures engage in a sharp dialogue of glance and gesture. The wide eyes turn in their sockets, and the enlarged hands make broad gestures. This kind of simplified motion, which is characteristic of Late Antique narrative art of Roman and Judeo-Christian subject matter alike, has great power to communicate without ambiguity.

But the Santa Maria Maggiore mosaics also reveal the heritage of classical art. The towns in the background of the *Parting of Abraham and Lot* and *Adoration of the Magi* mosaics would not be out of place in a Roman mural (FIG. 7-19, *left*) or on the Column of Trajan (FIG. 7-45C), and the biblical figures are modeled in light and dark, still loom with massive solidity, and cast shadows on the ground beneath a blue sky. Another century had to pass before Western Christian mosaicists commonly portrayed figures as flat images, rather than as three-dimensional bodies, finally rejecting the norms of classical art in favor of a style better suited to a focus on the spiritual instead of the natural world (see "Picturing the Spiritual World," page 260). Early Christian art, like Late Antique Roman art in general, vacillates between these two stylistic poles.

Ravenna and Thessaloniki

In the decades after 324, when Constantine founded Constantinople, the New Rome in the East, the pace of Christianization of the Roman Empire quickened. In 380, the emperor Theodosius I (r. 379–395) issued an edict finally establishing Christianity as the state religion. In 391, he enacted a ban against worship of the old Roman gods, and in 394, he abolished the Olympic Games, the enduring symbol of the classical world and its values.

Theodosius died in 395, and imperial power passed to his two sons, Arcadius (r. 395–408), who became emperor of the East, and Honorius (r. 395–423), emperor of the West. In 404, when the Visigoths, under their king, Alaric (r. 395–410), threatened to overrun Italy from the northwest, Honorius moved his capital from Milan to Ravenna, an ancient Roman city (perhaps founded by the Etruscans) near Italy's Adriatic coast, some 80 miles south of Venice. In 410, Alaric captured and sacked Rome, and in 476, Ravenna fell to Odoacer (r. 476–493), the first Germanic king of Italy. Odoacer was overthrown in turn by Theodoric (r. 471–526), king of the Ostrogoths, who established his capital at Ravenna in 493. Ravenna fell to the Byzantine emperor Justinian (r. 527–565) in 539, and the subsequent history of the city belongs with that of Byzantium and is treated in detail in the next chapter.

Mausoleum of Galla Placidia. The so-called Mausoleum of Galla Placidia, Honorius's half-sister, is a small *cruciform* (cross-shaped) structure (FIG. 8-22) with barrel-vaulted arms and a tower at the *crossing.* Built shortly after 425, almost a quarter century before Galla Placidia's death in 450, it is a little gem of Early Christian art and

8-22 Mausoleum of Galla Placidia (looking northeast), Ravenna, Italy, ca. 425.

This cruciform mausoleum with a domed crossing is an early example of the combination of central and longitudinal plans. The unadorned brick exterior encloses a rich ensemble of mosaics.

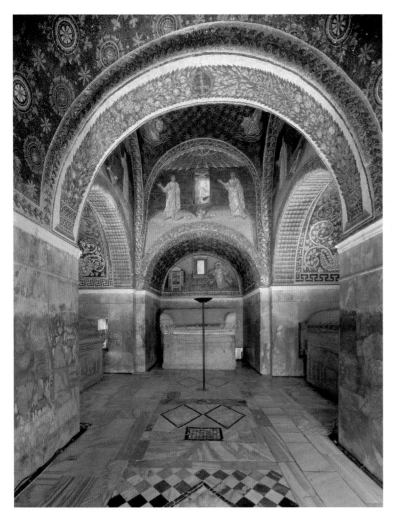

8-23 Interior of the Mausoleum of Galla Placidia (looking south), Ravenna, Italy, ca. 425.

Before Late Antiquity, mosaics were usually confined to floors. Inside the so-called Mausoleum of Galla Placidia, glass mosaics cover every square inch of the interior above the marble-faced walls.

architecture, but the real name of the undoubtedly wealthy and important person who was buried inside is not known. The mausoleum adjoined the narthex of the now greatly altered palace-church of Santa Croce (Holy Cross), which was also cruciform in plan. The building's cross arms are of unequal length, so the structure has a longitudinal orientation, unlike the centrally planned Santa Costanza (FIGS. 8-11 and 8-12), but because all four arms are very short, the emphasis is on the tall *crossing tower* with its internal dome. This unassuming Ravenna mausoleum thus represents one of the earliest successful fusions of the two basic Late Antique plans—the longitudinal, used for basilican churches, and the central, used primarily for baptisteries and mausolea. It introduced, on a small scale, a building type that was to have a long history in church architecture: the longitudinally planned building with a domed crossing, the form that the remodeled Saint Peter's would assume in the 17th century (FIG. 24-4).

The Mausoleum of Galla Placidia's unadorned brick exterior encloses one of the richest mosaic ensembles (FIG. 8-23) in Early Christian art. Glass mosaics cover every square inch of the interior surfaces above the marble-faced walls. Garlands and decorative medallions resembling snowflakes on a dark blue ground adorn the barrel vaults of the nave and cross arms. The dome of the tower has a large golden cross set against a star-studded sky. Representations of saints and apostles cover the other surfaces. At the end of the nave is a mosaic representing Saint Lawrence next to the gridiron on which he was tortured (see "Early Christian Saints," pages 246–247). The martyred saint carries a cross, suggesting that faith in Christ led to his salvation. Old and New Testament stories of salvation abound in Early Christian catacomb paintings, sarcophagus reliefs, and mosaics alike.

Christ in his role as Good Shepherd, another popular subject in Early Christian funerary art, appears in the lunette (FIG. 8-24) above the entrance. No earlier version of the Good Shepherd is as regal as this one. Instead of carrying a lamb on his shoulders (FIGS. 8-6, 8-7, and 8-8A), Jesus sits among his

8-24 *Christ as Good Shepherd*, mosaic from the entrance (north) wall of the Mausoleum of Galla Placidia, Ravenna, Italy, ca. 425.

Jesus sits among his flock, haloed and robed in gold and purple. The landscape and the figures, with their cast shadows, are the work of a mosaicist still rooted in the naturalistic classical tradition.

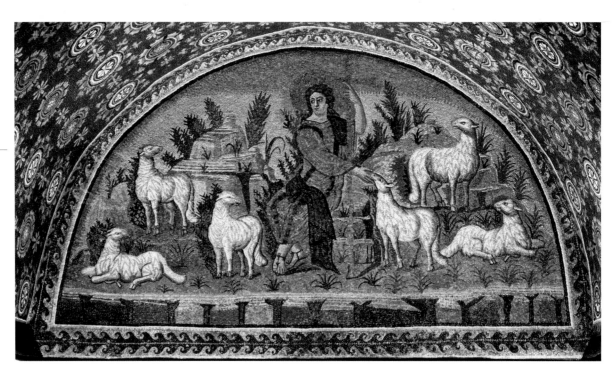

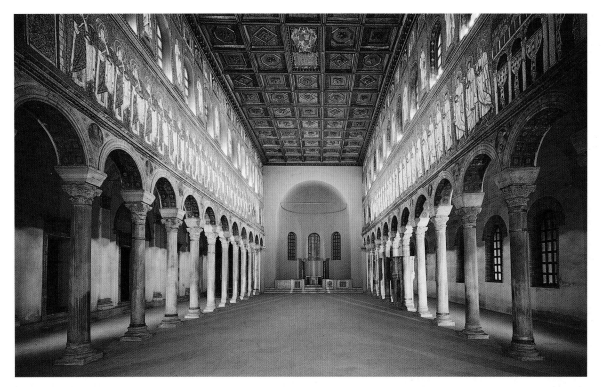

Theodoric, king of the Ostrogoths, established his capital at Ravenna in 493. His palace-church features an extensive series of mosaics depicting Hebrew prophets and scenes from the life of Christ.

flock, haloed and robed in gold and purple. To his left and right, the sheep are distributed evenly in groups of three. But their arrangement is rather loose and informal, and they occupy a carefully described landscape extending from foreground to background beneath a blue sky. As at Santa Maria Maggiore (FIG. 8-21), all the forms have three-dimensional bulk and are still deeply rooted in the classical tradition.

Sant'Apollinare Nuovo. Ravenna is famous for its treasure trove of Early Christian and Byzantine mosaics. About 30 years later than the Galla Placidia mosaics are those of Ravenna's Orthodox Baptistery (FIG. 8-24A). An especially large cycle of mosaics adorns the palace-church (FIG. 8-25) that Theodoric built soon after he settled in Ravenna. A three-aisled basilica originally dedicated to "Our Lord Jesus Christ," the church, probably constructed between 495 and 504, was rededicated in the ninth century as Sant'Apollinare Nuovo, when it acquired the relics of Saint Apollinaris. The rich mosaic decoration of the nave walls fills three zones. Only the upper two remain unchanged from Theodoric's time. Hebrew patriarchs and prophets stand between the clerestory windows. Above them, scenes from Christ's life alternate with decorative panels.

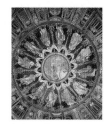

🔗 8-24A Orthodox Baptistery, Ravenna, ca. 458.

The *Miracle of the Loaves and Fishes* mosaic (FIG. 8-26) stands in sharp contrast to the 80-year-earlier mosaics of the Mausoleum of Galla Placidia. Jesus, beardless, in the imperial dress of gold and purple, and now distinguished by the cross-inscribed *nimbus* (halo)

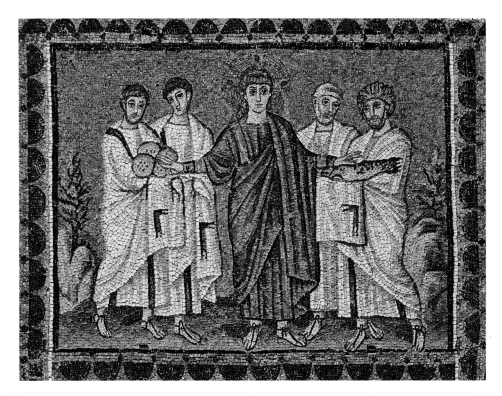

8-26 *Miracle of the Loaves and Fishes*, mosaic from the top register of the nave wall (above the clerestory windows in FIG. 8-25) of Sant'Apollinare Nuovo, Ravenna, Italy, early sixth century.

In contrast to FIG. 8-24, Jesus here faces directly toward the viewer. Blue sky has given way to the otherworldly splendor of heavenly gold, the standard background color for medieval mosaics.

Picturing the Spiritual World

The early-sixth-century mosaics of Sant'Apollinare Nuovo in Ravenna are but one example of a major stylistic shift in the art of Late Antiquity. Why did Early Christian artists begin to depict the sky as golden instead of blue? The answer is clear. These artists were seeking a means to conjure a spiritual world before the eyes of the faithful, not to represent the everyday world outside the sacred space of the church. In *Miracle of the Loaves and Fishes* (FIG. 8-26), for example, the solution the mosaicist adopted was to reduce the landscape setting, which the artist who decorated the Mausoleum of Galla Placidia so explicitly described (FIG. 8-24), to a few rocks and bushes enclosing the figure group like parentheses. The blue sky of the physical world gave way to the otherworldly splendor of heavenly gold.

The movement away from classical illusionism toward a more abstract style depicting the spiritual rather than the physical world occurred even earlier in the Eastern Roman Empire than in the West. Many of the features of the *Miracle of the Loaves and Fishes* mosaic appear in more advanced form and at least a century earlier in the mosaics of the dome of the Church of Hagios Georgios (Saint George) at Thessaloniki in northern Greece. The church, of the central-plan type, originally served as the mausoleum of the Roman emperor Galerius (r. 293–311), the tetrarchic Caesar of the East under Diocletian (FIG. 7-72). The tomb, which formed part of Galerius's palace complex at Thessaloniki, resembled in general form the mausoleum in Diocletian's palace (FIG. 7-73) at Split. When Christian architects converted the Thessaloniki mausoleum into a church in the late fourth or fifth century, they added an apse and a narthex and covered the huge dome (79′ 3″ in diameter) with two zones of mosaics.

The detail reproduced here (FIG. 8-27) comes from the lower band of mosaics. The upper band is poorly preserved. In the lower zone, eight pairs of over-life-size figures of saints with their arms raised in prayer (compare FIGS. 8-6 and 8-7) stand before two-story architectural fantasies that resemble Roman mural paintings (FIG. 7-19, *right*) and the facades of the rock-cut tombs (FIG. 7-53) of Petra. In this respect, the Thessaloniki mosaics are more closely tied to the classical past than are those of Sant'Apollinare Nuovo. Yet the Hagios Georgios figures and architecture alike have lost almost all substance, and it is increasingly difficult to imagine rounded torsos and limbs beneath the flat, curtainlike garments the saints wear.

A new aesthetic is on exhibit here, one quite foreign to classical art, with its worldly themes, naturalism, perspective illusionism, and modeling in light and shade. Indeed, the ethereal golden background suggests that these saints exist not on earth but in the palatial kingdom of Heaven far above the heads of the Christian worshipers below. This is precisely the impression the Early Christian mosaicists wished to create.

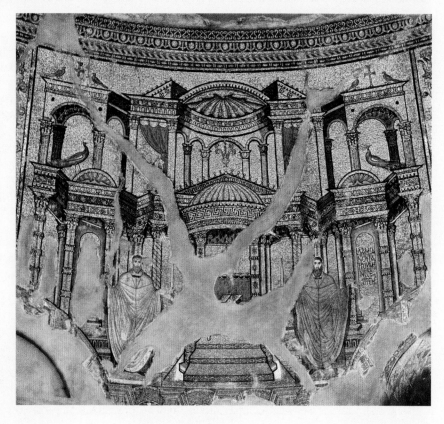

8-27 Two saints, detail of the mosaic frieze of the lower zone of the dome, Hagios Georgios (Church of Saint George), Thessaloniki, Greece, late fourth or early fifth century.

The dome mosaics of Hagios Georgios depict eight pairs of saints with their arms raised in prayer, standing before architectural fantasies suggesting the palatial kingdom of Heaven with its golden sky.

that signifies his divinity, faces directly toward the viewer. With extended arms, he directs his disciples to distribute to the great crowd the miraculously increased supply of bread and fish he has produced. Peter and Andrew are on Jesus's left; the young man to his right is probably John the Evangelist.

The mosaicist told the story with the least number of figures necessary to make its meaning explicit, aligning the figures laterally, moving them close to the foreground, and placing them in a shallow picture box. The composition, so different from those in the lunettes of the Mausoleum of Galla Placidia, is similar to that of the Samuel and David mural (FIG. 8-2) in the Dura-Europos synagogue two-and-a-half centuries earlier, illustrating once again that Early Christian artists inherited both classical naturalism and Late Antique abstraction from Roman art. But the Sant'Apollinare Nuovo mosaic, like those in the earlier Hagios Georgios (FIG. 8-27) in Thessaloniki, differs from the Dura murals as well as the Galla Placidia mosaics in having a golden background, which lifts the mosaic out of time and space and emphasizes the spiritual over the physical (see "Picturing the Spiritual World," above). As discussed in the next chapter, this new approach to representation would soon become the hallmark of Byzantine art, although classical naturalism also lived on in Byzantium for a millennium.

Late Antiquity

Soldier Emperors to the Sack of Rome 235–410

- The Second Commandment prohibition against worshiping images once led scholars to think that the Jews of the Roman Empire had no figural art, but the synagogue at Dura-Europos contains an extensive series of mural paintings illustrating episodes from the Hebrew Bible. Dura's baptistery contains the oldest surviving mural program in Christian art.

- Christ was crucified ca. 29, but very little Christian art or architecture survives from the first centuries of Christianity. "Early Christian art" refers to the earliest art of Christian content, not to the art of Christians at the time of Jesus.

- Early Christian art comes primarily from the catacombs of Rome. Painters decorated the walls and ceilings of the catacombs with frescoes, and wealthier Christians placed sarcophagi containing the remains of family members in catacomb galleries and cubicula. Both frescoes and sarcophagus reliefs featured a mix of Old and New Testament themes.

- Constantine's Edict of Milan of 313 granted Christianity legal status equal or superior to the cults of the traditional gods. The emperor was the first great patron of Christian art and built the first churches in Rome, including Old Saint Peter's.

- The models for the new Christian houses of worship were not Roman temples but civic basilicas, which were not associated with the old gods and could accommodate large congregations inside. Early Christian mausolea, such as Constantina's, were central-plan structures, which became standard for churches in Byzantium.

- Late Antique artists excelled in producing illuminated manuscripts and luxurious items for domestic use in silver and ivory, such as tableware, boxes, and diptychs, and decorated them with reliefs depicting both Christian and traditional Roman themes.

- In a Christian ceremony, Constantine dedicated Constantinople as the new capital of the Roman Empire in 330. He was baptized on his deathbed in 337.

- The emperor Theodosius I (r. 379–395) proclaimed Christianity the official religion of the Roman Empire in 380 and banned worship of the old Roman gods in 391. But some wealthy families, such as the Nicomachi and the Symmachi, continued to worship the old gods and commissioned artworks embodying the aesthetic ideals of the classical past.

- Honorius (r. 395–423) moved the capital of his Western Roman Empire to Ravenna in 404. Rome fell to the Visigothic king Alaric in 410.

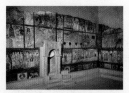

Synagogue, Dura-Europos,
ca. 245–256

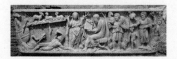

Santa Maria Antiqua sarcophagus,
ca. 270

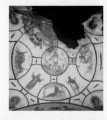

Catacomb of Saints Peter
and Marcellinus, Rome,
early fourth century

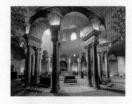

Santa Costanza, Rome,
ca. 337–351

Sack of Rome to Justinian 410–527

- In the fifth and sixth centuries, builders followed the pattern that Constantinian architects formulated for the first churches. Santa Sabina and Santa Maria Maggiore in Rome are characteristic examples.

- Mosaics became a major vehicle for the depiction of Christian themes in churches. Extensive mosaic cycles are preserved in Santa Maria Maggiore and especially at Ravenna in Sant'Apollinare Nuovo and the so-called Mausoleum of Galla Placidia. The latter is an early example of a domed longitudinal building.

- A new aesthetic gradually took hold. Classical naturalism yielded to a desire to depict the spiritual world. As in Hagios Georgios, wafer-thin figures seen against an ethereal golden background replaced the classical norm of weighty figures in a landscape beneath a blue sky.

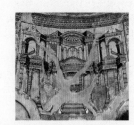

Hagios Georgios, Thessaloniki,
late fourth or early fifth century

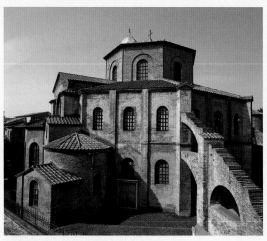

9-1a San Vitale is a central-plan church with an octagonal plan modeled on churches in Constantinople. Its austere facade gives no hint of its sumptuous marble- and mosaic-covered interior.

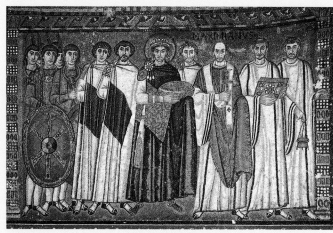

9-1b The apse mosaics celebrate the Byzantine emperor's dual political and religious roles. Justinian, clad in his purple imperial robe with a halo behind his head, is accompanied by Bishop Maximianus.

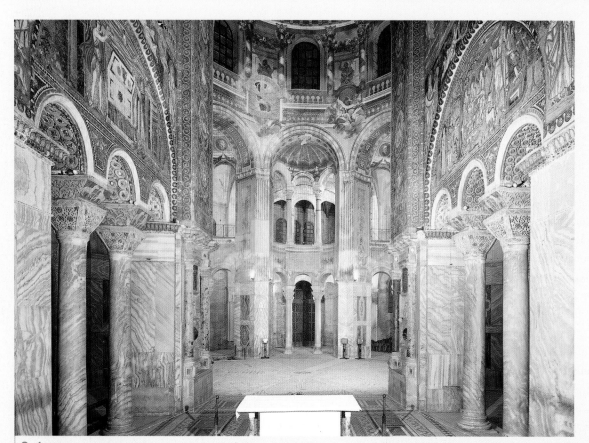

9-1 **Interior of San Vitale (looking west from the apse), Ravenna, Italy, 526–547.**

9-1c The haloed Byzantine empress Theodora holds the golden cup of wine for the Eucharist as her husband carries the golden platter with the bread. But neither she nor Justinian was ever in Ravenna.

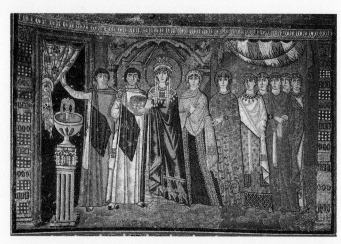

BYZANTIUM /9

Church and State United

San Vitale (FIG. 9-1) is the most spectacular building in Ravenna, the Byzantine Empire's outpost in northern Italy. Begun while Ravenna was ruled by the Ostrogoths, the church was completed less than a decade after the Byzantine army captured the city. Dedicated by Bishop Maximianus in 547 in honor of Saint Vitalis, the second-century Christian martyr who died at the hands of the Romans at Ravenna, the church makes an unforgettable impression on all who have entered it and marveled at its intricate design and magnificent mosaics.

The exterior's octagonal regularity is not readily apparent inside the centrally planned church. The design features two concentric octagons. The dome-covered inner octagon rises above the surrounding octagon to provide the interior with clerestory lighting. Eight large rectilinear piers alternate with curved, columned *exedrae,* pushing outward into the surrounding two-story ambulatory. A rich diversity of ever-changing perspectives greets visitors walking through the building. Arches looping over arches, curving and flattened spaces, and wall and vault shapes all seem to change constantly with the viewer's position. Natural light, filtered through alabaster-paned windows, plays over the glittering mosaics and glowing marbles covering the building's complex surfaces, producing a splendid effect.

San Vitale's mosaics, like the building itself, must be regarded as one of the greatest achievements of Byzantine art. The apse and choir decorations form a unified composition, whose theme is the holy ratification of Emperor Justinian's right to rule. In the apse vault, Christ sits on the orb of the world at the time of the Second Coming. On the choir wall to the left of the apse mosaic appears Justinian. The two are joined visually and symbolically by the imperial purple they wear and by their haloes. A dozen attendants accompany Justinian, paralleling Christ's 12 apostles. Thus the mosaic program underscores the dual political and religious roles of the Byzantine emperor. The laws of the Church and the laws of the State, united in the laws of God, manifest themselves in the person of the emperor, whose right to rule is God-given.

Justinian's counterpart on the opposite wall of the apse is his empress, Theodora, with her corresponding retinue. Both processions move into the apse, Justinian proceeding from left to right and Theodora from right to left, in order to take part in the Eucharist. Justinian carries the bowl containing the bread, Theodora the golden cup with the wine. Neither one ever visited Ravenna, however. Their participation in the liturgy at San Vitale is pictorial fiction. The mosaics are proxies for the absent sovereigns. Justinian is present because he was the head of the Byzantine state, and his appearance in the mosaic underscores that his authority extended over his territories in Italy.

THE CHRISTIAN ROMAN EMPIRE

In 324, when Constantine I (r. 306–337) founded Constantinople (Greek, "Constantine's city") on the site of ancient Byzantium, he legitimately could claim to be ruler of a united Roman Empire. But when Theodosius I (r. 379–395) died, he divided the Empire between his sons. Arcadius, the elder brother, became Emperor of the East, and Honorius, Emperor of the West. Arcadius ruled from Constantinople. After the sack of Rome in 410, Honorius moved the Western capital to Milan and later to Ravenna. Though not formally codified, Theodosius's division of the Empire (which paralleled Diocletian's century-earlier division of administrative responsibility) became permanent. Centralized government soon disintegrated in the Western half and gave way to warring kingdoms. The Eastern half of the Roman Empire, only loosely connected by religion to the West and with only minor territorial holdings there, had a long and complex history of its own. Centered at Constantinople—dubbed the New Rome—the Eastern Roman Empire remained a cultural and political entity for a millennium, until the last of a long line of Eastern Roman emperors, ironically named Constantine XI, died at Constantinople in 1453 in a futile attempt to defend the city against the Ottoman Turks (see "Ottoman Empire," page 309).

Historians refer to that eastern empire as Byzantium (MAP 9-1), employing Constantinople's original name, and use the term *Byzantine* to identify whatever pertains to Byzantium—its territory, its history, and its culture. The Byzantine emperors, however, did not use that term to define themselves. They called their empire Rome and themselves Romans. Though they spoke Greek and not Latin, the Eastern Roman emperors never relinquished their claim as the legitimate successors to the ancient Roman emperors (see "The Emperors of New Rome," page 267). During the long

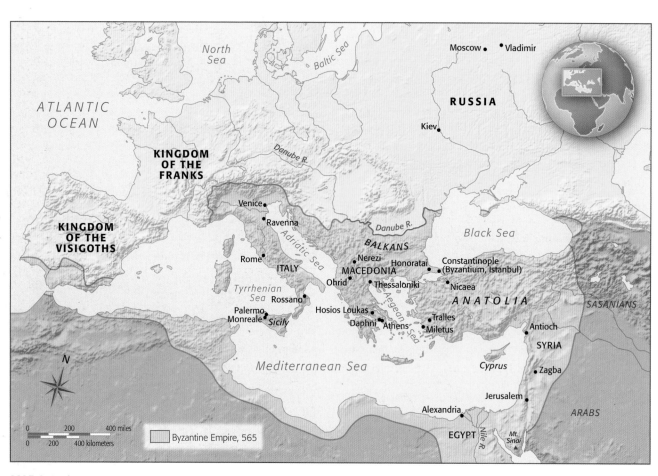

MAP 9-1 The Byzantine Empire at the death of Justinian in 565.

BYZANTIUM

324–726	843–1204	1261–1453
Early Byzantine	**Middle Byzantine**	**Late Byzantine**
■ Constantine founds Constantinople, 324 ■ Theodosius I erects an obelisk in the Constantinopolitan hippodrome, 390 ■ Justinian builds Hagia Sophia with a dome resting on pendentives, 532–537 ■ Maximianus dedicates the mosaic-rich San Vitale at Ravenna, 547 ■ Icon painting flourishes at Mount Sinai until Leo III bans picturing the divine in 726	■ Theodora repeals iconoclasm in 843 ■ Churches feature exterior walls with decorative patterning, Greek-cross plans, and domes on drums resting on pendentives or squinches ■ Ivory triptychs with carved figures become popular for personal prayer	■ Michael VIII recaptures Constantinople after the Crusader sack of 1204 ■ Late Byzantine artists decorate the Church of Christ in Chora with mural paintings ■ Constantinople falls to the Ottoman Turks in 1453

course of its history, Byzantium was the Christian buffer against the expansion of Islam into central and northern Europe, and throughout the Middle Ages, Europe felt its cultural influence. Byzantium Christianized the Slavic peoples of the Balkans and of Russia, giving them its Orthodox religion and alphabet, its literary culture, and its art and architecture. Byzantium's collapse in 1453 brought the Ottoman Empire into Europe as far as the Danube River, but Constantinople's fall had an impact even farther to the west. The flight of Byzantine scholars introduced the study of classical Greek to Italy after many centuries and helped inspire the new consciousness of antiquity that historians call the Renaissance.

Art historians divide the history of Byzantine art into three periods. The first, Early Byzantine, extends from the founding of Constantinople in 324 to the onset of *iconoclasm* (the destruction of images used in religious worship) in 726 under Emperor Leo III. The Middle Byzantine period begins with the renunciation of iconoclasm in 843 and ends with the Western Crusaders' occupation of Constantinople in 1204. Late Byzantine corresponds to the two centuries after the Byzantines recaptured Constantinople in 1261 until its final loss in 1453 to the Ottoman Turks.

EARLY BYZANTINE ART

The golden age of Early Byzantine art began with the accession of Justinian in 527, but important Byzantine artworks survive from the two centuries before Justinian's reign.

Before Justinian

Noteworthy among the pre-Justinianic examples of Byzantine art are the reliefs (FIG. 9-1A) honoring Theodosius I on the pedestal of the obelisk in the Constantinople *hippodrome,* as well as some superb carved ivories and illuminated manuscripts. They testify to the continuation of imperially commissioned political art and of private luxury art from the Late Antique West to Byzantium.

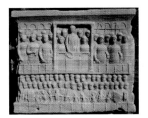

⚐ **9-1A** Obelisk of Theodosius, Constantinople, 390.

Archangel Michael. In the early sixth century, a master carver, probably at Constantinople, produced one of the largest extant Byzantine ivory panels (FIG. 9-2). It is probably the right half of a hinged diptych and depicts the archangel Michael. (The seven Christian archangels are distinct from and more important than other angels by virtue of having individual names.) The inscription opens with "Receive these gifts." The dedication may be a reference to the cross-surmounted orb of power the archangel once offered to a Byzantine emperor depicted on the missing diptych leaf. (Michael was the patron saint of Byzantine emperors, who often appear juxtaposed with him in Byzantine art.) The prototype for the archangel must have been a classical winged Victory, although Victory was personified as a woman in Greco-Roman art and usually carried a palm branch, as she does on a somewhat later Byzantine ivory (FIG. 9-4). The Christian artist here ingeniously adapted a classical personification and imbued it with new meaning.

The archangel's flowing drapery, which reveals the body's shape; the delicately incised wings; and the facial type and coiffure are further indications that the artist who carved this ivory was still working in the tradition of classical art. Nonetheless, this Byzantine

sculptor had little concern for the rules of naturalistic representation. The archangel dwarfs the architectural setting. Michael's feet, for example, rest on three steps at once, and his upper body, wings, and arms are in front of the column shafts, whereas his lower body is behind the column bases at the top of the receding staircase. These spatial ambiguities, of course, do not detract from the figure's striking beauty, but they do signify the emergence in Byzantium of the same aesthetic already noted in the Late Antique mosaics of Thessaloniki (FIG. 8-27). Here, as there, the Byzantine artist rejected the goal of most classical artists: to render the three-dimensional world in convincing and consistent fashion and to people that world with fully modeled figures firmly rooted on the ground. Michael seems more to float in front of the architecture than to stand in it.

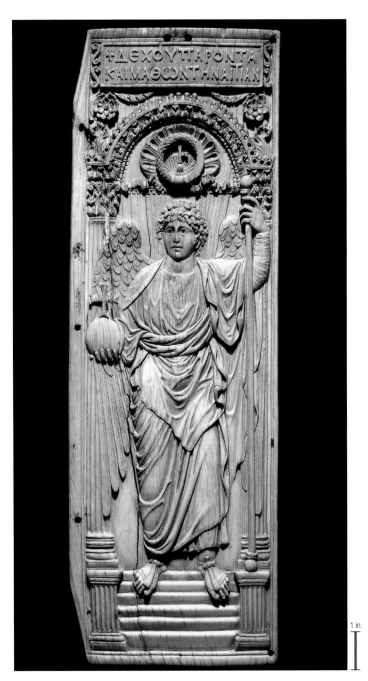

1 in.

9-2 Archangel Michael, right leaf of a diptych, early sixth century. Ivory, 1′ 5″ × 5½″. British Museum, London.

The sculptor who carved this unusually large Byzantine ivory panel modeled Michael on a classical winged Victory, but the archangel seems to float in front of the architecture rather than stand in it.

Vienna Dioskorides. The physical world was, however, the focus of one of the rare surviving early medieval secular books. In the mid-first century, a Greek physician named Dioskorides compiled an encyclopedia of medicinal herbs called *De materia medica*. An early-sixth-century copy of this medical manual, nearly a thousand pages in length, is in the Austrian National Library. The so-called *Vienna Dioskorides* was a gift from the people of Honoratai, near Constantinople, to Anicia Juliana, daughter of the short-lived Emperor of the West, Anicius Olybrius (r. 472). Anicia Juliana was a leading patron of the arts and had built a church dedicated to the Virgin Mary at Honoratai in 512. She also provided the funds to construct Saint Polyeuktos in Constantinople between 524 and 527. The excavated ruins of that church indicate that it was a domed basilica—an important forerunner of the pioneering design of Justinian's Hagia Sophia (FIG. 9-7).

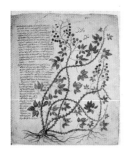

⊿ **9-2A** Blackberry bush, *Vienna Dioskorides,* ca. 512.

The *Vienna Dioskorides* contains 498 illustrations, almost all images of plants (FIG. 9-2A) rendered with a scientific fidelity to nature that stands in stark contrast to contemporaneous Byzantine paintings and mosaics of religious subjects. It is likely that the *Vienna Dioskorides* painters copied the illustrations as well as the text of a classical manuscript. One page, however, cannot be a copy—the dedication page (FIG. 9-3) featuring a portrait of Anicia Juliana in an eight-pointed star and circle frame. This earliest known illustrated dedication page shows Anicia Juliana enthroned between Magnanimity and Prudence, with a kneeling figure labeled Gratitude of the Arts at her feet. The princess holds a book in her left hand, probably this *De materia medica*. The shading and modeling of the figures, the heads seen at oblique angles, the rendering of the throne's footstool in perspective, and the use of personifications place this manuscript firmly in the classical tradition, an artistic mode that remained a key ingredient of Byzantine art throughout its long history.

Justinianic Art and Architecture

Historians and art historians alike regard the reign of Emperor Justinian (r. 527–565) as Byzantium's first golden age, during which the Christian Roman Empire briefly rivaled the old Roman Empire in power and extent (MAP 9-1). Justinian's generals, Belisarius and Narses, drove the Ostrogoths out of Italy, expelled the Vandals from the African provinces, beat back the Bulgars on the northern frontier, and held the Sasanians at bay on the eastern borders. At home, the emperor put down a dangerous rebellion of political and religious factions in the city (the Nika revolt of 532) and supervised the codification of Roman law in a great work known as the *Corpus juris civilis* (*Code of Civil Law*), which became the foundation of the law systems of many modern European nations. Justinian could claim, with considerable justification, to have revived the glory of Old Rome in New Rome.

At the beginning of the fourth century, Constantine recognized Christianity and became its first imperial sponsor. By the end of the century, Theodosius had established Christianity as the Roman Empire's official religion. It was Justinian, however, who proclaimed Christianity the Empire's only lawful religion, specifically the Orthodox Christian doctrine. In Orthodox Christianity, the central article of faith is the equality of the three aspects of the

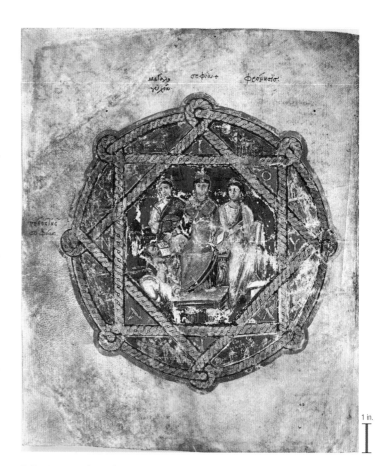

9-3 Anicia Juliana between Magnanimity and Prudence, folio 6 verso of the *Vienna Dioskorides,* from Honoratai, near Constantinople (Istanbul), Turkey, ca. 512. Tempera on vellum, 1′ 3″ × 1′ 11″. Österreichische Nationalbibliothek, Vienna.

In gratitude for her generosity, the people of Honoratai presented Anicia Juliana, a great art patron, with a book in which she appears enthroned with personifications of magnanimity and prudence.

Trinity of Father, Son, and Holy Spirit (as stated in Roman Catholic, Protestant, and Eastern Orthodox creeds today). All other versions of Christianity were heresies, especially the Arian, which asserted that the Father and Son were distinct entities and that the Father created the Son. Therefore, Christ was not equal to God. Also classified as a heresy was the Monophysite view that Christ had only one nature, which was divine, contrary to both the Orthodox and Arian belief that Christ had a dual divine-human nature. Justinian considered it his first duty not only to stamp out the few surviving polytheistic cults but also to crush all those who professed any Christian doctrine other than the Orthodox.

Barberini Ivory. Justinianic art—like Late Antique art in the West and the art of Theodosius (FIG. 9-1A) and his successors in Constantinople—was both religious and secular. A masterwork of political art is the ivory plaque known today as the *Barberini Ivory* (FIG. 9-4) because it was once part of the 17th-century collection (which also included the *Barberini Faun,* FIG. 5-85) of Cardinal Francesco Barberini (1597–1679) in Rome. Carved in five parts (one is lost), the panel shows at the center an emperor, usually identified as Justinian, riding triumphantly on a rearing horse, while a startled, half-hidden barbarian recoils in fear behind him. The dynamic twisting postures of both horse and rider and the motif of the spear-thrusting equestrian emperor are familiar motifs in Roman imperial works (see "The Emperors of New Rome," page 267), as are the bountiful Earth

The Emperors of New Rome

The emperors of Byzantium, the New Rome on the Bosporus, considered themselves the direct successors of the emperors of the Old Rome on the Tiber. Although they proclaimed Orthodox Christianity as the official state religion and suppressed all of Old Rome's polytheistic cults, the political imagery of Byzantine art displays a striking continuity between ancient Rome and medieval Byzantium. Artists continued to portray emperors sitting on thrones holding the orb of the earth in their hands, presiding over public entertainments (FIG. 9-1A), battling foes while riding on mighty horses (FIG. 9-4), and receiving tribute from defeated enemies. In the Early Byzantine period, the State also set up official portraits of the emperors in great numbers throughout the territories that Byzantium controlled. But, as was true of classical art, much of imperial Byzantine statuary is forever lost. Nonetheless, scholars have been able to reconstruct the general appearance of some of the lost portraits of the Byzantine emperors based on miniature versions of them on ivory reliefs such as the *Barberini Ivory* (FIG. 9-4) and descriptions in surviving texts.

One especially impressive portrait in the Roman imperial tradition, melted down long ago, depicted Justinian on horseback atop a grandiose column. Cast in glittering bronze, like the equestrian statue of Marcus Aurelius (FIG. 7-58) fashioned nearly 400 years earlier, it attested to the continuity between the art of Old Rome and that of New Rome, where pompous imperial images were commonly displayed at the apex of freestanding columns. (Compare FIG. 7-1, where a statue of Saint Peter has replaced a lost statue of Emperor Trajan.) Procopius of Caesarea (ca. 500–ca. 565), the historian of Justinian's reign, described the equestrian portrait:

> Finest bronze, cast into panels and wreaths, encompasses the stones [of the column] on all sides, both binding them securely together and covering them with adornment. . . . This bronze is in color softer than pure gold, while in value it does not fall much short of an equal weight of silver. At the summit of the column stands a huge bronze horse turned towards the east, a most noteworthy sight. . . . Upon this horse is mounted a bronze image of the Emperor like a colossus. . . . He wears a cuirass in heroic fashion and his head is covered with a helmet . . . and a kind of radiance flashes forth from there. . . . He gazes towards the rising sun, steering his course, I suppose, against the Persians. In his left hand he holds a globe, by which the sculptor has signified that the whole earth and sea were subject to him, yet he carries neither sword nor spear nor any other weapon, but a cross surmounts his globe, by virtue of which alone he has won the kingship and victory in war.

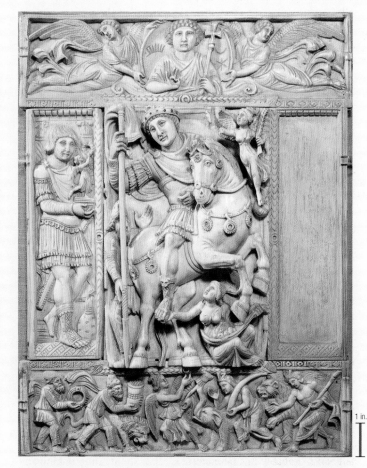

9-4 Justinian as world conqueror (*Barberini Ivory*), mid-sixth century. Ivory, 1′ 1½″ × 10½″. Musée du Louvre, Paris.

Classical style and motifs lived on in Byzantine art in ivories such as this one. Justinian rides a rearing horse accompanied by Victory and Earth personified. Above, Christ blesses the emperor.

> Stretching forth his right hand towards the regions of the East and spreading out his fingers, he commands the barbarians that dwell there to remain at home and not to advance any further.*

Statues such as this one are the missing links in an imperial tradition that never really died and that lived on also in the Holy Roman Empire (FIG. 11-12) and in Renaissance Italy (FIGS. 21-15 and 21-16).

*Cyril Mango, trans., *The Art of the Byzantine Empire, 312–1453: Sources and Documents* (reprint of 1972 ed., Toronto: Toronto University Press, 1986), 110–111.

(below the horse; compare FIG. 7-30) and palm-bearing Victory (flying in to crown the conqueror). Also borrowed from the art of Old Rome are the barbarians at the bottom of the plaque bearing tribute and seeking clemency. Accompanying them are a lion, elephant, and tiger—exotic animals native to Africa and Asia, sites of Justinianic conquest. At the left, a Roman soldier carries a statuette of another Victory, reinforcing the central panel's message. The source of the emperor's strength, however, comes not from his earthly armies but from God. The uppermost panel depicts two angels holding aloft a youthful image of Christ carrying a cross in his left hand. Christ

blesses Justinian with a gesture of his right hand, indicating approval of the emperor's rule.

Hagia Sophia. Like the emperors of Old Rome, Justinian was an ambitious builder. In Constantinople alone, he erected or restored more than 30 churches of the Orthodox faith. Procopius, the official chronicler of the Justinianic era, admitted that the emperor's extravagant building program was an obsession that cost his subjects dearly in taxation. But Justinian's monuments defined the Byzantine style in architecture forever after.

9-5 ANTHEMIUS OF TRALLES and ISIDORUS OF MILETUS, aerial view of Hagia Sophia (looking north), Constantinople (Istanbul), Turkey, 532–537.

Justinian's reign was the first golden age of Byzantine art and architecture. Hagia Sophia was the most magnificent of the more than 30 churches that Justinian built or restored in Constantinople alone.

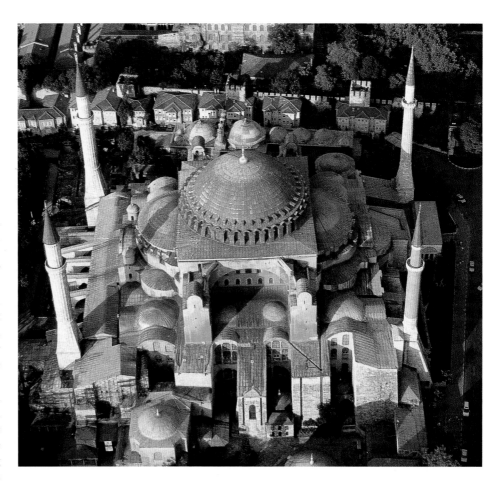

The emperor's most important project was the construction of Hagia Sophia (FIG. 9-5), the church of Holy Wisdom, in Constantinople. ANTHEMIUS OF TRALLES and ISIDORUS OF MILETUS, respectively a mathematician and a physicist (neither man an architect in the modern sense of the word), designed and built the church for Justinian between 532 and 537. They began work immediately after fire destroyed an earlier church on the site during the Nika riot in January 532. Justinian intended the new church to rival all other churches ever erected and even to surpass in scale and magnificence the Temple of Solomon in Jerusalem. The result was Byzantium's grandest building and one of the supreme accomplishments of world architecture.

Hagia Sophia's dimensions are formidable for any structure not made of steel. In plan (FIG. 9-6), it is about 270 feet long and 240 feet wide. The dome is 108 feet in diameter, and its crown rises some 180 feet above the pavement (FIGS. 9-7 and 9-8). (The first dome collapsed in 558. Its replacement required repair in the 9th and 14th centuries. The present dome is steeper and more stable than the original.) In scale, Hagia Sophia rivals the architectural wonders of Rome: the Pantheon (FIG. 7-49), the Baths of Caracalla (FIG. 7-65) and Diocletian (FIG. 7-66), and the Basilica Nova (FIG. 7-74). In exterior view (FIG. 9-5), the great dome dominates the structure, but the building's external aspects today are much changed from their original appearance. The huge buttresses are later additions to the Justinianic design, and after the Ottoman conquest of 1453, when Hagia Sophia became a *mosque*, the Turks constructed four towering *minarets* (see "The Mosque," page 299) at the corners of the former church. The building became a museum in 1935, but many in Turkey today wish to reconsecrate it as an Islamic shrine and reopen the building as a mosque for Muslim worship.

The characteristic Byzantine plainness and unpretentiousness of the exterior scarcely prepare visitors for the building's interior (FIG. 9-8). Paulus Silentiarius, a poet and *silentiary* (an usher responsible for maintaining silence in the palace) at Justinian's court, vividly described the original magnificence of Hagia Sophia's interior:

> Who . . . shall sing the marble meadows gathered upon the mighty walls and spreading pavement. . . . [There is stone] from the green flanks of Carystus [and] the speckled Phrygian stone, sometimes rosy mixed with white, sometimes gleaming with purple and silver flowers. There is a wealth of porphyry stone, too, besprinkled with little bright stars. . . . You may see the bright green stone of Laconia and the glittering marble

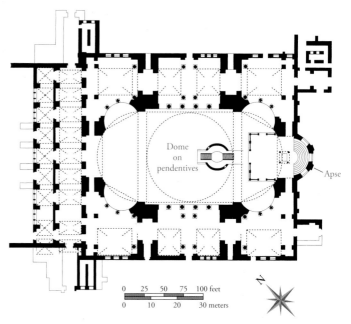

9-6 ANTHEMIUS OF TRALLES and ISIDORUS OF MILETUS, plan of Hagia Sophia, Constantinople (Istanbul), Turkey, 532–537.

In Hagia Sophia, Justinian's architects succeeded in fusing two previously independent architectural traditions: the vertically oriented central-plan building and the longitudinally oriented basilica.

with wavy veins found in the deep gullies of the Iasian peaks, exhibiting slanting streaks of blood-red and livid white; the pale yellow with swirling red from the Lydian headland; the glittering crocus-like golden stone [of Libya]; . . . glittering [Celtic] black [with] here and there an abundance of milk; the pale onyx with glint of precious metal; and

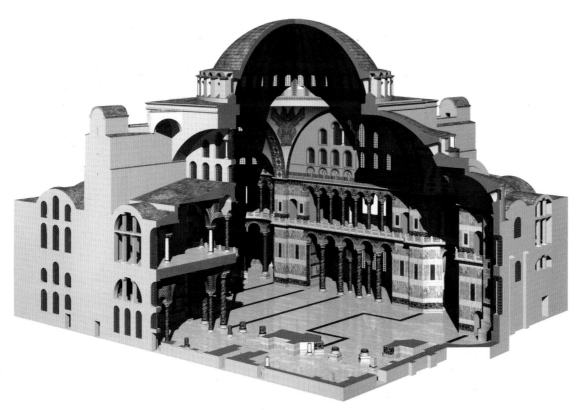

Hagia Sophia is a domed basilica. Buttressing the great dome are eastern and western half-domes whose thrusts descend, in turn, into smaller half-domes surmounting columned exedrae.

[Thessalian marble] in parts vivid green not unlike emerald. . . . It has spots resembling snow next to flashes of black so that in one stone various beauties mingle.[1]

The feature that distinguishes Hagia Sophia from equally lavishly revetted Roman buildings such as the Pantheon (FIG. 7-51) is the mystical quality of the light flooding the interior. The soaring canopy-like dome that dominates the inside as well as the outside of the church rides on a halo of light from windows in the dome's base. Visitors to Hagia Sophia from Justinian's time to today have been struck by the light within the church and its effect on the human spirit. The 40 windows at the base of the dome create the illusion that the dome rests on the light pouring through them.

Procopius observed that the dome looked as if it were suspended by "a golden chain from Heaven" and that "the space is not illuminated by the sun from the outside, but that the radiance is generated within, so great an abundance of light bathes this shrine all around."[2] Paul the Silentiary compared the dome to "the firmament which rests on air" and described the vaulting as covered with "gilded tesserae from which a glittering stream of golden rays pours abundantly and strikes men's eyes with irresistible force. It is as if one were gazing at the midday sun in spring."[3] Thus Hagia

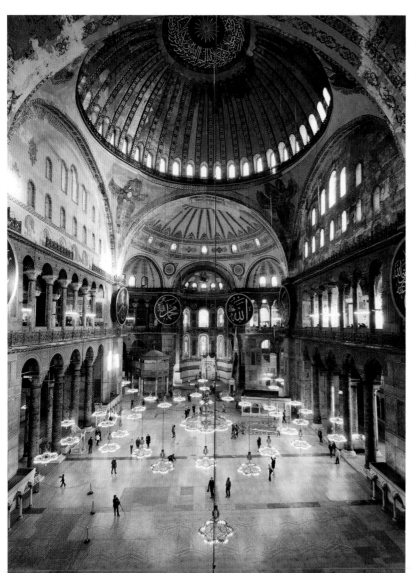

9-8 ANTHEMIUS OF TRALLES and ISIDORUS OF MILETUS, interior of Hagia Sophia (looking southwest), Constantinople (Istanbul), Turkey, 532–537.

Pendentive construction made possible Hagia Sophia's lofty dome, which seems to ride on a halo of light. A contemporary said that the dome seemed to be suspended by "a golden chain from Heaven."

Placing a Dome over a Square

Perhaps the most characteristic feature of Byzantine architecture is the use of a dome, which is circular at its base, over an interior space that is square in plan, as in the Justinianic church of Hagia Sophia (FIGS. 9-7 and 9-8) and countless later structures (for example, FIGS. 9-22, 9-23, and 9-26). Unlike other engineering marvels that the Byzantine Empire inherited from imperial Rome, the placement of a dome over a square was a problem that Byzantine builders had to solve themselves. Two innovative structural devices that became hallmarks of Byzantine engineering made this feat possible: *pendentives* and *squinches.*

In pendentive construction (from the Latin *pendere,* "to hang"), a dome rests on what is, in effect, a second, larger dome (FIG. **9-9**, *left*). The builders omit the top portion and four segments around the rim of the larger dome, producing four curved triangles, or pendentives. The pendentives join to form a ring and four arches whose planes bound a square. The pendentives and arches transfer the weight of the dome not to the walls but to the four piers from which the arches spring.

The first use of pendentives on a monumental scale was in Hagia Sophia (FIGS. 9-7 and 9-8) in the mid-sixth century, although Mesopotamian architects had experimented with pendentives earlier. In Roman and Early Christian central-plan buildings, such as the Pantheon (FIGS. 7-50 and 7-51) and Santa Costanza (FIG. 8-11), the domes spring directly from the circular top of a cylinder (FIG. 7-6).

The pendentive system is a dynamic solution to the problem of setting a round dome over a square, making possible a union of centralized

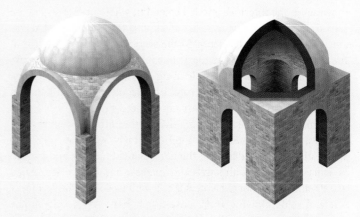

9-9 *Left:* dome on pendentives; *right:* dome on squinches (John Burge).

Pendentives (triangular sections of a sphere) make it possible to place a dome on a ring over a square. Squinches achieve the same goal by bridging the corners of the square to form an octagonal base.

and longitudinal (basilican) structures. A similar effect can be achieved using squinches (FIG. 9-9, *right*)—arches, corbels, or lintels—that bridge the corners of the supporting walls and form an octagon inscribed within a square. To achieve even greater height, a builder can rest a dome on a cylindrical drum that in turn rests on either pendentives or squinches, as in the 11th-century Church of the Dormition (FIG. 9-23) at Daphni, but the principle of supporting a dome over a square is the same.

Sophia has a vastness of space shot through with light, and a central dome that appears to be supported by the light it admits. In the sixth century, the lamps and incense used in the church services filled Hagia Sophia with particles that caught and reflected the sunlight, creating an atmosphere very different from what visitors experience today. Pseudo-Dionysius, perhaps the most influential mystic philosopher of the Justinianic age, wrote in *The Divine Names*: "Light comes from the Good and . . . light is the visual image of God."[4]

Pendentives. To achieve this illusion of a floating "dome of Heaven," Anthemius and Isidorus used *pendentives* (see "Placing a Dome over a Square," above) to transfer the weight from the great dome to the piers beneath rather than to the walls. With pendentives (FIG. 9-9, *left*), not only could the space beneath the dome be unobstructed, but scores of windows could puncture the walls. The pendentives created the impression of a dome suspended above, not held up by, walls. Experts today can explain the technical virtuosity of Justinian's builders, but it remained a mystery to their contemporaries. Procopius communicated the sense of wonderment experienced by those who entered Justinian's great church: "No matter how much they concentrate their attention on this and that, and examine everything with contracted eyebrows, they are unable to understand the craftsmanship and always depart from there amazed by the perplexing spectacle."[5]

By placing a hemispherical dome on a square base instead of on a circular base, as in the Pantheon (FIGS. 7-50 and 7-51),

Anthemius and Isidorus succeeded in fusing two previously independent and seemingly mutually exclusive architectural traditions: the vertically oriented central-plan building and the longitudinally oriented basilica. Hagia Sophia is, in essence, a domed basilica (FIG. 9-6)—a uniquely successful conclusion to several centuries of experimentation in church architecture. However, the thrusts of the pendentive construction at Hagia Sophia made external buttresses necessary, as well as huge internal northern and southern wall piers and eastern and western half-domes (FIG. 9-5). The semidomes' thrusts descend, in turn, into still smaller half-domes surmounting columned exedrae (FIGS. 9-7 and 9-8) that give a curving flow to the design.

The diverse vistas and screenlike ornamented surfaces mask the structural lines. The columnar arcades of the nave and second-story galleries have no real structural function. Like the walls they pierce, they are only part of a fragile "fill" between the huge piers. Structurally, although Hagia Sophia may seem Roman in its great scale and majesty, the organization of its masses is not Roman. The very fact that the "walls" in Hagia Sophia are concealed (and barely adequate) piers indicates that the architects sought Roman monumentality as an effect and did not design the building according to Roman principles. Hagia Sophia's eight great supporting piers are ashlar masonry, but the screen walls are brick, as are the vaults of the aisles and galleries and the dome and semicircular half-domes. Using brick in place of concrete was a further departure from Roman practice, and marks Byzantine architecture as a distinctive structural style.

The ingenious design of Hagia Sophia provided the illumination and the setting for the solemn liturgy of the Orthodox faith. The large windows along the rim of the great dome poured light down upon the interior's jeweled splendor, where priests staged the sacred spectacle. Sung by clerical choirs, the Orthodox equivalent of the Latin Mass celebrated the sacrament of the Eucharist at the altar in the apsidal sanctuary, in spiritual reenactment of Jesus's crucifixion. Processions of chanting priests, accompanying the patriarch (archbishop) of Constantinople, moved slowly to and from the sanctuary and the vast nave. The gorgeous array of their vestments (compare FIG. 9-35A) rivaled the interior's polychrome marbles, complementing the interior's finely wrought, gleaming candlesticks and candelabras; the illuminated books bound in gold or ivory and inlaid with jewels and enamels; and the crosses, sacred vessels, and processional banners. Each, with its great richness of texture and color, glowing in incense-filled shafts of light from the dome, contributed to the majestic ambience of Justinian's great church.

The nave of Hagia Sophia was reserved for the clergy, not the congregation. The laity, segregated by sex, had only partial views of the brilliant ceremony, the men from the shadows of the aisles, the women from the galleries. The emperor was the only layperson privileged to enter the sanctuary. When he participated with the patriarch in the liturgical drama, standing at the pulpit beneath the great dome, his rule was again sanctified and his person exalted. Church and State were symbolically made one (see "Church and State United," page 263). The church building was then the earthly image of the court of Heaven, its light the image of God and God's holy wisdom.

At Hagia Sophia, the intricate logic of Greek theology, the ambitious scale of Rome, the vaulting tradition of Mesopotamia, and the mysticism of the Orthodox Christian faith combined to create a building that is at once a summation of antiquity and a positive assertion of the triumph of Christianity.

Ravenna. In 493, Theodoric, the Ostrogoths' greatest king, chose Ravenna, an Etruscan, and later a Roman, city near the Adriatic coast of Italy south of Venice, as the capital of his kingdom, which encompassed much of the Balkans and all of Italy. During the short history of Theodoric's unfortunate successors, Ravenna's importance declined. But in 539, Justinian's general Belisarius captured the city, initiating an important new chapter in its history. Ravenna remained the Eastern Empire's foothold in Italy for two centuries, until the Lombards and then the Franks overtook it. During Justinian's reign, Ravenna enjoyed great prosperity at a time when repeated sieges, conquests, and sackings threatened the "eternal city" of Rome with extinction. As the seat of Byzantine dominion in Italy, Ravenna and its culture became an extension of Constantinople. Its art, even more than that of the Byzantine capital (where relatively little outside of architecture has survived), clearly reveals the transition from the Early Christian to the Byzantine style.

San Vitale. Construction of Ravenna's greatest shrine, San Vitale (FIGS. 9-1 and 9-10), began under Bishop Ecclesius (r. 522–532) shortly after Theodoric's death in 526. A wealthy citizen, Julianus Argentarius (Julian the Banker), provided the enormous sum of 26,000 *solidi* (gold coins), weighing in excess of 350 pounds, required to proceed with the work. San Vitale is unlike any of the Early Christian churches (FIG. 8-25) of Ravenna. It is not a basilica. Rather, it is centrally planned, like Justinian's churches in Constantinople, and it seems, in fact, to have been loosely modeled on the earlier Church of Saints Sergius and Bacchus there.

As already discussed (see "Church and State United," page 263), San Vitale's design features a dome-covered, clerestory-lit central space defined by piers alternating with curved, columned exedrae, creating an intricate eight-leafed plan (FIG. 9-11). The exedrae closely integrate the inner and outer spaces that otherwise would

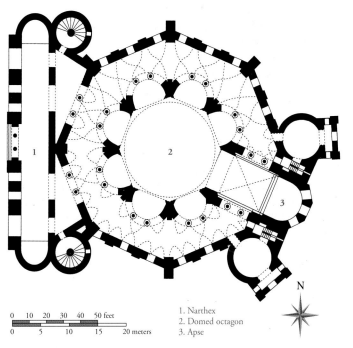

9-10 San Vitale (looking west), Ravenna, Italy, 526–547.

Justinian's general Belisarius captured Ravenna from the Ostrogoths. The city became the seat of Byzantine dominion in Italy. San Vitale honored Saint Vitalis, a second-century Ravenna martyr.

0 10 20 30 40 50 feet
0 5 10 15 20 meters

1. Narthex
2. Domed octagon
3. Apse

N

9-11 Plan of San Vitale, Ravenna, Italy, 526–547.

Centrally planned like Justinian's churches in Constantinople, San Vitale has a design featuring an off-axis narthex and two concentric octagons. A dome crowns the taller, inner octagon.

Apse (looking east) with mosaic of Christ between two angels, Saint Vitalis, and Bishop Ecclesius, San Vitale, Ravenna, Italy, 526–547.

In the apse vault, a youthful Christ, seated on the orb of the world at the time of the Second Coming, extends the gold martyr's wreath to Saint Vitalis. Bishop Ecclesius offers Christ a model of San Vitale.

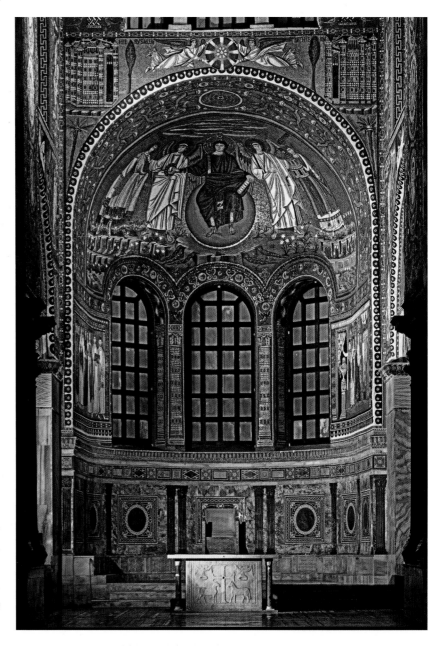

have existed simply side by side as independent units. A cross-vaulted *choir* preceding the apse interrupts the ambulatory and gives the plan some axial stability. Weakening this effect, however, is the off-axis placement of the narthex, whose odd angle (and that of the atrium that once preceded the narthex) is probably to be explained by the orientation of the preexisting streets in this section of Ravenna.

The mosaic- and marble-clad walls and vaults of San Vitale's interior (FIG. 9-1) are dazzling. In the apse vault (FIG. 9-12) is a vision of the Second Coming. Christ, youthful in the Early Christian tradition, sits atop the world and holds a scroll with seven seals (Rev. 5:1). The four rivers of Paradise flow beneath him, and rainbow-hued clouds float above. Christ extends the golden martyr's wreath to Vitalis, the patron saint of the church, whom an angel introduces. At Christ's left, another angel presents Bishop Ecclesius, who offers a model of San Vitale to the Savior. The arrangement recalls Christ's prophecy of the last days of the world: "And then shall they see the Son of Man coming in the clouds with great power and glory. And then shall he send his angels, and shall gather together his elect from the four winds, from the uttermost part of Heaven" (Mark 13:26–27).

Images and symbols covering the entire sanctuary express the single idea of Christ's redemption of humanity and the reenactment of it in the Eucharist.

9-13 **Justinian, Bishop Maximianus, and attendants, mosaic on the north wall of the apse, San Vitale, Ravenna, Italy, ca. 547.**

San Vitale's mosaics reveal the new Byzantine aesthetic. Justinian is foremost among the weightless and speechless frontal figures hovering before the viewer, their positions in space uncertain.

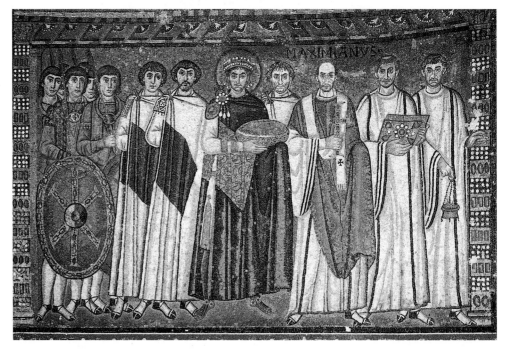

For example, the lunette mosaic over the two columns on the northern side of the choir depicts the story of Abraham and the three angels. Sarah, Abraham's wife, was 90 years old and childless when three angels visited Abraham. They announced that Sarah would bear a son, and she later miraculously gave birth to Isaac. Christians believe that the Old Testament angels symbolize the Holy Trinity. Immediately to the right in the lunette is the sacrifice of Isaac, a prefiguration of Christ's crucifixion (see "Old Testament Subjects in Christian Art," page 242).

Justinian and Theodora. The most distinctive elements of the mosaic program of San Vitale are the facing panels in the choir depicting Justinian and Theodora—even though neither the emperor nor empress ever entered San Vitale. The positions of the figures are all-important. They express the formulas of precedence and rank. In the Justinian mosaic (FIG. 9-13), the emperor is at the center, distinguished from the other dignitaries by his purple robe and halo, which connect him with the Savior in the vault above. At Justinian's left (at right in the mosaic) is Bishop Maximianus (r. 546–556), the man responsible for San Vitale's completion. (His magnificent ivory throne [FIG. 9-13A] is on display today in one of Ravenna's museums.) The mosaicist stressed the bishop's importance by labeling his figure with the only identifying inscription in the composition. (Some scholars think that Maximianus added the inscription and that the bishop represented was originally Ecclesius.)

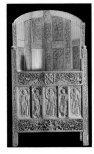

☑ **9-13A** Throne of Maximianus, ca. 546–556.

The artist divided the figures into three groups: the emperor and his staff; the clergy; and the imperial guard, bearing a shield with the *chi-rho-iota* (☧) monogram of Christ. Each group has a leader whose feet precede (by one foot overlapping) the feet of those who follow. The positions of Justinian and Maximianus are curiously ambiguous. Although the emperor appears to be slightly behind the bishop, the golden *paten* (large shallow bowl or plate for the Eucharist bread) he carries overlaps the bishop's arm. Thus, symbolized by place and gesture, the imperial and churchly powers are in balance. The emperor's paten, the bishop's cross, and the attendant clerics' book and censer produce a slow forward movement that strikingly modifies the scene's still formality. The artist placed nothing in the background, wishing the observer to understand the procession as taking place in this very sanctuary. Thus the emperor appears forever as a participant in the sacred rites and as the proprietor of this royal church and the ruler of the western territories of the Eastern Roman Empire.

The procession at San Vitale recalls but contrasts with that of Augustus and his entourage (FIG. 7-31) on the Ara Pacis, carved more than a half millennium earlier in Rome. There, the fully modeled marble figures have their feet planted firmly on the ground. The Roman officials—and their wives and children—talk among themselves, unaware of the viewer's presence. The emperor—the *princeps*—is first among equals. All is anecdote, all very human and of this world, even if the figures themselves conform to a classical ideal of beauty that cannot be achieved in reality. The frontal figures of the Byzantine mosaic who flank the central, haloed emperor hover, weightless and speechless, their positions in space uncertain. Tall, spare, angular, and elegant, they have lost the rather squat proportions characteristic of much Early Christian figural art. The garments fall straight, stiff, and thin from the narrow shoulders. The organic body has dematerialized, and, except for the heads, some of which seem to be portraits, viewers see a procession of solemn spirits gliding silently in the presence of the sacrament. Indeed, the theological basis for this approach to representation was the idea that the divine was invisible and that the purpose of religious art was to stimulate spiritual seeing (see "Picturing the Spiritual World," page 260). Theodulf of Orleans summed up this idea around 790: "God is beheld not with the eyes of the flesh but only with the eye of the mind."[6] The mosaics of San Vitale reveal this new Byzantine aesthetic, one very different from that of the classical world, but equally compelling. Byzantine art disparages matter and material values. It is an art in which blue sky has given way to heavenly gold, an art without solid bodies or cast shadows and with the perspective of Paradise, which is nowhere and everywhere.

The portraits in the Theodora mosaic (FIG. 9-14) exhibit the same stylistic traits as those in the Justinian mosaic, but the artist

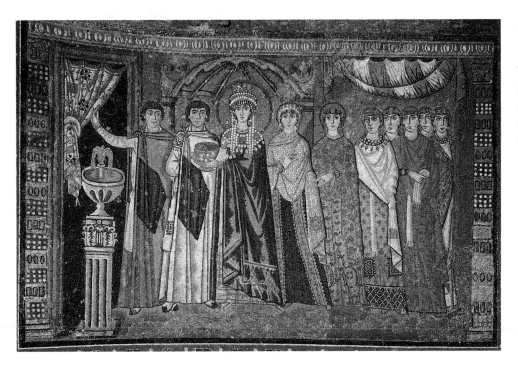

9-14 Theodora and attendants, mosaic on the south wall of the apse, San Vitale, Ravenna, Italy, ca. 547.

Justinian's counterpart on the opposite wall is the powerful Empress Theodora. Neither she nor Justinian ever visited Ravenna. San Vitale's mosaics are proxies for the absent sovereigns.

9-15 Saint Apollinaris amid sheep, apse mosaic, Sant'Apollinare in Classe, Ravenna, Italy, ca. 533–549.

Saint Apollinaris stands beneath Christ's cross, his arms raised in prayer. Although the scene is set in a landscape, the Byzantine artist rejected the classical illusionism of earlier mosaics (compare FIG. 8-23).

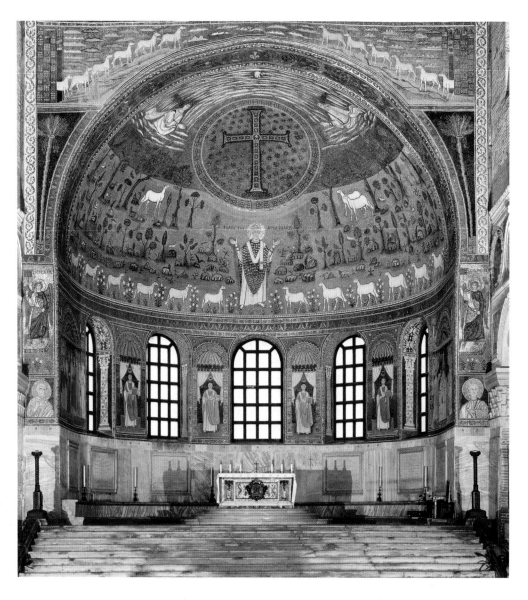

represented the women within a definite architecture, perhaps the atrium of San Vitale. The empress stands in state beneath an imperial canopy, waiting to follow the emperor's procession. An attendant beckons her to pass through the curtained doorway. That she is outside the sanctuary in a courtyard with a fountain and only about to enter attests that, in the ceremonial protocol, her rank was not quite equal to her consort's. But the very presence of Theodora at San Vitale is significant. She wielded enormous influence in the Byzantine state, as did many other Byzantine empresses (see "Born to the Purple: Empress Zoe," page 282). Of humble origin, Theodora, who was 15 years younger than Justinian, initially attracted his attention because of her beauty, but she soon became his most trusted adviser. John the Lydian, a civil servant at Constantinople at the time, described her as "the most intelligent of all and of all times."[7] For example, during the Nika revolt in Constantinople in 532, when all of her husband's ministers counseled flight from the city, Theodora, by the sheer force of her personality, persuaded Justinian and his generals to hold their ground—and they succeeded in suppressing the uprising. In the mosaic, the artist underscored Theodora's elevated rank by decorating the border of her garment with a representation of the three magi, suggesting that the empress belongs in the company of the three monarchs bearing gifts who approached the newborn Jesus.

Sant'Apollinare in Classe.   Until the ninth century, the Church of Sant'Apollinare in Classe housed the body of Saint Apollinaris, who died a martyr in Classe, Ravenna's port. The church itself is Early Christian in type, a basilica with a nave and flanking aisles, like Theodoric's palace-church (FIG. 8-25) dedicated to the same saint in Ravenna. As in the earlier church, the Justinianic building's exterior is plain and unadorned, but inside, sumptuous mosaics fill the apse (FIG. 9-15). The mosaic decorating the semidome above the apse was probably in place by the time of the church's dedication in 549. The mosaics of the framing arch and the figures between the windows are of later date.

Against a golden ground, a large medallion with a jeweled cross dominates the composition. This may represent the cross that Constantine erected on the hill of Calvary to commemorate the

martyrdom of Jesus. Visible just above the cross is the hand of God. On either side of the medallion, in the clouds, are the Old Testament prophets Moses and Elijah, who appeared before Jesus during his transfiguration (compare FIG. 9-16). Below these two figures are three sheep, symbols of the disciples John, Peter, and James, who accompanied Jesus to the foot of the mountain he ascended in order to converse with the prophets. Beneath, amid green fields with trees, flowers, and birds, stands the church's patron saint, Apollinaris. The mosaicist portrayed him in the Early Christian manner as an orant with uplifted arms (compare FIGS. 8-6 and 8-7). Accompanying Apollinaris are 12 sheep, perhaps representing the Christian congregation under the saint's protection. The composition is closely tied to the services enacted in the church. The sixth-century congregants saw, in hierarchical order from top to bottom, the hand of God, the symbols of Christ and his disciples, Apollinaris and his flock, and, presiding at the altar, Apollinaris's successor, the living bishop. Those attending the service were the bishop's sheep. Even the illiterate could make these visual associations.

Comparison of the Early Byzantine Sant'Apollinare in Classe mosaic with the Galla Placidia mosaic (FIG. 8-24) from the Early Christian period at Ravenna shows how the style and artists' approach to the subject changed during the course of a century. Both mosaics portray a human figure and some sheep in a landscape. But in Classe, in the mid-sixth century, the artist did not try to represent voluminous figures in a naturalistic setting, but instead treated the saint, the animals, and the plants as flat symbols, lined up side by side. The mosaicist carefully avoided overlapping in what must have been an intentional effort to omit all reference to the three-dimensional space of the material world and physical reality. Shapes have lost the volume seen in the earlier mosaic and instead are flat silhouettes with linear details. The effect is that of an extremely rich tapestry without illusionistic devices. This new Byzantine style became the ideal vehicle for conveying the extremely complex symbolism of the fully developed Christian dogma.

Mount Sinai. During Justinian's reign, almost continuous building activity took place, not only in Constantinople and Ravenna but throughout the Byzantine Empire. At about the time that mosaicists in Ravenna were completing their work at San Vitale and Sant'Apollinare in Classe, Justinian's builders were expanding an important early *monastery* (an enclosed compound for monks) at Mount Sinai in Egypt, where Moses received the Ten Commandments from God. Now called Saint Catherine's, the monastery marked the spot at the foot of the mountain where the Bible says that God first spoke to the Hebrew prophet from a burning bush.

Monasticism originated in Egypt in the third century and spread rapidly to Palestine and Syria in the East and as far as Ireland in the West. It began as a migration to the wilderness by those who sought a more spiritual way of life, far from the burdens, distractions, and temptations of town and city. In desert places, these refuge seekers lived austerely as hermits, in contemplative isolation, cultivating the soul's perfection. So many thousands fled the cities that the authorities became alarmed—noting the effect on the tax base, military recruitment, and business in general.

The origins of the monastic movement are associated with Saints Anthony and Pachomius in Egypt in the fourth century (see "Early Christian Saints," pages 246–247). By the fifth century, many of the formerly isolated monks had begun to live together within a common enclosure and to formulate regulations governing communal life under the direction of an abbot (see "Medieval Monasteries and Benedictine Rule," page 336). The monks typically lived in a walled monastery, an architectural complex that included the monks' residence (an alignment of single sleeping cells), an *oratory* (monastic church), a *refectory* (dining hall), a kitchen, storage and service quarters, and a guesthouse for pilgrims (FIG. 11-20).

Justinian rebuilt the monastery at Mount Sinai between 548 and 565 and constructed imposing walls around it. The site had been an important pilgrimage destination since the fourth century, and Justinian's fortress protected not only the monks but also the lay pilgrims during their visits. The Mount Sinai church was dedicated to the Virgin Mary, whom the Orthodox Church had officially recognized in the mid-fifth century as the Mother of God (*Theotokos*, "she who bore God" in Greek), putting to rest a controversy about the divine nature of Christ.

The mosaic in the church's apse is the *Transfiguration* (FIG. 9-16). Other mosaics in the church depict Moses receiving the Law and standing before the burning bush. Indeed, the various themes are

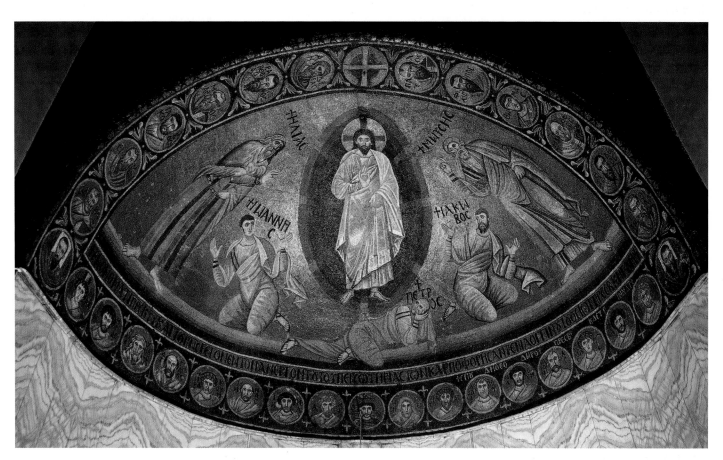

9-16 *Transfiguration,* mosaic in the apse of the Church of the Virgin, monastery of Saint Catherine, Mount Sinai, Egypt, ca. 548–565.

In this apse mosaic, unlike the one in Sant'Apollinare (FIG. 9-15), the artist swept away all traces of landscape for a depthless field of gold. The figures cast no shadows even though bathed in divine light.

The *Vienna Genesis*

The *Vienna Genesis* (FIGS. 9-17 and 9-17A) is a manuscript in codex format that was produced in a Constantinopolitan or possibly a Syrian workshop, using only the costliest materials. The preserved 48 folios (out of probably 96 originally) are fine vellum dyed with rich purple, the same dye used to give imperial cloth its distinctive color. The Greek text is in silver ink, long ago turned black. The illustrations are the work of several different painters. All were tasked with providing a picture to fill the lower half of each page, with the upper half reserved for the biblical text. Not surprisingly, the nature of the illustrations varies from painter to painter and the compositions reflect diverse sources. Many take the form of simple rectangular panels representing a single episode. Others, including the two reproduced here, show successive moments of the same story with the key figure or figures repeated in a single setting. On folio 12 the manuscript painter depicted events from the story of Jacob, which the viewer "reads" as the

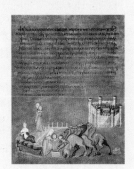

⬈ 9-17A Rebecca and Eliezer, *Vienna Genesis,* early sixth century.

narrative unfolds along a winding path beginning at the upper left, where Jacob leads his two wives and his 11 sons toward a bridge. The sons have more heads than bodies—a common way of suggesting a crowd in Late Antique art (compare FIG. 8-20). At the right, the main figures appear again crossing the bridge as they circle down into the lower zone where Jacob wrestles with the angel and then meets his brother, Esau. The family appears one more time at the lower left.

Art historians generally consider the paintings in the *Vienna Genesis* early examples of a method of pictorial storytelling called *continuous narration* (compare FIG. 7-43A), although here, as on the Column of Trajan frieze (FIG. 7-45), the figures move from place to place within the same frame. In the strictest definition of continuous narration, a single figure must appear more than once in the same space. What might be the model for this kind of presentation of the biblical story? Various answers have been proposed, but the most intriguing and convincing is that this painter's model was a Genesis manuscript in scroll form, which the artist adapted to the newer codex format. If so, the *Vienna Genesis,* the oldest preserved illustrated Bible book, is evidence for the existence of still earlier illustrated biblical texts in the form of long rotuli with both pictures and text revealed gradually as the reader unwinds the scroll.

9-17 The story of Jacob, folio 12 verso of the *Vienna Genesis,* early sixth century. Tempera, gold, and silver on purple vellum, 1′ ¼″ × 9 ¼″. Österreichische Nationalbibliothek, Vienna.

The Old Testament story of Jacob unfolds along a winding path and over bridges, with the chief figures appearing several times in the same illustration. The pictorial source may have been an illustrated scroll.

---

intertwined. In the apse, Moses reappears below Jesus with his disciples John, Peter, and James, and another Old Testament prophet, Elijah, here beholding the Savior transfigured into heat and light, paralleling the burning bush. The mosaicist depicted Jesus in a deep-blue *mandorla* (almond-shaped aureole of light), stressing the intense whiteness of Jesus's transfigured, spiritualized form, from which rays stream down on the disciples. The stately figures of the prophets and the static frontality of Jesus set off the frantic terror and astonishment of the gesticulating disciples. These distinctions dramatically contrast the eternal composure of heavenly beings with the distraught responses of the earthbound. At Mount Sinai, the mosaicist swept away all traces of landscape and architectural setting for a depthless field of gold, fixing the figures and their labels in isolation from one another. A rainbow band of colors graduating from yellow to blue bounds the golden field at its base. The relationship of the figures to this multicolor ground line is ambiguous. The artist placed some figures behind it, whereas others overlap it. The bodies cast no shadows, even though supernatural light streams over them. This is not the natural world that Jesus and his disciples inhabited. It is a world of mystical vision. The mosaicist subtracted all substance that might suggest the passage of time or motion through physical space, enabling the devout to contemplate the eternal and motionless world of religious truth (see "Picturing the Spiritual World," page 260).

Manuscript and Icon Painting

As in the Early Christian period, manuscript painting was an important art form during the Early Byzantine era. This period also marked the beginning of another Byzantine pictorial tradition with a long and distinguished history—icon painting.

Early Byzantine Books. The oldest well-preserved painted manuscript containing biblical scenes is the early-sixth-century *Vienna Genesis,* so called because it is today one of the treasures of the Austrian National Library in Vienna and contains the text of only the first book of the Old Testament (see "The *Vienna Genesis,*" page 276).

More popular than illustrated Old Testament books were Gospel books, which contained the texts of the four *Gospels* (see "Medieval Books," page 324). Two important Early Byzantine examples are the *Rossano Gospels* (FIG. 9-17B), contemporaneous with the *Vienna Genesis* and also featuring purple-dyed pages, and the somewhat later *Rabbula Gospels* (FIGS. 9-18 and 9-18A). The latter, written in Syriac by the monk Rabbula at the monastery of Saint John the Evangelist at Zagba in Syria, dates to 586 and boasts full-page paintings of the life of Jesus, especially scenes of his passion.

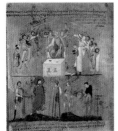

🔼 **9-17B** Christ before Pilate, *Rossano Gospels,* early sixth century.

The page depicting Christ's ascension (FIG. 9-18) shows Christ, bearded and surrounded by a mandorla, as in the Mount Sinai representation of the Transfiguration (FIG. 9-16), but here angels bear the mandorla aloft. Below, Mary, other angels, and various apostles look on. The artist set the figures into a mosaic-like frame (compare FIGS. 9-13 and 9-14), and many art historians think that the model for the manuscript page was a mural painting or mosaic in a Byzantine church somewhere in the Eastern Empire.

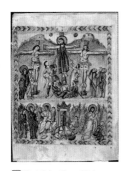

🔼 **9-18A** *Crucifixion and Resurrection, Rabbula Gospels,* 586.

The account of Christ ascending to Heaven is not part of the accompanying text of the *Rabbula Gospels* but comes from the book of Acts. In the latter, the Virgin is not present at the miraculous event. In the *Rabbula Gospels* representation, however, the Theotokos occupies a prominent position, central and directly beneath Christ. It is an early example of the important role the Mother of God played in medieval art, both in the East and in the West. Frontal, with a nimbus, and posed as an orant, Mary stands apart from the commotion all about her and looks out at the viewer. Other details also depart from the Gospel texts. Christ, for example, does not rise in a cloud. Rather, as in the vision of Ezekiel in the book of Revelation, he ascends in a mandorla above a fiery winged chariot. The chariot carries the symbols of the four evangelists—the man, lion, ox, and eagle (see "The Four Evangelists," page 331). This page therefore does not illustrate the Gospels. Rather, its purpose is to present one of the central tenets of Christian faith. Similar compositions appear on pilgrims' flasks from Palestine that were souvenir items reproducing important monuments visited. They reinforce the theory that the Byzantine painter based the *Ascension of Christ* in the *Rabbula Gospels* on a lost painting or mosaic in a major church.

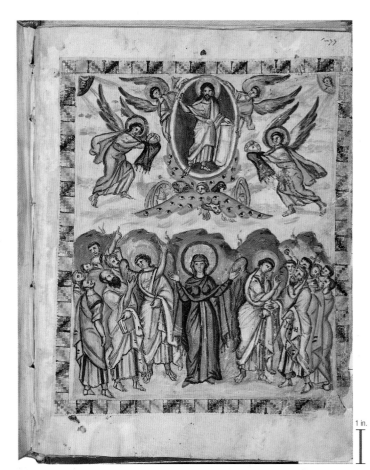

1 in.

9-18 *Ascension of Christ,* folio 13 verso of the *Rabbula Gospels,* from Zagba, Syria, 586. Tempera on parchment, 1′ 1″ × 10½″. Biblioteca Medicea-Laurenziana, Florence.

The Gospels do not mention the Virgin as witness to Christ's ascension. Her prominent position in the *Rabbula Gospels* is an early example of the important role that Mary played in medieval art.

Icons. Gospel books such as the *Rossano* and *Rabbula Gospels* played an important role in monastic religious life. So, too, did *icons,* which also figured prominently in private devotion (see "Icons and Iconoclasm," page 278). Unfortunately, few early icons survive. Two of the finest examples come from Saint Catherine's monastery at Mount Sinai. One represents Christ blessing the viewer (FIG. 19-18B), and the other the enthroned Theotokos (FIG. 9-19). The medium used for both icons is encaustic on wood, continuing a tradition of panel painting in Egypt that, like so much else in the Byzantine world, dates to the Roman Empire (FIGS. 7-60A, 7-61, 7-61A, and 7-62).

The smaller of the two illustrated icons (FIG. 9-19) is more ambitious in the number of figures depicted. In a composition reminiscent of the portrait of Anicia Juliana (FIG. 9-3) in the *Vienna Dioskorides,* the Sinai icon painter represented the enthroned Theotokos and Child with Saints Theodore and George. The two guardian saints intercede with the Virgin on the viewer's behalf. Behind them, two angels gaze upward to a shaft of light where the hand of God appears. The foreground figures are strictly frontal and have a solemn demeanor. Background details are few. The shallow forward plane of the picture dominates. Traces of the Greco-Roman illusionism noted in the Anicia Juliana portrait remain in the Virgin's rather personalized features, in her sideways glance, and in the posing of the angels' heads. But the painter rendered the saints' bodies in the new Byzantine manner.

Icons and Iconoclasm

Icons ("images" in Greek) are small portable paintings depicting Christ (FIG. **9-18B**), the Virgin, or saints (or a combination of all three, as in FIG. 9-19). Icons survive from as early as the fourth century. From the sixth century on, they became enormously popular in Byzantine worship, both public and private. Eastern Christians considered icons a personal, intimate, and indispensable medium for spiritual transaction with holy figures. Some icons (for example, FIG. 9-31) came to be regarded as wonder-working, and believers ascribed miracles and healing powers to them.

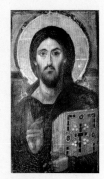

⏏9-18B Christ blessing, Mount Sinai, sixth century.

Icons were by no means universally accepted, however. From the beginning, many Christians were deeply suspicious of the practice of imaging the divine, whether on portable panels, on the walls of churches, or especially as statues that reminded them of ancient idols (FIGS. 8-8A and 8-8B). The opponents of Christian figural art had in mind the Old Testament prohibition of images that the Lord dictated to Moses in the Second Commandment: "Thou shalt not make unto thee any graven image or any likeness of anything that is in heaven above, or that is in the earth beneath, or that is in the water under the earth. Thou shalt not bow down thyself to them, nor serve them" (Exod. 20:4, 5). For example, early in the fourth century, Constantia, sister of Emperor Constantine, requested an image of Christ from Eusebius of Caesarea (ca. 263–339), the first great historian of the Christian Church. He rebuked her, referring to the Second Commandment:

> Can it be that you have forgotten that passage in which God lays down the law that no likeness should be made of what is in heaven or in the earth beneath? . . . Are not such things banished and excluded from churches all over the world, and is it not common knowledge that such practices are not permitted to us . . . lest we appear, like idol worshipers, to carry our God around in an image?*

Opposition to icons became especially strong in the eighth century, when the faithful often burned incense and knelt before the icons in prayer to seek protection or a cure for illness. Although their purpose was only to evoke the presence of the holy figures addressed in prayer, for many, the icons became identified with the personages represented. Icon veneration became confused with idol worship, and this brought about an imperial ban on the making not only of icons but of all sacred images, as well as edicts ordering the destruction of existing images (*iconoclasm*). The *iconoclasts* ("breakers of images") and the *iconophiles* ("lovers of images") became bitter and irreconcilable enemies. The anguish of the latter is evident in the following graphic description of the deeds of the iconoclasts, written in about 754:

> In every village and town one could witness the weeping and lamentation of the pious, whereas, on the part of the impious, [one saw] sacred things trodden upon, [liturgical] vessels turned to other use, churches scraped down and smeared with ashes because they contained holy images. And wherever there were venerable images of

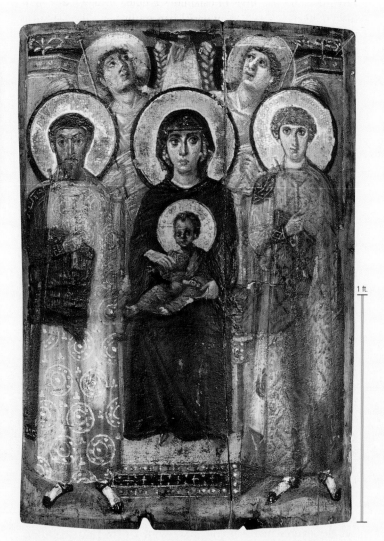

9-19 Virgin (Theotokos) and Child between Saints Theodore and George, icon, sixth or early seventh century. Encaustic on wood, 2′ 3″ × 1′ 7 3/8″. Monastery of Saint Catherine, Mount Sinai, Egypt.

Byzantine icons are the heirs to the Roman tradition of portrait painting on small wood panels, but their Christian subjects and their use as devotional objects broke sharply from classical models.

Christ or the Mother of God or the saints, these were consigned to the flames or were gouged out or smeared over.†

The consequences of iconoclasm for the study of Early Byzantine art are difficult to overstate. For more than a century, not only did the portrayal of Christ, the Virgin, and the saints cease, but the iconoclasts also destroyed countless works from the first several centuries of Christendom. For this reason, writing a history of Byzantine art before the ninth century presents a great challenge to art historians.

*Cyril Mango, trans., *The Art of the Byzantine Empire, 312–1453: Sources and Documents* (reprint of 1972 ed., Toronto: University of Toronto Press, 1986), 17–18.
†Ibid., 152.

Iconoclasm. The preservation of the Early Byzantine icons at the Mount Sinai monastery is especially fortuitous because in the seventh century, a series of calamities erupted in Egypt and Syria that indirectly caused an imperial ban on images. The Sasanians (FIGS. 2-28A and 2-29), chronically at war with Rome, swept into the Eastern provinces, and between 611 and 617 they captured the great cities of Antioch, Jerusalem, and Alexandria. The Byzantine emperor Heraclius (r. 610–641) had hardly defeated them in 627 when a new and overwhelming power appeared unexpectedly on the stage of history. The Arabs, under the banner of the new Islamic religion, conquered not only Byzantium's eastern provinces but also Persia itself, replacing the Sasanians in the age-old balance of power with the Christian West (see "The Rise and Spread of Islam," page 293). In a few years, the Arabs were launching attacks on Constantinople, and Byzantium was fighting for its life.

These were catastrophic years for the Eastern Roman Empire. They terminated once and for all the long story of imperial Rome, closed the Early Byzantine period, and inaugurated the medieval era of Byzantine history. The Byzantine Empire lost almost two-thirds of its territory and much of its population, wealth, and material resources. The shock of these events may have persuaded Emperor Leo III (r. 717–741) that God was punishing Byzantium for its idolatrous worship of icons by setting upon it the merciless armies of the infidel—an enemy that, moreover, shunned the representation not only of God but of all living things in holy places. Some scholars believe that another motivation for Leo's 726 ban on picturing the divine was to assert the authority of the State over the Church, especially the monasticism movement, which was growing rapidly. In any case, for more than a century, Byzantine artists produced little new religious figurative art. In place of images of holy figures, the iconoclasts used symbolic forms already familiar in Early Christian art—for example, the cross (FIG. 9-15).

MIDDLE BYZANTINE ART

In the late eighth and ninth centuries, a powerful reaction against iconoclasm set in. The case in favor of icons had been made forcefully earlier in the eighth century by Saint John of Damascus (ca. 675–ca. 749), who argued that the invisible God the Father had made an image of himself in the son Jesus and in humankind in general and that although icons were likenesses of holy figures, they were not identical to their prototypes. To oppose making images of holy figures was contrary to the actions of God. Two female regents in particular led the movement to restore image making in the Byzantine Empire: Empresses Irene in 780 and Theodora in 843, after the death of her husband, Theophilos (r. 829–842). Unlike Irene's short-lived repeal of the prohibition against icons, Theodora's opposition proved to be definitive and permanent and led to the condemnation of iconoclasm as a heresy.

Shortly thereafter, a new line of emperors, the Macedonian dynasty, resuscitated the Early Byzantine tradition of lavish imperial patronage of religious art and architecture and the making of images of Christ, the Virgin, and saints. Basil I (r. 867–886), head of the new dynasty, regarded himself as the restorer of the Roman Empire. He denounced as usurpers the Carolingian monarchs of the West who, since 800, had claimed the title "Roman Empire" for their realm (see "Carolingian Empire," page 328). Basil bluntly reminded their emissary that the only true emperor of Rome reigned in Constantinople. They were not Roman emperors but merely "kings of the Germans." Iconoclasm had forced Byzantine artists westward, where doubtless they found employment at the courts of these Germanic kings (see "Theophanu, a Byzantine Princess at the Ottonian Court," page 342). These Byzantine "refugees" strongly influenced the character of Western European art.

Architecture and Mosaics

The triumph of the iconophiles over the iconoclasts meant that Byzantine mural painters, mosaicists, book illuminators, ivory carvers, and metalworkers once again received plentiful commissions. Basil I and his successors also undertook the laborious and costly task of refurbishing the churches the iconoclasts had defaced and neglected.

Theotokos, Hagia Sophia. In 867, the Macedonian dynasty dedicated a new mosaic (FIG. 9-20) depicting the enthroned Virgin with the Christ Child in her lap in the apse of the Justinianic church of Hagia Sophia. In the vast space beneath the dome of the

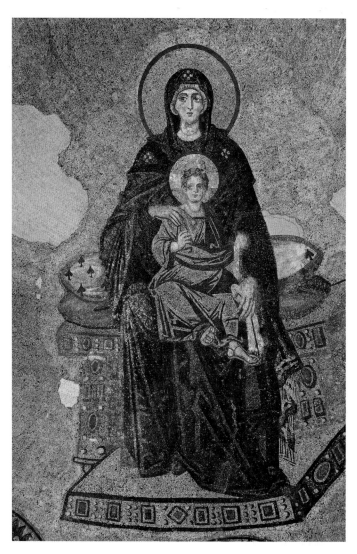

9-20 Virgin (Theotokos) and Child enthroned, mosaic in the apse of Hagia Sophia, Constantinople (Istanbul), Turkey, dedicated 867.

After the repeal of iconoclasm, Basil I dedicated a huge new mosaic in the apse of Hagia Sophia depicting the Virgin and Child enthroned. An inscription says that it replaced one that the iconoclasts destroyed.

great church, the figures look undersized, but the seated Theotokos is more than 16 feet tall. An accompanying inscription, now fragmentary, announced that "pious emperors" (the Macedonians) had commissioned the mosaic to replace one that the "impostors" (the iconoclasts) had destroyed. Some art historians think that this declaration may be purely rhetorical, however. There may not have been any comparable image of the Virgin and Child in the sixth-century apse.

Nonetheless, the ninth-century mosaic echoes the style and composition of surviving Early Byzantine artworks—for example, the Mount Sinai icon (FIG. 9-19) of the Theotokos, Christ, and saints. In the Hagia Sophia mosaic, however, the angular placement of the throne and footstool alleviate the strict frontality of Mother and (much older) Child. The Constantinopolitan artist rendered the furnishings in a perspective that, although imperfect, recalls once more the Greco-Roman roots of Byzantine art. The treatment of the folds of Christ's robes is, by contrast, even flatter and more schematic than in earlier mosaics. These seemingly contradictory stylistic features are not uncommon in Byzantine paintings and mosaics. What is most significant, however, about the image of the Theotokos and Christ Child in the Hagia Sophia apse is its very existence, marking the end of iconoclasm in the Byzantine Empire.

Hosios Loukas. Although the new emperors did not wait long to redecorate the churches of their predecessors, they undertook little new church construction in the decades after the renunciation of iconoclasm in 843. But in the 10th century and through the 12th, a number of monastic churches arose that are the flowers of Middle Byzantine architecture. They feature a brilliant series of variations on the domed central plan. From the exterior, the typical later Byzantine church building is a domed cube, with the dome rising above the square on a kind of cylinder or *drum*. The churches are small, vertical, and high shouldered, and, unlike earlier Byzantine buildings, have exterior wall surfaces decorated with vivid patterns, probably reflecting Islamic architecture.

The monastery of Hosios Loukas (Saint Luke; a local saint who died in 953, not the evangelist) in Greece, near ancient Delphi, boasts two churches. The main church, or *katholikon* (FIGS. 9-21 and 9-22, *bottom*), dates to the early 11th century. The other is the Church of the Theotokos (FIG. 9-22, *top*), built during the second half of the 10th century. The katholikon exemplifies church design during this second golden age of Byzantine art and architecture. Light stones framed by dark red bricks—the so-called *cloisonné* technique, a term borrowed from enamel work (see "Cloisonné," page 321)—make up the walls. The interplay of arcuated windows, projecting apses, and varying rooflines further enhances this surface dynamism. The plans of both Hosios Loukas churches show the form of a domed cross in square with four equal-length, vaulted cross arms (the *Greek cross*). The dome of the smaller Church of the Theotokos rests on pendentives. In the larger and later katholikon, the architect placed the dome over an octagon inscribed within a square, forming the octagon using squinches (FIG. 9-9, *right*), which play the same role as pendentives in making

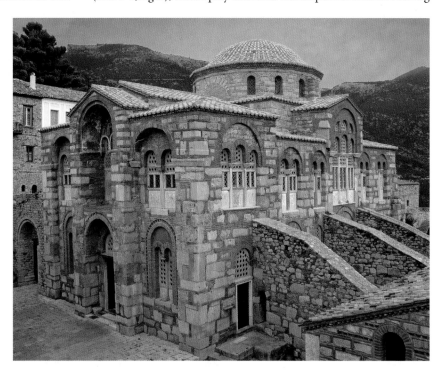

9-21 Katholikon (looking northeast), monastery of Hosios Loukas, Distomo, Greece, first quarter of 11th century.

Middle Byzantine churches typically are small and high shouldered, with a central dome on a drum, and exterior wall surfaces with decorative patterns, probably reflecting Islamic architecture.

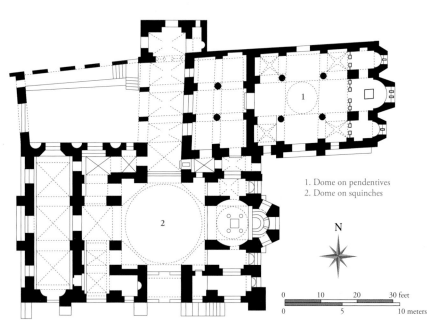

1. Dome on pendentives
2. Dome on squinches

N

0   10   20   30 feet
0   5   10 meters

9-22 Plan of the Church of the Theotokos (*top*) and the katholikon (*bottom*), monastery of Hosios Loukas, Distomo, Greece, second half of 10th and first quarter of 11th century, respectively.

The plans of the pair of Middle Byzantine churches at the monastery of Hosios Loukas in Greece feature a domed square at the center of a cross with four equal-length vaulted arms (the Greek cross).

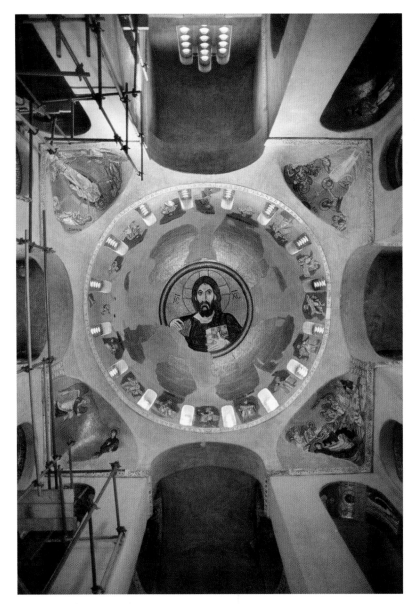

9-23 Interior of the Church of the Dormition (looking upward, into the dome), Daphni, Greece, ca. 1090–1100.

The Daphni dome rests on an octagon formed by squinches. At the center is a mosaic of Christ as Last Judge, which resembles a gigantic icon hovering dramatically in space above the awestruck worshiper below.

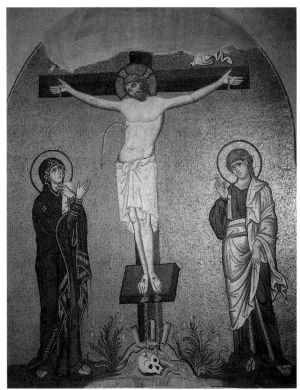

9-24 *Crucifixion,* mosaic in the north arm of the east wall of the Church of the Dormition, Daphni, Greece, ca. 1090–1100.

The Daphni *Crucifixion* is a subtle blend of Hellenistic style and the more abstract Byzantine manner. The Virgin Mary and Saint John point to Christ on the cross as if to a devotional object.

the transition from a square base to a round dome but create a different visual effect on the interior. This arrangement departs from the older designs, such as Santa Costanza's circular plan (FIG. 8-12), San Vitale's octagonal plan (FIG. 9-11), and Hagia Sophia's dome on pendentives rising from a square (FIG. 9-7). The katholikon's complex core lies within two rectangles, the outermost one forming the exterior walls. Thus, in plan from the center out, a circle-octagon-square-oblong series exhibits an intricate interrelationship that is at once complex and unified.

Daphni. Similar in general design to the katholikon of Hosios Loukas, but constructed at the end of the 11th century, is the monastic Church of the Dormition (from the Latin for "sleep," referring to Christ's receiving the soul of the Virgin Mary at the moment of her death; compare FIG. 13-48) at Daphni, west of Athens. As at Hosios Loukas, the Daphni church's interior (FIG. 9-23) creates a mystery out of space, surface, light, and dark. High and narrow, the

design forces the viewer's gaze to rise and revolve. The eye is drawn upward toward the dome, but much can distract it in the interplay of flat walls and concave recesses, wide and narrow openings, groin and barrel vaults, and illuminated and dark spaces. Middle Byzantine architects aimed for the creation of complex interior spaces with dramatically shifting perspectives.

At Daphni, the main elements of the late-11th-century pictorial program are intact, although the mosaics underwent restoration in the 19th century. Gazing down from on high in the dome is the fearsome image of Christ as *Pantokrator*—literally "ruler of all" in Greek, but usually applied to Christ in his role as Last Judge of humankind. The dome mosaic is the climax of an elaborate hierarchical mosaic program including several New Testament episodes below. The Daphni Pantokrator can be likened to a gigantic icon hovering dramatically in space. The image serves to connect the awestruck worshiper in the church below with Heaven through Christ. The Pantokrator theme was a common one in churches throughout the Byzantine Empire. A mosaic of the Pantokrator also adorned the dome of the Hosios Loukas katholikon. Today a painting replaces it.

Below the Daphni dome, on the wall beneath the barrel vault of one arm of the Greek cross, is a mosaic (FIG. 9-24) depicting Christ's death on the cross in a pictorial style characteristic of the posticonoclastic Middle Byzantine period. As in the Pantokrator mosaic in the dome, the Daphni *Crucifixion* is a subtle blend of the painterly naturalistic style of Late Antiquity and the later, more abstract and formalistic Byzantine style. The Byzantine artist

Born to the Purple: Empress Zoe

Although rarely rulers in their own right, Byzantine empresses often wielded great power and influence. Theodora (ca. 500–548) was Justinian's most trusted adviser. In 780, Irene (ca. 755–802) became regent for her 10-year-old son, Constantine VI (r. 780–797), and briefly repealed the imperial ban against icons.

In 843, another empress, Theodora (ca. 815–867), convened a religious council, which permanently put an end to iconoclasm. Theodora attained sainthood as a result.

The most influential Byzantine empress of the 11th century was Zoe Porphyrogenita (Greek, "born to the purple"), the elder daughter of Constantine VIII (r. 1025–1028). Born around 978, Zoe was not permitted to marry until just before her father's death, and she remained childless throughout her life. In 1028, Zoe married Romanos III Argyros (r. 1028–1034), whom Constantine favored as his successor, but she soon fell in love with another member of the court, with whom she may have plotted the drowning of Romanos in his bath. In any case, Zoe married Michael IV (r. 1034–1041) the same day, even though by law, widows were supposed to wait a full year before remarrying. Toward the end of Michael's reign, the couple adopted a son, Michael V (r. 1042), who succeeded his father and banished his adoptive mother to a convent. With the support of her subjects, Zoe returned to Constantinople, deposed the emperor, and ruled briefly in 1042 in her own name before marrying Constantine IX Monomachos (r. 1042–1054), who outlived her by four years. Thus four successive emperors of Byzantium owed their coronations to their marriage to, or adoption by, Zoe.

A mosaic portrait of Zoe and her last husband flanking the enthroned Christ (FIG. 9-25) adorns the east wall of the south gallery of Hagia Sophia. The emperor holds a purse, signifying the generous donation Constantine made to the church. Zoe holds a scroll, also a reference to her gifts to the church. Inscriptions next to the portraits describe Constantine as "pious emperor and king of the Romans"

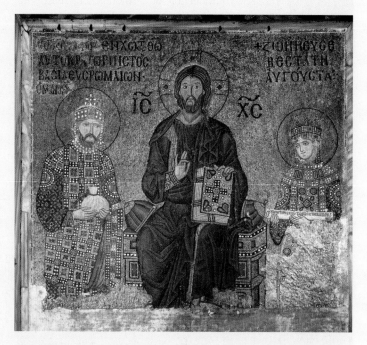

9-25 **Christ between Constantine IX Monomachos and Empress Zoe, mosaic on the east wall of the south gallery of Hagia Sophia, Constantinople (Istanbul), Turkey, ca. 1028–1035.**

Zoe, who was the wife of three emperors, here appears with the enthroned Christ and her third husband. Constantine IX's portrait replaced successive portraits of Zoe's previous two husbands.

and Zoe as "pious empress." Careful examination during conservation has revealed that the mosaic dates to the reign of Romanos and originally bore his portrait. Zoe twice asked the imperial artists to update the mosaic with new portraits and labels upon each of her subsequent marriages.

---

fully assimilated classicism's simplicity, dignity, and grace into a perfect synthesis with Byzantine piety and pathos. The figures have regained the classical organic structure to a surprising degree, particularly compared to figures from the Justinianic period (compare FIGS. 9-13 and 9-14). The style is a masterful adaptation of classical statuesque qualities to the linear Byzantine manner.

In quiet sorrow and resignation, the Virgin and Saint John flank the crucified Christ. A skull at the foot of the cross indicates Golgotha, the Place of the Skull. The artist needed nothing else to set the scene. Symmetry and closed space combine to convey the motionless and unchanging aspect of the deepest mystery of the Christian religion, as recalled in the ceremony of the Eucharist. The picture is not a narrative of the historical event of Jesus's execution, the approach taken by the carver of the Early Christian ivory panel (FIG. 8-16) examined in the previous chapter. Nor is Christ a triumphant, beardless youth, oblivious to pain and defiant of the laws of gravity. Rather, he has a tilted head and sagging body, and although the Savior is not overtly in pain, blood and water spurt from the wound that Longinus inflicted on him, as recounted in Saint John's Gospel. The Virgin and John point to the figure on the cross as if

to a devotional object. They act as intercessors between the viewer below and Christ, who, in the dome, appears as Last Judge of all humans. The mosaic decoration of the church is the perfect complement to Christian liturgy.

Empress Zoe. As did their Early Byzantine counterparts, Middle Byzantine mosaicists produced portraits of their imperial patrons for church interiors. Several such images grace the interior walls of Hagia Sophia (FIG. 9-8) in Constantinople. Perhaps the finest of these (FIG. 9-25) is on the east wall of the south gallery. It depicts Constantine IX and Zoe flanking the enthroned Christ. As in the much earlier imperial portraits (FIGS. 9-13 and 9-14) in San Vitale at Ravenna, the emperor and empress are haloed, but no longer is there a separation between the human and the divine, as in the sixth-century apse. Other Middle Byzantine mosaics depict the imperial couple flanking the Virgin.

Russia and the West. The Middle Byzantine revival of church building and of figural mosaics extended beyond the Greek-speaking East in the 10th to 12th centuries. The marriage of Anna, the sister of

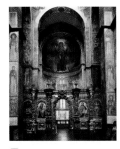

9-25A Saint Sophia, Kiev, begun 1037.

Basil II (r. 976–1025), to the Russian prince Vladimir (r. 980–1015) in 989 marked the introduction of Orthodox Christianity to Russia. Construction of the vast five-apse, 13-dome Cathedral of Saint Sophia (FIG. 9-25A) in Kiev followed within a half century. A resurgence of religious architecture and of the mosaicist's art also occurred in areas of the former Western Roman Empire where the ties with Constantinople were strongest. In the Early Byzantine period, Venice, about 80 miles north of Ravenna on the eastern coast of Italy, was a dependency of that Byzantine stronghold. In 751, Ravenna fell to the Lombards, who wrested control of most of northern Italy from Constantinople. Venice, however, became an independent power. Its *doges* (dukes) enriched themselves and the city through seaborne commerce, serving as the crucial link between Byzantium and the West.

San Marco, Venice. Venice had obtained the relics of Saint Mark from Alexandria in Egypt in 829, and shortly thereafter, the doges constructed the first Venetian shrine dedicated to the evangelist—a palace chapel and martyrium. Fire destroyed the ninth-century chapel in 976. The Venetians then built a second shrine on the site, but a grandiose new San Marco (FIG. 9-26) begun in 1063 by Doge Domenico Contarini (r. 1043–1071) replaced it. The model for Contarini's church was the Church of the Holy Apostles in Constantinople, built in Justinian's time. That shrine no longer exists, but its key elements were a cruciform plan with a central dome over the crossing and four other domes over the four equal arms of the Greek cross, as at San Marco. Because

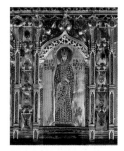

9-26A *Pala d'Oro*, San Marco, Venice, ca. 1105.

of its importance to the city, the doges filled the church's interior with lavish furnishings, such as the 10th-century *Pala d'Oro* (FIG. 9-26A) imported from Constantinople, and deposited there many of the treasures, including costly gold, silver, and enamel icons (FIG. 9-26B) brought back as booty from the Fourth

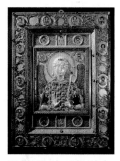

9-26B Archangel Michael icon, Venice, ca. 1100.

Crusade's sack of the Byzantine capital in 1204.

The interior (FIG. 9-26) of San Marco is, like its plan, Byzantine in effect. Light enters through a row of windows at the bases of all five domes, vividly illuminating a rich cycle of mosaics. Both Byzantine and local artists worked on San Marco's mosaics over the course of several centuries. Most of the mosaics date to the 12th and 13th centuries. Cleaning and restoration on a grand scale have returned the mosaics to their original splendor, enabling visitors to experience the full radiance of 40,000 square feet of mosaics covering all the walls, arches, vaults, and domes like a gold-brocaded figured fabric.

In the vast central dome, 80 feet above the floor and 42 feet in diameter, Christ ascends to Heaven in the presence of the Virgin Mary and the 12 apostles. In the great arch framing the church crossing are mosaics depicting Christ's crucifixion and resurrection and the liberation from death (Anastasis) of Adam and Eve, John the Baptist, and other biblical figures. The mosaics have explanatory labels in both Latin and Greek, reflecting Venice's position as the key link between Eastern and Western Christendom in the later Middle Ages. The insubstantial figures on the walls, vaults, and domes appear weightless, and they project no farther from their flat field than do the elegant Latin and Greek letters above them. Nothing here reflects on the world of matter, of solids, of light and shade, of perspective space. Rather, the mosaics reveal the mysteries of Christian faith.

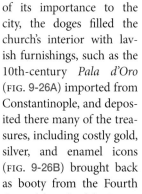

9-26 Interior of San Marco (looking east), Venice, Italy, begun 1063.

Modeled on a church in Constantinople, San Marco has a central dome over the crossing, four other domes over the arms of the Greek cross, and 40,000 square feet of Byzantine-style mosaics.

Norman Sicily. Matching Venetian success in the western Mediterranean were the Normans, the northern French descendants of the Vikings who, having driven the Arabs from Sicily, set up a powerful kingdom there. Although they were the enemies of Byzantium, the Normans, like the Venetians, integrated aspects of Byzantine culture into their own and even employed Byzantine artisans. They also incorporated in their monuments elements of the Islamic art of the Arabs they had defeated. The Normans' Palatine (Palace) Chapel (FIG. 9-26C) at Palermo with its prismatic (*muqarnas*) ceiling, a characteristic Muslim form (FIGS. 10-22 and 10-30), is one example of the rich interplay of Western Christian, Byzantine, and Islamic cultures in Norman Sicily.

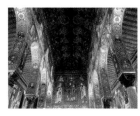

🖝 9-26C Cappella Palatina, Palermo, begun 1142.

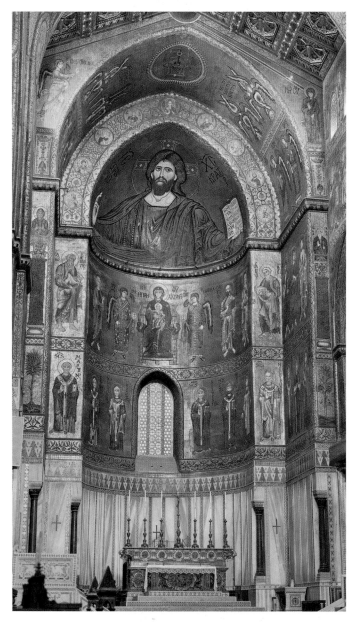

9-27 Pantokrator, Theotokos and Child, angels, and saints, mosaic in the apse of the cathedral of Monreale, Italy, ca. 1180–1190.

In centrally planned Byzantine churches, the image of the Pantokrator usually appears in the main dome, but Monreale's cathedral is a longitudinal basilica. The semidome of the apse is its only vault.

Monreale. The mosaics of the great basilican church of Monreale, not far from Palermo, are striking evidence of Byzantine influence. They rival those of San Marco in both quality and extent. One scholar has estimated that the Monreale mosaics required more than 100 million glass and stone tesserae. The Norman king William II (r. 1087–1100) paid for the mosaics, and the artists portrayed him twice in the church, continuing the theme of royal presence and patronage of the much earlier Ravenna portraits of Justinian and Theodora (FIGS. 9-13 and 9-14) at San Vitale and the Middle Byzantine portraits of Constantine IX and Zoe (FIG. 9-25) in Hagia Sophia. In one panel, William stands next to the enthroned Christ, who places his hand on William's crown. In the second, the king kneels before the Virgin and presents her with a model of the Monreale church.

The apse mosaics (FIG. 9-27) are especially impressive. The image of Christ as Pantokrator is in the vault. In Byzantium, the Pantokrator's image usually appears in the main dome (FIG. 9-23). But the Monreale church is a basilica, longitudinally planned in the Western tradition. The semidome of the apse, the only vault in the building and its architectural focus, was the logical choice for the most important element of the pictorial program. Below the Pantokrator in rank and dignity is the enthroned Theotokos, flanked by archangels and the 12 apostles, symmetrically arranged in balanced groups. Lower on the wall (and less elevated in the church hierarchy) are popes, bishops, and other saints. The artists observed the stern formalities of Byzantine style here, far from Constantinople. The Monreale mosaics, like those at San Marco (FIG. 9-26) in Venice and in the Palatine Chapel (FIG. 9-26C) in Palermo, testify to the stature of Byzantium and of Byzantine art in medieval Italy.

Ivory Carving and Painting

Middle Byzantine artists also produced costly carved ivories in large numbers. The three-part *triptych* replaced the earlier diptych as the standard format for ivory panels.

Harbaville Triptych. One example of this type is the *Harbaville Triptych* (FIG. 9-28), a portable shrine with hinged wings used for private devotion. Ivory triptychs were very popular—among those who could afford such luxurious items—and they often replaced icons for use in personal prayer. Carved on the wings of the *Harbaville Triptych,* both inside and out, are four pairs of full-length figures and two pairs of medallions depicting saints. A cross dominates the central panel on the back of the triptych (not illustrated). On the inside is a scene of *Deësis,* in which John the Baptist and the Theotokos appear as intercessors, praying on behalf of the viewer to the enthroned Savior. Below them are five apostles.

In contrast to the formality and solemnity usually associated with Byzantine art, visible in the mosaics of Ravenna and Monreale, a softer, more fluid style is displayed here. The figures may lack true classical contrapposto, but the looser stances (most stand on bases, as if freestanding statues) and three-quarter views of many of the heads relieve the hard austerity of the customary frontal pose. This more natural, classical spirit was a second, equally important stylistic current of the Middle Byzantine period, as it was in earlier centuries. The classical style also surfaced in mural painting and book illumination.

Nerezi. When the emperors lifted the ban against religious images and again encouraged religious painting at Constantinople, the impact was felt far and wide. The style varied from region

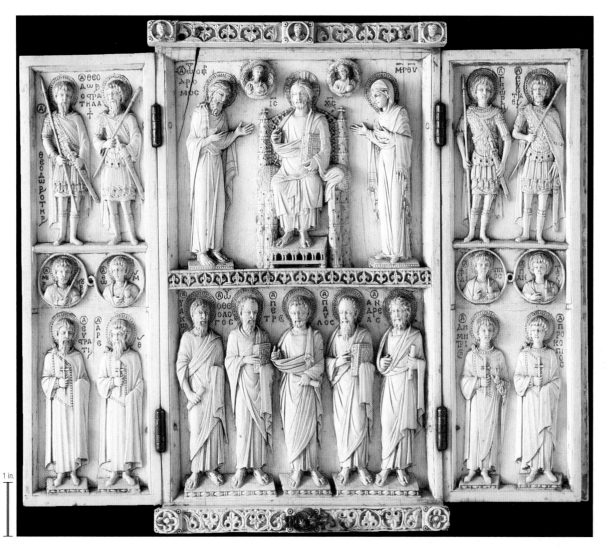

9-28 **Christ enthroned with saints (*Harbaville Triptych*), ca. 950. Ivory, central panel $9\frac{1}{2}'' \times 5\frac{1}{2}''$. Musée du Louvre, Paris.**

This small three-part shrine (triptych) with hinged wings was used for private devotion. The ivory carver depicted the figures with classical stances, in contrast to the frontal poses of most Byzantine figures.

1 in.

to region, but a renewed enthusiasm for picturing the key New Testament figures and events was universal. In 1164, at Nerezi in Macedonia, a member of the Comnenian imperial family sponsored the construction of the church of Saint Pantaleimon. Byzantine painters, possibly brought from Constantinople, embellished the church with murals of great emotional power. One of these, *Lamentation* (FIG. 9-29), is an image of passionate grief over the dead Christ. The artist captured Christ's followers in attitudes,

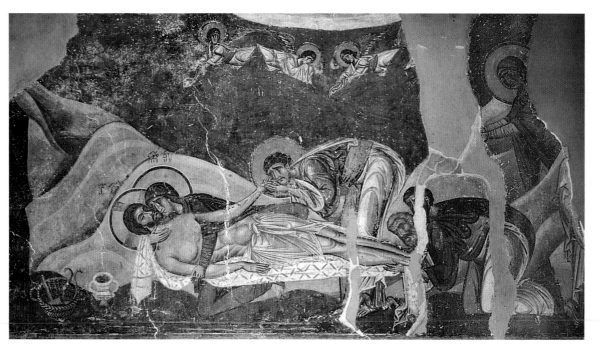

9-29 *Lamentation*, **wall painting, Saint Pantaleimon, Nerezi, Macedonia, 1164.**

Working in an alternate Byzantine mode, this Middle Byzantine painter staged the emotional lamentation over the dead Christ in a hilly landscape below a blue sky, and peopled it with fully modeled figures.

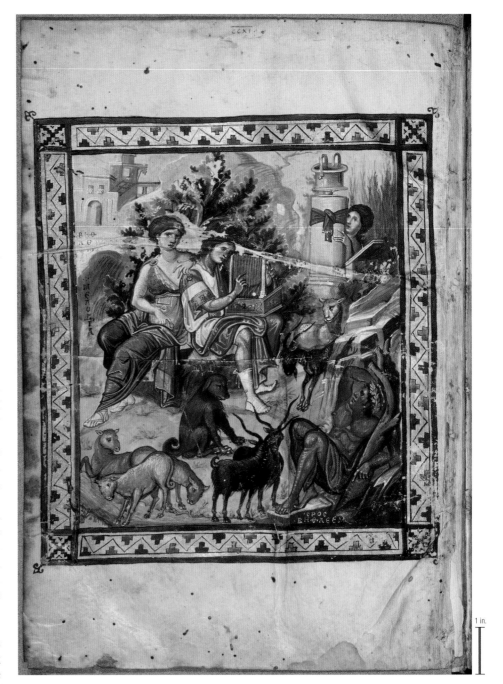

9-30 David composing the psalms, folio 1 verso of the *Paris Psalter,* ca. 950–970. Tempera on vellum, 1′ 2⅛″ × 10¼″. Bibliothèque nationale de France, Paris.

During the Macedonian Renaissance, Byzantine artists revived the classical style. This painter portrayed David as if he were a Greek hero, accompanied by Melody, Echo, and Bethlehem personified.

1 in.

expressions, and gestures of quite human bereavement. Joseph of Arimathea and the disciple Nicodemus kneel at his feet. Mary presses her cheek against her dead son's face. Saint John clings to Christ's left hand. In the Gospels, neither Mary nor John was present at the entombment of Christ. Their inclusion here, as elsewhere in Middle Byzantine art, intensified for the viewer the emotional impact of Christ's death.

The setting for this lamentation is a hilly landscape below a blue sky—a striking contrast to the abstract golden world of the mosaics favored for church walls throughout the Byzantine Empire. In order to make utterly convincing an emotionally charged realization of the theme, this artist instead staged the mourning scene in a more natural setting and peopled it with fully modeled actors. This alternate representational mode is no less Byzantine than the frontal, flatter figures more commonly associated with Byzantine art. In time, artists in Italy (FIG. 14-10) would emulate this more naturalistic style, giving birth to Renaissance art.

Paris Psalter. Another example of this classical-revival style is a page from a book of the Psalms of David. The so-called *Paris Psalter* (FIG. 9-30) in France's National Library reasserts the artistic values of the Greco-Roman past with astonishing authority. Art historians believe that the manuscript dates from the mid-10th century—the so-called Macedonian Renaissance, a time of enthusiastic and careful study of the language and literature of ancient Greece. It is not surprising that artists would once again draw inspiration from the Hellenistic naturalism of the pre-Christian Mediterranean world.

David, the psalmist, surrounded by sheep, goats, and his faithful dog, plays his harp in a rocky landscape with a town in the background. Similar settings appeared frequently in Pompeian murals. Befitting an ancient depiction of Orpheus, the Greek hero who could charm even inanimate objects with his music, allegorical figures accompany the Old Testament harpist. Melody looks over his shoulder, and Echo peers from behind a column. A reclining male figure points to a Greek inscription identifying him as representing the mountain of Bethlehem. These allegorical figures do not appear in the Bible. They are the stock population of Greco-Roman painting (compare Bethlehem to the personified Campus Martius in FIG. 7-56). Apparently, the artist had seen a work from Late Antiquity or perhaps earlier and partly translated it into a Byzantine pictorial idiom. In works such as this, Byzantine artists kept the classical style alive in the Middle Ages.

Vladimir Virgin. Nothing in Middle Byzantine art better demonstrates the rejection of the iconoclastic viewpoint than the painted icon's return to prominence. After the restoration of images, icons multiplied by the thousands to meet public and private demand. In the 11th century, the clergy began to display icons in hierarchical order (Christ, the Theotokos, John the Baptist, and then other saints, as on the *Harbaville Triptych*) in tiers on the *templon,* the low columnar screen separating the sanctuary from the main body of a Byzantine church.

The *Vladimir Virgin* (FIG. 9-31) is the most renowned Middle Byzantine icon produced in Russia. Unfortunately, the revered

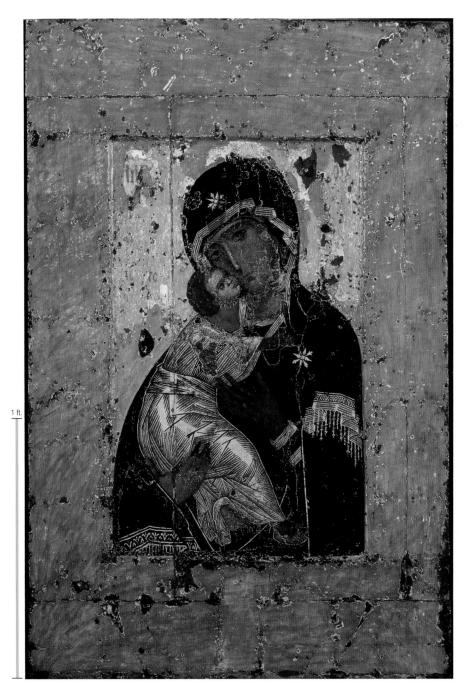

1 ft.

9-31 Virgin of Compassion icon (*Vladimir Virgin*), late 11th or early 12th century, with later repainting. Tempera on wood, 2′ 6½″ × 1′ 9″. Tretyakov Gallery, Moscow.

In this icon, the artist depicted Mary as the Virgin of Compassion, who presses her cheek against her son's as she contemplates his future. The reverse side shows the instruments of Christ's passion.

The icon of Vladimir, like most icons, has seen hard service. Placed before or above altars in churches or private chapels, the icon became blackened by the incense and smoke from candles burning before or below it. It was taken to Kiev (Ukraine) in 1131, then to Vladimir (Russia) in 1155 (hence its name), and finally, as a wonder-working image, to Moscow in 1395, to protect that city from Timur (Tamerlane) and his Mongol armies. The Russians believed that the sacred picture saved the city of Kazan from later Tartar invasions and all of Russia from the Poles in the 17th century. The *Vladimir Virgin* is a historical symbol of Byzantium's religious and cultural mission to the Slavic world.

LATE BYZANTINE ART

The Comnenians succeeded the Macedonians in the late 11th century, and during the new dynasty's rule, three events of fateful significance changed Byzantium's fortunes for the worse. The Seljuk Turks conquered most of Anatolia. The Byzantine Orthodox Church broke finally with the Church of Rome. And the Crusades brought the Latins (a generic term for the peoples of the West) into Byzantine lands on their way to fight for the Christian cross against the Saracens (Muslims) in the Holy Land (see "The Crusades," page 360).

Crusaders had passed through Constantinople many times en route to "smite the infidel"

image has been repainted many times, and only traces of the original surface remain. Descended from such works as the Mount Sinai icon (FIG. 9-19), the *Vladimir Virgin* clearly reveals the stylized abstraction resulting from centuries of working and reworking the conventional image. Probably the work of a painter from Constantinople, the *Vladimir Virgin* displays all the characteristic traits of the Early Byzantine icon of the Virgin and Child: the Virgin's long, straight nose and small mouth; the golden rays in the infant's drapery; the decorative sweep of the unbroken contour that encloses the two figures; and the flat silhouette against the golden ground. But this is a much more tender and personalized image of the Virgin than that in the Mount Sinai icon. Here, Mary is the Virgin of Compassion, who presses her cheek against her son's in an intimate portrayal of mother and child. A deep pathos infuses the image as Mary contemplates the future sacrifice of her son. (The back of the icon bears images of the instruments of Christ's passion.)

and had marveled at its wealth and magnificence. Envy, greed, religious fanaticism (the Latins called the Greeks "heretics"), and even ethnic enmity motivated the Crusaders when, during the Fourth Crusade in 1203 and 1204, the Venetians persuaded them to divert their expedition against the Muslims in Palestine and to attack Constantinople instead. They took the city, sacked it, and, as noted, brought back many of Constantinople's portable treasures to adorn San Marco in Venice. The historian Nicetas Choniates (1155–1216) expressed the feelings of the Byzantines of his era toward the Crusaders: "The accursed Latins would plunder our wealth and wipe out our race. . . . Between us there can be only an unbridgeable gulf of hatred. . . . They bear the Cross of Christ on their shoulders, but even the Saracens are kinder."[8]

The Latins set up kingdoms within Byzantium, notably in Constantinople itself. What remained of Byzantium split into three small states. The Palaeologans ruled one of these, the kingdom of Nicaea. In 1261, Michael VIII Palaeologus (r. 1259–1282) succeeded in

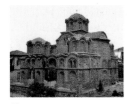

Saint Catherine, Thessaloniki, ca. 1280.

recapturing Constantinople. One of the gems of Late Byzantine architecture—the church dedicated to Saint Catherine (FIG. 9-31A) in Thessaloniki—dates to his reign. But Michael's empire was no more than a fragment, and even that disintegrated during the next two centuries. Isolated from the Christian West by Muslim conquests in the Balkans and besieged by Muslim Turks to the east, Byzantium sought help from the West. It was not forthcoming. In 1453, the Ottoman Turks, by then a formidable power, took Constantinople and brought to an end the long history of Byzantium. But despite the state's grim political condition under the Palaeologan dynasty, the arts flourished well into the 15th century.

Painting

During the 14th and 15th centuries, artists throughout the Byzantine world produced masterpieces of mural and icon painting rivaling those of the earlier periods. Four characteristic examples from the old capital of Constantinople and as far away as Russia illustrate the range and quality of painting during the Late Byzantine period.

Christ in Chora. Perhaps the best Late Byzantine fresco is the *Anastasis* (FIG. 9-32) in the apse of the *parekklesion* (side chapel, in this instance a funerary chapel) of the Church of Christ in Chora in Constantinople. The high quality of the painting is not surprising, because the church enjoyed the patronage of Theodore Metochites (1260–1332), grand deputy to Andronikos II Palaeologus (r. 1282–1328). One of many subsidiary subjects that made up the complex mosaic program of San Marco (FIG. 9-26) in Venice, the Anastasis episode is here central to a cycle of pictures portraying the themes of human mortality and redemption by Christ and of the intercession of the Virgin, both appropriate for a funerary chapel. Christ, trampling Satan and all the locks and keys of his prison house of Hell, raises Adam and Eve from their tombs. Looking on are John the Baptist, King David, and King Solomon on the left, and various martyr saints on the right. Christ, central and in a luminous mandorla, reaches out equally to a white-haired, bearded, prophet-like Adam and a matronly Eve, neither of whom resembles the youthful sinners of traditional representations of the first man and

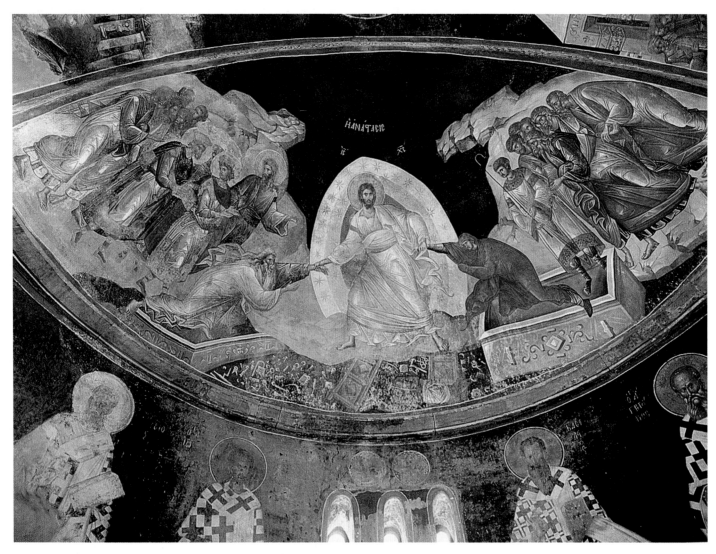

9-32 *Anastasis,* fresco in the apse of the parekklesion of the Church of Christ in Chora (now the Kariye Museum), Constantinople (Istanbul), Turkey, ca. 1310–1320.

In this Late Byzantine funerary chapel, Christ, a white apparition surrounded by a luminous mandorla, raises Adam and Eve from their tombs as John the Baptist and Kings David and Solomon look on.

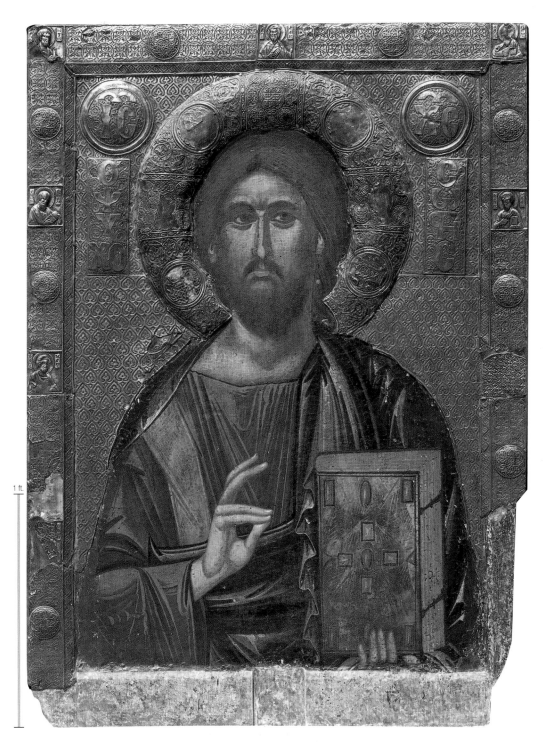

9-33 Christ as Savior of Souls, icon from Saint Clement, Ohrid, Macedonia, early 14th century. Tempera, linen, and silver on wood, 3′ $\frac{1}{4}$″ × 2′ 2$\frac{1}{2}$″. Icon Gallery of Saint Clement, Ohrid.

Notable for the lavish use of finely etched silver foil, this icon typifies Byzantine stylistic complexity. Christ's fully modeled head and neck contrast with the schematic linear folds of his garment.

Ohrid Icons. Icon painting may most intensely reveal Byzantine spirituality. In the Late Byzantine period, the Middle Byzantine templon developed into an *iconostasis* ("icon stand"), a high screen with doors. As its name implies, the iconostasis supported tiers of painted devotional images, which began to be produced again in large numbers, both in Constantinople and throughout the diminished Byzantine Empire.

One example (FIG. 9-33), notable for the lavish use of finely etched silver foil to frame the painted figure of Christ as Savior of Souls, dates to the beginning of the 14th century. It comes from the church of Saint Clement at Ohrid in Macedonia, which boasts many Late Byzantine icons imported from the capital. The painter of the Ohrid Christ, in a manner consistent with Byzantine art's conservative nature, adhered to an iconographical and stylistic tradition dating to the earliest icons from the monastery at Mount Sinai. As elsewhere (FIGS. 9-18B, 9-23, and 9-25), the Savior holds a bejeweled Bible in his left

woman. The action is dramatic, the gestures and movements forceful, especially those of the central figures. The background is deep blue instead of gold, but the figures cast no shadows. Nonetheless, the jagged abstractions of drapery found in many earlier Byzantine frescoes and mosaics are gone in a return to the fluid delineation of drapery characteristic of the long tradition of classical illusionism.

Throughout the centuries, Byzantine artists looked back to Greco-Roman illusionism. But unlike classical artists, Byzantine painters and mosaicists did not believe that the systematic observation of material nature should be the source of their representations of the eternal. They drew their images from a persistent and conventionalized vision of a spiritual world unsusceptible to change. That consistent vision is what unites works as distant in time as the sixth-century apse mosaic (FIG. 9-16) at Mount Sinai and the 14th-century fresco in the Church of Christ in Chora.

hand while he blesses the faithful with his right hand. The mixture of styles is typical of Byzantine painting. Note especially the juxtaposition of Christ's fully modeled head and neck, which reveal the Byzantine artist's Greco-Roman heritage, with the schematic linear folds of Christ's garment, which do not envelop the figure but rather seem to be placed in front of it.

Late Byzantine icons often have paintings on two sides because they were carried in processions. When the clergy brought the icons into the church, they did not mount them on the iconostasis but exhibited them on stands so that they could be viewed from both sides. The Ohrid icon of Christ has the Crucifixion on its reverse. Another double icon from Ohrid, also imported from Constantinople, represents the Virgin on the front as Christ's counterpart as Savior of Souls. On the reverse is the *Annunciation*, in which, with a commanding gesture of heavenly authority, the angel Gabriel

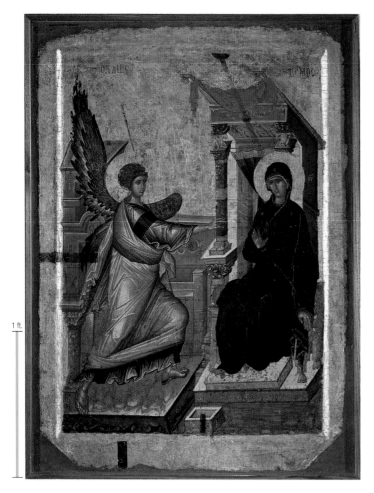

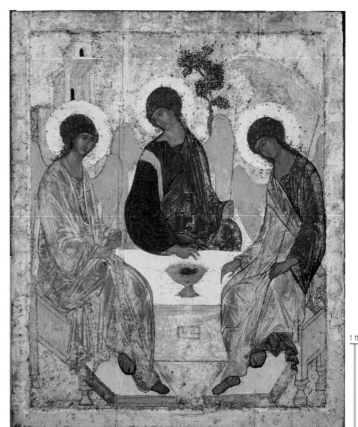

9-35 ANDREI RUBLYEV, *Three Angels* (Old Testament Trinity), ca. 1410. Tempera on wood, 4′ 8″ × 3′ 9″. Tretyakov Gallery, Moscow.

This exceptionally large icon featuring subtle line and vivid colors is one of the masterworks of Russian painting. It depicts the three angels who appeared to Abraham, prefiguring the Trinity.

9-34 *Annunciation,* reverse of a two-sided icon from the Church of the Virgin Peribleptos, Ohrid, Macedonia, early 14th century. Tempera and linen on wood, 3′ $\frac{5}{8}$″ × 2′ 2$\frac{3}{4}$″. Icon Gallery of Saint Clement, Ohrid.

Late Byzantine icons often have two painted sides because they were carried in processions. On this icon, the Virgin Mary appears on the front, and this *Annunciation* is on the back.

announces to Mary that she is to be the Mother of God (FIG. 9-34). She responds with a simple gesture conveying both astonishment and reluctance. The gestures and attitudes of the figures are again conventional, as are the highly simplified architectural props. The painter rendered the latter in inconsistent perspective derived from classical prototypes, but set the sturdy three-dimensional forms against an otherworldly golden sky, suggesting the sacred space in which the narrative unfolds. This icon therefore also exemplifies the diversity of stylistic sources that characterizes Byzantine art from its beginnings until the fall of Constantinople.

Andrei Rublyev.   Icon painting flourished also in Russia. Russian icons usually have strong patterns, firm lines, and intense contrasting colors, which serve to heighten the legibility of the icons in the wavering candlelight and clouds of incense that worshipers encountered in church interiors. For many art historians, Russian painting reached a climax in the work of ANDREI RUBLYEV (ca. 1370–1430). His nearly 5-foot-tall panel (FIG. 9-35) depicting the three Old Testament angels who appeared to Abraham is a work of great spiritual power. Painted during the tenure of Photius (FIG. 9-35A) as metropolitan (Orthodox archbishop) of Russia, it is an unsurpassed example of subtle line in union with what once were intensely vivid

colors, now faded. The angels sit about a table, each framed with a halo and sweeping wings, three nearly identical figures distinguished primarily by the color of their garments. The light linear play of the draperies sets off the tranquil demeanor of the figures. Juxtapositions of complementary hues add intensity to the coloration. The blue and green folds of the central figure's cloak, for example, stand out starkly against the deep-red robe and the gilded orange of the wings. In the figure on the left, the highlights of the orange cloak are an opalescent blue-green. The unmodulated saturation, brilliance, and purity of the color harmonies are the hallmark of Rublyev's style.

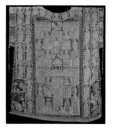

☑ **9-35A** Large sakkos of Photius, ca. 1417.

The Third Rome.   With the fall of Constantinople in 1453, Russia became Byzantium's self-appointed heir, defending Christendom against the infidel. The court of the tsar (derived from Caesar) declared, "Because the Old Rome has fallen, and because the Second Rome, which is Constantinople, is now in the hands of the godless Turks, thy kingdom, O pious Tsar, is the Third Rome. . . . Two Romes have fallen, but the Third stands, and there shall be no more."[9] Rome, Byzantium, Russia—Old Rome, New Rome, and Third Rome—were a continuum, spanning two-and-a-half millennia during which artists and architects produced many of the most significant paintings, sculptures, and buildings in the long history of art through the ages.

Byzantium

Early Byzantine Art 324–726

- Constantine I (r. 324–337) founded Constantinople on the site of the ancient Greek city of Byzantium in 324 and dedicated this "New Rome" to the Christian God in 330.

- Theodosius I (r. 379–395) erected an obelisk with imperial ceremonial scenes in the Constantinople hippodrome.

- The first golden age of Byzantine art was the result of the lavish patronage of Justinian (r. 527–565), who built or restored more than 30 churches in Constantinople, including Hagia Sophia, which rivaled the architectural wonders of Old Rome. A brilliant fusion of central and longitudinal plans, the church boasts a 180-foot-high dome resting on pendentives, but contemporaries viewed the dome as floating miraculously above the congregation.

- The seat of Byzantine power in Italy was Ravenna, which also prospered under Justinian. San Vitale, Ravenna's greatest church, is a domed octagonal building modeled on central-plan churches in Constantinople. Its mosaics celebrate the emperor's dual political and religious roles. The weightless, hovering, frontal figures against a golden background reveal the new Byzantine aesthetic.

- Justinian also rebuilt the monastery at Mount Sinai in Egypt. The preserved Sinai icons—portable devotional paintings depicting Christ, the Virgin, and saints—are the finest preserved from the Early Byzantine period.

- The art of manuscript illumination also flourished during the sixth century. Among the best examples are the *Vienna Genesis* and the *Rabbula Gospels.*

- In 726, Leo III (r. 717–741) enacted a ban against picturing the divine, initiating the era of iconoclasm (726–843) and the destruction of countless Early Byzantine artworks.

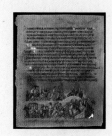

Hagia Sophia, Constantinople, 532–537

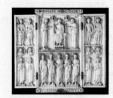

Vienna Genesis, early 6th century

Middle Byzantine Art 843–1204

- Empress Theodora repealed iconoclasm in 843. Basil I (r. 867–886) and his Macedonian dynasty successors installed new figural mosaics in Hagia Sophia, marking the triumph of the iconophiles over the iconoclasts.

- Ivory carving and manuscript painting were major art forms during the Middle Byzantine period, as during the preceding era. Hinged ivory shrines, such as the *Harbaville Triptych,* were popular for use in private prayer.

- The *Paris Psalter,* the finest preserved example of Macedonian Renaissance manuscript painting, is noteworthy for the conscious revival of classical naturalism.

- Middle Byzantine churches, such as the Church of the Theotokos and the katholikon at Hosios Loukas and the Church of the Dormition at Daphni, have highly decorative exterior walls and feature domes that rest on drums above the center of a Greek cross. The crowning element of interior mosaic programs was often a fearsome image of Christ as Pantokrator in the dome.

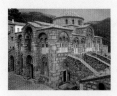

Harbaville Triptych, ca. 950

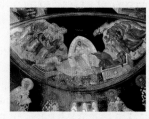

Katholikon, Hosios Loukas, ca. 1000–1025

Late Byzantine Art 1261–1453

- In 1204, Latin Crusaders sacked Constantinople, bringing to an end the Middle Byzantine era. In 1261, Michael VIII Palaeologus (r. 1259–1282) succeeded in recapturing the city. Constantinople remained in Byzantine hands until it fell to the Ottoman Turks in 1453.

- The Church of Christ in Chora contains important mural paintings of the Late Byzantine period. An extensive picture cycle portrays Christ as redeemer. In the apse, he raises Adam and Eve from their tombs.

- Late Byzantine icons were displayed in tiers on an iconostasis or on individual stands so that worshipers could see the paintings on both sides. Christ or the Virgin usually appeared on the front. The reverse depicted a narrative scene from the life of Christ.

Church of Christ in Chora, Constantinople, ca. 1310–1320

▼10-1a Islamic architecture draws on diverse sources. The horseshoe arches of the Córdoba mosque's prayer hall may derive from Visigothic architecture. The Arabs overthrew that Christian kingdom in 711.

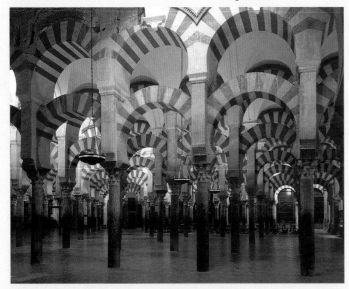

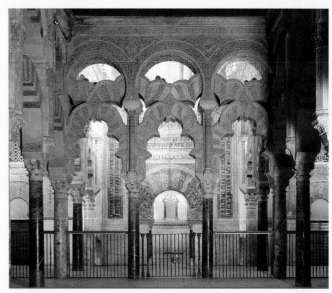

▲10-1b In the 10th century, al-Hakam II added a maqsura to the Córdoba mosque. The hall highlights Muslim architects' bold experimentation with curvilinear shapes and different kinds of arches.

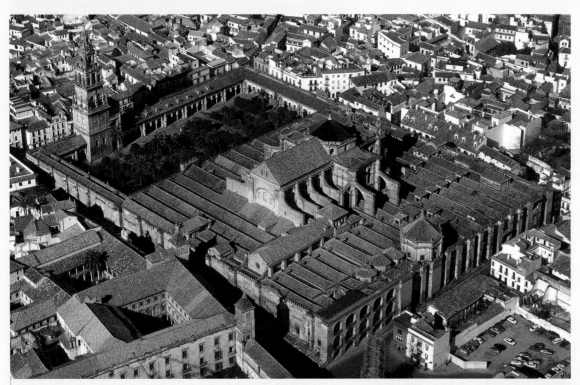

10-1 **Aerial view of the Great Mosque (looking north), Córdoba, Spain, 8th to 10th centuries; rededicated as the Cathedral of Saint Mary, 1236.**

▶10-1c Byzantine artists installed the mosaics in the mihrab dome in the Córdoba mosque, but the decorative patterns formed by the crisscrossing ribs and the multi-lobed arches are distinctly Islamic.

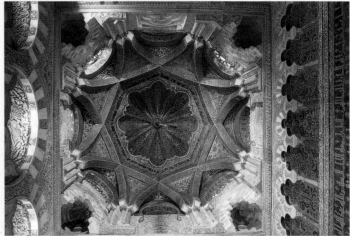

THE ISLAMIC WORLD /10

The Rise and Spread of Islam

At the time of Muhammad's birth around 570, the Arabian peninsula was peripheral to the Byzantine and Sasanian empires. The Arabs, nomadic herders and caravan merchants who worshiped many gods, resisted the Prophet's teachings of Islam, an Arabic word meaning "submission to the one God [*Allah* in Arabic]." Within a decade of Muhammad's death in 632, however, Muslims ("those who submit") ruled Arabia, Palestine, Syria, Iraq, and northern Egypt. From there, the new religion spread rapidly both eastward and westward (MAP 10-1).

With the rise of Islam also came the birth of a compelling new worldwide tradition of art and architecture. In the Middle East and North Africa, Islamic art largely replaced Late Antique art, the last phase of Greco-Roman art. In India, the establishment of Muslim rule at Delhi in the early 13th century brought Islamic art and architecture to South Asia. In fact, perhaps the most famous building in Asia, the Taj Mahal (FIG. 33-6) at Agra, is an Islamic mausoleum. At the opposite end of the then-known world, in Spain, the Arabs had overthrown the Christian kingdom of the Visigoths in 711. There, at Córdoba, Abd al-Rahman I (r. 756–788) founded a Spanish Muslim dynasty, which became the center of a brilliant court culture that profoundly influenced medieval Europe.

The jewel of the capital at Córdoba was its Great Mosque (FIG. 10-1), begun in 784 and enlarged several times during the 9th and 10th centuries until it eventually became one of the largest mosques in the western Islamic world (see "The Mosque," page 299). In 1236, Christians converted the shrine into a church after they captured the city from the Muslims. (The tallest part of the complex, at the center of the aerial view, is Córdoba's cathedral.)

A visual feast greets all visitors to the Córdoba mosque. The Muslim designers employed by al-Hakam II (r. 961–976) used overlapping horseshoe-shaped arches—which became synonymous with Islamic architecture in Europe—to adorn the eastern and western gates to the complex. Double rows of arches surmount the more than 500 columns and piers in the mosque's huge prayer hall. Even more elaborate multilobed arches on slender columns form dazzling frames for other areas of the mosque, especially in the *maqsura,* the hall reserved for the ruler, which at Córdoba connects the mosque to the palace. Crisscrossing ribs form intricate decorative patterns in the complex's largest dome. Walls covered with costly marbles and mosaics rival those of the most magnificent mosques of the Islamic heartland in ancient Mesopotamia.

The Great Mosque at Córdoba typifies Islamic architecture both in its conformity to the basic principles of mosque design and in its incorporation of distinctive regional forms.

EARLY ISLAMIC ART

The religion of Islam arose in Arabia early in the seventh century, after the Prophet Muhammad began to receive God's revelations (see "Muhammad and Islam," page 295). At that time, the Arabs were not major players on the world stage. Yet within little more than a century, the eastern Mediterranean, which Byzantium once ringed and ruled, had become an Islamic lake, and the armies of Muhammad's successors had subdued the Middle East, long the seat of Persian dominance and influence (MAP 10-1). The swiftness of the Islamic advance is among the wonders of world history. By 640, Muslims ruled Syria, Palestine, and Iraq. In 642, the Byzantine army abandoned Alexandria, marking the Muslim conquest of Lower (northern) Egypt. In 651, Islamic forces ended more than 400 years of Sasanian rule in Iran. All of North Africa was under Muslim control by 710. A victory at Jerez de la Frontera in southern Spain in 711 seemed to open all of western Europe to the Muslims. By 732, they had advanced north to Poitiers in France. There, however, an army of Franks under Charles Martel (r. 714–741), the grandfather of Charlemagne, opposed them successfully, halting Islamic expansion at the Pyrenees. In Spain, by contrast, the Muslim rulers of Córdoba (FIG. 10-1) flourished until 1031, and

not until 1492 did Islamic influence and power end in Iberia. That year, the army of King Ferdinand II of Aragon (r. 1479–1516) and Queen Isabella, the sponsors of Christopher Columbus's voyage to the New World, overthrew the Islamic rulers of Granada. In the East, the Muslims reached the Indus River by 751. Only in Anatolia did stubborn Byzantine resistance slow their advance. Relentless Muslim pressure against the shrinking Byzantine Empire eventually brought about its collapse in 1453, when the Ottoman Turks entered Constantinople.

Military might alone, however, cannot account for the irresistible and far-ranging sweep of Islam from Arabia to India to North Africa and Spain. That Islam endured in the lands that Muhammad's successors conquered can be explained only by the nature of the Islamic faith and its appeal to millions of converts. Islam remains today one of the world's great religions, with adherents on all continents. Its sophisticated culture has had a major influence around the globe. Arab scholars laid the foundations of arithmetic and algebra and made significant contributions to astronomy, medicine, and the natural sciences. During the 12th and 13th centuries, Christian scholars in the West eagerly studied Arabic translations of Aristotle and other ancient Greek writers. Arabic love lyrics and poetic descriptions of nature inspired the early French troubadours.

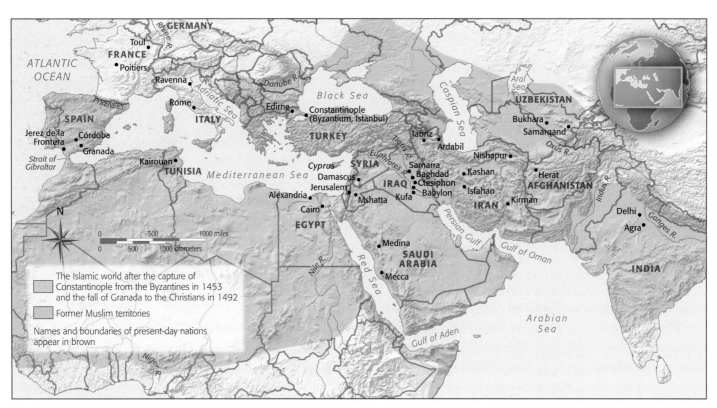

MAP 10-1 The Islamic world around 1500.

THE ISLAMIC WORLD

622–756	756–1453	1453–1924
■ Muhammad abandons Mecca for Medina in 622 ■ The Umayyads, the first Islamic dynasty, build the Dome of the Rock in Jerusalem and the Great Mosque in Damascus	■ The Abbasids produce the earliest Korans with Kufic calligraphy ■ The Spanish Umayyad dynasty builds the Great Mosque in its capital at Córdoba ■ The Nasrids construct magnificent palaces in the Alhambra ■ The Fatimid, Ayyubid, and Mamluk dynasties in Egypt are lavish art patrons	■ The Ottomans capture Byzantine Constantinople in 1453 and develop the domed central-plan mosque ■ Timurid book illumination flowers under Husayn Bayqara ■ Under Shah Tahmasp, Safavid artisans perfect the manufacture of cuerda seca and mosaic tiles

Muhammad and Islam

Muhammad, revered by Muslims as the Final Prophet in the line including Abraham, Moses, and Jesus, was a native of Mecca on the west coast of Arabia. Born around 570 into a family of merchants in the great Arabian caravan trade, Muhammad was critical of the polytheistic religion of his fellow Arabs. In 610, he began to receive the revelations of God through the archangel Gabriel. Opposition to Muhammad's message among the Arabs was strong and led to persecution. In 622, the Prophet and his followers abandoned Mecca for a desert oasis eventually called Medina ("City of the Prophet"). Islam dates its beginnings from this flight, known as the *Hijra* (Arabic, "emigration").*

Barely eight years later, in 630, Muhammad returned to Mecca with 10,000 soldiers. He took control of the city, converted the population to Islam, and destroyed all the idols. But he preserved as the Islamic world's symbolic center the small cubical building that had housed the idols, the *Kaaba* (from the Arabic for "cube"). The Arabs associated the Kaaba with the era of Abraham and Ishmael, the common ancestors of Jews and Arabs. Muhammad died in Medina in 632.

The essential tenet of Islam is acceptance of and submission to God's will. Muslims must live according to the rules laid down in the collected revelations communicated through Muhammad during his lifetime. The Koran, Islam's sacred book, codified by the Muslim ruler Uthman (r. 644–656), records Muhammad's revelations. The word *Koran* means "recitations"—a reference to Gabriel's instructions to Muhammad in 610 to "recite in the name of God." The Koran is composed of 114 *surahs* ("chapters") divided into verses.

The profession of faith in the one God—Allah—is the first of the Five Pillars of Islam binding all Muslims. In addition, the faithful must worship five times daily facing Mecca, give alms to the poor, fast during the month of Ramadan, and, once in a lifetime—if possible—make a pilgrimage to Mecca. The revelations in the Koran are not the only guide for Muslims. Muhammad's words and exemplary ways and customs—the *Hadith,* recorded in the *Sunnah* (the Prophet's "clear path")—offer models to all Muslims on ethical problems of everyday life. The reward for the faithful is Paradise.

Islam has much in common with Judaism and Christianity. Muslims think of their religion as a continuation, a completion, and in some sense a reformation of those other great monotheisms. For example, Islam incorporates many Hebrew biblical teachings, with their sober ethical standards and rejection of idol worship. But, unlike Jesus, Muhammad did not claim to be divine. Rather, he was God's messenger, the Final Prophet, who purified and perfected the common faith of Jews, Christians, and Muslims in one God. Islam also differs from Judaism and Christianity in its simpler organization. Muslims worship God directly, without a hierarchy of rabbis, priests, or saints acting as intermediaries.

In Islam, as Muhammad defined it, the union of religious and secular authority was even more complete than in Byzantium. Muhammad established a new social order, replacing the Arabs' old decentralized tribal one, and took complete charge of his community's temporal as well as spiritual affairs. After Muhammad's death, the *caliphs* (from the Arabic for "successor") continued this practice of uniting religious and political leadership in one ruler—and erected some of the most impressive buildings in the history of architecture, beginning with the late seventh-century Dome of the Rock in Jerusalem (FIG. 10-2).

*Muslims date events beginning with the Hijra in the same way that Christians reckon events from Christ's birth and the Romans before them began their calendar with Rome's founding by Romulus in 753 BCE. The Muslim year is, however, a 354-day year of 12 lunar months, and thus dates cannot be converted by simply adding 622 to Common Era dates.

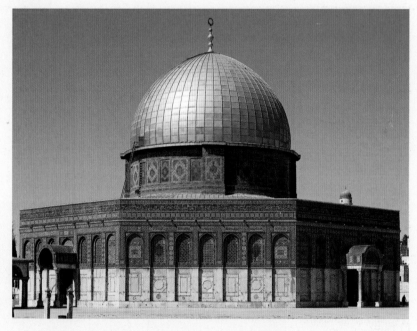

10-2 **Dome of the Rock (looking southwest), Jerusalem, 687–692.**

Abd al-Malik erected the Dome of the Rock to mark the triumph of Islam in Jerusalem on a site sacred to Muslims, Christians, and Jews. The shrine takes the form of an octagon with a towering dome.

Architecture

During the early centuries of Islamic history, the Muslim world's political and cultural center was the Fertile Crescent of ancient Mesopotamia (MAP 2-1), but with the rapid expansion of Muslim power, new dynasties were established far beyond the original sphere of influence of the caliphs of Damascus, the capital of modern Syria, and Baghdad, the capital of Iraq (see "Major Muslim Dynasties," page 297). Like other potentates before and after, the Muslim caliphs were builders on a grand scale. The first Islamic buildings, both religious and secular, are in the Middle East, but important early examples of Islamic architecture still stand also in North Africa, Spain, and Central Asia.

Jerusalem. The Muslims captured Jerusalem from the Byzantines in 638, and the first great Islamic building was erected there between 687 and 692 by the Umayyad caliph Abd al-Malik (r. 685–705). The Dome of the Rock (FIG. 10-2) rises from a huge

The Rock of the Dome of the Rock

Curiously, none of the inscriptions in the Dome of the Rock (FIGS. 10-2, 10-3, and 10-4) refer to the rock within the shrine, even though the rock is key to the meaning of the building. The structure was designed around it: the "footprint" of the central cylinder is a circle that exactly circumscribes the rock (which covers an underground cavern), and the entire shrine is a monumental frame for this presumably holy place. But what did the early Muslims regard as holy about that rock?

Several events and functions have been associated with the rock over time. Eventually, the site was thought to be the location of Adam's grave and the spot where Abraham prepared to sacrifice Isaac. The rock also later came to be identified with the place where Muhammad began his miraculous journey to Heaven (the *Miraj*) and then, on the same night, returned to his home in Mecca. Among the oldest ideas advanced is that what many believe are the traces of feet on the rock are God's footprints at the time of the creation of the world and that God will return to the same spot at the Last Judgment. Another early explanation is that the altar of the Temple of Solomon rested on the rock. The only certainty is that the Dome of the Rock is not a mosque, as is popularly thought.

One clue to the meaning of the shrine comes from the original mosaics. Against a lush vegetal background, Abd al-Malik's mosaicists depicted crowns, jewels, chalices, and other royal motifs—probably a reference to the triumph of Islam over the Byzantine and Persian empires. Inscriptions, mostly from the Koran, underscore Islam as the superior new monotheism, superseding both Judaism and Christianity in Jerusalem. Therefore, the essential meaning of the Dome of the Rock, whatever the significance of the rock itself, is that it is an architectural tribute to the triumph of Islam, marking the coming of the new religion to the city that had been, and still is, sacred to both Jews and Christians.

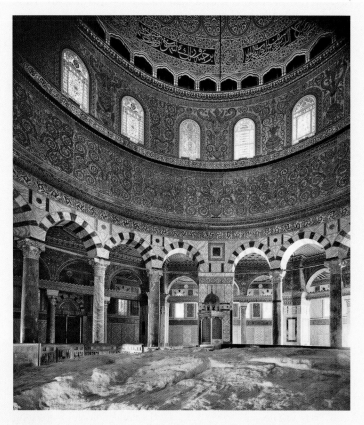

10-3 Interior of the Dome of the Rock, Jerusalem, 687–692.

The Dome of the Rock is a domed central-plan rotunda in the Late Antique tradition. At the center, below the dome, is the rocky outcropping later associated with Adam, Abraham, and Muhammad.

10-4 View into the dome of the Dome of the Rock, Jerusalem, 687–692.

The mosaics ringing the base of the dome inside the Dome of the Rock are largely intact and suggest the original appearance of the exterior walls, today covered with 16th-century ceramic tiles.

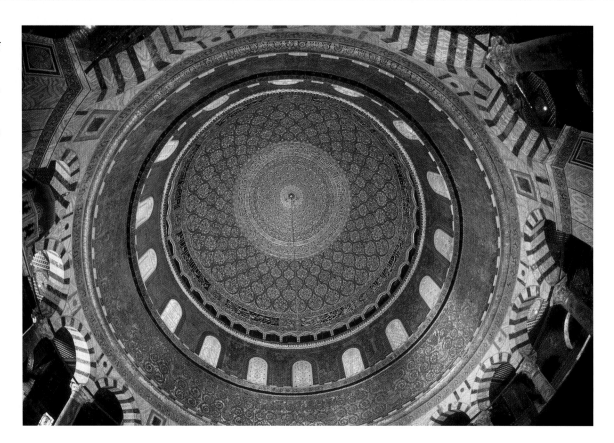

platform known as the Noble Enclosure, where in ancient times the Hebrews built the Temple of Solomon. The original temple was destroyed in 516 BCE. The Roman emperor Titus destroyed the rebuilt temple in 70 CE (FIG. 7-41). In its form, construction, and decoration, the Dome of the Rock is firmly in the Late Antique tradition of the Mediterranean world. It is a domed central-plan structure descended from the Pantheon (FIG. 7-49) in Rome and Hagia Sophia (FIG. 9-5) in Constantinople, but it more closely resembles the octagonal San Vitale (FIG. 9-10) in Ravenna. According to the historian Muhammad ibn Ahmad al-Muqaddasi (946–1000), who was born in Jerusalem, the inspiration for the Dome of the Rock was a neighboring Christian monument, the Anastasis Rotunda (FIG. 8-8C) of Constantine's Church of the Holy Sepulchre. Al-Muqaddasi also reported that Abd al-Malik judged the church to be so magnificent that it "dazzled Muslim minds," and therefore the caliph decided to construct an even greater shrine. The Christian domed rotunda bore a family resemblance to the roughly contemporaneous Constantinian mausoleum later rededicated as Santa Costanza (FIGS. 8-11 and 8-12) in Rome. Crowning the Islamic shrine is a 75-foot-tall double-shelled wood dome, which so dominates the elevation as to reduce the octagon to functioning visually merely as its base. This soaring, majestic unit creates a decidedly more commanding effect than that of similar Late Antique and Byzantine domical structures (compare FIG. 10-2 to FIGS. 9-5 and 9-10). The silhouettes of those domes are comparatively insignificant when seen from the outside.

The Dome of the Rock's exterior has been much restored. Tiling from the 16th century and later has replaced the original mosaics (see "Islamic Tilework," page 311). Yet the vivid, colorful patterning wrapping the walls like a textile is typical of Islamic ornamentation. It contrasts markedly with Byzantine brickwork and Greco-Roman

ART AND SOCIETY

Major Muslim Dynasties

Dynasty	Territory	Dates
Umayyad	Syria, Spain	661–750, 756–1031
Abbasid	Iraq	750–1258
Samanid	Uzbekistan	819–1005
Fatimid	Egypt	909–1171
Seljuk	Turkey, Iran	1060–1307
Ayyubid	Egypt	1171–1250
Nasrid	Spain	1232–1492
Mamluk	Egypt	1250–1517
Ilkhanid	Iran	1256–1353
Ottoman	Turkey, Greece, N. Africa	1281–1924
Timurid	Iran	1370–1501
Safavid	Iran	1501–1732

sculptured decoration. The rich mosaic ornamentation ringing the base of the dome (FIG. 10-4) is largely intact and suggests the original appearance of the exterior walls. But, whereas the formal roots of the design and decoration of the Dome of the Rock are easily established, the meaning and purpose of the shrine are much more difficult to determine (see "The Rock of the Dome of the Rock," page 296).

Damascus. The Umayyads transferred their capital from Mecca to Damascus in 661. There, Abd al-Malik's son, the caliph al-Walid (r. 705–715), purchased a Byzantine church dedicated to John the Baptist (formerly a Roman temple of Jupiter) and built an imposing new mosque for the expanding Muslim population (see "The Mosque," page 299). The Umayyads demolished the church, but they used the Roman precinct walls as a foundation for their construction. Like the Dome of the Rock, Damascus's Great Mosque (FIG. 10-5) owes much to Roman and Early Christian architecture. The Islamic builders incorporated stone blocks, columns, and capitals salvaged from the earlier structures on the land acquired by al-Walid. Pier arcades reminiscent of Roman aqueducts (FIG. 7-33) frame the courtyard. The *minarets*, two at the southern corners and one at the northern side of the enclosure—the earliest in the Islamic world—are modifications of the preexisting Roman square towers. The grand prayer hall, taller than the rest of the complex, is on the south side of the courtyard (facing Mecca). Its position recalls that of a Roman temple opening onto a forum (compare FIG. 7-12). The hall's facade, with its pediment and arches, also recalls Roman and

10-5 **Aerial view of the Great Mosque (looking southeast), Damascus, Syria, 706–715.**

The Umayyads constructed Damascus's Great Mosque after they transferred their capital from Mecca in 661. The mosque owes a debt to Late Antique architecture in its plan and decoration.

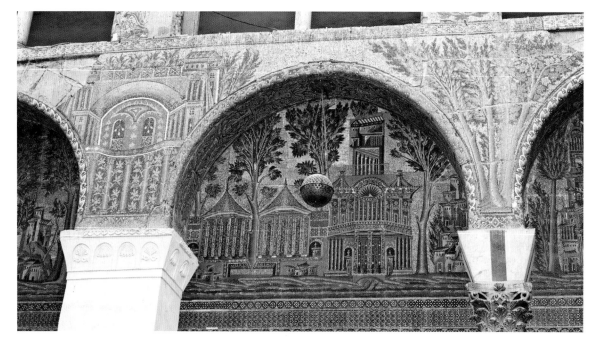

10-6 Detail of mosaics in the courtyard arcade of the Great Mosque, Damascus, Syria, 706–715.

The mosaics of the Great Mosque at Damascus are probably the work of Byzantine artists and include buildings and landscapes common in Late Antique art—but no zoomorphic forms.

Byzantine models. This basic plan was maintained throughout the long history of mosque architecture. The Damascus mosque synthesizes elements received from other cultures into a novel architectural unity, which includes the distinctive Islamic elements of *mihrab*, mihrab dome, *minbar*, and minaret.

An extensive cycle of glass mosaics once covered the walls and arcades (FIG. 10-6) of the Great Mosque. Throughout the complex, the mosaicists depicted palatial villas, trees, and gardens beside rivers. Like the architectural design of the mosque, the mosaics owe much to Roman, Early Christian, and Byzantine art. Indeed, the golden background suggests that they were the work of Byzantine mosaicists. The borders, consisting of stylized vegetal designs, also have parallels in Roman, Early Christian, and Byzantine ornamentation. But no zoomorphic forms, human or animal, appear in either the pictorial or the ornamental spaces. This is true also of the mosaics in the earlier Dome of the Rock (FIG. 10-4). Although there is no prohibition against figural art in the Koran, Islamic tradition, based on the Hadith, shuns the representation of fauna of any kind in sacred places. Accompanying (but now lost) inscriptions explained the world shown in the Damascus mosaics, suspended miragelike in a featureless field of gold, as an image of Paradise. The imagery is consistent with many passages from the Koran describing the gorgeous places of Paradise awaiting the faithful—gardens, groves of trees, flowing streams, and "lofty chambers." The notion of Paradise may also be an element of the iconography of the mosaics inside the Dome of the Rock.

Mshatta and Baghdad. The Umayyad caliphs maintained power for nearly a century, during which they constructed numerous palatial residences throughout their domains. Perhaps the most impressive was the palace (FIGS. 10-6A and 10-6B) at Mshatta in Jordan, datable just before 750 when, after years of civil war, the Abbasids, who claimed descent from Abbas, an uncle of Muhammad, overthrew the Umayyad caliphs. The new rulers moved the capital from

Damascus to a site in Iraq near the old Sasanian capital of Ctesiphon (FIG. 2-29). There the caliph al-Mansur (r. 754–775) established a new capital, Baghdad, which he called Madina al-Salam, the City of Peace. Laid out in 762 at a time that astrologers determined was favorable, Baghdad had a circular plan, about a mile-and-a-half in diameter, and came to be known as the Round City. The shape, which had precedents in ancient Assyria, Parthia, and Persia, signified that the new capital was the center of the universe. The city had a moat and four gates oriented to the four compass points. At the center was the caliph's palace.

No traces of al-Mansur's City of Peace remain today, but for almost 300 years, Baghdad was the hub of Arab power and of a brilliant Islamic culture. The Abbasid caliphs amassed great wealth and established diplomatic relations throughout the world, even with Charlemagne in Germany. They spent lavishly on art, literature, and science and were responsible for the translation of numerous Greek texts that otherwise would have been lost. In fact, many of these ancient works first became known in medieval Europe through their Arabic versions.

Kairouan. Several decades after the founding of Baghdad, the Abbasids constructed at Kairouan in Tunisia one of the best preserved early mosques (FIGS. 10-7 and 10-8). Its design—of the *hypostyle hall* type—most closely reflects the mosque's supposed precursor, Muhammad's house in Medina (see "The Mosque," page 299). Still in use today, the Kairouan mosque retains its carved wood minbar of 862, the oldest known. The huge precinct is some 450 by 260 feet. Built of stone, its walls have sturdy buttresses, square in profile. Lateral entrances on the east and west lead to an arcaded forecourt (FIG. 10-8, no. 7) resembling a Roman forum (FIG. 7-44), oriented north–south on axis with the mosque's impressive minaret (no. 8) and the two domes of the hypostyle prayer hall (no. 4). The first dome (no. 6)

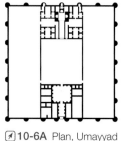

⊿ 10-6A Plan, Umayyad palace, Mshatta, ca. 740–750.

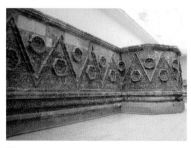

⊿ 10-6B Frieze, Umayyad palace, Mshatta, ca. 740–750.

The Mosque

Islamic religious architecture is closely related to Muslim prayer, an obligation laid down in the Koran for all Muslims. In Islam, worshiping can be a private act and requires neither prescribed ceremony nor a special locale. Only the *qibla*—the direction (toward Mecca) that Muslims face while praying—is important. But worship also became a communal act when the first Muslim community established a simple ritual for it. To celebrate the Muslim sabbath, which occurs on Friday, the community convened each Friday at noon, probably in the Prophet's house in Medina. The main feature of Muhammad's house was a large, square court with rows of palm trunks supporting thatched roofs along the north and south sides. The southern side, which faced Mecca, was wider and had a double row of trunks. After the prayer, the *imam,* or leader of collective worship, stood on a stepped pulpit, or *minbar,* set up in front of the southern (qibla) wall, and preached the sermon.

These features became standard in the Islamic house of worship, the *mosque* (from Arabic *masjid,* "a place of prostration"), where the faithful gather for the five daily prayers. The *congregational mosque* (also called the *Friday mosque* or *great mosque*) was ideally large enough to accommodate a community's entire population for the Friday noon prayer. An important feature both of ordinary mosques and of congregational mosques is the *mihrab* (FIG. 10-8, no. 2), a semicircular niche usually set into the qibla wall. Often a dome over the bay in front of the mihrab marked its position (FIGS. 10-5 and 10-8, no. 3). The niche was a familiar Greco-Roman architectural feature, generally enclosing a statue. Scholars still debate the mihrab's origin, purpose, and meaning in Islamic architecture. The niche originally may have honored the place where the Prophet stood in his house at Medina when he led communal worship.

In some mosques, a *maqsura* precedes the mihrab. The maqsura, the area generally reserved for the ruler or his representative, can be quite elaborate in form (FIG. 10-13). Many mosques also have one or more *minarets* (FIGS. 10-5, 10-7, 10-9, 10-26, and 10-29), towers used to call the faithful to worship. When the Muslims converted buildings of other faiths into mosques, they clearly signaled the change on the exterior by the construction of minarets (FIG. 9-5). *Hypostyle halls,* communal worship halls with roofs held up by a multitude of columns (FIGS. 10-8, no. 4, and 10-11), are characteristic features of early mosques. Later variations include mosques with four *iwans* (vaulted rectangular recesses), one on each side of the courtyard (FIGS. 10-15 and 10-16), and *central-plan* mosques with a single large dome-covered interior space (FIG. 10-27), as in Byzantine churches, some of which later became mosques (FIG. 9-8).

Today, despite many variations in design and detail (see, for example, the adobe-and-wood mosque in Mali [FIG. 19-10] and the Great Mosque in Xi'an [FIG. 34-5A], which is laid out like a Buddhist temple) and the employment of building techniques and materials unknown in Muhammad's day, the mosque's essential features remain unchanged. The orientation of all mosques everywhere, whatever their plan, is Mecca, and Muslims worship facing the qibla wall.

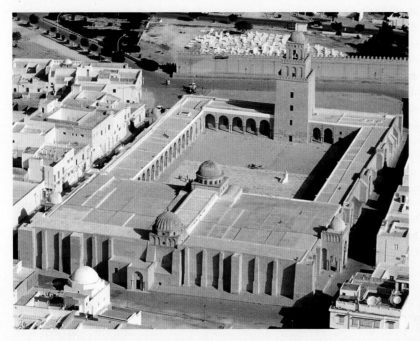

10-7 Aerial view of the Great Mosque (looking north), Kairouan, Tunisia, ca. 836–875.

The Great Mosque at Kairouan consists of a columnar prayer hall (with two domes) facing south toward Mecca, an arcaded forecourt resembling a Roman forum, and a minaret to call Muslims to worship.

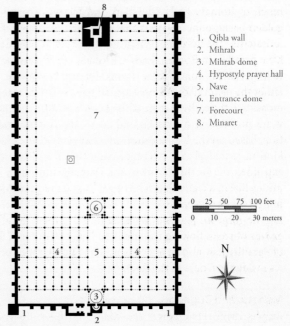

1. Qibla wall
2. Mihrab
3. Mihrab dome
4. Hypostyle prayer hall
5. Nave
6. Entrance dome
7. Forecourt
8. Minaret

| 0 | 25 | 50 | 75 | 100 feet |
| 0 | 10 | 20 | | 30 meters |

N

10-8 Plan of the Great Mosque, Kairouan, Tunisia, ca. 836–875.

Kairouan's Great Mosque is an early example of the type of mosque with a forecourt and a hypostyle prayer hall. The plan most closely resembles the layout of Muhammad's house in Medina.

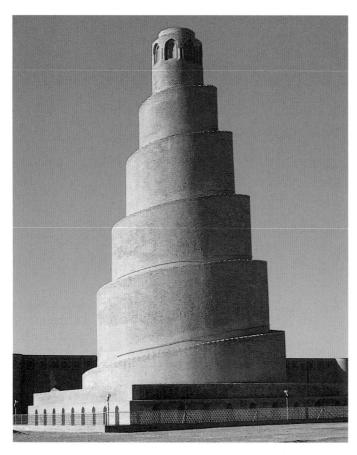

10-9 Malwiya Minaret (looking southwest), Great Mosque, Samarra, Iraq, 848–852.

The unique spiral Malwiya Minaret of the Abbasid caliph al-Mutawakkil's 45,000-square-yard Great Mosque at Samarra is more than 165 feet tall. It served to announce the presence of Islam in the Tigris Valley.

is over the entrance bay, the second (no. 3) over the bay that fronts the mihrab (no. 2) set into the *qibla* wall (no. 1). A raised nave (no. 5) connects the domed spaces and prolongs the north–south axis of the minaret and courtyard. Eight columned aisles flank the nave on either side, providing space for a large congregation.

Samarra. The three-story minaret of the Kairouan mosque is square in plan and believed to be a near-copy of a Roman lighthouse. Minarets take a variety of forms, however. Perhaps the most striking and novel is the spiral minaret (FIG. 10-9) of the Great Mosque at Samarra, Iraq, on the east bank of the Tigris River north of Baghdad. Samarra was the capital of the Abbasid caliph al-Mutawakkil (r. 847–861), who built the 45,000-square-yard mosque between 848 and 852. At the time of its construction, the Samarra mosque was the largest in the world. It boasts a perimeter wall with 44 semicircular towers and resembles a fortified city. The mosque's minaret, known as the *Malwiya* ("snail shell" in Arabic), is more than 165 feet tall. Although it now stands alone to the north of the sacred precinct, originally a bridge linked the minaret to the mosque. Its unique stepped spiral ramp increases in slope from bottom to top in order to keep each stage the same height. Once thought to be an ancient Mesopotamian ziggurat, the Samarra minaret inspired some European depictions of the biblical Tower of Babel (Babylon's ziggurat; see "Babylon, City of Wonders," page 50). Because the Malwiya is too tall to have been used to call Muslims to prayer, the Abbasids probably intended the tower, which is visible

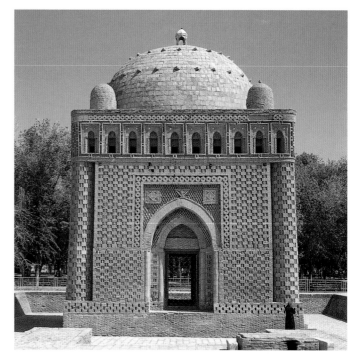

10-10 Mausoleum of the Samanids (looking west), Bukhara, Uzbekistan, early 10th century.

Grandiose tombs were almost unknown in the early Islamic period. The Samanid mausoleum at Bukhara is one of the oldest. Its dome-on-cube form had a long afterlife in Islamic funerary architecture.

from a considerable distance in the flat plain around Samarra, to announce the presence of Islam in the Tigris Valley (compare the early-13th-century Qutb Minar [FIG. 33-2, *left*] at Delhi). Unfortunately, Samarra's spiral minaret has suffered damage at the hands of various parties during the war in Iraq that began in 2003 and the conflict that continues today in the region.

Bukhara. While recognizing the ultimate authority of the Baghdad caliphs, the dynasties that oversaw the eastern realms of the Abbasid Empire enjoyed considerable independence. One of them, the Samanids (r. 819–1005), presided over the frontier beyond the Oxus River (Transoxiana) on the border with India. In the early 10th century, the Samanids erected an impressive domed brick mausoleum (FIG. 10-10) at Bukhara in modern Uzbekistan. Monumental tombs were virtually unknown in the early Islamic period. Muhammad had been opposed to elaborate burials and instructed his followers to bury him in a simple unmarked grave. In time, however, the Prophet's resting place in Medina acquired a wood screen and a dome. By the ninth century, Abbasid caliphs were laid to rest in dynastic mausolea.

The Samanid mausoleum at Bukhara is one of the earliest preserved tombs in the Islamic world. Constructed of baked bricks, it takes the form of a dome-capped cube with slightly sloping sides. With exceptional skill, the builders painstakingly shaped and placed the bricks to create a vivid and varied surface pattern. Some of the bricks form *engaged columns* (half-round, attached columns) at the corners. A brick *blind arcade* (a series of arches in relief, with blocked openings) runs around the upper part of the wall on all four sides. Inside, the walls are as elaborate as the exterior. The brick dome rests on arcuated brick squinches (FIG. 9-9, *right*) framed by engaged colonnettes. The dome-on-cube form would have a long and distinguished future in Islamic funerary architecture (FIGS. 10-25 and 33-6).

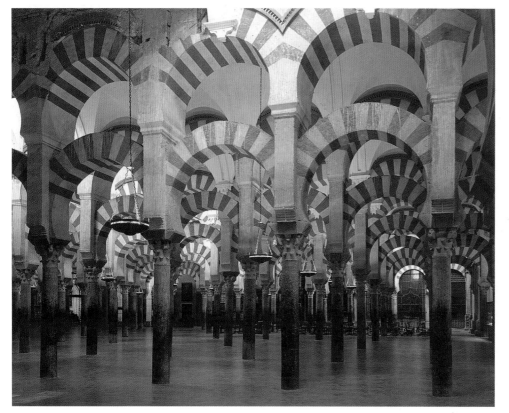

10-11 Prayer hall of the Mezquita (Great Mosque), Córdoba, Spain, 8th to 10th centuries.

Córdoba was the capital of the Spanish Umayyad dynasty. In the Great Mosque's hypostyle prayer hall, 36 piers and 514 columns support a unique series of double–tiered horseshoe-shaped arches.

The most important building project the Umayyad dynasty undertook at Córdoba was the erection of a great mosque (FIG. 10-1) on the site of a Visigothic church, thereby marking the triumph of Islam in Spain, as before in Jerusalem (see "The Rock of the Dome of the Rock," page 296). Begun in 784 by Abd al-Rahman I and enlarged several times during the next two centuries, Córdoba's *Mezquita* (Spanish, "mosque") eventually became one of the largest mosques in the Islamic West. Today, the hypostyle prayer hall (FIG. 10-11) has 36 piers and 514 columns topped by a unique system of double-tiered arches that carried a timber roof (later replaced by vaults). The two-story system was the builders' response to the need to raise the roof to an acceptable height using short columns that had been employed earlier in other structures, both Visigothic and Roman. The lower arches are horseshoe-shaped, a form perhaps adapted from earlier Mesopotamian architecture or of Visigothic origin (FIG. 11-10). In the West, the horseshoe arch quickly became closely associated with Muslim architecture. Visually, these arches seem to billow out like wind-blown sails, and they contribute greatly to the light and airy effect of the Córdoba mosque's interior.

Córdoba. At the opposite end of the Muslim world, Abd al-Rahman I (r. 756–788), the only Umayyad notable to escape the Abbasid massacre of his clan in Syria, fled in 750 to Spain, where the Arabs had overthrown the Christian Visigoths in 711. The Arab military governors accepted the fugitive as their overlord, and he founded the Spanish Umayyad dynasty, which lasted nearly three centuries. The capital of the Spanish Umayyads was Córdoba, which became the center of a brilliant culture rivaling that of the Abbasids at Baghdad and exerting major influence on the civilization of the Christian West (see "The Rise and Spread of Islam," page 293).

In 961, al-Hakam II (r. 961–976) became caliph. A learned man who amassed a library of 400,000 volumes, he immediately undertook major renovations to the mosque. His builders expanded the prayer hall, added a series of domes, and constructed imposing gates on the complex's eastern (FIG. 10-12) and western facades. The gates are noteworthy for their colorful masonry and intricate surface patterns, especially in the uppermost zone, with its series of overlapping horseshoe-shaped arches springing from delicate colonnettes.

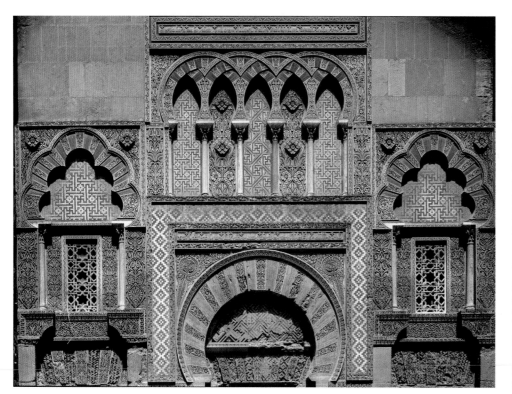

10-12 Detail of the facade of the east gate of the Mezquita (Great Mosque), Córdoba, Spain, 961–965.

The caliph al-Hakam II expanded and renovated Córdoba's Mezquita, adding new gates that feature intricate surface patterns of overlapping horseshoe-shaped arches and multilobed arches.

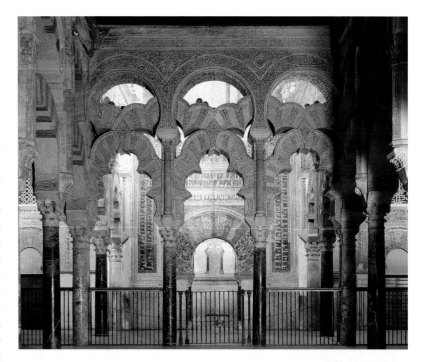

Reserved for the caliph, the maqsura of the Córdoba Mezquita connected the mosque to his palace. It is a prime example of Islamic experimentation with highly decorative multilobed arches.

Also dating to the caliphate of al-Hakam II is the mosque's extraordinary maqsura (FIG. 10-13), the area reserved for the caliph and connected to his palace by a corridor in the qibla wall. The Córdoba maqsura is a prime example of Islamic experimentation with highly decorative multilobed arches (which are subsidiary motifs in the contemporaneous gates; compare FIG. 10-12). The Muslim builders created rich and varied abstract patterns and further enhanced the magnificent effect of the complex arches by covering the walls with marbles and mosaics. Al-Hakam II wished to emulate the great mosaic-filled monuments that his Umayyad predecessors had erected in Jerusalem (FIG. 10-4) and Damascus (FIG. 10-6), and he brought the mosaicists and even the tesserae to Córdoba from Constantinople.

The same desire for decorative effect also inspired the design of the dome (FIG. 10-14) covering the area in front of the mihrab, one of the four domes built during the 10th century to emphasize the axis leading to the mihrab. The dome rests on an octagonal base of arcuated squinches. Crisscrossing ribs form an intricate pattern centered on two squares set at 45-degree angles to each other. The mosaics are the work of the same Byzantine artists responsible for the maqsura's decoration.

Isfahan. Muslim rulers built mosques of the hypostyle-hall type throughout their realms during the early centuries of the new religion, but other mosque plans gradually gained favor in certain regions (see "The Mosque," page 299). At Isfahan, the third-largest city in Iran today, the Abbasids constructed the first mosque, of hypostyle design, in that formerly Sasanian city during the eighth century. In the 11th century, the Seljuks, a Turkic people who had converted to Islam, built an extensive, though short-lived, empire (r. 1060–1307) that stretched eastward from Anatolia and included Iran. At that time, the Seljuk *sultan* (ruler) Malik Shah I (r. 1072–1092) made Isfahan his capital and transformed the Abbasid hypostyle mosque in stages. The Seljuk Friday Mosque (FIG. 10-15) underwent further modification over subsequent centuries, but still retains its basic 11th-century plan (FIG. 10-16), consisting of a large courtyard bordered by an arcade on each side, originally of one story. (The two-story arcade dates to the mid-15th century.) Four vaulted iwans open onto the courtyard, one at the center of each side. The

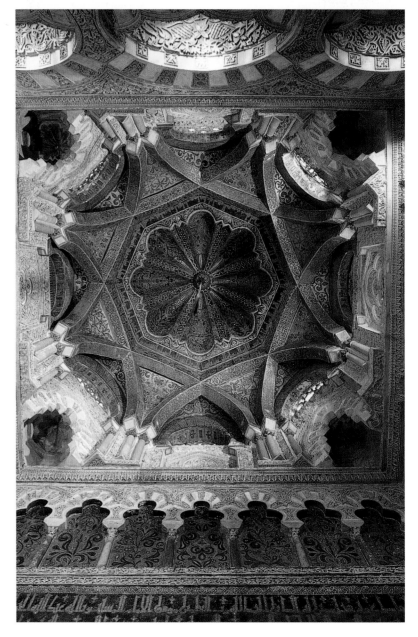

10-14 Dome in front of the mihrab of the Mezquita (Great Mosque), Córdoba, Spain, 961–965.

The dome in front of the Córdoba mihrab rests on an octagonal base of arcuated squinches. Crisscrossing ribs form an intricate decorative pattern. Byzantine artists fashioned the mosaic ornamentation.

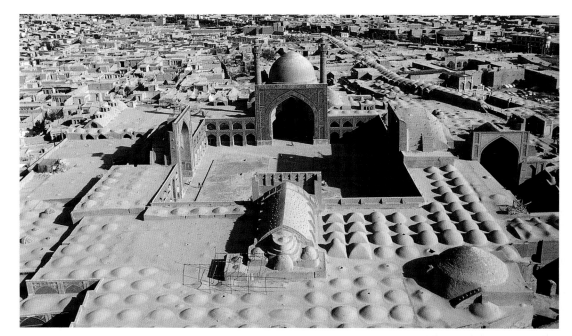

10-15 Aerial view of the Friday Mosque (looking southwest toward the qibla iwan), Isfahan, Iran, 11th to 17th centuries.

The typical Iranian mosque plan with four vaulted iwans and a courtyard was perhaps first used in this mosque, which Sultan Malik Shah I built in the late 11th century at the Seljuk capital of Isfahan.

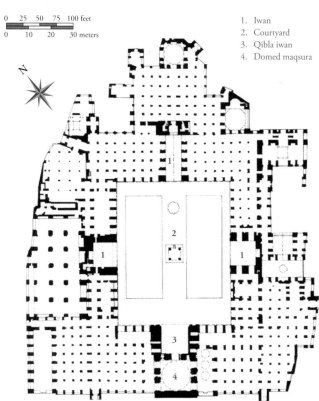

0   25   50   75   100 feet
0   10   20   30 meters

1. Iwan
2. Courtyard
3. Qibla iwan
4. Domed maqsura

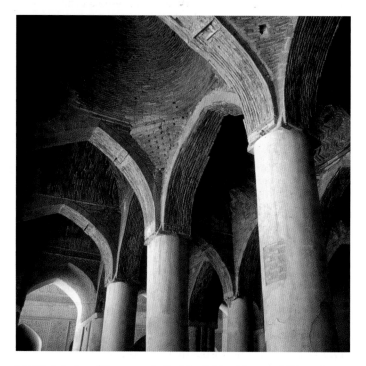

10-17 Interior of the prayer hall of the Friday Mosque, Isfahan, Iran, 11th to 12th centuries.

The vast prayer hall of Isfahan's Friday Mosque is of the hypostyle type and consists of simple columns without capitals. The unfluted shafts support about 200 brick vaults and domes on pointed arches.

10-16 Plan of the Friday Mosque, Isfahan, Iran, 11th to 17th centuries.

In Isfahan's Friday Mosque, as in other four-iwan mosques, the qibla iwan is the largest. Its size and the dome-covered maqsura in front of it indicate the proper direction to face for Muslim prayer.

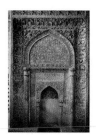

southwestern iwan (FIG. 10-16, no. 3) leads into a dome-covered room (no. 4) in front of the mihrab that functioned as a maqsura reserved for the sultan and his attendants. A second, stucco mihrab (FIG. 10-16A), the work of the renowned calligrapher HAYDAR (d. 1325), was

⊡**10-16A** Mihrab, Friday Mosque, Isfahan, 1310.

added to the winter prayer hall in 1310 under the Ilkhanid dynasty (r. 1256–1353). The hypostyle prayer hall (FIG. 10-17) is vast and features simple unfluted column shafts without capitals supporting about 200 small brick vaults and domes on *pointed arches*. It is uncertain whether Isfahan's Friday Mosque is the earliest example of a four-iwan mosque, but that plan became standard in Iranian religious architecture. In this type of mosque, the qibla iwan is always the largest. Its size (and the dome that often accompanied it) immediately indicated to worshipers the proper direction for prayer.

Luxury Arts

The furnishings of Islamic mosques and palaces reflect a love of sumptuous materials and rich decorative patterns. Muslim artisans masterfully worked ivory (FIG. 10-18), metal, wood, and glass into a great variety of objects for sacred spaces or the home.

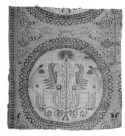

↗10-17A Silk textile, from Zandana, eighth century.

They used colored glass with striking effect in mosque lamps (FIG. 10-32) and produced ceramics (FIG. 10-21) of high quality in large numbers. Muslim metalworkers created elaborate ewers (FIG. 10-19), basins (FIG. 10-35), jewel cases, writing boxes, and other portable items (FIG. 10-36) made of bronze or brass, engraved, and inlaid with silver. Weavers used silk (FIGS. 10-17A) and wool (FIG. 10-31) to fashion textiles featuring both abstract and pictorial motifs.

Because wood is scarce in most of the Islamic world, the kinds of furniture used in the West—beds, tables, and chairs—are rare in Muslim buildings. The function of a room (eating or sleeping, for example) in an Islamic building is not defined by heavy furnishings and can be changed simply by rearranging the carpets and cushions.

Ivory. The centers of production for these luxurious art forms were usually the courts of the Muslim caliphs and sultans. One was Córdoba. Abd al-Rahman III (r. 912–961), a descendant of the founder of the Umayyad dynasty in Spain, became *emir* (ruler) when he was 22. In 929, he declared himself caliph, a title previously restricted to the Muslim rulers who controlled the holy cities of Mecca and Medina. During his nearly 50-year reign, he constructed a lavish new palace for himself and his successors at Medina al-Zahra, about five miles from Córdoba. The palace complex housed royal workshops for the production of luxury items for the caliph's family and for use as diplomatic gifts, including richly carved ivory boxes. Befitting their prospective owners, Spanish Umayyad ivory *pyxides* (singular, *pyxis*; a cylindrical box with a hemispherical lid) usually featured motifs symbolic of royal power and privilege, including hunting scenes and musical entertainments.

The pyxis shown here (FIG. 10-18) belonged to al-Mughira, the younger son of Abd al-Rahman III. The inscription carved at the

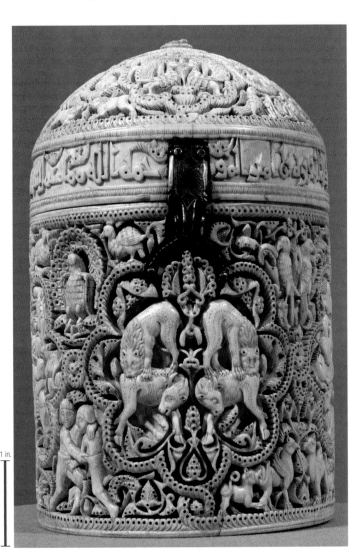

1 in.

10-18 Pyxis of al-Mughira, from Medina al-Zahra, near Córdoba, Spain, 968. Ivory, $5\frac{7}{8}''$ high. Musée du Louvre, Paris.

The royal workshops of Abd al-Rahman III produced luxurious objects such as this ivory pyxis decorated with hunting motifs and vine scrolls. It belonged to al-Mughira, the caliph's younger son.

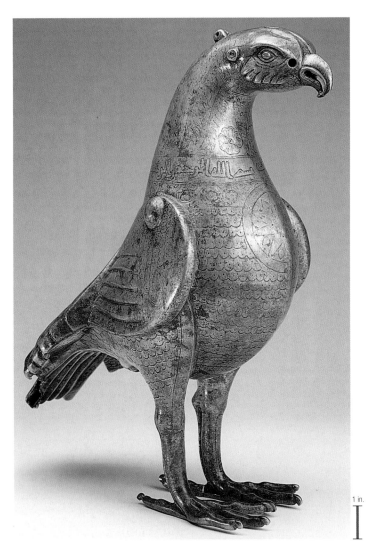

1 in.

10-19 SULAYMAN, ewer in the form of a bird, 796. Brass with silver and copper inlay, 1′ 3″ high. Hermitage, Saint Petersburg.

Signed and dated by its maker, this bird ewer resembles a freestanding statuette. The engraved decoration of the body combines natural feathers with abstract motifs and Arabic calligraphy.

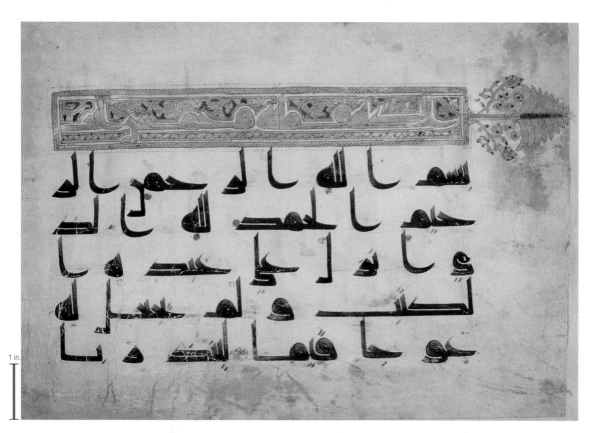

10-20 **Koran page with beginning of surah 18, 9th or early 10th century. Ink and gold on vellum, $7\frac{1}{4}'' \times 10\frac{1}{4}''$. Chester Beatty Library and Oriental Art Gallery, Dublin.**

The script used in the oldest-known Korans is the stately rectilinear Kufic. This page has five text lines and a palm-tree finial, but characteristically does not include depictions of animals or humans.

base of the lid is a prayer for the 18-year-old prince's well-being: "God's blessing, favors, and happiness to al-Mughira, son of the commander of the faithful [the standard epithet for caliphs], may God have mercy upon him, in the year 357 [968 CE]." The anonymous ivory carver decorated the pyxis with a rich array of animals amid lush vine scrolls surrounding four eight-lobed figural medallions. On one side, illustrated here, lions attack bulls, a motif with a long history originating in the ancient Middle East. The other motifs include riders, hunters, and musicians, royal themes appropriate for a caliph's son.

Metalwork. One striking example of early Islamic metalwork is the cast brass ewer (FIG. 10-19) in the form of a bird signed by SULAYMAN and dated 796. Some 15 inches tall, the ewer is nothing less than a freestanding statuette, although the holes between the eyes and beak function as a spout and betray its utilitarian purpose. The decoration on the body, which bears traces of silver and copper inlay, takes a variety of forms. In places, the incised lines seem to suggest natural feathers, but the rosettes on the neck, the large medallions on the breast, and the inscribed collar have no basis in anatomy. Similar motifs appear in Islamic textiles, pottery, and architectural tiles. The ready adaptability of motifs to various scales and techniques illustrates both the flexibility of Islamic design and its relative independence from its carrier.

Korans. In the Islamic world, the art of *calligraphy,* ornamental writing, held a place of honor. Muslim scribes wanted to reproduce the Koran's sacred words in a script as beautiful as human hands could contrive. Passages from the Koran adorned not only the fragile pages of books but also the walls of buildings—for example, in the mosaic band above the outer ring of columns inside the Dome of the Rock (FIGS. 10-3 and 10-4). The practice of calligraphy was itself a holy task and required long training. The scribe had to possess exceptional spiritual refinement. An ancient Arabic proverb proclaims, "Purity of writing is purity of soul." Only in China does calligraphy hold as elevated a position among the arts (see "Calligraphy and Inscriptions on Chinese Paintings," page 1061).

Arabic script predates Islam. It is written from right to left with certain characters connected by a baseline. Although the codification of the chief Islamic book, the sacred Koran, occurred in the mid-seventh century, the earliest preserved Korans date to the ninth century. Koran pages were either bound into books or stored as loose sheets in boxes. Most of the early examples feature texts written in the script form called *Kufic,* after the city of Kufa, one of the renowned centers of Arabic calligraphy. Kufic script—used also for the inscription on al-Mughira's 10th-century pyxis (FIG. 10-18)—is quite angular, with the uprights forming almost right angles with the baseline. As with Hebrew and other Semitic languages, the usual practice was to write in consonants only. But to facilitate recitation of the Koran, scribes often indicated vowels by red or yellow symbols above or below the line.

All of these features are present in a 9th- or early-10th-century Koran page (FIG. 10-20) now in Dublin and in the blue-dyed page (FIG. 10-20A) of a contemporaneous Koran now at Harvard University. The Dublin page carries the heading and opening lines of surah 18 of the Koran. The five text lines are in black ink with red vowels, below a decorative band incorporating the chapter title in gold and ending in a palm-tree *finial* (a crowning ornament). This approach to page design has parallels at the extreme

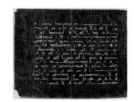

⊿ 10-20A *Blue Koran,* from Kairouan, 9th to mid-10th century.

northwestern corner of the then-known world—in the early medieval manuscripts of Britain and Ireland, where text and ornamentation were similarly united (FIG. 11-1). But the stylized human and animal forms that populate those Christian books never appear in Korans.

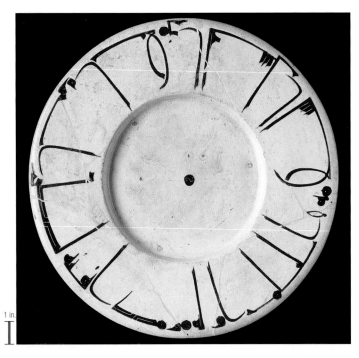

10-21 Dish with Arabic proverb, from Nishapur, Iran, 10th century. Painted and glazed earthenware, 1' 2½" diameter. Musée du Louvre, Paris.

An Arabic proverb in Kufic calligraphy is the sole decoration of this dish made for a cultured owner. It states that magnanimity, although bitter at first taste, is ultimately sweeter than honey.

Ceramics. Around the same time, potters in Nishapur in Iran and in Samarqand in Uzbekistan developed a simple but elegant type of glazed dish with calligraphic decoration. One of the best-preserved examples of *Samarqand ware* is a large dish (FIG. 10-21) from the Nishapur region in Khurasan province of northeastern Iran. To produce dishes such as this, the ceramists formed the shape from the local dark pink clay and then immersed the dish in a tub of white slip. When the slip dried, a painter-calligrapher wrote a Kufic text in black or brown paint around the flat rim of the dish, usually, as here, extending the angular letters both horizontally and vertically to create a circular border and to fill the full width of the rim. A transparent glaze, applied last, sealed the decoration and, after firing, gave the dish an attractive sheen.

The text on this dish is an Arabic proverb, which reads: "Knowledge is bitter-tasting at first, but in the end it is sweeter than honey. Good health [to the owner of this dish]." Because the Arabic words are so similar, recently some scholars have translated "knowledge" as "magnanimity." In either case, this and similar proverbs with practical advice for secular life would have appealed to cultured individuals such as successful merchants. The proverb's reference to food is, of course, highly appropriate for the decoration of tableware.

10-22 Muqarnas dome, Hall of the Abencerrajes, Palace of the Lions, Alhambra, Granada, Spain, 1354–1391.

The structure of this dome on an octagonal drum is difficult to discern because of the intricately carved stucco muqarnas. The prismatic forms reflect sunlight, creating the effect of a starry sky.

LATER ISLAMIC ART

In 1192, a Muslim army under the command of Muhammad of Ghor won a decisive battle at Tarain, which led to the formation in 1206 of an Islamic sultanate at Delhi and eventually to the greatest Muslim empire in Asia, the Mughal Empire. But no sooner did the Muslims establish a permanent presence in South Asia than the Mongols, who had invaded northern China in 1210, overthrew the Abbasid caliphs in Central Asia and Persia. Isfahan fell to the Mongols in 1236, Baghdad in 1258, and Damascus in 1260. Islamic art continued to flourish, however, and important new regional artistic centers emerged. The rest of this chapter treats the art and architecture of the Nasrids (1232–1492) in Spain, the Ayyubids (1171–1250) and Mamluks (1250–1517) in Egypt, the Timurids (1370–1501) and Safavids (1501–1732) in Iran, and the Ottomans (1281–1924) in Turkey. The Islamic art of South Asia is discussed in Chapter 33.

Architecture

In the early years of the 11th century, the Umayyad caliphs' power in Spain unraveled, and their palaces fell prey to Berber soldiers from North Africa. The Berbers ruled southern Spain for several generations, but could not resist the pressure of Christian forces from the north. Córdoba fell to the Christians in 1236, the same year that the Mongols captured Isfahan. From then until the final Christian triumph in 1492, the Nasrids, an Arab dynasty that had established its capital at Granada in 1232, ruled the remaining Muslim territories in Spain.

Alhambra. On a rocky spur at Granada, the Nasrids constructed a huge palace-fortress called the Alhambra ("the Red" in Arabic), named for the rose color of the stone used for its walls and 23 towers. By the end of the 14th century, the complex had a population of 40,000 and included at least a half dozen royal residences. Only two

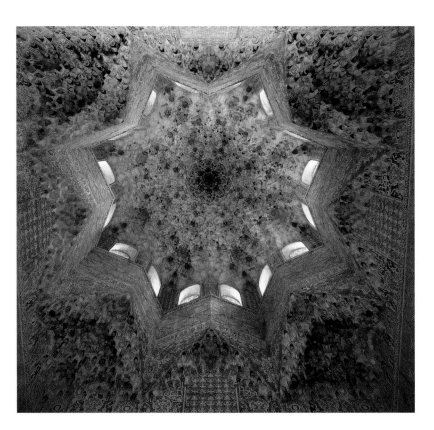

WRITTEN SOURCES

A Venetian Visitor to the Alhambra

In 1526, Andrea Navagiero (1483–1529), the Venetian ambassador to Spain, visited the Alhambra and wrote a vivid account of the Nasrid palace. He was especially impressed by the lavish use of marble for paving stones, the stucco ornamentation of vaults and ceilings, the use of windows to illuminate rooms, and the courtyard fountain in the Palace of the Lions.

> The Alhambra is enclosed by strong walls and is like a Castle, separate from the rest of the City, dominating nearly everything. . . . [M]ost of the area is occupied by a handsome Palace . . . very sumptuously made with fine marbles . . . on the floors rather than the walls . . . and very lovely halls with elegant windows and rather excellent Moorish workmanship adorning not only the walls but also the ceilings [FIG. 10-22]. These are part plaster with plenty of gilding and part ivory also with gilding. . . . [T]here is a most handsome fountain which, being made of various lions that spew water by mouth, gives the name to the Patio of the Lions [FIG. 10-23]. These Lions bear the basin of the fountain and they are made in such a way that, when they don't spew water, if a man speaks any word into the mouth of one of them, speaking in a low voice, if one then puts ear to the mouth of any of the other Lions, it appears to answer so that one hears whatever it was that was said. Among other things there are some handsome underground baths in this Palace, paved with the finest marble and with places to bathe oneself: and everything of marble and with light entering through the roof: with lots of glass, like eyes, all over.*

*D. Fairchild Ruggles, ed., *Islamic Art & Visual Culture: An Anthology of Sources* (Malden, Mass.: Wiley-Blackwell, 2011), 118.

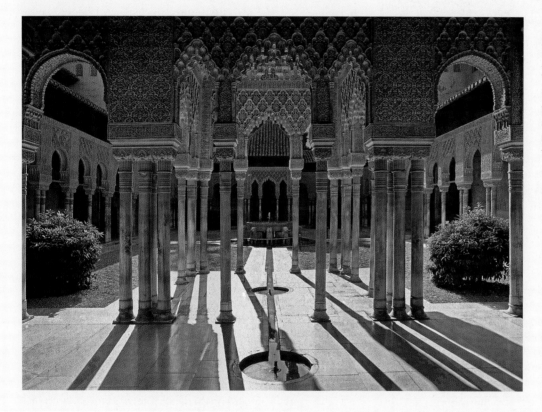

10-23 **Court of the Lions (looking east), Palace of the Lions, Alhambra, Granada, Spain, 1354–1391.**

The Nasrid Palace of the Lions takes its name from the fountain in this courtyard, a rare Islamic example of stone sculpture. Interwoven abstract ornamentation and Arabic calligraphy cover the stucco walls.

of these fared well over the centuries. Paradoxically, they owe their preservation to the Christian victors, who maintained a few of the buildings as trophies commemorating the expulsion of the Nasrids. The two palaces provide a vivid picture of court life in Islamic Spain before the Christian reconquest.

Visitors to the Alhambra today, as in the past, never fail to be impressed by the elaborate stucco walls and ceilings in the Nasrid palaces (see "A Venetian Visitor to the Alhambra," above). A spectacular example is the dome (FIG. 10-22) of the Hall of the Abencerrajes (a leading Spanish family) in the so-called Palace of the Lions. The dome rests on an octagonal drum supported by squinches and pierced by eight pairs of windows, but its structure is difficult to discern because of the intricate carved stucco decoration. Some 5,000 *muqarnas*—tier after tier of stalactite-like prismatic forms that seem aimed at denying the structure's solidity—cover the ceiling. The muqarnas catch and reflect sunlight as well as form beautiful abstract patterns. The lofty vault in this hall and others in the palace symbolize the dome of Heaven. The flickering light and shadows create the effect of a starry sky as the sun's rays glide from window to window during the day. To underscore the symbolism, the palace walls bear inscriptions with verses by the court poet Ibn Zamrak (1333–1393), who compared the Alhambra's lacelike muqarnas ceilings to "the heavenly spheres whose orbits revolve."

The Palace of the Lions takes its name from its courtyard (FIG. 10-23), which contains a fountain with 12 marble lions carrying a water basin on their backs. Colonnaded courtyards with fountains and statues have a long history in the Mediterranean world, especially in the houses and villas of the Roman Empire (FIG. 7-16A).

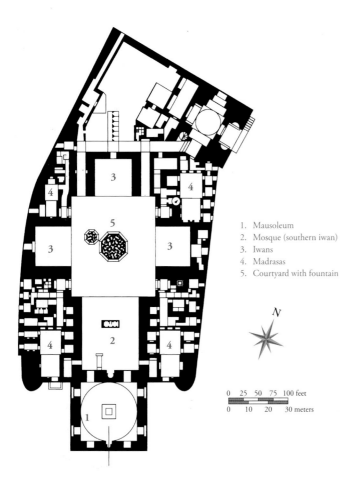

10-24 Plan of the madrasa-mosque-mausoleum complex of Sultan Hasan, Cairo, Egypt, begun 1356.

1. Mausoleum
2. Mosque (southern iwan)
3. Iwans
4. Madrasas
5. Courtyard with fountain

Sultan Hasan's Cairo complex included his tomb, four madrasas, and a mosque. The plan with four iwans opening onto a central courtyard derives from Iranian models (FIG. 10-16).

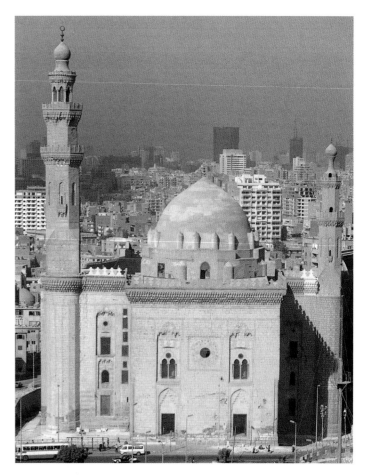

10-25 Madrasa-mosque-mausoleum complex of Sultan Hasan (looking northwest with the mausoleum in the foreground), Cairo, Egypt, begun 1356.

Hasan's mausoleum is a gigantic version of the earlier Samanid mausoleum (FIG. 10-10). Because of its location south of the complex's mosque, praying Muslims face the Mamluk sultan's tomb.

The Alhambra's lion fountain is an unusual instance of freestanding stone sculpture in the Islamic world, unthinkable in a sacred setting. But the design of the courtyard is distinctly Islamic and features many multilobed pointed arches and lavish stuccoed walls carved with interwoven abstract motifs and Arabic calligraphy. The palace was the residence of Muhammad V (r. 1354–1391), and its courtyards, lush gardens, baths, and luxurious carpets and other furnishings served to conjure the image of Paradise.

Cairo. After the Mongol conquests, the center of Islamic power moved from Baghdad to Egypt. The lords of Egypt at the time were former Turkish slaves—*mamluks* in Arabic—who converted to Islam. The capital of the Mamluk sultans was Cairo, which became the largest Muslim city of the late Middle Ages. The Mamluks were prolific builders, and Sultan Hasan, although not an important figure in Islamic history, was the most ambitious of all. He ruled briefly as a child and was deposed, but regained the sultanate from 1354 until his assassination in 1361.

Hasan's major building project in Cairo was a huge madrasa complex (FIGS. 10-24 and 10-25) on a plot of land about 8,000 square yards in area. A *madrasa* ("place of study" in Arabic) is a theological college devoted to the teaching of Islamic law. Hasan's complex was so large that it housed not only four madrasas for the study of the four major schools of Islamic law but also a mosque,

mausoleum, orphanage, and hospital, as well as shops and baths. Like all Islamic building complexes incorporating religious, educational, and charitable functions, this one depended on an endowment funded by rental properties. The income from these paid the salaries of attendants and faculty, provided furnishings and supplies such as oil for the lamps or free food for the poor, and supported scholarships for needy students.

The grandiose structure has a large central courtyard (FIG. 10-24, no. 5) with a fountain in the center and four vaulted iwans opening onto it, as in Iranian mosques (FIG. 10-16). In each corner of the main courtyard, between the iwans (FIG. 10-24, no. 3), is a madrasa (no. 4) with its own courtyard and four or five stories of rooms for the students. The largest iwan (no. 2) in the complex, on the southern side, served as a mosque. Contemporaries believed that the soaring vault over this iwan was taller than the arch of the Sasanian palace (FIG. 2-29) at Ctesiphon, which was then one of the most admired engineering feats in the world. Behind the qibla wall stands the sultan's mausoleum (FIGS. 10-24, no. 1, and 10-25), a gigantic version of the Samanid tomb (FIG. 10-10) at Bukhara but with two flanking minarets. The builders intentionally placed the dome-covered cube south of the mosque so that the prayers of the faithful facing Mecca would be directed toward Hasan's tomb. (The tomb houses only the bodies of the sultan's two sons, however. They could not recover their father's remains after his assassination.)

A muqarnas cornice crowns the exterior walls of Hasan's complex, and marble plaques of several colors cover the mihrab in the mosque and the walls of the mausoleum. The complex as a whole is relatively austere, however. Its massiveness and geometric clarity present a striking contrast to the filigreed elegance of the contemporaneous Alhambra (FIGS. 10-22 and 10-23) and testify to the diversity of regional styles within the Islamic world, especially after the end of the Umayyad and Abbasid dynasties.

Ottoman Empire. After the downfall of the Seljuks (FIGS. 10-15, 10-16, 10-16A, and 10-17), several local dynasties established themselves in Anatolia, among them the Ottomans, founded by Osman I (r. 1281–1326). Under Osman's successors, the Ottoman state expanded throughout vast areas of Asia, Europe, and North Africa. By the middle of the 15th century, the Ottoman Empire had become one of the great world powers.

The Ottoman emperors were lavish patrons of architecture, and the builders in their employ developed a new type of mosque, the core of which was a dome-covered square prayer hall. The combination of dome and square had an appealing geometric clarity and became the nucleus of all Ottoman architecture. At first used singly, the domed units came to be used in multiples, the distinctive feature of later Ottoman architecture.

After the Ottoman Turks conquered Constantinople (Istanbul) in 1453, they firmly established their architectural code. Hagia Sophia (FIG. 9-5) especially impressed the new lords of Constantinople. In some respects, Justinian's great church conformed to their own ideals, and they converted the Byzantine church into a mosque with minarets. But the longitudinal orientation of Hagia Sophia's interior (FIGS. 9-7 and 9-8) never satisfied Ottoman builders, and Anatolian development moved instead toward the central-plan mosque.

Sinan the Great. The first Ottoman central-plan mosques date to the 1520s, but the finest examples are the designs of the most famous Ottoman architect, SINAN (ca. 1491–1588), who worked for one of the greatest Ottoman sultans, Suleyman the Magnificent (r. 1520–1566; FIG. 10-25A). Sinan perfected the Ottoman architectural style. By his time, Ottoman builders almost universally employed the basic domed unit, which

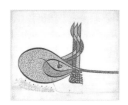

⌖ 10-25A Tughra of Suleyman the Magnificent, ca. 1555–1560.

could be multiplied, enlarged, or contracted as needed. Thus the typical 16th-century Ottoman mosque was a creative assemblage of domical units and artfully juxtaposed geometric spaces. Architects usually designed domes with an extravagant margin of structural safety that has since served them well in earthquake-prone Istanbul and other Turkish cities. (Vivid

demonstration of the sound construction of the Ottoman mosques came in August 1999, when a powerful earthquake centered 65 miles east of Istanbul toppled hundreds of modern buildings and killed thousands of people, but caused no damage to the centuries-old mosques.) Working within this architectural tradition, Sinan searched for solutions to the problems of unifying the additive elements and of creating a cavernous centralized space with harmonious proportions.

Sinan's vision found ultimate expression in the Mosque of Selim II (FIG. 10-26) at Edirne, which had been the capital of the Ottoman Empire from 1363 to 1453 and where Selim II (r. 1566–1574) maintained a palace. There, Sinan designed a mosque with a massive dome set off by four slender pencil-shaped minarets (each more than 200 feet high, among the tallest ever constructed). The dome's height surpasses that of Hagia Sophia's dome (see "Sinan the Great and the Mosque of Selim II," page 310). But it is the organization of the Edirne mosque's interior space that reveals Sinan's genius. The mihrab is recessed into an apselike alcove deep enough

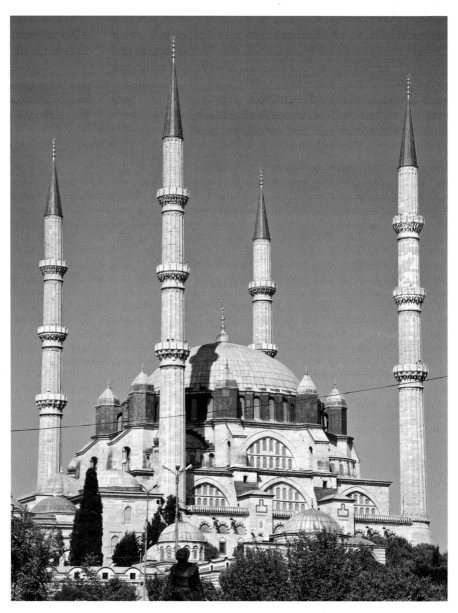

10-26 SINAN, **Mosque of Selim II (looking east), Edirne, Turkey, 1568–1575.**

The Ottomans developed a new type of mosque with a dome-covered square prayer hall. The dome of Sinan's Mosque of Selim II is taller than Hagia Sophia's (FIG. 9-5) and is an engineering triumph.

Sinan the Great and the Mosque of Selim II

Sinan, called Sinan the Great, was truly the greatest Ottoman architect. Born a Christian, he converted to Islam, served in the Ottoman government, and trained in engineering and the art of building while in the Ottoman army. Officials quickly recognized Sinan's talent and entrusted him with increasing responsibility until, in 1538, he became chief court architect for Suleyman the Magnificent (FIG. 10-25A), a generous patron of art and architecture. He retained that position for a half century. Tradition associates Sinan with hundreds of building projects, both sacred and secular, although he could not have been involved with all of them.

The capstone of Sinan's distinguished career was the Edirne mosque (FIGS. 10-26 and 10-27) of Suleyman's son, Selim II, which Sinan designed when he was almost 80 years old. In it, he sought to surpass the greatest achievements of Byzantine architects, just as Sultan Hasan's builders in Cairo (FIG. 10-25) attempted to rival and exceed the Sasanian architects of antiquity. Sa'i Mustafa Çelebi, Sinan's biographer, recorded the architect's accomplishment in his own words:

Sultan Selim Khan ordered the erection of a mosque in Edirne. . . . His humble servant [I, Sinan] prepared for him a drawing depicting, on a dominating site in the city, four minarets on the four corners of a dome. . . . Those who consider themselves architects among Christians say that in the realm of Islam no dome can equal that of the Hagia Sophia; they claim that no Muslim architect would be able to build such a large dome. In this mosque, with the help of God and the support of Sultan Selim Khan, I erected a dome six cubits higher and four cubits wider than the dome of the Hagia Sophia.*

The Edirne dome is, in fact, higher than Hagia Sophia's (FIGS. 9-5 and 9-8) when measured from its base, but its crown is not as far above the pavement as that of the dome of Justinian's church. Nonetheless, Sinan's feat won universal acclaim as an engineering triumph. The Ottomans considered the Mosque of Selim II proof that they finally had outshone the Christian emperors of Byzantium in the realm of architecture.

*Aptullah Kuran, *Sinan: The Grand Old Master of Ottoman Architecture* (Washington, D.C.: Institute of Turkish Studies, 1987), 168–169.

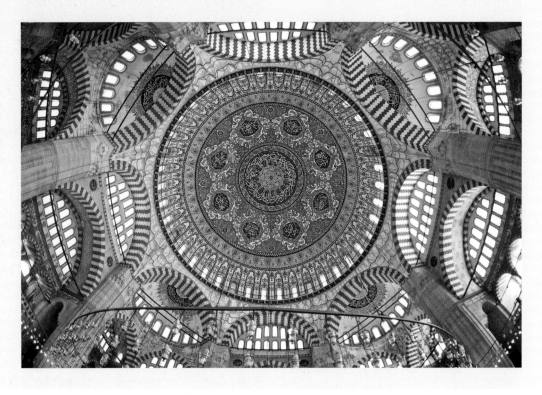

10-27 **SINAN**, view into the dome of the Mosque of Selim II, Edirne, Turkey, 1568–1575.

The interior of Sinan's Edirne mosque is a fusion of an octagon and a dome-covered square with four half-domes at the corners. The plan features geometric clarity and precise numerical ratios.

to permit window illumination from three sides, making the brilliantly colored tile panels of its lower walls sparkle as if with their own glowing light (FIG. 10-27). (In all, there are almost 300 windows in the Edirne mosque, which flood the interior with sunlight.) The plan of the main hall is an ingenious fusion of an octagon with the dome-covered square. The octagon, formed by the eight massive dome supports, is pierced by the four half-dome-covered corners of the square. The result is a fluid interpenetration of several geometric volumes that represents the culminating solution to Sinan's lifelong search for a vast yet unified interior space. Sinan's forms are clear and legible, like mathematical equations. Height, width, and masses relate to one another in a simple but effective ratio of 1:2,

and precise numerical ratios similarly characterize the complex as a whole. The forecourt of the building, for example, covers an area equal to that of the mosque proper. Most architectural historians regard the Mosque of Selim II as the climax of Ottoman architecture. Sinan proudly proclaimed it his masterpiece.

Isfahan. At the time that the Ottomans were establishing their empire in Turkey, Iran underwent a period of political upheaval until the arrival of the forces of Timur in the late 14th century. Isfahan, the former Seljuk capital, was, in fact, under siege in 1354 when the Madrasa Imami was constructed. Its mihrab is an early masterpiece of Iranian ceramic tilework (see "Islamic Tilework,"

Islamic Tilework

From the seventh century—when the Dome of the Rock (FIG. 10-2), the earliest major Islamic building, was constructed—to the present day, Muslim builders have used mosaics or ceramic tiles to decorate the walls and vaults of mosques, madrasas, palaces, and tombs.

The golden age of Islamic tilework was the 16th and 17th centuries. At that time, Muslim artists used two basic techniques to enliven the interiors of buildings with brightly colored tiled walls and to sheathe their exteriors with gleaming tiles that reflected the sun's rays.

In *mosaic tilework* (for example, FIGS. 10-28 and 10-29), potters fire large ceramic panels of single colors in the kiln and then cut them into smaller pieces and set the pieces in plaster in a manner similar to the laying of mosaic tesserae of stone or glass (see "Mosaics," page 256).

Cuerda seca tilework ("dry cord" tilework) was introduced in Umayyad Spain during the 10th century—hence its Spanish name even in Middle Eastern and Central Asian contexts.

Cuerda seca tiles (for example, FIG. 10-30) are polychrome and can bear complex geometric and vegetal patterns as well as Arabic script more easily than can mosaic tiles. They are also more economical to use because vast surfaces can be covered with large tiles much more quickly than they can with thousands of smaller mosaic tiles. But when builders use cuerda seca tiles to sheathe curved surfaces (vaults, domes, minarets), the ceramists must fire the tiles in the exact shape required—a daunting challenge, especially when the tiles must conform to complex muqarnas shapes.

Polychrome tiles have other drawbacks. Because the ceramists fire all the glazes at the same temperature, cuerda seca tiles are not as brilliant in color as mosaic tiles and do not reflect light the way the more irregular surfaces of tile mosaics do. The preparation of the multicolored cuerda seca tiles also requires greater care. To prevent the colors from running together during firing, the potters outline the motifs with cords containing manganese, which leaves a matte black line between the colors after firing.

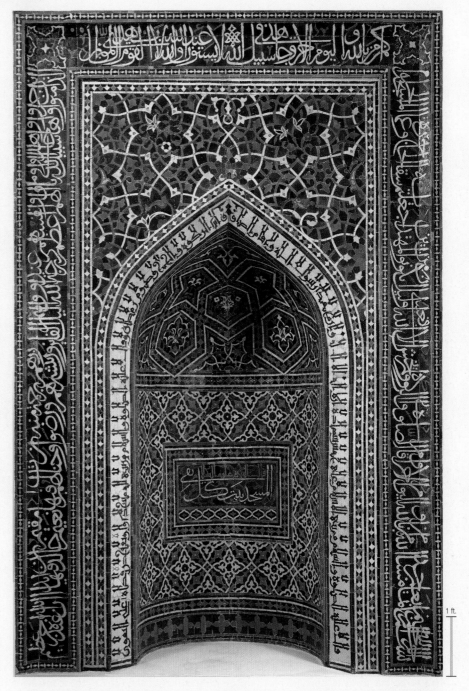

10-28 Mihrab, from the Madrasa Imami, Isfahan, Iran, ca. 1354. Glazed mosaic tilework, 11′ 3″ × 7′ 6″. Metropolitan Museum of Art, New York.

This Iranian mihrab is a masterpiece of mosaic tilework. Every piece had to be cut to fit its specific place in the design. It exemplifies the perfect aesthetic union of Islamic calligraphy and ornamentation.

above). As already noted, verses from the Koran appeared in the mosaics of the Dome of the Rock (FIGS. 10-3 and 10-4) in Jerusalem and in mosaics and other media on the walls of countless later Islamic structures. Indeed, some of the masterworks of Arabic calligraphy are not in manuscripts but on walls. The Madrasa Imami mihrab (FIG. 10-28), like the earlier mihrab (FIG. 10-16A) in the winter prayer hall of Isfahan's Friday Mosque, exemplifies the perfect aesthetic union between the Islamic calligrapher's art and abstract ornamentation. The pointed arch framing the mihrab niche bears an inscription from the Koran in Kufic, the stately rectilinear script employed for the earliest Korans (FIGS. 10-20 and 10-20A). Many supple cursive styles also make up the repertoire of Islamic calligraphy. One of these styles, known as *Muhaqqaq,* fills the mihrab's outer rectangular frame. The mosaic tile decoration on

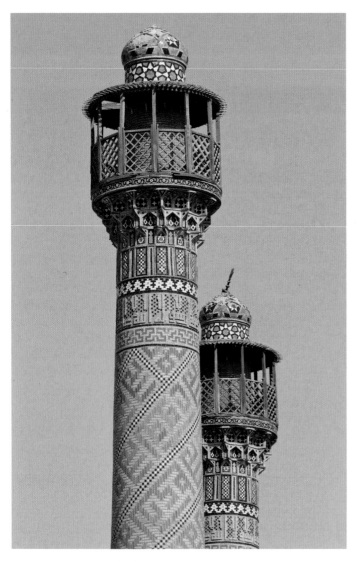

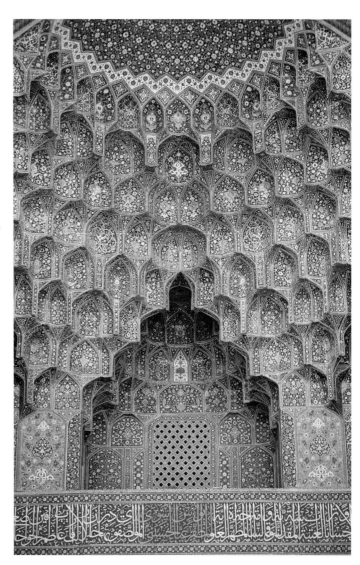

10-29 Mosaic tilework of the minarets of the qibla iwan of the Friday Mosque, Isfahan, Iran, 16th century.

The mosaic tilework of these twin minarets dates to the Safavid dynasty. Highly skilled artisans prepared small tiles of several colors and then placed them in geometric patterns on the curved surfaces.

10-30 Muqarnas tilework of the entrance portal of the Imam Mosque (formerly the Shah Mosque), Isfahan, Iran, 1611–1638.

The ceramists who produced the cuerda seca tiles of the muqarnas-filled portal to the Imam Mosque had to manufacture a wide variety of shapes with curved surfaces to cover the hall's arches and vaults.

the curving surface of the niche and the area above the pointed arch consists of tighter and looser networks of geometric and abstract floral motifs. The mosaic technique is masterful. Every piece had to be cut to fit its specific place in the mihrab—even the tile inscriptions. The ceramist smoothly integrated the subtly varied decorative patterns with the framed inscription in the center of the niche—proclaiming that the mosque is the domicile of the pious believer. The mihrab's outermost inscription—detailing the Five Pillars of Islamic faith (see "Muhammad and Islam," page 295)—serves as a fringelike extension, as well as a boundary, for the entire design. The unification of calligraphic and geometric elements is so complete that only the practiced eye can distinguish them. The artist transformed the architectural surface into a textile surface—the three-dimensional wall into a two-dimensional hanging—weaving the calligraphy into it as another cluster of motifs within the total pattern.

Imam Mosque. The art of ceramic tilework reached its peak in the 16th and 17th centuries in Iran and Turkey, when, for example,

the Ottomans replaced the exterior mosaics of the Dome of the Rock (FIG. 10-2) in Jerusalem with glazed tiles. In Iran, the Safavids (r. 1501–1732) ruled the ancient Persian domains formerly under the control of the Abbasids, Seljuks, and Timurids (FIG. 10-33). The Safavids installed the ceramic tile revetment on the walls, vaults, and minarets (FIG. 10-29) of the Seljuks' Friday Mosque (FIG. 10-15) at Isfahan and built the Imam Mosque (formerly the Shah, or Royal, Mosque) in the early 17th century, which boasts some of the finest examples of Iranian *cuerda seca* tilework. The use of glazed tiles has a long history in the Middle East. Even in ancient Mesopotamia, builders sometimes covered walls and gates with colorful baked bricks, as in Babylon's Ishtar Gate (FIG. 2-24), datable around 575 BCE.

In the Imam Mosque in Isfahan, Safavid tiles cover almost every surface. For the entrance portal (FIG. 10-30), the ceramists had to manufacture a wide variety of shapes with curved surfaces to sheathe the complex forms of the muqarnas-filled pointed half dome. The result was a technological triumph as well as a dazzling display of abstract decoration.

Luxury Arts

The tile-covered mosques of Isfahan, Sultan Hasan's madrasa complex in Cairo, and the architecture of Sinan the Great in Edirne are enduring testaments to the brilliant artistic culture of the Safavid, Mamluk, and Ottoman rulers of the Muslim world. Still, these are but some of the most conspicuous public manifestations of the greatness of later Islamic art and architecture (see Chapter 33 for the achievements of the Muslim rulers of India). In the smaller-scale, and often private, realm of the luxury arts, Muslim artists also excelled. From the vast array of manuscript paintings, ceramics, textiles, and metalwork, the six masterpieces illustrated here suggest both the range and the quality of the inappropriately dubbed Islamic "minor arts" of the 13th to 16th centuries.

Ardabil Carpets. The first of these artworks (FIG. 10-31) is by far the largest, one of a pair of carpets from Ardabil in Iran. The carpets come from the funerary mosque of Shaykh Safi al-Din (1252–1334), the founder of the Safavid line. The carpets date, however, to 1540—two centuries after the construction of the mosque, during the reign of Shah Tahmasp (r. 1524–1576; FIG. 33-5). Tahmasp elevated carpet weaving to a national industry and set up royal factories at Isfahan, Kashan, Kirman, and Tabriz. The name MAQSUD OF KASHAN appears as part of the design of the carpet illustrated here. Maqsud must have been the artist who supplied the master pattern to two teams of royal weavers (one for each of the two carpets). The carpet, almost 35 by 18 feet, consists of roughly 25 million knots, some 340 to the square inch. (Its twin has even more knots.)

The design consists of a central sunburst medallion, representing the inside of a dome, surrounded by 16 pendants. Mosque lamps (appropriate motifs for the Ardabil funerary mosque) hang from two pendants on the long axis of the carpet. The lamps are of different sizes. This may be an optical device to make the two appear equal in size when viewed from the end of the carpet at the room's threshold (the bottom end in FIG. 10-31). Covering the rich blue background are leaves and flowers attached to delicate stems that spread over the whole field. The entire composition presents the illusion of a heavenly dome with lamps reflected in a pool of water full of floating lotus blossoms. No human or animal figures appear, as befits a carpet intended for a mosque, although they can be found on other Islamic textiles used in secular contexts, both earlier (FIG. 10-17A) and later.

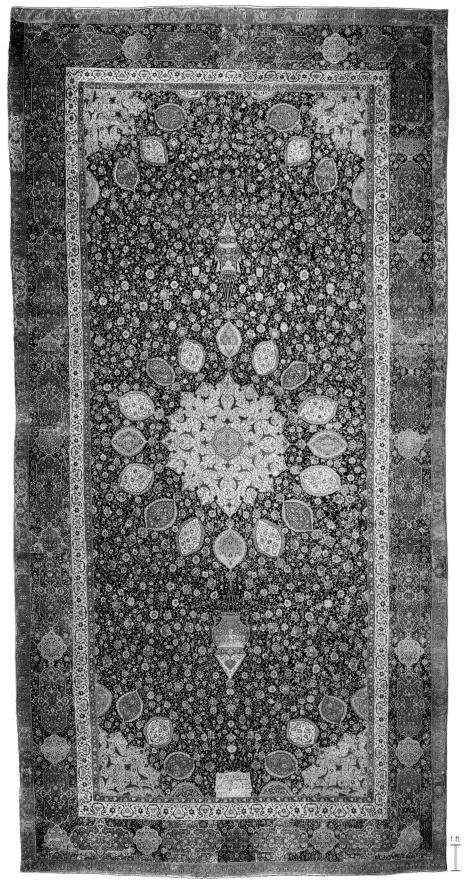

1 ft.

10-31 MAQSUD OF KASHAN, carpet from the funerary mosque of Shaykh Safi al-Din, Ardabil, Iran, 1540. Wool and silk, 34′ 6″ × 17′ 7″. Victoria & Albert Museum, London.

Maqsud of Kashan's enormous Ardabil carpet required roughly 25 million knots. It presents the illusion of a heavenly dome with mosque lamps reflected in a pool of water filled with floating lotus blossoms.

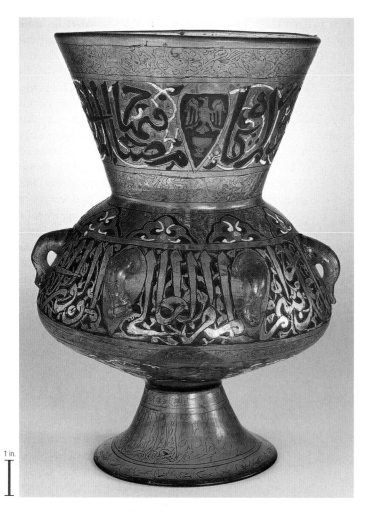

1 in.

10-32 Mosque lamp of Sayf al-Din Tuquztimur, from Egypt, 1340. Glass with enamel decoration, 1′ 1″ high. British Museum, London.

The enamel decoration of this glass mosque lamp includes a quotation from the Koran comparing God's light with the light in a lamp. The burning wick dramatically illuminated the sacred verse.

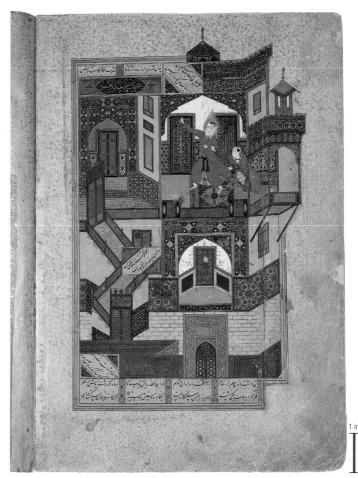

1 in.

10-33 BIHZAD, *Seduction of Yusuf,* folio 52 verso of the *Bustan* of Sultan Husayn Bayqara, from Herat, Afghanistan, 1488. Ink and colors on paper, $11\frac{7}{8}″ \times 8\frac{5}{8}″$. National Library, Cairo.

The most famous Timurid manuscript painter was Bihzad. This page displays vivid color, intricate decorative detailing, and a brilliant balance between two-dimensional patterning and perspective.

Mosque Lamps.   The kind of mosque lamps depicted on the Ardabil carpets were usually made of glass and lavishly decorated. Islamic artists perfected this art form, and fortunately, despite their exceptionally fragile nature, many examples survive, in large part because those who handled them did so with reverence and care. One of the finest is the mosque lamp (FIG. 10-32) made for Sayf al-Din Tuquztimur (d. 1345), an official in the court of the Mamluk sultan al-Nasir Muhammad (r. 1293–1341). The glass lamps hung on chains from mosque ceilings. The shape of Tuquztimur's lamp is typical of the period, consisting of a conical neck, a wide body with six vertical handles, and a tall foot. Inside, a small glass container held the oil and wick. The *enamel* decoration (colors fused to the surfaces) includes Tuquztimur's emblem—an eagle over a cup (Tuquztimur served as the sultan's cup-bearer)—and cursive Arabic calligraphy giving the official's name and titles as well as a quotation of the Koranic verse (24:35) that compares God's light with the light in a lamp. The lamplight dramatically illuminated that verse (and Tuquztimur's name).

Timurid *Bustan*.   In the late 14th century, a new Islamic empire arose in Central Asia under the leadership of Timur (r. 1370–1405), known in the Western world as Tamerlane. Timur, a successor of the Mongol conqueror Genghis Khan, quickly extended his dominions

to include Iran and parts of Anatolia. The Timurids, who ruled until 1501, were great patrons of art and architecture in Herat, Bukhara, Samarqand, and other cities. Herat in particular became a leading center for the production of luxurious books under the patronage of the Timurid sultan Husayn Bayqara (r. 1470–1506).

The most famous Persian painter of his age was BIHZAD, who worked at the Herat court before migrating to Tabriz. At Herat, he illustrated the sultan's copy of *Bustan* (*The Orchard*) by the Persian poet Sadi (ca. 1209–1292). One page (FIG. 10-33) represents a story in both the Bible and the Koran—the seduction of Yusuf (Joseph) by Potiphar's wife, Zulaykha. Bihzad dispersed Sadi's text throughout the page in elegant Arabic script in a series of beige panels. According to the tale as told by Jami (1414–1492), an influential mystic theologian and poet whose Persian text appears in blue in the white pointed arch of the composition's lower center, Zulaykha lured Yusuf into her palace and led him through seven rooms, locking each door behind him. In the last room she threw herself at Yusuf, but he resisted and was able to flee when the seven doors opened miraculously. Bihzad's painting of the story highlights all the stylistic elements that brought him great renown: vivid color, intricate decorative detailing suggesting luxurious textiles and tiled walls, and a brilliant balance between two-dimensional patterning and perspective depictions of balconies and staircases.

Bihzad's apprentices later worked for the Mughal court in India and introduced his distinctive style to South Asia (see "Humayun," page 1046).

Safavid *Shahnama*. The successors of the Timurids in Iran were the Safavids. Shah Tahmasp, the Safavid ruler who commissioned the Ardabil carpets (FIG. 10-31), was also a great patron of books. Around 1525, he commissioned an ambitious decade-long project to produce an illustrated 742-page copy of the *Shahnama* (*Book of Kings*). The *Shahnama*, the Persian national epic poem by Firdawsi (940–1025), recounts the history of Iran from creation until the Muslim conquest. Tahmasp's *Shahnama* contains 258 illustrations by many artists, including some of the most admired painters of the day. It was eventually presented as a gift to Selim II, the Ottoman sultan who was the patron of Sinan's mosque (FIGS. 10-26 and 10-27) at Edirne. The manuscript later entered a private collection in the West and ultimately was auctioned as a series of individual pages, destroying its integrity but underscoring that Western collectors viewed each page as an independent masterpiece.

The page reproduced here (FIG. 10-34) is the work of SULTAN-MUHAMMAD and depicts Gayumars, the legendary first king of Iran, and his court. According to tradition, Gayumars ruled from a mountaintop when humans first learned to cook food and clothe themselves in leopard skins. In Sultan-Muhammad's representation of the story, Gayumars presides over his court from his mountain throne. The king is surrounded by light amid a golden sky. His son and grandson perch on multicolored rocky outcroppings to the viewer's left and right, respectively. The court encircles the ruler and his heirs. All of the figures wear leopard skins. Dozens of human faces appear among the rocks, and many species of animals populate the lush landscape. According to the *Shahnama*, wild beasts became instantly tame in the presence of Gayumars. Sultan-Muhammad rendered the figures, animals, trees, rocks, and sky with an extraordinarily delicate touch. The sense of lightness and airiness permeating the painting is enhanced by its placement on the page—floating, off center, on a speckled background of gold leaf. The painter gave his royal patron a singular vision of Iran's fabled past.

Baptistère de Saint Louis. Metalwork was another early Islamic art form (FIG. 10-19) that continued to play an important role in the later period. An example of the highest quality is a brass basin (FIG. 10-35) from Egypt inlaid with gold and silver and signed—six times—by the Mamluk artist MUHAMMAD IBN AL-ZAYN. The basin, used for washing hands at official ceremonies, must have been fashioned for a specific

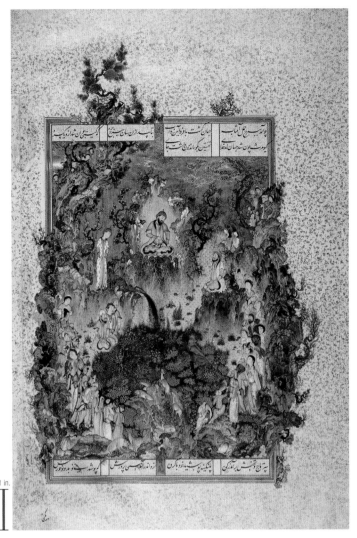

10-34 SULTAN-MUHAMMAD, *Court of Gayumars,* folio 20 verso of the *Shahnama* of Shah Tahmasp, from Tabriz, Iran, ca. 1525–1535. Ink, watercolor, and gold on paper, 1′ 1″ × 9″. Prince Sadruddin Aga Khan Collection, Geneva.

Sultan-Muhammad painted the legend of King Gayumars for the Safavid ruler Shah Tahmasp (FIG. 33-5). The off-center placement on the page enhances the sense of lightness permeating the painting.

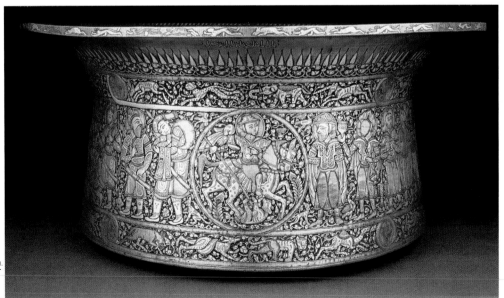

10-35 MUHAMMAD IBN AL-ZAYN, basin (*Baptistère de Saint Louis*), from Egypt, ca. 1300. Brass inlaid with gold and silver, $8\frac{3}{4}''$ high. Musée du Louvre, Paris.

Muhammad ibn al-Zayn proudly signed (six times) this basin used for washing hands at official ceremonies. The central band, inlaid with gold and silver, depicts Mamluk hunters and Mongol enemies.

Christian Patronage of Islamic Art

During the 11th through 13th centuries, large numbers of Christians traveled to Islamic lands, especially to the Christian holy sites in Jerusalem and Bethlehem, either as pilgrims or as Crusaders (see "Pilgrimages," page 350, and "The Crusades," page 360). Many returned with mementos of their journey, usually in the form of inexpensive mass-produced souvenirs. But some wealthy individuals commissioned local Muslim artists to produce custom-made pieces using costly materials.

A unique brass canteen (FIG. 10-36) inlaid with silver and decorated with scenes of the life of Jesus appears to be the work of a 13th-century Ayyubid metalsmith in the employ of a Christian patron. The canteen is a luxurious version of the "pilgrim flasks" that Christian visitors to the Holy Land often carried back to Europe. Four inscriptions in Arabic promise eternal glory, secure life, perfect prosperity, and increasing good luck to the canteen's unnamed owner, who, despite the Arabic words, must have been a Christian, because only a Christian would have commissioned a canteen engraved with New Testament subjects. The Madonna and infant Jesus appear enthroned in the central medallion, and three panels depicting events from the Gospels (see "The Life of Jesus in Art," pages 244–245) fill most of the band around the medallion. The narrative unfolds in a counterclockwise sequence (Arabic is read from right to left), beginning with the Nativity (at 2 o'clock) and continuing with the presentation in the temple (10 o'clock) and Jesus's entry into Jerusalem (6 o'clock). The scenes may have been chosen because the patron had visited their locales (Bethlehem and Jerusalem). Most scholars believe that the Muslim artist used

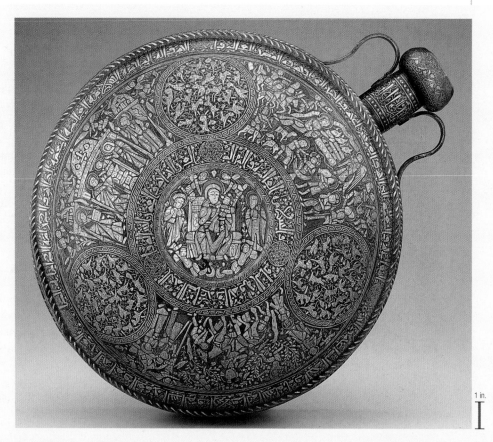

10-36 Canteen with episodes from the life of Jesus, from Syria, ca. 1240–1250. Brass, inlaid with silver, 1′ 2½″ high. Freer Gallery of Art, Washington, D.C.

This unique canteen is the work of an Ayyubid metalsmith in the employ of a Christian pilgrim to the Holy Land. The three scenes from the life of Jesus appear in counterclockwise sequence.

Syrian Christian manuscripts as the source for the canteen's Christian iconography. Many of the decorative details, however, are common in contemporary Islamic metalwork inscribed with the names of Muslim patrons. Whoever the owner was, the canteen testifies to the fruitful artistic interaction between Christians and Muslims in 13th-century Syria.

Mamluk patron. Some scholars think that a court official named Salar ordered the piece as a gift for his sultan, but no inscription identifies him. The central band depicts Mamluk hunters and Mongol enemies. Running animals fill the friezes above and below. Stylized vegetal forms of inlaid silver fill the background of all the bands and roundels. Figures and animals also decorate the inside and underside of the basin, which has long been known as the *Baptistère de Saint Louis*. The association with the famous French king (see "Louis IX, the Saintly King," page 398) is a myth, however.

Louis died before Muhammad ibn al-Zayn made the piece. Nonetheless, the *Baptistère*, taken to France long ago, was used in the baptismal rites of newborns of the French royal family as early as the 17th century.

Like the Zandana silk (FIG. 10-17A) in Toul Cathedral and a 13th-century inlaid brass canteen (FIG. 10-36) featuring scenes of the life of Jesus (see "Christian Patronage of Islamic Art," above), the *Baptistère de Saint Louis* testifies to the prestige of Islamic art well beyond the boundaries of the Islamic world.

The Islamic World

Umayyad Syria and Abbasid Iraq 661–1258

- The Umayyads (r. 661–750) were the first Islamic dynasty. They ruled from their capital at Damascus (Syria) until the Abbasids (r. 750–1258) overthrew them and established a new capital at Baghdad (Iraq).

- The first great Islamic building was the Dome of the Rock, a domed octagon commemorating the triumph of Islam in Jerusalem, which the Muslims captured from the Byzantines in 638.

- Umayyad and Abbasid mosques—for example, those in Damascus and Kairouan (Tunisia)—are of the hypostyle-hall type and incorporate arcaded courtyards and minarets. The mosaic decoration of early mosques was often the work of Byzantine artists, but excluded zoomorphic forms.

- The earliest preserved Korans date to the ninth century and feature Kufic calligraphy and decorative motifs, but no figural illustrations.

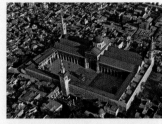

Great Mosque, Damascus, 706–715

Islamic Spain 756–1492

- Abd al-Rahman I established the Umayyad dynasty (r. 756–1031) in Spain when he escaped the Abbasid massacre of his clan in 750.

- The Umayyad capital was at Córdoba, where the caliphs constructed and expanded the Great Mosque between the 8th and 10th centuries. The mosque features horseshoe and multilobed arches and mosaic-covered domes resting on arcuated squinches.

- The last Spanish Muslim dynasty was the Nasrid (r. 1232–1492), whose capital was at Granada. The Alhambra is the best surviving example of Islamic palace architecture. It is famous for its courtyards, stuccoed walls, and arches and its muqarnas decoration on vaults and domes.

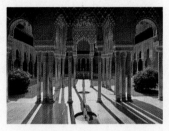

Court of the Lions, Alhambra, 1354–1391

Islamic Egypt 909–1517

- The Fatimids (r. 909–1171) established their caliphate at Cairo (Egypt) in 909. Their successors were the Ayyubids (r. 1171–1250) and the Mamluks (r. 1250–1517).

- The most ambitious Mamluk builder was Sultan Hasan, whose madrasa-mosque-mausoleum complex in Cairo derives from Iranian four-iwan mosque designs.

- Egyptian artists excelled in glassmaking, metalwork, and other luxury arts and produced magnificent mosque lamps and engraved basins.

Mosque lamp of Sayf al-Din Tuquztimur, 1340

Timurid and Safavid Iran and Central Asia 1370–1732

- The Timurid (r. 1370–1501) and Safavid (r. 1501–1732) dynasties, which ruled Iran and Central Asia for almost four centuries, were great patrons of art and architecture.

- The Timurid court at Herat (Afghanistan) employed the most skilled painters of the day, who specialized in illustrating books. The most famous manuscript painter was Bihzad.

- Persian painting also flourished in Safavid Iran under Shah Tahmasp (r. 1524–1576), who in addition set up royal carpet factories in several cities.

- The art of tilework reached its peak under the patronage of the Safavid dynasty. Builders of the time frequently used cuerda seca and mosaic tiles to cover the walls, minarets, vaults, and domes of mosques, madrasas, palaces, and tombs.

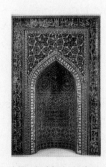

Mihrab, Madrasa Imami, Isfahan, ca. 1354

Ottoman Turkey 1281–1924

- Osman I (r. 1281–1326) founded the Ottoman dynasty in Turkey. By the middle of the 15th century, the Ottomans had become a fearsome power and captured Byzantine Constantinople in 1453.

- The greatest Ottoman architect was Sinan (ca. 1491–1588), who perfected the design of the domed central-plan mosque. His Mosque of Selim II at Edirne is also an engineering triumph. Its dome is taller than Hagia Sophia's.

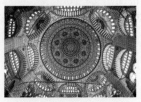

Sinan, Mosque of Selim II, Edirne, 1568–1575

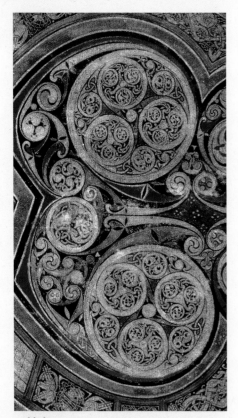

▲ **11-1a** In this opening page to the Gospel of Saint Matthew, the painter transformed the biblical text into abstract pattern, literally making God's words beautiful. The intricate design recalls early medieval metalwork.

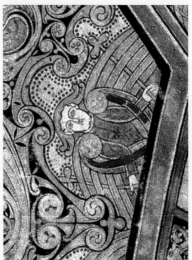

◀**11-1b** The *chi-rho-iota* page is not purely embellished script and abstract pattern. Three half-figures of winged angels appear to the left of *chi*, accompanying the Christogram as if accompanying Christ himself.

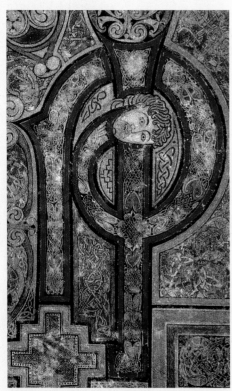

▲ **11-1c** The other figural elements on this page of the *Book of Kells* include a youthful long-haired male head growing out of the end of the curve in the Greek letter *rho*, intertwined with the letter *iota*.

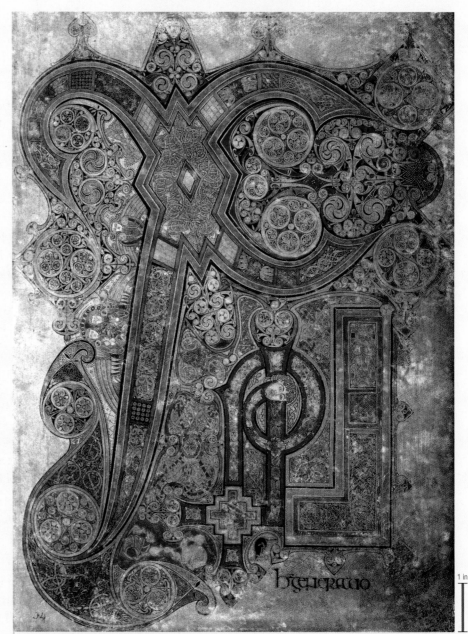

11-1 ***Chi-rho-iota*** **(XPI) page, folio 34 recto of the *Book of Kells*, probably from Iona, Scotland, late eighth or early ninth century. Tempera on vellum, 1′ 1″ × 9½″. Trinity College Library, Dublin.**

EARLY MEDIEVAL EUROPE /11

Missionaries and the Beauty of God's Words

The half millennium between 500 and 1000 was the great formative period of western medieval art, a time of significant innovation that produced some of the most extraordinary artworks in world history. The patrons of many of these works were Christian missionaries, who brought to the non-Christian peoples of the former northwestern provinces of the Roman Empire not only the Gospel but the culture of the Late Antique Mediterranean world, including the art of the book.

In Ireland, the most distant European outpost of the then-known world, the Christianization of the Celts began in the fifth century. By the end of the seventh century, monks at several Irish monasteries were producing magnificent illuminated books for use by the clergy but also to dazzle their converts, who could not read, with the beauty of God's words. The greatest of these early Irish books is the *Book of Kells,* which one commentator described in the *Annals of Ulster* for the year 1003 as "the chief relic of the western world." The manuscript (named after the monastery in central Ireland that once owned it) was probably the work of scribes and illuminators at the monastery at Iona. The monks kept the *Book of Kells* in an elaborate metalwork box, as befits a greatly revered "relic," and they most likely displayed it on the church altar.

The page reproduced here (FIG. 11-1) opens the account of the nativity of Jesus in the Gospel of Saint Matthew and is the passage read in church on Christmas Eve. The initial letters of Christ in Greek (XPI, *chi-rho-iota*) occupy nearly the entire page, although two words—*autem* (abbreviated simply as *h*) and *generatio*—appear at the lower right. Together they read: "Now this is how the birth of Christ came about." The illuminator transformed the holy words into extraordinarily intricate abstract designs that recall Celtic and Anglo-Saxon metalwork (compare FIG. 11-3A), but the page is not purely embellished script and abstract pattern. The letter *rho,* for example, ends in a youthful long-haired male head, and half-figures of winged angels appear to the left of *chi,* accompanying the Christogram as if accompanying Christ himself. When the priest Giraldus Cambrensis visited Ireland in 1185, he described a manuscript that, if not the *Book of Kells* itself, must have been very much like it:

> Fine craftsmanship is all about you, but you might not notice it. Look more keenly at it and you . . . will make out intricacies, so delicate and subtle, so exact and compact, so full of knots and links, with colors so fresh and vivid, that you might say that all this was the work of an angel, and not of a man. For my part, the oftener I see the book, the more carefully I study it, the more I am lost in ever fresh amazement, and I see more and more wonders in the book.[1]

In the early Middle Ages, the monasteries of northern Europe were both the repositories of knowledge in the midst of an almost wholly illiterate population and the greatest centers of art production.

EUROPE AFTER THE FALL OF ROME

Early medieval art* in western Europe (MAP 11-1) was the result of a unique fusion of the classical heritage of Rome's northwestern provinces, the cultures of the non-Roman peoples north of the Alps, and Christianity. Although the Romans called everyone who lived beyond their empire's frontiers "barbarians," many northerners had risen to prominent positions within the Roman army and government during Late Antiquity. Others established their own areas of rule, sometimes with Rome's approval, sometimes in opposition to imperial authority. Over the centuries, the various population groups merged, and a new order gradually replaced what had been the Roman Empire, resulting eventually in today's European nations.

As Rome's power waned, armed conflicts and competition for political authority became commonplace among the Huns, Vandals, Merovingians, Franks, Goths, and other non-Roman peoples of Europe. Once one group established itself in Italy or in one of Rome's European provinces, another often pressed in behind and compelled the first one to move on. The Visigoths, for example, who at one time controlled part of Italy and formed a kingdom in what is today southern France, were forced southward into Spain under pressure from the Franks, who had crossed the lower Rhine River and established themselves firmly in France, Switzerland, the Netherlands, and parts of Germany. The Ostrogoths moved from Pannonia (at the junction of modern Hungary, Austria, and the former Yugoslavia) to Italy. Their king, Theodoric, chose Ravenna as his capital in 493, only to have the city fall less than a century later to the Lombards, the last of the early Germanic powers to occupy land within the limits of the old Roman Empire. Anglo-Saxons controlled what had been Roman Britain. Celts inhabited France and parts of the British Isles, including Ireland. In Scandinavia, the seafaring Vikings held sway.

MEROVINGIANS AND ANGLO-SAXONS

Art historians do not know the full range of art and architecture that these non-Roman cultures produced. What has survived is probably not fully representative and consists almost exclusively of small portable "status symbols"—weapons and items of personal adornment such as bracelets, pendants, and belt buckles discovered in lavish burials. Earlier scholars, who viewed medieval art through a Renaissance lens, ignored these "minor arts" because of their small scale, seemingly utilitarian nature, and abstract ornamentation, and because their makers rejected the classical idea that naturalistic representation should be the focus of artistic endeavor. In

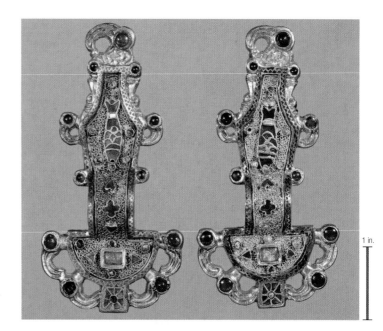

11-2 Pair of Merovingian looped fibulae, from Jouy-le-Comte, France, mid-sixth century. Silver gilt worked in filigree, with inlays of garnets and other stones, 4″ high. Musée d'archéologie nationale, Saint-Germain-en-Laye.

Early medieval jeweled fibulae were status symbols for elite patrons. This pair, probably owned by a Merovingian woman, features eagle heads and fish integrated into a highly decorative design.

the early Middle Ages, people regarded these objects, which often display a high degree of technical and stylistic sophistication, as treasures. The objects enhanced their owners' prestige and testified to the stature of those buried with them. In the great early (possibly seventh-century) Anglo-Saxon epic *Beowulf*, after Beowulf dies, his comrades cremate the hero and place his ashes in a huge *tumulus* (burial mound) overlooking the sea. As an everlasting tribute to Beowulf's greatness, they "buried rings and brooches in the barrow, all those adornments that brave men had brought out from the hoard after Beowulf died. They bequeathed the gleaming gold, treasure of men, to the earth."[2]

*The adjective *medieval* and the noun *Middle Ages* are very old terms stemming from an outmoded view of the roughly 1,000 years between the adoption of Christianity as the Roman Empire's official religion and the rebirth (Renaissance) of interest in classical antiquity. Earlier historians, following the lead of the humanist scholars of Renaissance Italy, viewed this period as a long and artistically crude interval between (in the middle of) two great civilizations. The force of tradition dictates the retention of both terms to describe this period and its art, although scholars long ago ceased to see medieval art as unsophisticated or inferior.

EARLY MEDIEVAL EUROPE

410–768	768–919	919–1024
Merovingian and Anglo-Saxon	**Hiberno-Saxon and Carolingian**	**Ottonian**
■ After the fall of Rome, Merovingian and Anglo-Saxon artists produce costly portable items of personal adornment featuring cloisonné ornamentation and intertwined animal-and-interlace patterns	■ Christian missionaries commission sumptuous illuminated manuscripts featuring full pages devoted to embellishing the word of God	■ Ottonian painters and sculptors produce illuminated manuscripts and ivory reliefs inspired by Late Antique and Byzantine sources
■ Anglo-Saxon kings are laid to rest in treasure-laden ship burials, a tradition reflected in the *Beowulf* saga	■ Charlemagne and his Carolingian successors (768–877) initiate a conscious revival of the art and culture of Early Christian Rome	■ Bishop Bernward adorns Saint Michael's at Hildesheim with bronze doors and a freestanding bronze column covered with figural reliefs
	■ Carolingian architects introduce the twin-tower west-work and modular plans for basilican churches	■ Ottonian architects introduce the alternate-support system and galleries into the naves of churches

Cloisonné

The most extraordinary item found in the Sutton Hoo tumulus is the purse cover shown in FIG. 11-3, a masterpiece of *cloisonné* ornamentation. The *Beowulf* saga refers to the warlords who honored the living and dead by giving them jewelry and other costly portable items as "treasure givers," and the cloisonné technique was a favored manufacturing process for their treasures.

The technique, however, is much older than the era of the Merovingian and Anglo-Saxon kings, and dates at least as early as the New Kingdom in Egypt.

Metalworkers produced cloisonné jewelry by soldering small metal strips, or *cloisons* (French for "partitions"), edge up, to a metal background, and then filling the compartments with semiprecious stones, pieces of colored glass, or glass paste fired to resemble sparkling jewels. The edges of the cloisons are an important part of the design.

Cloisonné is a cross between mosaic and stained glass (see "Mosaics," page 256, and "Stained-Glass Windows," page 392), but medieval artists used it only on a miniature scale. The decoration of the Sutton Hoo purse cover consists of seven cloisonné plaques within a cloisonné border—five plaques with human and animal figures and two with purely abstract ornament.

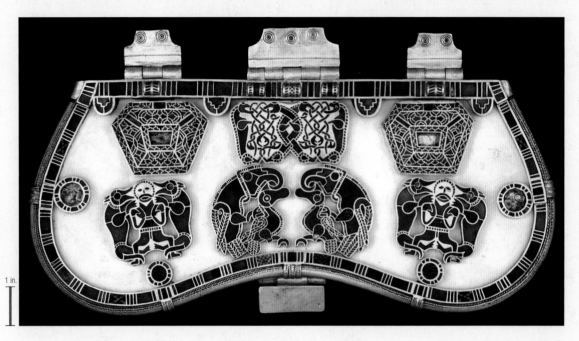

1 in.

11-3 Purse cover, from the Sutton Hoo ship burial in Suffolk, England, ca. 625. Gold, glass, and cloisonné garnets, $7\frac{1}{2}''$ wide. British Museum, London (gift of Mrs. E. M. Pretty).

This purse cover with cloisonné ornamentation comes from a treasure-laden royal burial ship. The combination of abstract interlace with animal figures is the hallmark of early medieval art in western Europe.

Merovingian Fibulae. Most characteristic, perhaps, of the prestige adornments of the early medieval period was the *fibula,* a decorative pin favored by the Romans (and the Etruscans before them; FIG. 6-2). Men and women alike used fibulae to fasten their garments. Made of bronze, silver, or gold, these pins often featured profuse decoration, sometimes incorporating inlaid precious or semiprecious stones. The pair of fibulae illustrated here (FIG. 11-2) formed part of a find of jewelry of the mid-sixth century, when Merovingian kings (r. 482–751), named for the founder of their line, Merovech, ruled large parts of what is now France. The pins, probably once the proud possession of a wealthy Merovingian woman, accompanied their owner into the afterlife. They resemble, in general form, the roughly contemporaneous but plain fibulae used to fasten the outer garments of some of the attendants flanking the Byzantine emperor Justinian in the apse mosaic (FIG. 9-13) of San Vitale in Ravenna. (Note how much more elaborate is the emperor's clasp. In Rome, Byzantium, and early medieval Europe alike, these fibulae were emblems of office and of prestige.)

Covering almost the entire surface of each of the Merovingian fibulae are decorative patterns adjusted carefully to the basic shape of the object. They thus describe and amplify the fibula's form and structure, becoming an organic part of the pin itself. Often the early medieval metalworkers so successfully integrated zoomorphic elements into this type of highly disciplined, abstract decorative design that the animal forms became almost unrecognizable. For example, the fibulae in FIG. 11-2 incorporate a fish just above the center of each pin. The looped forms at the top and around the edges are stylized eagles' heads with red garnets forming the eyes.

Sutton Hoo Ship Burial. In 1939, archaeologists uncovered a treasure-laden ship in a burial mound at Sutton Hoo, near the sea, in Suffolk, England. The Sutton Hoo ship never set out to sea. Rather, it is among the best examples of the early medieval tradition of burying great lords in ships with rich furnishings (see "Early Medieval Ship Burials," page 322). Among the many precious finds were a purse cover (FIG. 11-3) with gold, glass, and garnet *cloisonné* ornamentation (see "Cloisonné," above); a gold belt buckle (FIG. 11-3A); 10 silver bowls; a silver plate with the imperial stamp of the Byzantine emperor Anastasius I (r. 491–518); and 40 gold coins (perhaps to pay the 40

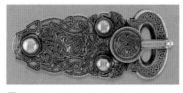

⬈**11-3A** Belt buckle, Sutton Hoo, ca. 625.

Early Medieval Ship Burials

The Vikings, famous for their prowess as shipbuilders and sailors, were not the only early medieval northern European civilization to bury their elite in sailing vessels, whether beneath grand earthen mounds or set adrift in the ocean. For example, the Anglo-Saxon *Beowulf* saga recounts the funeral of the warrior lord Scyld, whom his comrades laid to rest in a ship overflowing with arms and armor and costly adornments.

> They laid their dear lord, the giver of rings, deep within the ship by the mast in majesty; many treasures and adornments from far and wide were gathered there. I have never heard of a ship equipped more handsomely with weapons and war-gear, swords and corselets; on his breast lay countless treasures that were to travel far with him into the waves' domain.*

Two archaeological discoveries during the first half of the 20th century at Sutton Hoo (FIGS. 11-3 and 11-3A) in England and Oseberg (FIG. 11-4) in Norway confirmed that ship burials were not fictional literary inventions. Norwegian excavators discovered the Oseberg ship in 1904 in a burial mound near Tonsberg on the west coast of the Oslo fjord. Grave robbers had long before plundered the treasure of jewelry and metalwork presumably buried with the deceased, but most of the other furnishings of the ship were intact. These included five animal-head posts (FIG. 11-4A) of uncertain function found in the ship's burial chamber, dated ca. 834 based on analysis of the tree rings in the wood. The burial chamber also contained

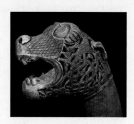

⌐↗⌐**11-4A** Animal-head post, Oseberg, ca. 834.

the remains of two women of different ages, clothing, furniture, and a four-wheeled cart. Scholars are uncertain whether the older woman, thought to be 60–70 years of age, or her younger companion, a woman about 50 years old, was the more important, the other possibly being her attendant, who may have been sacrificed to accompany her mistress into the afterlife. Also found aboard the Oseberg ship were the skeletons of 14 horses, three dogs, and an ox.

The ship itself is most likely about 15 years older than the burial and was a seaworthy vessel, but because of its relatively light construction, it probably was used only for coastal voyages. Fifteen pairs of holes for oars indicate that 30 rowers formed the crew of the Oseberg ship. The mast was about 28 feet tall. The vessel may have been a pleasure yacht belonging to a woman of high status. It has an elegant, elongated shape designed to cut through the water. Its sweeping lines end in a stylized sea serpent's head at the top of the prow. All along the border of the ship are carved reliefs of interlaced animals, the most characteristic motif in the Viking decorative repertoire.

11-4 Viking ship burial, Oseberg, Norway, ca. 820. Wood, 70′ 10⅜″ long.

This Viking burial ship features carved wood ornament with interlaced animals. In it were the remains of two women, 14 horses, three dogs, and an ox. There was probably also a treasure of jewelry and metalwork.

*Beowulf 36–42. Translated by Kevin Crossley-Holland (New York: Farrar, Straus & Giroux, 1968), 2–3.

oarsmen who would row the deceased across the sea on his final voyage). Also placed in the ship were two silver spoons inscribed "Saulos" and "Paulos," Saint Paul's names in Greek before and after his baptism. They may allude to a conversion to Christianity. Some historians have associated the ship with the East Anglian king Raedwald (r. 599?–625), who was baptized a Christian before his death in 625, but the identity of the king buried at Sutton Hoo is uncertain.

On the Sutton Hoo purse cover, four symmetrically arranged groups of figures make up the lower row. The end groups consist of a man standing between two beasts. He faces front, and they appear in profile. This heraldic type of grouping has a venerable heritage in the ancient world (FIG. 2-7), but must also have delivered a powerful contemporary message. It is a pictorial parallel to the epic sagas of the era in which heroes such as Beowulf battle and conquer horrific monsters. The two center groups represent eagles attacking ducks. The metalworker ingeniously composed the animal figures. For example, the convex beaks of the eagles (compare the Merovingian fibulae, FIG. 11-2) fit against the concave beaks of the ducks. The two figures fit together so snugly that they seem at first to be a single dense abstract design. This is true also of the man-and-animals motif.

Above these figures are three geometric designs. The outer ones are purely linear, although they also rely on color contrasts for their effect. The central design is an interlace pattern in which the interlacements evolve into writhing animal figures. Elaborate intertwining linear patterns are characteristic of many times and places, notably in the art of the Islamic world (see FIGS. 10-6B, 10-12, 10-13, and 10-23). But the combination of interlace with animal figures was uncommon outside the realm of the early medieval warlords. In fact, metalcraft with interlace patterns and other motifs beautifully integrated with animal forms was the premier art of the early Middle Ages in northwestern Europe. Interest in animal-based interlace patterns was so great that artists imitated the colorful effects of these jewelry designs in the painted decorations of manuscripts (FIGS. 11-1, 11-6, and 11-7), in the ornamentation of churches (FIG. 11-5), and in sculpture in stone and in wood (FIGS. 11-4 and 11-4A), the last an especially important medium of Viking art.

VIKINGS

In 793, the pre-Christian traders and pirates of Scandinavia known as Vikings (named after the *viks*—coves or harbors—of the Norwegian shoreline) landed in the British Isles. They destroyed the Christian monastic community on Lindisfarne Island off the Northumbrian (northeastern) coast of England. Shortly after, these Norsemen (North men) attacked the monasteries at Jarrow in England and on Iona Island, off the west coast of Scotland. (Monasteries were very attractive targets because they owned treasures but were undefended.) From then until the mid-11th century, the Vikings were the terror of western Europe. From their great ships, they seasonally harried and plundered harbors and river settlements. Their fast, seaworthy longboats took them on wide-ranging voyages, from Ireland eastward to Russia and westward to Iceland and Greenland and even, briefly, to Newfoundland in North America, long before Columbus arrived in the New World.

The Vikings were intent not merely on a hit-and-run strategy of destruction but also on colonizing the lands they conquered. Their exceptional talent for organization and administration, as well as for war, enabled them to acquire and govern large territories in Ireland, England, and France, as well as in the Baltic regions and Russia. For a while, in the early 11th century, the whole of England was part of a Danish empire. When Vikings settled in northern France in the early 10th century, their territory came to be called Normandy—home of the Norsemen who became Normans. (Later, a Norman duke, William the Conqueror, sailed across the English Channel and invaded and became the master of Anglo-Saxon England; FIG. 12-41.)

Oseberg Ship Burial. Much of the preserved art of the Viking sea-rovers consists of decoration of their great ships. Striking examples of Viking woodcarving come from a ship burial near the sea at Oseberg, Norway (see "Early Medieval Ship Burials," page 322). The ship (FIG. 11-4), discovered beneath an earthen mound as was the earlier Sutton Hoo vessel, is more than 70 feet long. The Oseberg burial contained the remains of two women. The size of the sleek ship alone and the wood vessel's lavishly carved ornamentation (FIG. 11-4A) attest to the importance of those laid to rest beneath the mound. The Oseberg ship also once must have carried many precious objects, which, unfortunately, robbers stole long before its modern discovery.

Stave Church, Urnes. By the 11th century, much of Scandinavia had become Christian, but Viking artistic traditions persisted. Nowhere is this more evident than in the decoration of the wood portal (FIG. 11-5) of the stave church (*staves* are wedge-shaped timbers placed vertically) at Urnes, Norway. The portal and a few staves are almost all that remain from the mid-11th-century church. Builders later incorporated these fragments into the walls of the 12th-century church. Gracefully elongated animal forms intertwine with flexible plant stalks and tendrils in spiraling rhythm. The effect of natural growth is astonishing, yet the designer subjected the organic forms to a highly refined abstract sensibility. The motifs include one large four-legged beast standing to the left of the portal, perhaps serving as a guardian. It bites, and is bitten by, one of the serpentine animals, and exemplifies the intertwining compositions favored by the non-Roman peoples north of the Alps before their conversion to Christianity.

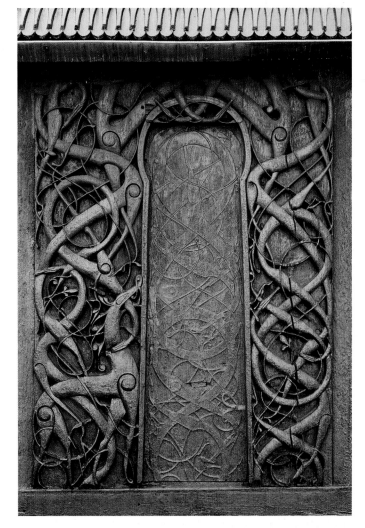

11-5 Wood portal of the stave church at Urnes, Norway, ca. 1050–1070.

By the 11th century, Scandinavia had become mostly Christian, but Viking artistic traditions persisted, as in the intertwining animal-and-plant decoration of this Norwegian church portal.

Medieval Books

Because of the central role that books played in the medieval Church, scribes in the monasteries of western Europe developed a large number of specialized types for priests, monks and nuns, and laypersons.

The primary sacred text came to be called the Bible ("the Book," in Greek), consisting of the Hebrew scriptures (the "Old Testament") and the Christian "New Testament," written in Greek. In the late fourth century, Saint Jerome (d. 420) produced the canonical Latin, or *Vulgate* ("vulgar," or common tongue), version of the Bible, which incorporates 46 Old and 27 New Testament books. Before the invention of the printing press in the 15th century, all books were handwritten. Bibles were major undertakings, labor-intensive and very expensive to produce. Consequently, few early medieval monasteries possessed a complete Bible. Instead, medieval codices consist of a section of the Bible, such as a single book (for example, the *Vienna Genesis,* FIGS. 9-17 and 9-17A) or a set of several books.

The *Pentateuch* contains the five books of the Hebrew Torah, beginning with the story of Adam and Eve (Genesis). The *Gospels* ("good news") are the New Testament works of Saints Matthew, Mark, Luke, and John (see "The Four Evangelists," page 331) and tell the story of Christ's life, death, and resurrection (see "The Life of Jesus in Art," pages 244–245). Medieval Gospel books often contain *canon tables*—a concordance, or matching, of the corresponding passages of the four Gospels, which Eusebius of Caesarea (d. ca. 339) compiled in the fourth century. *Psalters* (FIGS. 11-14A and 11-15) collect the 150 psalms of King David, written in Hebrew and translated into both Greek and Latin.

The Church also frequently employed other types of books. *Lectionaries* (FIGS. 11-12A and 11-32) contain passages from the Gospels reordered to appear in the sequence that priests read them during the celebration of Mass throughout the year. *Breviaries* include the texts required for monks' daily recitations. *Sacramentaries* incorporate the prayers that priests recite during Mass. *Benedictionals* contain bishops' blessings. In the later Middle Ages, scribes also created specialized books for the private devotions of the laity, patterned after monks' readers. The most popular was the *Book of Hours,* so called because it contains the prayers to be read at specified times of the day.

Medieval scribes produced many other types of books—compilations of saints' lives (*passionals*), theological treatises, secular texts on

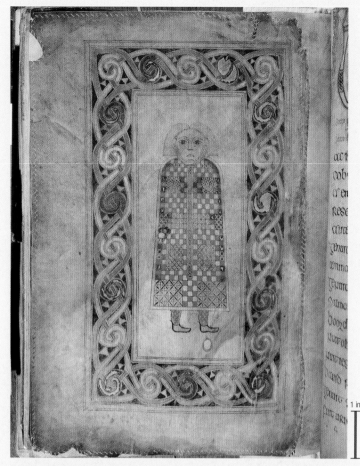

11-6 Man (symbol of Saint Matthew), folio 21 verso of the *Book of Durrow,* possibly from Iona, Scotland, ca. 660–680. Ink and tempera on parchment, $9\frac{5}{8}'' \times 6\frac{1}{8}''$. Trinity College Library, Dublin.

This early Hiberno-Saxon Gospel book has four pages devoted to the symbols of the four evangelists. The cloak of Saint Matthew's man resembles a cloisonné brooch filled with abstract ornamentation.

history and science, and even some classics of Greco-Roman literature—but these contained illustrations less frequently than did the various sacred texts.

HIBERNO-SAXON MONASTERIES

At the same time that powerful Merovingian, Anglo-Saxon, and Scandinavian warlords were amassing artworks dominated by abstract and animal motifs, Christian missionaries were establishing monasteries in northern Europe and sponsoring artworks of Christian content (see "Missionaries and the Beauty of God's Words," page 319). The early medieval art of these monasteries, however, differs dramatically from contemporaneous works produced in Italy and the Byzantine Empire. These Christian artworks are among the most distinctive ever created and testify to the fruitful fusion of native and imported artistic traditions.

In Ireland, in part because of their isolation, the Celts who converted to Christianity, although nominally subject to the Church of Rome, quickly developed a different form of monastic organization.

The monks often selected inaccessible and inhospitable places where they could carry on their duties far from worldly temptations and distractions. Before long, Irish monks, filled with missionary zeal, set up monastic establishments in Britain and Scotland. In 563, the most famous of these monks, Saint Columba (521–597), founded an important monastery on the Scottish island of Iona, where he successfully converted the native Picts to Christianity.

The Iona monastery became one of several major artistic centers of the early Middle Ages. Art historians called the art of these monasteries *Hiberno-Saxon* (Hibernia was the Roman name for Ireland) or *Insular* to denote the early medieval art of the Irish-English islands. The most distinctive products of the Hiberno-Saxon monasteries were illuminated Christian books, such as the *Book of Kells* (FIG. 11-1). Books were the primary vehicles in the effort to Christianize Britain, Scotland, and Ireland. They brought the word of God to a predominantly illiterate population, who regarded the monks' sumptuous volumes with awe. Books were scarce and jealously guarded treasures of the libraries and *scriptoria* (writing studios) of monasteries and major churches. Illuminated books are the most important extant monuments of the brilliant artistic culture that flourished in Ireland and Northumbria during the seventh and eighth centuries.

Book of Durrow. Among the earliest Hiberno-Saxon illuminated manuscripts is the *Book of Durrow,* a Gospel book (see "Medieval Books," page 324) that may have been written and decorated in the monastic scriptorium at Iona, although it has no documented provenance. In the late Middle Ages, it was in the monastery in Durrow, Ireland—hence its modern name. The Durrow Gospels already display one of the most characteristic features of Insular book illumination—full pages devoted neither to text nor to illustration but to pure embellishment. The Hiberno-Saxon painters must have felt that beautiful decoration lent prestige to books just as ornamental jewelry lent status to those who wore it. Interspersed between the Durrow text pages are so-called *carpet pages,* resembling textiles, made up of decorative panels of abstract and animal forms (compare FIG. 11-7). The *Book of Durrow* also contains pages on which the illuminator

enormously enlarged the initial letters of an important passage of sacred text and transformed those letters into elaborate decorative patterns (compare FIG. 11-1). Such manuscript pages have no precedents in Greco-Roman books. They reveal the striking independence of Insular artists from the classical tradition.

In the *Book of Durrow,* each of the four Gospel books has a carpet page facing a page dedicated to the symbol of the evangelist who wrote that Gospel. An elaborate interlace design similar to those found on contemporaneous belt buckles and brooches frames each symbol. These pages serve to highlight the major divisions of the text. The symbol of Saint Matthew (FIG. 11-6) is a man (more commonly represented later as winged; see "The Four Evangelists," page 331), but the only human parts that the artist—a seventh-century monk—chose to render are a schematic frontal head and two profile feet. A cloak of yellow, red, and green squares—resembling cloisons filled with intricate abstract designs and outlined in dark brown or black—envelops the rest of the "body." The *Book of Durrow* weds the abstraction of northern European early medieval personal adornment with the Christian pictorial imagery of Italy and Byzantium. The vehicle for the transmission of those Mediterranean forms was the illustrated book itself, which Christian missionaries brought to Ireland.

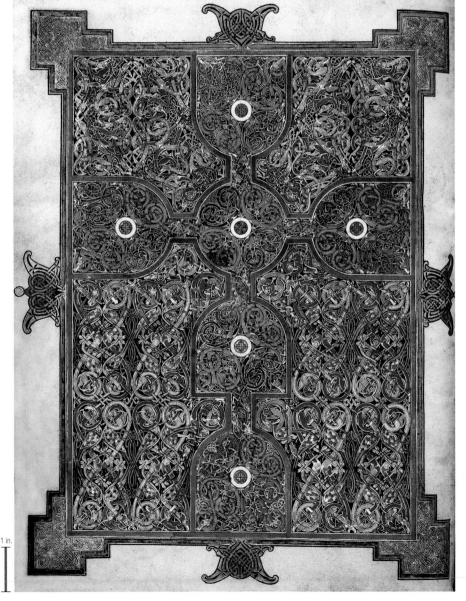

1 in.

Lindisfarne Gospels. The marriage between Christian imagery and the animal-and-interlace style of the northern warlords is evident in the cross-inscribed carpet page (FIG. 11-7) of the *Lindisfarne Gospels.* Produced in the Northumbrian monastery on Lindisfarne Island, the book contains several ornamental pages and exemplifies Hiberno-Saxon art at its best. According to a later *colophon* (an inscription, usually on the last page, providing information regarding a book's manufacture), Eadfrith, bishop of Lindisfarne between 698 and his death in 721, wrote the *Lindisfarne Gospels* "for God and Saint Cuthbert." Cuthbert's *relics* recently had been deposited in the Lindisfarne church (see "The Veneration of Relics," page 349).

The Lindisfarne carpet page features much more intricate patterning and detail than comparable ornamental pages in the *Book of Durrow.* Serpentine interlacements of fantastic animals devour each other, curling over and returning on their writhing, elastic shapes. The rhythm of expanding and contracting forms produces a vivid effect of motion and change, but the painter held it in check by the regularity of the design and by the dominating motif of the inscribed cross. The cross—the

11-7 Cross-inscribed carpet page, folio 26 verso of the *Lindisfarne Gospels,* from Northumbria, England, ca. 698–721. Tempera on vellum, 1′ 1½″ × 9¼″. British Library, London.

The cross-inscribed carpet page of the *Lindisfarne Gospels* exemplifies the way that Hiberno-Saxon illuminators married Christian imagery and the animal-and-interlace style of the early medieval warlords.

The Lindisfarne Saint Matthew

As is characteristic of illuminated medieval Gospel books (see "Medieval Books," page 324), portraits of the authors of the four accounts of Christ's life (see "The Four Evangelists," page 331) open each section of the *Lindisfarne Gospels*. The portrait of the evangelist Matthew (FIG. 11-8) in that manuscript differs sharply from the representation of Matthew's symbol in the earlier *Book of Durrow* (FIG. 11-6). Art historians agree that the model for the Lindisfarne illuminator was either an illustrated Gospel book that a Christian missionary brought with him from Italy or a northern manuscript modeled in turn on a representation in a Mediterranean book. Author portraits were familiar features of Greek and Latin books, and similar representations of seated philosophers or poets writing or reading (FIGS. 7-25, 7-70, and 8-7) abound in ancient art. The Lindisfarne Matthew sits in his study writing in a codex that he rests on his lap. A curtain sets the scene indoors, as in classical art (FIG. 5-58), and Matthew's seat is at an angle, which also suggests a Mediterranean model employing classical perspective.

However, the Northumbrian painter's goal was not to copy the assumed model faithfully. Instead, uninterested in volume, shading, and perspective—hallmarks of the pictorial illusionism of Greco-Roman painting—the Lindisfarne illuminator conceived the subject exclusively in terms of line and color. In the Hiberno-Saxon manuscript, the drapery folds are a series of sharp, regularly spaced, curving lines filled in with flat colors. The painter converted fully modeled forms bathed in light into the linear idiom of Insular art. The result is a vivid new vision of Saint Matthew.

Although it seems clear that a Late Antique or early medieval author portrait was the model for the Lindisfarne page depicting Saint Matthew composing his Gospel account, other aspects of the illumination present difficulties in interpretation. For example, the Hiberno-Saxon painter (or the scribe) added the identifying label for the evangelist by using a curious combination of Greek (*O Agios*, "saint [*hagios*]"—written, however, in Latin rather than Greek letters) and Latin (*Mattheus*). Why? Was the artist or scribe copying words from two different sources, or was the combination of Greek and Latin intentional, perhaps to lend the page the prestige of two classical languages? The former was the language of the New Testament, the latter of the Church of Rome. Latin dominates here, for the label accompanying Matthew's symbol, the winged man, is *imago hominis*, "image of the man."

More problematic is the identity of the third figure or, more precisely, the disembodied head and shoulders looking at Matthew from behind the curtain. Among the possibilities that various scholars have

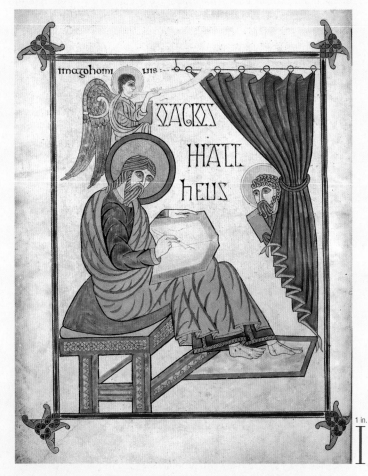

11-8 Saint Matthew, folio 25 verso of the *Lindisfarne Gospels*, from Northumbria, England, ca. 698–721. Tempera on vellum, $1' \frac{1}{2}'' \times 9\frac{1}{4}''$. British Library, London.

Portraits of the four authors frequently appeared in Gospel books. This Hiberno-Saxon depiction of the evangelist Matthew with his symbol derives directly or indirectly from an image in a Mediterranean book.

suggested are Christ and Saint Cuthbert. But a more convincing identification is the Old Testament prophet Moses. According to this suggestion, Moses is holding the closed book of the Old Testament in contrast with the open book of Matthew's New Testament. This is a common juxtaposition in medieval Christian art and thought.

all-important symbol of the imported religion—stabilizes the rhythms of the serpentines and, perhaps by contrast with its heavy immobility, seems to heighten the effect of motion. The illuminator placed the motifs in detailed symmetries, with inversions, reversals, and repetitions that the viewer must study closely in order to appreciate not only their variety but also their mazelike complexity. The animal forms intermingle with clusters and knots of line, and the whole design vibrates with energy. The color is rich yet cool. The painter adroitly adjusted shape and color to achieve a smooth and perfectly even surface.

As do most Hiberno-Saxon artworks, the Lindisfarne cross page displays the artist's preference for small, infinitely complex,

and painstaking designs. Even the Matthew symbol (FIG. 11-6) in the *Book of Durrow* reveals that the illuminator's concern was abstract design, not the depiction of the natural world. But exceptions exist. In some Insular manuscripts, the artists appear to have based their compositions on classical pictures in imported Mediterranean books (see "The Lindisfarne Saint Matthew," above).

High Crosses. The *Lindisfarne Gospels* is surpassed in richness only by the *Book of Kells,* which boasts an unprecedented number of full-page illuminations, including carpet pages, evangelist symbols, portrayals of the Virgin Mary and of Christ, New Testament narrative scenes, canon tables, and several instances of enlarged and

11-9 *High Cross of Muiredach* (east face), Monasterboice, Ireland, 923. Sandstone, 18′ high.

Early medieval Irish high crosses are exceptional in size. This cross probably marked Abbot Muiredach's grave and features themes well suited to a Christian burial: the Crucifixion and the Last Judgment.

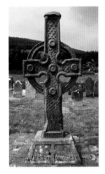

⬈ **11-9A** *South Cross,* Ahenny, late eighth century.

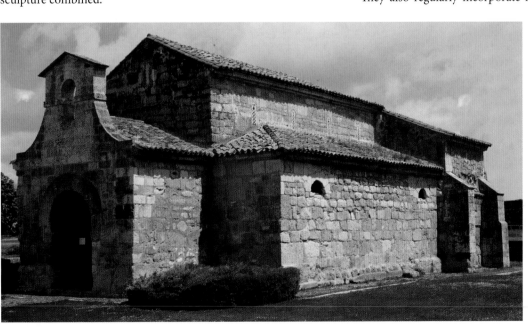

The *High Cross of Muiredach* (FIG. 11-9) at Monasterboice and the *South Cross* (FIG. 11-9A) at Ahenny are two of the largest and finest early medieval high crosses. The Monasterboice cross is larger and more unusual because of its extensive narrative relief decoration, which may have been inspired by the relief decoration of Early Christian stone sarcophagi that Irish missionaries encountered during their travels, although the subject matter is very different. An inscription on the bottom of the west face of the shaft asks a prayer for a man named Muiredach. Most scholars identify him as the influential Irish cleric of the same name who was abbot of Monasterboice and died in 923. The monastery he headed was one of Ireland's oldest, founded in the late fifth century. The cross probably marked the abbot's grave. Four arcs forming a circle connect the concave arms, which expand into squared terminals (compare FIG. 11-7). The circle intersecting the cross identifies the type as Celtic. At the center of the west side of Muiredach's cross is a depiction of the crucified Christ. On the east side (FIG. 11-9), the risen Christ stands as judge of the world, the hope of the dead. Below him is a depiction of the weighing of souls on scales (compare FIG. 3-1)—a theme that, two centuries later, sculptors of church portals (FIG. 12-1) pursued with extraordinary force.

VISIGOTHIC AND MOZARABIC ART

The Romans never ruled Ireland, but Spain was a province of the Roman Empire for hundreds of years. The Roman conquest brought new roads to the Iberian peninsula and new cities with Roman temples, fora, theaters, and aqueducts. The province also produced two of Rome's most important emperors—Trajan and Hadrian (FIG. 7-48). But in the early fifth century, the Roman cities fell to Germanic invaders, most notably the Visigoths, who had converted to Christianity. Many of the stone churches that the Visigoths built in the sixth and seventh centuries still stand.

Baños de Cerrato. An outstanding example is the small church of San Juan Bautista (Saint John the Baptist, FIG. 11-10) at Baños de Cerrato, which the Visigothic king Recceswinth (r. 649–672) constructed in 661 in thanksgiving for a cure after bathing in the waters there. The Visigothic churches are basilican in form, but often have multiple square apses. (The Baños de Cerrato church has three.) They also regularly incorporate horseshoe arches, a form usually associated with Islamic architecture (FIGS. 10-11 and 10-12) but that in Spain predates the Muslim conquest of 711.

embellished words from the Bible (for example, FIG. 11-1). Nonetheless, as magnificent to behold as the Hiberno-Saxon manuscripts are, they are still relatively small objects, as are the portable fibulae, purses, and other treasures coveted by early medieval patrons. In the Hiberno-Saxon world, the *high crosses* of Ireland and northern England, set up between the 8th and 10th centuries, are exceptional in their mass and scale. These majestic monuments, some more than 20 feet in height, loom large in the burial grounds adjoining Hiberno-Saxon monasteries. Freestanding and unattached to any architectural fabric, the high crosses have the imposing unity, weight, and presence of both building and statue—architecture and sculpture combined.

11-10 San Juan Bautista (looking northeast), Baños de Cerrato, Spain, 661.

This small three-aisled basilican church dedicated to Saint John the Baptist is typical of Visigothic architecture in Spain. It features three square apses and an entrance portal crowned by a horseshoe arch.

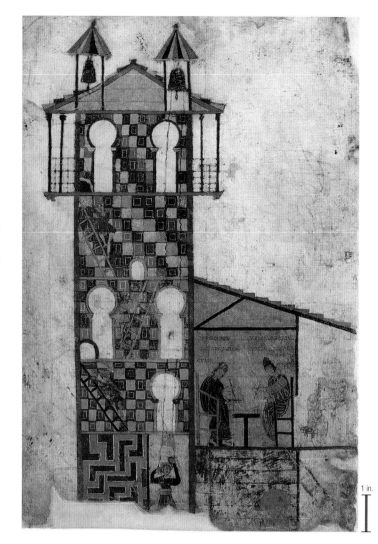

11-11 EMETERIUS, the tower and scriptorium of San Salvador de Tábara, colophon (folio 168) of the *Commentary on the Apocalypse* by Beatus, from Tábara, Spain, 970. Tempera on parchment, $1' 2\frac{1}{8}'' \times 10''$. Archivo Histórico Nacional, Madrid.

In this earliest known depiction of a medieval scriptorium, the painter carefully recorded the tower's Islamic-style glazed-tile walls and elegant windows with horseshoe arches, a Visigothic legacy.

1 in.

Tábara. Although the Islamic caliphs of Córdoba swept the Visigoths away (see "Córdoba," page 301), they never succeeded in gaining control of the northernmost parts of the peninsula. There, the Christian culture called *Mozarabic* (referring to Christians living in Arab territories) continued to flourish, as did some Jewish communities. One northern Spanish monk, Beatus (ca. 730–798), abbot of San Martín at Liébana, wrote *Commentary on the Apocalypse* around 776. This influential work was widely copied and illustrated in the monastic scriptoria of medieval Europe. One copy, produced in 970, is the work of scribes and painters at the monastery of San Salvador at Tábara in the kingdom of Léon. The colophon (FIG. 11-11) to the illustrated *Commentary* presents the earliest known depiction of a medieval scriptorium. Because the artist provided a composite of exterior and interior views of the building, it is especially informative.

At the left is a great bell tower with a monk on the ground floor ringing the bells. The painter carefully recorded the Islamic-style glazed-tile walls of the tower, its interior ladders, and its elegant windows with their horseshoe arches, the legacy of the Visigoths. To the right, in the scriptorium proper, three monks perform their respective specialized duties. The colophon identifies the two monks in the main room as the scribe Senior and the painter EMETERIUS. To the right, a third monk uses shears to cut sheets of parchment. The colophon also pays tribute to Magius, "the worthy master painter. . . . May he deserve to be crowned with Christ,"[3] who died before he could complete his work on the book. His pupil Emeterius took his place and brought the project to fruition. He probably was the painter of the colophon.

The colophon of another Beatus manuscript, dated 975 and today in Girona Cathedral, also names Emeterius as co-illuminator with the nun Ende, a "painter and servant of God." Ende's is one of the few recorded names of a woman artist in the early Middle Ages, a rarity also in the ancient world (see "Iaia of Cyzicus," page 223).

CAROLINGIAN EMPIRE

On Christmas Day of the year 800, Pope Leo III (r. 795–816) crowned Charles the Great (Charlemagne), king of the Franks since 768, as emperor of Rome (r. 800–814). In time, Charlemagne came to be seen as the first Holy (that is, Christian) Roman Emperor, a title that his successors did not formally adopt until the 12th century. The setting

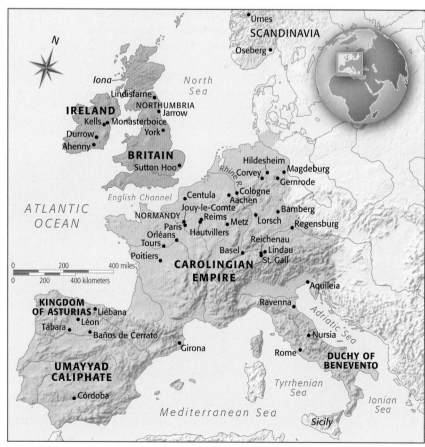

MAP 11-1 The Carolingian Empire at the death of Charlemagne in 814.

Charlemagne's *Renovatio Imperii Romani*

Charlemagne's official seal bore the phrase *renovatio imperii Romani* ("renewal of the Roman Empire"). As the pope's designated Roman emperor, Charlemagne sought to revive the glory of Early Christian Rome. He accomplished this in part through artistic patronage—commissioning imperial portrait statues (FIG. 11-12) and large numbers of illustrated manuscripts (FIGS. 11-12A and 11-13)—and by fostering a general revival of learning.

To make his empire as splendid as Rome's, Charlemagne invited to his court at Aachen the best minds and the finest artisans of western Europe and Byzantium. Among them were Theodulf of Orléans (d. 821), Paulinus of Aquileia (d. 802), and Alcuin (d. 804), master of the cathedral school at York, the center of Northumbrian learning. Alcuin brought Anglo-Saxon scholarship to the Carolingian court.

Charlemagne himself, according to Einhard (d. 840), his biographer, "most zealously cultivated the liberal arts, held those who taught them in great esteem, and conferred great honors upon them."* He could read and speak Latin fluently, in addition to Frankish, his native tongue, and understood Greek, although he did not speak it well. Einhard also reports that Charlemagne studied rhetoric and mathematics with the learned men whom he gathered around him. But he never learned to write properly. That was a task best left to professional scribes. In fact, one of Charlemagne's dearest projects was the recovery of the true text of the Bible, which, through centuries of errors in copying, had become quite corrupted. Various scholars undertook the great project, but Alcuin of York's revision of the Bible, prepared at the new monastery at Tours, became the most widely used.

Charlemagne's scribes also were responsible for the development of a new, more compact, and more easily written and legible version of Latin script called *Caroline minuscule*. The letters on this page are descendants of the alphabet that Carolingian scribes perfected. Later generations also owe to Charlemagne's patronage the restoration and copying of important classical texts. The earliest known manuscripts of many Greek and Roman authors are Carolingian in date.

*Einhard, *Life of Charlemagne,* 25. Translated by Samuel Epes Turner (New York: Harper, 1880), 61.

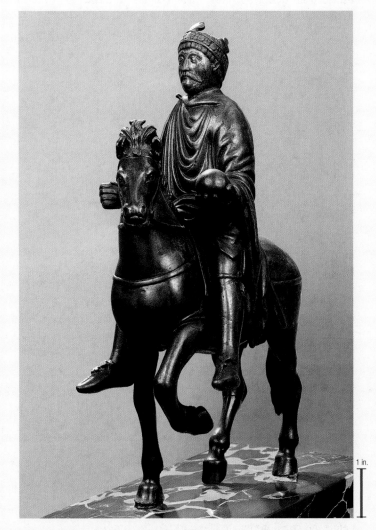

11-12 Equestrian portrait of Charlemagne or Charles the Bald, from Metz, France, ninth century. Bronze, originally gilt, 9½″ high. Musée du Louvre, Paris.

The Carolingian emperors sought to revive the glory and imagery of the Roman Empire. This equestrian portrait depicts a crowned emperor holding a globe, the symbol of world dominion.

---

for Charlemagne's coronation, fittingly, was Saint Peter's basilica (FIG. 8-9) in Rome, built by Constantine, the first Roman emperor to embrace Christianity. Born in 742, when northern Europe was still in chaos, Charlemagne consolidated the Frankish kingdom that his father and grandfather bequeathed him, defeated the Lombards in Italy (MAP 11-1), and laid claim to reviving the glory of the Roman Empire. He gave his name (Carolus Magnus in Latin) to an entire era, the *Carolingian* period.

The "Carolingian Renaissance" was a remarkable historical phenomenon, an energetic, brilliant *renovatio* of the art, culture, and political ideals of Early Christian Rome (see "Charlemagne's *Renovatio Imperii Romani,*" above). Charlemagne's (Holy) Roman Empire, waxing and waning for a thousand years and with many hiatuses, existed in central Europe until Napoleon destroyed it in 1806.

Sculpture and Painting

When Charlemagne returned home from his coronation in Rome, he ordered the transfer of an equestrian statue of the Ostrogothic king Theodoric from Ravenna to the Carolingian palace complex at Aachen. That portrait is lost, as is the grandiose gilded-bronze statue of the Byzantine emperor Justinian that once crowned a column in Constantinople (see "The Emperors of New Rome," page 267). But in the early Middle Ages, both statues stood as reminders of ancient Rome's glory and of the pretensions and aspirations of the medieval successors of Rome's Christian emperors.

Carolingian Portraiture. The portrait of Theodoric may have been the inspiration for a ninth-century bronze statuette (FIG. 11-12) of a Carolingian emperor on horseback. Charlemagne greatly admired Theodoric, the first Germanic ruler of Rome, and many scholars have identified the small bronze figure as Charlemagne himself. Others, however, think that it portrays his grandson, Charles the Bald (r. 840–877). The ultimate model for the statuette was the equestrian portrait of Marcus Aurelius (FIG. 7-58) in Rome. In the Middle Ages, people mistakenly thought that the bronze statue represented Constantine, another revered predecessor of Charlemagne and his Carolingian successors. Both the Roman and the medieval sculptors portrayed their emperor as overly large so that the ruler, not the horse, is the center of attention. But unlike Marcus Aurelius, who extends his right arm in a gesture of clemency to a foe who once cowered beneath the raised foreleg of his horse, Charlemagne (or Charles the Bald) is on parade. He wears imperial robes rather than a general's cloak, although his sheathed sword is visible. On his head is a crown, and in his outstretched left hand he holds a globe, a symbol of world dominion. The portrait proclaimed the renovatio of the Roman Empire's power and trappings.

Coronation Gospels. As noted, Charlemagne was a sincere admirer of learning, the arts, and classical culture, even before his coronation as emperor of Rome. He placed high value on books, both sacred and secular, importing many and sponsoring the production of far more. One of the earliest is the *Godescalc Lectionary* (FIG. **11-12A**), securely dated to 781 to 783, but the most famous is the early-ninth-century purple vellum *Coronation Gospels* (also known as the *Gospel Book of Charlemagne*), which has a text written in handsome gold letters. The major full-page illuminations, which show the four Gospel authors at work (see "The Four Evangelists," page 331), reveal that, compared with their Hiberno-Saxon counterparts, Carolingian manuscript painters brought a radically different stylistic sensibility to their work. For example, for the page depicting Saint Matthew (FIG. 11-13), the *Coronation Gospels* painter, in contrast to the Northumbrian illuminator who painted the portrait of the same evangelist in the *Lindisfarne Gospels* (FIG. 11-8), created shapes using color and modulation of light and shade, not line, and defined the massive drapery folds wrapped around Matthew's body by employing deft, illusionistic brushwork. The cross-legged chair, the lectern, and the saint's toga are familiar Roman accessories. In fact, this Carolingian evangelist portrait closely follows the format and style of Greco-Roman author portraits, as exemplified by the seated Menander (FIG. 7-25) at Pompeii. The *Coronation Gospels* landscape background also has many parallels in Roman painting, and the frame consists of the kind of acanthus leaves found in Roman temple capitals and friezes (FIG. 7-32). Almost nothing is known in the Hiberno-Saxon or Frankish world that could have prepared the way for this portrayal of Saint Matthew. If a Frankish, rather than an Italian or a Byzantine, artist painted the evangelist portraits of the *Coronation Gospels,* the Carolingian artist had fully absorbed the classical manner. Classical painting style was one of the many components of Charlemagne's program to establish Aachen as the capital of a renewed Christian Roman Empire.

Ebbo Gospels. The classical-revival style evident in the *Coronation Gospels* was by no means the only one that appeared suddenly in the Carolingian world. The painters of the court school

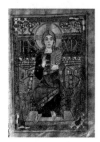

11-12A Christ enthroned, *Godescalc Lectionary,* 781–783.

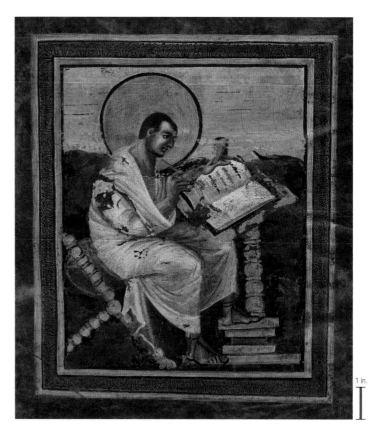

1 in.

11-13 Saint Matthew, folio 15 recto of the *Coronation Gospels* (*Gospel Book of Charlemagne*), from Aachen, Germany, ca. 800–810. Ink and tempera on vellum, full page 1′ $\frac{3}{4}″$ × 10″; detail 8$\frac{3}{4}″$ high. Schatzkammer, Kunsthistorisches Museum, Vienna.

The books produced for Charlemagne's court reveal the legacy of classical art (FIG. 7-25). The Carolingian painter used light, shade, and perspective in this representation of the evangelist at work.

and monastic scriptoria employed a wide variety of styles derived from Late Antique prototypes. Another Saint Matthew (FIG. 11-14), in a Gospel book produced for Archbishop Ebbo of Reims, may be an interpretation of an author portrait very similar to the one that the *Coronation Gospels* master used as a model. The *Ebbo Gospels* illuminator, however, replaced the classical calm and solidity of the *Coronation Gospels* evangelist with an energy approaching frenzy. Matthew (the winged man in the upper right corner identifies him) writes in frantic haste. His hair stands on end, his eyes open wide, the folds of his drapery writhe and vibrate, and the landscape behind him rears up alive. The painter even set the page's leaf border in motion. Matthew's face, hands, inkhorn, pen, and book are the focus of the composition. This presentation contrasts strongly with the settled pose of the Saint Matthew of the *Coronation Gospels,* with its even stress so that no part of the composition jumps out at viewers to seize their attention. Just as the painter of the *Lindisfarne Gospels* Matthew (FIG. 11-8) transformed a Mediterranean model into an original Hiberno-Saxon idiom, so the *Ebbo Gospels* artist translated a classical prototype into a new Carolingian style. This master painter brilliantly merged classical illusionism and the northern linear tradition.

Utrecht Psalter. One of the finest and most unusual medieval manuscripts—indeed, one of the most remarkable illustrated books

The Four Evangelists

Evangelist derives from the Greek word for "one who announces good news," namely the Gospel of Christ. The authors of the Gospels, the first four books of the New Testament, are Saints Matthew, Mark, Luke, and John, collectively known as the four evangelists. Two—Matthew and John—were also apostles (see "Early Christian Saints," pages 246–247). The Gospel books provide the authoritative account of the life of Jesus, differing in some details but together constituting the primary literary basis for the iconography of Christian art (see "The Life of Jesus in Art," pages 244–245). Each evangelist has a unique symbol derived from various biblical passages, including the accounts in Ezekiel (1:5–14) and the Apocalypse (4:6–8) describing the beasts that pulled the throne-chariot of God (FIG. 9-18).

- ■ **Matthew** was a tax collector in Capernaum before Jesus called him to become an apostle (FIGS. 24-17 and 25-7). Little else is known about him, and accounts differ as to how he became a martyr. Matthew's symbol is the winged man or angel (FIGS. 11-8 and 11-14), because his Gospel opens with a description of the human ancestry of Christ.
- ■ **Mark** was the first bishop of Alexandria in Egypt, where he suffered martyrdom. He was a companion of both Saint Peter and Saint Paul. One tradition says that Peter dictated the Gospel to Mark, or at least inspired him to write it. Because Mark's Gospel begins with a voice crying in the wilderness, his symbol is the lion, the king of the desert.
- ■ **Luke** was a disciple of Saint Paul, who refers to Luke as a physician. A later tradition says that Luke painted a portrait of the Virgin Mary and the Christ Child (FIGS. 20-1 and 23-14A). Consequently, late medieval painters' guilds often chose Luke as their patron saint. Luke's symbol is the ox, because his Gospel opens with a description of the priest Zacharias sacrificing an ox.
- ■ **John** was the apostle seated next to Jesus at the Last Supper (FIG. 22-4) and was the only disciple who witnessed Jesus's crucifixion (FIGS. 9-24 and 23-2). In addition to his Gospel, John was the author of the Apocalypse, the last book of the New Testament, which he wrote in exile on the Greek island Patmos (FIG. 25-32). The Apocalypse records John's visions of the end of the world, the Last Judgment, and the Second Coming. John's symbol is the eagle, the high-flying bird symbolizing the soaring style of his writing and his apocalyptic visions.

The four evangelists appear frequently in medieval art, especially in illuminated Gospel books, where they regularly serve as frontispieces to their respective Gospels, lending their authority to the accounts of

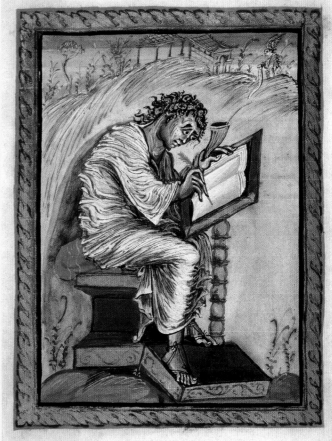

1 in.

11-14 Saint Matthew, folio 18 verso of the *Ebbo Gospels* (*Gospel Book of Archbishop Ebbo of Reims*), from the abbey of Saint Peter, Hautvillers, France, ca. 816–835. Ink and tempera on vellum, full page $10\frac{1}{4}'' \times 8\frac{3}{4}''$; detail $7\frac{3}{4}''$ high. Bibliothèque municipale, Épernay.

This Gospel author writes frantically, and the folds of his drapery writhe and vibrate. Even the landscape rears up alive. The painter merged classical illusionism with the northern European linear tradition.

Christ's life, death, and resurrection. Artists often represented them as seated authors, with or without their symbols (FIGS. I-8, 11-8, 11-13, and 11-14). In some instances, all four evangelists appear together (FIG. I-8). Frequently, both in painting and in sculpture, the evangelists are represented only by their symbols (FIGS. 9-13A, 11-6, 12-9, 12-11, 12-19, and 13-5).

of any date—is the *Utrecht Psalter* (FIGS. 11-14A and 11-15) from Saint Peter's abbey in Hautvillers, France. The text reproduces the psalms of King David in three columns of Latin capital letters in emulation of the script and page organization of ancient books. The artist illustrated each psalm with a pen-and-ink drawing stretching across the width of the page. Some scholars have argued that the costumes and other details indicate that the artist followed one or

more manuscripts created 400 years before. Even if the *Utrecht Psalter* is not a copy, the artist's intention was to evoke earlier artworks and to make the book appear ancient, a common aspiration in the age of Charlemagne. But whatever model the Carolingian artist used, it is unlikely to have included illustrations of the distinctive kind that appear throughout the *Utrecht Psalter* (see "How to Illustrate a Psalm," page 332).

How to Illustrate a Psalm

Illustrating a narrative, such as the life of Jesus, is a relatively straightforward task for an artist. Illustrating a psalm—a poem—presents a special problem because there is no story line, just verbal metaphors. The painter of the *Utrecht Psalter* (FIG. 11-14A) met this challenge brilliantly, bringing the psalmist's words to life by visualizing them literally with figures that move and gesticulate with nervous energy. (It has been suggested that this literal approach was intended to aid the book's owner in memorizing the psalms.)

The page illustrated here (FIG. 11-15) exemplifies this Carolingian artist's loose linear drawing style and genius for anecdotal detail, which characterize every illustration in the manuscript.

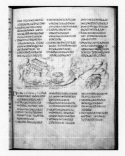

⤢ **11-14A** Psalm 23, *Utrecht Psalter,* ca. 820–835.

In Psalm 44 (Psalm 43 of the Vulgate text of the Carolingian era), the psalmist laments the plight of the oppressed Israelites. The accompanying illustration in the *Utrecht Psalter* closely follows the poetic text. For example, the psalm says "We are counted as sheep for slaughter." Consequently, in front of a walled city reminiscent of cities on the Column of Trajan (FIGS. 7-45, 7-45A, and 7-45C) in Rome and in Early Christian mosaics (FIGS. 8-20 and 8-21) and manuscripts (FIG. 9-17A), the artist drew some slain sheep fallen to the ground. At the left, the faithful grovel on the ground before a temple ("Our soul is bowed down to the dust; our belly cleaveth unto the earth"). To illustrate the passage in which six angels plead, "Awake, why sleepest thou, O Lord?" the artist depicted the Lord reclining in a canopied bed overlooking the slaughter below. But "the Lord" is Jesus, complete with cruciform halo, instead of David's Hebrew God. The drawing shows a vivid animation of much the same kind as the *Ebbo Gospels* Saint Matthew (FIG. 11-14). The bodies of the *Utrecht Psalter* figures are tense, with shoulders hunched and heads thrust forward. As in the *Ebbo Gospels,* even the earth heaves up around the figures.

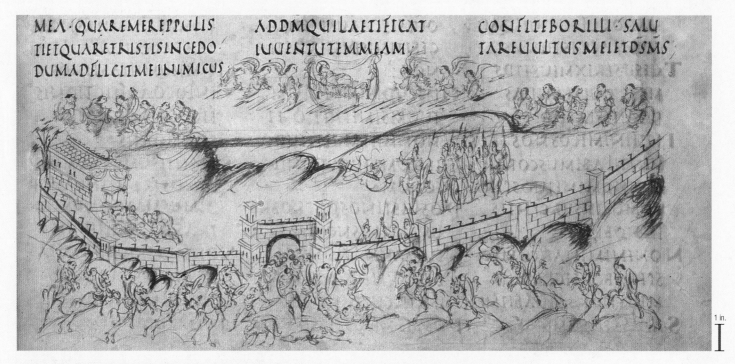

11-15 Psalm 44, detail of folio 25 recto of the *Utrecht Psalter,* from the abbey of Saint Peter, Hautvillers, France, ca. 820–835. Ink on vellum, full page, 1′ 1″ × 9 7/8″; detail, 4 1/2″ high. University Library, Utrecht.

The drawings in the *Utrecht Psalter* are rich in anecdotal detail and show figures acting out, literally, King David's psalms—the Carolingian artist's solution to the problem of illustrating poetic metaphors.

Lindau Gospels. The taste for costly portable objects, the hallmark of the art of the early medieval warlords, persisted under Charlemagne and his successors. The Carolingians commissioned numerous works employing luxurious materials, including book covers made of gold and jewels and sometimes also ivory or pearls. Gold and gems not only underscored the wealth of the owners but glorified the word of God and evoked the heavenly Jerusalem. One of the most lavishly decorated Carolingian book covers

(FIG. 11-16) is the one later added to the *Lindau Gospels.* The gold cover, fashioned in one of the workshops of Charles the Bald's court, is grand in conception. A youthful Christ in the Early Christian tradition, nailed to the cross, is the central motif. Surrounding Christ are pearls and jewels (raised on golden claw feet so that they can catch and reflect the light even more brilliantly and protect the delicate metal relief from denting). The statuesque, open-eyed figure, rendered in *repoussé* (hammered relief), recalls

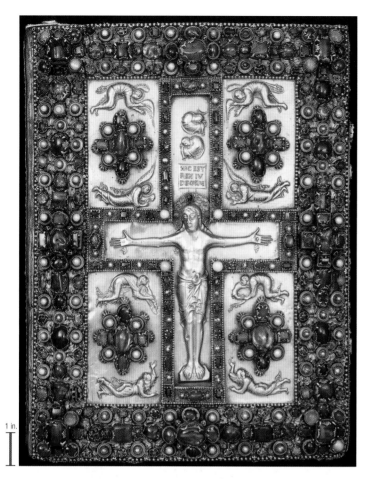

11-16 *Crucifixion,* front cover of the *Lindau Gospels,* from Saint Gall, Switzerland, ca. 870. Gold, precious stones, and pearls, 1′ 1⅜″ × 10⅜″. Pierpont Morgan Library, New York.

This gold-and-jeweled Carolingian book cover revives the Early Christian imagery of the youthful Christ (FIG. 8-16). The statuesque crucified Christ, heedless of pain, is classical in conception and style.

the beardless, unsuffering Christ of a fifth-century ivory plaque (FIG. 8-16) from Italy. By contrast, the four angels and the personifications of the moon and the sun above and the crouching figures of the Virgin Mary and Saint John (and two other figures of uncertain identity) in the quadrants below display the vivacity and nervous energy of the *Utrecht Psalter* figures (FIGS. 11-14A and 11-15). The *Lindau Gospels* cover highlights the stylistic diversity of early medieval art in Europe. Here, however, the translated figural style of the Mediterranean prevailed, in keeping with the classical tastes and imperial aspirations of the Frankish emperors of Rome.

Architecture

In his eagerness to reestablish the imperial past, Charlemagne also encouraged the use of Roman building techniques. In architecture, as in sculpture and painting, innovations made in the reinterpretation of earlier Roman Christian sources became fundamental to the subsequent development of northern European architecture. For his models, Charlemagne looked to Rome and Ravenna. One was the former heart of the Roman Empire, which he wanted to renew. The other was the long-term western outpost of Byzantine might and splendor, which he wanted to emulate in his own capital at Aachen, a site chosen because of its renowned hot springs.

Aachen. Charlemagne often visited Ravenna, and the equestrian statue of Theodoric he brought from there to display in his Aachen palace complex served as a model for Carolingian equestrian portraits (FIG. 11-12). Charlemagne also imported porphyry (purple marble) columns from Ravenna to adorn his Palatine Chapel (see "Charlemagne's Palatine Chapel at Aachen," page 334), and historians long have thought that he chose one of Ravenna's churches as the model for the new structure. The Aachen chapel's plan (FIG. 11-17, *left*)

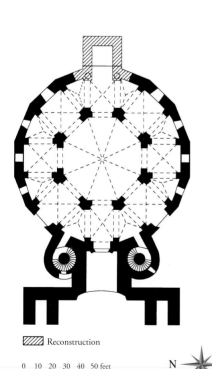

Reconstruction

0 10 20 30 40 50 feet
0 5 10 15 meters

N

11-17 Restored plan (*left*) and cutaway view (*right*) of the Palatine Chapel of Charlemagne, Aachen, Germany, 792–805 (John Burge).

Charlemagne sought to emulate Byzantine splendor in Germany. The plan of his Aachen chapel is based on that of San Vitale (FIG. 9-11) at Ravenna, but the architect omitted San Vitale's apse-like extensions.

Charlemagne's Palatine Chapel at Aachen

In his biography of Charlemagne, Einhard only briefly mentions the "beautiful church" the emperor built at his capital at Aachen, even though it was Einhard whom Charlemagne placed in charge of its construction. Unlike modern architectural historians, the scholarly monk, who held a position of prominence in Charlemagne's court, was not concerned with describing the innovative design of the interior vaulting (FIG. 11-18) or the facade (FIG. 11-19) of the Palatine Chapel (FIG. 11-17). As other medieval writers had done when commenting on buildings (see "Abbot Suger and the Rebuilding of Saint-Denis," page 383), Einhard focused on the extravagant gifts the emperor bestowed on the church and its clergy and attendants, which he cites as examples of Charlemagne's piety.

[Because of his devotion to the Christian religion, he built the Palatine Chapel at Aachen], which he adorned with gold and silver and lamps, and with rails and doors of solid brass. He had the columns and marbles for this structure brought from Rome and Ravenna, for he could not find such as were suitable elsewhere. . . . He provided it with a great number of sacred vessels of gold and silver, and with such a quantity of clerical robes that not even the doorkeepers, who fill the humblest office in the church, were obliged to wear their every-day clothes when in the exercise of their duties.*

Charlemagne, like Constantine in the fourth century, also lavished gifts upon the basilica dedicated to Saint Peter (FIG. 8-9) in Rome, where he was crowned emperor in 800.

He cherished the Church of St. Peter the Apostle at Rome above all other holy and sacred places, and heaped its treasury with a vast wealth of gold, silver, and precious stones. He sent great and countless gifts to the popes; and throughout his whole reign the wish that he had nearest at heart was to . . . defend and protect the Church of St. Peter, and to beautify and enrich it.[†]

*Einhard, *Life of Charlemagne*, 26. Translated by Samuel Epes Turner (New York: Harper, 1880), 63–64.
[†]Einhard, 27. Ibid., 64–65.

11-18 Interior of the Palatine Chapel of Charlemagne (looking east), Aachen, Germany, 792–805.

Charlemagne's chapel is the first vaulted medieval structure north of the Alps. The architect transformed the complexity and lightness of San Vitale's interior (FIG. 9-1) into simple, massive geometric form.

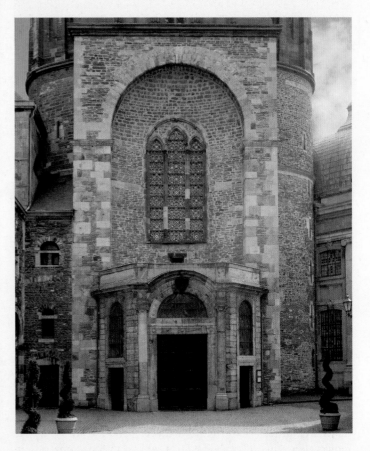

11-19 West facade of the Palatine Chapel of Charlemagne, Aachen, Germany, 792–805.

The innovative design of Charlemagne's palace chapel features cylindrical towers with spiral staircases flanking the entrance portal (compare FIG. 11-17), foreshadowing later medieval dual-tower church facades.

resembles San Vitale's (FIG. 9-11), and a direct relationship very likely exists between the two.

A comparison between the Carolingian chapel, the first vaulted structure of the Middle Ages north of the Alps, and its southern counterpart yields several insights. The Aachen plan is simpler. The architect omitted San Vitale's apselike extensions reaching from the central octagon into the ambulatory. At Aachen, the two main units stand in greater independence of each other. This solution may lack the subtle sophistication of the Byzantine building, but the Palatine Chapel gains geometric clarity. The photograph reproduced here (FIG. 11-18) shows that Charlemagne's builders converted the lightness and complexity of San Vitale's interior (FIG. 9-1) into the simple, massive geometry of the Aachen chapel.

The Carolingian conversion of a complex Byzantine prototype into a building that embodies robust strength and clear structural articulation foreshadows the architecture of the 11th and 12th centuries and the style called Romanesque (see "Romanesque," page 348). So, too, does the treatment of the Palatine Chapel's exterior, where two cylindrical towers with spiral staircases flank the entrance portal (FIGS. 11-17 and 11-19). This was a first step toward the great dual-tower facades of western European churches from the 10th century to the present. Above the portal, Charlemagne could appear in a large framing arch and be seen by those gathered in the atrium in front of the chapel. (The arcuated second-story window in FIG. 11-19 dates to the Gothic period; the plan in FIG. 11-17 includes only part of the atrium.) Directly behind the arch was Charlemagne's marble throne. From there he could peer down at the altar in the apse from a privileged position in his private gallery. Charlemagne's second-story gallery followed the model of the imperial gallery at Hagia Sophia (FIGS. 9-7 and 9-8) in Constantinople. The Palatine Chapel was in every sense a royal chapel. Charlemagne received the title of Roman emperor in Saint Peter's, but the coronation of his son and successor, Louis the Pious (r. 814–840), took place in the Palatine Chapel.

Saint Gall. The emperor was not the only important builder of the Carolingian age. With increased prosperity came the construction and expansion of many monasteries. A unique document, the ideal plan (FIG. 11-20) for a Benedictine monastery (see "Medieval Monasteries and Benedictine Rule," page 336) at Saint Gall in Switzerland, provides precious information about the design of Carolingian monastic communities. Haito, the abbot of Reichenau and bishop of Basel from 806 to 823, ordered the preparation of the plan and sent it around 819 to Gozbertus, abbot of Saint Gall from 816 to 836, as a guide for the rebuilding of the Saint Gall monastery. The design's fundamental purpose was to separate the monks from the laity (nonclergy) who also inhabited the community. Variations of the scheme may be seen in later monasteries all across western Europe.

Near the center, dominating everything, was the *oratory* (monastic church) with its *cloister,* a colonnaded courtyard not unlike the Early Christian atrium (FIG. 8-10) but situated to the side of the church instead of in front of its main portal. Reserved for the monks alone, the cloister, a kind of earthly paradise removed from the world at large, provided the peace and quiet necessary for contemplation. Clustered around the cloister were the most essential buildings: the dormitory, *refectory* (dining hall), kitchen, and storage rooms.

Other structures, including an infirmary, school, guesthouse, bakery, brewery, and workshops, filled the areas around this central core of church and cloister. In at least one Carolingian monastery, at Lorsch in Germany, a monumental freestanding gateway (FIG. 11-19A) stood in front of the church.

Haito invited the abbot of Saint Gall to adapt the plan as he saw fit, and indeed, the Saint Gall builders did not follow the Reichenau model precisely. Nonetheless, had the abbot wished, Haito's plan could have served as a practical guide for the Saint Gall masons because it

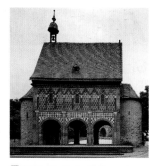

11-19A Torhalle, Lorsch, late eighth or ninth century.

was laid out using a *module* (standard unit) of 2.5 feet. The designer consistently employed that module, or multiples or fractions of it, for all elements of the plan. For example, the nave's width, indicated on the plan as 40 feet, is equal to 16 modules. Each monk's bed is 2.5 modules long, and the paths in the vegetable garden are 1.25 modules wide. Like so much else in the Carolingian Empire, this rational, indeed mathematical, approach to urban planning revived ancient Greek and Roman practice (see "Hippodamos's Plan for the Ideal City," page 154, and FIGS. 5-77 and 7-43).

The prototypes carrying the greatest authority for Charlemagne and his builders were those from the Christian phase of the Late Roman Empire. The widespread adoption of the Early Christian basilica, at Saint Gall and elsewhere, rather than the domed central plan of Byzantine churches, was crucial to the subsequent development of western European church architecture. Unfortunately, no Carolingian basilica has survived in its original form. Nevertheless, it is possible to reconstruct the appearance of some of them with fair accuracy—for example, the abbey of Saint-Riquier (FIG. 11-19B) at Centula, France, which an 11th-century illuminator reproduced in a now-lost manuscript.

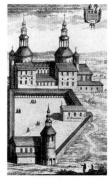

11-19B Saint-Riquier, Centula, 790–799.

Some Carolingian structures followed their Early Christian models quite closely. But in other instances, the ninth-century builders significantly modified the basilica plan, converting it into a much more complex form. The oratory at Saint Gall, for example, was essentially a traditional basilica, but it had features not found in any Early Christian church. Most obvious is the addition of a second apse on the west end of the building, perhaps to accommodate additional altars and to display relics (see "The Veneration of Relics," page 349). Whatever its purpose, this feature remained a characteristic regional element of German churches until the 11th century (compare FIGS. 11-22, 11-24, and 11-25).

Not quite as evident but much more important to the subsequent development of church architecture in northern Europe was the presence of a *transept* at Saint Gall, a very rare feature but one that characterized the two greatest Early Christian basilicas in Rome, Saint Peter's (FIGS. 8-9 and 8-10) and Saint Paul's, as well as the main church at the Centula abbey (FIG. 11-19B). The Saint Gall transept is as wide as the nave on the plan and was probably the same height. Early Christian builders had not been concerned with proportional relationships. On the Saint Gall plan, however, the various parts of the building relate to one another by a geometric scheme that ties them together into a tight and cohesive unit.

Medieval Monasteries and Benedictine Rule

Since Early Christian times, monks who established monasteries also made the rules governing communal life. The most significant of these monks was Benedict of Nursia (Saint Benedict, ca. 480–547), who founded the Benedictine Order in 529. By the ninth century, the "Rule" that Benedict wrote (*Regula Sancti Benedicti*) had become standard for all western European monastic communities, in part because Charlemagne had encouraged its adoption throughout the Frankish territories.

Saint Benedict believed that the corruption of the clergy that accompanied the increasing worldliness of the Church had its roots in the lack of firm organization and regulation. As he saw it, idleness and selfishness had led to neglect of the commandments of God and of the Church. The cure for this was communal association in an *abbey* under the absolute rule of an *abbot* whom the monks elected (or an *abbess* chosen by the nuns), who would ensure that the clergy spent each hour of the day in useful work and in sacred reading.

> Idleness is the enemy of the soul. Therefore, the brothers should have specified periods for manual labor as well as for prayerful reading.*

The emphasis on work and study and not solely on meditation and austerity is of great historical significance. Since antiquity, manual labor had been considered unseemly, the business of the lowborn or of slaves. Benedict raised it to the dignity of religion. The core idea of what many people today call the "work ethic" found early expression in Benedictine monasteries as an essential feature of spiritual life. By thus exalting the virtue of manual labor, Benedict not only rescued it from its age-old association with slavery but also recognized it as the way to self-sufficiency for the entire religious community.

Whereas some of Saint Benedict's followers emphasized spiritual "work" over manual labor, others, most notably the Cistercians (see "Bernard of Clairvaux," page 356), put Benedictine teachings about the value of physical work into practice. These monks reached into their surroundings and helped reduce the vast areas of daunting wilderness of early medieval Europe. They cleared dense forest teeming with wolves, bear, and wild boar; drained swamps; cultivated wastelands; and built roads, bridges, and dams, as well as monastic churches and their associated living and service quarters.

The ideal monastery (FIG. 11-20) provided all the facilities necessary for the conduct of daily life as well as "the Work of God"—a mill, bakery, infirmary, vegetable garden, and even a brewery—so that the monks would feel no need to wander outside its protective walls. Benedict's rules of conduct were very strict—for example:

> [The monks must] sleep clothed, and girded with belts or cords. . . . Thus the monks will always be ready to arise without delay when the signal is given; each will hasten to arrive at the Work of God before the others, yet with all dignity and decorum. . . . The oratory ought to be what it is called, and nothing else is to be done or stored there. After the Work of God, all should leave in complete silence and with reverence for God, so that a brother who may wish to pray alone will not be disturbed by the insensitivity of another. . . . The beds are to be inspected frequently by the abbot, lest private possessions be found there. A monk discovered with anything not given him by the abbot must be subjected to very severe punishment. In order

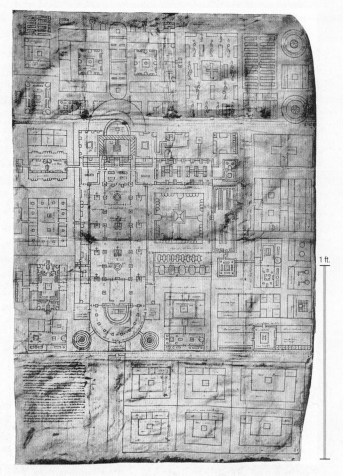

1 ft.

11-20 Schematic plan for a monastery, from Saint Gall, Switzerland, ca. 819. Red ink on parchment, 2′ 4″ × 3′ 8⅛″. Stiftsbibliothek, Saint Gall.

The purpose of this plan for an ideal, self-sufficient Benedictine monastery was to separate the monks from the laity. Near the center is the church with its cloister, the monks' earthly paradise.

that this vice of private ownership may be completely uprooted, the abbot is to provide all things necessary; that is, cowl, tunic, sandals, shoes, belt, knife, stylus, needle, handkerchief and writing tablets.†

As Benedict recognized, the monks were often scribes and scholars. In fact, the clergy had a monopoly on the skills of reading and writing in an age of almost universal illiteracy. Monastic communities were centrally important to the revival of learning. The libraries and scriptoria (FIG. 11-11), where the monks and nuns read, copied, illuminated, and bound books with ornamented covers, became centers of study. Monasteries were almost the sole repositories of what remained of the literary culture of the Greco-Roman world and early Christianity. Saint Benedict's requirements of manual labor and sacred reading came to include writing and copying books, studying music for chanting daily prayers, and—of great significance—teaching. The monasteries were the schools of the early Middle Ages as well as self-sufficient communities and production centers.

Rule of Saint Benedict, 48.1. Translated by Timothy Fry, *The Rule of St. Benedict in English* (Collegeville, Minn.: Liturgical Press, 1981), 69.
†*Rule of Saint Benedict*, 22.5–6; 52.1–3; 55.16–19. Translated by Fry, 49, 72, 76–77.

The Saint Gall plan also reveals another important feature of many Carolingian basilicas, including Saint-Riquier (FIG. 11-19B) at Centula: towers framing the end(s) of the church. Haito's plan shows only two towers, both cylindrical and on the west side of the church, as at Charlemagne's Palatine Chapel (FIGS. 11-17 and 11-19), but they stand apart from the church facade. If a tower existed above the crossing, the silhouette of Saint Gall would have shown three towers, altering the horizontal profile of the traditional basilica and identifying the church even from afar. Saint-Riquier had six towers.

Corvey. Other Carolingian basilicas had towers incorporated in the fabric of the west end of the building, thereby creating a grandiose unified facade greeting all those who entered the church. Architectural historians call this feature of Carolingian and some later churches the *westwork* (from the German *Westwerk,* "western entrance structure"). Early medieval writers referred to it as a *castellum* (Latin, "castle" or "fortress") or *turris* ("tower"). The major surviving example is the westwork (FIG. 11-21) of the abbey church at Corvey. The uppermost parts are 12th-century additions (easily distinguishable from the original westwork by the differing masonry technique). Stairs in each tower provided access to the upper stories. On the second floor is a two-story chapel with an aisle and a gallery on three sides. As at Aachen, the chapel opens onto the nave, and from it the visiting emperor and his entourage could watch and participate in the service below. Not all Carolingian westworks, however, served as seats reserved for the emperor. They also functioned as churches within churches, housing a second altar for special celebrations on major feast days. Boys' choirs stationed in the westwork chapel participated from above in the services conducted in the church's nave.

OTTONIAN EMPIRE

Louis the Pious laid Charlemagne to rest in the Palatine Chapel at Aachen in 814. Charlemagne had ruled for 46 years, but his empire survived him by fewer than 30. When Louis died in 840, his three sons—Charles the Bald, Lothair I, and Louis the German—divided the Carolingian Empire among themselves. After bloody conflicts, the brothers signed a treaty at Verdun in 843, partitioning the Frankish lands into western, central, and eastern areas, very roughly foreshadowing the later nations of France and Germany and a third realm corresponding to a long strip of land stretching from the Netherlands and Belgium to Rome. Intensified Viking incursions in the west helped bring about the collapse of the Carolingians. The empire's breakup into weak kingdoms, ineffectual against the invasions, brought a time of confusion to Europe. Complementing the Viking threat in the west were the invasions of the Magyars in the east and the plundering and piracy of the Saracens (Muslims) in the Mediterranean.

Only in the mid-10th century did the eastern part of the former empire consolidate under the rule of a new Saxon line of German emperors, called, after the names of the three most illustrious family members, the *Ottonians*. In Rome in 962, the pope crowned the first Otto, king of the Germans since 936, as "emperor of Rome," the title that Charlemagne's weak successors held during most of the previous century and that Otto retained until his death in 973. The Ottonian emperors made headway against the eastern invaders, remained free from Viking attacks, and not only preserved but also enriched the culture and tradition of the Carolingian period. The Church, which had become corrupt and disorganized, recovered in the 10th century under the influence of a

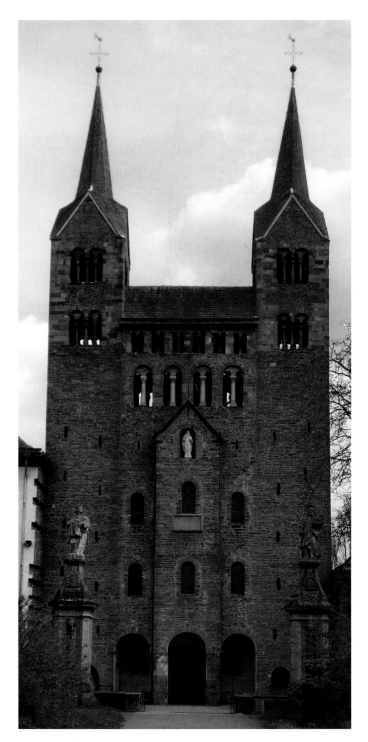

11-21 Westwork of the abbey church, Corvey, Germany, 873–885.

An important new feature of Carolingian church architecture was the westwork, a monumental western facade incorporating two towers. The sole example in its original form is the abbey church at Corvey.

Equalizing the widths of nave and transept automatically makes the area where they cross (the *crossing*) a square. Most Carolingian churches shared this feature. But in Haito's plan, the *crossing square* is also the unit of measurement for the remainder of the church plan. The transept arms are equal to one crossing square, the distance between transept and apse is one crossing square, and the nave is 4.5 crossing squares long. In addition, the two aisles are half as wide as the nave, integrating all parts of the church in a rational and orderly plan.

great monastic reform encouraged and sanctioned by the Ottonians. The new German emperors also cemented ties with Italy and the papacy as well as with Byzantium (see "Theophanu, a Byzantine Princess at the Ottonian Court," page 342). The Ottonian line ended in the early 11th century with the death of Henry II (r. 1002–1024).

Architecture

Ottonian architects followed the course of their Carolingian predecessors, building basilican churches with towering spires and imposing westworks, but they also introduced new features that would have a long future in Western church architecture.

Gernrode. The best-preserved 10th-century Ottonian basilica is Saint Cyriakus (FIG. 11-22) at Gernrode, begun in 961 and completed in 973. In the 12th century, a large apse replaced the western entrance, but the upper parts of the westwork, including the two cylindrical towers, are intact. The interior (FIG. 11-23), although heavily restored in the 19th century, retains its 10th-century character. Saint Cyriakus reveals how Ottonian architects enriched the Early Christian and Carolingian basilica. The church has a transept at the east with a square choir in front of the apse. The nave is one of the first in western Europe to incorporate a gallery between the ground-floor arcade and the clerestory, a design that became very popular in the succeeding Romanesque era. Scholars have reached

no consensus on the function of these galleries in Ottonian churches. They cannot have been reserved for women, as some think they were in Byzantium, because Saint Cyriakus is the centerpiece of a convent exclusively for nuns, founded the same year that construction of the church began. The galleries may have housed additional altars, as in the westwork at Corvey, or the singers in the church's choir. The Gernrode builders also transformed the nave arcade itself by adopting the *alternate-support system,* in which heavy square piers alternate with columns, dividing the nave into vertical units. The division continues into the gallery level, breaking the smooth rhythm of the all-column arcades of Early Christian and Carolingian basilicas and leading the eye upward. Later architects would carry this verticalization of the basilican nave much further (FIG. 13-20).

Hildesheim. Many of the most important architectural patrons of the Carolingian and Ottonian eras were not emperors but local church officials—for example, Abbot Gozbertus of Saint Gall (FIG. 11-20) and Abbot Angilbert of Centula (FIG. 11-19B)—although some of them had close ties with the imperial family. One of the great patrons of Ottonian art and architecture was Bishop Bernward (r. 993–1022) of Hildesheim, Germany, who also had imperial connections: he was the tutor of Otto III (r. 983–1002). Bernward, who made Hildesheim a center of learning, was the builder of the abbey church of Saint Michael (FIG. 11-24) there, and an eager scholar, a lover of the arts, and,

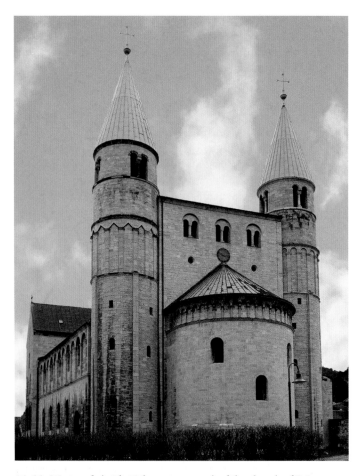

11-22 Westwork (with 12th-century apse) of the church of Saint Cyriakus, Gernrode, Germany, 961–973.

The impressive 10th-century two-tower facade of Saint Cyriakus was modified during the 12th century to incorporate an apse in place of a portal, but it is otherwise an intact Ottonian westwork.

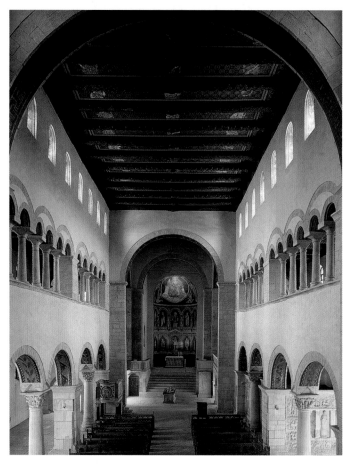

11-23 Nave (looking east) of the church of Saint Cyriakus, Gernrode, Germany, 961–973.

Ottonian builders modified the interior elevation of Early Christian basilicas. The Gernrode designer added a gallery above the nave arcade and adopted an alternate-support system of piers and columns.

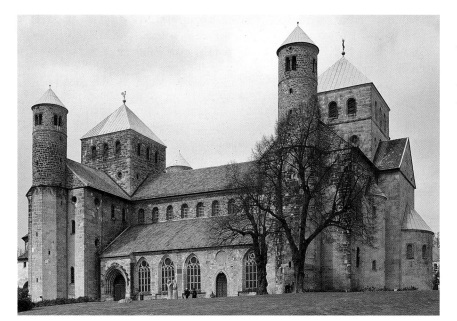

11-24 **Saint Michael's (looking northwest), Hildesheim, Germany, 1001–1031.**

Built by Bishop Bernward, a great art patron, Saint Michael's is a masterpiece of Ottonian basilica design. The church's two apses, two transepts, and multiple towers give it a distinctive profile.

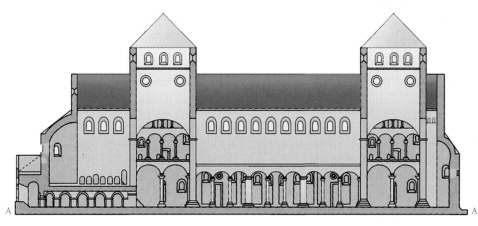

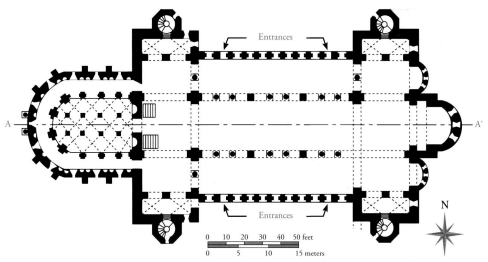

11-25 **Longitudinal section (*top*) and plan (*bottom*) of the abbey church of Saint Michael's, Hildesheim, Germany, 1001–1031.**

The entrances to Saint Michael's are on the side. Alternating piers and columns divide the space in the nave into vertical units. These features transformed the tunnel-like horizontality of Early Christian basilicas.

Entrances

A ——— A′

Entrances

| 0 | 10 | 20 | 30 | 40 | 50 feet |
| 0 | | 5 | | 10 | 15 meters |

N

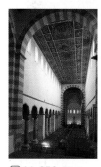

↗ **11-25A** Nave, Saint Michael's, Hildesheim, 1001–1031.

according to Thangmar of Heidelberg, his biographer, an expert craftsman and bronze-caster. In 1001, Bernward traveled to Rome as the guest of Otto III. During his stay, he studied at first hand the monuments of the ancient empire that the Carolingian and Ottonian emperors revered.

Constructed between 1001 and 1031 (and rebuilt after a bombing during World War II), Saint Michael's (FIG. 11-24) has a double-transept plan (FIG. 11-25, *bottom*), six towers, and a westwork. The two transepts create eastern and western centers of gravity. The nave (FIG. 11-25A) merely seems to be a hall connecting them.

Lateral entrances leading into the aisles from the north and south additionally make for an almost complete loss of the traditional basilican orientation toward the east. Some ancient Roman basilicas, such as the Basilica Ulpia (FIG. 7-44, no. 4) in the Forum of Trajan, also had two apses and entrances on the side, and Bernward probably was familiar with this variant basilican plan.

At Hildesheim, as in the plan of the monastery at Saint Gall (FIG. 11-20), the builders adopted a modular approach. The crossing squares, for example, are the basis for the nave's dimensions—three crossing squares long and one square wide. The placement

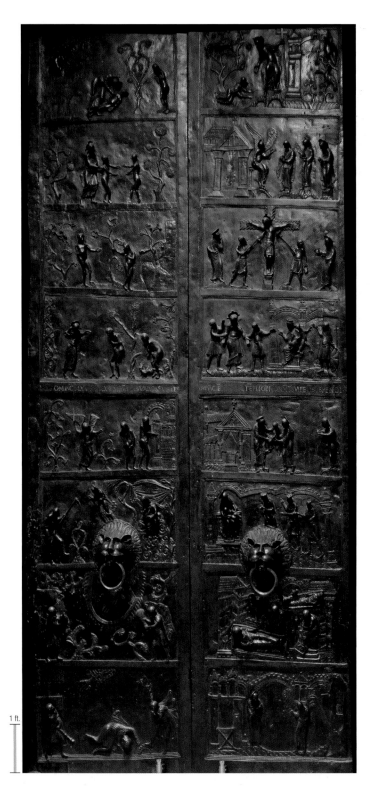

1 ft.

11-26 Doors with relief panels (Genesis, left door; life of Christ, right door), commissioned by Bishop Bernward for Saint Michael's, Hildesheim, Germany, 1015. Bronze, 15′ 5¾″ high. Römer- und Pelizaeus-Museum, Hildesheim.

Bernward's doors tell the story of Original Sin and redemption, and draw parallels between the Old and New Testaments, juxtaposing, for example, Eve nursing Cain with Mary and the infant Christ.

of heavy piers at the corners of each square gives visual emphasis to the three units. These piers alternate with pairs of columns (FIGS. 11-25 and 11-25A) as wall supports in a design similar to that of Saint Cyriakus (FIG. 11-23) at Gernrode.

Sculpture and Painting

In 1001, when Bishop Bernward was in Rome visiting the young Otto III, he resided in Otto's palace on the Aventine Hill in the neighborhood of Santa Sabina (FIGS. 8-18 and 8-19), an Early Christian church renowned for its carved wood doors (FIG. 8-19A). Those doors, decorated with episodes from both the Old and New Testaments, may have inspired the remarkable bronze doors that the bishop commissioned for his new church in Germany.

Hildesheim Doors. The doors (FIG. 11-26) to Saint Michael's, dated by inscription to 1015, are more than 15 feet tall. They are technological marvels, because the Ottonian metalworkers cast each door in a single piece with the figural sculpture. Carolingian sculpture, like most sculpture since Late Antiquity, consisted primarily of small-scale art executed in ivory and precious metals, often for book covers (FIG. 11-16). The Hildesheim doors are gigantic in comparison, but the 16 individual panels stem from this tradition.

Bernward placed the bronze doors in the portal to Saint Michael's that led from the cloister, where the monks would see them each time they entered the church. The panels of the left door illustrate highlights from Genesis, beginning with the creation of Eve (at the top) and ending with the murder of Abel, Adam and Eve's son, by his brother Cain (at the bottom). The right door recounts the life of Christ (reading from the bottom up), starting with the Annunciation and terminating with Noli me tangere, when Christ appears to Mary Magdalene after his resurrection (see "The Life of Jesus in Art," pages 244–245). Together, the doors tell the story of Original Sin and ultimate redemption, showing the expulsion from the Garden of Eden and the path back to Paradise through the Church. (Reliefs depicting additional episodes from Jesus's life decorate a bronze column [FIG. 11-26A] that Bernward also commissioned for Saint Michael's.) As in Early Christian times, the Ottonian clergy interpreted the Hebrew Bible as prefiguring the New Testament (see "Old Testament Subjects in Christian Art," page 242). For example, the Hildesheim designer juxtaposed the Fall of Adam and Eve on the left door with the Crucifixion on the right door. Eve nursing the infant Cain is opposite Mary with the Christ Child in her lap.

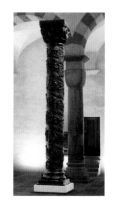

⬈**11-26A** Column, Saint Michael's, Hildesheim, ca. 1015–1022.

The composition of many of the scenes on the doors derives from Carolingian manuscript illumination, and the style of the figures has an expressive strength that brings to mind the illustrations in the *Utrecht Psalter* (FIGS. 11-14A and 11-15). For example, in the fourth panel (FIG. 11-27) from the top on the left door, God, portrayed as a man, accuses Adam and Eve after their fall from grace. He jabs his finger at them with the force of his whole body. The force is concentrated in the gesture, which becomes the psychic focus of the entire composition. The frightened pair crouch, not only to hide their shame but also to escape the lightning bolt of divine wrath. Each passes the blame—Adam pointing backward to Eve and Eve pointing downward to the deceitful serpent. The starkly flat setting throws into relief the gestures and attitudes of rage, accusation, guilt, and fear. The sculptor presented the story with simplicity, although with great emotional impact, as well as a flair for anecdotal detail. Adam and Eve both struggle to point with one arm while attempting to shield their bodies from view with the

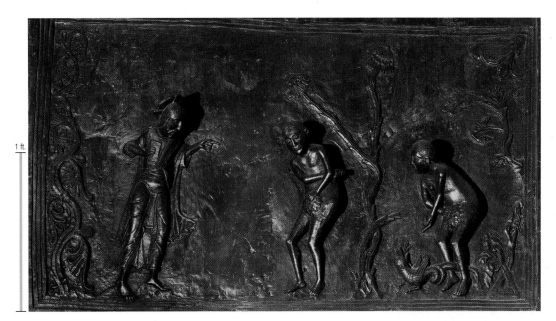

The Hildesheim bronze-caster recounted the story of Original Sin with a flair for anecdote. With vivid gestures, God accuses Adam, who passes the blame to Eve, who points in turn to the serpent.

other. With an instinct for expressive pose and gesture, the artist brilliantly communicated their newfound embarrassment at their nakedness and their unconvincing denials of wrongdoing.

Magdeburg Ivories. The figural panels of the bronze doors of Saint Michael's at Hildesheim constitute a unique ensemble, but they are not the only series of small-scale narrative relief panels made for display in an Ottonian church. Sixteen ivory plaques remain from a set of perhaps as many as 50 that once decorated the altar, pulpit, or another important item of church furniture in Magdeburg Cathedral. The cathedral housed the relics of Saint Mauritius (Maurice), a Christian army commander from Africa whom the Romans executed in Gaul during the third century when he refused to sacrifice to the old gods. Otto I transferred the saint's relics from France to Magdeburg in 960. A former monastic community on the eastern frontier of the Ottonian Empire, Magdeburg became an archbishopric in 968, the year Otto I dedicated the city's new cathedral. The 10th-century church burned down in 1207. The present cathedral is a Gothic replacement.

Most of the plaques depict scenes from the life of Christ. The one illustrated here (FIG. 11-28), however, features Otto I presenting Magdeburg Cathedral to Christ, who sits on a large wreath and extends his right hand to the emperor to indicate that he welcomes the gift. Ottonian representations of the emperor usually depict him as the central figure and of large stature (for example, FIG. 11-31), but the artist here represented the bearded and crowned Otto to one side and as small as a child. The age-old principle of hierarchy of scale dictated that the artist depict the only mortal as the smallest figure. Christ is largest, and the saints are intermediate in size. The two most prominent are Saint Peter, at the right holding the key to the kingdom of Heaven, and Saint Mauritius, who introduces the emperor to Christ. Art historians believe that the plaques are the work of ivory carvers in Milan, the leading city of Lombardy, which was part of Otto I's empire.

Otto II and Theophanu. On April 14, 972, Otto I arranged the marriage of his son, Otto II, to the Byzantine princess Theophanu (see "Theophanu, a Byzantine Princess at the Ottonian Court," page 342). The wedding secured the important political alliance between the Ottonian and Byzantine empires. Because the couple married in Rome with the pope administering the vows, the wedding reaffirmed the close relationship between the Ottonians and

the papacy. The marriage, commemorated on a contemporaneous ivory plaque (FIG. 11-29), also enhanced the already strong artistic and cultural ties between Germany and Constantinople.

Gero Crucifix. During the Ottonian period, interest in freestanding statuary, which had been exceedingly rare for the preceding half millennium, also revived. The outstanding example

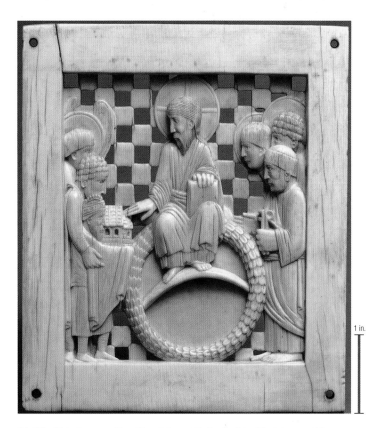

11-28 Otto I presenting Magdeburg Cathedral to Christ, panel from an altar or pulpit in Magdeburg Cathedral, Magdeburg, Germany, 962–968. Ivory, 5″ × 4½″. Metropolitan Museum of Art, New York (gift of George Blumenthal, 1941).

This ivory panel was affixed to an altar or pulpit dedicated by Otto I in Magdeburg Cathedral. It shows Saint Mauritius introducing the emperor to Christ, to whom Otto presents the new cathedral.

Theophanu, a Byzantine Princess at the Ottonian Court

The bishop of Mainz crowned Otto I king of the Saxons at Aachen in 936, but it was not until 962 that Pope John XII (r. 955–964) conferred the title of emperor of Rome upon him in Saint Peter's basilica. Otto, known as the Great, had ambitions to restore the glory of Charlemagne's Christian Roman Empire and to enlarge the territory under his rule. In 951, he defeated a Roman noble who had taken prisoner Adelaide, the widow of the Lombard king Lothar. Otto then married Adelaide, assumed the title of king of the Lombards, and extended his power south of the Alps. Looking eastward, in 972 he arranged the marriage of his son (and coemperor since 967), Otto II, to Theophanu (ca. 955–991), probably the niece of Emperor Nikephoros II Phokas (r. 963–969). Otto was 17 years old, his bride 16. They wed in Saint Peter's in Rome, with Pope John XIII (r. 965–972) presiding. When Otto the Great died the next year, Otto II became sole emperor (r. 973–983). The second Otto died in Italy a decade later and was buried in the atrium of Saint Peter's. His son, Otto III, only three years old at the time, nominally became king, but it was his mother, Theophanu, coregent with Adelaide until 985 and sole regent thereafter, who wielded power in the Ottonian Empire until her death in 991. Adelaide then served as regent until Otto III was old enough to rule on his own. He became emperor of Rome in 996 and died six years later.

Theophanu brought the prestige of Byzantium to Germany. Artistic ties between the Ottonian court and Constantinople became even stronger, and the Ottonians imported Byzantine luxury goods, including ivory plaques, in great quantities. One surviving ivory panel (FIG. 11-29) commemorates the marriage between Otto II and Theophanu. It shows Christ, central and the largest figure, extending both arms to bless the crowned emperor and his empress. (Otto appears much older than 17, consistent with his imperial stature.) The artist depicted all three standing rigidly and looking directly at the viewer. The frontality of the figures, the tripartite composition, and the style of carving suggest that the work is an import from Constantinople, as does the lengthy Greek dedicatory inscription. A few words are in Latin, however, and the inscription also identifies the donor—the tiny bowing figure clinging to Christ's stool—as an Italian bishop. Some art historians therefore think that the artist may have been an Ottonian ivory carver in Lombardy. Whoever made the plaque, the iconography is distinctively Byzantine, because the imagery declares that Otto's authority to rule comes directly from Christ, not from the pope. Whether of Byzantine or Ottonian manufacture, the ivory is an Ottonian commission in Byzantine style. The influence of Byzantine art is also evident in Ottonian manuscript painting (FIGS. 11-30A and 11-32).

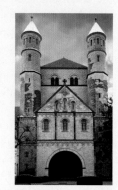

Theophanu also made her mark as a patron of ecclesiastical architecture, remodeling and expanding the towering westwork (FIG. 11-29A) of the abbey church of Saint Pantaleon in Cologne.

11-29A Saint Pantaleon, Cologne, 966–996.

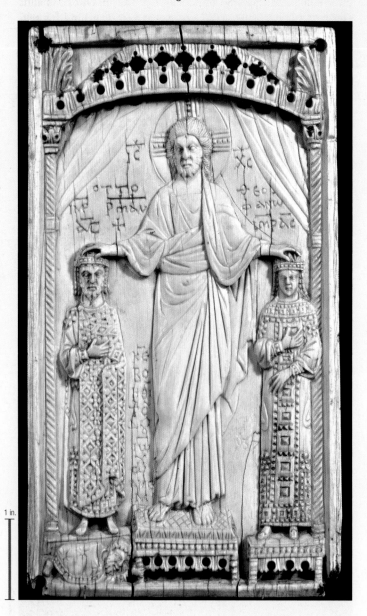

1 in.

11-29 Christ blessing Otto II and Theophanu, 972–973. Ivory, $7\frac{1}{8}" \times 4"$. Musée national du Moyen Âge, Paris.

Commemorating the marriage of Otto II and Theophanu, this ivory plaque is Byzantine in style and iconography. Theophanu came from Constantinople and promoted Byzantine art at the Ottonian court.

of Ottonian large-scale sculpture is the *crucifix* (FIG. 11-30) that Archbishop Gero (r. 969–976) commissioned and presented to Cologne Cathedral in 970. Carved in oak, then painted and gilded, the 6-foot-tall image of Christ nailed to the cross is both statue and *reliquary* (a shrine for sacred relics; see "The Veneration of Relics," page 349). A compartment in the back of the head held bread for the Eucharist. According to one story, a crack developed in the wood of Gero's crucifix, but miraculously healed. Similar tales of miracles surround many sacred Christian objects—for example, some Byzantine icons (see "Icons," page 278).

The *Gero Crucifix* presents a conception of Christ dramatically different from that seen on the *Lindau Gospels* cover (FIG. 11-16), with

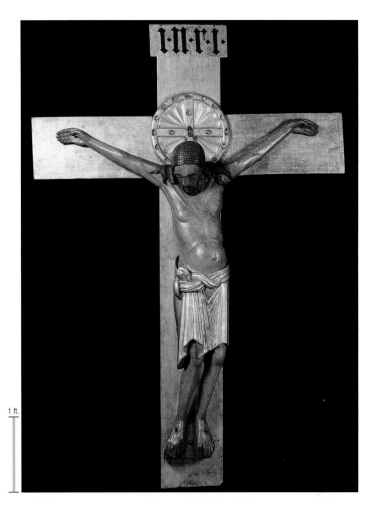

11-30 Crucifix commissioned by Archbishop Gero (*Gero Crucifix*), Cologne Cathedral, Cologne, Germany, ca. 970. Painted wood, height of figure 6′ 2″.

In this early example of the revival of large-scale sculpture in the Middle Ages, an Ottonian sculptor depicted with unprecedented emotional power the intense agony of Christ's ordeal on the cross.

its Early Christian imagery of the youthful Christ triumphant over death. Consistent with the strong Byzantine element in Ottonian art, the bearded Christ of the Cologne crucifix is more akin to Byzantine representations of the suffering Jesus (FIG. 9-24), but the emotional power of the Ottonian work is greater still. The sculptor depicted Christ as an all-too-human martyr. Blood streaks down his forehead from the (missing) crown of thorns. His eyelids are closed, his face is contorted in pain, and his body sags under its weight. The muscles stretch to their limit—those of the right shoulder and chest seem almost to rip apart. The halo behind Christ's head may foretell his subsequent resurrection, but the worshiper can sense only his pain. The *Gero Crucifix* is the most powerful characterization of intense agony of the early Middle Ages.

Gospel Book of Otto III.

In a Gospel book containing some of the finest early medieval paintings of the life of Christ (for example, FIG. 11-30A), one full-page representation (FIG. 11-31) stands apart from the rest. The page shows Otto III, son of Otto II and Theophanu, enthroned and

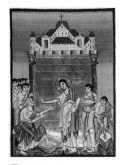

⬀ **11-30A** Jesus and Peter, *Gospel Book of Otto III*, 997–1000.

holding the scepter and cross-inscribed orb that signify his universal authority, conforming to a Christian imperial iconographic tradition that began with Constantine (FIG. 7-79, *right*). At the emperor's sides are the clergy and the barons (the Church and the State), both aligned in his support. On the facing page (not illustrated), also derived from ancient Roman sources, are female personifications of Slavinia, Germany, Gaul, and Rome—the provinces of the Ottonian Empire—bringing tribute to the young emperor.

Of the three Ottos, the last most fervently dreamed of a revived Christian Roman Empire. Indeed, it was his life's obsession. The boy-emperor was keenly aware of his descent from both German and Byzantine imperial lines, but he apparently was prouder of his Constantinopolitan than his German roots. He moved his court, with its Byzantine rituals, to Rome and there set up theatrically the symbols and trappings of Roman imperialism. Otto's romantic dream of imperial unity for Europe, the conceit behind his self-aggrandizing portrayal in the *Gospel Book of Otto III*, never materialized, however. He died prematurely, at age 21, and, at his request, was buried beside Charlemagne at Aachen.

Lectionary of Henry II.

Otto III's successor, Henry II, was the last Ottonian emperor. Of the artworks produced during his reign, the *Lectionary of Henry II* is the most noteworthy. A product of the leading Ottonian scriptorium at Reichenau, as was Otto III's Gospel book, Henry's lectionary (see "Medieval Books," page 324) was a gift to Bamberg Cathedral. In the full-page illumination of the announcement of Christ's birth to the shepherds, the angel has

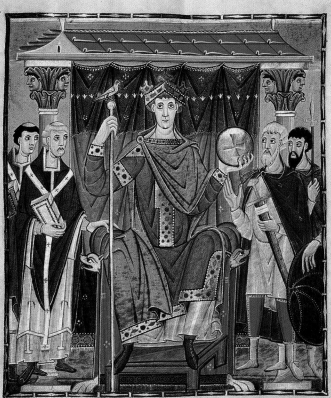

11-31 Otto III enthroned, folio 24 recto of the *Gospel Book of Otto III*, from Reichenau, Germany, 997–1000. Tempera on vellum, 1′ 1″ × 9¾″. Bayerische Staatsbibliothek, Munich.

Emperor Otto III, descended from both German and Byzantine imperial lines, appears in this Gospel book enthroned and holding the scepter and cross-inscribed orb signifying his universal authority.

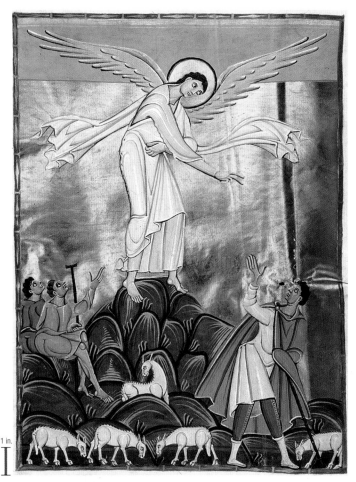

1 in.

11-32 Annunciation to the shepherds, folio in the *Lectionary of Henry II,* from Reichenau, Germany, 1002–1014. Tempera on vellum, full page 1′ 5″ × 1′ 1″; detail 10½″ high. Bayerische Staatsbibliothek, Munich.

The full-page illuminations in the *Lectionary of Henry II* fuse elements of Late Antique landscapes, the Carolingian-Ottonian anecdotal narrative tradition, and the gold background of Byzantine art.

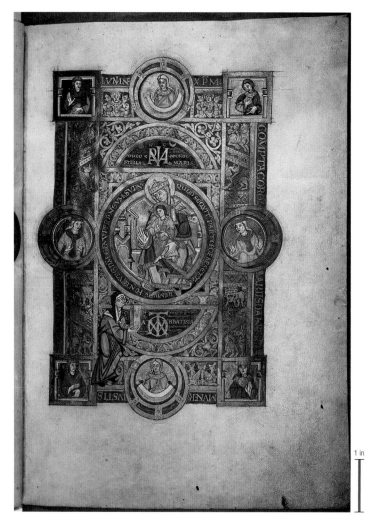

1 in.

11-33 Abbess Uta dedicating her codex to the Virgin, folio 2 recto of the *Uta Codex,* from Regensburg, Germany, ca. 1025. Tempera on parchment, 9⅝″ × 5⅛″. Bayerische Staatsbibliothek, Munich.

The *Uta Codex* illustrates the important role that women played both in religious life and as patrons of the arts. The dedicatory page shows Abbess Uta presenting her codex to the Virgin Mary.

just alighted on a hill, his still-beating wings rippling his draperies (FIG. 11-32). The angel looms immense above the startled and terrified shepherds, filling the golden sky. He extends his hand in a gesture of authority and instruction. Emphasized more than the message itself are the power and majesty of God's authority. The painting is a summation of the stylistic complexity of Ottonian art. It is a highly successful fusion of the Carolingian-Ottonian anecdotal narrative tradition, elements derived from Late Antique painting—for example, the rocky landscape setting with grazing animals (FIG. 8-24)—and the golden background of Byzantine book illumination and mosaic decoration.

Uta Codex. Another lectionary (FIG. 11-33), one of the finest Ottonian books produced for the clergy, as opposed to the imperial court, was the work of scribes and illuminators at Regensburg. Their patron was Uta, abbess of Niedermünster from 1003 to 1025, a leading nun well known in royal circles. Uta was instrumental in bringing Benedictine reforms to the Niedermünster convent, whose nuns were usually the daughters of the local nobility. Near the end of her life, she presented the nunnery with a sumptuous manuscript containing many full-page illuminations interspersed with Gospel readings, the so-called *Uta Codex.* The lectionary's case, fashioned of gold with jeweled and enamel decoration, also survives.

The dedicatory page (FIG. 11-33) at the front of the *Uta Codex* depicts the Virgin Mary with the Christ Child in her lap in the central medallion. Labeled *Virgo Virginum,* Virgin of Virgins, Mary is the model for Uta and the Niedermünster nuns. Uta is the full-length figure presenting a new book—this book—to the Virgin. An inscription accompanies the dedicatory image: "Virgin Mother of God, happy because of the divine Child, receive the votive offerings of your Uta of ready service."[4] The artist painted Uta last, superimposing her figure upon the design and carefully placing it so that Uta's head touches the Virgin's medallion but does not penetrate it, suggesting the interplay between, but also the separation of, the divine and human realms.

In many respects, the *Uta Codex* is more typical of the earlier medieval period and the succeeding Romanesque and Gothic eras than are the artworks and buildings commissioned by the Carolingian and Ottonian emperors. The Roman Empire, in revived form, may have lived on to 1002 at Otto III's court in Rome, but after Henry II's death in 1024, Rome's influence waned. Romanesque Europe found unity not politically but in a shared religious fervor, manifested most clearly in the launching of crusades to free the Holy Land from Muslim control (see "The Crusades," page 360).

Early Medieval Europe

Merovingians, Anglo-Saxons, and Vikings 5th to 10th Centuries

- After the fall of Rome in 410, the Merovingians, Anglo-Saxons, Franks, Goths, Vikings, and other non-Roman peoples competed for power in the former Roman northwestern provinces.

- Other than the ornamentation of ships used for burials, the surviving artworks of this period are almost exclusively small-scale status symbols, especially items of personal adornment, such as bracelets, pins, purses, and belt buckles, often featuring cloisonné decoration. A mixture of abstract and zoomorphic motifs appears on these portable treasures. Especially characteristic are intertwined animal-and-interlace patterns.

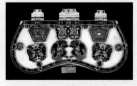

Purse cover, Sutton Hoo, ca. 625

Hiberno-Saxon Monasteries 6th to 10th Centuries

- Art historians call the Christian art of early medieval Britain and Ireland Hiberno-Saxon or Insular. The most important extant artworks are the illuminated manuscripts produced in the monastic scriptoria of Ireland and Northumbria—for example, the *Lindisfarne Gospels* and the *Book of Kells*.

- These Insular books feature folios devoted neither to text nor to illustration but to pure embellishment. "Carpet pages" consist of decorative panels of abstract and zoomorphic motifs. Some books also have full pages depicting the four evangelists or their symbols. Text pages often present the initial letters of important passages enlarged and transformed into elaborate decorative patterns.

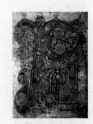

Book of Kells,
late eighth or ninth century

Carolingian Empire 768–877

- Charlemagne, king of the Franks since 768, expanded the territories he inherited from his father, and in 800, Pope Leo III crowned him emperor of Rome (r. 800–814). Charlemagne and his successors initiated a conscious revival of the art and culture of Early Christian Rome in their capital at Aachen.

- Carolingian sculptors revived the imperial Roman tradition of portraying rulers on horseback holding the orb of world power, as well as the Early Christian tradition of depicting Christ as a statuesque youth. The books that Carolingian artists produced sometimes featured magnificent jeweled covers (*Lindau Gospels*).

- Carolingian manuscripts merged the illusionism of classical painting with the northern European linear tradition, replacing the calm and solid figures of those models with figures that leap from the page with frenzied energy, as in the *Ebbo Gospels* and the *Utrecht Psalter.*

- Carolingian architects looked to Ravenna and Early Christian Rome for models, but transformed their sources, introducing, for example, the twin-tower western facade for basilicas at Corvey and elsewhere and employing strict modular plans for entire monasteries as well as individual churches, as seen in the plan of the Saint Gall monastery in Switzerland.

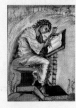

Ebbo Gospels, ca. 816–835

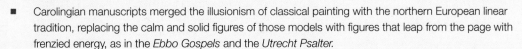

Abbey church, Corvey, 873–885

Ottonian Empire 919–1024

- In the mid-10th century, a new line of emperors, the Ottonians, consolidated the eastern part of Charlemagne's former empire and sought to preserve and enrich the culture and tradition of the Carolingian period.

- Like other early medieval artists, Ottonian artists excelled in producing small-scale artworks, especially ivory plaques with narrative reliefs, often influenced by Byzantine art. But Ottonian sculptors also revived the art of large-scale sculpture in such works as the *Gero Crucifix* and the bronze doors of Saint Michael's at Hildesheim. Ottonian painters combined motifs and landscape elements from Late Antique art with the golden backgrounds of Byzantine art.

- Ottonian architects built basilican churches incorporating the towering spires and imposing westworks of their Carolingian models, but introduced the alternate-support system and galleries into the nave.

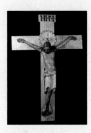

Gero Crucifix, ca. 970

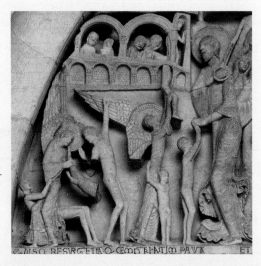

▶12-1a Above Autun Cathedral's portal, at the far left, a trumpet-blowing angel announces the Second Coming. Another obliging angel boosts one of the blessed over the fortified walls of Heaven.

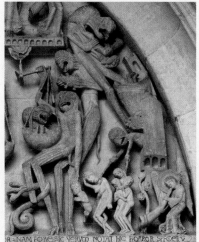

◀12-1b In Gislebertus's unforgettable rendition of Judgment Day, one of the Devil's agents shoves the damned headfirst into the dragon mouth of Hell while another demon drags four terrified souls in.

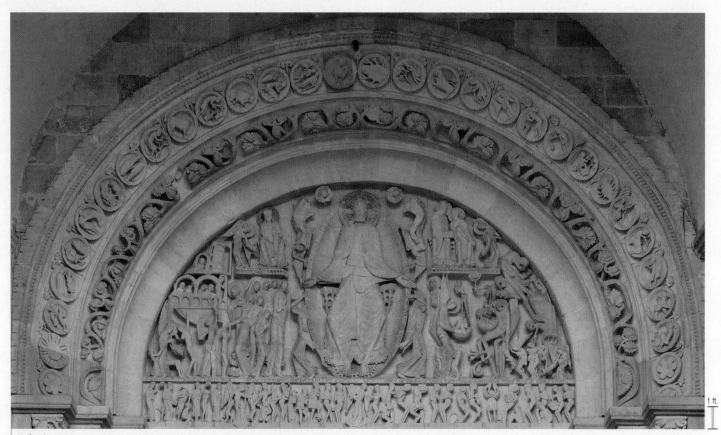

12-1 GISLEBERTUS, *Last Judgment*, west tympanum of Saint-Lazare, Autun, France, ca. 1120–1135. Marble, lintel 21′ wide.

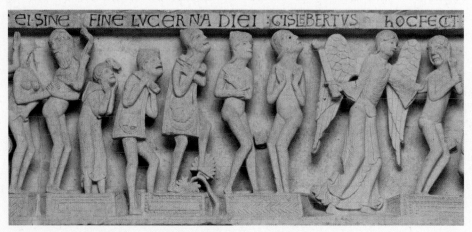

◀12-1c Below, the souls of the dead line up to await their fate. Two of the men carry the travel bags of pilgrims to Jerusalem and Santiago de Compostela, and consequently they can expect to be judged favorably.

ROMANESQUE EUROPE /12

The Blessed and the Damned on Judgment Day

As worshipers entered the western portal of the Burgundian cathedral of Saint-Lazare (Saint Lazarus) at Autun, they passed under a dramatic representation of the Last Judgment (FIG. 12-1) by the sculptor GISLEBERTUS. A renowned artist, he inscribed his name and also this message from the church's officials:

> I [Christ] alone arrange all things and crown the deserving. Punishment, with me as judge, holds in check those whom vice stimulates. Whoever is not seduced by an impious life will rise again in this way, and the light of day will shine on him forever. May this terror terrify those whom earthly error binds, for the horror of these images here in this manner truly depicts what will be.[1]

This warning echoes the sentiment expressed in a mid-10th-century copy of Beatus of Liébana's *Commentary on the Apocalypse.* There, the painter Magius (teacher of Emeterius; FIG. 11-11) explained the purpose of his work: "I have painted a series of pictures for the wonderful words of [the Apocalypse's] stories, so that the wise may fear the coming of the future judgment of the world's end."[2]

Few people in 12th-century France other than the clergy could read Gislebertus's message, but even the illiterate could, in the words of Saint Bernard of Clairvaux, "read in the marble" (see "Bernard of Clairvaux," page 356). Indeed, in the entire history of art, there is probably no more terrifying visualization of what awaits sinners than the one that Gislebertus invented for Autun Cathedral. Four trumpet-blowing angels announce the Second Coming of Christ, enthroned at the center, far larger than any other figure. He dispassionately presides over the separation of the blessed from the damned. At the left, an obliging angel boosts one of the saved into the heavenly city. Below, the dead line up to await their fate. Two of the men near the center of the lintel carry bags emblazoned with a cross and a shell. These are the symbols of pilgrims to Jerusalem and Santiago de Compostela, respectively (see "Pilgrimage Roads," page 350). Those who had made either difficult journey would be judged favorably. To their right, three small figures beg an angel to intercede on their behalf. The angel responds by pointing to the Judge above. On the right side are those who will be condemned to Hell. Giant hands pluck one poor soul from the group. Directly above is Gislebertus's unforgettable rendition of the weighing of souls (FIG. I-7; compare FIG. 11-9). Angels and the Devil's agents try to manipulate the balance for or against a soul. Hideous demons guffaw and roar. Their gaunt, lined bodies, with legs ending in sharp claws, writhe and bend like long, loathsome insects. A devilish creature, leaning from the dragon mouth of Hell (compare FIG. 11-9), drags souls in, while, above him, a howling demon shoves the damned headfirst into a furnace.

The Autun *Last Judgment* is one of the earliest examples of the rebirth of the art of large-scale sculpture in the Middle Ages, a hallmark of the age that art historians have dubbed *Romanesque* because of the extensive use of stone sculpture and vaulting in 11th- and 12th-century ecclesiastical architecture.

EUROPEAN CULTURE
IN THE NEW MILLENNIUM

"Romanesque." The Romanesque era is the first since Archaic and Classical Greece to take its name from an artistic style rather than from politics or geography. Unlike Carolingian and Ottonian art, named for emperors, or Hiberno-Saxon art, a regional term, *Romanesque* is a title that art historians invented to describe medieval art that appeared "Roman-like." Architectural historians first employed the adjective in the early 19th century to characterize European architecture of the 11th and 12th centuries. They noted that certain architectural elements of this period, principally barrel and groin vaults based on the round arch, resembled those of ancient Roman architecture. Thus the word distinguished most Romanesque buildings from earlier medieval timber-roofed structures, as well as from later Gothic churches with vaults resting on *pointed arches* (see "The Gothic Rib Vault," page 387). Scholars in other fields quickly borrowed the term. Today, "Romanesque" broadly designates the history and culture of western Europe between about 1050 and 1200. In fact, in terms of art and architecture, "Romanesque" is not one style of painting or sculpting or one way of constructing buildings but many regional styles and techniques with significant variations even within the artworks and buildings of a single region. To a certain extent, Romanesque art and architecture can be compared with the European Romance languages, which vary regionally but have a common core in Latin, the language of the Romans.

Towns and Churches. In the early Middle Ages, the focus of life was the *manor*, or estate, of a landholding *liege lord*, who might grant rights to a portion of his land to *vassals*. In this socioeconomic system, called *feudalism*, the vassals swore allegiance to their liege and rendered him military service in return for use of the land and the promise of protection. But in the Romanesque period, a sharp increase in trade encouraged the growth of towns and cities, which gradually displaced feudal estates as the backbone of late medieval European society. Feudal lords granted independence to the new towns in the form of charters, which enumerated the communities' rights, privileges, immunities, and exemptions beyond the feudal obligations that the vassals owed the lords. Often located on navigable rivers, the new urban centers naturally became the nuclei of networks of maritime and overland commerce.

Separated by design from the busy secular life of Romanesque towns were the monasteries (see "Medieval Monasteries," page 336) and their churches. During the 11th and 12th centuries, thousands of Christian houses of worship were remodeled or newly constructed. This immense building enterprise was in part a natural by-product of the rise of independent cities and the prosperity they enjoyed. But it also was an expression of the widely felt relief and thanksgiving that the conclusion of the first Christian millennium in the year 1000 had not brought an end to the world, as many had feared. In the Romanesque age, the construction of churches became almost an obsession. Raoul Glaber (ca. 985–ca. 1046), a monk who witnessed the coming of the new millennium, noted the beginning of it:

> [After the] year of the millennium, which is now about three years past, there occurred, throughout the world, especially in Italy and Gaul [France], a rebuilding of church basilicas. Notwithstanding, the greater number were already well established and not in the least in need, nevertheless each Christian people strove against the others to erect nobler ones. It was as if the whole earth, having cast off the old by shaking itself, were clothing itself everywhere in the white robe of the church.[3]

Pilgrims and Relics. The enormous investment in new and remodeled churches and their furnishings also reflected a significant increase in pilgrimage traffic in Romanesque Europe (see "Pilgrimage Roads in France and Spain," page 350, and MAP 12-1). Pilgrims, along with wealthy landowners, were important sources of funding for those monasteries that possessed the relics of revered saints (see "The Veneration of Relics," page 349). The monks of Sainte-Foy (FIG. 12-6A) at Conques, for example, used pilgrims' donations to pay for a magnificent cameo- and jewel-encrusted gold and silver reliquary (FIG. 12-2) to house the skull of Saint Faith. In fact, the clergy of the various monasteries vied with one another to provide the most magnificent settings for the display of their unique relics. They found justification for their lavish expenditures on buildings and furnishings in the Bible itself—for example, "Lord, I have loved the beauty of your house, and the place where your glory dwells" (Psalm 26:8). Traveling pilgrims fostered the growth of towns as well as monasteries. Pilgrimages were a major economic as well as conceptual catalyst for the art and architecture of the Romanesque period.

FRANCE AND NORTHERN SPAIN

As noted, although art historians use the adjective "Romanesque" to describe 11th- and 12th-century art and architecture throughout Europe, pronounced regional differences exist. This chapter examines in turn Romanesque France and Spain, the Holy Roman Empire, Italy, and Normandy and England.

Architecture and Architectural Sculpture

The regional diversity of the Romanesque period is particularly evident in architecture. For example, some Romanesque churches, especially in Italy, retained the timber roofs of their Early Christian

---

ROMANESQUE EUROPE

1000–1100	1100–1200
▪ The passing of the year 1000, the growth of towns, and the popularity of pilgrimages foster a surge in church construction	▪ Romanesque sculptors revive large-scale stone relief carving, especially on church facades, usually greeting worshipers with a vision of Christ as Last Judge
▪ Romanesque architects replace the timber roofs of churches with barrel vaults in the nave and groin vaults in the aisles	▪ Saint Bernard of Clairvaux opposes the proliferation of sculpture in churches
▪ Churches along the pilgrimage roads to Santiago de Compostela feature radiating chapels in ambulatories and transepts	▪ Manuscript illumination flourishes in the scriptoria of Cluniac monasteries
▪ The *Bayeux Tapestry* commemorates the Norman conquest of England in 1066	▪ Pilgrimages give impetus to the manufacture of costly reliquaries
	▪ Architects in Normandy and England introduce groin vaulting in church naves in conjunction with a three-story elevation (arcade-tribune-clerestory)

The Veneration of Relics

The cult of *relics* was not new in the Romanesque era. For centuries, Christians had traveled to sacred shrines housing the body parts of, or objects associated with, the holy family or the saints. The faithful had long believed that bones, clothing, instruments of martyrdom, and the like had the power to heal body and soul. In the 11th and 12th centuries, however, the veneration of relics reached a high point, prompting the devout to undertake often dangerous pilgrimages to hallowed shrines in Jerusalem, in Rome, and throughout western Europe (see "Pilgrimage Roads in France and Spain," page 350). Churches vied with one another not only for the possession of relics but also in the magnificence of the containers (*reliquaries*) that preserved and protected them.

The case of the relics of Saint Faith (Sainte Foy, in French), an early-fourth-century child martyr who refused to pay homage to the Roman gods, is a telling example. A monk from the abbey church at Conques (FIG. 12-6A) stole the saint's skull from the nearby abbey of Agen around 880. The monks justified the act as *furta sacra* ("holy theft"), claiming that Saint Faith herself wished to move.

The reliquary (FIG. 12-2) they provided to house the saint's remains is one of the most sumptuous ever produced. It takes the form of an enthroned statuette of the martyr. Fashioned of gold leaf and silver gilt over a wood core, the reliquary prominently features inset jewels and cameos of various dates—the accumulated donations of pilgrims and church patrons over many years. The saint's oversize head is a reworked ancient Roman *parade helmet*—a masklike helmet worn by soldiers on special ceremonial occasions and not part of standard battle dress. The monks added a martyr's crown to the ancient helmet. The rear of the throne bears an image of Christ on the cross engraved in rock crystal, establishing a parallel between Christ's martyrdom and Saint Faith's.

Reflecting the Romanesque passion for relics, *The Song of Roland*, an 11th-century epic poem recounting a historical battle of 778 between Charlemagne's rear guard and the Saracens, describes Durendal, the extraordinary sword that the hero Roland wielded, as follows:

> Ah, Durendal, fair, hallowed, and devote,
> What store of relics lie in thy hilt of gold!
> St Peter's tooth, St Basil's blood, it holds,
> Hair of my lord St Denis, there enclosed,
> Likewise a piece of Blessed Mary's robe.*

In view of the keen competition among Romanesque monasteries and cities for the possession of saints' relics, the author of the 12th-century *Pilgrim's Guide to Santiago de Compostela* saw fit to include comments on authenticity. For example, about Saint James's tomb, the guidebook states:

> May therefore the imitators from beyond the mountains blush who claim to possess some portion of him or even his entire relic. In fact, the body of the Apostle is here in its entirety, divinely lit by paradisiacal carbuncles, incessantly honored with immaculate and soft perfumes, decorated with dazzling celestial candles, and diligently worshipped by attentive angels.†

*173.2344–2348. Translated by Dorothy L. Sayers, *The Song of Roland* (New York: Penguin, 1957), 141.
†Translated by William Melczer, *The Pilgrim's Guide to Santiago de Compostela* (New York: Italica Press, 1993), 127.

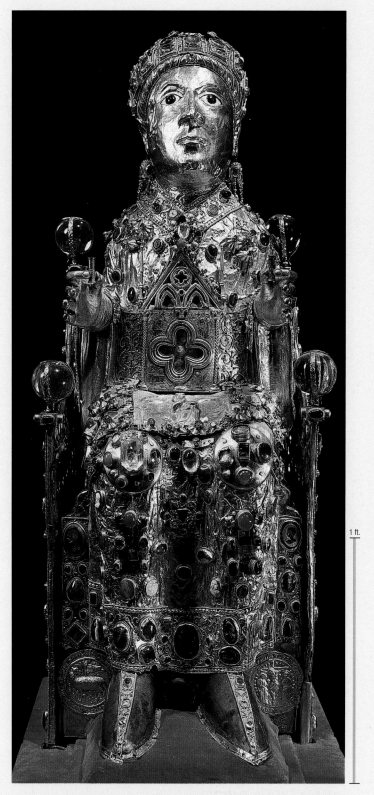

1 ft.

12-2 Reliquary statue of Sainte Foy (Saint Faith), late 10th to early 11th century with later additions. Gold, silver gilt, jewels, and cameos over a wood core, 2′ 9½″ high. Treasury, Sainte-Foy, Conques.

This enthroned image containing the skull of Saint Faith is one of the most lavish Romanesque reliquaries. The head is an ancient Roman helmet, and the cameos are donations from pilgrims.

Pilgrimage Roads in France and Spain

In the Romanesque era, pilgrimage was the most conspicuous feature of public devotion, proclaiming pilgrims' faith in the power of saints and hope for their special favor. The major shrines—Saint Peter's and Saint Paul's in Rome and the Church of the Holy Sepulcher in Jerusalem—drew pilgrims from all over Europe, just as Muslims journeyed from afar to Mecca (see "Muhammad and Islam," page 295). For the sake of salvation, pilgrims braved bad roads and hostile wildernesses where robbers preyed on innocent travelers. The journeys could take more than a year to complete—when they were successful. People often undertook pilgrimage as an act of repentance or as a last resort in their search for a cure for some illness or disability. Hardship and austerity were means of increasing pilgrims' chances for the remission of sin or of disease. The distance and peril of the pilgrimage were measures of the reward that pilgrims sought and of the sincerity of their repentance.

For those with insufficient time or money to make a pilgrimage to Rome or Jerusalem (in short, most people), holy destinations could be found closer to home. In France, for example, the church at Vézelay (FIG. 12-15) housed the bones of Mary Magdalene. Pilgrims could view Saint Lazarus's remains at Autun (FIG. 12-1), Saint Saturninus's at Toulouse (FIG. 12-5), Saint Faith's at Conques (FIGS. 12-2 and 12-6A), and Saint Martin's at Tours (see "The Veneration of Relics," page 349). Each of these great shrines was also an important way station en route to the most hallowed shrine in western Europe, the tomb of Saint James at Santiago de Compostela (FIG. 12-6B) in northwestern Spain.

Large crowds of pilgrims paying homage to saints placed a great burden on the churches possessing their relics and led to changes in church design, principally longer and wider naves and aisles; transepts and ambulatories with additional chapels (FIG. 12-6); and second-story galleries (FIGS. 12-6B and 12-7). Pilgrim traffic also established the routes that later became the major avenues of commerce and communication in western Europe. The popularity of pilgrimages gave rise to travel guides that, like modern guidebooks, provided pilgrims with information not only about saints and shrines but also about roads, accommodations, food, and drink. How widely circulated these handwritten books were is a matter of debate, but the information they provide is invaluable.

The most famous Romanesque guidebook described the four roads leading to Santiago de Compostela through Arles and Toulouse, Conques and Moissac, Vézelay and Périgueux, and Tours and Bordeaux (MAP 12-1). Saint James (see "Early Christian Saints," pages 246–247) was the symbol of Christian resistance to Muslim expansion in western Europe, and his relics, discovered in the ninth century, drew pilgrims to Santiago de Compostela from far and wide. The guidebook's anonymous 12th-century author, possibly Aimery Picaud, a Cluniac monk, was himself a well-traveled pilgrim. The text states that the author wrote the guide "in Rome, in the lands of Jerusalem, in France, in Italy, in Germany, in Frisia and mainly in Cluny."* Pilgrims reading the guidebook learned about the saints and their shrines at each stop along the way to Spain. Saint Saturninus of Toulouse, for example, endured a martyr's death at the hands of the Romans when he

> was tied to some furious and wild bulls and then precipitated from the height of the citadel. . . . His head crushed, his brains knocked out, his whole body torn to pieces, he rendered his worthy soul to Christ. He is buried in an excellent location close to the city of Toulouse where a large basilica [FIG. 12-5] was erected by the faithful in his honor.†

*Translated by William Melczer, *The Pilgrim's Guide to Santiago de Compostela* (New York: Italica Press, 1993), 133.
†Ibid., 103.

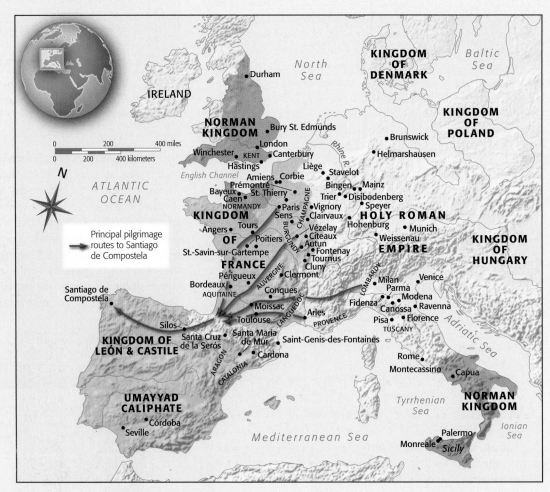

MAP 12-1 Western Europe around 1100.

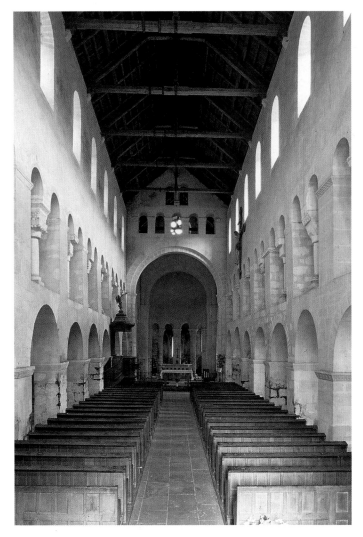

12-3 Interior of Saint-Étienne (looking east), Vignory, France, 1050–1057.

The timber-roofed abbey church at Vignory reveals a kinship with the three-story naves of Ottonian churches (FIG. 11-23), which also feature an alternate-support system of piers and columns.

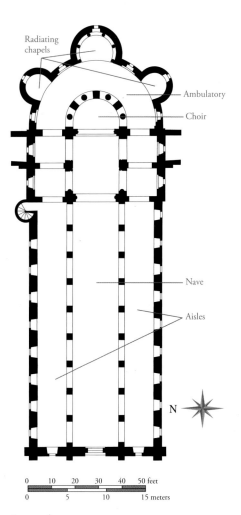

12-4 Plan of Saint-Étienne, Vignory, France, 1050–1057.

The innovative plan of the east end of the abbey church of Saint Stephen features an ambulatory around the choir and three semicircular radiating chapels opening onto it for the display of relics.

predecessors long after stone vaulting had become commonplace elsewhere. Even in France and northern Spain, home of many of the most innovative instances of stone vaulting, some Romanesque architects continued to build timber-roofed churches.

Vignory. The mid-11th-century church of Saint-Étienne (Saint Stephen) at Vignory in the Champagne region of central France has strong ties to Carolingian-Ottonian architecture, but incorporates features that became common only in later Romanesque buildings. The interior (FIG. 12-3) reveals a kinship with the three-story timber-roofed churches of the Ottonian era—for example, Saint Cyriakus (FIG. 11-23) at Gernrode. At Vignory, however, the second story is not a true *tribune* (gallery over the aisle opening onto the nave) but rather a screen with alternating piers and columns opening onto very tall flanking aisles. The east end of the church, by contrast, has an innovative plan (FIG. 12-4) with an ambulatory around the choir and three semicircular chapels opening onto it. These *radiating chapels* probably housed the church's relics, which the faithful could view without disturbing a service in progress by entering the choir, where the officiating priest performed the sacred rites at the main altar.

Other 11th-century churches—for example, Sant Vicenç (FIG. 12-4A) at Cardona, Spain, and Saint-Philibert (FIG. 12-4B) at Tournus, France—are noteworthy as early Romanesque examples of stone vaulting, and in that respect are more advanced than the timber-roofed Saint-Étienne. But the Vignory church is among the first to incorporate stone sculpture, one of the Romanesque period's defining features. At Vignory, however, the only sculpture is the relief decoration of the capitals of the ambulatory and false tribunes, where abstract and vegetal ornamentation, lions, and other four-legged beasts are the exclusive motifs (compare FIG. 12-10, *right*).

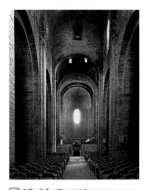

12-4A Sant Vicenç, Cardona, ca. 1029–1040.

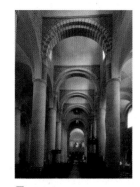

12-4B Saint-Philibert, Tournus, ca. 1060.

12-5 Aerial view of Saint-Sernin (looking northwest), Toulouse, France, ca. 1070–1120.

Pilgrimages were a major economic catalyst in the Romanesque era. The clergy vied to provide magnificent settings for the display of holy relics. Toulouse was a major stop on the road to Santiago de Compostela.

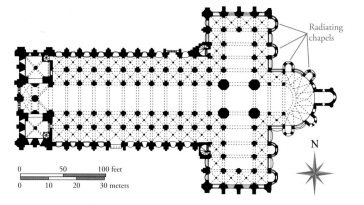

Toulouse. Dwarfing the Vignory, Cardona, and Tournus churches is the immense stone-vaulted basilica of Saint-Sernin (Saint Saturninus; FIG. 12-5) at Toulouse. Construction began around 1070 to honor the city's first bishop, a martyr saint of the mid-third century. Toulouse was an important stop on the pilgrimage road through southwestern France to Santiago de Compostela (see "Pilgrimage Roads," page 350). Large congregations gathered at the shrines along the major pilgrimage routes, and the unknown architect designed Saint-Sernin to accommodate them. The grand scale of the building is apparent in the aerial view reproduced here, which includes automobiles, trucks, and nearly invisible pedestrians. The church's 12th-century exterior is still largely intact, although the two towers of the western facade (FIG. 12-5, *left*) were never completed, and the prominent crossing tower dates to the Gothic and later periods.

Saint-Sernin's plan (FIG. 12-6) closely resembles those of the churches of Sainte-Foy (FIG. 12-6A) at Conques, Saint James (FIG. 12-6B) at Santiago de Compostela, and Saint-Martin at Tours, and exemplifies what has come to be called the "pilgrimage church" type. At Toulouse, the builders increased the length of the nave, doubled the side aisles, and added a transept, ambulatory, and radiating chapels to provide additional space for pilgrims and the clergy. Radiating chapels opening onto an ambulatory had been introduced earlier in Vignory's abbey church (FIG. 12-4), but at Toulouse the chapels are greater in number and open onto the transept as well as the ambulatory.

The Saint-Sernin plan is extremely regular and geometrically precise. The crossing square, flanked by massive piers and marked off by heavy arches, served as the module for the entire church. Each nave bay, for example, measures exactly one half of the crossing square, and each aisle bay measures exactly one quarter.

12-6 Plan of Saint-Sernin, Toulouse, France, ca. 1070–1120 (after Kenneth John Conant).

Increased traffic led to changes in church design. "Pilgrimage churches" have longer and wider naves and aisles, as well as transepts and ambulatories with radiating chapels for viewing relics.

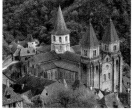

12-6A Sainte-Foy, Conques, mid-11th to early 12th century.

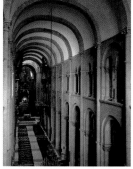

12-6B Saint James, Santiago de Compostela, ca. 1075–1120.

The builders employed similar simple ratios throughout the church. The first suggestion of this kind of planning scheme in medieval Europe was the Saint Gall monastery plan (FIG. 11-20) almost three centuries earlier. The Toulouse solution was a crisply rational and highly refined realization of an idea first seen in Carolingian architecture. This approach to design became increasingly common in the Romanesque period.

The Burning of Canterbury Cathedral

The perils of wood construction were the subject of frequent commentary among chroniclers of medieval church history. In some cases, the Christian houses of worship burned over and over again in the course of a single century and repeatedly had to be extensively repaired or completely rebuilt. In September 1174, for example, Canterbury Cathedral, which had been dedicated only 44 years earlier, was accidentally set ablaze and destroyed. Gervase of Canterbury (1141–1210), who entered the monastery there in 1163 and wrote a history of the archbishopric from 1100 to 1199, provided in his *Chronica* a vivid eyewitness account of the disastrous fire:

[D]uring an extraordinarily violent south wind, a fire broke out before the gate of the church, and outside the walls of the monastery, by which three cottages were half destroyed. From thence, while the citizens were assembling and subduing the fire, cinders and sparks carried aloft by the high wind were deposited upon the church, and being driven by the fury of the wind between the joints of the lead, remained there among the half-rotten planks, and shortly glowing with increased heat, set fire to the rotten rafters; from these the fire was communicated to the larger beams and their braces, no one yet perceiving or helping. For the well-painted ceiling below, and the sheet-lead covering above, concealed between them the fire that had arisen within. . . . But beams and braces burning, the flames arose to the slopes of the roof; and the sheets of lead yielded to the increasing heat and began to melt. Thus the raging wind, finding a freer entrance, increased the fury of the fire. . . . And now that the fire had loosened the beams from the pegs that bound them together, the half-burnt timbers fell into the choir below upon the seats of the monks; the seats, consisting of a great mass of woodwork, caught fire, and thus the mischief grew worse and worse. And it was marvelous, though sad,

to behold how that glorious choir itself fed and assisted the fire that was destroying it. For the flames multiplied by this mass of timber, and extending upwards full fifteen cubits [about 25 feet], scorched and burned the walls, and more especially injured the columns of the church. . . . In this manner the house of God, hitherto delightful as a paradise of pleasures, was now made a despicable heap of ashes, reduced to a dreary wilderness.*

*Translated by Robert Willis, quoted in Elizabeth Gilmore Holt, *A Documentary History of Art*, 2d ed. (Princeton, N.J.: Princeton University Press, 1981), 1:52–54.

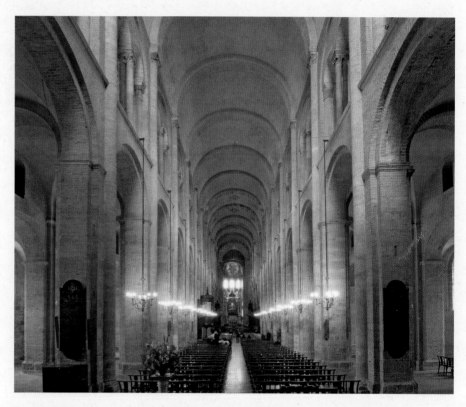

12-7 Interior of **Saint-Sernin** (looking east), Toulouse, France, ca. 1070–1120.

Saint-Sernin's stone compound piers and barrel vaults in the nave, and the groin vaults in the tribune galleries, helped prevent the kind of disastrous fire that destroyed Canterbury Cathedral.

Another telling feature of Saint-Sernin's design is the insertion of tribunes opening onto the nave over the inner aisles (FIG. 12-7), a feature also of the nave (FIG. 12-6B) of the church of Saint James at Santiago de Compostela. These galleries housed overflow crowds on special occasions and played an important role in buttressing the nave's continuous semicircular cut-stone barrel vault, in contrast to the fire-prone timber roof over the nave (FIG. 12-3) of the smaller abbey church at Vignory (see "The Burning of Canterbury Cathedral," above). Groin vaults (indicated by Xs on the plan, FIG. 12-6; compare FIG. 7-6) in the tribunes as well as in the ground-floor aisles absorbed the pressure exerted by the barrel vault along the entire length of the nave and transferred the main thrust to the thick outer walls (see "Stone Vaulting in Romanesque Churches," page 354).

The builders of Saint-Sernin were not content merely to buttress the massive nave vault. They also carefully coordinated the design of the vault with that of the nave arcade below and with the modular plan of the building as a whole. The nave elevation (FIG. 12-7), which features *engaged columns* (attached half-columns) embellishing the piers marking the corners of the bays, fully reflects the church's geometric floor plan (FIG. 12-6). Architectural historians refer to piers with columns or pilasters attached to their rectangular cores as *compound piers*. At Saint-Sernin, the engaged columns rise from the bottom of the compound piers to the vault's *springing* (the lowest stone of an arch) and continue across the nave as *transverse arches*. As a result, the Saint-Sernin nave gives the impression of being numerous identical vertical volumes of space placed one behind the other, marching down the building's length

Stone Vaulting in Romanesque Churches

After fire destroyed Canterbury Cathedral in 1174, the monks resolved to build a new church more impervious to fire. They summoned a master builder from Sens, a French city 75 miles southeast of Paris, to supervise the construction of the replacement cathedral. Gervase, the Canterbury monk who wrote an account of the fire (see "The Burning of Canterbury Cathedral," page 353) reported that the first task William of Sens tackled was "the procuring of stone from beyond the sea."*

Substituting stone vaulting for timber roofing in the nave, transept, and aisles was the best available solution to the problem of building a fire-resistant church. However, many architectural historians believe that a quest for fireproof structures was not the primary rationale for introducing stone barrel and groin vaults in Romanesque churches, although that was no doubt one of the attractions of masonry construction in an age when candles and lamps provided interior illumination. Other factors probably played a greater role in the decision to make the enormous investment of time and funds required. The rapid spread of stone vaulting throughout Romanesque Europe—beginning at Cardona (FIG. 12-4A), Tournus (FIG. 12-4B), Santiago de Compostela (FIG. 12-6B), Toulouse (FIG. 12-7), Cluny (FIG. 12-8), Speyer (FIG. 12-21), and Milan (FIG. 12-23), as much as a century before the new Canterbury Cathedral—was more likely the result of a desire to provide a suitably majestic setting for the display of relics as well as enhanced acoustics for the Christian liturgy and the music accompanying it.

Some contemporaneous texts, in fact, comment on the visual impact of costly stone vaults. For example, in 1150 at Angers in northwestern France, a church chronicler explained what the bishop sought to achieve by replacing the timber roof of his cathedral with stone vaults: "[He] took down the timber beams of the nave of the church, threatening to fall from sheer old age, and began to build stone vaults of wondrous effect."[†] Stone vaulting was an aesthetic solution to a different kind of problem than protecting churches from destruction by fire.

*Translated by Robert Willis, quoted in Elizabeth Gilmore Holt, *A Documentary History of Art,* 2d ed. (Princeton, N.J.: Princeton University Press, 1981), 1:54.
[†]Translated by John Hooper Harvey, *The Medieval Architect* (London: Waylan, 1972), 39.

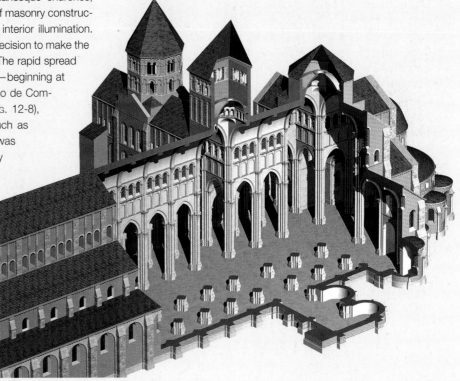

12-8 Restored cutaway view of the third abbey church ("Cluny III"; looking northeast), Cluny, France, 1088–1130 (John Burge).

Cluny III was the largest church in Europe for 500 years. It had a 500-foot-long, three-story (arcade-tribune-clerestory) nave, four aisles, radiating chapels, and slightly pointed stone barrel vaults.

in orderly procession. Saint-Sernin's spatial organization corresponds to and renders visually the plan's geometric organization. The articulation of the building's exterior walls (FIG. 12-5), where buttresses frame each bay, also reflects the segmentation of the nave. This rationally integrated scheme, with repeated units decorated and separated by moldings, would have a long future in European church architecture.

Cluny.   Architectural historians are fortunate that several important late-11th-century churches still stand, but the greatest of them all does not. In 909, William the Pious, duke of Aquitaine (r. 893–918), donated land near Cluny in Burgundy to a community of reform-minded Benedictine monks under the leadership of Berno of Baume (d. 927). Because William waived his feudal rights to the land, the abbot of Cluny was obligated only to the pope in Rome, an exceptional privilege. Berno founded a new order

at Cluny according to the rules of Saint Benedict (see "Medieval Monasteries and Benedictine Rule," page 336). Under Berno's successors, the Cluniac monks became famous for their scholarship, music, and art. Their influence and wealth grew rapidly, and they built a series of ever more elaborate monastic churches at Cluny.

Abbot Hugh of Semur (1024–1109) began construction of the third church at Cluny in 1088. Called Cluny III by architectural historians, the building has largely vanished, but it is possible to reconstruct what it looked like (FIG. 12-8). When work concluded in 1130, Cluny III was the largest church in Europe, and it retained that distinction for almost 500 years until the completion of the new Saint Peter's (FIG. 24-4) in Rome in the early 17th century. Contemporaries considered Cluny III a place suitable for angels to dwell if they lived on earth. The church had a bold and influential design, with a barrel-vaulted nave, four aisles, and radiating chapels, as at Saint-Sernin (FIGS. 12-6 and 12-7), but with a three-story

A SECOND OPINION

The Rebirth of Large-Scale Sculpture in Romanesque Europe

With some notable exceptions, such as Irish high crosses (FIGS. 11-9 and 11-9A), stone sculpture had almost disappeared from the art of western Europe during the early Middle Ages. The revival of stonecarving in the 11th century at Toulouse (FIG. 12-9) and Saint-Genis-des-

Fontaines (FIG. 12-9A) in southern France and at Silos (FIG. 12-9B) in northern Spain is a hallmark of the Romanesque age—and one reason that the period is aptly named. The inspiration for

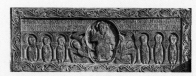

12-9A Saint-Genis-des-Fontaines, 1019–1020.

stone sculpture no doubt came, at least in part, from the abundant remains of ancient statues and reliefs throughout Rome's northwestern provinces. Yet these models had been available for centuries and therefore cannot explain the sudden proliferation of stone sculpture in Romanesque churches. Why did Romanesque church officials decide to revive the art of stone sculpture in the 11th century?

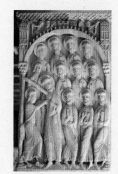

12-9B Santo Domingo, Silos, ca. 1090–1100.

Many art historians have noted that the reemergence of large-scale stone sculpture coincided with the introduction of stone vaulting in early Romanesque churches. But medieval builders had erected stone-walled basilicas and towering stone westworks for centuries, even if the structures bore timber ceilings and roofs. The earliest Romanesque sculptures, in fact, appear in timber-roofed churches, such as Saint-Étienne (FIG. 12-3) at Vignory. Therefore, the addition of stone vaults to basilican churches cannot account for the resurgence of stonecarving in the Romanesque period. But just as stone vaulting reflects the greater prosperity of the age, so too does the decoration of churches with large-scale sculptures. Both are consistent with the widespread desire in the Romanesque period to beautify the house of God and make it, in the words of Gervase of Canterbury, "a paradise of pleasures."

The popularity of stone sculpture in the 12th century also reflects the changing role of many churches in western Europe. In the early Middle Ages, most churches served small monastic communities, and the worshipers were primarily or exclusively clergy. With the rise of towns in the Romanesque period, churches, especially those on the major pilgrimage routes, increasingly served the lay public. The display of sculpture both inside and outside Romanesque churches was a means of impressing—and educating—a new and largely illiterate audience.

Portal sculptures, especially those with Christ as the central motif (FIGS. 12-1, 12-11, 12-12B, 12-14, and 12-15), communicated a very important message. These entryways reflect the belief, dating to Early Christian times, that Christ is the door to salvation ("I am the door; who enters through me will be saved"—John 10:9). An inscription on the tympanum of the late-11th-century monastic church of Santa Cruz de la Serós in Spain made this message explicit: "I am the eternal door. Pass through me faithful ones. I am the source of life."

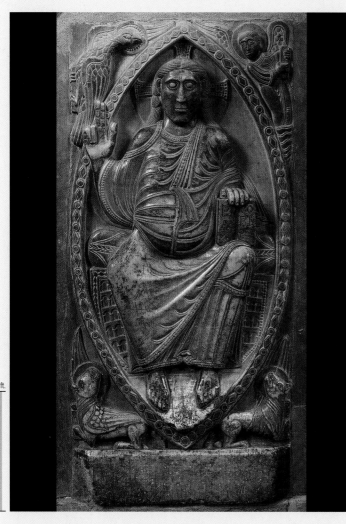

1 ft.

12-9 BERNARDUS GELDUINUS, *Christ in Majesty,* relief in the ambulatory of Saint-Sernin (FIG. 12-5), Toulouse, France, ca. 1096. Marble, 4′ 2″ high.

One of the earliest series of large Romanesque figural stone reliefs decorated the pilgrimage church of Saint-Sernin. The models were probably metal or ivory Carolingian and Ottonian book covers.

nave elevation (arcade-tribune-clerestory) and vaults with pointed arches, which became typical of French church architecture only in the Gothic age (see "The Gothic Rib Vault," page 387). With a nave more than 500 feet long and more than 100 feet high (both dimensions are about 50 percent greater than the comparable dimensions of Saint-Sernin), it exemplified the grandiose scale of the new stone-vaulted Romanesque churches and was a symbol of the power and prestige of the Cluniac order.

Bernardus Gelduinus. The Cluniac monks were also the primary patrons of stone sculpture in the Romanesque era, but it is Saint-Sernin that boasts one of the earliest precisely dated medieval series of large-scale Romanesque figural reliefs—a group of seven marble slabs representing Christ, angels, and apostles (see "The Rebirth of Large-Scale Sculpture in Romanesque Europe," above). An inscription on the altar states that the reliefs date to the year 1096 and identifies the artist as BERNARDUS GELDUINUS. Today, the

Bernard of Clairvaux on Cloister Sculpture

The most influential theologian of the Romanesque era was Bernard of Clairvaux (1090–1153). A Cistercian monk and abbot of the monastery he founded at Clairvaux in northern Burgundy, he embodied not only the reforming spirit of the Cistercian order but also the new religious fervor awakening throughout Europe. Bernard's impassioned eloquence made him a celebrity and drew him into the stormy politics of the 12th century. He intervened in high matters of both Church and State, defended and sheltered embattled popes, counseled kings, denounced heretics, and preached Crusades against the Muslims (see "The Crusades," page 360)—all in defense of papal Christianity and spiritual values. The Church declared Bernard a saint in 1174, barely two decades after his death.

In a letter Bernard wrote in 1127 to William, abbot of Saint-Thierry, he complained about the rich outfitting of non-Cistercian churches in general and, in particular, the sculptural adornment of monastic cloisters, such as those at Silos (FIG. 12-9B) and Moissac (FIGS. 12-10 and 12-10A).

> I will overlook the immense heights of the places of prayer, their immoderate lengths, their superfluous widths, the costly refinements, and painstaking representations which deflect the attention . . . of those who pray and thus hinder their devotion. . . . But so be it, let these things be made for the honor of God . . . [But] in the cloisters, before the eyes of the brothers while they read—what . . . are the filthy apes doing there? The fierce lions? The monstrous centaurs? The creatures, part man and part beast? The striped tigers? The fighting soldiers? The hunters blowing horns? You may see many bodies under one head, and conversely many heads on one body. On one side the tail of a serpent is seen on a quadruped, on the other side the head of a quadruped is on the body of a fish. Over there an animal has a horse for the front half and a goat for the back. . . . Everywhere so plentiful and astonishing a variety of contradictory forms is seen that one would rather read in the marble than in books, and spend the whole day wondering at every single one of them than in meditating on the law of God. Good God! If one is not ashamed of the absurdity, why is one not at least troubled at the expense?*

*Bernard of Clairvaux, *Apologia* 12.28–29. Translated by Conrad Rudolph, *The "Things of Greater Importance": Bernard of Clairvaux's* Apologia *and the Medieval Attitude toward Art* (Philadelphia: University of Pennsylvania Press, 1990), 279, 283.

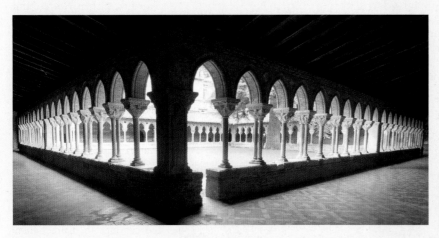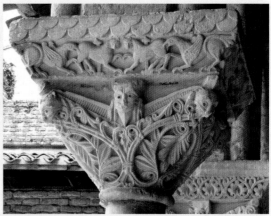

12-10 General view (*left*; looking southeast) and historiated capital (*right*) of the cloister of Saint-Pierre, Moissac, France, ca. 1100–1115.

The revived tradition of stonecarving probably began with historiated capitals. The most extensive preserved ensemble of sculptured early Romanesque capitals is in the Moissac cloister.

sculptures adorn the church's ambulatory wall, but their original location is unknown. In the view of some scholars, the reliefs once formed part of a shrine dedicated to Saint Saturninus that stood in the *crypt* (a vaulted underground chamber) of the grand pilgrimage church. Others believe that the plaques once decorated a choir screen or an exterior portal. The relief illustrated here (FIG. 12-9), *Christ in Majesty,* is the centerpiece of the group. Christ sits in a mandorla, his right hand raised in blessing, his left hand resting on an open book inscribed *Pax vobis* ("Peace unto you"). The signs of the four evangelists (see "The Four Evangelists," page 331) occupy the corners of the slab. Art historians debate the sources of Bernardus's style, but the composition could have been used earlier for

a Carolingian or Ottonian work in metal or ivory, perhaps a book cover. The polished marble has the gloss of both materials, and the sharply incised lines and ornamentation of Christ's aureole are characteristic of pre-Romanesque metalwork.

Moissac. The abbey of Saint-Pierre (Saint Peter) at Moissac in southwestern France joined the Cluniac order in 1047 and was an important stop along the pilgrimage route to Santiago de Compostela. Enriched by the gifts of pilgrims and noble benefactors, the monks adorned their church with one of the most extensive series of relief sculptures in Romanesque Europe. The oldest are in the cloister (FIG. 12-10). *Cloister* (from the Latin word *claustrum,* "enclosed place") connotes being shut away from the world. Architecturally, the medieval church cloister expressed the seclusion of the spiritual life, the *vita contemplativa* ("contemplative life"), as opposed to the *vita activa* ("active life") of the lay population. At Moissac, as elsewhere, the cloister provided the monks (and nuns) with a foretaste of Paradise. In its garden or the timber-roofed columnar walkway framing the garden, they could read their devotions, pray, meditate, and carry on other activities in a beautiful and centrally located space. The cloisters of the 12th century are monuments to the vitality, popularity, and influence of monasticism at its peak.

Moissac's cloister sculpture program consists of large figural reliefs (FIG. 12-10A) on the piers as well as *historiated capitals* (capitals ornamented with carved figures; FIG. 12-10, *right*) on the columns. The 76 capitals alternately crown single and paired column shafts. They are variously decorated, some with abstract patterns, many with biblical scenes or scenes from the lives of saints, others with fantastic

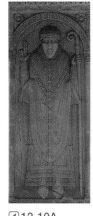

12-10A Abbot Durandus, Moissac, ca. 1000–1115.

monsters of all sorts—basilisks, griffins, lizards, gargoyles, and more. *Bestiaries*—collections of illustrations of real and imaginary animals—became very popular in the Romanesque age. The monstrous forms were reminders of the chaos and deformity of a world without God's order. Medieval artists delighted in inventing composite multiheaded beasts and other fantastic creations. Historiated capitals were also a feature of Moissac's mother church, Cluny III, and were common in Cluniac monasteries.

Not everyone shared the Cluniac monks' enthusiasm for stone sculpture. One group of Benedictine monks founded a new order at Cîteaux in eastern France in 1098. The Cistercians (from the Latin name for Cîteaux) split from the Cluniac order to return to the strict observance of the rules of Saint Benedict (see "Medieval Monasteries and Benedictine Rule," page 336), changing the color of their robes from Cluniac black to unbleached white. These White Monks emphasized productive manual labor, and their systematic farming techniques stimulated the agricultural transformation of Europe.

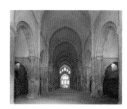

12-10B Notre-Dame, Fontenay, 1139–1147.

The Cistercian movement expanded with astonishing rapidity. Within a half century, the White Monks had established more than 500 monasteries. Their churches, such as Notre-Dame at Fontenay (FIG. 12-10B), are uniformly austere. The Cistercians rejected figural sculpture as a distraction from their devotions. The most outspoken Cistercian critic of church sculpture was Abbot Bernard of Clairvaux (see "Bernard of Clairvaux on Cloister Sculpture," page 356).

Bernard directed his tirade against figural sculpture primarily at monks who allowed the carvings to distract them from their meditations. But at Moissac (FIG. 12-11) and other Cluniac churches, the most extensive sculptural ensembles adorned those parts of the church open to the laity, especially the facade. Saint-Pierre's

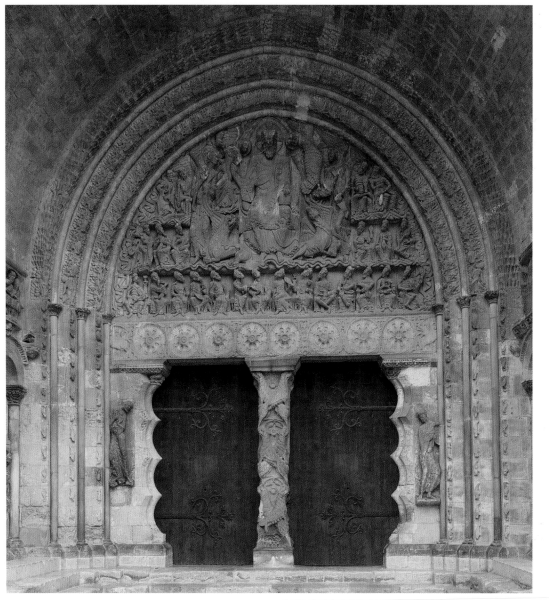

12-11 South portal of Saint-Pierre, Moissac, France, ca. 1115–1135.

A vision of the Second Coming of Christ on Judgment Day greets worshipers entering Saint-Pierre at Moissac. Accompanying Christ in the tympanum are the 24 elders and the symbols of the four evangelists.

The Romanesque Church Portal

One of the most significant and distinctive features of Romanesque art is the revival of stone sculpture (see "The Rebirth of Large-Scale Sculpture," page 355). Large-scale carved biblical figures were extremely rare in Christian art before the year 1000. But in the late 11th and early 12th centuries, rich ensembles of figural reliefs began to appear again, most often in the grand stone portals (FIGS. 12-11 and 12-12B) through which the faithful had to pass. Sculpture had been employed in church doorways before. For example, carved wood doors (FIG. 8-19A) greeted Early Christian worshipers as they entered Santa Sabina in Rome, and Ottonian bronze doors (FIG. 11-26) decorated with Old and New Testament scenes marked the entrance from the cloister to the church of Saint Michael's at Hildesheim. But these were exceptions, and in the Romanesque era (and during the Gothic period that followed), sculpture usually appeared in the area *around,* rather than *on,* the doors.

Shown in FIG. **12-12** are the parts of church portals that Romanesque sculptors regularly decorated with figural reliefs:

■ *Tympanum* (FIGS. 12-1, 12-11, 12-12B, and 12-15), the prominent semicircular *lunette* above the doorway proper, comparable in importance to the triangular *pediment* of a Greco-Roman temple
■ *Voussoirs* (FIG. 12-15), the wedge-shaped blocks that together form the **archivolts** of the arch framing the tympanum
■ *Lintel* (FIGS. 12-1, 12-9A, 12-15, and 12-15C), the horizontal beam above the doorway
■ *Trumeau* (FIGS. 12-11 and 12-13), the center post supporting the lintel in the middle of the doorway
■ *Jambs* (FIG. 12-11), the side posts of the doorway

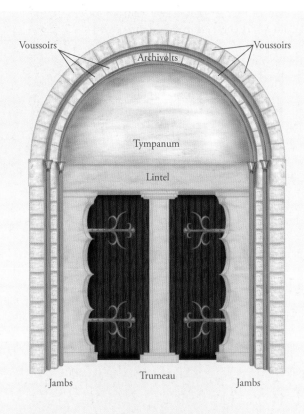

12-12 **The Romanesque church portal (John Burge).**

The clergy considered the church doorway to be the beginning of the path to salvation through Christ. Many Romanesque churches feature didactic figural reliefs above and beside the entrance portals.

richly decorated south portal faces the town square, and features figural and decorative reliefs in its tympanum, voussoirs, lintel, trumeau, and jambs (see "The Romanesque Church Portal," above).

The focus of the sculptural program of the Moissac portal is the tympanum depicting the Second Coming of Christ as king and judge of the world in its last days—a subject chosen to underscore the role of the church as the path to Heaven (see "The Rebirth of Large-Scale Sculpture," page 355). As befits his majesty, the enthroned Christ is at the center, reflecting a compositional rule followed since Early Christian times. Flanking him are the signs of the four evangelists and attendant angels holding scrolls to record human deeds for judgment. Completing the design are 24 figures of crowned musicians. They are the 24 elders who accompany Christ as the kings of this world and make music in his praise. Each turns to face the enthroned judge, much as would the courtiers of a medieval monarch in attendance on their lord. Two courses of wavy lines symbolizing the clouds of Heaven divide the elders into three tiers.

Variations on the theme of the Second Coming adorn the tympana of many Romanesque churches, but the style of these sculptures is quite diverse. The figures of the Moissac tympanum contrast sharply with those of the earlier Saint-Sernin ambulatory reliefs (FIG. 12-9) and the Silos pier reliefs (FIG. 12-9B), as well as with the contemporaneous tympana at Autun (FIGS. 12-1 and 12-14) and Vézelay (FIG. 12-15), the later reliefs on the facade of

Notre-Dame-la-Grande (FIG. 12-12A) at Poitiers and Saint Trophîme (FIG. 12-12B) at Arles, and even the pier reliefs (FIG. 12-10A) of the Moissac cloister. The extremely elongated bodies of the angels recording each soul's fate, the cross-legged dancing pose of Saint Matthew's angel, and the jerky, hinged movement of the elders' heads are characteristic of the nameless Moissac master's style of representing the human figure. The zigzag and dovetail lines of the draperies, the band-like folds of the torsos, the bending back of the hands against the body, and the wide cheekbones are also common features of this distinctive style. The animation of the individual figures, however, contrasts with the stately monumentality of the composition as a whole, producing a dynamic tension in the tympanum.

The jambs and central post (trumeau) of the Moissac portal (FIG. 12-11) have scalloped contours, a borrowing from Spanish Islamic architecture (compare FIGS. 10-11 and 10-12). Six roaring interlaced lions on

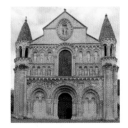

⏴12-12A
Notre-Dame-la-Grande, Poitiers, ca. 1130–1150.

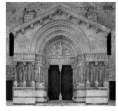

⏴12-12B
Saint-Trophîme, Arles, mid-12th century.

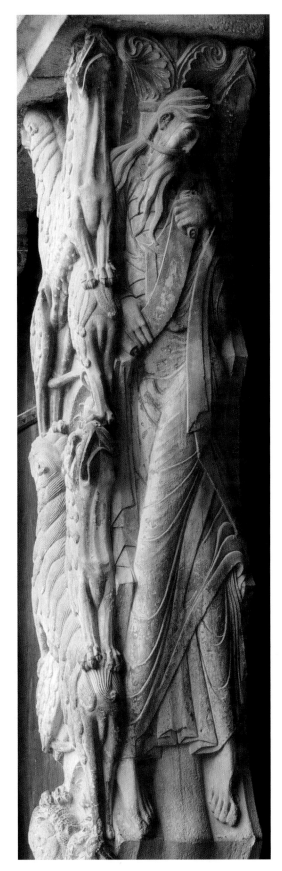

12-13 Old Testament prophet (Jeremiah or Isaiah?), right side of the trumeau of the south portal (FIG. 12-11) of Saint-Pierre, Moissac, France, ca. 1115–1130.

This animated prophet displays the scroll recounting his vision. His position below the apparition of Christ as Last Judge is in keeping with the tradition of pairing Old and New Testament themes.

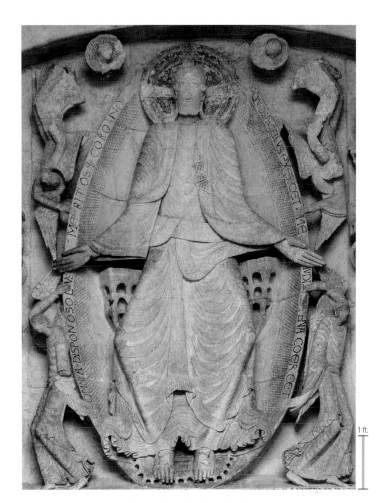

12-14 GISLEBERTUS, Christ, detail of *Last Judgment*, west tympanum (FIG. 12-1) of Saint-Lazare, Autun, France, ca. 1120–1135. Detail, 8′ 9″ high.

Christ presides over the separation of the blessed from the damned in Gislebertus's dramatic vision of the Last Judgment (FIG. 12-1), designed to terrify those guilty of sin and beckon them into the church.

the front of the trumeau greet worshipers as they enter the church. The notion of placing fearsome images at the gateways to important places is of very ancient origin (compare FIGS. 2-18A, 2-20, 4-19, 5-16, and 6-9). In the Middle Ages, lions were the church's ideal protectors because people believed that lions slept with their eyes open.

On the trumeau's right face is a prophet (FIG. 12-13)—identified by some scholars as Jeremiah, and as Isaiah by others—who displays a scroll bearing his prophetic vision. His position below the apparition of Christ as the apocalyptic judge (compare FIG. 12-14) is yet another instance of the pairing of Old and New Testament themes, in keeping with an iconographic tradition established in Early Christian times (see "Old Testament Subjects in Christian Art," page 242). The prophet's figure is very tall and thin, in the manner of the tympanum angels, and, like Matthew's angel, he executes a cross-legged step. The animation of the body reveals the passionate nature of the soul within. The flowing lines of the drapery folds ultimately derive from manuscript illumination (compare FIG. 12-16A) and here play gracefully around the elegant figure. The long, serpentine locks of hair and beard frame an arresting image of the dreaming mystic. The prophet seems entranced by his vision of what is to come, the light of ordinary day unseen by his wide eyes.

The Crusades

In 1095, Pope Urban II (r. 1088–1099) delivered a stirring sermon at the Council of Clermont in which he called for an assault on the Holy Land:

> [Y]our brethren who live in the East are in urgent need of your help . . . [because] the Turks and Arabs have attacked them. . . . They have killed and captured many, and have destroyed the churches . . . I, or rather the Lord, beseech you as Christ's heralds . . . to persuade all people of whatever rank, foot-soldiers and knights, poor and rich, to carry aid promptly to those Christians and to destroy that vile race from the lands of our friends. . . . All who die by the way . . . shall have immediate remission of sins. . . . Let those who go not put off the journey, but rent their lands and collect money for their expenses . . . [and] eagerly set out on the way with God as their guide.*

Between 1095 and 1190, Christians launched three great Crusades from France. The *Crusades* ("taking of the Cross") were mass armed pilgrimages whose stated purpose was to wrest the Christian shrines of the Holy Land from Muslim control. Similar vows bound Crusaders and pilgrims. All those who set out for the Holy Land hoped not only to atone for sins and win salvation but also to glorify God and extend the power of the Church. The joint action of the papacy and the mostly French feudal lords in this type of holy war strengthened papal authority over the long run and created an image of Christian solidarity.

The symbolic embodiment of the joining of religious and secular forces in the Crusades was the Christian warrior—the fighting priest, or the priestly fighter. From the early medieval warrior evolved the Christian knight, who fought for the honor of God rather than in defense of his chieftain. The first and most typical of the crusading knights were the Knights Templar. After the Christian conquest of Jerusalem in 1099, they stationed themselves next to the Dome of the Rock (FIG. 10-2)—that is, on the site of Solomon's Temple, the source of their name. Their mission was to protect pilgrims visiting the recovered Christian shrines. Formally founded in 1118, the Knights Templar order received the blessing of Bernard of Clairvaux, who gave them a rule of organization based on that of his own Cistercians. Bernard justified their militancy by declaring that "the knight of Christ" is "glorified in slaying the infidel . . . because thereby Christ is glorified," and the Christian knight then wins salvation. The Cistercian abbot saw the Crusades as part of the general reform of the Church and as the defense of the supremacy of Christendom. He himself called for the Second Crusade in 1147 at Vézelay (FIG. 12-15). For the Muslims, however, the Crusaders were nothing more than violent invaders who slaughtered the population of Jerusalem (Jewish as well as Muslim) when they took the city in July 1099.

In the end, the Muslims expelled the Christian armies, and the Crusaders failed miserably in their attempt to regain the Holy Land. Today, there are few reminders of the Crusader occupation save for fortified castles such as the Krak des Chevaliers (FIG. 12-15A) near Homs in Syria. But in western Europe, the Crusades had a much greater impact by increasing the power and prestige of the towns. Italian port cities such as Pisa (FIG. 12-29) thrived on the commercial opportunities presented by the transportation of Crusaders overseas. Many communities purchased their charters from the barons who owned their land when the latter needed to finance their campaigns in the Holy Land. This gave rise to a middle class of merchants and artisans to rival the power of the feudal lords and the great monasteries—an economic and societal change of enormous consequence for the later history of Europe.

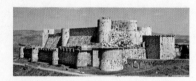

12-15A Krak des Chevaliers, Homs, 1142–1170.

*As recorded by Fulcher of Chartres (1059–ca. 1127). Translated by O. J. Thatcher and E. H. McNeal, quoted in Roberta Anderson and Dominic Aidan Bellenger, eds., *Medieval Worlds: A Sourcebook* (New York: Routledge, 2003), 88–90.

12-15 *Pentecost* and *Mission of the Apostles,* tympanum of the center portal of the narthex of La Madeleine, Vézelay, France, 1120–1132.

In the tympanum of the church most closely associated with the Crusades, light rays emanating from Christ's hands instill the Holy Spirit in the apostles, whose mission is to convert the world's heathens.

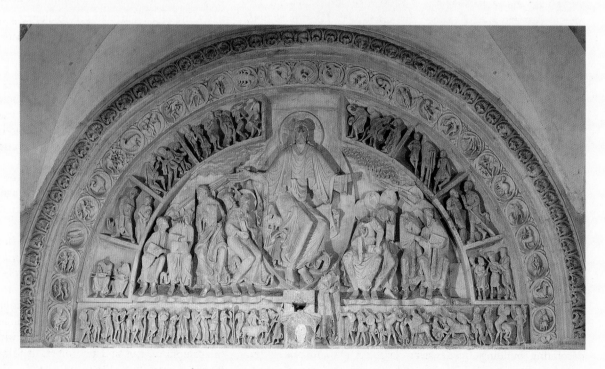

Vézelay. At the same time that Gislebertus and his assistants were at work on the tympanum (FIGS. 12-1 and 12-14), nave (FIG. 12-15B), and north portal (FIG. 12-15C) of Saint-Lazare at Autun, a team of stonecarvers was decorating the nearby church of La Madeleine (Mary Magdalene; FIG. 12-15) at Vézelay. Vézelay is more closely associated with the Crusades (see "The Crusades," page 360) than any other church in Europe. Pope Urban II had intended to call for the launching of the First Crusade at Vézelay in 1095, but he delivered the sermon at Clermont instead. In 1147, at Vézelay, Bernard of Clairvaux called for the Second Crusade, and King Louis VII of France took up the cross there. The Magdalene church at Vézelay was also the place from which King Richard the Lionhearted of England and King Philip Augustus of France set out in 1190 on the Third Crusade.

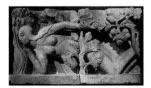

⊕**12-15B** GISLEBERTUS, *Suicide of Judas,* Autun, ca. 1120–1135.

⊕**12-15C** GISLEBERTUS, *Eve,* Autun, ca. 1120–1135.

The major element of the sculptural program of La Madeleine at Vézelay is the tympanum (FIG. 12-15) of the central portal of the church's narthex, in which worshipers entering the church see a representation of the Pentecost and the mission of the apostles. As related in Acts 1:4–9, Christ foretold that the 12 apostles would receive the power of the Holy Spirit and become witnesses of the truth of the Gospels throughout the world. The light rays emanating from Christ's hands represent the instilling of the Holy Spirit in the apostles (Acts 2:1–42) at the Pentecost (the seventh Sunday after Easter). The apostles (see "Early Christian Saints," pages 246–247), holding the Gospel books, receive their spiritual assignment to preach the Gospel to all nations. The Christ figure is a splendid linear design in which the drapery folds shoot out in rays, break into quick zigzag rhythms, and spin into whorls, wonderfully conveying the spiritual light and energy flowing from the Savior over and into the equally animated apostles. The overall composition, as well as the detailed treatment of the figures, contrast with the much more sedate representation of the Second Coming (FIG. 12-11) at Moissac. There, a grid of horizontal and vertical lines contains almost all the figures. The sharp differences between the two tympana highlight the regional diversity of Romanesque art, as well as the personal style of different master sculptors.

The world's heathen, the objects of the apostles' mission, appear on the Vézelay lintel below and in eight compartments around the tympanum. The portrayals of the yet-to-be-converted constitute a medieval anthropological encyclopedia. Present are the legendary giant-eared Panotii of India; Pygmies (who require ladders to mount horses); and a host of other races, some characterized by a dog's head, others by a pig's snout, and still others by flaming hair. The assembly of agitated figures also includes hunchbacks, mutes, the blind, and the lame. Humanity, still suffering, awaits the salvation to come. As at Moissac (FIG. 12-11), Autun (FIG. 12-1), and Saint-Trophîme (FIG. 12-12B) in Arles, the sculptured tympanum of the entrance portal established God's omnipotence and presented the Church as the road to salvation (see "The Rebirth of Large-Scale Sculpture," page 355).

Painting and Other Arts

Unlike the practices of placing vaults over naves and aisles and decorating building facades with large-scale stone reliefs, the art of painting needed no "revival" in the Romanesque period.

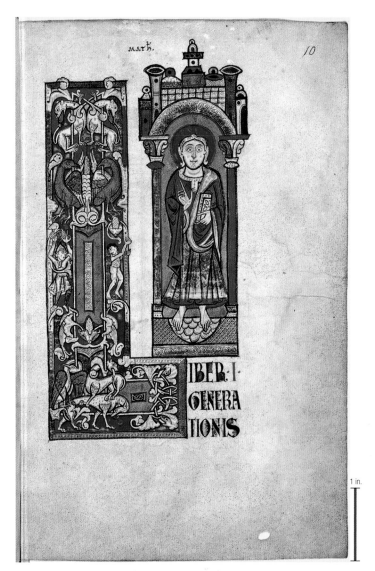

12-16 Initial *L* and Saint Matthew, folio 10 recto of the *Codex Colbertinus,* probably from the abbey of Saint-Pierre, Moissac, France, ca. 1100. Tempera on vellum, $7\frac{1}{2}'' \times 4''$. Bibliothèque nationale de France, Paris.

Probably produced in the Moissac scriptorium, the *Codex Colbertinus* illuminations are stylistically similar to the contemporaneous cloister sculptures (FIG. 12-10A) of that Cluniac monastery.

Monasteries produced illuminated manuscripts in large numbers in the early Middle Ages, and the Roman tradition of mural painting had never died. But the quantity of preserved frescoes and illustrated books from the Romanesque era is unprecedented.

Codex Colbertinus. In addition to sponsoring the costliest sculptural programs of the Romanesque age, Cluniac monasteries produced many of the finest and most ornate illuminated manuscripts, including the *Codex Colbertinus* (FIG. 12-16) and the *Corbie Gospels* (FIG. 12-16A), both of which are closely related stylistically to the relief sculptures of Saint-Pierre at Moissac.

The *Codex Colbertinus* is, in fact, probably the work of scribes and painters in the Moissac scriptorium, and it is contemporaneous with the column capitals and pier reliefs of Saint-Pierre's cloister (FIGS. 12-10 and 12-10A). The

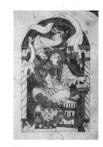

⊕**12-16A** *Corbie Gospels,* ca. 1120.

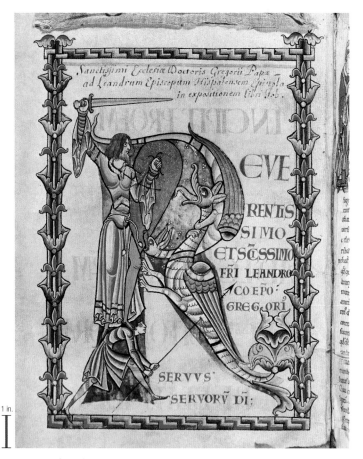

12-17 Initial *R* with knight fighting dragons, folio 4 verso of the *Moralia in Job,* from Cîteaux, France, ca. 1115–1125. Ink and tempera on vellum, 1′ 1¾″ × 9¼″. Bibliothèque municipale, Dijon.

Ornamented initials date to the Hiberno-Saxon era, but this illuminator translated the theme into Romanesque terms. The duel between knight and dragons symbolized a monk's spiritual struggle.

major illuminations in the manuscript are the full pages featuring historiated initials and evangelist portraits. The opening page (FIG. 12-16) of the Gospel according to Saint Matthew includes both the large initial letter *L* of *Liber* ("book") and a generic portrait of the author. Matthew holds a book in his left hand and raises his right hand in a gesture of blessing. He stands frontally between a pair of columns supporting an arch. On one of the Moissac piers, Abbot Durandus (FIG. 12-10A) is similarly framed. The two figures are similar in other respects as well—for example, in the way both artists depicted the robed men with dangling feet.

The letter *L* has no equivalent in the Moissac sculptures, but the real and imaginary animals and birds with long, twisted necks that inhabit the initial have parallels in Saint-Pierre's cloister capitals. The intertwining forms attest to the long afterlife of the animal-and-interlace style of the illuminated books (FIG. 11-7) of the Hiberno-Saxon period.

Moralia in Job. Another major Romanesque scriptorium was at the abbey of Cîteaux, mother church of the Cistercian order. Just before Bernard of Clairvaux joined the monastery in 1112, the monks completed work on an illuminated copy of Saint Gregory's *Moralia in Job*. It is an example of Cistercian illumination that predates Bernard's passionate opposition to monastic figural art, which in 1134 resulted in a Cistercian ban on elaborate paintings in manuscripts as well as sculptural ornamentation in monasteries. In sharp

contrast to the Cluniac monks at Moissac and other monasteries, the Cistercians prohibited full-page illustrations in their books, and even initial letters had to be nonfigurative and of a single color.

The historiated initial illustrated here (FIG. 12-17) clearly would have been in violation of Bernard's ban had it not been painted two decades before his prohibitions took effect. A knight, his squire, and two roaring dragons form an intricate letter *R*, the initial letter of the salutation *Reverentissimo*. This page is the opening of Gregory's letter to "the most revered" Leandro, bishop of Seville, Spain. The knight is a slender, regal figure who raises his shield and sword against the dragons, while the squire, crouching beneath him, runs a lance through one of the monsters. Although the clergy viewed the duel between knight and dragons as an allegory of the spiritual struggle of monks against the Devil for the salvation of souls, Bernard opposed this kind of illumination, just as he condemned carvings of monstrous creatures and "fighting soldiers" on cloister capitals (see "Bernard of Clairvaux," page 356).

Ornamented initials date to the Hiberno-Saxon period (FIG. 11-1), but in the *Moralia in Job,* the artist translated the theme into Romanesque terms. The page with the initial *R* may be a reliable picture of a medieval baron's costume. The typically French Romanesque banding of the torso and partitioning of the folds are evident, but the master painter deftly avoided stiffness and angularity. The partitioning here accentuates the knight's verticality and elegance and the thrusting action of his servant. The flowing sleeves add a spirited flourish to the swordsman's gesture. The knight, handsomely garbed, cavalierly wears no armor and calmly aims a single stroke, unmoved by the ferocious dragons lunging at him.

Saint-Savin-sur-Gartempe. Although the art of fresco painting (see "Fresco," page 428) never died in early medieval Europe, the murals (not true frescoes, however) of the Benedictine abbey church of Saint-Savin-sur-Gartempe have no Carolingian or Ottonian parallels, because the paintings decorate the stone barrel vault of the church's nave (FIG. 12-18). Saint-Savin is a *hall church*—a church where the aisles are approximately the same height as the nave. The tall windows in the aisles of a hall church provide more illumination to the nave than do the smaller windows in churches having low aisles and tribunes. The abundant light streaming into the church may explain why the monks chose to decorate the nave's barrel vault with paintings. (They also painted the nave piers to imitate rich veined marble.)

The subjects of Saint-Savin's nave paintings all come from the Pentateuch—for example, *Tower of Babel* (FIG. 12-18, *right*), in which the Babylonian ziggurat is represented as a Romanesque tower with engaged columns being constructed in the presence of a haloed Christ-like God. New Testament themes appear in the transept, ambulatory, and chapels, where the painters also depicted the lives of Saint Savin and another local saint. The elongated, agitated, cross-legged figures have stylistic affinities both to the reliefs of southern French portals (FIG. 12-13) and to illuminated manuscripts such as the *Corbie Gospels* (FIG. 12-16A) and the *Moralia in Job* (FIG. 12-17).

Santa María de Mur. In the Romanesque period, northern Spain, home to the great pilgrimage church of Saint James (FIG. 12-6B) at Santiago de Compostela, was one of the most important regional artistic centers. In fact, Catalonia, in northeastern Spain, boasts more Romanesque mural paintings today than anywhere else. Especially impressive is the *Christ in Majesty* fresco (FIG. 12-19), now in Boston, that once filled the apse of Santa María de Mur, a monastery church not far from Lérida. The formality, symmetry, and placement of the figures are Byzantine (compare FIGS. 9-16 and

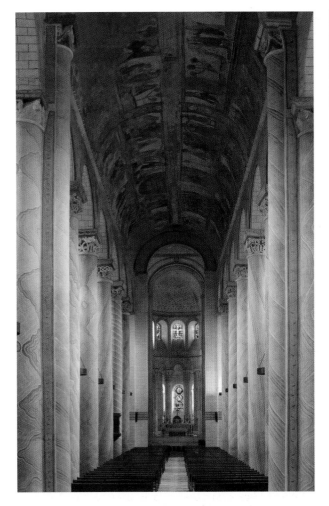

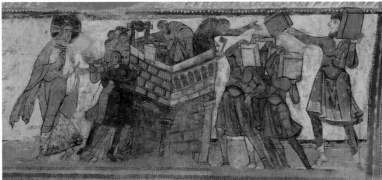

12-18 Nave (*left*; looking east) and detail (*above*) of *Tower of Babel* on the painted vault of the abbey church of Saint-Savin, Saint-Savin-sur-Gartempe, France, late 11th century.

Saint-Savin is a hall church with aisles approximately the same height as the nave. The tall aisle windows provide ample illumination for the Old Testament paintings on the nave's barrel vault.

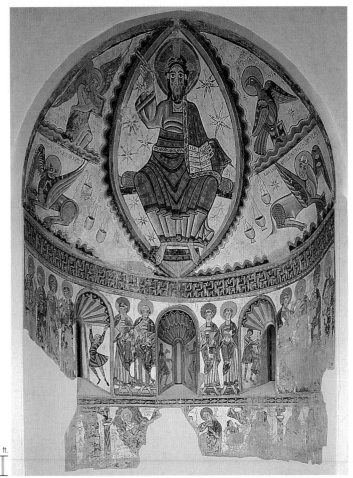

9-28), but the Spanish artist rejected Byzantine mosaic in favor of direct painting on plaster-coated walls.

The iconographic scheme in the semidome of the apse echoes the themes of the stone reliefs in the tympana of contemporaneous French (FIGS. 12-1 and 12-12B) and Spanish Romanesque church portals. The signs of the four evangelists flank Christ in a star-strewn mandorla. Seven lamps between Christ and the evangelists' signs symbolize the seven Christian communities where Saint John addressed his revelation of the Apocalypse at the beginning of his book (Rev. 1:4, 12, 20). Below stand apostles, paired off in formal frontality, as in the Monreale Cathedral apse (FIG. 9-27). The Spanish painter rendered the principal figures with partitioning of the drapery into volumes, here and there made tubular by local shading, and stiffened the irregular shapes of pliable cloth into geometric patterns. The overall effect is one of simple, strong, and even blunt directness of statement, reinforced by harsh, bright color, appropriate for a powerful icon.

Morgan Madonna. Despite the widespread use of stone relief sculptures to adorn church portals, resistance to the creation of statues in the round—in any material—continued in the Romanesque period. The avoidance of anything that might be construed as an idol was still the rule, in keeping with the Second Commandment. Freestanding statues of Christ, the Virgin Mary, and the saints were still quite rare two centuries after Archbishop Gero commissioned a life-size painted wood figure of the crucified Christ (FIG. 11-30) for Cologne Cathedral. The veneration of relics, however, brought with it a demand for small-scale images of the holy family and saints to be placed on the chapel altars of the churches along the pilgrimage roads. Reliquaries in the form of saints (FIG. 12-2) or parts of saints (FIG. 12-28), tabletop crucifixes, and wood devotional figurines began to be produced in great numbers.

One popular type, a specialty of the workshops of Auvergne, France, was a painted wood statuette depicting the Virgin Mary

12-19 *Christ in Majesty,* apse, Santa María de Mur, near Lérida, Spain, mid-12th century. Fresco, 24′ high. Museum of Fine Arts, Boston.

In this fresco, formerly in the apse of Santa María de Mur, Christ appears in a mandorla between the four evangelists' signs. The fresco resembles French and Spanish Romanesque tympanum reliefs.

1 ft.

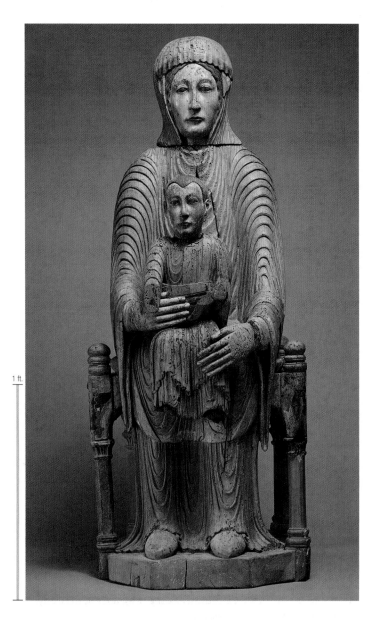

The veneration of relics created a demand for small-scale images of the holy family and saints to be placed on chapel altars. This painted wood statuette depicts the Virgin as the "throne of wisdom."

with the Christ Child in her lap. The *Morgan Madonna* (FIG. 12-20), so named because it once belonged to the American financier and collector J. Pierpont Morgan, is one example. The type, known as the *sedes sapientiae* (Latin, "throne of wisdom"), is a western European freestanding version of the Byzantine Theotokos theme popular in icons and mosaics (FIGS. 9-19 and 9-20). Christ holds a Bible in his left hand and raises his right arm in blessing (both hands are broken off). He is the embodiment of the divine wisdom contained in holy scripture. His seated mother is in turn the throne of wisdom because her lap is the Christ Child's throne. As in Byzantine art, both Madonna and Child sit rigidly upright and are strictly frontal, emotionless figures. But the intimate scale, the gesture of benediction, the once-bright coloring of the garments, and the soft modeling of the Virgin's face make this mother-and-son pair seem much less remote than its Byzantine counterparts.

HOLY ROMAN EMPIRE

The Romanesque successors of the Ottonians were the Salians (r. 1027–1125), a dynasty of Franks. They ruled an empire corresponding roughly to present-day Germany and the Lombard region of northern Italy (MAP 12-1). Like their predecessors, the Salian emperors were important patrons of art and architecture, although the monasteries of the Holy Roman Empire, as elsewhere in Romanesque Europe, remained great centers of artistic production.

Architecture

Traditional histories of Romanesque art and architecture usually present France as the center of innovation and other regions as peripheral. But, especially in terms of the technology of constructing large buildings, the architects of the Holy Roman Empire seem to have led the way (see "How to Illuminate a Nave," page 365).

Speyer. Construction of Speyer Cathedral (FIGS. 12-21 and 12-22) in the German Rhineland, far from the pilgrimage routes of southern France and northern Spain, began in 1030. The church was the burial place of the Holy Roman emperors until the beginning of the 12th century, and funding for the building campaign came from imperial patrons, not traveling pilgrims and local landowners. Speyer, like all cathedrals, was also the seat (*cathedra* in Latin) of the powerful local bishop. In its earliest form, the church, begun by Conrad II (r. 1027–1039) when Speyer had a population of only 500, was a timber-roofed structure. When Henry IV (r. 1056–1105)

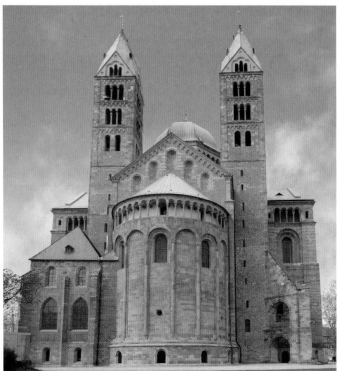

12-21 **East end of Speyer Cathedral, Speyer, Germany, ca. 1082–1105.**

Speyer Cathedral is the largest Romanesque church in the world. Its east end features twin 234-foot spires, blind windows and arches, and open arcuated galleries in the apse and transept wings.

How to Illuminate a Nave

The barrel-vaulted naves of Saint James (FIG. 12-6B) at Santiago de Compostela, Saint-Sernin (FIG. 12-7) at Toulouse, Cluny III (FIG. 12-8), and Notre-Dame (FIG. 12-10B) at Fontenay admirably met French and Spanish Romanesque architects' goals of making the house of the Lord beautiful and providing excellent acoustics for church services. In addition, they were relatively fireproof compared with timber-roofed structures such as Saint-Étienne (FIG. 12-3) at Vignory (see "Stone Vaulting in Romanesque Churches," page 354). But the barrel vaults often failed in one critical requirement: they did not provide adequate lighting for the nave.

Due to the great outward thrust that barrel vaults exert along their full length, even when pointed (FIGS. 12-8 and 12-10B) instead of semicircular, a clerestory is difficult to construct. (The Santiago de Compostela, Toulouse, and Fontenay designers did not even attempt to introduce a clerestory, although their counterparts at Cluny III succeeded.) In designing churches, the central aim of Romanesque architects in the Holy Roman Empire (and in Normandy and England; FIGS. 12-34 and 12-36) was to develop a masonry vault system that admitted light and was also aesthetically pleasing.

Covering the nave with groin vaults instead of barrel vaults became the solution. Ancient Roman builders had used the groin vault widely, because they realized that its concentration of thrusts at four supporting points enabled them to introduce clerestory windows (FIGS. 7-6, 7-66, and 7-74). Concrete, which could be poured into forms, where it solidified into a homogeneous mass (see "Roman Concrete Construction," page 186), made the gigantic Roman groin vaults possible. But the technique of mixing concrete had been forgotten in the Middle Ages.

The technical problems of building groin vaults of cut stone and heavy rubble, which have very little cohesive quality, at first limited their use to the covering of small areas, such as the individual bays of the aisles of the pilgrimage churches at Santiago de Compostela (FIG. 12-6B) and Toulouse (FIG. 12-7). During the 11th century, however, masons in the Holy Roman Empire at Speyer (FIGS. 12-21 and 12-22) and elsewhere, using cut stone blocks held together with mortar, developed a groin vault of impressive dimensions.

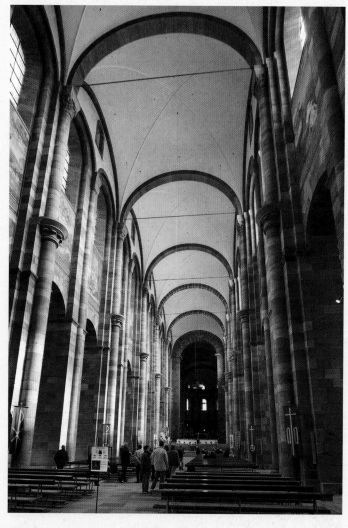

12-22 Interior of Speyer Cathedral (looking east), Speyer, Germany, begun 1030; nave vaults, ca. 1082–1105.

The imperial cathedral at Speyer is one of the earliest examples of the use of groin vaulting in a nave. Groin vaults made possible the insertion of large clerestory windows above the nave arcade.

rebuilt the cathedral between 1082 and 1105, his masons covered the nave (FIG. 12-22) with stone groin vaults. The large clerestory windows above the nave arcade provided ample light to the interior. Architectural historians disagree about where the first comprehensive use of groin vaulting occurred in Romanesque times, and nationalistic concerns sometimes color the debate. But no one doubts that the large groin vaults covering the nave of Speyer Cathedral represent one of the most daring and successful engineering experiments of the time. The nave is 45 feet wide, and the crowns of the vaults are 107 feet above the floor.

Speyer Cathedral employs an alternate-support system in the nave, as in the Ottonian churches of Saint Cyriakus (FIG. 11-23) at Gernrode and Saint Michael's (FIGS. 11-25 and 11-25A) at Hildesheim. At Speyer, however, the alternation continues all the way up into the vaults, with the nave's more richly molded compound piers marking the corners of the groin vaults. Speyer's interior shows the same striving for height and the same compartmentalized effect seen at Santiago de Compostela (FIG. 12-6B) and Toulouse (FIG. 12-7), but by virtue of the alternate-support system, the rhythm of the Speyer nave is a little more complex. Because each compartment has its own vault, the impression of a sequence of vertical spatial blocks is even more convincing.

The exterior (FIG. 12-21) of Speyer Cathedral, with its multiple towers reaching to the sky, reveals the heritage of Ottonian church design (compare FIGS. 11-22, 11-24, and 11-29A). Constructed of red sandstone ashlar blocks from Rhineland quarries, the cathedral is the largest Romanesque church in the world, befitting the grandiose ambitions of the church's imperial patrons. Speyer Cathedral's east end is noteworthy not only for its twin 234-foot spires echoing the pair on the westwork at the opposite end of the church but also for the pleasing and much-emulated combination of blind arcades and open arcuated galleries in the apse and two transept wings.

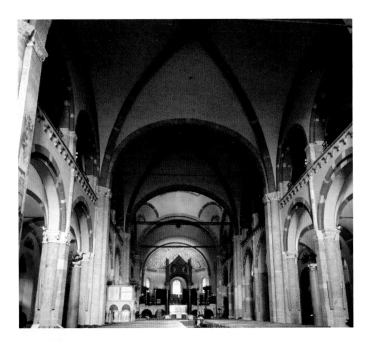

12-23 Interior of Sant'Ambrogio (looking east), Milan, Italy, late 11th to early 12th century.

Sant'Ambrogio reveals the architectural ties between Lombardy and Germany. Each groin-vaulted nave bay corresponds to two aisle bays. The alternate-support system complements this modular plan.

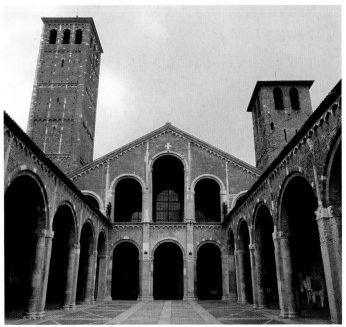

12-24 Atrium of Sant'Ambrogio (looking east), Milan, Italy, late 11th to early 12th century.

With its atrium and low, broad proportions, Sant'Ambrogio recalls Early Christian basilicas, but two prominent bell towers flank the narthex. There is also an octagonal tower over the nave's east end.

Milan. After Charlemagne crushed the Lombards in 773, German kings ruled Lombardy, and the Rhineland and northern Italy cross-fertilized each other artistically. No scholarly agreement exists as to which source of artistic influence, the German or the Lombard, was dominant in the Romanesque age. The question, no doubt, will remain the subject of controversy until the construction date of Sant'Ambrogio (FIGS. 12-23 and 12-24) in Milan can be established unequivocally. The church, erected in honor of Saint Ambrose (d. 397), Milan's first bishop, is the central monument of Lombard Romanesque architecture. Some scholars think that the church was a prototype for Speyer Cathedral, but Sant'Ambrogio is a remarkable building whether or not it was a model for Speyer's builders.

The Milanese church has a nave (FIG. 12-23) and two aisles, but no transept. Each bay consists of a full square in the nave flanked by two small squares in each aisle, all covered with groin vaults. The main vaults are slightly domical, rising higher than the transverse arches. The windows in the octagonal dome over the last bay—probably here, as elsewhere, a reference to the dome of Heaven—provide the major light source for the otherwise rather dark interior. (The building lacks a clerestory.) The emphatic alternate-support system perfectly reflects the geometric regularity of the plan. The lighter pier moldings stop at the gallery level, and the heavier ones rise to support the main vaults. At Sant'Ambrogio, the compound piers even continue into the ponderous vaults, which have supporting arches, or *ribs,* along their groins. The groin vaults of Sant'Ambrogio are one of the first instances in the history of architecture of *rib vaulting,* a key characteristic of mature Romanesque and later Gothic churches (see "The Gothic Rib Vault," page 387).

Sant'Ambrogio is also noteworthy because it has an *atrium* (FIG. 12-24) in the Early Christian tradition (FIGS. 8-9 and 8-10), one of the last to be built, and a two-story narthex pierced by arches on both levels. Two *campaniles* (Italian, "bell towers") join the building on the west. The shorter one dates to the 11th century,

and the taller north campanile is a 12th-century addition. Over the nave's east end is an octagonal tower that recalls the crossing towers of Ottonian churches (FIG. 11-24).

The regional diversity of Romanesque architecture quickly becomes evident by comparing the proportions of Sant'Ambrogio with those of Speyer Cathedral (FIGS. 12-21 and 12-22), Saint James (FIG. 12-6B) at Santiago de Compostela, and Saint-Sernin (FIGS. 12-5 and 12-7) at Toulouse. The Milanese building does not aspire to the soaring height of the French, Spanish, and German churches. Save for the later of the two towers, Sant'Ambrogio's proportions are low and broad and remain close to those of Early Christian basilicas. Italian architects, even those working within the orbit of the Holy Roman Empire, had firm roots in the venerable Early Christian style and never sought the verticality found in northern European architecture, not even during the Gothic period.

Painting and Other Arts

The number and variety of illuminated manuscripts dating to the Romanesque era attest to the great demand for illustrated religious tomes in abbeys throughout Europe. The extraordinarily productive scribes and painters who created these books were almost exclusively monks and nuns working in the scriptoria of those same isolated religious communities. Some of the best manuscripts, however, were produced for the nobility, as during the Carolingian and Ottonian eras.

Hildegard of Bingen. Among the most interesting German religious manuscripts is the *Scivias* (*Know the Ways* [*Scite vias*] *of God*) of Hildegard of Bingen. Hildegard was a nun who eventually became the abbess of the convent at Disibodenberg in the Rhineland (see "Romanesque Countesses, Queens, and Nuns," page 367). The manuscript, lost in 1945, exists today only in a facsimile (FIG. 12-25). The

Romanesque Countesses, Queens, and Nuns

Romanesque Europe was still a man's world, but women could and did have power and influence. Countess Matilda of Canossa (1046–1115), who ruled Tuscany after 1069, was sole heiress of vast holdings in northern Italy. She was a key figure in the political struggle between the popes and the German emperors who controlled Lombardy. With unflagging resolution, she defended the reforms of Pope Gregory VII (r. 1073–1085) and at her death willed most of her lands to the papacy.

More famous and more powerful was Eleanor of Aquitaine (1122–1204), wife of Henry II of England. She married Henry after the annulment of her marriage to Louis VII, king of France. She was queen of France for 15 years and queen of England for 35 years. During that time she bore three daughters and five sons. Two became kings: Richard I (the Lionhearted) and John. She supported her sons when they rebelled against their father, for which Henry imprisoned her. Released at Henry's death, she lived on as dowager queen, managing England's government and King John's holdings in France.

Of quite different stamp was Hildegard of Bingen (1098–1179), the most prominent nun of the 12th century and one of the greatest religious figures of the Middle Ages. Hildegard was born into an aristocratic family that owned large estates in the German Rhineland. At a very early age, she began to have visions. When she was eight, her parents placed her in the Benedictine *double monastery* (for monks and nuns) at Disibodenberg. She became a nun at 15. In 1141, God instructed Hildegard to disclose her visions to the world:

> It happened that, in the eleven hundred and forty-first year of the Incarnation of the Son of God, Jesus Christ, when I was forty-two years and seven months old, Heaven was opened and a fiery light of exceeding brilliance came and permeated my whole brain, and inflamed my whole heart and my whole breast, not like a burning but like a warming flame, as the sun warms anything its rays touch. And immediately I knew the meaning of the exposition of the Scriptures, namely the Psalter, the Gospel and the other catholic volumes of both the Old and the New Testaments. . . . I heard a voice from Heaven saying to me, "Cry out therefore, and write thus!"*

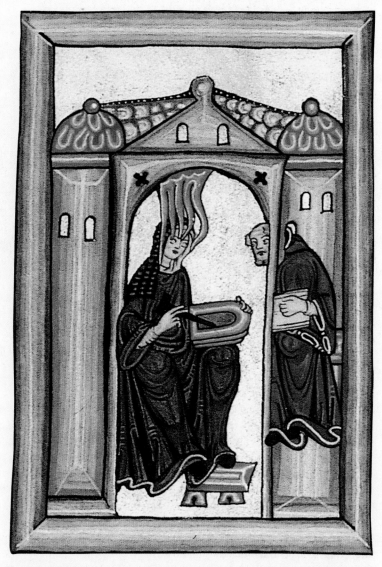

12-25 **Hildegard reveals her visions, detail of a facsimile of a lost folio in the Rupertsberger *Scivias* by Hildegard of Bingen, from Trier or Bingen, Germany, ca. 1150–1179. Abbey of St. Hildegard, Rüdesheim/Eibingen.**

Hildegard of Bingen, the most prominent nun of her time, experienced divine visions, shown here as five tongues of fire entering her brain. She also composed music and wrote scientific treatises.

Before then, Hildegard had revealed her visions only to close confidants at the monastery. One of them was the monk Volmar, and Hildegard chose to dictate her visions to him for posterity (FIG. 12-25). No less a figure than Bernard of Clairvaux certified in 1147 that her visions were authentic, and Archbishop Heinrich of Mainz joined in the endorsement. In 1148, the Cistercian pope Eugenius III (r. 1145–1153) formally authorized Hildegard "in the name of Christ and Saint Peter to publish all that she had learned from the Holy Spirit." At this time, Hildegard became the abbess of a new convent built for her near Bingen. As reports of Hildegard's visions spread, kings, popes, barons, and prelates sought her counsel. All of them were attracted by her spiritual insight into the Christian faith. In addition to her visionary works—the most important of which is the *Scivias*—Hildegard wrote two scientific

treatises. *Physica* is a study of the natural world, and *Causae et curae* (*Causes and Cures*) is a medical encyclopedia. Hildegard also composed the music and wrote the lyrics of 77 songs, which appeared under the title *Symphonia*.

Hildegard was the most famous Romanesque nun, but she was by no means the only learned woman of her age. A younger contemporary, Herrad (d. 1195), abbess of Hohenburg, was also the author of an important medieval encyclopedia. Herrad's *Hortus deliciarum* (*Garden of Delights*) is a history of the world intended for instructing the nuns under her supervision, but it reached a much wider audience.

*Translated by Mother Columba Hart and Jane Bishop, in Elizabeth Spearing, ed., *Medieval Writings on Female Spirituality* (New York: Penguin, 2002), 9, 11.

original probably was written and illuminated at the monastery of Saint Matthias at Trier between 1150 and Hildegard's death in 1179, but it is possible that Hildegard supervised production of the book at Bingen. The *Scivias* contains a record of Hildegard's vision of the divine order of the cosmos and of humankind's place in it. The vision came to her as a fiery light pouring into her brain from the open vault of Heaven.

On the opening page (FIG. 12-25) of the *Scivias,* Hildegard sits within the monastery walls, her feet resting on a footstool. The representation of Hildegard writing echoes those of the evangelists in the *Coronation Gospels* (FIG. 11-13) and *Ebbo Gospels* (FIG. 11-14). The *Scivias* page is a link in a chain of author portraits with roots in classical antiquity (FIG. 7-25). The Romanesque artist showed Hildegard experiencing her divine vision by depicting five long tongues of fire emanating from above and entering her brain, just as she describes the experience in the accompanying text. Using a wax tablet resting on her left knee, Hildegard immediately sets down what has been revealed to her. Nearby, the monk Volmar, Hildegard's confessor, stands ready to copy into a book everything she wrote. Here, in a singularly dramatic context, is a picture of the essential nature of ancient and medieval book manufacture—individual scribes copying and recopying texts by hand (compare FIG. 11-11). The most labor-intensive and costliest texts, such as Hildegard's *Scivias,* also were illuminated (see "Manuscript Illumination," page 252). They required the collaboration of skilled painters—for example, the Weissenau monk RUFILLUS, who placed a portrait of himself at work (FIG. 12-25A) in a *passional* (book of saints' lives).

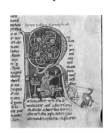

🔎 **12-25A**

RUFILLUS, initial *R,* ca. 1170–1200.

Gospels of Henry the Lion.

Until his cousin Emperor Frederick Barbarossa (r. 1152–1190) confiscated his vast landholdings, the Guelph nobleman Henry the Lion (1129–1195), duke of Saxony from 1142 to 1180 and duke of Bavaria from 1156 to 1180, was one of the most powerful figures in the Holy Roman Empire. Best known for his crusades against the Slavs and his founding of Munich, Henry was the builder of Brunswick Cathedral and a great patron of the arts. The *Gospels of Henry the Lion,* which he commissioned in 1188 for the high altar of the cathedral, contains 24 full-page paintings among its 50 illuminations. Produced at the monastery Henry established at Helmarshausen, his *Gospels* carry on the imperial tradition of the Ottonians (FIG. 11-32). One page (FIG. 12-26) commemorates Henry's marriage on February 1, 1168, to Matilda Plantagenet (1156–1189), daughter of King Henry II of England and Eleanor of Aquitaine—or, more precisely, the couple's spiritual coronation. From above, Christ presides over the bestowing of crowns, which are placed on the heads of Henry and Matilda by two hands emerging from Heaven. The duke and duchess hold jeweled crosses and wear rich robes. Flanking them are Henry's Guelph ancestors and English royalty. Among the saints witnessing the coronation is Thomas Becket. On the dedication page of the manuscript, the scribe describes Henry as "the descendant of Charlemagne. To him alone would England entrust Matilda." In the richness of its coloration and the complexity of its composition, Henry's coronation page has few equals in Romanesque manuscript painting.

Rainer of Huy.

Among Henry the Lion's other commissions was an over-life-size bronze statue of a lion for his capital at

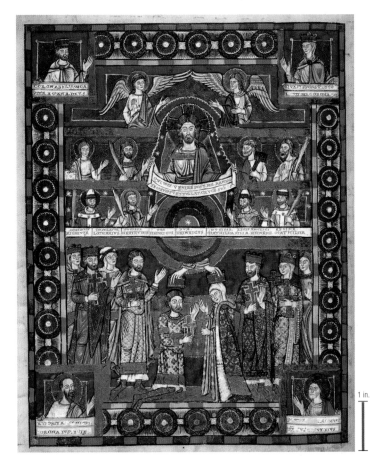

1 in.

12-26 **Coronation of Henry and Matilda, folio 171 verso of the** ***Gospels of Henry the Lion,*** **from the Benedictine abbey at Helmarshausen, Germany, 1188. Tempera on parchment, 9″ × 6″. Herzog August Bibliothek, Wolfenbüttel.**

Two hands from Heaven crown Henry, duke of Saxony and Bavaria, and Matilda, daughter of Henry II of England, in the presence of Guelph and English ancestors and of saints, including Thomas Becket.

Brunswick. Indeed, in the Romanesque era, skilled metalworkers were much in demand in the Holy Roman Empire. One whose name is recorded was RAINER OF HUY, a bronzeworker from the Meuse River region in Belgium, an area renowned for its metalwork. Art historians have attributed an 1118 bronze baptismal font (FIG. 12-27) to him. Made for Notre-Dame-des-Fonts in Liège, the bronze basin rests on the foreparts of a dozen oxen. The oxen refer to the "molten sea . . . on twelve oxen" cast in bronze for King Solomon's temple (1 Kings 7:23–25). The Old Testament story prefigured Jesus's baptism (medieval scholars equated the oxen with the 12 apostles), which is appropriately the central scene on the Romanesque font.

In his work, Rainer, like so many earlier artists in the Holy Roman Empire beginning in Carolingian times, revived the classical style and the classical spirit. His sculpted figures are softly rounded, with idealized bodies and faces and heavy, clinging drapery. Rainer even represented one figure (at the left in FIG. 12-27) in a three-quarter view from the rear, a popular motif in classical art. Some of the figures, including Jesus himself, are undressed, which is also common in Greco-Roman art, whereas nudity is very rare in the art of the Middle Ages. Adam and Eve (FIGS. 8-8, 11-27, 12-15C, and 12-31) are exceptions, but medieval artists usually depicted the first man and woman as embarrassed by their nudity, the opposite of the high value the classical world placed on the beauty of the human body.

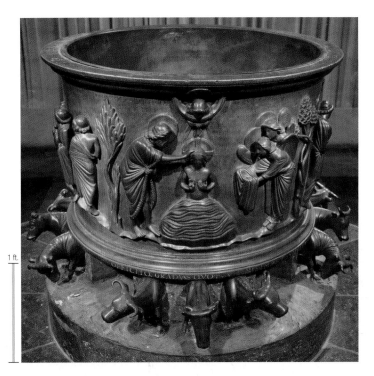

12-27 RAINER OF HUY, *Baptism of Christ,* baptismal font from Notre-Dame-des-Fonts, Liège, Belgium, 1118. Bronze, 2′ 1″ high. Saint-Barthélémy, Liège.

In the work of Rainer of Huy, the classical style and the classical spirit lived on in the Holy Roman Empire. His Liège baptismal font features idealized figures and even a nude representation of Jesus.

Saint Alexander. The reliquaries of Saint Faith (FIG. 12-2) and of Saint Alexander (FIG. 12-28), a hallowed pope (Alexander II, r. 1061–1073), are among the most sumptuous of the Romanesque age, a time when churches vied to possess the most important relics and often expended large sums on their containers (see "The Veneration of Relics," page 349). Made in 1145 for Abbot Wibald of Stavelot in Belgium, Saint Alexander's reliquary takes the form of an almost-life-size head, fashioned in beaten (repoussé) silver with bronze gilding for the hair. The idealized head resembles portraits of youthful Roman emperors such as Augustus (FIG. I-10) and Constantine (FIG. 7-78), and the Romanesque metalworker may have used an ancient sculpture as a model. The saint wears a collar of jewels and enamel plaques around his neck. Enamels and gems also adorn the box on which the head is mounted. The reliquary rests on four bronze dragons—mythical animals of the kind populating Romanesque cloister capitals. Not surprisingly, Bernard of Clairvaux was as critical of lavish church furnishings like the reliquaries of Saints Faith and Alexander as he was of Romanesque cloister sculpture:

> [Men's] eyes are fixed on relics covered with gold and purses are opened. The thoroughly beautiful image of some male or female saint is exhibited and that saint is believed to be the more holy the more highly colored the image is. People rush to kiss it, they are invited to donate, and they admire the beautiful more than they venerate the sacred. . . . O vanity of vanities, but no more vain than insane! The Church . . . dresses its stones in gold and it abandons its children naked. It serves the eyes of the rich at the expense of the poor.[4]

The central plaque on the front of the Stavelot reliquary depicts Pope Alexander, who was *canonized* (declared a saint) after his

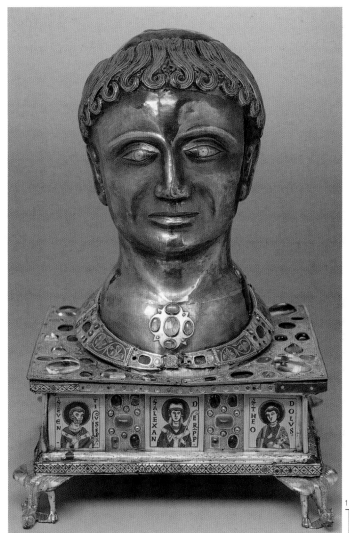

12-28 Head reliquary of Saint Alexander, from the abbey church, Stavelot, Belgium, 1145. Silver repoussé (partly gilt), gilt bronze, gems, pearls, and enamel, 1′ 5½″ high. Musées royaux d'Art et d'Histoire, Brussels.

The Stavelot reliquary is typical in its use of costly materials. The combination of an idealized classical head with Byzantine-style enamels underscores the stylistic diversity of Romanesque art.

death. Saints Eventius and Theodolus flank him. The nine plaques on the other three sides represent female allegorical figures—Wisdom, Piety, and Humility among them. Although a local artist produced these enamels in the Meuse River region, the models were surely Byzantine. Saint Alexander's reliquary underscores the multiple sources of Romanesque art, as well as its stylistic diversity. Not since antiquity had people journeyed as extensively as they did in the Romanesque period, and artists regularly saw works of wide geographic origin. Abbot Wibald himself exemplified the well-traveled 12th-century clergyman. He was abbot of Montecassino in southern Italy and took part in the Second Crusade. Frederick Barbarossa sent him to Constantinople to arrange Frederick's wedding to the niece of the Byzantine emperor Manuel Comnenus. (Two centuries before, another German emperor, Otto II, married the Byzantine princess Theophanu, who promoted Byzantine style in the Holy Roman Empire; see "Theophanu," page 342.)

ITALY

Nowhere is the regional diversity of Romanesque art and architecture more readily apparent than in Italy, where the ancient Roman and Early Christian heritage was strongest. Although Tuscany—the ancient Etruscan heartland (MAP 6-1)—and other regions south of Lombardy were part of the territory of the Salian emperors, Italy south of Milan represented a distinct artistic zone during the Romanesque period.

Architecture and Architectural Sculpture

Italian Romanesque architects adhered closely to the Early Christian basilican type of church, and consequently designed buildings that were for the most part structurally less experimental than those erected in Germany and Lombardy.

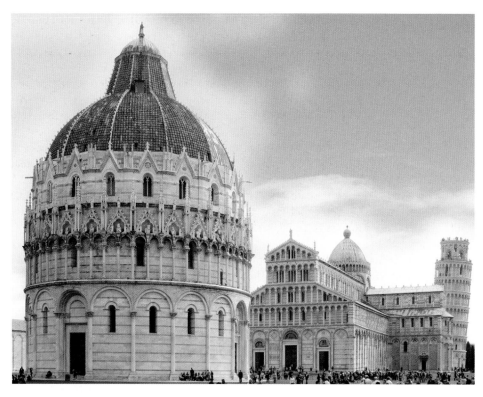

12-29 Cathedral complex (looking northeast), Pisa, Italy; cathedral begun 1063; baptistery begun 1153; campanile (FIG. 12-29A) begun 1174.

Pisa's cathedral more closely resembles Early Christian basilicas than structurally more experimental French and German Romanesque churches. Separate bell towers and baptisteries are Italian features.

Pisa. The cathedral complex (FIG. 12-29) at Pisa dramatically testifies to the prosperity the busy maritime city enjoyed. The spoils of a naval victory over the Saracens off Palermo in Sicily in 1062 provided the funds for the Pisan building program. The cathedral, its freestanding bell tower, and the baptistery, where infants and converts were initiated into the Christian community, present a rare opportunity to study a coherent group of three Romanesque buildings. Save for the upper portion of the baptistery, with its remodeled Gothic exterior, the three structures are stylistically homogeneous.

Construction of Pisa Cathedral began first—in 1063, the same year that work began on San Marco (FIG. 9-26) in Venice, another powerful maritime city. The cathedral is large, with a nave and four aisles, and is one of the most impressive and majestic Romanesque churches. The Pisans, according to a document of the time, wanted their bishop's church not only to be a monument to the glory of God but also to bring credit to the city. At first glance, Pisa Cathedral resembles an Early Christian basilica with a timber roof, columnar arcade, and clerestory. But the broadly projecting transept with apses, the crossing dome, and the facade's multiple arcaded galleries distinguish it as Romanesque. So too does the rich marble *incrustation* (wall decoration consisting of bright panels of different colors, as in the Pantheon's interior, FIG. 7-51). The cathedral's campanile, detached in the standard Italian fashion, is Pisa's famous Leaning Tower (FIG. 12-29A). Graceful arcaded galleries mark the tower's stages and repeat the cathedral facade's motif, effectively relating the round campanile to its mother building.

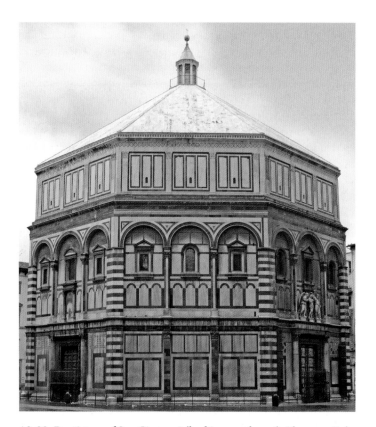

12-29A Leaning Tower, Pisa, begun 1174.

Florence. The public understandably thinks of Florence as a Renaissance city (MAP 21-1), but it was already an important independent city-state in the Romanesque period. The gem of

12-30 Baptistery of San Giovanni (looking northwest), Florence, Italy, dedicated 1059.

The Florentine baptistery is a domed octagon descended from Roman and Early Christian central-plan buildings. The distinctive Tuscan Romanesque marble paneling stems from Roman wall designs.

Florentine Romanesque architecture is the baptistery (FIG. 12-30) of San Giovanni (Saint John), the city's patron saint. Pope Nicholas II (r. 1059–1061) dedicated the building in 1059. It thus predates Pisa's baptistery (FIG. 12-29, *left*), but construction of the Florentine baptistery continued into the next century. Both baptisteries face their city's cathedral. Freestanding baptisteries are unusual, and these Tuscan examples reflect the significance the Florentines and Pisans attached to baptismal rites. On the day of a newborn child's anointment, the citizenry gathered in the baptistery to welcome a new member into their community. Baptisteries therefore were important civic, as well as religious, structures. Some of the most renowned artists of the late Middle Ages and the Renaissance provided the Florentine and Pisan baptisteries with pulpits (FIG. 14-2), bronze doors (FIGS. 14-20, 21-2, 21-3, 21-9, and 21-10), and mosaics.

The simple and serene classicism of San Giovanni's design recalls ancient Roman architecture. The baptistery stands in a direct line of descent from the Pantheon (FIGS. 7-49 and 7-51); imperial mausolea (such as Diocletian's; FIG. 7-73, *center right*); the Early Christian Santa Costanza (FIGS. 8-12 and 8-13) and Anastasis Rotunda (FIG. 8-8C); the Byzantine San Vitale (FIGS. 9-1 and 9-10); and other Roman and Christian central-plan structures, including Charlemagne's Palatine Chapel (FIGS. 11-17 and 11-18) at Aachen. The distinctive Tuscan Romanesque marble incrustation adorning the walls of Florence's baptistery and the slightly later church of San Miniato al Monte (FIGS. 12-30A and 12-30B) stems ultimately from Roman wall designs (FIGS. 7-17 and 7-51). (The ancient tradition of decorating walls with frescoes also survived in Romanesque

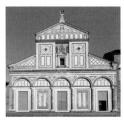

12-30A Façade, San Miniato al Monte, Florence, begun ca. 1062.

Italy—for example, at Sant'Angelo in Formis, FIG. 12-30C.) The simple oblong and arcuated panels of the baptistery assert the building's structural lines and its elevation levels. In plan, San Giovanni is a domed octagon, wrapped on the exterior by an elegant arcade, three arches to a bay. It has three entrances, one each on the north, south, and east sides. On the west side, an oblong sanctuary replaces the original semicircular apse. The domical vault is some 90 feet in diameter, its construction a feat remarkable for its time.

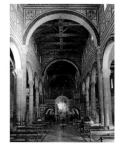

12-30B Nave, San Miniato al Monte, Florence, ca. 1062–1090.

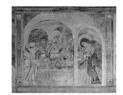

12-30C Sant'Angelo in Formis, near Capua, ca. 1085.

Modena. Although Italian Romanesque churches are far more conservative structurally than their counterparts in France, Spain, and the Holy Roman Empire, church officials in all regions adorned the facades of their buildings with stone sculpture. In fact, one of the first examples of fully developed narrative relief sculpture in Romanesque art is the marble frieze (FIG. 12-31) on the facade of Modena Cathedral in northern Italy. Carved around 1110, it represents scenes from Genesis set against an architectural backdrop of a type common on Roman and Early Christian sarcophagi, which were plentiful in the region. The segment illustrated here, *Creation and Temptation of Adam and Eve* (Gen. 2, 3:1–8), repeats the theme employed almost exactly a century earlier on Bishop Bernward's bronze doors (FIGS. 11-26 and 11-27) at Hildesheim. At Modena, as at Saint Michael's and Saint-Lazare at Autun (FIG. 12-15C), the faithful entered the Lord's house with a reminder of Original Sin and the suggestion that the only path to salvation is through Christ.

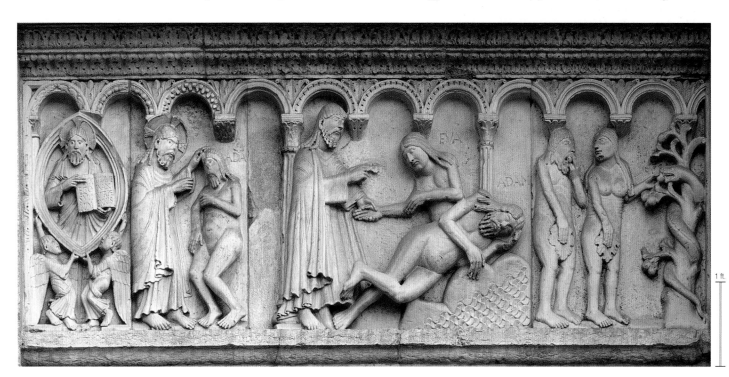

12-31 WILIGELMO, *Creation and Temptation of Adam and Eve,* detail of the frieze on the west facade, Modena Cathedral, Modena, Italy, ca. 1110. Marble, 3′ high.

For Modena's cathedral, Wiligelmo represented scenes from Genesis against an architectural backdrop of a type common on Roman and Early Christian sarcophagi, which were plentiful in the area.

On the Modena frieze, Christ is at the far left, framed by a mandorla held up by angels—a variation on the motif of the Saint-Sernin ambulatory relief (FIG. 12-9; compare FIG. 12-9A and the Autun tympanum, FIG. 12-14). The creation of Adam, then Eve, and the serpent's temptation of Eve are to the right. The relief carving is high, and some parts are almost entirely in the round. The frieze is the work of a master craftsman whose name, WILIGELMO, appears in an inscription on another relief on the facade. There he boasts, "Among sculptors, your work shines forth, Wiligelmo." The inscription is also an indication of how proud Wiligelmo's patrons were to obtain the services of such an accomplished sculptor for their city's cathedral, as doubtless were Gislebertus's patrons at Autun (FIGS. 12-1 and 12-14), who also displayed the sculptor's name on their church's facade.

Fidenza. The reawakening of interest in stone sculpture in the round also is evident in northern Italy, where the sculptor

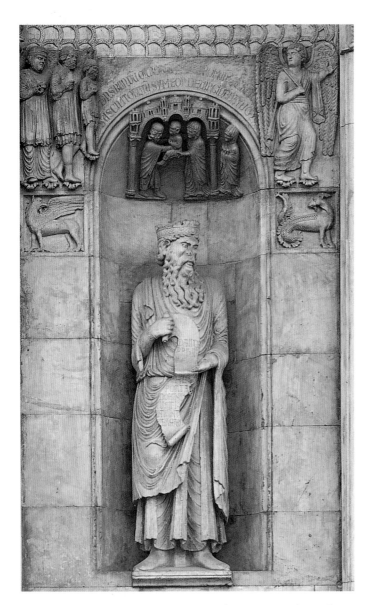

12-32 BENEDETTO ANTELAMI, *King David,* statue in a niche on the west facade of Fidenza Cathedral, Fidenza, Italy, ca. 1180–1190.

Benedetto Antelami's *King David* on the facade of Fidenza Cathedral is a rare example of life-size freestanding statuary in the Romanesque period. The style is unmistakably rooted in Greco-Roman art.

BENEDETTO ANTELAMI was active in the last quarter of the 12th century. Several reliefs by his hand exist, including Parma Cathedral's pulpit and the portals of that city's baptistery. But his most unusual works are the two life-size marble statues of biblical figures he carved for the west facade of Fidenza Cathedral. Antelami's *King David* (FIG. 12-32) seems confined within his niche. His elbows are kept close to his body. Absent is the weight shift that is the hallmark of classical statuary, yet the sculptor's conception of this prophet is unmistakably rooted in Greco-Roman art. Comparison of the Fidenza *David* with the prophet on the Moissac trumeau (FIG. 12-13), who also displays an unfurled scroll, reveals how much the Italian sculptor freed his figure from its architectural setting. Other sculptors did not immediately emulate Antelami's classical approach to portraying figures in stone. But the idea of placing freestanding statues in niches would be taken up again in Italy by Early Renaissance sculptors (FIGS. 21-4, 21-5, and 21-6).

NORMANDY AND ENGLAND

After their conversion to Christianity in the early 10th century, the Vikings (FIGS. 11-4 and 11-4A) settled on the northern coast of France in present-day Normandy. Almost at once, they proved themselves not only aggressive warriors but also skilled administrators and builders, active in Sicily (FIGS. 9-26C and 9-27) as well as in northern Europe.

Architecture

The Normans quickly developed a distinctive Romanesque architectural style that became the major source of French Gothic architecture.

Caen. Most critics consider the abbey church of Saint-Étienne at Caen the masterpiece of Norman Romanesque architecture. Begun by William of Normandy (William the Conqueror; FIGS. 12-40 and 12-41) in 1067, work must have advanced rapidly, because the Normans buried the duke in the church in 1087. Saint-Étienne's west facade (FIG. 12-33) is a striking design rooted in the tradition of Carolingian and Ottonian westworks (compare FIGS. 11-21, 11-22, and 11-29A), but it reveals a new unified organizational scheme. Four large buttresses divide the facade into three bays corresponding to the nave and aisles. Above the buttresses, the towers also display a triple division and a progressively greater piercing of their walls from lower to upper stages. (The culminating spires are a Gothic addition.) The three-part composition extends throughout the facade, both vertically and horizontally, organizing it into a close-knit, well-integrated composition consistent with the careful and methodical planning of the entire structure.

The original design of Saint-Étienne called for a timber roof, as originally at Speyer Cathedral. But the Caen nave (FIG. 12-34) has compound piers with simple engaged half-columns alternating with piers with half-columns attached to pilasters. When the Normans decided to install groin vaults around 1115, the existing alternating compound piers in the nave proved a good match. Those piers soar all the way to the vaults' springing. Their branching ribs divide the large square-vault compartments into six sections—a *sexpartite vault* (FIG. 12-35). The vaults rise high enough to provide room for clerestory windows. The resulting three-story elevation, with its large arched openings, enables ample light to reach the interior (see "How to Illuminate a Nave," page 365). It also makes the nave

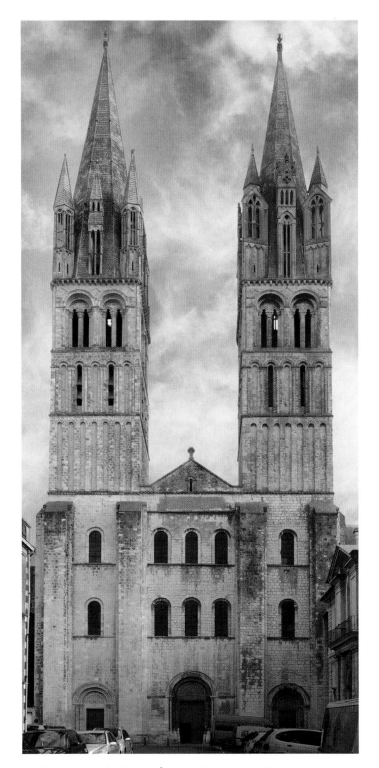

12-33 West facade of Saint-Étienne, Caen, France, begun 1067.

The division of Saint-Étienne's facade into three parts corresponding to the nave and aisles reflects the methodical planning of the entire structure. The towers also have three sections.

appear taller than it is. As in the Milanese church of Sant'Ambrogio (FIG. 12-23), the Norman building has rib vaults. The diagonal and transverse ribs form a structural skeleton that partially supports the still fairly massive paneling between them. But despite the heavy masonry, Saint-Étienne's large windows and reduced interior wall surface give the nave a light and airy quality unusual in the Romanesque period.

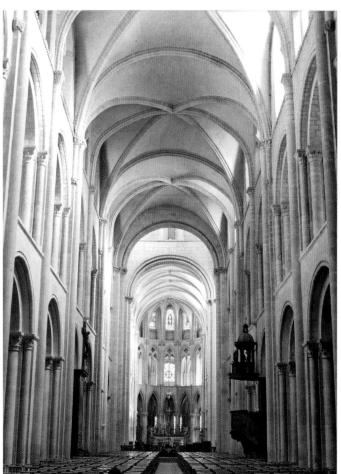

12-34 Interior of Saint-Étienne (looking east), Caen, France, vaulted ca. 1115–1120.

The groin vaults of Saint-Étienne make clerestory windows possible. The three-story elevation with its large arched openings provides ample light and makes the nave appear taller than it is.

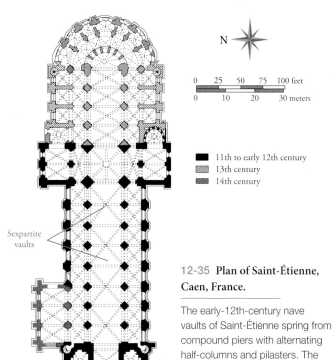

Sexpartite vaults

12-35 Plan of Saint-Étienne, Caen, France.

The early-12th-century nave vaults of Saint-Étienne spring from compound piers with alternating half-columns and pilasters. The diagonal and transverse ribs divide the vaults into six compartments.

0   25   50   75   100 feet
0   10   20   30 meters

■ 11th to early 12th century
▨ 13th century
▦ 14th century

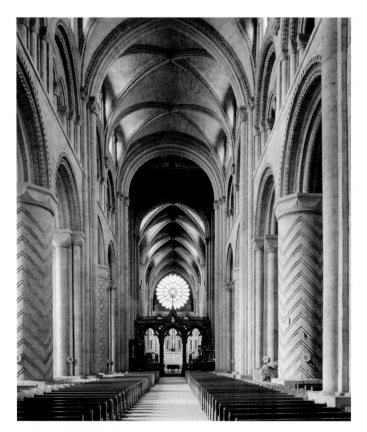

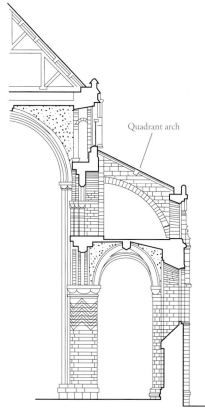

12-36 Interior (*left*; looking east) and lateral section (*right*) of Durham Cathedral, Durham, England, begun ca. 1093.

Durham Cathedral boasts the first examples of rib groin vaults placed over a three-story nave. The builders replaced groin vaults in the tribune with quadrant arches as buttresses of the nave vaults.

Quadrant arch

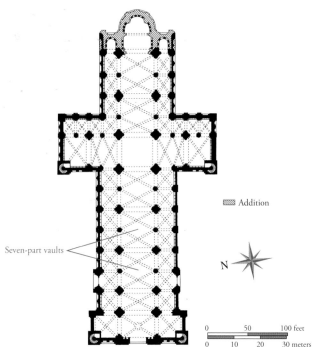

Seven-part vaults

Addition

N

| 0 | | 50 | | 100 feet |
| 0 | 10 | 20 | | 30 meters |

12-37 Plan of Durham Cathedral, Durham, England (after Kenneth John Conant).

Durham Cathedral is typically English in its long, slender proportions. In the nave, simple pillars alternate with compound piers that support the transverse arches of the seven-part groin vaults.

Durham. William of Normandy's conquest of Anglo-Saxon England in 1066 began a new epoch in English history. In architecture, it signaled the importation of Norman Romanesque building and design methods. Durham Cathedral (FIGS. 12-36 and 12-37)

sits majestically on a cliff overlooking the Wear River in northern England, the centerpiece of a monastery, church, and fortified-castle complex on the Scottish frontier. Unlike Speyer Cathedral and Saint-Étienne, Durham Cathedral, begun around 1093—before the remodeling of the Caen church—was a vaulted structure from the outset. Consequently, the pattern of the ribs of the nave's groin vaults corresponds perfectly to the design of the arcade below. Each seven-part nave vault covers two bays. Large, simple pillars ornamented with abstract designs (diamond, chevron, and cable patterns, all originally painted) alternate with compound piers that carry the transverse arches of the vaults. The pier-vault relationship scarcely could be more visible or the building's structural rationale better expressed.

The bold surface patterning of the pillars in the Durham nave is a reminder that the raising of imposing stone buildings such as the Romanesque churches of England and Normandy required more than just the talents of master designers. A corps of expert masons had to transform rough stone blocks into the precise shapes necessary for their specific place in the church's fabric. Although thousands of simple quadrangular blocks make up the great walls of these buildings, the stonecutters also had to produce large numbers of blocks of far more complex shapes. To cover the nave and aisles, the masons had to carve blocks with concave faces to conform to the curve of the vault. Also required were blocks with projecting moldings for the ribs, blocks with convex surfaces for the pillars or with multiple profiles for the compound piers, and so forth. It was an immense undertaking, and it is no wonder that medieval building campaigns often lasted for decades.

Durham Cathedral's plan (FIG. 12-37) is typically English in its long, slender proportions. It does not employ the modular scheme with the same care and logic seen at Caen. But in other ways, this English church is even more innovative than the French church.

The Durham builders employed the earliest known example of a rib groin vault placed over a three-story nave. In the nave's western parts, completed before 1130, the rib vaults have pointed arches, bringing together for the first time two key elements that determined the structural evolution of Gothic architecture (see "The Gothic Rib Vault," page 387). Also of great significance is the way the English builders buttressed the nave vaults. The lateral section (FIG. 12-36, *right*) exposes the simple *quadrant arches* (arches whose curve extends for one quarter of a circle's circumference) that take the place of groin vaults in the Durham tribune. The structural descendants of these quadrant arches are the *flying buttresses* that are another hallmark of the mature Gothic solution to church construction (see "High Gothic Cathedrals," page 389, and FIG. 13-11).

Painting and Other Arts

Many of the finest illustrated manuscripts of the Romanesque age were the work of monks in English scriptoria, following in the tradition of Hiberno-Saxon book production.

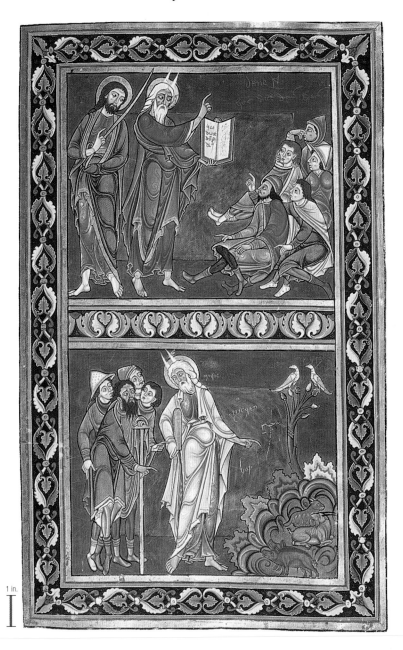

1 in.

Bury Bible. Produced at the Bury Saint Edmunds abbey in England around 1135, the *Bury Bible* (FIG. 12-38) exemplifies the luxurious illumination common to the large Bibles produced in wealthy Romanesque abbeys not subject to the Cistercian restrictions on painted manuscripts. These costly books lent prestige to monasteries that could afford them (see "Medieval Books," page 324). The artist responsible for the *Bury Bible* is known: MASTER HUGO, who was also a sculptor and metalworker. With Gislebertus (FIG. 12-1), Bernardus Gelduinus (FIG. 12-9), Rufillus (FIG. 12-25A), Rainer of Huy (FIG. 12-27), Wiligelmo (FIG. 12-31), and Benedetto Antelami (FIG. 12-32), Hugo was one of the small but growing number of Romanesque artists who signed their works or whose names others recorded. In the 12th century, artists—illuminators as well as sculptors—increasingly began to identify themselves. Although most medieval artists remained anonymous, the contrast of the Romanesque period with the early Middle Ages is striking.

Hugo apparently was a secular artist, one of the emerging class of professional artists and artisans who depended for their livelihood on commissions from well-endowed monasteries. These artists resided in towns rather than within secluded abbey walls, and they traveled frequently to find work. They were the exception, however, and most Romanesque scribes and illuminators continued to be monks and nuns working anonymously in the service of God. The Benedictine rule, for example, specified that "artisans in the monastery . . . are to practice their craft with all humility, but only with the abbot's permission. If one of them becomes puffed up by his skillfulness in his craft, . . . he is to be removed from practicing his craft and not allowed to resume it unless, after manifesting his humility, he is so ordered by the abbot."[5] Some monks,

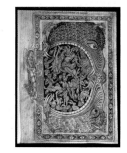

⌐ **12-38A** *Winchester Psalter,* ca. 1145–1155.

however, produced illuminated volumes not for use in the abbey but on royal commission—for example, the *Winchester Psalter* (FIG. 12-38A).

One page (FIG. 12-38) of the *Bury Bible* shows two scenes from Deuteronomy framed by symmetrical leaf motifs in softly glowing harmonized colors. In the upper register, Master Hugo painted *Moses Expounding the Law,* in which he represented the prophet with horns, consistent with Saint Jerome's translation of the Hebrew word that also means "rays" (compare Michelangelo's similar conception of the Hebrew prophet, FIG. 22-14). The lower panel portrays Moses pointing out the clean and unclean beasts. The gestures are slow and gentle and have quiet dignity. The figures of Moses and Aaron seem to glide. This presentation is quite different

12-38 MASTER HUGO, *Moses Expounding the Law,* folio 94 recto of the *Bury Bible,* from Bury Saint Edmunds, England, ca. 1135. Ink and tempera on vellum, 1′ 8″ × 1′ 2″. Corpus Christi College, Cambridge.

Master Hugo was a rare Romanesque lay artist, one of the emerging class of professional artists and artisans who depended for their livelihood on commissions from wealthy monasteries.

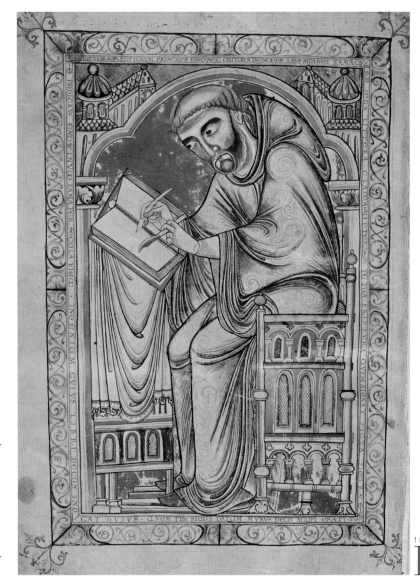

12-39 EADWINE THE SCRIBE(?), *Eadwine the Scribe at work,* folio 283 verso of the *Eadwine Psalter,* from Christ Church Priory, Canterbury, England, ca. 1160–1170. Ink and tempera on vellum, 1′ 8¼″ × 1′ 4¼″. Trinity College, Cambridge.

Although he humbly offered his book as a gift to God, the English monk Eadwine added an inscription to his portrait declaring himself "the prince of scribes" whose fame would endure forever.

1 in.

from the abrupt emphasis and jerky movement seen in earlier Romanesque paintings. The movements of the figures appear more integrated and smooth. Yet patterning remains in the multiple divisions of the draped limbs, the lightly shaded volumes connected with sinuous lines and ladderlike folds. Hugo still thought of the drapery and the body as somehow the same. The frame has a quite definite limiting function, and the painter carefully fit the figures within it.

Eadwine Psalter. The *Eadwine Psalter* is the masterpiece of an English monk known as EADWINE THE SCRIBE. It contains 165 illustrations, many of them variations of those in the Carolingian *Utrecht Psalter* (FIGS. 11-14A and 11-15). The last page (FIG. 12-39), however, presents a rare picture of a Romanesque artist at work (compare FIG. 12-25A). The style of the Eadwine portrait resembles that of the *Bury Bible,* but although the patterning is still firm (notably in the cowl and the thigh), the drapery falls more softly and follows the movements of the body beneath it. Here, the abstract patterning seen in many Romanesque painted and sculpted garments yielded slightly, but clearly, to more naturalistic representation. The Romanesque artist's instinct for decorating the surface remained, however, as is apparent in the gown's whorls and spirals. Significantly, the artist painted those interior lines very lightly so that they would not conflict with the functional lines containing them.

The "portrait" of Eadwine—it is probably a generic type and not a specific likeness—is in the long tradition of author portraits in ancient and medieval art (FIGS. 7-25, 11-8, 11-13, 11-14, and 12-25), although the true author of the *Eadwine Psalter* is King David. Eadwine exaggerated his importance by likening himself to an evangelist writing his Gospel and by including an inscription within the inner frame identifying himself and proclaiming *scriptorum princeps ego* ("I am the prince of scribes"). He declares that the excellence of his work will cause his fame to endure forever, and consequently he can offer his book as an acceptable gift to God. Eadwine may have been concerned for his fame, as were other Romanesque sculptors and painters who signed their works, but these artists, whether clergy or laity, were as yet unaware of the concepts of "fine art" and "fine artist." To them, their work existed not for its own sake but for God's. Nonetheless, works such as this one are an early sign of a new attitude toward the role of the artist in society that presages the reemergence in the Renaissance of the classical notion of individual artistic genius.

Bayeux Tapestry. The most famous work of English Romanesque art is neither a book nor Christian in subject. The so-called *Bayeux Tapestry* (FIGS. 12-40 and 12-41) is unique in medieval art. It is an embroidered fabric—not, in fact, a woven tapestry—made of wool sewn on linen (see "Embroidery and Tapestry," page 377). Closely related to Romanesque manuscript illumination, its borders contain the kinds of real and imaginary animals found in contemporaneous books, and an explanatory Latin text sewn in thread accompanies many of the pictures.

Some 20 inches high and about 230 feet long, the *Bayeux Tapestry* is a continuous, friezelike pictorial narrative of a crucial moment in England's history and of the events leading up to it. The Norman defeat of the Anglo-Saxons at Hastings in 1066 brought England under the control of the Normans, uniting all of England and much of France under one rule. The dukes of Normandy became the kings of England. Commissioned by Bishop Odo, the half brother of the conquering Duke William, the embroidery may have been sewn by women at the Norman court. Many art historians, however, believe that it was the work of English stitchers in Kent, where Odo was earl after the Norman conquest. Odo donated the work to Bayeux Cathedral (hence its nickname), but it is uncertain whether it was originally intended

Embroidery and Tapestry

The most famous embroidery of the Middle Ages is, ironically, known as the *Bayeux Tapestry* (FIGS. 12-40 and 12-41). Embroidery and tapestry are related—but different—means of decorating textiles. *Tapestry* designs are woven on a loom as part of the fabric. *Embroidery* patterns are sewn onto fabrics with threads.

The needleworkers who fashioned the *Bayeux Tapestry* were either Norman or English women. They employed eight colors of dyed wool yarn—two varieties of blue, three shades of green, yellow, buff, and terracotta red—and two kinds of stitches. In *stem stitching,* short overlapping strands of thread form jagged lines. *Laid-and-couched work* creates solid blocks of color. In the latter technique, the needleworker first lays down a series of parallel and then of cross stitches. Finally, the stitcher tacks down the crosshatched threads using *couching* (knotting).

On the *Bayeux Tapestry,* the embroiderers left the natural linen color exposed for the background, human flesh, building walls, and other "colorless" design elements. Stem stitches define the contours of figures and buildings and delineate interior details, such as facial features, body armor, and roof tiles. The clothing, animal bodies, and other solid areas are laid-and-couched work.

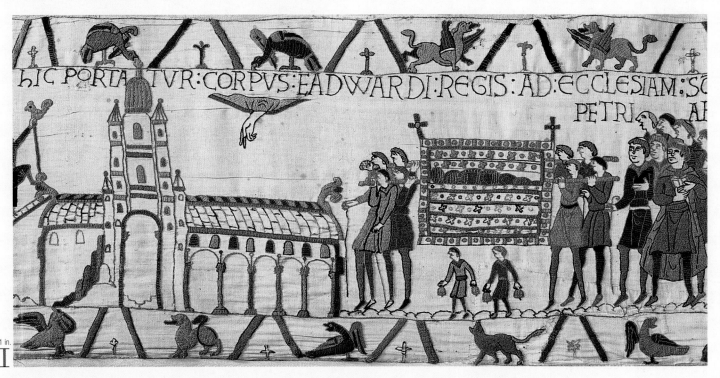

12-40 Funeral procession to Westminster Abbey, detail of the *Bayeux Tapestry,* from Bayeux Cathedral, Bayeux, France, ca. 1070–1080. Embroidered wool on linen, 1′ 8″ high (entire length of fabric 229′ 8″). Centre Guillaume le Conquérant, Bayeux.

The *Bayeux Tapestry* is really an embroidery. The needleworkers employed eight colors of dyed wool yarn and sewed the threads onto linen using both stem stitching and laid-and-couched work.

for display in the church's nave, where the theme would have been a curious choice.

The events that precipitated the Norman invasion of England are well documented. In 1066, Edward the Confessor (r. 1042–1066), the Anglo-Saxon king of England, died. The Normans believed that Edward had recognized William of Normandy as his rightful heir. But the crown went to Harold, earl of Wessex, the king's Anglo-Saxon brother-in-law, who had sworn an oath of allegiance to William. The betrayed Normans, descendants of the seafaring Vikings, boarded their ships, crossed the English Channel, and crushed Harold's forces.

Illustrated here are two episodes of the epic tale as represented in the *Bayeux Tapestry.* The first detail (FIG. 12-40) depicts King Edward's funeral procession. The hand of God points the way to the church in London where he was buried—Westminster Abbey, consecrated on December 28, 1065, just a few days before Edward's death. The church was one of the first Romanesque buildings erected in England, and the embroiderers took pains to record its main features, including the lofty crossing tower and the long nave with tribunes. There, William was crowned king of England on Christmas Day, 1066. (The coronation ceremony for every English monarch since then also has taken place in Westminster Abbey.)

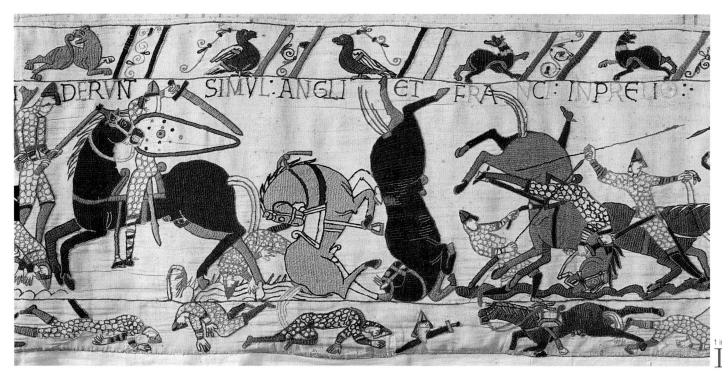

12-41 Battle of Hastings, detail of the *Bayeux Tapestry,* from Bayeux Cathedral, Bayeux, France, ca. 1070–1080. Embroidered wool on linen, 1′ 8″ high (entire length of fabric 229′ 8″). Centre Guillaume le Conquérant, Bayeux.

The *Bayeux Tapestry* is unique in medieval art. Like the scroll-like frieze of the Column of Trajan (FIG. 7-45) and other historical narratives in Roman art, it depicts contemporaneous events in full detail.

The second detail (FIG. 12-41) shows the Battle of Hastings in progress. The Norman cavalry cuts down the English defenders. Filling the lower border are the dead and wounded, although the upper register continues the animal motifs of the rest of the embroidery. The Romanesque artists co-opted some of the characteristic motifs of Greco-Roman battle scenes—for example, the horses with twisted necks and contorted bodies (compare FIG. 5-70)—but rendered the figures in the Romanesque manner. Linear patterning and flat color replaced classical three-dimensional volume and modeling in light and dark hues.

The *Bayeux Tapestry* stands apart from all other Romanesque artworks in depicting in full detail an event at a time shortly after it occurred, recalling the historical narratives of ancient Roman art. Art historians have often likened the Norman embroidery to the scroll-like frieze of the Column of Trajan (FIG. 7-45). Like the Roman account, the story told on the textile is the conqueror's version of history, a proclamation of national pride.

As in the ancient frieze, the narrative is not confined to battlefield successes. It is a complete chronicle of events. Included are the preparations for war, with scenes depicting the felling and splitting of trees for ship construction, the loading of equipment onto the vessels, the cooking and serving of meals, and so forth. In this respect, the *Bayeux Tapestry* is the most *Roman*-esque work of Romanesque art.

Romanesque Europe

France and Northern Spain

- *Romanesque* takes its name from the Roman-like barrel and groin vaults based on round arches employed in many European churches built between 1050 and 1200. Romanesque vaults, however, are made of stone, not concrete. The largest Romanesque church was at Cluny in France.

- Numerous churches sprang up along the pilgrimage roads leading to the shrine of Saint James at Santiago de Compostela in northwestern Spain. These churches were large enough to accommodate the huge crowds of pilgrims who came to view the sacred relics displayed in the radiating chapels off the ambulatory and transept.

- The Romanesque period also brought the revival of large-scale stone relief sculpture in cloisters and especially in church portals, where, as at Autun, scenes of Christ as Last Judge often greeted the faithful as they entered what the clergy considered the doorway to the road to salvation.

- The leading patrons of Romanesque sculpture and painting were the monks of the Cluniac order. By contrast, the Cistercians, under the leadership of Bernard of Clairvaux, condemned figural art in both churches and religious books.

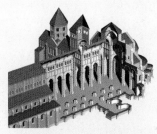

Abbey church, Cluny, 1088–1130

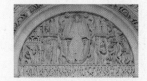

Saint-Lazare, Autun, ca. 1120–1135

Holy Roman Empire

- In the Romanesque period, the Salian dynasty (r. 1027–1125) ruled an empire corresponding roughly to present-day Germany and northern Italy. Henry the Lion (1129–1195), duke of Saxony and Bavaria, was also a major art patron.

- Architects in the Holy Roman Empire built structurally innovative churches. Speyer Cathedral and Sant'Ambrogio in Milan are two of the earliest examples of the use of groin vaults in naves.

- In Belgium, sculptors excelled in metalwork, producing costly reliquaries of silver, jewels, and enamel, such as that containing the remains of Pope Alexander II. Rainer of Huy, one of several Romanesque artists whose name is known, cast a baptismal font in a single piece.

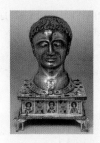

Reliquary of Saint Alexander, Stavelot, 1145

Italy

- The regional diversity of Romanesque art and architecture is especially evident in Italy, where the heritage of ancient Rome and Early Christianity was strongest.

- Romanesque churches and baptisteries in Pisa and Florence have timber roofs, in contrast to the vaulted interiors of northern European buildings. The exteriors often feature marble paneling of different colors. Church campaniles were usually freestanding, as were baptisteries, which took the form of independent central-plan buildings facing the cathedral.

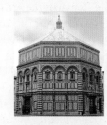

Baptistery, Florence, dedicated 1059

Normandy and England

- After their conversion to Christianity in the early 10th century, the Vikings settled on the northern coast of France. From there, Duke William of Normandy crossed the channel and conquered England in 1066. The *Bayeux Tapestry* chronicles that war—a unique example of contemporaneous historical narrative art in the Middle Ages.

- Norman and English Romanesque architects introduced new features to church design that later greatly influenced French Gothic architecture. Saint-Étienne at Caen and Durham Cathedral are the earliest examples of the use of rib groin vaults over a three-story (arcade-tribune-clerestory) nave. The Durham builders also experimented with quadrant arches in the tribune to buttress the nave vaults.

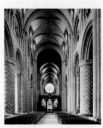

Durham Cathedral, begun ca. 1093

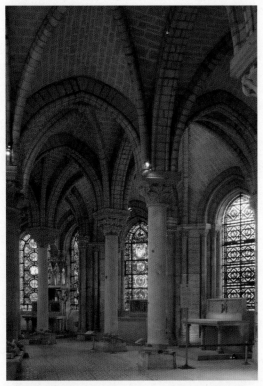

▼ **13-1a** Gothic architecture was born at Saint-Denis, the burial place of the martyr saint who brought Christianity to Gaul. The church's east end was dedicated by Abbot Suger, the founding spirit of the Gothic style.

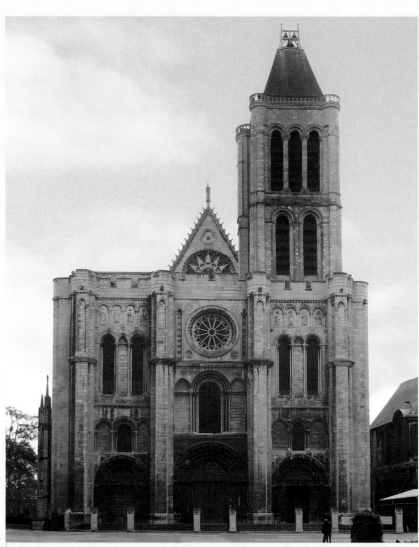

13-1 **Abbey church, Saint-Denis, France, remodeled beginning in 1135; east end dedicated in 1144.**

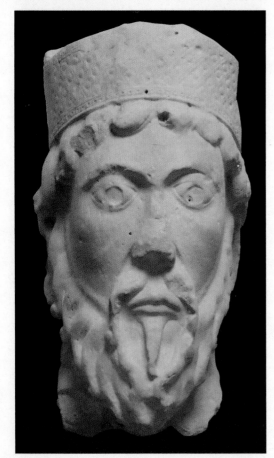

▲ **13-1b** The figural sculptures of Saint-Denis's west facade are largely destroyed, but a few fragments are preserved, including this head of an Old Testament prophet, usually identified as Moses.

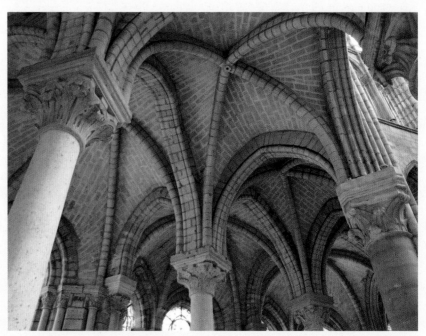

▲ **13-1c** In the ambulatory and radiating chapels dedicated in 1144, exceptionally light-weight vaults spring from slender columns. Colored-glass windows transform natural light into divine light.

GOTHIC EUROPE NORTH OF THE ALPS /13

The Birth of Gothic

On June 11, 1144, King Louis VII of France, Queen Eleanor of Aquitaine, five archbishops, and other dignitaries attended the dedication by Abbot Suger of the new choir of the abbey church of Saint-Denis (FIG. 13-1). Saint-Denis was the official church of the French monarchy and the burial place of Saint Dionysius (Denis in French), the missionary who brought Christianity to Gaul and died a martyr's death there in the third century. Architectural historians pinpoint the birth of the style that later came to be called *Gothic* to 1144 and identify Suger as its founding spirit.

Although later Gothic churches would reach far greater heights, both literally and figuratively, most of the essential elements of the new architectural style are present at Saint-Denis. The west facade, for example, which welcomes worshipers into the church, is very different in character from its Romanesque predecessors. The unknown designer introduced a large round window over the central portal and punctured the rest of the wall surfaces to a greater degree, creating a lighter effect by breaking up the facade with a larger number of voids. Figural sculpture (unfortunately mostly destroyed during the French Revolution of the late 18th century) adorned all three portals, and narrative reliefs decorated the three tympana (the Last Judgment in the central tympanum, episodes from the life of Saint Denis in the flanking portals). The most innovative aspect of the portals, however, was the introduction of figures attached to the columns in the jambs, the first step toward the revival of freestanding statuary in the later Middle Ages.

More remarkable still is the articulation of the church's east end, where exceptionally lightweight vaults spring from slender columns in the ambulatory and radiating chapels, replacing the thick walls that separated Romanesque chapels. The lightness of the vaults also enabled the builders to open up the outer walls with colored-glass windows that, in the minds of contemporary observers, transformed natural light into divine light.

Born at Saint-Denis in the region around Paris called the Île-de-France, Gothic architecture is one of the towering achievements in the history of world architecture, and it was so recognized at the time. The Gothic style quickly came to be called *opus francigenum* ("French work") or, more simply, *opus modernum* ("modern work"), and Gothic churches were admired and emulated throughout Europe as stone and glass images of the City of God, the Heavenly Jerusalem. The extraordinary technological and aesthetic achievement that Gothic architecture represents was the unique product of an era of economic prosperity and deep spirituality, but the Gothic style lives on in countless chapels, academic buildings, and residence halls on college campuses today.

"GOTHIC"

Just as the term *Romanesque* never appears in 11th-and 12th-century documents, the adjective *Gothic* was never used by those who witnessed the erection of *opus modernum* churches during the 12th, 13th, and 14th centuries. But unlike "Romanesque," "Gothic" is not the invention of modern architectural historians. It owes its origin to Giorgio Vasari (1511–1574; see "Giorgio Vasari's *Lives*," page 648), who employed the term for the first time in his *Introduction to the Three Arts of Design* (1550). Vasari attributed late medieval art and architecture to the Goths, whom he regarded as responsible for both the downfall of Rome and the dissolution of the classical style in art and architecture. Vasari's assessment of "Gothic" art was quite negative. In his treatise, he called Gothic art "monstrous and barbarous," echoing a view already voiced a century earlier by the influential Renaissance artist Lorenzo Ghiberti (1378–1455), who in his *Commentaries* described the Middle Ages as a period of decline. "Gothic," like "medieval" (that is, the era between the "good art" of classical antiquity and the Renaissance revival of the classical style), is an unfortunate if unavoidable label completely out of sync with both late medieval and modern views of the Gothic era as one of the high points in the history of Western art and architecture.

The great artistic innovations of the Gothic age were, as in the Romanesque period, made possible by the widespread prosperity and favorable climate that Europe enjoyed in the 12th and 13th centuries. This was a time of profound change in European society. The focus of both intellectual and religious life shifted definitively from monasteries in the countryside to rapidly expanding cities. In these new urban centers, prosperous merchants made their homes and formed *guilds* (professional associations), scholars founded the first modern universities, and vernacular literature (written in the local spoken languages rather than in Latin), especially courtly romances, exploded in popularity. Although the papacy was at the height of its power, and Christian knights still waged Crusades against the Muslims, the independent nation-states of modern Europe were beginning to take shape.

In fact, many regional variants existed within European Gothic, just as distinct regional styles characterized the Romanesque period. Therefore, this chapter deals only with contemporaneous developments in three major regions north of the Alps—France, England, and the Holy Roman Empire (MAP 13-1). The art and architecture

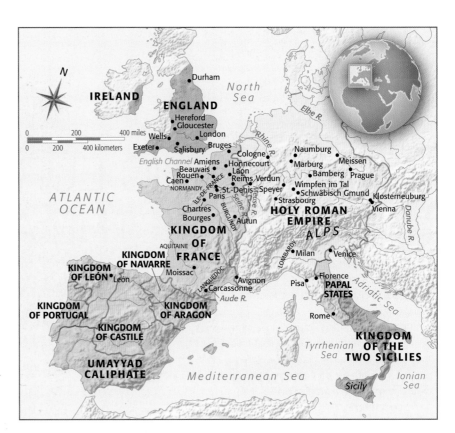

MAP 13-1 Europe around 1200.

of 13th- and 14th-century Italy are the subject of Chapter 14. The Gothic style spread beyond these areas, however, reaching, for example, Eastern Europe and Scandinavia.

FRANCE

What contemporaries called *opus francigenum* was born in the Île-de-France, and the earliest manifestation of the new style appeared a few miles north of Paris at the abbey of Saint-Denis (see "The Birth of Gothic," page 381). The story of Gothic art and architecture told here therefore also begins in northern France.

Architecture, Sculpture, and Stained Glass

Saint-Denis. According to legend, after his execution on Montmartre (Martyr's Hill) in Paris, Saint Dionysius, the Christian martyr who was the city's first bishop, miraculously stood up and marched to his grave north of Paris carrying his severed head in his

---

GOTHIC EUROPE

1140–1194	1194–1300	1300–1500
Early Gothic	**High Gothic**	**Late Gothic**
▪ Abbot Suger begins rebuilding the French royal abbey church at Saint-Denis with stained-glass windows and rib vaults on pointed arches ▪ At Saint-Denis and Chartres Cathedral, jamb statues of Old Testament kings and queens adorn all three portals of the west facade ▪ The builders of Laon Cathedral insert a triforium as the fourth story in the nave elevation	▪ The rebuilt Chartres Cathedral sets the pattern for High Gothic churches: four-part nave vaults braced by external flying buttresses, three-story elevation (arcade, triforium, clerestory), and stained-glass windows in place of heavy masonry ▪ At Chartres and Reims in France, at Naumburg in Germany, and elsewhere, statues become more independent of their architectural setting ▪ Manuscript illumination moves from monastic scriptoria to urban lay workshops, especially in Paris	▪ The Flamboyant style in France and the Perpendicular style in England emphasize surface embellishment over structural clarity. Characteristic features are delicate webs of flamelike tracery and fan vaults with pendants resembling stalactites ▪ The humanization of holy figures in statuary continues, especially in Germany, where sculptors dramatically record the suffering of Jesus

Abbot Suger and the Rebuilding of Saint-Denis

Abbot Suger of Saint-Denis (ca. 1081–1151) rose from humble parentage to become the right-hand man of both Louis VI (r. 1108–1137) and Louis VII (r. 1137–1180). When the latter, accompanied by Queen Eleanor, left Paris to join the Second Crusade (1147–1149), Suger served as regent of France. From his youth, Suger wrote, he had dreamed of the possibility of embellishing Saint-Denis (FIG. 13-1), the church in which most French monarchs since Merovingian times had been buried. Within 15 years of becoming abbot of Saint-Denis, Suger began rebuilding the abbey's Carolingian basilica. In his time, the French monarchy's power, except for scattered holdings, extended over an area not much larger than Paris and its environs, but the kings had pretensions to rule all of France. Suger aimed to increase the prestige of both his abbey and the monarchy by rebuilding France's royal church in grand fashion.

Suger wrote three treatises about his activities as abbot. Together they furnish a uniquely rich and detailed description of the role of an abbot as a patron of art and architecture. In one important passage, he enumerated the special qualities of the new east end (FIGS. **13-2** and **13-3**) dedicated in 1144:

[I]t was cunningly provided that—through the upper columns and central arches which were to be placed upon the lower ones built in the crypt—the central nave of the old [Carolingian church] should be equalized, by means of geometrical and arithmetical instruments, with the central nave of the new addition; and, likewise, that the dimensions of the old side-aisles should be equalized with the dimensions of the new side-aisles, except for that elegant and praiseworthy extension in [the form of] a circular string of chapels, by virtue of which the whole [church] would shine with the wonderful and uninterrupted light of most luminous windows, pervading the interior beauty.*

The abbot's brief discussion of Saint-Denis's new ambulatory and chapels is key to understanding Early Gothic (ca. 1140–1194) French architecture. Suger wrote at much greater length, however, about his church's glorious gem-studded and gold furnishings. Here, for example, is his description of the *altar frontal* (the decorated panel on the front of the altar) in the choir:

Into this panel, which stands in front of [Saint Denis's] most sacred body, we have put . . . about forty-two marks of gold [and] a multifarious wealth of precious gems, hyacinths, rubies, sapphires, emeralds and topazes, and also an array of different large pearls.†

The costly furnishings and the light-filled space caused Suger to "delight in the beauty of the house of God" and "called [him] away from external cares." The new church made him feel as if he were "dwelling . . . in some strange region of the universe which neither exists entirely in the slime of the earth nor entirely in the purity of Heaven." In Suger's eyes, his splendid new church, permeated with light and outfitted with precious gems and gold, was a way station on the road to Paradise, which "transported [him] from this inferior to that higher world."§ He regarded a lavish investment in art as a spiritual aid, not as an undesirable distraction for the pious monk, as did Bernard of Clairvaux (see "Bernard of Clairvaux," page 356). Suger's forceful justification of art in

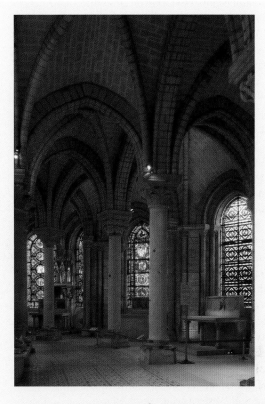

13-2 Ambulatory and radiating chapels (looking northeast), abbey church, Saint-Denis, France, 1140–1144.

Abbot Suger's remodeling of Saint-Denis marked the beginning of Gothic architecture. Rib vaults with pointed arches spring from slender columns. Stained-glass windows admit divine lux nova.

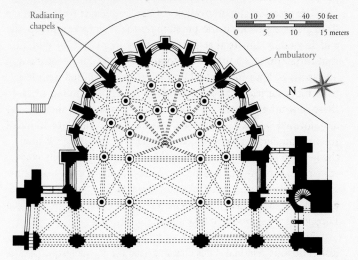

13-3 Plan of the east end, abbey church, Saint-Denis, France, 1140–1144 (after Sumner Crosby).

The innovative plan of the east end of Saint-Denis dates to Abbot Suger's lifetime. By using exceptionally light rib vaults, the builders were able to eliminate the walls between the radiating chapels.

the church was very much in accord with the spirit of the Gothic age, which witnessed the proliferation of costly stained-glass windows and painted stone sculptures in the cathedrals of France in particular and in Europe more generally.

*Translated by Erwin Panofsky, *Abbot Suger on the Abbey Church of Saint-Denis and Its Art Treasures,* 2d ed. (Princeton: Princeton University Press, 1979), 101.
†Ibid., 55.
§Ibid., 65.

hands. In the seventh century, a Benedictine community of monks settled on the site of the saint's burial and founded an abbey there that they named Saint-Denis in honor of Dionysius. Two centuries later, the monks constructed a basilica at Saint-Denis, which housed the saint's tomb and those of nearly all the French kings dating back to the sixth century, as well as the crimson battle flag said to have belonged to Charlemagne. The Carolingian basilica became France's royal church, the very symbol of the monarchy—just as Speyer Cathedral (FIGS. 12-21 and 12-22) was the burial place of the German rulers of the Holy Roman Empire.

Abbot Suger. By 1122, when Suger, one of the Saint-Denis abbey's monks, became abbot of Saint-Denis, the old church was in disrepair and had become too small to accommodate the growing number of pilgrims who came to see the tomb of the saint and those of the French kings. Suger also believed that the basilica was of insufficient grandeur to serve as the official church of the French monarchy. Therefore, around 1135, the abbot began a major campaign to rebuild the church. He started by erecting a new west facade (FIG. 13-1). In his account of the building campaign (see "Abbot Suger and the Rebuilding of Saint-Denis," page 383), Suger mentioned that he imported masons and craftsmen from different regions to execute his vision of a grandiose new church for the patron saint of France. Indeed, the church's facade combines the tripartite design of Norman Romanesque churches, such as Saint-Étienne (FIG. 12-33) at Caen, with the richly sculptured portals of the early-12th-century churches of Burgundy (for example, Autun and Vézelay, FIGS. 12-1 and 12-15) and the "pilgrimage churches" of southwestern France (for example, Moissac, FIG. 12-11).

As at Caen, pier buttresses divide the Saint-Denis facade into three sections corresponding to the church's nave and flanking aisles. (There are also three stories in the lower facade and three in the towers. Three is a sacred number in Christian theology—the Trinity of God the Father, Jesus Christ, and the Holy Spirit.) But for Suger's facade, the designer introduced a large *rose window* over the central portal, which is wider and taller than the aisle portals, and also punctured much of the rest of the wall surface, creating a lighter effect than that of the typical Romanesque facade.

In contrast to the carved decoration of Moissac, Autun, and most other Romanesque facades, at Saint-Denis figural sculpture adorned all three portals across the front of the church. Narrative reliefs decorated the three tympana and the archivolts. Most notably, the jambs featured figures of Old Testament kings, queens, and prophets (FIG. 13-3A) attached to columns. These *jamb statues* referred to the royal lineage of Christ but also to the kings and queens of France, not surprising for the official church of the French monarchy and the burial site of its kings. Unfortunately, Suger's statues were in large part destroyed during an 18th-century remodeling and later by vandalism during the French Revolution against the hereditary monarchy, but they set the pattern for Gothic sculpture in the Île-de-France for the next century. Old engravings record the facade's appearance, which closely approximated that of the slightly later Royal Portal (FIGS. 13-5 and 13-6) of Chartres Cathedral.

Work began on the east end (FIGS. 13-2 and 13-3) of Saint-Denis in 1140. Because the French considered the old church a relic in its own right, the new choir had to conform to the dimensions of

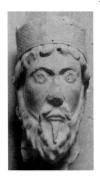

⬀ **13-3A** Moses, west facade, Saint-Denis, ca. 1137–1140.

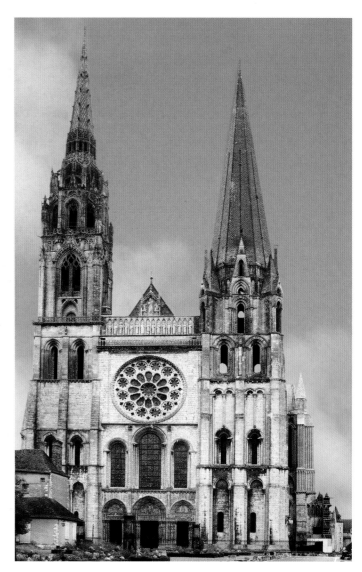

13-4 West facade of Chartres Cathedral, Chartres, France, ca. 1145–1155.

The Early Gothic west facade was all that remained of Chartres Cathedral after the 1194 fire. The design still has much in common with Romanesque facades. The rose window is an example of plate tracery.

the crypt below it. Nevertheless, the remodeled east end of Saint-Denis (Suger died before he could transform the nave) represented a sharp departure from past practice. Innovative rib vaults resting on pointed arches (see "The Gothic Rib Vault," page 387) cover the ambulatory and chapels. These pioneering, exceptionally lightweight vaults spring from slender columns in the ambulatory and from the thin masonry walls framing the chapels. The lightness of the vaults enabled the builders to eliminate the walls between the chapels as well as open up the outer walls with *stained-glass* windows (see "Stained-Glass Windows," page 392). Suger and his contemporaries marveled at the "wonderful and uninterrupted light" pouring in through the "most luminous windows." The abbot called the colored light *lux nova* ("new light"). Saint-Denis's pointed-arch vaulting and stained-glass windows, both of which had precedents in the Romanesque era, became hallmarks of French Gothic architecture.

Royal Portal, Chartres. The innovative idea of placing jamb statues in the portals of the Saint-Denis abbey church was adopted immediately afterward at the Cathedral of Notre-Dame at Chartres, also in the Île-de-France. Work on the west facade (FIG. 13-4)

⬀ Every thumbnail image has a corresponding full-size MindTap Bonus Image and content in the MindTap reader for this chapter.

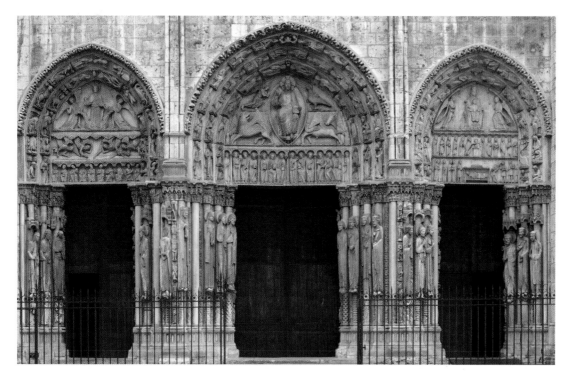

The sculptures of the Royal Portal proclaim the majesty and power of Christ. The tympana depict, from left to right, Christ's ascension, the Second Coming, and the infant Jesus in the lap of the Virgin Mary.

wisdom" (FIG. 12-20). But the Virgin appears more frequently on the Chartres facade than she does in the sculptural programs of any Romanesque church portal. At Chartres, Mary assumes a central role, a position she maintained throughout the Gothic period, during which time her cult achieved its greatest popularity. As the mother of the Savior, she stood compassionately between the Last Judge and the horrors of Hell, interceding for all her faithful (compare FIG. 13-39B). Worshipers in the later 12th and 13th centuries sang hymns to the Virgin and dedicated great cathedrals to her. Soldiers carried her image into battle on banners, and Mary's name joined Saint Denis's as part of the French kings' battle cry. The Virgin became the spiritual lady of chivalry, and the Christian knight dedicated his life to her. The severity of Romanesque themes stressing the Last Judgment yielded to the gentleness of Gothic art, in which Mary is the kindly queen of Heaven.

Jamb Statues. Statues of Old Testament kings and queens (FIG. 13-6) occupy the jambs flanking each doorway of the Royal Portal. They are the royal ancestors of Christ and, both figuratively and literally, support the New Testament figures above the doorways. They wear 12th-century clothes, and medieval observers may have

began around 1145, very likely employing some of the same stonemasons and sculptors who worked at Saint-Denis. Like the Saint-Denis facade (FIG. 13-1), the west front of Chartres retains the fortress-like look of many Romanesque churches, but features a large rose window and a greater number of openings in the solid masonry wall as well as extensive figural sculpture in its triple entrance. Chartres's Royal Portal (FIG. 13-5; so named because of the figures of kings and queens flanking its three doorways, as at Saint-Denis) constitutes the most complete surviving ensemble of Early Gothic sculpture. Thierry of Chartres, chancellor of the Cathedral School of Chartres from 1141 until his death 10 years later, may have conceived the complex iconographical program. The archivolts of the right portal, for example, depict the seven female personifications of the liberal arts with the learned men of antiquity at their feet. The figures celebrate the revival of classical scholarship in the 12th century and symbolize human knowledge, which Thierry and other leading intellectuals of the era believed led to true faith (see "Paris, the New Center of Medieval Learning," page 388).

The sculptures of the Royal Portal proclaim the majesty and power of Christ. To unite the three doorways both visually and thematically, the sculptors carved episodes from the lives of the Virgin (Notre Dame, "Our Lady") and Christ on the capitals, which form a kind of frieze linking one entrance to the next (FIG. 13-5). Christ's ascension into Heaven appears in the tympanum of the left portal. All around, in the archivolts, are the signs of the zodiac and scenes representing the various labors of the months of the year. They are symbols of the cosmic and earthly worlds. The Second Coming of Christ is the subject of the central tympanum, as at Moissac (FIG. 12-11). The signs of the four evangelists, the 24 elders of the Apocalypse, and the 12 apostles appear around Christ or on the lintel. In the tympanum of the right portal, Christ appears in the lap of the Virgin Mary. Scenes of the Savior's childhood fill the lintel below, where Jesus appears on an altar, connecting the sculptures at the church entrance with the symbolic sacrifice of the Eucharist within.

The Virgin in Gothic France. The depiction of Mary in the right tympanum recalls Byzantine representations of the Theotokos (FIGS. 9-19 and 9-20), as well as the Romanesque "throne of

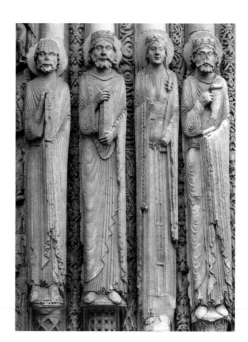

13-6 Jamb statues of Old Testament figures on the right side of the central doorway of the Royal Portal (FIG. 13-5), Chartres Cathedral, Chartres, France, ca. 1145–1155.

The biblical kings and queens of the Royal Portal are the royal ancestors of Christ. These Early Gothic jamb statues display the first signs of a new interest in naturalism in European sculpture.

regarded them as images of the kings and queens of France. (This was the motivation for vandalizing the comparable figures at Saint-Denis during the French Revolution; compare FIG. 13-3A.) The figures stand rigidly upright with their elbows held close against their torsos. The linear folds of their garments—inherited from the Romanesque style, along with the elongated proportions—generally echo the vertical lines of their column shafts. In this respect, Gothic jamb statues differ significantly from classical *caryatids* (compare FIGS. 5-17 and 5-54). The Gothic figures are *attached* to columns. The classical statues *replaced* the columns. The Chartres (and Saint-Denis) jamb statues are therefore technically high reliefs. Nonetheless, the statues of the kings and queens stand out from the plane of the wall and display signs of a new interest in naturalism on the part of medieval sculptors, noticeable particularly in the heads, where kindly human faces replace the masklike features of most Romanesque figures. At Chartres, a personalization of appearance began that led first to idealized images of the perfect Christian and finally, by 1400, to the portraiture of specific individuals. The sculptors of the Royal Portal figures initiated an era of artistic concern with personality and individuality.

Laon Cathedral. Both Chartres Cathedral and the abbey church of Saint-Denis had lengthy construction histories, and only small portions of those structures date to the Early Gothic period. Laon Cathedral (FIGS. 13-7 and 13-8), however, begun about 1190 and finished shortly after 1200, provides a comprehensive picture of French church architecture of the second half of the 12th century. Characteristically, the Laon design retains some features of earlier Romanesque churches, notably the alternate-support system of the nave arcade (above the piers, alternating bundles of three and five shafts frame the aisle bays) and large sexpartite rib vaults, as at Caen (FIG. 12-34). Significantly, however, Laon's rib vaults all rest on pointed arches, a rare occurrence in the Romanesque era and a feature that became one of the essential elements of Early Gothic architecture (see "The Gothic Rib Vault," page 387). An important new feature of the Laon nave is the *triforium*: the band of arcades below the clerestory (FIGS. 13-7 and 13-15a). The triforium occupies the space corresponding to the exterior strip of wall covered by the sloping timber roof above the galleries. The insertion of the triforium into the Romanesque three-story nave elevation reflected a growing desire to break up all continuous wall surfaces. The new horizontal zone produced the characteristic four-story Early Gothic interior elevation: nave arcade, tribune gallery, triforium, and clerestory with single *lancets* (tall, narrow windows ending in pointed arches).

Laon Cathedral's west facade (FIG. 13-8) signals an even more pronounced departure from the Romanesque style still lingering at Saint-Denis (FIG. 13-1) and Chartres (FIG. 13-4). Typically Gothic are the huge central rose window, the deep porches

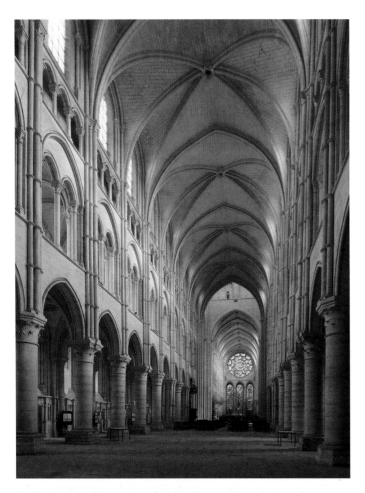

13-7 Interior of Laon Cathedral (looking northeast), Laon, France, begun ca. 1190.

The insertion of a triforium at Laon broke up the nave wall and produced the characteristic four-story Early Gothic nave elevation (FIG. 13-15a): arcade, tribune gallery, triforium, and clerestory.

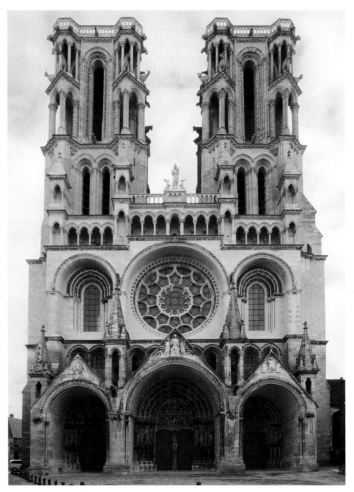

13-8 West facade of Laon Cathedral, Laon, France, begun ca. 1190.

The huge central rose window, the deep porches in front of the doorways, and the open structure of the towers distinguish Laon Cathedral's Early Gothic facade from Romanesque church facades.

The Gothic Rib Vault

The ancestors of the Gothic *rib vault* are the Romanesque vaults found at Caen (FIG. 12-34), Durham (FIG. 12-36, *left*), and elsewhere. The rib vault's distinguishing features are the crossed, or diagonal, arches under its groins. These arches form the *armature,* or skeletal framework, for constructing the vault. Gothic vaults (for example, FIGS. 13-2, 13-7, and 13-21) generally have thinner *vaulting webs* (the masonry between the ribs) than found in typical Romanesque vaults. But the chief difference between the two types of vaults is the *pointed arch,* an integral part of the Gothic skeletal armature. The first wide use of pointed (or *ogival*) arches was in Sasanian architecture (FIG. 2-29), and Islamic builders later adopted them. French Romanesque architects (FIGS. 12-10B and 12-11) probably borrowed the form from Muslim Spain or, less likely, Norman Sicily and passed it to their Gothic successors. Pointed arches enabled Gothic builders to make the crowns of all the vaults approximately the same level, regardless of the space to be vaulted. Romanesque architects could not achieve this with semicircular arches.

The drawings in FIG. 13-9 illustrate this key difference. In FIG. 13-9a, the rectangle *ABCD* is an oblong nave bay to be vaulted. *AC* and *DB* are the diagonal ribs; *AB* and *DC,* the transverse arches; and *AD* and *BC,* the nave arcade's arches. If the architect uses semicircular arches (*AFB, BJC,* and *DHC*), their radii and, therefore, their heights (*EF, IJ,* and *GH*) will be different, because the width of a semicircular arch determines its height. The result will be a vault (FIG. 13-9b) with higher transverse arches (*DHC*) than the arcade's arches (*CJB*). The vault's crown (*F*) will be still higher. If the builder uses pointed arches (FIG. 13-9c), the transverse (*DLC*) and arcade (*BKC*) arches can have the same heights (*GL* and *IK* in FIG. 13-9a). The result will be a Gothic rib vault where the points of the arches (*L* and *K*) are at the same level as the vault's crown (*F*).

A major advantage of the Gothic vault is its flexibility, which enables the vaulting of compartments of varying shapes, as at Saint-Denis (FIGS. 13-1b, 13-2, and 13-3). Pointed arches also channel the weight of the vaults more directly downward than do semicircular arches. The vaults therefore require less buttressing to hold them in place, in turn making it possible for the stonemasons to open up the walls and place large windows beneath the arches. Because pointed arches also lead the eyes upward, they make the vaults appear taller than they are. In FIG. 13-9, the crown (*F*) of both the Romanesque (*b*) and Gothic (*c*) vaults is the same height from the pavement, but the Gothic vault seems taller. Both the physical and visual properties of rib vaults with pointed arches aided Gothic builders in their quest for soaring height in church interiors (FIG. 13-15).

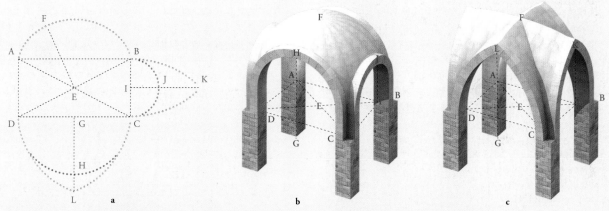

13-9 Diagram (*a*) and drawings of rib vaults with semicircular (*b*) and pointed (*c*) arches (John Burge).

Pointed arches channel the weight of the rib vaults more directly downward than do semicircular arches, requiring less buttressing. Pointed arches also make the vaults appear taller than they are.

in front of the doorways, and the open structure of the towers. A comparison of the facades of Laon Cathedral and Saint-Étienne (FIG. 12-33) at Caen reveals a much deeper penetration of the wall mass in the later building. At Laon, as in Gothic architecture generally, the operating principle was to reduce sheer mass and replace it with intricately framed voids.

Notre-Dame, Paris. About 1130, Louis VI moved his official residence to Paris, spurring much commercial activity and a great building boom, including the erection of a modern cathedral worthy of the new intellectual capital of Europe (see "Paris, the New Center of Medieval Learning," page 388).

Notre-Dame (FIG. 13-10) occupies a picturesque site on an island in the Seine River called the Île-de-la-Cité. The Gothic church, which replaced a large Merovingian basilica, has a complicated building history. The choir and transept were in place by 1182, the nave by about 1225, and the facade not until 1250 to 1260. Sexpartite vaults cover the nave, as at Laon. The original elevation (the builders modified the design as work progressed) had four stories, but the scheme (FIG. 13-15b) differed from Laon's (FIG. 13-15a). In each bay, in place of the triforium over the gallery, was a stained-glass *oculus* (small round window), opening up the wall below the clerestory lancet. As a result, windows filled two of the four stories, further reducing the masonry area.

The innovative architectural device that made this possible was the *flying buttress,* an external buttress that springs from the lower roofs over the aisles and ambulatory and counters the outward thrust of the nave vaults. Gothic builders had introduced flying buttresses as early as 1150 in a few smaller churches, but at Notre-Dame in Paris, they circle a great urban cathedral. The internal

Paris, the New Center of Medieval Learning

A few years before the formal consecration of the altar of the Cathedral of Notre-Dame (FIG. 13-10) in Paris, Philip II Augustus (r. 1180–1223) succeeded to the throne. Philip brought the feudal barons under his control and expanded the royal domains to include Normandy in the north and most of Languedoc in the south, laying the foundation for the modern nation of France. Renowned as "the maker of Paris," he gave the city its walls, paved its streets, and built the palace of the Louvre (now one of the world's great museums) to house the royal family.

One result of the urbanization of Paris that had enormous consequences for the later history of Europe was the emergence of cities as the centers of scholarship and teaching, displacing monasteries in this role. Although Rome remained the religious center of Western Christendom, the Île-de-France and Paris in particular became its intellectual capital as well as the leading artistic center of the Gothic world. The University of Paris attracted the best minds from all over Europe. Virtually every thinker of note in the Gothic age at some point studied or taught in Paris.

Even in the Romanesque period, Paris was a center of learning. Its Cathedral School professors, known as Schoolmen, developed the philosophy called *Scholasticism*. The greatest of the early Schoolmen was Peter Abelard (1079–1142), a champion of logical reasoning. Abelard and his contemporaries had been introduced to the writings of the Greek philosopher Aristotle through the Arabic scholars of Islamic Spain. Abelard applied Aristotle's system of rational inquiry to the interpretation of religious belief. Until the 12th century, both clergy and laymen considered truth the exclusive property of divine revelation as given in the holy scriptures. But the Schoolmen, using Aristotle's method, sought to demonstrate that reason alone could lead to certain truths. Their goal was to prove the central articles of Christian faith by argument (*disputatio*). In Scholastic argument, the Schoolmen stated a possibility, then cited an authoritative view in objection, next reconciled the positions, and, finally, offered a reply to each of the rejected original arguments.

One of Abelard's greatest critics was Bernard of Clairvaux (see "Bernard of Clairvaux," page 356), who believed that Scholasticism was equivalent to questioning Christian dogma. Although Bernard succeeded in 1140 in having the Church officially condemn Abelard's doctrines, the Schoolmen's philosophy developed systematically until it became the dominant Western philosophy of the late Middle Ages. By the 13th century, the Schoolmen of Paris already had organized as a professional guild of master scholars, separate from the numerous Church schools overseen by the bishop of Paris. The structure of the Parisian guild served as the model for many other European universities.

The greatest advocate of Abelard's Scholasticism was Thomas Aquinas (1225–1274), an Italian Dominican friar who was declared a saint in 1323. Aquinas settled in Paris in 1244. There, the German theologian Albertus Magnus (d. 1280) instructed him in Aristotelian philosophy. Aquinas went on to become an influential teacher at the University of Paris. His most famous work, *Summa Theologica* (*Compendium of Theology*; left unfinished at his death), is a model of the Scholastic approach to knowledge. Aquinas divided his treatise into books, the books into questions, the questions into articles, each article into objections with contradictions and responses, and, finally, answers to the objections. He set forth five ways to prove the existence of God by rational argument. Aquinas's work remains the foundation of contemporary Catholic teaching.

13-10 **Notre-Dame (looking northwest), Paris, France, begun 1163; nave and flying buttresses, ca. 1180–1200; remodeled after 1225.**

King Philip II initiated a building boom in Paris, which quickly became the intellectual capital of Europe. Notre-Dame in Paris was the first great cathedral built using flying buttresses.

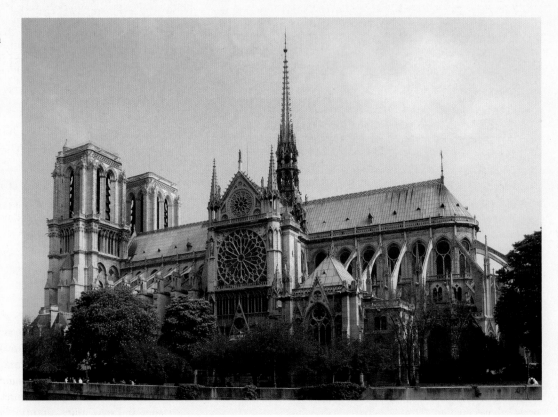

High Gothic Cathedrals

The great cathedrals erected throughout Europe in the later 12th and 13th centuries are the enduring symbols of the Gothic age. They are eloquent testimonies to the extraordinary skill of the architects, engineers, carpenters, masons, sculptors, glassworkers, and metalsmiths who constructed and embellished them. Most of the architectural components of Gothic cathedrals appeared in earlier structures, but Gothic architects combined them in new ways. The essential ingredients of their formula for constructing churches in the opus modernum style were rib vaults with pointed arches, flying buttresses, and huge colored-glass windows. These three features and the most important other terms used in describing Gothic buildings are listed and defined here and illustrated in FIG. 13-11.

- **Pinnacle** (FIG. 13-11, no. 1) A sharply pointed ornament capping the piers or flying buttresses; also used on cathedral facades.
- **Flying buttresses** (2) Masonry struts that transfer the thrust of the nave vaults across the roofs of the side aisles and ambulatory to a tall pier rising above the church's exterior wall.
- **Vaulting web** (3) The masonry blocks (the *web*) filling the area between the ribs of a groin vault.
- **Diagonal rib** (4) In plan, one of the ribs forming the X of a groin vault. In FIG. 13-9, the diagonal ribs are the lines *AC* and *DB*.
- **Transverse rib** (5) A rib crossing the nave or aisle at a 90-degree angle (lines *AB* and *DC* in FIG. 13-9).
- **Springing** (6) The lowest stone of an arch; in Gothic vaulting, the lowest stone of a diagonal or transverse rib.
- **Clerestory** (7) The windows below the vaults in the nave elevation's uppermost level. By using flying buttresses and rib vaults with pointed arches, Gothic architects could build huge clerestory windows and fill them with stained glass held in place by ornamental stonework called *tracery.*
- **Oculus** (8) A small round window.
- **Lancet** (9) A tall, narrow window crowned by a pointed arch.
- **Triforium** (10) The story in the nave elevation consisting of arcades, usually *blind arcades* but occasionally filled with stained glass.

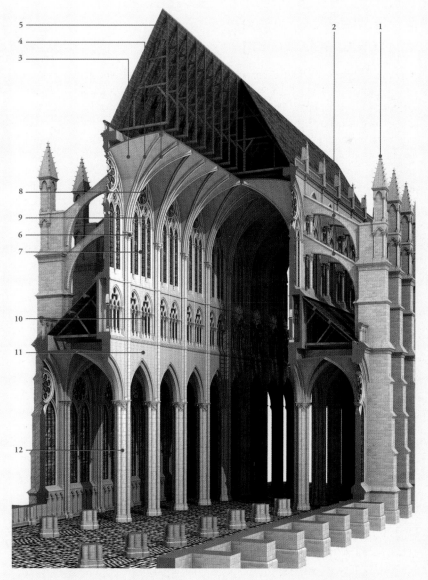

13-11 Cutaway view of a High Gothic cathedral based on Amiens Cathedral (FIGS. 13-15*d* and 13-20) (John Burge).

The major elements of the High Gothic formula for constructing a church in the opus modernum style are rib vaults with pointed arches, flying buttresses, and stained-glass windows.

- **Nave arcade** (11) The series of arches supported by piers separating the nave from the side aisles.
- **Compound pier (cluster pier) with shafts (responds)** (12) A pier with a group, or cluster, of attached shafts, or responds, extending to the springing of the vaults.

quadrant arches (FIG. 12-36, *right*) beneath the aisle roofs at Durham, also employed at Laon, perform a similar function and may be regarded as precedents for exposed Gothic flying buttresses. The combination of precisely positioned flying buttresses and rib vaults with pointed arches was the ideal solution to the problem of constructing lofty naves with huge windows (see "High Gothic Cathedrals," above, and FIG. 13-11).

Chartres after 1194. Churches burned frequently in the Middle Ages (see "The Burning of Canterbury Cathedral," page 353), and church officials often had to raise money unexpectedly for new building campaigns. In contrast to monastic churches, which usually were small and often could be completed quickly, urban cathedrals had construction histories that frequently extended over decades and sometimes centuries, and required a large workforce

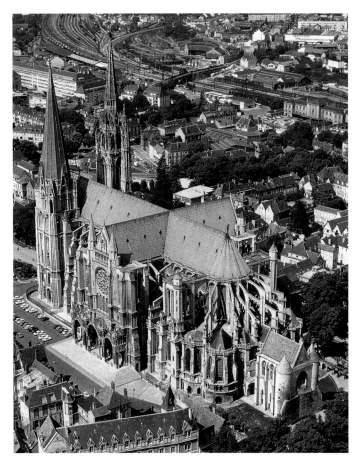

13-12 Aerial view of Chartres Cathedral (looking northwest), Chartres, France, as rebuilt after 1194.

Architectural historians consider the rebuilt Chartres Cathedral the earliest example of High Gothic architecture. The sculptures of its two transept porches are also prime examples of High Gothic style.

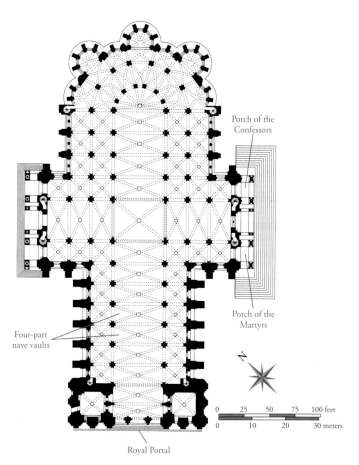

13-13 Plan of Chartres Cathedral, Chartres, France, as rebuilt after the 1194 fire (after Paul Frankl).

The Chartres plan—in which one square (instead of two) in each aisle flanks a single rectangular unit in the nave with a four-part vault—became the norm for High Gothic church architecture.

of quarriers, masons, sculptors, glaziers, and metalsmiths. Financing for building projects depended largely on taxation and donations, and sometimes the clergy offered *indulgences* (pardons for sins committed) to those who helped underwrite the enormous cost of erecting a large urban cathedral. A shortfall of funds often caused an interruption in the building program. Unforeseen events, such as wars, famines, or plagues, or friction between the town and cathedral authorities would also often halt construction, which then might not resume for years. At Reims in 1323, the townspeople revolted against their heavy tax burden and stormed the bishop's residence, driving him out of the city and suspending work on the cathedral for three years. A notable exception to the rule was the rebuilding of Chartres Cathedral (FIG. 13-12) after the devastating fire of 1194, which took a relatively short 27 years.

Chartres Cathedral's mid-12th-century west facade (FIG. 13-4) and the masonry of the crypt to the east were the only sections left standing after the 1194 conflagration. The crypt housed the most precious relic of Chartres—the mantle of the Virgin, which miraculously survived the fire. For reasons of piety and economy, the builders used the crypt for the foundation of the new structure. The retention of the crypt and west facade determined the new church's dimensions but not its plan or elevation. Architectural historians generally consider the post-1194 Chartres Cathedral the first High Gothic (1194–1300) building.

The Chartres plan (FIG. 13-13) reveals a new kind of organization. Rectangular nave bays replaced the square bays with

sexpartite vaults and the alternate-support system, still present in Early Gothic churches such as Laon Cathedral (FIG. 13-7). The new system, in which a single square in each aisle (rather than two, as before) flanks a single rectangular unit in the nave, became the High Gothic norm.

A change in vault design and the abandonment of the alternate-support system usually accompanied this new bay arrangement. The High Gothic nave vault, which covered only one bay and therefore could be braced more easily than its Early Gothic predecessor, had only four parts. The combined visual effect of these changes was to unify the interior (FIG. 13-14), because the nave now consisted of a sequence of identical units. The level crowns of the successive nave vaults, which pointed arches made possible, enhanced this effect.

Another key features of the 1194 Chartres Cathedral, as in the earlier Paris Cathedral (FIG. 13-10), was the incorporation of flying buttresses. These external buttresses enabled the builders to eliminate the tribune above the aisle, which had partially braced Romanesque and Early Gothic naves (compare FIG. 13-15c with FIGS. 13-15a and 13-15b). The new High Gothic three-story nave elevation consisted of arcade, triforium, and clerestory with greatly enlarged windows. The Chartres windows are almost as tall as the main arcade and consist of double lancets with a single crowning oculus. The strategic placement of flying buttresses made possible a nave elevation in which the voids take up more space than the solid masonry.

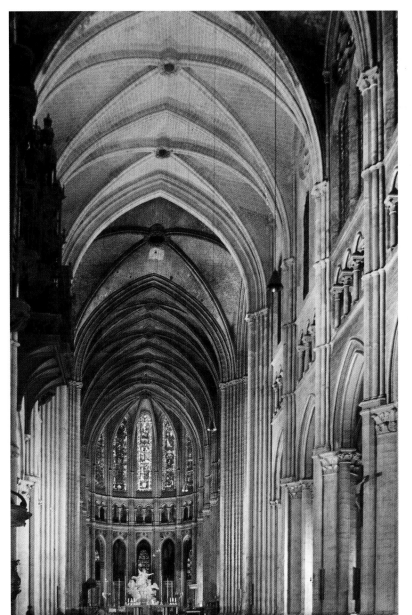

13-14 Interior of Chartres Cathedral (looking east), Chartres, France, begun 1194.

Chartres Cathedral established the High Gothic model also in its three-story elevation consisting of nave arcade, triforium, and clerestory with stained-glass windows almost as tall as the main arcade.

Chartres Stained Glass. Despite the vastly increased size of its clerestory windows, the Chartres nave (FIG. 13-14) is not drenched with light. This seeming contradiction is the result of the use of colored glass for the windows instead of clear glass. The purpose of the Chartres stained-glass windows was not to illuminate the interior with bright sunlight but to transform natural light into Suger's mystical lux nova (see "Stained-Glass Windows," page 392). Chartres Cathedral retains almost the full complement of its original stained glass, paid for by workers' guilds (FIG. 13-16) and royalty (FIG. 13-18) alike. Although the tinted windows have a dimming effect, they transform the character of the church's interior in dramatic fashion. Gothic buildings that no longer have their original stained-glass windows give a false impression of what their designers intended.

One Chartres window that survived the fire of 1194 is the tall single lancet called *Notre Dame de la Belle Verrière*

13-15 Nave elevations of four French Gothic cathedrals at the same scale (John Burge).

Gothic naves evolved from a four-story elevation (arcade, tribune gallery, triforium, clerestory) to a three-story elevation (without tribune). The height of the vaults also increased dramatically.

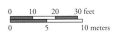

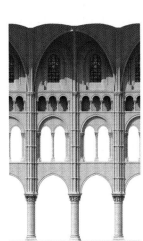

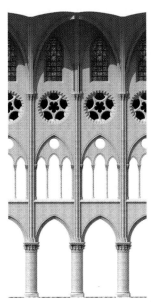

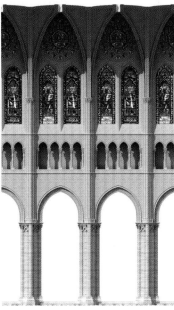

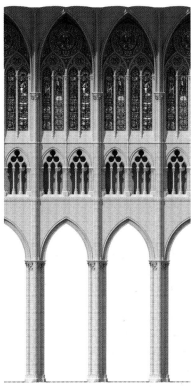

a Laon
height of nave, 80′; width of nave, 37′6″; ratio, 2.13:1

b Paris
height of nave, 115′; width of nave, 40′; ratio, 2.88:1

c Chartres
height of nave, 120′; width of nave, 45′6″; ratio, 2.64:1

d Amiens
height of nave, 144′; width of nave, 48′; ratio, 3.00:1

Stained-Glass Windows

Stained-glass windows, although not a Gothic invention, are almost synonymous with Gothic architecture. No other age produced windows of such rich color and beauty. The technology of manufacturing colored glass is very old, however. Egyptian artists excelled at fashioning colorful glass objects for both home and tomb, and archaeologists have uncovered thousands of colored-glass artifacts at Greco-Roman sites. But Gothic artists used stained glass in new ways. In earlier eras, the clergy introduced color and religious iconography into church interiors mainly with mural paintings and mosaics, often with magnificent effect. Stained-glass windows differ from mosaics and frescoes in one all-important respect. They do not conceal walls. They replace them. Moreover, they transmit rather than reflect light, filtering and transforming natural sunlight.

Abbot Suger called this colored light lux nova (see "Abbot Suger," page 383). Suger's contemporary, Hugh of Saint-Victor (1096–1141), a prominent Parisian theologian, also commented on the mystical quality of stained-glass windows: "Stained-glass windows are the Holy Scriptures . . . and since their brilliance lets the splendor of the True Light pass into the church, they enlighten those inside."* William Durandus (ca. 1230–1296), bishop of Mende in southern France, expressed a similar sentiment at the end of the 13th century: "The glass windows in a church are Holy Scriptures, which expel the wind and the rain, that is, all things hurtful, but transmit the light of the True Sun, that is, God, into the hearts of the faithful."†

According to Suger, the 12th-century stained-glass windows of Saint-Denis (FIG. 13-2) were "painted by the exquisite hands of many masters from different regions,"§ proving that the art was well established at that time. In fact, colored-glass windows appeared in some churches as early as the fourth century, and several sophisticated Romanesque examples of figural stained-glass windows survive.

The manufacture of these windows was costly and labor-intensive. A German Benedictine monk named Theophilus recorded the full process around 1100. First, the master designer drew the exact composition of the planned window on a wood panel, indicating all the linear details and noting the colors for each section. Glassblowers provided flat sheets of glass of different colors to *glaziers* (glassworkers), who cut the windowpanes to the required size and shape with special iron shears. Glaziers produced an even greater range of colors by *flashing* (fusing one layer of colored glass to another). Next, painters added details such as faces, hands, hair, and clothing in enamel by tracing the master design on the wood panel through the colored glass. Then they heated the painted glass to fuse the enamel to the surface. Next, the glaziers "leaded" the various fragments of glass—that is, they joined them by strips of lead called *cames*. The *leading* not only held the pieces together but also separated the colors to heighten the effect of the design as a whole. The distinctive character of Romanesque and Gothic stained-glass windows is largely the result of this combination of fine linear details with broad, flat expanses of color framed by black lead. Finally, the glaziers strengthened the completed window with an armature of iron bands, which in the 12th century formed a grid over the entire design (FIG. 13-17). In the 13th century, the bands followed the outlines of the medallions and of the surrounding areas (FIGS. **13-16**, 13-18, and 13-26).

The form of the stone frames for the stained-glass windows also evolved. At Saint-Denis (FIG. 13-1) and Laon (FIG. 13-8), and on Chartres Cathedral's 12th-century west facade (FIG. 13-4), *plate tracery* holds the rose window in place. The glass fills only the "punched holes" in the heavy ornamental stonework. *Bar tracery*, a later development, used first at Reims (FIGS. 13-24 and 13-24A), is much more slender. The stained-glass windows of the Chartres transepts (FIG. 13-18) and on the facades of the cathedrals of Amiens (FIG. 13-22) and Reims fill almost the entire opening, and the stonework is unobtrusive, resembling delicate leading more than masonry wall.

*Hugh of Saint-Victor, *Speculum de mysteriis ecclesiae,* sermon 2.
†William Durandus, *Rationale divinorum officiorum,* 1.1.24. Translated by John Mason Neale and Benjamin Webb, *The Symbolism of Churches and Church Ornaments* (Leeds: T. W. Green, 1843), 28.
§Translated by Erwin Panofsky, *Abbot Suger on the Abbey Church of Saint-Denis and Its Art Treasures,* 2d ed. (Princeton: Princeton University Press, 1979), 73.

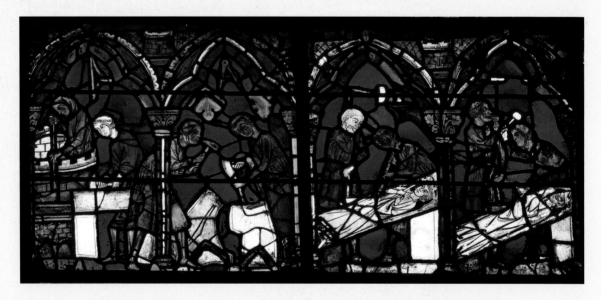

13-16 **Stonemasons and sculptors, detail of a stained-glass window in the northernmost radiating chapel in the ambulatory, Chartres Cathedral, Chartres, France, ca. 1200–1220.**

Glaziers made stained-glass windows by fusing layers of colored glass, joining the pieces with lead strips, and painting the details in enamel. The windows transformed natural light into divine light.

(*Our Lady of the Beautiful Window*, FIG. 13-17). The central section with a red background, which depicts the Virgin Mary enthroned with the Christ Child in her lap, dates to about 1170. High Gothic glaziers added framing angels seen against a blue ground (not included in FIG. 13-17) when they reinstalled the window in the south aisle of the 13th-century choir. Mary is here the beautiful young queen of Heaven, haloed, crowned, and accompanied by the dove of the Holy Spirit. Comparing this Virgin and Child with the enthroned Theotokos and Child (FIG. 9-20) of Hagia Sophia highlights not only the greater severity and aloofness of the Byzantine image but also the sharp difference between the light-reflecting mosaic medium and Gothic light-filtering stained glass. Gothic and Byzantine builders used light to transform the material world into the spiritual, but in opposite ways. In Gothic architecture, light entered from outside the building through a screen of stone-set colored glass. In Byzantine architecture, light reflected off myriad glass tesserae set into the thick masonry wall.

Chartres Cathedral's 13th-century Gothic windows are even more spectacular than the *Belle Verrière* because the introduction of flying buttresses made it possible for builders to plan from the outset on filling entire walls with stained glass. The north transept's immense rose window (approximately 43 feet in diameter) and tall

lancets (FIG. 13-18) were the gift of Queen Blanche of Castile (FIG. 13-32) around 1220. The royal motifs of yellow castles on a red ground and yellow *fleur-de-lis*—three-petaled iris flowers (compare FIG. 25-24), France's royal floral emblem—on a blue ground fill the eight narrow windows in the rose's lower *spandrels*. The iconography is also fitting for a queen. The enthroned Virgin and Child appear in the *roundel* at the center of the rose, which resembles a gem-studded book cover or cloisonné brooch. Around her are four doves of the Holy Spirit and eight angels. Twelve square panels contain images of Old Testament kings, including David and Solomon (at the 12 and 1 o'clock positions, respectively). These are the royal ancestors of Christ. Isaiah (11:1–3) had prophesied that the Messiah would come from the family of the patriarch Jesse, father of David. The genealogical "tree of Jesse" is a familiar motif in medieval art. Below, in the lancets, are Saint Anne and the baby Virgin (see "Early Christian Saints," pages 246–247). Flanking them are four of Christ's Old Testament ancestors (Melchizedek, David, Solomon, and Aaron), echoing the royal genealogy of the rose but at a larger scale. Many Gothic

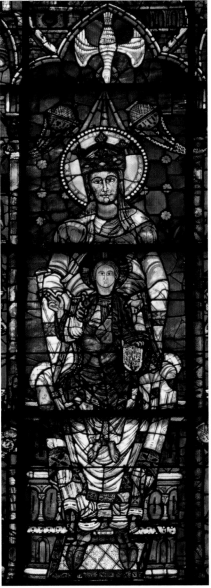

13-17 Virgin and Child and angels (*Notre Dame de la Belle Verrière*), detail of a window in the south wall of the choir of Chartres Cathedral, Chartres, France, ca. 1170. Stained glass, 12′ 9″ high.

This stained-glass window miraculously survived the devastating Chartres fire of 1194. It has an armature of iron bands forming a grid over the entire design, an Early Gothic characteristic.

1 ft.

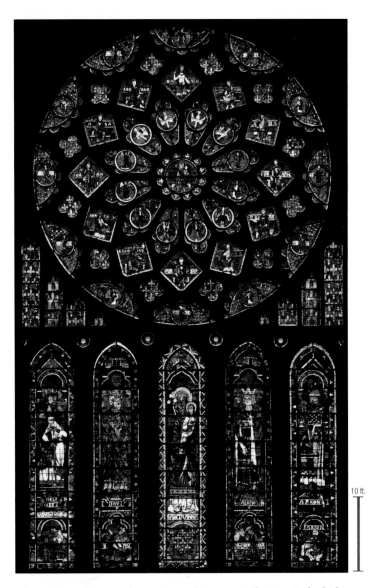

10 ft.

13-18 Rose window and lancets, north transept, Chartres Cathedral, Chartres, France, ca. 1220. Stained glass, rose window 43′ in diameter.

Immense stained-glass rose and lancet windows, held in place by an intricate armature of bar tracery, fill almost the entire facade wall of the High Gothic north transept of Chartres Cathedral.

13-19 Saint Theodore, jamb statue in the left portal of the Porch of the Martyrs, south transept, Chartres Cathedral, Chartres, France, ca. 1230.

Although the statue of Theodore is still attached to a column, the setting no longer determines its pose. The High Gothic sculptor portrayed the saint in a contrapposto stance, as in classical statuary.

stained-glass windows also present narrative scenes, and their iconographical programs are often more complex than those of the sculptured church portals. (The representation of masons and sculptors at work in FIG. 13-16, for example, is the lowest section of a lancet dedicated to the life of Caraunus—Chéron in French—a legendary local sixth-century martyr who was probably the patron saint of the Chartres stonemasons' guild.)

Almost the entire mass of wall opens up into stained glass, held in place by an intricate stone armature of bar tracery and filling the church with lux nova that changes in hue and intensity with the hours. Here, the Gothic passion for luminous colored light led to a most daring and successful attempt to subtract all superfluous material bulk just short of destabilizing the structure. That this vast, complex fabric of stone-set glass has maintained its structural integrity for almost 800 years attests to the Gothic builders' engineering genius.

Chartres South Transept. The sculptures adorning the portals of the two Chartres transepts erected after the 1194 fire are also prime examples of the new High Gothic spirit. Unlike the Early Gothic portals of its west facade (compare FIGS. 13-4 and 13-12), the Chartres transept portals project forcefully from the church, following the innovative form of the west facade portals of Laon (FIG. 13-8) and Paris (FIG. 13-10) Cathedrals. Similarly, the jamb statues of saints (FIGS. 13-19 and 13-19A) in the transepts, which date from 1220 to 1230, are more independent from the architectural framework. The figures still stand in front of the jamb columns, but are carved separately from them. The architectural setting does not determine their poses as much as it did on the west portals (FIG. 13-6).

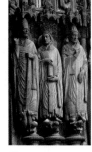

⟐13-19A
Porch of the Confessors, Chartres, ca. 1220–1230.

The masterpiece of the south transept is the figure of Saint Theodore (FIG. 13-19), the martyred warrior on the left jamb of the left portal (the Porch of the Martyrs). The statue embodies the great changes that French sculpture had undergone since the Royal Portal jamb figures of the mid-12th century. The High Gothic sculptor portrayed Theodore as the ideal Christian knight, clothing him in the cloak and chain-mail armor of 13th-century Crusaders. The handsome, long-haired youth holds his spear firmly in his right hand and rests his left hand on his shield. He turns his head to the left and swings out his hip to the right. The body's resulting torsion and pronounced sway recall ancient Greek statuary, especially the contrapposto stance of Polykleitos's *Spear Bearer* (FIG. 5-41). The stylistic transformation that occurred in 13th-century French Gothic sculpture echoes the revolutionary developments in ancient Greek sculpture during the transition from the Archaic to the Classical style and could appropriately be described as a second "Classical revolution."

Amiens Cathedral. Chartres Cathedral is one of the most influential buildings in the history of architecture. Its builders set a pattern that many other Gothic architects followed, even if they refined the details. Construction of Amiens Cathedral began in 1220 while work was still in progress at Chartres. The architects were ROBERT DE LUZARCHES, THOMAS DE CORMONT, and RENAUD DE CORMONT. The survival of the names of these and other Gothic architects no doubt reflects the enormous prestige that accrued to all associated with the great cathedrals of the Gothic age. The Amiens builders finished the cathedral's nave (FIG. 13-20) by 1236 and the radiating chapels by 1247, but work on the choir (FIG. 13-21) continued until almost 1270. The Amiens elevation (FIGS. 13-15d and 13-20) derived from the High Gothic formula of Chartres (FIGS. 13-14 and 13-15c). Amiens Cathedral's proportions are more slender, however, and the number and complexity of the lancet windows in both its clerestory and its triforium are greater. The whole design reflects the Amiens builders' confident use of the complete High Gothic structural vocabulary: the rectangular-bay system, the four-part rib vault, and an external buttressing system that made possible the almost complete elimination of heavy masses and thick weight-bearing walls. At Amiens, the concept of skeletal architecture reached full maturity. The remaining stretches of wall seem to serve no purpose other than to provide a weather screen for the interior.

Amiens Cathedral is one of the most impressive examples of French Gothic architects' obsession with constructing ever-taller naves. Using their new skeletal frames of stone, French builders attempted goals almost beyond limit, pushing to new heights with increasingly slender supports. The nave vaults at Laon rise to a height of about 80 feet; at Paris, 115 feet; and at Chartres, 120 feet. Those at Amiens are 144 feet above the floor (FIG. 13-20). The most daring quest for exceptional height occurred at Beauvais (FIG. I-3), where the choir vaults are 157 feet high—but the builders never completed the cathedral. The Beauvais vaults are unstable and require additional buttressing today.

At Amiens, the lines of the vault ribs converge at the colonnettes and speed down the shell-like walls to the compound piers. Almost every part of the superstructure has its corresponding element below. The overall effect is of effortless strength, of a buoyant lightness not normally associated with stone architecture. Viewed directly from below, the choir vaults (FIG. 13-21) resemble a canopy, tentlike and suspended from bundled masts. The light flooding in from the clerestory makes the vaults seem even more insubstantial. The effect recalls another great building, one utterly

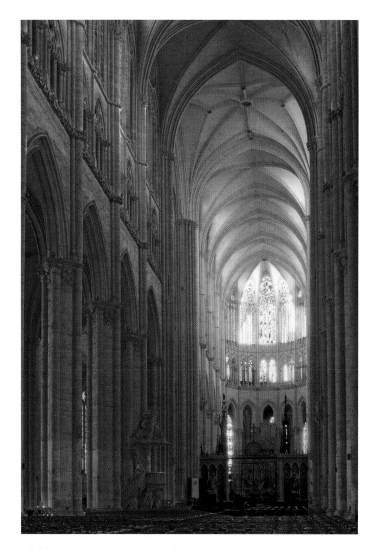

13-20 ROBERT DE LUZARCHES, THOMAS DE CORMONT, and RENAUD DE CORMONT, interior of Amiens Cathedral (looking east), Amiens, France, begun 1220.

The concept of skeletal architecture reached full maturity in the nave and choir of Amiens Cathedral. The four-part nave vaults on pointed arches rise an astounding 144 feet above the floor (FIG. 13-15*d*).

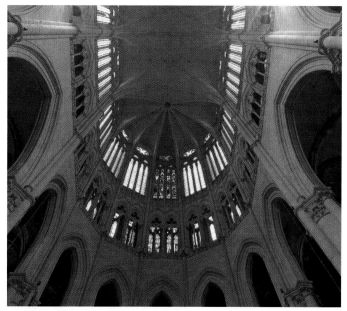

13-21 ROBERT DE LUZARCHES, THOMAS DE CORMONT, and RENAUD DE CORMONT, vaults, clerestory, and triforium of the choir of Amiens Cathedral, Amiens, France, begun 1220.

The Amiens choir vaults resemble a canopy on bundled masts. The light entering from the clerestory and triforium creates a buoyant lightness not normally associated with stone architecture.

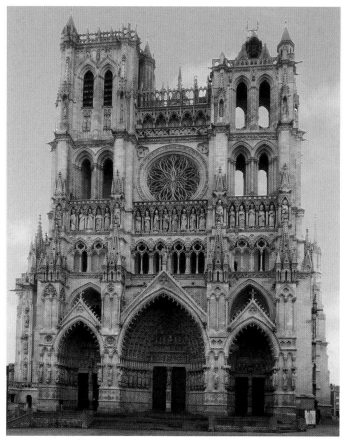

13-22 ROBERT DE LUZARCHES, THOMAS DE CORMONT, and RENAUD DE CORMONT, west facade of Amiens Cathedral, Amiens, France, begun 1220.

The deep piercing of the Amiens facade left few surfaces for decoration, but sculptors covered the remaining ones with colonnettes, pinnacles, and rosettes that nearly dissolve the structure's masonry.

different from Amiens but where light also plays a defining role: Hagia Sophia (FIG. 9-8) in Constantinople. The designers of Amiens Cathedral, too, reduced the building's physical mass through structural ingenuity and daring, but in the High Gothic basilica, unlike the domed Byzantine church, light further dematerializes what remains.

Work began on the Amiens west facade (FIG. 13-22) at the same time as the nave (1220). Its lower parts reflect the influence of Laon Cathedral (FIG. 13-8) in the spacing of the funnel-like, gable-covered portals. At Amiens, however, the builders punctured the upper parts of the facade to an even greater degree. The deep piercing of walls and towers left few areas for decoration, but sculptors covered the remaining surfaces with a network of colonnettes, arches, pinnacles, rosettes, and other decorative stonework that visually screens and nearly dissolves the structure's solid core. Sculpture also extends to the areas above the portals, especially the band of statues (the *kings' gallery*) running the full width of the facade directly below the rose window (with 15th-century tracery). The uneven towers were later additions. The shorter one dates from the 14th century, the taller one from the 15th century.

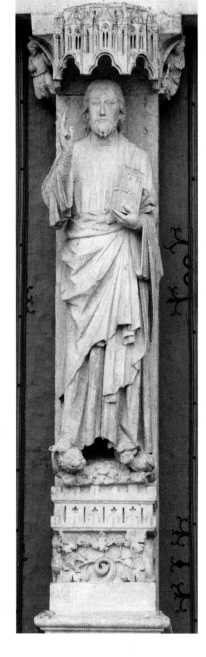

13-23 Christ (*Beau Dieu*), trumeau statue of the central doorway of the west facade, Amiens Cathedral, Amiens, France, ca. 1220–1235.

The *Beau Dieu* blesses all who enter Amiens Cathedral. He tramples a lion and a dragon symbolizing the evil forces in the world. This benevolent Gothic Christ gives Christian worshipers hope in salvation.

Beau Dieu. Greeting worshipers as they enter the cathedral is the statue on the central doorway's trumeau that the French call the *Beau Dieu* (*Beautiful God*; FIG. 13-23). The High Gothic sculptor fully modeled Christ's figure, enveloping his body with massive drapery folds cascading from his waist. Compared with the kings and queens (FIG. 13-6) of the Royal Portal, the *Beau Dieu* is almost independent of its architectural setting. Nonetheless, the statue is still attached to the trumeau, and the sculptor placed an architectural canopy over Christ's head. The canopy mimics the east end of a 13th-century cathedral with a series of radiating chapels boasting elegant lancet windows in the latest Gothic style.

Above the *Beau Dieu* is the great central tympanum with the representation of Christ as Last Judge. The trumeau Christ does not strike terror into sinners, however. Instead, he blesses those who enter the church and tramples a lion and a dragon symbolizing the evil forces in the world. This image of Christ gives humankind hope in salvation. The Amiens *Beau Dieu* exemplifies the bearded, benevolent Gothic image of Christ that replaced the youthful Early Christian Christ (FIGS. 8-8A and 8-8B) and the stern Byzantine Pantocrator (FIG. 9-23) as the preferred representation of the Savior in later European art. The handsome figure's quiet grace and grandeur also contrast sharply with the emotional intensity of the twisting Romanesque prophet (FIG. 12-13) carved in relief on the Moissac trumeau.

Reims Cathedral. Construction of Reims Cathedral in the heart of France's Champagne wine district began about a decade before work commenced at Amiens. Dedicated to the Virgin Mary, Reims Cathedral occupies a special place in the history of France

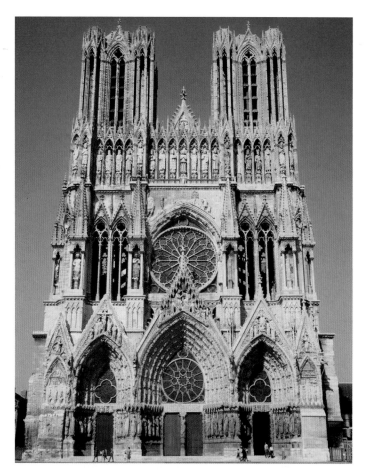

13-24 JEAN D'ORBAIS, JEAN LE LOUP, GAUCHER DE REIMS, and BERNARD DE SOISSONS, west facade of Reims Cathedral, Reims, France, ca. 1211–1290.

Reims Cathedral's facade reveals High Gothic architects' desire to replace heavy masonry with intricately framed voids. Stained-glass windows, not stone reliefs, fill the three tympana.

as well as in the history of architecture. Since 496 it has been the site of all French kings' coronations. The architects were JEAN D'ORBAIS, JEAN LE LOUP, GAUCHER DE REIMS, and BERNARD DE SOISSONS. The last two were primarily responsible for the west facade (FIG. 13-24), where they carried the High Gothic style of Amiens still further, both architecturally and sculpturally. The Amiens and Reims facades, although similar, display some significant differences. The kings' gallery of statues at Reims is *above* the great rose window, and the figures stand in taller and more

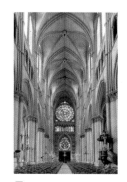

13-24A Interior of Reims Cathedral, begun 1211.

ornate frames. In fact, the builders "stretched" every detail of the facade. The openings in the towers and those to the left and right of the rose window are taller, narrower, and more intricately decorated, and they more closely resemble the elegant lancets of the clerestory within (FIG. 13-24A). A pointed arch also frames the rose window itself, and the pinnacles over the portals are taller and more elaborate than those at Amiens. Most striking, however, is the treatment of the tympana over the doorways, where the builders inserted stained-glass windows instead of the stone relief sculptures

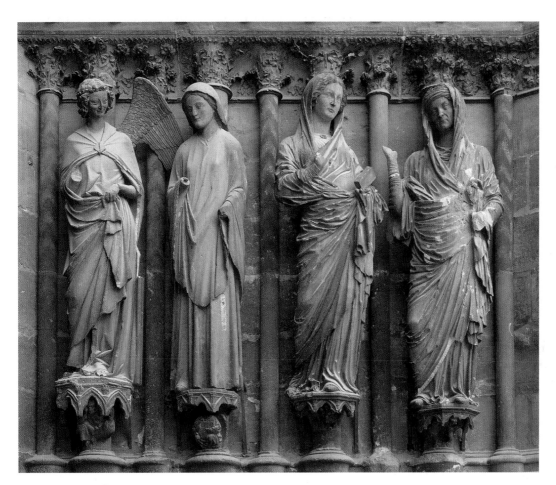

13-25 *Annunciation* and *Visitation,* jamb statues on the right side of the central doorway of the west facade of Reims Cathedral, Reims, France, ca. 1230–1255.

Several sculptors working in diverse styles carved the Reims jamb figures, but all resemble free-standing statues, with bodies and arms in motion. The biblical figures gesture and engage in dialogue.

that adorned earlier facades. The contrast with Romanesque heavy masonry construction (FIG. 12-33) is extreme. No less noteworthy, however, is the rapid transformation of the Gothic facade since the 12th-century designs of Saint-Denis (FIG. 13-1) and Chartres (FIG. 13-4) and even Laon (FIG. 13-8).

Reims Cathedral is also a prime example of the High Gothic style in sculpture. The statues and reliefs of the west facade celebrate the Virgin Mary. Above the central gable, Mary is crowned as queen of Heaven. On the trumeau, she is the youthful Mother of God above reliefs depicting Original Sin. (Many medieval theologians considered Mary the new Eve, who, through her son, Jesus, the new Adam, can guide the way to redemption.) The jamb statues to Mary's left and right relate episodes from the infancy cycle (see "The Life of Jesus in Art," pages 244–245), including the Annunciation and Visitation (FIG. 13-25). The statues appear completely detached from their architectural background because the sculptors shrank the supporting columns into insignificance. The columns in no way restrict the free and easy movements of the full-bodied figures. These 13th-century jamb statues contrast strikingly with those of the Early Gothic Royal Portal (FIG. 13-6), where the background columns occupy a volume equal to that of the figures.

The Reims statues also vividly illustrate how long it frequently took to complete the sculptural ornamentation of a large Gothic cathedral. Sculptural projects of this magnitude normally required decades to complete and entailed hiring many sculptors, often working in diverse styles. Art historians believe that three different sculptors carved the four statues in FIG. 13-25 at different times during the quarter century from 1230 to 1255. The Visitation group (*right*) is the work of one of the many artists of the era—in

Germany and Italy as well as France—who must have studied classical statuary. Reims was an ancient Roman city. The heads of both Mary and Saint Elizabeth resemble Roman portraits, and the rich folds of the garments they wear also recall Roman sculpted figures (FIG. 7-60). The Gothic statues closely approximate the classical naturalistic style, and feature postures in which the swaying of the hips is much more pronounced than in the Chartres Saint Theodore (FIG. 13-19). The right legs of the Reims figures bend, and the knees press through the rippling folds of the garments. The sculptor also set the holy figures' arms in motion. Mary and Elizabeth look at each other and engage in a dialogue using gestures. In the Reims Visitation group, the formerly isolated Gothic jamb statues became actors in a biblical narrative.

The statues in the Annunciation group (FIG. 13-25, *left*) also stand free from their architectural setting, but they are products of different workshops. Mary is a slender figure with severe drapery. This artist preferred broad expanses of fabric to the multiplicity of folds of the Visitation Mary. The angel Gabriel, the latest of the four statues, exhibits the elegant style of the Parisian court at the middle of the 13th century (compare FIG. 13-34). Gabriel has a much more elongated body and is far more animated than his neighbors. He pivots gracefully, almost as if dancing, and smiles broadly. Like a courtier, Gabriel exudes charm. Mary, in contrast, is serious and introspective and does not respond overtly to the news the angel has brought.

Sainte-Chapelle. The stained-glass windows inserted into the portal tympana of Reims Cathedral exemplify the wall-dissolving High Gothic architectural style. The architect of Sainte-Chapelle

Louis IX, the Saintly King

The royal patron behind the Parisian Rayonnant court style (FIG. 13-26) of Gothic art and architecture was King Louis IX (1215–1270; r. 1226–1270), grandson of Philip Augustus (see "Paris, the New Center of Medieval Learning," page 388). Louis inherited the throne when he was only 12 years old, so until he reached adulthood 6 years later, his mother, Blanche of Castile (FIG. 13-32), granddaughter of Eleanor of Aquitaine (see "Romanesque Countesses, Queens, and Nuns," page 367), served as France's regent.

The French regarded Louis as the ideal king. In 1297, only 27 years after Louis's death, Pope Boniface VIII (r. 1294–1303) declared the king a saint. In his own time, Louis was revered for his piety, justice, truthfulness, and charity. His almsgiving and his donations to religious foundations were extravagant. He especially favored the *mendicant* (begging) orders, the Dominicans and Franciscans (see "Mendicant Orders," page 423), because he admired their poverty, piety, and self-sacrificing disregard of material things.

Louis launched two unsuccessful Crusades (see "The Crusades," page 360), the Seventh (1248–1254, when in her son's absence, Blanche was again French regent) and the Eighth (1270). He died in Tunisia during the latter. As a crusading knight who lost his life in the service of the Church, Louis personified the chivalric virtues of courage, loyalty, and self-sacrifice. Saint Louis united in his person the best qualities of the Christian knight, the benevolent monarch, and the holy man. He became the model of medieval Christian kingship.

Louis's political accomplishments were also noteworthy. He subdued the unruly French barons, and between 1243 and 1314, no one seriously challenged the crown. He negotiated a treaty with King Henry III (r. 1216–1272) of England, France's traditional enemy. Such was Louis's reputation for integrity and just dealing that he served as arbiter in at least a dozen international disputes. So successful was he as peacekeeper that despite civil wars through most of the 13th century, international peace prevailed.

Under Saint Louis, medieval France was at its most prosperous, and its art and Rayonnant architecture were admired and imitated throughout Europe.

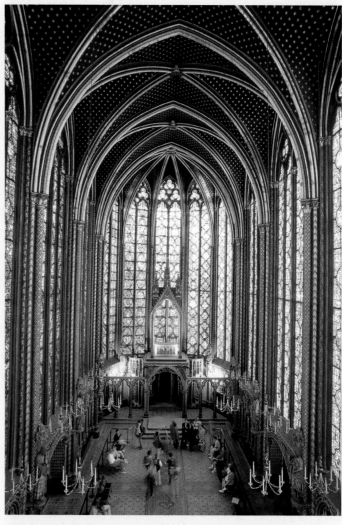

13-26 Interior of the upper chapel (looking southeast), Sainte-Chapelle, Paris, France, 1243–1248.

At Louis IX's Sainte-Chapelle, the architect succeeded in dissolving the walls to such an extent that 6,450 square feet of stained glass account for more than three-quarters of the Rayonnant Gothic structure.

in Paris extended this style to an entire building (FIG. 13-26). Louis IX (see "Louis IX, the Saintly King," above) built the chapel on the Île-de-la-Cité near Notre-Dame as a repository for the crown of thorns and other relics of Christ's passion that he had purchased in 1239 from his cousin Baldwin II (r. 1228–1261), the Latin emperor of Constantinople. Sainte-Chapelle is a masterpiece of the architectural style Louis favored—the High Gothic *Rayonnant* ("radiant") style, which dominated the second half of the 13th century. The chapel's architect carried the dissolution of walls and the reduction of the bulk of the supports to the point that some 6,450 square feet of stained glass make up more than three-quarters of the structure. The supporting elements are hardly more than large *mullions* (vertical stone bars). The emphasis is on the extreme slenderness of the architectural forms and on linearity in general. Although the building required restoration in the 19th century (after suffering damage during the French Revolution), it retains most of its original 13th-century stained glass. Sainte-Chapelle's enormous windows filter

the light and fill the interior with an unearthly rose-violet atmosphere. Approximately 49 feet high and 15 feet wide, they were the largest designed up to their time.

Virgin of Paris. The "court style" of Sainte-Chapelle has its pictorial parallel in the mannered elegance of the roughly contemporaneous Gabriel of the Reims Annunciation group (FIG. 13-25, *left*), but the style long outlived Saint Louis and his royal artists and architects. An example of the court style in Late Gothic (ca. 1300–1500) sculpture is the early-14th-century statue known as the *Virgin of Paris* (FIG. 13-27) because of its location in Paris Cathedral (FIG. 13-10). The sculptor portrayed Mary in an exaggerated S-curve posture typical of Late Gothic sculpture. She is a worldly queen and wears a heavy, gem-encrusted crown. The princely Christ Child reaches toward his young mother. The tender, anecdotal characterization of mother and son seen here is a later manifestation of the humanization of the portrayal of religious figures in Gothic sculpture that began at Chartres

Virgin and Child
(*Virgin of Paris*), Notre-
Dame, Paris, France,
early 14th century.

Late Gothic sculpture is
elegant and mannered.
Here, the solemnity of Early
and High Gothic religious
figures gave way to a tender,
anecdotal portrayal of Mary
and Jesus as royal mother
and son.

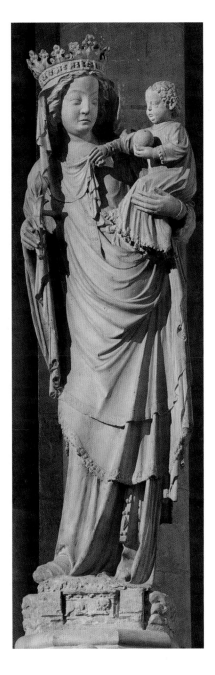

and developed especially in Germany (FIGS. 13-49 and 13-52). The tone of Late Gothic statuary is very different from the solemnity of most High Gothic figures, just as Late Classical Greek statues of the Olympian gods (compare FIG. 13-27 with FIG. 5-63) differ from High Classical depictions.

Saint-Maclou, Rouen. French Late Gothic architecture also represents a departure from the norms of High Gothic. The transition from Rayonnant architecture to the so-called *Flamboyant* style (named for the flamelike appearance of its pointed bar tracery) occurred in the 14th century. The new manner reached its florid maturity nearly a century later in Rouen, the capital of Normandy, in the church of Saint-Maclou (FIG. 13-28). The church is intimate in scale (only about 75 feet high and 180 feet long) compared with the grandiose 13th-century cathedrals, and its facade contrasts sharply with the High Gothic style (FIGS. 13-22 and 13-24). The five portals (two of them false doors) are not aligned but form a convex arc. Ornate gables crown the doorways, pierced through and filled with wiry, "flickering" Flamboyant tracery. Made up of curves and countercurves forming brittle decorative webs, the ornate Late Gothic tracery masks the building's structure. The transparency of the pinnacles over the doorways enables visitors to see the central rose window and the flying buttresses, even though they are set well back from the facade. The overlapping of all features, pierced as they are, confuses the structural lines and produces a bewildering complexity of views that is the hallmark of the Flamboyant style.

Carcassonne. The Gothic period may have been the age of the great cathedrals, but widespread prosperity also stimulated the construction of major secular buildings such as town halls, palaces, and private residences. In a time of frequent warfare, the feudal

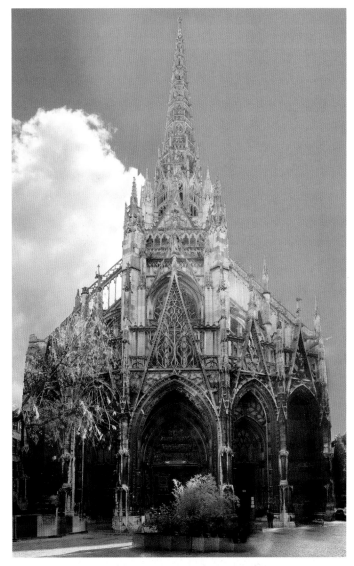

13-28 West facade of Saint-Maclou, Rouen, France, ca. 1500–1514.

Saint-Maclou is the masterpiece of Late Gothic Flamboyant architecture. Its ornate tracery of curves and countercurves forms brittle decorative webs that mask the small church's structure.

barons often constructed fortified castles in places that enemies could not easily reach. Sometimes thick defensive wall circuits or *ramparts* enclosed entire late medieval towns, such as Carcassonne (FIG. 13-29) in Languedoc in southern France. In time, however, purely defensive wars became obsolete due to the invention of artillery and improvements in siege craft. The fortress era gradually passed, and throughout Europe, once-mighty ramparts fell into ruin.

Carcassonne, once the regional center of resistance to the northern forces of royal France, is the best-preserved example of a Gothic fortified town. Heavily restored in the 19th century by EUGÈNE VIOLLET-LE-DUC (1814–1879; the architect responsible also for the restoration of Paris Cathedral, FIG. 13-10), Carcassonne occupies a site on a hill bounded by the Aude River. Fortified since Roman times, it has Visigothic walls dating from the 6th century, reinforced in the 12th century. *Battlements* (low parapets) with *crenellations* (composed of alternating solid *merlons* and open *crenels*) protected guards patrolling the stone ring surrounding the town. Carcassonne might have been forced to surrender, but could not easily be taken by storm. Within the town's double walls was a fortified castle (FIG. 13-29, *right*) with a massive

A SECOND OPINION

Gothic Cathedrals and Gothic Cities

The southern French walled city of Carcassonne (FIG. 13-29) can serve to underscore that the traditional approach to the study of Gothic cathedrals is deceiving. Rather than isolated and self-contained religious shrines, Gothic churches, especially the bishop's church, were integral components of their cities. Architectural historians are increasingly shifting their focus from individual buildings to the overall urban environment, although, unlike Gothic churches, no Gothic city is preserved in anything like its original form. However, a great deal is known about the general character of Gothic cities and the role of the cathedral in the urban environment.

Gothic cathedrals, in vivid contrast to the oratories of earlier medieval monasteries, were not sharply segregated from the secular world. Quite the contrary. Some, like Salisbury Cathedral (FIG. 13-40), stood majestically on vast green lawns, but most stood at the intersection of major streets in their respective cities, often with houses and shops crowding them on every side. As a rule, the cathedral was the largest and most richly ornamented building in a Gothic city, but civic and guild halls (FIG. 13-30), hospitals, and even palatial private residences (FIG. 13-31) competed with the bishop's church for attention—and in some cases for the claim to being the tallest structure in the city.

Secular life even extended into what is usually thought of as an inviolable sacred sanctuary. The Gothic cathedral was by no means exclusively a place of worship. Meetings of civic councils were so commonly held in the nave and aisles of spacious cathedrals that many towns never felt the need to erect administrative buildings. Cathedrals often were the place where lawsuits and other judicial proceedings were held. Reims Cathedral (FIG. 13-24) in France and Westminster Abbey (FIGS. 12-40 and 13-45) in England were where all French and English monarchs were crowned. It was not unusual for merchants to conduct business in cathedrals. At Chartres (FIG. 13-14), for example, wine merchants set up their stalls in the nave and later in the crypt of the cathedral dedicated to the Virgin. In the Gothic cathedral, the spiritual and secular worlds met and merged.

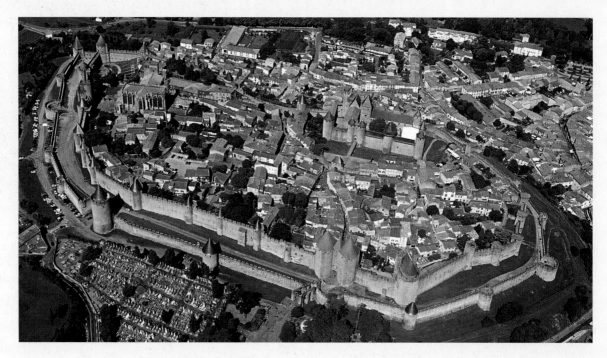

13-29 Aerial view of the fortified town of Carcassonne (looking west), France. Bastions and towers, 12th to 13th centuries, restored by EUGÈNE VIOLLET-LE-DUC in the 19th century.

Carcassonne provides a rare glimpse of what was once a familiar sight in Gothic France: a tight complex of castle, cathedral, and town with a crenellated and towered wall circuit for defense.

attached *keep,* a secure tower that could serve as a place of last refuge. Balancing that center of secular power was the bishop's seat, the Cathedral of Saint-Nazaire (FIG. 13-29, *left*). The small church, built between 1269 and 1329, was possibly the work of an architect brought in from northern France. In any case, Saint-Nazaire's builders were certainly familiar with the latest developments in architecture in the Île-de-France. Today, Carcassonne provides a rare glimpse of what was once a familiar sight in Gothic France: a tightly contained complex of castle, cathedral, and town within towered walls (see "Gothic Cathedrals and Gothic Cities," above).

Guild Hall, Bruges. One of the many signs of the growing urbanization of life in the late Middle Ages was the erection of monumental meeting halls and warehouses for the increasing number of craft guilds being formed throughout Europe. An early example is the imposing market and guild hall (FIG. 13-30) of the clothmakers of Bruges, begun in 1230. Situated in the city's major square, the hall testifies to the important role of artisans and merchants in Gothic Europe. The design combines features of military construction (the corner watchtowers with their crenellations) and ecclesiastical architecture (lancet windows with crowning oculi). The uppermost, octagonal portion of the tower with its flying buttresses and pinnacles dates to the 15th century, but even the original two-story tower is taller than the rest of the building. Lofty towers, a common feature of late medieval guild and town halls, were designed to compete for attention and prestige with the towers of city cathedrals (compare FIGS. 14-16 and 14-19B).

House of Jacques Coeur. The new class of wealthy merchants who rose to prominence throughout Europe in the late Middle

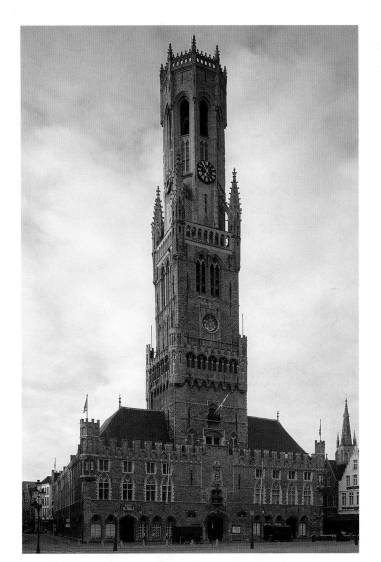

13-30 Hall of the cloth guild (looking south), Bruges, Belgium, begun 1230.

The Bruges cloth guild's meeting hall is an early example of a new type of secular architecture in the late Middle Ages. Its lofty tower competed for attention with the towers of the cathedral.

Ages may not have accumulated fortunes equaling those of the hereditary royalty and nobility, but they still wielded enormous power and influence. The career of the French financier Jacques Coeur (1395–1456) illustrates the ways that enterprising private citizens could win—and quickly lose—wealth and power. Coeur had banking houses in every city of France and many cities abroad. He employed more than 300 agents and competed with the great trading republics of Italy. His merchant ships filled the Mediterranean, and with the papacy's permission, he imported spices and textiles from Muslim lands to the east. He was the treasurer of King Charles VII (r. 1422–1461) of France and a friend of Pope Nicholas V (r. 1447–1455). In 1451, however, his enemies framed him on an absurd charge of having poisoned Agnès Sorel (1422–1450), the king's mistress. The judges who sentenced Coeur to prison and confiscated his vast wealth and property were among those who owed him money. Coeur escaped in 1454 and made his way to Rome, where the pope warmly received him. He died of fever while leading a fleet of papal war galleys in the eastern Mediterranean.

Jacques Coeur's great townhouse still stands in his native city of Bourges. Built between 1443 and 1451 (with special permission to encroach upon the town ramparts), it is the best-preserved example of Late Gothic domestic architecture. The house's plan is irregular, with the units arranged around an open courtyard (FIG. 13-31). The service areas (maintenance shops, storage rooms, servants' quarters, and baths—a rare luxury in any home until the 20th century) occupy the ground level. The upper stories house the great hall and auxiliary rooms used for offices and family living rooms. Over the main entrance is a private chapel. One of the towers served as a treasury. The exterior and interior facades have steep pyramidal roofs of different heights. Decorative details include Flamboyant tracery and large pointed-arch stained-glass windows. An elegant canopied niche facing the street once housed a royal equestrian statue. A comparable statue of Coeur on horseback dominated the facade opening onto the interior courtyard. Jacques Coeur's house is both a splendid example of Late Gothic architecture and a monumental symbol of the period's new secular spirit.

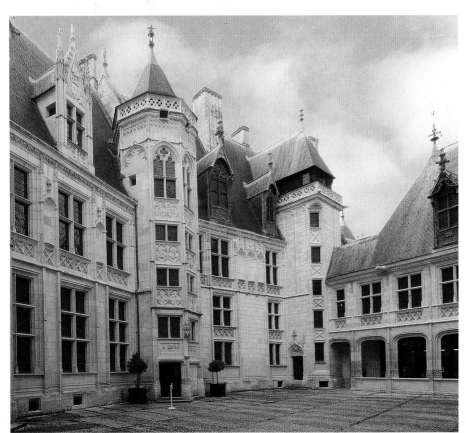

13-31 Inner facade and courtyard of the house of Jacques Coeur, Bourges, France, 1443–1451.

The townhouse of the wealthy Bourges financier Jacques Coeur is the leading example of Late Gothic domestic architecture and a symbol of the period's new secular spirit. The home features elaborate tracery.

Gothic Book Production

The Florentine poet Dante Alighieri (1265–1321) referred to Paris in his *Divine Comedy* (ca. 1310–1320) as the city famed for the art of illumination.* During the Gothic period, book production shifted from monastic scriptoria to urban workshops of professional artists—and Paris boasted the most and best. These new for-profit secular businesses sold their products to the royal family, scholars, and prosperous merchants. The Parisian shops were the forerunners of modern publishing houses.

Not surprisingly, some of the finest extant Gothic books belonged to the French monarchy (FIGS. 13-32, 13-34, 13-35, 13-36, and 13-36A). Louis IX in particular was an avid collector of both secular and religious books. He and his royal predecessors and successors amassed a vast library that is today the core of France's national library.

One of the many books the royal family commissioned is a moralized Bible now in the Pierpont Morgan Library. *Moralized Bibles* are heavily illustrated, each page pairing paintings of Old and New Testament episodes with explanations of their moral significance. Louis's mother, Blanche of Castile, ordered the Morgan Bible during her regency (1226–1234) for her teenage son. The dedication page (FIG. **13-32**) has a costly gold background and depicts Blanche and Louis enthroned beneath triple-lobed arches and miniature cityscapes. The latter are comparable to the architectural canopies above the heads of contemporaneous French portal statues (FIGS. 13-19 and 13-23). With vivid gestures, Blanche instructs the young Louis, underscoring her superior position. (The prominence of Mary as queen of Heaven in Gothic art parallels the rising influence of secular queens in Gothic Europe.) Below Blanche and Louis are a monk and a professional lay scribe. The older clergyman instructs the scribe, who already has divided his page into two columns of four roundels each, a format often used for the paired illustrations of moralized Bibles. The inspiration for such pages filled with circular frames was probably the roundels of stained-glass windows, such as those of Louis's own Sainte-Chapelle (FIG. 13-26).

The picture of Gothic book production on the dedication page of Blanche of Castile's Bible is a very abbreviated one, as is the view of a Spanish monastic scriptorium discussed earlier (FIG. 11-11). Indeed, the manufacturing processes used in the professional workshops of 13th-century Paris and the monastery of 10th-century Tábara did not differ significantly. Book production involved many steps and required numerous specialized artists, scribes, and assistants of varying skill levels. The Benedictine abbot Johannes Trithemius (1462–1516) described the way books were still made in his day in his treatise *In Praise of Scribes*:

> If you do not know how to write, you still can assist the scribes in various ways. One of you can correct what another has written. Another can add the rubrics [headings] to the corrected text. A third can add initials and signs of division. Still another can arrange the leaves and attach the binding. Another of you can prepare the covers, the leather, the buckles and clasps. All sorts of assistance can be offered the scribe to help him pursue his work without interruption. He needs many things which can be prepared by others: parchment cut, flattened and ruled for script, ready ink and pens. You will always find something with which to help the scribe.[†]

Preparation of the illuminated pages also involved several hands. Some artists, for example, specialized in painting borders or initials. Only the workshop head or one of the most advanced assistants would

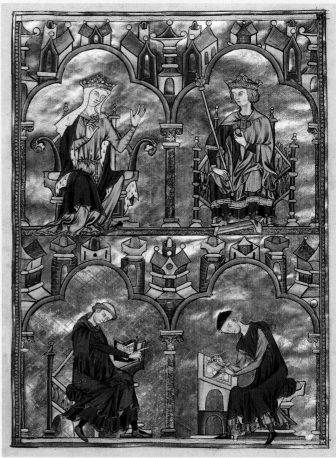

13-32 Blanche of Castile, Louis IX, and two monks, dedication page (folio 8 recto) of a moralized Bible, from Paris, France, 1226–1234. Ink, tempera, and gold leaf on vellum, 1′ 3″ × 10½″. Pierpont Morgan Library, New York.

The dedication page of this royal book depicts Saint Louis, his mother and French regent Blanche of Castile, a monk, and a lay scribe at work on the paired illustrations of a moralized Bible.

paint the main figural scenes. Given this division of labor and the assembly-line nature of Gothic book production, it is astonishing how uniform the style is on a single page, as well as from page to page, in most illuminated manuscripts. One Parisian book of special interest in this regard is the *Belleville Breviary* (FIG. 13-36), which gives the name of the workshop head, Jean Pucelle, and those of some of his assistants in a memorandum at the end of the manuscript recording the payment they received for their work. Inscriptions in other Gothic illuminated books regularly state the production costs—the prices paid for materials, especially gold, and for the execution of initials, figures, flowery script, and other embellishments. By this time, however, although the cost of materials was still the major factor determining a book's price, individual skill and "brand name" also played a significant role. In the Gothic age, urban workshops of professional scribes and painters ended the centuries-old monopoly of the Church in book production.

*Dante, *Divine Comedy,* Purgatory, 11.81.
[†]Translated by Roland Behrendt, *Johannes Trithemius, In Praise of Scribes: De laude scriptorum* (Lawrence, Kansas: Coronado Press, 1974), 71.

Book Illumination and Luxury Arts

Paris's claim as the intellectual center of Gothic Europe (see "Paris," page 388) did not rest solely on the stature of its university faculty and the reputation of its architects, masons, sculptors, and glaziers. The city was also a renowned center for the production of fine books, such as the Bible (FIG. 13-32) that once belonged to Blanche of Castille (see "Gothic Book Production," page 402).

God as Creator. Another Bible produced in Paris during the 1220s features a magnificent frontispiece: *God as Creator of the World* (FIG. 13-33). Above the illustration, the scribe wrote (in French rather than Latin): "Here God creates heaven and earth, the sun and moon, and all the elements." The painter depicted God in the process of creating the world, shaping the universe with the aid of a compass. Within the perfect circle already created are the spherical sun and moon and the unformed matter that will become the earth once God applies the same geometric principles to it. In contrast to the biblical account of creation, in which God created the sun, moon, and stars after the earth had been formed, and made the world by sheer force of will and a simple "Let there be" command, this Gothic Bible portrays God systematically creating the universe using geometrical principles.

Indeed, geometry played an important symbolic as well as practical role in Gothic art and architecture. Gothic artists, architects, and theologians alike thought that the triangle, for example, embodied the Trinity of God the Father, Christ, and the Holy Spirit. The circle, which has neither a beginning nor an end, symbolized the eternity of the one God. The book of Revelation (21:12–21) describes the Heavenly Jerusalem as a walled city in the form of a perfect square with 12 gates. When Gothic architects based their designs on the art of geometry, building their forms out of abstract shapes laden with symbolic meaning, they believed they were working according to the divinely established laws of nature.

Psalter of Saint Louis. The gold backgrounds of the frontispieces of Blanche of Castille's Bible and of the *God as Creator* Bible are unusual and have no parallel in the figural decoration of Gothic stained-glass windows. But the radiance of stained glass probably inspired the glowing color of other 13th-century Parisian illuminated manuscripts. In some cases, masters in the same urban workshop produced both glass and books. Many art historians believe that the *Psalter of Saint Louis* (FIG. 13-34) is one of several books produced in Paris for Louis IX by artists associated with those who made the stained glass for his Sainte-Chapelle (FIG. 13-26). Certainly, the painted architectural setting in Louis's book of psalms

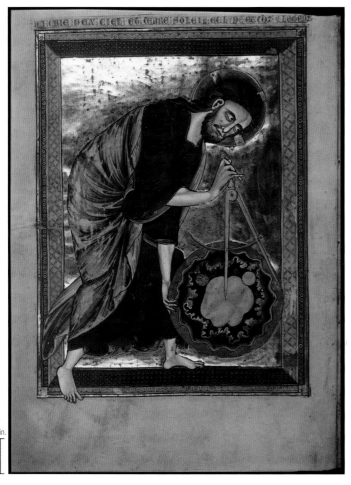

1 in.

13-33 *God as Creator of the World,* folio 1 verso of a moralized Bible, from Paris, France, ca. 1220–1230. Ink, tempera, and gold leaf on vellum, 1′ 1½″ × 8¼″. Österreichische Nationalbibliothek, Vienna.

Paris boasted renowned workshops for the production of illuminated manuscripts. In this book, the artist portrayed God in the process of creating the universe using a Gothic builder's compass.

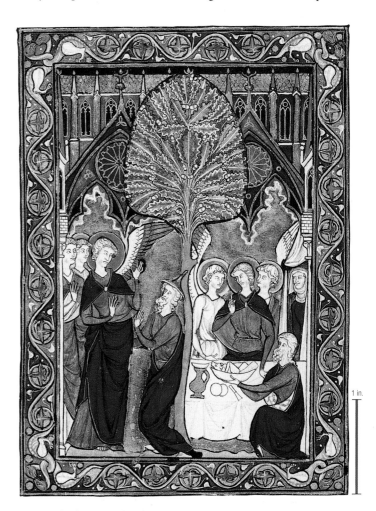

1 in.

13-34 *Abraham and the Three Angels,* folio 7 verso of the *Psalter of Saint Louis,* from Paris, France, 1253–1270. Ink, tempera, and gold leaf on vellum, 5″ × 3½″. Bibliothèque nationale de France, Paris.

The architectural settings in the *Psalter of Saint Louis* reflect the lightness and transparency of Rayonnant royal buildings such as Sainte-Chapelle (FIG. 13-26). The colors emulate stained glass.

reflects the pierced screenlike lightness and transparency of royal Rayonnant buildings such as Sainte-Chapelle. The intense colors, especially the blues, emulate stained glass, and the lines in the borders resemble leading. The gables, pierced by rose windows with bar tracery, are standard Rayonnant architectural features.

The page from the *Psalter of Saint Louis* shown here, *Abraham and the Three Angels* (FIG. 13-34), illustrates the Old Testament story that Christians believe prefigures the Trinity (see "Old Testament Subjects in Christian Art," page 242). Two episodes appear on the same page, separated by the tree of Mamre mentioned in the Bible. At the left, Abraham greets the three angels. In the other scene, he entertains them while his wife, Sarah, peers at them from a tent. The figures' delicate features and the linear wavy strands of their hair have parallels in Blanche of Castile's Bible (FIG. 13-32),

as well as in Parisian stained glass. The elegant proportions, facial expressions, theatrical gestures, and swaying poses are characteristic of the Parisian court style admired throughout Europe. Compare, for example, the angel in the left foreground with the Gabriel statue (FIG. 13-25, *left*) of the Reims Annunciation group.

Breviary of Philippe le Bel. As did a few Romanesque painters (FIGS. 12-25A, 12-38, and 12-39), some Gothic manuscript illuminators signed their work. The names of others appear in royal accounts of payments made and similar official documents. One of the artists who produced books for the French court was MASTER HONORÉ, whose Parisian workshop was on the street known today as rue Boutebrie. Honoré illuminated a *breviary* (see "Medieval Books," page 324) for Philippe le Bel (Philip the Fair, r. 1285–1314) in 1296. On the page illustrated here (FIG. 13-35), Honoré painted two Old Testament scenes involving David. In the upper panel, Samuel anoints the youthful David (compare FIG. 8-2). Below, while King Saul looks on, David prepares to aim his slingshot at his most famous opponent, the giant Goliath (who already touches the wound on his forehead). Immediately to the right, David slays Goliath with his sword.

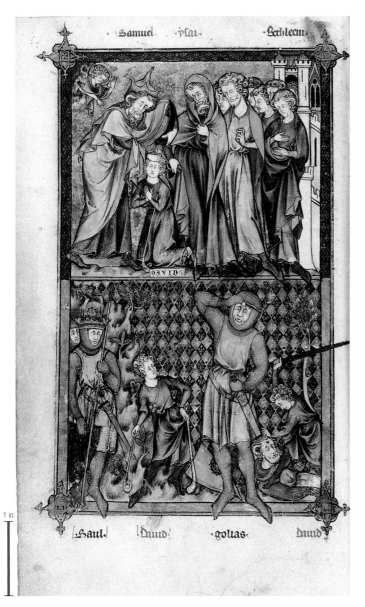

1 in.

13-35 MASTER HONORÉ, *Samuel Anointing David* and *Battle of David and Goliath*, folio 7 verso of the *Breviary of Philippe le Bel,* from Paris, France, 1296. Ink and tempera on vellum, $7\frac{7}{8}'' \times 4\frac{7}{8}''$. Bibliothèque nationale de France, Paris.

Master Honoré was one of the Parisian lay artists who produced books for the French monarchy. His figures are noteworthy for their sculptural volume and the play of light and shade on their bodies.

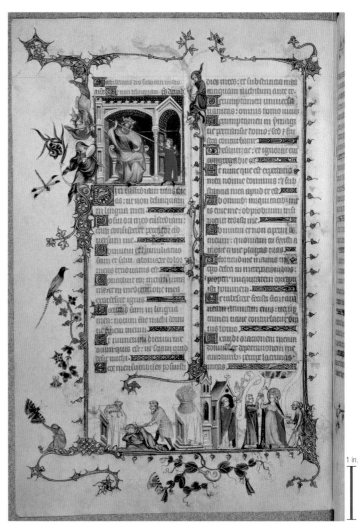

1 in.

13-36 JEAN PUCELLE, *David before Saul*, folio 24 verso of the *Belleville Breviary,* from Paris, France, ca. 1325. Ink and tempera on vellum, $9\frac{1}{2}'' \times 6\frac{3}{4}''$. Bibliothèque nationale de France, Paris.

Pucelle's fully modeled figures in architectural settings rendered in convincing perspective reveal his study of contemporaneous painting in Italy. He was also a close observer of plants and fauna.

Master Honoré's linear treatment of hair, his figures' delicate hands and gestures, and their elegant swaying postures are typical of Parisian painting of the time. This painter, however, was much more interested than most of his colleagues in giving his figures sculptural volume and showing the play of light on their bodies. Nonetheless, Honoré showed little concern for locating his figures in space. The Goliath panel in Philippe's breviary has a textilelike decorative background, and the feet of the artist's figures regularly overlap the border. Although Master Honoré explored naturalism in figure painting, he still approached the art of book illumination as a decorator of two-dimensional pages. He did not embrace the classical notion that a painting should be an illusionistic window into a three-dimensional world.

Belleville Breviary. David and Saul also are the subjects of a miniature painting at the top left of an elaborately decorated text page (FIG. 13-36) in the *Belleville Breviary*, which JEAN PUCELLE of Paris painted around 1325. In this manuscript and the Book of Hours (FIG. 13-36A) he illuminated for Queen Jeanne d'Evreux (1310–1371), wife of Charles IV (r. 1322–1328), Pucelle outdid Honoré and other French artists by placing his fully modeled figures in three-dimensional architectural settings rendered in convincing perspective. For example, he painted Saul as a weighty figure

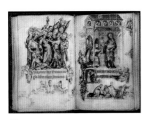

▶13-36A PUCELLE, *Hours of Jeanne d'Evreux*, ca. 1325–1328.

seated on a throne seen in three-quarter view, and he meticulously depicted the receding coffers of the barrel vault over the young David's head. Similar "stage sets" already had become commonplace in Italian painting, and art historians believe that Pucelle visited Italy and studied Duccio di Buoninsegna's work (FIGS. 14-1, 14-11, 14-11A, and 14-12) in Siena. Pucelle's (or an assistant's) renditions of plants, a bird, butterflies, a dragonfly, a fish, a snail, and a monkey also reveal a keen interest in and close observation of the natural world. Nonetheless, in the *Belleville Breviary*, the text still dominates the figures, and the artist (and his patron) delighted in ornamental flourishes, fancy initial letters, and abstract patterns. In that respect, comparisons with panel paintings such as Duccio's are inappropriate. Pucelle's breviary remains firmly in the tradition of book illumination.

Villard de Honnecourt. One of the most intriguing Parisian manuscripts preserved today was not a book sold to the royal family or, in fact, to any customer. It was instead a personal sketchbook compiled by VILLARD DE HONNECOURT, an early 13th-century master mason. The pages of drawings include plans of choirs with radiating chapels and sketches of church towers, lifting devices, a sawmill, stained-glass windows, and other subjects of obvious interest to architects and masons. Also sprinkled liberally throughout the pages are pictures of religious and worldly figures as well as animals, some realistic and others purely fantastic. On the page reproduced here (FIG. 13-37), Villard demonstrated the value of the "art of geometry" to artists, showing how both natural forms and buildings are based on simple geometric shapes such as the square, circle, and triangle (compare FIG. 13-33). Even when he claimed that he drew his animals from nature, Villard composed his figures around a skeleton not of bones but of abstract geometric forms. Geometry was, in Villard's words, "strong help in drawing figures." He also added a cautionary note for others to read: "In these four

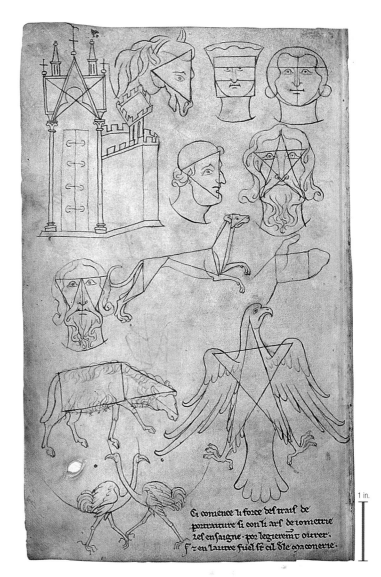

1 in.

13-37 VILLARD DE HONNECOURT, figures based on geometric shapes, folio 18 verso of a sketchbook, from Paris, France, ca. 1220–1235. Ink on vellum, $9\frac{1}{4}'' \times 6''$. Bibliothèque nationale de France, Paris.

On this page from his private sketchbook, the 13th-century master mason Villard de Honnecourt sought to demonstrate that simple geometric shapes are the basis of both natural forms and buildings.

leaves are some figures from the discipline of geometry. But to become familiar with it [the art of geometry], it is necessary to pay careful attention. Whoever wishes to know about [it] must work at each one."[1]

Virgin of Jeanne d'Evreux. In addition to commissioning illuminated manuscripts, the royal family also patronized goldsmiths, silversmiths, and other artists specializing in the production of luxury works in metal and enamel for churches, palaces, and private homes. Especially popular were statuettes of sacred figures, which the wealthy purchased either for private devotion or as gifts to churches. The Virgin Mary was a favored subject, reflecting her increased prominence in the iconography of Gothic portal sculpture.

Perhaps the finest of these costly statuettes is the large silver-gilt figurine known as the *Virgin of Jeanne d'Evreux*. The French queen donated this image of the Virgin and Child to the royal abbey church of Saint-Denis in 1339. Mary stands on a rectangular

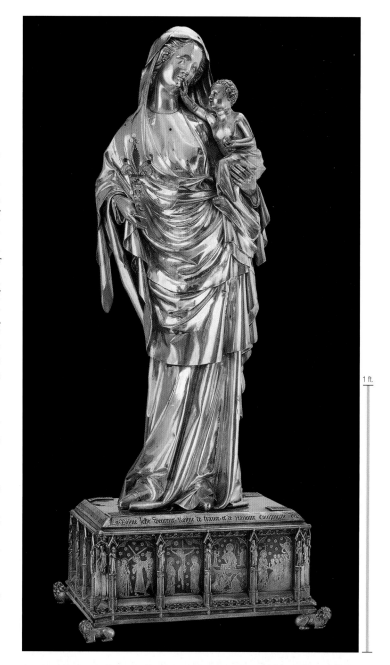

13-38 *Virgin of Jeanne d'Evreux,* from the abbey church of Saint-Denis, France, 1339. Silver gilt and enamel, 2′ 3½″ high. Musée du Louvre, Paris.

Queen Jeanne d'Evreux donated this costly reliquary-statuette to the royal abbey of Saint-Denis (FIG. 13-1). The intimate human characterization of the holy figures recalls that of the *Virgin of Paris* (FIG. 13-27).

base decorated with enamel scenes of Christ's passion (FIG. 13-38). (Some art historians think the enamels are Jean Pucelle's work.) But no hint of grief about her son's future appears in the beautiful young Mary's face. The Christ Child, also without a care in the world, playfully reaches for his mother. The elegant proportions of the two figures, Mary's emphatic swaying posture, the heavy drapery folds, and the intimate human characterization of mother and son are also features of the roughly contemporaneous *Virgin of Paris* (FIG. 13-27). The sculptor of large stone statues and the royal silversmith working at small scale approached the representation of the Virgin and Child in a similar fashion. In both instances, Mary appears not only as the mother of Christ but also as the queen of Heaven. The Saint-Denis Mary originally had a crown on her head, and the scepter she holds is in the form of the fleur-de-lis (compare FIG. 13-18). The statuette also served as a reliquary. The Virgin's scepter contained hairs believed to come from Mary's head.

Castle of Love. Gothic artists produced luxurious objects for secular as well as religious contexts. Sometimes they decorated these costly pieces with stories of courtly love inspired by the romantic literature of the day, such as the account of Lancelot and Queen Guinevere, wife of King Arthur of Camelot. The French poet Chrétien de Troyes recorded their love affair in the late 12th century.

An interesting object of this type is a woman's jewelry box adorned with ivory relief panels. The theme of the panel illustrated here (FIG. 13-39) is related to the allegorical poem *Romance of the Rose* by Guillaume de Lorris, written around 1225 to 1235 and completed by Jean de Meung between 1275 and 1280. At the left, the sculptor carved the allegory of the siege of the Castle of Love. Gothic knights attempt to capture love's fortress by shooting flowers from their bows and hurling baskets of roses over the walls from catapults. Among the castle's defenders is Cupid, who aims

13-39 *Castle of Love,* lid of a jewelry box, from Paris, France, ca. 1330–1350. Ivory and iron, 4½″ × 9¾″. Walters Art Museum, Baltimore.

French Gothic artists also created luxurious objects for homes. Adorning this jewelry casket are ivory reliefs inspired by the romantic literature of the day. Knights joust and storm the Castle of Love.

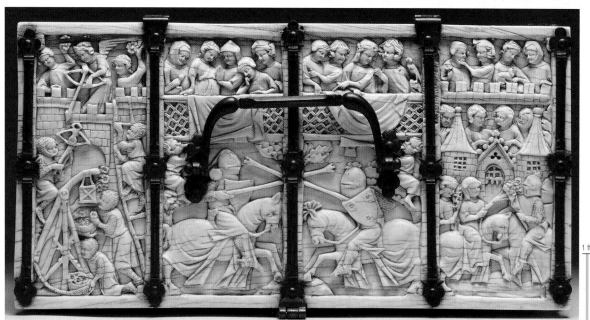

his arrow at one of the knights while a comrade scales the walls on a ladder. In the lid's central sections, two knights joust on horseback. Several maidens survey the contest from a balcony and cheer the knights on as trumpets blare. A youth in the crowd holds a hunting falcon. The sport was a favorite pastime of the leisure class in the late Middle Ages. At the right, the victorious knight receives his prize (a bouquet of roses) from a chastely dressed maiden on horseback. The scenes on the sides of the box include the legend of the unicorn—a white horse with a single ivory horn, a medieval allegory of female virtue. Only a virgin could attract the rare animal, and any woman who could do so thereby demonstrated her moral purity. Although religious themes monopolized artistic production for churches in the Gothic age, secular themes figured prominently in private contexts. Unfortunately, very few examples of the latter survive.

OPUS FRANCIGENUM OUTSIDE FRANCE

In 1269, the prior (deputy abbot) of the church of Saint Peter at Wimpfen im Tal in the German Rhineland hired "a very experienced architect who had recently come from the city of Paris" to rebuild his monastery church.[2] The architect reconstructed the church *opere francigeno* ("in the French manner")—that is, in the Gothic style,

the opus modernum, of the Île-de-France (see "The Birth of Gothic," page 381). A French architect may also have designed the Cathedral of Santa María (FIG. 13-39A) at Léon in northern Spain, begun in 1254. In the Czech Republic, Saint Vitus Cathedral in Prague, begun in 1344, closely emulates French Gothic architecture. The spread of the Gothic style had begun almost as soon as the "modern style" emerged in northern France, but in the second half of the 13th century, the French Gothic style

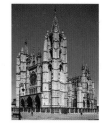

⏏13-39A Santa María, Léon, begun 1254.

became dominant throughout the Continent. European architecture did not, however, turn Gothic all at once or even uniformly. Almost everywhere, patrons and builders modified the court style of the Île-de-France according to local preferences. Because the old Romanesque traditions lingered on in many places, each area, marrying its local Romanesque design to the new style, developed its own brand of Gothic architecture.

England

The influence of French Gothic artistic and architectural styles in England began with William the Conqueror and the Norman invasion of 1066 (FIG. 12-41) and continued in the Gothic period. But just as the Romanesque architecture of Normandy and England has a distinctive character, so too do English artworks (for example, RICHARD DE BELLO'S *mappamundi* in Hereford Cathedral, FIG. 13-39B) and buildings. English Gothic churches, such as the cathedrals at Salisbury, Wells, Exeter, and Gloucester, cannot be mistaken for French ones.

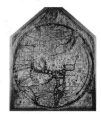

⏏13-39B Mappamundi of Henry III, ca. 1277–1289.

Salisbury Cathedral. The English Gothic style reflects an aesthetic sensibility quite different from French Gothic in emphasizing linear pattern and horizontality instead of structural logic and verticality. Salisbury Cathedral (FIG. 13-40), begun in 1220—the same year that work started on Amiens Cathedral (FIG. 13-22)—embodies these essential characteristics. The building campaign lasted about 40 years. The two cathedrals, both dedicated to the Virgin Mary, are thus also almost exactly contemporaneous, and the differences between them are revealing. Although

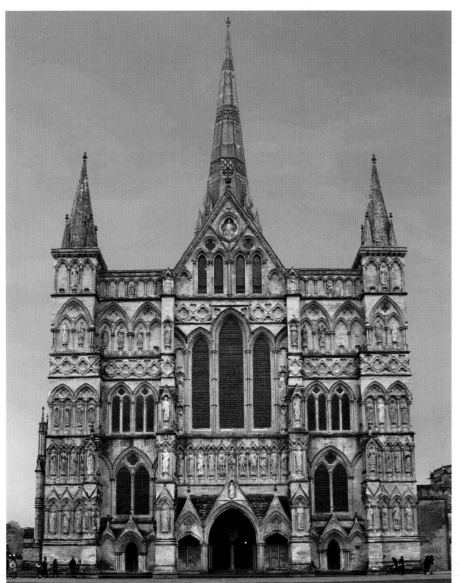

13-40 **West facade of Salisbury Cathedral, Salisbury, England, 1220–1265.**

Exhibiting the distinctive regional features of English Gothic architecture, Salisbury Cathedral has a squat facade that is wider than the building behind it. The architect used flying buttresses sparingly.

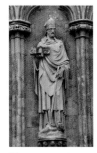

⏏**13-40A** Bishop Poore, Salisbury Cathedral, 1868–1869.

Salisbury's facade incorporates some of the superficial motifs of French Gothic architecture—for example, lancet windows and blind arcades with pointed arches as well as statuary in shallow niches (FIG. 13-40A)—it presents a striking contrast to French High Gothic designs (FIGS. 13-22 and 13-24). The English facade is a squat screen in front of the nave, wider than the building behind it. The architect did not seek to match the soaring height of French facades or try to make the facade correspond to the three-part division of the interior (nave and two aisles). Salisbury's height is also modest compared with that of Amiens and Reims. Because height was not a decisive factor in the English building, the architect used flying buttresses sparingly.

Equally distinctive is Salisbury Cathedral's long rectilinear plan (FIG. 13-41), with its double transept and square eastern end. The latter feature was characteristic of Cistercian (FIG. 12-10B) and English churches since Romanesque times. The interior (FIG. 13-42)—although Gothic in its three-story elevation, pointed arches, four-part rib vaults, compound piers, and the tracery of the triforium—conspicuously departs from the French Gothic style. The pier colonnettes stop at the springing of the nave arches and do not connect with the vault ribs (compare FIGS. 13-20, 13-21, and 13-24A). Instead, the vault ribs rise from *corbels* in the triforium, producing a strong horizontal emphasis. Underscoring this horizontality is the rich color contrast between the light stone of the walls and vaults and the dark marble (from the Isle of Purbeck in southeastern England) used for the triforium moldings and corbels, compound pier responds, and other details. In short, French Gothic architecture may have inspired the design of Salisbury Cathedral, but its builders transformed the French style in accordance with English taste.

Wells Cathedral. The elaboration of architectural pattern for its own sake had long been a distinguishing feature of English architecture. The decorative motifs on the Romanesque piers of Durham Cathedral (FIG. 12-36, *left*) are an early example. An especially interesting example is found in the nave (FIG. 13-43) of Wells Cathedral, where William Joy solved a structural problem in a unique and aesthetically pleasing way (see "The Scissors Arches of Wells Cathedral," page 409).

Exeter and Gloucester. The pier, wall, and vault elements, still relatively simple at Salisbury, became increasingly complex in the 14th century in what

13-42 Interior of Salisbury Cathedral (looking east), Salisbury, England, 1220–1258.

Salisbury Cathedral's interior differs from contemporaneous French Gothic designs in the strong horizontal emphasis of its three-story elevation and the use of dark Purbeck marble for moldings.

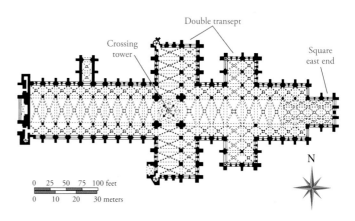

13-41 Plan of Salisbury Cathedral, Salisbury, England, 1220–1258.

The long rectilinear plan of Salisbury Cathedral, with its double transept and square eastern end, is typically English. The four-part rib vaults of the nave follow the Chartres model (FIG. 13-13).

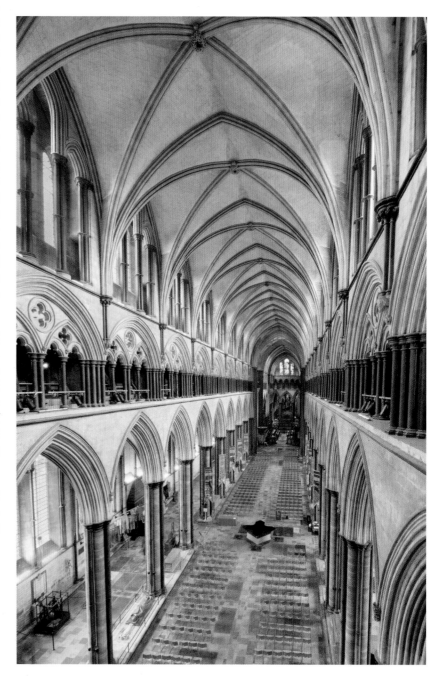

The Scissors Arches of Wells Cathedral

Begun earlier than the nave of Salisbury Cathedral (FIG. 13-42), Wells Cathedral's 67-foot-tall nave (FIG. 13-43), built between 1192 and 1230

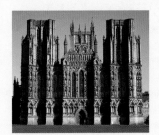

by ADAM LOCK, is also an outstanding example of the Early English Gothic architectural style. (The later facade, FIG. 13-43A, is the work of THOMAS NORREYS.) As in Salisbury, the design closely reflects developments in France, but has the distinctive "look" of English naves with moldings that divide the elevation into three horizontal bands—nave arcade, triforium (without tracery), and clerestory—capped by four-part rib vaults with pointed arches.

⚐ **13-43A** West facade, Wells Cathedral, begun ca. 1230.

The present form of the nave is almost unaltered from the 13th century, with one important exception. Between 1314 and 1322, the cathedral's crossing tower was heightened, adding unwelcome pressure to the piers below. The church authorities feared that the tower would collapse. To avert that outcome, in 1338 master mason WILLIAM JOY buttressed the piers at the crossing by inserting what are known as *scissors arches* across the width of the nave and on the two adjacent sides where the nave intersects the transept. The scissors arches that Joy designed consist of a wide pointed arch somewhat taller than the nave arcade, topped by an inverted arch beneath the vault ribs. He also inserted oculi in the spandrels between the two arches, lightening the scissors both visually and literally. The introduction of these elegant curvilinear forms enhanced the beauty of the nave while solving the structural problem of preventing the collapse of the central spire.

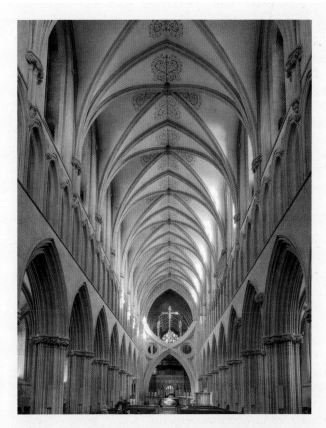

13-43 ADAM LOCK, nave of Wells Cathedral (looking east), Wells, England, 1192–1230; scissors arches added by WILLIAM JOY, 1338.

To avert the collapse of the tower erected in the early 14th century over the crossing of the nave and transept of Wells Cathedral, Joy designed structurally sound and aesthetically pleasing scissors arches.

architectural historians call the *Decorated* style—exemplified by the nave of Exeter Cathedral (FIG. 13-43B), designed by THOMAS OF WITNEY—culminating in the *Perpendicular* style, a masterpiece of which is the choir (FIG. 13-44) of Gloucester Cathedral. The latter church was originally constructed in the late 11th century, but its choir was remodeled about a century after Salisbury under Edward III (r. 1327–1377),

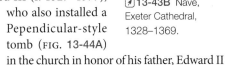

⚐ **13-43B** Nave, Exeter Cathedral, 1328–1369.

who also installed a Pependicular-style tomb (FIG. 13-44A) in the church in honor of his father, Edward II (r. 1307–1327). The Perpendicular style takes

13-44 Choir of Gloucester Cathedral (looking east), Gloucester, England, 1332–1357.

The Perpendicular style of English Late Gothic architecture takes its name from the pronounced verticality of its linear details. The multiplication of ribs in the vaults is also a characteristic feature.

⚐ **13-44A** Tomb of Edward II, Gloucester, ca. 1330–1335.

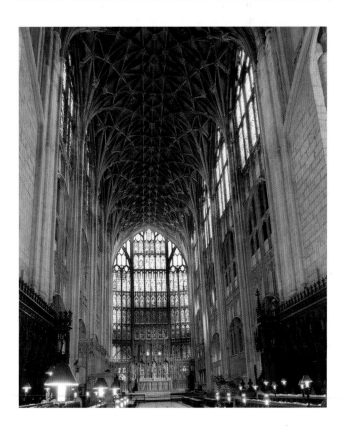

its name from the pronounced verticality of its decorative details, in contrast to the horizontal emphasis of Salisbury and Early English Gothic.

A single enormous window divided into tiers of small windows of similar shape and proportion fills the characteristically square east end of Gloucester Cathedral. At the top, two slender lancets flank a wider central section that also ends in a pointed arch. The design has much in common with the screen facade of Salisbury Cathedral, but the proportions are different. Vertical, as opposed to horizontal, lines dominate. In the choir wall, the architect also erased Salisbury's strong horizontal accents, as the vertical wall elements lift directly from the floor to the vaulting, unifying the walls with the vaults in the French manner. The vault ribs, which designers had begun to multiply soon after Salisbury, are at Gloucester a dense thicket of entirely ornamental strands serving no structural purpose. The choir, in fact, does not have any groin vaults at all but a continuous Romanesque barrel vault with applied Gothic ornamentation. In the Gloucester choir, the taste for decorative surfaces triumphed over structural clarity.

Chapel of Henry VII. The decorative, structure-disguising qualities of the Perpendicular style became even more pronounced in its late phases. The primary example (FIG. 13-45) is the early-16th-

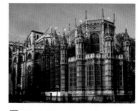

13-45A Chapel of Henry VII, London, 1503–1519.

century ceiling of the chapel of Henry VII (FIG. 13-45A) adjoining Westminster Abbey in London. Here, ROBERT and WILLIAM VERTUE turned the earlier English linear play of ribs into a kind of architectural embroidery. The architects pulled the ribs into distinctly English *fan vaults* (vaults with radiating ribs forming a fanlike pattern) with large hanging *pendants* resembling stalactites. The vault looks as if it had been some organic mass hardened in the process of melting. Intricate tracery resembling lace overwhelms the cones hanging from the ceiling. The chapel represents the dissolution of structural Gothic into decorative fancy. The architects released the Gothic style's original lines from their function and multiplied them into the uninhibited architectural virtuosity and theatrics of the Perpendicular style. A parallel phenomenon in France is the Flamboyant style of Saint-Maclou (FIG. 13-28) at Rouen.

Holy Roman Empire

As part of his plan to make his new church at Saint-Denis an earthly introduction to the splendors of Paradise (see "Abbot Suger," page 383), Suger selected artists from the Meuse River region in present-day Belgium to fashion for the choir a magnificent crucifix on an elaborate base decorated with 68 enamel scenes pairing Old and New Testament episodes. The Mosan (Meuse) region had long been famous for the quality of its metalworkers and enamelers (FIGS. 12-27 and 12-28). Indeed, as Suger's treatises demonstrate, in the Middle Ages, the artists who worked at small scale with precious metals, ivory, and jewels produced the most admired objects in a church, far more important in the eyes of contemporaries than the painted jamb figures and tympanum reliefs that are the focus of modern histories of medieval art. The loss of Suger's crucifix and all of the other costly items he described is therefore especially unfortunate.

Nicholas of Verdun. The leading Mosan artist of the late 12th and early 13th centuries was NICHOLAS OF VERDUN. In 1181, Nicholas completed work on a gilded-copper and enamel *ambo* (a pulpit for biblical readings) for the Benedictine abbey church at Klosterneuburg, near Vienna in Austria. After a fire damaged the pulpit in 1330, the church hired artists to convert what remained into an *altarpiece*. The pulpit's sides became the wings of a *triptych* (three-part altarpiece). The 14th-century artists also added 6 scenes to Nicholas's original 45. The *Klosterneuburg Altar* in its final form (FIG. 13-45B) has a central row of enamels depicting New Testament episodes, beginning with the Annunciation, and bearing

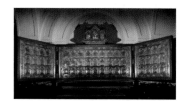

13-45B *Klosterneuburg Altar*, refashioned after 1330.

the label *sub gracia*, or the world "under grace"—that is, after the coming of Christ. The upper and lower registers contain Old Testament scenes labeled, respectively, *ante legem*, "before the law" that Moses received on Mount Sinai, and *sub lege*, "under the law" of the Ten Commandments. In this scheme, prophetic Old Testament events appear above and below the New Testament episodes they prefigure. For example, framing the annunciation to Mary of the

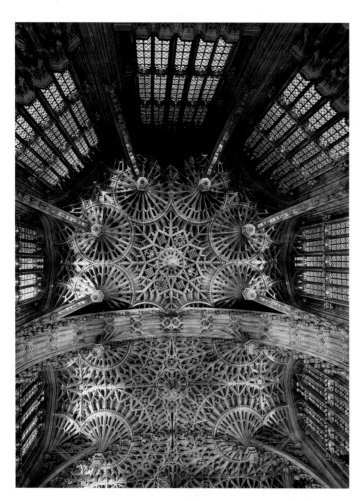

13-45 ROBERT and WILLIAM VERTUE, fan vaults of the chapel of Henry VII, Westminster Abbey, London, England, 1503–1519.

The chapel of Henry VII is the primary example of the decorative and structure-disguising qualities of the Perpendicular style in the use of fan vaults with lacelike tracery and pendants resembling stalactites.

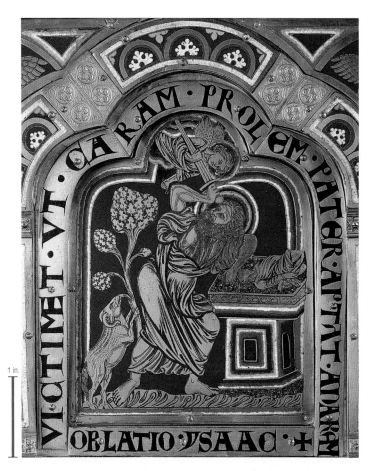

Nicholas of Verdun was the leading artist of the Meuse River region, renowned for its enamel- and metalwork. His gold figures twist and turn and stand out vividly from the blue enamel background.

coming birth of Jesus are enamels of angels announcing the births of Isaac and Samson. In the central section of the triptych, the Old Testament counterpart of Christ's crucifixion is Abraham's sacrifice of Isaac (FIG. 13-46), a parallel already established in Early Christian times in both art (FIG. 8-8, *top left*) and literature (see "Old Testament Subjects in Christian Art," page 242). Here, the angel flies in at the last moment to grab the blade of Abraham's sword before he can slay the bound Isaac on the altar.

Nicholas of Verdun's Klosterneuburg enamels may give an idea of the appearance of the Old and New Testament enamels on the lost Saint-Denis crucifix. Universally admired, Mosan enamels and metalwork were instrumental in the development of the French Gothic figural style. The gold figures stand out vividly from the blue enamel background. The biblical actors twist and turn, make emphatic gestures, and wear garments almost overwhelmed by the intricate linear patterns of their folds.

Sculpted versions of the Klosterneuburg figures appear on the huge reliquary in Cologne Cathedral known as the *Shrine of the Three Kings* (FIG. 13-47). Around 1190, Philip von Heinsberg, archbishop of Cologne from 1167 to 1191, commissioned Nicholas of Verdun to create the shrine to contain the relics of the three magi acquired by Holy Roman Emperor Frederick Barbarossa (r. 1155–1190) in the conquest of Milan in 1164. Possession of the three kings' relics, which the emperor donated to Cologne Cathedral, gave the archbishop and his successors the right to crown German kings. Nicholas's reliquary, made of silver and bronze with ornamentation in enamel and gemstones, is one of the most luxurious

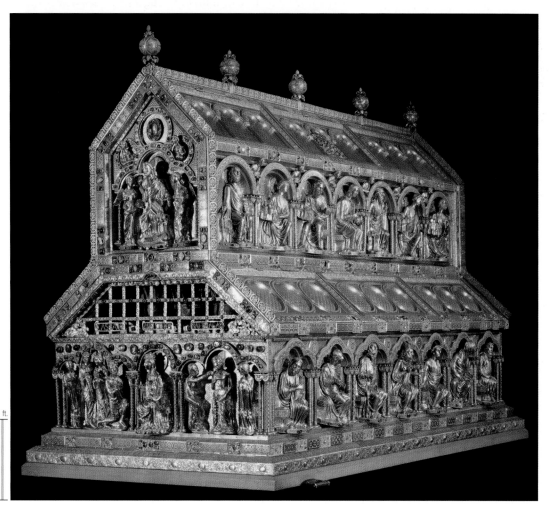

13-47 NICHOLAS OF VERDUN, *Shrine of the Three Kings,* begun ca. 1190. Silver, bronze, enamel, and gemstones, $5'\,8'' \times 6' \times 3'\,8''$. Cologne Cathedral, Cologne.

This huge reliquary in the form of a basilican church is fashioned of silver and bronze with ornamentation in enamel and gemstones. It contains Cologne Cathedral's relics of the three magi.

13-48 *Death of the Virgin,* tympanum of the left doorway of the south transept, Strasbourg Cathedral, Strasbourg, France, ca. 1230.

Stylistically akin to the Visitation statues (FIG. 13-25, *right*) of Reims Cathedral, the figures in Strasbourg's south-transept tympanum express profound sorrow through dramatic poses and gestures.

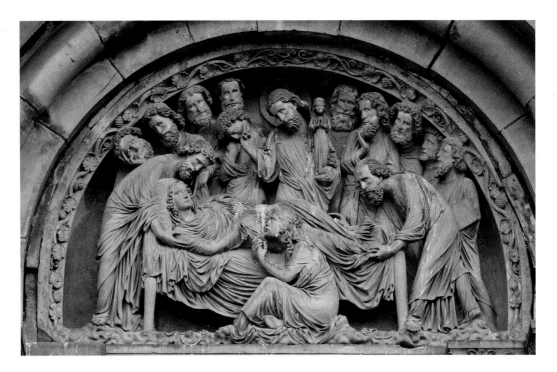

ever fashioned, especially considering its size: 6 feet long and almost as tall. The shape resembles that of a basilican church. Repoussé figures of the Virgin Mary, the three magi, Old Testament prophets, and New Testament apostles in arcuated frames are variations of those on the Klosterneuburg pulpit. The deep channels and tight bunches of drapery folds are hallmarks of Nicholas's style.

The *Klosterneuburg Altar* and *Shrine of the Three Kings,* together with Suger's treatises on the furnishings of Saint-Denis, help people today visualize how magnificently outfitted medieval church interiors were. The sumptuous small-scale objects exhibited in the choir and chapels, which also housed the church's most precious relics, played a defining role in creating an otherworldly atmosphere for Christian ritual. These Gothic examples continued a tradition dating to the Roman emperor Constantine and the first imperial patronage of Christianity (see "Old Saint Peter's," page 248).

Strasbourg Cathedral. About the time that Nicholas of Verdun was at work on the *Klosterneuburg Altar,* construction began on a new cathedral for Strasbourg in present-day France, then an important city in the German Rhineland ruled by the successors of the Ottonian dynasty. The apse, choir, and transepts, begun in 1176, were in place by around 1230. Stylistically, these sections of Strasbourg Cathedral are Romanesque. But the reliefs of the two south-transept portals are fully Gothic and reveal the same interest in the antique style seen in contemporaneous French sculpture, especially that of Reims, as well as in the earlier work of Nicholas of Verdun. By the mid-13th century, artists throughout Europe were producing antique-looking statuary and relief sculpture.

Filling the left tympanum is a representation of the death of the Virgin (FIG. 13-48). A comparison of the Strasbourg Mary on her deathbed with the Mary of the Reims Visitation (FIG. 13-25, *right*) shows the stylistic kinship of the Strasbourg and Reims masters. The 12 apostles gather around the Virgin, forming an arc of mourners well suited to the semicircular frame. The sculptor adjusted the heights of the figures to fit the available space (the apostles at the right are the shortest) and, as in many depictions of crowds in the history of art, some of the figures have no legs or feet. At the center, Christ receives his mother's soul (the doll-like figure he holds in his left hand). Mary Magdalene, wringing her hands in grief, crouches

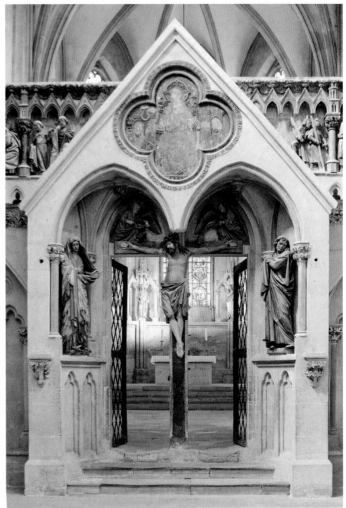

13-49 NAUMBURG MASTER, *Crucifixion,* west choir screen of Naumburg Cathedral, Naumburg, Germany, ca. 1249–1255. Painted limestone, life size.

The emotional pathos of the crucified Christ and the mourning Virgin and Saint John are characteristic of German medieval sculpture. The choir screen is also notable for its preserved coloration.

beside the deathbed. The sorrowing figures express emotion in varying degrees of intensity, from serene resignation to gesturing agitation. The sculptor organized the figures both by dramatic pose and gesture and by the rippling flow of deeply incised drapery passing among them like a rhythmic electric pulse. The sculptor's objective was to imbue the sacred figures with human emotions and to stir emotional responses in observers. In Gothic France, as already noted, art became increasingly humanized and natural. In the Holy Roman Empire, artists carried this humanizing trend even further by emphasizing passionate drama.

Naumburg Cathedral. During his tenure as bishop (1242–1272), Dietrich II of Wettin completed the rebuilding of the Romanesque cathedral at Naumburg in northern Germany. The church had two choirs, and the western choir, which Dietrich commissioned, was the most distinctive aspect of the project. The bishop built the choir as a memorial to 12 donors of the original 11th-century church. The artist who oversaw this project, known as the NAUMBURG MASTER, directed the team of sculptors responsible for the monumental screen (FIG. 13-49) that functioned as a portal to the western choir. Based loosely on contemporaneous church portals with trumeau and jamb statues, the Naumburg screen includes life-size figures of Christ on the cross and of the distraught Virgin Mary and John the Evangelist. John, openly crying, turns his head away, unable to look at the suffering Christ (FIG. 13-49A). Mary also does not look at her son, but she faces and gestures toward the approaching worshipers, suggesting that she can intercede on their behalf at the Last Judgment (compare FIG. 13-39B).

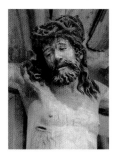

⬀ **13-49A** Detail of *Crucifixion,* Naumburg, ca. 1249–1255.

The statues in the choir, which portray the 12 original donors (some of whom were the bishop's ancestors), were carved by the same workshop. Two of the figures (FIG. 13-50) stand out from the group of solemn men and women because of their exceptional quality. They represent the *margrave* (military governor) Ekkehard II of Meissen and his wife, Uta. The statues are attached to columns and stand beneath architectural canopies, following the pattern of French Gothic portal statuary, but they project from the architecture more forcefully and move more freely than contemporaneous French jamb figures. The period garments and the individualized features and personalities of the margrave and his wife give the impression that they posed for the Naumburg Master, although the subjects lived well before the sculptor's time. Ekkehard, the intense knight, contrasts with the beautiful and aloof Uta. With a wonderfully graceful gesture, she draws the collar of her cloak partly across her face while she gathers up a soft fold of drapery with a jeweled, delicate hand. The sculptor subtly revealed the shape of Uta's right arm beneath her cloak and rendered the fall of drapery folds with an accuracy suggesting that the Naumburg Master used a living model. The two statues are convincing images of real people, even if they bear the names of aristocrats whom the artist never met. By the mid-13th century, in the Holy Roman Empire as well as in England (FIG. 13-44A) and elsewhere, life-size statues of secular personages had found their way into churches.

The Naumburg choir screen and donor statues are also remarkable because, as indoor sculptures, they have retained much of their color, whereas almost all the statues on church exteriors, exposed to sun and rain for centuries, have lost their original paint. The statues

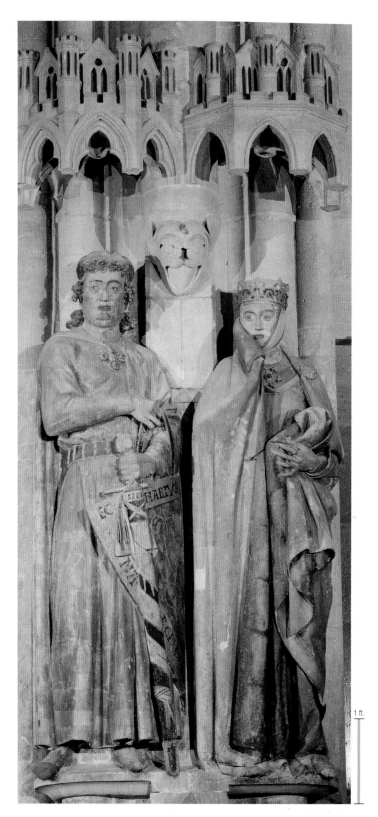

13-50 NAUMBURG MASTER, *Ekkehard and Uta,* statues in the west choir, Naumburg Cathedral, Naumburg, Germany, ca. 1249–1255. Painted limestone, Ekkehard 6′ 2″ high.

The period costumes and individualized features of these donor statues give the impression that Ekkehard and Uta posed for the Naumburg Master, but they lived long before the sculptor's time.

give visitors to the Naumburg choir today an excellent idea of the original appearance of the portal sculptures of Romanesque and Gothic churches.

Bamberg Rider. Somewhat earlier in date than the Naumburg donor figures is the *Bamberg Rider* (FIG. 13-51), the oldest preserved large-scale equestrian statue of the Middle Ages. For centuries, this statue has been mounted against a pier in Bamberg Cathedral beneath an architectural canopy that frames the rider's body but not his horse. Scholars debate whether the statue was made for this location or moved there, perhaps from the church's exterior. Whatever the statue's original location, it revives the imperial imagery of Byzantium (see "The Emperors of New Rome," page 267) and the Carolingian Empire (FIG. 11-12), derived in turn from ancient Roman statuary (FIG. 7-58).

Unlike Ekkehard and Uta, the *Bamberg Rider* seems to be a true portrait of a living person. Some art historians believe that it represents a Holy Roman emperor, perhaps Frederick II (r. 1220–1250), who was a benefactor of Bamberg Cathedral. The many other identifications include Saint George and one of the three magi, but a historical personality is most likely the subject. The placement of a portrait of a Holy Roman emperor in the cathedral would have underscored the unity of Church and State in 13th-century Germany. The artist carefully represented the rider's costume, the high

saddle, and the horse's trappings, and turned the rider's head toward the observer, as if presiding at a review of his troops. The torsion of this figure—and its size relative to the framing canopy—asserts its independence from its architectural setting. The Naumburg Master took a similar approach to the design of his figures in the Naumburg Cathedral choir (FIGS. 13-49 and 13-50).

Röttgen Pietà. The 13th-century donor statues at Naumburg and the *Bamberg Rider* stand in marked contrast to a haunting 14th-century German painted wood statuette (FIG. 13-52) of the Virgin Mary holding the dead Christ in her lap. As does the *Crucifixion* (FIGS. 13-49 and 13-49A) of Naumburg's west choir, this *Pietà* (Italian, "pity" or "compassion") reflects the increased interest during the 13th and 14th centuries in humanizing biblical figures and in the suffering of Jesus and the grief of his mother and followers. This expressed emotionalism accompanied the shift toward the representation of the human body in motion. As the figures of the church portals began to twist on their columns, then move within their niches, and then stand independently, their details became more outwardly related to the human audience as indicators of recognizable human emotions.

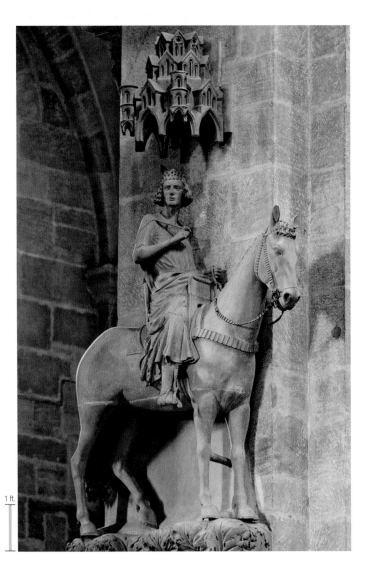

13-51 Equestrian portrait (*Bamberg Rider*), statue in the east choir, Bamberg Cathedral, Germany, ca. 1235–1240. Sandstone, 7′ 9″ high.

Probably a portrait of a German emperor, perhaps Frederick II, the *Bamberg Rider* revives the imagery of the Carolingian Empire. The French-style architectural canopy cannot contain the statue.

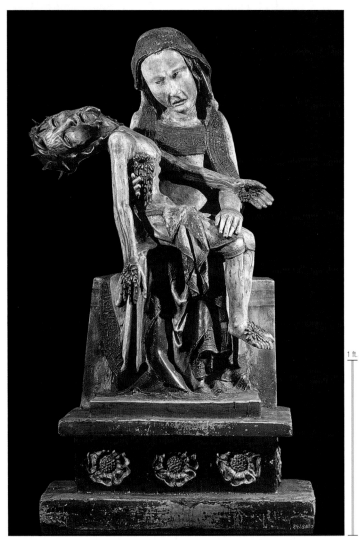

13-52 *Röttgen Pietà*, from the Rhineland, Germany, ca. 1300–1325. Painted wood, 2′ 10½″ high. Rheinisches Landesmuseum, Bonn.

This statuette of the Virgin grieving over the distorted dead body of Christ in her lap reflects the increased interest during the 13th and 14th centuries in the Savior's suffering and the Virgin's grief.

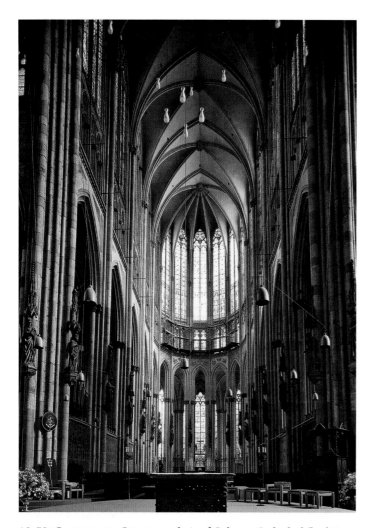

13-53 GERHARD OF COLOGNE, choir of Cologne Cathedral (looking east), Cologne, Germany, completed 1322.

Cologne Cathedral's nave is 422 feet long. Its 150-foot-high choir is a taller variation on the Amiens Cathedral choir (FIGS. 13-20 and 13-21). Both exemplify Gothic architects' quest for height.

The sculptor of the *Röttgen Pietà* (named after a collector) portrayed Christ as a stunted, distorted human wreck, stiffened in death and covered with streams of blood gushing from a huge wound. The Virgin, who cradles him in her lap as if he were a child, is the very image of maternal anguish, her oversized face twisted in an expression of unbearable grief. This statue expresses nothing of the serenity of Romanesque (FIG. 12-20) and earlier Gothic (FIG. 13-17) depictions of Mary. Nor does it have anything in common with the aloof, iconic images of the Theotokos with the infant Jesus in her lap common in Byzantine art (FIGS. 9-19 and 9-20). Here the artist forcibly confronts the devout with an appalling icon of agony, death, and sorrow. The work calls out to the horrified believer, "What is your suffering compared to this?"

Cologne Cathedral. The architecture of the Holy Roman Empire remained conservatively Romanesque well into the 13th century. By mid-century, though, the French Gothic style began to have a profound influence. Cologne Cathedral (FIGS. 13-53 and 13-53A), begun in 1248 under the direction of GERHARD OF COLOGNE, boasts a 150-foot-high choir that is a skillful variation of the design of the Amiens Cathedral choir (FIGS. 13-20 and 13-21), with double lancets in the triforium and tall, slender single windows

in the clerestory above and choir arcade below. Completed in the 14th century but according to Gerhard's plans, the choir expresses the Gothic quest for height even more emphatically than do many French Gothic buildings. Despite the cathedral's seeming lack of substance, proof of its stability came during World War II, when the city of Cologne suffered heavy aerial bombardments. The church survived the war by virtue of its Gothic skeletal design. Once the first few bomb blasts blew out

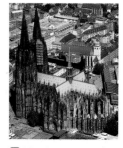

13-53A Cologne Cathedral, begun 1248.

all of its windows, subsequent explosions had no adverse effects, and the skeleton remained intact and structurally sound.

Saint Elizabeth, Marburg. A different type of design, also probably of French origin (FIG. 12-18, *left*) but developed especially in Germany, is the *Hallenkirche* (hall church), in which the height of the aisles is the same as the height of the nave. Hall churches, consequently, have no tribune, triforium, or clerestory. An early German example of this type is the church of Saint Elizabeth (FIG. 13-54) at Marburg, built between 1235 and 1283. It

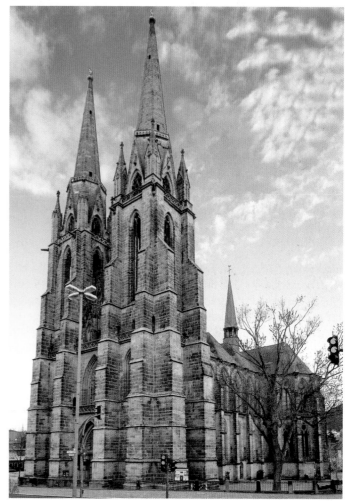

13-54 Saint Elizabeth (looking northeast), Marburg, Germany, 1235–1283.

The facade of this German church has two spire-capped towers in the French manner, but no tracery arcades or portal sculpture. There are also no flying buttresses ringing the building's flanks and east end.

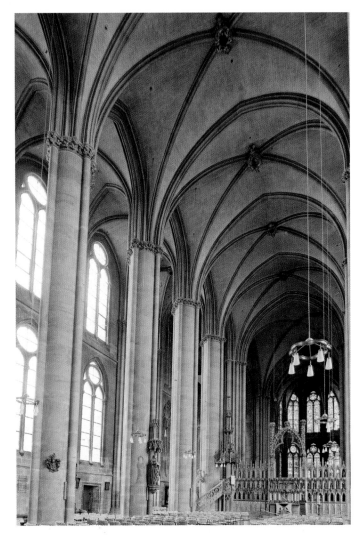

13-55 Interior of Saint Elizabeth (looking east), Marburg, Germany, 1235–1283.

This German church is an early example of a Hallenkirche, in which the aisles are the same height as the nave. Because of the tall windows in the aisle walls, sunlight brightly illuminates the interior.

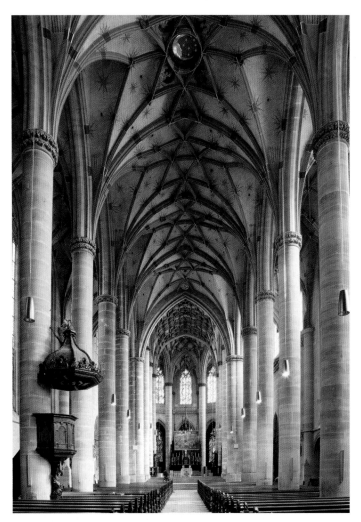

13-56 PETER PARLER, choir (looking east) of Heiligkreuzkirche (Church of the Holy Cross), Schwäbisch Gmünd, Germany, begun 1351.

As at Exeter and Gloucester in England, the vaults of this German church are structurally simple but visually complex. The multiplication of ribs characterizes Late Gothic architecture throughout Europe.

incorporates French-inspired rib vaults with pointed arches and tall lancet windows. The facade has two spire-capped towers in the French manner, but no tracery arcades or portal sculpture. Because the aisles provide much of the bracing for the nave vaults, the exterior of Saint Elizabeth is without the dramatic parade of flying buttresses typically circling French Gothic churches. But the Marburg interior (FIG. 13-55), lighted by double rows of tall windows in the aisle walls, is more unified and free flowing, less narrow and divided, and more brightly illuminated than the interiors of most French and English Gothic churches.

Heinrich and Peter Parler. A later German hall church is the Heiligkreuzkirche (Church of the Holy Cross) at Schwäbisch Gmünd, begun in 1317 by HEINRICH PARLER (ca. 1290–ca. 1360). Heinrich was the founder of a family of architects who worked in Germany and later in northern Italy. His name first surfaces in the early 14th century, when he played a role in supervising the construction of Cologne Cathedral (FIGS. 13-53 and 13-53A). Work continued on the Schwäbisch Gmünd church into the 16th century, but the nave was substantially complete when one of Heinrich's sons, PETER PARLER (1330–1399), began work on the choir (FIG. 13-56) in 1351.

As in the nave of the church, the choir aisles are as tall as the central space. The light entering the choir through the large windows in the aisle walls and in the chapels ringing the choir provides ample illumination for the clergy conducting services. It also enables worshipers to admire the elaborate patterns of the vault ribs. The multiplication of ribs in this German church is consistent with 14th-century taste throughout Europe and has parallels in the Flamboyant style of France and especially the Perpendicular style of England. As in the nave (FIG. 13-43B) of Exeter Cathedral and the choir (FIG. 13-44) of Gloucester Cathedral, the choir vaults at Schwäbisch Gmünd are structurally simple but visually complex. Parler's vaults form an elegant canopy for the severe columnar piers from which they spring, creating a very effective contrast.

One of Peter Parler's brothers, named Heinrich after their father, was also an architect. He was among those who formed a committee in 1386 to advise the Milanese on the design and construction of their new cathedral. The case of the Parler family underscores both the dramatic increase in the number of recorded names of artists and architects during the Gothic period, and the international character of Gothic art and architecture, despite sometimes pronounced regional variations.

Gothic Europe

France

- Most scholars regard Saint-Denis as the birthplace of Gothic art and architecture. There, Abbot Suger used rib vaults with pointed arches to rebuild the Carolingian royal church and filled the ambulatory windows with stained glass. On the west facade, Suger introduced sculpted figures in the portal jambs, a feature that appeared soon after on the Royal Portal of Chartres Cathedral. Saint-Denis, the west facade of Chartres, and Laon Cathedral are the key monuments of Early Gothic (1140–1194) architecture.

- After a fire in 1194, Chartres Cathedral was rebuilt with flying buttresses, four-part nave vaults, and a three-story elevation of nave arcade, triforium, and clerestory. These features set the pattern for High Gothic (1194–1300) cathedrals. French architects sought to construct naves of soaring height. The vaults of Amiens Cathedral are 144 feet high.

- Flying buttresses made possible the introduction of huge stained-glass windows. High Gothic windows employed delicate lead cames and bar tracery. The colored glass converted natural sunlight into divine light (Suger called it lux nova), dramatically transforming the character of church interiors.

- High Gothic jamb statues differ markedly from their Early Gothic predecessors in their more open composition and asymmetrical stances. In the Chartres transepts, at Reims, and elsewhere, the sculpted figures not only move freely but sometimes engage in dialogue with their neighbors.

- In the 13th century, Paris was the intellectual capital of Europe and home to numerous workshops of professional lay artists specializing in the production of luxurious illuminated manuscripts. These urban for-profit ancestors of modern publishing houses usurped the role of monastic scriptoria.

- The High Gothic Rayonnant court style of Louis IX and his Saint-Chapelle in Paris gave way in the Late Gothic (1300–1500) period to the Flamboyant style, in which flamelike tracery formed brittle decorative webs, as at Saint-Maclou in Rouen.

- The prosperity of the era also led to a boom in civic and private architecture. Important examples are the fortified circuit wall of Carcassonne, the hall of the cloth guild in Bruges, and the house of the financier Jacques Coeur in Bourges.

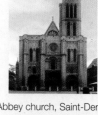

Abbey church, Saint-Denis, begun ca. 1135

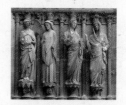

Reims Cathedral, ca. 1230–1255

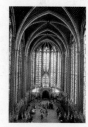

Sainte-Chapelle, Paris, 1243–1248

England

- The Parisian Gothic style spread rapidly throughout Europe during the 13th century, but many regional styles developed, as in the Romanesque period. English Gothic churches, such as Salisbury Cathedral, differ from their French counterparts in their wider and shorter facades, square east ends, double transepts, sparing use of flying buttresses, and horizontal emphasis of the nave.

- Especially characteristic of English Gothic architecture is the elaboration of architectural patterns, which often disguise the underlying structure of the buildings. For example, the fan vaults of the chapel of Henry VII at Westminster Abbey in London transform the logical rib vaults of French buildings into decorative fancy in the Late Gothic Perpendicular style.

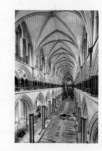

Salisbury Cathedral, 1220–1258

Holy Roman Empire

- Nicholas of Verdun was the leading artist of the Meuse River region, an area renowned for enamel- and metalwork. Nicholas's altars and shrines provide an idea of the sumptuous nature of the furnishings of Gothic churches. His innovative figural style influenced the development of Gothic sculpture.

- German architects eagerly embraced the French Gothic architectural style at Cologne Cathedral and elsewhere. German originality manifested itself most clearly in the Gothic period in sculpture, which often featured emotionally charged figures in dramatic poses and also revived the art of portraiture. Statues of historical figures are key elements of the sculptural programs of Naumburg and Bamberg Cathedrals.

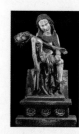

Röttgen Pietà, ca. 1300–1325

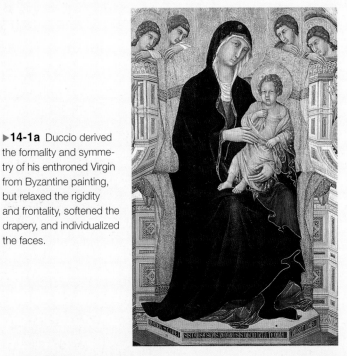

▶**14-1a** Duccio derived the formality and symmetry of his enthroned Virgin from Byzantine painting, but relaxed the rigidity and frontality, softened the drapery, and individualized the faces.

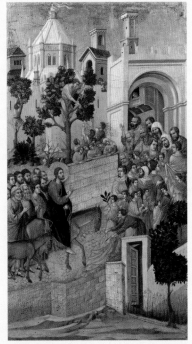

◀**14-1b** The Sienese master's panel depicting Jesus's entry into Jerusalem retains the golden sky of Byzantine painting but features fully modeled figures, anecdotal detail, and a cityscape rendered in perspective.

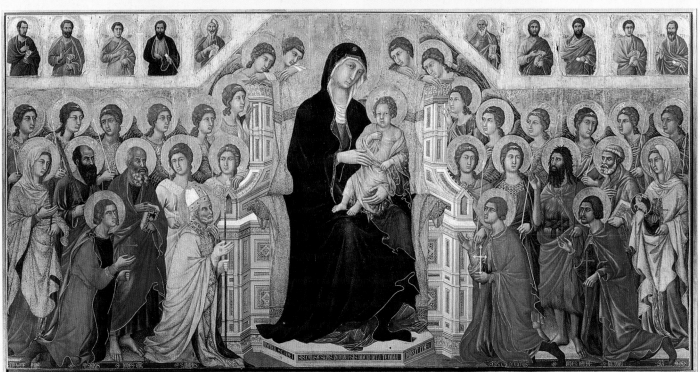

1 ft.

14-1 **DUCCIO DI BUONINSEGNA**, *Virgin and Child Enthroned with Saints*, principal panel of the front of the *Maestà* altarpiece, from Siena Cathedral, Siena, Italy, 1308–1311. Tempera and gold leaf on wood, 7′ × 13′. Museo dell'Opera del Duomo, Siena.

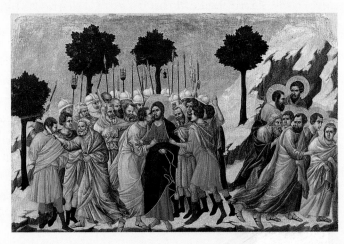

▶**14-1c** In this dramatic depiction of Judas's betrayal of Jesus, the actors display a variety of individual emotions. Duccio here took a decisive step toward the humanization of religious subject matter.

LATE MEDIEVAL ITALY **14**

Duccio di Buoninsegna

Art historians debate whether the art of Italy between 1200 and 1400 is the last phase of medieval art or the beginning of the rebirth (*renaissance,* in French) of Greco-Roman naturalism. All agree, however, that these two centuries mark a major turning point in the history of Western art and that one of the pivotal figures of this age was the Sienese painter Duccio di Buoninsegna (active ca. 1278–1318). Duccio's masterwork is the huge (13-foot-high) *Maestà* (*Virgin Enthroned in Majesty*) in Siena Cathedral, commissioned in 1308 and completed in 1311. The altarpiece consists of a central panel (FIG. 14-1) with the dedicatory inscription, surmounted by seven pinnacles, and a *predella,* or raised shelf, of panels at the base.

The main panel on the front of the *Maestà* represents the Virgin enthroned as queen of Heaven amid angels and saints. Duccio derived the gold background, the composition's formality and symmetry, and the figures and facial types of the principal angels and saints from Byzantine tradition. But the artist relaxed the strict frontality and rigidity of the figures. They turn to each other in quiet conversation. Further, Duccio individualized the faces of the four patron saints of Siena (Ansanus, Savinus, Crescentius, and Victor) kneeling in the foreground, who perform their ceremonial gestures without stiffness. Similarly, he softened the usual Byzantine hard body outlines and drapery patterning. The folds of the garments, particularly those of the female saints at both ends of the panel, fall and curve loosely. This is a feature familiar in French Gothic works (FIG. 13-38) and is a mark of the artistic dialogue between Italy and northern Europe in the 14th century.

In contrast to the main panel, the predella and the back (FIG. 14-11) of the *Maestà* present an extensive series of narrative panels of different sizes and shapes, beginning with the annunciation of Jesus's birth to Mary and culminating with the Savior's resurrection and other episodes following his crucifixion. The New Testament scenes—for example, *Entry into Jerusalem* and *Betrayal of Jesus*—reveal Duccio's powers as a pictorial storyteller. Although the backgrounds, with their golden skies and rock formations, remain conventional, the style of the figures inhabiting these city- and landscapes has changed radically from Byzantine art. Duccio modeled the figures with a range of tonalities from light to dark, and arranged their draperies convincingly. Especially striking is the way the figures react to events. Through posture, gesture, and even facial expression, they display a variety of emotions. In these panels, Duccio took a decisive step toward the humanization of religious subject matter, a key feature of Italian Renaissance art.

DUECENTO
(13TH CENTURY)

When the Italian humanists of the 16th century condemned the art of the late Middle Ages in northern Europe as "Gothic" (see "Gothic," page 382), they did so by comparing it with the contemporaneous art of Italy (MAP 14-1), which consciously revived the classical* art of antiquity. Italian Renaissance artists and scholars regarded medieval artworks as distortions of the noble art of the Greeks and Romans. However, interest in the art of classical antiquity was not entirely absent during the medieval period, even in France, the origin and center of the Gothic style. For example, on the west front of Reims Cathedral, the 13th-century statues of Christian saints and angels (FIG. 13-25) reveal the unmistakable influence of ancient Roman art on French sculptors. Nevertheless, the classical revival that took root in Italy during the 13th and 14th centuries was much more pervasive and longer lasting.

Sculpture

Italian admiration for classical art surfaced early on at the court of Frederick II, King of Sicily (r. 1197–1250) and Holy Roman Emperor (r. 1220–1250). Frederick's nostalgia for Rome's past grandeur fostered a revival of classical sculpture in Sicily and southern Italy during the 13th century (the *Duecento*, the 1200s) not unlike the classical *renovatio* ("renewal") that Charlemagne encouraged in Germany and France four centuries earlier (see "Charlemagne's *Renovatio Imperii Romani*," page 329).

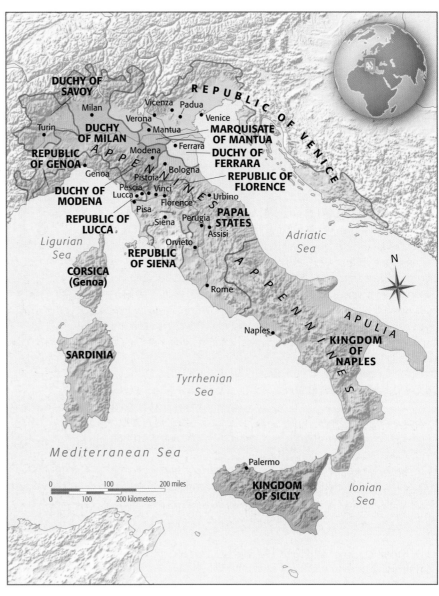

MAP 14-1 Italy around 1400.

Nicola Pisano. The sculptor Nicola d'Apulia (Nicholas of Apulia), better known as NICOLA PISANO (active ca. 1258–1278) after his adopted city (see "Italian Artists' Names," page 421), received his early training in southern Italy during Frederick's rule. In 1250, Nicola traveled northward and eventually settled in Pisa. Then at the height of its political and economic power, the maritime city was a magnet for artists seeking lucrative commissions. Nicola

*In *Art through the Ages,* the adjective "Classical," with uppercase C, refers specifically to the Classical period of ancient Greece, 480–323 BCE. Lowercase "classical" refers to Greco-Roman antiquity in general—that is, the period treated in Chapters 5, 6, and 7.

specialized in carving marble reliefs and may have been the inventor of a new kind of church furniture—the monumental stone *pulpit* (raised platform from which priests delivered sermons) with wraparound narrative reliefs depicting biblical themes and supports in the form of freestanding statues.

Nicola fashioned the first such pulpit (FIG. 14-2) in 1260 for Pisa's century-old baptistery (FIG. 12-29, *left*). Some elements of the pulpit's design carried on medieval traditions—for example, the *trefoil* (triple-curved) arches (compare FIG. 13-32) and the lions supporting some of the columns—but Nicola also incorporated classical elements. The large capitals with two rows of thick overlapping leaves crowning

Italian Artists' Names

In contemporary societies, people have become accustomed to a standardized method of identifying individuals, in part because of the proliferation of official documents such as driver's licenses, passports, and student identification cards. Modern names consist of given names (names selected by the parents) and family names, although the order of the two (or more) names varies from country to country. In China, for example, the family name precedes the given name.

This kind of regularity in names was not, however, the norm in premodern Italy. Many individuals were known by their place of birth or adopted hometown. Nicola Pisano (FIGS. 14-2 and 14-3) was "Nicholas the Pisan," Giulio Romano was "Julius the Roman," and Domenico Veneziano was "Dominic the Venetian." Leonardo da Vinci ("Leonard from Vinci") hailed from the small town of Vinci, near Florence (MAP 14-1). Art historians therefore refer to these artists by their given names, not the names of their towns. (The title of Dan Brown's best-selling novel should have been *The Leonardo Code,* not *The Da Vinci Code.*)

Nicknames were also common. Giorgione was "Big George." People usually referred to Tommaso di Cristoforo Fini as Masolino ("Little Thomas") to distinguish him from his more famous pupil Masaccio ("Brutish Thomas"). Guido di Pietro was called Fra Angelico ("Angelic Friar"). Cenni di Pepo is remembered as Cimabue (FIG. 14-6), which means "bull's head."

The format of names was also impermanent and could be changed at will. This flexibility has resulted in significant challenges for historians, who often must deal with archival documents and other records referring to the same artist by different names.

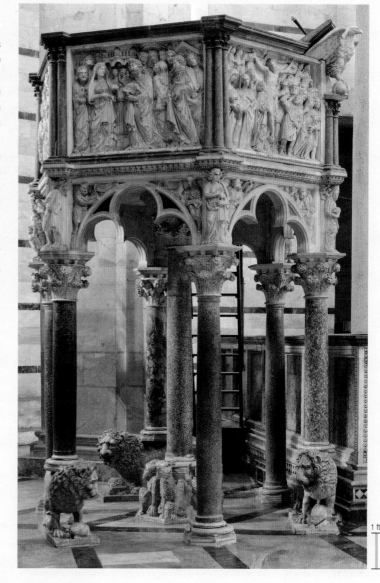

14-2 NICOLA PISANO, pulpit of the baptistery, Pisa, Italy, 1259–1260. Marble, 15′ high.

The Pisa baptistery pulpit by Nicola Pisano (Nicholas of Pisa) retains many medieval features—for example, trefoil arches—but many of the figures derive from ancient Roman relief sculptures.

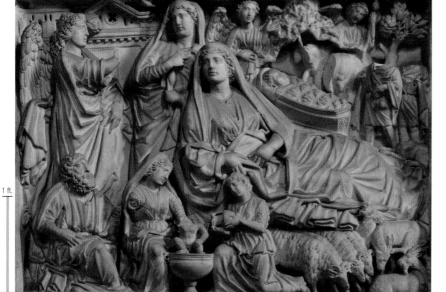

the columns are a Gothic variation of the Corinthian capital (FIG. 5-73). The arches are round, as in Roman architecture, rather than pointed (*ogival*), as in Gothic buildings. Also, each of the large rectangular relief panels resembles the sculptured front of a Roman *sarcophagus* (coffin; for example, FIG. 7-69).

The densely packed large-scale figures of the individual panels also seem to derive from the compositions found on Roman sarcophagi. One of the six panels (FIG. 14-3) of the baptistery pulpit

14-3 NICOLA PISANO, Annunciation, Nativity, and adoration of the shepherds, relief panel on the pulpit of the baptistery, Pisa, Italy, 1259–1260. Marble, 2′ 10″ × 3′ 9″.

Classical sculptures inspired the faces, beards, coiffures, and draperies as well as the bulk and weight of Nicola's figures. The Nativity Madonna resembles lid figures on Roman sarcophagi.

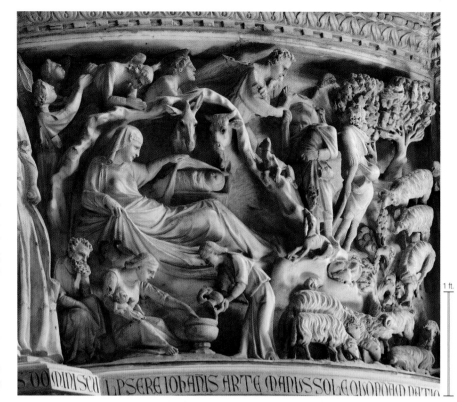

14-4 GIOVANNI PISANO, Nativity and annunciation to the shepherds, relief panel on the pulpit of the cathedral, Pisa, Italy, 1302–1310. Marble, 2′ 10 3/8″ × 3′ 7″.

The French Gothic style had a greater influence on Giovanni Pisano, Nicola's son. Giovanni arranged his figures loosely and dynamically. The Virgin is less remote and gazes tenderly at her newborn son.

depicts scenes from the infancy cycle of Christ (see "The Life of Jesus in Art," pages 244–245), including the Annunciation (top left), Nativity (center and lower half), and adoration of the shepherds (top right). Mary appears twice, stunned by the angel's news in the Annunciation and reclining after giving birth in the Nativity, where her posture and drapery are reminiscent of those of the lid figures on Etruscan (FIG. 6-5) and Roman (FIG. 7-60) sarcophagi. The face types, beards, and coiffures, as well as the bulk and weight of Nicola's figures, also reveal the influence of classical relief sculpture. Art historians have even been able to pinpoint the models of some of the pulpit figures, including the reclining Virgin, in Roman sculptures in Pisa.

Giovanni Pisano. Nicola's son, GIOVANNI PISANO (ca. 1250–ca. 1314), likewise became a sought-after sculptor of church pulpits. His career extended into the early 14th century, when he carved (singlehandedly, according to an inscription) the marble pulpit in Pisa's cathedral (FIG. 12-29, *center*). The pulpit is the largest known example of the type. It boasts nine curved narrative panels, including, in addition to the subjects that Giovanni's father represented, scenes from the life of John the Baptist. The Nativity and annunciation to the shepherds panel (FIG. 14-4) offers a striking contrast to Nicola's quiet, dignified presentation of the religious narrative. The younger sculptor arranged the figures loosely and dynamically, with Mary depicted as a much more relaxed and less remote mother who does not impassively watch her servants wash her newborn son but rather pulls back his blanket to gaze tenderly at him. The angels that announce the birth of the Savior to the shepherds twist and bend in excited animation. Giovanni's slender and sinuous shepherds, unlike Nicola's stockier figures, do not yet share in the miraculous event, but one can imagine their animated gestures when, moments later, they will view the swaddled Christ Child. The father worked in the classical tradition, the son in a style derived from French Gothic. These styles were two of the three most important ingredients in the formation of the distinctive and original art of 14th-century Italy.

Painting and Architecture

The third major stylistic element in late medieval Italian art was the Byzantine tradition. Throughout the Middle Ages, the Byzantine style dominated Italian painting, but its influence was especially strong after the fall of Constantinople in 1204, which precipitated a migration of Byzantine artists to Italy.

Bonaventura Berlinghieri. One of the leading painters working in the Italo-Byzantine style, or *maniera greca* (Italian, "Greek manner"), was BONAVENTURA BERLINGHIERI (active ca. 1235–1244)

of Lucca. His most famous work is the *Saint Francis Altarpiece* (FIG. 14-5) in the church of San Francesco (Saint Francis) in Pescia. Painted in 1235 using *tempera* on wood panel (see "Tempera and Oil Painting," page 574), the altarpiece honors Saint Francis of Assisi, whose most important shrine (FIG. 14-5A) was at Assisi itself. The Pescia altarpiece highlights the increasingly prominent role of religious orders in late medieval Italy (see "The Great Schism, Mendicant Orders, and Confraternities," page 423). Saint Francis's Franciscan order worked diligently to impress on the public the saint's valuable example and to demonstrate the order's commitment to teaching and to alleviating suffering. Berlinghieri's altarpiece, painted only nine years after Francis's death, is the earliest securely dated representation of the saint.

Berlinghieri depicted Francis wearing the costume later adopted by all Franciscan monks: a coarse clerical robe tied at the waist with a rope. The saint displays the *stigmata*—marks resembling Christ's wounds—that miraculously appeared on his hands and feet. Flanking Francis are two angels, whose frontal poses, prominent halos, and lack of modeling reveal the Byzantine roots of Berlinghieri's style. So, too, does the use of *gold leaf* (gold beaten into tissue-paper-thin sheets, then applied to surfaces), which emphasizes the image's flatness and otherworldly, spiritual nature.

Appropriately, Berlinghieri's panel focuses on the aspects of the saint's life that the Franciscans wanted to promote, thereby making visible (and thus more credible) the legendary life of this holy man. Saint Francis believed that he could get closer to God by rejecting worldly goods, and to achieve this he stripped himself bare in a public square and committed himself to a strict life of fasting, prayer, and meditation. His followers considered the appearance of stigmata on Francis's hands and feet (clearly visible in the saint's frontal image, which resembles a Byzantine icon; compare FIG. 9-18A) as God's blessing, and viewed Francis as a second Christ. Fittingly, four of the six narrative scenes along the sides of the panel depict miraculous healings, connecting Saint Francis even more emphatically to Christ. The narrative scenes provide an

The Great Schism, Mendicant Orders, and Confraternities

In 1305, the College of Cardinals (the collective body of all cardinals) elected a French pope, Clement V (r. 1305–1314), who settled in Avignon. Subsequent French popes remained in Avignon, despite their announced intentions to return to Rome. Understandably, the Italians, who saw Rome as the rightful capital of the universal Church, resented the Avignon papacy. The conflict between the French and the Italians resulted in the election in 1378 of two popes—Clement VII, who

resided in Avignon (and who does not appear in the Catholic Church's official list of popes), and Urban VI (r. 1378–1389), who remained in Rome. Thus began what became known as the Great Schism. After 40 years, Holy Roman Emperor Sigismund (r. 1410–1437) convened a council that resolved this crisis by electing a new Roman pope, Martin V (r. 1417–1431), who was acceptable to both the Avignonese and Roman branches of the Church.

The pope's absence from Italy during much of the 14th century contributed to an increase in the prominence of monastic orders. The Augustinians, Carmelites, and Servites became very active, ensuring a constant religious presence in the daily life of Italians, but the largest and most influential monastic orders were the *mendicants* (begging friars)—the Franciscans, founded by Francis of Assisi (ca. 1181–1226; FIGS. 14-5 and 14-5A), and the Dominicans, founded by the Spaniard Dominic de Guzmán (ca. 1170–1221). As did other monks, the

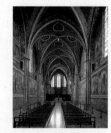

14-5A San Francesco, Assisi, 1228–1253.

mendicant friars renounced all worldly goods and committed themselves to spreading God's word, performing good deeds, and ministering to the sick and dying. But unlike the many monks who resided in rural and often isolated monasteries, the mendicants lived in the heart of cities and preached to large urban crowds. The Dominicans, in particular, contributed significantly to establishing urban educational institutions. The Franciscans and Dominicans became very popular in Italy because of their concern for the poor and the personal relationship with God that they encouraged common people to cultivate.

Although both mendicant orders worked for the glory of God, a degree of rivalry nevertheless existed between the two. For example, in Florence they established their churches on opposite sides of the city—Santa Croce (FIG. I-4), the Franciscan church, on the eastern side, and the Dominicans' Santa Maria Novella (FIG. 14-5B) on the western (MAP 21-1).

Confraternities, organizations consisting of laypersons who dedicated themselves to strict religious observance, also grew in popularity during the 14th and 15th centuries. The mission of confraternities included tending the sick,

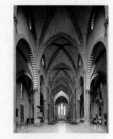

14-5B Santa Maria Novella, Florence, begun ca. 1246.

burying the dead, singing hymns, and performing other good works. The confraternities as well as the mendicant orders continued to play an important role in Italian religious life through the 16th century. The numerous artworks they commissioned and the monastic churches they built have ensured their enduring legacy.

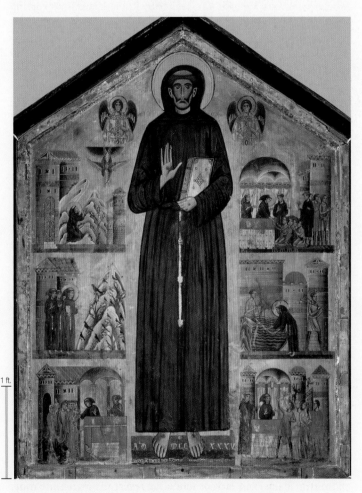

14-5 BONAVENTURA BERLINGHIERI, *Saint Francis Altarpiece,* San Francesco, Pescia, Italy, 1235. Tempera on wood, 5′ × 3′.

Berlinghieri painted this altarpiece in the Italo-Byzantine style, or maniera greca, for the mendicant (begging) order of Franciscans. It is the earliest securely dated portrayal of Saint Francis of Assisi.

active contrast to the stiff formality of the large central image of Francis. At the upper left, taking pride of place at the saint's right, Francis receives the stigmata. Directly below, the saint preaches

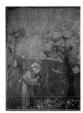

14-5C ST. FRANCIS MASTER, *Francis Preaching to the Birds,* ca. 1290–1300.

to the birds, a subject that also figures prominently in the fresco program (FIG. 14-5C) of San Francesco at Assisi, the work of a painter whom art historians call the SAINT FRANCIS MASTER. These and the scenes depicting Francis's miracle cures strongly suggest that Berlinghieri's source was one or more Byzantine illuminated manuscripts (compare FIGS. 9-17B, 9-18, and 9-18A) with biblical narrative scenes.

Cimabue. One of the first artists to break from the Italo-Byzantine style that dominated 13th-century Italian painting was Cenni di Pepo, better known as CIMABUE (ca. 1240–1302). Cimabue challenged some of the major conventions of late medieval art in pursuit of a closer approximation of the appearance of the natural world—the core of the classical naturalistic tradition. He painted *Madonna Enthroned with Angels and Prophets* (FIG. 14-6) for Santa Trinità (Holy Trinity) in Florence, the Benedictine church near the Arno River built between 1258 and 1280. The composition and the gold background reveal the painter's reliance on Byzantine models (compare FIG. 9-19). Cimabue also used the gold embellishments common to Byzantine art for the folds of the Madonna's robe, but they are no longer merely decorative patterns. In his panel, they enhance the three-dimensionality of the drapery. Furthermore,

Cimabue constructed a deeper space for the Madonna and the surrounding figures to inhabit than was common in Byzantine art. The Virgin's throne, for example, is a massive structure that Cimabue convincingly depicted as receding into space. The overlapping bodies of the angels on each side of the throne and the half-length prophets who look outward or upward from beneath it reinforce the sense of depth.

Pietro Cavallini. The leading Roman painter at the end of the 13th century was Pietro dei Cerroni, known as PIETRO CAVALLINI (ca. 1240–ca. 1340), or "Little Horse" (see "Italian Artists' Names," page 421), who his son said lived to age 100. Cavallini enjoyed the patronage of Pope Nicholas III (r. 1277–1280), who commissioned him to restore the Early Christian frescoes in San Paolo fuori le Mura (Saint Paul Outside-the-Walls) in Rome. Cavallini's careful study and emulation of those Late Antique paintings must have profoundly influenced his later work, which unfortunately survives only in fragments. Around 1290, Cavallini received two important commissions for churches in Trastevere, on the west bank of the Tiber near the Vatican. He produced mosaics depicting the life of the Virgin for Santa Maria in Trastevere, and painted a fresco cycle of Old and New Testament scenes in Santa Cecilia in Trastevere, of which only part of his *Last Judgment* (FIG. 14-7) survives, but what remains confirms his stature as an innovative artist of the highest order (see "Pietro Cavallini," page 425).

TRECENTO (14TH CENTURY)

In the 14th century (the *Trecento,* or 1300s), Italy consisted of numerous independent city-states, each corresponding to a geographic region centered on a major city (MAP 14-1). Most of the city-states, such as Venice, Florence, Lucca, and Siena, were republics—constitutional oligarchies governed by executive bodies, advisory councils, and special commissions. Other powerful 14th-century states included the Papal States, the Kingdom of Naples, and the duchies of Milan, Modena, Ferrara, and Savoy. As their names indicate, these states were politically distinct from the republics, but all the states shared in the prosperity of the period. The sources of wealth varied from state to state. Italy's port cities expanded maritime trade, whereas the economies of other cities depended on banking or the manufacture of arms or textiles.

Black Death. The outbreak of the Black Death (bubonic plague) in the late 1340s threatened this prosperity, however. Originating in China, the Black Death swept across Europe. The most devastating natural disaster in European history, the Black Death eliminated between 25 and 50 percent of the Continent's population in about five years. The plague devastated Italy's inhabitants. In large Italian cities, where people lived in relatively close proximity, the death tolls climbed as high as 50 to 60 percent of the population. The Black Death also had a significant effect on art. It stimulated religious bequests and encouraged the commissioning of devotional images. The focus on sickness and death also led to a burgeoning in hospital construction.

Renaissance Humanism. Another significant development in 14th-century Italy was the blossoming of a vernacular literature (written in the commonly spoken language instead of Latin), which dramatically affected Italy's intellectual and cultural life. Latin remained the official language of Church liturgy and state

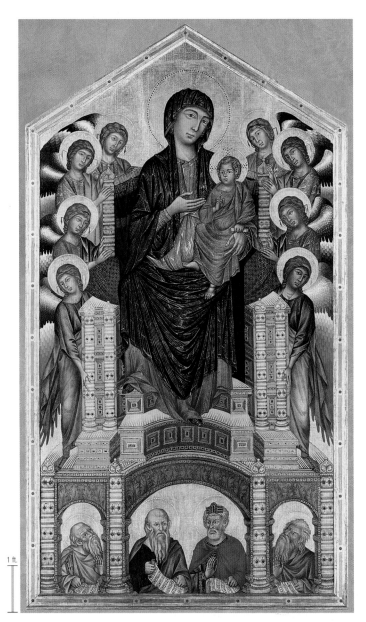

14-6 CIMABUE, *Madonna Enthroned with Angels and Prophets,* from Santa Trinità, Florence, ca. 1280–1290. Tempera and gold leaf on wood, 12′ 7″ × 7′ 4″. Galleria degli Uffizi, Florence.

Cimabue was one of the first artists to break away from the *maniera greca.* Although he relied on Byzantine models, the Italian master depicted the Madonna's massive throne as receding into space.

1 ft.

Pietro Cavallini

The authors of the most important Renaissance commentaries on Italian art of the 13th and 14th centuries were all Florentines, and civic pride doubtless played a role in attributing the reorientation of the art of painting to Florentine artists, especially Giotto (FIG. 14-9). Giorgio Vasari (1511–1574), the "father of art history" (see "Vasari's *Lives*," page 648), lauded Giotto as the first to make a definitive break from the maniera greca of late medieval Italian painting and to return to the naturalism of the ancients. But the stylistic revolution that Giotto represents was not solely his creation. Other artists paved the way for the Florentine master in the mural program of San Francesco at Assisi (FIGS. 14-5A and 14-5C) and in the churches of Rome. One of them was Pietro Cavallini, who has not received the recognition he deserves because his extant works are few and poorly preserved and because of the enduring influence of Vasari's artist biographies. Art historians, however, now recognize Cavallini as a pioneering figure in the creation of the Renaissance style in Italy.

In Cavallini's *Last Judgment* fresco (FIG. **14-7**) in Santa Cecilia in Trastevere, Christ appears at the center of the upper zone flanked by angels. The Virgin Mary is to his right and John the Baptist to his left (FIG. 14-7, *top*). Six enthroned apostles to each side (FIG. 14-7, *bottom*) complete the friezelike composition. Below the Savior is an altar with the instruments of his martyrdom (cross, nails, Longinus's spear, and so on). To the left of the altar (the Savior's right side), angels present to Christ those about to be saved, while the agents of the Devil (on his left) claim the damned. The theme is familiar from Romanesque portal sculpture (FIG. 12-1), but here it appears inside the church on the entrance (west) wall as the culmination of the biblical cycle painted on the nave walls.

Cavallini's apostles sit on deep thrones seen in perspective. Both the disciples and their thrones face inward toward Christ, uniting both sides of the composition with the central figure. The apostles' garments have deep folds that catch the light. Light also illuminates the figures' faces. Cavallini used light effectively to create volume and mass, a radical departure from the maniera greca, but the light does not come from a uniform source, and the apostles appear against a neutral dark background. Giotto carried Cavallini's innovations further, but the Roman painter deserves the loftier reputation that art historians are beginning to grant him.

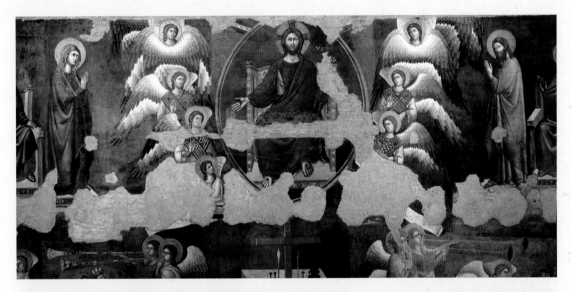

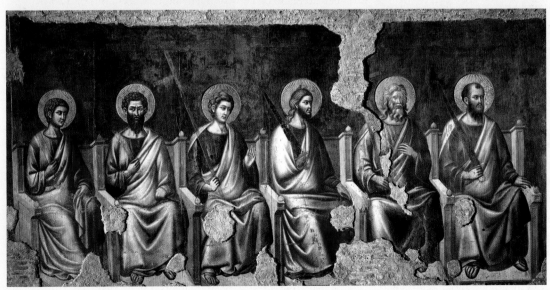

14-7 PIETRO CAVALLINI, **Christ flanked by angels** (*top*) **and apostles** (*bottom*), two details of the *Last Judgment* fresco on the west wall of the nave of Santa Cecilia in Trastevere, Rome, Italy, ca. 1290–1295.

A pioneer in the representation of fully modeled figures seen in perspective with light illuminating their faces and garments, Pietro Cavallini of Rome may have influenced Giotto di Bondone (FIG. 14-9).

documents. However, the creation of an Italian vernacular litera-ture (based on the Tuscan dialect common in Florence) expanded the audience for philosophical and intellectual concepts because of its greater accessibility. Dante Alighieri (1265–1321, author of *The Divine Comedy*), the poet and scholar Francesco Petrarch (1304–1374), and Giovanni Boccaccio (1313–1375, author of *Decameron*) were most responsible for establishing this vernacular literature.

The development of easily accessible literature was one impor-tant sign that the essentially religious view that had dominated Europe during the Middle Ages was about to change dramati-cally in what historians call the *Renaissance*. Although religion continued to occupy a primary position in the lives of Europe-ans, a growing concern with the natural world, the individual, and humanity's worldly existence characterized the Renaissance period—the 14th through 16th centuries. The word *renaissance* in French and English (*rinascità* in Italian) refers to a "rebirth" of art and culture. A revived interest in classical cultures—indeed, the veneration of classical antiquity as a model—was central to this rebirth. The notion that the Renaissance represented the restoration of the glorious past of Greece and Rome gave rise to the concept of the "Middle Ages" as the era falling between antiquity and the Renaissance.

Fundamental to the development of the Italian Renaissance was *humanism,* which emerged during the 14th century and became a central component of Italian art and culture in the 15th and 16th centuries. Humanism was more a code of civil conduct, a theory of education, and a scholarly discipline than a philosophi-cal system. The chief concerns of Italian humanists, as their name suggests, were human values and interests as distinct from—but not opposed to—religion's otherworldly values. Humanists pointed to classical cultures as particularly praiseworthy. This enthusiasm for antiquity involved study of Latin literature, especially the ele-gant Latin of Cicero (106–43 BCE) and the Augustan age (27 BCE–14 CE), and a conscious emulation of what proponents believed were the Roman civic virtues. These included self-sacrificing service to the state, participation in government, defense of state institutions (especially the administration of justice), and stoic indifference to personal misfortune in the performance of duty. With the help of a new interest in and knowledge of Greek, the humanists of the late 14th and 15th centuries recovered a large part of Greek as well as Roman literature and philosophy that had been lost, left unnoticed, or cast aside in the Middle Ages. Indeed, classical cultures provided humanists with a model for living in this world, a model primarily of human focus derived not from an authoritative and traditional religious dogma but from reason.

Ideally, humanists sought no material reward for services ren-dered. The sole reward for heroes of civic virtue was fame, just as the reward for leaders of the holy life was sainthood. For the edu-cated, the lives of heroes and heroines of the past became models of conduct as important as the lives of the saints. Petrarch wrote a book on illustrious men, and his colleague Boccaccio comple-mented it with 106 biographies of famous women—from Eve to Joanna, queen of Naples (r. 1343–1382). Both Petrarch and Boccac-cio were renowned in their own day as poets, scholars, and men of letters—their achievements equivalent in honor to those of the heroes of civic virtue. In 1341 in Rome, Petrarch received the lau-rel wreath crown, the ancient symbol of victory and merit. The humanist cult of fame emphasized the importance of creative indi-viduals and their role in contributing to the renown of the city-state and of all Italy.

Giotto

Celebrated in his own day as the first Renaissance painter, GIOTTO DI BONDONE (ca. 1266–1337) is a towering figure in the history of art. Scholars still debate the sources of the Florentine painter's style, but one formative influence must have been Cimabue, whom Vasari identified as Giotto's teacher, while noting that the pupil eclipsed his master by abandoning the "crude maniera greca" (see "Vasari's *Lives*," page 648). The 13th-century murals of San Francesco at Assisi (FIGS. 14-5A and 14-5C) and those of Pietro Cavallini in Rome (FIG. 14-7) may also have influenced Giotto—although some schol-ars believe that the young Giotto himself was one of the leading painters of the Assisi church. French Gothic sculpture (which Giotto may not have seen but which was certainly familiar to him from the work of Giovanni Pisano, who had spent time in Paris) and ancient Roman art probably also contributed to Giotto's artistic education. Yet no mere synthesis of these varied influences could have produced the significant shift in artistic approach that has led some scholars to describe Giotto as the father of Western pictorial art.

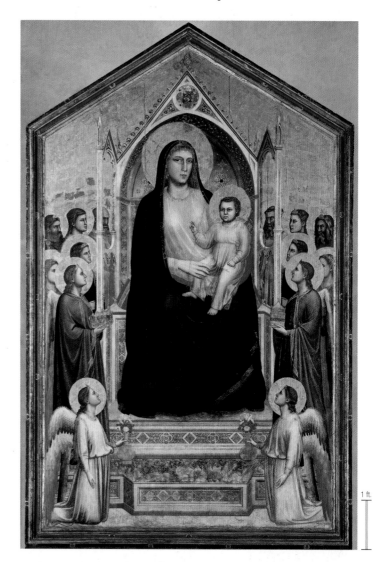

14-8 GIOTTO DI BONDONE, *Madonna Enthroned* (*Ognissanti Madonna*), from the Chiesa di Ognissanti (All Saints' Church), Flor-ence, ca. 1310. Tempera and gold leaf on wood, 10′ 8″ × 6′ 8″. Galleria degli Uffizi, Florence.

The *Ognissanti Madonna* retains the gold background of Byzantine art, but Giotto revived classical naturalism by giving his figures substance and bulk, in contrast to the maniera greca of Cimabue (FIG. 14-6).

Madonna Enthroned. On nearly the same great scale as Cimabue's enthroned Madonna (FIG. 14-6) is Giotto's panel (FIG. 14-8) depicting the same subject, painted for the high altar of Florence's Church of the Ognissanti (All Saints). Although still portrayed against the traditional gold background, Giotto's Madonna sits on her Gothic throne with the unshakable stability of an ancient marble goddess (compare FIG. 7-30). Giotto replaced Cimabue's slender Virgin, fragile beneath the thin ripplings of her drapery, with a weighty, queenly mother. In Giotto's painting, the Madonna's body is not lost—indeed, it is asserted. Giotto even showed Mary's breasts pressing through the thin fabric of her white undergarment. Gold highlights have disappeared from her heavy robe. Giotto aimed instead to construct a figure with substance and bulk—qualities suppressed in favor of a spiritual immateriality in Byzantine and Italo-Byzantine art. The different approaches of teacher and pupil can also be seen in the angels flanking the Madonna's throne. Cimabue stacked his angels to fill the full height of the panel. Giotto's statuesque angels stand on a common level,

leaving a large blank area above the heads of the background figures. The *Ognissanti Madonna* marks the end of medieval painting in Italy and the beginning of a new naturalistic approach to art.

Arena Chapel. Giotto's masterwork is the mural cycle of the Arena Chapel (FIG. 14-9) in Padua, which takes its name from an adjacent ancient Roman arena (amphitheater). A banker, Enrico Scrovegni, built the chapel on a site adjacent to his palace and consecrated it in 1305, in the hope that the chapel would atone for the moneylender's sin of usury. Some scholars have suggested that Giotto may also have been the chapel's architect, because its design so perfectly suits its interior decoration. The rectangular hall has only six windows, all in the south wall, which provide ample

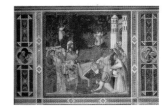

🔼 **14-9A** GIOTTO, *Entry into Jerusalem,* ca. 1305.

illumination for the frescoes that fill the almost unbroken surfaces of the other walls.

In 38 framed scenes (FIGS. 14-9A, 14-10, and 14-10A), Giotto presented one of the most impressive and complete Christian pictorial cycles ever rendered. The narrative unfolds on the north and south walls in three zones, reading from top to bottom: in the top level are the lives of the Virgin and her parents, Joachim and Anna; in the middle zone, the life and mission of Jesus; and, in the lowest level, the Savior's passion and resurrection. Below, imitation marble veneer—reminiscent of ancient Roman *revetment* (FIG. 7-51), which Giotto may have seen—alternates with personified virtues and vices painted in *grisaille* (monochrome grays, often used for modeling in paintings) to resemble sculpture. On the west wall above the chapel's entrance is Giotto's dramatic *Last Judgment,* in which Scrovegni appears among the saved, kneeling as he presents his chapel to the Virgin. (Christ as Last Judge is also the culminating scene of Cavallini's late-13th-century fresco cycle [FIG. 14-7] in Santa Cecilia in Trastevere in Rome. In fact, Giotto's enthroned apostles are strikingly similar to Cavallini's.) The chapel's vaulted ceiling is blue, an azure sky dotted with golden stars symbolic of Heaven. Medallions bearing images of Christ, Mary, and various prophets also appear on the vault. Giotto painted the same blue in the backgrounds of the narrative panels on the walls below. The color thereby functions as a unifying agent for the entire decorative scheme.

Giotto set his goal as emulating the appearance of the natural world—the approach championed by the ancient Greeks and Romans but largely abandoned in the Middle Ages in favor of representing spiritual rather than physical reality (see "Picturing the Spiritual World," page 260). Subtly scaled to the chapel's space, Giotto's stately

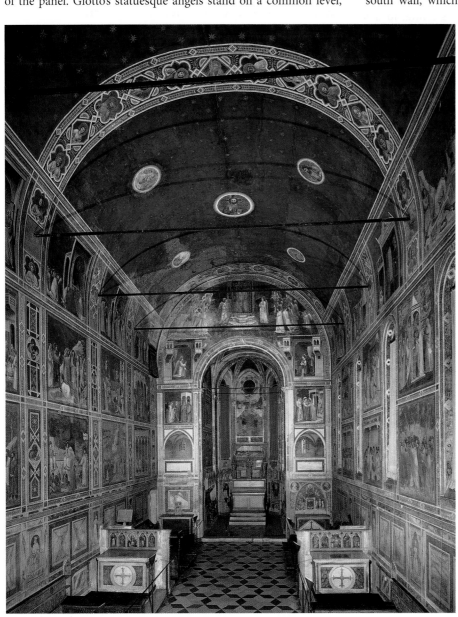

14-9 GIOTTO DI BONDONE, interior of the Arena Chapel (Cappella Scrovegni; looking west), Padua, Italy, 1305–1306.

Giotto's 38 panels in the Arena Chapel depict the lives of the Virgin, her parents, and Jesus. Enrico Scrovegni built the chapel in order to atone for his sin of moneylending and earn a place in Heaven.

Fresco Painting

Fresco painting has a long history, particularly in the Mediterranean region, where the Minoans (FIGS. 4-7, 4-8, 4-9, 4-9A, and 4-10) used it as early as the 17th century BCE. *Fresco* (Italian for "fresh") is a mural-painting technique involving the application of permanent limeproof pigments, diluted in water, on freshly laid lime plaster. Because the surface of the wall absorbs the pigments as the plaster dries, fresco is one of the most durable painting techniques. The stable condition of the ancient Minoan frescoes, as well as those found at Pompeii (FIGS. 7-18, 7-22, 7-24, 7-24A, and 7-25) and other Roman sites (FIGS. 7-19, 7-20, 7-21, and 7-54A), in San Francesco (FIGS. 14-5A and 14-5C) at Assisi, the Roman church of Santa Cecilia in Trastevere (FIGS. 14-7), and in the Arena Chapel (FIGS. 14-9, 14-9A, 14-10, and 14-10A) at Padua, testify to the longevity of this painting method. The colors have remained vivid (although dirt and soot have often necessitated cleaning—most famously in the Vatican's Sistine Chapel; FIGS. 22-18B and 22-18C) because of the chemically inert pigments the artists used.

This *buon fresco* ("true" fresco) process is time-consuming and demanding and requires several layers of plaster. Although buon fresco methods vary, generally the artist (or, more precisely, an apprentice in the master's workshop) prepares the wall with a rough layer of lime plaster called the *arriccio* (brown coat). The artist then transfers the composition to the wall, usually by drawing directly on the arriccio with a burnt-orange pigment called *sinopia* (most popular during the 14th century), or by transferring a *cartoon* (a full-size preparatory drawing). Cartoons increased in usage in the 15th and 16th centuries, largely replacing sinopia underdrawings. Finally, the painter lays the *intonaco* (painting coat) smoothly over the drawing in sections (called *giornate*—Italian for "days") only as large as the artist expects to complete in that session. (In Giotto's *Lamentation* [FIG. 14-10], for example, it is easy to distinguish the various giornate.) The buon fresco painter must apply the colors quickly, because once the plaster is dry, it will no longer absorb the pigment. Any unpainted areas of the intonaco after a session must be cut away so that fresh plaster can be applied for the next giornata.

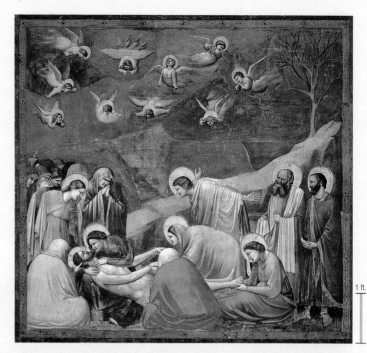

14-10 GIOTTO DI BONDONE, *Lamentation*, Arena Chapel (Cappella Scrovegni; FIG. 14-9), Padua, Italy, ca. 1305. Fresco, 6′ 6¾″ × 6′ ¾″.

Giotto painted *Lamentation* in several sections, each corresponding to one painting session, or giornata. Artists employing the buon fresco technique must complete each section before the plaster dries.

In addition to the buon fresco technique, artists used *fresco secco* ("dry" fresco). Fresco secco involves painting on dried lime plaster, the method the ancient Egyptians employed (FIGS. 3-28 and 3-28A). Although the finished product visually approximates buon fresco, the plaster wall does not absorb the pigments, which simply adhere to the surface, so fresco secco is not as permanent as buon fresco.

In areas of high humidity, such as Venice with its streets of water, fresco was less appropriate because moisture is an obstacle to the drying process.

and slow-moving half-life-size figures (as in *Entry into Jerusalem*, FIG. 14-9A) act out the religious dramas convincingly and with great restraint. The biblical actors are sculpturesque, simple, and weighty, often *foreshortened* (seen from an angle) and modeled with light and shading in the ancient manner. They convey individual emotions through their postures and gestures. Constructing the illusion of a weighty, three-dimensional body also requires constructing the illusion of a space sufficiently ample to contain that body, and Giotto achieved that goal as well in the Arena Chapel frescoes (see "Fresco Painting," above). The new interest in naturalism definitively displaced the maniera greca in Italy, inaugurating an age some scholars call "early scientific" by establishing the accurate reproduction of the visible world as a central, if not the sole, aim of artists. By stressing the preeminence of sight for gaining knowledge of the world, Giotto and his successors contributed to the foundation of empirical science.

Lamentation. The panel in the lowest zone of the north wall, *Lamentation* (FIG. 14-10), illustrates particularly well the revolutionary nature of Giotto's style. In the presence of boldly foreshortened angels, seen head-on with their bodies receding into the background and darting about in hysterical grief, a congregation mourns over the dead Savior just before his entombment. Mary cradles her son's body. Mary Magdalene looks solemnly at the wounds in Christ's feet. Saint John the Evangelist throws his arms back dramatically. Giotto arranged a shallow stage for the figures, bounded by a thick diagonal rock incline defining a horizontal ledge in the foreground. Though narrow, the ledge provides firm visual support for the figures. The rocky setting recalls the landscape of a 12th-century Byzantine mural (FIG. 9-29) at Nerezi in Macedonia. Here, the steep slope leads the viewer's eye toward the picture's dramatic focal point at the lower left.

The postures and gestures of Giotto's figures convey a broad spectrum of grief. They range from Mary's almost fierce despair to the passionate outbursts of Mary Magdalene and John to the philosophical resignation of the two disciples at the right and the mute sorrow of the two hooded mourners in the foreground.

In *Lamentation,* a single event provokes a host of individual responses in figures that are convincing presences both physically and psychologically. Painters before Giotto rarely attempted, let alone achieved, this combination of naturalistic representation, compositional complexity, and emotional resonance.

The formal design of *Lamentation*—the way that Giotto grouped the figures within the constructed space—is worth close study. Each group has its own definition, and each contributes to the rhythmic order of the composition. The strong diagonal of the rocky ledge, with its single dead tree (the tree of knowledge of good and evil, which withered after Adam and Eve's Original Sin), concentrates the viewer's attention on the heads of Christ and his mother, which Giotto positioned dynamically off center. The massive bulk of the seated mourner in the painting's left corner arrests and contains all movement beyond Mary and her dead son. The placement of the seated mourner at the right establishes a relation with the center figures, who, by gazes and gestures, draw the viewer's attention back to Christ's head. Figures seen from the back, which are frequent in Giotto's compositions (compare *Betrayal of Jesus,* FIG. 14-10A), represent

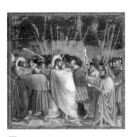

▣ 14-10A GIOTTO, *Betrayal of Jesus,* ca. 1305.

an innovation in the movement away from the Italo-Byzantine style. These figures emphasize the foreground, aiding the visual placement of the intermediate figures farther back in space. This device, the very contradiction of Byzantine frontality, in effect puts viewers behind the "observer figures," who, facing the action as spectators, reinforce the sense of stagecraft as a model for painting. Also markedly different from the *maniera greca* is Giotto's habit of painting incomplete figures cut off by the composition's frame, a feature also of his Ognissanti Madonna (FIG. 14-8).

Giotto's new devices for depicting spatial depth and body mass could not, of course, have been possible without his management of light and shade. He shaded his figures to indicate both the direction of the light illuminating their bodies and the shadows (the diminished light), thereby giving the figures volume. In *Lamentation,* light falls upon the upper surfaces of the figures (especially the two central bending figures) and passes down to dark in their garments, separating the volumes one from the other and pushing one to the fore, the other to the rear. The gradual transition from light from a single steady source—not shown in the picture—to shade was the first step toward the development of *chiaroscuro* (the use of contrasts of dark and light to produce modeling) in later Renaissance painting.

The stagelike settings made possible by Giotto's innovations in perspective and lighting suited perfectly the dramatic narrative that the Franciscans emphasized then as a principal method for educating the faithful in their religion. In this new age of humanism, the old stylized presentations of the holy mysteries had evolved into *mystery plays* offered at church portals and in city squares. (Eventually, confraternities also presented more elaborate religious dramas called *sacre rappresentazioni*—"holy representations.") The great increase in popular sermons to huge city audiences prompted a public taste for narrative, recited as dramatically as possible. The arts of illusionistic painting, of drama, and of sermon rhetoric with all their theatrical flourishes developed simultaneously and were mutually influential. Giotto's art masterfully synthesized dramatic narrative, holy lesson, and truth to human experience in a visual idiom of his own invention, accessible to all.

Siena

Among 14th-century Italian city-states, the Republics of Siena and Florence were the most powerful. Both were urban centers of bankers and merchants with widespread international contacts and large sums available for the commissioning of artworks (see "Artists' Guilds, Artistic Commissions, and Artists' Contracts," page 430).

Duccio. The works of Duccio di Buoninsegna are the supreme examples of 14th-century Sienese art. The artist's most famous commission, the immense *Maestà* altarpiece (FIG. 14-1), replaced a much smaller painting of the Virgin Mary on the high altar of Siena Cathedral (FIG. 14-13A). The Sienese believed that the Virgin had brought them victory over the Florentines at the Battle of Monteperti in 1260, and she was the focus of the religious life of the republic. When Duccio and his assistants completed the prestigious commission in 1311, the entire city celebrated. Shops closed, and the bishop led a great procession of priests, civic officials, and the populace at large in carrying the altarpiece from Duccio's studio outside the city gate through the *Campo* (literally "field"—Siena's main *piazza,* or plaza), past the town hall (FIG. 14-16), and up to its home on Siena's highest hill. So great was Duccio's stature that the church's officials permitted him to include his name in the dedicatory inscription on the front of the altarpiece on the Virgin's footstool: "Holy Mother of God, be the cause of peace for Siena and of life for Duccio, because he painted you thus."

Painted in tempera front and back, the work unfortunately can no longer be seen in its entirety, because of its dismantling in subsequent centuries. Many of Duccio's panels are on display today as single masterpieces, scattered among the world's museums. The main panel (FIG. 14-1) reveals Duccio's interest in the naturalism increasingly embraced by Trecento painters. Nonetheless, Duccio understood that his *Maestà* would be the focus of worship in Siena's largest and most important church, its cathedral, the seat of the bishop of Siena, and that the altarpiece should be an object holy in itself. The Sienese master recognized how the role of the artwork in liturgical ritual limited his experimentation in depicting narrative action and producing illusionistic effects by modeling forms and adjusting their placement in pictorial space, as Giotto had done in the Arena Chapel a few years before.

Instead, the queen of Heaven panel is a miracle of color composition and texture manipulation, unfortunately not fully revealed in photographs. Close inspection of the original reveals what the Sienese artist learned from other sources. In the 13th and 14th centuries, Italy was the distribution center for the great silk trade from China and the Middle East (see "Silk and the Silk Road," page 477). After processing the silk in Lucca and Florence, the Italians exported the precious fabric throughout Europe to satisfy an immense market for elegant dress. (Dante, Petrarch, and many other humanists decried the appetite for luxury in costume, which to them represented a decline in civic and moral virtue.) People throughout Europe (Duccio and other artists among them) prized fabrics from China, Persia, Byzantium, and the Islamic world. In his depiction of the enthroned Virgin among saints, Duccio created the glistening and shimmering effects of textiles, adapting the motifs and design patterns of exotic materials. Complementing the sumptuous fabrics and the (lost) gilded wood frame are the halos of the holy figures, which feature tooled decorative designs in gold leaf (*punchwork*). But, as did Giotto in his *Ognissanti Madonna* (FIG. 14-8), Duccio eliminated almost all the gold patterning of the

Artists' Guilds, Artistic Commissions, and Artists' Contracts

The structured organization of economic activity during the 14th century, when Italy had established a thriving international trade and held a commanding position in the Mediterranean world, extended to many trades and professions. *Guilds* (associations of master craftspeople, apprentices, and tradespeople), which had emerged during the 12th century, became prominent. These associations not only protected members' common economic interests against external pressures, such as taxation, but also provided them with the means to regulate their internal operations (for example, training apprentices and assuring high-quality work).

Because of today's international open art market, the notion of an "artists' union" may seem strange. The general public tends to think of art as the creative expression of an individual artist. However, artists did not always enjoy this degree of freedom. Historically, they rarely undertook projects without receiving a specific commission. The patron contracting for the artist's services could be a civic group, religious institution, private individual, or even the artists' guild itself. Guilds, although primarily business organizations, also contributed to their city's religious and artistic life by subsidizing the building and decoration of numerous churches and hospitals. For example, the wool manufacturers' guild oversaw the start of Florence Cathedral (FIGS. 14-19 and 14-19A) in 1296, and the wool merchants' guild supervised the completion of its dome (FIG. 21-29A). The guild of silk manufacturers and goldsmiths provided the funds to build Florence's foundling hospital, the Ospedale degli Innocenti (FIG. 21-30).

Monastic orders, confraternities, and the Vatican were also major art patrons. In addition, wealthy families and individuals—for example, the Paduan banker Enrico Scrovegni (FIG. 14-9)—commissioned artworks for a wide variety of reasons. Besides the aesthetic pleasure these patrons derived from art, the images often also served as testaments to the patron's piety, wealth, and stature. (In Scrovegni's case, he hoped that building the Arena Chapel and decorating it with biblical frescoes would outweigh his sins as a moneylender and earn him a place in Heaven.) Because artworks during this period were the product of service contracts, a patron's needs or wishes played a crucial role in the final form of any painting, sculpture, or building.

Some early contracts between patrons and artists still exist. Patrons normally asked artists to submit drawings or models for approval, and they expected that the artists they hired would adhere closely to the approved designs. The contracts usually stipulated certain conditions, such as the insistence on the artist's own hand in the production of the work, the quality of pigment and amount of gold leaf or other costly materials to be used, the deadline for completion, the amount and timing of payment, and the penalties for failure to meet the contract's terms.

A few extant 13th- and 14th-century painting contracts are especially illuminating. Although they may specify the subject to be represented, these binding legal documents always focus on the financial aspects of the commission and the responsibilities of the painter to the patron (and vice versa). For example, in a contract dated November 1, 1301, between Cimabue (FIG. 14-6) and another artist

and the Hospital of Santa Chiara in Pisa, the artists agree to supply an altarpiece

> with colonnettes, tabernacles, and predella, painted with histories of the divine majesty of the Blessed Virgin Mary, of the apostles, of the angels, and with other figures and pictures, as shall be seen fit and shall please the said master of or other legitimate persons for the hospital.*

Other terms of the Santa Chiara contract specify the size of the panel and require the artists to use gold and silver gilding for parts of the altarpiece.

The contract for an altarpiece's frame was usually a separate document, because it necessitated employing the services of a master carpenter. For example, on April 15, 1285, the leading painter of Siena, Duccio di Buoninsegna (FIGS. 14-1, 14-11, 14-11A, and 14-12), signed a contract with the rectors of the Confraternity of the Laudesi, the lay group associated with the Dominican church of Santa Maria Novella (FIG. 14-5B) in Florence. The contract specified only that Duccio was to provide the painting, not its frame—and it imposed conditions that the painter had to meet if he was to be paid.

> [The rectors] promise . . . to pay the same Duccio . . . as the payment and price of the painting of the said panel that is to be painted and done by him in the way described below . . . 150 lire of the small florins. . . . [Duccio, in turn, promises] to paint and embellish the panel with the image of the blessed Virgin Mary and of her omnipotent Son and other figures, according to the wishes and pleasure of the lessors, and to gild [the panel] and do everything that will enhance the beauty of the panel, his being all the expenses and the costs. . . . If the said panel is not beautifully painted and it is not embellished according to the wishes and desires of the same lessors, they are in no way bound to pay him the price or any part of it.[†]

Sometimes patrons furnished the materials and paid artists by the day instead of a fixed amount. That was the arrangement Duccio made on October 9, 1308, when he agreed to paint the *Maestà* (FIG. 14-1) for the high altar of Siena Cathedral.

> Duccio has promised to paint and make the said panel as well as he can and knows how, and he further agreed not to accept or receive any other work until the said panel is done and completed. . . . [The church officials promise] to pay the said Duccio sixteen solidi of the Sienese denari as his salary for the said work and labor for each day that the said Duccio works with his own hands on the said panel . . . [and] to provide and give everything that will be necessary for working on the said panel so that the said Duccio need contribute nothing to the work save his person and his effort.[§]

In all cases, the artists worked for their patrons and could count on being compensated for their talents and efforts only if the work they delivered met the standards of those who ordered it.

*Translated by John White, *Duccio: Tuscan Art and the Medieval Workshop* (London: Thames & Hudson, 1979), 34.
†Translated by James H. Stubblebine, *Duccio di Buoninsegna and His School* (Princeton, N.J.: Princeton University Press, 1979), 1: 192.
§Ibid., 201.

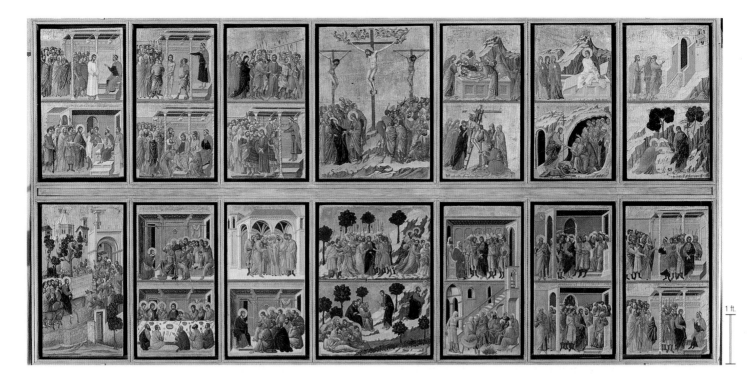

14-11 DUCCIO DI BUONINSEGNA, 14 panels illustrating the passion of Jesus, back of the *Maestà* altarpiece (FIG. 14-1), from Siena Cathedral, Siena, Italy, 1308–1311. Tempera and gold leaf on wood, 7′ × 13′. Museo dell'Opera del Duomo, Siena.

On the back of the *Maestà* altarpiece, Duccio painted Jesus's passion in 24 scenes on 14 panels, beginning with *Entry into Jerusalem* (FIG. 14-11A), at the lower left, through *Noli me tangere,* at top right.

figures' garments in favor of creating three-dimensional volume. Traces remain only in the Virgin's red dress.

In the narrative panels on the back of the *Maestà,* however, Duccio was free to pursue a greater degree of innovation in the representation of anecdotal narratives set in landscapes and the interiors of buildings. The section reproduced here (FIG. 14-11), consisting of 26 scenes in 14 panels, relates the events of Christ's passion. The largest scene, at top center, depicts the Savior's crucifixion—a highly appropriate choice for an altarpiece in front of which the Sienese bishop celebrated Mass, the ritual reenactment of Christ's sacrifice. Duccio drew the details of his scenes from the accounts in all four Gospels. The viewer reads the pictorial story in zigzag fashion, beginning with *Entry into Jerusalem* (FIG. 14-11A) at the lower left. The narrative ends with Christ's appearance to Mary Magdalene (*Noli me tangere*) at the top right. Duccio consistently dressed Jesus in blue robes in most of the panels, but beginning with *Transfiguration,* the Savior's garment is gilded, reviving a stylistic feature of the maniera greca for its symbolic value.

One of the finest panels from Duccio's passion cycle is *Betrayal of Jesus,* in which the Sienese master represented several episodes of the event—the betrayal of Jesus by Judas's false kiss, the disciples fleeing in terror, and Peter cutting off the ear of the high priest's servant (FIG. 14-12; compare FIG. 14-10A). Duccio carefully differentiated among the anger of Peter, the malice of Judas (echoed in the faces of the

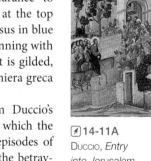

🖊 14-11A
DUCCIO, *Entry into Jerusalem,* 1308–1311.

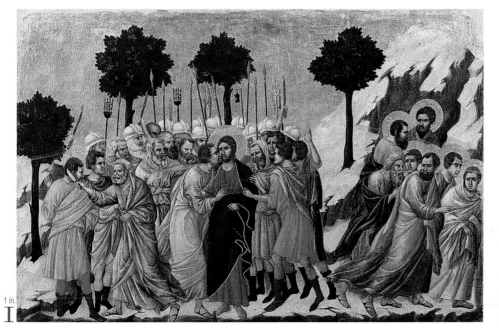

14-12 DUCCIO DI BUONINSEGNA, *Betrayal of Jesus,* panel on the back (FIG. 14-11) of the *Maestà* altarpiece (FIG. 14-1), from Siena Cathedral, Siena, Italy, 1308–1311. Tempera and gold leaf on wood, 1′ 10$\frac{1}{2}$″ × 3′ 4″. Museo dell'Opera del Duomo, Siena.

In his panel depicting Judas betraying Jesus with a kiss, Duccio brilliantly captured various human emotions—the anger of Peter, the malice of Judas, and the timidity of the fleeing apostles.

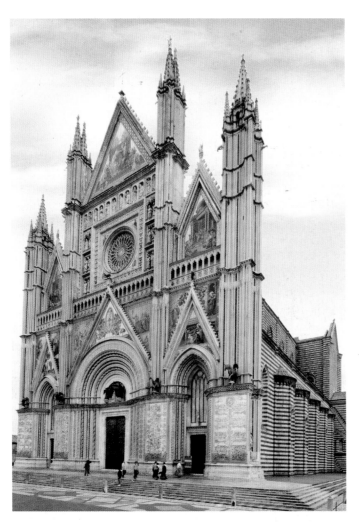

14-13 LORENZO MAITANI, Orvieto Cathedral (looking northeast), Orvieto, Italy, begun 1310.

The pointed gables over the doorways, the rose window, and the large pinnacles derive from French Gothic architecture, but the facade of Orvieto Cathedral masks a traditional timber-roofed basilica.

throng about Jesus), and the apprehension and timidity of the fleeing disciples. These figures are actors in a religious drama that the artist interpreted in terms of thoroughly human actions and reactions. In this and the other narrative panels—for example, *Entry into Jerusalem* (FIG. 14-11A), a theme treated also by Giotto in the Arena Chapel (FIG. 14-9A)—Duccio made a seminal contribution to the Renaissance humanization of biblical themes.

Orvieto Cathedral. While Duccio was working on the *Maestà* altarpiece for Siena's most important church, a Sienese architect, LORENZO MAITANI (ca. 1255–1330), received the commission to design Orvieto's cathedral (FIG. 14-13). The Orvieto facade, like

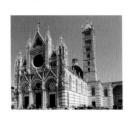

14-13A Siena Cathedral, begun ca. 1226.

the earlier facade of Siena Cathedral (FIG. 14-13A), begun by Giovanni Pisano (FIG. 14-4), highlights the appeal of the vocabulary of French Gothic art and architecture in Italy at the end of the 13th and beginning of the 14th century. Characteristically French are the pointed gables over Orvieto Cathedral's three doorways, the rose window and statues in niches in the kings' gallery of the

upper zone, and the four large pinnacles dividing the facade into three bays. The outer pinnacles serve as miniature substitutes for the tall northern European west-front towers. Adorning the four piers flanking the three portals are elaborate reliefs representing, from left to right, Old Testament scenes, the Tree of Jesse, New Testament scenes, and the Last Judgment. The individual episodes of the stories fill the spaces between tree branches. Both compositionally and iconographically, the Orvieto reliefs derive from the French Late Gothic tradition.

Maitani's facade, however, is a Gothic overlay masking a marble-revetted basilican structure in the Tuscan Romanesque tradition, as the three-quarter view of the cathedral in FIG. 14-13 reveals. Few Italian architects fully embraced the Gothic style. The Orvieto facade resembles a great altar screen. Its single plane may be covered with carefully placed Gothic carved and painted decoration, but in principle, Orvieto Cathedral belongs with Pisa Cathedral (FIG. 12-29) and other earlier Italian buildings, rather than with the French cathedrals at Amiens (FIG. 13-22) and Reims (FIG. 13-24). Inside, the Orvieto church has a timber-roofed nave with a two-story elevation (columnar arcade and clerestory) in the Early Christian manner (compare FIGS. 8-18 and 8-25). Both the chancel arch framing the apse and the nave arcade's arches are round as opposed to pointed.

Simone Martini. Duccio's successors in the Sienese school also produced innovative works. SIMONE MARTINI (ca. 1285–1344) was a pupil of Duccio's and may have assisted him in painting the *Maestà* altarpiece. Martini was a close friend of Petrarch's, and the poet praised him highly for his portrait of "Laura" (the woman to whom Petrarch dedicated his sonnets). Martini worked for the French kings in Naples and Sicily and, in his last years, produced paintings for the papal court at Avignon, where he came in contact with French painters. By adapting the elegant and luxuriant patterns of the Gothic style to Sienese art and, in turn, by acquainting painters north of the Alps with the Sienese style, Martini was instrumental in creating the so-called *International Gothic* style. This new style swept Europe during the late 14th and early 15th centuries because it appealed to the aristocratic taste for brilliant colors, lavish costumes, intricate ornamentation, and themes involving splendid processions (compare FIG. 21-17).

The Saint Ansanus altarpiece (FIG. 14-14) that Martini created for Siena Cathedral (FIG. 14-13A) features radiant colors, fluttering lines, and weightless elongated figures in a spaceless setting—all hallmarks of the artist's style. The complex etiquette of the European chivalric courts probably inspired Martini's presentation of Gabriel bringing his message to the Virgin. The angel has just alighted, the breeze of his passage lifting his mantle, his glittering wings still beating. The gold of his splendid gown signals that he has descended from Heaven to announce the coming birth of the son of God. The Virgin, putting down her book of devotions, shrinks shyly from Gabriel's reverent bow—an appropriate act in the presence of royalty. Mary draws about her the deep-blue, golden-hemmed mantle, colors befitting the queen of Heaven. Between the two figures is a vase of white lilies, symbolic of the Virgin's purity. Despite Mary's modest reserve and the tremendous import of the angel's message, the scene subordinates drama to court ritual, and structural experimentation to surface splendor. The intricate tracery of the richly tooled (reconstructed) French Gothic–inspired frame and the elaborate punchwork halos (by then a characteristic feature of Sienese panel painting) enhance the tactile magnificence of the altarpiece.

Simone Martini and his student and assistant, LIPPO MEMMI (active ca. 1317–1350), signed the *Annunciation* panel and dated it

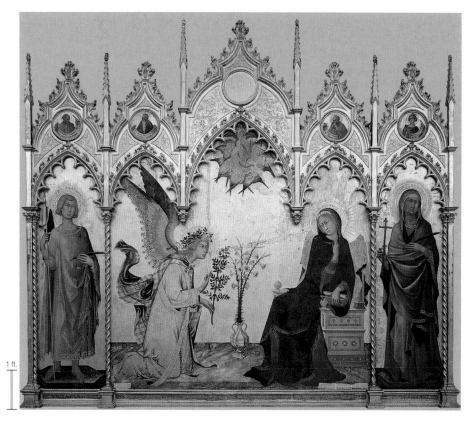

14-14 Simone Martini and Lippo Memmi, *Annunciation,* from the altar of Saint Ansanus, Siena Cathedral, Siena, Italy, 1333 (frame reconstructed in the 19th century). Tempera and gold leaf on wood, center panel 10′ 1″ × 8′ 8¾″. Galleria degli Uffizi, Florence.

A pupil of Duccio's, Simone Martini was instrumental in the creation of the International Gothic style. Its hallmarks are radiant colors, flowing lines, and weightless figures in golden, spaceless settings.

is often difficult to distinguish the master's hand from those of assistants, especially if the master corrected or redid part of the pupil's work (see "Artistic Training in Renaissance Italy," page 434).

Pietro Lorenzetti. Another of Duccio's students, Pietro Lorenzetti (ca. 1280–1348), contributed significantly to the general experiments in pictorial realism taking place in 14th-century Italy. Surpassing even his renowned master, Lorenzetti achieved a remarkable degree of spatial illusionism in his *Birth of the Virgin* (FIG. 14-15), a large *triptych* (three-part panel painting) created for the altar of Saint Savinus in Siena Cathedral (FIG. 14-13A). Lorenzetti

(1333). The latter's contribution to the altarpiece is still a matter of debate, but most art historians believe that he painted the two lateral saints (Ansanus at left, Margaret at right). These figures, which are reminiscent of the jamb statues of Gothic church portals, have greater solidity and lack the linear elegance of Martini's central pair. Given the nature of medieval and Renaissance workshop practices, it

painted three of the pilasters dividing the altarpiece into three sections as though they were the ends of the walls extending back into the painted space. Viewers seem to look through the frame (added later) into a boxlike stage, where the event takes place. That the second pilaster from the right cuts across a figure, blocking part of it from view, strengthens the illusion of spatial recession. In subsequent centuries, artists exploited this use of architectural elements to enhance the illusion of painted figures acting out a drama a mere few feet away. This kind of pictorial illusionism characterized ancient Roman mural painting (FIGS. 7-18 and 7-19, *right*), but had not been practiced in Italy for a thousand years.

The setting for *Birth of the Virgin* also represented a marked step in the advance of worldly realism. Unlike in other altarpieces of this era, the figures in Lorenzetti's painting are not seen against an otherworldly gold background. Instead, the Sienese master painted a detailed interior of an upper-class Italian home of the period, complete with floor tiles and fabrics whose receding lines enhance the sense of depth. Lorenzetti removed the front walls of the house to enable the viewer to peer inside, where Saint Anne (see "Early Christian Saints," pages 246–247) props herself up wearily as the midwives wash the newborn Virgin and the women bring gifts. Anne, like Nicola Pisano's Nativity Virgin (FIG. 14-3),

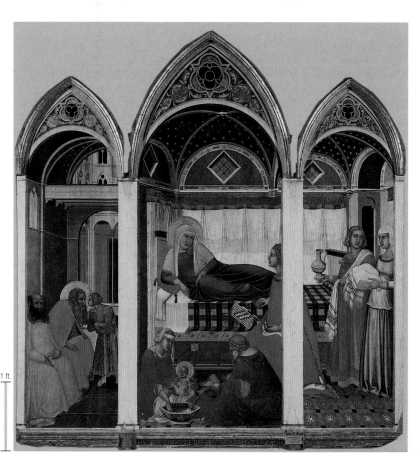

14-15 Pietro Lorenzetti, *Birth of the Virgin,* from the altar of Saint Savinus, Siena Cathedral, Siena, Italy, 1342. Tempera on wood, 6′ 1″ × 5′ 11″. Museo dell'Opera del Duomo, Siena.

In this triptych, Pietro Lorenzetti revived the pictorial illusionism of ancient Roman murals and painted three of the pilasters dividing the panel as if they were walls extending back into the pictorial space.

Artistic Training in Renaissance Italy

In Italy during the 14th through 16th centuries, training to become a professional artist capable of earning membership in the appropriate guild was a laborious and lengthy process. Aspiring artists started their training at an early age, anytime from 7 to 15 years old. Their fathers would negotiate an arrangement with a master artist whereby each youth lived with that master for a specified number of years, usually five or six. During that time, the boys served as apprentices to the master of the workshop, learning the trade. (This living arrangement served as a major obstacle for women who wished to become professional artists, because it was inappropriate for young girls to live in a male master's household.) The guilds supervised this rigorous training. They wanted not only to ensure their professional reputations by admitting only the most talented members but also to control the number of artists (and thereby limit competition). Toward this end, they frequently tried to regulate the number of apprentices working under a single master.

The skills that apprentices learned varied with the type of studio they joined. Those apprenticed to painters learned to grind pigments, draw, prepare wood panels for painting, gild, and lay plaster for fresco. Sculptors in training learned to manipulate different materials—wood, stone, clay, or bronze—although many sculpture workshops specialized in only one or two of these materials. For stone carving, apprentices learned their craft by blocking out the master's designs for statues. As their skills developed, apprentices took on increasingly difficult tasks.

Cennino Cennini (ca. 1370–1440) explained the value of this apprenticeship system and, in particular, the advantages for young artists in studying and copying the works of older masters, in an influential book published in 1400, *Il libro dell'arte* (*The Handbook of Art*):

> Having first practiced drawing for a while, . . . take pains and pleasure in constantly copying the best things which you can find done by the hand of great masters. And if you are in a place where many good masters have been, so much the better for you. But I give you this advice: take care to select the best one every time, and the one who has the greatest reputation. And, as you go on from day to day, it will be against nature if you do not get some grasp of his style and of his spirit. For if you undertake to copy after one master today and after another one tomorrow, you will not acquire the style of either one or the other, and you will inevitably,

through enthusiasm, become capricious, because each style will be distracting your mind. You will try to work in this man's way today, and in the other's tomorrow, and so you will not get either of them right. If you follow the course of one man through constant practice, your intelligence would have to be crude indeed for you not to get some nourishment from it. Then you will find, if nature has granted you any imagination at all, that you will eventually acquire a style individual to yourself, and it cannot help being good; because your hand and your mind, being always accustomed to gather flowers, would ill know how to pluck thorns.*

After completing their apprenticeships, artists entered the appropriate guilds. For example, painters, who ground pigments, joined the guild of apothecaries. Sculptors were members of the guild of stoneworkers, and goldsmiths entered the silk guild, because metalworkers often stretched gold into threads wound around silk for weaving. Guild membership served as certification of the artists' competence, but did not mean they were ready to open their own studios. New guild-certified artists usually served as assistants to master artists, because until they established their reputations, they could not expect to receive many commissions, and the cost of establishing their own workshops was high. In any case, this arrangement was not permanent, and workshops were not necessarily static enterprises. Although well-established and respected studios existed, workshops could be organized around individual masters (with no set studio locations) or organized for a specific project, especially an extensive decoration program.

Generally, assistants to painters were responsible for gilding frames and backgrounds, completing decorative work, and, occasionally, rendering architectural settings. Artists regarded figures, especially those central to the represented subject, as the most important and difficult parts of a painting, and the master reserved these for himself. Sometimes assistants painted secondary or marginal figures, but only under the master's close supervision. That was probably the case with Simone Martini's *Annunciation* (FIG. 14-14), in which the master painted the Virgin and angel, whereas his assistant, Lippo Memmi, was probably responsible for the flanking saints.

*Translated by Daniel V. Thompson Jr., *Cennino Cennini, The Craftsman's Handbook* (Il Libro dell'arte) (New York: Dover, 1960; reprint of 1933 ed.), 14–15.

---

resembles a reclining figure on the lid of a Roman sarcophagus (FIG. 7-60). At the left, in a side chamber, Joachim eagerly awaits news of the delivery. Lorenzetti's altarpiece is as noteworthy for the painter's careful inspection and recording of details of the everyday world as for his innovations in spatial illusionism.

Palazzo Pubblico. Not all Sienese painting of the early 14th century was religious in character. One of the most important fresco cycles of the period (FIG. 14-17A) was a civic commission for Siena's *Palazzo Pubblico* ("public palace" or city hall; FIG. 14-16). Siena was a proud commercial and political rival of Florence. The secular center of the community, the civic meeting hall in the main

square (the Campo), was almost as great an object of civic pride as the city's cathedral (FIG. 14-13A). The Palazzo Pubblico has a slightly concave facade (to conform to the irregular shape of the Campo) and a gigantic tower visible from miles around (compare FIGS. 13-30 and 14-19B). The imposing building and tower must have earned the admiration of Siena's citizens as well as of visitors to the city, inspiring in them respect for the republic's power and success. The tower served as a lookout over the city and the countryside around it and as a bell tower (*campanile*) for ringing signals of all kinds to the populace. Siena, like other Italian city-states, had to defend itself against neighboring cities and often against kings and emperors. In addition, it had to secure itself against internal upheavals common in the

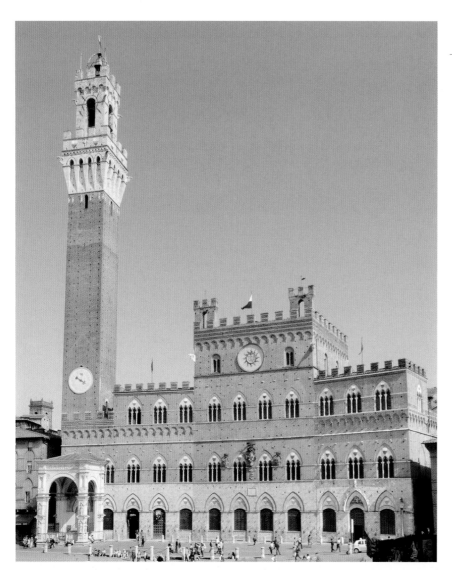

14-16 Palazzo Pubblico (looking east), Siena, Italy, 1288–1309.

Siena's Palazzo Pubblico has a concave facade and a gigantic tower visible for miles around. The tower served as both a defensive lookout over the countryside and a symbol of the city-state's power.

history of the Italian city-republics. Class struggle, feuds among rich and powerful families, and even uprisings of the whole populace against the city governors (known as "the Nine" in Siena) were constant threats in medieval Italy. The heavy walls and *battlements* (fortified *parapets*) of the Sienese town hall eloquently express how frequently the city governors needed to defend themselves against their own citizens. The Palazzo Pubblico tower, out of reach of most missiles, incorporates *machicolated galleries* (galleries with holes in their floors to enable defenders to dump stones or hot liquids on attackers below) built out on *corbels* (projecting supporting architectural members) for defense of the tower's base.

Ambrogio Lorenzetti. The painter entrusted with the major fresco program in the Palazzo Pubblico was Pietro Lorenzetti's younger brother, AMBROGIO LORENZETTI (ca. 1290–1348). In the frescoes (FIGS. 14-17 and 14-18) Ambrogio produced for Siena's city hall, he elaborated his brother's advances in illusionistic representation in spectacular fashion, while giving visual form to Sienese civic concerns in a series of groundbreaking allegorical paintings (see "Cityscapes and Landscapes as Allegories," page 436).

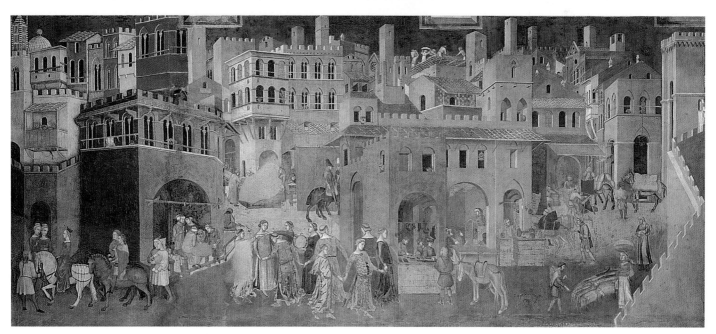

14-17 AMBROGIO LORENZETTI, *Peaceful City,* detail from *Effects of Good Government in the City and in the Country,* east wall of the Sala della Pace (FIG. 14-17A) in the Palazzo Pubblico (FIG. 14-16), Siena, Italy, 1338–1339. Fresco.

In the Hall of Peace of Siena's city hall, Ambrogio Lorenzetti painted an illusionistic panorama of a bustling 14th-century city. The fresco is an allegory of good government in the Sienese republic.

Cityscapes and Landscapes as Allegories

During the 14th century, the citizens of Italy's leading cities often endured violent party struggles and the overthrow and reinstatement of govern-

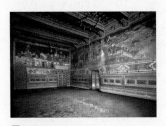

14-17A Sala della Pace, Siena, 1338–1339.

ments. The turbulent politics of the era are the backdrop for Ambrogio Lorenzetti's commission to paint allegories of the effects of good and bad government on the walls of the Sala della Pace (Hall of Peace; FIG. 14-17A) of Siena's Palazzo Pubblico (FIG. 14-16). The Sienese leaders ("the Nine") who paid for the frescoes had undertaken the "ordering and reformation of the whole city and countryside of Siena," but it was left to Lorenzetti to determine how to portray the abstract notions of just and unjust government. His solution was not to invent personifications of good and bad government but to create vast views of life in the city and in the surrounding Tuscan countryside as allegories of the *effects* of good and bad government.

Peaceful City (FIG. 14-17) is a panoramic view of Siena, with its clustering palaces, markets, towers, churches, streets, and walls, reminiscent of the townscapes of ancient Roman murals at Pompeii and elsewhere (FIG. 7-19, *left*), but Lorenzetti could not have seen them because they lay buried beneath volcanic ash (see "An Eyewitness Account of the Eruption of Mount Vesuvius," page 191). The city's traffic moves peacefully,

guild members ply their trades and crafts, and radiant maidens, clustered hand in hand, perform a graceful circling dance. Dances were regular features of festive springtime rituals. Here, dancing also serves as a metaphor for a peaceful commonwealth. The artist fondly observed the life of his city, and its architecture gave him an opportunity to apply Sienese artists' rapidly growing knowledge of perspective.

In *Peaceful Country* (FIG. 14-18), Ambrogio's representation of the countryside beyond Siena's walls, the painter presented a bird's-eye view of the undulating Tuscan terrain—its villas, castles, plowed farmlands, and peasants engaged in their occupations at different seasons of the year. Although it is an allegory, not a snapshot of the Tuscan countryside on a specific day, Lorenzetti's *Peaceful Country,* like his *Peaceful City,* has the character of a portrait of a specific place and environment. *Peaceful Country* is one of the first examples of landscape painting in Western art since antiquity (FIG. 7-20).

Security personified hovers above the hills and fields, unfurling a scroll promising safety to all who live under the rule of law—that is, the law administered by the Nine, who met in this room to oversee Sienese affairs. The Nine had the power to enforce their laws by imposing penalties, including even capital punishment. As a warning to those who might defy the Nine, Security carries a model of a gallows with a hanged criminal.

The Nine, however, could not protect Siena's citizens from the bubonic plague sweeping through Europe in the mid-14th century. The Black Death killed thousands of Sienese and may have ended the careers of the Lorenzetti brothers. Both Pietro and Ambrogio disappear from historical records in 1348.

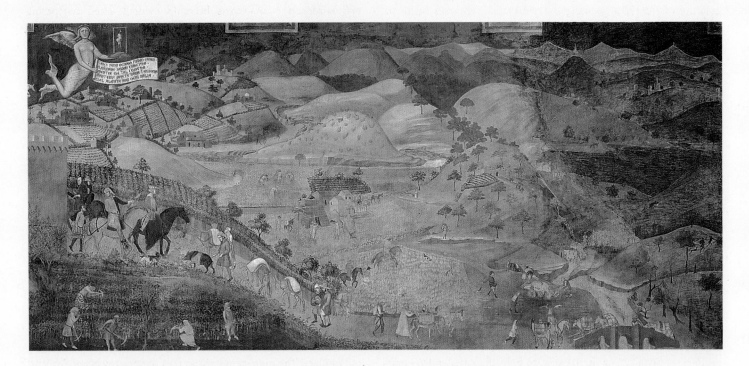

14-18 AMBROGIO LORENZETTI, *Peaceful Country,* detail from *Effects of Good Government in the City and in the Country,* east wall of the Sala della Pace (FIG. 14-17A) in the Palazzo Pubblico (FIG. 14-16), Siena, Italy, 1338–1339. Fresco.

To portray the concept of good government in the countryside, Ambrogio Lorenzetti painted a sweeping view of Tuscan hills—one of the first instances of landscape painting in Western art since antiquity.

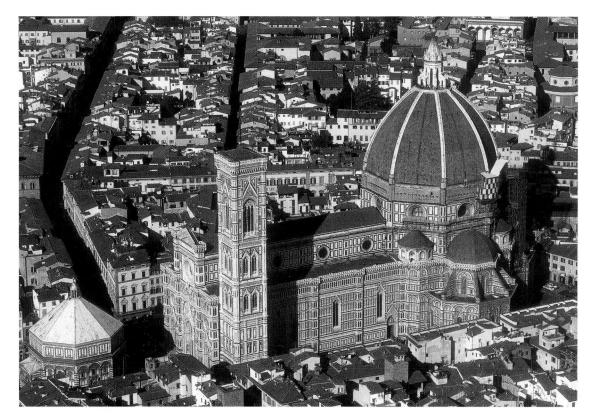

14-19 ARNOLFO DI CAMBIO and others, aerial view of Santa Maria del Fiore (and the Baptistery of San Giovanni; looking northeast), Florence, Italy, begun 1296. Campanile designed by GIOTTO DI BONDONE, 1334.

The Florentine Duomo's marble revetment carries on the Tuscan Romanesque architectural tradition, linking this basilican church more closely to Early Christian Italy than to Gothic France.

Florence

Like Siena, the Republic of Florence was a dominant city-state during the 14th century. The historian Giovanni Villani (ca. 1276–1348), for example, described Florence as "the daughter and the creature of Rome," suggesting a preeminence inherited from the Roman Empire. Florentines were fiercely proud of what they perceived as their economic and cultural superiority. Florence controlled the textile industry in Italy, and the republic's gold *florin* was the standard coin of exchange everywhere in Europe.

Santa Maria del Fiore. Florentines translated their pride in their predominance into such landmark buildings as Santa Maria del Fiore (Saint Mary of the Flower; FIGS. 14-19 and 14-19A), Florence's cathedral, the site of the most important religious observances in the city. ARNOLFO DI CAMBIO (ca. 1245–1302) began work on the cathedral (*Duomo* in Italian) in 1296, three years before he received the commission to build the city's town hall, the Palazzo della Signoria (FIG. 14-19B).

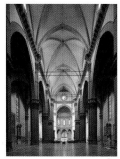

⌐ **14-19A** Florence Cathedral, begun 1296.

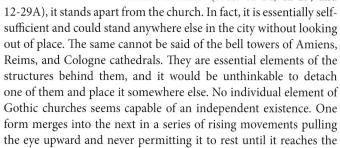

⌐ **14-19B** Palazzo della Signoria, Florence, 1299–1310.

Intended as the "most beautiful and honorable church in Tuscany," the cathedral reveals the competitiveness that Florentines felt with cities such as Siena (FIG. 14-13A) and Pisa (FIG. 12-29). Church authorities planned for the Duomo to hold the city's entire population, and although its capacity is only about 30,000 (Florence's population at the time was slightly less than 100,000), the building seemed so large that even Leon Battista Alberti, the renowned 15th-century Italian architect (see "Alberti's *On the Art of Building*," page 620), commented that it seemed to cover "all of Tuscany with its shade." The builders ornamented the cathedral's surfaces, in the old Tuscan fashion, with marble geometric designs, matching the revetment to that of the facing 11th-century Romanesque baptistery of San Giovanni (FIGS. 12-30 and 14-19, *left*).

The vast gulf separating Santa Maria del Fiore from its northern European counterparts becomes evident when comparing the Florentine church with the High Gothic cathedrals of Amiens (FIG. 13-22), Reims (FIG. 13-24), and Cologne (FIG. 13-53A). Gothic architects' emphatic stress on the vertical produced an awe-inspiring upward rush of unmatched vigor and intensity. The French and German buildings express organic growth shooting heavenward, as the pierced, translucent stone tracery of the spires merges with the atmosphere. Florence Cathedral, by contrast, clings to the ground and has no aspirations to flight. All emphasis is on the horizontal elements of the design, and the building rests firmly and massively on the ground. The clearly defined simple geometric volumes of the cathedral show no tendency to merge either into each other or into the sky.

Giotto di Bondone designed the Duomo's campanile in 1334. In keeping with Italian tradition (FIGS. 12-24, 12-29, and 12-29A), it stands apart from the church. In fact, it is essentially self-sufficient and could stand anywhere else in the city without looking out of place. The same cannot be said of the bell towers of Amiens, Reims, and Cologne cathedrals. They are essential elements of the structures behind them, and it would be unthinkable to detach one of them and place it somewhere else. No individual element of Gothic churches seems capable of an independent existence. One form merges into the next in a series of rising movements pulling the eye upward and never permitting it to rest until it reaches the

14-20 ANDREA PISANO, south doors of the Baptistery of San Giovanni (FIG. 12-30), Florence, Italy, 1330–1336. Gilded bronze, doors 16′ × 9′ 2″; individual panels 1′ 7$\frac{1}{4}$″ × 1′ 5″.

Andrea Pisano's bronze doors have 28 panels with figural reliefs in French Gothic quatrefoil frames. The lower eight depict Christian virtues. The rest represent the life of John the Baptist.

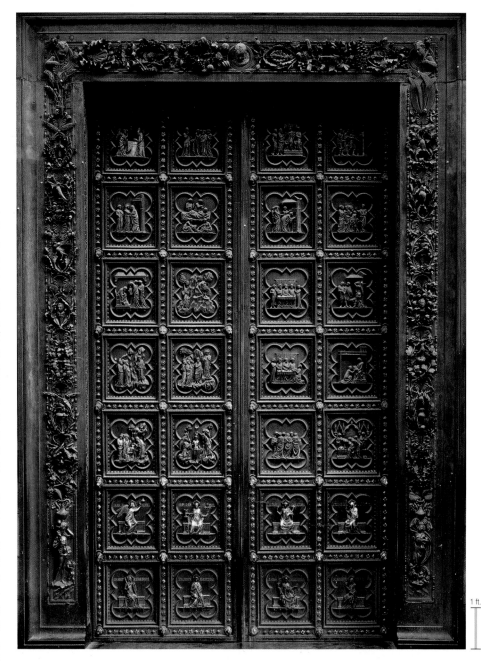

1 ft.

sky. The Florentine campanile is entirely different. Neatly subdivided into cubic sections, Giotto's tower is the sum of its component parts. Not only could this tower be removed from the building without adverse effects, but also each of the parts—cleanly separated from each other by continuous moldings—seems capable of existing independently as an object of considerable aesthetic appeal. This compartmentalization is reminiscent of the Romanesque style, but it also forecasts the ideals of Renaissance architecture. Artists hoped to express structure in the clear, logical relationships of the component parts and to produce self-sufficient works that could exist in complete independence. Compared with northern European towers, Giotto's campanile has a cool and rational quality more appealing to the intellect than to the emotions.

The facade of Florence Cathedral was not completed until the 19th century, and then in a form much altered from its original design. In fact, until the 17th century, Italian builders exhibited little concern for the facades of their churches, and dozens remain unfinished to this day. One reason for this may be that Italian architects did not conceive the facades as integral parts of the structures but rather, as in the case of Orvieto Cathedral (FIG. 14-13), as screens that could be added to the church exterior at any time.

Andrea Pisano. A generation after work began on Santa Maria del Fiore, the Florentines decided also to beautify their 11th-century baptistery (FIGS. 12-30 and 14-19, *left*) with a set of bronze doors (FIG. 14-20) for the south entrance to the building. The sponsors were the members of Florence's guild of wool importers, who competed for business and prestige with the wool manufacturers' association, an important sponsor of the cathedral building campaign. The wool importers' guild hired ANDREA PISANO (ca. 1290–1348), a native of Pontedera in the territory of Pisa—unrelated to Nicola and Giovanni Pisano (see "Italian Artists' Names," page 421)—to create the doors. Andrea designed 28 bronze panels for the doors, each cast separately, of which 20 depict episodes from the life of John the Baptist, to whom the baptistery was dedicated. Eight panels (at the bottom) represent personified Christian virtues. The *quatrefoil* (four-lobed, cloverlike) frames are of the type used earlier for reliefs flanking the doorways of Amiens Cathedral (FIG. 13-22), suggesting that French Gothic sculpture was one source of Andrea's style. The gilded figures stand on projecting ledges in each quatrefoil. Their proportions and

flowing robes also reveal a debt to French sculpture, but the compositions, both in general conception (small groups of figures in stagelike settings) and in some details, owe a great deal to Giotto, for whom Andrea had earlier executed reliefs for the cathedral's campanile, perhaps according to Giotto's designs.

The wool importers' patronage of the baptistery did not end with this project. In the following century, the guild paid for the even more prestigious east doors (FIG. 21-10), directly across from the cathedral's west facade, and also for a statue of John the Baptist on the facade of Or San Michele. The latter was a multipurpose building housing a 14th-century tabernacle (FIG. 14-20A) by ANDREA ORCAGNA (active ca. 1343–1368) featuring the painting *Madonna and Child Enthroned with Saints* by BERNARDO DADDI (active ca. 1312–1348).

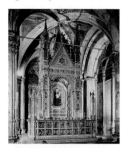

14-20A ORCAGNA, Or San Michele tabernacle, 1355–1359.

Pisa

Siena and Florence were inland centers of commerce. Pisa was one of Italy's port cities, which, with Genoa and Venice, controlled the rapidly growing maritime avenues connecting western Europe with the lands of Islam, with Byzantium and Russia, and with China. As prosperous as Pisa was as a major shipping power, however, it was not immune from the disruption that the Black Death wreaked across all of Italy and Europe in the late 1340s. Concern with death, a significant theme in art even before the onset of the plague, became more prominent in the years after midcentury.

Camposanto. *Triumph of Death* (FIGS. 14-21 and 14-22) is a tour de force of death imagery. The creator of this immense fresco measuring more than 18 by 49 feet remains disputed. Some art historians attribute the work to FRANCESCO TRAINI (active ca. 1321–1363), while others argue for BUONAMICO BUFFALMACCO (active ca. 1315–1336). Painted on one wall of the Camposanto (Holy Field), the enclosed burial ground adjacent to Pisa's cathedral (FIG. 12-29), the fresco captures the horrors of death, and forces viewers to confront their mortality. The painter rendered each scene with naturalism and emotive power. In the left foreground (FIG. 14-21), stylish young aristocrats mounted on fine horses encounter three coffin-encased corpses in differing stages of decomposition. As the horror of the confrontation with death strikes them, the ladies turn away with delicate disgust, while a gentleman holds his nose. (The animals, horses and dogs, sniff excitedly.) At

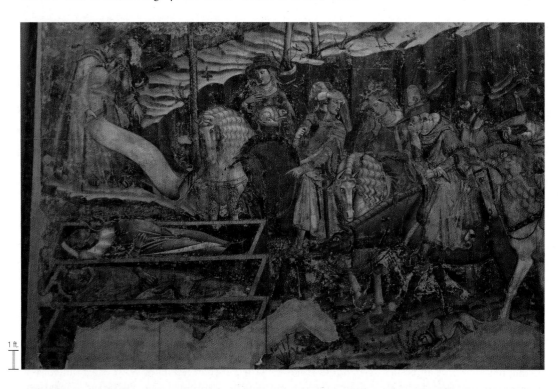

14-21 FRANCESCO TRAINI or BUONAMICO BUFFALMACCO, riders discover three corpses, detail of *Triumph of Death*, Camposanto, Pisa, Italy, 1330s. Full fresco, 18′ 6″ × 49′ 2″.

Befitting its location on a wall in Pisa's Camposanto, the enclosed burial ground adjacent to the cathedral, this fresco captures the horrors of death and forces viewers to confront their mortality.

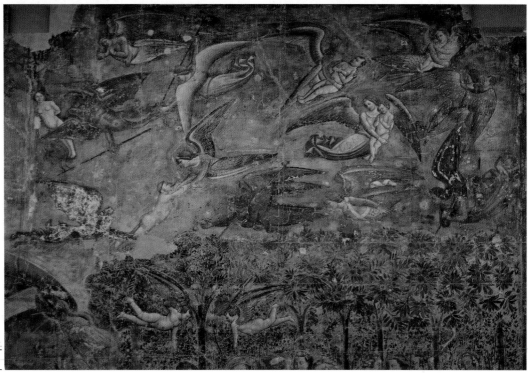

14-22 FRANCESCO TRAINI or BUONAMICO BUFFALMACCO, angels and demons vie for souls, detail of *Triumph of Death*, Camposanto, Pisa, Italy, 1330s. Full fresco, 18′ 6″ × 49′ 2″.

Above a scene of the good life of music and feasting in an orange grove, angels and demons struggle for the souls of the corpses in this dramatic vision of the triumph of death in Pisa's major cemetery.

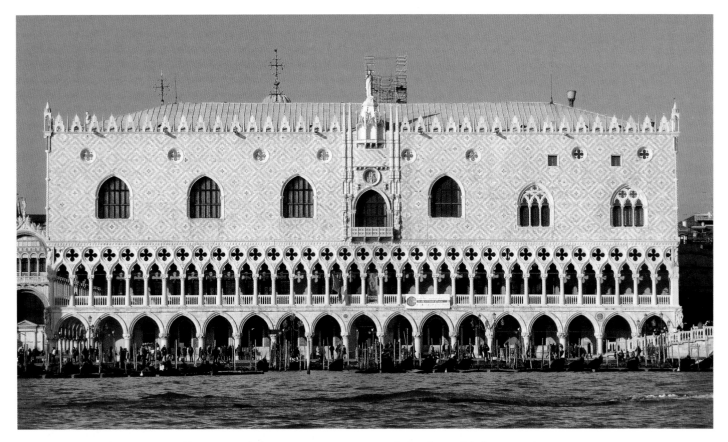

14-23 Doge's Palace (looking north), Venice, Italy, begun ca. 1340–1345; expanded and remodeled, 1424–1438.

The delicate patterning in cream- and rose-colored marbles, the pointed and ogee arches, and the quatrefoil medallions of the Doge's Palace constitute a Venetian variation of northern Gothic architecture.

the far left, Marcarius, an early hermit saint, unrolls a scroll bearing an inscription commenting on the folly of pleasure and the inevitability of death. On the far right (FIG. 14-22), ladies and gentlemen ignore dreadful realities, occupying themselves in an orange grove with music and amusements while all around them angels and demons reminiscent of the grieving angels of Giotto's *Lamentation* (FIG. 14-10) struggle for the souls of the corpses heaped in the foreground.

In addition to these direct and straightforward scenes, the mural contains details conveying more subtle messages. For example, the painter depicted those who appear unprepared for death—and thus unlikely to achieve salvation—as wealthy and reveling in luxury. Given that the Dominicans—an order committed to a life of poverty (see "Mendicant Orders," page 423)—played a role in designing this fresco program, this imagery surely was a warning against greed and lust.

Venice

One of the wealthiest cities of late medieval Italy—and of Europe—was Venice, renowned for its streets of water. Situated on a lagoon on the northeastern coast of Italy, Venice was secure from land attack and could rely on a powerful navy for protection against invasion from the sea. Internally, Venice was a tight corporation of powerful families that, for centuries, provided stable rule by a long series of *doges* (dukes) and fostered economic growth.

Doge's Palace. The Venetian republic's seat of government was the Doge's Palace (FIG. 14-23), situated on the Grand Canal adjacent to Venice's most important church, San Marco (FIG. 9-26). Begun around 1340 to 1345 and significantly remodeled after 1424, Venice's ducal palace was the most ornate public building in medieval Italy. In a stately march, the first level's short and heavy columns support rather severe pointed arches that look strong enough to carry the weight of the upper structure. Their rhythm doubles in the upper arcades, where more slender columns carry ogee arches (made up of double-curving lines), which terminate in flamelike tips between medallions pierced with quatrefoils. Each story is taller than the one beneath it, the topmost as high as the two lower arcades combined. Yet the building does not look top-heavy. This is due in part to the complete absence of articulation in the top story and in part to the walls' delicate patterning in cream- and rose-colored marbles, which makes them appear paper thin. The palace in which Venice's dukes conducted state business represents a delightful and charming variant of Late Gothic architecture. Colorful, decorative, light and airy in appearance, their Venetian palace is ideally suited to the unique Italian city that floats between water and air.

Late Medieval Italy

Duecento (13th Century)

- Diversity of style characterizes the art of 13th-century Italy, with some artists working in the *maniera greca*, or Italo-Byzantine style, some in the mode of Gothic France, and others in the newly revived classical naturalistic tradition.

- The leading painters working in the Italo-Byzantine style were Bonaventura Berlinghieri and Cimabue, whose most famous pupil was Giotto di Bondone. Both drew inspiration from Byzantine icons and illuminated manuscripts. Berlinghieri's *Saint Francis Altarpiece* is the earliest dated portrayal of Saint Francis of Assisi, who died in 1226.

- Trained in southern Italy in the court style of Frederick II (r. 1197–1250), Nicola Pisano was a master sculptor who settled in Pisa and carved pulpits incorporating marble panels that, both stylistically and in individual motifs, derive from ancient Roman reliefs. Nicola's son, Giovanni Pisano, whose career extended into the 14th century, also was a sculptor of church pulpits, but his work more closely reflects French Gothic sculpture.

- At the end of the 13th century, in Rome and Assisi, Pietro Cavallini and other fresco painters created mural programs foreshadowing the revolutionary art of Giotto.

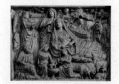

Berlinghieri, *Saint Francis Altarpiece*, 1235

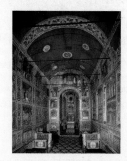

Nicola Pisano, Pisa Baptistery pulpit, 1259–1260

Trecento (14th Century)

- During the 14th century, Italy suffered the most devastating natural disaster in European history—the Black Death—but it was also the time when Renaissance humanism took root. Although religion continued to occupy a primary position in Italian life, scholars and artists became increasingly concerned with the natural world.

- Art historians from Giorgio Vasari in the 16th century to today regard Giotto di Bondone of Florence as the first Renaissance painter. His masterpiece is the extensive series of frescoes adorning the interior of the Arena Chapel in Padua, where he established himself as a pioneer in pursuing a naturalistic approach to representation, which was at the core of the classical tradition in art. The Renaissance marked the rebirth of classical values in art and society.

- The greatest master of the Sienese school of painting was Duccio di Buoninsegna, whose *Maestà* retains many elements of the *maniera greca*. However, Duccio relaxed the frontality and rigidity of his figures, and in the *Maestà*'s narrative scenes took a decisive step toward humanizing religious subject matter by depicting actors displaying individual emotions.

- Secular themes also came to the fore in 14th-century Italy, most notably in Ambrogio Lorenzetti's frescoes for Siena's Palazzo Pubblico. His representations of the city and its surrounding countryside are among the first landscapes in Western art since antiquity.

- The prosperity of the 14th century led to many major building campaigns, both religious and secular, including new cathedrals in Florence, Siena, and Orvieto, and new administrative palaces in Florence, Siena, and Venice. The city halls of both Florence and Siena are fortress-like structures with battlements—eloquent testimonies to the internal and external conflicts of the era.

- The 14th-century architecture of Italy underscores the regional character of late medieval art. Orvieto Cathedral's facade, for example, incorporates many elements of the French Gothic vocabulary, but it is a screen masking a timber-roofed structure in the Early Christian tradition with round arches in the nave arcade. By contrast, Florence's Duomo (Santa Maria del Fiore) is a vaulted and domed basilica.

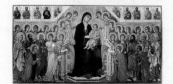

Giotto, Arena Chapel, Padua, 1305–1306

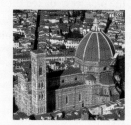

Duccio, *Maestà*, Siena Cathedral, 1308–1311

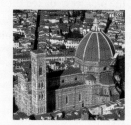

Duomo, Florence, begun 1296

INTRODUCTION

1. Quoted in George Heard Hamilton, *Painting and Sculpture in Europe, 1880–1940*, 6th ed. (New Haven: Yale University Press, 1993), 345.
2. Quoted in *Josef Albers: Homage to the Square* (New York: Museum of Modern Art, 1964), n.p.

CHAPTER 2

1. Translated by Claudia E. Suter, *Gudea's Temple Building: The Representation of an Early Mesopotamian Ruler in Text and Image* (Groningen: Styx, 2000), 57.
2. Translated by Françoise Tallon, in Prudence O. Harper et al., *The Royal City of Susa* (New York: Metropolitan Museum of Art, 1991), 132.

CHAPTER 3

1. The chronology adopted in this chapter is that of John Baines and Jaromír Malék, *Atlas of Ancient Egypt* (Oxford: Oxford University Press, 1980), 36–37. The division of kingdoms is that of, among others, Mark Lehner, *The Complete Pyramids* (New York: Thames & Hudson, 1997), 89, and David P. Silverman, ed., *Ancient Egypt* (New York: Oxford University Press, 1997), 20–39.
2. Translated by James P. Allen, *The Ancient Egyptian Pyramid Texts* (Atlanta, Ga.: Society of Biblical Literature, 2005), 31.
3. Ibid., 57.
4. Ibid., 56.

CHAPTER 4

1. Homer, *Iliad*, 2. 466–649. Translated by E. V. Rieu, *Homer: The Iliad* (Harmondsworth: Penguin, 1950), 32–36.

CHAPTER 5

1. Diodorus Siculus, *Library of History*, 1.91.
2. Pausanias, *Description of Greece*, 5.16.1.
3. Plutarch, *Life of Pericles*, 12.
4. Pliny, *Natural History*, 34.74.
5. Plutarch, *Life of Pericles*, 13.4.
6. Pliny, *Natural History*, 36.20.
7. Lucian, *Amores*, 13–14; *Imagines*, 6.
8. Plutarch, *Moralia*, 335A–B. Translated by J. J. Pollitt, *The Art of Ancient Greece: Sources and Documents* (New York: Cambridge University Press, 1990), 99.
9. Pliny, *Natural History*, 34.88.

CHAPTER 7

1. Livy, *History of Rome*, 25.40.1–3.
2. Juvenal, *Satires*, 3.171.
3. Ibid., 3.225, 232.

CHAPTER 9

1. Paulus Silentiarius, *Descriptio Sanctae Sophiae*, 617–646. Translated by Cyril Mango, *The Art of the Byzantine Empire, 312–1453: Sources and Documents* (reprint of 1972 ed., Toronto: University of Toronto Press, 1986), 85–86.
2. Procopius, *De aedificiis*, 1.1.23ff. Translated by Mango, 74.
3. Paulus Silentiarius, 489, 668. Translated by Mango, 83, 86.
4. Translated by Colin Luibheid, *Pseudo-Dionysius: The Complete Works* (New York: Paulist Press, 1987), 68ff.
5. Procopius, 1.1.23ff. Translated by Mango, 75.
6. *Libri Carolini* 4.2. Translated by Herbert L. Kessler, *Spiritual Seeing: Picturing God's Invisibility in Medieval Art* (Philadelphia: University of Pennsylvania Press, 2000), 119.
7. John the Lydian, *De magistratibus populi romani* 3.69. Quoted in Paolo Cesaretti, *Theodora: Empress of Byzantium* (New York: Vendome Press, 2001), 269.
8. Nina G. Garsoïan, "Later Byzantium," in John A. Garraty and Peter Gay, eds., *The Columbia History of the World* (New York: Harper and Row, 1972), 453.
9. Ibid., 460.

CHAPTER 11

1. Translated by Françoise Henry, *The Book of Kells* (New York: Knopf, 1974), 165.
2. *Beowulf* 3162–3164, translated by Kevin Crossley-Holland (New York: Farrar, Straus & Giroux, 1968), 119.
3. Translated by John W. Williams, in *The Art of Medieval Spain A.D. 500–1200* (New York: Metropolitan Museum of Art, 1993), 156.
4. Translated by Adam S. Cohen, *The Uta Codex* (University Park: Pennsylvania University Press, 2000), 11, 41.

CHAPTER 12

1. Translated by Calvin B. Kendall, *The Allegory of the Church: Romanesque Portals and Their Verse Inscriptions* (Toronto: University of Toronto Press, 1998), 207.
2. Translated by John Williams, *A Spanish Apocalypse: The Morgan Beatus Manuscript* (New York: Braziller, 1991), 223.
3. Translated by Charles P. Parkhurst Jr., in Elizabeth G. Holt, *A Documentary History of Art* (Princeton, N.J.: Princeton University Press, 2nd ed., 1981), 1:18.
4. Bernard of Clairvaux, *Apologia* 12.28. Translated by Conrad Rudolph, *The "Things of Greater Importance": Bernard of Clairvaux's* Apologia *and the Medieval Attitude toward Art* (Philadelphia: University of Pennsylvania Press, 1990), 281, 283.
5. *Rule of Saint Benedict*, 57.1–3. Translated by Timothy Fry, *The Rule of St. Benedict in English* (Collegeville, Minn.: Liturgical Press, 1981), 77–78.

CHAPTER 13

1. Translated by Carl F. Barnes Jr., *The Portfolio of Villard de Honnecourt: A New Critical Edition and Color Facsimile* (Paris: Bibliothèque nationale de France, 2009), 127.
2. Paul Frankl, *The Gothic: Literary Sources and Interpretation through Eight Centuries* (Princeton, N.J.: Princeton University Press, 1960), 55.

GLOSSARY

NOTE: *Text page references are in parentheses.*
References to bonus image online essays are in pink.

abacus—The uppermost portion of the *capital* of a *column,* usually a thin slab. (116)

abbess—See *abbey.* (336)

abbey—A religious community under the direction of an abbot (for monks) or an abbess (for nuns). (336)

abbot—See *abbey.* (336)

abrasion—The rubbing or grinding of stone or another material to produce a smooth finish. (66)

abstract—Nonrepresentational; forms and colors arranged without reference to the depiction of an object. (22)

acropolis—Greek, "high city." In ancient Greece, usually the site of the city's most important temple(s). (115)

ad catacumbas—Latin, "in the hollows." See *catacombs.* (240)

additive light—Natural light, or sunlight, the sum of all the wavelengths of the visible *spectrum.* See also *subtractive light.* (7)

additive sculpture—A kind of sculpture *technique* in which materials (for example, clay) are built up or "added" to create form. (11)

aesthetics—The branch of philosophy that addresses the nature of beauty, especially in art. (1)

agora—An open square or space used for public meetings or business in ancient Greek cities. (137)

aisle—The portion of a *basilica* flanking the *nave* and separated from it by a row of *columns* or *piers.* (12, 191, 249)

ala (pl. **alae**)—One of a pair of rectangular recesses at the back of the *atrium* of a Roman *domus.* (193)

altar frontal—A decorative panel on the front of a *church* altar. (383)

altarpiece—A panel, painted or sculpted, situated above and behind an altar. See also *retable.* (410)

alternate-support system—In *church* architecture, the use of alternating wall supports in the *nave,* usually *piers* and *columns* or *compound piers* of alternating form. (338)

Amazonomachy—In Greek mythology, the battle between the Greeks and Amazons. (135)

ambo—A *church pulpit* for biblical readings. (410)

ambulatory—A covered walkway, outdoors (as in a *church cloister*) or indoors; especially the passageway around the *apse* and the *choir* of a *church.* In Buddhist architecture, the passageway leading around the *stupa* in a *chaitya hall.* (250)

amphiprostyle—A *classical* temple *plan* in which the *columns* are placed across both the front and back but not along the sides. (115)

amphitheater—Greek, "double theater." A Roman building type resembling two Greek theaters put together. The Roman amphitheater featured a continuous elliptical *cavea* around a central *arena.* (192)

amphora—An ancient Greek two-handled jar used for general storage purposes, usually to hold wine or oil. (108)

amulet—An object worn to ward off evil or to aid the wearer. (61)

Anastasis—Greek, "resurrection." In Byzantine art, the representation of Christ's descent into limbo. (245)

ankh—The Egyptian sign of life. (79)

antae—The molded projecting ends of the walls forming the *pronaos* or *opisthodomos* of an ancient Greek temple. (115)

ante legem—Latin, "before the law." In Christian thought, the period before Moses received the Ten Commandments. See also *sub lege.* (410)

apadana—The great audience hall in ancient Persian palaces. (51)

aphros—Greek, "foam." (107)

apostle—Greek, "messenger." One of the 12 disciples of Jesus. (246)

apotheosis—Elevated to the rank of gods, or the ascent to Heaven. (209)

apotropaic—Capable of warding off evil. (118)

apoxyomenos—Greek, "athlete scraping oil from his body." (146)

apse—A recess, usually semicircular, in the wall of a building, commonly found at the east end of a *church.* (28, 133, 212, 249)

aqueduct—A channel for carrying water, often elevated on *arches.* (205)

arcade—A series of *arches* supported by *piers* or *columns.* (54, 206, 249, 270, 300)

arch—A curved structural member that spans an opening and is generally composed of wedge-shaped blocks (*voussoirs*) that transmit the downward pressure laterally. See also *thrust.* (50)

Archaic—The artistic style of 600–480 BCE in Greece, characterized in part by the use of the *composite view* for painted and *relief* figures and of Egyptian stances for *statues.* (112)

Archaic smile—The smile that appears on all *Archaic* Greek *statues* from about 570 to 480 BCE. The smile is the Archaic sculptor's way of indicating that the person portrayed is alive. (113)

architrave—The *lintel* or lowest division of the *entablature;* also called the epistyle. (116)

archivolt—The continuous molding framing an *arch.* In *Romanesque* and *Gothic* architecture, one of the series of concentric bands framing the *tympanum.* (358)

arcuated—*Arch*-shaped. (50)

arcuated lintel—A *lintel* with alternating horizontal and *arcuated* sections. (217)

arena—In a Roman *amphitheater,* the central area where bloody *gladiator* combats and other boisterous events took place. (192)

armature—The crossed, or diagonal, *arches* that form the skeletal framework of a *Gothic rib vault.* In sculpture, the framework for a clay form. (11, 387)

arriccio—In *fresco* painting, the first layer of rough lime plaster applied to the wall. (428)

arringatore—Italian, "orator." (178)

ashlar masonry—Carefully cut and regularly shaped blocks of stone used in construction, fitted together without mortar. (64)

atlantid—A male figure that functions as a supporting *column* or *pier.* See also *caryatid.* (3-23A)

atlatl—A device that enables hunters to throw a spear farther and with greater velocity. (19)

atmospheric perspective—See *perspective.* (197)

atrium (pl. **atria**)—The central reception room of a Roman *domus* that is partly open to the sky. Also, the open, *colonnaded* court in front of and attached to a Christian *basilica.* (193, 248)

attic—The uppermost story of a building, *triumphal arch,* city gate, or *aqueduct.* (205)

attribute—(n.) The distinctive identifying aspect of a person—for example, an object held, an associated animal, or a mark on the body. (v.) To make an *attribution*. (6, 246)

attribution—Assignment of a work to a maker or makers. (6)

augur—A Roman priest who determined the will of the gods from the flight of birds and whose attribute is the *lituus*. (165)

augustus—Latin, "majestic" or "exalted." (201)

aula—An ancient Roman audience hall. (231)

autem generatio—Latin, "now this is how the birth of Christ came about." (319)

axial plan—See *plan*. (74)

axis mundi—Latin, "axis of the world." In South Asia, a tall pillar planted deep in the ground, connecting earth and sky. (50)

baldacchino—A canopy on *columns*, frequently built over an altar. The term derives from *baldacco*. (250)

baldric—A sashlike belt worn over one shoulder and across the chest to support a sword. (224)

baptism—The Christian bathing ceremony in which an infant or a convert becomes a member of the Christian community. (244)

baptistery—In Christian architecture, the building used for *baptism*, usually situated next to a *church*. Also, the designated area or hall within a *church* for baptismal rites. (237)

bar tracery—See *tracery*. (392)

Baroque/baroque—The traditional blanket designation for European art from 1600 to 1750. Uppercase *Baroque* refers to the art of this period, which features dramatic theatricality and elaborate ornamentation in contrast to the simplicity and orderly rationality of *Renaissance* art, and is most appropriately applied to Italian art. Lowercase *baroque* describes similar stylistic features found in the art of other periods—for example, the *Hellenistic* period in ancient Greece. The term derives from *barroco*. (156)

barrel vault—See *vault*. (186)

base—In ancient Greek architecture, the molded projecting lowest part of *Ionic* and *Corinthian columns*. (*Doric* columns do not have bases.) (51, 152)

basilica (adj. **basilican**)—In Roman architecture, a public building for legal and other civic proceedings, rectangular in plan, with an entrance usually on a long side. In Christian architecture, a *church* somewhat resembling the Roman basilica, usually entered from one end and with an *apse* at the other. (190, 248)

bas-relief—See *relief*. (12)

battlement—A low parapet at the top of a circuit wall in a fortification. (399, 435)

beam—A horizontal structural member that carries the load of the superstructure of a building; a timber *lintel*. (28)

beatification—The declaration by the Catholic Church of a person as *beatus*; a preliminary stage in the process of *canonization*. (246)

beatus—Latin, "blessed." (246)

ben-ben—A pyramidal stone; an emblem of the Egyptian god Re. (60)

benedictional—A Christian religious book containing bishops' blessings. (324)

bent-axis plan—A *plan* that incorporates two or more angular changes of direction, characteristic of Sumerian architecture. (33)

bestiary—A collection of illustrations of real and imaginary animals. (357)

bilateral symmetry—Having the same *forms* on either side of a central axis. (66)

bilingual vases—Experimental Greek vases produced for a short time in the late sixth century BCE; one side featured *black-figure* decoration, the other *red-figure*. (121)

black-figure painting—In early Greek pottery, the silhouetting of dark figures against a light background of natural, reddish clay, with linear details *incised* through the silhouettes. (111)

blind arcade—An *arcade* having no true openings, applied as decoration to a wall surface. (54, 300, 389)

block statue—In ancient Egyptian sculpture, a cubic stone image with simplified body parts. (75)

Book of Hours—A Christian religious book for private devotion containing prayers to be read at specified times of the day. (324)

boss—A circular knob. (11-3A)

breviary—A Christian religious book of selected daily prayers and Psalms. (324, 404)

bucranium (pl. **bucrania**)—Latin, "bovine skull." A common motif in classical architectural ornament. (1-15A)

buon fresco—See *fresco*. (91, 428)

burin—A pointed tool used for *engraving* or *incising*. (17)

bust—A freestanding sculpture of the head, shoulders, and chest of a person. (12)

buttress—An exterior masonry structure that opposes the lateral *thrust* of an *arch* or a *vault*. A pier buttress is a solid mass of masonry. A flying buttress consists typically of an inclined member carried on an arch or a series of arches and a solid buttress to which it transmits lateral thrust. (186)

Byzantine—The art, territory, history, and culture of the Eastern Christian Empire and its capital of Constantinople (ancient Byzantium). (264)

caduceus—See *kerykeion*. (107)

caementa—Latin, "small stones." A key ingredient of Roman *concrete*. (186)

caldarium—The hot-bath section of a Roman bathing establishment. (225)

caliph(s)—Islamic rulers, regarded as successors of Muhammad. (295)

calligraphy—Greek, "beautiful writing." Handwriting or penmanship, especially elegant writing as a decorative art. (305)

came—A lead strip in a *stained-glass* window that joins separate pieces of colored glass. (392)

campanile—A bell tower of a *church*, usually, but not always, freestanding. (366, 434, 12-29A)

campo—Italian, "field." (429)

canon—A rule (for example, of proportion). The ancient Greeks considered beauty to be a matter of "correct" proportion and sought a canon of proportion, for the human figure and for buildings. The fifth-century BCE sculptor Polykleitos wrote the *Canon*, a treatise incorporating his formula for the perfectly proportioned *statue*. Also, a *church* official who preaches, teaches, administers sacraments, and tends to pilgrims and the sick. (68, 134, 144, 12-25A)

canon table—A concordance, or matching, of the corresponding passages of the four *Gospels* as compiled by Eusebius of Caesarea in the fourth century. (324)

canonization (adj. **canonized**)—The declaration by the Catholic Church of a person as a *saint* after his or her death, often as a *martyr*. (246, 14-5A)

canopic jars—In ancient Egypt, the four jars containing the lungs, liver, stomach, and intestines of the deceased removed during mummification. (61)

capital—The uppermost member of a *column*, serving as a transition from the *shaft* to the *lintel*. In *classical* architecture, the form of the capital varies with the *order*. (51, 62, 115)

Capitolium—An ancient Roman temple dedicated to the gods Jupiter, Juno, and Minerva. (190)

caput mundi—Latin, "head (capital) of the world." (182)

cardo—The north-south street in a Roman town, intersecting the *decumanus* at right angles. (189)

Caroline minuscule—The alphabet that *Carolingian* scribes perfected, from which the modern English alphabet was developed. (329)

Carolingian—Pertaining to the empire of Charlemagne (Latin, "Carolus Magnus") and his successors. (329)

carpet page—In early medieval manuscripts, a decorative page resembling a textile. (325)

cartography—The art of mapmaking. (13-39B)

cartoon—In painting, a full-size preliminary drawing from which a painting is made. (428)

carving—A sculptural *technique* in which the artist cuts away material (for example, from a stone block) in order to create a *statue* or a *relief.* (11)

caryatid—A female figure that functions as a supporting *column.* See also *atlantid.* (386, 3-23A)

castellum—See *westwork.* (336)

casting—A sculptural *technique* in which the artist pours liquid metal, plaster, clay, or another material into a *mold.* When the material dries, the sculptor removes the cast piece from the mold. (11)

castrum—A Roman military encampment. (211)

catacombs—Subterranean networks of rock-cut galleries and chambers designed as cemeteries for the burial of the dead. (240)

cathedra—Latin, "seat." See *cathedral.* (248, 364, 9-13A)

cathedral—A bishop's *church.* The word derives from *cathedra,* referring to the bishop's chair. (9-13A)

causeway—A raised roadway. (64)

cavea—Latin, "hollow place or cavity." The seating area in ancient Greek and Roman theaters and *amphitheaters.* (151)

cella—The chamber at the center of an ancient temple; in a *classical* temple, the room (Greek, *naos*) in which the *cult statue* usually stood. (33, 115, 117)

centaur—In ancient Greek mythology, a creature with the front or top half of a human and the back or bottom half of a horse. (105)

centauromachy—In ancient Greek mythology, a battle between the Greeks and *centaurs.* (120)

central plan—See *plan.* (250, 299)

cestrum—A small spatula used in *encaustic* painting. (223, 5-63A)

chancel arch—The arch separating the chancel (the *apse* or *choir*) or the *transept* from the *nave* of a basilica or *church.* (231, 249)

chantry—An endowed chapel for the chanting of the *Mass* for the founder of the chapel. (13-44A)

chaplet—A metal pin used in hollow-casting to connect the *investment* with the clay core. (129)

charun—An Etruscan death demon. (177)

chiaroscuro—In drawing or painting, the treatment and use of light and dark, especially the gradations of light that produce the effect of *modeling.* (429)

chimera—A monster of Greek invention with the head and body of a lion and the tail of a serpent. A second head, that of a goat, grows out of one side of the body. (174)

chisel—A tool with a straight blade at one end for cutting and shaping stone or wood. (18)

chiton—A Greek tunic, the essential (and often only) garment of both men and women, the other being the *himation,* or mantle. (114)

chlamys—A woollen Greek cloak. (5-47A)

choir—The space reserved for the clergy and singers in the *church,* usually east of the *transept* but, in some instances, extending into the *nave.* (12, 272)

Christ—Savior. From Latin Christus and Greek Christos, "the anointed one." (244)

Christogram—The monogram comprising the three initial letters (chi-rho-iota) of Christ's name in Greek. (234, 251)

chronology—In art history, the dating of art objects and buildings. (2)

chryselephantine—Fashioned of gold and ivory. (135, 4-13A)

church—Christian house of worship. (249)

cire perdue—See *lost-wax process.* (128)

cista (pl. **cistae**)—An Etruscan cylindrical container made of sheet bronze with cast handles and feet, often with elaborately engraved bodies, used for women's toiletry articles. (175)

city-state—An independent, self-governing city. (31)

Classical/classical—The art and culture of ancient Greece between 480 and 323 BCE. Lowercase *classical* refers more generally to Greco-Roman art and culture. (125)

claustrum—Latin, "enclosed place." See *cloister.* (356)

clerestory—The *fenestrated* part of a building that rises above the roofs of the other parts. The oldest known clerestories are Egyptian. In Roman *basilicas* and medieval *churches,* clerestories are the windows that form the *nave's* uppermost level below the timber ceiling or the *vaults.* (75, 186, 249, 389)

cliens—Latin, "client." A Roman who owes allegiance to a *patronus.* (193)

cloison—French, "partition." A cell made of metal wire or a narrow metal strip soldered edge-up to a metal base to hold *enamel,* semiprecious stones, pieces of colored glass, or glass paste fired to resemble sparkling jewels. (321)

cloisonné—A decorative metalwork *technique* employing *cloisons*; also, decorative brickwork in later Byzantine architecture. (280, 321)

cloister—A *monastery* courtyard, usually with covered walks or *ambulatories* along its sides. (335, 356)

cluster pier—See *compound pier.* (389)

codex (pl. **codices**)—Separate pages of *vellum* or *parchment* bound together at one side; the predecessor of the modern book. The codex superseded the *rotulus.* In *Mesoamerica,* a painted and inscribed book on long sheets of bark paper or deerskin coated with fine white plaster and folded into accordion-like pleats. (252)

coffer—A sunken panel, often ornamental, in a *vault* or a ceiling. (216)

collage—A composition made by combining on various materials a flat surface, such as newspaper, wallpaper, printed text and illustrations, photographs, and cloth. (8)

colonnade—A series or row of *columns,* usually spanned by *lintels.* (71)

colonnette—A thin *column.* (197)

colophon—An inscription, usually on the last page, giving information about a book's manufacture. In Chinese painting, written texts on attached pieces of paper or silk. (325)

column—A vertical, weight-carrying architectural member, circular in cross-*section* and consisting of a *base* (sometimes omitted), a *shaft,* and a *capital.* (10, 50)

complementary colors—Those pairs of *colors,* such as red and green, that together embrace the entire *spectrum.* The complement of one of the three *primary colors* is a mixture of the other two. (7)

compose—See *composition.* (7)

Composite capital—A capital combining *Ionic* volutes and *Corinthian* acanthus leaves, first used by the ancient Romans. (209)

composite view—A convention of representation in which part of a figure is shown in profile and another part of the same figure is shown frontally; also called twisted perspective. (22)

composition—The way in which an artist organizes *forms* in an artwork, either by placing shapes on a flat surface or arranging forms in space. (7)

compound pier—A *pier* with a group, or cluster, of attached *shafts,* or *responds,* especially characteristic of *Gothic* architecture. (353, 389)

conceptual representation—The representation of the fundamental distinguishing properties of a person or object, not the way a figure or object appears in space and light at a specific moment. See also *composite view.* (27)

concrete—A building material invented by the Romans and consisting of various proportions of lime mortar, volcanic sand, water, and small stones. (185)

confraternity—In Late Antiquity, an association of Christian families pooling funds to purchase property for burial. In late medieval Europe, an organization founded by laypersons who dedicated themselves to strict religious observances. (241, 14-20A)

congregational mosque—A city's main *mosque,* designed to accommodate the entire Muslim population for the Friday noonday prayer. Also called the great mosque or Friday mosque. (299)

connoisseur—An expert in *attributing* artworks to one artist rather than another. More generally, an expert on artistic *style.* (6)

consuls—In the Roman Republic, the two chief magistrates. (183)

continuous narration—The depiction of the same figure more than once in the same space at different stages of a story. (276, 7-43A)

contour line—In art, a continuous *line* defining the outer shape of an object. (7)

contrapposto—The disposition of the human figure in which one part is turned in opposition to another part (usually hips and legs one way, shoulders and chest another), creating a counterpositioning of the body about its central axis. Sometimes called "weight shift" because the weight of the body tends to be thrown to one foot, creating tension on one side and relaxation on the other. (132)

corbel—A projecting wall member used as a support for some element in the superstructure. Also, *courses* of stone or brick in which each course projects beyond the one beneath it. Two such walls, meeting at the topmost course, create a *corbeled arch* or *corbeled vault*. (408, 435)

corbeled arch—An *arch* formed by the piling of stone blocks in horizontal *courses*, cantilevered inward until the blocks meet at a *keystone*. (97)

corbeled dome—A *dome* formed by the piling of stone blocks in successive circles of horizontal *courses*, cantilevered inward to form a conical dome. (97)

corbeled vault—A *vault* formed by the piling of stone blocks in horizontal *courses*, cantilevered inward until the two walls meet in an *arch*. (27, 97)

Corinthian capital—A more ornate form than *Doric* or *Ionic*; it consists of a double row of acanthus leaves from which tendrils and flowers grow, wrapped around a bell-shaped *echinus*. Although this *capital* is often cited as the distinguishing feature of the Corinthian *order*, in strict terms no such order exists. The Corinthian capital is a substitute for the standard capital used in the Ionic order. (152)

cornice—The projecting, crowning member of the *entablature* framing the *pediment*; also, any crowning projection. (116)

cornucopia—Horn of plenty. (7-58A)

couching—Knotting. See *embroidery*. (377)

crenel—See *crenellation*. (399)

crenellation—Alternating solid merlons and open crenels in the notched tops of walls, as in *battlements*. (399)

cross vault—See *vault*. (186)

crossing—The space in a *cruciform church* formed by the intersection of the *nave* and the *transept*. (257, 337)

crossing square—The area in a *church* formed by the intersection (*crossing*) of a *nave* and a *transept* of equal width, often used as a standard *module* of interior proportion. (337)

crossing tower—The tower over the *crossing* of a *church*. (258)

crucifix—A freestanding sculptural representation of Christ on the cross. (342)

cruciform—Cross-shaped. (257)

Crusades—In medieval Europe, armed pilgrimages aimed at recapturing the Holy Land from the Muslims. (360)

crypt—A *vaulted* space under part of a building, wholly or partly underground; in *churches*, normally the portion under an *apse*. (356)

cubiculum (pl. **cubicula**)—A small cubicle or bedroom that opened onto the *atrium* of a Roman *domus*. Also, a chamber in an Early Christian *catacomb* that served as a mortuary chapel. (193, 241)

cuerda seca—A type of *polychrome* tilework used in decorating Islamic buildings. (311)

cuirass—A military leather breastplate. (188)

cult statue—The *statue* of the deity that stood in the *cella* of an ancient temple. (101, 115)

cuneiform—Latin, "wedge-shaped." A system of writing used in ancient Mesopotamia, in which wedge-shaped characters were produced by pressing a *stylus* into a soft clay tablet, which was then baked or otherwise allowed to harden. (33)

cuneus (pl. **cunei**)—In ancient Greek and Roman theaters and *amphitheaters*, the wedge-shaped section of stone benches separated by stairs. (151)

cupola—An exterior architectural feature composed of a *drum* with a shallow cap; a *dome*. (9-31A)

cutaway—An architectural drawing that combines an exterior view with an interior view of part of a building. (12)

Cycladic—The prehistoric art of the Aegean Islands around Delos, excluding Crete. (87)

Cyclopean masonry—A method of stone construction, named after the mythical *Cyclopes*, using massive, irregular blocks without mortar, characteristic of the Bronze Age fortifications of Tiryns and other *Mycenaean* sites. (96)

Cyclops (pl. **Cyclopes**)—In Greek mythology, a one-eyed giant. (96)

cylinder seal—A cylindrical piece of stone usually about an inch or so in height, decorated with an *incised* design, so that a raised pattern is left when the seal is rolled over soft clay. In the ancient Near East, documents, storage jars, and other important possessions were signed, sealed, and identified in this way. Stamp seals are an earlier, flat form of seal used for similar purposes. (37)

damnatio memoriae—The Roman decree condemning those who ran afoul of the Senate. Those who suffered damnatio memoriae had their memorials demolished and their names erased from public inscriptions. (209)

deacon—A *church* official charged with distributing alms to the poor. (247)

Decorated—The more ornate phase of English Gothic architecture, which flourished from about 1270 to 1370, succeeded by the Perpendicular style. (409)

decumanus—The east-west street in a Roman town, intersecting the *cardo* at right angles. (189)

decursio—The ritual circling of a Roman funerary pyre. (220)

Deësis—Greek, "entreaty to God." In Byzantine art, an image of Christ flanked by two figures, often the Virgin Mary and John the Baptist, who intercede on behalf of humankind. (284)

demos—Greek, "the people," from which the word *democracy* derives. (106)

demotic—Late Egyptian writing. (58)

denarius—The standard Roman silver coin from which the word *penny* ultimately derives. (189)

diagonal rib—See *rib*. (389)

diaphragm arch—A transverse, wall-bearing *arch* that divides a *vault* or a ceiling into compartments, providing a kind of firebreak. (12-30A)

dictator—In the Roman Republic, the supreme magistrate with extraordinary powers, appointed during a crisis for a specified period. Julius Caesar eventually became *dictator perpetuo*, dictator for life. (183)

dictator perpetuo—See *dictator*. (189)

dipteral—See *peristyle*. (115)

diptych—A two-paneled painting or *altarpiece*; also, an ancient Roman, Early Christian, or Byzantine hinged writing tablet, often of ivory and carved on the external sides. (253)

disciplina Etrusca—Latin, "Etruscan [religious] practice." (6-2A)

diskobolos—Greek, "discus thrower." (130)

disputatio—Latin, "logical argument." The philosophical methodology used in *Scholasticism*. (388)

documentary evidence—In art history, the examination of written sources in order to determine the date of an artwork, the circumstances of its creation, or the identity of the artist(s) who made it. (3)

doge—Italian (Venetian dialect), "duke." (283, 440)

dome—A hemispherical *vault*; theoretically, an *arch* rotated on its vertical axis. In *Mycenaean* architecture, domes are beehive-shaped. (27)

dominus et deus—Latin, "lord and god." (211)

domus—A Roman private house. (193)

Doric—One of the two systems (or *orders*) invented in ancient Greece for articulating the three units of the *elevation* of a classical building—the platform, the *colonnade*, and the superstructure (*entablature*). The Doric order is characterized by, among other features, *capitals* with funnel-shaped *echinuses*, *columns* without *bases*, and a *frieze* of *triglyphs* and *metopes*. See also *Ionic*. (115)

doryphoros—Greek, "spear bearer." (131)

double monastery—A *monastery* for both monks and nuns. (367)

dressed masonry—Stone blocks shaped to the exact dimensions required, with smooth faces for a perfect fit. (64, 205)

dromos—The passage leading to a *tholos tomb*. (98)

drum—One of the stacked cylindrical stones that form the *shaft* of a *column*. Also, the cylindrical wall that supports a *dome*. (116, 280)

dry masonry—A mortarless stone construction *technique* in which the stones are held in place by their own weight. (25)

Duecento—Italian, "200"—that is, the 13th century (the 1200s) in Italy. (420)

duomo—Italian, "cathedral." (437)

echinus—The convex element of a *capital* directly below the *abacus*. (116)

elevation—In architecture, a head-on view of an external or internal wall, showing its features and often other elements that would be visible beyond or before the wall. (12)

embroidery—The *technique* of sewing threads onto a finished ground to form contrasting designs. Stem stitching employs short overlapping strands of thread to form jagged lines. Laid-and-couched work creates solid blocks of color. (377, 9-35A)

emir—A Muslim ruler. (304)

enamel—A decorative coating, usually colored, fused onto the surface of metal, glass, or ceramics. (314)

encaustic—A painting *technique* in which pigment is mixed with melted wax and applied to the surface while the mixture is hot. (111, 223)

engaged column—A half-round *column* attached to a wall. See also *pilaster*. (62, 177, 300, 353)

engraving—The process of *incising* a design in hard material, often a metal plate (usually copper); also, the *print* or impression made from such a plate. (17)

ensi—Sumerian, "ruler." (39)

entablature—The part of a building above the *columns* and below the roof. The entablature has three parts: *architrave, frieze,* and *pediment*. (116)

entasis—The convex profile (an apparent swelling) in the *shaft* of a *column*. (117)

Eucharist—In Christianity, the partaking of the bread and wine, which believers hold to be either Christ himself or symbolic of him. (245)

eunuch—A castrated male. (2-5A)

evangelist—One of the four authors (Matthew, Mark, Luke, John) of the New Testament *Gospels*. (247, 329)

exedra (pl. **exedrae**)—Recessed area, usually semicircular. (198, 263)

extramural—Outside the walls (of a city). (170)

facade—Usually, the front of a building; also, the other sides when they are emphasized architecturally. (54)

faience—A low-fired opaque glasslike silicate. (94)

fan vault—See *vault*. (410)

fauces—Latin, "jaws." In a Roman *domus,* the narrow foyer leading to the *atrium*. (193)

felicior—Latin, "luckier." (211)

fenestration (adj. **fenestrated**)—The arrangement of the windows of a building. (186)

feudalism—The medieval political, social, and economic system held together by the relationship between landholding *liege lords* and the *vassals* who were granted tenure of a portion of their land and in turn swore allegiance to the liege lord. (348)

fibula (pl. **fibulae**)—A decorative pin, usually used to fasten garments. (167, 321)

findspot—Place where an artifact was found; *provenance*. (18)

finial—A crowning ornament. (305)

First Style mural—The earliest style of Roman *mural* painting. The aim of the artist was to imitate, using painted *stucco relief,* the appearance of costly marble panels. (194)

flagellate—To whip. (245)

Flamboyant—A Late French *Gothic* style of architecture superseding the *Rayonnant* style and named for the flamelike appearance of its pointed bar *tracery*. (194)

flashing—In making *stained-glass* windows, fusing one layer of colored glass to another to produce a greater range of *colors*. (302)

fleur-de-lis—A three-petaled iris flower; the royal flower of France. (393)

florin—The denomination of gold coin of *Renaissance* Florence that became an international currency for trade. (437)

flute or fluting—Vertical channeling, roughly semicircular in cross-*section* and used principally on *columns* and *pilasters*. (51, 71, 116)

flying buttress—See *buttress*. (12, 375, 389)

folio—A page of a manuscript or book. (257)

foreshortening (adj. **foreshortened**)—The use of *perspective* to represent in art the apparent visual contraction of an object that extends back in space at an angle to the perpendicular plane of sight. (10, 44, 123, 428)

form—In art, an object's shape and structure, either in two dimensions (for example, a figure painted on a surface) or in three dimensions (such as a *statue*). (7)

formal analysis—The visual analysis of artistic *form*. (7)

forum (pl. **fora**)—The public square of an ancient Roman city. (189)

foundry—A workshop for casting metal. (129)

Fourth Style mural—In Roman *mural* painting, the Fourth Style marks a return to architectural *illusionism,* but the architectural vistas of the Fourth Style are irrational fantasies. (197)

freedmen, freedwomen—In ancient and medieval society, men and women who had been freed from servitude, as opposed to having been born free. (190)

freestanding sculpture—See *sculpture in the round*. (12)

fresco—Painting on lime plaster, either dry (dry fresco, or fresco secco) or wet (true, or buon, fresco). In the latter method, the pigments are mixed with water and become chemically bound to the freshly laid lime plaster. Also, a painting executed in either method. (428)

fresco secco—See *fresco*. (76, 91)

Friday mosque—See *congregational mosque*. (299)

frieze—The part of the *entablature* between the *architrave* and the *cornice*; also, any sculptured or painted band. See *register*. (31, 115, 116)

frigidarium—The cold-bath section of a Roman bathing establishment. (225)

fundator quietis—Latin, "bringer of peace." (233)

furta sacra—Latin, "holy theft." (349)

garbha griha—Hindi, "womb chamber." In Hindu temples, the *cella,* the holy inner sanctum often housing the god's image or *symbol*. (460)

genre—A *style* or category of art; also, a kind of painting that realistically depicts scenes from everyday life. (5)

Geometric—The *style* of Greek art during the ninth and eighth centuries BCE, characterized by *abstract* geometric ornament and schematic figures. (108)

gigantomachy—In ancient Greek mythology, the battle between gods and giants. (118)

giornata (pl. **giornate**)—Italian, "day." The section of plaster that a *fresco* painter expects to complete in one session. (428)

gladiator—An ancient Roman professional fighter, usually a slave, who competed in an *amphitheater*. (207)

glaze (adj. **glazed**)—A vitreous coating applied to pottery to seal and decorate the surface; it may be colored, transparent, or opaque, and glossy or *matte*. In *oil painting*, a thin, transparent, or semitransparent layer applied over a *color* to alter it slightly. (47, 110)

glazier—A glassworker. (392)

gold leaf—Gold beaten into tissue-paper-thin sheets that then can be applied to surfaces. (422)

gorgon—In ancient Greek mythology, a hideous female demon with snake hair. Medusa, the most famous gorgon, was capable of turning anyone who gazed at her into stone. (118)

Gospels—The four New Testament books that relate the life and teachings of Jesus. (277, 324)

Gothic—Originally a derogatory term named after the Goths, used to describe the history, culture, and art of western Europe in the 12th to 14th centuries. Typically divided into periods designated Early (1140–1194), High (1194–1300), and Late (1300–1500). (381)

Gothic Revival—See *Neo-Gothic.* (13-53A)

granulation—A decorative *technique* in which tiny metal balls (granules) are fused to a metal surface. (167)

great mosque—See *congregational mosque.* (299)

Greek cross—A cross with four arms of equal length. (280)

griffin—An eagle-headed winged lion. (52, 93, 10-6B)

grisaille—A *monochrome* painting done mainly in neutral grays to simulate sculpture. (427, 13-36A)

groin—The edge formed by the intersection of two barrel *vaults.* (186)

groin vault—See *vault.* (186, 364)

ground line—In paintings and *reliefs,* a painted or carved baseline on which figures appear to stand. (21, 31)

guild—An association of merchants, craftspersons, or scholars in medieval and *Renaissance* Europe. (382, 430)

Hadith—The words and exemplary deeds of the Prophet Muhammad. (295)

hagios (fem. **hagia**)—Greek, "saint." (326)

hall church—See *Hallenkirche.* (362)

Hallenkirche—German, "hall *church.*" A *church* design favored in Germany, but also used elsewhere, in which the *aisles* rise to the same height as the *nave.* (415)

haruspex (pl. **haruspices**)—An Etruscan priest who foretells events by studying animal livers. (6-13A)

head cluster—An abbreviated way of representing a crowd by painting or carving many heads close together, usually with too few bodies for the number of heads. (256)

Helladic—The prehistoric art of the Greek mainland (*Hellas* in Greek). (87)

Hellas—The ancient name of Greece. (87, 106)

Hellenes (adj. **Hellenic**)—The name the ancient Greeks called themselves as the people of *Hellas.* (106)

Hellenistic—The term given to the art and culture of the roughly three centuries between the death of Alexander the Great in 323 BCE and the death of Queen Cleopatra in 30 BCE, when Egypt became a Roman province. (153)

henge—An arrangement of *megalithic* stones in a circle, often surrounded by a ditch. (28)

heraldic composition—A *composition* that is symmetrical on either side of a central figure. (36)

herm—A sculpted head on a quadrangular *pillar.* (133)

Hiberno-Saxon—An art *style* that flourished in the *monasteries* of the British Isles in the early Middle Ages. Also called Insular. (324)

hierarchy of scale—An artistic convention in which greater size indicates greater importance. (11, 31)

hieroglyph—A *symbol* or picture used to confer meaning in *hieroglyphic* writing. (57)

high cross—A tall early medieval Irish freestanding stone cross. (327)

high relief—See *relief.* (12, 67)

Hijra—The flight of Muhammad from Mecca to Medina in 622, the year from which Islam dates its beginnings. (295)

himation—An ancient Greek mantle worn by men and women over the *chiton* and draped in various ways. (114)

Hippodamian plan—A city *plan* devised by Hippodamos of Miletos ca. 466 BCE, in which a strict grid was imposed on a site, regardless of the terrain, so that all streets would meet at right angles. (154)

hippodrome—A *stadium* for horse racing. (265, 9-1A)

historiated—Ornamented with representations, such as plants, animals, or human figures, that have a narrative—as distinct from a purely decorative—function. (357)

historiated capital—A *capital* with a carved figural ornament. (357)

honos—Latin, "honor." Personified as a seminude male youth in Roman art. (211)

hubris—Greek, "arrogant pride." (142)

hue—The name of a *color.* See also *primary colors, secondary colors,* and *complementary colors.* (7)

humanism—In the *Renaissance,* an emphasis on education and on expanding knowledge (especially of *classical* antiquity), the exploration of individual potential and a desire to excel, and a commitment to civic responsibility and moral duty. (426)

hydria—An ancient Greek three-handled water pitcher. (144)

hypaethral—A building having no *pediment* or roof, open to the sky. (154)

hypostyle hall—A hall with a roof supported by *columns.* (75, 298, 299)

icon—A portrait or image; especially in *Byzantine churches,* a panel with a painting of sacred personages that are objects of veneration. In the visual arts, a painting, a piece of sculpture, or even a building regarded as an object of veneration. (277)

iconoclasm—The destruction of religious or sacred images. In Byzantium, the period from 726 to 843 when there was an imperial ban on such images. The destroyers of images were known as iconoclasts. Those who opposed such a ban were known as iconophiles. (265, 278)

iconoclast—See *iconoclasm.* (278)

iconography—Greek, the "writing of images." The term refers both to the content, or subject, of an artwork and to the study of content in art. It also includes the study of the symbolic, often religious, meaning of objects, persons, or events depicted in works of art. (5)

iconophile—See *iconoclasm.* (278)

iconostasis—Greek, "icon stand." In Byzantine *churches,* a screen or a partition, with doors and many tiers of *icons,* separating the sanctuary from the main body of the church. (289)

illuminare—Latin, "to adorn, ornament, or brighten." (252)

illuminated manuscript—A luxurious handmade book with painted illustrations and decorations. (252)

illusionism (adj. **illusionistic**)—The representation of the three-dimensional world on a two-dimensional surface in a manner that creates the illusion that the person, object, or place represented is three-dimensional. See also *perspective.* (8)

imago (pl. **imagines**)—In ancient Rome, a portrait-mask of an ancestor displayed in the *atrium* of a *domus.* (187)

imago hominis—Latin, "image of the man." The *symbol* of the *evangelist* Matthew. (326)

imam—In Islam, the leader of collective worship. (299)

imperator—Latin, "commander in chief," from which the word *emperor* derives. (201)

impluvium—In a Roman *domus,* the basin located in the *atrium* that collected rainwater. (193)

in antis—In ancient Greek architecture, the area between the *antae.* (115)

incise—To cut into a surface with a sharp instrument, especially to decorate metal and pottery. (17)

incrustation—Wall decoration consisting of bright panels of different *colors.* (206, 370)

indulgence—A religious pardon for a sin committed. (390)

insula (pl. **insulae**)—In Roman architecture, a multistory apartment house, usually made of brick-faced *concrete;* also refers to an entire city block. (218)

Insular—See *Hiberno-Saxon.* (324)

intensity—See *color.* (7)

interaxial—The distance between the center of the lowest *drum* of a *column* and the center of the next. Also called the intercolumniation. (134)

intercolumniation—See *interaxial.* (134)

internal evidence—In art history, the examination of what an artwork represents (people, clothing, hairstyles, and so on) in order to determine its date. Also, the examination of the *style* of an artwork to identify the artist who created it. (3)

International Gothic—A *style* of 14th- and 15th-century painting begun by Simone Martini, who fused the French *Gothic* manner with Sienese art. This style appealed to the aristocracy because of its brilliant *color,* lavish costumes, intricate ornamentation, and themes involving splendid processions of knights and ladies. (432)

intonaco—In *fresco* painting, the last layer of smooth lime plaster applied to the wall; the painting layer. (428)

investiture—Ceremony in which a ruler receives the authority to govern. (2-17A)

investment—In hollow-casting, the final clay *mold* applied to the exterior of the wax model. (129)

Ionic—One of the two systems (or *orders*) invented in ancient Greece for articulating the three units of the *elevation* of a *classical* building: the platform, the *colonnade,* and the superstructure (*entablature*). The Ionic order is characterized by, among other features, *volutes, capitals, columns* with *bases,* and an uninterrupted *frieze.* (115)

iwan—In Islamic architecture, a *vaulted* rectangular recess opening onto a courtyard. (54)

jamb statue—A *statue,* usually attached to a *column,* set against the *jamb* of a *Gothic church* portal. (384)

jambs—In architecture, the side posts of a doorway. (358)

ka—In ancient Egypt, the immortal human life force. (57)

Kaaba—Arabic, "cube." A small cubical building in Mecca, the symbolic center of the Islamic world. (295)

katholikon—The main *church* in a Greek Orthodox *monastery.* (280)

keep—A fortified tower in a castle that served as a place of last refuge. (400)

kerykeion—In ancient Greek mythology, a serpent-entwined herald's rod (Latin, *caduceus*), the attribute of Hermes (Roman Mercury), the messenger of the gods. (107)

ketos—Greek, "sea dragon." (241)

keystone—See *voussoir.* (177)

khan—Arabic, "lord." (10-25A)

kings' gallery—The band of *statues* running the full width of the *facade* of a *Gothic cathedral* directly above the *rose window.* (395)

kiva—A square or circular underground structure that is the spiritual and ceremonial center of *Pueblo* Indian life. (1-15A)

kline (pl. **klinai**)—A couch or funerary bed. A type of *sarcophagus* with a reclining portrait of the deceased on its lid. (222)

Koran—Islam's sacred book, composed of *surahs* (chapters) divided into verses. (295)

kore (pl. **korai**)—Greek, "young woman." An *Archaic* Greek *statue* of a young woman. (111)

kouros (pl. **kouroi**)—Greek, "young man." An *Archaic* Greek *statue* of a young man. (112)

krater—An ancient Greek wide-mouthed bowl for mixing wine and water. (102, 108)

Kufic—An early form of Arabic script, characterized by angularity, with the uprights forming almost right angles with the baseline. Named after the city of Kufa. (305)

kylix—An ancient Greek drinking cup with a wide bowl and two horizontal handles. (5-24A)

labrys—*Minoan* double ax. (89)

labyrinth—Maze. The English word derives from the mazelike plan of the *Minoan* palace at Knossos. (89)

lady chapel—A chapel within an English church dedicated to "Our Lady," the Virgin Mary. (13-45A)

laid-and-couched work—See *embroidery.* (377)

lamassu—Assyrian guardian in the form of a man-headed winged bull or lion. (47)

lancet—In *Gothic* architecture, a tall narrow window ending in a *pointed arch.* (386, 389)

landscape—A picture showing natural scenery, without narrative content. (5, 93)

Late Antique—The non-*naturalistic* artistic *style* of the Late Roman Empire. (225)

lateral section—See *section.* (12)

leading—In the manufacture of *stained-glass* windows, the joining of colored glass pieces using lead *cames.* (392)

lectionary—A book containing passages from the *Gospels,* arranged in the sequence that they are to be read during the celebration of religious services, including the *Mass,* throughout the year. (330)

lekythos (pl. **lekythoi**)—A flask containing perfumed oil; lekythoi were often placed in Greek graves as offerings to the deceased. (142)

libation—The pouring of liquid as part of a religious ritual. (35)

liber—Latin, "book." (386)

liberator urbis—Latin, "liberator of the city." (233)

liege lord—In *feudalism,* a landowner who grants tenure of a portion of his land to a *vassal.* (348)

line—The extension of a point along a path, made concrete in art by drawing on or chiseling into a *plane.* (7)

linear perspective—See *perspective.* (196)

lintel—A horizontal *beam* used to span an opening. (28, 358)

liturgy (adj. **liturgical**)—The official ritual of public worship. (249)

lituus—The curved staff carried by an *augur.* (165)

loculus (pl. **loculi**)—An opening in the wall of a gallery in the *catacombs* in which the remains of the deceased were deposited. (241)

loggia—A gallery with an open *arcade* or a *colonnade* on one or both sides. (14-20A)

longitudinal plan—See *plan.* (249)

longitudinal section—See *section.* (12)

lost-wax process—A bronze-*casting* method in which a figure is modeled in wax and covered with clay; the whole is fired, melting away the wax (French, *cire perdue*) and hardening the clay, which then becomes a *mold* for molten metal. Also called the cire perdue process. (129)

low relief—See *relief.* (12)

lunette—A semicircular area (with the flat side down) in a wall over a door, niche, or window; also, a painting or *relief* with a semicircular frame. (241, 7-54A)

lux nova—Latin, "new light." Abbot Suger's term for the light that enters a *Gothic church* through *stained-glass* windows. (384)

machicolated gallery—A gallery in a defensive tower with holes in the floor to allow stones or hot liquids to be dumped on enemies below. (435)

madrasa—An Islamic theological college adjoining and often containing a *mosque.* (308)

malwiya—Arabic, "snail shell." (300)

mamluk—Arabic, "slave." Also the name of the Muslim dynasty of former Turkish slaves that ruled Egypt from 1250 to 1517. (308)

mandorla—An almond-shaped *nimbus* surrounding the figure of Christ or other sacred figure. In Buddhist Japan, a lotus-petal-shaped nimbus. (276)

maniera greca—Italian, "Greek manner." The Italo-*Byzantine* painting *style* of the 13th century. (425)

manor—In *feudalism,* the estate of a *liege lord.* (348)

manuscript—From the Latin *manu scriptus*; a handwritten book. (252)

mappamundi—Latin, "cloth of the world." A medieval world map. (407, 13-39A)

maqsura—In some *mosques,* a screened area in front of the *mihrab* reserved for a ruler. (293, 299)

margrave—Military governor of the Holy Roman Empire. (413)

martyr—A person who chooses to die rather than deny his or her religious belief. See also *saint.* (241, 246)

martyrium (pl. **martyria**)—A shrine to a Christian *martyr.* (248)

mass—The bulk, density, and weight of matter in *space.* (8)

Mass—The Catholic and Orthodox ritual in which believers understand that Christ's redeeming sacrifice on the cross is repeated when the priest consecrates the bread and wine in the *Eucharist.* (245)

mastaba—Arabic, "bench." An ancient Egyptian rectangular brick or stone structure with sloping sides erected over a subterranean tomb chamber connected with the outside by a shaft. (61)

matins—In Christianity, early morning prayers. (13-36A)

mausoleum (pl. **mausolea**)—A monumental tomb. The name derives from the mid-fourth-century BCE tomb of Mausolos at Halikarnassos, one of the Seven Wonders of the ancient world. (230, 248, 5-63C)

maximus—Latin, "greatest." (182)

meander—An ornament, usually in bands but also covering broad surfaces, consisting of interlocking geometric motifs. An ornamental pattern of contiguous straight lines joined usually at right angles. (108)

medium (pl. **media**)—The material (for example, marble, bronze, clay, *fresco*) in which an artist works; also, in painting, the vehicle (usually liquid) that carries the pigment. (7)

megalith (adj. **megalithic**)—Greek, "great stone." A large, roughly hewn stone used in the construction of monumental prehistoric structures. (7)

megaron—The large reception hall and throne room in a *Mycenaean* palace, fronted by an open, two-*columned* porch. (96, 4-18A)

melior—Latin, "better." (211)

mendicants—In medieval Europe, friars belonging to the Franciscan and Dominican orders, who renounced all worldly goods, lived by contributions of laypersons (the word *mendicant* means "beggar"), and devoted themselves to preaching, teaching, and doing good works. (398, 423)

menorah—In antiquity, the Jewish sacred seven-branched candelabrum. (210)

merlon—See *crenellation*. (399)

Mesolithic—The "middle" Stone Age, between the *Paleolithic* and the *Neolithic* ages. (23)

Messiah—The savior of the Jews prophesied in Hebrew scripture. Christians believe that Jesus of Nazareth was the Messiah. (244)

metope—The square panel between the *triglyphs* in a *Doric frieze*, often sculpted in *relief*. (115, 116)

mezquita—Spanish, "mosque." (301)

mihrab—A semicircular niche set into the *qibla* wall of a *mosque*. (298)

mina—A unit of ancient Mesopotamian currency equal to 1/50 *shekel*. (45)

minaret—A distinctive feature of *mosque* architecture, a tower from which the faithful are called to worship. (133, 268, 297, 299)

minbar—In a *mosque*, the *pulpit* on which the *imam* stands. (298, 299)

Minoan—The prehistoric art of Crete, named after the legendary King Minos of Knossos. (87)

Minotaur—The mythical beast, half man and half bull, that inhabited the *labyrinth* of the *Minoan* palace at Knossos. (86)

Miraj—The ascension of the Prophet Muhammad to Heaven. (296)

module (adj. **modular**)—A basic unit of which the dimensions of the major parts of a work are multiples. The principle is used in sculpture and other art forms, but it is most often employed in architecture, where the module may be the dimensions of an important part of a building, such as the diameter of a *column*. (335)

mold—A hollow form for *casting*. (11)

molding—In architecture, a continuous, narrow surface (projecting or recessed, plain or ornamented) designed to break up a surface, to accent, or to decorate. (82)

monastery—A group of buildings in which monks live together, set apart from the secular community of a town. (275)

monasticism—The religious practice in which monks live together in a *monastery* set apart from the secular community of a town. (247, 275)

monochrome (adj. **monochromatic**)—One *color*. (197)

monolith (adj. **monolithic**)—A stone *column shaft* that is all in one piece (not composed of *drums*); a large, single block or piece of stone used in *megalithic* structures. Also, a colossal *statue* carved from a single piece of stone. (72, 116)

monotheism—The worship of one all-powerful god. (237)

Moralized Bible—A heavily illustrated Bible, each page pairing paintings of Old and New Testament episodes with explanations of their moral significance. (402)

mors—Latin, "death." (13-39B)

mortuary temple—In Egyptian architecture, a temple erected for the worship of a deceased *pharaoh*. (64)

mosaic—Patterns or pictures made by embedding small pieces (*tesserae*) of stone or glass in cement on surfaces such as walls and floors; also, the *technique* of making such works. (256)

mosaic tilework—An Islamic decorative *technique* in which large ceramic panels are fired, cut into smaller pieces, and set in plaster. (311)

moschophoros—Greek, "calf bearer." (112)

mosque—The Islamic building for collective worship. From the Arabic word *masjid,* meaning a "place for bowing down." (268, 299)

Mozarabic—Referring to the Christian culture of northern Spain when Islamic *caliphs* ruled southern Spain. (328)

Muhaqqaq—A cursive *style* of Islamic *calligraphy*. (311)

mullion—A vertical member that divides a window or that separates one window from another. (398)

mummification—A *technique* used by ancient Egyptians to preserve human bodies so that they may serve as the eternal home of the immortal *ka*. (61)

mummy—An embalmed Egyptian corpse; see *mummification*. (61)

muqarnas—Stucco decorations of Islamic buildings in which stalactite-like forms break a structure's solidity. (284, 307, 9-26C)

mural—A wall painting. (16)

muralist—A *mural* painter. (20)

Mycenaean—The prehistoric art of the Late *Helladic* period in Greece, named after the citadel of Mycenae. (87)

mystery play—A dramatic enactment of the holy mysteries of the Christian faith, performed at *church* portals and in city squares. (12-38A)

naos—See *cella*. (115)

narthex—A porch or vestibule of a *church*, generally *colonnaded* or *arcaded* and preceding the *nave*. (249)

natatio—The swimming pool in a Roman bathing establishment. (225)

naturalism (adj. **naturalistic**)—The *style* of painted or sculpted representation based on close observation of the natural world that was at the core of the *classical* tradition. (15)

nave—The central area of an ancient Roman *basilica* or of a *church*, demarcated from *aisles* by *piers* or *columns*. (191, 249)

nave arcade—In *basilica* architecture, the series of *arches* supported by *piers* or *columns* separating the *nave* from the *aisles*. (249, 389)

necropolis—Greek, "city of the dead." A large burial area or cemetery. (62)

nemes—In ancient Egypt, the linen headdress worn by the *pharaoh*, with the *uraeus* cobra of kingship on the front. (65)

Neolithic—The "new" Stone Age. (23)

Nereids—Sea nymphs; daughters of the Greek god Nereus. (251)

niello—A black metallic alloy. (99)

nimbus—A *halo* or aureole appearing around the head of a holy figure to signify divinity. (259)

nomarch—Egyptian, "great overlord." A regional governor during the Middle Kingdom. (3-16A)

Nun—In ancient Egypt, the primeval waters from which the creator god emerged. (60)

nymphs—In *classical* mythology, female divinities of springs, caves, and woods. (107)

obelisk—A tall four-sided *monolithic pillar* with a pyramidal top—symbolic of the Egyptian sun god Re. (72)

oculus (pl. **oculi**)—Latin, "eye." The round central opening of a *dome*. Also, a small round window in a *Gothic cathedral*. (186, 387, 389, 14-5B)

ogee arch—An *arch* composed of two double-curving lines meeting at a point. (440, 13-44A)

ogive (adj. **ogival**)—The diagonal *rib* of a *Gothic vault*; a pointed, or Gothic, *arch*. (387, 421)

opere francigeno—See *opus francigenum*. (407)

opisthodomos—In ancient Greek architecture, a porch at the rear of a temple, set against the blank back wall of the *cella*. (115)

optical representation—The representation of people and objects seen from a fixed viewpoint. (27)

optimus—Latin, "best." (211)

opus francigenum—Latin, "French work." Architecture in the *style* of *Gothic* France; *opere francigeno* (adj.), "in the French manner." (381)

opus modernum—Latin, "modern work." The late medieval term for *Gothic* art and architecture. Also called *opus francigenum*. (381)

opus reticulatum—An ancient Roman method of facing *concrete* walls with lozenge-shaped bricks or stones to achieve a netlike ornamental surface pattern. (11-19A)

oracle—A prophetic message. (5-16A)

orant—In Early Christian art, a figure with both arms raised in the ancient gesture of prayer. (241)

oratory—The *church* of a Christian *monastery*. (275)

orchestra—Greek, "dancing place." In ancient Greek theaters, the circular piece of earth with a hard and level surface on which the performance took place. (151)

order—In *classical* architecture, a *style* represented by a characteristic design of the *columns* and *entablature*. See also *superimposed orders*. (116)

Orientalizing—The early phase of *Archaic* Greek art (seventh century BCE), so named because of the adoption of forms and motifs from ancient Mesopotamia, Persia, and Egypt. See also *Daedalic*. (109)

orthogonal plan—The imposition of a strict grid *plan* on a site, regardless of the terrain, so that all streets meet at right angles. See also *Hippodamian plan*. (154)

Ottonian (adj.)—Pertaining to the empire of Otto I and his successors. (337)

pala—A panel placed behind and over the altar in a *church*. (9-26A)

palaestra—An ancient Greek and Roman exercise area, usually framed by a *colonnade*. In Greece, the palaestra was an independent building; in Rome, palaestras were also frequently incorporated into a bathing complex. (131, 225)

palazzo pubblico—Italian, "public palace." City hall. (434)

palette—A thin board with a thumb hole at one end on which an artist lays and mixes *colors*; any surface so used. Also, the colors or kinds of colors characteristically used by an artist. In ancient Egypt, a slate slab used for preparing makeup. (20, 59)

Pantokrator—Greek, "ruler of all." Christ as ruler and judge. (281)

papyrus—A plant native to Egypt and adjacent lands used to make paperlike writing material; also, the material or any writing on it. (57)

parade helmet—A masklike helmet worn by Roman soldiers on special ceremonial occasions. (349)

parapet—A low, protective wall along the edge of a balcony, roof, or bastion. (140, 435)

parchment—Lambskin prepared as a surface for painting or writing. (252)

parekklesion—The side chapel in a *Byzantine church*. (288)

parthenos—Greek, "virgin." The epithet of Athena, the virgin goddess. (107)

passage grave—A prehistoric tomb with a long stone corridor leading to a burial chamber covered by a great *tumulus*. (27)

passio—Latin, "suffering." (245)

passional—A Christian book containing the lives of *saints*. (324, 368)

Passover—The annual feast celebrating the release of the Jews from bondage to the *pharaohs* of Egypt. (244)

paten—A large shallow bowl or plate for the bread used in the *Eucharist*. (273)

patrician—A Roman freeborn landowner. (183)

patron—The person or entity that pays an artist to produce individual artworks or employs an artist on a continuing basis. (6)

patronus—Latin, "patron." A freeborn Roman, often a slave owner, to whom a *cliens* of lesser stature owes allegiance. (193)

Pax Augustus—Latin, "Augustan Peace." (201)

Pax Romana—Latin, "Roman Peace." (201)

pax vobis—Latin, "peace unto you." (356)

pebble mosaic—A *mosaic* made of irregularly shaped stones of various *colors*. (148, 256)

pectoral—An ornament on the chest. (167)

pediment—In *classical* architecture, the triangular space (gable) at the end of a building, formed by the ends of the sloping roof above the *colonnade*; also, an ornamental feature having this shape. (115, 116)

pendant—The large hanging terminal element of a *Gothic* fan *vault*. (410)

pendentive—A concave, triangular section of a hemisphere, four of which provide the transition from a square area to the circular base of a covering *dome*. Although pendentives appear to be hanging (pendant) from the dome, they in fact support it. (270)

Pentateuch—The first five books of the Old Testament. (237)

peplos (pl. **peploi**)—A simple, long, belted garment of wool worn by women in ancient Greece. (114)

period style—See *style*. (3)

peripteral—See *peristyle*. (115)

peristyle—In *classical* architecture, a *colonnade* all around the *cella* and its porch(es). A peripteral colonnade consists of a single row of *columns* on all sides; a dipteral colonnade has a double row all around. (115)

Perpendicular—An English Late *Gothic style* of architecture distinguished by the pronounced verticality of its decorative details. (409)

personal style—See *style*. (4)

personification—An *abstract* idea represented in bodily form. (5)

perspective—A method of presenting an illusion of the three-dimensional world on a two-dimensional surface. In linear perspective, the most common type, all parallel lines or surface edges converge on one, two, or three vanishing points located with reference to the eye level of the viewer (the horizon line of the picture), and associated objects are rendered smaller the farther from the viewer they are intended to seem. Atmospheric, or aerial, perspective creates the illusion of distance by the greater diminution of *color* intensity, the shift in color toward an almost neutral blue, and the blurring of contours as the intended distance between eye and object increases. (3)

pharaoh (adj. **pharaonic**)—An ancient Egyptian king. (71)

phersu—A masked man who appears in scenes of Etruscan funerary games. (165)

phoibos—Greek, "radiant." The epithet of the Greek god Apollo. (107)

physical evidence—In art history, the examination of the materials used to produce an artwork in order to determine its date. (2)

piazza—Italian, "plaza." (429)

pictograph—A picture, usually stylized, that represents an idea; also, writing using such means; also, painting on rock. See also *hieroglyphic*. (31)

pier—A vertical, freestanding masonry support. (12)

Pietà—A painted or sculpted representation of the Virgin Mary mourning over the body of the dead Christ. (245, 414)

pilaster—A flat, rectangular, vertical member projecting from a wall of which it forms a part. It usually has a *base* and a *capital* and is often *fluted*. (141, 177)

pillar—Usually a weight-carrying member, such as a *pier* or a *column*; sometimes an isolated, freestanding structure used for commemorative purposes. (72, 3-23A)

pinakotheke—Greek, "picture gallery." An ancient Greek building for the display of paintings on wood panels. (138)

pinnacle—In *Gothic churches*, a sharply pointed ornament capping the *piers* or flying *buttresses*; also used on *church facades*. (389)

plan—The horizontal arrangement of the parts of a building or of the buildings and streets of a city or town, or a drawing or diagram showing such an arrangement. In an axial plan, the parts of a building are organized longitudinally, or along a given axis; in a central plan, the parts of the structure are of equal or almost equal dimensions around the center. (12)

plane—A flat surface. (7)

plate tracery—See *tracery*. (392)

plebeian—The Roman social class that included small farmers, merchants, and freed slaves. (183)

pointed arch—A narrow *arch* of pointed profile, in contrast to a semicircular arch. (3, 303, 348, 387, 12-10B)

polis (pl. **poleis**)—An independent *city-state* in ancient Greece. (106)

polytheism—The belief in multiple gods. (237)

pontifex maximus—Latin, "chief priest" (of the Roman state religion). (201)

portico—A roofed *colonnade*; also an entrance porch. (155)

post-and-lintel system—A system of construction in which two posts support a *lintel*. (28)

predella—The narrow ledge on which an *altarpiece* rests on an altar. (419)

prefiguration—In Early Christian art, the depiction of Old Testament persons and events as prophetic forerunners of Christ and New Testament events. (241)

primary colors—Red, yellow, and blue—the *colors* from which all other colors may be derived. (7)

princeps—Latin, "first citizen." The title Augustus and his successors as Roman emperor used to distinguish themselves from Hellenistic monarchs. (201, 273)

pronaos—The space, or porch, in front of the *cella*, or naos, of an ancient Greek temple. (115)

proportion—The relationship in size of the parts of persons, buildings, or objects, often based on a *module*. (10)

propylaia—Greek, "gates." (138)

prostyle—A *classical* temple *plan* in which the *columns* are only in front of the *cella* and not on the sides or back. (115)

protome—The head, forelegs, and part of the body of an animal. (51)

provenance—Origin or source; *findspot*. (3, 87)

pseudoperipteral—In Roman architecture, a pseudoperipteral temple has a series of *engaged columns* all around the sides and back of the *cella* to give the appearance of a *peripteral colonnade*. (184)

pulpit—A raised platform in a *church* or *mosque* on which a priest or *imam* stands while leading the religious service. (420)

punchwork—Tooled decorative work in *gold leaf*. (429)

pylon—The wide entrance gateway of an Egyptian temple, characterized by its sloping walls. (74)

pylon temple—An Egyptian temple entered through a monumental *pylon*, typical of the New Kingdom. (74)

pyxis (pl. **pyxides**)—A cylindrical container with a hemispherical lid. (304)

qibla—The direction (toward Mecca) that Muslims face when praying. (299)

quadrant arch—An *arch* whose curve extends for one-quarter of a circle's circumference. (375)

quatrefoil—A shape or *plan* in which the parts assume the form of a cloverleaf. (438)

radiating chapels—In medieval *churches*, chapels for the display of *relics* that opened directly onto the *ambulatory* and the *transept*. (351)

radiocarbon dating—A method of measuring the decay rate of carbon isotopes in organic matter to determine the age of organic materials such as wood and fiber. (16)

raking cornice—The *cornice* on the sloping sides of a *pediment*. (116)

ramparts—Defensive wall circuits. (399)

Rayonnant—The "radiant" style of *Gothic* architecture, dominant in the second half of the 13th century and associated with the French royal court of Louis IX at Paris. (398)

recto—The front side of a manuscript *folio*. (252)

red-figure painting—In later Greek pottery, the silhouetting of red figures against a black background, with painted linear details; the reverse of *black-figure painting*. (122)

refectory—The dining hall of a Christian *monastery*. (275, 335)

regional style—See *style*. (3)

register—One of a series of superimposed bands or *friezes* in a pictorial narrative, or the particular levels on which motifs are placed. (31)

relics—The body parts, clothing, or objects associated with a holy figure, such as the Buddha or Christ or a Christian *saint*. Also, in Africa, the bones of ancestors. (248)

relief—In sculpture, figures projecting from a background of which they are part. The degree of relief is designated high, low (bas), or sunken. In the last, the artist cuts the design into the surface so that the highest projecting parts of the image are no higher than the surface itself. See also *repoussé*. (12)

relief sculpture—See *relief*. (12)

relieving triangle—In *Mycenaean* architecture, the triangular opening above the *lintel* that serves to lighten the weight to be carried by the lintel itself. (97, 98)

reliquary—A container for holding *relics*. (342, 349)

Renaissance—French, "rebirth." The term used to describe the history, culture, and art of 14th- through 16th-century western Europe during which artists consciously revived the *classical* style. (419, 426)

renovatio—Latin, "renewal." During the *Carolingian* period, Charlemagne sought to revive the culture of ancient Rome (*renovatio imperii Romani*). (329, 420)

renovatio imperii Romani—See *renovatio*. (329)

repoussé—Formed in *relief* by beating a metal plate from the back, leaving the impression on the face. The metal sheet is hammered into a hollow *mold* of wood or some other pliable material and finished with a graver. See also *relief*. (53, 99, 251, 332)

res gestae—Latin, "achievements." (7-40A)

respond—An engaged *column, pilaster,* or similar element that either projects from a *compound pier* or some other supporting device or is bonded to a wall and carries one end of an *arch*. (389)

reverentissimo—Latin, "most revered." (362)

revetment—In architecture, a wall covering or facing. (186, 427)

rhyton—A drinking vessel. (53)

rib—A relatively slender, molded masonry *arch* that projects from a surface. In *Gothic* architecture, the ribs form the framework of the *vaulting*. A diagonal rib is one of the ribs that form the X of a *groin vault*. A transverse rib crosses the *nave* or *aisle* at a 90-degree angle. (12, 366)

rib vault—A *vault* in which the diagonal and transverse *ribs* compose a structural skeleton that partially supports the masonry *web* between them. (366, 387)

ridge beam—The *beam* running the length of a building below the peak of the gabled roof. (117)

rinascità—Italian, "rebirth." (426)

Romanesque—"Roman-like." A term used to describe the history, culture, and art of medieval western Europe from ca. 1050 to ca. 1200. (347, 348, 382)

rose window—A circular *stained-glass* window. (384)

roundel—See *tondo*. (393)

rustication (adj. **rusticated**)—To give a rustic appearance by roughening the surfaces and beveling the edges of stone blocks to emphasize the joints between them. Rustication is a *technique* employed in ancient Roman architecture, and was also popular during the *Renaissance*, especially for stone *courses* at the ground-floor level. (205, 14-19B)

sacra rappresentazione (pl. **sacre rappresentazioni**)—Italian, "holy representation." A more elaborate version of a *mystery play* performed for a lay audience by a *confraternity*. (429)

sacramentary—A Christian religious book incorporating the prayers that priests recite during *Mass*. (324)

saint—From the Latin word *sanctus,* meaning "made holy by God." Applied to persons who suffered and died for their Christian faith or who merited reverence for their Christian devotion while alive. In the Roman Catholic Church, a worthy deceased Catholic who is canonized by the pope. (241)

sakkos—The tunic worn by a *Byzantine* priest. (9-35A)

Samarqand ware—A type of Islamic pottery produced in Samarqand and Nishapur in which the ceramists formed the shape of the vessel from dark pink clay and then immersed it in a tub of white slip, over which they painted ornamental or *calligraphic* decoration and which they sealed with a transparent *glaze* before firing. (306)

sanctuary—A sacred site for ritual activity; a religious complex centered on a temple. (34)

sanctus—Latin, "holy." (246)

sarcophagus (pl. **sarcophagi**)—Greek, "consumer of flesh." A coffin, usually of stone. (85, 421)

saturation—See *color.* (7)

satyr—A Greek mythological follower of Dionysos having a man's upper body, a goat's hindquarters and horns, and a horse's ears and tail. (158)

scarab—An Egyptian gem in the shape of a beetle. (61)

Scholasticism—The *Gothic* school of philosophy in which scholars applied Aristotle's system of rational inquiry to the interpretation of religious belief. (388)

school—A chronological and stylistic classification of works of art with a stipulation of place. (6)

scissors arches—A pair of *arches* resembling scissors, comprising an inverted arch above a traditional arch; used in the nave of Wells Cathedral in the 14th century. (409)

screen facade—A *facade* that does not correspond to the structure of the building behind it. (12-12A)

scriptorium (pl. **scriptoria**)—The writing studio of a *monastery.* (325)

sculpture in the round—Freestanding figures, *carved* or *modeled* in three dimensions. (12)

Second Style mural—The *style* of Roman *mural* painting in which the aim was to dissolve the confining walls of a room and replace them with the illusion of a three-dimensional world constructed in the artist's imagination. (194)

secondary colors—Orange, green, and purple, obtained by mixing pairs of *primary colors* (red, yellow, blue). (7)

section—In architecture, a diagram or representation of a part of a structure or building along an imaginary *plane* that passes through it vertically. Drawings showing a theoretical slice across a structure's width are lateral sections. Those cutting through a building's length are longitudinal sections. See also *elevation* and *cutaway.* (12)

sedes sapientiae—Latin, "throne of wisdom." A *Romanesque* sculptural type depicting the Virgin Mary with the Christ Child in her lap. (364)

senate—Latin senatus, "council of elders." The Senate was the main legislative body in Roman constitutional government. (183)

serdab—A small concealed chamber in an Egyptian *mastaba* for the *statue* of the deceased. (61)

Severe Style—The Early *Classical style* of Greek sculpture, ca. 480–450 BCE. (126)

sexpartite vault—See *vault.* (372)

shaft—The tall, cylindrical part of a *column* between the *capital* and the *base.* (51, 116, 389)

shaman (adj. **shamanic**)—A religious leader who gains access to the world of spirits through trances. (17)

shekel—A unit of ancient Mesopotamian currency. (45)

signoria—Italian, "lordship." The governing body of medieval and *Renaissance* Florence. (14-19B)

silentiary—An usher responsible for maintaining silence in the *Byzantine* imperial palace in Constantinople. (268)

sinopia—A burnt-orange pigment used in *fresco* painting to transfer a *cartoon* to the *arriccio* before the artist paints the plaster. (428)

siren—In ancient Greek mythology, a creature that was part bird and part woman. (111)

sistrum—An Egyptian percussion instrument or rattle. (95)

skene—Greek, "stage." The stage of a *classical* theater. (151)

skenographia—Greek, "scene painting"; the Greek term for *perspective* painting. (196)

skiagraphia—Greek, "shadow painting." The Greek term for shading, said to have been invented by Apollodoros, an Athenian painter of the fifth century BCE. (148)

slip—A mixture of fine clay and water used in ceramic decoration. (119)

socii—Latin, "allies." (191)

solidus (pl. **solidi**)—A *Byzantine* gold coin. (271)

space—In art history, both the actual area that an object occupies or a building encloses and the *illusionistic* representation of space in painting and sculpture. (8)

spandrel—The roughly triangular space enclosed by the curves of adjacent *arches* and a horizontal member connecting their vertexes; also, the space enclosed by the curve of an *arch* and an enclosing right angle. The area between the arch proper and the framing *columns* and *entablature.* (209, 393)

spectrum—The range or band of visible *colors* in natural light. (7)

sphinx—A mythical Egyptian beast with the body of a lion and the head of a human. (65)

spolia—Latin, "spoils." Older *statues* and *reliefs* reused in *Late Antique* monuments. (250)

springing—The lowest stone of an *arch,* resting on the *impost block.* In *Gothic vaulting,* the lowest stone of a diagonal or transverse *rib.* (353, 389)

spur wall—A short wall extending from the principal wall outward to a *column* or *pilaster.* (3-6A)

squinch—An architectural device used as a transition from a square to a polygonal or circular base for a *dome.* It may be composed of *lintels, corbels,* or *arches.* (270)

stained glass—In *Gothic* architecture, the colored glass used for windows. (12, 384)

stamp seal—See *cylinder seal.* (37)

statue—A three-dimensional sculpture. (12)

stave—A wedge-shaped timber; vertically placed staves embellish the architectural features of a building. (323)

stele (pl. **stelae**)—A *carved* stone slab used to mark graves or to commemorate historical events. (39)

stem stitching—See *embroidery.* (377)

stigmata—In Christian art, the wounds Christ received at his crucifixion that miraculously appear on the body of a *saint.* (422)

still life—A picture depicting an arrangement of inanimate objects. (5, 199)

stoa—In ancient Greek architecture, an open building with a roof supported by a row of *columns* parallel to the back wall. A covered *colonnade* or *portico.* (155)

Stoic—A philosophical school of ancient Greece, named after the *stoas* in which the philosophers met. (154)

strategos—Greek, "general." (133)

strigil—A tool ancient Greek athletes used to scrape oil from their bodies after exercising. (147)

stringcourse—A raised horizontal *molding,* or band, in masonry. Its principal use is ornamental, but it usually reflects interior structure. (11-19A)

stucco—A type of plaster used as a coating on exterior and interior walls. Also used as a sculptural *medium.* (184)

stylistic evidence—In art history, the examination of the *style* of an artwork in order to determine its date or the identity of the artist. (3)

stylobate—The uppermost course of the platform of a *classical* Greek temple, which supports the *columns.* (116)

stylus—A needlelike tool used in *engraving* and *incising*; also, an ancient writing instrument used to inscribe clay or wax tablets. (32, 199)

sub gracia—Latin, "under grace." In Christian thought, the period after the coming of Christ. (410)

sub lege—Latin, "under the law." In Christian thought, the period after Moses received the Ten Commandments and before the coming of Christ. See also *sub gracia*. (410)

subtractive light—The painter's light in art; the light reflected from pigments and objects. See also *additive light*. (7)

subtractive sculpture—A kind of sculpture *technique* in which materials are taken away from the original mass; *carving*. (11)

sultan—A Muslim ruler. (302)

sunken relief—See *relief*. (79)

Sunnah—The collection of the Prophet Muhammad's moral sayings and descriptions of his deeds. (295)

surah—A chapter of the *Koran*, divided into verses. (295)

symbol—An image that stands for another image or encapsulates an idea. (5)

symmetria—Greek, "commensurability of parts." Polykleitos's treatise on his *canon* of proportions incorporated the principle of symmetria. (131)

symposium (pl. **symposia**)—An ancient Greek banquet attended solely by men (and female servants and prostitutes). (108, 144)

synagogue—Jewish house of worship. (237)

taberna—In Roman architecture, a single-room shop usually covered by a *barrel vault*. (214)

tablinum—The study or office in a Roman *domus*. (193)

tapestry—A weaving *technique* in which the *weft* threads are packed densely over the *warp* threads so that the designs are woven directly into the fabric. (337)

tattoo—A permanent design on the skin produced using indelible dyes. The term derives from the Tahitian, Samoan, and Tongan word *tatau* or *tatu*. (13)

technique—The processes artists employ to create *form*, as well as the distinctive, personal ways in which they handle their materials and tools. (7)

tempera—A *technique* of painting using pigment mixed with egg yolk, glue, or casein; also, the *medium* itself. (224, 422)

templon—The columnar screen separating the sanctuary from the main body of a *Byzantine church*. (286)

tephra—The volcanic ash produced by the eruption on the *Cycladic* island of Thera. (92)

tepidarium—The warm-bath section of a Roman bathing establishment. (225)

terminus ante quem—Latin, "point [date] before which." (2)

terminus post quem—Latin, "point [date] after which." (2)

tesara—Greek, "four." (120)

tessera (pl. **tesserae**)—Greek, "cube." A tiny stone or piece of glass cut to the desired shape and size for use in forming a *mosaic*. (149, 256)

tetrarch—One of four corulers. (229)

tetrarchy—Greek, "rule by four." A type of Roman government established in the late third century CE by Diocletian in an attempt to foster order by sharing power with potential rivals. (229)

texture—The quality of a surface (rough, smooth, hard, soft, shiny, dull) as revealed by light. In represented texture, a painter depicts an object as having a certain texture even though the pigment is the real texture. (8)

theatron—Greek, "place for seeing." In ancient Greek theaters, the slope overlooking the *orchestra* on which the spectators sat. (151)

Theotokos—Greek, "she who bore God." The Virgin Mary, the mother of Jesus. (255, 275)

Third Style mural—In Roman *mural* painting, the *style* in which delicate linear fantasies were sketched on predominantly *monochromatic* backgrounds. (197)

tholos (pl. **tholoi**)—A temple with a circular *plan*. Also, the burial chamber of a *tholos tomb*. (99, 151, 185)

tholos tomb—In *Mycenaean* architecture, a beehive-shaped tomb with a circular plan. (98)

thrust—The outward force exerted by an *arch* or a *vault* that must be counterbalanced by a *buttress*. (186)

tinscvil—Etruscan, "gift to [the god] Tinia." (174)

toga—The garment worn by an ancient Roman male citizen. (174)

tonality—See *color*. (7)

tondo (pl. **tondi**)—A circular painting or *relief* sculpture. (224, 7-47A, 10-17A)

Torah—The Hebrew religious scroll containing the *Pentateuch*. (237)

torque—The distinctive necklace worn by the Gauls. (157)

tramezzo—A screen placed across the *nave* of a *church* to separate the clergy from the lay audience. (14-5B)

transept—The part of a *church* with an axis that crosses the *nave* at a right angle. (248, 335)

transverse arch—An *arch* separating one *vaulted bay* from the next. (353)

transverse barrel vault—In medieval architecture, a semicylindrical *vault* oriented at a 90-degree angle to the *nave* of a *church*. (12-4B)

transverse rib—See *rib*. (389)

treasury—In ancient Greece, a small building set up for the safe storage of *votive offerings*. (118)

Trecento—Italian, "300"—that is, the 14th century (the 1300s) in Italy. (424)

trefoil—A cloverlike ornament or symbol with stylized leaves in groups of three. (420, 13-45B)

tria—Greek, "three." (121)

tribune—In *church* architecture, a gallery over the inner *aisle* flanking the *nave*. (351)

triclinium (pl. **triclinia**)—The dining room of a Roman *domus*. (6-9A)

triforium—In a *Gothic cathedral*, the *blind arcaded* gallery below the *clerestory*; occasionally, the *arcades* are filled with *stained glass*. (386)

triglyph—A triple projecting, grooved member of a *Doric frieze* that alternates with *metopes*. (116)

trilithon—A pair of *monoliths* topped with a *lintel*; found in *megalithic* structures. (28)

Trinity—In Christianity, God the Father, his son Jesus Christ, and the Holy Spirit. (244)

tripod—An ancient Greek deep bowl on a tall three-legged stand. (153, 222)

triptych—A three-paneled painting, ivory plaque, or *altarpiece*. Also, a small, portable shrine with hinged wings used for private devotion. (284, 410, 433)

triumphal arch—In Roman architecture, a freestanding *arch* commemorating an important event, such as a military victory or the opening of a new road. (209)

trumeau—In *church* architecture, the *pillar* or center post supporting the *lintel* in the middle of the doorway. (358)

tubicen—Latin, "trumpet player." (157)

tug—Turkish, "horse's tail." (10-25A)

tughra—The official signature of an Ottoman emperor. (10-25A)

tumulus (pl. **tumuli**)—Latin, "burial mound." In Etruscan architecture, tumuli cover one or more subterranean multichambered tombs cut out of the local tufa (limestone). Tumuli are also characteristic of the Japanese Kofun period of the third and fourth centuries CE. (27, 170, 320)

tunnel vault—See *vault*. (186)

turris—See *westwork*. (336)

Tuscan column—The standard type of Etruscan *column*. It resembles ancient Greek *Doric* columns but is made of wood, is *unfluted*, and has a *base*. Also a popular motif in *Renaissance* and *Baroque* architecture. (168)

twisted perspective—See *composite view*. (22)

tympanum (pl. **tympana**)—The space enclosed by a *lintel* and an *arch* over a doorway. (358)

typology—In Christian theology, the recognition of concordances between events, especially between episodes in the Old and New Testaments. (242)

uraeus—An Egyptian cobra; one of the emblems of *pharaonic* kingship. (65)

ushabti—In ancient Egypt, a figurine placed in a tomb to act as a servant to the deceased in the afterlife. (61)

valley temple—The temple closest to the Nile River, associated with each of the Old Kingdom pyramids at Gizeh in ancient Egypt. (64)

value—See *color*. (7)

vanishing point—See *perspective*. (196)

vanth—An Etruscan female winged demon of death. (177)

vassal—In *feudalism*, a person who swears allegiance to a *liege lord* and renders him military service in return for tenure of a portion of the lord's land. (348)

vault (adj. **vaulted**)—A masonry roof or ceiling constructed on the *arch* principle, or a concrete roof of the same shape. A barrel (or tunnel) vault, semicylindrical in cross-*section*, is in effect a deep arch or an uninterrupted series of arches, one behind the other, over an oblong space. A quadrant vault is a half-barrel vault. A groin (or cross) vault is formed at the point at which two barrel vaults intersect at right angles. In a ribbed vault, there is a framework of *ribs* or arches under the intersections of the vaulting sections. A sexpartite vault is one whose ribs divide the vault into six compartments. A fan vault is a vault characteristic of English *Perpendicular Gothic* architecture, in which radiating ribs form a fanlike pattern. (12, 54)

vaulting web—See *web*. (387, 389)

velarium—In a Roman *amphitheater*, the cloth awning that could be rolled down from the top of the *cavea* to shield spectators from sun or rain. (192)

vellum—Calfskin prepared as a surface for writing or painting. (252)

venationes—Ancient Roman wild animal hunts staged in an *amphitheater*. (207)

veristic—True to natural appearance; super-realistic. (188)

verso—The back side of a manuscript *folio*. (252)

vik—Old Norse, "cove." (323)

Villanovan—The earliest period of Etruscan art, contemporaneous with the *Geometric* period in Greece (ca. 900–700 BCE), named after an archaeological site near Bologna. (165)

Virgo Virginum—Latin, "Virgin of Virgins"—that is, the Virgin Mary. (344)

virtus—Latin, "valor." Personified as an *Amazon*-like woman in Roman art. (211)

vita activa—Latin, "active life." The daily life of the laity, as opposed to the *vita contemplativa* of monastic life. (357)

vita contemplativa—Latin, "contemplative life." The secluded spiritual life of monks and nuns. (357)

vizier—An Egyptian *pharaoh's* chief administrator. (3-12A)

volume—The *space* that *mass* organizes, divides, or encloses. (8)

volute—A spiral, scroll-like form characteristic of the ancient Greek *Ionic* and the Roman *Composite capital*. (51)

votive offering—A gift of gratitude to a deity. (31)

voussoir—A wedge-shaped stone block used in the construction of a true *arch*. The central voussoir, which sets the arch, is called the *keystone*. (177, 358)

Vulgate—Common tongue; spoken medieval Latin. (324)

wanax—Mycenaean king. (96)

web—The masonry blocks that fill the area between the *ribs* of a *groin vault*. Also called vaulting web. (387)

wedjat—The eye of the Egyptian falcon-god Horus, a powerful *amulet*. (60)

weld—To join metal parts by heating, as in assembling the separate parts of a *statue* made by *casting*. (12)

Westwerk—German, "western entrance structure." (336)

westwork—The *facade* and towers at the western end (*Westwerk*) of a medieval *church*, principally in Germany. In contemporaneous documents, the westwork is called a castellum (Latin, "castle" or "fortress") or turris ("tower"). (336)

white-ground painting—An ancient Greek vase-painting *technique* in which the pot was first covered with a *slip* of very fine white clay, over which black *glaze* was used to outline figures, and diluted brown, purple, red, and white were used to color them. (141)

ziggurat—In ancient Mesopotamian architecture, a tiered platform for a temple. (43)

This list of books is very selective, but comprehensive enough to satisfy the reading interests of the beginning art history student and general reader. Significantly expanded from the previous edition, the 15th edition bibliography can also serve as the basis for undergraduate research papers. The resources listed range from works that are valuable primarily for their reproductions to those that are scholarly surveys of schools and periods or monographs on individual artists. The emphasis is on recent in-print books and on books likely to be found in college and municipal libraries. No entries for periodical articles appear, but the bibliography begins with a list of some of the major journals that publish art historical scholarship in English.

Selected Periodicals

African Arts
American Art
American Indian Art
American Journal of Archaeology
Antiquity
Archaeology
Archives of American Art
Archives of Asian Art
Ars Orientalis
Art Bulletin
Art History
Art in America
Art Journal
Artforum International
Artnews
Burlington Magazine
Gesta
History of Photography
Journal of Egyptian Archaeology
Journal of Roman Archaeology
Journal of the Society of Architectural Historians
Journal of the Warburg and Courtauld Institutes
Latin American Antiquity
October
Oxford Art Journal
Women's Art Journal

General Studies

Baxandall, Michael. *Patterns of Intention: On the Historical Explanation of Pictures.* New Haven, Conn.: Yale University Press, 1985.

Bindman, David, ed. *The Thames & Hudson Encyclopedia of British Art.* London: Thames & Hudson, 1988.

Boström, Antonia. *The Encyclopedia of Sculpture.* 3 vols. London: Routledge, 2003.

Broude, Norma, and Mary D. Garrard, eds. *The Expanding Discourse: Feminism and Art History.* New York: Harper Collins, 1992.

Bryson, Norman. *Vision and Painting: The Logic of the Gaze.* New Haven, Conn.: Yale University Press, 1983.

Bryson, Norman, Michael Ann Holly, and Keith Moxey. *Visual Theory: Painting and Interpretation.* New York: Cambridge University Press, 1991.

Burden, Ernest. *Illustrated Dictionary of Architecture.* 2d ed. New York: McGraw-Hill, 2002.

Büttner, Nils. *Landscape Painting: A History.* New York: Abbeville, 2006.

Carrier, David. *A World Art History and Its Objects.* University Park: Pennsylvania State University Press, 2012.

Chadwick, Whitney. *Women, Art, and Society.* 5th ed. New York: Thames & Hudson, 2007.

Cheetham, Mark A., Michael Ann Holly, and Keith Moxey, eds. *The Subjects of Art History: Historical Objects in Contemporary Perspective.* New York: Cambridge University Press, 1998.

Chilvers, Ian, and Harold Osborne, eds. *The Oxford Dictionary of Art.* 3d ed. New York: Oxford University Press, 2004.

Corbin, George A. *Native Arts of North America, Africa, and the South Pacific: An Introduction.* New York: Harper Collins, 1988.

Crouch, Dora P., and June G. Johnson. *Traditions in Architecture: Africa, America, Asia, and Oceania.* New York: Oxford University Press, 2000.

Curl, James Stevens. *Oxford Dictionary of Architecture and Landscape Architecture.* 2d ed. New York: Oxford University Press, 2006.

Davis, Whitney. *A General Theory of Visual Culture.* Princeton, N.J.: Princeton University Press, 2011.

Duby, Georges, ed. *Sculpture: From Antiquity to the Present.* 2 vols. Cologne: Taschen, 1999.

Encyclopedia of World Art. 17 vols. New York: McGraw-Hill, 1959–1987.

Evers, Bernd, and Christof Thoenes. *Architectural Theory from the Renaissance to the Present.* Cologne: Taschen, 2011.

Fielding, Mantle. *Dictionary of American Painters, Sculptors, and Engravers.* 2d ed. Poughkeepsie, N.Y.: Apollo, 1986.

Fine, Sylvia Honig. *Women and Art: A History of Women Painters and Sculptors from the Renaissance to the 20th Century.* Rev. ed. Montclair, N.J.: Alanheld & Schram, 1978.

Fleming, John, Hugh Honour, and Nikolaus Pevsner. *The Penguin Dictionary of Architecture and Landscape Architecture.* 5th ed. New York: Penguin, 2000.

Frazier, Nancy. *The Penguin Concise Dictionary of Art History.* New York: Penguin, 2000.

Freedberg, David. *The Power of Images: Studies in the History and Theory of Response.* Chicago: University of Chicago Press, 1989.

Gaze, Delia, ed. *Dictionary of Women Artists.* 2 vols. London: Routledge, 1997.

Hall, James. *Dictionary of Subjects and Symbols in Art.* 2d ed. Boulder, Colo.: Westview, 2008.

Harris, Anne Sutherland, and Linda Nochlin. *Women Artists: 1550–1950.* Los Angeles: Los Angeles County Museum of Art; New York: Knopf, 1977.

Hauser, Arnold. *The Sociology of Art.* Chicago: University of Chicago Press, 1982.

Hults, Linda C. *The Print in the Western World: An Introductory History.* Madison: University of Wisconsin Press, 1996.

Kemp, Martin. *The Science of Art: Optical Themes in Western Art from Brunelleschi to Seurat.* New Haven, Conn.: Yale University Press, 1990.

Kirkham, Pat, and Susan Weber, eds. *History of Design: Decorative Arts and Material Culture, 1400–2000.* New Haven, Conn.: Yale University Press, 2013.

Kostof, Spiro, and Gregory Castillo. *A History of Architecture: Settings and Rituals.* 2d ed. Oxford: Oxford University Press, 1995.

Kultermann, Udo. *The History of Art History.* New York: Abaris, 1993.

Le Fur, Yves, ed. *Musée du Quai Branly: The Collection. Art from Africa, Asia, Oceania, and the Americas.* Paris: Flammarion, 2009.

Lucie-Smith, Edward. *The Thames & Hudson Dictionary of Art Terms.* 2d ed. New York: Thames & Hudson, 2004.

Moffett, Marian, Michael Fazio, and Lawrence Wadehouse. *A World History of Architecture.* Boston: McGraw-Hill, 2004.

Morgan, Anne Lee. *Oxford Dictionary of American Art and Artists.* New York: Oxford University Press, 2008.

Murray, Peter, and Linda Murray. *The Penguin Dictionary of Art and Artists.* 7th ed. New York: Penguin, 1998.

Nelson, Robert S., and Richard Shiff, eds. *Critical Terms for Art History.* Chicago: University of Chicago Press, 1996.

Nici, John B. *Famous Works of Art—And How They Got That Way.* New York: Rowman & Littlefield, 2015.

Pazanelli, Roberta, ed. *The Color of Life: Polychromy in Sculpture from Antiquity to the Present.* Los Angeles: J. Paul Getty Museum, 2008.

Penny, Nicholas. *The Materials of Sculpture.* New Haven, Conn.: Yale University Press, 1993.

Pevsner, Nikolaus. *A History of Building Types.* London: Thames & Hudson, 1987. Reprint of 1979 ed.

———. *An Outline of European Architecture.* 8th ed. Baltimore: Penguin, 1974.

Pierce, James Smith. *From Abacus to Zeus: A Handbook of Art History.* 7th ed. Upper Saddle River, N.J.: Pearson Prentice Hall, 1998.

Placzek, Adolf K., ed. *Macmillan Encyclopedia of Architects.* 4 vols. New York: Macmillan, 1982.

Podro, Michael. *The Critical Historians of Art.* New Haven, Conn.: Yale University Press, 1982.

Pollock, Griselda. *Vision and Difference: Femininity, Feminism, and Histories of Art.* London: Routledge, 1988.

Pregill, Philip, and Nancy Volkman. *Landscapes in History Design and Planning in the Eastern and Western Traditions.* 2d ed. Hoboken, N.J.: Wiley, 1999.

Preziosi, Donald, ed. *The Art of Art History: A Critical Anthology.* New York: Oxford University Press, 1998.

Read, Herbert. *The Thames & Hudson Dictionary of Art and Artists.* Rev. ed. New York: Thames & Hudson, 1994.

Reid, Jane D. *The Oxford Guide to Classical Mythology in the Arts 1300–1990s.* 2 vols. New York: Oxford University Press, 1993.

Rogers, Elizabeth Barlow. *Landscape Design: A Cultural and Architectural History.* New York: Abrams, 2001.

Roth, Leland M. *Understanding Architecture: Its Elements, History, and Meaning.* 2d ed. Boulder, Colo.: Westview, 2006.

Schama, Simon. *The Power of Art.* New York: Ecco, 2006.

Slatkin, Wendy. *Women Artists in History: From Antiquity to the 20th Century.* 4th ed. Upper Saddle River, N.J.: Prentice Hall, 2000.

Squire, Michael. *The Art of the Body: Antiquity and Its Legacy.* New York: Oxford University Press, 2011.

Steer, John, and Antony White. *Atlas of Western Art History: Artists, Sites, and Monuments from Ancient Greece to the Modern Age.* New York: Facts on File, 1994.

Stratton, Arthur. *The Orders of Architecture: Greek, Roman, and Renaissance.* London: Studio, 1986.

Summers, David. *Real Spaces: World Art History and the Rise of Western Modernism.* London: Phaidon, 2003.

Sutcliffe, Antony. *Paris: An Architectural History.* New Haven, Conn.: Yale University Press, 1996.

Sutton, Ian. *Western Architecture: From Ancient Greece to the Present.* New York: Thames & Hudson, 1999.

Trachtenberg, Marvin, and Isabelle Hyman. *Architecture, from Prehistory to Post-Modernism.* 2d ed. Upper Saddle River, N.J.: Prentice Hall, 2003.

Turner, Jane, ed. *The Dictionary of Art.* 34 vols. New ed. New York: Oxford University Press, 2003.

Watkin, David. *A History of Western Architecture.* 5th ed. London: Laurence King, 2011.

Wescoat, Bonna D., and Robert G. Ousterhout, eds. *Architecture of the Sacred: Space, Ritual, and Experience from Classical Greece to Byzantium.* New York: Cambridge University Press, 2012.

West, Shearer. *Portraiture.* New York: Oxford University Press, 2004.

Wittkower, Rudolf. *Sculpture Processes and Principles.* New York: Harper & Row, 1977.

Wren, Linnea H., and Janine M. Carter, eds. *Perspectives on Western Art: Source Documents and Readings from the Ancient Near East through the Middle Ages.* New York: Harper & Row, 1987.

Zaczek, Iain. *A Chronology of Art.* New York: Thames & Hudson, 2018.

Zijlmans, Kitty, and Wilfried van Damme, eds. *World Art Studies: Exploring Concepts and Approaches.* Amsterdam: Valiz, 2008.

Ancient Art, General

Aruz, Joan, and Ronald Wallenfels, eds. *Art of the First Cities: The Third Millennium BC from the Mediterranean to the Indus.* New York: Metropolitan Museum of Art, 2003.

Beard, Mary, and John Henderson. *Classical Art: From Greece to Rome.* New York: Oxford University Press, 2001.

Boardman, John, ed. *The Oxford History of Classical Art.* New York: Oxford University Press, 1997.

Boardman, John. *The World of Ancient Art.* London: Thames & Hudson, 2006.

Chitham, Robert. *The Classical Orders of Architecture.* 2d ed. Boston: Architectural Press, 2005.

Clayton, Peter A., and Martin J. Price, eds. *The Seven Wonders of the Ancient World.* New York: Routledge, 1988.

Connolly, Peter, and Hazel Dodge. *The Ancient City: Life in Classical Athens and Rome.* New York: Oxford University Press, 1998.

De Grummond, Nancy Thomson, ed. *An Encyclopedia of the History of Classical Archaeology.* 2 vols. Westport, Conn.: Greenwood, 1996.

Dunbabin, Katherine. *Mosaics of the Greek and Roman World.* New York: Cambridge University Press, 1999.

Gates, Charles. *Ancient Cities: The Archaeology of Urban Life in the Ancient Near East and Egypt, Greece, and Rome.* 2d ed. London: Routledge, 2011.

Grossman, Janet Burnett. *Looking at Greek and Roman Sculpture in Stone: A Guide to Terms, Styles, and Techniques.* Los Angeles: J. Paul Getty Museum, 2003.

Kampen, Natalie B., ed. *Sexuality in Ancient Art.* New York: Cambridge University Press, 1996.

Lexicon Iconographicum Mythologiae Classicae. 10 vols. Zurich: Artemis, 1981–1999.

Ling, Roger. *Ancient Mosaics.* Princeton, N.J.: Princeton University Press, 1998.

Lloyd, Seton, and Hans Wolfgang Muller. *Ancient Architecture: Mesopotamia, Egypt, Crete.* New York: Electa/Rizzoli, 1980.

Malacrino, Carmelo. *Constructing the Ancient World: Architectural Techniques of the Greeks and Romans.* Los Angeles: J. Paul Getty Museum, 2010.

Marconi, Clemente, ed. *The Oxford Handbook of Greek and Roman Art and Architecture.* New York: Oxford University Press, 2014.

Oleson, John Peter, ed. *The Oxford Handbook of Engineering and Technology in the Classical World.* New York: Oxford University Press, 2008.

Oliphant, Margaret. *The Atlas of the Ancient World: Charting the Great Civilizations of the Past.* New York: Simon & Schuster, 1992.

Onians, John. *Classical Art and the Cultures of Greece and Rome.* New Haven, Conn.: Yale University Press, 1999.

Renfrew, Colin, and Paul G. Bahn. *Archaeology: Theories, Methods, and Practices.* London: Thames & Hudson, 1991.

Stillwell, Richard, William L. MacDonald, and Marian H. McAllister, eds. *The Princeton Encyclopedia of Classical Sites.* Princeton, N.J.: Princeton University Press, 1976.

Trigger, Bruce. *Understanding Early Civilizations: A Comparative Study.* New York: Cambridge University Press, 2003.

Ward-Perkins, John B. *Cities of Ancient Greece and Italy: Planning in Classical Antiquity.* Rev. ed. New York: Braziller, 1987.

Wolf, Walther. *The Origins of Western Art: Egypt, Mesopotamia, the Aegean.* New York: Universe, 1989.

CHAPTER 1
Art in the Stone Age

Aujoulat, Norbert. *Lascaux: Movement, Space, and Time.* New York: Abrams, 2005.

Bahn, Paul G. *The Cambridge Illustrated History of Prehistoric Art.* New York: Cambridge University Press, 1998.

———. *Cave Art: A Guide to the Decorated Ice Age Caves of Europe.* London: Frances Lincoln, 2007.

Bahn, Paul G., and Jean Vertut. *Journey through the Ice Age.* Berkeley: University of California Press, 1997.

Beltrán, Antonio, ed. *The Cave of Altamira.* New York: Abrams, 1999.

Berhgaus, Guner. *New Perspectives on Prehistoric Art.* Westport, Conn.: Praeger, 2004.

Burl, Aubrey. *Great Stone Circles.* New Haven, Conn.: Yale University Press, 1999.

Chauvet, Jean-Marie, Eliette Brunel Deschamps, and Christian Hillaire. *Dawn of Art: The Chauvet Cave.* New York: Abrams, 1996.

Chippindale, Christopher. *Stonehenge Complete.* 3d ed. New York: Thames & Hudson, 2004.

Clottes, Jean. *Cave Art.* London: Phaidon, 2008.

———. *Chauvet Cave: The Art of Earliest Times.* Salt Lake City: University of Utah Press, 2003.

———. *What Is Paleolithic Art? Cave Paintings and the Dawn of Human Creativity.* Chicago: University of Chicago Press, 2016.

Cunliffe, Barry, ed. *The Oxford Illustrated Prehistory of Europe.* New York: Oxford University Press, 2001.

Guthrie, R. Dale. *The Nature of Paleolithic Art.* Chicago: University of Chicago Press, 2005.

Hodder, Ian. *The Leopard's Tale: Revealing the Mysteries of Çatalhöyük*. London: Thames & Hudson, 2006.

Kenyon, Kathleen M. *Digging up Jericho*. New York: Praeger, 1974.

Leroi-Gourhan, André. *The Dawn of European Art: An Introduction to Paleolithic Cave Painting*. Cambridge: Cambridge University Press, 1982.

Marshack, Alexander. *The Roots of Civilization: The Cognitive Beginnings of Man's First Art, Symbol and Notation*. 2d ed. Wakefield, R.I.: Moyer Bell, 1991.

Pfeiffer, John E. *The Creative Explosion: An Inquiry into the Origins of Art and Religion*. New York: Harper & Row, 1982.

Renfrew, Colin, ed. *British Prehistory: A New Outline*. London: Noyes, 1975.

Ruspoli, Mario. *The Cave of Lascaux: The Final Photographs*. New York: Abrams, 1987.

Scarre, Chris. *Exploring Prehistoric Europe*. New York: Oxford University Press, 1998.

Wainwright, Geoffrey. *The Henge Monuments: Ceremony and Society in Prehistoric Britain*. London: Thames & Hudson, 1990.

White, Randall. *Prehistoric Art: The Symbolic Journey of Humankind*. New York: Abrams, 2003.

Whitley, David S. *Cave Paintings and the Human Spirit: The Origin of Creativity and Belief*. Amherst, N.Y.: Prometheus, 2009.

CHAPTER 2
Ancient Mesopotamia and Persia

Akurgal, Ekrem. *Art of the Hittites*. New York: Abrams, 1962.

Allen, Lindsay. *The Persian Empire*. Chicago: University of Chicago Press, 2005.

Amiet, Pierre. *Art of the Ancient Near East*. New York: Abrams, 1980.

Ascalone, Enrico. *Mesopotamia: Assyrians, Sumerians, Babylonians*. Berkeley and Los Angeles: University of California Press, 2007.

Bahrani, Zainab. *Art of Mesopotamia*. New York: Thames & Hudson, 2017.

———. *The Graven Image: Representation in Babylonia and Assyria*. Philadelphia: University of Pennsylvania Press, 2003.

Bienkowski, Piotr, and Alan Millard, eds. *Dictionary of the Ancient Near East*. Philadelphia: University of Pennsylvania Press, 2000.

Collins, Paul. *Assyrian Palace Sculptures*. Austin: University of Texas Press, 2008.

Collon, Dominique. *Ancient Near Eastern Art*. Berkeley: University of California Press, 1995.

———. *First Impressions: Cylinder Seals in the Ancient Near East*. 2d ed. London: British Museum, 1993.

———. *Near Eastern Seals*. Berkeley: University of California Press, 1990.

Crawford, Harriet. *Sumer and the Sumerians*. 2d ed. New York: Cambridge University Press, 2004.

———, ed. *The Sumerian World*. London: Routledge, 2013.

———. *Ur: The City of the Moon God*. London: Bloomsbury Academic, 2015.

Curatola, Giovanni, ed. *The Art and Architecture of Mesopotamia*. New York: Abbeville, 2007.

Curtis, John E. *Ancient Persia*. Cambridge, Mass.: Harvard University Press, 1990.

Curtis, John E., and Julian E. Reade. *Art and Empire: Treasures from Assyria in the British Museum*. New York: Metropolitan Museum of Art, 1995.

Curtis, John E., and Nigel Tallis, eds. *Forgotten Empire: The World of Ancient Persia*. Berkeley: University of California Press, 2005.

Finkel, Irving L., and Michael J. Seymour, eds. *Babylon*. New York: Oxford University Press, 2008.

Foster, Benjamin R., and Karen Polinger Foster. *Civilizations of Ancient Iraq*. Princeton, N.J.: Princeton University Press, 2009.

Frankfort, Henri. *The Art and Architecture of the Ancient Orient*. 5th ed. New Haven, Conn.: Yale University Press, 1996.

Ghirshman, Roman. *The Arts of Ancient Iran: From Its Origins to the Time of Alexander the Great*. New York: Golden, 1964.

———. *Persian Art: The Parthian and Sassanian Dynasties, 249 BC–AD 651*. New York: Golden, 1962.

Gunter, Ann C., ed. *Investigating Artistic Environments in the Ancient Near East*. Washington, D.C.: Arthur M. Sackler Gallery, 1990.

Harper, Prudence O., Joan Aruz, and Françoise Tallon, eds. *The Royal City of Susa: Ancient Near Eastern Treasures in the Louvre*. New York: Metropolitan Museum of Art, 1992.

Leick, Gwendolyn. *Mesopotamia: The Invention of the City*. New York: Penguin, 2003.

Lloyd, Seton. *The Archaeology of Mesopotamia: From the Old Stone Age to the Persian Conquest*. London: Thames & Hudson, 1984.

Macqueen, James G. *The Hittites and Their Contemporaries in Asia Minor*. Rev. ed. New York: Thames & Hudson, 1986.

Meyers, Eric M., ed. *The Oxford Encyclopedia of Archaeology in the Near East*. 5 vols. New York: Oxford University Press, 1997.

Moortgat, Anton. *The Art of Ancient Mesopotamia*. New York: Phaidon, 1969.

Oates, Joan. *Babylon*. Rev. ed. London: Thames & Hudson, 1986.

Parrot, André. *The Arts of Assyria*. New York: Golden, 1961.

———. *Sumer: The Dawn of Art*. New York: Golden, 1961.

Porada, Edith. *Man and Images in the Ancient Near East*. Wakefield, R.I.: Moyer Bell, 1995.

Porada, Edith, and Robert H. Dyson. *The Art of Ancient Iran: Pre-Islamic Cultures*. Rev. ed. New York: Greystone, 1969.

Postgate, J. Nicholas. *Early Mesopotamia: Society and Economy at the Dawn of History*. London: Routledge, 1992.

Potts, Daniel T. *The Archaeology of Elam: Formation and Transformation of an Ancient Iranian State*. New York: Cambridge University Press, 1999.

Reade, Julian E. *Assyrian Sculpture*. Cambridge, Mass.: Harvard University Press, 1999.

———. *Mesopotamia*. Cambridge, Mass.: Harvard University Press, 1991.

Roaf, Michael. *Cultural Atlas of Mesopotamia and the Ancient Near East*. New York: Facts on File, 1990.

Russell, John M. *Sennacherib's Palace without Rival at Nineveh*. Chicago: University of Chicago Press, 1991.

Saggs, H.W.F. *Babylonians*. London: British Museum, 1995.

Sasson, Jack M., ed. *Civilizations of the Ancient Near East*. 4 vols. New York: Scribner, 1995.

Snell, Daniel C. *Life in the Ancient Near East: 3100–332 BC*. New Haven, Conn.: Yale University Press, 1997.

Strommenger, Eva, and Max Hirmer. *5,000 Years of the Art of Mesopotamia*. New York: Abrams, 1964.

Suter, Claudia E. *Gudea's Temple Building: The Representation of an Early Mesopotamian Ruler in Text and Image*. Groningen: Styx, 2000.

Van de Mieroop, Marc. *The Ancient Mesopotamian City*. New York: Oxford University Press, 1997.

Winter, Irene J. *On Art in the Ancient Near East*. 2 vols. Leiden: Brill, 2010.

Zettler, Richard L., and Lee Horne. *Treasures from the Royal Tombs of Ur*. Philadelphia: University of Pennsylvania Museum of Archaeology and Anthropology, 1998.

CHAPTER 3
Egypt from Narmer to Cleopatra

Allen, James P., ed., *Egyptian Art in the Age of the Pyramids*. New York: Abrams, 1999.

Arnold, Dieter. *Building in Egypt: Pharaonic Stone Masonry*. New York: Oxford University Press, 1991.

Arnold, Dorothea. *The Royal Women of Amarna*. New York: Metropolitan Museum of Art, 1996.

Baines, John, and Jaromír Málek. *Atlas of Ancient Egypt*. New York: Facts on File, 1980.

Bard, Kathryn A., ed. *Encyclopedia of the Archaeology of Ancient Egypt*. London: Routledge, 1999.

———. *An Introduction to the Archaeology of Ancient Egypt*. Oxford: Blackwell, 2007.

Bianchi, Robert S. *Cleopatra's Egypt: Age of the Ptolemies*. Brooklyn: Brooklyn Museum, 1988.

Capel, Anne K., and Glenn E. Markoe, eds. *Mistress of the House, Mistress of Heaven: Women in Ancient Egypt*. New York: Hudson Hills, 1996.

D'Auria, Sue, Peter Lacovara, and Catharine H. Roehrig. *Mummies and Magic: The Funerary Arts of Ancient Egypt*. Boston: Museum of Fine Arts, 1988.

Dodson, Aidam, and Salima Ikram. *The Tomb in Ancient Egypt*. New York: Thames & Hudson, 2008.

Emberling, Geoff. *Nubia: Ancient Kingdoms of Africa*. Princeton, N.J.: Princeton University Press, 2011.

Hawass, Zahi. *Valley of the Golden Mummies*. New York: Abrams, 2000.

Ikram, Salima, and Aidan Dodson. *The Mummy in Ancient Egypt: Equipping the Dead for Eternity*. New York: Thames & Hudson, 1998.

Kemp, Barry J. *Ancient Egypt: Anatomy of a Civilization*. 2d ed. New York: Routledge, 2006.

Kozloff, Arielle P., and Betsy M. Bryan. *Egypt's Dazzling Sun: Amenhotep III and His World*. Cleveland: Cleveland Museum of Art, 1992.

Lange, Kurt, and Max Hirmer. *Egypt: Architecture, Sculpture, and Painting in Three Thousand Years*. 4th ed. London: Phaidon, 1968.

Lehner, Mark. *The Complete Pyramids: Solving the Ancient Mysteries*. New York: Thames & Hudson, 1997.

Málek, Jaromír. *Egypt: 4,000 Years of Art*. New York: Phaidon, 2003.

———. *Egyptian Art*. London: Phaidon, 1999.

Redford, Donald B. *Akhenaton, the Heretic King.* Princeton, N.J.: Princeton University Press, 1984.

———, ed. *The Oxford Encyclopedia of Ancient Egypt.* 3 vols. New York: Oxford University Press, 2001.

Reeves, C. Nicholas. *The Complete Tutankhamun: The King, the Tomb, the Royal Treasure.* London: Thames & Hudson, 1990.

Robins, Gay. *The Art of Ancient Egypt.* Rev. ed. Cambridge, Mass.: Harvard University Press, 2008.

———. *Egyptian Painting and Relief.* Aylesbury: Shire, 1986.

———. *Proportion and Style in Ancient Egyptian Art.* Austin: University of Texas Press, 1994.

———. *Women in Ancient Egypt.* London: British Museum, 1993.

Romer, John. *Valley of the Kings: Exploring the Tombs of the Pharaohs.* New York: Holt, 1994.

Russmann, Edna R. *Egyptian Sculpture: Cairo and Luxor.* Austin: University of Texas Press, 1989.

Schäfer, Heinrich. *Principles of Egyptian Art.* Rev. ed. Oxford: Clarendon, 1986.

Schulz, Regina, and Matthias Seidel, eds. *Egypt: The World of the Pharaohs.* Cologne: Könemann, 1999.

Shafer, Byron E., ed. *Temples of Ancient Egypt.* Ithaca, N.Y.: Cornell University Press, 1997.

Shaw, Ian, and Paul Nicholson. *The Dictionary of Ancient Egypt.* London: British Museum, 1995.

Smith, William Stevenson, and William Kelly Simpson. *The Art and Architecture of Ancient Egypt.* Rev. ed. New Haven, Conn.: Yale University Press, 1998.

Snape, Steven. *Ancient Egyptian Tombs: The Culture of Life and Death.* Oxford: Wiley-Blackwell, 2011.

Taylor, John H. *Journey through the Afterlife: The Ancient Egyptian Book of the Dead.* Cambridge, Mass.: Harvard University Press, 2010.

Tiradritti, Francesco. *Egyptian Wall Paintings.* New York: Abbeville, 2008.

Weeks, Kent R. *The Treasures of Luxor and the Valley of the Kings.* Vercelli: White Star, 2005.

———, ed. *Valley of the Kings.* Vercelli: White Star, 2001.

Wenke, Robert J. *The Ancient Egyptian State: The Origins of Egyptian Culture (c. 8000–2000 BC).* New York: Cambridge University Press, 2009.

Wildung, Dietrich. *Egypt: From Prehistory to the Romans.* Cologne: Taschen, 1997.

Wilkinson, Toby. *The Egyptian World.* London: Routledge, 2009.

CHAPTER 4
The Prehistoric Aegean

Andreadaki-Vlazaki, Maria, ed. *From the Land of the Labyrinth: Minoan Crete 3000–1100 B.C.* New York: Alexander S. Onassis Public Benefit Foundation, 2008.

Barber, R.L.N. *The Cyclades in the Bronze Age.* Iowa City: University of Iowa Press, 1987.

Betancourt, Philip P. *A History of Minoan Pottery.* Princeton, N.J.: Princeton University Press, 1965.

———. *Introduction to Aegean Art.* New York: Institute for Aegean Prehistory, 2007.

Cadogan, Gerald. *Palaces of Minoan Crete.* London: Methuen, 1980.

Castleden, Rodney. *Mycenaeans.* London: Routledge, 2005.

Chadwick, John. *The Mycenaean World.* New York: Cambridge University Press, 1976.

Cline, Eric H., ed. *The Oxford Handbook of the Bronze Age Aegean.* New York: Oxford University Press, 2010.

Cullen, Tracey, ed. *Aegean Prehistory: A Review.* Boston: Archaeological Institute of America, 2001.

Demargne, Pierre. *The Birth of Greek Art.* New York: Golden, 1964.

Dickinson, Oliver P.T.K. *The Aegean Bronze Age.* New York: Cambridge University Press, 1994.

Doumas, Christos. *Thera, Pompeii of the Ancient Aegean: Excavations at Akrotiri, 1967–1979.* New York: Thames & Hudson, 1983.

———. *The Wall-Paintings of Thera.* Athens: Thera Foundation, 1992.

Fitton, J. Lesley. *Cycladic Art.* 2d ed. Cambridge, Mass.: Harvard University Press, 1999.

———. *The Discovery of the Greek Bronze Age.* London: British Museum, 1995.

Forsyth, Phyllis Young. *Thera in the Bronze Age.* New York: Peter Lang, 1997.

Getz-Preziosi, Patricia. *Sculptors of the Cyclades: Individual and Tradition in the Third Millennium BC.* Ann Arbor: University of Michigan Press, 1987.

Graham, James W. *The Palaces of Crete.* Princeton, N.J.: Princeton University Press, 1987.

Hampe, Roland, and Erika Simon. *The Birth of Greek Art: From the Mycenaean to the Archaic Period.* New York: Oxford University Press, 1981.

Higgins, Reynold. *Minoan and Mycenaean Art.* Rev. ed. New York: Thames & Hudson, 1997.

Hood, Sinclair. *The Arts in Prehistoric Greece.* New Haven, Conn.: Yale University Press, 1992.

Immerwahr, Sarah A. *Aegean Painting in the Bronze Age.* University Park: Pennsylvania State University Press, 1990.

MacGillivray, J. A. *Minotaur: Sir Arthur Evans and the Archaeology of the Minoan Myth.* New York: Hill and Wang, 2000.

Marinatos, Nanno. *Art and Religion in Thera: Reconstructing a Bronze Age Society.* Athens: Mathioulakis, 1984.

Marinatos, Spyridon, and Max Hirmer. *Crete and Mycenae.* London: Thames & Hudson, 1960.

McDonald, William A., and Carol G. Thomas. *Progress into the Past: The Rediscovery of Mycenaean Civilization.* 2d ed. Bloomington: Indiana University Press, 1990.

McEnroe, John. *Architecture of Minoan Crete: Constructing Identity in the Aegean Bronze Age.* Austin: University of Texas Press, 2010.

Preziosi, Donald, and Louise A. Hitchcock. *Aegean Art and Architecture.* New York: Oxford University Press, 1999.

Schofield, Louise. *The Mycenaeans.* London: British Museum, 2007.

Shaw, Joseph W. *Elite Minoan Architecture: Its Development at Knossos, Phaistos, and Malia.* Philadelphia: INSTAP Academic Press, 2015.

———. *Minoan Architecture: Materials and Techniques.* Padua: Centro di Archeologia Cretese, 2009.

Shelmerdine, Cynthia W., ed. *The Cambridge Companion to the Aegean Bronze Age.* New York: Cambridge University Press, 2008.

Taylour, Lord William. *The Mycenaeans.* London: Thames & Hudson, 1990.

Vermeule, Emily. *Greece in the Bronze Age.* Chicago: University of Chicago Press, 1972.

Warren, Peter. *The Aegean Civilizations: The Making of the Past.* New York: Peter Bedrick, 1989.

CHAPTER 5
Ancient Greece

Arias, Paolo. *A History of One Thousand Years of Greek Vase Painting.* New York: Abrams, 1962.

Ashmole, Bernard. *Architect and Sculptor in Classical Greece.* New York: New York University Press, 1972.

Barletta, Barbara A. *The Origins of the Greek Architectural Orders.* New York: Cambridge University Press, 2001.

Berve, Helmut, Gottfried Gruben, and Max Hirmer. *Greek Temples, Theatres, and Shrines.* New York: Abrams, 1963.

Biers, William. *The Archaeology of Greece: An Introduction.* 2d ed. Ithaca, N.Y.: Cornell University Press, 1996.

Boardman, John. *Athenian Black Figure Vases.* Rev. ed. New York: Thames & Hudson, 1991.

———. *Athenian Red Figure Vases: The Archaic Period.* New York: Thames & Hudson, 1988.

———. *Athenian Red Figure Vases: The Classical Period.* New York: Thames & Hudson, 1989.

———. *Early Greek Vase Painting, 11th–6th Centuries BC.* New York: Thames & Hudson, 1998.

———. *Greek Sculpture: The Archaic Period.* Rev. ed. New York: Thames & Hudson, 1985.

———. *Greek Sculpture: The Classical Period.* New York: Thames & Hudson, 1987.

———. *Greek Sculpture: The Late Classical Period and Sculpture in Colonies and Overseas.* New York: Thames & Hudson, 1995.

———. *The Parthenon and Its Sculpture.* Austin: University of Texas Press, 1985.

Camp, John M. *The Archaeology of Athens.* New Haven, Conn.: Yale University Press, 2001.

Carpenter, Thomas H. *Art and Myth in Ancient Greece.* New York: Thames & Hudson, 1991.

Charbonneaux, Jean, Roland Martin, and François Villard. *Archaic Greek Art.* New York: Braziller, 1971.

———. *Classical Greek Art.* New York: Braziller, 1972.

———. *Hellenistic Art.* New York: Braziller, 1973.

Clark, Andrew J., Maya Elston, and Mary Louise Hart. *Understanding Greek Vases: A Guide to Terms, Styles, and Techniques.* Los Angeles: J. Paul Getty Museum, 2002.

Cohen, Beth, ed. *The Colors of Clay: Special Techniques in Athenian Vases.* Los Angeles: J. Paul Getty Museum, 2006.

Cohn, Ada. *The Alexander Mosaic: Stories of Victory and Defeat.* New York: Cambridge University Press, 1997.

Coldstream, J. Nicholas. *Geometric Greece: 900–700 BC.* 2d ed. London: Routledge, 2003.

Coulton, J. J. *Ancient Greek Architects at Work.* Ithaca, N.Y.: Cornell University Press, 1982.

Donohue, A. A. *Greek Sculpture and the Problem of Description.* New York: Cambridge University Press, 2005.

Fullerton, Mark D. *Greek Art.* New York: Cambridge University Press, 2000.

Gunter, Ann C. *Greek Art and the Orient.* New York: Cambridge University Press, 2009.

Haynes, Denys E. L. *The Technique of Greek Bronze Statuary.* Mainz: von Zabern, 1992.

Houser, Caroline. *Greek Monumental Bronze Sculpture.* New York: Vendome, 1983.

Hurwit, Jeffrey M. *The Acropolis in the Age of Pericles.* New York: Cambridge University Press, 2004.

———. *The Art and Culture of Early Greece, 1100–480 BC.* Ithaca, N.Y.: Cornell University Press, 1985.

———. *The Athenian Acropolis: History, Mythology, and Archaeology from the Neolithic Era to the Present.* New York: Cambridge University Press, 1999.

Jenkins, Ian. *Greek Architecture and Its Sculpture.* Cambridge, Mass.: Harvard University Press, 2006.

———. *The Parthenon Frieze.* Austin: University of Texas Press, 1994.

Jones, Mark Wilson. *Origins of Classical Architecture: Temples, Orders, and Gifts to the Gods in Ancient Greece.* New Haven, Conn.: Yale University Press, 2014.

Junker, Klaus. *Interpreting the Images of Greek Myths: An Introduction.* New York: Cambridge University Press, 2012.

Keesling, Catherine M. *The Votive Statues of the Athenian Acropolis.* New York: Cambridge University Press, 2008.

Lawrence, Arnold W., and R. A. Tomlinson. *Greek Architecture.* Rev. ed. New Haven, Conn.: Yale University Press, 1996.

Martin, Roland. *Greek Architecture: Architecture of Crete, Greece, and the Greek World.* New York: Electa/Rizzoli, 1988.

Mattusch, Carol C. *Classical Bronzes: The Art and Craft of Greek and Roman Statuary.* Ithaca, N.Y.: Cornell University Press, 1996.

———. *Greek Bronze Statuary from the Beginnings through the Fifth Century BC.* Ithaca, N.Y.: Cornell University Press, 1988.

Mee, Christopher. *Greek Archaeology.* Hoboken, N.J.: Wiley-Blackwell, 2011.

Mee, Christopher, and Tony Spawforth. *Greece: An Oxford Archaeological Guide.* New York: Oxford University Press, 2001.

Morris, Sarah P. *Daidalos and the Origins of Greek Art.* Princeton, N.J.: Princeton University Press, 1992.

Neer, Richard T. *The Emergence of the Classical Style in Greek Sculpture.* Chicago: University of Chicago Press, 2010.

———. *Greek Art and Archaeology: A New History, c. 2500–150 BCE.* New York: Thames & Hudson, 2011.

Osborne, Robin. *Archaic and Classical Greek Art.* New York: Oxford University Press, 1998.

Palagia, Olga, ed. *Greek Sculpture: Functions, Materials, and Techniques in the Archaic and Classical Periods.* New York: Cambridge University Press, 2006.

———. *The Pediments of the Parthenon.* Leiden: E. J. Brill, 1993.

Palagia, Olga, and Jerome J. Pollitt. *Personal Styles in Greek Sculpture.* New York: Cambridge University Press, 1996.

Pedley, John Griffiths. *Greek Art and Archaeology.* 4th ed. Upper Saddle River, N.J.: Prentice Hall, 2007.

———. *Sanctuaries and the Sacred in the Ancient Greek World.* New York: Cambridge University Press, 2005.

Petrakos, Vasileios. *Great Moments in Greek Archaeology.* Los Angeles: J. Paul Getty Museum, 2007.

Pollitt, Jerome J. *Art and Experience in Classical Greece.* New York: Cambridge University Press, 1972.

———. *Art in the Hellenistic Age.* New York: Cambridge University Press, 1986.

———. *The Art of Ancient Greece: Sources and Documents.* 2d ed. New York: Cambridge University Press, 1990.

Pugliese Carratelli, G. *The Greek World: Art and Civilization in Magna Graecia and Sicily.* New York: Rizzoli, 1996.

Reeder, Ellen D., ed. *Pandora: Women in Classical Greece.* Baltimore: Walters Art Gallery, 1995.

Rhodes, Robin F. *Architecture and Meaning on the Athenian Acropolis.* New York: Cambridge University Press, 1995.

Richter, Gisela M. *The Portraits of the Greeks.* Rev. ed. by R.R.R. Smith. Ithaca, N.Y.: Cornell University Press, 1984.

Ridgway, Brunilde S. *The Archaic Style in Greek Sculpture.* 2d ed. Chicago: Ares, 1993.

———. *Fifth-Century Styles in Greek Sculpture.* Princeton, N.J.: Princeton University Press, 1981.

———. *Fourth-Century Styles in Greek Sculpture.* Madison: University of Wisconsin Press, 1997.

———. *Hellenistic Sculpture I: The Styles of ca. 331–200 BC.* Madison: University of Wisconsin Press, 1990.

———. *Hellenistic Sculpture II: The Styles of ca. 200–100 BC.* Madison: University of Wisconsin Press, 2000.

———. *Prayers in Stone: Greek Architectural Sculpture.* Berkeley: University of California Press, 1999.

———. *Roman Copies of Greek Sculpture: The Problem of the Originals.* Ann Arbor: University of Michigan Press, 1984.

———. *The Severe Style in Greek Sculpture.* Princeton, N.J.: Princeton University Press, 1970.

Robertson, Martin. *The Art of Vase-Painting in Classical Athens.* New York: Cambridge University Press, 1992.

———. *A History of Greek Art.* Rev. ed. 2 vols. New York: Cambridge University Press, 1986.

———. *A Shorter History of Greek Art.* New York: Cambridge University Press, 1981.

Shapiro, H. Alan. *Art and Cult in Athens under the Tyrants.* Mainz: von Zabern, 1989.

———. *Myth into Art: Poet and Painter in Classical Greece.* New York: Routledge, 1994.

Smith, R.R.R. *Hellenistic Sculpture.* New York: Thames & Hudson, 1991.

Smith, Tyler Jo, and Dimitris Plantzos, eds. *A Companion to Greek Art.* Hoboken, N.J.: Wiley-Blackwell, 2012.

Spawforth, Tony. *The Complete Greek Temples.* London, Thames & Hudson, 2006.

Spivey, Nigel. *Greek Art.* London: Phaidon, 1997.

———. *Greek Sculpture.* New York: Cambridge University Press, 2013.

Stansbury-O'Donnell, Mark D. *A History of Greek Art.* Hoboken, N.J.: Wiley-Blackwell, 2015.

———. *Looking at Greek Art.* New York: Cambridge University Press, 2011.

———. *Pictorial Narrative in Ancient Greek Art.* New York: Cambridge University Press, 1999.

Stewart, Andrew. *Art, Desire, and the Body in Ancient Greece.* New York: Cambridge University Press, 1997.

———. *Art in the Hellenistic World: An Introduction.* New York: Cambridge University Press, 2014.

———. *Classical Greece and the Birth of Western Art.* New York: Cambridge University Press, 2008.

———. *Greek Sculpture: An Exploration.* 2 vols. New Haven, Conn.: Yale University Press, 1990.

Stuttard, David. *Parthenon: Power and Politics on the Acropolis.* London: British Museum, 2013.

Whitley, James. *The Archaeology of Ancient Greece.* New York: Cambridge University Press, 2001.

Wycherley, Richard E. *How the Greeks Built Cities.* New York: Norton, 1976.

CHAPTER 6
The Etruscans

Banti, Luisa. *The Etruscan Cities and Their Culture.* Berkeley: University of California Press, 1973.

Barker, Graeme, and Tom Rasmussen. *The Etruscans.* Oxford: Blackwell, 1998.

Boethius, Axel. *Etruscan and Early Roman Architecture.* 2d ed. New Haven, Conn.: Yale University Press, 1978.

Bonfante, Larissa, ed. *Etruscan Life and Afterlife: A Handbook of Etruscan Studies.* Detroit: Wayne State University Press, 1986.

Brendel, Otto J. *Etruscan Art.* 2d ed. New Haven, Conn.: Yale University Press, 1995.

Cristofani, Mauro. *The Etruscans: A New Investigation.* London: Orbis, 1979.

De Grummond, Nancy Thomson. *Etruscan Myth, Sacred History, and Legend.* Philadelphia: University of Pennsylvania Museum, 2006.

De Grummond, Nancy Thomson, and Ingrid Edlund-Berry, eds. *The Archaeology of Sanctuaries and Ritual in Etruria.* Portsmouth, R.I.: Journal of Roman Archaeology, 2011.

De Grummond, Nancy Thomson, and Lisa Pieraccini, eds. *Caere.* Austin: University of Texas Press, 2016.

De Grummond, Nancy Thomson, and Erika Simon. *The Religion of the Etruscans.* Austin: University of Texas Press, 2006.

Hall, John F. *Etruscan Italy: Etruscan Influences on the Civilizations of Italy from Antiquity to the Modern Era.* Bloomington: Indiana University Press, 1996.

Haynes, Sybille. *Etruscan Civilization: A Cultural History.* Los Angeles: J. Paul Getty Museum, 2000.

Heurgon, Jacques. *Daily Life of the Etruscans.* London: Weidenfeld & Nicolson, 1964.

Izzet, Vedia. *The Archaeology of Etruscan Society.* New York: Cambridge University Press, 2007.

Lulof, Patricia S., and Iefke van Kampen, eds. *Etruscans: Eminent Women, Powerful Men.* Zwolle, the Netherlands: W Books, 2011.

Pallottino, Massimo. *The Etruscans.* Harmondsworth: Penguin, 1978.

Richardson, Emeline. *The Etruscans: Their Art and Civilization.* Rev. ed. Chicago: University of Chicago Press, 1976.

Ridgway, David, and Francesca Ridgway, eds. *Italy before the Romans.* New York: Academic, 1979.

Shipley, Lucy. *The Etruscans (Lost Civilizations).* London: Reaktion, 2017.

Spivey, Nigel. *Etruscan Art.* New York: Thames & Hudson, 1997.

Spivey, Nigel, and Simon Stoddart. *Etruscan Italy: An Archaeological History.* London: Batsford, 1990.

Sprenger, Maja, Gilda Bartoloni, and Max Hirmer. *The Etruscans: Their History, Art, and Architecture.* New York: Abrams, 1983.

Steingräber, Stephan. *Abundance of Life: Etruscan Wall Painting.* Los Angeles: J. Paul Getty Museum, 2006.

Torelli, Mario, ed. *The Etruscans.* New York: Rizzoli, 2001.

Turfa, Jean Macintosh, ed. *The Etruscan World.* London: Routledge, 2013.

CHAPTER 7
The Roman Empire

Aldrete, Gregory S. *Daily Life in the Roman City: Rome, Pompeii, and Ostia.* Westport, Conn.: Greenwood, 2004.

Anderson, James C., Jr. *Roman Architecture and Society.* Baltimore: Johns Hopkins University Press, 1997.

Andreae, Bernard. *The Art of Rome.* New York: Abrams, 1977.

Barton, Ian M., ed. *Roman Domestic Buildings.* Exeter: University of Exeter Press, 1996.

———. *Roman Public Buildings.* 2d ed. Exeter: University of Exeter Press, 1995.

Bianchi Bandinelli, Ranuccio. *Rome: The Center of Power: Roman Art to AD 200.* New York: Braziller, 1970.

———. *Rome: The Late Empire: Roman Art AD 200–400.* New York: Braziller, 1971.

Borg, Barbara E., ed. *A Companion to Roman Art.* Hoboken, N.J.: Wiley-Blackwell, 2015.

Brendel, Otto J. *Prolegomena to the Study of Roman Art.* New Haven, Conn.: Yale University Press, 1979.

Claridge, Amanda. *Rome: An Oxford Archaeological Guide.* 2d ed. New York: Oxford University Press, 2010.

Clarke, John R. *Art in the Lives of Everyday Romans: Visual Representation and Non-Elite Viewers in Italy, 100 B.C.–A.D. 315.* Berkeley: University of California Press, 2003.

———. *The Houses of Roman Italy, 100 BC–AD 250.* Berkeley: University of California Press, 1991.

Coarelli, Filippo. *Rome and Environs: An Archaeological Guide.* Berkeley and Los Angeles: University of California Press, 2007.

Cornell, Tim, and John Matthews. *Atlas of the Roman World.* New York: Facts on File, 1982.

D'Ambra, Eve. *Roman Art.* New York: Cambridge University Press, 1998.

———, ed. *Roman Art in Context.* Upper Saddle River, N.J.: Prentice Hall, 1994.

Dobbins, John J., and Pedar W. Foss, eds. *The World of Pompeii.* London: Routledge, 2007.

Dyson, Stephen L. *Rome: A Living Portrait of an Ancient City.* Baltimore: Johns Hopkins University Press, 2010.

Fejfer, Jane. *Roman Portraits in Context.* New York: Walter de Gruyter, 2008.

Friedland, Elise A., ed. *The Oxford Handbook of Roman Sculpture.* New York: Oxford University Press, 2015.

Gazda, Elaine K., ed. *Roman Art in the Private Sphere.* Ann Arbor: University of Michigan Press, 1991.

Grant, Michael. *Cities of Vesuvius: Pompeii and Herculaneum.* Harmondsworth: Penguin, 1976.

Hannestad, Niels. *Roman Art and Imperial Policy.* Aarhus: Aarhus University Press, 1986.

Henig, Martin, ed. *A Handbook of Roman Art.* Ithaca, N.Y.: Cornell University Press, 1983.

Kent, John P. C., and Max Hirmer. *Roman Coins.* New York: Abrams, 1978.

Kleiner, Diana E. E. *Roman Sculpture.* New Haven, Conn.: Yale University Press, 1992.

Kleiner, Diana E. E., and Susan B. Matheson, eds. *I Claudia: Women in Ancient Rome.* New Haven, Conn.: Yale University Art Gallery, 1996.

Kleiner, Fred S. *A History of Roman Art.* Enhanced ed. Belmont, Calif.: Wadsworth, 2010.

Kraus, Theodor. *Pompeii and Herculaneum: The Living Cities of the Dead.* New York: Abrams, 1975.

Lancaster, Lynne. *Concrete Vaulted Construction in Imperial Rome.* New York: Cambridge University Press, 2006.

Ling, Roger. *Roman Painting.* New York: Cambridge University Press, 1991.

L'Orange, Hans Peter. *The Roman Empire: Art Forms and Civic Life.* New York: Rizzoli, 1985.

MacCormack, Sabine G. *Art and Ceremony in Late Antiquity.* Berkeley: University of California Press, 1981.

MacDonald, William L. *The Architecture of the Roman Empire I: An Introductory Study.* Rev. ed. New Haven, Conn.: Yale University Press, 1982.

———. *The Architecture of the Roman Empire II: An Urban Appraisal.* New Haven, Conn.: Yale University Press, 1986.

———. *The Pantheon: Design, Meaning, and Progeny.* Cambridge, Mass.: Harvard University Press, 1976.

Marder, Tod A., and Mark Wilson Jones, eds. *The Pantheon: From Antiquity to the Present.* New York: Cambridge University Press, 2015.

Mattusch, Carol C., ed. *Pompeii and the Roman Villa: Art and Culture around the Bay of Naples.* New York: Thames & Hudson, 2008.

Mazzoleni, Donatella. *Domus: Wall Painting in the Roman House.* Los Angeles: J. Paul Getty Museum, 2004.

McKay, Alexander G. *Houses, Villas, and Palaces in the Roman World.* Ithaca, N.Y.: Cornell University Press, 1975.

Meiggs, Russell. *Roman Ostia.* New York: Oxford University Press, 1985. Reprint of 1973 ed.

Nash, Ernest. *Pictorial Dictionary of Ancient Rome.* 2d ed. 2 vols. New York: Praeger, 1962.

Pollitt, Jerome J. *The Art of Rome, 753 BC–AD 337: Sources and Documents.* Rev. ed. New York: Cambridge University Press, 1983.

Potter, T. W. *Roman Italy.* Berkeley and Los Angeles: University of California Press, 1990.

Richardson, Lawrence, Jr. *A New Topographical Dictionary of Ancient Rome.* Baltimore: Johns Hopkins University Press, 1992.

———. *Pompeii: An Architectural History.* Baltimore: Johns Hopkins University Press, 1988.

Sear, Frank. *Roman Architecture.* Rev. ed. Ithaca, N.Y.: Cornell University Press, 1989.

Stambaugh, John E. *The Ancient Roman City.* Baltimore: Johns Hopkins University Press, 1988.

Stamper, John W. *The Architecture of Roman Temples: The Republic to the Middle Empire.* New York: Cambridge University Press, 2005.

Stewart, Peter. *The Social History of Roman Art.* New York: Cambridge University Press, 2008.

Taylor, Rabun. *Roman Builders.* New York: Cambridge University Press, 2003.

Toynbee, Jocelyn M. C. *Death and Burial in the Roman World.* London: Thames & Hudson, 1971.

Wallace-Hadrill, Andrew. *Herculaneum: Past and Future.* London: Frances Lincoln, 2011.

———. *Houses and Society in Pompeii and Herculaneum.* Princeton, N.J.: Princeton University Press, 1994.

Ward-Perkins, John B. *Roman Architecture.* New York: Electa/Rizzoli, 1988.

———. *Roman Imperial Architecture.* 2d ed. New Haven, Conn.: Yale University Press, 1981.

Wilson-Jones, Mark. *Principles of Roman Architecture.* New Haven, Conn.: Yale University Press, 2000.

Wood, Susan. *Roman Portrait Sculpture AD 217–260.* Leiden: E. J. Brill, 1986.

Yegül, Fikret. *Baths and Bathing in Classical Antiquity.* Cambridge, Mass.: MIT Press, 1992.

Zanker, Paul. *Pompeii: Public and Private Life.* Cambridge, Mass.: Harvard University Press, 1998.

———. *The Power of Images in the Age of Augustus.* Ann Arbor: University of Michigan Press, 1988.

———. *Roman Art.* Los Angeles: J. Paul Getty Museum, 2010.

Zanker, Paul, and Bjorn Ewald. *Living with Myths: The Imagery of Roman Sarcophagi.* New York: Oxford University Press, 2012.

CHAPTER 8
Late Antiquity

Bowersock, G. W., Peter Brown, and Oleg Grabar, eds. *Late Antiquity: A Guide to the Postclassical World.* Cambridge, Mass.: Harvard University Press, 1998.

Brody, Lisa R., and Gail L. Hoffman, eds. *Dura Europos: Crossroads of Antiquity*. Chestnut Hill, Mass.: McMullen Museum of Art, Boston College, 2010.

Chi, Jennifer Y., and Sebastian Heath, eds. *Edge of Empires: Pagans, Christians, and Jews at Roman Dura-Europus*. Princeton, N.J.: Princeton University Press, 2011.

Cioffarelli, Ada. *Guide to the Catacombs of Rome and Its Surroundings*. Rome: Bonsignori, 2000.

Dresken-Weiland, Jutta. *Mosaics of Ravenna: Image and Meaning*. Regensburg: Schnell & Steiner, 2016.

Elsner, Jaś. *Art and the Roman Viewer: The Transformation of Art from the Pagan World to Christianity*. New York: Cambridge University Press, 1995.

———. *Imperial Rome and Christian Triumph*. New York: Oxford University Press, 1998.

Fine, Steven. *Art and Judaism in the Greco-Roman World: Toward a New Jewish Archaeology*. New York: Cambridge University Press, 2005.

Finney, Paul Corby. *The Invisible God: The Earliest Christians on Art*. New York: Oxford University Press, 1994.

Grabar, André. *The Beginnings of Christian Art, 200–395*. London: Thames & Hudson, 1967.

———. *Christian Iconography*. Princeton, N.J.: Princeton University Press, 1980.

Gutmann, Joseph. *Sacred Images: Studies in Jewish Art from Antiquity to the Middle Ages*. Northampton, Mass.: Variorum, 1989.

Janes, Dominic. *God and Gold in Late Antiquity*. New York: Cambridge University Press, 1998.

Jensen, Robin Margaret. *Understanding Early Christian Art*. New York: Routledge, 2000.

Koch, Guntram. *Early Christian Art and Architecture*. London: SCM, 1996.

Krautheimer, Richard. *Rome, Profile of a City: 312–1308*. Princeton, N.J.: Princeton University Press, 1980.

Krautheimer, Richard, and Slobodan Ćurčić. *Early Christian and Byzantine Architecture*. 4th ed. New Haven, Conn.: Yale University Press, 1986.

Lazaridou, Anastasia, ed. *Transition to Christianity: Art of Late Antiquity, 3rd–7th Century AD*. New York: Onassis Cultural Center, 2011.

Lowden, John. *Early Christian and Byzantine Art*. London: Phaidon, 1997.

Malbon, Elizabeth Struthers. *The Iconography of the Sarcophagus of Junius Bassus*. Princeton, N.J.: Princeton University Press, 1991.

Mathews, Thomas P. *The Clash of Gods: A Reinterpretation of Early Christian Art*. Rev. ed. Princeton, N.J.: Princeton University Press, 1999.

Milburn, Robert. *Early Christian Art and Architecture*. Berkeley: University of California Press, 1988.

Nicolai, Vincenzo Fiocchi, Fabrizio Bisconti, and Danilo Mazzoleni. *The Christian Catacombs of Rome: History, Decoration, Inscriptions*. Regensburg: Schnell & Steiner, 2006.

Peppard, Michael. *The World's Oldest Church: Bible, Art, and Ritual at Dura-Europos, Syria*. New Haven, Conn.: Yale University Press, 2016.

Perkins, Ann Louise. *The Art of Dura-Europos*. Oxford: Clarendon, 1973.

Poeschke, Joachim. *Italian Mosaics, 300–1300*. New York: Abbeville, 2010.

Rutgers, Leonard V. *Subterranean Rome: In Search of the Roots of Christianity in the Catacombs of the Eternal City*. Leuven: Peeters, 2000.

Spier, Jeffrey, ed. *Picturing the Bible: The Earliest Christian Art*. New Haven, Conn.: Yale University Press, 2007.

Thunø, Erik. *The Apse Mosaic in Early Medieval Rome: Time, Network, and Repetition*. New York: Cambridge University Press, 2015.

Volbach, Wolfgang, and Max Hirmer. *Early Christian Art*. New York: Abrams, 1962.

Webb, Matilda. *The Churches and Catacombs of Early Christian Rome: A Comprehensive Guide*. Brighton: Sussex Academic Press, 2001.

Webster, Leslie, and Michelle Brown, eds. *The Transformation of the Roman World, AD 400–900*. Berkeley: University of California Press, 1997.

Weitzmann, Kurt, ed. *Age of Spirituality: Late Antique and Early Christian Art, Third to Seventh Century*. New York: Metropolitan Museum of Art, 1979.

———. *Late Antique and Early Christian Book Illumination*. New York: Braziller, 1977.

Weitzmann, Kurt, and Herbert L. Kessler. *The Frescoes of the Dura Synagogue and Christian Art*. Washington, D.C.: Dumbarton Oaks, 1990.

Wharton, Annabel Jane. *Refiguring the Post-Classical City: Dura Europos, Jerash, Jerusalem, and Ravenna*. New York: Cambridge University Press, 1996.

CHAPTER 9
Byzantium

Barber, Charles. *Figure and Likeness: On the Limits of Representation in Byzantine Iconoclasm*. Princeton, N.J.: Princeton University Press, 2002.

Borsook, Eve. *Messages in Mosaic: The Royal Programmes of Norman Sicily*. Oxford: Clarendon, 1990.

Cormack, Robin. *Byzantine Art*. New York: Oxford University Press, 2000.

———. *Icons*. Cambridge, Mass.: Harvard University Press, 2007.

———. *Painting the Soul: Icons, Death Masks, and Shrouds*. London: Reaktion, 1997.

———. *Writing in Gold: Byzantine Society and Its Icons*. New York: Oxford University Press, 1985.

Cormack, Robin, and Maria Vassiliki. *Byzantium, 330–1453*. London: Royal Academy of Arts, 2008.

Cutler, Anthony. *The Hand of the Master: Craftsmanship, Ivory, and Society in Byzantium, 9th–11th Centuries*. Princeton, N.J.: Princeton University Press, 1994.

Deliyannis, Deborah Mauskopf. *Ravenna in Late Antiquity*. New York: Cambridge University Press, 2010.

Demus, Otto. *The Mosaic Decoration of San Marco, Venice*. Chicago: University of Chicago Press, 1990.

Dresken-Weiland, Jutta. *Mosaics of Ravenna: Image and Meaning*. Regensburg: Schnell & Steiner, 2016.

Evans, Helen C. *Byzantium: Faith and Power (1261–1557)*. New York: Metropolitan Museum of Art, 2004.

Evans, Helen C., and William D. Wixom, eds. *The Glory of Byzantium: Art and Culture of the Middle Byzantine Era AD 843–1261*. New York: Metropolitan Museum of Art, 1997.

Freely, John. *Byzantine Monuments of Istanbul*. New York: Cambridge University Press, 2004.

Grabar, André. *The Golden Age of Justinian: From the Death of Theodosius to the Rise of Islam*. New York: Odyssey, 1967.

Grabar, André, and Manolis Chatzidakis. *Greek Mosaics of the Byzantine Period*. New York: New American Library, 1964.

James, Liz, ed. *Art and Text in Byzantine Culture*. New York: Cambridge University Press, 2007.

Kleinbauer, W. Eugene. *Hagia Sophia*. London: Scala, 2004.

Lowden, John. *Early Christian and Byzantine Art*. London: Phaidon, 1997.

Maguire, Eunice Dauterman, and Henry Maguire. *Other Icons: Art and Power in Byzantine Secular Culture*. Princeton, N.J.: Princeton University Press, 2007.

Maguire, Henry. *Art and Eloquence in Byzantium*. Princeton, N.J.: Princeton University Press, 1981.

———. *The Icons of Their Bodies: Saints and Their Images in Byzantium*. Princeton, N.J.: Princeton University Press, 1996.

Mainstone, Rowland J. *Hagia Sophia: Architecture, Structure, and Liturgy of Justinian's Great Church*. 2d ed. New York: Thames & Hudson, 2001.

Mango, Cyril. *Art of the Byzantine Empire, 312–1453: Sources and Documents*. Toronto: University of Toronto Press, 1986. Reprint of 1972 ed.

———. *Byzantine Architecture*. New York: Electa/Rizzoli, 1985.

Mark, Robert, and Ahmet S. Cakmak, eds. *Hagia Sophia from the Age of Justinian to the Present*. New York: Cambridge University Press, 1992.

Mathews, Thomas F. *Byzantium: From Antiquity to the Renaissance*. New York: Abrams, 1998.

McClanan, Anne. *Representations of Early Byzantine Empresses: Image and Empire*. New York: Palgrave Macmillan, 2002.

Ousterhout, Robert. *Master Builders of Byzantium*. Princeton, N.J.: Princeton University Press, 2000.

Patricios, Nicholas. *The Sacred Architecture of Byzantium: Art, Liturgy and Symbolism in Early Christian Churches*. New York: I. B. Tauris, 2013.

Pelikan, Jaroslav. *Imago Dei: The Byzantine Apologia for Icons*. Princeton, N.J.: Princeton University Press, 1990.

Poeschke, Joachim. *Italian Mosaics, 300–1300*. New York: Abbeville, 2010.

Rodley, Lyn. *Byzantine Art and Architecture: An Introduction*. New York: Cambridge University Press, 1994.

Von Simson, Otto G. *Sacred Fortress: Byzantine Art and Statecraft in Ravenna*. Princeton, N.J.: Princeton University Press, 1986.

Weitzmann, Kurt. *The Icon*. New York: Dorset, 1987.

———. *Illustrations in Roll and Codex*. Princeton, N.J.: Princeton University Press, 1970.

CHAPTER 10
The Islamic World

Allan, James, and Sheila R. Canby. *Hunt for Paradise: Court Arts of Safavid Iran 1501–76*. Geneva: Skira, 2004.

Atil, Esin. *The Age of Sultan Suleyman the Magnificent*. Washington, D.C.: National Gallery of Art, 1987.

Baker, Patricia L. *Islam and the Religious Arts*. London: Continuum, 2004.

———. *Islamic Textiles*. London: British Museum, 1995.

Blair, Sheila S. *Islamic Calligraphy.* Edinburgh: Edinburgh University Press, 2008.

Blair, Sheila S., and Jonathan Bloom. *The Art and Architecture of Islam 1250–1800.* New Haven, Conn.: Yale University Press, 1994.

Bloom, Jonathan M., and Sheila S. Blair. *The Grove Encyclopedia of Islamic Art and Architecture.* New York: Oxford University Press, 2009.

———. *Islamic Arts.* London: Phaidon, 1997.

Brend, Barbara. *Islamic Art.* Cambridge, Mass.: Harvard University Press, 1991.

Canby, Sheila R. *Persian Painting.* London: British Museum, 1993.

Dodds, Jerrilynn D., ed. *Al-Andalus: The Art of Islamic Spain.* New York: Metropolitan Museum of Art, 1992.

Ettinghausen, Richard, Oleg Grabar, and Marilyn Jenkins-Madina. *The Art and Architecture of Islam, 650–1250.* Rev. ed. New Haven, Conn.: Yale University Press, 2001.

Ferrier, Ronald W., ed. *The Arts of Persia.* New Haven, Conn.: Yale University Press, 1989.

Frishman, Martin, and Hasan-Uddin Khan. *The Mosque: History, Architectural Development, and Regional Diversity.* New York: Thames & Hudson, 1994.

George, Alain. *The Rise of Islamic Calligraphy.* London: Saqi, 2010.

Goodwin, Godfrey. *A History of Ottoman Architecture.* 2d ed. New York: Thames & Hudson, 1987.

Grabar, Oleg. *The Alhambra.* Cambridge, Mass.: Harvard University Press, 1978.

———. *The Dome of the Rock.* Cambridge, Mass.: Harvard University Press, 2006.

———. *The Formation of Islamic Art.* Rev. ed. New Haven, Conn.: Yale University Press, 1987.

———. *Islamic Visual Culture, 1100–1800.* New York: Ashgate, 2006.

———. *Masterpieces of Islamic Art: The Decorated Page from the 8th Century to the 17th Century.* New York: Prestel, 2009.

Grube, Ernst J. *Architecture of the Islamic World: Its History and Social Meaning.* 2d ed. New York: Thames & Hudson, 1984.

Hattstein, Markus, and Peter Delius, eds. *Islam: Art and Architecture.* Cologne: Könemann, 2000.

Hillenbrand, Robert. *Islamic Architecture: Form, Function, Meaning.* Edinburgh: Edinburgh University Press, 1994.

———. *Islamic Art and Architecture.* New York: Thames & Hudson, 1999.

Irwin, Robert. *The Alhambra.* Cambridge, Mass.: Harvard University Press, 2004.

———. *Islamic Art in Context: Art, Architecture, and the Literary World.* New York: Abrams, 1997.

Michell, George, ed. *Architecture of the Islamic World.* New York: Thames & Hudson, 1978.

Mozzati, Luca. *Islamic Art: Architecture, Painting, Calligraphy, Ceramics, Glass, Carpets.* New York: Prestel, 2010.

Necipoglu, Gulru. *The Age of Sinan: Architectural Culture in the Ottoman Empire.* Princeton, N.J.: Princeton University Press, 2005.

Petruccioli, Attilio, and Khalil K. Pirani, eds. *Understanding Islamic Architecture.* London: Routledge, 2002.

Porter, Venetia. *Islamic Tiles.* London: British Museum, 1995.

Robinson, Frank. *Atlas of the Islamic World.* Oxford: Equinox, 1982.

Ruggles, D. Fairchild, ed. *Islamic Art & Visual Culture: An Anthology of Sources.* Malden, Mass.: Wiley-Blackwell, 2011.

Schimmel, Annemarie. *Calligraphy and Islamic Culture.* New York: New York University Press, 1984.

Stierlin, Henri. *Islam I: Early Architecture from Baghdad to Cordoba.* Cologne: Taschen, 1996.

———. *Islamic Art and Architecture from Isfahan to the Taj Mahal.* New York: Thames & Hudson, 2002.

Tadgell, Christopher. *Four Caliphates: The Formation and Development of the Islamic Tradition.* London: Ellipsis, 1998.

Ward, Rachel M. *Islamic Metalwork.* New York: Thames & Hudson, 1993.

Welch, Anthony. *Calligraphy in the Arts of the Islamic World.* Austin: University of Texas Press, 1979.

Medieval Art, General

Alexander, Jonathan J. G. *Medieval Illuminators and Their Methods of Work.* New Haven, Conn.: Yale University Press, 1992.

The Art of Medieval Spain, AD 500–1200. New York: Metropolitan Museum of Art, 1993.

Benton, Janetta Rebold. *Art of the Middle Ages.* New York: Thames & Hudson, 2002.

Binski, Paul. *Painters (Medieval Craftsmen).* Toronto: University of Toronto Press, 1991.

Calkins, Robert G. *Illuminated Books of the Middle Ages.* Ithaca, N.Y.: Cornell University Press, 1983.

———. *Medieval Architecture in Western Europe: From AD 300 to 1500.* New York: Oxford University Press, 1998.

Coldstream, Nicola. *Masons and Sculptors (Medieval Craftsmen).* Toronto: University of Toronto Press, 1991.

———. *Medieval Architecture.* New York: Oxford University Press, 2002.

Cross, Frank L., and Livingstone, Elizabeth A., eds. *The Oxford Dictionary of the Christian Church.* 3d ed. New York: Oxford University Press, 1997.

De Hamel, Christopher. *A History of Illuminated Manuscripts.* Oxford: Phaidon, 1986.

———. *Scribes and Illuminators (Medieval Craftsmen).* Toronto: University of Toronto Press, 1992.

Doig, Allan. *Liturgy and Architecture: From the Early Church to the Middle Ages.* New York: Ashgate, 2008.

Heller, Ena Giurescu, and Patricia C. Pongracz. *Perspectives on Medieval Art: Learning through Looking.* New York: Museum of Biblical Art, 2010.

Holcomb, Melanie, ed. *Pen and Parchment: Drawing in the Middle Ages.* New York: Metropolitan Museum of Art, 2009.

Hourihane, Colum, ed. *The Grove Encyclopedia of Medieval Art and Architecture.* New York: Oxford University Press, 2012.

Kessler, Herbert L. *Seeing Medieval Art.* Toronto: Broadview, 2004.

———. *Spiritual Seeing: Picturing God's Invisibility in Medieval Art.* Philadelphia: University of Pennsylvania Press, 2000.

Lasko, Peter. *Ars Sacra, 800–1200.* 2d ed. New Haven, Conn.: Yale University Press, 1994.

Martin, Therese, ed. *Reassessing the Roles of Women as 'Makers' of Medieval Art and Architecture.* Leiden: Brill, 2012.

Murray, Peter, and Linda Murray. *The Oxford Companion to Christian Art and Architecture.* New York: Oxford University Press, 1996.

Pelikan, Jaroslav. *Mary through the Centuries: Her Place in the History of Culture.* New Haven, Conn.: Yale University Press, 1996.

Prache, Anne. *Cathedrals of Europe.* Ithaca, N.Y.: Cornell University Press, 1999.

Raguin, Virginia Chieffo. *Stained Glass from Its Origins to the Present.* New York: Abrams, 2003.

Ross, Leslie. *Medieval Art: A Topical Dictionary.* Westport, Conn.: Greenwood, 1996.

Schütz, Bernard. *Great Cathedrals.* New York: Abrams, 2002.

Sekules, Veronica. *Medieval Art.* New York: Oxford University Press, 2001.

Snyder, James, Henry Luttikhuizen, and Dorothy Verkerk. *Art of the Middle Ages.* 2d ed. Upper Saddle River, N.J.: Prentice Hall, 2006.

Stokstad, Marilyn. *Medieval Art.* 2d ed. Boulder, Colo.: Westview, 2004.

Tasker, Edward G. *Encyclopedia of Medieval Church Art.* London: Batsford, 1993.

CHAPTER 11
Early Medieval Europe

Alexander, Jonathan J. G. *Insular Manuscripts, Sixth to the Ninth Century.* London: Miller, 1978.

The Art of Medieval Spain, AD 500–1200. New York: Metropolitan Museum of Art, 1993.

Backhouse, Janet, D. H. Turner, and Leslie Webster, eds. *The Golden Age of Anglo-Saxon Art, 966–1066.* Bloomington: Indiana University Press, 1984.

Bandmann, Günter. *Early Medieval Architecture as Bearer of Meaning.* New York: Columbia University Press, 2005.

Barral i Altet, Xavier. *The Early Middle Ages: From Late Antiquity to AD 1000.* Cologne: Taschen, 1997.

Brown, Katharine Reynolds, Dafydd Kidd, and Charles T. Little, eds. *From Attila to Charlemagne.* New York: Metropolitan Museum of Art, 2000.

Brown, Michelle P. *The Lindisfarne Gospels: Society, Spirituality, and the Scribe.* Toronto: University of Toronto Press, 2003.

Carver, Martin. *Sutton Hoo: A Seventh-Century Princely Burial Ground and Its Context.* London: British Museum, 2005.

Collins, Roger. *Early Medieval Europe, 300–1000.* New York: St. Martin's, 1991.

Conant, Kenneth J. *Carolingian and Romanesque Architecture, 800–1200.* 4th ed. New Haven, Conn.: Yale University Press, 1992.

Davis-Weyer, Caecilia. *Early Medieval Art, 300–1150: Sources and Documents.* Toronto: University of Toronto Press, 1986. Reprint of 1971 ed.

Diebold, William J. *Word and Image: An Introduction to Early Medieval Art.* Boulder, Colo.: Westview Press, 2000.

Dodwell, Charles R. *Anglo-Saxon Art: A New Perspective.* Ithaca, N.Y.: Cornell University Press, 1982.

———. *The Pictorial Arts of the West, 800–1200.* New Haven, Conn.: Yale University Press, 1993.

Farr, Carol. *The Book of Kells: Its Function and Audience*. London: British Library, 1997.

Garrison, Eliza. *Ottonian Imperial Art and Portraiture: The Artistic Patronage of Otto III and Henry II*. Burlington, Vt.: Ashgate, 2012.

Graham-Campbell, James. *Viking Art*. New York: Thames & Hudson, 2013.

Harbison, Peter. *The Golden Age of Irish Art: The Medieval Achievement 600–1200*. New York: Thames & Hudson, 1999.

Henderson, George. *From Durrow to Kells: The Insular Gospel-Books, 650–800*. London: Thames & Hudson, 1987.

Hubert, Jean, Jean Porcher, and Wolfgang Fritz Volbach. *The Carolingian Renaissance*. New York: Braziller, 1970.

———. *Europe of the Invasions*. New York: Braziller, 1969.

Mayr-Harting, Henry. *Ottonian Book Illumination: An Historical Study*. 2 vols. London: Miller, 1991–1993.

McClendon, Charles. *The Origins of Medieval Architecture: Building in Europe, AD 600–900*. New Haven, Conn.: Yale University Press, 2005.

Meehan, Bernard. *The Book of Kells*. London: Tate, 2002.

Megaw, Ruth, and John Vincent Megaw. *Celtic Art: From Its Beginning to the Book of Kells*. New York: Thames & Hudson, 1989.

Mütherich, Florentine, and Joachim E. Gaehde. *Carolingian Painting*. New York: Braziller, 1976.

Nees, Lawrence J. *Early Medieval Art*. New York: Oxford University Press, 2002.

Nordenfalk, Carl. *Celtic and Anglo-Saxon Painting: Book Illumination in the British Isles, 600–800*. New York: Braziller, 1977.

O'Brien, Jacqueline, and Peter Harbison. *Ancient Ireland: From Prehistory to the Middle Ages*. New York: Oxford University Press, 2000.

Richardson, Hilary, and John Scarry. *An Introduction to Irish High Crosses*. Dublin: Mercier, 1990.

Stalley, Roger. *Early Medieval Architecture*. New York: Oxford University Press, 1999.

Webster, Leslie. *Anglo-Saxon Art*. Ithaca, N.Y.: Cornell University Press, 2012.

Wilson, David M. *From Viking to Crusader: Scandinavia and Europe 800–1200*. New York: Rizzoli, 1992.

Wilson, David M., and Ole Klindt-Jensen. *Viking Art*. 2d ed. Minneapolis: University of Minnesota Press, 1980.

CHAPTER 12
Romanesque Europe

Armi, C. Edson. *Masons and Sculptors in Romanesque Burgundy: The New Aesthetics of Cluny III*. 2 vols. University Park: Pennsylvania State University Press, 1983.

Ashley, Kathleen, and Marilyn Deegan. *Being a Pilgrim: Art and Ritual on the Medieval Routes to Santiago*. Burlington, Vt.: Lund Humphries, 2009.

Bagnoli, Martina, Holger A. Kleiner, C. Griffith Mann, and James Robinson, eds. *Treasures of Heaven: Saints, Relics, and Devotion in Medieval Europe*. New Haven, Conn.: Yale University Press: 2010.

Barral i Altet, Xavier. *The Romanesque: Towns, Cathedrals, and Monasteries*. Cologne: Taschen, 1998.

Burnett, Charles, and Peter Dronke. *Hildegard of Bingen: The Context of Her Thought and Art*. London: Warburg Institute, 1998.

Cahn, Walter. *Romanesque Bible Illumination*. Ithaca, N.Y.: Cornell University Press, 1982.

———. *Romanesque Manuscripts: The Twelfth Century*. 2 vols. London: Miller, 1998.

Conant, Kenneth J. *Carolingian and Romanesque Architecture, 800–1200*. 4th ed. New Haven, Conn.: Yale University Press, 1992.

Demus, Otto. *Romanesque Mural Painting*. New York: Thames & Hudson, 1970.

Dodwell, Charles R. *The Pictorial Arts of the West, 800–1200*. New Haven, Conn.: Yale University Press, 1993.

Fergusson, Peter. *Architecture of Solitude: Cistercian Abbeys in Twelfth-Century Europe*. Princeton, N.J.: Princeton University Press, 1984.

Fernie, Eric. *Romanesque Architecture*. New Haven, Conn.: Yale University Press, 2014.

Folda, Jaroslav. *The Art of the Crusaders in the Holy Land, 1098–1187*. New York: Cambridge University Press, 1995.

———. *Crusader Art*. London: Lund Humphries, 2008.

Grape, Wolfgang. *The Bayeux Tapestry: Monument to a Norman Triumph*. New York: Prestel, 1994.

Hearn, Millard F. *Romanesque Sculpture: The Revival of Monumental Stone Sculpture in the Eleventh and Twelfth Centuries*. Ithaca, N.Y.: Cornell University Press, 1981.

Hourihane, Colum, ed. *Romanesque Art and Thought in the Twelfth Century*. Princeton, N.J.: Index of Christian Art, 2008.

Kahn, Deborah, ed. *The Romanesque Frieze and Its Spectator*. London: Miller, 1992.

Kendall, Calvin B. *The Allegory of the Church: Romanesque Portals and Their Verse Inscriptions*. Toronto: University of Toronto Press, 1998.

Kubach, Hans E. *Romanesque Architecture*. New York: Electa, 1988.

Male, Émile. *Religious Art in France: The Twelfth Century*. Rev. ed. Princeton, N.J.: Princeton University Press, 1978.

Minne-Sève, Viviane, and Hervé Kergall. *Romanesque and Gothic France: Architecture and Sculpture*. New York: Abrams, 2000.

Nichols, Stephen G. *Romanesque Signs: Early Medieval Narrative and Iconography*. New Haven, Conn.: Yale University Press, 1983.

Nordenfalk, Carl. *Early Medieval Book Illumination*. New York: Rizzoli, 1988.

Petzold, Andreas. *Romanesque Art*. New York: Abrams, 1995.

Schapiro, Meyer. *The Sculpture of Moissac*. New York: Thames & Hudson, 1985.

Seidel, Linda. *Legends in Limestone: Lazarus, Gislebertus, and the Cathedral of Autun*. Chicago: University of Chicago Press, 1999.

Stalley, Roger. *Early Medieval Architecture*. New York: Oxford University Press, 1999.

Tate, Robert B., and Marcus Tate. *The Pilgrim Route to Santiago*. Oxford: Phaidon, 1987.

Toman, Rolf, ed. *Romanesque: Architecture, Sculpture, Painting*. Cologne: Könemann, 1997.

Wilson, David M. *The Bayeux Tapestry: The Complete Tapestry in Color*. New York: Thames & Hudson, 2004.

Zarnecki, George, Janet Holt, and Tristram Holland, eds. *English Romanesque Art, 1066–1200*. London: Weidenfeld & Nicolson, 1984.

CHAPTER 13
Gothic Europe North of the Alps

Barnes, Carl F. *The Portfolio of Villard de Honnecourt*. New York: Ashgate, 2009.

Binski, Paul. *Becket's Crown: Art and Imagination in Gothic England, 1170–1300*. New Haven, Conn.: Yale University Press, 2004.

Bony, Jean. *The English Decorated Style: Gothic Architecture Transformed, 1250–1350*. Ithaca, N.Y.: Cornell University Press, 1979.

———. *French Gothic Architecture of the Twelfth and Thirteenth Centuries*. Berkeley: University of California Press, 1983.

Branner, Robert, ed. *Chartres Cathedral*. New York: Norton, 1969.

———. *Manuscript Painting in Paris during the Reign of St. Louis*. Berkeley: University of California Press, 1977.

———. *St. Louis and the Court Style in Gothic Architecture*. London: Zwemmer, 1965.

Brown, Sarah, and David O'Connor. *Glass-Painters (Medieval Craftsmen)*. Toronto: University of Toronto Press, 1991.

Camille, Michael. *Gothic Art: Glorious Visions*. New York: Abrams, 1996.

———. *The Gothic Idol: Ideology and Image-Making in Medieval Art*. New York: Cambridge University Press, 1989.

Courtenay, Lynn T., ed. *The Engineering of Medieval Cathedrals*. Aldershot: Scolar, 1997.

Crosby, Sumner McKnight. *The Royal Abbey of Saint-Denis from Its Beginnings to the Death of Suger, 475–1151*. New Haven, Conn.: Yale University Press, 1987.

Erlande-Brandenburg, Alain. *The Cathedral: The Social and Architectural Dynamics of Construction*. New York: Cambridge University Press, 1994.

———. *Gothic Art*. New York: Abrams, 1989.

Favier, Jean. *The World of Chartres*. New York: Abrams, 1990.

Fitchen, John. *The Construction of Gothic Cathedrals: A Study of Medieval Vault Erection*. Chicago: University of Chicago Press, 1981.

Frankl, Paul. *The Gothic: Literary Sources and Interpretations through Eight Centuries*. Princeton, N.J.: Princeton University Press, 1960.

Frankl, Paul, and Paul Crossley. *Gothic Architecture*. New Haven, Conn.: Yale University Press, 2000.

Frisch, Teresa G. *Gothic Art 1140–c. 1450: Sources and Documents*. Toronto: University of Toronto Press, 1987. Reprint of 1971 ed.

Gerson, Paula, ed. *Abbot Suger and Saint-Denis*. New York: Metropolitan Museum of Art, 1986.

Givens, Jean A. *Observation and Image-Making in Gothic Art*. New York: Cambridge University Press, 2004.

Grodecki, Louis. *Gothic Architecture*. New York: Electa/Rizzoli, 1985.

Grodecki, Louis, and Catherine Brisac. *Gothic Stained Glass, 1200–1300*. Ithaca, N.Y.: Cornell University Press, 1985.

Jantzen, Hans. *High Gothic: The Classic Cathedrals of Chartres, Reims, Amiens*. Princeton, N.J.: Princeton University Press, 1984.

Male, Émile. *Religious Art in France: The Thirteenth Century*. Rev. ed. Princeton, N.J.: Princeton University Press, 1984.

Minne-Sève, Viviane, and Hervé Kergall. *Romanesque and Gothic France: Architecture and Sculpture.* New York: Abrams, 2000.

Murray, Stephen. *Notre Dame, Cathedral of Amiens: The Power of Change in Gothic.* New York: Cambridge University Press, 1996.

Nussbaum, Norbert. *German Gothic Church Architecture.* New Haven, Conn.: Yale University Press, 2000.

Panofsky, Erwin. *Abbot Suger on the Abbey Church of St. Denis and Its Art Treasures.* 2d ed. Princeton, N.J.: Princeton University Press, 1979.

Perkinson, Stephen. *The Likeness of the King: A Prehistory of Portraiture in Late Medieval France.* Chicago: University of Chicago Press, 2009.

Prina, Francesca. *The Story of Gothic Architecture.* New York: Prestel, 2011.

Radding, Charles M., and William W. Clark. *Medieval Architecture, Medieval Learning.* New Haven, Conn.: Yale University Press, 1992.

Recht, Roland. *Believing and Seeing: The Art of Gothic Cathedrals.* Chicago: University of Chicago Press, 1999.

Rudolph, Conrad. *Artistic Change at St-Denis: Abbot Suger's Program and the Early Twelfth-Century Controversy over Art.* Princeton, N.J.: Princeton University Press, 1990.

Sauerländer, Willibald, and Max Hirmer. *Gothic Sculpture in France, 1140–1270.* New York: Abrams, 1973.

Scott, Robert A. *The Gothic Enterprise: A Guide to Understanding the Medieval Cathedral.* Berkeley and Los Angeles: University of California Press, 2003.

Simson, Otto G. von. *The Gothic Cathedral: Origins of Gothic Architecture and the Medieval Concept of Order.* 3d ed. Princeton, N.J.: Princeton University Press, 1988.

Toman, Rolf, ed. *The Art of Gothic: Architecture, Sculpture, Painting.* Cologne: Könemann, 1999.

Williamson, Paul. *Gothic Sculpture, 1140–1300.* New Haven, Conn.: Yale University Press, 1995.

Wilson, Christopher. *The Gothic Cathedral: The Architecture of the Great Church, 1130–1530.* London: Thames & Hudson, 1990.

CHAPTER 14
Late Medieval Italy

Bomford, David. *Art in the Making: Italian Painting before 1400.* London: National Gallery, 1989.

Borsook, Eve, and Fiorelli Superbi Gioffredi. *Italian Altarpieces 1250–1550: Function and Design.* Oxford: Clarendon, 1994.

Bourdua, Louise. *The Franciscans and Art Patronage in Late Medieval Italy.* New York: Cambridge University Press, 2004.

Cole, Bruce. *Sienese Painting: From Its Origins to the Fifteenth Century.* New York: Harper Collins, 1987.

Derbes, Anne. *Picturing the Passion in Late Medieval Italy: Narrative Painting, Franciscan Ideologies, and the Levant.* New York: Cambridge University Press, 1996.

Derbes, Anne, and Mark Sandona, eds. *The Cambridge Companion to Giotto.* New York: Cambridge University Press, 2004.

Flores d'Arcais, Francesca. *Giotto.* 2d ed. New York: Abbeville, 2012.

Hills, Paul. *The Light of Early Italian Painting.* New Haven, Conn.: Yale University Press, 1987.

Maginnis, Hayden B. J. *Painting in the Age of Giotto: A Historical Reevaluation.* University Park: Pennsylvania State University Press, 1997.

———. *The World of the Early Sienese Painter.* University Park: Pennsylvania State University Press, 2001.

Malafarina, Gian Franco, ed. *The Basilica of St. Francis in Assisi.* New York: Thames & Hudson, 2014.

Meiss, Millard. *Painting in Florence and Siena after the Black Death.* Princeton, N.J.: Princeton University Press, 1976.

Moskowitz, Anita Fiderer. *Italian Gothic Sculpture, c. 1250–c. 1400.* New York: Cambridge University Press, 2001.

———. *Nicola & Giovanni Pisano: The Pulpits: Pious Devotion, Pious Diversion.* London: Harvey Miller, 2006.

Norman, Diana, ed. *Siena, Florence, and Padua: Art, Society, and Religion 1280–1400.* New Haven, Conn.: Yale University Press, 1995.

Poeschke, Joachim. *Italian Frescoes: The Age of Giotto, 1280–1400.* New York: Abbeville, 2005.

Pope-Hennessy, John. *Italian Gothic Sculpture.* 3d ed. Oxford: Phaidon, 1986.

Stubblebine, James H. *Duccio di Buoninsegna and His School.* Princeton, N.J.: Princeton University Press, 1979.

White, John. *Art and Architecture in Italy: 1250–1400.* 3d ed. New Haven, Conn.: Yale University Press, 1993.

———. *Duccio: Tuscan Art and the Medieval Workshop.* London: Thames & Hudson, 1979.

The author and publisher are grateful to the proprietors and custodians of various works of art for photographs of these works and permission to reproduce them in this book. Sources not included in the captions are listed here.

NOTE: All references in the following credits are to figure numbers unless otherwise indicated.

Introduction—I-1 and I-1a–c: The Trustees of the British Museum/Art Resource, NY; **I-2:** AKG-Images; **I-3:** Interior view of the choir, begun after 1284/ French School, (13th century)/PAUL MAEYAERT/Beauvais Cathedral, Beauvais, France/Bridgeman Images; **I-4:** AKG-Images; **I-5:** Board of Trustees, National Gallery of Art, Washington; **I-6:** Art © Estate of Ben Shahn/Licensed by VAGA, New York, NY. Photo: Whitney Museum of American Art, New York. (gift of Edith and Milton Lowenthal in memory of Juliana Force); **I-7:** Jonathan Poore/ Cengage Learning; **I-8:** AKG-Images; **I-9:** © The Metropolitan Museum of Art. Image source: Art Resource, NY; **I-10:** Fred S. Kleiner; **I-11:** © 2011 The Josef and Anni Albers Foundation/Artists Rights Society (ARS), New York. Photo: © Whitney Museum of American Art; **I-12:** National Gallery, London/Art Resource, NY; **I-13:** © 2011 Museum of Fine Arts, Boston. 11.4584; **I-14:** bpk, Berlin/Staatsgemäldesammlungen, Munich, Germany/Art Resource, NY; **I-15:** Jürgen Liepe, Berlin; **I-16:** Nimatallah/Art Resource, NY; **I-17:** Scala/Art Resource, NY; **I-18:** Cengage Learning; **I-19 (left):** National Library of Australia; **I-19 (right):** The New Zealanders /George L. Craik. London, 1830. Rex Nan Kivell Collection NK1277.

Chapter 1—1-1 and 1-1a–c: Jean Vertut; **1-1A:** Dr. Paul G. Bahn; **Map 1-1:** Cengage Learning; **1-2:** With permission: Namibia Archaeological Trust; **1-3:** AKG-Images; **1-4:** Erich Lessing/Art Resource, NY; **1-4A:** RMN-Grand Palais/ Art Resource, NY; **1-5:** Venus with a horn, from Laussel in the Dordogne (stone)/ Prehistoric/Musee des Antiquites Nationales, St. Germain-en-Laye, France/ Bridgeman Images; **1-5A:** Louis de Seille/Courtesy Jean Clottes; **1-6:** Jean Vertut; **1-7:** RMN-Grand Palais/Art Resource, NY; **1-8:** Jean Vertut; **1-9:** Jean Vertut; **1-9A:** AKG-Images; **1-10:** Jean Vertut; **1-11:** French Ministry of Culture and Communication, Regional Direction for Cultural Affairs-Rhone-Alpes region, Regional Department of Archaeology; **1-12:** © Michele Burgess/Alamy; **Map 1-2:** Cengage Learning; **1-13:** Zev Radovan www.biblelandpictures.com; **1-14:** Leemage/Getty Images; **1-15:** Erich Lessing/Art Resource, NY; **1-15A:** John Swogger/Catalhoyuk Kazi Evi Kucukkoy Cumra/Konya; **1-16:** DEA/M. Seemuller/De Agostini Picture Library/Getty Images; **1-17:** Dagli Orti/REX/Shutterstock; **1-17A:** Göran Burenhult/The Image Works; **1-18:** Bob Krist/Getty Images; **1-19:** John Burge/Cengage Learning; **1-20:** Jonathan Poore/Cengage Learning.

Chapter 2—2-1 and 2-1a–c: Erich Lessing/Art Resource, NY; **2-2:** Richard Ashworth/Robert Harding; **Map 2-1:** Cengage Learning; **2-3:** Cengage Learning; **2-4:** AKG-Images/Bildarchiv Steffens; **2-5:** Erich Lessing/Art Resource, NY; **2-5A:** Hirmer Fotoarchiv, Munich; **2-6:** The Trustees of the British Museum/Art Resource, NY; **2-7:** University of Pennsylvania Museum of Archaeology and Anthropology, Philadelphia; **2-8:** Fred S. Kleiner; **2-9:** The Trustees of the British Museum/Art Resource, NY; **2-10:** The Trustees of The British Museum/Art Resource, NY; **2-11:** RMN-Grand Palais/Art Resource, NY; **2-12:** Scala/Art Resource, NY; **2-13:** RMN-Grand Palais/Art Resource, NY; **2-14:** University of Pennsylvania Museum of Archaeology and Anthropology, Philadelphia; **2-15:** Silvio Fiore/SuperStock; **2-16:** Erich Lessing/Art Resource, NY; **2-17:** Erich Lessing/ Art Resource, NY; **2-17A:** Erich Lessing/Art Resource, NY; **2-17B:** Erich Lessing/ Art Resource, NY; **2-18:** RMN-Grand Palais/Art Resource, NY; **2-18A:** © Iberfoto/The Image Works; **2-18B:** Vase, Style I, from Susa, Iran, 5000–4000 BC (ceramic), Mesopotamian/Louvre, Paris, France/Giraudon/The Bridgeman Art Library; **2-19:** RMN-Grand Palais/Art Resource, NY; **2-19A:** Cengage Learning; **2-20:** Fred S. Kleiner; **2-21:** © The Trustees of The British Museum/Art Resource, NY; **2-22:** © The Trustees of The British Museum/Art Resource, NY; **2-22A:** Fred S. Kleiner; **2-23:** Fred S. Kleiner; **2-24:** Bildarchiv Preussischer Kulturbesitz/Art Resource, NY; **2-25 (top):** robertharding/Superstock; **2-25 (bottom):** age fotostock/ SuperStock; **2-26:** Fred S. Kleiner; **2-27:** David Poole/Robert Harding Picture Library; **2-28:** Scala/Art Resource, NY; **2-28A:** © MARKA/Alamy; **2-29:** Gérard Degeorge/AKG-Images.

Chapter 3—3-1 and 3-1a–c: © The Trustees of the British Museum/Art Resource, NY; **Map 3-1:** © 2018 Cengage Learning; **3-1A:** J. E. Quibell and F. W.

Geen, Hierakonpolis vol. 2 (London 1902) p. 76/Egyptian Museum; **3-2:** Werner Forman/Art Resource, NY; **3-3:** Werner Forman/Art Resource, NY; **3-4:** Cengage Learning; **3-5:** AKG-Images; **3-6:** Cengage Learning; **3-6A:** Juergen Ritterbach/ Alamy **3-7:** Erich Lessing/Art Resource, NY; **3-8:** Yann Arthus-Bertrand; **3-9:** Cengage Learning; **3-10:** Courtesy of the Semitic Museum, Harvard University; **3-11:** Jon Arnold Images Ltd/Alamy; **3-12:** Araldo de Luca; **3-12A:** Erich Lessing/ Art Resource, NY; **3-13:** Photograph © 2011 Museum of Fine Arts, Boston. 11.1738; **3-13A:** AKG-Images; **3-14:** Erich Lessing/Art Resource, NY; **3-14A:** Jürgen Liepe, Berlin; **3-14B:** DEA Picture Library/Getty Images; **3-15:** Jean Vertut; **3-16:** Men herding sheep and cattle from the Mastaba Chapel of Ti, Old Kingdom (wall painting), Egyptian 5th Dynasty (c. 2494–2345 BC)/Saqqara, Memphis, Egypt/The Bridgeman Art Library; **3-16A:** Photograph © 2011 Museum of Fine Arts, Boston; **3-17:** Purchase: William Rockhill Nelson Trust; **3-18:** DEA/G. Sioen/Getty Images; **3-19:** /AKG-Images; **3-20:** DeAgostini/DeAgostini/Superstock; **3-21:** © The Metropolitan Museum of Art/Art Resource, NY; **3-22:** Scala/ Art Resource, NY; **3-23:** G. Aunion Juan/Alamy; **3-23A:** Upperhall Ltd/robertharding/Getty Images; **3-24:** Jean Claude Golvin; **3-24A:** Yann Arthus-Bertrand; **3-25:** Peter Horree/Alamy; **3-26:** Peter Horree/Alamy; **3-27:** bpk, Berlin/Aegyptisches Museum, Staatliche Museen, Berlin, Germany/Juergen Liepe/Art Resource, NY; **3-28:** © The Trustees of The British Museum/Art Resource, NY; **3-28A:** © The Trustees of The British Museum/Art Resource, NY; **3-29:** Araldo de Luca; **3-30:** Vladimir Wrangel/Shutterstock; **3-31:** Aegyptisches Museum, Staatliche Museen, Berlin, Germany/Art Resource, NY; **3-32:** Fred S. Kleiner; **3-33:** The innermost coffin of the king, from the Tomb of Tutankhamun (c. 1370–1352 BC) New Kingdom (gold inlaid with semi-precious stones) (for detail see 343642), Egyptian 18th Dynasty (c. 1567–1320 BC)/Egyptian National Museum, Cairo, Egypt/Photo © Boltin Picture Library/The Bridgeman Images; **3-34:** Robert Harding/robertharding/Getty Images; **3-35:** Dagli Orti/REX/Shutterstock; **3-36:** Fred S. Kleiner; **3-37:** Jürgen Liepe, Berlin; **3-38:** Yann Arthus-Bertrand.

Chapter 4—4-1: Nimatallah/Art Resource, NY; **4-1a:** Sarcophagus from Hagia Triada, Phaistos, Crete (Greece), detail from decoration, Minoan Civilization, 15th century BC/De Agostini Editore/Bridgeman Images; **4-1b:** Aghia Triadha (Hagia Triada) sarcophagus, detail, parade of bidders/De Agostini Editore/ Bridgeman Images; **4-1c:** Aghia Triadha (Hagia Triada) sarcophagus, detail, parade of bidders/De Agostini Editore/Bridgeman Images; **Map 4-1:** © 2018 Cengage Learning; **4-2:** Erich Lessing/Art Resource, NY; **4-3:** Dagli Orti/REX/ Shutterstock; **4-4:** John Burge; **4-5:** Cengage Learning; **4-6:** Roger Wood/Getty Images; **4-7:** Courtesy Saskia Ltd., © Dr. Ron Wiedenhoeft; **4-8:** DEA/G. Dagli Orti/De Agostini Picture Library/Getty Images; **4-9:** Fred S. Kleiner; **4-9A:** AKG-Images; **4-10:** Leemage/Getty Images; **4-11:** Studio Kontos/Photostock; **4-12:** Scala/Art Resource, NY; **4-13:** Dagli Orti/REX/Shutterstock; **4-13A:** British School at Athens; **4-14:** Erich Lessing/Art Resource, NY; **4-15:** Cengage Learning; **4-16:** Studio Kontos/Photostock; **4-17:** Cengage Learning; **4-18:** Constantinos Iliopoulos/Alamy; **4-18A:** Dagli Orti/REX/Shutterstock; **4-19:** villorejo/Alamy; **4-20:** Fred S. Kleiner; **4-21:** Vanni Archive/Getty Images; **4-21A:** Fred S. Kleiner; **4-22:** Joe Vogan/Alamy; **4-23:** Dagli Orti/REX/Shutterstock; **4-24:** Erich Lessing/ Art Resource, NY; **4-25:** Nimatallah/Art Resource, NY; **4-26:** Fred S. Kleiner; **4-27:** AKG-Images.

Chapter 5—5-1: Carolyn Clarke/Alamy; **5-1a:** Fred S. Kleiner; **5-1b:** Royal Ontario Museum; **5-1c:** Fred S. Kleiner; **Map 5-1:** © 2018 Cengage Learning; **5-2:** The Metropolitan Museum of Art/Art Resource, NY; **5-2A:** Nimatallah/Art Resource, NY; **5-3:** © The Metropolitan Museum of Art/Art Resource, NY; **5-4:** Photograph © 2011 Museum of Fine Arts, Boston; **5-5:** Copyright the Trustees of The British Museum; **5-5A:** 2005 Trustees of Dartmouth College; **5-6:** RMN-Grand Palais/Art Resource, NY; **5-7:** © The Metropolitan Museum of Art. Image source: Art Resource, NY; **5-8:** Nimatallah/Art Resource, NY; **5-9:** DEA/G. Dagli Orti/Getty Images; **5-10:** Nimatallah/Art Resource, NY; **5-11:** Marie Mauzy/Art Resource, NY; **5-12:** © 2018 Cengage Learning; **5-13:** John Burge/Cengage Learning; **5-14:** Fred S. Kleiner; **5-15:** Cengage Learning; **5-16:** Vanni/Art Resource, NY; **5-16A:** DEA Picture Library/Getty Images; **5-17:** Cengage Learning; **5-18:** Nimatallah/Art Resource, NY; **5-19:** Canali Photobank; **5-19A:** Scala/Art Resource, NY; **5-20:** Scala/Art Resource, NY; **5-20A:** © The Trustees of The British Museum/Art Resource, NY; **5-21:** Photograph © 2011 Museum of Fine Arts, Boston; **5-22:** Photograph © 2011 Museum of Fine Arts, Boston; **5-23:** Attic red-figure calyx-krater depicting Herakles wrestling with Antaeus, from Cervetri, c. 510 BC (ceramic) (see also 92569)/Euphronios, (fl.c. 520–500 BC)/Louvre, Paris, France/Bridgeman Images; **5-23A:** Scala/Ministero per i Beni e le Attività culturali/Art Resource, NY; **5-24:** Courtesy Saskia Ltd., © Dr. Ron Wiedenhoeft;

5-24A: © Royal Museums of Art and History, Brussels; **5-25:** Marie Mauzy/Art Resource, NY; **5-26 (left):** Courtesy Saskia Ltd., © Dr. Ron Wiedenhoeft; **5-26 (right):** Cengage Learning; **5-27:** DEA/G. Dagli Orti/Getty Images; **5-28:** Saskia Ltd., © Dr. Ron Wiedenhoeft; **5-29:** SASKIA Ltd. Cultural Documentation. © Dr. Ron Wiedenhoeft; **5-30:** Fred S. Kleiner; **5-31:** Dagli Orti/REX/Shutterstock; **5-32:** Studio Kontos/Photostock; **5-33:** AKG-Images/John Hios; **5-33A:** Vanni Archive/Art Resource, NY; **5-34:** Dagli Orti/REX/Shutterstock; **5-35:** Marie Mauzy/Art Resource, NY; **5-36:** Scala/Art Resource, NY; **5-37:** Cengage Learning, 2014; **5-38:** Vanni Archive/Art Resource, NY; **5-39:** Nimatallah/Art Resource, NY; **5-40:** Scala/Art Resource, NY; **5-41:** Scala/Ministero per i Beni e le Attività culturali/Art Resource, NY; **5-42:** Fred S. Kleiner; **5-43:** Yann Arthus-Bertrand; **5-44:** Cengage Learning; **5-45:** Cengage Learning, 2014; **5-46:** Royal Ontario Museum; **5-47:** Fred S. Kleiner; **5-47A:** Fred S. Kleiner; **5-48:** Fred S. Kleiner; **5-49:** Fred S. Kleiner; **5-49A:** Fred S. Kleiner; **5-49B:** Fred S. Kleiner; **5-49C:** Fred S. Kleiner; **5-50A:** Fred S. Kleiner; **5-50 (top):** Fred S. Kleiner; **5-50 (middle):** Studio Kontos/Photostock; **5-50 (bottom):** Fred S. Kleiner; **5-51:** © Constantinos Iliopoulos/Alamy; **5-52:** Fred S. Kleiner; **5-53:** Cengage Learning, 2014; **5-54:** Fred S. Kleiner; **5-55:** Fred S. Kleiner; **5-56:** Marie Mauzy/Art Resource, NY; **5-57:** Nimatallah/Art Resource, NY; **5-58:** Scala/Art Resource, NY; **5-58A:** Scala/Art Resource, NY; **5-59:** RMN-Grand Palais/Art Resource, NY; **5-60:** Scala/Art Resource, NY; **5-61:** Fred S. Kleiner; **5-62:** Scala/Art Resource, NY; **5-62A:** Photograph © 2011 Museum of Fine Arts, Boston; **5-63:** Statue of Hermes and the Infant Dionysus, c. 330 BC (parian marble), Praxiteles (c. 400–c. 330 BC)/Archaeological Museum, Olympia, Archaia, Greece/Bridgeman Images; **5-63A:** © The Metropolitan Museum of Art/Art Resource, NY; **5-63B:** Archaeological Receipts Fund; **5-63C:** Nevit Dilmen; **5-64:** Marie Mauzy/Art Resource, NY; **5-65:** Canali Photobank; **5-66:** Fred S. Kleiner; **5-67:** Art Resource, NY; **5-68:** AKG-Images/De Agostini Picture Lib./G. Dagli Orti; **5-69:** The Rape of Persephone, from the Tomb of Persephone (wall painting), Macedonian School/Vergina, Macedonia, Greece/The Bridgeman Art Library; **5-70:** Canali Photobank; **5-71:** Duby Tal/Albatross/Alamy; **5-72:** Fred S. Kleiner; **5-73:** Vanni/Art Resource, NY; **5-74:** Fred S. Kleiner; **5-75:** Yann Arthus-Bertrand; **5-76:** Cengage Learning; **5-77:** John Burge/Cengage Learning; **5-78:** Melvyn Longhurst/Alamy; **5-79:** bpk, Bildagentur/Antikensammlung, Staatliche Museen, Berlin, Germany/Resource, NY; **5-80:** bpk, Berlin/Antikensammlung, Staatliche Museen, Berlin, Germany/Johannes Laurentius/Art Resource, NY; **5-81:** Araldo de Luca/Fine Art/Corbis; **5-82:** Araldo de Luca/Fine Art/Corbis; **5-83:** The Victory of Samothrace (Parian marble) (see also 92583 & 94601-03 & 154093), Greek, (2nd century BC)/Louvre, Paris, France/Giraudon/The Bridgeman Art Library; **5-84:** RMN-Grand Palais/Art Resource, NY; **5-84A:** Nimatallah/Art Resource, NY; **5-84B:** © The Metropolitan Museum of Art/Art Resource, NY; **5-85:** Saskia Ltd.; **5-86:** Erich Lessing/Art Resource, NY; **5-87:** © The Metropolitan Museum of Art/Art Resource, NY; **5-88:** Ny Carlsberg Glyptotek, Copenhagen; **5-89:** Araldo de Luca/Fine Art Premium/Corbis; **5-90:** Fred S. Kleiner.

Chapter 6—6-1: BeBa/Iberfoto/The Image Works; **6-1a:** Scala/Art Resource, NY; **6-1b:** AKG-Images; **6-1c:** Scala/Art Resource, NY; **Map 6-1:** 2018 Cengage Learning; **6-2:** Hirmer Fotoarchiv; **6-2A:** Cengage Learning; **6-3:** Model of an Etruscan temple, reconstruction, 4th–5th century BC (plastic)/Institute of Etruscology, University of Rome, Italy/The Bridgeman Art Library; **6-4:** Araldo de Luca/Fine Art/Corbis; **6-5:** Araldo de Luca/Fine Art/Corbis; **6-6:** Fred S. Kleiner; **6-7:** Scala/Art Resource, NY; **6-7A:** Cengage Learning; **6-8:** Leemage/Getty Images; **6-9:** © BeBa/Iberfoto/The Image Works; **6-9A:** AKG-Images; **6-10:** Hirmer Fotoarchiv, Munich; **6-11:** Fred S. Kleiner; **6-12:** Scala/Art Resource, NY; **6-13:** Araldo de Luca/Fine Art/Corbis; **6-13A:** Back of a bronze mirror decorated with a scene showing an old man examining the liver of an animal, bears the name of Chalenas (Greek soothsayer) early 4th century BC/Vatican Museums and Galleries, Vatican City, Italy/The Bridgeman Art Library; **6-14:** Jonathan Poore/Cengage Learning; **6-15:** John Burge/Cengage Learning; **6-16:** Gianni Dagli Orti/Corbis; **6-16A:** Photograph © 2011 Museum of Fine Arts, Boston. 1975.799; **6-17:** Scala/Art Resource, NY.

Chapter 7—7-1: Jonathan Poore/Cengage Learning; **7-1a–c:** Fred S. Kleiner; **Map 7-1:** 2018 Cengage Learning; **7-2:** Charles & Josette Lenars/Encyclopedia/Corbis; **7-3:** Fred S. Kleiner; **7-4:** Fred S. Kleiner; **7-5:** Cengage Learning; **7-6:** John Burge; **7-7:** Araldo de Luca/Corbis; **7-8:** Fred S. Kleiner; **7-9:** Fred S. Kleiner; **7-9A:** Fred S. Kleiner; **7-10:** The American Numismatic Society; **7-10A:** Universal Images Group/Art Resource, NY; **7-11:** Fred S. Kleiner; **7-12:** Alinari/Art Resource, NY; **7-13:** Guido Alberto Rossi/AGE Fotostock; **7-14:** Erich Lessing/Art Resource, NY; **7-15:** John Burge/Cengage Learning; **7-16:** View from the atrium to the peristyle, House of the Vettii, Pompeii (photo)/Bildarchiv Steffens (First Account)/Bridgeman Images; **7-16A:** Araldo De Luca; **7-17:** Wayne Howes/Photographer's Direct; **7-18:** Scala/Art Resource, NY; **7-19:** © The Metropolitan Museum of Art/Art Resource, NY; **7-20:** Fred S. Kleiner; **7-21:** © The Metropolitan Museum of Art/Art Resource, NY; **7-22:** Canali Photobank; **7-23:** Fred S. Kleiner; **7-24:** Scala/Art Resource, NY; **7-24A:** Scala/Art Resource, NY; **7-25:** Fred S. Kleiner; **7-26:** Canali Photobank; **7-27:** Scala/Art Resource, NY; **7-28:** Ny Carlsberg Glyptotek; **7-29:** Fred S. Kleiner; **7-30:** Fred S. Kleiner; **7-31:** Sasika Ltd. Cultural Documentation; **7-32:** Fred S. Kleiner; **7-33:** Jonathan Poore/Cengage Learning; **7-34:** Fred S. Kleiner; **7-34A:** Canali Photobank; **7-35:** Cengage Learning, 2016; **7-36:** Robert Harding Picture Library; **7-37:** Fred S. Kleiner; **7-38:** Ny Carlsberg Glyptotek, Copenhagen; **7-39:** Fred S. Kleiner; **7-40:** Jonathan Poore/Cengage Learning; **7-40A:** Jonathan Poore/Cengage Learning; **7-41:** Fred S. Kleiner; **7-42:** Fred S. Kleiner; **7-43:** © Google Maps; **7-43A:** Scala/Art Resource, NY; **7-44:** John Burge/Cengage Learning; **7-44A:** Scala/Art Resource, NY; **7-45:** Fred S. Kleiner; **7-45A:** Fred S. Kleiner; **7-45B:** Fred S. Kleiner; **7-45C:** Fred S. Kleiner; **7-46:** Jonathan Poore/Cengage Learning; **7-47:** Fred S. Kleiner; **7-47A:** Jonathan Poore/Cengage Learning; **7-48:** Fred S. Kleiner; **7-49:** Fred S. Kleiner; **7-50:** John Burge/Cengage Learning; **7-51:** Martin Child/SuperStock; **7-52:** Fred S. Kleiner; **7-53:** Jon Sparks/Encyclopedia/Corbis; **7-53A:** Fred S. Kleiner; **7-54:** Scala/Art Resource, NY; **7-54A:** Andrea Matone; **7-55:** Erich Lessing/Art Resource, NY; **7-56:** Fred S. Kleiner; **7-57:** Fred S. Kleiner; **7-58:** Fred S. Kleiner; **7-58A:** Araldo de Luca/Fine Art/Corbis; **7-59:** Sarcogaphus, Italy, Roman empire, c. 100-125. Greek marble, L. 210 cm. © Cleveland Museum of Art. Gift of the John Trust, 1928.856; **7-60:** Scala/Art Resource, Inc.; **7-60A:** © The Trustees of The British Museum/Art Resource, NY; **7-60B:** Mummy portrait of a young woman, from Hawara, Egypt, ca. 110–120 CE. Encaustic on wood, 1′ 5 1/4″ × 1′ 1 3/8″. Royal Museum of Scotland, Edinburgh; **7-61:** The Trustees of The British Museum; **7-62:** bpk, Berlin/Antikensammlung, Staatliche Museen, Berlin, Germany, Art Resource, NY; **7-63:** Fred S. Kleiner; **7-64:** Araldo de Luca; **7-65:** Cengage Learning; **7-66:** Scala/Art Resource, NY; **7-67:** Fred S. Kleiner; **7-67A:** Fred S. Kleiner; **7-68:** © The Metropolitan Museum of Art/Art Resource, NY; **7-69:** Fred S. Kleiner; **7-70:** Scala/Art Resource, NY; **7-71:** Jessica Nitschke, Cengage Learning; **7-72:** Fred S. Kleiner; **7-73:** Fred S. Kleiner; **7-74 (top):** Jonathan Poore/Cengage Learning; **7-74 (bottom):** John Burge/Cengage Learning; **7-75:** Jonathan Poore/Cengage Learning; Learning; **7-76:** Fred S. Kleiner; **7-77:** Jonathan Poore/Cengage Learning; **7-78:** Jonathan Poore/Cengage Learning; **7-79:** The American Numismatic Society; Staatliche Munzsammlung.

Chapter 8—8-1: Erich Lessing/Art Resource, NY; **8-1a:** Art Resource, NY; **8-1b:** Cengage Learning; **8-1c:** Dr. Stephanie Smith; **Map 8-1:** Cengage Learning; **8-2:** Art Resource, NY; **8-3:** Cengage Learning; **8-4:** Dr. Stephanie Smith; **8-4A:** Marco Simola/Photographer's Direct; **8-5:** Scala/Art Resource, NY; **8-6:** foto Pontificia Commissione per l'Archeologia Sacra; **8-7:** Fred S. Kleiner; **8-8:** Scala/Art Resource, NY; **8-8A:** Fred S. Kleiner; **8-8B:** Courtesy Saskia Ltd., © Dr. Ron Wiedenhoeft; **8-8C:** AP Photo/Tsafrir Abayov; **8-9:** John Burge/Cengage Learning; **8-10:** 2018 Cengage Learning; **8-11:** Jonathan Poore/Cengage Learning; **8-12:** Cengage Learning; **8-13:** Jonathan Poore/Cengage Learning; **8-13A:** Canali Photobank, Italy; **8-14:** © The Trustees of the British Museum; **8-15:** Biblioteca Apostolica Vaticana; **8-16:** The Trustees of The British Museum/Art Resource, NY; **8-17:** Victoria and Albert Museum, London; **8-18:** Jonathan Poore/Cengage Learning; **8-19:** Jonathan Poore/Cengage Learning; **8-19A:** AKG-Images; **8-19B:** Jonathan Poore/Cengage Learning; **8-20:** The left hand apse arch ("Triumphal Arch") with the Nativity and the Adoration of the Magi/Painton Cowen/Bridgeman Images; **8-21:** Jonathan Poore/Cengage Learning; **8-22:** Fred S. Kleiner; **8-23:** Cameraphoto Arte, Venice/Art Resource, NY; **8-24:** Scala/Art Resource, NY; **8-24A:** The Baptism of Christ surrounded by the Apostles, from the vault of the central dome (mosaic), Byzantine, (5th century AD)/Battistero Neoniano, Ravenna, Italy/Giraudon/The Bridgeman Art Library; **8-25:** Scala/Art Resource, NY; **8-26:** Scala/Art Resource, NY; **8-27:** Ma Hirmer/ Hirmer Verlag GMBH.

Chapter 9—9-1: DEA/A Dagli Orti/AGE Fotostock; **9-1a–c:** Canali Photobank, Italy; **Map 9-1:** 2018 Cengage Learning; **9-1A:** Mark Johnson; **9-2:** British Museum/HIP/Art Resource, NY; **9-2A:** Österreichische Nationalbibliothek, Vienna; **9-3:** Osterreichische Nationalbibliothek; **9-4:** Réunion des Musées Nationaux/Art Resource, NY; **9-5:** Images & Stories/Alamy; **9-6:** John Burge/Cengage Learning; **9-7:** John Burge/Cengage Learning; **9-8:** David Pearson/Alamy; **9-9:** Cengage Learning; **9-10:** DEA/A Dagli Orti/AGE Fotostock; **9-11:** Cengage Learning; **9-12:** Alfredo Dagli Orti/Art Resource, NY; **9-13:** Canali Photobank; **9-13A:** Dagli Orti/REX/Shutterstock; **9-14:** Canali Photobank; **9-15:** Scala/Art Resource, NY; **9-16:** Studio Kontos/Photostock; **9-17:** Osterreichische Nationalbibliothek, Vienna; **9-17A:** Österreichische Nationalbibliothek, Vienna, Bildarchiv. folio 7 recto of the Vienna Genesis; **9-17B:** Scala/Art Resource, NY; **9-18:** Firenze, Biblioteca Medicea Laurenziana, Ms. Laur. Plut. 1.56, c. 13v; **9-18A:** Scala/Art Resource, NY; **9-18B:** Christ Pantocrator, 6th century (encaustic on panel)/Monastery of Saint Catherine, Mount Sinai, Egypt/Ancient Art and Architecture Collection Ltd./The Bridgeman Art Library; **9-19:** Ronald Sheraton/Danita Delimont Stock Photography; **9-20:** Funkystock/age fotostock/SuperStock; **9-21:** © Fred S. Kleiner; **9-22:** Cengage Learning; **9-23:** Vanni/Art Resource, NY; **9-24:** Studio Kontos/Photostock; **9-25:** Erich Lessing/Art Resource, NY; **9-25A:** Kurt and Rosalia Scholz/SuperStock; **9-26:** Alinari/Art Resource, NY; **9-26A:** Cameraphoto Arte, Venice/Art Resource, NY; **9-26B:** Werner Forman/Art Resource, NY; **9-26C:** Fred S. Kleiner; **9-27:** Scala/Art Resource, NY; **9-28:** Réunion des Musées Nationaux/Art Resource, NY; **9-29:** © Josephine Powell; **9-30:** Snark/Art Resource, NY; **9-31:** Scala/Art Resource, NY; **9-31A:** Orthodox World; **9-32:** Werner Forman/Art Resource, NY; **9-33:** Stojan Saveski, Republic of Macedonia; **9-34:** Erich Lessing/Art Resource, NY; **9-35:** Scala/Art Resource, NY; **9-35A:** State Historical Cultural Museum, Moscow, Kremlin.

Chapter 10—10-1: Album/Oronoz/Album/SuperStock; **10-1a:** © Bednorz-Images; **10-1b:** © Bednorz-Images; **10-1c:** Adam Woolfit/Robert Harding Picture Library; **Map 10-1:** © Cengage Learning; **10-2:** Stefano Baldini/AGE Fotostock; **10-3:** Erich Lessing/Art Resource, NY; **10-4:** Richard Nowitz Photography/Getty Images; **10-5:** Gerard Degeorge/AKG-Images; **10-6:** B.O'Kane/Alamy; **10-6A:** Cengage Learning; **10-6B:** Fred S. Kleiner; **10-7:** Guido Alberto Rossi; **10-8:** Cengage Learning; **10-9:** Malwiya minaret of the Great Mosque, Samarra, Iraq, 848-852 (photo)/Bildarchiv Steffens (First Account)/Bridgeman Images; **10-10:** © E. Simanor/Robert Harding Picture Library; **10-11:** © Bednorz-Images; **10-12:** Decorative scheme above the doorway in the east facade, part of the extension built by al-Hakam II, 961–66 (photo)/Mezquita (Great Mosque) Cordoba, Spain/The Bridgeman Art Library; **10-13:** © Bednorz-Images; **10-14:** Adam Woolfit/Robert Harding Picture Library; **10-15:** Aerial view of the Jameh Mosque,

Isfahan, Iran, built 11th/12th century (photo)/Bildarchiv Steffens (First Account)/ Bridgeman Images; **10-16:** Cengage Learning; **10-16A:** Duffour/Andia/Alamy; **10-17:** Adrian Weston/ Alamy; **10-17A:** Musée Lorrain, Nancy, France/photo G. Mangin; **10-18:** Erich Lessing/Art Resource, NY; **10-19:** The State Hermitage Museum, St. Petersburg; **10-20:** The Trustees of the Chester Beatty Library, Dublin; **10-20A:** Unknown Artist, folio from a qur'an: sura 2: 229–mid 231 (recto), sura 2: 231–begin 233 (verso). Ink, color, gold, and silver on vellum dyed blue; 28.73 × 37.62 cm (11 5/16″ × 14 13/16″) Harvard Art Museum, Arthur M. Sackler Museum, Francis H. Burr Memorial Fund, 1967.23 Photo: Katya Kallsen © President and Fellows of Harvard College **10-21:** Réunion des Musées Nationaux/Art Resource, NY; **10-22:** Toyohiro Yamada /Taxi/Getty Images; **10-23:** Mauritius/SuperStock.com; **10-24:** Cengage Learning; **10-25:** Hans Georg Roth/ Getty Images; **10-25A:** The Metropolitan Museum of Art/Art Resource, NY; **10-26:** Bernardo Ricci Armani/Getty Images; **10-27:** Bernardo Ricci Armani/ Getty Images; **10-28:** © The Metropolitan Museum of Art/Art Resource, NY; **10-29:** dbtravel /dbimages/Alamy; **10-30:** Boisvieux Christophe/hemis.fr/Hemis/ Alamy; **10-31:** Victoria & Albert Museum, London/Art Resource, NY; **10-32:** © The Trustees of The British Museum; **10-33:** Erich Lessing/Art Resource, NY; **10-34:** The Court of Gayumars (2005.1.165; M200) © Aga Khan Trust for Culture Geneva; **10-35:** Réunion des Musées Nationaux/Art Resource, NY; **10-36:** Freer Gallery of Art Washington, DC, Purchase, F1941.10.

Chapter 11—11-1 and 11-1a–c: Album/Art Resource, NY; **11-2:** Réunion des Musées Nationaux/Art Resource, NY; **11-2A:** The Trustees of The British Museum/Art Resource, NY; **11-3:** The Trustees of The British Museum/Art Resource, NY; **11-4:** Universal History Archive/Getty Images; **11-4A:** HIP/Art Resource, NY; **11-5:** Erich Lessing/Art Resource, NY; **11-6:** MS 57 fol.21v The Man, symbol of St. Matthew the Evangelist, introductory page to the Gospel of St. Matthew, Irish, from Durrow, County Offaly (vellum)/© The Board of Trinity College, Dublin, Ireland/The Bridgeman Art Library; **11-7:** British Library Board/ Robana/Art Resource, NY; **11-8:** British Library Board/Robana/Art Resource, NY; **11-9:** Michael Jenner/Getty Images; **11-9A:** Michael Jenner/Robert Harding; **11-10:** Jonathan Poore; **11-11:** Album/Oronoz/Album/SuperStock; **Map 11-1:** 2018 Cengage Learning; **11-12:** Equestrian statue of Charlemagne (747–814) (bronze) (see also 28028), French School, (8th century)/Louvre, Paris, France/ Giraudon/The Bridgeman Art Library; **11-12A:** AKG-Images; **11-13:** Kunsthistorisches Museums, Wien; **11-14:** DEA/G. Dagli Orti/Getty Images; **11-15:** Utrecht, University Library, Ms. 32, fol. 25r; **11-15A:** Utrecht, University Library, Ms. 32, fol. 25r; **11-16:** The Pierpont Morgan Library/Art Resource, NY; **11-17:** Cengage Learning, 2016; **11-17 (top):** Cengage Learning, 2016; **11-17 (bottom):** Cengage Learning, 2016; **11-18:** Bildarchiv Steffens/The Bridgeman Art Library International; **11-19:** Jonathan Poore/Cengage Learning; **11-19A:** Hirmer Verlag; **11-19B:** Plan of the Benedictine Abbey of Saint-Riquier in 1673 (engraving), French School (17th century)/Bibliotheque Nationale, Paris, France/Giraudon/ The Bridgeman Art Library; **11-20:** AKG-Images; **11-21:** Jonathan Poore/Cengage Learning; **11-22:** Jonathan Poore/Cengage Learning; **11-23:** Jonathan Poore/ Cengage Learning; **11-24:** © Bednorz-Images; **11-25A:** Jonathan Poore/Cengage Learning; **11-25 (top):** Jonathan Poore/Cengage Learning; **11-25 (bottom):** Jonathan Poore/Cengage Learning; **11-26:** Hubertus Blume/Alamy; **11-26A:** Jonathan Poore/Cengage Learning; **11-27:** Erich Lessing/Art Resource, NY; **11-28:** The Metropolitan Museum of Art/Art Resource, NY; **11-29:** Réunion des Musées Nationaux/Art Resource, NY; **11-29A:** Jonathan Poore/Cengage Learning; **11-30:** © Rheinisches Bildarchiv Köln, rba_c000008; **11-30A:** Bayerische Staatsbibliothek, Munich; **11-31:** Bayerische Staatsbibliothek, Munich; **11-32:** Bayerische Staatsbibliothek, Munich; **11-33:** Bayerische Staatsbibliothek, Munich.

Chapter 12—12-1: 2018 Cengage Learning; **12-1a–c:** Jonathan Poore/Cengage Learning; **12-2:** DEA/A. Dagli Orti/Getty Images; **Map 12-1:** DEA/A. Dagli Orti/ Getty Images; **12-3:** Claude Huber; **12-4:** Cengage Learning; **12-4A:** Interior of the Collegiate Church of Saint Vincent, Cardona (photo)/Inglesia de San Vicente de Cardona, Catalunya, Spain/Photo © AISA/The Bridgeman Art Library; **12-4B:** Jonathan Poore/Cengage Learning; **12-5:** AKG-Images; **12-6:** Cengage Learning; **12-6A:** Jonathan Poore/Cengage Learning; **12-6B:** AKG-Images/Andrea Jemolo; **12-7:** Jonathan Poore/Cengage Learning; **12-8:** Cengage Learning; **12-9:** Jonathan Poore/Cengage Learning; **12-9A:** Koenemann GmbH/Photo: Achim Bednorz; **12-9B:** The Incredulity of St Thomas (photo), Spanish School, (12th century)/ Santo Domingo de Silos, Castilla y Leon, Spain/John Bethell/The Bridgeman Art Library; **12-10A:** Jonathan Poore/Cengage Learning; **12-10 (left):** Jonathan Poore/Cengage Learning; **12-10 (right):** Fred S. Kleiner; **12-11:** Jonathan Poore/ Cengage Learning; **12-12:** John Burge/Cengage Learning; **12-12A:** Jonathan Poore/Cengage Learning; **12-12B:** © Bednorz-Images; **12-13:** Jonathan Poore/ Cengage Learning; **12-14:** Jonathan Poore/Cengage Learning; **12-15:** Jonathan Poore/Cengage Learning; **12-15A:** © Peter Horree/Alamy; **12-15B:** Jonathan Poore/Cengage Learning; **12-15C:** Jonathan Poore/Cengage Learning; **12-16:** Bibliothèque Nationale, Paris; **12-16A:** Giraudon/Art Resource, NY; **12-17:** Erich Lessing/Art Resource, NY; **12-18 (left):** Jonathan Poore/Cengage Learning; **12-18 (right):** Jonathan Poore/Cengage Learning; **12-19:** Photograph © 2011 Museum of Fine Arts, Boston. 21.1285; **12-20:** © The Metropolitan Museum of Art/Art Resource, NY; **12-21:** Jonathan Poore/Cengage Learning; **12-22:** Jonathan Poore/ Cengage Learning; **12-23:** Fred S. Kleiner; **12-24:** Fred S. Kleiner; **12-25:** Abtei St. Hildegard; **12-26:** World History Archive/Superstock; **12-27:** AKG-Images/ Bildarchiv Monheim; **12-28:** Photograph Speldoorn © Musées royaux d'Art et d'Histoire—Brussels; **12-29:** Jonathan Poore/Cengage Learning; **12-29A:** Jonathan Poore/Cengage Learning; **12-30:** Jonathan Poore/Cengage Learning; **12-30A:** Jonathan Poore/Cengage Learning; **12-30B:** Jonathan Poore/Cengage Learning; **12-30C:** Canali Photobank, Milan, Italy; **12-31:** © Bednorz-Images; **12-32:** © Bednorz-Images; **12-33:** Jonathan Poore/Cengage Learning; **12-34:** Jonathan Poore/Cengage Learning; **12-35:** Cengage Learning; **12-36 (left):** Heritage Image Partnership Ltd/Alamy; **12-36 (right):** Cengage Learning; **12-37:** Cengage Learning; **12-38:** The Master and Fellows of Corpus Christi College, Cambridge; **12-38A:** © British Library Board. All Rights Reserved/The Bridgeman Art Library; **12-39:** The Bridgeman Art Library; **12-40:** By special permission of the City of Bayeux; **12-41:** By special permission of the City of Bayeux.

Chapter 13—13-1 and 13-1a–b: Jonathan Poore/Cengage Learning; **13-1c:** Fred S. Kleiner; **Map 13-1:** Cengage Learning; **13-2:** Jonathan Poore/Cengage Learning; **13-3:** Jonathan Poore/Cengage Learning; **13-4:** Jonathan Poore/Cengage Learning; **13-5:** Jonathan Poore/Cengage Learning; **13-6:** Jonathan Poore/ Cengage Learning; **13-7:** Jonathan Poore/Cengage Learning; **13-8:** Jonathan Poore/Cengage Learning; **13-9:** Jonathan Poore/Cengage Learning; **13-10:** Jonathan Poore/Cengage Learning; **13-11:** John Burge/Cengage Learning; **13-12:** Universal Images Group North America LLC/DeAgostini/Alamy; **13-13:** Cengage Learning; **13-14:** Album/Oronoz/Album/Superstock; **13-15:** Album/Oronoz/ Album/Superstock; **13-16:** Jonathan Poore/Cengage Learning; **13-17:** Jonathan Poore/Cengage Learning; **13-18:** Jonathan Poore/Cengage Learning; **13-19:** Four martyr saints, column figures from the west door of the south portal, c. 1220 (stone)/Peter Willi/Chartres Cathedral, Chartres, France/Bridgeman Images; **13-19A:** Jonathan Poore/Cengage Learning; **13-20:** Jonathan Poore/Cengage Learning; **13-21:** Jonathan Poore/Cengage Learning; **13-22:** Jonathan Poore/ Cengage Learning; **13-23:** Jonathan Poore/Cengage Learning; **13-24:** SEF/Art Resource, NY; **13-24A:** Jonathan Poore/Cengage Learning; **13-25:** Jonathan Poore/Cengage Learning; **13-26:** AKG-Images; **13-27:** Jonathan Poore/Cengage Learning; **13-28:** Jonathan Poore/Cengage Learning; **13-29:** Guido Alberto Rossi; **13-30:** © Bednorz-Images; **13-31:** Jonathan Poore/Cengage Learning; **13-32:** The Morgan Library & Museum/Art Resource, NY; **13-33:** Österreichische Nationalbibliothek, Vienna; **13-34:** Bibliotheque Nationale; **13-35:** Bibliotheque Nationale; **13-36:** Snark/Art Resource, NY; **13-36A:** The Metropolitan Museum of Art, The Cloisters Collection, 1954 (54.1.2). Image © The Metropolitan Museum; **13-37:** Bibliotheque Nationale; **13-38:** Réunion des Musées Nationaux/Art Resource, NY; **13-39:** The Walters Art Museum; **13-39A:** AKG-Images/Schütze/Rodemann; **13-39B:** Richard de Bello(?), Mappamundi (world map) of Henry III, ca. 1277–1289. Tempera on vellum, 5′ 2″ × 4′ 4″. Hereford Cathedral, Hereford, England; **13-40:** Jonathan Poore/Cengage Learning; **13-40A:** Jonathan Poore/ Cengage Learning; **13-41:** Cengage Learning; **13-42:** Jonathan Poore/Cengage Learning; **13-43:** Jonathan Poore/Cengage Learning; **13-43A:** Jonathan Poore/Cengage Learning; **13-43B:** Jonathan Poore/Cengage Learning; **13-44:** Jonathan Poore/ Cengage Learning; **13-44A:** Jonathan Poore/Cengage Learning; **13-45:** Werner Foreman Archive Ltd./Art Resource; **13-45A:** Jonathan Poore/Cengage Learning; **13-45B:** Erich Lessing/Art Resource, NY; **13-46:** Erich Lessing/Art Resource, NY; **13-47:** Erich Lessing/Art Resource, NY; **13-48:** Jonathan Poore/Cengage Learning; **13-49:** Jonathan Poore/Cengage Learning; **13-49A:** Jonathan Poore/Cengage Learning; **13-50:** Jonathan Poore/Cengage Learning; **13-51:** Jonathan Poore/Cengage Learning; **13-52:** Erich Lessing/Art Resource, NY; **13-53:** AKG-Images/De Agostini Picture Lib./W. Buss; **13-53A:** www.webaviation.co.uk; **13-54:** Jonathan Poore/Cengage Learning; **13-55:** Jonathan Poore/Cengage Learning; **13-56:** Jonathan Poore/Cengage Learning.

Chapter 14—14-1 and 14-1a–c: Scala/Art Resource, NY; **Map 14-1:** Cengage Learning;**14-2:** Jonathan Poore/Cengage Learning; **14-3:** Jonathan Poore/Cengage Learning; **14-4:** Jonathan Poore/Cengage Learning; **14-5:** Scala/Art Resource, NY; **14-5A:** Alinari/Art Resource, NY; **14-5B:** Photo by Ralph Lieberman; **14-5C:** Erich Lessing/Art Resource, NY; **14-6:** Scala/Ministero per i Beni e le Attività culturali/Art Resource, NY; **14-7 (top):** Leemage/Getty Images; **14-7 (bottom):** White Images/Scala/Art Resource, NY; **14-8:** Thekla Clark/Getty Images; **14-9:** Scala/Art Resource, NY; **14-9A:** AKG-Images; **14-10:** Scala/Art Resource, NY; **14-10A:** Alinari/Art Resource, NY; **14-11:** Scala/Art Resource, NY; **14-11A:** Scala/Art Resource, NY; **14-12:** Scala/Art Resource, NY; **14-13:** Jonathan Poore/ Cengage Learning; **14-13A:** Jonathan Poore/Cengage Learning; **14-14:** Canali Photobank; **14-15:** Alinari/Art Resource, NY; **14-16:** Jonathan Poore/Cengage Learning; **14-17:** Scala/Art Resource, NY; **14-17A:** Scala/Art Resource, NY; **14-18:** Scala/Art Resource, NY; **14-19:** Alinari/Art Resource, NY; **14-19A:** Scala/ Art Resource, NY; **14-19B:** Jonathan Poore/Cengage Learning; **14-20:** South Door of the Baptistry of San Giovanni, 1336 (bronze), Pisano, Andrea (1270–1349)/ Baptistery, Florence, Italy/The Bridgeman Art Library; **14-20A:** Scala/Art Resource, NY; **14-21:** Jonathan Poore/Cengage Learning; **14-22:** Jonathan Poore/ Cengage Learning; **14-23:** Fred. S. Kleiner.

lamassu (man-headed winged bull), from the citadel of Sargon II, Dur Sharrukin (modern Khorsabad), 47, *47*

Lamentation (Giotto di Bondone), Arena Chapel (Cappella Scrovegni), Padua, 428–429, *428*, 440

Lamentation (Grünewald), 14-9A

Lamentation, wall painting, Saint Pantaleimon, Nerezi, 285–286, *285*, 428, 12-30C

landscapes, 5, 9; Ancient Greece, 142–143, 148; Ancient Mesopotamia and Persia, 42; early Christian art, 252, 258–259, 260; Etruscan, 173; Italian late medieval art, *423*, *431*; Minoan, *92*, 93, *103*; Roman art, 197–198

landscape with swallows (*Spring Fresco*), Akrotiri, *92*, 93, *103*

Laocoön and his sons (Athanadoros, Hagesandros, and Polydoros of Rhodes), 161–162, *161*

Laon Cathedral, 386–387, *386*, 390, *391*, 392, 394, 395, 397

large sakkos of Photius, 290, *290*, 9-35A

Lars Pulena sarcophagus, Tarquinia, *176*, 177–178

Lascaux cave paintings (France), *14*, 15, 20–23; Axial Gallery, 22, *22*, 1-9A; Hall of the Bulls, *14*, 15, 20, 22, 1-9A; rhinoceros, wounded man, and disemboweled bison, 22–23, *22*; running horse, 22, *22*, 1-9A

Last Judgment: Italian Quattrocento Renaissance, 11; Italian Trecento, 424, 425, *425*, 427; in Romanesque art, 5, 6, 12, *346*, *347*, 12-15C

Last Judgment (Cavallini), Santa Cecilia, Travestere, Rome, 424, 425, *425*, 427

Last Judgment (Gislebertus), Saint-Lazare, 5, 6, 11, 12, *346*, *347*, 12-15C

Last Supper, 245, 246–247

late Antiquity art, 236–261, *238*; early Christian art, 236–251; ivory carving, 252–254; luxury arts, 251–254; manuscript illumination, 252

late Byzantine art, 265, 287–290

late Classical Greek art, 163; architecture of, 151–153; painting, 141–144; sculpture, 145–147

late medieval Italian art, 418–441

late Minoan (New Palace) period, 88

later Islamic art, 306–316; architecture, 306–312; luxury arts, 313–316; mosque lamps, 314, *314*

late Roman Empire art, 223–234, *229*

Laussel (France), woman holding a bison horn, 18–19, *18*, 1-5A

Leaning Tower, Pisa, 370, *370*, 12-29A

Lectionary of Henry II, 343–344, *344*

Leo III (Pope), 265, 279, 328

León (Spain), Santa María Cathedral, 407, *407*, 13-39A

Leonardo da Vinci, 421

Lepcis Magna, Libya, Chariot procession of Septimius Severus, relief from the attic of the Arch of Septimius Severus, 225, *225*, 239

Lérida (Spain), Santa María de Mur, 362–363, *363*

Le Tuc d'Audoubert (France), 19; cave paintings, 19; two bison reliefs, 19, *19*

Liber pontificalis, or *Book of the Pontiffs (Popes)*, 250

Lindau Gospels, 332–333, *333*

Lindisfarne Gospels, 325–326, *325*, *326*, 330, 342

Lion Gate, Hattusa, 45, *45*, 2-18A

Lion Gate, Mycenae, 97, 98–99, *98*, 101, 2-18A

Lion Hunt (Rubens), 10, *10*

Lock, Adam, Wells Cathedral, 409, *409*

London (England), Westminster Abbey, *377*, 400, 410, *410*, 13-45A

Lorenzetti, Ambrogio: *Effects of Good Government in the City and in the Country*, Sala della Pace in the

Palazzo Pubblico, Siena, 435, *435*, 436, 14-17A; *Peaceful City*, detail from *Effects of Good Government in the City and in the Country*, Sala della Pace, Palazzo Pubblico, Siena, 435, *435*, 436; *Peaceful Country*, detail from *Effects of Good Government in the City and in the Country*, Sala della Pace, Palazzo Pubblico, Siena, 436, *436*

Lorenzetti, Pietro, *Birth of the Virgin*, from the altar of Saint Savinus, Siena Cathedral, Siena, 433, *433*

Lorenzo the Magnificent. See Medici

Louis IX, Saint (king of France), 398, 402, 403

Ludovisi Battle Sarcophagus, 227–228, *227*

Luxor (Egypt), 115, 3-24A. See also Thebes (Egypt)

luxury arts: Gothic, 405–407; Islamic, 304–306, 313–316; late Antiquity, 251–254

Luzarches, Robert de, 394; Amiens Cathedral, *389*, *391*, 392, 394–395, *395*, 432, 437, 438

Lysikrates, Choragic Monument of Lysikrates, Athens, 152–153, *153*

Lysippides Painter, Achilles and Ajax playing a dice game, Orvieto, 121, *121*

Lysippos of Sikyon, 147, 157, 161; *Apoxyomenos* (*Scraper*), 146–147, *146*; portrait of Alexander the Great, 147–148; weary Herakles (Farnese Hercules), 147, *147*, 226

M

La Madeleine (France), bison licking its flank, fragmentary spear-thrower, 19–20, *19*

Madonna and Child Enthroned with Saints (Bernardo Daddi), Or San Michele, Florence, 438, *438*, 14-20A

Madonna Enthroned (*Ognissanti Madonna*) (Giotto di Bondone), Chiesa di Ognissanti (All Saints' Church), Florence, *426*, 427, 429

Madonna Enthroned with Angels and Prophets, Santa Trinità (Holy Trinity), Florence (Cimabue), 424, *424*, 427, 430

Madrasa Imami, Isfahan, 310–312, *311*

madrasa-mosque-mausoleum complex of Sultan Hasan, Cairo, 308–309, *308*

Maestà altarpiece (Duccio), Siena Cathedral, *418*, 419, 429, 430, 431–432, *431*, 14-11A

Magdeburg (Germany) ivories, 341, *341*

Magdeburg Cathedral, 341, *341*

La Madeleine, Vézelay, 360, *360*, 361

La Magdeleine (France) (cave) reclining woman, 19, *19*, 21, 1-5A

Maison Carrée (Square House), Nîmes, 204, *204*

Maitani, Lorenzo, Orvieto Cathedral, 432, *432*

Makapansgqat (South Africa), water-worn pebble resembling a human face, 16, *16*, 1-1A

male harp player, from Keros (Cyclades), 88, *88*

Malwiya Minaret, Great Mosque, Samarra, 300, *300*

man (symbol of Saint Matthew), folio 21 verso of the *Book of Durrow* (possibly from Iona, Scotland), *324*, 325

Mantiklos Apollo, Thebes, 109–111, *109*, 112

man with portrait busts of his ancestors, from Rome, 187, *187*

Maori of Aotearoa (New Zealand), facial moko (tattoos), 13, *13*

Mappamundi of Henry III (Richard de Bello), Hereford Cathedral, 407, *407*, 13-39B

Maqsud of Kashan, 313; carpet from the funerary mosque of Shaykh Safi al-Din, Ardabil, 313, *313*

Maqsura of the Mezquita (Great Mosque), Córdoba, 302, *302*

Marcus Aurelius (Roman emperor), 183, 200, 219, 221, *221*, 223, 224, 237, 330, 7-47A, 7-58A

Marine Style octopus flask, Palaikastro, 94, *94*

Mark, Saint, 229, 247, 283, 331, 12-16A. See also four evangelists

Markets of Trajan (Apollodorus of Damascus), Rome, 184, *184*, 213–214, *213*, 214, 230

Martini, Simone, 432–433; *Annuciation* panel, Saint Ansanus altarpiece, Siena Cathedral, Siena, 432–433, *433*, 434; Saint Ansanus altarpiece, Siena Cathedral, Siena, 432, *433*

Mary Magdalene, 361; in Byzantine art, 277, *277*, 9-18A; in early Christian art, 245, 247; early medieval art, 340; in Gothic art, 412; in Italian 14th century art, 431; in late medieval Italian art, 428; relics of, 350; in Romanesque art, 362

Marzabotto, city plan, 167, *167*, 6-2A

Masaccio (Tommaso di ser Giovanni di Mone Cassai), 421; *Holy Trinity*, 14-5B; *Tribute Money*, 246

mastabas, 61, 62, 64

Master Honoré, *Samuel Anointing David* and *Battle of David and Goliath*, *Breviary of Philippe le Bel*, 404–405, *404*

Master Hugo, *Moses Expounding the Law*, folio 94 recto of the *Bury Bible* (from Bury Saint Edmunds), 375–376, *375*

Matthew, Saint, 247, 325–326, *326*, 330, *330*, 331, *331*

Mau, August, "Pompeian Styles," 194–198

Mausoleum, Halikarnassos, 145, *145*, 5-63C

Mausoleum of Galla Placidia, Ravenna, 257–259, *257*, *258*, 260, 8-24A

Mausoleum of the Samanids, Bukhara, 300, *300*

Maxentius (Roman emperor), 230, 232, 233, 234

medieval books, 324–325. See also illuminated manuscripts

Medina al-Zahra, 304; Pyxis of al-Mughira, 304–305, *304*

Megaron, Palace of Nestor, Pylos, 98, *98*, 4-18A

Melfi sacrophagus, 222, *222*

Melos (Greece), Aphrodite (*Venus de Milo*), 158, *158*

Memmi, Lippo, 432–433; *Annuciation* panel, Saint Ansanus altarpiece, Siena Cathedral, Siena, 432–433, *433*

Menander portrait, Pompeii, 199, *199*

Menkaure (pharaoh of Egypt), 63, 67, *67*; pyramid of, 65

Mentuemhet portrait statue, Karnak, 81–82, *81*

Merovingian art, 320–321, *320*

Merovingian looped fibulae, Jouy-le-Comte, 320, *320*

Mesolithic art, 23

Mesopotamia, *24map*, *32map*, 34

Mesopotamian art, 24, 32–50, 60

metalwork: Aegean, 95, 99–100, *99*, 4-13A, 4-21A; African, 12; Akkadian, 40; Carolingian, 329, *329*, 330; early medieval pre-Christian, 319, 321–323, *321*, 11-3A; Etruscan, 175–177, *175*; Gothic, 409, *409*, 13-43A; Greek, 129, *129*; Islamic, 305, 315–316; Romanesque, 368

metopes, 125–126, *126*, 135, *135*

Mezquita (Great Mosque), Córdoba, 301, *301*, 302

Michelangelo Buonarroti, 161; basilica, Saint Peter's, Rome, 329, 334, 342; remodeling of Baths of Caracalla, *226*; unfinished statues, 11, *11*

middle Byzantine art, 265, 279–287; architecture of, 279–280; mosaics in, 279–280

mihrab, Friday Mosque, Isfahan, 303, *303*, 10-16A

mihrab, from the Madrasa Imami, Isfahan, 311–312, *311*

mihrab of the Mezquita (Great Mosque), Córdoba, 302, *303*

Milan (Italy), 264, 354, 366, 424; Sant'Ambrogio, 366, *366*

Mildenhall Treasure, 251–252, *251*

Miniature Ships Fresco, Akrotiri, 93, *93*, 4-9A

Minoan art, 84, *84*, 85–87, 88–90; architecture, 88–90; ceremony of bull-leaping, 91, *91*; painting, 90–92, *91*, 428; palaces, 88–90, *90*; pottery, 93–94, *94*; sculpture, 94–95

Minoan sarcophagus, *84*, 85

Minoan woman or goddess (*La Parisienne*), from the palace, Knossos (Crete), 90–91, *90*

Miracle of the Loaves and Fishes, Sant'Apollinare Nuovo (Orthodox Baptistery), Ravenna, 259–260, *260*

Miracles of Jesus, 259–260, *260*

Mission of the Apostles, La Madeleine, Vézelay, 360, *360*

Mnesikles, Propylaia, Acropolis, Athens, 138, *138*

model of the hypostyle hall, temple of Amen-Re, Karnak, 19th Dynasty, *74*, 75

model of the pyramid complex, Gizeh, 65

Modena Cathedral, 371, *371*, 372, 12-15C

Moissac (France), 350, 356, 372; *Codex Colbertinus*, 361–362, *361*; Saint-Pierre, 356–359, *356*, *357*, 358, *359*, 361, *361*, 362

Monastery of Hosios Loukas, Distomo, 280–281, *280*

Monreale cathedral, 284, *284*, 9-26A

Monterozzi necropolis, Tarquinia, 172–173, *172*, *173*, 6-9A

Moralia in Job, Cîteaux, 362, *362*

Morgan Madonna, Auvergne, 363–364, *364*

mortuary precinct of Djoser (Imhotep), Saqqara, 62, *62*, 63, 3-6A

mortuary temple of Hatshepsut, Deir el-Bahri, 71–73, *71*, *72*, 73

mosaic in the ambulatory vault of Santa Costanza, Rome, 250, *251*

mosaics: in ancient Greek art, 148, *148*; in Byzantine art, 262, 263, 279–280, 283, 284; in early Christian art, 256–257, 259–260, 272–276; in Islamic art, 312; in middle Byzantine art, 279–280; in Roman art, 192–193, 198, *262*, 273–274, *273*

Moses, 275–276, *380*, 384, *384*, 13-3A

Moses, west façade, Saint-Denis, *380*, 384, 13-3A

mosque lamp of Sayf al-Din Tuquztimur, 314, *314*

Mosque of Selim II (Sinan the Great), Edirne, 309–310, *309*, *310*

Mount Sinai (Egypt): Christ blessing, 278, *278*, 9-18B; Monastery of Saint Catherine, 275–276, *275*, 278, *278*, 279, 280, 287, 289, 9-18B

Mozarabic art, 327–328

Mshatta (Jordan), 298; Umayyad Palace, 298, *298*, 10-6A, 10-6B

Muhammad, 293, 294, 295, 300

Muhammad ibn al-Zayn, basin, *Baptistère de Saint Louis*, 315–316, *315*

mummy case of Artemidorus, 222–223, *222*, 7-60A

mummy portrait of a priest of Serapis, Hawara, 223, *223*

Muqarnas decoration, 307; dome, Hall of the Abencerrajes, Alhambra, *306*, 307; tilework of the entrance portal of the Imam Mosque, Isfahan, 312, *312*